How to use your Connected Casebook

Step 1: Go to **www.CasebookConnect.com** and redeem your access code to get started.

Access Code:  STXT96941798870

Step 2: Go to your **BOOKSHELF** and select your Connected Casebook to start reading, highlighting, and taking notes in the margins of your e-book.

Step 3: Select the **STUDY** tab in your toolbar to access a variety of practice materials designed to help you master the course material. These materials may include explanations, videos, multiple-choice questions, flashcards, short answer, essays, and issue spotting.

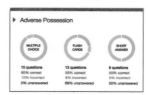

Step 4: Select the **OUTLINE** tab in your toolbar to access chapter outlines that automatically incorporate your highlights and annotations from the e-book. Use the My Notes area for copying, pasting, and editing your book notes or creating new notes.

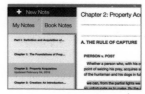

Step 5: If your professor has enrolled your class, you can select the **CLASS INSIGHTS** tab and compare your own study center results against the average of your classmates.

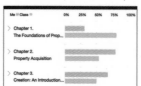

Is this a used casebook? Access code already scratched off?

You can purchase the Digital Version and still access all of the powerful tools listed above.
Please visit CasebookConnect.com and select Catalog to learn more.

PLEASE NOTE: Each access code can only be used once. This access code will expire one year after the discontinuation of the corresponding print title and must be redeemed before then. CCH reserves the right to discontinue this program at any time for any business reason. For further details, please see the Casebook Connect End User Agreement.

PIN: 9111149523

32149

CONTRACTS

ASPEN CASEBOOK SERIES

CONTRACTS

CASES, DISCUSSION, AND PROBLEMS

Fourth Edition

Brian A. Blum
Lewis & Clark Law School

Amy C. Bushaw
Lewis & Clark Law School

 Wolters Kluwer

2 3 4 5 6 7 8 9 0

ISBN 978-1-4548-6835-4

Library of Congress Cataloging-in-Publication Data

Names: Blum, Brian A., author. | Bushaw, Amy C., 1958- author.
Title: Contracts : cases, discussion, and problems / Brian A. Blum (Lewis & Clark Law School), Amy C. Bushaw (Lewis & Clark Law School).
Description: Fourth edition. | New York : Wolters Kluwer, [2017] | Series: Aspen casebook series
Identifiers: LCCN 2016056685 | ISBN 9781454868354
Subjects: LCSH: Contracts—United States. | LCGFT: Casebooks
Classification: LCC KF801.A7 B58 2017 | DDC 346.7302/2—dc23
LC record available at https://lccn.loc.gov/2016056685

About Wolters Kluwer Legal & Regulatory U.S.

Wolters Kluwer Legal & Regulatory U.S. delivers expert content and solutions in the areas of law, corporate compliance, health compliance, reimbursement, and legal education. Its practical solutions help customers successfully navigate the demands of a changing environment to drive their daily activities, enhance decision quality and inspire confident outcomes.

Serving customers worldwide, its legal and regulatory portfolio includes products under the Aspen Publishers, CCH Incorporated, Kluwer Law International, ftwilliam.com and MediRegs names. They are regarded as exceptional and trusted resources for general legal and practice-specific knowledge, compliance and risk management, dynamic workflow solutions, and expert commentary.

SUMMARY OF CONTENTS

CONTENTS

10 PROMISSORY ESTOPPEL   341

15   CONTRACT INTERPRETATION AND CONSTRUCTION   569

18 CONDITIONS AND PROMISES 725

Our Approach to the Fourth Edition

We are grateful to have had the privilege of developing and refining the book through successive editions and have enjoyed teaching from it. We think that our approach and selection of materials has worked well, and we are gratified to have received positive comments on the book from our own students as well as from professors who have adopted it and students who have used it at other schools. In revising for the fourth edition, we have maintained the tone, style, and approach of the book while incorporating new ideas for teaching the subject and making selective changes to the book to update and enhance it, based on our own experience and suggestions from others. Although we have kept most of the cases that were in the third edition, we have added or substituted new interesting and compelling cases. We have also retained most of the problems from the third edition, but have added many new problems, including a number based on material that was previously in the form of notes. A new feature of this book is the addition of self-assessment multiple choice questions for each chapter, located at the end of the book.

Our philosophy and approach in writing this book has always been to present materials that are challenging and interesting but at the same time readable, clear, and accessible to students. Edited court opinions form the foundation of this book. We combine those opinions with full interconnecting explanatory text and with questions and problems designed to encourage students to think about and apply the legal principles raised by the cases or by other materials in the assignment. We and our students have found that the combination of text, court opinions, questions, and problems allows for more focused class preparation and enhances class discussion. We have therefore been careful, in revising this book for its fourth edition, to preserve what we consider to be the strongly beneficial features of the book and to adhere to its philosophy and approach. In each of the following sections, we outline the changes we have made in the fourth edition.

Our General Philosophy and Approach

Even a casual browsing of this book will reveal that it does not follow the traditional form of a casebook. It is not simply a collection of edited court opinions, extracts from law journal articles, and citations. Rather, it is an interwoven combination of explanatory text, edited court opinions, notes, questions, and problems. Throughout, we intend to provide a coherent and guided treatment of the subject of contract law and, more generally, of legal reasoning, argument, philosophy, and practice. In adopting this approach, we attempt to give students a sufficiently complete set of readings for each class assignment to enable them to prepare effectively for a rich and challenging class discussion.

The law is infinitely complex. We welcome the complexities and subtleties of contract law and recognize that it presents many questions that have no ready answers. However, we believe that there is no need to aggravate the law's complexity by keeping students in the dark about matters that, if presented clearly, can help them focus on more challenging issues, understand central rules, learn to apply principles and policies of law, and develop a sense of the overall structure and purpose of doctrine. We are confident that this book amply challenges any student but that it does so without creating undue confusion and consequent frustration. Having taught from this book for many years, we are convinced that this approach allows students to reach a subtler and more sophisticated appreciation of contract law and analysis.

This book is designed to foster, and to make more rewarding and effective, the collaborative discourse between the professor and students and among students. In our experience, the conversation is deeper, and the experience more enjoyable and enlightening, if the reading prepares students by providing context, background, and basic information and explanation that helps them understand the issues that will be tackled in class discussion. Although the book provides considerably more information and explanation than is commonly found in casebooks, this does not preempt class discussion or spoon-feed the students. On the contrary, it allows them to attain a level of knowledge and understanding before entering the classroom that greatly enhances their ability to make a meaningful contribution to class discussion and to engage in the kind of critical thinking and rigorous analysis that is so vital to an understanding of the law.

The Use of Case Analysis as a Teaching Tool

We continue to use the widely accepted pedagogy of case analysis as our principal teaching tool. Mastery of case analysis is fundamental, and it must be taught thoroughly to any person who aims to function as a lawyer in our legal system. We have edited cases carefully and sometimes quite rigorously to keep them to a manageable length and to focus the students' attention on the issues relevant to class discussion. In addition to using edited court opinions as principal cases, we also recount the facts and decisions of other cases to form the basis of problems.

We focus primarily on modern cases, and include a significant number of very recent ones. We believe in presenting modern cases because students find them more relevant and have more confidence that the opinions provide up-to-date expositions of the law. This is not to say that we disregard those older cases that remain superb teaching tools or that have become so well known that they have achieved iconic status. You will find a number of these cherished cases in the book. However, where we include an older case, we make a point of providing contextual discussion or a newer case as well so that students are able to appreciate the older case's relationship to the current state of the law.

Apart from their value as analytical tools, cases are also narratives. They tell stories about real people and actual events. A good story helps brighten what might otherwise be a dry discourse. We therefore try to include cases, where possible, with provocative and interesting facts. If the facts are funny or outrageous, or if they involve a well-known public figure or a timely social issue, so much the better.

The Use of Questions and Problems

We include questions on most cases or groups of cases. The questions are designed to aid the students' preparation for class by drawing their attention to difficult or crucial aspects of the doctrine and encouraging them to think about discussion points. Students should be able to answer every question from information provided in the book. Often, there is no one right answer to a question; thoughtful analysis can lead to different points of view.

We use problems to supplement or extrapolate from associated principal cases or to raise issues that may be covered more effectively by a problem. Some problems test students' understanding of, or their ability to apply, principles drawn from the preceding case. Others are connected to textual explanation and are used instead of a principal case to allow students to apply the principles expounded in the text to a new factual situation, or to test understanding of the text. Some problems are based on reported cases summarized in the text, while others present hypothetical facts. Often problems call on students to consider how particular issues should be handled in practice, and periodically they present legal issues in a planning or transactional context. Some of the problems are relatively quick and simple while others require more complex analysis. Most problems are open to more than one analysis and require students to articulate and justify their resolution of the problem.

Self-Assessment Questions

We have added new self-assessment multiple choice questions to this edition of the book. The purpose of these questions is give students a means of self-testing their understanding of the materials after completing each chapter of the book. There are self-assessment questions and answers for each chapter of the book, located at the end of the book.

The Purpose of the Interconnecting Text

The cases, problems, and questions are bound together by interconnecting text throughout the book. It concisely introduces and explains concepts, places materials in context, and informs an exploration of the genuinely subtle and challenging aspects of contract law. We try to make the text clear and concrete, so it often includes explanatory examples or hypotheticals. Exposition is also used to incorporate commentary, criticism, and theoretical perspectives from legal scholarship. Also, because we believe that it is vital for students to see the relationship among the many topics that form contract law, we use the text, problems, and questions to help students discover the connections and analogies among different aspects of the course.

The Exploration of Issues Beyond Contract Law

While we devote most of our effort to drawing out the principles, policies, norms, and theory of contract law, we make it a point to go beyond this primary subject matter to explore the broader legal and societal fabric of which contract law forms an inseparable part. We pay particular attention to legal process, analysis, and argument. We raise litigation and procedural questions to help students to realize that procedural issues can significantly affect the resolution of contract disputes and to encourage students to discover connections between their contracts and their civil procedure courses. As much as possible, we have integrated issues of legal ethics into our discussion. Where the cases are conducive to the introduction of other themes, such as agency, consumer protection, or the relationship between contract and tort, we take the opportunity to raise them.

Planning and Drafting Issues

Our primary focus on cases means that most contract issues appear through the lens of litigation. However, it is important to realize that most contracts do not end up in litigation. In this edition, we continue our approach of including questions and problems that raise transactional issues and that shift focus from doctrinal analysis or dispute resolution to provide exposure to the practical skills involved in advising clients, negotiating and drafting contracts.

Standard Contracts and Contracting Via Technology

Because standard contracts are so prevalent, we place particular emphasis on them throughout the book. As part of this focus, we pay close attention to the process of contracting through communications technology, including Internet-based contracts.

Remedies

Disputes over contracts almost always involve a "bottom line." One of the parties seeks the payment of damages or some other remedy from the other. Contract remedies are therefore a major aspect of contract law. We follow the traditional organization of the contracts course by beginning with the formation of contracts and focusing on remedies toward the end of the book, in Chapters 20 and 21. However, the entire book is written with sensitivity to remedial issues, and we raise them throughout. Therefore, students will have acquired a basic knowledge of remedies even before reaching the more intensive exposure to remedies in Chapters 20 and 21. This should be particularly helpful in shorter courses, where there is not enough time to cover remedies in detail. For courses where there is more time to allocate to remedies, but not enough to cover Chapters 20 and 21 fully, we have divided those chapters into smaller, self-contained units so that shorter assignments can be made. We are aware that some professors prefer to begin the contracts course with remedies and we have therefore designed Chapters 20 and 21 so that students do not need to have studied other topics before working with them.

Sales of Goods

Some contracts courses do not cover sales of goods under the Uniform Commercial Code (UCC) Article 2 in detail or at all, and defer a significant portion of the coverage of sales of goods to an upper-class course. We do cover sales of goods throughout this book but have attempted to make the book adaptable so that a professor who wishes to limit the students' exposure to sales of goods can do so. Our treatment includes discussion of applicable UCC Article 2 provisions in each chapter, and we regularly compare UCC provisions to analogous rules of general contract law. We have found that a thorough treatment of sales of goods alongside common law contracts works well. It makes students constantly aware that sales of goods may be subject to different rules and allows the students to contrast those rules with the common law as we progress through the course. It also helps them appreciate the influence of the UCC on the development of the common law.

We include in the materials the text of the applicable provisions of Article 2 of the UCC, together with relevant general provisions from Article 1.[1] We have found that students appreciate having all the relevant statutory material in the book. They do not need a separate statutory supplement. (However, some

---

[1] Article 1 was revised in 2001. That revision has been widely enacted by states, and it is used in this book. There was an attempt to revise Article 2 in 2003, but the revision was not enacted by any state and was eventually abandoned. Other than a brief mention to alert students to this history, we do not deal with the failed effort to amend Article 2.

professors still prefer to assign a statutory supplement that sets out the entire text and Official Comments of these articles.)

Global Perspectives

To introduce students to a global perspective on contract law, we include notes at the end of most chapters on the UNIDROIT Principles of International Commercial Contracts (Third Edition, promulgated in 2010) and the United Nations Convention on Contracts for the International Sale of Goods (CISG). The notes are brief and merely expose students in broad terms to the similarities and differences between domestic law and the law that may be applicable to transactions across international borders. We also refer to comparative law perspectives where we feel that it is illuminating to do so.

We have enjoyed writing this fourth edition. We hope that others enjoy it too and find it enlightening, supportive, and challenging.

Brian Blum
Amy Bushaw

February 2017

ACKNOWLEDGMENTS

We owe thanks to many people who helped us with this book in all of its four editions. We have had able research assistance from several Lewis & Clark students. Our students in successive contracts classes have challenged, encouraged, and informed us by their reactions to these materials. We have also received welcome and helpful comments and suggestions from colleagues who have adopted this book and sometimes from their students as well. We thank them for having taken the trouble to communicate with us.

We are grateful for the guidance, enthusiasm, and excellent editorial, publication, and postpublication work by many members of staff at Wolters Kluwer. Provisions from the Restatement, Second, of Contracts and the Official Text of the Uniform Commercial Code (copyright © by the American Law Institute) are reprinted with permission.

To enhance the readability of cases and to minimize distractions, we have followed a number of editing conventions in our reproduction of court opinions:

1. We have eliminated all citations that we feel are not needed for teaching purposes. Although we indicate omission of text from an opinion by ellipsis, we do not indicate the omission of citations in cases.

2. We have eliminated footnotes in cases without indication. We have retained only those footnotes that we consider useful or necessary for teaching purposes. In many places, we have added our own footnotes to opinions as explanations or comments on the case. Within cases, our footnotes conclude with the abbreviation "EDS." to distinguish them from the court's footnotes. We have renumbered footnotes in cases so that all footnotes in each chapter are consecutive.

3. Where appropriate to reduce length or complexity, we have substituted our own summaries of the facts of cases or of discussion in opinions. Our own text within cases is enclosed in square brackets.

4. We have brought some uniformity to divergent citation forms in the cases, but some inconsistencies remain because of citation practices or rules in different jurisdictions.

5. We have altered paragraph breaks in opinions where readability called for this adjustment.

6. We have corrected obvious typographical or grammatical errors in opinions without indication.

CONTRACTS

CHAPTER 1

Introduction to Contracts

A | AN INTRODUCTION TO THE STUDY OF CONTRACT LAW

1. The Legal Definition of Contract

Even as they enter law school, most students have a pretty good idea of what contracts are and of the pervasive role they play in daily life. This book examines the rules, principles, and concepts of the law that govern the making of contracts, their performance, and enforcement. The word "contract" may be used in lay language to describe any form of agreement or consensual relationship. In law, however, the word is used more narrowly to <u>signify a legal relationship</u> that must have specific qualities and consequences. Section 1 of the Restatement, Second, of Contracts[1] defines "contract" as "a promise or a set of promises for the breach of which the law gives a remedy, or the performance of which the law in some way recognizes as a duty." Admittedly, this is rather a vague definition that seems to raise more questions than it answers. However, it does suggest a number of key factors that must be present for an arrangement to qualify as a contract. Specifically, a contract is an exchange relationship, created by agreement between two or more parties, containing at least one promise, and recognized as enforceable in law. In a few types of transactions (covered by a rule known as the Statute of Frauds), the agreement must be recorded

---

[1] The Restatement, Second, of Contracts is a highly influential text that sets out principles of contract law. It is described more fully in Section A.4.b.

either in <u>writing</u> or <u>electronically</u> to qualify as a legally enforceable contract, but in most cases an <u>oral agreement is sufficient</u> and no particular formalities are needed.

2. The Sources, Nature, and Traditions of Contract Law

a. The Roots of Contract Law

[margin note: Contracts developed late in law history]

Contract law occupies such a predominant role in our modern legal system that it is hard to imagine that this has not always been so. However, the law of contracts as a coherent, systematic body of rules developed quite late in the history of our law and did not take the form recognizable today until the latter part of the nineteenth century. The classifications of legal categories that are familiar to us today—such as contracts, torts, and property—were not recognized in early English common law.[2] Early law was very formalistic. To sue, the plaintiff had to fit his claim into one of a number of established writs (often called "forms of action"), and if the facts of the case did not fit into a writ, no relief was available. Certain writs did exist for types of claims that we would classify as contracts today, but these were very narrow and did not cover the situation in which a plaintiff sought to enforce an executory contract—that is, one that he had not yet fully performed.

[margin note: writ → form of action]

During the Middle Ages English courts began to recognize that the breach of an executory agreement should give rise to a legal action. Because no form of action existed for such suits, courts adapted one of the forms of action available for tort to serve the purpose of enforcing contractual promises. The form used was known as "trespass on the case," a form of action that lay for injury resulting from wrongful nonviolent action. (Trespass on the case was distinguished from trespass, which lay for torts involving violence.) The courts began the process of expansion by including in the writ of trespass on the case situations in which a person undertook to perform a duty and then performed it improperly, thereby causing harm. In its original form, the writ covered only wrongful performance ←(misfeasance), and did not extend to include failure to perform altogether (nonfeasance). Because liability for this variety of trespass on the case was based on a promise—an agreed assumption of a duty—the cause of action became known as "assumpsit" (Latin for "he has taken up" the duty). In time, liability for the breach of an executory contract expanded beyond improper performance to cover failure to perform at all. The action of assumpsit became the foundation of what eventually grew, by slow development over many centuries, into what we now recognize as the general cause of action for breach of contract. When

[margin note: trespass on the case]

[margin note: wrongful performance]

[margin note: failure to perform]

---

[2] The term "common law" is explained below.

the British settled the American colonies, they brought this growing but still rudimentary collection of rules and principles with them, and it formed the basis of colonial law and ultimately state contract law.[3]

Because contract law was developed by courts in performing their ongoing function of deciding cases, its evolution was not systematic or neatly organized. By the nineteenth century, many of the rules and principles that form the basis of modern contract law had been formulated, but they had not yet been comprehensively organized into a coherent compendium. The work of constructing such a compilation of the law of contracts of the kind that we would expect to find today in an authoritative treatise was begun not much more than a century ago. We will return to the work of these nineteenth-century jurists shortly in our overview of the theoretical themes of contract law in Section A.5. But first we will briefly introduce the sources and nature of contract law in our legal system.

b. Contract as State Law Applied in Both State and Federal Courts

Except in some very narrow and specific circumstances (for example, where the federal government enters contracts subject to federal procurement statutes or has enacted a particular law in the exercise of its power to regulate interstate commerce), contracts are governed by state law. Therefore, there is no single and unified law of contracts in the United States. Rather, there are as many separate and distinct systems of contract law as there are states and territories. A practitioner must be concerned with the law of contracts applicable in the specific state that governs the transaction, but law schools, whose students may end up practicing anywhere in the country, must adopt a wider view. We therefore teach contracts as if it is a national law. For the most part, this works out well, because the law in every state (except Louisiana[4]) derives from the same source—the common law of England. As the law has developed in each state, it is influenced by what happens in other states and by nationwide trends in economic and social philosophy. Therefore, while the individual state systems of contract law may vary in matters of detail, they share a core of rules and

so many types of contract law

* *all 49 states come from the common law of england*

---

[3] Much has been written on the history of the law of contracts. For students who are interested in reading more detailed, but brief and manageable accounts of this history, we recommend E. Allan Farnsworth, *Contracts* 9-19 (4th ed. 2004), and John E. Murray, Jr., *Murray on Contracts* 4-11 (5th ed. 2011). For those with a deeper interest in the historical development of contract law in this country, a classic work is Lawrence M. Friedman, *Contract Law in America* (U. Wis. Press 1965).

[4] Before it became a U.S. Territory, Louisiana was colonized successively by Spain and France. As a result, Civilian law was well established in Louisiana by the time of statehood. In the early nineteenth century, Louisiana codified its law, drawing on its Spanish and French legal traditions and influenced heavily by the Code Napoléon. (The Code Napoléon and the meaning of the term "Civilian" are explained in the text.) Although Louisiana is the only state whose law is not derived from the law of England, many of its legal rules are very similar to those of other states. This is partly because the underlying legal systems of England and continental Europe often deal with issues in similar ways, and partly because states influence each other in the development of the law.

principles that permit generalization. This is particularly true at the level of fundamental values, reasoning, and analysis.

Although most contract suits must be brought in state court, and federal courts do not have jurisdiction to hear them, some contract suits do fall within the jurisdiction of a federal court. A federal court may have jurisdiction over a contracts case for one of a number of reasons. It acquires diversity jurisdiction if the parties are citizens of different states and the amount in controversy exceeds the statutory minimum. Federal courts also have jurisdiction if the federal government is a party to the contract, if the suit arises under a federal procedure such as bankruptcy, or if it involves a federal question. Where a federal court hears a contract suit, it commonly applies the law of the state whose law governs the transaction.

c. The Meaning of "Common Law"

(i) "Common Law" Denotes Our Legal System as a Whole. In England, the term "common law" developed to distinguish the body of English national law common to all of England from local law and custom. (Note that we refer to English common law. It is incorrect to speak of "British" common law because Scotland's legal system is distinct from England's.) As mentioned earlier, the law of contracts, like all American law, is based on the common law of England, transplanted to America by the colonists and used by the colonies—and later by the states—as the basis of their legal systems. This also happened in most of the other colonies established by Great Britain around the world. This legacy has generally survived. As a result, England, the United States, Canada, Australia, India, and many other countries that used to be part of the British Empire share the common law legal tradition.

A second great legal tradition derives from continental Europe. It has its basis in ancient Roman law, and is called "Civilian" or "civil law" in recognition of its roots in the Roman Civil Code, called the *Corpus Juris Civilis*. Over the centuries, continental scholars expanded and built on the Roman law base to create the modern Civilian system. One of the most important features of the system is its comprehensive codification. During the nineteenth century, European countries created massive codes, reducing the entire body of national law into legislative form. The preeminent codifications were accomplished in France (the Code Napoléon) and Germany, and these were used as models in many other countries. All of continental Europe, as well as many countries that were colonies of European powers, adopted codes. However, the use of these codes was not confined to countries that followed the Roman law tradition. Because the codes were so comprehensive and coherent, they were attractive models for countries that wished to modernize their legal systems. As a result, most countries in the world other than those that were part of the British sphere imported one or another of the European codifications as their basic legal framework.

[handwritten margin note: common → court heavy civil → rely on codes]

Although common law and civil law have many similarities in concepts and in substantive rules, they differ quite significantly in many ways. As you might imagine, the most important differences lie in the underlying style and concept of the systems. The common law places great reliance on the role of courts as participants in the creation of law, while the civil law focuses heavily on the code as the source of law and subordinates the judicial lawmaking role. This difference in approach permeates each system and emerges in many different ways.

(ii) "Common Law" Is Used Within Our Legal System to Distinguish Judge-Made Law from Legislation and to Describe an Approach to Legal Analysis. While "common law" describes our legal system as a whole, it is also used within our legal system in two related narrower senses. First, it distinguishes those areas of the law that derive principally from judicial decision rather than from statute. In this sense, contracts is a common law subject because most of its rules are not found in legislation, but have been developed by courts. This does not mean that there are no statutes governing contracts. Indeed, many do exist, of which Article 2 of the Uniform Commercial Code, discussed in Chapter 2, is a prime example. However, judge-made law predominates in the field. (By contrast, tax law, created by and based on the Internal Revenue Code—legislation passed by Congress—is classified as a statutory subject.) Second, "common law" describes an approach to the analysis and development of the law. Even in an area governed by statute, the courts play a vital role in interpreting and developing the law by applying general rules to specific cases. As a result, gaps in the law are filled and legal principles are expounded through the process of judicial decision making. Judicial interpretations of statutes are thus themselves a source of law.

[handwritten margin note: there are contract laws but most of the feild come from judges]

The use of judicial opinions as a means of studying the law is partly explained by the importance of judge-made law in our system. However, cases do not simply serve the purpose of setting out legal doctrine. A treatise could do this more efficiently. Opinions also teach legal argument and analysis, and provide concrete illustrations of the application of law to resolve disputes, show the relationship between law and fact, and provide insight into the many considerations that must be taken into account in formulating and applying the law. Because the courts' lawmaking power is so fundamental a part of our legal system, the doctrine of precedent serves a pivotal role in our law.

[handwritten margin note: precedent is pivotal]

3. The Doctrine of Precedent and Case Analysis

a. The Doctrine of Precedent

[handwritten note: ★decide the case before you]

In a system in which judges have no lawmaking role (as is generally true of most courts in Civilian systems), the court's sole function is to decide the case before it, thereby resolving the dispute between the parties. However, if as in common law systems, the court's opinion establishes or reaffirms legal rules, its reach goes beyond the immediate parties. The opinion creates generally applicable law that has a binding effect on everyone within the jurisdiction, and must be followed in future cases involving other parties but substantially similar facts—that is, the opinion creates a precedent. This is the doctrine of precedent (described in Latin as *stare decisis*, meaning "to stand with what has been decided"). For this reason, court opinions constitute a primary source of law and are published.

The operation of precedent has many complexities that we do not attempt to explore in this introductory note. We confine ourselves to a few broad general principles that you may find helpful as you begin to analyze cases:

1. Not every court is senior enough to establish precedent. For example, decisions of trial courts do not usually create precedents; only the decisions of appellate courts have binding force. (This explains why most of the opinions that you will read are delivered by appellate courts. In fact, in most states, trial court opinions are not published.)

2. Appellate courts do not officially publish (report) every opinion that they issue. In both the federal and state systems, courts are selective in deciding which opinions are worthy of being published in the official court reports, and rules of court may contain guidelines to be followed by courts in deciding which of their opinions should be reported. In the days before the creation of online databases such as Westlaw and Lexis, it was very difficult to find unreported decisions. However, with the advent of these databases, unreported decisions have become accessible. (You will find a number of such cases in this book, which have only the Westlaw citation and a note that the case is not officially reported.) The precedential weight of unreported decisions varies from one jurisdiction to another, and some court rules limit the use of unreported cases in briefs.

3. Precedents do not bind every court. The force of a precedent depends on the jurisdiction in which it is decided and the jurisdiction whose law it applies.

The effect of precedent is illustrated in the following example. Say that Sally Conn and Chip Micro live in the state of Cyberia. (We use a fictional state in this example to provide a generalized sketch of the judicial structure of a state.) Sally has formed a startup high-technology business, and Chip is a genius inventor. Sally and Chip agree orally that Sally will employ Chip for two years to work on a new product that Sally is developing. Sally reneges on this agreement and Chip sues her for damages in a Cyberia trial court. Because both parties live in Cyberia and the agreement was entered there, Cyberia law governs the transaction.[5]

---

[5] The question of which jurisdiction's law governs a particular transaction (called choice of law) is complex and is beyond the scope of this book. Choice of law—the determination of the state law that must be applied to resolve a legal issue—is different from the question of which court has jurisdiction to hear the case. Therefore, although a state court often does apply the law of its own state in resolving the case, it sometimes happens that the law governing the transaction is the law of another state. For purposes of our introduction to the doctrine of precedent, we use the least complicated situation of a court applying its own state's law.

Upon being served with Chip's complaint, Sally makes a motion before the trial court for dismissal of his suit. Sally denies that she entered into a legally binding contract with Chip and claims that even if the parties did intend a contractual commitment, their oral agreement lacks the formalities required by law for enforcement as a contract.[6] After hearing argument on the legal issue involved in the motion to dismiss, the trial court agrees with Sally. The court finds that because the agreement could not be performed within a year of its making, it had to be recorded in writing or in retrievable electronic form and signed by Sally to be legally enforceable as a contract. Therefore, even if the parties did make the agreement alleged by Chip, the agreement was oral and unenforceable. Accordingly, the trial court awards judgment to Sally, dismissing Chip's suit.

Chip feels the trial court was wrong and he decides to appeal its decision. Like most states, Cyberia has a judicial structure consisting of two levels of appellate court. Appeals from the decision of a trial court must first be made to the Cyberia Court of Appeals, the state's lower appellate court. Thereafter, there is the possibility of an appeal to the Cyberia Supreme Court, the state's highest court, provided that the Supreme Court agrees to hear the appeal. (The Supreme Court does not review every case appealed to it. It selects only those cases that it considers legally significant or otherwise worthy of its consideration. The party who wishes to appeal to the Supreme Court must file a process, commonly called a writ of certiorari or a writ of review, requesting the Supreme Court to hear the appeal. If the court decides to hear the case, it grants the writ.)

The Court of Appeals, applying Cyberia law, upholds the trial court. The precedent set by the Court of Appeals is absolutely binding only on courts in Cyberia that are inferior to the Court of Appeals. In any case that arises in the future in the state involving the point of law on which the Court of Appeals has pronounced in this case, the trial court must apply the rule of law established by the Court of Appeals. Although the Court of Appeals is, in a sense, also bound by its own decision and is expected to follow its own precedents, it has the power to overrule them if it concludes that they are wrong.

The Cyberia Supreme Court is not bound by the precedent set by the Court of Appeals. Of course, if Chip appealed the decision further to the Cyberia Supreme Court and the Supreme Court accepted the appeal, the court could reverse the decision of the lower court in this case. If Chip does not appeal to the Supreme Court, the rule, as settled by the Court of Appeals, remains the law until such time as the Court of Appeals considers a future case raising the same legal rule and overrules its prior decision, or a future case makes its way to the Supreme Court. If the Supreme Court does hear a future case involving the rule established by the Court of Appeals, the Supreme Court may agree with the Court of Appeals' view of the law and give its stamp of authority to the

---

[6] Although oral contracts are generally enforceable, certain kinds of contracts, such as a contract that cannot be performed within a year of its making, must be recorded and signed by the party against whom enforcement is sought. (The record and signature may be in a hard-copy or electronic form.) This formal requirement, known as the Statute of Frauds, is discussed in Chapter 8.

precedent, or it may disagree and establish a different rule. That rule then binds all courts in the state. As is true of the Court of Appeals, the Supreme Court will normally follow its own precedents, but it has the power to overrule them if persuaded that they are wrong. In all cases (except those involving constitutional interpretation) the legislature has the final say on what the legal rule should be. If the legislature disagrees with a legal rule established by judicial precedent, including Supreme Court precedent, it has the power to pass a statute that changes the rule.

As noted above, precedents are binding only in the state over which the court has jurisdiction. Although the decision of the Cyberia Supreme Court binds the courts in that state, it has no binding effect in another state. Therefore, if a similar issue later arose in a court in another state, the courts of that other state have no duty to follow the Cyberia precedent. However, if the issue has not been settled by binding precedent in the other state, its courts may consult the Cyberia decision (as well as any from additional states) as persuasive authority.

Many opinions are long and involve complex facts and several legal issues. It can therefore be difficult to pinpoint exactly what part of the opinion is binding precedent. It is only the rule or holding of the case (in Latin, *ratio decidendi*, roughly translated as "the reason for the decision") that constitutes the binding part of the precedent. This is the narrowest and most crucial part of the opinion, the articulation of the rule that is directly applicable to the facts of the case and is needed to resolve it. In addition to expressing the rule that disposes of the case, a court commonly expounds more widely on the law—for example, by indicating how the case might have been decided had the facts been different. This part of the opinion, called *obiter dictum* (roughly translated as "said in passing" and usually stated in abbreviated form as "dictum") has persuasive force, but is not the law.

Appellate courts sit in panels or en banc (that is, the case is decided by a group of judges). Quite often, the panel is not unanimous. One or more judges may dissent from the majority opinion or may concur in it. (Although in lay usage "concurrence" means agreement, it has a different meaning in the judicial context. The concurring judge agrees with the conclusion reached by the majority but disagrees with or wishes to express a qualification on the rationale for that conclusion.) Where dissenting or concurring opinions are published, they are merely of persuasive weight. The majority opinion establishes the rule of the case.

Questions following the *Kakaes* case in this chapter and the *Audio Visual Artistry* case in Chapter 2 focus on the use and force of precedent. However, you should not stop thinking about precedent thereafter, and should constantly be conscious of the precedential authority on which an opinion is based, and the precedential effect of that opinion on subsequent cases.

b. Reading and Briefing Cases

It is not enough just to extract the legal doctrine expounded in a case. To study a case properly, you must pay careful attention to the facts on which the court's decision is based, the procedural context in which it is decided, and any broader policy considerations that might motivate the decision. To properly understand a judicial opinion, you must be conscious of the court's rationale, its disposition of the parties' arguments, and the scope of its decision. You also need to go beyond the confines of the opinion itself, to evaluate it critically, explore its possible permutations, and seek its relationship to broader themes of the law. A common method of studying a case is to brief it—that is, to write notes on it in an organized way to take account of all the case's salient aspects. The exact form that a brief takes is influenced by the case itself and by the student's individual learning style. However we offer some general guidelines that will help you to think about what you should be extracting from your study of a case:

1. *Get the parties straight.* Make sure you know who is suing whom and what their relationship is. Although you need to know which party is the plaintiff and which is the defendant, it helps to avoid confusion if you make sure that you know, apart from the parties' relationship in the litigation, what their relationship was in the transaction that is being litigated. (For example, if the case involves a sale, is the plaintiff the buyer or the seller?)

2. *Identify what is being claimed in the case.* Take note of the cause (or causes) of action on which the plaintiff bases the suit as well as the remedy sought. Determine who wins the case and why.

3. *Take note of the procedural posture of the case, including the history of the lawsuit.* The procedural context of the opinion is an important ingredient in interpreting it. For example, an opinion delivered on some preliminary motion before trial must be read differently from one rendered after trial. In an appellate case, identify the disposition in the lower court (or courts). Take note of the stage the case had reached at the time of the appeal and the decision that is being appealed.

4. *Take careful note of the facts of the case.* Facts are crucial to the decision, and the scope and effect of an opinion cannot be properly understood without careful examination of the facts on which it is based. In its opinion, the court sets out the facts that it accepts for the purpose of the opinion, and also indicates if those facts are agreed to by the parties, disputed but established at trial, or based on preliminary (and as yet unproved) allegations. Of course, not every fact mentioned by the court is central or even relevant to the case, so you also need to interpret the opinion to evaluate the relative importance of each fact.

5. *Identify the legal issues involved.* Identify each legal issue that is presented by the case. Some cases hinge on a single question of law, but others involve more than one issue. If more than one legal issue is discussed, you should try to decide which are central, forming the rule of the case, and which are dicta.

6. *Analyze all the argumentation in the opinion.* Study and evaluate not only the court's argument, but also any other arguments (such as those of the lower courts, the parties, or a dissenting or concurring judge) that may be set out in

the opinion, and that offer supporting, alternative, or contrasting views. Take note of the use of authoritative and persuasive precedent, reasoning, and any expressed or underlying policy rationales.

7. *Evaluate the opinion critically.* Having studied the court's disposition as well as any other arguments advanced, form a view of the case. Do you agree with the reasoning or the result or both? Articulate why you agree or disagree. (Yes, you are allowed to disagree with the court, even though the judge is wise and vastly experienced and you are just a first-year law student.)

8. *Consider whether the case ties into other concepts that you have studied.* Of course, this will be difficult to do at the beginning, but as you proceed with your study of law, you will find that there are many analogies and themes that interweave and interconnect, not only in the law of contracts, but in the law as a whole. We will often raise these connections in the text and questions, but you should be thinking about this on your own as well.

c. Learning the Law Through Cases and Problems

The study of law through cases has been used in American law schools for over a century, albeit with a shifting emphasis. The focus on case law has been so enduring because it offers a great opportunity to explore the rules, principles, and policies of the law in the context of real disputes. Cases provide a concrete, fact-based context that exposes the methodology of legal argument and analysis. Such instruction forms the basis of what is needed not only by the litigator but also by the lawyer who helps in planning and facilitating contractual relationships. By anticipating what might go wrong, a lawyer can help avoid future disputes. In addition to cases, we use problems to allow you to engage in exercises of legal methodology by analyzing facts and applying legal rules in order to resolve hypothetical disputes.

There is a drawback to a strong focus on cases. It tends to be oriented toward litigation and may therefore not be attentive enough to other important lawyering skills such as client counseling, negotiation, and drafting. Many lawyers spend their time trying to solve problems, facilitate transactions, and avoid litigation. Much legal work relating to contracts is concerned with forming and performing them, not with fighting over them. The vast majority of contracts do not end up in court. Most are made and consummated without friction. Where one party does not perform as promised or a dispute arises, the problem is commonly resolved without recourse to litigation—by negotiation, a consensual termination of the relationship, or extrajudicial dispute resolution. Even if matters get to the stage of bringing suit, cases are frequently settled before or during trial. Of those cases that are tried, even a smaller number are appealed. Therefore, a course that is based largely on the study of appellate court opinions—in some ways, the very worst examples of the breakdown of the relationship—could provide a skewed perspective of what really happens in most transactions.

It should also be noted that most cases that reach the level of appeal concern legal issues that are uncertain. Competent and ethical attorneys do not waste their clients' money by recommending extended litigation and appeals unless there is at least a tenable argument to be made in support of a client's position. Because casebooks concentrate on appellate cases, particularly on cases that present interesting issues, students could quite easily form the impression that the whole of contract law is an ambiguous mess in which every question has at least two contending answers. It is therefore worth cautioning that there are many situations that do not result in litigation simply because the rights and duties of the parties are clear.

You should bear these concerns in mind as you explore the cases in this book. We regularly draw them to your attention through text, questions, and problems which will give you the opportunity of thinking beyond litigation to matters of planning, counseling, drafting, and informal dispute resolution.

4. The Role of Scholarly Commentary

a. The Influence of Scholarly Writing

While court opinions contain authoritative discussions of the law, they are, of course, not the only source of legal commentary. In studying and seeking to understand the law, lawyers (including professors and judges) and law students rely heavily on the work of scholars who write books and articles to explain, analyze, debate, and theorize on the law. Unlike court opinions, these scholarly texts do not make law—they cannot bind a court. (They are commonly called "secondary authority.") However, good, thoughtful commentary is persuasive and is often cited and discussed in court opinions. In this text, we keep the citation of secondary authority to a minimum but periodically refer to significant books and articles. There are, however, four comprehensive treatments of contract law that have had dominant influence over the last century, and these are singled out for mention in this introduction.

The first, originally written in the 1920s, is Professor Samuel Williston's multivolume *Treatise on the Law of Contracts.* Williston was surely the most influential contracts scholar of his day, and his treatise, as well as his work on the Restatement of Contracts, mentioned below, did more than any other secondary commentary to formulate and set the tone for contract law in the twentieth century. In the 1950s another legendary scholar of contract law, Professor Arthur Corbin, published his own multivolume treatise, *Corbin on Contracts.* Corbin built on Williston's foundations but significantly departed from his basic philosophy of law.[7] Corbin's work has had a profound and continuing

---

[7] The differing philosophies of Williston and Corbin are briefly described in Section A.5.

influence on the development of contract law. Currently, the preeminent comprehensive treatise on contract law is *Contracts* by Professor E. Allan Farnsworth, who was also centrally involved in the drafting of the Restatement, Second, of Contracts.[8] The Restatement, Second, of Contracts (referred to from now on as the Restatement, Second) is the fourth commentary on this list. It is not a typical treatise and therefore merits further explanation.

b. The Restatement, Second → 1981

The original Restatement of Contracts was published in 1932 by the American Law Institute (ALI), a prestigious national organization formed for the purpose of creating compilations of legal rules in various common law fields. The model chosen by the ALI for the Restatement of Contracts (and other Restatements) was to structure the book in a way that makes it look more like a statute than a treatise. It sets out rules of contract law in statutory form—that is, in numbered sections, with each section being followed by commentary and illustrations. Williston was the Reporter (the principal drafter) for the Restatement of Contracts, and Corbin was a primary adviser. The Restatement of Contracts was immensely influential and was constantly cited by cases. By the 1950s the ALI decided that the Restatement needed to be updated, and work was begun on the Restatement, Second. Its initial Reporter was Professor Robert Braucher, who was succeeded by Farnsworth during the course of drafting. Corbin continued as an advisor until his death. The Restatement, Second, was published in 1981.

Like the original Restatement, the Restatement, Second, continues to be very influential, as you will notice from the number of times that you see it cited in the cases. It follows the format and organization of the original Restatement but seeks to update the rules and commentary to reflect developments since the 1930s. The rules in the Restatement, Second, are generally based on decided cases, but they do not necessarily represent the law as it exists in any particular jurisdiction. As we have already noted, contracts are governed by state law, and some variations occur between states. In some areas, the authors of the Restatement, Second, based their rule on what the majority of courts have decided, but in others they adopted a less well-established rule because they felt it was the best rule; that is, the Restatement, Second, does not necessarily "restate" clearly established law. Sometimes it articulates the law as it exists in most states, but sometimes it expresses what the drafters considered to be the best rule, even though it may not be widely recognized by courts.

---

[8] Two other well-respected modern treatises on contract law are Joseph M. Perillo, *Calamari and Perillo on Contracts* (6th ed. 2009), and John E. Murray, Jr., *Murray on Contracts* (5th ed. 2011).

↑ for commercial transactions

One of the significant influences in the drafting of the Restatement, Second, was the enactment of the Uniform Commercial Code (UCC)[9] in the period following the publication of the original Restatement. The drafters believed that, in many situations, the reforms relating to sales of goods in UCC Article 2 should *sale of goods* be adopted by the courts in relation to other contracts. They therefore drafted many sections of the Restatement, Second, so as to conform to the equivalent provisions in Article 2. This has influenced courts in their development of common law principles so that the common law has drawn closer to Article 2. You will notice this trend as this course proceeds.

bound to UCC not to restatement

It is worth stressing again (because students often forget this) that although the Restatement, Second, reads like a statute, with numbered sections and language in statutory form, it is not a statute; it is a treatise. Therefore, although courts give it great deference and often rely on it as persuasive authority, it is not the same as the UCC, which forms the basis of statutes enacted into law by state legislatures. While courts are bound to follow statutes such as the UCC where the transaction is governed by the statute, they are not constrained to adopt the position taken by the Restatement, Second.

5. Theoretical Perspectives on Contract Law

The law is composed of many rules, but it is much more than a collection of rules. Because the law is a means through which society seeks to achieve desired ends, legal rules must be understood in light of the law's underlying purposes. Therefore, as important as it is to know the rules of law, an examination confined to those rules is superficial and cannot produce true insight into what the law is really about. We must go further and look at the more fundamental questions: Why are the rules as they are? What societal goals do they and should they seek to achieve? Are they the most effective rules for achieving those aims? Are the rules just and morally justifiable? Do the rules, as a whole, form a coherent and rational system for dealing with the interactions that they govern? In short, every time we study a topic in this course, we must be conscious not only of being able to describe what the rules are, but also to consider the policies

have to think about where the law came from

that generate the rules, and to think about the normative questions that justify the rules or that may form the basis for challenging them. As you may expect, many judges and scholarly commentators have written on the policy and jurisprudence of the law of contracts. These writings show that there is sometimes wide agreement, but also often strong disagreement on the nature and underlying purposes of contract law and on the means that it should employ to achieve optimal societal benefits. This introduction attempts, in very broad

---

[9] The UCC is introduced in Chapter 2. It was drafted for the purpose of unifying state law relating to various commercial transactions and has been enacted as a statute by state legislatures. Article 2 of the UCC governs sales of goods.

Contract law has values & rules

terms, to give you a brief initial overview of some of the thinking on these issues over the last century. This survey is quite generalized and abstract, but it will at least alert you to the fact that contract law embodies values as well as rules, and that there are different ways of seeing its role and ultimate goals.

Jurisprudential thinkers have been pondering the moral underpinnings and social value of contract law for many centuries; however, we will begin our survey in late-nineteenth-century America. This was the era known as the "classical period" of American contract law, when the great work of systematizing the law was first undertaken. By that time, many fundamental ideas about contract had been established: the ability to enter into contracts and the right to be bound only by voluntarily and consensual undertakings—that is, freedom of contract—was firmly grounded, not only in the common law, but in the U.S. Constitution.[10] Contract was seen as an exercise of free will by autonomous parties acting pursuant to their right to order their private relationships by agreement. It was also well understood that the right to make and demand enforcement of contracts carried with it the correlative legal and moral duty to keep contractual promises. Although contracts were recognized as private arrangements between the parties involved, it had long been settled that the state played a vital role in setting the rules that governed these relationships and provided a mechanism for enforcing them.

State played a role in setting rules

The classical conception of contract was built on these foundations, but it was molded by two philosophical strains that had become dominant by the late nineteenth century. One was based on then-current economic theory and the other derived from a conception of the role and nature of law and government. Belief in capitalism and the virtues of a free market were the economic underpinnings of classicism. Laissez-faire[11] economic theories had taken root by this time, extolling the free market and frowning upon government regulation. Classicists felt that too much regulation of contracts, either by legislatures or by courts, would not only undermine freedom of contract but would interfere with the wealth-maximizing power of a free market. Therefore, the law should give parties wide leeway to order their relationships as they saw fit. This meant that legislatures should not enact laws that burdened or restricted contracting, and that courts should give effect to the expressed will of the parties in the absence of a clear showing that a party had been forced or tricked into manifesting assent to a contract by outrageously dishonest or coercive behavior.

push for less government involvement in contracts

---

[10] The two provisions of the U.S. Constitution that bear most directly on freedom of contract are the due process clause, U.S. Const. amend. V and XIV, and the contracts clause, U.S. Const. art. 1, §10. The due process clause, which prohibits federal and state government from depriving persons of "life, liberty, or property, without due process of law" protects the ability to enter into relationships and the right not to be held to relationships that are not formed voluntarily. The contracts clause, which prohibits states from passing any law "impairing the Obligation of Contracts," protects the right to judicial enforcement of contracts. Quite apart from federal protection, freedom of contract is also guaranteed in many state constitutions.

[11] "Laissez-faire," translated as "allow to do," means that the government should abstain from regulating the actions of citizens, especially in the marketplace.

In combination with this attitude toward the market, the classicists viewed law in formalistic terms (and are therefore sometimes described as "formalists"). They saw the law as a logical, self-contained system of interlocking rules. These rules are firm, ascertainable, and rationally related, so that a judge can find them by recourse to or reasoning from prior cases, and can then apply them with minimal judicial invention or policymaking. The adjudication of contract disputes therefore involves little more than the rather mechanical process of finding and applying the correct rule. Classicists placed great value on the certainty and predictability of legal rules. They felt that if rules were clear, the resolution of disputes would be more predictable, thus allowing contracting parties to feel more secure in their transactions. In this way, contract law would facilitate market activity. The great systematizing of contract law, mentioned in Section A.2, was a reflection of this belief that the law could be arranged and stated in the form of clear principles. In fact, one of the great early classicists, Christopher Columbus Langdell (dean of the Harvard Law School and the first law professor to write a casebook) went so far as to describe the law as a science.[12] Williston, whose work was introduced in Section A.4, is the preeminent scholar of the late classical period. His focus on identifying and expounding on an integral system of contract rules to be applied by courts underlies his treatise and is a basic foundation of the original Restatement of Contracts.

As a practical matter, the classical approach tended to have a quite strict rule orientation, with particular emphasis on the interpretation of written documents and other objective (observable) indications of contractual intent. Its ultimate effect was to strongly favor the enforcement of transactions at their face value. Philosophically, classicists saw this as a positive value, because a focus on formalism ensured that parties would be held to manifested intent, thus promoting security of transactions and stability in the marketplace. To critics of classicism, its disadvantage was glaringly obvious: It tended towards rigidity, paid insufficient attention to underlying questions of fairness, limited the discretion of the judge to take account of other policy concerns, and was likely to favor the interests of the economically powerful over those who might need judicial protection from overreaching.

The classical conception of law began to erode during the early decades of the twentieth century, as the economy became increasingly more complex, and powerful enterprises proliferated. People became more concerned about the social and economic dimensions of commercial interactions between parties of disparate power and sophistication. Legal commentators and judges increasingly questioned the premise that the law could be encompassed in a system of clear rules to be applied by courts in mechanistic fashion. The critics considered

---

[12] Langdell's principal works were his contracts casebook and a treatise titled *A Summary of the Law of Contracts*, which was appended to the casebook. A passage from the preface of his casebook, in which he describes law as a science, is quoted in Grant Gilmore, *The Death of Contract* 13 (Ronald K.L. Collins ed., 2d ed., Ohio St. U. Press 1995). (Professor Gilmore was himself a giant of contract and commercial law. *The Death of Contract*, based on a series of lectures, is one of the most influential and enduring essays on contract law.)

not realistic in practice

tends to lead to skewed & unfair results

such formalism to be based on an unrealistic theoretical model, divorced from what was really happening in the marketplace and the courts. They were skeptical of the classicist view that law consisted of neutral principles and criticized the classical orientation toward "black letter" rules as rigid and often leading to skewed and unfair results. These commentators advocated a much broader and more fluid approach that examined rules in the entire societal context and took into account the realities of the marketplace, the relationship of the parties, and the decision-making process of the courts. They understood, through the growing influence of the social sciences, that law is very much an instrument of public policy applied by judges who are not immune from the influence of their own political predilections. This broader view of the law allows for greater flexibility in rules, which inevitably undermines the certainty and predictability so cherished by the classicists.

law is an instrument of public policy

realism

rules were less rigid & open to more judicial opinion

Because it emphasizes the realistic study of law in action, this philosophy is known as legal realism. Legal realism offered a vital new insight into the law that has formed the basis of enduring premises of legal analysis and judicial process. Although it was a bold departure from classical thought, it was not revolutionary. Realists continued to accept and work within the framework of rules and principles established by the classicists while softening the rules' hard edges and treating them as much more fluid and subject to greater judicial discretion. Corbin was one of the preeminent advocates of this new approach, as was Professor Karl Llewellyn, whose contribution is discussed in Chapter 2. The Restatement of Contracts, with Williston as its Reporter but with Corbin's deep involvement, reflects this transition. The work on the Restatement proceeded through the 1920s and culminated in publication in 1932, by which time realism had already begun to eclipse classicism as the prevailing philosophy. As a collaboration between leading figures in these two opposing schools, the Restatement exhibits values derived from both.[13]

Restatement includes Classicism & realism

In addition to this focus on a realistic view of law, the 1920s and 1930s saw a change in the general attitude to the role of government in commercial transactions. The excesses of laissez-faire economics during the nineteenth century showed that too much faith in the free market tended to favor the predations of the powerful. Legislatures realized that freedom of contract needed to be tempered with social responsibility. In response, they began to enact laws that regulated specific kinds of contracts that had become most susceptible to overreaching and advantage-taking by parties with overbearing power.

The concept of law advanced by the legal realists (as well as by associated schools of thought that emphasized the social role of law) has become firmly established as the mainstream of contract jurisprudence and underlies most modern court opinions as well as much commentary, including the

---

[13] Professor Gilmore observes that the antithetical points of view held by Williston and Corbin give the Restatement a ". . . schizophrenic quality which makes . . . [it], viewed historically, the fascinating document which it is." Gilmore, *The Death of Contract, supra* note 12, at 66.

today: neoclassicism

Restatement, Second. Current mainstream thinking is sometimes called neo-classicism to reflect the fact that it is based on but has moved away from the classical model. However, the strong formalism of the classicists is no longer commonplace. While it is occasionally found in recent opinions, you are more likely to encounter it in older cases.

This does not mean that everyone is a neoclassicist today. There are a number of modern philosophical schools that have challenged neoclassical thinking, arguing that a realistic view of law may provide understanding of the world as it exists, but furnishes few if any tools with which to challenge or improve it. Instead, these schools have adopted alternative analyses that describe the law from varied perspectives and emphasize different normative values. Some writers adopt a consent theory of contract. They see the consensual aspect of contract as central, so that rules of law should be built around the core value of assent. Some writers favor a promissory theory of contract that places great stress on the morality of keeping promises and promotes the sanctity of promise as the true moral and legal justification of rules of contract law. Some writers argue for a relational theory of contracts in which rules take into account that most contracts are not discrete, one-time transactions but are part of an ongoing series of dealings between parties who have a long-term relationship. They fault traditional theory *pay attention* for paying insufficient attention to the overall relationship of the parties, resulting *to the* in rules that disregard the dynamics of the relationship on matters such as con-*relationship* tract formation and dispute resolution. The Critical Legal Studies movement *of the parties* adopts a radical approach to contract law. This school examines the effect of contract law on the economic or political underdog and criticizes traditional thinking as an instrument of dominant economic interests. It calls for the "deconstruction" of current rules and their replacement by principles that are more altruistic. Other writers, some of whom have views that are related to those of the Critical Legal Studies movement, focus on the effect of traditional contract law on specific classes of people, such as women and ethnic minorities, whose interests traditionally have not been served by the law.

The Law and Economics movement focuses on economic efficiency as the *economic* yardstick for measuring the efficacy and propriety of contract rules. In some *efficiency are* respects, the proponents of an economics-based approach have embraced the *the measure of* earlier laissez-faire philosophy and place faith in free market mechanisms to *how contract* motivate the behavior of contracting parties in a way that maximizes value *law was doing* for them and for society. The basic idea is that if the law facilitates, rather *law facilitates* than interferes with, the operation of the market, the parties will place their *the market* own value on transactions, and allocate resources optimally. This will result in efficient transactions and the greatest good for society as a whole. The Law and Economics approach has been controversial. Its opponents argue that the economic analysis of law often relies too heavily on theoretical market models and assumptions about human behavior that may not represent reality. In addition, its opponents contend that the approach tends to focus too strongly on economic efficiency at the expense of other values, such as fairness or protection of the weak.

└→ may focus too much on economics

One of the reactions to the Law and Economics movement has been the development of a school of thought known as Behavioral Law and Economics. Scholars who write from this perspective recognize that the model of a rational decision-maker, so central to the economic analysis of law, is an artificial construct. Real people are seldom capable of rational decision-making because their decisions are too heavily influenced by emotion, fallible memory, and inadequate understanding of information. To correct for this problem, these scholars attempt to take more account of actual decision-making behavior, as revealed by empirical study.

As you pursue your study of contract law, you may develop your own theories of what the law's underlying purpose is or should be. Law is dynamic and changes in response to debate over its goals and effects. Attention to theory not only enriches academic study; it also allows lawyers to be more effective counselors and advocates.

6. International Perspectives on Contract Law

Although our focus is on the domestic law of contracts in the United States, we will periodically refer briefly to the equivalent (and sometimes different) rules of contract law that you might find in transactions that cross national borders. It is beyond the scope of the first-year contracts course to discuss in any detail contracts between parties who are located in different countries. However, because international commerce is such an important aspect of modern business, it is helpful to be aware from the outset that the approach to and the rules governing contracts in the international setting may not be the same as those established for the purely domestic setting. (We should emphasize the words "may not" because the law of an American state could apply to an international transaction, either because the parties selected the law of that state as the governing law or because it is otherwise applicable under international principles of choice of law.) Where we refer to international principles, we do so in short text notes that are intended to provide only basic and general comparisons between the legal rules and principles that you study in this course and those that you might find in transnational contracts.

In these periodic notes, we will refer to two documents. The first is a treaty, the United Nations Convention on Contracts for the International Sale of Goods *contracts for the international sale of goods* (the CISG). This treaty applies only to contracts involving the sale of goods, and it is introduced in Chapter 2. The United States has ratified the CISG, and, as a treaty of the United States, it has binding force in every state in relation to transactions that fall within its scope.

The second is the UNIDROIT Principles of International Commercial Contracts. This publication is similar in its effect to the Restatement, Second. It is **not a treaty* not a treaty, but rather an influential scholarly publication, intended to reflect general rules applicable to international commercial transactions. It was drafted under the auspices of the International Institute for the Unification of Private Law (abbreviated in French as UNIDROIT) and first promulgated in final form in 1994. UNIDROIT adopted updated editions of the Principles in 2004 and again in

2010. In creating the Principles, the drafters examined the rules of contract law from several countries (including the United States) and attempted to cull common principles and best solutions for the purpose of articulating a rational and broadly accepted set of rules that could be applied to international transactions. The UNIDROIT Principles are not binding law, but they may be applied by agreement of the parties or might be useful as persuasive authority where a court or arbitrator seeks guidance on how to resolve an international dispute.

pull common principles & best practice

B WHAT MAKES AN AGREEMENT INTO A CONTRACT

In Section A.1 we quoted the definition of "contract" from the Restatement, Second: "a promise or a set of promises for the breach of which the law gives a remedy, or the performance of which the law in some way recognizes as a duty." We then identified the hallmarks of a legally recognized contract—an exchange relationship created by agreement between two or more parties, containing at least one promise, and recognized as enforceable in law. We now survey these elements.

creates a relationship

An exchange relationship. A contract is more than the spoken words of agreement or the document recording what was agreed. Once a contract is formed, a relationship exists in which the parties commit themselves to each other for a common enterprise. The relationship may be intended to be short (for example, a purchase of goods to be delivered and paid for later that same day), or it may be intended to last for a long time (for example, a ten-year lease of office space). It may be a discrete, one-time transaction entered into by parties who have not contracted with each other before and do not expect to have future dealings, or it may be one of many transactions entered into by parties who deal with each other regularly.

purpose of relationship

The purpose of the relationship is exchange—a reciprocal arrangement in which each party gives up something to get something else from the other. The function of contract law is to facilitate these exchanges. As we will see when we deal with consideration doctrine in Chapter 9, an agreement that lacks any element of exchange (for example, an agreement that one person will make a gift to another) does not qualify as a contract.

if there is no exchange, there is no contract

Created by agreement. A contract is created by agreement. There must, of course, be at least two parties to this agreement, but there could be many parties to it—multiparty contracts are common. The voluntary nature of contract is fundamental. We can call a relationship a contract only if both parties, in the exercise of free will, intend to make a contract and consent to enter it. Freedom of contract—which includes both the power to choose whether or not to make a contract and the power to assent to its terms—is a central policy of our law. As we will see later, the question of what constitutes contractual intent and assent can be quite intricate, but consent remains a vital premise of contract.

* must be voluntary - consent

Containing at least one promise. Although exchange is an indispensable component of a contract, it is not enough on its own to give rise to a contract. For a transaction to be a contract, at least one of the parties must have made a promise—that is, must have committed to do something or refrain from doing something in the future. If no future commitment is made, the law of contracts, which is concerned with the enforcement of promises, has no role to play in the relationship. In most cases, of course, it is not just one but both of the parties who make commitments, but only one promise is needed to qualify the relationship as a contract.

Recognized as enforceable in law. A basic purpose of contract law is to enforce contract obligations—that is, contractual promises become the law between the parties, binding the party who made them and giving the party to whom they are made the right to employ the power of the state, through its courts,[14] to enforce them. Only a small number of contracts ever end up in litigation, but the right of recourse to legal process gives contractual obligations great weight. Parties who enter contracts know that they undertake a serious commitment and realize that its breach could result in a lawsuit and a judicially imposed remedy. The legal recognition and enforcement of contract obligations are crucial attributes of contract law. Without these attributes, there would be no ultimate recourse to law where social or economic pressure is not enough to motivate a party to honor his commitment. This would diminish reliability and predictability in commercial dealings. Legal recognition of contractual promises distinguishes them from other promises, such as a promise to a spouse to clean up the garage this weekend or to a friend to show up for his boring party.

The remedies available to a party for the enforcement of contractual obligations are a crucial aspect of the law of contracts. We defer a detailed discussion of remedies to Chapters 20 and 21 of this book. However, the issue of remedy—what relief an aggrieved party might expect from a court in the event of breach and litigation—is the crucial "bottom line" both in structuring the transaction and in dealing with any dispute that arises under it. Therefore, we constantly draw your attention to remedies throughout this book (beginning with the case in this chapter) so that you will begin to build a familiarity with remedial principles and concepts from the outset.

---

[14] Many contracts contain arbitration clauses that oblige the parties to resolve disputes and seek remedies through the process of arbitration, rather than by litigation before a court. We discuss arbitration clauses later. In short, arbitrators are private individuals appointed as provided in the contract, and the process of arbitration may be quicker and less formal than litigation. Arbitration provisions usually bind the parties to the arbitrator's decision. Nevertheless, even where a dispute is resolved by arbitration, any enforcement of that award against a recalcitrant party is accomplished through the enforcement power of the courts.

THE ENFORCEMENT OF CONTRACTS: AN INTRODUCTION TO REMEDIES

In Section B, we identified legal enforceability as a fundamental attribute of contract. In this section we introduce the meaning and scope of enforcement in more detail. As noted in Section B, where parties make a contract, each of them has the right to seek legal redress if the other fails to perform her contractual undertakings as promised. In most situations, of course, a party who complains about a breach of contract will first attempt to rectify the problem without suing. However, if it comes to the point that discussion, negotiation, and other informal attempts to resolve the problem are unsuccessful, legal enforceability means that the aggrieved party can sue to seek a remedy for the breach. Generally, the plaintiff seeks to preserve the financial gain anticipated from the contract. Sometimes he tries to do this by asking the court to order the defendant to perform. But more commonly, the plaintiff asks the court for monetary compensation to restore the financial advantage that has been lost as a result of the breach. It is the desire for this remedy, and the economic decision that it is worth litigating to get it, that usually motivates a party to initiate suit. *make up the difference of what's lost*

Most contracts are economic relationships. People usually enter into contracts for the purpose of gaining something of economic value. Therefore, when a contract is breached, the loss to the victim of the breach is usually financial or economic in nature. Of course, this is not necessarily the only negative impact of a breach of contract. The breach could, and often does, cause disappointment, anger, inconvenience, or other emotional or sentimental ill effects. However, it is a firm and well-established principle of contract law that any remedy granted for breach of contract focuses only on repairing the economic harm of the breach and does not aim to compensate for any of its noneconomic consequences. *contracts don't aim to compensate for anything that's not money*

1. Damages or Specific Performance: An Introduction to the Distinction Between Law and Equity

One might assume that where a party breaches a contract, the most direct and logical remedy would be for the court to order the defendant to perform what she promised. This is known as an order for specific performance. However, partly as a result of the Anglo-American legal tradition, and partly for policy reasons, specific performance is not the preferred remedy for breach of contract. It is available only in limited situations, and the standard remedy for breach of contract is an award of monetary damages.

Historically, the preference for damages over specific performance derives from a very old jurisdictional distinction in English law. When modern courts

— sue when informal remedies don't work

plaintiff wants to keep the gain as is laid out in the contract

specific performance ↳ not the preferred remedy

distinguish "law" from "equity," they are alluding to this ancient jurisdictional distinction. (This is a distinction that spans the whole common law system, so you will encounter it in contract topics beyond contract remedies, and in many other areas of the law.) During the early period of English common law, court procedures were rigid and formalistic. Courts of law could grant relief only if the plaintiff could fit his claim into one of a narrow selection of writs, and the court could grant only the relief provided for in the writ. The writ relating to contract claims provided only for the remedy of money damages. However, the monarch had the power to ameliorate any harsh results of this formalistic system. He or she had the royal prerogative to do justice between subjects by granting a remedy that was not available in a court. The monarch delegated this function to the chancellor, the highest royal official. So, for example, in a contracts case, the chancellor could order specific performance even though the law courts could not.

As the number of petitions to the chancellor grew, it became necessary to create a full-time court, which came to be known as the Court of Chancery or the Court of Equity. The Court of Equity existed alongside the Courts of Law. As the two separate sets of courts evolved, a dual system developed in which each had a distinct jurisdictional boundary and each followed its own rules and principles.

Because the Court of Equity was intended to intervene only where the law courts could not provide proper relief, a petitioner had to establish, as a prerequisite to invoking Chancery jurisdiction, that the remedy available at law was inadequate. In the case of contract remedies, this meant that the petitioner had to show that an award of damages at law would not properly compensate him. This could be, for example, because it would be too difficult to prove damages, or because the promised performance was so unique that a money award could not compensate for his loss. In addition, because the petitioner was invoking the chancellor's prerogative to grant a remedy on equitable grounds, the petitioner also had to establish that he had acted fairly in the transaction, and that justice, fairness, and the public good would best be served by the granting of relief.

This dual system of law courts and equity courts entered American law when the colonies (and, after independence, the states) adopted the common law of England as the basis of their legal systems. By the beginning of the twentieth century the jurisdictional distinction between law and equity was abolished both in England and in most American states. Judicial reform in most states and in the federal court system merged legal and equitable jurisdiction into a single set of courts. However, even though the same courts exercised both legal and equitable jurisdiction, courts have continued to draw the traditional distinction between suits based in law and those based in equity. There has been a gradual erosion of the firm lines of the division between legal and equitable principles and remedies, but the traditional distinctions still exist in many areas of the law. In relation to contract remedies, courts still largely follow the rule that the equitable remedy of specific performance is not available unless the plaintiff can show that the legal remedy of damages is inadequate and the equities favor specific enforcement.

Tradition may be a justification for following a practice, but tradition alone is not usually a sufficient reason for preserving rules and principles that no longer make sense. Therefore, the courts' continued adherence to the law-equity distinction must be explained on rational grounds as well. A common policy explanation for continuing to treat specific performance as the exceptional remedy is that damages are usually a more efficient and less burdensome means of rectifying the harm caused by a breach of contract. Of course, not everyone agrees with this rationale, and there has been much debate over the years on the question of the proper principles to use in deciding on the most appropriate remedy. We will explore this rationale later in the course, when we focus more fully on remedies.

In the next case, the court refuses an order of specific performance, and instead awards damages to the plaintiff. The purpose of contract damages is to award a sum of money to the victim of the breach to compensate him for the loss of the economic gain that he reasonably expected from the contract. They are intended to give the victim of the breach the benefit of his bargain by requiring the breaching party to pay him the amount of money that will place him in the financial position that he would have been in had the contract been performed as agreed. These damages are therefore known as "expectation" or "benefit of the bargain" damages. Questions following the case allow you to consider the rationale for awarding damages instead of specific performance and the nature of the damages that might best achieve the goal of adequately compensating the plaintiff for his loss.

The case is decided by the District of Columbia Court of Appeals. Because the District of Columbia is a federal area, not within any state, there are no state courts in the District. However, the District of Columbia has its own court system in which the District of Columbia Superior Court is the trial court and the District of Columbia Court of Appeals is the equivalent of a state supreme court.

KAKAES v. GEORGE WASHINGTON UNIVERSITY

790 A.2d 581 (2002)
District of Columbia Court of Appeals

SCHWELB, Associate Judge.

This case . . . arises from the refusal of George Washington University to award tenure to the plaintiff, Professor Apostolos K. Kakaes, who had been on a "tenure accruing" track at the University since his appointment in September 1987 as an Assistant Professor in the Department of Electrical Engineering and Computer Science (EECS). . . . [A] non-jury trial was held before . . . [the Superior Court].

[handwritten margin note: money]

[handwritten margin note: contract is the faculty code]

After hearing extensive testimony which established that the University had failed to provide Dr. Kakaes with timely notice, as required by the Faculty Code, of its decision to deny tenure, and after further proceedings relating to the issue of relief, the judge declined to order the University to grant Dr. Kakaes tenure. The judge held instead that Kakaes was entitled to an award of damages in the amount of $75,018, as well as costs and interest. Dr. Kakaes appeals, contending that the contract between the parties required the University to grant him tenure and that the amount of damages awarded by the judge was inadequate. We affirm.

[handwritten margin note: remedy]

*[handwritten margin note: * need to be notified by june 30 of the final year in your term]*

[handwritten margin note: court costs]

... Section IV.A.3.1.c of the University's Faculty Code, which constitutes the contract between the parties ... provides in pertinent part that "[a] faculty member of the rank of assistant professor or higher who will not be granted tenure at the end of the final year of his or her maximum term of appointment shall be so notified in writing no later than June 30 preceding the year in which his or her appointment will expire. ... Any such faculty member who is not so notified shall acquire tenure at the end of the term." On June 28, 1993, the University's vice president, Roderick French, wrote a letter to Dr. Kakaes advising him that "you will not be granted tenure at the conclusion of your current appointment." In the same letter, however, Vice President French further advised Dr. Kakaes: "The President and I are in the process of transmitting the report of the Executive Committee to the Board of Trustees for its consideration. You will be notified of the outcome as soon as possible." In a separate letter written on the same date to the Chairman of the EECS department, Vice President French wrote that "[b]y so informing [Dr. Kakaes], the question of [his] ultimate tenuring or termination remains to be resolved."

On October 22, 1993, Dr. Kakaes brought suit against the University for breach of contract, alleging that he had not been provided the timely notice required by the Faculty Code of the decision to deny him tenure.[15] ... [The trial judge] found that University had breached its contract with Dr. Kakaes, but she declined to order the University to grant him tenure. This appeal followed.

[handwritten margin note: he claims this to be]

Dr. Kakaes relies on the provision of the Faculty Code quoted ... [above], which states, in pertinent part, that if timely notice has not been given, then "[a]ny such faculty member who is not so notified shall acquire tenure at the end of the term." Kakaes contends that the contract specifies the remedy for its breach—namely, the award of tenure—and that, by what he considers the plain language of the contract, he is entitled to specific performance, and therefore to tenure. We do not agree.

We note in the first instance that the provision that the faculty member "shall acquire tenure at the end of the term" need not necessarily be construed as specifying a remedy. A reasonable alternative reading is that the University has contractually obligated itself to grant tenure in such cases, but that the

---

[15] On February 10, 1994, while Dr. Kakaes's suit was pending, the Board of Trustees voted to deny him tenure.

* bench trial

contract does not identify the relief available to a plaintiff in the event that the University breaches that obligation. Under this construction of the Faculty Code, the trial judge would be entirely justified in awarding monetary damages rather than ordering the University to award Dr. Kakaes tenure. It is "axiomatic" that equitable relief will not be granted where the plaintiff has a complete and adequate remedy at law. *District of Columbia v. Wical Ltd. P'ship*, 630 A.2d 174, 184 (D.C.1993) (quoting *Marshall v. District of Columbia*, 458 A.2d 28, 29 (D.C.1982)); *accord, District of Columbia v. N. Washington Neighbors, Inc.*, 336 A.2d 828, 829 (D.C.1975) (*per curiam*). Dr. Kakaes has not shown why damages would not provide him with full and complete relief, and at least in the absence of a provision specifying an equitable remedy, award of legal relief is the entirely appropriate norm.

But even if the contract is construed as specifying a grant of tenure as the remedy for its breach, the result will not be different. The trial judge addressed this issue in some detail:

The plaintiff is not entitled to be reinstated as a faculty member at GW, nor is he entitled to the granting of tenure. While plaintiff relies upon Article IV.A.3.1.c. of the Faculty Code, which the court found had been breached, as support for his claim to a position as a tenured professor, plaintiff's argument ignores a substantial body of law disfavoring such a remedy, that is, enforcement of a personal service contract, particularly in the university employment area. *Greene v. Howard Univ.*, 271 F. Supp. 609, 615 (D.D.C.1967), *aff'd in pertinent part*, [134 U.S. App. D.C. 81,] 412 F.2d 1128 (D.C. Cir. 1969) ("A contract to hire a teacher may not be enforced by specific performance"). *See also Howard Univ. v. Best*, 547 A.2d 144, 146–47, 154 n. 10, 157 (D.C.1988); *Tucker v. Warfield*, [73 App. D.C. 278, 280–81 & n. 3,] 119 F.2d 12, 13–14 & n. 3 (D.C. Cir. 1941). . . . "It would be intolerable for the courts to interject themselves and to require an educational institution to hire or maintain on its staff a professor or instructor whom it deemed undesirable and did not wish to employ." *Greene v. Howard Univ.*, 271 F. Supp. at 615. Indeed, specifically addressing the issue raised in this case, the D.C. Court of Appeals echoed this view in *Howard Univ. v. Best, supra*: "The requirement for clear and satisfactory proof of the custom and practice of a University, in determining the reasonable expectations of the parties, reflects public policy concerns that indefinite tenure not occur by default." 547 A.2d at 154. *See also Cusumano v. Ratchford*, 507 F.2d 980, 986 (8th Cir. 1974), *cert. denied*, 423 U.S. 829, 96 S. Ct. 48, 46 L. Ed. 2d 46 (1975) ("It cannot serve the public welfare or promote the best interests of the University or its professional staff to have a body of teachers . . . *the permanent tenures of whom rest upon administrative neglect or oversight. . . .*") (emphasis added).

Our review of the trial judge's decision not to require the University to grant Dr. Kakaes tenure is deferential. "Specific performance is an extraordinary equitable remedy, the denial or granting of which is within the sound and informed discretion of the trial court." *Drazin v. Am. Oil Co.*, 395 A.2d 32, 34 (D.C.1978). The judge's discretion extends to the denial of specific performance even where, as Dr. Kakaes alleges here, the parties have provided in their contract for a particular remedy. As one commentator has written under the heading "Provisions For Specific Relief Are Not Binding,"

> [t]he Second Restatement of Contracts maintains that parties to a contract cannot vary by agreement the requirement that damages be inadequate in order to obtain equitable relief. Supporting this position are numerous opinions in which courts have stated that a clause in a contract providing for specific performance or an injunction does not by itself bind a court to grant the agreed remedy.

Edward Yorio, *Contract Enforcement: Specific Performance and Injunctions*, §19.2.1, at 441 (1989) [hereinafter *Contract Enforcement*]. It is true that there has been some scholarly criticism of the courts' reluctance to grant specific performance where there is an adequate remedy at law; "[some] commentators argue that the parties to a contract are in a better position than a judge to determine the remedy that serves their respective interests most satisfactorily." *Contract Enforcement, supra,* §19.2.2, at 442. We agree in principle that "[i]ndividuals usually benefit when left free to maximize their own interests in negotiating the terms of a contract. But *the principle of equitable discretion rests on the premise that courts ought to consider and reflect other interests in devising a system of contract remedies.*" §19.2.3, at 444 (emphasis added).

parties are in a better position to decide than the law

In the present case, we agree with the trial judge that there is a public interest in avoiding the grant of tenure by default. Administrative errors and oversights should not result in a tenured appointment for a person whom the responsible University officials consider unsuitable to receive it. Generally speaking, in the words of Judge Holtzoff, "[a] contract to hire a teacher may not be enforced by specific performance." *Greene, supra,* 271 F. Supp. at 615. We therefore conclude that the trial judge did not abuse her discretion in declining to require the University to grant tenure to Professor Kakaes.

Turning to the issue of damages, the trial judge first noted that the University's failure to provide Dr. Kakaes, prior to June 30, 1993, with a final decision as to tenure left him "with insufficient time, after learning for certain that his job was ending, to secure another position." It was for this harm, according to the judge, that Dr. Kakaes was entitled to receive damages. The judge continued:

> In light of these circumstances and the nature of the damages evidence presented at trial by plaintiff, the court finds that plaintiff has only proven that he is entitled to an award for the actual reduction of income from GW which plaintiff suffered in 1994—$38,459.00 (as his position ended on May 30, 1994 and he did not receive a continued GW salary for the latter half of 1994),—and in the first half of the next year, 1995, the first year after he was actually given a legally sufficient notice of the university's decision—$36,599.00. Because of the plaintiff's choice to pursue non-academic employment thereafter, and the increased earnings from his extremely lucrative business endeavors after leaving GW, the court has determined that he is not entitled to any award for later years of lost GW employment. Instead, the court has determined that its award of damages must be limited to the amount necessary

to make the plaintiff whole, and to place him in the same position he would have been in had GW not breached the notice provision of the code. Nor is plaintiff entitled to any award of attorneys' fees, as he has failed to establish that the university's defenses in this case were presented in bad faith. . . .

Dr. Kakaes testified on his own behalf and attempted to "compare what my actual income was to what my actual income would have been had I been [at the University]." Dr. Kakaes presented no expert testimony, and the trial judge expressed considerable skepticism regarding Kakaes' own credibility as a witness. The judge, as the trier of fact, was free to either credit or disregard Dr. Kakaes' opinion as to his calculation of damages.

We recognize that the predicate for denying equitable relief to Dr. Kakaes was that he had a full and adequate remedy at law. Nevertheless, the burden was on him to prove the extent of his damages. His failure to present expert testimony was problematical, for the task of projecting a person's lost earnings lends itself to clarification by expert testimony because it involves the use of statistical techniques and requires a broad knowledge of economics. . . . The decision whether or not to require expert testimony is within the discretion of the trial court, whose ruling should be sustained unless clearly erroneous. Without expert testimony, the trial judge was unpersuaded by the plaintiff's lay testimony, and we cannot say that her findings were clearly wrong. Accordingly, we conclude that Dr. Kakaes has failed to demonstrate any reversible error on the part of the trial judge with respect to the quantum of damages.

For the foregoing reasons, the judgment of the trial court is affirmed.

■ QUESTIONS

(1) The court cites several cases as authority for its refusal to award specific performance to Dr. Kakaes. Which, if any, are binding precedent and which are merely persuasive precedent?

(2) The court quotes from a book written by Edward Yorio, which includes a citation to the Restatement, Second, of Contracts. What proposition does this commentary support, and what is its authoritative weight? → *persuasive*

people should be able to contract for their own remedy

■ PROBLEM 1.1

Say that six months after *Kakaes* was decided, the District of Columbia Superior Court had to decide a case in which Donna Primo, a famous musician, reneged on a contract to perform as the lead attraction at a music festival. She gave notice to the festival organizers of her intention not to perform one month before the concert was to take place. The

bound by Kakaes precedent

organizers had sold out all the tickets to the concert, primarily because Donna was the principal performer. It is not possible to find another performer of her stature so soon before the festival, so if she does not honor her contract, the festival probably will have to be cancelled, the organizers will lose a fortune, and thousands of fans will be disappointed. On the other hand, it would not be particularly burdensome for Donna to perform. She routinely gives such performances, which she can do without much effort, and she reneged only because she felt that she had booked too many appearances and wanted some time off.

Is *Kakaes* on point as a precedent? To what extent does it determine how the Superior Court must decide Donna's case?

she will need to pay damages

■ QUESTIONS

(1) As the introductory text to this section indicates, to obtain an award of specific performance, the plaintiff must show that the legal remedy of damages is inadequate and that the equities favor specific enforcement. In *Kakaes*, the court found damages to be an adequate remedy. What if they were not? Say, for example, that the plaintiff was not an electrical engineer and computer scientist, but a history professor. He can show that there are no means of pursuing the profession of an historian outside of an academic institution, and that because the denial of tenure is regarded very negatively in academia, George Washington University's refusal of tenure would effectively ensure that he would never be able to get another academic position.

Would or should this change the court's thinking on whether specific performance is called for? What role should the equities of the case play in the decision?

(2) Apparently the university decided not to grant tenure to Dr. Kakaes, but failed to give him the required notice of termination. We are not told why the university did not wish to grant tenure to him. What if it was shown that Dr. Kakaes was well qualified to receive tenure, and that the university had no legitimate grounds to deny it to him? Do you think that this would have changed the court's decision not to grant him specific performance?

(3) Why was the court not persuaded by the argument that specific performance should be granted because the contract itself provided for this remedy? Should not the parties to a contract be able to specify the remedy to be granted to one of them in the event of a breach by the other?

■ PROBLEM 1.2

Seller owned an exquisite condominium on the 30th floor of a prestigious residential tower. The condominium had a commanding view of the city, the river, and the mountains that lay beyond the city. She contracted to sell it to Buyer for $2.5 million. Shortly after the contract of sale was signed, but before the transaction closed, a condominium on the same floor, with the same view, sold for $2.75 million, and Seller realized that she had underpriced her condominium. She therefore reneged on the contract.

She immediately contracted to sell the condominium to another buyer for $2.8 million. There are no other condominiums available on the same side of the building, but Buyer can buy a condominium of the same size and floor plan on the same floor, on the other side of the building. That condominium overlooks the rather ugly industrial area of the city, with no view of the river or mountains. Because the view is less attractive, the price of this other condominium is $2 million.

Buyer seeks an order of specific performance. Should the court grant it?

2. Expectation Damages

Although the court refused to grant on order of specific performance to Dr. Kakaes, which would have compelled the university to tenure him, it did award damages to him, based on his actual loss of income resulting from the breach. As noted above, the purpose of contract damages is to give the victim of the breach the benefit of his bargain by compensating him for the economic gain that he lost as a result of the breach of contract.

■ QUESTIONS

(1) Although the court does not make it entirely clear, it sounds like Dr. Kakaes did not secure another academic position after the university terminated his employment, but that he instead pursued non-academic employment that was "extremely lucrative." If, in fact, he earned more money from this non-academic work, why is he entitled to any damages at all?

(2) Assume that upon being denied tenure by the university, Dr. Kakaes found a position as an assistant professor at another university in the District of Columbia area. He took up employment in that position two months after leaving George Washington University. The other university pays less than

George Washington, so his annual salary is $2,000 less than he would have earned had he stayed at George Washington. What should his damages be?

(3) At the end of the opinion, the court indicates that Dr. Kakaes lost the opportunity of proving higher damages because the trial court did not find his testimony credible, and that he may have succeeded in claiming more damages had he been able to establish them by expert testimony. Can you divine from the opinion what these additional damages might have been, and why the plaintiff may have been entitled to them if proved? *Cost of looking for a new job*

incidental damages

Litigation can be very expensive. One might therefore assume that if a person sues successfully for enforcement of a contract, the winning plaintiff should be able to recover not only expectation damages, but also the legal fees he incurred in suing for them. However, while this is true in many countries, the well-established rule of American law is that each party is responsible for his own attorneys' fees and the loser does not have to pay the winner's attorneys' fees. In a portion of the opinion that we omitted from the edited version of the case, the court follows this rule by refusing to award attorneys' fees to Dr. Kakaes. The court does point to one exception to the usual rule: Attorneys' fees may be awarded against a losing party who asserted a claim or defense vexatiously or in bad faith. Attorneys' fees may also be available if provided for in the contract or by statute. The inability to recover the costs of litigation can have a significant impact on the economic viability of litigation, so that the damages awarded may fall far short of compensating for the loss once the plaintiff's legal costs have been paid out of any award.

The calculation of expectation damages differs from case to case, and it can get very complex. In *Kakaes*, the plaintiff was awarded damages equivalent to the amount that he would have earned had he been given proper notice of the university's decision not to grant tenure to him. In many cases, a common measure of expectation damages is the added cost of a substitute transaction: Where the defendant fails to perform its obligation under a contract and the plaintiff is able to enter into a substitute transaction, his expectation damages can usually be measured by determining the cost of a substitute transaction and deducting the contract price from that cost. In other words, the plaintiff is awarded a sum of money that is equal to the extra cost of entering into a new transaction for a similar performance in substitution for the performance promised by the defendant. Even where the plaintiff does not actually enter into a substitute transaction, the market value of a substitute may be used to determine the plaintiff's expectation under the contract. Problems 1.3 and 1.4 illustrate substitutionary expectation damages.

■ PROBLEM 1.3

As in Problem 1.2, Seller owned the exquisite 30th-floor condominium with the spectacular view, which she contracted to sell to Buyer for $2.5 million. She reneged on the contract when a neighboring condominium sold for $2.75 million and she discovered that she had underpriced her own condominium. She immediately resold the condominium to another buyer for $2.8 million. There were no other condominiums available on the higher floors of the building, but there was a condominium of the same size and floor plan on the third floor of the building. That condominium had no view at all and was shaded most of the day by surrounding tall buildings. As a result it was much cheaper. Buyer decided to buy it, and paid $1.5 million for it.

(a) What expectation damages, if any, has Buyer suffered?
(b) Buyer is very distressed about the lack of view and the gloomy darkness of the condominium. Should Buyer be able to claim damages to compensate him for the disappointment of having to settle for this less desirable home?

■ PROBLEM 1.4

Expectant Enterprises, Inc. entered into a contract with Cutrate Construction Co. under which Cutrate agreed to renovate an office building for Expectant for a price of $4 million. Cutrate failed to begin work on time and told Expectant that it had no intention of performing. This was a clear breach of contract by Cutrate. Expectant had not made any payment to Cutrate. Expectant immediately contacted other contractors to solicit bids for the work. The best bid it could get was for $4.5 million. Expectant accepted the bid, and work began immediately. However, there was a month's delay in starting the job because of the time needed to obtain bids and to negotiate the substitute contract. As a result, the renovation of the office building was completed a month after the completion date specified in Expectant's contract with Cutrate, and Expectant lost $50,000 in rent that it would have obtained for that month.

What are Expectant's expectation damages?

3. The Method of Enforcing an Award of Damages

Where a court awards specific performance, the award is an order of the court. As such, the court can compel performance as ordered. In some situations, the court can have the order executed by a public official. For example, if the court orders specific performance of a contract to sell real property (such as the contract in Problem 1.2), the court can have the order enforced by commanding the sheriff or some other official to transfer title to the plaintiff by executing and recording a deed of transfer in the deeds registry, and to evict the defendant from the property. Where it is not possible to enforce the order in this way, the court can use its contempt power to compel the defendant to perform; that is, if the defendant refuses to perform voluntarily, the court can fine or even imprison him until he obeys the order. In some cases (such as Donna's case in Problem 1.1), supervision to ensure that the defendant performs properly can be quite difficult, especially where the standards for determining adequate performance are more subjective and difficult to quantify.

Where the court awards damages, the enforcement mechanism is not as powerful. An award of damages is merely an adjudication that the defendant owes the stated amount of money to the plaintiff. It is not a court order, and payment cannot be compelled by the court's contempt power. If the defendant does not pay the judgment voluntarily, the plaintiff must attempt to enforce it by collecting the money from property of the defendant. To do this, the plaintiff has the clerk of the court issue a writ instructing the sheriff (or an equivalent officer) to find and seize property of the defendant and to sell it at public auction to generate proceeds to pay the judgment. If the defendant has no property that can be seized, there is little that the plaintiff can do. As a practical matter, this is a crucial consideration for anyone who wishes to sue for damages. Even if he wins, the victory will be hollow if the defendant does not have the money or property to satisfy the judgment.

CHAPTER 2

Sales of Goods

 ## A AN INTRODUCTION TO ARTICLE 2

1. The Creation of the Uniform Commercial Code

Contracts for the sale of goods are very common, and we will encounter them often. They differ in an important respect from other contracts because they are governed by a statute, Article 2 of the Uniform Commercial Code (UCC).

As noted in Chapter 1, most contracts are governed by rules and principles of common law, as developed by courts over many centuries. However, there are some areas in which legislatures have enacted statutory rules that apply to contracts generally or to particular types of contracts. Sometimes these statutes merely codify common law principles (that is, incorporate into statutory form rules that are already established at common law), and sometimes they enact new rules that change or add to rules that previously existed at common law. For example, a legislature may enact statutory provisions requiring that contracts for consumer goods or services have certain provisions designed to protect consumers or to inform them clearly of their rights and obligations; or to regulate certain types of contracts within a particular industry, such as the insurance industry; or to forbid terms in contracts that exploit workers or discriminate against workers based on age, race, or gender. Even where such statutes are enacted, the common law rules of contract law apply to the transactions in question to the extent that they are not displaced by the statutory provisions.

Since the early twentieth century, contracts for the sale of goods have been governed by statute. During the latter years of the nineteenth century, there was growing sentiment in favor of unifying state commercial law. Many scholars, practitioners, and judges believed that the variations in commercial law among the states created confusion and uncertainty in and impeded interstate commerce. As a result of this concern, state legislatures sponsored an organization, The National Conference of Commissioners on Uniform State Laws (NCCUSL), which commonly uses the shorter name, Uniform Law Commission (ULC). (We continue to call it by its original name, NCCUSL.) The task of NCCUSL is to draft uniform model statutes and recommend them to state legislatures for adoption. NCCUSL is not itself a legislative body. Its role is to draft proposed laws, which are then considered by state legislatures. The laws do not take effect in a state unless enacted by the state legislature. Upon its formation, NCCUSL, under the leadership of its Reporter, Professor Williston, immediately began work on drafting a uniform model sales law based on an English statute that had been enacted a few years earlier. The model law, called the Uniform Sales Act, was completed in 1906 and subsequently enacted by many state legislatures.

By the 1940s the Sales Act needed updating, and NCCUSL, in collaboration with the American Law Institute (ALI—the body responsible for drafting the Restatements), embarked on an extensive project to revise the law of sales and to expand its efforts at unifying commercial law by drafting model laws covering other types of commercial transactions. NCCUSL and ALI completed this work in the 1950s and published their final draft of the text of the UCC, a comprehensive uniform law governing several types of commercial transactions, including sales of goods.

When NCCUSL and ALI publish their final draft of a model law, they are said to "promulgate" the model law, and the final draft is known as the "Official Text." However, it must be stressed again that the promulgation of the Official Text of a model law does not make it the law. At that stage it is just a legislative proposal addressed to the states by NCCUSL and ALI. For the Official Text to become law in a state, the state legislature must adopt it by enacting it as a statute of the state. In the years following promulgation of the Official Text, the UCC was enacted in every state except Louisiana. (As noted in Chapter 1, Louisiana is a Civilian jurisdiction with its own commercial code. It did adopt parts of the UCC but did not enact Article 2.)

The goal of NCCUSL and ALI in promulgating a model law is to have every state enact the law as drafted. If only some states enact the model law, or if states change it when enacting it, the benefit of uniformity is lost or diminished. When states originally enacted the UCC, they did adopt it largely in the form in which it was promulgated. However, some legislatures did make changes. Although a practitioner must be careful of nonuniform enactments in a particular jurisdiction, we will not be concerned with them but will rely on the Official Text of the UCC, as promulgated by NCCUSL and ALI, as a representation of the actual law, as it may be found in most states.

2. The UCC Provisions Covered in This Course: Articles 1 and 2

Although the UCC has 11 Articles, we are concerned with only two of them: Article 2, which covers sales of goods, and Article 1, which sets out general provisions that apply to all transactions covered by the UCC, including sales of goods. Although most of the rules pertaining to sales of goods are found in Article 2, it is important not to forget Article 1, whose provisions are also directly relevant. Many of the words and phrases used in Article 2 (and elsewhere in the UCC) are defined in Article 1. In addition, Article 1 sets out general statements of purpose, policy, interpretation, and approach.

3. Revisions of the UCC

NCCUSL and ALI recognized that the UCC, like other statutes, requires updating and adjustment. Were this to be left solely to state legislatures, uniformity would quickly erode as different states altered their versions of the UCC over time. To try to ensure uniform amendments to the UCC, NCCUSL and ALI created a procedure to review the various Articles of the UCC and to draft amendments, which would then be presented to state legislatures for enactment. This process is slow. It usually takes NCCUSL and ALI years to formulate revisions before they are finally promulgated as amendments to the Official Text. Thereafter, state legislatures have to be persuaded to enact the amendments. NCCUSL and ALI have promulgated changes to several Articles over the years, and state legislatures have generally, but not always, enacted them. For the purposes of this course, we are concerned only with work done on Articles 1 and 2.

NCCUSL and ALI extensively revised the Official Text of Article 1 in 2001 and that of Article 2 in 2003. Most states have adopted the 2001 revisions of Article 1, so we can generally assume that the Official Text of Article 1, as revised in 2001, is an accurate representation of the law as enacted by the states. Therefore, whenever Article 1 is quoted or cited in this book, we use the 2001 Official Text. (Some states that adopted the 2001 revision of Article 1 did not adopt all of its revisions. As noted in Section 1, we do not take account of any nonuniform adoptions in a particular state, but a practitioner must be sure to consult the actual statute of the state whose law governs the transaction.) The 2003 revision of Article 2 was a failure. The revisions were controversial when promulgated, and NCCUSL and ALI were not successful in persuading any state to adopt them. It was unclear for many years whether the revised version of Article 2 would ever become law. That uncertainty was resolved in 2011, when NCCUSL and ALI withdrew their support for the revision. As a result, the Official Text of Article 2 remains largely as it was before the failed revision. While some states have made relatively small variations in the Official Text when adopting it as the law of the state, the Official Text accords substantially with the state law on sales of goods. We can therefore be confident that it does generally represent the actual law applicable throughout the United States.

4. The Style and Jurisprudence of the UCC

While the old Uniform Sales Act was a product of classical thinking, the UCC is a strong expression of legal realism, which was the prevailing philosophy at the time of its drafting. Professor Karl Llewellyn the dominant force in drafting Article 2 and one of the most important participants in the drafting of the UCC as a whole, was a firm legal realist. He rejected the notion that law could consist of a set of "black letter" rules that could be mechanically applied to the resolution of disputes. He saw law as a means of achieving societal ends, to be drafted so that it reflects how people actually act and gives effect to their reasonable expectations. In the commercial field, he considered custom and usage of the marketplace to be the yardstick for creating rules that mirrored reality and sought to draft rules that were sensitive to commercial practice and that would allow courts to remain responsive to it in applying the rules. To this end, Llewellyn believed in broadly written provisions that expressed key general principles but that left room for flexibility in the adjudication of cases. As you come across Article 2 provisions in the course of this book, you will see how heavily this attitude weighed in its drafting.

law should be written broadly then leave room for clarify by courts

The UCC itself expresses this approach in many areas. However, it is most clearly articulated in UCC 1-103(a). This section is part of Article 1, which, as mentioned above, applies throughout the UCC and expresses general principles and approaches to be followed by courts in dealing with all Articles of the UCC.

UCC 1-103(a). CONSTRUCTION OF [UNIFORM COMMERCIAL CODE][1] TO PROMOTE ITS PURPOSES AND POLICIES . . .

(a) [The Uniform Commercial Code] must be liberally construed and applied to promote its underlying purposes and policies, which are:

purpose of UCC

(1) to simplify, clarify, and modernize the law governing commercial transactions;

(2) to permit the continued expansion of commercial practices through custom, usage, and agreement of the parties; and

(3) to make uniform the law among the various jurisdictions.

---

[1] The phrase [Uniform Commercial Code] is bracketed in the Official Text to indicate that a state may substitute its own statutory title for these words upon enacting the UCC.

5. Working with Article 2

[handwritten: law when it's enacted by state legislature]

It must be stressed that Article 2, a state statute, is very different from the Restatement, Second, which, although written to look like a statute, with its rules set out in sections, is just persuasive secondary authority. Article 2, as enacted by a state legislature, is the law. It binds courts, which must apply it where a sale of goods is involved. As a statute, its force is greater than that of judicial precedent. Therefore, if a provision of Article 2 is inconsistent with a principle of the common law of contracts, as established by judicial precedent, the Article 2 provision prevails.

[handwritten margin: statute > precedent for enforceability]

This does not mean that the application of Article 2 is simply a matter of finding the right rule and plugging it into the facts to reach a nice, clean result. As we discussed in Chapter 1, we have passed the stage of believing that any laws, whether derived from judicial precedent or from a statute, can be applied with such mechanical ease. Most sections of Article 2 are written in broad terms, leaving plenty of room for interpretation and reasoning to reach results in specific cases. Therefore, a large body of both binding and persuasive precedent, frequently presenting different or contradictory approaches, has grown up in the interpretation of the provisions of Article 2.

[handwritten margin: precedent has grown around Art. 2]

Furthermore, just because the law relating to the sale of goods is governed by statute does not mean that common law principles are irrelevant. In fact, the common law of contracts continues to have considerable importance in transactions involving the sale of goods. There are two reasons for this.

First, many rules in the UCC are not much different from those of common law. In part this is because many UCC provisions are codifications of rules that exist under common law, or are at least based on common law principles. There has also been movement in the other direction: Because the UCC presented a modern approach when it was promulgated, it has steadily influenced courts in developing the common law, so many differences that existed at the time the UCC was first drafted have disappeared or have become less marked. This influence has also affected commentators, who in turn have persuaded courts. As noted in Chapter 1, the Restatement, Second, has many provisions modeled on Article 2.

[handwritten margin: with most people using it, therefore there are less differences in law]

[handwritten: common law is supplemental]

Second, UCC 1-103(b) (one of the general provisions of Article 1) states that common law principles supplement Code provisions unless displaced by them. Therefore, where the UCC does not deal with a particular aspect of the law or does not deal with it fully enough, the court must look to common law to resolve the issue. The drafters of Article 2 deliberately declined to enact provisions in areas where they felt that common law principles were adequate, so there are significant areas of contract law that are not covered in Article 2. Also, the open-ended drafting style of Article 2 often leaves much scope for the use of common law rules in extrapolating from or refining the statutory language. Therefore, the common law interweaves with the provisions of Article 2, sometimes to fill gaps left by the statute and sometimes to build on what the statute says. The cardinal principle to be followed by courts in doing this is to ensure that common law rules are applied consistently to supplement but not to undermine the Code provisions.

6. The Organization of Article 2 and the Citation of Code Sections

The UCC consists of several Articles, each governing specified types of commercial transactions. For example, beyond Article 2, Article 2A deals with leases of goods, Articles 3 and 4 deal with commercial instruments (such as checks and promissory notes) and banking, and Article 9 deals with the manner of acquiring an interest in personal property as security for a debt. We are concerned only with Article 2, which deals with sales of goods, and with Article 1, which contains definitions and general principles that apply in Article 2 as well as in all other Articles of the UCC.

Each Article of the UCC is divided into parts, and each part consists of a number of sections on related topics. The standard form of citing a UCC section is to cite the number of the Article, followed by a hyphen or period and the section number. In this book, we use the hyphen. For example, if we refer to section 102 of Article 2, we cite it as UCC 2-102. However, when courts apply the UCC, the citation may not look exactly like this, because courts commonly cite to it in the form that it has been enacted in the state statute. For example, suppose that the UCC section in issue is UCC 2-102. In a Connecticut case, the court would cite the section as Conn. Gen. Stat. §42a-2-102. This shows that the UCC has been incorporated into the Connecticut statutes under Title 42a. If the case emanated from New Jersey, the citation would be to that state's statutes: N.J.S.A. 12A:2-102. However, it is usually not difficult to identify the corresponding section in the Official Text because most state statutes incorporate the section numbers used in the Official Text.

7. The Official Comments to the UCC

When the drafters wrote the UCC, they wrote an "Official Comment" to each section. These comments, which can be quite lengthy, explain the sections, set out the reasoning for the rules, provide examples, and embellish the rather sparse statutory language. Although the comments are not part of the statute, and are therefore not "the law," they have been tremendously influential. Courts routinely cite them in interpreting the sections, and it is sometimes hard to remember that they are really just persuasive in nature.

B THE SCOPE OF ARTICLE 2

sales

UCC 2-102 states, "[T]his Article applies to transactions in goods. . . ." Although the section uses the broader word "transactions," you may treat that word as meaning "sales" for our purposes. UCC 2-105(1) defines "goods" to mean ". . . all things (including specially manufactured goods) which are movable at the time of identification to the contract for sale. . . ." UCC 2-106(1) defines a sale as ". . . the passing of title from the seller to the buyer for a price. . . ."

not for services

If a transaction is clearly a pure sale of goods (for example, the buyer purchases groceries at a supermarket) Article 2 unquestionably applies. Likewise, if the contract consists purely of the rendition of services (for example, the buyer of the groceries employs a cook to prepare her meals), Article 2 does not apply to it. However, some transactions include both the sale of goods and the provision of services. (For example, the customer at a restaurant is both buying the food ordered and paying for the service of having it prepared and served to her at her table.)

As noted in Section A.5, in many respects, the rules in Article 2 are the same as those in the common law. This is because many Article 2 provisions are codifications of common law, many common law rules have evolved to conform to Article 2, and common law principles supplement Article 2 provisions under UCC 1-103(b) where Article 2 does not displace them. As a result, in many situations the decision of whether to apply the common law or Article 2 has no practical significance—the result would be the same whether the common law or Article 2 applied. However, in some cases it is crucial to resolve the question of scope because there is a significant difference between the common law and Article 2. The next case deals with the question of what law should govern a hybrid transaction, and it also indicates some situations in which the resolution of a case would be different under the common law and Article 2.

hybrid transaction

AUDIO VISUAL ARTISTRY v. TANZER

403 S.W.3d 789 (2012)
Tennessee Court of Appeals

STAFFORD, Judge.

This is a breach of contract case. Appellant/Homeowner contracted with Appellee for the installation of a "smart home" system. After myriad problems arose, Appellant fired Appellee, who filed the instant lawsuit to collect the unpaid balance for equipment and installation. The trial court determined that the primary purpose of the parties' agreement was the sale of goods and applied Article 2 of the Uniform Commercial Code. . . . Appellant appeals, arguing that the trial court erred in applying the UCC. . . .

On or about March 26, 2004, Appellant Stephen Tanzer and Appellee Audio Video Artistry ("AVA") entered into discussions for the sale and installation of electronic and entertainment equipment in Mr. Tanzer's home. AVA is a residential entertainment and communications firm specializing in custom design projects. . . . [It offers] state-of-the-art home theater, multi-room music and television, lighting control and phone/intercom systems. The sale, installation, and integration of these systems for the creation of a "smart home" (also known as "domotics") is AVA's specialty. . . . [In March 2004, AVA, represented by one of its owners, Chris Rogers, submitted a written proposal to Tanzer to install 6 "independent" zones of music consisting of 13 rooms and related equipment to switch, power, and control the music system; a phone system throughout the house with door communications; a lighting control system throughout the house to include 64 standard wattage (600w) loads; and network wiring for television, phone, music, and computers throughout the home. The systems pricing for this work (i.e., the total price of $78,567.13) was broken out in the original proposal as follows: Equipment, $56,375.00; labor/programming, $9,880.00; cable and parts, $5,660.00; and tax, $6,652.13.]

On September 22, 2004, AVA and Mr. Tanzer entered into a written contract, which incorporates the original proposal, adding an additional "seventh zone" for music, and also adding seven automated shades. These shades were included as a "purchase incentive" at no cost to Mr. Tanzer. The contract provides that, in the event the shades do not work in an acceptable fashion, Mr. Tanzer would receive an additional $8,400 credit. The contract further contemplates that Mr. Tanzer's needs and desires for the "smart system" would likely evolve during the course of the project; therefore, the contract specifically provides that "[v]erbal agreements throughout the life of the project may also be honored as part of this contract and will be documented by AVA."

As originally contemplated, the contract called for a Concierge whole-house audio system. The audio/visual items were to be integrated via the Crestron system, which would allow Mr. Tanzer to play music in the seven, independently-controlled music "zones." Remote control "touch-panels" would control and integrate DVD, television, music, and other smart home functions. The contract further included a Lutron automated lighting system, which would be integrated into the Crestron system, along with an intercom/phone/whole house networking system.

At the time the parties entered their contract, construction had just commenced on Mr. Tanzer's home. The home is not a usual residence; rather, it is an approximately 15,000 square foot, $3.5 million build. Because of the size and scope of the project, AVA was to install certain wiring and equipment during the construction process. Pre-wiring began on the house as the framing went in, but equipment installation and programming of the smart system did not begin in earnest until March, 2006. Mr. Tanzer and his family moved into the home in April, 2006.

During the project, and as contemplated in the contract, the original scope of work was changed and AVA performed additional work. One significant change was the decision to use an Escient music system in lieu of the Concierge music system. Mr. Rogers allegedly represented to Mr. Tanzer, after the job had begun, that the Escient system was better able to do what Mr. Tanzer wanted, i.e., stream music from his PC, which was not a function that the Concierge system offered. AVA agreed to sell and install the Escient system for the same price as the Concierge system. Later, an art frame and shade were also added to conceal the television in the sitting room. The "art shade" is a custompainted, frame-mounted piece of artwork on canvas, which can be rolled down to conceal a television at the push of a button. Other changes related to the Crestron touch panels, which were changed from radio-frequency panels to Wi-Fi panels (Crestron came out with a Wi-Fi product before installation commenced). The Wi-Fi panels were changed at the same cost as that previously quoted for the radio-frequency panels. Another change was the switch in the music distribution equipment, which would allow for future expansion of the system. Further changes included equipment for the media room and five additional pairs of speakers. AVA also integrated the pool system, the alarm system, and the HVAC system with the Crestron control system.

Mr. Tanzer eventually became unsatisfied with AVA's work. . . . [He claimed that he was still having trouble with the functionality of the system fifteen months after its installation, AVA's attempts to fix problems were ineffective, and new problems arose every time AVA tinkered with the system.] To compound these alleged issues, in July, 2006, the basement of the house flooded, damaging the media room. A year later, in July of 2007, while AVA was allegedly still trying to "debug" the system, the home was struck by lightning. The power surge from the lightning caused damage to the Crestron processor and Ethernet card. Although the damaged components had no warranty against "Acts of God," it is not disputed that AVA replaced them without additional charge. In August 2007, Mr. Tanzer fired AVA and requested a final billing. . . . [The bill reflected a total project cost of $119,402.15 (increased from the original proposal because of changes to the system) and an outstanding balance of $43,824.55. Tanzer disputed this balance, and AVA filed this suit in November 2007 for breach of contract. Tanzer denied any liability and counterclaimed for damages, alleging that it was AVA which breached the contract. A crucial issue in the case was whether the transaction was governed by UCC Article 2. It was important to resolve this to determine whether provisions of Article 2 relating to a buyer's right to reject or revoke acceptance of goods that did not conform to the contract, and the buyer's right to offset damages for defective goods were applicable.[2] The trial court held that Article 2 did apply to the transaction. It held that AVA was entitled to payment of the balance of

---

[2] It is not necessary to concern yourself about these issues at this stage. The buyer's right to reject or revoke acceptance of nonconforming goods is discussed in Chapter 19, and the buyer's right to damages for defective goods that have been accepted is discussed in Chapter 20. For the present, it is sufficient to note that Article 2 has specific provisions relating to these issues, which would be applicable only if Article 2 governed the transaction. —EDS.

[handwritten margin note: article 2 does apply here]

the contract price, less an offset due to Tanzer for a portion of the equipment that he rejected, and for damages for defects in equipment that he accepted. The Court of Appeals agreed that Article 2 did apply to the transaction and affirmed the judgment of the trial court. We include here only that portion of the opinion relating to the question of whether Article 2 applies to the transaction.]

Mr. Tanzer asserts that the trial court erred in applying UCC Article 2 to his contract with AVA. Specifically, Mr. Tanzer argues that thrust of the contract is for services and not for the sale of goods such that common-law breach of contract principles apply. We begin our analysis with 67 Am. Jur. 2d *Sales* §37, which provides:

> Article 2 [of the UCC] applies to transactions in goods but does not apply to construction contracts or contracts for the rendition of services. However, the existence of a sale in and of itself does not automatically implicate the Uniform Commercial Code. In many cases, a contract or transaction may involve both the transaction of a sale and the rendition of services, presenting a "mixed" or hybrid transaction or contract. To determine whether such "mixed" or "hybrid" contracts are governed by Article 2, a court must examine the whole transaction and look to the essence or main objective of the parties' agreement or the primary or overall purpose of the transaction.
>
> Ordinarily, a court determines whether a mixed contract for goods and services is subject to Article 2 by considering whether the contract, reasonably stated, is for goods with labor incidentally involved or for services with goods incidentally involved. The question is generally one of fact, involving a consideration of the contract in its entirety. Depending upon whether the contract or transaction is predominantly for the sale of goods or the rendition of services, Article 2 applies to the entire contract or not at all.

[handwritten margin note: goods w/ labor incidentally involved]

[handwritten note: all or nothing]

As further discussed in 1 Stephen W. Ramp & Katherine Simpson Allen, *Tennessee Practice: Uniform Commercial Code Forms* §2-106 (2d ed. 2002):

> A sale is the passing of title from the seller to the buyer for a price. Courts will consider the substance of the transaction rather than how the parties chose to label the transaction. Where the service component of a contract for sale overrides the goods aspect of the transaction it will not fall within Article 2 once the transaction is determined to be a service and not a sale.

The question of whether UCC Article 2 or common-law contract principles apply is important . . . [for a number of reasons. For example, Article 2 provides that unless there is an express disclaimer, the goods sold are subject to implied warranties, it has a statute of limitations that requires the sales contract to be memorialized in a writing or record, it has a statute of limitations that differs from the common law, and it makes provision for remedies for both buyers and sellers.]

One of the earliest cases to adopt the predominant purpose test was *Bonebrake v. Cox*, 499 F.2d 951 (8th Cir. 1974), which involved a contract for the sale and installation of pre-fabricated bowling equipment. The *Bonebrake* Court noted that such hybrid contracts are legion and then proposed its test: "The test for inclusion or exclusion is not whether they are mixed, but granting that they are mixed, whether their predominant factor, their thrust, their purpose, reasonably stated, is the rendition of service, with goods incidentally involved (e.g., contract with artist for painting), or is a transaction of sale, with labor incidentally involved (e.g., installation of a water heater in a bathroom)." In *Bonebrake*, the court concluded that the goods element predominated, thus invoking the rules of Article 2, including the warranty provisions.

the contract is mixed is enough

In the case of *Pass v. Shelby Aviation*, 2000 WL 388775 (Tenn. App. 2000), Tennessee adopted and applied the *Bonebrake* predominant purpose test. Applying the test, the *Pass* Court determined that a mixed transaction of goods and services was "predominantly the provision of a service, not subject to the warranty provisions of the UCC." In that case, Max E. Pass, Jr., and his wife, Martha N. Pass, were both killed when their aircraft, piloted by Mr. Pass, crashed outside of Opelika, Alabama. Approximately four-and-one-half months prior to the fatal flight, Mr. Pass had taken the aircraft to defendant, Shelby Aviation, Inc., for inspection and service. During the servicing, Shelby Aviation replaced both rear wing attach point brackets on the plane. After the crash, the administrators of the Pass's estates filed a lawsuit against Shelby Aviation. The suit alleged that the rear wing brackets, which were sold and installed by Shelby Aviation, were defective and asserted claims for breach of . . . express and implied warranties under Article 2 of the UCC. . . . This Court determined that the predominant purpose test was the appropriate test to apply because it looks at the transaction as a whole. In applying the test, the Court stated: "In order to determine whether the predominant purpose of a mixed transaction is the sale of goods or the provision of a service, we examine the language of the parties' contract, the nature of the business of the supplier of the goods and services, the reason the parties entered into the contract (i.e. what each bargained to receive), and the respective amounts charged under the contract for goods and for services. None of these factors alone is dispositive. The party seeking application of the UCC bears the burden of proof to show that the predominant purpose of the contract was the sale of goods." In concluding that the foregoing relevant factors should be considered in determining the choice of law for mixed contracts for sales of goods and service, the *Pass* Court relied upon an Indiana Supreme Court Case, *Insul-Mark Midwest, Inc. v. Modern Materials, Inc.*, 612 N.E.2d 550 (Ind. 1993) [which formulated the test on the same terms]. . . .

① *language of contract/nature of business,*
③ *reason the contract was entered in to*
④ *amount charged for goods v. services*

Applying the foregoing principles, the *Pass* Court determined that "the invoice clearly emphasizes the repair and inspection aspects of the transaction, indicating that the predominant purpose was the sale of service, with the sale of goods incidental to that service." Further, the overall nature of Shelby Aviation's business was service rather than the sale of parts, and "Mr. Pass took the plane to Shelby Aviation primarily to have a service performed, i.e., the annual inspection." Finally, the court looked to allocation of costs between goods and services. . . . [The costs of the goods was only 37 percent of the total price.

The court concluded that the predominant purpose of the transaction was the provision of a service rather than the sale of goods, so that the warranty provisions of Article 2 were not applicable.]

From *Pass*, we understand that, in applying the predominant purpose test, the court looks to four factors:

predominant purpose test

(1)   the language of the contract;
(2)   the nature of the business of the supplier of goods and services;
(3)   the reason the parties entered into the contract; and
(4)   the amounts paid for the rendition of the services and goods, respectively.

We now turn to address each of these factors based on the evidence contained in the record to determine whether the trial court correctly found that the contract at issue in this case predominantly involves the sale of goods such that UCC Article 2 is applicable.

The first factor set out by the *Pass* Court requires us to look "to the language of the contract, in light of the situation of the parties and the surrounding circumstances. Specifically, [the court] looks to the terms describing the performance of the parties, and the words used to describe the relationship between the parties." Contractual language that refers to the transaction as a "purchase," for example, or identifies the parties as the "buyer" and "seller," indicates that the transaction is for goods rather than services.

Turning to the contract between Mr. Tanzer and AVA, we first note that it is titled "Systems Sale and Installation Contract." From the plain language, it is clear that this is a hybrid contract, contemplating both the sale of goods and the installation of the goods. The question, then, is whether the language, when viewed in context, indicates the predominant purpose of the contract.

language of the contract

Throughout the contract, Mr. Tanzer is referred to as the "purchaser," a term that connotes a sale of goods contract. In various sections, the contract states that: (1) "[p]er this contract, AVA agrees to deliver and install **equipment** included in the proposal;" (2) "AVA retains ownership of the **equipment** until contract is paid in full;" (3) "Delays . . . by parties other than AVA that prohibit proper installation of **delivered equipment** shall not delay payment . . . ;" (4) "Prices are subject to change on items . . . between the time of execution of this contract and the **delivery of goods**;" (5) "All **pre-paid goods** shall be delivered at the price agreed;" (6) "Model numbers may change . . . therefore **Product** delivered may not . . . be the same model number agreed to in the Proposal;" and (7) "Final installation of most **electronic hardware** corresponds with purchaser['s] actual move-in date. . . ." (Emphases added). As noted in *Bonebrake*, "equipment" is a term of art, which is "peculiar [to the sale of goods.]" Furthermore, the contract incorporates, by reference, the earlier proposal, which sets out the specific equipment that AVA would install in the Tanzer home.

inter alia
↳ among other things

In his brief, Mr. Tanzer urges this Court to read the disputed contract as a construction or building contract based, *inter alia,* upon the fact that the equipment and installation occurred during the building process and the items installed allegedly became part of the completed home. In support of his argument, Mr. Tanzer relies upon the case of *Aluminum Vinyl Sales Company v. Woerz,* 1993 WL 367125 (Tenn. App. 1993). *Woerz* involved a contract for the installation of vinyl siding on a home. In pertinent part, the *Woerz* Court stated:

> The Uniform Commercial Code does not apply to a contract for the rendition of services or to construction contracts. The subject matter of the contract before us is to furnish "all the materials and labor necessary for" the installation of vinyl siding to the entire exterior of Defendant's house. A contract to furnish a movable thing and affix it to the freehold is not a contract for the sale of goods, but one to furnish materials and affix them to the freehold by work and labor, and, until the materials are affixed, title to the materials does not pass.

↳ service contract

Despite Mr. Tanzer's reading of *Woerz*, we cannot extend its holding so far as to conclude that it stands for the proposition that any and all contracts that contemplate the sale of goods, which are installed in a home or affixed to realty, are to be construed as predominantly service contracts. . . . [Rather, if the product consisted of goods that were identifiable, tangible and movable before installation and, once installed, constitute only a small portion of a total building, they remain goods, covered by Article 2. The court cites cases giving examples such as electrical equipment, water heaters, and air conditioners. The court concludes that the mere fact that the components were installed in Tanzer's house did not alter their identity as movable goods.]

In addition to the plain language of the contract, the court may also consider the nature of the seller's business. It is not disputed in the record that AVA is in the business of design and sale of custom, state-of-the-art, home theater, multi-room music/television/lighting control, and phone/intercom systems. AVA does not manufacture or promote one brand of product; rather, it sells and installs products from various manufacturers. From our review of the record, it appears that AVA's "design" role really constitutes a determination of what goods the customer needs and what integration system(s) will work to link the various components. In this sense, the "integration" of the whole system is done by the controlling system, i.e., Escient, Concierge, Crestron, Lutron. The sale of these respective systems is, in the opinion of this Court, similar to the sale of an integrated computer system. The installation and service that AVA performs is incidental to the overarching purpose of its business, which is to sell "smart home" components.

The third factor instructs the court to consider the final product the purchaser bargained to receive, and whether it may be described as a good or a service. Whether the purchaser sought to procure a good or a service by entering into the subject contract is a strong indication of the predominant purpose of the contract. As discussed above, even in cases where labor and services were contemplated by the parties to be an integral part of the contract, courts have still held that Article 2 applies. Turning to the record in the instant case, in his answer, Mr. Tanzer admits that he contracted for electronic equipment. It is not

nature of business ↓ sell smart home components

reason for contract ↓ wanted a smart home

disputed that AVA orders all of the equipment it sells from the manufacturer or from the distributor. In other words, none of the equipment was "constructed" at Tanzer's home; it was merely installed there. The record further indicates that the equipment maintained its characteristics as personalty and was never rendered immovable from the residence. In support of this conclusion, Mr. Tanzer presented a spreadsheet at trial, which indicated all of the equipment he was willing to return to AVA. The fact that Mr. Tanzer could return this equipment supports a finding that it had not become a permanent improvement to his realty. The fact that the original proposal, which was incorporated into the contract, breaks apart the costs of the "equipment," i.e., tangible goods, from the cost of "cable/misc. parts," i.e., materials also supports a finding that Mr. Tanzer bargained for the purchase of equipment, and that the services rendered by AVA in connection with that sale, including delivery and installation, were necessary but incidental to the ultimate purpose of the contract, i.e., to obtain the various components and the integration system that would link them.

The final factor to be considered is the respective amounts charged under the contract for the goods and services. If the cost of the goods is but a small portion of the overall contract price, such fact would increase the likelihood that the services portion predominates. Conversely where the charge for goods exceeds that for services, the contract is more likely to be for goods. In this case, the trial court found that the costs of labor and services were "insignificant" compared to the cost of the equipment. As set out above, under the original contract, equipment sales constituted $56,375 of the total price of $71,915 (before taxes); on the other hand, labor accounted for only $9,880. In the final invoice, equipment totaled $89,640.03 of the total contract price of $109,830.03 (before taxes), with labor constituting only $13,260.00. Viewed as a percentage, equipment constitutes roughly 82% of the final contract price. Accordingly, this factor weighs heavily in favor of a finding that the contract was predominantly for the sale of goods.

Based upon the foregoing, we conclude that all four of the *Pass* factors favor the trial court's conclusion that the instant contract was predominantly for the sale of goods. Accordingly, we conclude that the trial court did not err in applying UCC Article 2 to this transaction.

■ QUESTIONS

(1) Look at each of the authorities cited in the case. Are they binding or persuasive? Would your answer be the same if this case was before a Tennessee trial court?

(2) Assume that in a case decided after *Audio Visual Artistry*, a Tennessee trial court has to decide if a contract to sell and install an integrated computer system (that is, a contract to supply the computer and all related equipment and

to set up the system so that it is operational) is predominantly a sale of goods. What is the precedential weight of *Audio Visual Artistry*?

———————

Here are a few things to keep in mind in relation to the proper scope of UCC Article 2:

(1) *An alternative test for deciding scope.* Like most recent cases, *Audio Visual Artistry* applies the predominant purpose test to decide if the transaction is governed by the common law or Article 2. Once the predominant purpose is determined, either the common law or Article 2 is applied to the transaction as a whole. There is an alternative test that is less commonly used in recent cases. It is known as the "gravamen" test. Under that test, the court does not decide the predominant purpose of a hybrid transaction, but rather breaks it into separate components and applies Article 2 to that portion of the contract that involves a sale of goods, and the common law to the non-sale portion. For example, if the gravamen test had been used in *Audio Visual Artistry*, the court would have applied Article 2 to resolve any dispute relating to the equipment itself, and would have applied the common law to any dispute relating to the installation and other services pertaining to the operation of the equipment. The probable reason why most courts have followed the predominant purpose test rather than the gravamen test is because it can be very awkward, and in some cases completely unworkable, to try to break up the contract and to apply different legal rules to the separate parts of it.

(2) *A different scope issue: goods versus real property.* In *Audio Visual Artistry* the court was concerned whether the predominant purpose of the transaction was a sale of goods or services. Because the components of the system were incorporated into the house, the case hints at another scope issue that could arise where goods are so incorporated into real property that they lose their identity as goods and become part of the real property. This issue does not come up in this case because the components were clearly goods at the crucial time. To qualify as goods under UCC 2-105, the things must be movable at the time of identification to the contract, which occurred before they were incorporated into the real property.

■ PROBLEM 2.1

Dazzle Carpet Co., Inc. is a carpet cleaning company. It cleans carpets with equipment that it takes to the customer's premises. The carpet cleaning equipment is filled with a mixture of water and a special solvent, patented by Dazzle. The steam produced by the mixture dissolves dirt on the carpet, which is then vacuumed up by the cleaning machine. The cost of the solvent constitutes about 10 percent of the price of the cleaning service. The rest of the price covers labor charges. Dazzle wishes UCC Article 2 to apply to its transactions, so it includes language in its standard contract that refers to itself as "the seller" and to the customer as "the buyer." The contract specifically states, "The parties agree that this is a contract for the sale of goods, subject to UCC Article 2." Is this enough to make Article 2 applicable to Dazzle's transactions?

[handwritten annotation: → no look in to the nature of the sale not exclusively language]

As noted earlier, it may not matter to decide which law applies to a hybrid transaction, because the rules of Article 2 and the common law are the same with regard to the aspect of the transaction that is subject to dispute. However, in some cases the rules of Article 2 and the common law diverge, so it is important to decide which applies. As *Audio Visual Artistry* indicates, the difference between the common law and Article 2 in that case related to specific provisions of Article 2 that deal with a buyer's right to reject or revoke acceptance of goods and the buyer's remedy for goods that have been accepted. Here are some other examples:

[handwritten annotation: implied warranties]

(1) Article 2 provides for implied warranties, which may not be available under common law. This was the issue in the *Pass* case, discussed in *Audio Visual Artistry*.

[handwritten annotation: needs to be written or recorded]

(2) Article 2 contains a statute of frauds which requires that many contracts for the sale of goods be memorialized in a writing or record. Therefore, an oral contract for the sale of goods may not be enforceable. Although some common law contracts are also subject to a statute of frauds, many are not.[3] As a result, a determination that an oral contract is not a sale of goods could mean that it is enforceable, but a determination that it is a sale of goods may make it unenforceable.

(3) To ensure that claims are litigated within a reasonable time after they arise, the law requires a plaintiff to commence suit on a claim within a stated period after the right to sue on the claim accrues. This is known as the statute of limitations. If a plaintiff fails to commence suit within the period prescribed by the statute of limitations, the claim becomes unenforceable in a court, and any suit on the claim will be dismissed. The period of the statute of limitations varies depending on the nature of the claim. In most states, the statute of limitations for contract claims is six years or more. However, if the contract is a sale of goods subject to UCC Article 2, the UCC prescribes a shorter statute of limitations—in most circumstances it is four years. Therefore, if a plaintiff

[handwritten annotation: statute of limitations → have to file claims in a preperscribed period]

[handwritten annotation: 6 years or more - states Art. 2 - 4 years]

---

[3] The statute of frauds is discussed in Chapter 8.

waits, say, five years to sue on the contract, a determination that it is a sale of goods would preclude suit on the claim.

This is what happened in *Bruel & Kjaer v. Village of Bensenville*, 969 N.E.2d 445 (Ill. App. 2012). The court had to decide whether a contract to sell noise-monitoring and radar equipment, together with the provision of certain services—including the provision of software, the installation of the equipment, and the servicing of the equipment—was predominantly a sale of goods or a contract for services. The court found that the contract was predominantly a sale of goods. As a result, it was subject to the Article 2 four-year statute of limitations, rather than the common law ten-year statute of limitations. Because the seller had waited more than four years to sue the buyer for the balance of the contract price, its suit was time-barred under the shorter Article 2 limitation period, and its claim was dismissed.

sale of goods

■ PROBLEM 2.2

Last year, the state Supreme Court had to decide if an oral dealership agreement was predominantly a sale of goods. The agreement in question was entered into between a television manufacturer and an appliance retailer, and it gave the retailer the exclusive right to sell the manufacturer's products in a defined territory. Under the agreement, the retailer would buy the televisions from the manufacturer for resale to its own customers. It would maintain an inventory of those products and would provide services such as promoting the products and servicing them for customers. The television manufacturer breached the agreement by appointing competing dealers in the retailer's exclusive territory. The retailer sued the manufacturer. The crucial question was whether the dealership agreement was a sale of goods because if it was, the oral agreement was unenforceable under the Article 2 statute of frauds. The court held that although the agreement had several service aspects, these services were ancillary to the predominant purpose of the contract, which was the retailer's purchase of the televisions for resale to its customers. As a result, the court held the oral agreement to be unenforceable.

The following case is now being litigated in the trial court: Blithe Spirit, Inc., a liquor distributor, sued Moonshine Malt, Inc., a whiskey distillery, for breach of an alleged oral distributorship agreement. In its complaint, Blithe alleged that Moonshine entered into a contract appointing Blithe as the sole distributor of its products in the state. The agreement provided that Blithe would solicit orders from liquor stores for Moonshine's products. Blithe would then transmit those orders to Moonshine, who would deliver and bill directly to the stores, and would then pay Blithe a commission. Blithe alleged that Moonshine breached the agreement by refusing to accept any orders for whiskey from Blithe's customers. Moonshine answered the complaint by denying that it had made any contract with Blithe. It also moved for dismissal of the case on the ground that the complaint did not allege a written agreement, as would be required for enforcement of the alleged contract under the statute of frauds provided for in Article 2. Blithe responded to the motion by asserting that the contract was not a sale of goods and therefore not subject to Article 2's statute of frauds.

Accept Blithe's factual allegations as true. Resolve the motion to dismiss.

C THE APPLICABILITY OF ARTICLE 2 TO SALES OF INTANGIBLE RIGHTS, ESPECIALLY SOFTWARE AND OTHER INTELLECTUAL PROPERTY

Because "goods" are defined in UCC 2-105(1) to mean movable things, it is clear that intangible rights do not qualify as goods. However, the treatment of intangible rights to intellectual property, protected by the right-holder's copyright or patent, has never been definitively settled. It has long been clear that when intellectual property is incorporated into a tangible product, that product is goods. Therefore, where a novel is published in book form, or music or a movie is published on a CD or DVD, the physical object—the book, CD, or DVD—is goods. This is true even though the real value of the object lies not in the paper or plastic of which it is made but in the creative work that the object incorporates. However, even though title of the physical object (the book, CD, or DVD) passed to the buyer upon sale, this does not mean that the buyer also became the owner of the intellectual content. As the owner of a book, the buyer may keep it, scribble in it, sell it, or tear it to pieces. However, he may not do as he wishes with the content of the book, which is subject to copyright laws that restrict the buyer's right to reproduce it or otherwise use it in a manner not authorized by the holder of the copyright. Many courts have adopted the same approach to software that is incorporated into a movable physical object (such as a computer program on a disk) or a program installed in goods (such as a car, home appliance, or digital camera) that is required to make the item operate.

However, intellectual property is often not delivered in corporeal form. Books, music, movies, and software are commonly sold on and downloaded from the Internet or otherwise transmitted electronically from the seller to the buyer. This raises two difficult questions relating to the applicability of Article 2. First, is this kind of property goods? Second, even if it can be

no definite answer on patents

IP is usually not delivered in a physical way (ex. book, CD)

characterized as goods, has there actually been a sale? Recall that UCC 2-106(1) defines a sale as the passage of title from the seller to the buyer for a price. When intellectual property is transmitted electronically, there is no physical object for which title passes. Rather, the property is provided to the recipient under a license, which confers a right, usually granted with restrictions and limitations, to use the property in a particular way, for a stated purpose, and for a finite period.

transferred by license, not title

These questions have not been answered definitively. Article 2 was enacted long before technology made commerce of this kind possible and attempts by NCCUSL and ALI to develop uniform legislation to deal with the issue have not succeeded. Some years ago, these bodies promulgated the Uniform Computer Information Transactions Act (UCITA), which would have governed the sale and licensing of certain computer-related intellectual property. However, the proposed uniform law was controversial, not well received, and had few adoptions by states. NCCUSL and ALI attempted, again, in the unsuccessful effort to revise Article 2 in 2003, to clarify the applicability of Article 2 to the transfer of rights to use intellectual property. The proposed amendments to Article 2 would have expressly excluded from Article 2 the electronic transfer of "information" that is not incorporated into a tangible product. However, as explained in Section A.3, NCCUSL and ALI did not succeed in getting any state to adopt the revised version of Article 2, and it never became the law. As a result, the question of whether Article 2 applies to a transfer of intellectual property in electronic form continues to be dealt with by courts under the original broad and nonspecific scope provisions of Article 2. Some courts find Article 2 applicable, while others do not, holding principles of intellectual property or the common law of contracts to be more apposite. The next case provides an example of scope analysis in a contract involving website design and associated services.

UCITA

some judges find Art. 2 applicable, some don't

CONWELL v. GRAY LOON OUTDOOR MARKETING GROUP, INC.

906 N.E.2d 805 (2009)
Indiana Supreme Court

SHEPARD, Chief Justice.

As the Internet becomes a ubiquitous presence in American commerce, the nation's courts work to find satisfactory legal frameworks for resolving the disputes that inevitably arise. In this suit between a business enterprise and the marketing firm that created and hosted its website, we conclude that the Uniform Commercial Code does not apply and that the web design firm may collect for its work under principles of common law contract. . . . We affirm the trial court's judgment for the marketing firm.

disposition

In November 2003, Piece of America was a limited partnership pursuing the sale of novelty packages: one-square-inch parcels of land in each of the fifty states. . . . To market and sell its products, Piece of America sought to establish a website. None of the partners had any sophistication in Internet technologies or website design, so they approached Gray Loon Marketing, which provides various marketing and communication services, to design and publish its website. In September 2003, Gray Loon gave POA a design proposal for the website and an estimated price of $8,080. Among other things, Gray Loon's proposal for POA's package stated, "It is Gray Loon's philosophy that clients have purchased goods and services from us and that inherently means ownership of those goods and services as well." . . .

[Piece of America agreed to the proposal and the parties executed a contract at the end of 2003. Shortly thereafter, Gray Loon designed and launched the site, which it hosted. Piece of America paid Grey Loon in full for this work. In April 2004 Piece of America entered into a second agreement with Gray Loon for modifications to the site. Unlike the initial contract, this agreement was oral, and the parties never discussed the price of the additional work. Gray Loon executed the changes, but Piece of America failed to pay for this work despite repeated demands. Grey Loon therefore took the website offline in October 2004 and instituted suit against Piece of America for payment of its design and hosting fees. The trial court and court of appeals, applying UCC Article 2, decided that the oral contract was valid under Article 2.[4] The Supreme Court held that the lower courts were incorrect in finding that the transaction was governed by UCC Article 2. Nevertheless, it affirmed the judgment in favor of Grey Loon on the basis that the oral contract was binding under common law principles.]

you can't apply art. 2, but the web designer win

A web page consists of computer programming that is decoded by an Internet browser to show the "graphic user interface" that ranges from a simple combination of graphics and text to interactive applications. For our purposes, there are essentially two aspects of a website: the content that the pages on a website display and the programming that encodes it in such a way for a browser to interpret. In some web design relationships, the hiring party provides all content while the designer simply translates it into a format appropriate for viewing in the World Wide Web. On other occasions, the hiring party provides a vision and a goal for the site and the designer creates both the content and the programming. The latter characterization seems to fit the facts here, though POA provided some content.

↳ here POA only provided the goal. all the content was grey loon

---

[4] The Article 2 sections relevant in the case were UCC 2-201, the statute of frauds, and UCC 2-305, which states that it is not necessary for the parties to settle on a price in their contract if they intend the sale to be at a reasonable or market price. The lower courts upheld the contract on the basis that the oral agreement was enforceable because it was covered by exceptions to the statute of frauds, and that UCC 2-305 validated the contract despite the absence of an express price. —Eds.

The website at issue here was distributed by Gray Loon for free to any Internet user who directed an Internet browser to POA's domain. Piece of America paid Gray Loon to author and to distribute (or "host") the website files via its server, making it available to any computer connected through the Internet. Piece of America could have bifurcated these two tasks and hired a third party to host the site or to design it. If it had hired a third company to host the site for distribution over the Internet, it would have had to transfer the files to the other company's servers. Gray Loon could have copied them to a disk and physically delivered it or transferred the files over the Internet using any number of methods. . . .

Indiana's U.C.C. Article 2 "applies to transactions in goods." Ind. Code. §26-1-2-102 (2008). Goods "means all things (including specially manufactured goods) which are movable at the time of identification to the contract for sale, other than the money in which the price is to be paid, investment securities and things in action." Ind. Code §26-1-2-105 (2008).

Where close questions arise about whether a transaction involved the transfer of goods or performance of services, courts commonly choose one or the other by asking what was the "predominant thrust." *Compare, e.g., Ogden Martin Systs. of Indianapolis, Inc. v. Whiting Corp.*, 179 F.3d 523, 530-531 (7th Cir. 1999) (predominant thrust of installation of solid waste handling cranes was the goods), and *Insul-Mark Midwest, Inc. v. Modern Materials, Inc.*, 612 N.E.2d 550, 556 (Ind. 1993) (predominant thrust of coating of screws was the service).

Arguably, software could be treated as a good, or not, depending on how it is created or transmitted. Where software is contained in a tangible medium, especially when produced on a mass scale, courts have had a difficult time placing software into the established categories. Unsurprisingly, this challenge has prompted suggestions that a new legal paradigm may be needed. . . . Happily, this case does not include any of the aspects (like the legal effect of an agreement to transfer software on a tangible medium) that have complicated resolution of the U.C.C.'s applicability in some cases reported in the literature. We thus can address the goods/services question rather cleanly.

Our Court of Appeals has decided at least two cases on whether software is a good. Piece of America points us to a decision from two decades ago, *Data Processing Servs., Inc. v. L.H. Smith Oil Corp.*, 492 N.E.2d 314 (Ind. Ct. App. 1986). *Data Processing Services* involved custom software used in the operations of an oil company. The court determined that the sale . . . [of] customized computer software was not a sale for goods. It said the transaction was "more analogous to a client seeking a lawyer's advice or a patient seeking medical treatment." It further stated: "While a tangible end product, such as floppy disks, hard disks, punch cards or magnetic tape used as a storage medium for the program may be involved incidentally in this transaction, it is the skill and knowledge of the programmer which is being purchased in the main, not the devices by which this skill and knowledge is placed into the buyer's computer. The means of transmission is not the essence of the agreement." The Court of Appeals treated the agreement as a contract for services because that is how the language of the contract suggested the parties themselves understood it; they used terms such as "to act," and treated the object of the contract as the programmer's knowledge, skill, and ability. . . .

In a more recent case, the Court of Appeals considered a contract that licensed one software company to use another's software modules in its own end product. *Olcott Int'l & Co., Inc. v. Micro Data Base Sys., Inc.*, 793 N.E.2d 1063, 1071 (Ind. Ct. App. 2003). In concluding that U.C.C. Article 2 applied to the contract, the Court of Appeals relied on both parties' acquiescence in that conclusion and reasoned that because the agreement involved pre-existing, standardized software modules, they were goods rather than services. . . .

On the surface, these cases might suggest that customized software is a service while pre-made software is a good, but when courts try to pour new wine into old legal bottles, we sometimes miss the nuances. It would be a mistake, for instance, to treat software as a good simply because it was contained in a tangible medium that fits within that category. This would conflate the sale of a book with the sale of its intellectual content, suggesting that the purchaser of the book might be buying a right to general use of the expressions contained in the volume.

A website created under arrangements calling for the designer to fashion, program, and host its operation on the designer's server is neither tangible nor moveable in the conventional sense. To be sure, one can copy a website using tangible, movable objects such as hard drives, cables, and disks. These objects are in themselves just as certainly goods, but it does not necessarily follow that the information they contain classifies as goods as well. The arrangement between POA and Gray Loon contemplated a custom design for a single customer and an ongoing hosting relationship. As such, conventional "predominant thrust" doctrine suggests that the U.C.C. did not apply. . . .

■ QUESTIONS

(1) The court remarks that where software is contained in a mass-produced tangible medium, "courts have had a difficult time placing software into the established categories." However, it observes that because this case does not include any of the complicating aspects that have challenged courts, the goods/services question can be addressed "rather cleanly." What do you think this means? *they made all the content*

(2) The court warns against conflating the sale of a book with the sale of its intellectual content. Why is this a concern?

(3) The original written contract contained the language, "It is Gray Loon's philosophy that clients have purchased goods and services from us and that inherently means ownership of those goods and services as well." Did this language have any influence on the outcome of the case? Should it have any influence? Should parties be able to determine the question of scope by providing for it in the contract?

■ PROBLEM 2.3

Meg A. Byte bought a video camera online for $350. The physical components of the camera—a small plastic shell and the internal mechanisms to operate the camera—represent just a small fraction of the price. The real value incorporated into the camera is the program that allows the camera to record high-quality images. When Meg bought the camera from the seller's website, she also bought a separate software program to enable her to edit her movies on her computer, and a separate two-year extended warranty and service agreement to cover any repairs to her camera. A few days after she placed her order, Meg received a package in the mail that included the camera, a printed version of the extended warranty and service agreement, and a numerical "product key" for the software. The software for the editing program was not physically delivered to Meg. Instead, the "product key" enabled her to download it from the website to her computer.

  To what extent, if at all, does Article 2 apply to this transaction?

D   MERCHANTS AND ARTICLE 2

A party's status as a merchant under Article 2 is a source of confusion to students, so we introduce it early to clarify it and explain its scope.

  The first point to emphasize is that Article 2 applies to every transaction that qualifies as a sale of goods, no matter who the parties might be. For example, it applies to a householder's sale of her used goods at a garage sale or through a classified advertisement in a newspaper or on the Internet; to a store's sale of goods to a consumer; and to a supplier's sale of raw materials to a manufacturer. It is the nature of the transaction as a sale of goods, not the identity or occupation of the parties, that determines whether Article 2 applies. However, there are a few provisions in Article 2 that impose special rules or standards on a merchant. Some of these provisions apply only if both parties to the sale qualify as merchants. Others apply to the merchant party even if the other party is not a merchant. "Merchant" is defined in UCC 2-104(1):

UCC 2-104(1). DEFINITIONS: "MERCHANT" . . .

  "Merchant" means a person who deals in goods of the kind or otherwise by his occupation holds himself out as having knowledge or skill peculiar to the practices or goods involved in the transaction or to whom such

[handwritten margin note, left:] special rules on a merchant but art. 2 doesn't go in to specify who it applies to

[handwritten note, bottom:] having knowledge or skills particular to the goods in a transaction

knowledge /skill is attributed to employment

knowledge or skill may be attributed by his employment of an agent or broker or other intermediary who by his occupation holds himself out as having such knowledge or skill.

———————

This definition is wider than what one might understand in common usage. It contains two alternative bases for determining if a person is a merchant. The first defines a merchant as a person who deals in goods of the kind involved in the transaction—that is, he routinely buys and sells them. The second expands the definition beyond this to include one who may not deal in goods of the kind, but who, by occupation, holds himself out (that is, represents to a reasonable person) as having knowledge or skill peculiar to either the goods or the practices involved in the transaction. The Official Comment to UCC 2-104 indicates that this more

distinguishes casual v. professional

general definition of merchant distinguishes a casual or occasional buyer or seller (such as a consumer) from a professional in business who is expected to have familiarity with this type of transaction. Therefore, for example, a clothing retailer is clearly a merchant who deals in goods of the kind with regard to clothing that he buys and sells. However, he may also qualify as a merchant with regard to goods that he does not buy and sell, such as to shop fittings, computer software and hardware to track inventory and sales, and office supplies used in the business. He may qualify as a merchant with regard to these goods because by occupation he has knowledge and skill with regard to the goods or practices involved in the transaction. Conversely, he would likely not qualify as a merchant with regard to the sandwich that he buys each day to eat for lunch at his desk. UCC 2-104(1) also treats a person as a merchant if she is represented in the transaction by an agent or intermediary who, by occupation, holds out such knowledge or skill. If a party qualifies as a merchant, a few sections of Article 2 impose a different rule or standard (typically a higher standard) on her. By far, most provisions of Article 2 do not refer to merchants at all, which means that most of Article 2 makes no distinction between sales that involve a merchant and sales that do not. It is only where a section specifically refers to merchants that there is a different rule for them. Some of these sections create a special rule in sales "between merchants"—that is, where both parties to the transaction are merchants. Others apply a special rule to the merchant party, even if the other party is not a merchant. In the following case, the section that has a special rule for a merchant is UCC 2-403, which deals with the question of what happens when a person entrusted with the owner's goods violates that trust by selling them unlawfully to a third party. We do not study UCC 2-403 in this course, so it is used here only to illustrate the application of UCC 2-104. You will see other examples of special rules that apply only to merchants or between merchants as we proceed through the course. Again, it is important to remember that merchant status is only relevant in those sections that specifically prescribe a special rule applicable to a merchant or between merchants.

ZARETSKY v. WILLIAM GOLDBERG DIAMOND CORP.

69 F. Supp. 3d 386 (2014)
United States District Court, Southern District of New York

SCHEINDLIN, District Judge.

This case concerns the ownership of a 7.44 carat pear-shaped diamond, which is currently being held by the Gemological Institute of America ("GIA"), pending determination of title. In February 2003, the owner of the diamond—the William Goldberg Diamond Corporation ("WGDC")—consigned it, along with other items, to Derek Khan, a well-known celebrity fashion stylist. The purpose of the consignment—which reflected an ongoing arrangement between Khan and WGDC, and between Khan and other established jewelers—was for Khan to "adorn his celebrity clients" with high-end jewelry, in preparation for "special events and fashion shoots." The arrangement was governed by a Consignment Agreement, which made clear that Khan had no freestanding authority to "sell, pledge, hypothecate, or otherwise dispose of the [diamond]," but that he *could* sell the diamond "if and when [he] . . . received from [WGDC] a separate invoice." In other words, Khan was only authorized to sell the diamond if WGDC approved the sale, and set out specific terms, prior to any sale.

Typically, after WGDC consigned a piece of jewelry to Khan, he would "return the jewelry to WGDC . . . within a few days of the celebrity event." After the February 2003 consignment, however, Khan failed to return the diamond in a timely manner, prompting WGDC to become suspicious and, eventually, file a police report. On March 17, 2003, the diamond surfaced in the legitimate market, when Louis Newman—a New York diamond merchant—submitted the diamond to the GIA for certification, which was issued on March 25, 2003. In late 2003, the diamond was purchased by Stanley & Sons—another New York diamond merchant—on behalf of Frank and Donna Walsh (the "Walshes"). Some years later, the Walshes conveyed the diamond to plaintiffs, their children.

WGDC argues that because Khan stole the diamond, he could not hold title in the diamond—nor transfer title to it—as a matter of law. Therefore, WGDC argues that it is the rightful owner of the diamond. On the other hand, plaintiffs argue that Khan was not a thief, but rather an entrusted merchant who held "voidable title" in the diamond—and was therefore capable of transferring title—under the Uniform Commercial Code ("UCC"). When the Walshes purchased the diamond in 2003, plaintiffs argue that their parents acquired good title to the diamond, which was subsequently transferred to them. Therefore, plaintiffs contend that WGDC is no longer the owner of the diamond as a matter of law. . . .

Both sides moved for summary judgment on their respective legal theories. For the reasons set forth below, plaintiffs' motion is granted and WGDC's is denied.

Under New York law,[5] ... [while a thief cannot acquire title to stolen property, a person to whom property is entrusted by its owner acquires voidable, as opposed to void, title, and therefore can pass good title to a third party.] Section 2-403(2) of New York's UCC provides that "[a]ny entrusting of ... goods to a merchant who deals in goods of that kind gives [the merchant] power to transfer all rights of the entrustor to a buyer in the ordinary course of business." In other words, if an owner entrusts his property to a merchant, he is estopped from seeking replevin, down the line, against a good faith purchaser for value—even if the sale was the product of "fraud punishable as larcenous under the criminal law." (UCC 2-403(1)).

The purpose of the merchant entrustment rule is to "enhance the reliability of commercial sales by merchants who deal in the kind of goods sold by shifting the risk of resale to one who leaves his property with a merchant." Put otherwise, the rule is meant to protect "buyers in the ordinary course of business"[6] by making owners—not purchasers—shoulder the financial risk associated with fraudulent transactions. If an owner "knowingly delivers property into the possession of a merchant, he assumes the risk of the merchant's acting unscrupulously by selling the property without the owner's consent to an innocent purchaser." This puts the onus on owners to carefully "select the merchant to whom they entrust their property."

The applicability of the entrustment rule depends on whether an entrustee is a "merchant," which the UCC defines in two ways. *First,* an entrustee is a "merchant" if he "deals in goods of the kind." *Second,* an entrustee is a merchant if "by his occupation," he "holds himself out as having knowledge or skill peculiar to the practices or goods involved in the transaction."

There is no dispute that WGDC voluntarily consigned the diamond to Khan, or that the Consignment Agreement set the terms of their arrangement. The parties' disagreement pertains to the *reason* for the consignment. WGDC maintains that it entrusted the diamond to Khan for the sole and limited purpose of Khan, a fashion stylist, adorning his celebrity clients. Plaintiffs, in contrast, argue that Khan had conditional authority to sell the diamond, and that he therefore operated as a broker for WGDC. If true, this would make Khan a "merchant" under the UCC's first definition: It would mean that Khan dealt in jewelry.

---

[5] Note that this case is before a federal court which applies state law—the law of New York. As explained in Section A.2.b of Chapter 1, contracts are governed by state law but in some situations, federal courts have jurisdiction to hear contracts cases. In this case, the basis of the court's jurisdiction is diversity of citizenship—the parties are citizens of different states and the amount at issue is large enough to satisfy the minimum required. Although the federal court has jurisdiction to adjudicate the case, it applies the law of the state that governs the transaction. —EDS.

[6] This is a term of art used in the UCC. *See* N.Y.U.C.C. §2-104(1) (defining "buyer in the ordinary course of business" as "a person that buys goods in good faith, without knowledge that the sale violates the rights of another person in the goods, and in the ordinary course from a person, other than a pawnbroker, in the business of selling goods of that kind").

The nature of Khan's and WGDC's relationship is a disputed question of fact ... [but the court does not have to resolve that] because even if WGDC is right about its relationship with Khan, he still qualifies as a "merchant" under the UCC's *second* definition. "By his occupation," Khan clearly "[held] himself out as having knowledge or skill peculiar to the practices or goods involved in the transaction." Therefore, the merchant entrustment rule applies, and WGDC is estopped from seeking replevin against plaintiffs.

WGDC offers two arguments against this construction of "merchant." *First*, it repeatedly emphasizes that Khan was a fashion stylist, not a jeweler, so whatever his knowledge or skill regarding jewelry, it was not by virtue of his occupation. This argument fails. Put simply, fashion stylists often *do*—and the record makes clear that Khan, in fact, did—have "knowledge or skill peculiar to [jewelry]." At the time of the diamond's consignment, Khan made his living preparing celebrities for events and fashion shoots, a job that required him to provide jewelry to certain celebrities or other well-known individuals, for whom he was employed as a personal stylist. Obviously, "by [this] occupation," Khan must have "[held] himself out as having knowledge or skill" about jewelry—specifically, knowledge about jewelry as a category of accessory, and skill in the selection of jewelry for fashion purposes. That is why WGDC (and others) consigned their jewelry to him.

Second, WGDC argues that Khan did not hold himself out as having the specific type of "knowledge or skill" necessary to make him a "merchant." According to WGDC, Khan was in no way involved in the diamond or jewelry industries, either at the wholesale or retail level. He did not purchase, sell, or resell diamonds or other jewelry. He was not a dealer in diamonds; nor did he otherwise engage in the selling purchasing, lending, or marketing of diamonds or other jewelry. But even if all this is true, nothing in the language of the UCC suggests that the phrase "knowledge or skill peculiar to the practices or goods involved in the transaction" necessarily refers to knowledge of, or skills related to, the *business* dimension of those "practices or goods." If anything, the UCC's bifurcated definition of "merchant" cuts the other way. That the UCC differentiates between "deal[ing] in goods" and possessing "knowledge or skill [about] goods" suggests that the latter definition is not exclusively concerned with business knowledge.

Khan obviously had "knowledge [and] skill[s]" related to jewelry. Absent explicit guidance from New York courts, I conclude that Khan's particular type of "knowledge [and] skill[s]"—related to aesthetics, not business—is covered by the UCC's broad definition. WGDC has not identified any case that holds otherwise. And more importantly, rejecting this broad definition would undermine the spirit of the merchant entrustment rule, which aims to protect purchasers by shifting the risk of loss through fraudulent transfer to the owner of the goods, who can select the merchant to whom he entrusts his property. The rationale behind the rule, in other words, is to enhance confidence in commercial transactions by protecting the innocent purchaser who buys from a merchant dealing in goods of that kind—which counsels in favor of giving "merchant" a broad definition, to the benefit of purchasers, not owners.

It is undisputed that plaintiffs came into the possession of the diamond innocently. And it is also clear that if the merchant entrustment rule applies—to protect plaintiffs' innocent acquisition—WGDC will be left to bear an unfortunate liability. Such is the nature of a case like this, where the true perpetrator—Khan—is beyond the Court's grasp. There can be no doubt that Khan's actions were larcenous. However, because he falls within the broad definition of "merchant" set out in the UCC, his larceny did not preclude him from passing title. I conclude, therefore, that plaintiffs are the rightful owners of the diamond.

■   ■   ■

WGDC appealed the district court's grant of summary judgment in favor of the plaintiffs. In *Zaretsky v. William Goldberg Diamond Corp.*, 820 F.3d 513 (2d Cir. 2016) the Court of Appeals for the Second Circuit reversed the district court's judgment for the plaintiffs and granted summary judgment to WGDC. The Court of Appeals did not disagree with the district court's conclusion that Kahn qualified as a merchant under UCC 2-104(1) because by his occupation, he held himself out as "having knowledge or skill peculiar to the practices or goods involved in the transaction." Rather, the basis for overruling the district court's grant of summary judgment to the plaintiffs was that the entrustment provision in UCC 2-403(2), by its terms, applies only where the goods have been entrusted to a "merchant who deals in goods of that kind." Therefore, even though Kahn may have been a merchant under the second alternative basis set out in the definition (having knowledge or skill peculiar to the practices or goods involved in the transaction), he did not qualify as a merchant for purposes of UCC 2-403(2), which specifically gives the power to transfer rights in entrusted goods only to one who qualifies as a merchant under the first alternative basis of the definition—he must deal in goods of that kind. As you can see from reading the district court's opinion, the district judge expressly declined to decide if Kahn dealt in jewelry.

The court of appeals then discussed what it means to "deal in" goods. Although it found no definitive interpretation of that term by the New York Court of Appeals, it concluded, based on persuasive authority from other courts, that a person can only be said to deal in the goods that are in issue in the case if he regularly engages in sales of goods of that kind. Under that definition, the Court of Appeals held that the plaintiffs had not raised a triable issue of fact as to Khan's capacity to transfer title under section 2–403(2) because there was no evidence that he regularly sold diamonds or other high-end jewelry.

■ PROBLEM 2.4

After she bought her video camera, Meg A. Byte shot an amazing video of her dog performing very clever tricks with a Frisbee. When Meg showed the video to her friends, they praised it highly and suggested that she make copies and sell them. Meg used her computer program to edit the video and to burn it onto DVDs. She then rented a stall at a local crafts fair, at which she sold several of the DVDs. Meg is an accountant by profession, and this is the only time that she has participated in a crafts fair or sold DVDs.

Does Article 2 apply to Meg's DVD sales? If so, does she qualify as a merchant, either as a person who deals in goods of that kind, or who, by occupation, holds herself out as having knowledge and skill peculiar to the practices or goods involved in the transaction?

E INTERNATIONAL SALES OF GOODS AND THE CISG

In Chapter 1, Section A.6, we mention the United Nations Convention on Contracts for the International Sale of Goods (the CISG). As noted in that section, our focus in this course is on the domestic law of contracts as it applies to transactions entered into between parties who are both located in the United States. However, to provide some exposure to international perspectives on contracts law, we periodically refer to equivalent rules and principles of the law of contracts that might be encountered in transactions that cross national borders. In the context of the international sales of goods, the CISG often provides the law governing the transaction.

The CISG is an international convention that was adopted at a diplomatic conference in Vienna, convened by the United Nations Commission on International Trade Law (UNCITRAL) in 1980. (Because the CISG was adopted in Vienna, it is sometimes referred to as the Vienna Convention.) It is a multilateral treaty that binds nations who have become signatories to it by ratifying it. At present, at least 70 countries, including the United States, have done so. As a treaty of the United States, the CISG is the law in every state and it has the effect of a statute applicable to transactions that fall within its scope.

Article 1(1) of the CISG sets out the scope of its application. It states that the convention applies, for instance, "to contracts of sale of goods between parties whose places of business are in different States" (by which is meant countries), both of which countries are "Contracting States" (that is, countries that have ratified the convention).[7] In addition, Article 2(a) generally excludes consumer sales from the convention, so it does not come into effect unless the transaction is commercial in nature. This usually means that both parties are commercial entities involved in the export-import trade. Article 3(2) of the CISG states that the Convention "does not apply to contracts in which the preponderant part of the obligations of the party who furnishes the goods consists in the supply of labour or other services." Unlike UCC 2-102, which is silent on how hybrid trans-actions are to be treated, the CISG makes specific provision for dealing with those transactions by using a test akin to the "predominant purpose" test.

If the CISG applies, its provisions supersede those of UCC Article 2. There-fore, if a court in the United States adjudicates a dispute that is subject to the CISG, the court will apply it, and not the UCC, as the governing law. As one might expect, because the UCC was one of the sources consulted in drafting the CISG, many of the rules adopted by the CISG are quite similar to those found in UCC Article 2. However, this is not always so, as you will see later in this book.

In addition to the fact that the parties' businesses must be in different sig-natory countries, there is a further limitation on the applicability of the CISG. Article 6 provides that the parties may validly agree to exclude the application of the CISG in its entirety, or, even if they do not completely exclude it, they may provide in their agreement for rules different from those set out in the CISG.

---

[7] In some circumstances contemplated by Article 1, the CISG applies even if one of the parties is located in a country that has not ratified the Convention. In all cases, however, the CISG applies only where the transaction is transnational—that is, the parties are located in different countries.

CHAPTER 3

Contractual Assent and the Objective Test

A THE OBJECTIVE STANDARD FOR DETERMINING ASSENT

Contracts are formed by mutual consent. Both parties must intend to enter the contract and they must agree on its terms. This cannot happen, no matter how much each party desires the contract, unless they express their individual intentions to each other. Communication, usually by words but sometimes by conduct, is vital to the formation of a contract. The problem is that words or actions do not always accurately and precisely convey the state of mind of the utterer. Even if they do, they may not be properly understood by the person to whom they are expressed. As a result, there could be an outward appearance of agreement, even though the parties' subjective states of mind may not be in accord. Legal assent to a contract is determined not by trying to ascertain if the parties subjectively believed that they had an agreement but by having regard to their apparent intent as shown by their overt acts and words. Because these manifestations of assent are observable to the other party, they are described as "objective" to distinguish them from the purely internal or "subjective" state of mind of the actor.

Because courts rely primarily on evidence of outward manifestations of intent when determining the existence and terms of a contract, a person could be bound to a contract if her words and actions, reasonably interpreted, indicate assent, even though she did not mean to make it or to make it on the apparent terms. At first impression, this may seem to undermine the consensual nature of contract by imposing obligations on a party in the absence of true assent. A subjective test of agreement, making contracts dependent on a shared

[handwritten margin note: approval / permission]

[handwritten margin note: if your actions show assent you could be bound]

63

intent to be bound, best serves to insulate a person from unintended obligations. However, too heavy a focus on the actual state of the mind of a party is neither good policy nor good practice. As a matter of policy, the objective test recognizes that full and perfect assent is not the only value to be served by contract law. Economic interaction cannot be efficiently maintained unless a person manifesting contractual intent is held accountable for the reasonable reliance placed on her words and actions by the party to whom her intent was manifested. As a practical matter, the proof of subjective intent is dependent on the party's self-interested and often unverifiable testimony on the state of her own mind. Observable, objective indications of intention are more likely to be reliable.

Although there is historical evidence that common law courts have always placed emphasis on objective manifestations of assent, the nineteenth century saw a movement in the direction of favoring a subjective test of assent. This approach was based on the idea that because contract is based on consent, there can be no true contract unless both parties had the will to enter it. There is scholarly controversy over the extent to which this "will theory" of contract was actually followed by courts,[1] but one can find nineteenth-century opinions in which courts took the idea of assent quite literally and held that a contract could only be formed if there was a true "meeting of the minds"—a conscious and deliberate agreement between the parties gauged from their subjective intentions.

This subjectivist trend was completely at odds with the formalist classical conception of the role of contract law. The law could not facilitate and ensure the security of transactions if it did not hold a party accountable to his outward manifestation of assent. It would defeat the reasonable expectations of the other party and undermine the security of transactions as a whole if courts based assent on what a party actually thought rather than on what he reasonably seemed to have intended by his words or conduct. Toward the end of the nineteenth century, writers and courts began to assert the objective test very forcefully. Surely one of the most famous and frequently quoted expressions of this attitude is the passage written by Judge Learned Hand in *Hotchkiss v. National City Bank of New York*, 200 F. 287, 293 (S.D.N.Y. 1911):

> . . . A contract has, strictly speaking, nothing to do with the personal, or individual, intent of the parties. A contract is an obligation attached by the mere force of law to certain acts of the parties, usually words, which ordinarily accompany and represent a known intent. If, however, it were proved by twenty bishops that either party, when he used the words, intended something else than the usual meaning which the law imposes upon them, he would still be held, unless there were some mutual mistake, or something else of the sort. . . .

---

[1] For one article that summarizes this debate and concludes that the objective test was always central to the common law, and that the "will theory" was just a brief flirtation with subjectivity, see Joseph M. Perillo, *The Origins of the Objective Theory of Contract Formation and Interpretation*, 69 Fordham L. Rev. 427 (2000).

Another is an observation made by Justice Oliver Wendell Holmes in his compilation of lectures on the common law, published in 1881: "The law has nothing to do with the actual state of the parties' minds. In contract, as elsewhere, it must go by externals, and judge parties by their conduct."[2]

Many modern courts are not as rigid in their focus on objective manifestations of intent. Although they continue to emphasize objective indicia of assent, they are often willing to find some relevance in evidence of what a party may have thought or believed.

MORALES v. SUN CONSTRUCTORS, INC.

541 F.3d 218 (2008)
United States Court of Appeals, Third Circuit[3]

CHAGARES, Circuit Judge.

This case requires us to determine whether an arbitration clause in an employment agreement is enforceable where one party is ignorant of the language in which the agreement is written.

Juan Morales (Morales) was employed by Sun Constructors, Inc. (Sun). The employment relationship between Morales and Sun was governed by a signed employment agreement (the Agreement) that contained an arbitration clause. Morales was terminated by Sun, and he filed a wrongful termination suit against his former employer in the District Court of the Virgin Islands. Sun moved to stay the proceedings pending arbitration, but the District Court denied the motion, finding that Morales signed the Agreement without realizing it contained an arbitration clause. The Agreement was written in English, a language Morales cannot understand, and the District Court concluded that the arbitration clause was unenforceable because Morales did not assent to the clause. On appeal, Sun argues that Morales is bound by the entire Agreement, even if he is ignorant of its terms. We agree and will reverse the decision of the District Court and remand the case with instructions to enter a stay pending arbitration.

Appellee Morales is a Spanish-speaking welder who resides in St. Croix, United States Virgin Islands. Welders like Morales were in high demand by appellant Sun, and Morales acknowledged: "[Sun] needed me. It was an emergency. . . . They needed to start work, so they were under pressure." On April 15, 2004, after Morales

---

[2] Oliver Wendell Holmes, *The Common Law* 309 (Little, Brown & Co. 1881).

[3] It so happens that this case and most of the other cases in this chapter are before federal courts. You will find federal courts dealing with contracts cases in other chapters of this book as well. Remember, as explained in Section A.2.b of Chapter 1, that in most cases contracts are governed by state law and contract disputes are tried by state courts. However, in some circumstances federal courts have jurisdiction to hear contracts cases, such as where the parties are citizens of different states and the amount in controversy is sufficient to satisfy the prescribed minimum requirement for diversity jurisdiction. Even though a federal court deals with the case, it applies the governing state contract law.

had passed a written exam, in English,[4] Sun hired him and required him to attend a 2½-hour orientation conducted entirely in English and to sign an hourly employment agreement. Five paragraphs of the Agreement (paragraphs 12 through 16) pertained to arbitration and covered nearly 8 of the 13 pages of the Agreement. The Sun employee who conducted the orientation, Mr. Langner, asked Jose Hodge (Hodge), a bilingual applicant who was also present at the orientation, and whom Morales knew, to explain to Morales what Langner was saying and help him fill out the documents. Hodge testified that he generally understands about eighty-five percent of what is said and written in English. He also stated that Morales did not ask him what he was signing and that he did not specifically explain the arbitration clause to Morales. Mr. Langner stated that he did explain the arbitration provisions in English and that, during the orientation, Hodge was speaking to Morales in a foreign language. The Agreement governed the employment relationship between Morales and Sun for the entirety of the relationship.

On April 6, 2005, Sun fired Morales . . . [for] a violation of safety standards. Morales filed a wrongful termination suit against Sun in the District Court on December 20, 2006, seeking relief under eight causes of action all covered by the Agreement's arbitration clause. The District Court determined that mutual assent to the arbitration clause did not exist and denied Sun's motion to stay the proceedings pending arbitration. This appeal followed. . . .

The Federal Arbitration Act (FAA), 9 U.S.C. §§1-16, provides that arbitration agreements are "enforceable to the same extent as other contracts," and establishes a strong federal policy in favor of the resolution of disputes through arbitration. However, [under 9 U.S.C. §2] arbitration provisions may be attacked "under such grounds as exist at law or in equity for the revocation of a contract."

When determining whether the parties agreed to arbitrate a certain matter courts generally should apply ordinary state-law principles that govern the formation of contracts. It is well-settled under the Restatement (Second) of Contracts (the Restatement) that mutual assent between parties is necessary for the formation of a contract. *See* Restatement §17. While mutual assent "is sometimes referred to as a 'meeting of the minds,'" Restatement §17 cmt. c, this phrase must not be construed too literally. Acceptance is measured not by the parties' subjective intent, but rather by their outward expressions of assent. As the Restatement explains: "The parties to most contracts give actual as well as apparent assent, but it is clear that a mental reservation of a party to a bargain does not impair the obligation he purports to undertake. The phrase used here, therefore, is 'manifestation of mutual assent.'" . . .

[*Williston on Contracts* §4:19 (4th ed. 2008) explains:]

According to the objective theory of contract formation, what is essential is not assent, but rather what the person to whom a manifestation is made is justified as regarding as

---

[4] The court does not explain how Morales could pass a written exam in English if he could not understand it. —Eds.

assent. Thus, if an offeree, in ignorance of the terms of an offer, so acts or expresses itself as to justify the other party in inferring assent, and this action or expression was of such a character that a reasonable person in the position of the offeree should have known it was calculated to lead the offeror to believe that the offer had been accepted, <u>a contract will be formed in spite of the offeree's ignorance of the terms of the offer</u>. The most common illustration of this principle is the situation when one who is ignorant of the language in which a document is written, or who is illiterate, executes a writing proposed as a contract under a mistake as to its contents. Such a person is bound, in the absence of fraud, if the person does not require the document to be read to him. . . . *[handwritten: → bound even if you don't read it]*

[left margin handwritten: if your actions make a regular person assume you've accepted then ignorance is irrelevant]

Arbitration agreements in the employment context are not exempt from this principle. *See, e.g., Booker v. Robert Half Int'l, Inc.,* 315 F. Supp. 2d 94, 101 (D.D.C. 2004) (stating that "[f]ailure to read or understand an arbitration agreement, or an employer's failure to explain it, simply will not constitute 'special circumstances' warranting relieving an employee from compliance with the terms of an arbitration agreement that she signed").

*[left margin handwritten: no ignorance *]*

Morales, in essence, requests that this Court create an exception to the objective theory of contract formation where a party is <u>ignorant of the language</u> in which a contract is written. We decline to do so. In the absence of fraud, the fact that an offeree cannot read, write, speak, or understand the English language is immaterial to whether an English-language agreement the offeree executes is enforceable. . . . Morales is not claiming fraud and he is not alleging that Sun misrepresented the contents of the Agreement to him. Further, there is no evidence that Sun tried to hide the arbitration clause; indeed, it comprised about one-half of the Agreement.

It was <u>Morales' obligation to ensure he understood the Agreement before signing.</u> Morales did not ask Hodge to translate the document word-for-word or ask to take the Agreement home and have it translated, notwithstanding the fact that he testified that, in the past, he had paid someone to translate documents for him. Morales did not even request a copy of the employment contract, a demand Sun has indicated it would have granted without dispute. Moreover, in the almost one year that Morales worked for Sun, he never questioned the terms of the Agreement. Morales' signature manifested his assent to the entire Agreement, and he is bound by the arbitration clause therein. . . .

[left margin handwritten: disposition]

For the foregoing reasons, the judgment of the District Court will be reversed and the case remanded for the District Court to enter a stay pending arbitration.

■   ■   ■

Morales shows that modern courts still <u>focus on objective evidence</u>. Does this mean that subjective evidence, offered by a party to describe what she was thinking at the time of making the objective manifestation, is entirely irrelevant and inadmissible? The role and relevance of subjective testimony is addressed in the next case.

SR INTERNATIONAL BUSINESS INSURANCE CO., LTD. v. WORLD TRADE CENTER PROPERTIES, LLC

467 F.3d 107 (2006)
United States Court of Appeals, Second Circuit

WALKER, Circuit Judge.

These are appeals from judgments following two separate phases of a jury trial to adjudicate whether the coordinated terrorist attacks of September 11, 2001—whereby two jetliners separately crashed into the twin towers of the World Trade Center ("WTC"), destroying both buildings—constituted one or two "occurrences" under the terms of multiple insurance contracts. The parties are entities with varying property interests in the WTC (the "Silverstein Parties") and the insurance companies they retained to provide approximately $3.5 billion in multi-layered insurance on a "per occurrence" basis. At issue in the overall litigation is whether the Silverstein Parties can recover in the aggregate up to $3.5 billion, for one occurrence, or up to $7 billion, for two occurrences, under the terms of more than thirty separate insurance contracts that together provide the total coverage. The parties do not dispute that the destruction of the WTC resulted in a loss that greatly exceeds $3.5 billion. [Shortly after the attack, SR International, one of the insurers, filed suit against the Silverstein Parties, seeking a judicial declaration that the damage to the WTC was one insurance loss under its policy. The Silverstein Parties counterclaimed against all the insurers, seeking a declaration that the attacks were more than one occurrence.[5] Multiple motions and trials ensued, resulting in judgments against some of the insurers and in favor of others.]

The resolution of the broad question presented in these appeals—whether the coordinated attacks constituted one or two occurrences—is complicated by the fact that, as of September 11, 2001, the Silverstein Parties were still in the midst of negotiating final property insurance coverage for the WTC. Silverstein Properties had only recently entered into a long-term lease for the WTC and, with one exception, none of the many insurers that it had retained to provide property insurance coverage had issued a final insurance policy. Instead, these insurers had issued temporary binders or slips, which provide interim insurance coverage until a final policy is either issued or refused. These fully enforceable, interim insurance contracts or binders are a product of necessity: They serve as

in between finalized insurance policies

---

[5] The remedy sought by the Silverstein parties is a declaratory judgment. In asking the court for a declaratory judgment, the party asks the court to give a judgment declaring the rights and obligations of the parties. Where the court issues a declaratory judgment, it does not make any monetary award. It simply answers the legal issue posed in the case. For this reason, a declaratory judgment is not the norm in contracts cases, where the party initiating litigation usually wishes to get more than a declaration of rights by the court, and also seeks an award of damages to compensate for loss caused by the breach. However, a declaratory judgment can be a useful device where, as in this case, all that is needed is a declaration of rights. —Eds.

a "quick and informal device to record the giving of protection pending the execution and delivery of a more conventionally detailed policy of insurance." *Employers Commercial Union Ins. Co. v. Firemen's Fund Ins. Co.*, 45 N.Y.2d 608, 613, 412 N.Y.S.2d 121, 384 N.E.2d 668, 670 (1978). Because, in this case, the binders left the term "occurrence" undefined, the resolution of the broad question presented in these appeals required an individualized inquiry to determine what each pair of parties—the insured Silverstein Parties and each insurer—intended for the word "occurrence" to mean in each binder. . . . [The court noted that this individualized inquiry would seek to ascertain the parties' intentions by examining extrinsic evidence such as what was stated by the parties in negotiations, the content of policy forms exchanged during the negotiations, and the customary terms used by the insurer. The court's opinion is complex, and deals with many aspects of the litigation. For our purposes, we focus on only one aspect of the opinion, relating to the trial court's admission of subjective evidence of intent.]

The Silverstein parties argue that the district court abused its discretion when it permitted several of the insurers' witnesses to testify as to which form they thought they had bound to during the course of the parties' negotiations. They contend that this testimony should have been excluded as impermissible evidence of the insurers' uncommunicated subjective intent. They further contend that the admission of "such self-serving testimony constituted prejudicial error and requires a new trial."

"The cardinal principle for the construction and interpretation of insurance contracts—as with all contracts—is that the intentions of the parties should control." *Newmont Mines Ltd. v. Hanover Ins. Co.*, 784 F.2d 127, 135 (2d Cir. 1986). Under New York law, this is accomplished by looking to "the objective manifestations of the intent of the parties as gathered by their expressed words and deeds." *Brown Bros. Elec. Contractors, Inc. v. Beam Constr. Corp.*, 41 N.Y.2d 397, 399, 393 N.Y.S.2d 350, 361 N.E.2d 999, 1001 (1977). The parties' communicated expressions are interpreted objectively to give effect to the "reasonable expectations" of the parties, not necessarily their actual expectations. *Id.* at 400, 393 N.Y.S.2d 350, 361 N.E.2d 999; *see also Mencher v. Weiss*, 306 N.Y. 1, 7, 114 N.E.2d 177 (1953) ("[T]he manifestation of a party's intention rather than the actual or real intention is ordinarily controlling"). Thus, it has been said that "the existence of a binding contract is not dependent on the subjective intent of either [party]." *Brown Bros. Elec.*, 41 N.Y.2d at 399, 393 N.Y.S.2d 350, 361 N.E.2d 999.

Although a party's uncommunicated subjective intent cannot supply the ultimate meaning of an ambiguous contract, it is quite another thing to hold that such evidence is wholly irrelevant and inadmissible for other purposes. *Cf.* Fed. R. Evid. 401 (stating that evidence is relevant if it has "*any* tendency to make the existence of *any* fact that is of consequence to the determination of the action more probable or less probable than it would be without the evidence" (emphasis added)). Under the objective theory of contract, the parties' "reasonable expectations" are determined based on an objective understanding of the "attendant circumstances [in which the agreement was made], the situation of the parties, and the objectives they were striving to attain." *Brown Bros. Elec.*, 41 N.Y.2d at 400, 393 N.Y.S.2d 350, 361 N.E.2d 999 (citations omitted); *see also Rudman v. Cowles Commc'ns, Inc.*, 30 N.Y.2d 1, 11, 330 N.Y.S.2d 33, 280 N.E.2d 867 (1972) (stating that, when a contract is ambiguous, "the court may and should look to the prior negotiations [of the parties] to determine what was intended"); *Kitching v. Brown*, 180 N.Y. 414, 420, 73 N.E. 241 (1905) ("One of the familiar rules applicable to the interpretation of ambiguous covenants and agreements is to ascertain, as nearly as may be, the situation of the parties, their surroundings and circumstances, the occasion and apparent object of their stipulations, and from all these sources to gather the meaning and intent of their language"). At least with respect to a negotiated agreement, a party's subjective understanding, while not controlling, may shed light on the state of those negotiations and could bear on that party's objective actions. *See Kabil Devs. Corp. v. Mignot*, 279 Or. 151, 566 P.2d 505 (1977) (stating that "a factfinder might well believe that what a party thought he was doing would show in what he did").

In this case, the jury was asked to determine whether the parties intended for . . . [a standard form contract exchanged during the negotiations] to govern during the binder period. We think that the insurers' subjective understandings were relevant insofar as they provided the jury with an understanding of the state of the parties' negotiations and helped to explain the parties' overt actions. For example, the fact that an insurer thought that it had bound to the . . . form might help to explain the changes that it made to the interim binder. As a result, we conclude that the district court did not abuse its discretion when it permitted some of the insurers' witnesses to testify as to which form they thought that they had bound, "as long as the jury was not misled into treating this testimony, in its context, as something more than evidence bearing on the behavior and the perceptions of the parties to the negotiation." *Kabil*, 279 Or. at 158, 566 P.2d 505.

We do not believe that the jury was so misled in this case. The district court gave an appropriate limiting instruction:

> A party's intent that is not communicated to the other party has no bearing; only the intent indicated by words and acts that are made known to the other party may be considered. You may recall that I permitted some witnesses to testify about their own understanding and assumptions about certain events even though they did not communicate those understandings and assumptions to another party. That testimony was received only to help explain the witness's own actions and statements. However, a witness's own understandings that are not communicated to another party cannot change the meaning of statements and acts that are communicated to that other party.

Accordingly, we reject the Silverstein parties' claims of error regarding subjective intent evidence.

■   ■   ■

[handwritten: used as supplement to objective evidence]

In *SR International*, the issue was whether subjective evidence should have been admitted to supplement the objective evidence of what was intended by the parties. The probative weight of the subjective evidence lay in the fact that it was consistent with and not contradictory to the objective evidence. The following problem raises the question of how subjective evidence should be treated if there is a clash between a party's outward manifestations of assent (words and conduct) and his testimony about what he thought when he made those manifestations.

■ PROBLEM 3.1

Nadia Borrower owns a small business, which was in financial difficulty and could not pay its operating expenses. She approached Nora Lender for a loan of $100,000. Nora agreed to lend Nadia the money provided that Nadia's husband, Ray, signed a suretyship agreement, under which he guaranteed payment of the debt and committed to pay it if she defaulted. Nora prepared and gave Nadia the suretyship agreement, to be signed and returned before the loan was advanced. Nadia took it home that night and gave it to Ray, saying, "I need you to sign this." Ray was engrossed in playing a game on his iPad. Without taking his eyes off the screen, he distractedly asked Nadia, "What's this?" She replied, "It's some paperwork for my business loan." "Oh, whatever," said Ray as he took the paper and, glancing momentarily from the screen, scribbled his signature on it without reading it. Nadia took the signed form back to Nora the next day and received the loan. Despite the new funds, Nadia could not turn her business around, and it failed a few weeks later, causing her to default on the loan. Nora demanded payment from Ray under the suretyship agreement. Ray argued that he never agreed to guarantee Nadia's debt. When he signed the paper, he was distracted and did not really know what he was signing. Had he realized what it was, he would have refused to sign it.[6]

In *SR International* the court indicates that even under the objective test, evidence of subjective state of mind can have probative value. Do you think that Ray's testimony of his state of mind is entitled to any probative weight in determining whether he intended to enter the contract?

[handwritten: → not after morales w/ ignorance]

---

[6] The moral of this story, to paraphrase the immortal words of Shakespeare's Polonius, is "Nadia Borrower Nora Lender be; for loan oft loses both itself and friend, and borrowing dulls the edge of husband, Ray."

THE DETERMINATION OF OBJECTIVE MEANING: THE REASONABLE PERSON CONSTRUCT

The objective test holds a party accountable for her words or actions by looking at her outward manifestations to determine her assent. However, it does not do this simply by accepting the other party's actual understanding of these manifestations. To do that would be just to adopt the hearer's subjective understanding in preference over the utterer's. The purely subjective understanding of the party to whom the manifestation is made is no more relevant to its objective meaning than the subjective intent of the party who made it. Therefore, the objective test requires that the manifestations be interpreted reasonably. Stated differently, the law is generally concerned with protecting a party's expectations based on her reliance on a manifestation only to the extent that her reliance was reasonable. This raises the question of how the factfinder (the jury, or if no jury is used, the judge) reaches a reasonable interpretation.

reliance must be reasonable

The classicists tended to see reasonableness in more abstract terms: The factfinder, as an impartial observer of the evidence of the parties' interaction, can decide the reasonable meaning of what was said or done. Contemporary courts have moved away from this rather detached view and define reasonableness within the entire context of the transaction. They therefore ask not what a reasonable interpretation of a manifestation might be in the abstract, but what it might be from the perspective of the party who observed it, taking into account his attributes (such as experience, training, and commercial sophistication), the background information that he possessed, the relationship between the parties, and the context of the transaction. Accordingly, subjective elements are not entirely excluded from the test of reasonableness. This orientation is appropriate because the objective test is, after all, aimed at protecting the reasonable expectations of the particular party involved in the transaction. Think about this as you try to resolve the following problem.

subjective is not completely excluded

■ PROBLEM 3.2

One of the provisions in the loan agreement between Nora and Nadia stated "The funds lent under this agreement may be used solely for the payment of the operating expenses of Nadia's business, and may not be used for Nadia's personal expenses." Nadia used $10,000 to pay for a business trip to Asia, during which she attempted to negotiate sales of her product with several potential customers. (Nadia worked hard on the trip and spent no time on recreational activities.) Nora claims that this was a breach of the contract. She meant the term "operating expenses" to cover only the routine expenses of keeping the business in operation, such as salaries, purchases of inventory, and payments to the lessor for rent. Nadia denies having breached the contract. In her understanding, the expenses of travel for the purpose of attracting business are "operating expenses." How is this dispute to be resolved? What role does the evidence of subjective understanding play in its resolution? What contextual facts would you look for to assist in resolving the meaning of "operating expenses"?

disagreement on what the other meant by "operating expenses"

negotiations, other business contracts, course of usage

C THE DUTY TO READ

1. The Duty to Read Standard Terms

In *Morales v. Sun Constructors*, Morales was held to his manifestation of assent, even though he did not really know and understand the terms to which he signified assent. Language was a barrier to Morales's true assent, yet the court made it clear that he could not avoid his commitment to arbitrate on this ground. In essence, if he did not know what he was agreeing to, he had the responsibility to find out before manifesting his agreement. Although the court did not actually use the phrase in the opinion, a party's accountability for knowledge of a contract's terms is often called a "duty to read." Where parties negotiate all the terms of the agreement, they are more likely to know the terms to which they have agreed. However, where a contract is on standard terms, drafted by one of the parties and presented to the other, there is a much stronger likelihood that the nondrafting party may not take the time and trouble to read and comprehend the terms that have been presented. For this reason, a party's accountability for his assent to unread terms is most likely to arise where the contract is on standard, predrafted terms. These terms may be presented in a variety of ways—for example, on a printed memorandum of agreement, on a website, on product packaging, or on posted notices.

we have a duty to read contracts

JAMES v. McDONALD'S CORPORATION

417 F.3d 672 (2005)
United States Court of Appeals, Seventh Circuit

RIPPLE, Circuit Judge.

[McDonald's conducted a promotional game called "Who Wants to Be a Millionaire." Customers were given game cards when they made purchases at McDonald's restaurants. Most cards had low-value food prizes, but a few were grand prize cards worth $1 million. Linda James received a game card when she purchased fries at a McDonald's restaurant. She claimed that it was a grand prize card, which McDonald's denied. Thereafter, it became known that grand prize cards had been stolen by employees of the firm who had handled the promotion. James sued McDonald's, claiming that it had fraudulently refused to honor her winning card and that it had fraudulently induced members of the public to buy its products by failing to disclose that the odds of winning were less than represented. McDonald's moved to compel Ms. James to arbitrate her claim under an arbitration clause contained in the rules of the game. The clause stated that as a condition of participating in the game, a participant agrees that all disputes arising out of the game or relating to prizes awarded will be resolved by final and binding arbitration under the rules of the American Arbitration Association and the Federal Arbitration Act. The opinion therefore does not deal with the merits of Ms. James's claim. The issue is simply whether she is bound by the arbitration provision set out in the terms of the promotion. The district court granted the motion to compel arbitration made by McDonald's. Ms. James did not initiate the arbitration proceedings but instead applied to the district court for reconsideration of her claim. The district court refused and dismissed her claim. Ms. James appealed on the basis that she never agreed to the arbitration provision, so that the district court erred by ordering her to submit her claims to arbitration.] . . .

McDonald's presented evidence, credited by the district court, that the Official Rules were posted openly in participating restaurants. The rules were posted near the food counter, on the back of in-store tray liners and near the drive-thru window. Also, the french fry cartons to which game cards were affixed had language directing participants to see the Official Rules for details. . . .

The FAA provides that a "written provision in any . . . contract . . . to settle by arbitration" any future controversy arising out of such contract "shall be valid, irrevocable, and enforceable, save upon such grounds as exist at law or in equity for the revocation of any contract." 9 U.S.C. §2. . . . [The court notes that the purpose of the FAA is to advance a liberal federal policy favoring arbitration agreements. Courts should resolve any doubts in favor of arbitration.] However, a party can be compelled to arbitrate only those matters that she has agreed to submit to arbitration. . . . An agreement to arbitrate is treated like any other contract. . . . If there is no contract there is to be no forced

no contract → no forced arbitration

look to state law on formation of contracts

arbitration. . . . In deciding whether the parties agreed to arbitrate a certain matter, federal courts generally should rely on state contract law governing the formation of contracts. . . .

Ms. James contends that she should not be forced to arbitrate her claims because she never entered into an agreement to arbitrate her dispute. She submits that she was not aware of the Official Rules, much less that the rules deprived her of a jury trial. For the same reasons, Ms. James contends that, if there was an agreement to arbitrate, it is unconscionable and should not be enforced. To support her position, Ms. James submits that one cannot assume that she knew of, and accepted, the arbitration clause in the Official Rules simply because she ate at a McDonald's restaurant. She maintains that customers cannot be expected to read every container of food they purchase in order to know that they are entering a contract. Rather, she submits that it was McDonald's burden to assure her understanding of, and willingness to be bound by, the arbitration provision.

Certainly, as Ms. James urges, a contract includes only terms on which the parties have agreed. *See ProCD, Inc. v. Zeidenberg*, 86 F.3d 1447, 1450 (7th Cir. 1996). However, one of the things that Ms. James agreed to by participating in the "Who Wants to be a Millionaire" game was to follow the game's rules in order to win the promised prize. As a general rule, a participant in a prize-winning contest must comply with the terms of the contest's rules in order to form a valid and binding contract with the contest promoter. The promoter's obligation is limited by the terms of the offer, including the conditions and rules of the contest that are made public. . . . [The district court] found that the Official Rules were "clearly and undisputably identified to [Ms. James] as being part of the contest." It is axiomatic that a contest normally has rules regarding eligibility to win the promised prize. Moreover, Ms. James cannot claim, on the one hand, that a valid contract obligates McDonald's to redeem her prize and, on the other hand, argue that no contract binds her to the contest rules. A contest participant cannot pick and choose among the terms and conditions of the contest; the rules stand or fall in their entirety.

participation in a contest means complying with its rules

can't choose the terms

Outside the promotional-contest context, this court has held that parties are bound to an arbitration provision even if they did not read the provision. For instance, in *Hill v. Gateway 2000, Inc.*, 105 F.3d 1147 (7th Cir.), *cert. denied*, 522 U.S. 808, 118 S. Ct. 47, 139 L. Ed. 2d 13 (1997), the purchasers of a computer conceded that they had noticed the terms printed inside the box in which their computer was shipped. However, they maintained that they had not read it closely enough to see the arbitration clause. We held that the arbitration clause was enforceable because the purchasers had the opportunity to return the computer after reading the terms.[7] We stated that "[a] contract need not be read to

---

[7] In Both *ProCD* and *Hill*, the question was whether a party could be bound to terms that were not made available to him at the time of the purchase of the goods but only became apparent later. We deal with that issue in Chapter 6. This was not an issue in *James*. —EDS.

be effective; people who accept take the risk that the unread terms may in retrospect prove unwelcome." [S]ee also ProCD, 86 F.3d at 1452 (binding consumer to arbitration clause printed inside box of software because consumer had the opportunity to return the software after reading the terms). In *Hill*, we explained that

> [p]ractical considerations support allowing vendors to enclose the full legal terms with their products. Cashiers cannot be expected to read legal documents to customers before ringing up sales. If the staff at . . . the other end of the phone for direct-sales operations such as Gateway's had to read the four-page statement of terms before taking the buyer's credit card number, the droning voice would anesthetize rather than enlighten many potential buyers. Others would hang up in a rage over the waste of their time. And oral recitation would not avoid customers' assertions (whether true or feigned) that the clerk did not read term X to them, or that they did not remember or understand it.

Hill, 105 F.3d at 1149; *see also ProCD*, 86 F.3d at 1451. The situation faced by McDonald's presents an apt comparison. To require McDonald's cashiers to recite to each and every customer the fourteen pages of the Official Rules, and then have each customer sign an agreement to be bound by the rules, would be unreasonable and unworkable. The Official Rules were identified to Ms. James as part of the contest, and that identification is sufficient in this case to apprise her of the contents of the rules. . . .

The district court concluded that the law required it to compel Ms. James to arbitrate her claims. Once it so ordered, it was incumbent upon Ms. James to abide by the district court's ruling and not to continue submitting arguments that the district court already had determined were meritless. . . . [T]he district court did not clearly abuse its discretion in dismissing Ms. James' case with prejudice. . . . [W]e affirm the judgment of the district court.

■ QUESTIONS

(1) In Chapter 1, we distinguish a contract from an instantaneous exchange, which does not qualify as a contract. In *James*, there was a simple and instantaneous exchange of fries for cash. Why is this a contract at all?

(2) Is the transaction in *James* a sale of goods? If so, why does the court not mention UCC Article 2?

(3) One of the questions raised in both *James* and *Morales* was whether the term was sufficiently brought to the attention of the nondrafting party. Identify the passages in both cases in which the court alludes to and disposes of this concern.

(4) How important was it that McDonald's had plastered the game's rules in almost every conceivable place? Do you think that the court may have been less inclined to hold Ms. James to the arbitration provision if it could be found only in tiny print on the back of the little game card?

(5)   The term at issue in *James* was an arbitration clause. What if it was not an arbitration provision but rather a clause that read, "By participating in this game, the participant undertakes to buy two McDonald's hamburgers every day for a month." Do you think that the court would have found that provision binding on Ms. James? *[handwritten: probably]* * *[handwritten: unconscionable clauses]*

As mentioned at the beginning of this section, the "duty to read" is often associated with standard, predrafted contracts of the kind involved in *James* and *Morales*. Standard contracts are commonplace in the modern economy. In countless transactions, the parties do not enter real negotiations and do not draft the terms of their contract from scratch. Rather, the parties use a standard, preprinted form that sets out contract terms drafted for all transactions of this kind or, as occurred in *James*, has the standard terms printed on a ticket, invoice, notice, or other writing given to or made available to the other party. With the burgeoning of Internet-based contracting in recent years, many standard contracts are not printed on paper but are set out on the website of one of the parties to the transaction. We focus on this form of standard contract in Section C.4.

[handwritten margin note: contract may be drafted by a third party] A standard contract may have been drafted by someone who is not a party to the contract (such as a form that is available from a trade organization or in a book or online), or it may have been drafted by one of the parties. Although some standard terms are fair and evenhanded, others are deliberately geared to serve the interests of the drafting party. Because standard contracts are so prevalent, you will encounter them quite often in the cases that you will study. In many cases, the fact that the contract was on a standard form has no legal relevance. There is nothing inherently wrong with standard contracts, and courts routinely enforce them, using the doctrines that apply to contracts generally. However, sometimes the manner in which a party presents standard terms, or the self-serving or unfair content of those terms, does raise questions of whether the other party should be held *[handwritten margin note: may be unenforceable if the terms are unreasonable]* to them. Some of these concerns are raised in passing in *James* and *Morales*, but they do not present a problem in these cases, so they are not the central focus of the courts' analysis. We examine these issues in detail later. In the interim, it is worth noting what they are:

1. The issue raised in questions 3 and 4 following *James* is whether the term was sufficiently brought to the attention of the nondrafting party. We consider this issue further in the context of electronic contracting in Section C.4, and it comes up again in Chapters 6 and 13. *[handwritten: → not right or reasonable]*

2. Another question is whether the term is unconscionable. Ms. James asserted that the clause was unconscionable and should not be enforced for that reason, but she did not press the unconscionability argument, and the court does not address this assertion. It merely alludes to it in passing. We discuss the doctrine of unconscionability in Chapter 13. In essence, a court may use the doctrine to refuse enforcement of a contract or a term of a contract that is

[handwritten left margin: ① party used unfair bargaining strategies ② resulting contract is unfair]

oppressive and unfair. Generally, for a party to obtain relief on grounds of unconscionability, she must establish both that the other party used improper or unfair bargaining tactics and that the resulting contract or the disputed term is unfair.

3. A third issue, fraud, is alluded to in both *James* and *Morales*. The court in *Morales* merely noted that no fraud was alleged. Ms. James claimed that McDonald's had fraudulently induced customers to play its promotional game by failing to disclose that winning cards had been stolen. Of course, this claim was not addressed by the court because it would have been dealt with by the arbitrator had Ms. James submitted to arbitration. We explore fraud in Chapter 13. For the present, we merely note that even where a party manifests assent to a contract, she can avoid it on grounds of fraud if the other party deliberately made a false representation (which could include a nondisclosure of information) with the intention of inducing her to enter the contract and she was in fact so induced.

[handwritten left margin: when you assent, you can get out of it if there's fraud]

2. Arbitration and Forum Selection Provisions in Standard Contracts

[handwritten: federal arbitration act]

a. Arbitration Provisions

[handwritten: ↳ neither party can sue in court]

It is no strange coincidence that the terms challenged in both *James* and *Morales* were arbitration clauses. As you read through this book, you will find several more cases in which an arbitration clause is in issue. Arbitration provisions have become increasingly common in both negotiated and standard contracts. Arbitration is a form of dispute resolution that is less formal than litigation before a court. Where parties agree to arbitrate, neither can sue in court to enforce the contract. Instead, they must have the dispute resolved by an arbitrator (or a panel of arbitrators), a private person appointed by the parties or by some other means provided for in the contract. The arbitrator's decision is binding on the parties.

Because court dockets are very crowded and litigation takes a long time, arbitration offers the prospect of a speedier and less expensive resolution of the dispute. For this reason, as the courts indicate in both *James* and *Morales*, where it is established that the parties entered into a valid and enforceable agreement to arbitrate, there is a general policy in favor of enforcing that agreement. This policy in favor of arbitration is expressed in many state statutes and also in the Federal Arbitration Act, 9 U.S.C. §§1-16 (FAA), which expressly upholds the validity of an agreement to arbitrate, unless there are grounds to invalidate it under general principles of contract law.[8] It must be emphasized that the policy

*[handwritten left margin: *tend to be faster & cheaper]*

*[handwritten: *courts favor enforcing arbitration]*

---

[8] We further discuss the FAA and the grounds for challenging the enforceability of an arbitration provision when we deal with the doctrine of unconscionability in Chapter 13, Section F.

in favor of compelling arbitration only applies where the parties have validly agreed to submit their dispute to arbitration. Therefore, in most cases in which a party resists a demand to arbitrate a dispute, the basis is that the party never actually assented to the apparent agreement to arbitrate. In the context of standard contracts, the argument that there was no assent usually boils down to whether the provision was fairly and reasonably brought to the notice of the party who signified apparent assent to it.

[handwritten: argument of no assent]

The fact that both James and Morales challenged the arbitration provision makes it apparent that a contracting party may not always see arbitration as being in her best interest. An agreement to arbitrate deprives a party of the right to litigate before a court and subjects her to a less formal dispute resolution process that may provide less protection of her interests or, in some cases, may be less accessible and convenient. Notwithstanding, a party who manifests assent to an arbitration agreement is bound by it unless she can establish a basis in contract law for challenging the validity or enforceability of the agreement.

*[handwritten: * to get out of it you must prove the validity & enforceability challenge]*

b. Arbitration Provisions That Bar Class Actions

Many arbitration provisions not only compel the parties to submit disputes to binding arbitration, but also confine the nondrafting party (typically the customer or consumer) to making claims only on her own behalf, and forbid her from commencing or participating in a class action.

Where a large group of people have similar claims against a defendant, a member of that group may initiate a class action against the defendant in which she asserts not only her own claim, but also those of all other members of the identified class. In consumer transactions or other transactions in which the individual claims of members of the class are too small to make litigating them economically feasible, a class action allows the representative plaintiffs to sue for the aggregate amount of all the claims of the class, which could be a very large amount. If the plaintiff wins the suit, the award, less attorneys' fees, will be distributed among members of the class. Although the actual benefit that individual class members may receive from the distribution is often quite small, the liability of the defendant could be very significant. The perceived societal benefit of such class actions is that, by making the aggregation of claims possible, they allow consumers and small claimants to hold the defendant accountable for conduct that cannot be discouraged or challenged effectively by an individual's suit.

[handwritten: class action makes economic sense]

[handwritten: hold big companies accountable]

It should therefore be no surprise that large corporations who enter into numerous similar transactions with members of the public do not like class actions. An easy way to deflect them is to include a provision in a standard contract that not only requires claims to be arbitrated, but also precludes class actions. In _AT&T Mobility LLC v. Concepcion_, 131 S. Ct. 1740 (2011) the U.S. Supreme Court held that a provision in an arbitration clause that waived

typically waive the right to a class action suit

the right to institute a class action is consistent with the policy of enforcing arbitration agreements, because arbitration is not suited to the classwide resolution of disputes. Of course, the same principle applies here as applies to arbitration provisions generally: The waiver of the right to institute a class action is binding only if it was validly assented to.

c. Forum Selection Clauses

↳ *in a specific jurisdiction*

A forum selection clause is a provision in a contract in which the parties agree that any dispute arising out of the transaction will be resolved by the courts of a specified jurisdiction. Forum selection clauses are often found in standard contracts where a corporation that enters into many transactions across the country specifies that any dispute arising out of a transaction must be litigated in the courts of the state in which the corporation has its head office. The reason, of course, is that the corporation wishes for the convenience and savings of dealing with any litigation at the place most convenient to it. Where the customer or consumer lives elsewhere, the burden of having to litigate the claim in the specified distant jurisdiction can be substantial.

multi state companies

Provided that the forum selection clause is fundamentally fair and has been mutually agreed to by the parties in a valid contract, a court will enforce it. Again, where the forum selection clause is in a standard contract, enforceability depends upon whether the clause was clear and fairly presented to the party to be bound.

3. Boxtop and Shrinkwrap Terms

A number of colorful words and phrases have entered the contracts vocabulary to describe situations that have become familiar in modern commerce. We introduce two of them—"boxtop" and "shrinkwrap"—here. Another two words—"clickwrap" and "browsewrap"—are introduced in Section C.4, and one more phrase—"rolling contracts"—is introduced in Chapter 6.

One way the seller of a product can present its standard terms is by printing them on the product's packaging. If the terms are printed on the exterior of the packaging and discernable before opening the packaging (such as terms printed on the box containing the product), they are known as "boxtop" terms. Alternatively, the terms could be included inside the package, say, in a printed insert or user's manual packaged with the product, or in electronic form on software included in the package. These terms are not apparent on the external packaging but are seen only when the packaging is opened. Terms of this kind are called "shrinkwrap" terms. (The name derives from the fact that products are commonly encased in a layer of protective plastic wrap, which must be torn open before the terms are accessible.) Provided that "boxtop" or "shrinkwrap" terms are presented to the buyer at the time of contracting, the buyer's "duty to read" those terms is determined under the same principles as those applicable to other standard terms. However, the analysis becomes more complicated if the terms are not readily apparent to or available to the buyer at the time of contracting. This issue is discussed in Chapter 6.

■ **PROBLEM 3.3**

An electronics store conducted a clearance sale of discontinued TV sets, which it offered for sale at a 30 percent discount. The boxes containing the discounted TV sets had a bright orange sticker affixed that read: "This product does not have the capacity to receive high-definition or 3D transmissions. It is priced for quick, final sale and is nonreturnable." The sticker was three inches by two inches in size, and the print was in 14-point black boldface type. A customer picked up the box, paid for it, and took it home. He did not notice the sticker.

(a) Can the customer return the TV after he discovers that it cannot receive high-definition or 3D transmissions?

(b) Would your answer change if, instead of being set out on the bright orange sticker on the box, the term was displayed or referred to in the following alternative ways?

(i) There was no notice on the box, but instead the term was contained in 12-point normal type on a four-inch-by-six-inch card, attached to the shelf on which the TV was displayed.

(ii) The bright orange sticker on the box read, in 14-point black boldface type, "Note: This sale is subject to special terms, available on request from a sales representative." If asked, the sales representative would have given the customer a printed sheet of paper setting out the term quoted at the beginning of this problem.

4. The Duty to Read Standard Terms in a Web-Based Transaction: Clickwrap and Browsewrap Terms

Anyone who has bought goods or services on the Internet is surely aware of two things. First, web-based transactions are almost always subject to standard terms that have been drafted by the owner of the website. Second, those standard terms are typically made available on the website and can be easily accessed by the buyer. If the standard terms are of any length, they are not likely to be displayed on the screen on which the buyer places the order. Instead, they must be accessed by clicking on a link or by scrolling through a box that appears on the screen before the order can be placed. For example, a buyer visits an airline's website to book a flight. The buyer selects the flight and clicks on a button to book it. Before she can complete the purchase, a pop-up window appears with the airline's standard terms. To read the standard terms, the buyer must scroll down in the window. Regardless of whether she actually reads the terms, the buyer cannot submit the booking until she checks a box or clicks a button on the pop-up screen that signifies her acceptance of the standard terms. Terms on a website that are set up in this way, so that the buyer has to indicate assent before placing her order, are known as "clickwrap" terms. Alternatively, the website may make the terms available to the buyer through a link, but it may not actually require the buyer to take any affirmative steps to indicate assent. Terms set out in this way are called "browsewrap" terms. The next case deals with the question of assent to browsewrap terms. As you will see, the "duty to read" is affected by the degree to which the terms are reasonably clear and conspicuous so that they may fairly be expected to come to the attention of the nondrafting party.

NGUYEN v. BARNES & NOBLE INC.

763 F.3d 1171 (2014)
United States Court of Appeals, Ninth Circuit

NOONAN, Circuit Judge.

Barnes & Noble, Inc. ("Barnes & Noble") appeals the district court's denial of its motion to compel arbitration against Kevin Khoa Nguyen ("Nguyen") pursuant to the arbitration agreement contained in its website's Terms of Use. In order to resolve the issue of arbitrability, we must address whether Nguyen, by merely using Barnes & Noble's website, agreed to be bound by the Terms of Use, even though Nguyen was never prompted to assent to the Terms of Use and never in fact read them. We agree with the district court that Barnes & Noble did not provide reasonable notice of its Terms of Use, and that Nguyen therefore did not unambiguously manifest assent to the arbitration provision contained therein. . . . We therefore affirm the district court's denial of Barnes & Noble's motion to compel arbitration and to stay court proceedings.

The underlying facts are not in dispute. Barnes & Noble is a national bookseller that owns and operates hundreds of bookstores as well as the website "www.barnesandnoble.com". In August 2011, Barnes & Noble, along with other retailers across the country, liquidated its inventory of discontinued Hewlett–Packard Touchpads ("Touchpads"), an unsuccessful competitor to Apple's iPad, by advertising a "fire sale" of Touchpads at a heavily discounted price. Acting quickly on the nationwide liquidation of Touchpads, Nguyen purchased two units on Barnes & Noble's website on August 21, 2011, and received an email confirming the transaction. The following day, Nguyen received another email informing him that his order had been cancelled due to unexpectedly high demand. Nguyen alleges that, as a result of "Barnes & Noble's representations, as well as the delay in informing him it would not honor the sale," he was "unable to obtain an HP Tablet during the liquidation period for the discounted price," and was "forced to rely on substitute tablet technology, which he subsequently purchased . . . [at] considerable expense."

In April 2012, Nguyen filed this lawsuit in California Superior Court on behalf of himself and a putative class of consumers whose Touchpad orders had been cancelled, alleging that Barnes & Noble had engaged in deceptive business practices and false advertising in violation of both California and New York law. Barnes & Noble removed the action to federal court and moved to compel arbitration under the Federal Arbitration Act ("FAA"), arguing that Nguyen was bound by the arbitration agreement in the website's Terms of Use.

The website's Terms of Use are available via a "Terms of Use" hyperlink located in the bottom left-hand corner of every page on the Barnes & Noble website, which appears alongside other hyperlinks labeled "NOOK Store Terms," "Copyright," and "Privacy Policy." These hyperlinks also appear underlined and set in green typeface in the lower lefthand corner of every page in the online checkout process.

Nguyen neither clicked on the "Terms of Use" hyperlink nor actually read the Terms of Use. Had he clicked on the hyperlink, he would have been taken to a page containing the full text of Barnes & Noble's Terms of Use, which state, in relevant part: "By visiting any area in the Barnes & Noble.com Site, creating an account, [or] making a purchase via the Barnes & Noble.com Site . . . a User is deemed to have accepted the Terms of Use." Nguyen also would have come across an arbitration provision, which . . . [committed him to resolve any claim arising out of the transaction by binding arbitration. It also confined him to bringing only claims on his own behalf, and precluded him from instituting class action proceedings.]

Nguyen contends that he cannot be bound to the arbitration provision because he neither had notice of nor assented to the website's Terms of Use. Barnes & Noble, for its part, asserts that the placement of the "Terms of Use" hyperlink on its website put Nguyen on constructive notice of the arbitration agreement. Barnes & Noble contends that this notice, combined with Nguyen's subsequent use of the website, was enough to bind him to the Terms of Use. The district court disagreed, and Barnes & Noble now appeals. . . .

The FAA, 9 U.S.C. §1 *et seq.*, requires federal district courts to stay judicial proceedings and compel arbitration of claims covered by a written and enforceable arbitration agreement. *Id.* §3. The FAA limits the district court's role to determining whether a valid arbitration agreement exists, and whether the agreement encompasses the disputes at issue. The parties do not quarrel that Barnes & Noble's arbitration agreement, should it be found enforceable, encompasses Nguyen's claims. The only issue is whether a valid arbitration agreement exists.

In determining whether a valid arbitration agreement exists, federal courts apply ordinary state law principles that govern the formation of contracts. . . . Here, the parties agree that the validity of the arbitration agreement is governed by New York law. . . . For the reasons that follow, we hold that Nguyen did not enter into Barnes & Noble's agreement to arbitrate.

"While new commerce on the Internet has exposed courts to many new situations, it has not fundamentally changed the principles of contract." *Register.com, Inc. v. Verio, Inc.,* 356 F.3d 393, 403 (2d Cir. 2004). One such principle is the requirement that "[m]utual manifestation of assent, whether by written or spoken word or by conduct, is the touchstone of contract." *Specht v. Netscape Commc'ns Corp.,* 306 F.3d 17, 29 (2d Cir. 2002) (applying California law).

Contracts formed on the Internet come primarily in two flavors: "clickwrap" (or "click-through") agreements, in which website users are required to click on an "I agree" box after being presented with a list of terms and conditions of use; and "browsewrap" agreements, where a website's terms and conditions of use are generally posted on the website via a hyperlink at the bottom of the screen. Barnes & Noble's Terms of Use fall in the latter category. "Unlike a clickwrap agreement, a browsewrap agreement does not require the user to manifest assent to the terms and conditions expressly . . . [a] party instead gives his assent simply by using the website." *Hines v. Overstock.com, Inc.,* 668 F. Supp. 2d 362, 366–67 (E.D.N.Y.2009). Indeed, in a pure-form browsewrap agreement, the website will contain a notice that by merely using the services of, obtaining information from, or initiating applications within the website, the user is agreeing to and is bound by the site's terms of service. Thus, by visiting the website—something that the user has already done—the user agrees to the Terms of Use not listed on the site itself but available only by clicking a hyperlink. The defining feature of browsewrap agreements is that the user can continue to use the website or its services without visiting the page hosting the browsewrap agreement or even knowing that such a webpage exists. Because no affirmative action is required by the website user to agree to the terms of a contract other than his or her use of the website, the determination of the validity of the browsewrap contract depends on whether the user has actual or constructive knowledge of a website's terms and conditions.

Were there any evidence in the record that Nguyen had actual notice of the Terms of Use or was required to affirmatively acknowledge the Terms of Use before completing his online purchase, the outcome of this case might be different. Indeed, courts have consistently enforced browsewrap agreements where the user had actual notice of the agreement. But where, as here, there is no evidence that the website user had actual knowledge of the agreement, the validity of the browsewrap agreement turns on whether the website puts a reasonably prudent user on inquiry notice of the terms of the contract. Whether a user has inquiry notice of a browsewrap agreement, in turn, depends on the design and content of the website and the agreement's webpage. Where the link to a website's terms of use is buried at the bottom of the page or tucked away in obscure corners of the website where users are unlikely to see it, courts have refused to enforce the browsewrap agreement. *See, e.g., Specht, 306 F.3d at 23* (refusing to enforce terms of use that "would have become visible to plaintiffs only if they had scrolled down to the next screen"); *In re Zappos.com,* 893 F. Supp. 2d at 1064 ("The Terms of Use is inconspicuous, buried in the middle to bottom of every Zappos.com webpage among many other links, and the website never directs a user to the Terms of Use"); *Van Tassell* [*v. United Mktg. Grp., LLC,* 795 F. Supp. 2d [790,] 792-93 [(N.D. Ill. 2011)] (refusing to enforce arbitration clause in browsewrap agreement that was only noticeable after a "multi-step process" of clicking through non-obvious links); *Hines,* 668 F. Supp. 2d at 367 (plaintiff "could not even see the link to [the terms and conditions] without scrolling down to the bottom of the screen—an action that was not required to effectuate her purchase"). On the other hand, where the website contains an explicit textual notice that continued use will act as a manifestation of the user's intent to be bound, courts have been more amenable to enforcing browsewrap agreements. *See, e.g., Cairo, Inc. v. Crossmedia Servs., Inc.,* No. 04–04825, 2005 WL 756610, at *2, *4-5 (N.D. Cal. Apr. 1, 2005) (enforcing forum selection clause in website's terms of use where every page on the website had a textual notice that read: "By continuing past this page and/or using this site, you agree to abide by the Terms of Use for this site, which prohibit commercial use of any information on this site"). *But see Pollstar v. Gigmania, Ltd.,* 170 F. Supp. 2d 974, 981 (E.D. Cal. 2000) (refusing to enforce browsewrap agreement where textual notice appeared in small gray print against a gray background). In short, the conspicuousness and placement of the "Terms of Use" hyperlink, other notices given to users of the terms of use, and the website's general design all contribute to whether a reasonably prudent user would have inquiry notice of a browsewrap agreement.

Barnes & Noble argues that the placement of the "Terms of Use" hyperlink in the bottom left-hand corner of every page on the Barnes & Noble website, and its close proximity to the buttons a user must click on to complete an online purchase, is enough to place a reasonably prudent user on constructive notice. It is true that the location of the hyperlink on Barnes & Noble's website distinguishes this case from *Specht,* the leading authority on the enforceability of browsewrap terms under New York law. There, the Second Circuit refused to enforce an arbitration provision in a website's licensing terms where the hyperlink to the terms was located at the bottom of the page, hidden below the "Download" button that users had to click to initiate the software download. Then-Second Circuit Judge Sotomayor, writing for the panel, held that "a reference to the existence of license terms on a submerged screen is not sufficient to place consumers on inquiry or constructive notice of those terms." By contrast, here the "Terms of Use" link appears either directly below the relevant button a user must click on to proceed in the checkout process or just a few inches away. On some pages, the content of the webpage is compact enough that a user can view the link without scrolling. On the remaining pages, the hyperlink is close enough to the "Proceed with Checkout" button that a user would have to bring the link within his field of vision in order to complete his order.

But the proximity or conspicuousness of the hyperlink alone is not enough to give rise to constructive notice, and Barnes & Noble directs us to no case law that supports this proposition.[9] The most analogous case the court was able to locate is *PDC Labs., Inc. v. Hach Co.,* an unpublished district court order cited by neither party. No. 09–1110, 2009 WL 2605270 (C.D.Ill. Aug. 25, 2009). There, the "Terms [and Conditions of Sale] were hyperlinked on three separate pages of the online . . . order process in underlined, blue, contrasting text". The court held that "[t]his contrasting text is sufficient to be considered conspicuous," thereby placing a reasonable user on notice that the terms applied. *Id.* It also observed, however, that the terms' conspicuousness was reinforced by the language of the final checkout screen, which read, "STEP 4 of 4: *Review terms,* add any comments, and submit order,'" and was followed by a hyperlink to the Terms.

As in *PDC*, the checkout screens here contained "Terms of Use" hyperlinks in underlined, color-contrasting text. But *PDC* is dissimilar in that the final screen on that website contained the phrase "Review terms." This makes *PDC* distinguishable, despite the court's explanation that the blue contrasting hyperlinks were sufficiently conspicuous on their own. . . .

In light of the lack of controlling authority on point, and in keeping with courts' traditional reluctance to enforce browsewrap agreements against individual consumers,[10] we therefore hold that where a website makes its terms of use available via a conspicuous hyperlink on every page of the website but otherwise provides no notice to users nor prompts them to take any affirmative action to demonstrate assent, even close proximity of the hyperlink to relevant buttons users must click on—without more—is insufficient to give rise to constructive notice. While failure to read a contract before agreeing to its terms does not relieve a party of its obligations under the contract, the onus must be on website owners to put users on notice of the terms to which they wish to bind consumers. Given the breadth of the range of technological savvy of online purchasers, consumers cannot be expected to ferret out hyperlinks to terms and conditions to which they have no reason to suspect they will be bound.

Barnes & Noble's argument that Nguyen's familiarity with other websites governed by similar browsewrap terms, including his personal website "www.kevinkhoa.com," gives rise to an inference of constructive notice is also of no moment. Whether Nguyen has experience with the browsewrap agreements

---

[9] Indeed, in cases where courts have relied on the proximity of the hyperlink to enforce a browsewrap agreement, the websites at issue have also included something more to capture the user's attention and secure her assent. *See, e.g., 5381 Partners LLC v. Sharesale.com, Inc.*, No. 12–CV–4263 JFB AKT, 2013 WL 5328324, at *7 (E.D.N.Y. Sept. 23, 2013) (in addition to hyperlink that appeared adjacent to the activation button users had to click on, website also contained a text warning near the button that stated "By clicking and making a request to Activate, you agree to the terms and conditions in the [agreement]"); *Zaltz*[v. *JDATE*], 952 F. Supp. 2d [439], 451-52 [(E.D.N.Y. 2013)] (users required to check box confirming that they had reviewed and agreed to website's Terms and Conditions, even though hyperlink to Terms and Conditions was located on the same screen as the button users had to click on to complete registration).

[10] *See* Woodrow Hartzog, *Website Design as Contract*, 60 Am. U.L. Rev. 1635, 1644 (2011) (observing that courts "tend to shy away from enforcing browsewrap agreements that require no outward manifestation of assent"); Lemley, [*Terms of Use*,] 91 Minn. L.Rev. [459,] 472-77 [(2006)]("An examination of the cases that have considered browsewraps in the last five years demonstrates that the courts have been willing to enforce terms of use against corporations, but have not been willing to do so against individuals").

found on other websites such as Facebook, LinkedIn, MySpace, or Twitter, has no bearing on whether he had constructive notice of Barnes & Noble's Terms of Use. There is nothing in the record to suggest that those browsewrap terms are enforceable by or against Nguyen, much less why they should give rise to constructive notice of Barnes & Noble's browsewrap terms. . . .

We hold that Nguyen had insufficient notice of Barnes & Noble's Terms of Use, and thus did not enter into an agreement with Barnes & Noble to arbitrate his claims. Affirmed.

FELDMAN v. GOOGLE, INC.

513 F. Supp. 2d 229 (2007)
United States District Court, Eastern District of Pennsylvania

GILES, District Judge.

[Feldman, a lawyer, purchased Internet advertising from Google's "AdWords" program. Under the program, the advertising fee that Google charged Feldman depended on the number of times that searchers clicked on his advertisement. Feldman alleged that some competitor or prankster committed "click fraud" by clicking repeatedly on his advertisement for the purpose of driving up the price that he had to pay Google for the advertising. Feldman did not claim that Google was complicit in this fraud, but contended that Google did not take adequate measures to warn him of it or prevent it. He sued Google in federal court in Pennsylvania for a refund of the advertising charges that he had overpaid as a result of the "click fraud" and for damages. Google moved to have the case transferred to the federal court in Santa Clara, California, on the grounds that Feldman had agreed to that venue by assenting to a standard forum selection clause when he placed his order for the advertising.] . . .

It is undisputed that advertisers, including Plaintiff, were required to enter into an AdWords contract before placing any ads or incurring any charges. To open an AdWords account, an advertiser had to have gone through a series of steps in an online sign-up process. To activate the AdWords account, the advertiser had to have visited his account page, where he was shown the AdWords contract. Toward the top of the page displaying the AdWords contract, a notice in bold print appeared and stated, "**Carefully read the following terms and conditions.** If you agree with these terms, indicate your assent below." The terms and conditions were offered in a window, with a scroll bar that allowed the advertiser to scroll down and read the entire contract. The contract itself included the preamble and seven paragraphs, in twelve-point font. The contract's preamble, the first paragraph, and part of the second paragraph were clearly visible before scrolling down to read the rest of the contract. The preamble, visible at first impression, stated that consent to the terms listed in the Agreement constituted a binding agreement with Google. A link to a printer-friendly version of the contract was offered at the top of the contract window for the advertiser who would rather read the contract printed on paper or view it on a full-screen instead of scrolling down the window.

At the bottom of the webpage, viewable without scrolling down, was a box and the words, "**Yes,** I agree to the above terms and conditions." The advertiser had to have clicked on this box in order to proceed to the next step. If the advertiser did not click on "**Yes,** I agree . . ." and instead tried to click the "Continue" button at the bottom of the webpage, the advertiser would have been returned to the same page and could not advance to the next step. If the advertiser did not agree to the AdWords contract, he could not activate his account, place any ads, or incur any charges. Plaintiff had an account activated. He placed ads and charges were incurred. . . .

[The court found that even if Feldman did not read the terms and had no actual knowledge of them (which he claimed to be the case), the terms were set out clearly and visibly in the scrollable text box. He therefore had reasonable notice of them, had a duty to read them, and bound himself to them by signifying his assent by clicking the "I agree" button.]

■ QUESTIONS

(1) In the *Specht* case, cited and discussed in *Barnes & Noble*, the court held that the customer did not receive reasonable notice of the arbitration provision because the link to the standard terms was "submerged" and not visible unless the customer scrolled down, beyond the download button, to a portion of the webpage that was not immediately visible on the screen. By contrast, Barnes & Noble's website had a link to the standard terms in the bottom left-hand corner of every page, close to the buttons that the customer had to click to complete the purchase. Why was that not good enough? What should Barnes & Noble have done to assure adequate notice of the terms?

(2) Barnes & Noble argued that Nguyen was familiar with websites and should have expected that there were standard terms. It might also be argued that because arbitration provisions are so common, a reasonable consumer might expect the standard terms to include an arbitration provision. The court was not persuaded that this was sufficient to give Nguyen constructive notice of the term. Why not? Do you agree with the court?

(3) Assume that a website sets up its standard terms in clickwrap form so that the customer has to click an "I agree" button before placing his order. Furthermore, the user is compelled to scroll down the text of the standard terms in the pop-up box because the "I agree" button does not become operational until after the user has done this. This would seem to assure that a court would hold the user to manifested assent, even if the user did not actually read the terms and had no idea what they said. As a matter of policy, is it in the public interest to allow the owner of the website to impose its terms on the user in this way?

■ PROBLEM 3.4

Spider's Web Sales, Inc. operates a website on which it sells a variety of consumer products. Its website contains a link to its standard terms, which appears on the page on which the customer submits her order after selecting the goods to be purchased. The link is preceded by the following words in capitalized boldface, "This transaction is subject to standard terms that will bind you, including an arbitration clause and a forum selection clause. You must read these terms by clicking on the link below before placing your order, and you will not be able to complete your purchase until you have done so." The customer merely has to click on the link before she can submit her order. There is no "I agree" button, and she does not have to signify assent to the terms.

When the customer clicks on the link, a page appears containing 24 terms, written in small print, so they can all fit onto a single screen. The body of text is a dense block, with no headings, boldface, or otherwise highlighted portions. The terms cover every conceivable subject, including a warranty limitation, the return policy, a disclaimer of liability for damages caused by defects in the goods, a waiver of the right to initiate a class action, a lengthy arbitration provision detailing the arbitration procedure, and a forum selection clause. No effort was made to draft the terms in language that makes them readily clear and accessible to a person without legal training. Do you think that the customer would be (or should be) bound by the arbitration and forum selection provisions? In considering this question, bear in mind that the broad principles relating to the duty to read and adequate notice of terms, articulated by the courts in *Morales v. Sun Constructors* and *James v. McDonald's Corporation*, apply to contracts entered into on the Internet.

■ PROBLEM 3.5

Your client, a startup web-based business is just about to launch its website from which it will sell bedding, tableware, and other household accessories. Your client has consulted you about drafting a standard contract that would bind all customers. You have discussed what standard terms should be included and have settled on and drafted a return policy, a limited express warranty, a disclaimer of liability, an arbitration clause, and a forum selection clause. What will you advise your client with regard to the manner in which these standard terms should be displayed and presented to customers who order on the website?

TRICKY JOKES

Most people are serious when they manifest the intention to enter a contract. Any miscommunication of intent, or divergence between subjective intent and objective manifestation of intent, is usually caused by inadvertence, carelessness, or inability to communicate accurately. However, once in a while it happens that one party's manifestation of assent to a contract is not intended by that party to be taken seriously. Under the objective test, the court will be concerned not with that party's subjective understanding that the manifestation was not serious but with the other party's reasonable understanding of the manifestation. The moral of the story, as shown by the next two beloved cases, is that if you are going to kid around, you should not be too subtle about it.

courts understanding

LUCY v. ZEHMER

196 Va. 493, 84 S.E.2d 516 (1954)
Virginia Supreme Court of Appeals

BUCHANAN, Justice.

[The court sets out the facts of the case and the testimony of the parties at considerable length. For the sake of economy, we summarize and redact the factual portion of the opinion while attempting to preserve the colorful testimony offered at trial, as quoted in the opinion.

A. H. Zehmer and his wife, Ida S. Zehmer, owned a tract of land known as the Ferguson Farm. Various people, including W. O. Lucy, had made offers to buy the farm over the years, but Zehmer had consistently refused to sell it. Lucy and Zehmer had known each other for about 15 to 20 years. On the night of December 20, 1952, the Saturday night before Christmas, Lucy visited Zehmer at his business premises—a restaurant that Zehmer operated along with a filling station and motor court. Lucy brought a partially filled bottle of whiskey with him, and they had a few drinks. After a short while, their conversation turned to the Ferguson Farm. About a half-hour later, at the conclusion of this conversation, Lucy left the restaurant with a piece of paper—a blank guest check, on the back of which was written, in Zehmer's hand, "We hereby agree to sell to W. O. Lucy the Ferguson Farm complete for $50,000.00, title satisfactory to buyer." The writing was signed by A. H. Zehmer and Ida S. Zehmer. Lucy claimed that the Zehmers had sold the farm to him, but Zehmer asserted that the transaction was not serious. It was nothing more than a joke: Zehmer did not believe that Lucy could raise $50,000, and he was just trying to call Lucy's bluff. On the next day, Lucy arranged with his brother to contribute half the price of the property for a half interest in it, checked the title, and notified Zehmer that he was ready to close. Zehmer refused to proceed, asserting that he had never agreed to sell

drunk sold his farm

the farm to Lucy. ($50,000 was apparently a good price for the farm, and Zehmer did not argue that Lucy had obtained an unduly good deal.)

sued for specific performance

Lucy sued the Zehmers for specific performance.[11] He testified at the trial, as did Mr. and Mrs. Zehmer and a waitress who was present in the restaurant at the time. The evidence was conflicting. Lucy testified that he asked Zehmer if he had sold the Ferguson farm, and Zehmer replied that he had not. Lucy said, "I bet you wouldn't take $50,000.00 for that place." Zehmer replied, "Yes, I would too; you wouldn't give fifty." Lucy said he would and asked Zehmer to write up an agreement to that effect. Zehmer took a restaurant check on which he wrote, "I do hereby agree to sell. . . ." When Lucy pointed out to him that Mrs. Zehmer would also have to sign the agreement, he tore up the first note and wrote it out again in the form quoted above. He then signed it and asked Mrs. Zehmer, who was about ten feet away at the other end of the counter, to sign it as well. Zehmer gave the writing to Lucy, who offered him $5. Zehmer refused, saying, "You don't need to give me any money, you got the agreement there signed by both of us." Lucy also testified that he suggested the provision about title examination, and Zehmer said he would sell the farm "complete, everything there."

offered signing money?

Zehmer testified that both he and Lucy had many drinks. He could see that Lucy was "pretty high." He said to Lucy, "Boy, you got some good liquor, drinking, ain't you?" Lucy then offered him a drink. "I was already high as a Georgia pine, and didn't have any more better sense than to pour another great big slug out and gulp it down, and he took one too." (In his testimony, Lucy conceded that the parties had had a few drinks but said neither was intoxicated.) Zehmer said that he and Lucy had argued for a while over whether Lucy had $50,000 in cash to enable him to buy the farm. Zehmer told Lucy that he did not believe he had the cash. Lucy told him that if he didn't believe that, he should "sign that piece of paper here and say you will take $50,000.00 for the farm." Thereupon, Zehmer "just grabbed the back off of a guest check there" and "scribbled this thing off." During the course of his testimony, Zehmer looked at the writing and exclaimed, "Great balls of fire, I got 'Firgerson' for Ferguson. I have got 'satisfactory' spelled wrong. I don't recognize that writing if I would see it, wouldn't know it was mine." Zehmer also testified that when he first gave the writing to his wife to sign, she refused to sign it but relented after Zehmer told her that he

---

[11] We introduce the remedy of specific performance in Chapter 1. As explained there, specific performance is an equitable remedy under which a court grants an order compelling the defendant to perform the contract. The performance in *Lucy* was the transfer of land, and the order compelled Zehmer to effect transfer against payment of the purchase price. If Zehmer failed to transfer the land voluntarily, the court would authorize the sheriff to record the transfer in the deeds registry and evict Zehmer from possession of the land. Although an order of specific performance would seem to be the most accurate means of giving the plaintiff his precise expectation, monetary damages are the norm, for the reasons explained in Chapter 1. As an equitable remedy, specific performance is available only where the plaintiff can show that the legal remedy of money damages would not adequately compensate for the breach, and that, overall, the equities favor specific relief. Despite this general preference for money damages, courts have traditionally been much more willing to grant specific performance of contract to sell real property, based on the traditional but now rather questionable supposition that land is unique, and its loss can therefore not be adequately compensated by money damages. We discuss specific performance in more detail in Chapter 21. —Eds.

wife only signed after husband told her it was a joke

was "just needling" Lucy—that the writing "didn't mean a thing in the world," and he was not selling the farm. Zehmer then took the piece of paper back to Lucy ". . . and I was still looking at the dern thing. I had the drink right there by my hand, and I reached over to get a drink, and he said, 'Let me see it.' He reached and picked it up, and when I looked back again, he had it in his pocket, and he dropped a five dollar bill over there, and he said, 'Here is five dollars payment on it.' . . . I said, 'Hell no, that is beer and liquor talking. I am not going to sell you the farm. I have told you that too many times before.'"

Mrs. Zehmer testified that during most of the conversation between Lucy and Zehmer, she was at the back of the restaurant helping the waitress to get things ready for next day. She heard most of the conversation but did not pay much attention until her husband came up to her to get her to sign the paper. When Zehmer asked her if she wanted to put her name on the paper, she initially said no but then signed it when Zehmer told her in an undertone, "It is nothing but a joke." She claimed that only one paper had been written and that the "I hereby agree to sell" had been altered to read "we." She said that she could tell that Lucy had been drinking and told her husband, "You should have taken him home," to which he replied, "Well, I am just about as bad off as he is."

The waitress testified that when Lucy first came in, "he was mouthy." She was cleaning up the restaurant and was not attentive to the discussions between Lucy and Zehmer. She said they were laughing and joking and "appeared to be drinking right much." She heard part of their exchange about the farm. She was aware that they squabbled about whether Lucy had enough money for the farm and thought that Lucy kept raising his offer until it reached $50,000. She saw Zehmer write something down on a piece of paper, which Lucy pocketed, tendering $5 that Zehmer did not accept. She said that Zehmer told Lucy he didn't want his money "because he didn't have enough money to pay for his property and wasn't going to sell his farm."]

*main point is whether Lucy had $50,000

. . . The defendants insist that the evidence was ample to support their contention that the writing sought to be enforced was prepared as a bluff or dare to force Lucy to admit that he did not have $50,000; that the whole matter was a joke; that the writing was not delivered to Lucy and no binding contract was ever made between the parties. It is an unusual, if not bizarre, defense. When made to the writing admittedly prepared by one of the defendants and signed by both, clear evidence is required to sustain it.

In his testimony Zehmer claimed that he "was high as a Georgia pine," and that the transaction "was just a bunch of two doggoned drunks bluffing to see who could talk the biggest and say the most." That claim is inconsistent with his attempt to testify in great detail as to what was said and what was done. It is contradicted by other evidence as to the condition of both parties, and rendered of no weight by the testimony of his wife that when Lucy left the restaurant she suggested that Zehmer drive him home. The record is convincing that Zehmer was not intoxicated to the extent of being unable to comprehend the nature and consequences of the instrument he executed, and hence that instrument is not to be invalidated on that ground. It was in fact conceded by defendants' counsel

holding

in oral argument that under the evidence Zehmer was not too drunk to make a valid contract.[12]

The evidence is convincing also that Zehmer wrote two agreements, the first one beginning "I hereby agree to sell." Zehmer first said he could not remember about that, then that "I don't think I wrote but one out." Mrs. Zehmer said that what he wrote was "I hereby agree," but that the "I" was changed to "We" after that night. The agreement that was written and signed is in the record and indicates no such change. Neither are the mistakes in spelling that Zehmer sought to point out readily apparent. — *no spelling mistakes*

The appearance of the contract, the fact that it was under discussion for forty minutes or more before it was signed; Lucy's objection to the first draft because it was written in the singular, and he wanted Mrs. Zehmer to sign it also; the rewriting to meet that objection and the signing by Mrs. Zehmer; the discussion of what was to be included in the sale, the provision for the examination of the title, the completeness of the instrument that was executed, the taking possession of it by Lucy with no request or suggestion by either of the defendants that he give it back, are facts which furnish persuasive evidence that the execution of the contract was a serious business transaction rather than a casual, jesting matter as defendants now contend. . . .

If it be assumed, contrary to what we think the evidence shows, that Zehmer was jesting about selling his farm to Lucy and that the transaction was intended by him to be a joke, nevertheless the evidence shows that Lucy did not so understand it but considered it to be a serious business transaction and the contract to be binding on the Zehmers as well as on himself. The very next day he arranged with his brother to put up half the money and take a half interest in the land. The day after that he employed an attorney to examine the title. The next night, Tuesday, he was back at Zehmer's place and there Zehmer told him for the first time, Lucy said, that he wasn't going to sell and he told Zehmer, "You know you sold that place fair and square." After receiving the report from his attorney that the title was good he wrote to Zehmer that he was ready to close the deal. Not only did Lucy actually believe, but the evidence shows he was warranted in believing, that the contract represented a serious business transaction and a good faith sale and purchase of the farm.

In the field of contracts, as generally elsewhere, "We must look to the outward expression of a person as manifesting his intention rather than to his

_____

[12] In claiming that the parties were too drunk to assent to a contract, Zehmer raises a defense of incapacity, which we study in Chapter 14. This passage gives you foresight into one of the limitations of the objective test. Even if a party manifests assent to a contract, the court may go behind that manifestation to examine the party's subjective state of mind where the party is suffering from a mental disease or incapacity (which could be induced by alcohol or drug abuse) that prevents him from understanding the transaction or acting rationally in entering it. Zehmer did not succeed in that argument in this case because the court did not believe that he was inebriated enough to qualify as incapacitated. —EDS.

[handwritten margin notes: trying to say the terms were changed; 1) contract exists; 2) discussion; 3) re-done terms; 4) signatures; 5) completeness; lucy saw it as serious; days passed before they said it was a joke]

must look at actions over intentions

secret and unexpressed intention. The law imputes to a person an intention corresponding to the reasonable meaning of his words and acts.' *First Nat. Bank v. Roanoke Oil Co.*, 169 Va. 99, 114, 192 S.E. 764, 770. At no time prior to the execution of the contract had Zehmer indicated to Lucy by word or act that he was not in earnest about selling the farm. They had argued about it and discussed its terms, as Zehmer admitted, for a long time. . . . [T]here had been what appeared to be a good faith offer and a good faith acceptance, followed by the execution and apparent delivery of a written contract. Both said that Lucy put the writing in his pocket and then offered Zehmer $5 to seal the bargain. Not until then, even under the defendants' evidence, was anything said or done to indicate that the matter was a joke. Both of the Zehmers testified that when Zehmer asked his wife to sign he whispered that it was a joke so Lucy wouldn't hear and that it was not intended that he should hear.

* mental assent not necessary

reasoning

The mental assent of the parties is not requisite for the formation of a contract. If the words or other acts of one of the parties have but one reasonable meaning, his undisclosed intention is immaterial except when an unreasonable meaning which he attaches to his manifestations is known to the other party. An agreement or mutual assent is of course essential to a valid contract but the law imputes to a person an intention corresponding to the reasonable meaning of his words and acts. If his words and acts, judged by a reasonable standard, manifest an intention to agree, it is immaterial what may be the real but unexpressed state of his mind. So a person cannot set up that he was merely jesting when his conduct and words would warrant a reasonable person in believing that he intended a real agreement. Whether the writing signed by the defendants and now sought to be enforced by the complainants was the result of a serious offer by Lucy and a serious acceptance by the defendants, or was a serious offer by Lucy and an acceptance in secret jest by the defendants, in either event it constituted a binding contract of sale between the parties.

Defendants contend further, however, that even though a contract was made, equity should decline to enforce it under the circumstances. These circumstances have been set forth in detail above. They disclose some drinking by the two parties but not to an extent that they were unable to understand fully what they were doing. There was no fraud, no misrepresentation, no sharp practice and no dealing between unequal parties. The farm had been bought for $11,000 and was assessed for taxation at $6,300. The purchase price was $50,000. Zehmer admitted that it was a good price. There is in fact present in this case none of the grounds usually urged against specific performance.

holding

The complainants are entitled to have specific performance of the contract sued on. The decree appealed from is therefore reversed and the cause is remanded for the entry of a proper decree requiring the defendants to perform the contract in accordance with the prayer of the bill.

disposition   Reversed and remanded.

wants a harrier jet from the pepsi commercial

LEONARD v. PEPSICO, INC.

88 F. Supp. 2d 116 (S.D.N.Y. 1999), aff'd, 210 F.3d 88 (2d Cir. 2000)
United States District Court, Southern District of New York

WOOD, District Judge.

leonard wants specific performance

pepsi granted summary judgement

Plaintiff brought this action seeking, among other things, specific performance of an alleged offer of a Harrier jet, featured in a television advertisement for defendant's "Pepsi Stuff" promotion. Defendant has moved for summary judgment. For the reasons stated below, defendant's motion is granted. This case arises out of a promotional campaign conducted by defendant, the producer and distributor of the soft drinks Pepsi and Diet Pepsi. The promotion, entitled "Pepsi Stuff," encouraged consumers to collect "Pepsi Points" from specially marked packages of Pepsi or Diet Pepsi and redeem these points for merchandise featuring the Pepsi logo. Before introducing the promotion nationally, defendant conducted a test of the promotion in the Pacific Northwest from October 1995 to March 1996. A Pepsi Stuff catalog was distributed to consumers in the test market, including Washington State. Plaintiff is a resident of Seattle, Washington. While living in Seattle, plaintiff saw the Pepsi Stuff commercial that he contends constituted an offer of a Harrier jet.

commercial

... The commercial opens upon an idyllic, suburban morning, where the chirping of birds in sun-dappled trees welcomes a paperboy on his morning route. As the newspaper hits the stoop of a conventional two-story house, the tattoo of a military drum introduces the subtitle, "MONDAY 7:58 AM." The stirring strains of a martial air mark the appearance of a well-coiffed teenager preparing to leave for school, dressed in a shirt emblazoned with the Pepsi logo, a red-white-and-blue ball. While the teenager confidently preens, the military drumroll again sounds as the subtitle "T-SHIRT 75 PEPSI POINTS" scrolls across the screen. Bursting from his room, the teenager strides down the hallway wearing a leather jacket. The drumroll sounds again, as the subtitle "LEATHER JACKET 1450 PEPSI POINTS" appears. The teenager opens the door of his house and, unfazed by the glare of the early morning sunshine, puts on a pair of sunglasses. The drumroll then accompanies the subtitle "SHADES 175 PEPSI POINTS." A voiceover then intones, "Introducing the new Pepsi Stuff catalog," as the camera focuses on the cover of the catalog.

The scene then shifts to three young boys sitting in front of a high school building. The boy in the middle is intent on his Pepsi Stuff Catalog, while the boys on either side are each drinking Pepsi. The three boys gaze in awe at an object rushing overhead, as the military march builds to a crescendo. The Harrier jet is not yet visible, but the observer senses the presence of a mighty plane as the extreme winds generated by its flight create a paper maelstrom in a classroom devoted to an otherwise dull physics lesson. Finally, the Harrier jet swings into view and lands by the side of the school building, next to a bicycle rack. Several students run for cover, and the velocity of the wind strips one hapless faculty member down to his underwear. While the faculty member is being deprived of his dignity, the voiceover announces: "Now the more Pepsi you drink, the more great stuff you're gonna get."

The teenager opens the cockpit of the fighter and can be seen, helmet-less, holding a Pepsi. Looking very pleased with himself, the teenager exclaims, "Sure beats the bus," and chortles. The military drumroll sounds a final time, as the following words appear: "HARRIER FIGHTER 7,000,000 PEPSI POINTS." A few seconds later, the following appears in more stylized script: "Drink Pepsi—Get Stuff." With that message, the music and the commercial end with a triumphant flourish.

Inspired by this commercial, plaintiff set out to obtain a Harrier jet. Plaintiff explains that he is "typical of the 'Pepsi Generation' . . . he is young, has an adventurous spirit, and the notion of obtaining a Harrier jet appealed to him enormously." . . . Although plaintiff initially set out to collect 7,000,000 Pepsi Points by consuming Pepsi products, it soon became clear to him that he "would not be able to buy (let alone drink) enough Pepsi to collect the necessary Pepsi Points fast enough." . . . [However, the rules of the promotion allowed a consumer to buy the additional Pepsi Points needed to redeem a prize for ten cents each, provided that at least 15 original Pepsi Points were sent in with the order. He managed to raise about $700,000.] On or about March 27, 1996, plaintiff submitted an Order Form, fifteen original Pepsi Points, and a check for $700,008.50. Plaintiff appears to have been represented by counsel at the time he mailed his check; the check is drawn on an account of plaintiff's first set of attorneys. At the bottom of the Order Form, plaintiff wrote in "1 Harrier jet" in the "Item" column and "7,000,000" in the "Total Points" column. In a letter accompanying his submission, plaintiff stated that the check was to purchase additional Pepsi Points "expressly for obtaining a new Harrier jet as advertised in your Pepsi Stuff commercial."

On or about May 7, 1996, defendant's fulfillment house rejected plaintiff's submission and returned the check, explaining that: "The item that you have requested is not part of the Pepsi Stuff collection. It is not included in the catalogue or on the order form, and only catalogue merchandise can be redeemed under this program. The Harrier jet in the Pepsi commercial is fanciful and is simply included to create a humorous and entertaining ad. We apologize for any misunderstanding or confusion that you may have experienced and are enclosing some free product coupons for your use." . . .

[Further correspondence followed in which Plaintiff's counsel threatened suit if the jet was not delivered, and PepsiCo's reasserted that the ad was clearly a joke, as would be obvious to any reasonable person. PepsiCo took the initiative by instituting suit in federal district court for a declaratory judgment stating that it had no obligation to furnish plaintiff with a Harrier jet.[13] In response, Leonard instituted his own suit against PepsiCo in a state court. After a

---

[13] As in *SR International*, the remedy sought here by PepsiCo is a declaratory judgment. PepsiCo has not suffered any monetary loss as a result of Leonard's actions, so it does not seek any economic compensation from him. It simply wishes the court to award a judgment declaring that it has no liability to Leonard, and

[handwritten: joined the cases ↑]

procedural scuffle, the suits were consolidated. PepsiCo moved for summary judgment. The issue in the case was whether PepsiCo had made an offer to Leonard and other members of the public, either in its TV commercial, or in a printed brochure setting out the details of the Pepsi Points promotion. If PepsiCo did make an offer, then it would be contractually bound to deliver the jet to Leonard upon his acceptance of the offer in his letter redeeming his Pepsi Points. In dealing with this issue, the court addresses two principal arguments. The one that we include here involves the question of whether the TV commercial was a serious manifestation of contractual intent, or just a joke. The second, which we defer to our discussion of offers in Chapter 4, deals with the question of whether, assuming PepsiCo's manifestation of intent was serious, and not reasonably understood as a joke, its TV commercial or its printed Pepsi Points brochure constituted an offer that would bind PepsiCo upon acceptance by a member of the public.]

[handwritten left margin: did pepsi make an offer?]

[handwritten left margin: ① serious offer or ② is the commercial brochure an offer?]

Plaintiff's understanding of the commercial as an offer must . . . be rejected because the Court finds that no objective person could reasonably have concluded that the commercial actually offered consumers a Harrier jet. In evaluating the commercial, the Court must not consider defendant's subjective intent in making the commercial, or plaintiff's subjective view of what the commercial offered, but what an objective, reasonable person would have understood the commercial to convey. If it is clear that an offer was not serious, then no offer has been made. [*Corbin on Contracts*, §1.11 at 30 states:]

[handwritten left margin: consider what an objective reasonable person would assume]

> What kind of act creates a power of acceptance and is therefore an offer? It must be an expression of will or intention. It must be an act that leads the offeree reasonably to conclude that a power to create a contract is conferred. This applies to the content of the power as well as to the fact of its existence. It is on this ground that we must exclude invitations to deal or acts of mere preliminary negotiation, and acts evidently done in jest or without intent to create legal relations.

An obvious joke, of course, would not give rise to a contract. On the other hand, if there is no indication that the offer is "evidently in jest," and that an objective, reasonable person would find that the offer was serious, then there may be a valid offer. See *Lucy v. Zehmer*, 196 Va. 493, 84 S.E.2d 516, 518, 520 (1954) (ordering specific performance of a contract to purchase a farm despite defendant's protestation that the transaction was done in jest as "just a bunch of two doggoned drunks bluffing"). . . . Plaintiff's insistence that the commercial appears to be a serious offer requires the Court to explain why the commercial is funny. Explaining why a joke is funny is a daunting task; as the essayist E.B. White has remarked, "Humor can be dissected, as a frog can, but the thing dies

---

instituting suit for a declaratory judgment allows it to take the initiative in bringing the case to court, even before Leonard sues. An additional advantage it gets by initiating the litigation is that, within reasonable limits, it has more control over the venue of the case. —EDS.

in the process...." The commercial is the embodiment of what defendant appropriately characterizes as "zany humor."

First, the commercial suggests, as commercials often do, that use of the advertised product will transform what, for most youth, can be a fairly routine and ordinary experience. The military tattoo and stirring martial music, as well as the use of subtitles in a Courier font that scroll terse messages across the screen, such as "MONDAY 7:58 AM," evoke military and espionage thrillers. The implication of the commercial is that Pepsi Stuff merchandise will inject drama and moment into hitherto unexceptional lives. The commercial in this case thus makes the exaggerated claims similar to those of many television advertisements: that by consuming the featured clothing, car, beer, or potato chips, one will become attractive, stylish, desirable, and admired by all. A reasonable viewer would understand such advertisements as mere puffery, not as statements of fact, and refrain from interpreting the promises of the commercial as being literally true.

[margin note: exaggerated claims are understood to be part of advertising]

Second, the callow youth featured in the commercial is a highly improbable pilot, one who could barely be trusted with the keys to his parents' car, much less the prize aircraft of the United States Marine Corps. Rather than checking the fuel gauges on his aircraft, the teenager spends his precious pre-flight minutes preening. The youth's concern for his coiffure appears to extend to his flying without a helmet. Finally, the teenager's comment that flying a Harrier jet to school "sure beats the bus" evinces an improbably insouciant attitude toward the relative difficulty and danger of piloting a fighter plane in a residential area, as opposed to taking public transportation.

[margin note: no teenager would actually be a pilot]

Third, the notion of traveling to school in a Harrier jet is an exaggerated adolescent fantasy. In this commercial, the fantasy is underscored by how the teenager's schoolmates gape in admiration, ignoring their physics lesson. The force of the wind generated by the Harrier jet blows off one teacher's clothes, literally defrocking an authority figure. As if to emphasize the fantastic quality of having a Harrier jet arrive at school, the jet lands next to a plebeian bike rack. This fantasy is, of course, extremely unrealistic. No school would provide landing space for a student's fighter jet, or condone the disruption the jet's use would cause.

[margin note: not a real method for getting to school]

Fourth, the primary mission of a Harrier jet, according to the United States Marine Corps, is to "attack and destroy surface targets under day and night visual conditions." Manufactured by McDonnell Douglas, the Harrier jet played a significant role in the air offensive of Operation Desert Storm in 1991. The jet is designed to carry a considerable armament load, including Sidewinder and Maverick missiles. As one news report has noted, "Fully loaded, the Harrier can float like a butterfly and sting like a bee—albeit a roaring 14-ton butterfly and a bee with 9,200 pounds of bombs and missiles." In light of the Harrier jet's well-documented function in attacking and destroying surface and air targets, armed reconnaissance and air interdiction, and offensive and defensive anti-aircraft warfare, depiction of such a jet as a way to get to school in the morning is

[margin note: the jet is a marine tool]

clearly not serious even if, as plaintiff contends, the jet is capable of being acquired "in a form that eliminates [its] potential for military use."

Fifth, the number of Pepsi Points the commercial mentions as required to "purchase" the jet is 7,000,000. To amass that number of points, one would have to drink 7,000,000 Pepsis (or roughly 190 Pepsis a day for the next hundred years—an unlikely possibility), or one would have to purchase approximately $700,000 worth of Pepsi Points. The cost of a Harrier jet is roughly $23 million dollars, a fact of which plaintiff was aware when he set out to gather the amount he believed necessary to accept the alleged offer. Even if an objective, reasonable person were not aware of this fact, he would conclude that purchasing a fighter plane for $700,000 is a deal too good to be true. . . .

In light of the obvious absurdity of the commercial, the Court rejects plaintiff's argument that the commercial was not clearly in jest. . . . [The court granted summary judgment to PepsiCo.[14]]

a humorous number of points is required

---

[14] It seems that Leonard is not the only civilian who has sought to acquire a Harrier jet. A report appeared on several Internet news sites in February 2011 of a seven-year-old boy in London who bought a Harrier on eBay by clicking a "buy it now" button on the website. Apparently, the jet had been retired by the Royal Air Force and bought by a dealer, which offered it for sale on eBay for £69,999. When the boy's father discovered what his son had done, he canceled the purchase, explaining that his son could not afford the jet on his allowance. (The price of the jet was lower than the value indicated in *Leonard* because it was no longer airworthy.) —EDS.

CHAPTER 4

The Offer

A THE PROCESS OF CONTRACT FORMATION

1. The Offer and Acceptance Model

[handwritten: offer made by offeror]

According to the classical structure, a contract is formed by an exchange of communications in which a transaction proposed by one party is accepted by the other. The proposal is called an offer, and the person who makes it is the offeror. The signification of assent by the party to whom the offer is made (the offeree) is called an acceptance. Sometimes a contract may be formed after just a single set of communications, such as where the offer is immediately accepted. In other cases, a contract may be made only after some haggling takes place. For example, the offeree may decline the offer and propose a transaction on different terms (this is called a counteroffer), which the original offeror may accept. The classicists concentrated on developing a set of rules to govern the process of contract formation. The rules seek to cover the details of this exchange of communications, prescribing the qualities and legal effect of an offer and the various responses to it. These rules, while made more flexible by the tenets of legal realism, still constitute the foundation and structure of our rules of contract formation.

You should recognize at the outset that the offer and acceptance model fits some fact situations well but is very strained and artificial in others. This means that it cannot always be the only or definitive means of analyzing formation issues. However, even where it cannot be dispositive, the offer and acceptance model still serves as a reference point for the analysis. This will become apparent as we proceed. Our first task is to learn the basic rules and principles.

[handwritten: offer is not the only way to form a contract]

101

Where parties undertake the process of contract formation, their communications are often fluid. It can therefore be quite artificial to try to separate issues relating to the offer from those relating to acceptance. Nevertheless, this is a convenient organization for the purpose of studying contract formation. We therefore focus on offer issues in this chapter and on acceptance issues in Chapter 5. However, you will find that some questions relating to acceptance creep into our discussion of offers in this chapter, and some questions of offer linger in Chapter 5. We conclude our discussion of offer and acceptance in Chapter 6 by looking at particular concerns that arise where offer and acceptance takes place through the use of electronic communications or standard forms.

2. An Overview of the Process of Contract Formation

We begin, in this chapter, by looking at the offer—the firm proposal to enter into a contract. This is the first stage in contract formation under the classical conception. However, before doing that it is useful to trace the process of contract formation briefly so that you can see this discussion in context and can anticipate some of the acceptance issues that we cover in Chapter 5.

Once an offer has been made, the next stage involves the offeree's reaction to it. If she accepts the offer, a contract comes into effect immediately upon acceptance, without any further action required by the offeror. The hallmark of an offer is that it gives the offeree the power to make the decision on whether or not there will be a contract. If a proposal is written in a way that does not give this power to the recipient, but keeps the final decision in the hands of the person who made the proposal, it is simply not an offer. To accept the offer, the offeree must not only signify assent to a contract on the terms proposed by the offer, but must do so within the time and in accordance with the procedure prescribed by the offeror or, in the absence of such instructions, a time and procedure that is reasonable under the circumstances. It is therefore useful to think of acceptance as having both a substantive aspect (assent to the contract terms) and a procedural aspect (communication of that assent in the proper time and manner).

If the offeree does not accept the offer within the specified or reasonable time that it is open for acceptance, the offer is rejected. It falls away, and no contract is created. An offeree may expressly reject an offer, but (except in very limited circumstances discussed later) she does not need to do anything to reject. If she just ignores the offer, her inaction is a rejection.

An offeree who has some interest in entering into a transaction with the offeror but does not like the terms proposed by the offeror could respond to the offer by making a counteroffer. This is, in legal effect, a new offer by the offeree that constitutes a rejection of the offeror's original offer and the substitution of a new one in its place. The original offeror now becomes the offeree under the *titles change with a counteroffer*

counteroffer and can accept or reject it. Alternatively, he could respond by making his own counteroffer, which would return the power of acceptance to the original offeree. The exchange of counteroffers could go on for some time, until the parties reach an agreement or the negotiations collapse.

– fixed time limit of what is "reasonable"

Although an offer has a period of duration, either fixed by the offeror or for a reasonable time, the offeror usually has the ability to cut short the time for acceptance by revoking the offer. As a general rule, as long as the offer has not yet been accepted, the offeror can cancel it even before its time has expired.[1] To do this, the offeror must notify the offeree that the offer is revoked.

B THE NATURE AND QUALITIES OF AN OFFER

1. The Definition of "Offer" at Common Law

Restatement definition

The Restatement, Second §24 defines "offer" as "the manifestation of willingness to enter into a bargain, so made as to justify another person in understanding that his assent to that bargain is invited and will conclude it." This follows the traditional formulation in which one of the parties (the offeror) makes an offer, indicating intent to enter into a contract on the proposed terms. As Restatement, Second §24 indicates, the hallmark of an offer, distinguishing it from a mere proposal initiating or continuing negotiations, is that the recipient of the offer (the offeree) must reasonably understand that the offeror has given her the

offeree must know that agreeing begins a contract

initiative to create the contract by accepting the offer. That is, the wording and context of the offer must make it clear to the reasonable offeree that her acceptance will bind the parties immediately, without the offeror having the opportunity to make the final decision. If the reasonable sense of the proposal is that the offeror retains the right to make the final decision, the proposal is not an offer; it is merely an invitation to the recipient to negotiate or to make an offer to the person making the proposal.

If the person making the proposal expresses his intent clearly, it is quite easy to tell whether he intends his communication to be an offer or merely a solicitation for an offer. However, communications are often not that clear, and their reasonable meaning must be determined by the process of interpretation, as discussed in Section B.3.

*offer must retain the power with the offeree

---

[1] There is an exception to this rule: Under the proper circumstances, an offeror may make a binding commitment not to revoke the offer before it lapses. Such a promise is called an "option" or a "firm offer," which is studied in Chapter 11.

2. Offers Under UCC Article 2

UCC Article 2 does not contain a definition of an offer or any rules that specifically address offers. It is not unusual to find that the UCC is silent on an issue of contract law. As mentioned in Chapter 2, the UCC is not intended to be a comprehensive codification of every single rule and principle of law that pertains to commercial transactions. The drafters of the UCC included in it only those provisions that they considered essential to express, and left other questions for resolution under common law. This general approach is articulated in UCC 1-103(b).

UCC 1-103(b). . . . APPLICABILITY OF SUPPLEMENTAL PRINCIPLES OF LAW

Unless displaced by the particular provisions of [the Uniform Commercial Code], the principles of law and equity . . . supplement its provisions.

Although it does not deal specifically with offers, Article 2 has two general provisions—UCC 2-204 and 2-206—that set out the approach to be adopted by courts in resolving offer and acceptance issues. These provisions reflect the philosophy of Karl Llewellyn and the other legal realists who drafted the UCC. They call for a realistic evaluation of the facts of the transaction that focuses not on technical rules, but on the question of whether an agreement was in fact made. At the time that the UCC was drafted, this approach may have been much more liberal than that used by courts in relation to contracts governed by common law. However, most modern courts adopt a similar attitude in deciding formation issues relating to common law contracts.

UCC 2-206 deals with acceptance issues, and we will study it in Chapters 5 and 6. UCC 2-204 sets out the broad general principles to be followed by courts in resolving formation issues. UCC 2-204 reads as follows:

UCC 2-204. FORMATION IN GENERAL

(1) A contract for sale of goods may be made in any manner sufficient to show agreement, including conduct by both parties which recognizes the existence of such a contract.

(2) An agreement sufficient to constitute a contract for sale may be found even though the moment of its making is undetermined.

(3) Even though one or more terms are left open a contract for sale does not fail for indefiniteness if the parties have intended to make a contract and there is a reasonably certain basis for giving an appropriate remedy.

3. Interpreting the Intent of a Communication to Determine Whether It Is an Offer

As discussed in Chapter 3, contracts are created by the communication of intent through outward manifestations, which must be given the meaning reasonably understood by the party to whom they were communicated. When a court deals with a dispute over the meaning of manifestations by words or conduct, it must interpret that meaning. Where there is no other relevant evidence, the process of interpretation may involve little more than hauling out a dictionary and looking up the meaning of words as they are used in the communication as a whole. This is sometimes referred to as "plain meaning" interpretation or interpretation within the "four corners" of the document. However, where there is relevant contextual evidence extrinsic to the document, proper interpretation may require that the meaning of the words or conduct be evaluated within that entire context. As a rule of thumb, if no such contextual evidence exists, interpretation is considered a matter of law for the judge to decide. However, if contextual evidence exists, the ascertainment of meaning may become a factual matter more properly handled by a jury.

Because the existence and terms of contracts are so fundamentally reliant on the meaning of the parties' communications, interpretation is a constant theme in contract law. It is therefore fitting that we begin our discussion of offer and acceptance by looking at two cases in which the courts had to decide whether a proposal for a transaction, addressed to a specific party and setting out the terms of the exchange, should be interpreted as an offer. In reading the cases, pay attention to the sources used by the court to determine meaning. How important is the plain meaning of the words used? Is there any evidence concerning the circumstances in which the communication was made? If so, what weight is given to those circumstances?

FLETCHER-HARLEE CORP. v. POTE CONCRETE CONTRACTORS, INC.

482 F.3d 247 (2007)
United States Court of Appeals, Third Circuit

AMBRO, Circuit Judge.

This is a cautionary tale of offer, acceptance, [and] commercial practice. . . . In the construction industry, general contractors compete for work by submitting bids detailing how they will complete the project, the materials they will use, the time it will take, and the price they will charge. To prepare these bids, general contractors in turn solicit bids from more specialized subcontractors. It is well understood in the industry that bids at both levels are

bids are firm offers

"firm offers."[2] In other words, subcontractors submit bids expecting to be held to their terms if selected. General contractors rely on subcontractors' bids to create a single-priced package of work. A subcontractor's subsequent refusal to honor its bid wreaks havoc on the general contractor's bid and can quickly turn a profitable project into a financial "black hole."

Since the advent of legal realism, building the law around commercial practice has been a goal of common law courts. It stems from principles of judicial restraint: judges recognize that the repeat players in an industry often are more capable of setting the industry's ground rules than they are. Thus, we use relevant commercial practice to aid us in interpreting contracts. *See* Restatement (Second) of Contracts §202 (1981).[3]

interpret contracts by their plain language

As this case demonstrates, however, there is a contract-law principle more powerful than commercial practice: we interpret documents in accord with their plain language. *Id.* at §203(b) ("[E]xpress terms are given greater weight than . . . usage of trade."). When the text of a subcontractor's bid, which would typically be a firm offer, specifically states that it is not one, we must follow that text. Therefore, we cannot allow a general contractor who purports to accept such a bid to sue for breach of contract. . . .

Fletcher-Harlee Corp., a general contractor, solicited bids from subcontractors on various aspects of a building project for which it intended to compete. In keeping with industry custom, Fletcher-Harlee's solicitation letter stipulated that bids must be held open for a minimum of 60 days and that subcontractors must agree to be accountable for the prices and proposals submitted. In response, Pote Concrete Contractors, Inc. submitted a written price quotation for providing the concrete for the project. Pote's "bid," however, did not conform to Fletcher-Harlee's terms; rather, it stipulated that its price quotation was for informational purposes only, did not constitute a "firm offer," and should not be relied on. Pote's response further stated that Pote did not agree to be held liable for any of the terms it submitted.

not a firm offer ←

The terms that Pote submitted were the most favorable, and, for reasons not apparent from the record, Fletcher-Harlee relied on them in preparing its general bid despite Pote's stated limitations.[4] Pote was quite serious about those limitations, and, when Fletcher-Harlee won the bid and tried to reduce Pote's terms to a written contract, it raised the price. This increase pushed Pote's bid

---

[2] A firm offer is one that cannot be revoked for a specified or reasonable period. That is, the offeror gives the offeree a stated or reasonable time in which to accept the offer and promises that the offer will not be withdrawn during that period. We discuss firm offers in Chapter 11. Do not worry about the requirements for and nature of firm offers for now. For present purposes, our focus is on the question of whether an offer was made at all. —Eds.

[3] Restatement, Second §202 sets out general principles of interpretation. We discuss it more fully in Chapter 15. Among other things, it recognizes that a manifestation of intent should be interpreted, whenever possible, within the context of the parties' transaction, including any usage of the trade of which the parties are members. As the court suggests, the Restatement, Second, places strong emphasis on commercial practice as a source of rules that apply to the contract. The same is true of UCC Article 2. —Eds.

[4] The disclaimer language was in normal print in the last paragraph of Pote's one-page submission letter. Fletcher-Harlee does not argue that it was worded or presented in a deceptive manner.

above the next lowest one, and so Fletcher-Harlee ended up using a different concrete subcontractor and spending over $200,000 more than expected.

Fletcher-Harlee sued Pote in District Court for breach of contract. . . . [The District Court granted Pote's motion to dismiss the suit on the basis that the facts pled did not support the contract cause of action.] Fletcher-Harlee now appeals to us. . . . For the reasons that follow, we affirm.

posture

disposition

As any first-year law student knows,[5] an offer and its acceptance are required to form a contract, and so we must decide how to characterize each of the communications between the parties. Fletcher-Harlee solicited a bid from Pote. In its solicitation letter, Fletcher-Harlee stipulated that bids should be held open for 60 days and that the subcontractor would be held liable for the terms of the bid. Was this letter an offer? Probably not. The document itself is not in the record, but we suspect that it was merely a request to submit an offer. "An offer is the manifestation of willingness to enter into a bargain, so made as to justify another person in understanding that his assent to that bargain is invited and will conclude it." Restatement (Second) of Contracts §24 (1981). Here, a subcontractor would understand that submitting a bid would not "conclude" the matter; rather, the general contractor would have to accept the bid to do so. The Restatement and New Jersey caselaw characterize solicitations like this one not as offers, but as invitations to make offers. Restatement (Second) of Contracts §26 cmt. d (1981). . . .

initial letter, not an offer

Second, Pote submitted to Fletcher-Harlee the terms on which it could complete the work. Was this an acceptance? Obviously not. Even if the Fletcher-Harlee communication were an offer, Pote's response could be no more than a counteroffer because its terms were materially different from those in the solicitation letter. . . . Restatement (Second) of Contracts §59 (1981) ("A reply to an offer which purports to accept it but is conditional on the offeror's assent to terms additional to or different from those offered is not an acceptance but is a counter-offer"). More importantly, because the submission expressly disclaimed Pote's intention to be bound, it could not be an offer. As quoted above, an offer is made when the offeree is justified in thinking that "his assent . . . will conclude" the deal. Restatement (Second) of Contracts §24 (1981). Here, the very terms of Pote's letter state that Fletcher-Harlee's assent would not. No offer and no acceptance mean no contract. The District Court properly dismissed Fletcher-Harlee's breach of contract claim. . . .

Pote's response was a counter offer

posture

While Pote may have exhausted any goodwill it had by bucking industry custom, the language of the disclaimer is so plain that we have no choice but to enforce it. . . . We thus affirm the District Court's dismissal of Fletcher-Harlee's complaint.

■ ■ ■

---

[5] Well, if you did not know this before, you know it now. —EDS.

It is common for a business that supplies goods or services to give a potential customer a price quotation or estimate, indicating the price it will charge for the goods or services and the terms on which it will provide them. Unless the language of the quote or estimate clearly indicates whether or not it is intended as an offer, there can be difficulties in determining its legal effect. The next case indicates that ambiguity in intention can result in a dispute over the nature of a price quotation, even where the parties are commercially and legally sophisticated.

price quote v.
offer

BABCOCK & WILCOX COMPANY v. HITACHI AMERICA, LTD.

406 F. Supp. 2d 819 (2005)
United States District Court, Northern District of Ohio

GWIN, District Judge.

issue
π claim
quotee had warranty lines; purchase order didn't
★ was the quote an offer

[Plaintiff Babcock & Wilcox Company ("B & W") contracted with Defendant Hitachi America, Ltd. ("Hitachi") for the design and supply of an emissions reduction system, known as a Selective Catalytic Reduction System ("SCR system"), that B & W installed at a coal-fired electrical power plant in Kansas City, Missouri. The principal function of the system was to convert nitrogen oxide into nitrogen and water vapor, thus reducing the nitrogen oxide emissions from the power plant. The parties concede that they entered into this contract and Hitachi delivered the SCR system, which B & W installed in the plant. Therefore, the question in the case is not whether a contract was concluded but what its terms were. After the SCR system was installed, B & W experienced trouble with it and claimed that the system did not conform to performance guarantees and warranties. The dispute centers on whether a price quotation given by Hitachi to B & W was an offer, subsequently accepted by a purchase order from B & W. If the price quotation was an offer, terms set out in the quotation relating to performance guarantees, warranty disclaimers, and remedies would have been included in the contract. However, if the quotation was not an offer, the purchase order would be the offer, and the contract would not include terms in the quotation that were not incorporated into the purchase order. This would have an impact on the extent and nature of the performance guarantees and the remedy for any breach.

both wanted summary judgment

B & W sued Hitachi for breach of contract. Hitachi filed a partial motion for summary judgment to resolve the scope of the contract and to identify its precise performance guarantee and warranty provisions. B & W filed a response and cross-motion for partial summary judgment, similarly limiting the issue to the question of what terms became part of the contract.]

... Negotiations as to the precise terms of the contract between the parties began some time in June 1999 and continued well into the following year. During this time, the parties sent several proposals or similar communications to each other, as described below. The parties dispute what interpretation the Court should attach to the communications. Specifically, each party claims that the B & W-Hitachi contract arose at a different point during the negotiations. As a result, the parties disagree on the precise terms of the contract, specifically as relates to the applicable performance guarantee, warranty, and remedy provisions. B & W first contacted Hitachi near June 28, 1999, when it issued a Request for Quotation to Hitachi and another vendor for the design and supply of the catalyst for the SCR system. . . . [In July 1999, Hitachi sent a partially completed proposal to B & W, followed by successive revised proposals. The proposal most relevant to the case was sent by Hitachi to B & W on December 9, 1999. It consisted of a one-page cover letter which was the price quotation, together with attachments that set out warranty, indemnification, and liability limitation terms, a performance guarantee, and technical specifications. (The court sometimes refers to these documents collectively as the "Price Quotation," and sometimes merely as the "proposal.")] Hitachi maintains that this proposal was an offer that B & W later accepted with its June 15, 2000 purchase order. In contrast, B & W claims the proposal was merely one communication in a series of initial negotiations.

The Hitachi Price Quotation lists a price for the catalyst, as well as a proposed delivery date and payment terms. Hitachi expressly limited the validity of the quote until December 10, 1999. After that time, it was subject to Hitachi's confirmation. Paragraph 6 of the quote sets forth a general performance guarantee, and . . . [attached proposed warranty, indemnification, and limitation of liability terms. The parties continued to correspond over the next several months, negotiating various terms that remained open, including the price. These terms were eventually settled in June 2000.]

[O]n June 15, 2000, B & W issued a detailed purchase order ("Purchase Order") for the catalyst. B & W contends that this document was an offer rather than an acceptance. In support, it points to language appearing at the start of the "Terms and Conditions" section that refers to the Purchase Order as an offer and sets forth means of acceptance. Specifically, under the heading, "Acceptance," the Purchase Order states:

> (a) This order is Buyer's offer to Seller and does not constitute an acceptance by Buyer of any offer to sell, quotation or proposal. Any reference to such offer to sell, quotation or proposal is solely for the purpose of incorporating the description and specifications of the goods and services contained therein to the extent that such description and specifications do no [sic] conflict with the description and specifications on the face of this order. This order consists only of the terms contained herein and on the face of this order and any supplements, specifications or other documents expressly incorporated herein by reference.
>
> (b) By acknowledging receipt of this order (or by shipping the goods or performing the services called for by this order) Seller agrees to the terms or conditions of sale contained in this order. Any additional or different terms or conditions contained in any acknowledgment of this order by Seller shall be deemed objected

[handwritten margin note: hitachi thinks the proposal was the offer]

[handwritten margin note: B & W thinks the purchase order is the offer]

to by Buyer without need of further notice of objection and shall be of no effect nor in any circumstance binding upon Buyer unless accepted by Buyer in writing. Acceptance or rejection by Buyer of any such additional terms or conditions shall not constitute an acceptance of any other additional term or condition.

Hitachi maintains that the "Terms and Conditions" referenced above are merely form language, appearing on the seventh and last page of the Purchase Order. Hitachi further claims that the true intent of the parties was that the Purchase Order constitute an acceptance of Hitachi's December 9, 1999 proposal. As a result, Hitachi claims that the terms and conditions relating to warranty and performance guarantee that it proposed in the December 9 letter are controlling. Indeed, the B & W Purchase Order does reference the Hitachi Price Quotation . . . [and incorporates specified provisions of Hitachi's quote and accompanying documents, including its performance guarantees. However, the purchase order sets forth additional and more extensive warranties than those contained in Hitachi's Price Quotation.] After receiving the B & W Purchase Order, Hitachi apparently reviewed the terms of the order. According to B & W, Hitachi neither objected to nor raised any concern about the terms and conditions stated in the Purchase Order. In response, Hitachi points out that it did not sign the acknowledgment form that accompanied the Purchase Order. However, it is apparently the general practice of Hitachi not to sign such forms. Irregardless, Hitachi did ship the goods requested under that Purchase Order sometime during the latter half of 2001.

Subsequently, B & W experienced trouble with the SCR system, allegedly stemming from either a catalyst defect or an insufficient supply of catalyst. When Hitachi refused to provide extra catalyst, B & W had to turn to an outside vendor. B & W now sues Hitachi for its alleged failure to provide catalyst conforming to Hitachi's proffered performance guarantees. The Court does not, however, at this point deal with Hitachi's actual liability, if any. Rather, the Court's present task is to discern the nature and scope of the contract between B & W and Hitachi. . . .

Neither party in the instant matter disputes the existence of a contract between B & W and Hitachi. Instead, their dispute lies in the nature and scope of this contract. . . . [Hitachi claims that its Price Quotation was the offer, which B & W accepted by its Purchase Order, but B & W contends that its Purchase Order represented was the offer, which Hitachi accepted by shipping the catalyst.]

As discussed below, the Court ultimately finds that the December 9, 1999 proposal was not an offer and does not represent the B & W-Hitachi contract. Instead, the B & W Purchase Order, issued six months after the December 9, 1999 proposal, constitutes the offer and memorialization of the contract. . . . Ohio courts define an offer as a "manifestation of willingness to enter into a bargain, so made as to justify another person in understanding that his assent to that bargain is invited and will conclude it." *Leaseway Distribution Centers, Inc. v. Dep't of Admin. Services*, 49 Ohio App. 3d 99, 550 N.E.2d 955, 961 (1988) (quoting Restatement

(Second) of Contracts §24 (1981)). The Sixth Circuit has stated that a price quotation typically "'is considered an invitation for an offer, rather than an offer to form a binding contract.'" *Dyno Construction Co. v. McWane, Inc.*, 198 F.3d 567, 572 (6th Cir. 1999). Along these same lines, it is most often the buyer's purchase order, submitted in response to such a quotation, that constitutes the offer.

There are situations where courts find that a price quotation is sufficiently detailed as to amount to an offer. The inclusion of items such as a "description of the product, price, quantity, and terms of payment may indicate that the price quotation is an offer rather than a mere invitation to negotiate." *Dyno Construction Co.*, 198 F.3d at 572. However, "the determination of the issue depends primarily upon the intention of the person communicating the quotation as demonstrated by all of the surrounding facts and circumstances." *Id.* Thus, for example, in *Dyno Construction Co.*, the Sixth Circuit held that the defendant seller's price quotation for iron pipe and fittings was not an offer and that no contract was formed when the plaintiff buyer told the defendant to order the requested pipe. The court focused on the fact that the price quote contained words such as "estimate" and "please call," stating that these expressions indicated intent to engage in further negotiations. Additionally, the quotation stated nothing about the terms of payment, place of delivery, or time of performance, though it did include a description of the materials, prices, and quantities. . . . Similarly, in *Mecanique C.N.C., Inc.* [*v. Durr Environmental, Inc.*, 304 F. Supp. 2d 971 (S.D. Ohio 2004)] the plaintiff sent a letter to the defendant containing a price quotation for the fabrication and installation of duct work in an SCR system comparable to the system involved in the present case. There, the United States District Court for the Southern District of Ohio held that the letter did not constitute an offer because, among other reasons, it lacked certain details such as terms of payment and time of performance. Additionally, the Court found that the letter's closing statement, "Hoping the above meets your entire satisfaction . . . ," indicated that the plaintiff intended the letter only to encourage further negotiations rather than result in a binding contract.

In contrast to the cases described above, the Sixth Circuit has under certain circumstances held that a price quotation constituted an offer. In *Mead Corp. v. McNally-Pittsburg Mfg.*, 654 F.2d 1197 (6th Cir. 1981), the plaintiff buyer solicited bids from several manufacturers for the construction of a coal washing plant, sending each manufacturer a bid package containing technical bid specifications and general conditions. In response, the defendant seller sent a bid proposal. The proposal contained a description of the offered price and delivery schedule for the project, as well as several noted exceptions to the conditions the buyer listed in its bid package. Specifically, the defendant proposed its own terms regarding limitation of liability. The parties continued negotiations, resolving all issues except for limitation of liability. Subsequently, the plaintiff sent a purchase order to the defendant. The purchase order explicitly incorporated the terms and conditions of the defendant's proposal, but also stated in form language that the purchase order was an offer and was governed only by the terms contained within the order. The court ultimately found that the defendant's bid proposal, rather than the plaintiff's subsequent purchase order, constituted the offer. It cited the fact that the plaintiff determined, upon receiving the defendant's proposal, to deal with the defendant as the desired manufacturer. Moreover, the plaintiff issued the purchase order "upon the heels of the negotiations" regarding the bid proposal, and the word "confirmation" appeared in all capital letters on page two of the purchase order. Additionally, the court noted that because the purchase order incorporated the terms and conditions of the defendant's proposal, the purchase order indicated assent to those terms.

po mirrored language of proposal, indicating assent

In all of the above cases, with the exception of *Mead*, the courts focused on the appearance and contents of the price quotation itself in order to ascertain the parties' intentions. More specifically, these courts looked at factors such as what terms were included, whether there was language on the quotation evincing the intent that it form an offer, or along the same lines whether there was language suggesting the quote was a mere communication in an ongoing negotiation. Notably, in *Mead*, the Court placed less focus on the details of the price quotation and increased focus on the actions of the parties in relation to the documents. Still, just as in the other cases, the court's ultimate focus appears to have been the intention of the parties. Essentially, in each case, the court must look to the totality of the circumstances to ascertain this intent.

ultimate focus is on intentions

In this case, Defendant Hitachi relies heavily on the Sixth Circuit's holding in *Mead*, arguing that the facts of that case are almost identical to the facts currently before the court. Indeed, the cases are similar in skeletal frame. Just as occurred in *Mead*, here B & W sent Hitachi a bid package containing certain product specifications, as well as detailed terms and conditions. After several months of communications, Hitachi sent the December 9, 1999 proposal. Like the letter at issue in *Mead*, Hitachi's letter also contained proposed warranty and limitation of liability terms. B & W responded to this proposal with an expression of intent to purchase the catalyst from Hitachi, and thereafter the parties continued to negotiate the specific contract terms. The Court additionally notes that Hitachi's December 9, 1999 proposal . . . was fairly detailed [and] . . . contained a lengthy description of the catalyst and of certain performance guarantees. Rounding out these specifications, the price quotation includes a quoted price of $2,488,117 for the catalyst, the date of delivery, a description of payment terms, and a statement that the quote would be valid for one day and would thereafter be subject to Hitachi's confirmation. These aspects of the quote tend to weigh in favor of Hitachi's argument that it amounted to an offer.

matching facts

However, the Court finds that despite the detailed nature of the proposal and the similarities between *Mead* and the present case, there are important facts in this case showing that the intentions of the parties were that Hitachi's December 9, 1999 proposal was merely an invitation for further negotiation. First, the language of the December 9 letter indicated that it called for further negotiation. Specifically, the correspondence is labeled a "price quotation" and closes with the statement, "If you have any questions or comments after reviewing this quotation please contact us." Consistent with the tone of this letter, the parties engaged in further negotiations for a period of six months after Hitachi issued the proposal. Moreover, the letter's proposal of additional terms,

including warranty and limitation of liability clauses is phrased in such a manner as to indicate the terms are far from firm, but rather are <u>suggested for
inclusion in a future contract</u>. Hitachi does not simply include these terms as
part of the price quote, but rather references them in a "comments" section,
stating, "[w]e *would also like to* add the attached limitation of liability . . ."
and "[w]e *would like to* substitute the attached warranty clause" (emphasis
added). The clauses thus operate as a starting point for negotiations rather
than as terms of the proposal. . . . [This intention is reinforced by correspondence following the quote, which indicates] that while B & W intended to eventually enter into a contract with Hitachi, B & W still considered the parties to be
in negotiations at that point.[6] . . .

these clauses are starting points

In addition to this evidence, the B & W Purchase Order itself further bolsters
B & W's position that the December 9, 1999 proposal was a price quotation, and
that the Purchase Order constitutes the actual offer. The Purchase Order contains a <u>complete and apparently final statement of all of the terms</u>, providing a
detailed description of the catalyst quantity, price, payment terms, delivery specifications, and various other terms. In addition to the standard boilerplate
terms and conditions appearing on page seven of the Purchase Order, it also
references certain <u>additional warranties and performance guarantees.</u> Moreover,
<u>the Purchase Order explicitly states that it is an offer and that Hitachi's accep-
tance is conditioned on the terms stated therein</u>. While such language is not
controlling, it is some evidence of the parties' intentions. *See Mead*, 654 F.2d at
1203 (stating that while such language is not dispositive of the parties' intentions, the court looks to the totality of the circumstances). Unlike the purchase
order in *Mead*, which contained similar boilerplate language, there is nothing on
the B & W Purchase Order, such as the word "confirmation," that would indicate
the boilerplate language is not applicable.

the language of the po is final *explicitly states it an offer

Finally, the Court notes that while the parties engaged in months of additional negotiations after Hitachi issued the December 9, 1999 letter, the parties
apparently ceased negotiations after B & W issued the Purchase Order. The
mere fact that the parties engaged in such extensive negotiations during that
period, involving not only issues of warranty and liability, but also the more
basic issue of catalyst price, shows the December 9, 1999, letter was nothing
more than one of several communications sent for the purpose of negotiating a
future agreement. Similarly, the fact that negotiations ceased after B & W issued
the Purchase Order shows <u>the parties viewed this document to be the true
memorialization of the parties' contract.</u>

negotiations stopped after purchase order

The Court thus finds the totality of the circumstances indicate that neither
party intended the December 9, 1999 Price Quotation to constitute an offer.
Instead, the intention of the parties appears only to have been to continue

[6] The Court notes that even if it did find Hitachi's December 9, 1999 proposal to be an offer, the time to accept
that offer was expressly limited to December 10, 1999. B & W did not respond until nearly two weeks later. At
that point, the alleged offer would have been inoperable.

negotiations until a mutually acceptable agreement could be forged. Further-more, the Court finds that the B & W Purchase Order constituted the offer and that Hitachi accepted this offer by shipping the goods pursuant to the explicit instructions of the Purchase Order regarding method of acceptance. . . .

■ QUESTIONS

(1) In both *Fletcher-Harlee* and *Babcock & Wilcox* the dispute is whether a bid or price quotation constituted an offer. In *Fletcher-Harlee* this question is crucial to determining whether a contract existed at all. In *Babcock & Wilcox*, the parties are not disputing the existence of a contract, so why does it matter whether the offer came from Hitachi or B & W? *determines final terms*

(2) The court states that price quotations are typically considered to be solicitations rather than offers, but that there are situations in which a price quotation is detailed enough to amount to an offer. It suggests that the degree of specific detail in the quotation, and the lack of qualifying language indicating tentativeness or a desire to keep negotiating, are important indicators that an offer is intended. Clearly, Hitachi's proposal had enough detail to satisfy the requirement of specificity, so what factors persuaded the court to conclude *no finite language, future negotiations* ← that it was merely a solicitation? Did the most important factors arise from qualifying language in the price quotation itself, or from the conduct of the parties subsequent to the price quotation?

(3) It turns out that the performance guarantees, warranties, and disclaimers in the price quotation were more favorable to Hitachi than the equivalent terms in the purchase order. What should Hitachi have done if it wished to ensure that its more favorable terms were part of the contract? *counter offer*

(4) The catalyst sold under this contract is goods. The court recognizes this and does in fact apply UCC Article 2 in dealing with other aspects of the case that are not included in the portion of the opinion set out here. However, the court does not apply or even mention UCC 2-204. Is that a serious omission? Do you think that anything in UCC 2-204 would have changed either the analysis or the result? *maybe!*

■ PROBLEM 4.1

Seller owned a vacant half-acre lot in his neighborhood. He was thinking of selling it and mentioned this to his neighbor, who expressed interest in buying it. About six months later, Seller sent an e-mail to the neighbor stating, "I have decided to sell the lot. I am thinking of putting it on the market for $150,000. Are you still interested in buying it?" On the same day, the neighbor sent a message in reply, stating, "Yes. $150,000 is fine. I have the funds available and can close as soon as you are ready. Let me know who will handle the escrow." Has an offer been made here? If so, by whom?

■ PROBLEM 4.2

Before Seller in Problem 4.1 sent his e-mail message, he showed it to you, his attorney. You asked if he intended the message to be an offer. Redraft the message based on the following alternative responses:

(a) Seller replied that he did not intend an offer—he just wanted to let the neighbor know that he was planning to sell so that the neighbor could make an offer if he wished.

(b) Seller replied that he did intend the message to be an offer. (Do you need any further information to redraft the message? If so, what must you find out from Seller?)

C IS AN ADVERTISEMENT AN OFFER OR A SOLICITATION?

1. What Makes a Proposal an Offer Rather Than a Solicitation?

offer v. solicitation

In *Fletcher-Harlee* and *Babcock & Wilcox*, the communications were addressed to a specific person. *Lefkowitz* and *Harris*, summarized below, and *Leonard*, which follows them, all involve advertisements addressed to the public at large. Where a proposal is disseminated so widely, it is less likely to be seen as an offer, but it might still qualify as one. To decide whether or not it is an offer, the court must ascertain the reasonable meaning of the communication by the same process of interpretation in context.

need to decide the reasonable meaning of communication

In *Lefkowitz v. Great Minneapolis Surplus Store*, 251 Minn. 188, 86 N.W.2d 689 (1957), the defendant store published two advertisements in a Minneapolis newspaper: The first, published on April 6, stated "Saturday 9 A.M. Sharp. 3 Brand New Fur Coats Worth to $100.00. First Come First Served $1 Each." The second, published on April 13, said "Saturday 9 A.M. . . . 1 Black Lapin Stole Beautiful, worth $139.50—$1.00. First Come First Served." On the Saturday following the publication of the first advertisement, Lefkowitz, the plaintiff, arrived at the store before anyone else, tendered his dollar and demanded the coat. The store refused to sell it, stating that it was a "house rule" that the offer was intended for women only and sales would not be made to men. On the Saturday after the second advertisement, Lefkowitz was again first at the

expectation damages

store and sought to buy the stole. The store refused to sell it to him, saying that Lefkowitz knew the house rule.

damages were advertised value

Lefkowitz sued the store for damages, calculated on the basis of the advertised value of the coat and stole, less the $1.00 price. The trial court awarded him damages of $138.50 for the stole. (It disallowed damages for the coat on evidentiary grounds.[7]) On appeal, the store argued that it should not be held liable for damages because no contract was ever made. It contended that the advertisement was not an offer, which would become a contract when a customer signified intent to buy the advertised item. Rather, the advertisement was merely a solicitation in which the store invited customers to make an offer, which the store could itself accept or reject. This meant that the store's refusal to sell the items to Lefkowitz was a rejection of his offer, so no contract came into being.

△ claim →

The court conceded the conventional view that advertisements are commonly construed as invitations to the public to make offers. However, an advertisement could be an offer if, interpreted in context, it would lead a reasonable prospective buyer to understand that an offer was intended. The court affirmed the trial court's judgment, holding that in this case, the advertisements were offers:

ads are typically seen as solicitations for offers

performance was promised in exchange for something requested

The test of whether a binding obligation may originate in advertisements addressed to the general public is "whether the facts show that some performance was promised in positive terms in return for something requested." 1 Williston, *Contracts* (Rev. ed.) §27. . . . [W]here the offer is clear, definite, and explicit, and leaves nothing open for negotiation, it constitutes an offer, acceptance of which will complete the contract. Whether in any individual instance a newspaper advertisement is an offer rather than an invitation to make an offer depends on the legal intention of the parties and the surrounding circumstances. We are of the view on the facts before us that the offer by the defendant of the sale of the Lapin fur was clear, definite, and explicit, and left nothing open for negotiation. The plaintiff having successfully managed to be the first one to appear at the seller's place of business to be served, as requested by the advertisement, and having offered the stated purchase price of the article, he was entitled to performance on the part of the defendant.

clear, definite, explicit & no negotiations left

offer here is clear in the advertisement

In *Harris v. Time, Inc.*, 191 Cal. App. 3d 449 (1987), the court also found an advertisement, in this case in the form of a mass mailing, to be an offer. Time sent out a large number of letters promoting subscriptions to "Fortune"

---

[7] The trial court disallowed damages for the coat on the grounds that Lefkowitz had not proved them adequately. To prove his damages, he had relied on the values stated in the advertisement. Although the ad for the stole stated that it was "worth $139.50," the ad for the coat stated that it was worth "to $100." The trial court found (and the supreme court agreed) that the "to" in the coat ad made the value too imprecise to prove damages. Had the court wanted to award damages, it probably could have done so by finding the words "worth to $100" were sufficient proof, in the absence of contrary evidence, to establish damages with reasonable certainty.

magazine. One of them was received by Joshua Gnaizda, a three-year old. The front of the envelope had two see-through windows that partially revealed the flyer inside the envelope. One of them showed Joshua's name and address, and the other revealed a picture of a calculator watch and the statement: "JOSHUA A. GNAIZDA, I'LL GIVE YOU THIS VERSATILE NEW CALCULATOR WATCH FREE Just for Opening this Envelope Before Feb. 15, 1985." When Joshua's mother opened the envelope, it appeared that the see-through window had not revealed the full text of the flyer. Printed below the picture of the calculator watch, and not viewable through the see-through window, were the additional words: "AND MAILING THIS CERTIFICATE TODAY!" The certificate clearly made Joshua eligible for the watch only if he purchased a subscription to Fortune magazine. It was Time's ill fortune that Joshua's father happened to be a public interest attorney. Instead of just throwing the junk mail away, he demanded a calculator watch from Time, Inc. When the company refused, he initiated a class action[8] against Time on behalf of Joshua and all other recipients of the mailing. The plaintiffs alleged breach of contract and other causes of action. They claimed a declaration that all recipients of the mailer were entitled to receive the promised item, an injunction against future similar mailings, compensatory damages in an amount equal to the value of the item, and $15 million punitive damages to be awarded to a fund devoted to consumer education and protection. Time demurred to the complaint for failure to state a cause of action. Its objection to the contract cause of action was that its letter did not constitute an offer. The trial court sustained the demurrer. The California Court of Appeals found that the letter was an offer. The court said:

Time argues there was no contract because the text of the unopened mailer amounted to a mere advertisement rather than an offer. It is true that advertisements are not typically treated as offers, but merely as invitations to bargain. There is, however, a fundamental exception to this rule: an advertisement can constitute an offer . . . if it calls for performance of a specific act without further communication and leaves nothing for further negotiation. (*Lefkowitz v. Great Minneapolis Surplus Store* (1957), 251 Minn. 188, 86 N.W.2d 689, 691). This is a basic rule of contract law, contained in the Restatement Second of Contracts and normally encountered within the first few weeks of law school. . . . The text of Time's unopened mailer was . . . an offer. . . . Time was not in the same position as a seller merely advertising price; the proper analogy is to a seller promising to give something to a customer in exchange for the customer's act of coming to *the store at a specified time*. (*Lefkowitz v. Great Minneapolis Surplus Store*, supra, 86 N.W.2d 689.) . . .

[8] Class actions are explained in Section C.2.b of Chapter 3. As a reminder, a class action is a form of suit in which a small group of named plaintiffs (in this case Joshua and two others) commence an action not only for their own benefit but also for that of a much larger group of people (all addressees of Time's mailer) who are too numerous to be joined individually as plaintiffs. One of the advantages of a class action in a suit like this, where individual damage awards would be negligible, is that it allows a claim to be made for the total damages suffered by the entire class.

[handwritten margin note: de minimus non curat lex → trivial matters]

*[handwritten margin note: * time won but just because the suit was a waste of time]*

Although the court held the letter to be an offer, Time escaped liability on other grounds. The court affirmed the dismissal of the suit on the basis of the maxim *de minimis non curat lex* (the law disregards trifles). Although it decried the nuisance of junk mail, the court considered the suit an absurd waste of the court's and lawyers' time and taxpayers' money. The court noted that Time's advertisement did no harm beyond momentary annoyance to the recipients and concluded that the appropriate response would be to throw it away rather than take up the scarce resources of an overburdened judicial system. In short, although Time won in the end, the basis of the victory revealed a serious flaw in its advertising technique.

The facts and part of the opinion in *Leonard v. PepsiCo* are set out in Chapter 3. In that portion of the opinion, the court concluded that PepsiCo was not legally bound to deliver a Harrier jet to Leonard because a reasonable person would understand its TV commercial to be a joke. As we note in Chapter 3, there was another issue in the case: Did PepsiCo even make an offer to consumers in either its TV commercial or its Pepsi Stuff catalog? We now reproduce the portion of the opinion that deals with that question. We do not restate the facts of the case to the extent that they are set out in Chapter 3.

[handwritten margin note: makes the offer]

LEONARD v. PEPSICO, INC.

88 F. Supp. 2d 116 (S.D.N.Y. 1999), aff'd, 210 F.3d 88 (2d Cir. 2000)
United States District Court, Southern District of New York

WOOD, District Judge.

[handwritten margin note: pepsi got summary judgement]

Plaintiff brought this action seeking, among other things, specific performance of an alleged offer of a Harrier jet, featured in a television advertisement for defendant's "Pepsi Stuff" promotion. Defendant has moved for summary judgment. For the reasons stated below, defendant's motion is granted. . . . [In addition to the TV commercial, PepsiCo published a Pepsi Stuff catalog.] The Catalog features youths dressed in Pepsi Stuff regalia or enjoying Pepsi Stuff accessories, such as "Blue Shades" ("As if you need another reason to look forward to sunny days"), "Pepsi Tees" ("Live in 'em. Laugh in 'em. Get in 'em"), "Bag of Balls" ("Three balls. One bag. No rules."), and "Pepsi Phone Card" ("Call your mom!"). The Catalog specifies the number of Pepsi Points required to obtain promotional merchandise. The Catalog includes an Order Form which lists, on one side, fifty-three items of Pepsi Stuff merchandise redeemable for Pepsi Points. Conspicuously absent from the Order Form is any entry or description of a Harrier jet. The amount of Pepsi Points required to obtain the listed merchandise ranges from 15 (for a "Jacket Tattoo" ("Sew 'em on your jacket, not your arm.")) to 3300 (for a "Fila Mountain Bike" ("Rugged. All-terrain. Exclusively for Pepsi.")). It should be noted that plaintiff objects to the implication that because an item was not shown in the Catalog, it was unavailable.

The rear foldout pages of the Catalog contain directions for redeeming Pepsi Points for merchandise. These directions note that merchandise may be ordered "only" with the original Order Form. The Catalog notes that in the event that a consumer lacks enough Pepsi Points to obtain a desired item, additional Pepsi Points may be purchased for ten cents each; however, at least fifteen original Pepsi Points must accompany each order. [The plaintiff submitted an order form with 15 original Pepsi Points and a check for $700,008.50 and filled out the order form to show that he was claiming the Harrier jet. When PepsiCo refused to deliver the jet, this litigation ensued, and PepsiCo moved for summary judgment on its request for a declaration that it had no obligation to furnish the jet.]

The question of whether or not a contract was formed is appropriate for resolution on summary judgment. As the Second Circuit has recently noted, "Summary judgment is proper when the 'words and actions that allegedly formed a contract [are] so clear themselves that reasonable people could not differ over their meaning.'" *Krumme v. Westpoint Stevens, Inc.*, 143 F.3d 71, 83 (2d Cir. 1998). . . .

[handwritten: summary judgement is ok when reasonable minds can't disagree]

The general rule is that an advertisement does not constitute an offer. The Restatement (Second) of Contracts §26 comment b explains that:

[handwritten: generally - ads ≠ offers]

Advertisements of goods by display, sign, handbill, newspaper, radio or television are not ordinarily intended or understood as offers to sell. The same is true of catalogues, price lists and circulars, even though the terms of suggested bargains may be stated in some detail. It is of course possible to make an offer by an advertisement directed to the general public (see §29), but there must ordinarily be some language of commitment or some invitation to take action without further communication.

*[handwritten: * invitation to take action]*

Similarly, a leading treatise [1 *Corbin on Contracts* §2.4, at 116-17 (rev. ed. 1993)] notes that:

It is quite possible to make a definite and operative offer to buy or sell goods by advertisement, in a newspaper, by a handbill, a catalog or circular or on a placard in a store window. It is not customary to do this, however; and the presumption is the other way. . . . Such advertisements are understood to be mere requests to consider and examine and negotiate; and no one can reasonably regard them as otherwise unless the circumstances are exceptional and the words used are very plain and clear.

[handwritten: words must be plain & clear to be an offer]

New York courts adhere to this general principle. An advertisement is not transformed into an enforceable offer merely by a potential offeree's expression of willingness to accept the offer through, among other means, completion of an order form. In *Mesaros v. United States*, 845 F.2d 1576 (Fed. Cir. 1988), for example, the plaintiffs sued the United States Mint for failure to deliver a number of Statue of Liberty commemorative coins that they had ordered. When demand for the coins proved unexpectedly robust, a number of individuals who had sent in their orders in a timely fashion were left empty-handed. The court began by noting the "well-established" rule that advertisements and order forms are "mere notices and solicitations for offers which create no power of acceptance in the recipient." The spurned coin collectors could not maintain a breach of contract action because no contract would be formed until the advertiser accepted the order form and processed payment. Under these principles, plaintiff's letter of March 27, 1996, with the Order Form and the appropriate number of Pepsi Points, constituted the offer. There would be no enforceable contract until defendant accepted the Order Form and cashed the check.

no contract until advertiser accepts the order form

The exception to the rule that advertisements do not create any power of acceptance in potential offerees is where the advertisement is "clear, definite, and explicit, and leaves nothing open for negotiation." In that circumstance, "it constitutes an offer, acceptance of which will complete the contract." *Lefkowitz v. Great Minneapolis Surplus Store*, 251 Minn. 188, 86 N.W.2d 689, 691 (1957). . . .

The present case is distinguishable from *Lefkowitz*. First, the commercial cannot be regarded in itself as sufficiently definite, because it specifically reserved the details of the offer to a separate writing, the Catalog. The commercial itself made no mention of the steps a potential offeree would be required to take to accept the alleged offer of a Harrier jet. The advertisement in *Lefkowitz*, in contrast, identified the person who could accept. Second, even if the Catalog had included a Harrier jet among the items that could be obtained by redemption of Pepsi Points, the advertisement of a Harrier jet by both television commercial and catalog would still not constitute an offer. As the *Mesaros* court explained, the absence of any words of limitation such as "first come, first served," renders the alleged offer sufficiently indefinite that no contract could be formed. "A customer would not usually have reason to believe that the shopkeeper intended exposure to the risk of a multitude of acceptances resulting in a number of contracts exceeding the shopkeeper's inventory." Farnsworth, [*Contracts*] at 242. There was no such danger in *Lefkowitz*, owing to the limitation "first come, first served." The Court finds, in sum, that the Harrier jet commercial was merely an advertisement. . . . [The court grants summary judgment to PepsiCo.]

Commercial had no details on how to accept
— lefkowitz just needed to open the mail

■   ■   ■

Lefkowitz, Harris, and *Leonard* all recite the conventional rule, also expressed in the Restatement, Second, and many contracts treatises, that advertisements are normally not to be treated as offers and that they only become such if they are written in a way that takes them out of the general rule. That is, the conventional rule is that advertisements are usually assumed not to be offers. However, some advertisements are exceptions to this rule because they are clear, definite, explicit, and leave nothing open for negotiation. A reasonable person would understand them to commit the advertiser to a contract immediately once a member of the targeted audience performs an act of acceptance by

ads are not offers unless they are written as a may making them an offer

ad needs word of limitation

conduct or communication. One of the factors that the court relied on in *PepsiCo* to distinguish *Lefkowitz* was that the advertisement in *Lefkowitz* contained words of limitation ("first come, first served"). The court, quoting Farnsworth, *Contracts*, indicates that this is significant. It reasoned that the absence of words of limitation would suggest that the advertisement is not an offer, because an advertiser cannot be assumed to risk receiving acceptances beyond its capacity to supply the advertised goods or services. The next case calls into question whether the conventional rule makes sense, and also explains why words of limitation in a communication might be relevant to the question of whether it is an offer.

SATERIALE v. R.J. REYNOLDS TOBACCO COMPANY

697 F.3d 777 (2012)
United States Court of Appeals, Ninth Circuit

FISHER, Circuit Judge.

rewards program with Camel Cash

R.J. Reynolds Tobacco Company (RJR) operated a customer rewards program, called Camel Cash, from 1991 to 2007. Under the terms of the program, RJR urged consumers to purchase Camel cigarettes, to save Camel Cash certificates included in packages of Camel cigarettes, to enroll in the program and, ultimately, to redeem their certificates for merchandise featured in catalogs distributed by RJR. . . . RJR initiated the Camel Cash customer loyalty program in 1991. RJR represented on Camel Cash certificates, packages of Camel cigarettes and in the media that customers who saved the certificates—called C-Notes—could exchange them for merchandise according to terms provided in a catalog. The C-Notes stated:

> USE THIS NEW C-NOTE AND THE C-NOTES YOU'VE BEEN SAVING TO GET THE BEST GOODS CAMEL HAS TO OFFER. CALL 1-800-CAMEL CASH (1800-266-3522) for a free catalog. Offer restricted to smokers 21 years of age or older. Value 1/1000 of 1¢. Offer good only in the USA, and void where restricted or prohibited by law. Check catalog for expiration date. Limit 5 requests for a catalog per household.

. . . The plaintiffs are 10 individuals who joined the Camel Cash program by purchasing RJR's products and filling out and submitting signed registration forms to RJR. RJR sent each plaintiff a unique enrollment number that was used in communications between the parties. These communications included catalogs RJR distributed to the plaintiffs containing merchandise that could be obtained by redeeming Camel Cash certificates. From time to time, RJR issued a new catalog with merchandise offered in exchange for Camel Cash, either upon request, or by mailing catalogs to consumers enrolled in the program. The number of Camel Cash certificates needed to obtain merchandise varied from as little as 100 to many thousands. This encouraged consumers to buy more packages of cigarettes together with Camel Cash and also to save or obtain Camel Cash certificates to redeem them for more valuable items. RJR honored the program from 1991 to 2006, and during that time Camel's share of the cigarette market nearly doubled, from approximately 4 percent to more than 7 percent. In October 2006, however, RJR mailed a notice to program members announcing that the program would terminate as of March 31, 2007. . . . [The termination notice stated that although the program was ending, customers would still be able to redeem existing C-Notes through March 2007. However, RJR did not honor this undertaking, and stopped redeeming certificates in October 2006. The plaintiffs were therefore unable to redeem the certificates that they had saved, and they commenced a class action against RJR, alleging various causes of action, including breach of contract. The trial court dismissed the suit. The Court of Appeals reversed the dismissal of the contract claim on the basis that the plaintiffs' complaint did make out a cause of action in contract. One of the contract issues was whether the C-Notes constituted offers, which the plaintiffs had accepted by buying the packs of camel cigarettes. We include that portion of the opinion.]

An offer is the manifestation of willingness to enter into a bargain, so made as to justify another person in understanding that his assent to that bargain is invited and will conclude it. The determination of whether a particular communication constitutes an operative offer, rather than an inoperative step in the preliminary negotiation of a contract, depends upon all the surrounding circumstances. The pertinent inquiry is whether the individual to whom the communication was made had reason to believe that it was intended as an offer. The issue here is whether the C-Notes, read in isolation or in combination with the catalogs, may have constituted an offer. . . . RJR argues that its C-Notes, whether read in isolation or in combination with the catalogs, were not offers, but invitations to make an offer. RJR relies on the common law's general rule that "[a]dvertisements of goods by display, sign, handbill, newspaper, radio or television are not ordinarily intended or understood as offers to sell." *Restatement, Second §26 cmt. b.* RJR emphasizes that two judicial decisions have applied this general rule to customer rewards programs similar to the Camel Cash program, *see Leonard v. PepsiCo, Inc.,* 88 F. Supp. 2d 116, 122–27 (S.D.N.Y.1999); *Alligood v. Procter & Gamble Co.,* 72 Ohio App. 3d 309, 594 N.E.2d 668, 668–70 (1991) (per curiam), and urges us to apply the rule here as well. We decline to do so.

First, it is not clear that the common law rule upon which RJR relies applies under California law. *See Donovan v. RRL Corpn.,* 109 Cal. Rptr. 2d 807, 27 P.3d at 710 (Cal. 2001) (stating that "[t]his court has not previously applied the common law rules upon which defendant relies, including the rule that advertisements generally constitute invitations to negotiate rather than offers," observing that "such rules . . . have been criticized on the ground that they are inconsistent with the reasonable expectations of consumers and lead to haphazard results," citing Melvin Aron Eisenberg, *Expression Rules in Contract Law and Problems of Offer and Acceptance,* 82 Cal. L. Rev. 1127, 1166–72 (1994), and concluding that "[i]n the present case . . . we need not consider the viability of the black-letter rule regarding the interpretation of advertisements").

Second, even assuming California law incorporates the common law rule, that rule includes an exception for offers of a reward, including offers of a reward for the redemption of coupons. As a leading contract law treatise explains,

> It is very common, where one desires to induce many people to action, to offer a reward for such action by general publication in some form. A statement that plausibly makes an offer of this kind must be reasonably interpreted according to its terms and the surrounding circumstances. If the statement, properly interpreted, calls for the performance or commencement of performance of specific acts, action in accordance with such an interpretation will close a contract or make the offer irrevocable. There are many cases of an offer of a reward for the capture of a person charged with crime, for desired information, for the return of a lost article, for the winning of a contest, or *for the redemption of coupons*. In addition, advertisements placed by buyers inviting sellers to ship goods without prior communication are clear cases of offers. The contracts so made are almost always unilateral.

Corbin on Contracts (hereinafter Corbin) §2.4 (2012) (emphasis added) (footnotes omitted). RJR does not discuss this exception, relying instead on *Leonard* and *Alligood*. Several courts, however, have applied the exception to customer rewards programs . . . [in cases involving coupons on soap wrappers, reward points obtained by purchasing Marlboro cigarettes, and reward miles awarded for flying on American Airlines.] Like these courts, we see no justification for applying the general common law rule, rather than the common law exception, to circumstances such as those presented here. The common law rule that advertisements ordinarily do not constitute offers arose to address a specific problem—the potential for over-acceptance—not applicable here. Professor Farnsworth explains that an offer ordinarily does not exist

> when a proposal for a limited quantity has been sent to more persons than its maker could accommodate. . . . Otherwise, supposing a shopkeeper were sold out of a particular class of goods, thousands of members of the public might crowd into the shop and demand to be served, and each one would have a right of action against the proprietor for not performing his contract. A customer would not usually have reason to believe that the shopkeeper intended exposure to the risk of a multitude of acceptances resulting in a number of contracts exceeding the shopkeeper's inventory.

E. Allan Farnsworth, *Contracts* (hereinafter Farnsworth) §3.10, at 134 (4th ed. 2004). This problem arises in the case of ordinary advertisements for the sale of goods or services, but not here. First, RJR's ostensible purpose in promoting the Camel Cash program was not to sell a limited inventory, but to induce as many consumers as possible to purchase Camel cigarettes. Second, RJR could not have been trapped into a situation in which acceptances exceeded inventory. RJR

[margin note: they control the inventory]

alone decided how many C-Notes to distribute, so it exercised absolute control over the number of acceptances. As Farnsworth explains, "if the very nature of a proposal restricts its maker's potential liability to a reasonable number of people, there is no reason why it cannot be an offer." *Id.* at 135.

[margin note: they can't be excused as an offer, just because everyone was exposed to the ad]

For these reasons, we find no reason to presume that RJR's communications did not constitute an offer merely because they were addressed to the general public in the form of advertisements. The operative question under California law, therefore, is simply "whether the advertiser, in clear and positive terms, promised to render performance in exchange for something requested by the advertiser, and whether the recipient of the advertisement reasonably might have concluded that by acting in accordance with the request a contract would be formed." *Donovan,* 109 Cal. Rptr. 2d 807, 27 P.3d at 710. Construing the complaint in the light most favorable to the plaintiffs, and drawing all reasonable inferences from the complaint in the plaintiffs' favor, we conclude that

[margin note: holding]

the plaintiffs have adequately alleged the existence of an offer to enter into a unilateral contract, whereby RJR promised to provide rewards to customers who purchased Camel cigarettes, saved Camel Cash certificates and redeemed their certificates in accordance with the catalogs' terms.

[margin note: repeatedly used the word]

We reach this conclusion in light of the totality of the circumstances surrounding RJR's communications to consumers: the repeated use of the word "offer" in the C-Notes; the absence of any language disclaiming the intent to be bound; the inclusion of specific restrictions in the C-Notes ("Offer restricted to smokers 21 years of age or older"; "Offer good only in the USA, and void where restricted or prohibited by law"; "Check catalog for expiration date"; "Limit 5 requests for a catalog per household"); the formal enrollment process, through which consumers submitted registration forms and RJR issued enrollment numbers; and the substantial reliance expected from consumers.[9] *Donovan* explains that under the common law "advertisements have been held to constitute offers where they invite the performance of a specific act without further communication and leave nothing for negotiation." 109 Cal. Rptr. 2d 807, 27 P.3d at 710. These requirements are satisfied here. RJR's alleged offer invited the performance of specific acts (saving C-Notes and redeeming them for rewards in accordance with the catalog) without further communication, and leaving

---

[9] The plaintiffs' substantial reliance distinguishes this case from cases involving garden-variety advertisements. To take advantage of the Camel Cash program, consumers were expected to purchase Camel cigarettes and accumulate Camel Cash certificates for a period of weeks, months or even years. [The complaint alleges] that "[t]he number of Camel Cash certificates needed to obtain merchandise . . . varied from as little as one hundred to many thousands," and noted that RJR "further encouraged plaintiffs and other Class members to collect their Camel Cash (as opposed to redeeming them as soon as possible) because merchandise listed in defendant's catalogs for redemption by a greater number of coupons was disproportionately more valuable than the merchandise which could be redeemed by fewer coupons". Citing an offer for a reward as an example, Corbin explains that "a proposal is likely to be deemed to be an offer if it is foreseeable that the addressee of the proposal will rely upon it." Corbin §2.2. This is so because a member of the public is unlikely to undertake substantial reliance in the absence of a binding commitment from the offeror—i.e., on the mere chance that the offeror will perform.

nothing for negotiation. . . . We reverse dismissal of the plaintiffs' breach of contract [claim]. . . .

Disposition

■ ■ ■

People usually assume that a merchant is committing itself to sell the advertised item at the stated price, and most retailers would consider it important—for reasons of good customer relations, even if not because of a legal obligation—to have the advertised products available at the advertised price. It is possible that customs of the marketplace could give rise to the reasonable expectation that an advertisement does create a binding obligation on the advertiser.[10]

This reasonable expectation could be bolstered by legislation that imposes the obligation on an advertiser to advertise truthfully and to have the advertised goods available at the stated price. Indeed, in many cases claiming that an advertiser was contractually bound by the advertisement, the plaintiff has an alternative cause of action based on an alleged violation of a statute prohibiting deceptive advertising. To curb deceptive advertising (such as "bait and switch"[11] advertising or untruthful claims) and other dishonest business practices, Congress and state legislatures have enacted statutes that impose obligations on advertisers to advertise truthfully and to have advertised goods and services available. This legislation has a direct impact on the obligations of an advertiser in that it imposes liability on the advertiser for false advertising and creates an alternative statutory cause of action in favor of members of the public who are aggrieved by the false advertisement.

However, the legislation may also have an indirect impact on the question of whether an advertisement can reasonably be understood to be an offer. The very existence of this statutory regulation could create the reasonable expectation in the marketplace that the advertisement is an offer. For example, in *Donovan v. RRL Corp.*, 26 Cal. 4th 261, 27 P.3d 702 (2001), one of the cases cited in *Sateriale*, a car dealer erroneously advertised a car for about $10,000 less than what the dealer had paid for it. The customer insisted on buying the car for the advertised price, and sued when the dealer refused to sell it at that price. The California Vehicle Code, which regulates advertisements for

---

[10] The court cites Professor Melvin Eisenberg's article, *Expression Rules in Contract Law and Problems of Offer and Acceptance*, 82 Cal. L. Rev. 1127, 1166-1173 (1994). In that article, Professor Eisenberg argues that a person who reads an advertisement normally has the reasonable expectation that the advertiser is committed to sell the advertised item at the price stated in the advertisement. For this reason, although courts often cite the conventional rules that an advertisement is not an offer, they commonly find that the advertisement at issue is an exception to the rule. Professor Jay Feinman and Mr. Stephen Brill, *Is an Advertisement an Offer? Why It Is, and Why It Matters*, 58 Hastings L.J. 61 (2006) make a similar argument and conclude that the conventional rule should be the opposite—that advertisements should be assumed to be offers unless it is clear that they are not so intended.

[11] "Bait and switch" is a practice in which a seller entices customers to visit its store by advertising an item at a bargain price. The seller does not intend to sell that item but hopes that once the customer is in the store, he can be persuaded to buy another more expensive or less desirable item.

motor vehicles, makes it a violation for a dealer to fail to sell a vehicle at the advertised price while the vehicle remains unsold. The court agreed with the dealer that the Code made the refusal to sell merely a violation subjecting the dealer to disciplinary action; it was not intended to supplant the common law of contracts. Nevertheless, the court held that the existence of the statute affected consumer expectations, so that a reasonable purchaser, knowing that a dealer would offend the statute by not selling the car as advertised, would consider the advertisement to be an offer.[12]

■ QUESTIONS

(1)   What had been your perception of the binding force of advertisements before you read this section of the book? How does your experience square with the conventional rule that advertisements are generally not offers, unless special circumstances indicate otherwise?

(2)   It was a significant fact in *Leonard* that the jet was not included in the catalog. Say that the plaintiff had ordered an item that was in the catalog (for example, the dirt bike), but PepsiCo declined to redeem the order because it was out of stock. Would the court in *Leonard* still have found that PepsiCo had made no offer? Do you think that the court in *Sateriale* would have agreed?

■ PROBLEM 4.3

PepsiCo persuaded the court that its advertisement was not an offer, but Great Minneapolis Surplus Store, Time, Inc., and RJR did not. Your client, a ski lodge, plans to place advertisements in newspapers and magazines in which it promotes a "February Special" room rate at a 30 percent discount. What language should your client include in the advertisements to ensure that they do not constitute offers?

[handwritten margin note: while supplies last, no limitations]

2. The Remedial Issues in *Lefkowitz, Harris,* and *Leonard*

The opinion in *Sateriale* does not indicate what remedy the plaintiffs were seeking. The other three cases in this section are more informative on the question

---

[12] Although the court found that the dealer had made an offer which had been accepted by the plaintiff, it allowed the dealer out of the contract on the grounds that it would be unfair to hold the dealer to the mistaken price.

of remedy. The relief sought in *Lefkowitz* is a typical expectation damages claim for the difference between the market price of the promised goods and the contract price of $1.00. The remedies sought in *Harris* are more complicated. In addition to claiming compensatory damages, the suit also seeks other relief, including a declaratory judgment, an injunction, and punitive damages. As noted in Chapter 3, in *Leonard*, PepsiCo initiated the litigation, seeking a declaratory judgment, and Leonard responded by suing PepsiCo for specific performance. Gnaidza and Leonard did not obtain any of the remedies they sought, of course, and we cannot say that the court would have granted them had the plaintiffs' causes of action not been dismissed. However, this is a good opportunity to explain each of the remedies briefly.

A declaratory judgment is explained in Chapter 3. In essence, the plaintiff does not claim monetary relief or for an order compelling or prohibiting action but merely asks the court to give a judgment declaring the rights and obligations of the parties. Most plaintiffs in contracts cases do wish for either damages or specific performance, so a declaratory judgment is usually not enough to provide relief. However, the remedy is useful where the plaintiff can accomplish its ends simply by the court's resolution of the parties' rights and obligations. (Of course, in *Harris* the plaintiff sought both a declaratory judgment and a money judgment.) *Leonard* illustrates another possible use of the declaratory judgment. PepsiCo, the potential defendant, anticipated the action threatened by Leonard. Instead of waiting for Leonard to sue, PepsiCo took the initiative and itself commenced suit, asking the court to declare that it was not liable to Leonard. The declaratory judgment procedure was useful to PepsiCo because the company had no claim against Leonard for compensatory relief but wanted to resolve the issue of its legal liability to him. (By suing first, it also got the advantage of selecting the venue of the suit, but there are limits on a potential defendant's ability to use the declaratory judgment procedure for this strategic end.)

An injunction is a court order either compelling the defendant to take specified action or forbidding it from taking specified action. An injunction requiring the defendant to take action is called a "mandatory" injunction, and one forbidding action is called "prohibitory." An injunction is an equitable remedy, like specific performance—in fact, an order for specific performance is essentially a form of mandatory injunction compelling the act of performing the contract. By contrast, the injunction sought in *Harris* was prohibitory. As an equitable remedy, it is available only where the plaintiff can show that there is no remedy at law that will provide adequate relief. If an injunction is granted, disobedience is contempt of court. In *Harris*, the plaintiffs combine a claim for damages for harm that has already occurred (Time's alleged breach of contract) with a claim for an order restraining future conduct.

Punitive damages may be awarded in addition to compensatory damages for the purpose of punishing the defendant and making an example of its conduct to discourage others from behaving in the same way. Punitive damages are therefore only appropriate where the defendant has engaged in conduct that merits punishment—the defendant has injured the plaintiff by acting deliberately and maliciously, or at least with wanton recklessness. Although the claim in *Harris* called for the damages to be paid into a consumer protection fund, this is unusual. Punitive damages are normally recovered by the plaintiff, adding to her gain from the litigation. Punitive damages are most commonly awarded in cases involving intentional or reckless torts or violations of duty under a statute that provides for such an award. In contrast, contract remedies are strongly focused on compensation and, as a matter of policy, courts do not consider it appropriate to punish a party for breach of contract, even if that breach was intentional. Therefore, punitive damages are very rarely allowed in contracts cases. In the few cases in which they are granted, the breach of contract usually constitutes the kind of action that also qualifies as a tort. Notice that in *Harris*, the plaintiff sued not only in contract, but also for unfair advertising and fraud. In some circumstances, these causes of action may permit recovery of punitive damages. In Chapter 21 we address more fully the limited availability of punitive damages in contract cases.

■ QUESTION

In *Leonard v. PepsiCo*, Leonard's claim was for specific performance. Based on what you have read about this remedy up to now, do you think that he would have been granted an order of specific performance if he had won on the merits?

D   OFFER AND ACCEPTANCE THROUGH ELECTRONIC MEDIA, ESPECIALLY BY AUTOMATED MEANS (ELECTRONIC AGENTS)

Of course, contracting by electronic communication was unknown when the common law rules of offer and acceptance were formulated. Even Article 2, although drafted in the twentieth century, predated the widespread use of computers in business transactions. In many respects, the original rules do not need to be specifically changed to take account of electronic communication because they can be applied as a matter of course to them. For example, questions of whether an offer was made can be resolved in the same way, whether the offeror's communication is oral, written on paper, sent by e-mail, printed in a newspaper, or posted on a website. Similarly, most of the rules governing acceptance can be applied without difficulty where the response to the offer is electronic.

However, there are some situations in which contemporary forms of electronic transactions do not fit comfortably into the traditional mold, and legislative guidance is helpful. One of these areas is the employment by one or both parties of technology that has been programmed to execute transactions automatically. For example, a seller sets up a website to sell its goods. It is programmed to conduct the transaction without a human operator so that it accepts orders from visitors to the website, provided that the electronic order form is completed in the correct way. It is possible that a buyer may employ similar automated means of transacting, say, by having a computerized inventory system that orders more stock from designated suppliers when inventory drops to a prescribed level. Such transactions raise the issue of whether an objective manifestation of actual human assent, at the point of contract formation, is necessary to form a contract.

To deal with this issue and other matters relating to electronic commerce (such as the recognition of electronic signatures, discussed in Chapter 8), The National Conference of Commissioners on Uniform State Laws (NCCUSL, which also uses the name Uniform Law Commission, or ULC) approved the Uniform Electronic Transactions Act (UETA) in 1999. Like the UCC, this is a uniform model law that must be enacted by states to become effective. UETA has been widely enacted by states and other U.S. Jurisdictions—49 at the time of this writing. In addition to this state law, Congress enacted the Electronic Signatures in Global and National Commerce Act (E-SIGN) in 2000. These statutes cover similar ground, and many of their provisions are similarly worded. E-SIGN §7002 defers to state law, provided that the state has enacted UETA or a closely equivalent statute. UETA and E-SIGN are applicable to all contracts, including sales of goods.[13]

Where a party uses automated means of entering into transactions, UETA §14 recognizes the machine as an "electronic agent" of the party, which is defined by UETA §2(6) as "a computer program or an electronic or other automated means used independently to initiate an action or respond to electronic records or performances in whole or in part, without review or action by an individual." (E-SIGN §7006(3) is to the same effect.) UETA §14 expresses general principles of formation where one party or both parties use an electronic agent. It states, in essence, that parties can form a contract by the interaction of electronic agents, even if no individual operated or reviewed the electronic agent's actions or the resulting agreement. It also recognizes that a contract may be formed where one of the parties uses an electronic agent and the other does not. The human party must have the means to agree to or refuse the transaction and must reasonably understand that his actions will lead to a contract. Official Comment 1 to §14 indicates that the section is intended to recognize that a contract can be formed by machines functioning as electronic agents and to negate a claim that the absence of human intent at the time of contract formation precludes creation of a contract. The relevant time for determining the manifested intent of a party who uses an electronic agent is when the machine is programmed and placed in use. (E-SIGN §7001(h) likewise recognizes contracting through an electronic agent.)

---

[13] When they proposed revisions to UCC Article 2 in 2003, NCCUSL and ALI added a number of provisions to Article 2 that would have duplicated the UETA provisions on electronic agents. Because of the failure of the proposed revision, there have not been any provisions relating to electronic agents added to UCC Article 2. However, since UETA and E-SIGN apply to sales of goods, UCC Article 2 did not need to be amended for the purpose of recognizing electronic agents.

E OFFERS UNDER THE UNIDROIT PRINCIPLES AND CISG

General principles of international contracting practices are set out in the UNI-DROIT Principles, introduced in Chapter 1. Recall that they do not have the force of law. The parties to an international transaction might adopt them in their contract, or they may be of persuasive force, akin to the Restatement, Second, to a court or arbitrator adjudicating an international contract dispute. They seek to express general, widely recognized principles applicable to international contracts. Article 2.1.1 provides that "[a] contract may be concluded either by the acceptance of an offer or by conduct of the parties that is sufficient to show agreement." Article 2.1.2 defines an offer as a proposal to conclude a contract that is "sufficiently definite and indicates the intention of the offeror to be bound in case of acceptance."

By contrast, as explained in Section E of Chapter 2, the CISG is a treaty and it has the force of law in U.S. jurisdictions with regard to international sales of goods that fall within its scope. Article 14(1) treats a proposal as an offer if it is "sufficiently definite and indicates the intention of the offeror to be bound in case of acceptance." To be sufficiently definite, the proposal must indicate the goods and must expressly or impliedly fix or provide for the determination of the price and quantity. Article 14(2) follows the same assumption as the common law with regard to offers, such as advertisements, that are not addressed to a specific offeree. The proposal is to be treated merely as an invitation to make offers unless the proposal clearly indicates a contrary intent.

CHAPTER 5

Acceptance

A GENERAL PRINCIPLES OF ACCEPTANCE

Some offers, such as the advertisements in *Lefkowitz* and *Sateriale* (described in Chapter 4, Section C), may be addressed to the public at large. However, most offers are addressed to a specific person or group of people. It is the offeror's right to direct the offer to whomever he chooses, and it may be accepted only by the person or persons designated in the offer. If, upon receiving an offer, the offeree wishes to enter the contract proposed by the offeror, she must signify her assent to it. The offeree's manifestation of assent to the offer is called the "acceptance." Because contracts are based on mutual assent, the acceptance must be a knowing, voluntary, and deliberate act. However, assent is measured by an objective standard, so the question of whether the offeree accepted the offer is determined with regard to the reasonable meaning of her response, rather than by what she may have thought or meant. (As always, this objective standard is not absolute because there are doctrines to protect a party from inadvertent conduct or from oppression or trickery.) The reasonable meaning of the offeree's manifestations is determined by the same process of interpretation as is applied to the offer.

The general approach to acceptance is set out in Restatement, Second §30 and in UCC 2-206(1)(a):

RESTATEMENT, SECOND §30. FORM OF ACCEPTANCE INVITED

(1) An offer may invite or require acceptance to be made by an affirmative answer in words, or by performing or refraining from performing a

specified act, or may empower the offeree to make a selection of terms in his acceptance.

(2) Unless otherwise indicated by the language or the circumstances, an offer invites acceptance in any manner and by any medium reasonable in the circumstances.

UCC 2-206(1)(a). OFFER AND ACCEPTANCE IN FORMATION OF CONTRACT

(1) Unless otherwise unambiguously indicated by the language or circumstances

(a) an offer to make a contract shall be construed as <u>inviting acceptance in any manner</u> and <u>by any medium reasonable in the circumstances</u> . . .

The general principles indicated by these provisions, both at common law and under Article 2, are that the offeror has considerable control over the manner in which an offer may be effectively accepted. If the offeror asserts this control by specifying how acceptance must occur, an offeree can accept effectively only by complying with the prescribed method. If the offeror has not been so exacting in specifying the manner of acceptance, a standard of reasonableness governs the question of whether the method of acceptance was appropriate and effective.

As is true with offers, Article 2 does not cover the rules of acceptance in any detail. Instead, it largely confines itself to expressing broad principles, leaving the detailed rules to common law. Recall that the common law applies to sales of goods by virtue of UCC 1-103(b), which provides that principles of law and equity supplement the UCC provisions unless displaced by particular provisions of the UCC. Because Article 2 says so little about acceptance, common law is widely applicable to the acceptance of an offer to sell goods. Therefore, the issues in this chapter are usually resolved in the same way in a sale of goods as they would be in a contract under common law.[1]

We begin this discussion of acceptance by summarizing the basic general principles that are commonly applied by courts in deciding whether an offer has been accepted. This text note is followed by some problems that allow you to work with these general principles and (in Section B) by some cases that apply them.

---

[1] UCC 2-207, which deals with additional terms in an acceptance or confirmation, is an exception to this general statement. We deal with UCC 2-207 in Chapter 6.

1. The Acceptance Must Be Communicated to the Offeror

Because the objective test requires the manifestation of intent to accept, the offeree's decision to accept is not usually effective until it has been communicated to the offeror. "Communication" is a term of art in this context. As explained below, under some circumstances the offeree's manifestation of acceptance may become effective as soon as it is dispatched, even if it is not actually received by the offeror in time or at all.

[handwritten margin note: ① must be communicated ② must be in compliance with the terms laid out]

2. The Acceptance Must Be in Compliance with Any Instructions in the Offer Relating to the Manner and Method of Acceptance → if there are any

Consider the following simple offer: "I offer to sell you my house for $400,000. To accept this offer, you must deliver your written, signed acceptance to me by 6 P.M. on Friday, June 3." It is useful to think of an offer as having two components. One may be described as substantive. The substantive portion of the offer consists of the actual terms of the contract proposed in the offer. In this offer, it is the language "I offer to sell you my house for $400,000." The other component may be described as procedural. This is the part of the offer that sets out any instructions that the offeror may wish to give the offeree on how to go about accepting the offer. In this offer it is the second sentence that requires delivery of a written, signed acceptance by 6 P.M. on Friday, June 3. As we discuss in Chapter 4, an offer must have the substantive component. A communication cannot qualify as an offer without it. However, the procedural component is not essential to the validity of the offer. An offeror may not care about how the offer is to be accepted and may provide no instructions on that at all. To the extent that the offer does not set out the time and manner of acceptance, the offeree may accept it within a reasonable time, and the communication of acceptance may be by any mode and in any manner that is reasonable. However, if the offer does specify any procedural requirements for acceptance, they must be complied with for the acceptance to be effective.

[handwritten margin note: — substantive offer → actual terms proposed; procedural → how to accept the offer; not essential to an offer]

Even where an offer does set out instructions for acceptance, the requirements may be more or less detailed and more or less mandatory. The extent to which an offer contains exact instructions for acceptance depends on the degree of control that the offeror wishes to retain over the acceptance process. An offeror who gives no instructions regarding the time or method of acceptance probably does not care how the offer is accepted as long as he gets the contract that he proposes. He is willing to leave it to the offeree to select a convenient and reasonable means of communicating acceptance. However, an offeror who wishes to maintain some control over the way the offer can be effectively accepted may give quite precise instructions, which may serve one or more of several different purposes. For example, the instructions may be designed to clearly limit the life of the offer, or to ensure that the offeror knows immediately if the offer has been accepted, or to prescribe a means of communication that the offeror considers reliable, or to provide written proof of acceptance.

The offeror has the right to specify the time and procedure for acceptance. Even if the offeree's response does not seek to change the substantive terms of the proposed contract, the response may fail as an acceptance if the offeree fails to follow the prescribed acceptance procedure or accepts after the offer's expiration. It is sometimes easy to tell that an attempt at acceptance is procedurally ineffective. For example, in the above example, the offer stated that acceptance must occur in a signed writing delivered to the offeror by 6 P.M. on June 3. A response, even on affirmative terms, would not qualify as an acceptance if the offeree attempted to accept on June 4 or called the offeror before 6 P.M. on June 3 and accepted orally. However, sometimes it is more difficult to decide if proper procedures have been followed. Often, the answer depends on a reasonable interpretation of the language of the offer in context. Courts are influenced by the degree of specificity and firmness in the offer's instructions and by the general assumption that, unless the language of the offer indicates otherwise, the offeror cares more about making the contract than about the exact method of forming it. As a result, unless the offer makes it clear that a particular form and method of acceptance is absolutely required (an exclusive method of acceptance), a response that does not precisely conform to instructions could be effective provided that it is reasonable, is consistent with the manner prescribed in the offer, and is no less protective of the offeror's rights. As mentioned previously, flexibility in evaluating the effect of the response is greatest where the offer is silent on the procedure for acceptance, so that the offeree may accept within a reasonable time in any way that is reasonable in the circumstances.

3. The Acceptance Must Not Vary the Terms of the Contract Proposed in the Offer

As stated above, to be an effective acceptance, the offeree's response must accept the substantive terms of the offer. If it indicates disagreement with any of the offer's terms or proposes different terms, it is not an acceptance; it is a rejection. Depending on its language, it could also be a counteroffer—that is, a refusal to enter a contract on the offeror's terms combined with a proposal by the former offeree (who now becomes the offeror) to contract on different terms.

In some cases it is obvious that a response is not an acceptance; rather, it is a counteroffer. For example, it would clearly be a counteroffer if, in response to the offer to sell the house for $400,000, the buyer delivered a signed letter to the seller on June 2 that read, "I do wish to buy your house but not for $400,000. I will give you $375,000 for it." In other cases, the import of the response is not as clear. Say, for example, the buyer responded, "I accept your offer, the transaction to close on or before August 1." This could be a counteroffer in that it appears to introduce a term relating to the date of closing that was absent from the offer. However, this may not be a new term—it could have been implicit in the offer or in accordance with usage that governs the transaction. If this is the case, the response could qualify as an acceptance.

if it's not a new term than it's not a counter offer

Sometimes, where a term set out in an acceptance deviates from that proposed in the offer, the difference may not be significant. Many older cases required exact correspondence between the offer and acceptance. If the response sought to alter the terms of the proposed contract in any way, it was not an acceptance. (This is known as the "mirror image" or "ribbon matching" rule.) Modern cases tend not to be as rigid. A response at variance with the offer may nevertheless qualify as an acceptance, provided that the offeree's intent to contract is apparent and the variations are not material—that is, they do not significantly depart from the offer. (Because the acceptance cannot bind the offeror to terms that differ from the offer, any nonmaterial variations in the acceptance are not part of the contract, which is formed on the offeror's terms.)

modern cases don't require perfect mirroring

At common law, if the response to an offer does propose terms sufficiently different to preclude it from being an acceptance, the response operates as a rejection of the offer and a counteroffer; that is, the original offer terminates and the offeree's response becomes a new offer, which the original offeror can accept if she so desires. Because the nonconforming response is a rejection of the original offer, the offeree cannot resuscitate the offer by retracting the different terms. Once an offer is rejected, it is no longer effective, and the offeree cannot thereafter accept it if she changes her mind, even if the time period specified in the offer for acceptance has not yet ended. (UCC Article 2 has some specific rules that deal with this situation, which we study in Chapter 6.)

if there are material differences then its a counter offer

* once the offer is rejected, its done

4. The Acceptance Must Occur While the Offer Is Still in Effect: Lapse or Termination of the Offer

Offers do not last forever. They are of limited duration and come to an end either at the time of expiration specified in the offer or, if no expiry date is specified, after a reasonable time. If an offeree does not accept the offer before it lapses, the offeree's inaction constitutes a rejection of the offer. The offer may state the period during which it is open for acceptance by specifying a definite date, as in the above example, in which the offer stated, "You must deliver your written, signed acceptance to me by 6 P.M. on Friday, June 3." Alternatively, the offer might state that it is open for a measurable period. ("This offer must be accepted within one week of its receipt.") If an offer specifies its duration, determining the date of its lapse is relatively straightforward—it comes to an end when the specified period ends. Obviously, the more precisely the duration is stated, the less likely that there will be disputes over its meaning and the need

* by date specified or a reasonable time

for interpretation. If the offer does not specify its duration, it is deemed to remain open for a reasonable time, which is determined in light of the circumstances of the transaction.

Where the offeree communicates an unequivocal intent to accept the offer, but does so after the offer has lapsed, a court may treat the ineffective acceptance as a new offer by the offeree. That is, even though the attempt to accept came after the offer ended, the offeree's positive response to the offer indicates that the offeree has the intent to enter a contract on the terms proposed in the offer. It may therefore be reasonable to treat the response as a new offer[2] by the former offeree, which can then be accepted by the offeror. In effect, this means that an offeror who decides to overlook a late communication of acceptance may still agree to form the contract.

Even before an offer comes to an end by the lapse of time, it may terminate as a result of action by either the offeror or the offeree. As we have discussed, action by the offeree terminates the offer if he rejects it, either by making a counteroffer or by an outright rejection. The offeror may also terminate the offer before its lapse date by revoking it; that is, if the offeror changes his mind after making the offer and decides that he no longer wishes to contract with the offeree, he can revoke the offer at any time before it has been accepted.[3] The revocation only becomes effective when it is communicated to the offeree. Either she must have received notice of revocation from the offeror (direct revocation) or she must have reliably learned in some other way that the offer is no longer open for acceptance (indirect revocation). Unless the offer qualifies as an option or firm offer (introduced in Section E), any commitment that the offeror may have made to keep it open for a stated period is not binding on him.

There is one further event that will terminate an offer before the stated or reasonable time for acceptance has expired: the death or mental incapacity of the offeror. A contract, once formed, is not usually terminated if one of the parties dies or becomes mentally incompetent. The contractual rights and duties of the deceased or incompetent party pass to his estate or legal custodian. However, it is a long-standing rule that if the offeror dies or becomes mentally incompetent between the time that the offer is made and the time that it is accepted, the offer lapses. This rule applies even if the offeree did not know or have reason to know of the intervening death or disability. The rule is justified on the basis that no contract can be created if the offeror has lost the ability to form contractual intent before acceptance. It is hard to reconcile this approach with the objective test of assent, but the rule survives nevertheless.

---

[2] Courts sometimes characterize a late acceptance as a counteroffer. This is not, strictly speaking, correct. A counteroffer is both a rejection of an existing offer and a new offer by the offeree. Because the original offer no longer exists, there is no existing offer to reject, so the response is more accurately regarded as a new offer.

[3] There are some narrow exceptions to this rule: For instance, the offeror may not revoke the offer if he has granted a valid option to the offeree. This is introduced in Sections E and F and is explored in some detail in Chapter 11.

default

5. The Effective Date of Acceptance and the "Mailbox" Rule

An acceptance takes effect when it is communicated to the offeror. Where the parties are in each other's presence it is usually not difficult to decide when the acceptance is communicated. The recipient hears the communication of acceptance as soon as it is manifested by speaking. However, when parties are not in instantaneous communication (assume that they are at a distance and corresponding by mail), there is a lag between the dispatch and receipt of the manifestation of acceptance. It can sometimes be important to determine which of these two events constitutes the legally effective acceptance. For example, say that an offer is open for acceptance until 6 P.M. on Friday, June 3. The offeree mails a letter of acceptance to the offeror on the morning of June 3, but it arrives in the offeror's mail on June 4. Because an attempt to accept after the expiry of the offer fails as an acceptance, fixing the effective date of the acceptance becomes crucial. A contract was created if the act of mailing the letter constitutes acceptance, but there is no contract if acceptance did not occur until the offeror actually received the letter.

The effective date of noninstantaneous communication of an acceptance is governed by the "mailbox" rule.[4] This rule, devised in a simpler era when mail was really the only effective means of communication between distant parties, provides that where the mail is an expressly or impliedly authorized or reasonable medium of acceptance, a properly stamped and addressed acceptance takes effect when deposited in the mail. It must be stressed that the "mailbox" rule is a default rule—an offeror who does not want it to apply can simply avoid it by specifying in the offer that acceptance will only be effective on receipt. However, where the offer makes no such specification and the offeree does accept by mail, the acceptance takes effect on mailing, provided that the letter is properly addressed and stamped and the mail is either an authorized or a reasonable means of communicating acceptance under the circumstances. It would be reasonable to use the mail, for example, where the offer itself is sent by mail or otherwise where use of the mail is customary and may be reasonably expected. Over the years, courts have advanced various rationales for the "mailbox" rule. Restatement, Second §63, comment a, justifies the rule on the simple basis that once the acceptance has been mailed, the offeree should be able to rely on its legal effectiveness.

Although the "mailbox" rule originated in the context of mail, courts have had to update the rule through the years to adapt it to new means of

Mailbox rule - contract begins when the letter is put in the mailbox

---

[4] Note that this discussion deals only with the effective date of an acceptance, and only describes the application of the "mailbox" rule to an acceptance. The rule does not cover the offeree's rejection of an offer or the offeror's revocation of an offer. Rejections and revocations are effective only on receipt. This note also does not cover the tangled situations that occur where an offeree first rejects an offer and then changes her mind and accepts it, or first accepts and then rejects it. In this type of situation, it may be appropriate not to apply the "mailbox" rule to protect the reasonable reliance of the offeror.

phone is = to face to face

communication, whether older forms of technology such as the teletype or telephone (treated by Restatement, Second §64 as the same as contracting face-to-face) or more contemporary forms of electronic communication such as fax, e-mail, and text messaging. In addition, even where people send communications in physical form, the use of private carriers or couriers is a common alternative to mail.

mail

what is the communication more like? face to face or mail?

In deciding whether acceptance through one of these new media is effective on dispatch or receipt, courts have considered whether the form of communication is more analogous to an instantaneous face-to-face discussion or to correspondence by mail. If one evaluates electronic communications on this basis, it becomes apparent that there is no easy and universal answer to the question of whether the mailbox rule should be applied to electronic means of communication. When people communicate electronically, say by e-mail, fax, or text message, they are not usually in each other's presence, and the communication is effected through a system controlled by a third party, such as the Internet service provider or telephone company. In this respect, electronic communications have some of the hallmarks of the mail. Unlike the mail, electronic communications are often instantaneous. However, they may not be if there are delays or disruptions in the communications system.

■ PROBLEM 5.1

General Construction, Inc., contracted to replace the windows of an office building. It needed to use scaffolding to perform the work, which it estimated would take two months. On April 1, it called Equipment Suppliers, Inc., and requested a price quote for renting the scaffolding for two months, beginning on May 1. On April 3, Equipment Suppliers' president visited the site. After inspecting the building and determining the amount of scaffolding required, he filled out and signed a standard form "proposal," which he handed to the representative of General Construction. The proposal offered to supply the scaffolding on the site for two months, beginning on May 1 and ending on July 1. The proposal showed a total price of $20,000, made up of two months' rent of $10,000 per month. The proposal concluded, "If the terms of this proposal are acceptable to you, please sign it in the space provided and return it to us as soon as possible." The space provided in the proposal for the customer's signature was a line at the bottom of the page that looked like this:

I accept this proposal _____ _____
                                    (signature)   (date)

General Construction decided immediately that it would accept Equipment Suppliers' proposal. However, because of a demanding work schedule, its president did not get around to filling in and signing the acceptance blank on the proposal until April 11. On April 12, General Construction had one of its clerks hand-deliver the signed document to Equipment Suppliers. On April 13, Equipment Suppliers called General Construction's president and told her that the response to the proposal came too late and that it was not able to supply the scaffolding. Was the response too late? How would you go about deciding this question?

returne

what's a reasonable amount of time?
↳ jury question

depends on the circumstance

■ PROBLEM 5.2

The proposal is the same as in Problem 5.1. As before, General Construction was handed it on April 3. That evening, General Construction's president realized that its estimate of two months for the work was too low, and that it would need the scaffolding for three months. The president therefore amended the proposal by scratching out the words "two months" and "July 1" and substituting "three months" and "August 1." She also changed the figure $20,000 to $30,000. She signed the proposal in the space provided and had a clerk deliver it by hand to Equipment Suppliers on April 4. Equipment Suppliers never acknowledged receipt or communicated further. *no acceptance of the counteroffer*

(a) Equipment Suppliers did not deliver the scaffolding on May 1, and when General Construction called to ask why, Equipment Suppliers responded that it had no scaffolding available and denied having a contract with General Construction. General Construction had to obtain scaffolding from another company in a hurry, and the best price it could find was $12,000 per month for three months. Does General Construction have a claim against Equipment Suppliers for the excess rental of $2,000 per month? If so, can it claim this amount for two months or three months?

(b) Assume that Equipment Suppliers did deliver the scaffolding on May 1. On July 1, its workers arrived to remove it. When General Construction protested that it had rented the scaffolding until August 1, Equipment Suppliers disagreed and insisted the scaffolding must be returned because it was needed for another job. Is Equipment Suppliers legally justified to demand the return of the scaffolding? *no*

performance began = acceptance

B

INTERPRETATION OF THE SUBSTANTIVE AND PROCEDURAL REQUIREMENTS OF ACCEPTANCE

R O T H v. M A L S O N

67 Cal. App. 4th 552, 79 Cal. Rptr. 2d 226 (1998)
California Court of Appeal

SIMS, Acting Presiding Judge.

[In July 1995, Malson, the seller (defendant), placed a parcel of 23.8 acres of real property on the market for a price of $47,600. On October 25, 1995, Roth, the buyer (plaintiff), executed a standard "Sales Agreement and Deposit Receipt" form offering to buy the property for $41,650, escrow to close within 30 days of acceptance. On November 2, 1995, the seller executed a standard form counteroffer to the buyer's original offer, changing the price to $44,000 but otherwise retaining all the terms in the buyer's original offer. The counteroffer stated that it would expire if not accepted by November 8, 1995. The counteroffer document contained blanks for a response by the counterofferee. To accept it, the counterofferee merely had to sign and date a blank line headed "Acceptance." Immediately below this blank, separated by a solid black line, there was a second blank labeled in bold print "Counter to Counter Offer" in which the counterofferee could write any proposed counteroffer that he wanted to make.

On November 6, 1995, the buyer sought to accept the counteroffer. However, instead of simply signing and dating the blank in the "Acceptance" area of the form, he signed and dated the portion labeled "Counter to Counter Offer." On the lines provided for "Changes/Amendments," he handwrote "Price to be $44,000.00 as above. Escrow to close on or before Dec. 6, 1995. All cash." The line for an expiration date for the "Counter to Counteroffer" was left blank. The buyer returned the form to the seller's agent by the November 8 deadline. In his deposition, the buyer said that he meant to communicate an acceptance, but he signed in the wrong place by mistake.

On November 16, 1995, the seller rejected the buyer's "counter to counteroffer." In December 1995 the buyer sued the seller for specific performance and damages. Both parties applied for summary judgment. The buyer argued that his response to the seller's counteroffer was an acceptance. Although he mistakenly signed in the "Counter to Counter Offer" space and wrote terms in the "Changes/Amendments" blank on the form, the terms written there did not change anything in the seller's counteroffer.

The trial court granted summary judgment in favor of the seller on the grounds that the buyer's response to the counteroffer was not a valid unqualified acceptance. The buyer appealed.]

. . . The sole issue presented by plaintiff on appeal is whether plaintiff's signature on the counteroffer form constituted an acceptance creating a contract. If it did not, then defendant is entitled to summary judgment because he has negated a necessary element of plaintiff's case—the existence of a contract. . . . The trial court concluded no contract was formed because plaintiff's "Counter to Counter Offer" was a qualified acceptance of defendant's counteroffer. We agree with the trial court and shall affirm the judgment in favor of defendant.

Plaintiff contends the trial court erred in granting summary judgment to defendant because plaintiff gave an absolute, unqualified acceptance—in substance though not in form—to defendant's counteroffer and thereby formed a binding contract. Plaintiff argues that, because his response to defendant's counteroffer did not really change any of the terms of the counteroffer, plaintiff's writing actually constituted an acceptance of defendant's counteroffer. Since the parties have so assumed, we also will assume for the sake of argument that plaintiff's response to the counteroffer did not vary any terms of the proposal. We disagree with plaintiff's position. . . .

[An acceptance must be absolute and unqualified. A qualified acceptance is a new offer. Under the objective test, the court must determine the reasonable meaning of the response to an offer.] Here, in responding to defendant's counteroffer, plaintiff's response on its face presented itself as a counter-counteroffer. [We disagree, with plaintiff's argument that] . . . because his "Changes/Amendments" did not really change or amend anything, his response should be construed as an acceptance rather than a counter-counteroffer. . . . [Plaintiff did not simply write] "I accept" in the space denominated "counteroffer." Rather, plaintiff inserted express terms (denominated "Changes/Amendments") that required the parties to the transaction and their agents to analyze whether the terms of the counter-counteroffer in fact matched up with the terms of the counteroffer. Viewing the counter-counteroffer in its entirety and objectively, the counter-counteroffer called for a response from the seller before a contract would be formed. In the absence of a response from defendant, no contract was formed. This principle is sound. There is no reason to put the parties or the courts in the position of comparing and contrasting terms (described as "Changes/Amendments") to determine whether there is any material variance when a response to a counteroffer is on its face presented as a counter-counteroffer. We agree with the trial court in this case, which stated in its ruling on summary judgment:

> Wisely, the real estate industry has developed standardized forms for the use by the general public in buying and selling real estate. [The form used here] provide[s] easily understood information and procedures to facilitate the transfer of real property between buyer and seller. As an added boon, litigation is, no doubt, minimized. Yet people still manage to create problems, intentionally or unintentionally. This case is a perfect example. The buyer, having deliberately or unintentionally, signed the form in the wrong place, now seeks to enforce the "agreement." Can any reasonable person ignore the possibility that a plaintiff who seeks to enforce such an "agreement" in his favor would not use his actions to avoid the purchase if it

were not in his favor. This potential for game-playing must be avoided at all costs. The form was clear. The facts are clear. Plaintiff did not absolutely and clearly accept the counteroffer.

Plaintiff considers it significant that his response to defendant's counter-offer did not give a deadline (as did the original offer and the counteroffer), which assertedly demonstrates that plaintiff was communicating an acceptance rather than a counter-counteroffer. We disagree. The absence of a deadline does not make plaintiff's response an acceptance rather than a counter-counteroffer. Similarly, we reject plaintiff's argument that the fact he responded before the counteroffer's deadline shows he was communicating an acceptance rather than a counter-counteroffer. Also unpersuasive is plaintiff's argument that his response should be construed as an acceptance because he signed the document at the bottom, which is "where most people sign documents."

Plaintiff claims California courts have defined a qualified acceptance as one which varies the terms of the original offer, thereby constituting a counteroffer. However, the cited authority, *Ten Winkel v. Anglo California S. Co.* (1938), 11 Cal. 2d 707, 81 P.2d 958, merely said that the written acceptance at issue in that case, "in that it varied the terms of the original offer, at most constituted a qualified acceptance and in effect constituted a counteroffer on the part of the original offeree. . . ." (Id. at p. 717.) *Ten Winkel* thus did not make variance of terms a sine qua non of a qualified acceptance.

Plaintiff claims Civil Code section 1651 supports his case, because it states written clauses prevail over printing, and therefore we must disregard the printing on the document which characterizes plaintiff's response as a counter-counter-offer rather than an acceptance. According to plaintiff, the handwritten parts show a contract was formed. However, even assuming for the sake of argument that Civil Code section 1651 applies to determinations whether a contract exists, as opposed to interpretation of an existing contract (a point disputed by defendant), the statute does not save plaintiff in this case. Plaintiff asks us to disregard the printed words "Counter to Counter Offer" and "Changes/Amendments." However, Civil Code section 1651 calls for disregard of printed portions only when written and printed portions are repugnant. An example of repugnant provisions is where one provision allows prepayment and another prohibits prepayment. Here, plaintiff fails to point to any handwritten provisions which actually conflict with printed provisions. Plaintiff's signature and handwritten remarks are not so repugnant with the printed portions of the form as to compel disregard of the printed words, even accepting plaintiff's claim that his handwritten remarks did not vary the terms of the proposed agreement. Moreover, disregard of the printed words in this case would leave the written words in a vacuum. Thus, we conclude Civil Code section 1651 does not apply in this case.

Plaintiff argues our conclusion gives the contract an unreasonable interpretation, in violation of Civil Code section 1643, which provides: "A contract must receive such an interpretation as will make it lawful, operative, definite, reasonable, and capable of being carried into effect, if it can be done without violating the intention of the parties." However, the issue here is not contract interpretation but rather the determination whether a contract exists. The statute itself contains the qualifier concerning the intention of the parties; thus, the statute is not violated if the objective manifestations of the parties' intent disclose lack of acceptance of an offer to make a contract.

We conclude the trial court properly entered summary judgment in favor of defendant. . . .

RAYE, Judge, dissenting.

I respectfully dissent. . . . The majority accurately summarizes the applicable principles and I have no quarrel with their explication of them. . . . [However, the majority fails] to apply them to the standard form agreement before us. Their bright line standard . . . is enticing—judicial decisionmaking becomes a simple matter of inspecting boxes on standard forms—but runs counter to the reasonable expectation of the parties, an overarching standard which heretofore has governed our decisionmaking in this area.

. . . [A]n acceptance must manifest an unconditional agreement to all the terms of the offer and an intention to be bound thereby. . . . [It] must not change, add to, or qualify the terms of the offer . . . [and] must be clear, positive and unambiguous. . . . [The acceptance in this case satisfies these requirements.]

Language is inherently susceptible to misunderstanding. Ambiguity abounds. For that reason the early common law required particular incantations to make an offer and formulaic expressions to accept. There is virtue in such an approach. However, the modern rule is otherwise. . . . Indeed, the trend, as exemplified by the Uniform Commercial Code, is toward even greater liberality in the construction of purported offers and acceptances. Whatever the merit of bright line formulations, the law reflects a preference for case-by-case determinations. Contract formation is not a matter of form but substance; there are no magic words and no magic forms essential to the creation of binding agreement.

Except for their use of a standard form agreement, the parties herein engaged in a classic offer and acceptance transaction. Stripped of the captions, boxes and other adornments, and subject to certain terms and conditions not relevant here, the writing at the heart of this dispute sets forth an offer to sell a 23.8-acre parcel for $44,000 with escrow to close within 30 days. Appellant expressed in writing a willingness to buy the parcel, reaffirming two critical terms: the purchase price ("Price to be $44,000 as above") and the date of closing ("escrow to close on or before December 6, 1995"). . . . [T]he majority concludes that despite the fact appellant's acceptance merely reiterated the terms of the offer, it was ineffective. . . . [A]ppellant's fate was sealed when he elected to convey his acceptance with words written in a box captioned "Counter to Counter Offer." . . .

The majority concludes that by placing the language of acceptance in a preprinted block captioned "Counter to Counter Offer," appellant's purported acceptance did not express an intent to be bound but rather called for a response from defendant. The majority is simply wrong. The appellant's handwritten language merely reaffirms the offer. The only other language in the box is preprinted and also reaffirms the offer: "Buyer accepts all other terms and conditions in the above counter offer." Had appellant's handwriting been intended as a true counter to respondent's counteroffer it is reasonable to expect that appellant would have filled in the blank space provided for insertion of an expiration date. That space remains blank. No response was required.

[The use of standard forms is efficient and should be encouraged. However,] . . . the trial court and the majority would treat the forms as sacrosanct and penalize those with the temerity to depart from the boxes provided. As the trial court bemoans, despite the convenience of standardized forms, "people still manage to create problems." Perhaps so. Nonetheless, our task is to ascertain their intentions from their language and conduct. The language and actions of the appellant clearly reflect an intent to accept respondent's offer; no other construction is plausible. For that reason, I dissent.

■ QUESTIONS

(1) Is the problem with the alleged acceptance in this case substantive or procedural? That is, did Roth, the buyer, fail to agree with the substantive terms of the seller's counteroffer, or did he fail to follow the correct procedure in seeking to communicate his acceptance?

(2) Much of the discussion in the majority and dissenting opinions concerns Roth's intent in responding to the counteroffer. Of course, this intent is based not on his subjective state of mind—what he may actually have intended—but on his objective manifestation of intent, as it would have been reasonably understood by Malson. Weigh all the arguments made by Roth in urging that his response to the counteroffer should reasonably be interpreted as an acceptance. Do you find the resolution of the majority or the dissent more persuasive? Do you see echoes of classicism versus realism in this case, decided nearly a century after the debate began?

TRINITY HOMES, LLC v. FANG

Not reported in S.E.2d, 63 Va. Cir. 409, 2003 WL 22699791 (2003)
Virginia Circuit Court

JACOBSON, Judge.

. . . The primary issue in this cause is the status and/or effect of an alleged facsimile transmission by Damon Stewart (Stewart), the agent for Trinity Homes, L.L.C. and Seabring Development, L.L.C. (Complainants) . . . to T.H. Nicholson, III (Nicholson), the agent for Ching Seng Fang and Carol S. Fang (Defendants), of the Agreement for Purchase & Sale of Real Estate (Agreement) dated June 17,

2002. . . . Stewart alleges that he placed the Agreement in his facsimile machine, dialed the number for Nicholson, pushed the button to start the facsimile and then went on an errand. The facsimile machine utilized by Stewart was not a modern version and did not provide any verification that a facsimile was being transmitted and/or that such facsimile was received. There are no phone records relative to the alleged transmission of the facsimile transmission by Stewart. Shortly after the time Stewart alleged he forwarded the facsimile to Nicholson, he received a phone call from Nicholson indicating that Defendants did not wish to sell the property nor enter into a contract with Complainants for that purpose.

Initially, it is necessary to consider whether facsimile (fax) transmissions are similar to or should be treated the same as [mailed letters under] the Mailbox Rule in regard to the acceptance of a contract. The Mailbox Rule was enunciated in *Adams v. Linsdell*, 106 Eng. Rep. 250 (K.B.1818). The Mailbox Rule states that once an offeree has dispatched his acceptance, it is too late for the offeror to revoke the offer. The Mailbox Rule has been accepted in most American jurisdictions and by the Restatement of Contracts §63 (Restatement). The Restatement addresses the issue of the application of the Mailbox Rule to electronic communication in §64, which states: "Acceptance given by telephone or other medium of substantially instantaneous two-way communication is governed by the principles applicable to acceptances where the parties are in the presence of each other." This is, therefore, a two-prong test: (1) the communication must be "substantially instantaneous"; and (2) the communication must be two-way. "The rationale of the Restatement's position is that when parties are conversing using 'substantially instantaneous two-way communication,' they are, in essence, in each other's presence." Shawn E. Tuma & Christopher R. Ward, *Contracting Over the Internet in Texas*, 52 Baylor L. Rev. 381, 393 (2000).

To be substantially instantaneous, the transmission must occur within a few seconds, or, at most, within a minute or two. For a communication to be two-way, one party must be able to "determine readily whether the other party is aware of the first party's communications, through immediate verbal response or, when the communication is face-to-face, through nonverbal cues." Michael S. Baum & Henry H. Perritt, Jr., *Electronic Contracting, Publishing and EDI Law* 321 (1991). Further, if a communication is not two-way, "the offeror will not know exactly when the offeree accepts and may attempt to revoke the offer after the offeree has already sent his instantaneous acceptance to the offeror[]. . . . In such a situation, the Mailbox Rule should continue to apply and the contract should be considered accepted upon dispatch of the offeree's acceptance." Tuma & Ward, *supra*, at 393.

The Supreme Court of Oklahoma considered this issue in *Osprey LLC v. Kelly-Moore Paint Co.*, 984 P.2d 194 (Ok. 1999). In *Osprey*, the plaintiff leased commercial property to the defendant. The lease required that the defendant provide notice of its intent to renew the lease at least six months prior to the expiration of the lease, and notice was to be given in writing and delivered personally or through registered first class mail. The defendant attempted to extend the lease by faxing a renewal letter on the last day of the notification period.

The plaintiff denied receiving the fax, despite a fax record and telephone record confirming the transmission. Applying the Mailbox Rule, the court held that the faxed notice of the lease renewal was sufficient to timely exercise the lease renewal option because the notice was in writing, and the delivery of the notice by fax transmission served the same purpose of the authorized methods of delivery. The court stated specifically: "the fax log and telephone records show that the notice was properly transmitted to Osprey. Transmitting the fax *was like mailing an acceptance under the Mailbox Rule*, where an offer is accepted when it is deposited in the mail." *Id.* at 200 (emphasis added); *cf.* Tuma & Ward, *supra*, at 393 n. 58 (citing *Western Union Tel. Co. v. Fletcher*, 208 S.W. 748, 751 (Tex. Civ. App. 1919)) ("The telegraph is considered an instantaneous form of communication but is only a one-way form to which the Mailbox Rule does apply").

This Court concludes that the Mailbox Rule is applicable in the instant cause and thus the issue is one of fact—whether or not the facsimile transmission of . . . [the agreement] was actually forwarded or transmitted by Stewart to Nicholson. As previously indicated, Stewart's fax machine was apparently one of early vintage and provided no verification of the transmission. . . . Unlike in the *Osprey* case there was no fax log and/or telephone records to show that the fax was properly transmitted to Nicholson. Stewart cannot say with certainty if the fax actually went through other than to say that he placed the fax in the fax machine, turned it on and then left before viewing and/or verifying its transmission. Further, Stewart did not recall looking at the fax machine by or through which the . . . [agreement] allegedly was transmitted, when he returned later in the afternoon from his errand. The burden is on the Complainants to prove by preponderance of the evidence that the fax transmission of . . . [the agreement] was actually made and accomplished. The Court in considering the totality of the evidence and the totality of the circumstances, finds and concludes that the burden has not been met nor satisfied and finds for the Defendants.

■ PROBLEM 5.3

The court cites *Osprey LLC v. Kelly-Moore Paint Co.*, 984 P.2d 194 (Okla. 1999) as authority for the application of the mailbox rule to fax transmissions. *Osprey* involved a dispute over a renewal option in a lease. One of the issues in *Osprey* was whether the option to renew the lease (that is, the offer) permitted acceptance by fax. The lease provided that if the lessee decided to exercise the renewal option, acceptance of the option "shall be in writing and may be delivered either personally or by depositing the same in United States mail, first class postage prepaid, registered or certified mail, return receipt requested." The court rejected the lessor's claim that the option had not been properly exercised and held that the notice of acceptance was effective. The court reasoned:

may does not exclude other methods of acceptance

"Shall" is ordinarily construed as mandatory and "may" is ordinarily construed as permissive. The contract clearly requires that notice "shall" be in writing. The provision for delivery, either personally or by certified or registered mail, uses the permissive "may" and it does not bar other modes of transmission which are just as effective. The purpose of providing notice by personal delivery or registered mail is to insure the delivery of the notice, and to settle any dispute which might arise between the parties concerning whether the notice was received. A substituted method of notice which performs the same function and serves the same purpose as an authorized method of notice is not defective. . . . The fax provided immediate written communication similar to personal delivery and, like a telegram, would be timely if it were properly transmitted before the expiration of the deadline to renew. Kelly-Moore's [the lessee's] use of the fax served the same function and the same purpose as the two methods suggested by the lease and it was transmitted before the expiration of the deadline to renew. Under these facts, we hold that the faxed or facsimile delivery of the written notice to renew the commercial lease was sufficient to exercise timely the renewal option of the lease. . . .

(a) Do you agree with the court's interpretation? Can you come up with a different "plain meaning" for this provision?

(b) Despite the rather exacting language of the clause in the contract, the court found in *Osprey* that the response by fax was a permissible mode of acceptance. Is there a way that the lessor (offeror) could have drafted the provision to ensure that personal delivery or mail were the exclusive methods of exercising the option (that is, accepting the offer to renew the lease)?

"must be by" *may only be*

(c) Do you agree with the court that a fax performs the same function and serves the same purpose as personal delivery or certified or registered mail? *yes (even faster than mail)*
    * *depends on the circumstance*

■ PROBLEM 5.4

Some (but not all) courts seem to make great efforts to interpret the offer's procedural requirements for acceptance as broadly as possible, so as to validate acceptances that may not qualify as such on a stricter interpretation. *Osprey* appears to be such a case. *Keller v. Bones*, 260 Neb. 202, 615 N.W.2d 883 (2000) is another. Keller made an offer to the Boneses to buy a ranch. The offer stated that it would lapse if not accepted by July 21, 1997, at 5 P.M. It also stated that "[u]pon execution by Seller, this agreement shall become a binding contract." The sellers decided to accept the offer and signed it just before 5 P.M. on July 21. However, they did not communicate their acceptance to the buyer until 5:12 P.M., when their real estate agent called the buyer and left a voicemail informing him of the acceptance. On the next day, the sellers received an offer from someone else and asked the buyer if they could "back out" of the sale. The buyer declined. The sellers then refused to go through with the sale to the buyer. The buyer sued the sellers for specific performance.

The lower courts granted summary judgment to the sellers on the grounds that they never accepted the buyer's offer—although they signified their acceptance by signing the offer before the deadline, acceptance is only effective on communication, and communication occurred only after the deadline. The Supreme Court reversed the summary judgment. It agreed that acceptance must usually be communicated to become effective. However, the terms of the buyer's offer required only that the offer be *signed* before the deadline, not that it be communicated by that time. In reaching this conclusion, the court relied on the language in the offer which stated that the agreement would become binding "upon execution by the seller." Because the court interpreted the deadline to apply to the act of signing, rather than the act of communicating acceptance, it was sufficient that notice of acceptance be given to the buyer within a reasonable time, and the voicemail message, left 12 minutes after the deadline, constituted reasonable notice.

(a)   Do you agree with the court? Do you think that the buyer really intended his deadline to apply to the act of signing rather than communicating acceptance? If not, how should the buyer have worded his offer?

(b)   Do the summaries of *Osprey* and *Keller* suggest any factors that might have influenced the courts to be flexible in their interpretations of the procedural requirements for acceptance? Are there any such factors in *Trinity*?

C   INADVERTENT MANIFESTATION OF ACCEPTANCE

The objective test focuses on the offeree's manifestation of assent rather than on her actual state of mind. Therefore, in deciding if an offer was accepted, courts focus on the reasonable understanding of the offeree's words or conduct in response to the offer and not on what the offeree may have thought or subjectively intended. However, in rare cases, that subjective intent may be relevant: Where an offeree, unaware of an offer, inadvertently acts in a way that signifies assent to an offer, it may push the objective test too far to find that conduct to be an acceptance. Even though the offeree appears, by her actions, to accept an offer, her assent cannot be readily inferred from that conduct if it is shown that she did not even know that the offer existed. As you may expect, this problem does not come up very often—in most cases it is not even conceivable that an offeree could appear to accept an offer without knowing about it. However, there are some situations in which this occurs. Most commonly, but not always, they involve public offers of reward.

Restatement, Second §23 states the general principle in rather abstract terms: "It is essential to a bargain that each party manifest assent with reference to the manifestation of the other." A more concrete illustration of this principle is provided by a well-known case, *Glover v. Jewish War Veterans of United States, Post No. 58*, 68 A.2d 233 (D.C. Mun. App. 1949). The Jewish War Veterans posted an offer of reward for information resulting in the "apprehension and conviction of the persons guilty of the murder" of one of its members. Acting on information that one of the killers was the boyfriend of Ms. Glover's daughter, the police questioned Ms. Glover about his whereabouts. Although she did not know where he was, she gave the police information that enabled them to find and arrest him. He was ultimately convicted of the murder. At the time that she was questioned by the police, Ms. Glover did not know of the reward. She only found out about it a few days afterward. Ms. Glover claimed the reward, but the court held that she was not entitled to it. The court reasoned that it is impossible for a person to accept an offer unless she knows of its existence. Therefore, because Ms. Glover was not aware of the reward when she spoke to the police, her apparent manifestation of assent to the offer—her conduct in providing the information—was inadvertent and cannot be treated as an acceptance of the reward offer.[5] (The offer of a reward was an offer for a unilateral contract, in which the offeree accepts the offer not by making a promise to perform what is required by the offer but by rendering that performance. This is explained in Section F.)

In the next case, the court discusses the issue of inadvertent manifestation of acceptance in the context of an employment relationship. After you read the case, consider whether it really involved an inadvertent manifestation of acceptance.

---

[5] The court noted that where the offer of a reward is made by the government, courts generally do not require that the claimant knows of the reward when furnishing the information. However, the court declined to follow that rule where the reward offer was by a private body.

ANDERSON v. DOUGLAS & LOMASON COMPANY

540 N.W.2d 277 (1995)
Iowa Supreme Court

TERNUS, Justice.

Defendant, Douglas & Lomason Company (DLC), discharged plaintiff, Terry Anderson, for taking a box of pencils. Anderson responded with a breach-of-contract action claiming DLC failed to follow progressive discipline policies contained in the employee handbook. The district court granted DLC's motion for summary judgment, which argued, in part, that the handbook did not constitute a contract. Anderson appealed....

On Anderson's first day of work at DLC he attended a six hour orientation session for new employees. He was informed that DLC had a progressive discipline policy and he was given a fifty-three page employee handbook which included these policies. Anderson read only the first few pages of the handbook; he admits he never read the provisions on progressive discipline. DLC fired Anderson after three years of employment. His termination was based on an incident which occurred as he was leaving the plant one day. Company personnel stopped his pickup and asked to search it. Anderson gave permission and the workers found a box of company pencils. As a result, they also asked to search his home and garage. Anderson consented and a subsequent search revealed no company property. However, that same day, DLC asked Anderson to resign. He refused and was immediately fired. Anderson responded by filing this breach-of-contract action against DLC. He claims DLC did not follow the progressive discipline policies outlined in its handbook for unauthorized possession of company property. These progressive discipline policies require a written warning for the first offense, a three-day suspension without pay for the second offense, and discharge for the third offense. Because this was not Anderson's third offense, he claims DLC could not fire him. DLC filed a motion for summary judgment claiming the handbook did not constitute a contract and therefore Anderson was employed at will. First, DLC contended the handbook was never communicated to or accepted by Anderson because he did not read it. Second, DLC argued the handbook was not definite enough to constitute an offer. DLC cited two reasons for its vagueness claim: the handbook contains no written guarantees that discharge will occur only for cause or under certain conditions—the rules are mere guidance; and the manual contains a written disclaimer. The district court granted the employer's summary judgment motion without explanation in a calendar entry.... [This extract from the opinion omits the court's discussion of the second argument, on which the employer ultimately prevailed.]

The central issue presented by this dispute is whether DLC's issuance of a handbook created an employment contract. This question arises because Iowa employment relationships are presumed to be at will: In the absence of a valid employment contract either party may terminate the relationship without consequence. . . . Despite the universal acceptance of the employment-at-will doctrine, legislatures and courts have restricted its application. For example, federal labor law gave rise to union contracts that include just cause discharge provisions. Reflecting the perceived need to protect employees from the harshness of the at-will doctrine, courts began to erode the doctrine with exceptions. These exceptions generally fell within three categories: (1) discharges in violation of public policy, (2) discharges in violation of employee handbooks constituting a unilateral contract, and (3) discharges in violation of a covenant of good faith and fair dealing. . . . [The court recognizes that the requirement that an employer follow progressive disciplinary procedures can restrict the employer's right to discharge an employee at will, if they are part of the employment contract.] We must now determine whether Anderson's handbook constitutes an enforceable contract. If it does not, we presume the parties intended a contract at will. . . . [The court notes that an employee handbook can create a contract where the handbook constitutes the offer, which the employee accepts by performance in embarking on the employment. For a contract to arise, the handbook must be sufficiently definite in its terms to create an offer, and it must be communicated to and accepted by the employee.] As with any contract, the party who seeks recovery on the basis of a unilateral[6] contract has the burden to prove the existence of a contract. Therefore, Anderson has the burden to prove DLC's handbook created an enforceable contract. We begin our analysis with a discussion of the communication aspect of the acceptance element of Anderson's claim.

Anderson read only a few pages of the employee manual; he did not read the provisions on progressive discipline. DLC contends that under these circumstances, there can be no acceptance. We disagree. DLC distributed its employee handbook to new employees. We think Anderson's receipt of the handbook is sufficient communication. Under traditional contract analysis, an offer is not effective until it reaches the offeree. Restatement (Second) of Contracts §51, cmt. a (1981) ("it is ordinarily essential to the acceptance of the offer that the offeree know of the proposal made"); *cf. Iowa Malleable Iron Co. v. Iowa Employment Sec. Comm'n*, 195 N.W.2d 714, 718 (Iowa 1972) ("one cannot be deemed to have declined an offer never communicated to him"). The reason for the rule is clear: The offeree must know of the offer before there can be mutual assent.

The most common illustration of the application of this rule is the general offer of a reward. The reward-giver, or offeror, bargains for performance, not a reciprocal promise; sometimes the performance is rendered without knowledge

---

[6] As mentioned in the text preceding this case, a unilateral contract is one in which acceptance occurs by actually rendering the performance required by the contract, rather than by promising to perform in the future. This is explained in Section F. —Eds.

of the offer. Some courts resolve this issue using the traditional law of contracts: "There can be no contract unless the claimant when giving the desired information knew of the offer of the reward and acted with the intention of accepting such offer; otherwise the claimant gives the information not in the expectation of receiving a reward but rather out of a sense of public duty or other motive unconnected with the reward." *Glover v. Jewish War Veterans*, 68 A.2d 233, 234 (D.C. 1949). Courts adopting this traditional approach do so because "it is impossible for an offeree actually to assent to an offer unless he knows of its existence." *Glover*, 68 A.2d at 234 (quoting Williston, §33, at 47). On the other hand, one authority has suggested knowledge of a reward-offer need not be a prerequisite to acceptance:

> It is probable, indeed, that the chief reason for enforcing a promise is that it has induced the promisee to act in reliance upon it. One who has rendered a service without knowledge of an offered promise has not so acted. But the chief reason is not necessarily the only reason for enforcing a promise. If it seems fair to the courts to enforce a promise when the promisor has received the desired equivalent, even though the one rendering it knew nothing of the promise and rendered the service from other motives, there is no sufficient reason for refusing to call that enforceable promise a contract.

1 Joseph M. Perillo, *Corbin on Contracts* §3.5, at 328 (rev. ed. 1993).

Iowa case law on rewards has not addressed this issue. However, we have adopted the traditional position with respect to unilateral contracts in general, that the offeree's performance must have been induced by the promise made. Nevertheless, for reasons that follow, we decline to follow the traditional requirement that knowledge of the offer is a prerequisite to acceptance in the limited context of employee handbook cases. . . . We believe important policies, which are confined to employee handbook cases, dictate a narrow divergence.

Where a contract is based upon an employee handbook distributed to all employees, the contract is not an individually negotiated agreement; it is a standardized agreement between the employer and a class of employees. We analogize to the interpretation of standardized contracts: "A standardized agreement 'is interpreted wherever reasonable as treating alike all those similarly situated, without regard to their knowledge or understanding of the standard terms of the writing.'" *Kinoshita v. Canadian P. Airlines, Ltd.*, 68 Haw. 594, 724 P.2d 110, 116-17 (1986) (quoting Restatement (Second) of Contracts §211(2) (1981)). Therefore, we hold it unnecessary that the particular employee seeking to enforce a promise made in an employee manual have knowledge of the promise. Although this holding is a departure from traditional 'bargain-theory' contract analysis, we think it produces "the salutary result that all employees, those who read the handbook and those who did not, are treated alike." E. Allan Farnsworth, *Developments in Contract Law During the 1980's: The Top Ten*, 41 Case W.

Res. L. Rev. 203, 209 (1990). Moreover, our deviation from traditional contract theory is consistent with the spirit of the judicially created at-will presumption: It is a common law presumption created in response to statutory and societal demands. . . .

[The court notes that its decision is supported by case law from other jurisdictions, in which courts have bound an employer to comply with its handbook promises, whether or not the employee knew of them. The court therefore finds that the employee's lack of knowledge of the progressive discipline provisions of the handbook did not preclude his acceptance of the employer's offer. However, the court ultimately finds in favor of the employer on the other issue in the case, that the handbook was not definite enough to constitute an offer. The court therefore finds that Anderson was employed at will and affirms the trial court's summary judgment in favor of the employer.]

■ QUESTIONS

(1) There is a significant factual difference between *Anderson* and *Glover*: When Mrs. Glover performed the act that apparently manifested acceptance, she did not know at all that an offer had been made. However, Mr. Anderson knew that his employment was subject to the handbook, and he simply did not read it.

 (a) Did the *Anderson* court mischaracterize the case as involving an inadvertent manifestation of acceptance?

 (b) If Mr. Anderson did not manifest acceptance inadvertently, what is the correct legal principle to apply? Is this a duty to read case, like those that we studied in Chapter 3? We would probably conclude that it is, if it was the employer who was seeking to bind the employee to a term in the handbook (such as an arbitration provision), and the employee raised the argument that he had not read the term. However, in this case, it is the employee who seeks to enforce a term that he failed to read. What is the most persuasive rationale for binding the employer to its handbook?

(2) In *Anderson*, the court refuses to treat Mr. Anderson's acceptance as inadvertent because it considers this resolution to be unfair and contrary to public policy. This makes sense because the reason for not holding a person to an inadvertent manifestation of acceptance is that it would be unfair to bind that person to a contract where he had no idea that an offer had been made and his conduct, coincidentally, gave the offeror the impression that he had accepted. However, in both *Anderson* and *Glover* the offeree is not seeking protection from inadvertently entering an unwanted contract, but rather seeks to enforce the contract. On this principle, do you think that *Glover* should have been decided differently?

SILENCE AS ACCEPTANCE

As a general rule, an offeree does not have to take affirmative steps to reject an offer. He can reject it simply by not responding to it. An offeror cannot change this general rule by writing the offer in a way that compels the offeree to respond to avoid being bound. Therefore, even if an offer states, "A contract will come into effect unless you notify me of your rejection of my offer by not later than 6 P.M. on Friday, September 1," the offeree can ignore the offer and will not be committed to a contract by her silence. This general rule is reflected in Comment a to Restatement, Second §69, which states that an offeror does not ordinarily have the power to cause the silence of the offeree to operate as acceptance.

There are some narrow exceptions to this rule, set out in §69. Silence or inaction may operate as acceptance where the parties have a relationship under which it is reasonable for the offeree to notify the offeror if he does not intend to accept. Silence may also signify assent if the offeree takes advantage of services offered with the reasonable opportunity to reject them and reason to know that they were offered with the expectation of compensation. Where property is offered, the offeree could be bound, even in the absence of a communication of acceptance to the offeror, if he acts toward the property in a manner inconsistent with the offeror's ownership of it.[7] Finally, the rule that an offer may not be accepted by silence is for the protection of the offeree, so it does not apply if the offeror has indicated that the offer may be accepted by inaction and the offeree does intend to accept the offer by remaining silent.

P R I D E v. L E W I S

179 S.W.3d 375 (2005)
Missouri Court of Appeals

ULRICH, Presiding Judge.

Larry L. Lewis appeals the judgment of the Circuit Court . . . finding that he breached a real estate contract and ordering him to pay damages in the amount of $20,900.00. . . . Mr. Lewis . . . contends . . . [that] the trial court's finding that a contract had been entered into was against the weight of the evidence because

---

[7] To counter abusive selling practices, legislatures have enacted statutes that qualify the rule that the offeree may accept by acting inconsistently with the offeror's ownership. A federal statute, 39 U.S.C. §3009, provides that if a commercial entity mails unordered merchandise (defined as merchandise mailed without the prior expressed request or consent of the recipient), the recipient may treat it as a gift and may use, keep, or discard it without any obligation to the sender. The sender is obliged to attach to the merchandise a conspicuous statement informing the recipient of this and is prohibited from mailing a bill to the recipient for the merchandise. A number of states have equivalent statutes that provide a similar rule for unordered merchandise delivered by means other than the mail.

the sellers presented a counteroffer, thereby extinguishing Mr. Lewis's offer, and neither Mr. Lewis nor his wife accepted the counteroffer. . . . [The court agrees with Lewis and reverses the judgment of the trial court.]

Andrew and Joyce Kay Pride, husband and wife, owned a house located in Nodaway County. In 2002, they moved to a farm and placed the house for sale with Priority One Realty. The house sat empty for some time; Mr. and Mrs. Pride then found a tenant to rent the house until such time as it sold. The tenant rented the house for a sum of $450 per month. In April 2003, Mr. and Mrs. Pride were informed that Mr. Lewis made an offer to purchase the house for $55,000, with earnest money in the amount of $1500. During this time, Mr. Lewis was married to Issoline Lewis. The first contract offered by Mr. Lewis through his realtor required Mr. and Mrs. Pride to owner finance the transaction. This offer was rejected by Mr. and Mrs. Pride. Mr. Lewis's realtor then presented a second contract. Mr. and Mrs. Pride's realtor presented them with the second contract, already signed by Mr. Lewis and his realtor. This contract specified conventional bank financing would be used. The contract stated that Mr. and Mrs. Pride were selling the house to Larry and Issoline Lewis. Mr. Lewis signed the contract on April 9, 2003. His realtor also signed the contract, although the date is not indicated. Mrs. Lewis never signed the contract. Mr. and Mrs. Pride, as well as their realtor, signed the real estate contract on April 11, 2003. Upon signing the contract, Mr. and Mrs. Pride informed their tenant that she would have to vacate the house by June 1, 2003. The contract provided by Mr. Lewis had a closing date of May 15, 2003. Mr. and Mrs. Pride changed this date, by hand, to June 1, 2003. This change was initialed by Mr. and Mrs. Pride, but not by Mr. Lewis or Mrs. Lewis.

Mr. and Mrs. Pride became aware that there was a problem with closing on the property in June, when the closing was scheduled to occur. They, along with their realtor, were prepared to close on the property but neither Mr. Lewis, Mrs. Lewis, nor their realtor ever appeared. Mr. and Mrs. Pride's realtor contacted Mr. Lewis's realtor and was informed that Mr. Lewis had not responded to phone calls or otherwise communicated with his realtor. Mr. Lewis testified that he thought "they were going to try to [close] early June, and that's the last I knew." He further testified that he had been travelling and had attempted to contact his real estate agent a couple of times but, upon not reaching her, "opted to wait and let them contact me." When the closing with Mr. Lewis failed to occur, Mr. and Mrs. Pride sent him a letter notifying him of his default and their electing not to take the $1500 earnest money as damages.

After the closing with Mr. Lewis failed to occur, Mr. and Mrs. Pride re-listed the house with a realtor. Before Mr. Lewis made his offer, the house's listing price had changed several times; when the house was listed again, after the closing with Mr. Lewis failed to occur, the house was listed for $55,000 and the price never changed. The house sold in June 2004 for $40,000. This was the highest offer Mr. and Mrs. Pride received for the house. During the additional year the house was for sale, Mr. and Mrs. Pride were unable to secure another tenant to rent the property.

The two contracts offered by Mr. Lewis and the contract wherein the house actually sold for $40,000 were the only three offers ever made for the property. Mr. and Mrs. Pride's realtor testified that the house may have been worth only $40,000 when the offer for $40,000 was made and the subsequent sale occurred.

Mr. and Mrs. Pride sued Mr. Lewis for breach of contract. They sought damages for the difference between the $55,000 contract price with Mr. Lewis and the $40,000 for which the house actually sold, for the lost rent the year they were unable to find another tenant, and for attorney's fees, as provided in the contract. The trial court entered judgment in favor of Mr. and Mrs. Pride and awarded them $20,900 in damages. . . . Mr. Lewis's timely appeal followed.

. . . Mr. Lewis argues that the trial court's finding that a contract had been entered into was against the weight of the evidence. He contends that when Mr. and Mrs. Pride changed the closing date, they made a counteroffer for the sale of the real estate. He further argues that, because neither he nor his wife signed or initialed the change in closing date, he never accepted the counteroffer and thus there was no contract. Before a plaintiff can establish a breach of contract, he or she must first establish the existence of a contract. Any acceptance that includes new or variant terms from the offer presented amounts to a counteroffer and a rejection of the original offer. The unequivocal acceptance of the offer is fundamental to the existence of a contract. Mr. Lewis contends that Mr. and Mrs. Pride made a counteroffer when they changed the closing date from May 15, 2003, to June 1, 2003. While both Mr. and Mrs. Pride initialed this change, it was undisputed at trial that neither Mr. nor Mrs. Lewis initialed the change to the contract. Mr. and Mrs. Pride acknowledge that changing the closing date amounted to a counteroffer.

The question is, was the counteroffer ever accepted? Mr. Lewis argues that he never accepted this counteroffer, and, thus, there was no contract. Mr. and Mrs. Pride argue that Mr. Lewis accepted their counteroffer through his conduct and failure to act. They specifically list three facts that manifest Mr. Lewis's acceptance of their counteroffer. They are: (1) Mr. Lewis never contacted his real estate agent, Mr. or Mrs. Pride, the Pride's real estate agent, or anyone else to reject the counteroffer; (2) Mr. Lewis knew the closing was to take place in early June; and (3) Mr. Lewis never sought the return of his earnest money. As a general rule, silence or inaction cannot constitute acceptance of an offer. Absent a duty to speak, silence may not be translated into acceptance merely because the offeror attaches that effect to it. Inaction or silence does not evidence any intention of the offeree.

This general rule does have exceptions, however. Acceptance of an offer or counteroffer does not always have to be made through explicit spoken or written word. *Citibank (South Dakota), N.A. v. Wilson*, 160 S.W.3d 810, 813 (Mo. App. W.D. 2005). An offer may be accepted by conduct or failure to act. *Id.* This is the rule of law upon which Mr. and Mrs. Pride rely. They claim that Mr. Lewis's conduct and failure to act amount to an acceptance of their counteroffer. While this statement of the law is accurate, it is of no avail in this case. This rule applies primarily to instances where services are rendered and the party benefited by the services is aware of the terms upon which the services are offered. *Id.* "If this party receives the benefit of the services in silence, when there was a reasonable opportunity to reject them, this party is manifesting assent to the terms proposed and thus accepts the offer." *Id.* (internal citations and quote marks omitted). *See also Moore v. Kuehn*, 602 S.W.2d 713, 718 (Mo. App. E.D. 1980) (stating that an offer may be accepted through conduct "[w]here the offeree with reasonable opportunity to reject offered goods or services takes the benefit of them under circumstances which would indicate to a reasonable man that they were offered with the expectation of compensation"). These cases involve benefits or services being conferred or actions taken in accordance with the proposed agreement in such a manner that the other party is justified in assuming the offer has been accepted. *See, e.g., Wilson*, 160 S.W.3d at 813 (finding acceptance of offer when credit card company mailed patron a revised agreement, patron was informed that the revised agreement was binding unless she cancelled her account within thirty days and did not use her credit card, and patron continued to use her credit card thus manifesting her acceptance of the revised agreement); *E.A.U., Inc.*, 794 S.W.2d at 686 (finding acceptance of offer where offeree referred offeror to third party for third party's approval of change, where offeree indicated it would be agreeable to any change authorized by third party, and where offeror notified offeree it had obtained third party's approval and offeree failed to reject the change).

The case relied upon by Mr. and Mrs. Pride for the rule of law that conduct may amount to acceptance of an offer is *Environmental Waste Management, Inc. v. Industrial Excavating & Equipment, Inc.*, 981 S.W.2d 607, 612 (Mo. App. W.D. 1998). This case is similar to the above examples in that the offeree received the benefit of services in silence, knowing the terms upon which they were offered and having the opportunity to decline the services, and thus was deemed to have accepted the terms of the offer. *Id.* In *Environmental Waste Management, Inc.*, the plaintiff sent the defendant a letter wherein its prices for contaminated soil removal were listed. The defendant allowed the plaintiff to remove contaminated soil, but then refused to pay the prices listed in the letter. The plaintiff subsequently sued for breach of contract and the court held that, by allowing the plaintiff to remove the contaminated soil, the defendant accepted the offer in the letter. *Id.*

Mr. and Mrs. Pride advance the similarity of this case. Mr. Lewis did not accept services or benefits under the terms of an agreement and later claim never to have accepted the agreement. This case is not analogous. As noted, *supra*, Mr. Lewis had no duty to reject the counteroffer. Further, while Mr. Lewis failed to request the refund of his earnest money, this is not sufficient to create a binding contract. Mr. and Mrs. Pride argue that: "Logic would indicate that a person would desire the return of their earnest money if they believed that no contract had ever been in existence." Maybe so; but almost no testimony regarding this was presented at trial. Mr. Lewis may have believed that the earnest money was nonrefundable. Perhaps he did not want to encounter the hostility of having it refunded. Whatever his reason, the fact that he failed to request the return of the earnest money does not make this case one where Mr. Lewis received a benefit or services under a proposed agreement.

The last evidence Mr. and Mrs. Pride advance as indicative of Mr. Lewis's acceptance of the counteroffer is the fact that he was aware the closing date was in early June. While this certainly weighs in favor of Mr. and Mrs. Pride, it is not sufficient for the trial court to find that Mr. Lewis had accepted the counteroffer resulting in a binding contract. Mr. Lewis could have been clearer with respect to the fact that he was rejecting the counteroffer. He may have known that Mr. and Mrs. Pride assumed their counteroffer had been accepted and were proceeding accordingly. Perhaps as a courtesy he should have informed Mr. and Mrs. Pride that he did not accept their counteroffer. Regardless of whether he breached cultural mores, Mr. Lewis had no legal duty to act or explicitly reject the counteroffer. Mr. and Mrs. Pride erroneously assumed that silence was equivalent to acceptance. This case does not fit with the line of cases holding that an offeree's conduct or failure to act amounted to acceptance of an offer. Mr. and Mrs. Pride should have secured Mr. Lewis's acceptance to the counteroffer before advancing the transaction. This court cannot create a contract where one did not exist, especially given the importance of an unequivocal acceptance of the offer.

Mr. and Mrs. Pride made a counteroffer when they changed the closing date in the real estate sales contract. Because the counteroffer was never accepted by Mr. or Mrs. Lewis, a contract was never formed. The judgment of the trial court is reversed.

REVOCATION OF AN OFFER

Unless an offer qualifies as an option, the offeror is free to revoke it at any time before it is effectively accepted. The offeror has the power to revoke even if the offer states that it will be kept open for a specific period of time. We deal with options in Chapter 11. We defer them until then because consideration is generally required for an option (as the courts state in both of the following opinions), and options cannot be properly understood until consideration has been studied. For the present, this means, in simple terms, that unless an offeror receives something (for example, a payment of money) in exchange for the promise to keep the offer open, he is not bound by that promise and can terminate the offer by revoking it at any time before it is accepted.

HENDRICKS v. BEHEE

786 S.W.2d 610 (1990)
Missouri Court of Appeals

FLANIGAN, Presiding Judge.

Plaintiff Steve L. Hendricks, d/b/a Hendricks Abstract & Title Co., instituted this interpleader action against defendants Eugene Behee, Artice Smith, and Pearl Smith. Plaintiff was the escrowee of $5,000 which had been paid by defendant Behee as a deposit accompanying Behee's offer to purchase real estate owned by defendants Artice Smith and Pearl Smith, husband and wife, in Stockton, Missouri. A dispute between Behee and the Smiths as to whether their dealings resulted in a binding contract prompted the interpleader action. Behee filed a crossclaim against the Smiths. After a nonjury trial, the trial court awarded plaintiff $997.50 to be paid out of the $5,000 deposit. None of the parties challenges that award. The trial court awarded the balance of $4,002.50 to defendant Behee. Defendants Smith appeal. In essence the Smiths contend that the dealings between them and Behee ripened into a contract and entitled the Smiths to the balance of $4,002.50, and that the trial court erred in ruling otherwise.

After Behee, as prospective buyer, and the Smiths, as prospective sellers, had engaged in unproductive negotiations, Behee, on March 2, 1987, made a written offer of $42,500 for the real estate and $250 for a dinner bell and flower pots. On March 3 that offer was mailed to the Smiths, who lived in Mississippi, by their real estate agent. There were two real estate agents involved. The trial court found that both were the agents of the Smiths, and that finding has not been disputed by the Smiths in this appeal. For simplicity, the two agents will be considered in this opinion as one agent who acted on behalf of the Smiths.

On March 4 the Smiths signed the proposed agreement in Mississippi. Before Behee was notified that the Smiths had accepted the offer, Behee withdrew the offer by notifying the real estate agent of the withdrawal. That paramount fact is conceded by this statement in the Smiths' brief: "On either March 5, 6 or 7, 1987, Behee contacted [the Smiths' real estate agent] and advised her that he desired to withdraw his offer to purchase the real estate. Prior to this communication, Behee had received no notice that his offer had been accepted by the Smiths."

There is no contract until acceptance of an offer is communicated to the offeror. An uncommunicated intention to accept an offer is not an acceptance. When an offer calls for a promise, as distinguished from an act, on the part of the offeree, notice of acceptance is always essential. A mere private act of the offeree does not constitute an acceptance. Communication of acceptance of a contract to an agent of the offeree is not sufficient and does not bind the offeror. Unless the offer is supported by consideration, an offeror may withdraw his offer at any time before acceptance and communication of that fact to him. To be effective, revocation of an offer must be communicated to the offeree before he has accepted.

Notice to the agent, within the scope of the agent's authority, is notice to the principal, and the agent's knowledge is binding on the principal. Before Behee was notified that the Smiths had accepted his offer, Behee notified the agent of the Smiths that Behee was withdrawing the offer. The notice to the agent, being within the scope of her authority, was binding upon the Smiths. Behee's offer was not supported by consideration and his withdrawal of it was proper. The judgment is affirmed.

▪ QUESTION

The Smiths are the sellers of the property, and Behee is the buyer. However, they are all defendants. What is the role of the plaintiff, Hendricks, and what relief is being sought by whom?

▪ PROBLEM 5.5

(a)   On March 1 the offeror mailed a written offer to the offeree. The offer said nothing about the time or manner of acceptance. The offeree received it on March 2. On March 4 the offeror changed his mind and mailed a revocation of the offer to the offeree. It was received by the offeree on March 6. In the interim, on March 5 the offeree had mailed an acceptance to the offeror. The acceptance was received on March 7. Do the parties have a contract?

(b)   The facts are the same as in question (a), except that the offer stated, "This offer will remain open for acceptance until March 10. Your written acceptance must be received by me on or before that date." Do the parties have a contract?

Hendricks expresses the rule that a revocation must be communicated. Until it is communicated, it does not take effect. The mailbox rule does not apply to a revocation, which must be received by the offeree to be effective. This means that an offeror who wishes to prevent acceptance must take care to ensure that the revocation comes to the offeree's attention before any effective acceptance. However, even if the offeror fails to do that, the offer will terminate if, before he accepts, the offeree reliably hears of its withdrawal from another source. This is sometimes called "indirect revocation."

Dickinson v. Dodds, a nineteenth-century English case, is one of the best-known cases on indirect revocation. However, there is some question over whether the case really stands for the proposition for which it has become famous. In *The Death of Contract*, Professor Gilmore argued that the decision in *Dickinson* was really based on the subjective test of assent—the court found no contract because, by the time the offeree decided to accept, the offeror had already changed his mind, and there was therefore no "meeting of the minds." Gilmore says that Williston and the classicists twisted the case to fit the objective theory.[8] There is language in the opinion of Lord Justice James, set out below (and also in the opinion of Lord Justice Mellish, which is not included here) that supports Gilmore's reading of the case. Be this as it may, the facts of the case, viewed in light of an objectivist interpretation, still serve as a great illustration of the principle of indirect revocation.

DICKINSON v. DODDS

2 Ch. Div. 463 (1876)
Court of Appeal

direct v. indirect revocation

In June, 1874, the defendant, John Dodds, who was the owner of certain house property at Croft, near Darlington, was in treaty with the plaintiff, Mr. George Dickinson, for the sale thereof to him, and on Wednesday the 10th of that month he signed and delivered to him the following document: "I hereby agree to sell to Mr. George Dickinson, C.E., the whole of the dwelling-house, garden ground, stabling and outbuildings thereto belonging, situate at Croft, belonging to me . . . for the sum of £800. As witness my hand this 10th day of June, 1874." Dickinson, however, desiring time to consider the matter, added the following postscript, which was also signed by Dodds. "P.S. This offer to be left over until Friday, 9 o'clock A.M., 12th of June, 1874."

In the afternoon of the following day, the plaintiff having heard that Dodds had been offering the property to Thomas Allan, left at the house of a Mrs. Burgess, where Dodds was then staying, a written acceptance of the offer. This, however, appears not to have been delivered to him. On the following morning, Friday, the 12th, before nine o'clock, the plaintiff met Dodds at the railway station, and gave him a written acceptance of the offer, which, however, he refused to accept, saying the plaintiff was too late as he had already sold the property. The plaintiff then filed his bill against Dodds and Thomas Allan, with whom he had on the 11th of June entered into a formal contract for the sale of the property, for specific performance, and other relief. The defendants claimed that the contract to leave the offer over was founded on no consideration, and could not be enforced. The cause was heard before Bacon, V.C., and his Lordship

---

[8] Grant Gilmore, *The Death of Contract* 31-33 (Ronald K.L. Collins ed., 2d ed., Ohio St. U. Press 1995).

holding that as the offer had been accepted before any notice of withdrawal had been given, a binding contract had been entered into, decreed specific performance accordingly. The defendants appealed.

JAMES, Lord Justice.

In this case the defendant, Mr. Dodds, signed a memorandum which was made out by the plaintiff, Mr. George Dickinson. . . . This document though beginning "I hereby agree to sell" was nothing but an offer, and was only intended to be an offer, because unless both sides had then agreed there was no agreement then made; it was in effect and substance as if he had said "I hereby offer to sell." Then Mr. Dickinson, the plaintiff, being minded not to complete the bargain at that time, added this postscript, which the defendant signed: "This offer to be left over until Friday, 9 o'clock A.M., 12th June, 1874."

no consideration

There was no consideration given for the undertaking or promise to keep the property unsold until nine o'clock on Friday morning, but apparently Mr. Dickinson was of opinion, and Mr. Dodds probably was also of opinion, that he was bound. But it is clear settled law, settled on one of the clearest principles, that this offer being a mere *nudum pactum* was not binding, and that at any moment before a complete acceptance of the offer by Mr. Dickinson, Dodds was as free as Dickinson himself.

Well, that being the state of things, it is, nevertheless, said that the only mode in which he could assert that freedom was by actually and distinctly saying "I withdraw that offer." It appears to me that there is no authority for the proposition that there must be an express and actual withdrawal or what is called a retraction of the offer, because before there can be an agreement it must appear that the two minds were at one at some one moment of time, that is to say, that there was an offer continuing up to the time of the acceptance, and accepted at that time. If there was not that continuing offer, then the acceptance comes to nothing. Of course it may well be that the one man is bound in some way or other to let the other man know that his mind with regard to the offer has been changed; but in this case beyond all question the plaintiff, Mr. Dickinson, knew as clearly that Mr. Dodds was no longer minded to sell the property—as if Dodds had gone to him and told him in so many words, "I withdraw the offer."

Dickinson's own account of the transaction is that he determined to accept the offer on the morning of the 11th of June, 1874, Thursday; but being engaged in business, and fully understanding and believing that he had until Friday the power to accept the offer, he did not on the morning of Thursday signify his acceptance of the offer to the defendant John Dodds. However, in the afternoon of Thursday, about 5 P.M., he was informed by a friend that he had accidentally been that morning to the office of Mr. Wooler, the defendant's solicitor, and had there heard that the defendant John Dodds had on that morning been at the office of the said Mr. Wooler, and had in some way or other, but how, in particular, was not represented to the plaintiff, been offering the said property, or agreeing to sell the said property, to the defendant Thomas Allan, and the plaintiff then immediately hastened to the place of residence of the defendant John Dodds, at Croft aforesaid, and enquired for, but could not find him, and he then and there left with the mother-in-law of the said John Dodds a formal acceptance of the said offer.

It is to my mind quite clear that before there was any acceptance by Dickinson he was perfectly aware that Dodds had changed his mind, and had in fact agreed to sell the property to Allan. It is impossible, therefore, to say that there was that continuance of the same mind between the two parties which is essential in point of law to the making of an agreement. I am of opinion, therefore, that Dickinson has failed to prove that there was any binding contract between Dodds and himself.

■ QUESTIONS

(1) Dickinson made two attempts to accept the offer. He delivered a formal acceptance to Dodds's mother-in-law on Thursday and then attempted to deliver another to Dodds himself on Friday morning. Neither was effective because Dickinson's knowledge of the sale preceded both attempts. Would Dickinson's acceptance delivered to Dodds's mother-in-law have been effective if it had been delivered before he received the information?

(2) The court says that Dickinson had heard that Dodds had "been offering . . . or agreeing to sell" the property to Allan. Should it make a difference whether he heard that Dodds was offering to sell the property, or agreeing to sell it?

■ PROBLEM 5.6

Anna Septimus, a college professor, intended to take a sabbatical in Greece during the spring semester, from January 1 to May 1. During the prior November she began to look for someone to take care of her house while she would be away. She placed an advertisement for a house sitter on the bulletin board in the student union. Roger Lodger, a student, responded to the notice, and Anna took him to see the house on November 10. Anna specified the period during which Roger would live in the house; they discussed what Roger would have to do to take care of the house; and Anna proposed the rent she wanted, suitably reduced to take account of Roger's duties. At the end of their meeting, Anna said, "Well, the job is yours if you want it." Roger replied, "Let me think about it for a couple of days. I will get back to you." Anna responded, "Okay, but don't delay, because if you don't want to do it, I have other people interested. Come by my office to let me know."

On November 12 Roger made up his mind to take the house-sitting job. A couple of days later, on November 14, he went to Anna's office to tell her. Anna was not there, so Roger told the secretary that he had come to see Anna about taking care of her house. The secretary replied, "Oh, I believe that she has found someone to do that." Notwithstanding, Roger left a note for Anna reading, "Dear Anna, I came by to see you today about the house-sitting arrangement. I am available and would like to do it. Sincerely, Roger."

Anna had indeed found someone else to take care of her house. On November 15 she wrote a note to Roger saying, "Roger, Thanks for your interest. As my secretary told you, I do now have a house sitter and no longer need you to do it. Regards, Anna." Roger insists that he has a contract with Anna. Is he correct?

F ACCEPTANCE BY PERFORMANCE: UNILATERAL CONTRACTS

1. The Distinction Between Unilateral and Bilateral Contracts

We have seen that an offeror has the power to prescribe the way in which his offer is to be accepted. If he wishes, he can control the manner of acceptance very tightly by specifying the action required to manifest acceptance. He can firmly regulate such things as the period within which acceptance must occur, the medium through which it must be communicated, the form it must take, and the stage at which it will become effective. We have also seen that offerors sometimes do exercise this power to control acceptance by setting out the prescribed method of acceptance in detail, but sometimes they do not. Where the method of acceptance is not fully specified in the offer, the offeree can accept by any reasonable method consistent with and fairly contemplated by the offer.

As part of his power to specify the method of acceptance, an offeror can call for the acceptance to be signified by any act that he chooses. For example, Algie, a homeowner, had requested Rufus, a roofer, to give him a quote for cleaning his moss-infested roof. After inspecting it on June 1, Rufus wrote out and handed to Algie an offer to clean his roof for a price of $1,500. The offer specified that the work would be performed on June 20, and it stated that Algie must make advance payment of the $1,500 by June 19. The offer also stated, "If you wish to accept this offer, you must sign it in the space provided below and return the original to me at the above address by not later than 6 P.M. on June 6." Rufus has set out the action that Algie must take to accept the offer, and in so doing has prescribed a mode of acceptance that Algie must follow to accept the offer. The only significance of Algie's act of signing and returning the letter is that it communicates his intent to enter the contract. It is not part of his performance under the contract, which is the payment of the price of $1,500. The same would be true if Rufus's offer called for some other act to signify acceptance, for example, if it specified that to accept the offer Algie must make a personal appearance at Rufus's home at 6 P.M. on June 6 and tap dance on the front porch. The tap dancing is merely symbolic—a designated method of manifesting assent. In both these illustrations, if Algie performs the act of acceptance as prescribed, a contract is created in which Algie promises to pay the price of $1,500 by June 19 and Rufus promises to clean the roof on June 20. This contract is described as bilateral because at the time of Algie's acceptance, a contract is formed under which both parties have made promises to be performed at a future date.

However, say that Rufus's offer had stated, "The price of the work must be paid in advance by June 6. To accept this offer, you must deliver the $1,500 in cash to me in person by June 6. This is the only way in which you can accept this offer." The nature of the act of acceptance has changed. It is no longer merely a manifestation of intent but is also the full completion of Algie's performance under the contract; that is, Algie's act of acceptance is his act of performance. Where this occurs, the contract is described as unilateral because the offeree's performance is complete at the point of contract formation, and only the offeror's performance remains outstanding when the contract is created. We can confidently characterize Rufus's offer as calling for a unilateral contract in the second example because he made it very clear that Algie could accept only by rendering his performance under the contract; that is, full performance of Algie's contract obligation is the exclusive means of acceptance. Where the offeror does not specify clearly that the only way to accept is to render the contractual performance, courts follow the usual approach to interpreting an offer: An offer is not taken to require an exclusive mode of acceptance unless, on a reasonable interpretation of the language and circumstances, this is clearly its intent. For example, say that Rufus's offer stated that the price must be paid by June 19 and that the offer must be accepted by June 6. However, it did not specify the mode of acceptance. Algie would be able to accept by manifesting assent by promise on June 6, creating a bilateral contract, or by paying by June 6, in effect creating a unilateral contract. (Because Rufus's offer allows acceptance either by promise or by rendering the contractual performance called for in the offer, it is conventional to describe the offer as calling for a bilateral contract. Although a unilateral contract may result if Algie chooses to accept by performance, that result is not mandated by the terms of the offer.)

In sum, the distinction between bilateral and unilateral contracts can be confusing. It helps to avoid confusion if you recognize that the distinction relates to the mode of acceptance. It is really just an application of the rules relating to the procedural requirements of the offer, discussed in Section A.2. In most situations, offers call for a bilateral contract; that is, offers usually

assent, then promise to perform

contemplate that if the offeree chooses to accept the offer, she may follow whatever procedure is appropriate to signify acceptance. Once that procedure has been completed by words or conduct indicating that the offeree has agreed to be bound on the terms called for in the offer, a bilateral contract is created under which both parties promise to perform in the future. Most contracts must by nature be bilateral because they contemplate that performance of both parties will take place in the future, after the contract has been made, and it is not even practicable for the offeree to accept by a completed act of performing his contract obligations. However, where an offer calls for a simple, one-time performance by the offeree, there is a stronger possibility that acceptance by fully performing that obligation is feasible and may either be required or permitted by the offer. In this situation, the offer must be interpreted to see if it merely allows acceptance by performance or—expressly or by clear implication—requires it as the exclusive mode of acceptance. As you can see, unilateral does not mean one-sided in the usual sense of the word. (A one-sided transaction, in which only one party promises something and the other does or promises nothing in return, does not qualify as a contract at all, as we will see when dealing with the concept of consideration.) Rather, unilateral is a term of art that describes a type of contract in which the obligation of one party is completely performed at the point of formation and all that remains is the promise of performance by the other.

■ PROBLEM 5.7

Algie requested Rufus, a roofer, to give him a quote for cleaning the moss-infested roof of his house. After inspecting it on June 1, Rufus wrote out and handed to Algie an offer to clean his roof for a price of $1,500. The offer specified that the work would be performed on June 20. It stated, "Ten percent of the price of the work, $150, must be paid in advance by June 6 and the balance of the price is due before commencement of the work on June 20. To accept this offer, you must pay the deposit of $150 in cash to me in person by June 6. This is the only way in which you can accept this offer."

Does the offer call for a unilateral or bilateral contract?

unilateral contracts— reward

still has to be performed

Probably, the most common kind of offer calling for a unilateral contract is an offer of a reward for performing some action, in which the offeror clearly does not seek a promise to perform the action, but must reasonably be understood to intend that the offer may be accepted only by actual performance of the action. One form of reward case involves a public advertisement offering a reward for providing information (such as the offer in *Glover v. Jewish War Veterans of United States*,[9] calling for information leading to the apprehension and conviction of a murderer) or the return of lost property. Another is an offer by a merchant for a reward or prize to induce members of the public to buy or use the merchant's products—such as the "Camel Cash" program described in *Sateriale v. R.J. Reynolds Tobacco Co.* or (had PepsiCo actually made an offer) the "Pepsi Points" program in *Leonard v. PepsiCo*.[10] The next case, an early example of this genre, is one of the icons of contract law.

CARLILL v. CARBOLIC SMOKE BALL CO.

1 Q.B. 256 (1892)
Court of Appeal

Appeal from a decision of HAWKINS, Justice.

The defendants, who were the proprietors and vendors of a medical preparation called "The Carbolic Smoke Ball," inserted in the Pall Mall Gazette of November 13, 1891, and in other newspapers, the following advertisement:

> £100 reward will be paid by the Carbolic Smoke Ball Company to any person who contracts the increasing epidemic influenza, colds, or any disease caused by taking cold, after having used the ball three times daily for two weeks according to the printed directions supplied with each ball. £1000 is deposited with the Alliance Bank, Regent Street, shewing our sincerity in the matter.
>
> During the last epidemic of influenza many thousand carbolic smoke balls were sold as preventives against this disease, and in no ascertained case was the disease contracted by those using the carbolic smoke ball.
>
> One carbolic smoke ball will last a family several months, making it the cheapest remedy in the world at the price, 10s., post free. The ball can be refilled at a cost of 5s. Address, Carbolic Smoke Ball Company, 27, Princes Street, Hanover Square, London.

The plaintiff, a lady, on the faith of this advertisement, bought one of the balls at a chemist's, and used it as directed, three times a day, from November 20, 1891, to January 17, 1892, when she was attacked by influenza. Hawkins, J., held that she was entitled to recover the £100. The defendants appealed.

Per LINDLEY, Lord Justice.

... We must first consider whether this was intended to be a promise at all, or whether it was a mere puff which meant nothing. Was it a mere puff? My answer

---

[9] Discussed in Section C of this chapter on inadvertent manifestation of acceptance.
[10] Both cases are discussed in Section C of Chapter 4.

they even said they meant it

very clear

to that question is "No," and I base my answer upon this passage: "£1000 is deposited with the Alliance Bank, shewing our sincerity in the matter." Now, for what was that money deposited or that statement made except to negative the suggestion that this was a mere puff and meant nothing at all? The deposit is called in aid by the advertiser as proof of his sincerity in the matter—that is, the sincerity of his promise to pay this £100 in the event which he has specified. I say this for the purpose of giving point to the observation that we are not inferring a promise; there is the promise, as plain as words can make it.

Then it is contended that it is not binding. In the first place, it is said that it is not made with anybody in particular. Now that point is common to the words of this advertisement and to the words of all other advertisements offering rewards. They are offers to anybody who performs the conditions named in the advertisement, and anybody who does perform the condition accepts the offer. In point of law this advertisement is an offer to pay £100 to anybody who will perform these conditions, and the performance of the conditions is the acceptance of the offer. . . .

performing the conditions laid out is the contract acceptance

We, therefore, find here all the elements which are necessary to form a binding contract enforceable in point of law. . . . It appears to me, therefore, that the defendants must perform their promise, and, if they have been so unwary as to expose themselves to a great many actions, so much the worse for them.

■   ■   ■

Because one can never have enough of *Leonard v. PepsiCo*, here is the portion of the court's opinion in which it discusses *Carlill*. Recall that Leonard's claim against PepsiCo failed because the court held that PepsiCo had never made an offer at all—the TV commercial was a joke (see Chapter 3), and neither the commercial nor the catalog could be construed as offers (see Chapter 4). Nevertheless, the court did discuss the question of whether, had an offer been made, the "Pepsi Stuff" promotion would have constituted a unilateral offer to the public.

L E O N A R D v. P E P S I C O , I N C .

88 F. Supp. 2d 116 (S.D.N.Y. 1999), aff'd 210 F.3d 88 (2d Cir. 2000)
United States District Court, Southern District of New York

WOOD, District Judge.

. . . In opposing the . . . motion [for summary judgment] the plaintiff largely relies on a . . . species of unilateral offer, involving public offers of a reward for performance of a specified act. Because these cases generally involve public declarations regarding the efficacy or trustworthiness of specific products, one court has aptly characterized these authorities as "prove me wrong" cases. See *Rosenthal v. Al Packer Ford*, 374 A.2d 377, 380 (Md. Ct. Spec. App. 1977).

The most venerable of these precedents is the case of *Carlill v. Carbolic Smoke Ball Co.*, 1 Q.B. 256 (Court of Appeal, 1892), a quote from which heads plaintiff's memorandum of law: "[I]f a person chooses to make extravagant promises ... he probably does so because it pays him to make them, and, if he has made them, the extravagance of the promises is no reason in law why he should not be bound by them." *Carbolic Smoke Ball*, 1 Q.B. at 268 (Bowen, L.J.).

[handwritten margin note: just because its a big promise does'it mean you're not bound to it]

Long a staple of law school curricula, *Carbolic Smoke Ball* owes its fame not merely to "the comic and slightly mysterious object involved," A. W. Brian Simpson, *Quackery and Contract Law: Carlill v. Carbolic Smoke Ball Company* (1893), in *Leading Cases in the Common Law* 259, 281 (1995), but also to its role in developing the law of unilateral offers. The case arose during the London influenza epidemic of the 1890s. Among other advertisements of the time, for Clarke's World Famous Blood Mixture, Towle's Pennyroyal and Steel Pills for Females, Sequah's Prairie Flower, and Epp's Glycerine Jube-Jubes, see Simpson, *supra*, at 267, appeared solicitations for the Carbolic Smoke Ball. . . .

Affirming the lower court's decision, Lord Justice Lindley began by noting that the advertisement was an express promise to pay £100 in the event that a consumer of the Carbolic Smoke Ball was stricken with influenza.[11] The advertisement was construed as offering a reward because it sought to induce performance, unlike an invitation to negotiate, which seeks a reciprocal promise. As Lord Justice Lindley explained, "advertisements offering rewards ... are offers to anybody who performs the conditions named in the advertisement, and anybody who does perform the condition accepts the offer." *Id.* at 262; *see also id.* at 268 (Bowen, L.J.). Because Mrs. Carlill had complied with the terms of the offer, yet contracted influenza, she was entitled to £100.

[handwritten margin note: sought performance not negotiation]

Like *Carbolic Smoke Ball*, the decisions relied upon by plaintiff involve offers of reward. In *Barnes v. Treece*, 549 P.2d 1152 (Wash. Ct. App. 1976), for example, the vice-president of a punchboard distributor, in the course of hearings before the Washington State Gambling Commission, asserted that, "I'll put a hundred thousand dollars to anyone to find a crooked board. If they find it, I'll pay it." Plaintiff, a former bartender, heard of the offer and located two crooked punchboards. Defendant ... repudiated the offer. The court ruled that the offer was valid and that plaintiff was entitled to his reward. The plaintiff in this case also cites cases involving prizes for skill (or luck) in the game of golf. See *Las Vegas Hacienda v. Gibson*, 359 P.2d 85 (Nev. 1961) (awarding $5,000 to plaintiff, who successfully shot a hole-in-one); *see also Grove v. Charbonneau Buick-Pontiac, Inc.*, 240 N.W.2d 853 (N.D. 1976) (awarding automobile to plaintiff, who successfully shot a hole-in-one).

---

[11] Although the Court of Appeal's opinion is silent as to exactly what a carbolic smoke ball was, the historical record reveals it to have been a compressible hollow ball, about the size of an apple or orange, with a small opening covered by some porous material such as silk or gauze. The ball was partially filled with carbolic acid in powder form. When the ball was squeezed, the powder would be forced through the opening as a small cloud of smoke. *See* Simpson, *supra*, at 262-63. At the time, carbolic acid was considered fatal if consumed in more than small amounts. *See id.* at 264.

Other "reward" cases underscore the distinction between typical advertisements, in which the alleged offer is merely an invitation to negotiate for purchase of commercial goods, and promises of reward, in which the alleged offer is intended to induce a potential offeree to perform a specific action, often for noncommercial reasons. In *Newman v. Schiff*, 778 F.2d 460 (5th Cir. 1985), for example, the Fifth Circuit held that a tax protestor's assertion that, "If anybody calls this show . . . and cites any section of the code that says an individual is required to file a tax return, I'll pay them $100,000," would have been an enforceable offer had the plaintiff called the television show to claim the reward while the tax protestor was appearing. The court noted that, like *Carbolic Smoke Ball*, the case "concerns a special type of offer: an offer for a reward." *James v. Turilli, 473* S.W.2d 757 (Mo. Ct. App. 1971), arose from a boast by defendant that the "notorious Missouri desperado" Jesse James had not been killed in 1882, as portrayed in song and legend, but had lived under the alias "J. Frank Dalton" at the "Jesse James Museum" operated by none other than defendant. Defendant offered $10,000 "to anyone who could prove me wrong." The widow of the outlaw's son demonstrated, at trial, that the outlaw had in fact been killed in 1882. On appeal, the court held that defendant should be liable to pay the amount offered. . . .

In the present case, the Harrier jet commercial did not direct that anyone who appeared at Pepsi headquarters with 7,000,000 Pepsi Points on the Fourth of July would receive a Harrier jet. Instead, the commercial urged consumers to accumulate Pepsi Points and to refer to the Catalog to determine how they could redeem their Pepsi Points. The commercial sought a reciprocal promise, expressed through acceptance of, and compliance with, the terms of the Order Form. . . .

[handwritten margin note: commercial sought negotiations, not a reward]

■ QUESTION

Of course, as the claimed offer of the Harrier jet was just a joke, it was no offer at all. But what about the items that were actually featured in the catalog? Assuming that the catalog itself constitutes an offer rather than a mere solicitation, do you think that the court is correct in characterizing the "Pepsi Stuff" catalog as an offer allowing for acceptance by promise but not by performance? Does this distinction matter? If so, why?

■ PROBLEM 5.8

Recall *Sateriale v. R.J. Reynolds Tobacco Co.* in Chapter 4. The court held that by promoting the "Camel Cash" customer loyalty program, RJR had made an offer to its customers. In a portion of the opinion not reproduced in our edited version of the case, the court considered whether the offer made by RJR was for a unilateral or bilateral contract. It held that the offer was for a unilateral contract. Although RJR had made a promise to its customers to redeem the certificates, the customers made no return promise to RJR. True, the customers had to do something to get their rewards: They had to buy the cigarettes and complete and submit the "Camel Cash" certificates to RJR. However, the customers neither promised to buy the cigarettes nor to submit the certificates—they just had to do this as a condition of getting the rewards.

(a)   Since this was an offer for a unilateral contract, what was the act of acceptance? What was the act of acceptance in *Carlill*?

(b)   In *Sateriale* the court makes the distinction between a promise to do something and a mere condition of becoming entitled to getting the performance promised by the other party. What does this mean? Why is the distinction important to the characterization of a contract as unilateral or bilateral?

▇ PROBLEM 5.9

(a)   Review the discussion of *Lefkowitz v. Great Minneapolis Surplus Store* and *Harris v. Time, Inc.* in Chapter 4. Are the offers in those two cases for unilateral contracts? Why or why not?

(b)   We indicated in the introductory text in Section C that *Glover v. Jewish War Veterans* involved a unilateral contract. Why is that contract properly classified as unilateral?

▇ PROBLEM 5.10

Harms v. Northland Ford Dealers, 602 N.W.2d 58, 1999 S.D. 143 (1999) is one of a number of reported cases involving the offer of a prize for hitting a hole-in-one during a golf tournament. Northland Ford was a sponsor of a golf tournament and had agreed with the organizers to provide a prize of a new Ford Explorer to the first golfer who hit a hole-in-one at the eighth hole. Jennifer Harms was a participant in the tournament. She registered for the tournament with the golf club, but had not had any dealings with Northland. Northland parked a Ford Explorer on the course next to a poster announcing the prize. The poster contained no information about the rules governing the award of the prize. These rules, as settled by the club and Northland, required all golfers, whether male or female, to tee off from the men's tee box to qualify for the prize. However, because of poor communication and coordination among the organizers, this rule was not announced to the participants in the tournament. Harms did hit a hole-in-one from the eighth tee, but she hit it from the women's tee box. Northland refused to award the prize to her on the grounds that she had not hit the ball from the men's tee.

The South Dakota Supreme Court upheld an award of summary judgment against Northland in favor of Harms. It held that under the objective test, Northland was bound by the rules that were manifested to the players and could not refuse to award the prize based on rules that it had not announced. In the absence of information to the contrary, participants in the competition would reasonably understand that the usual rule—women tee off from the women's tee—was in force. On the issue of offer and acceptance, the court characterized the offer as calling for a unilateral contract, to be accepted by the offeree's performance.

(a) Do you agree with the court that this was a unilateral contract? If so, why is the contract unilateral rather than bilateral? *her performance was the hole in one*

(b) Northland Ford made the offer to all tournament participants by placing the Ford Explorer and poster on the course. The above description of the case suggests that the act of hitting the hole-in-one was the act of performance and acceptance. However, even for a skilled golfer, actually getting a hole-in one is quite fortuitous. Therefore, do you think that it is the act of actually getting a hole-in-one that is the acceptance, or could the acceptance take place earlier? *can't revoke once performance has begun just the act of a hole-in-one*

(c) Say that when Jennifer and her golfing partner arrived at the eighth hole, Jennifer said "I feel really lucky today. I bet that I'll hit a hole-in-one here." Her partner replied, "I bet you $100 that you won't." Jennifer answered, "You're on." Assuming that a wager is legally enforceable in the state, is this a unilateral or bilateral contract? *accept by promise bilateral - acceptance and then future promise to pay the $100*

2. Performance as an Exclusive or Permissive Method of Acceptance

In the examples and cases discussed so far, it seemed relatively clear that the offeror required the offeree to accept by rendering the contract performance; that is, the performance was the exclusive mode of acceptance. However, in many situations the offer is not that clear. Acceptance by performance seems to be both possible and desired, but it is not necessarily the exclusive manner of acceptance. The offer could be interpreted to permit acceptance either by per-formance or by a signification of assent that would create a promise. As mentioned in Section F.1, the general approach to such situations is that unless the offer clearly requires acceptance to be only by performance, it can be accepted either by performance or promise. (Conversely, unless the offer clearly requires acceptance only by promise, it can be accepted by either promise or performance.) This is in accord with the broader principle that unless a method of acceptance is unambiguously prescribed as exclusive, the offeree may accept by any method that is consistent with the terms of the offer and is reasonable.

*[handwritten margin note: * offer must expressly say that performance is the only way]*

[handwritten note: terms & reasonable]

▇ PROBLEM 5.11

On August 15, the offeror writes a letter to the offeree stating, "I have decided to sell my first edition of *David Copperfield*. As you have expressed interest in buying it, I offer to sell it to you for $500,000. I will deliver the book to you on Friday, September 1. If you would like the book, you must deliver a cashier's check for $500,000 to me in person by August 25."

The offeree receives the letter on August 17. She immediately writes back saying, "I received your offer today. I accept. I will bring the cashier's check to you as requested on August 25."

The offeror received this response in the mail on August 19. He has changed his mind about selling the book and would like to withdraw his offer. Is it too late to revoke?

[handwritten note: yes no expression saying the check is the only way to accept]

3. Shipment as Acceptance of an Offer to Buy Goods

[handwritten margin note: language must be unambiguous]

UCC 2-206(1)(a), quoted in Section A, makes it clear that unless the language or circumstances otherwise unambiguously indicate, an offer is to be construed as inviting acceptance in any reasonable manner and medium. Performance, in the form of shipment of the goods ordered in the offer, is therefore usually an effective form of acceptance. UCC 2-206(1)(b) deals with this situation:

[handwritten note: shipment is an effective form of acceptance]

UCC 2-206(1)(b). OFFER AND ACCEPTANCE IN FORMATION OF CONTRACT

(1) Unless otherwise unambiguously indicated by the language or circumstances

...(b) an order or other offer to buy goods for prompt or current shipment shall be construed as inviting acceptance either by a prompt promise to ship or by the prompt or current shipment of conforming or non-conforming goods, but such a shipment of non-conforming goods does not constitute an acceptance if the seller seasonably notifies the buyer that the shipment is offered only as an accommodation to the buyer.

[handwritten margin note: nonconforming goods is not an acceptance only if the seller tells the buyer that the shipment is to serve as an accommodation]

■ PROBLEM 5.12

(a) Charlotte Anne's Chemical Concoctions, Inc., manufactures pharmaceutical products. Al Chemist owns a pharmacy. After consulting Charlotte Anne's price list, Al sent Charlotte Anne a fax on May 1 stating, "I would like to order 1,000 carbolic smoke balls at $5 per ball, as per your price list. Please confirm that you have the balls at that price and can deliver within 10 days." On May 3 Charlotte Anne mailed a letter to Al stating, "Thanks for your order. The smoke balls will be shipped immediately." The letter was received by Al on May 6. In the interim, on May 4, Al, assuming that Charlotte Anne had ignored his fax, bought the balls elsewhere. Does he have a contract with Charlotte Anne? *[handwritten: no, it was not an offer so shipment is not acceptance]*

[handwritten margin note: we don't know that delivery made it in 10 days ★most courts would find a contract here]

(b) The fax sent by Al is the same as in (a). On receiving the fax on May 1, Charlotte Anne immediately shipped the smoke balls to Al with a bill for $5,000. On May 2, before the shipment arrived, Al sent another fax to Charlotte Anne stating, "I no longer need smoke balls. Disregard my fax of yesterday." Do the parties have a contract? *[handwritten: yes]* *[handwritten: was still no offer]*

(c) The fax sent by Al on May 1 did not read as stated in question (a). It said instead, "I wish to buy 1,000 carbolic smoke balls at $5 per ball, as per your price list. Please ship immediately. Payment terms: 30 days." Charlotte Anne shipped the order on May 2. However, the company mistakenly sent 1,000 carbolic smoke suppositories instead of smoke balls.[12] When the suppositories arrived at Al's warehouse on May 3, Al rejected them as not in conformity with the contract. Al then purchased smoke balls from another manufacturer at $7 each and claimed the excess price of the substitutes from Charlotte Anne as damages for breach of contract. Charlotte Anne contends that Al has no claim for damages because no contract was ever made; that the company's shipment of the wrong goods was a counteroffer, which Al never accepted. Is this a good argument?

[handwritten margin note: there's a contract that's been accepted by shipping nonconforming goods]

[handwritten margin note: its a nonconforming good]

---

[12] In *Leonard v. PepsiCo*, Judge Wood was kind enough to explain the manner in which a smoke ball is administered. As to this item, you will have to rely on your imagination.

> (d) Would your answer to question (c) be different if the shipment of the suppositories was not an error, but deliberate: On receiving the order, Charlotte Anne had no smoke balls in stock. The company therefore shipped the suppositories with a note that read, "We do not have the smoke balls in stock at present, so we are sending you the suppositories instead. They are the same price and work just as well."

?

4. Communication of Acceptance by Performance

communication of offer takes place, or performance of a unilateral contract

Where the offeree accepts by promise, we have seen that the acceptance only becomes effective once the prescribed act of communication to the offeror takes place. However, the acceptance of a unilateral contract is accomplished immediately on performance. If performance is of a kind that is rendered directly to the offeror in his presence, he will, as a matter of course, receive communication of the acceptance as it takes place. However, where, as in *Carlill*, the performance takes place outside the offeror's presence, he may not know that the offer has been accepted unless he is told. Must the offeree do anything to notify the offeror of the acceptance? *↳ may not know of acceptance until told*

no need for Carlill to notify of acceptance by performance

After finding that the offer could be accepted by performance, the court in *Carlill* addressed the question of whether Mrs. Carlill had the obligation to notify Carbolic Smoke Ball Co. of the fact that she had accepted its offer by using the ball. The court concluded that, given the tone of the advertisement and the nature of the transaction, the best view was that the offeror had implicitly dispensed with the need for notification. Even if it had not, notification need not be given before or at the time of acceptance; it could be given some time afterwards, provided that the offeror had not revoked the offer in the interim. *↳ as long as it hasn't been revoked*

notice of acceptance is not normally required

unless ① requested ② reasonable time has passed to deem it lapsed

Both UCC 2-206(2) and Restatement, Second §54 deal with the offeree's obligation to notify the offeror of an acceptance by performance. UCC 2-206 states, "Where the beginning of a requested performance is a reasonable mode of acceptance an offeror who is not notified of acceptance within a reasonable time may treat the offer as having lapsed before acceptance." Restatement, Second §54 has an equivalent rule. It provides that notice is not generally necessary to make an acceptance by performance effective unless the offer requests notification. However, if an offeree has reason to know that the offeror has no adequate, reasonably prompt, and reliable means of learning of the performance, the offeree has the duty to exercise reasonable diligence to notify the offeror of acceptance. Unless the offeror in fact learns of the performance within a reasonable time or has dispensed with notice, failure to notify the offeror discharges the offeror's contractual duty.

5. Acceptance of an Offer by an Act That Cannot Be Accomplished Instantaneously

In many of the cases we have looked at so far, the act of performance—the payment of cash, the opening of an envelope, or the furnishing of information— could be accomplished instantly. However, some performances take a period of time to complete. Such a performance can be the subject of a unilateral contract, but because performance will take some time to complete, Restatement, Second §§45 and 62 protect the offeree from the risk that the offeror will revoke the offer after performance has begun but before it is complete. Section 45 applies where the offer requires performance as the exclusive mode of acceptance (that is, it mandates a unilateral contract), and §62 applies where the offer permits acceptance either by promise or performance.

acceptance of performance can take time
* protected from revokation once performance has started

RESTATEMENT, SECOND §45. OPTION CONTRACT CREATED BY PART PERFORMANCE OR TENDER

* option contract is made
– conditional on completion
or
– tender of performance by the terms
* no promissory option

(1) Where an offer invites an offeree to accept by rendering a performance and does not invite a promissory acceptance, an option contract is created when the offeree tenders[13] or begins the invited performance or tenders a beginning of it.

(2) The offeror's duty of performance under any option contract so created is conditional on completion or tender of the invited performance in accordance with the terms of the offer.

Note that the language of Restatement, Second §45 specifically covers only the situation where the offer "... invites an offeree to accept by rendering a performance and does not invite a promissory acceptance." That is, it applies only where the offer prescribes acceptance by performance as the exclusive mode of acceptance, and the offer does not permit promissory acceptance as an alternative. As noted earlier, the law usually assumes that the offeror is indifferent to the mode of acceptance unless the language of the offer, in context, clearly indicates that the method of acceptance is exclusive. Where the offer is not clearly intended to prescribe performance as the exclusive mode of acceptance but may be accepted either by performance or by a promise, Restatement, Second §62 applies rather than §45:

---

[13] An offeree tenders performance when he demonstrates that he is willing, ready, and able to perform. This means that where the offeree's performance requires the cooperation of the offeror, an option is created as soon as the offeree tenders performance, even if the offeror does not provide the cooperation necessary for performance to begin. —Eds.

RESTATEMENT, SECOND §62. EFFECT OF PERFORMANCE BY OFFEREE WHERE OFFER INVITES EITHER PERFORMANCE OR PROMISE

acceptance by performance

(1) Where an offer invites an offeree to choose between acceptance by promise and acceptance by performance, the tender or beginning of the invited performance or a tender of a beginning of it is an acceptance by performance.

(2) Such an acceptance operates as a promise to render complete performance.

———————

The next problem focuses on the different results that may follow depending on which analysis applies.

■ PROBLEM 5.13

On August 1, Webster D. Ziner, a designer of web pages, was consulted by Paul O. Alto, who wished to have a website designed for his new high-tech business. During the meeting, the parties worked out specifications for what was needed for the site and what Webster's fee would be. Webster indicated that the design work would take one month. The parties agreed that Paul would think further about the proposed project and would let Webster know if he wanted to go ahead with it. Webster made it clear that he did not make an offer at this stage and Paul concedes this.

On August 5, Paul sent an e-mail to Webster offering him the work on the terms discussed. The e-mail made no specific mention of a mode of acceptance but simply ended by stating, "Begin as soon as you can. I expect the completed work in about a month." On August 6 Webster began work. On August 8 he received an offer of a more lucrative project. Will he be in breach of contract if he decides to scrap the project for Paul?

contract accepted

G THE OFFER AND ACCEPTANCE MODEL IN PERSPECTIVE

The concept that contracts are formed through offer and acceptance is long-established. This model of contract formation conceives of a process in which the parties exchange a series of communications, either by correspondence or in a face-to-face interaction, in the hope of ultimately creating a contract. There can be as few as two communications—just an offer and an acceptance, or there can be several—for example, a solicitation that elicits an offer, responded to by a counteroffer, which is ultimately accepted. Although the model provides a handy framework for analyzing contract formation, it is just a model and does not necessarily represent what actually happens in every real-life situation.

Sometimes it is very difficult to unravel the interactions between the parties to identify exactly when an offer was created and which party made it. For example, where the parties reach an agreement during the course of a meeting at which they negotiate, each may have made proposals, counterproposals, and concessions relating to different aspects of their relationship until they achieved a final consensus. In other situations, for example, where the contract is executed in a rather mechanical way by one party signifying assent to standard terms proffered by the other, the idea of proposals dickered back and forth seems almost quaint. Nevertheless, the offer and acceptance model does provide a framework for analyzing formation issues.

Offer and acceptance issues do not arise in every contract dispute. They are most likely to be relevant in two situations, both of which are illustrated by the cases in this chapter. The first is where the parties dispute whether a contract has been formed at all. The second involves cases where the parties may agree that a contract was formed (or the court resolves the dispute on formation in favor of finding a contract), but the parties disagree on its terms. The question of what the offer was and what the acceptance was could be crucial to deciding if the ultimate contract terms were those proposed by one party or the other. If neither of these questions are in issue (that is, neither party disputes the existence of the contract or its content), it likely will not matter which party was the offeror and which the offeree or when exactly the contract came into being.[14]

ACCEPTANCE UNDER THE UNIDROIT PRINCIPLES AND THE CISG

The principles of contract formation that are set out in Chapter 2 of the UNI-DROIT Principles recognize that a contract is formed by the process of offer and acceptance. The approach to offer and acceptance is broad yet sparse. For example, the Principles have no detailed rules on what constitutes an acceptance, but just provide in general terms that an acceptance is a statement or other conduct indicating assent to the offer. Silence or inaction does not in itself constitute an acceptance. The acceptance must be made within the time fixed

---

[14] There is a third situation in which it may be crucial to decide who made the offer and who accepted it, but this situation is beyond the scope of this book and is just mentioned briefly here: The law of the jurisdiction in which the contract was created usually governs the transaction. A contract is created at the place where the offer is accepted. Therefore, where the parties are located in different states and the law of those states concerning the matter in dispute is different, the question of what constituted acceptance may determine which law applies. The choice of law could have a significant impact on the result of the case.

by the offeror, or if no time is specified, within a reasonable time. Communications, including the acceptance and any revocation, become effective only when they reach the recipient; that is, the mailbox rule does not apply.

Contract formation is dealt with in Articles 14 to 24 of the CISG, which take very much the same approach as, and use language similar to, the UNIDROIT Principles. The CISG also does not follow the mailbox rule but treats communications as effective only when received. The offeree assents to the offer by a statement or conduct indicating assent, not by silence or inaction. A reply to the offer that contains additions or other material changes to the offer is not an acceptance but a counteroffer.

Conflicting Standard Terms, the Battle of the Forms, and Late Notice of Standard Terms

 A ## THE COMMON LAW APPROACH TO CONFLICTING STANDARD TERMS

As we discuss in previous chapters, the use of standard forms is commonplace in contemporary contractual relationships. Up to now, we have focused largely on situations in which one of the parties has presented standard terms, and the question is whether the other party is bound by them. However, it may happen that both parties use standard terms, which are contained in their communications with each other. Because each of the parties has drafted its standard terms to serve its own interests, it could happen that there is a conflict between the standard terms. If the parties are not paying attention to these terms, they may not notice the conflict at the time of entering the transaction. When they later discover it, they may find that the conflict in the standard terms results in the failure of contract formation, or, if a contract was formed, in a dispute over whose terms became part of the contract. In this section we describe how the common law approaches this problem. In Section B we examine the very different approach to the problem adopted by UCC Article 2.

The following example illustrates a situation in which there is a conflict between standard terms in forms used by parties in seeking to enter a contract, and it explains the common law approach to such a conflict. Bricks & Mortar, Inc. (B&M) owns and operates several office buildings. It does not employ its own property maintenance staff but instead enters into contracts with specialist firms to perform these services on its properties. When B&M orders these services, it sends a form headed "Purchase Order" to the firm whose services it seeks to use. This purchase order is B&M's offer to the service firm, and it is the standard form used by B&M for all transactions of this kind. It has blanks in which B&M fills out the details of this particular transaction, such as the name and address of the service company, the description of the services to be performed, the price, and the payment terms. The form also has preprinted "boilerplate" terms—standard terms that B&M's attorney has drafted in advance and which B&M desires to have applicable in every transaction. For example, B&M wishes to ensure that the service provider accepts liability for and indemnifies B&M for any loss or damage caused by the service provider's employees to the person or property of third parties. It therefore includes a standard term in the purchase order that states as much.

On the occasion in issue in this example, B&M sends a purchase order to Leaf Disposal Services, Inc. (LD) in which B&M offers to employ LD to remove fallen leaves from its property during the months of November and December. Upon receiving the purchase order, LD just looks at the terms that B&M filled out and pays no attention to the preprinted terms. (Commonly, the filled-in terms are the only terms that really interest the offeree, who is focusing on getting the work and does not have the time or resources to examine the printed terms in the purchase order or the desire to risk losing business by haggling over those terms.) LD determines that it is able to perform the requested service for the price stated and decides to accept B&M's offer. LD has its own standard form that it uses to signify acceptance of offers of work. The form, headed "Order Acknowledgment," was drafted by its attorneys. It has a blank space in which LD inserts the particulars of the job, and it also includes standard preprinted terms that are designed to serve LD's interests. One of the printed terms states that LD assumes no liability for loss or damage caused by its employees to third parties, and that B&M indemnifies LD against any such claims. LD fills out the blank space, describing the services, price, and payment arrangements exactly in accordance with B&M's purchase order, and returns the acknowledgment to B&M. Like LD, B&M has no time or inclination to read boilerplate, so it pays no attention to the standard printed terms in the acknowledgment. Because neither party has reviewed and compared the standard language in the forms, they do not notice the conflict and assume that they have a contract.

Under traditional common law rules, LD has not accepted the offer. Traditional common law requires the acceptance to be a "mirror image" of the offer, and a response with a term different from the offer is not an acceptance; it is a rejection and counteroffer. As a result, no contract resulted from the exchange of the forms. Even though the conflict between offer and acceptance is in the boilerplate, the boilerplate is nevertheless objectively intended to be part of the proposed contract, and the purported acceptance varies the terms of the offer. (We say "traditional" here to remind you that a modern court may not apply the "mirror image" rule with great rigidity, so a response with terms at variance with the offer could be an acceptance as long as the variation is not significant. However, if the terms in the offeree's response depart in any significant way from those of the offer, the response does not qualify as an acceptance.)

The result of treating LD's response as a counteroffer depends on whether or not LD begins to perform after the exchange of the forms. If LD fails to perform, its counteroffer constituted a rejection of B&M's offer, and B&M never accepted the counteroffer, so no contract was formed. B&M would therefore have no recourse against LD for failing to perform. However, if LD did begin to perform and B&M accepted that performance, B&M's acquiescence in that performance would be treated as an acceptance of LD's counteroffer by conduct. This means that a contract does exist, but it is on LD's terms, so that if LD's employees cause injury or damage to a third party, its disclaimer of liability and indemnity provision would govern. This is called the "last shot" rule because it has the effect of giving precedence to the terms in the last communication before performance began. As we discuss in Section B, the drafters of Article 2 considered the common law approach to be unsound, so they devised a different treatment of conflicting forms in UCC 2-207.

B THE BATTLE OF THE FORMS—UCC 2-207

1. The Rationale and Aim of UCC 2-207

As part of the nontechnical approach to offer and acceptance, the drafters of the UCC sought to reform the law's treatment of contract formation where one or both parties use standard forms to communicate the offer and acceptance or to confirm an oral or informal agreement. The result of this effort is UCC 2-207. Although it is not, by its language, restricted to formation issues involving standard forms, it is most commonly associated with transactions of that kind.

Although UCC 2-207 could apply when only one party uses standard terms, it contemplates that in many commercial transactions between businesses, both parties have drafted standard terms which they exchange at the time of contract formation. Because the standard terms used by each party are likely drafted to protect its own interests, there is a strong possibility of conflict between the forms. UCC 2-207 is meant to provide a means of resolving such conflicts, hence its nickname, "battle of the forms."

The typical situation contemplated by UCC 2-207 is similar to that described in the example in Section A. In summary (to place the example in the context of a sale of goods): The buyer wishes to buy goods from the seller. It orders the goods (that is, it makes an offer to buy the goods) by sending its standard-form purchase order to the seller, which has blanks for the details of this particular transaction as well as preprinted boilerplate terms. For example, if the buyer wishes to ensure that it gets a warranty whenever it buys goods, it might include in its purchase order preprinted wording that reads, "The seller warrants that all goods purchased under this order are free of defects. Defective goods may be returned to the seller for a full refund within 90 days of delivery."

Upon receiving the purchase order, the seller (without reading the buyer's boilerplate) sends back its acknowledgement form with the intention of accepting the buyer's offer. The seller's response accords with the buyer's purchase order with regard to the transaction-specific terms such as the description of the goods, price, and delivery terms, but it also contains the seller's preprinted terms. One of these terms states, that the goods are sold "as is," and expressly disclaims any warranty on the seller's part. The seller sends this order acknowledgment to the buyer, intending it to be an acceptance. The buyer, like the seller, does not pay attention to the standard terms in the communication received. Because neither party has reviewed and compared the standard language in the forms, they think that they have a contract. As noted in Section A, the result of this exchange of forms at common law would depend on whether there had been performance after the seller sent its form to the buyer. If not, the seller's response would be an unaccepted counteroffer, so no contract would have been created. If so, the buyer's acquiescence in the seller's performance would be treated as assent to the counteroffer by conduct, so the resulting contract would be on the seller's terms.

Common law

The drafters of the UCC considered these results to be irrational where inadvertent dissonance between the offer and acceptance arises simply because the parties were using standard forms designed to favor their own interests and were not actively negotiating over or even reading these terms. The drafters therefore created UCC 2-207 to provide for a different approach to these situations. In doing so, they avoided the effects of the "mirror image" and "last shot" rules of common law in standard-form contracting.

Although UCC 2-207 has overcome the "mirror image" and "last shot" rules, it is poorly drafted. As you will see below, it is confusing and difficult to read. Not surprisingly, it has generated problems of interpretation and application.[1] We begin by setting out UCC 2-207 and explaining its structure and component parts.

2. The Structure and Operation of UCC 2-207

UCC 2-207. ADDITIONAL TERMS IN ACCEPTANCE OR CONFIRMATION

definite & seasonal in a reasonable time even if terms are different

(1) A definite and seasonable expression of acceptance or a written confirmation which is sent within a reasonable time operates as an acceptance even though it states terms additional to or different from those offered or

---

[1] In our introduction of Article 2 in Chapter 2, we mentioned that ALI and NCCUSL (ULC) developed a revised version of Article 2 in 2003. The proposed revision ultimately failed because states were not willing to adopt it. Nevertheless, it is interesting to note that the 2003 proposed revision of Article 2 recognized and sought to address the difficulties in UCC 2-207 by streamlining it and making it more coherent. Because the effort to redraft UCC 2-207 failed, we are stuck with the clumsy original drafting.

agreed upon, unless acceptance is expressly made conditional on assent to the additional or different terms.

(2) The additional terms are to be construed as proposals for addition to the contract. Between merchants such terms become part of the contract unless:

(a) the offer expressly limits acceptance to the terms of the offer;

(b) they materially alter it; or

(c) notification of objection to them has already been given or is given within a reasonable time after notice of them is received.

objection must be within a reasonable time

(3) Conduct by both parties which recognizes the existence of a contract is sufficient to establish a contract for sale although the writings of the parties do not otherwise establish a contract. In such case the terms of the particular contract consist of those terms on which the writings of the parties agree, together with any supplementary terms incorporated under any other provisions of this Act.

a. Acceptance Under UCC 2-207

→ rejects mirror image

UCC 2-207(1) rejects the "mirror image" rule by stating that a response to an offer containing different or additional terms could qualify as an acceptance, provided that it can reasonably be interpreted as showing intent to accept. To be an acceptance, it must express the intent to accept in definite terms and must accord with the transaction-specific terms in the offer. It must also be communicated "seasonably"—within the time stated for acceptance, or if no time is specified, within a reasonable time. If the response does not constitute a definite or seasonable expression of acceptance, no contract is created by the exchange of these two forms.

must show express intent to accept

UCC 2-207(1) contains language that has led to much confusion and difficulty in relation to the question of whether a response is an acceptance. UCC 2-207(1) provides that a response with additional or different terms is not to be treated as an acceptance if "acceptance is expressly made conditional on assent to the additional or different terms." If the response expressly makes acceptance of the offer conditional on assent to the additional or different terms in the response, the response is not an acceptance. Therefore, no contract is created by the exchange of these two forms. For a contract to arise, the offeror must expressly accept the terms of the response, or there must be some further action by the parties that clearly shows that they did in fact form a contract.

The purpose of this provision is to enable an offeree to use specific language in its response to make sure that the response will not be treated as an acceptance. The problem with the provision is that it applies even where the "expressly conditional" language is set out in a standard preprinted term in the response. As a result, the existence of boilerplate language in the offeree's form could preclude the formation of a contract even though the form on its face appears to be a definite and seasonable expression of acceptance. This result is ironic, since the whole purpose of UCC 2-207 is to underplay the impact of boilerplate terms.

As long as the response is treated as an acceptance, even though it does not match the offer exactly because it contains terms additional to or different from those in the offer, the exchange of forms does create a contract. The question of what happens to those terms must then be resolved. This question is dealt with in UCC 2-207(2), discussed in Section B.2.c.

b. Acceptance Distinguished from Confirmation in UCC 2-207

UCC 2-207(1) has a second drafting inelegancy. It clumsily combines two different situations by referring to both an expression of acceptance and a written confirmation following the formation of a contract. Where the court is dealing with a response to an offer, it is concerned with whether the response is an acceptance at all and, if so, whether any different or additional terms in the acceptance become part of the contract. However, where the parties have already made a contract orally or informally and one or both of them send a written confirmation, there is no issue of whether a contract was formed. The sole question is whether any terms in the confirmation, different from or additional to those initially agreed on, become part of the contract. The poor drafting of UCC 2-207(1) obscures this distinction. The best way to deal with the reference to a written confirmation in UCC 2-207(1) is to recognize that this reference does not really belong in that subsection at all: The purpose of UCC 2-207(1) is to determine whether a contract has been formed, and in a situation where a party is sending a confirmation, this question has already been answered. Therefore, whether we are dealing with a response that has been determined to be an acceptance with additional terms, or with a confirmation, we have passed the initial question of whether a contract exists and have reached the second stage of the inquiry—whether the terms put forward by one of the parties (whether as part of an acceptance or as part of a confirmation) should be included in the contract. This question is addressed in UCC 2-207(2). As you will see, the answer to this question under UCC 2-207(2) is often "no."

c. The Treatment of Additional and Different Terms in an Acceptance Under UCC 2-207(2)

UCC 2-207(2) comes into effect only if the response to the offer qualifies as an acceptance or if the terms are in a confirmation. The subsection treats any additional terms that are contained in the acceptance or confirmation as proposals for addition to the contract.

Note that UCC 2-207(1) refers to both additional and different terms, but UCC 2-207(2) mentions only additional terms and makes no reference to different terms. It has never been completely clear what makes a term different, rather than additional, so this question itself has caused interpretational difficulty. Roughly speaking, a term that merely adds new matter to the offer is additional, but a term that contradicts or alters the terms of the offer is more properly classified as different.

The reason for not mentioning different terms in Subsection (2) is obscure. It is quite possible the omission was simply an oversight, and some courts have treated it as such. Those courts apply Subsection (2) to both additional and different terms. Other courts have taken the omission at its face value and have held that different terms are not covered by Subsection (2). This approach requires the court to come up with some other way to handle different terms, which usually results in discarding them altogether. Apart from this brief mention of the distinction, we largely disregard it and focus on the section's treatment of additional terms.

UCC 2-207(2) is written in deceptively positive terms. It states that as between merchants, the additional terms become part of the contract unless stated conditions are satisfied. However, the positive tone of the subsection is misleading because the conditions will be satisfied in most cases in which the terms have any importance. The general rule, therefore, is that significant additional or different terms contained in an acceptance seldom become part of the contract. As a result, the contract is usually on the terms set out in the offer. (Some courts have not favored the offeror in this way, where the acceptance contains terms that conflict with those in the offer. These courts have adopted the approach that excludes from the contract all terms, both in the offer and the acceptance, that are in conflict. These terms cancel each other out, and the resulting gap is filled by "gap fillers"—statutory default terms supplied by the UCC—or, if the UCC does not have a default term on that issue, by any applicable default rule supplied by common law. This approach to conflicting terms in the offer and acceptance is called the "knockout" rule.)

For a proposed term in an acceptance to become part of the contract, all of four requirements must be satisfied. If any of these are not met, the proposed term falls away. First, the term can become part of the contract under UCC 2-207(2) only if the offer and acceptance are "between merchants." This means that both parties must be merchants, and if either does not qualify for that status, the term does not enter the contract absent express agreement to that term. We introduced the merchant status in Section D of Chapter 2. Recall that UCC 2-104(1) defines a merchant in two different ways. A merchant is either a person who deals in goods of the kind involved in the transaction, or a person who otherwise, by occupation, holds himself out as having knowledge or skill peculiar to the practices or goods involved in the transaction. The Official Comment to UCC 2-104 distinguishes a professional in a field from a casual or inexperienced party, and explains that merchant status might depend on specialized knowledge as to the goods, or to business practices, or both. It contemplates a broad scope of "merchant" for purposes of UCC 2-207 by indicating that even a person who does not deal in goods of the kind could be a merchant if he is in business and buys or sells goods in connection with that business—he likely holds himself out as having "knowledge or skill peculiar to the practices . . . involved in the transaction."

Nevertheless, while the definition of "merchant" is broad enough to cover transactions by businesses that do not routinely buy or sell the particular type of goods involved, the "between merchants" restriction in UCC 2-207 does cut down the application of the subsection so that it does not apply if one of the parties is a consumer or a person who is a casual buyer or seller.

central issue

Even if both parties are merchants, the term does not become part of the contract if it materially alters the contract as set out in the offer. The concept of materiality comes up in several places in this book. In essence, a term is material if it relates to an important aspect of the transaction; that is, the term is central to the contract and is one of the significant benefits that a party reasonably bargained for in making it. Quite apart from a term's significance to the bargained-for contractual benefit, Official Comments 4 and 5 to UCC 2-207 link materiality to surprise and hardship, suggesting that a term would qualify as material if it is not reasonably expected (is not adequately brought to the attention of a party and departs from standard practices and usage or from a course of dealings between the parties) and would impose a significant burden on the adversely affected party. Materiality is a question of interpretation to be decided in light of the language of the contract and the surrounding circumstances. One should therefore avoid the temptation of jumping to conclusions about whether a term is material. Notwithstanding, there are some terms that are pretty obviously material in most cases, such as the existence of a warranty on goods or the availability of usual remedies for breach. Other terms may be less obviously material, and a more careful examination of the contract in context is needed to decide their importance. The requirement that the term in the acceptance does not materially alter the contract means that an offeree who includes an important additional or different term in his response will not succeed in holding the offeror to that term. This really leaves nothing more than relatively unimportant terms as possibilities for inclusion in the contract.

relates to an important aspect of the transaction

obviously material

Even if the transaction is between merchants and the term is not material, it still will not enter the contract either if the offeror has stated in the offer that acceptance is limited to terms of the offer (which, again, ironically, can be accomplished by a boilerplate term in the offer) or if the offeror gives the offeree notification of objection to the term before or within a reasonable time after notice of the term is received.

As mentioned previously, the general effect of UCC 2-207(2) is to exclude many new terms in an acceptance: If the offeree's response to an offer is treated as an acceptance, his attempt to alter the terms proposed by the offeror in any material way is futile. This means, in essence, that most material aspects of contracts are on the offeror's terms. If both the offeror and the offeree are using standard forms, the result is quite random and really just favors the offeror's boilerplate over the offeree's.

most material elements are in the offeror's terms

d. Conduct Recognizing a Contract Under UCC 2-207(3)

UCC 2-207(3) applies where no contract was formed through the communications exchanged by the parties, but they went ahead and performed anyway. This may occur where, say, the response to the offer is not a definite or seasonable expression of acceptance, or it contains language making acceptance expressly conditional on assent to its additional or different terms. The offeror may not realize that the response is not an acceptance, so he may perform on the assumption that a contract exists on the terms that he offered. If the offeree accepts the performance, it makes no sense to say that the parties did not intend a contract. We are therefore not concerned here with whether a contract was formed. The conduct of the parties makes it clear that a contract was in fact created. However, if a dispute should later arise as to whether a term in one of the party's communications became part of the contract, the court needs to resolve the conflicting communications to decide this question.

At common law, the "last shot" rule would lead to a contract on the offeree's terms. Under the objective test, it would not matter that the offeror was not aware of the new term when she performed. Her performance manifests assent to the offeree's terms; that is, the result of the "last shot" rule is to treat the final communication as a counteroffer accepted by conduct so that the terms in the last communication sent would always end up being the terms of the contract. To avoid this random result, Subsection (3) provides that where the writings do not establish a contract but the parties' subsequent conduct demonstrates that a contract was made, the contract should be based on those terms on which the communications agree. Conflicting terms in the writings are discarded, and any gaps are filled by statutory gap fillers supplied by Article 2.

last shot rule

e. Application of UCC 2-207

Having set out the basic framework and operation of UCC 2-207, we include a couple of cases to illustrate how courts deal with formation questions under the section. The cases are followed by a set of problems to allow you to apply UCC 2-207.

LIVELY v. IJAM, INC.

114 P.3d 487 (2005)
Oklahoma Court of Civil Appeals

GOODMAN, Presiding Judge.

[Lively, an Oklahoma resident, filed a small claims affidavit in Tulsa County District Court on November 8, 2002. . . . Lively, the owner of a small business, was approached by a client who asked him to purchase a computer on its behalf. He found a computer advertised on a website operated by IJAM and an associated company. He did not order it online but called and ordered it by phone. He received the laptop in April 1999. It malfunctioned a short while later, and he returned it to Defendants for repair. Defendants never returned it to him. Lively initiated suit in small claims court in Oklahoma for return of the computer or its value. Defendants sought to dismiss the suit for lack of jurisdiction on the basis that the parties had agreed that Georgia courts would have exclusive jurisdiction over any disputes arising out of the sale. The alleged agreement was contained in a forum selection clause printed on the back of the invoice that accompanied the laptop. The trial court assumed jurisdiction and entered judgment in favor of Lively for the value of the laptop. The issue on appeal is whether the forum selection clause was part of the contract.]

. . . [Defendants] assert the trial court erred when it refused to enforce the forum selection clause contained in the invoice. . . . Lively did not receive the invoice containing the forum selection clause until he received the computer. . . .

Title 12A O.S.2001, §2-204(1) states: "A contract for sale of goods may be made in any manner sufficient to show agreement, including conduct by both parties which recognizes the existence of such a contract." If after a contract is formed, additional terms are proposed by one of the parties, "[t]he additional terms are to be construed as proposals for addition to the contract." 12A O.S.2001, §2-207(2). If both parties to a contract are merchants, §2-207(2) provides that the additional "terms become part of the contract unless: (a) the offer expressly limits acceptance to the terms of the offer; (b) they materially alter it; or (c) notification of objection to them has already been given or is given within a reasonable time after notice of them is received." . . .

In *Old Albany Estates, Ltd. v. Highland Carpet Mills, Inc.*, 1979 OK 144, 604 P.2d 849, the Oklahoma Supreme Court concluded that a contract for the sale of carpet existed prior to the delivery of the carpet or the receipt of an invoice by the buyer. The invoice given to the buyer after the first payment was made contained a warranty disclaimer which required the buyer to submit any claim against the seller within ten days after delivery. The seller asserted that the terms in the invoice were additional terms that became part of the contract because the buyer accepted the carpet. The Oklahoma Supreme Court disagreed, finding that a contract of sale existed prior to the delivery of the carpet or buyer's receipt of the invoice. Citing §2-207, it noted that the disclaimer could not become part of the contract because it materially altered the contract and the buyer never agreed to the alteration. The Court found that the disclaimer did not become a part of the contract by the buyer's mere act of accepting the carpet. The Court stated, "The fact plaintiff accepted the goods has no effect on this conclusion as a contract already existed; acceptance of the carpet was not necessary to create it."

Similarly, we find that a contract of sale existed between Defendants and Lively prior to the receipt of the invoice. Lively had already paid for the computer before it was shipped and a contract existed before Lively opened the box and found the invoice. Therefore, the question presented here is whether the

[handwritten margin note: issue]

[handwritten margin note: lively was not a merchant; additional must be agreed to—keeping the computer is not agreeing]

[handwritten margin note: hard to tell if lively is a merchant]

terms of the invoice, including the forum selection clause, became part of the contract. Any analysis under §2-207(2) must begin with a determination of whether both parties to the contract were merchants. If we assume that Lively is not a merchant, §2-207 requires that we treat the provisions of the invoice as "proposals for addition to the contract." In *Klocek v. Gateway, Inc.*, 104 F. Supp. 2d 1332 (D. Kan. 2000), a federal district court concluded that a purchaser, who was not a merchant, did not accept the "standard terms and conditions" which were included in the package containing the computer that the purchaser purchased from the seller. The court found that, under §2-207, the . . . additional or different terms only became a part of the contract if the buyer expressly agreed to the terms. The court concluded that the buyer did not expressly agree to those terms merely by keeping the computer for a specified time. If we consider Lively to be a consumer and not a merchant, we must reach a similar conclusion. There is no indication that Lively expressly accepted the terms and, therefore, the terms of the invoice did not become part of the contract. The forum selection clause does not apply under these facts.

The provisions of §2-207 may also be applied if Lively was considered to be a merchant. However, because this is a small claims action, the record is sparse, and we cannot definitively determine if Lively qualifies as a merchant. Under 12A O.S.2001, §2-104, a merchant is described as "a person who deals in goods of the kind or otherwise by his occupation holds himself out as having knowledge or skill peculiar to the practices or goods involved in the transaction. . . ." In an affidavit submitted to the trial court, Lively stated, "I am knowledgeable in computers and computer software and, additionally, work as a computer technician for local businesses." In that same affidavit, Lively described how he purchased the laptop for a client.

If we assume that Lively is a merchant, we are compelled to reach the same conclusion—that the terms are not part of the contract—but for different reasons. Under §2-207(2), additional terms become a part of the contract unless, among other reasons, the terms materially alter the contract. Other jurisdictions have concluded that forum selection clauses are material terms to a contract. *See, e.g.* . . . *Hugo Boss Fashions, Inc. v. Sam's European Tailoring, Inc.*, 293 A.D.2d 296, 742 N.Y.S.2d 1 (2002) (finding that invoice containing forum selection clause and waiver of jury [trial] materially altered the parties' oral contract for sale of goods); *Product Components, Inc. v. Regency Door and Hardware, Inc.*, 568 F. Supp. 651 (S.D. Ind. 1983) ("forum selection clauses contained in seller's acknowledgment form and invoice materially altered the parties' contract"). . . .

In *Licitra v. Gateway, Inc.*, 189 Misc. 2d 721, 734 N.Y.S.2d 389 (N.Y. City Civ. Ct. 2001), a New York Court found that the buyer of a personal computer was not bound by an agreement which arrived with the computer. It concluded that the terms of the agreement should not be enforced merely because the buyer chose to retain the computer he purchased from the seller. The Court stated, "It is obviously a 'take or leave it' situation since the terms of the 'Agreement' are not negotiable and no opportunity or procedure is established to amend or question the terms." We agree with the reasoning of these courts and find that a forum selection clause materially altered the contract between Defendants and Lively. Therefore, we find that the forum selection clause was not part of the contract.

holding

In summary, the forum selection clause contained in the invoice does not alter the terms of the contract between Lively and Defendants. Lively is not bound by any terms contained therein. Since jurisdiction over Defendants is not contractually decided, we must determine if jurisdiction can be obtained by personal jurisdiction. . . .

disposition

[The court reverses and remands the case because the trial court had not properly determined that it had personal jurisdiction over Defendants.]

■ QUESTIONS

(1)   The court says that it could not determine definitively from the record if Lively was a merchant, and so provides alternative analyses based on whether he was or was not a merchant. However, the facts do give us clues as to whether he is likely to qualify as a merchant. Based on these clues, would you characterize him as a merchant?   *yes*

(2)   The court concludes, purely on the basis of precedents from other jurisdictions, that the forum selection clause does materially alter the contract. In *Quality Wood Designs, Inc. v. Ex-Factory, Inc.*, 40 F. Supp. 3d 1137, 1149-1150 (D. S. Dak. 2014) the court noted that courts are divided on whether a forum selection clause is a material alteration. The court identified the elements of surprise and hardship, referred to in Official Comments 4 and 5 to UCC 2-207, as factors that influence courts in deciding whether the forum selection clause is a material alteration. Surprise likely would result if the forum selection clause was neither customary nor encountered previously in a course of dealing between the parties. Hardship would be present if litigating in the selected court would not simply be inconvenient, but would be unduly burdensome for the nondrafting party. Based on these considerations, do you agree that the forum selection provision should be treated as material?

surprise v. hardship

POLYTOP CORPORATION v. CHIPSCO, INC.

826 A.2d 945 (2003)
Rhode Island Supreme Court

PER CURIAM.

posture

. . . The plaintiff, Polytop Corporation (plaintiff or Polytop), appeals from a Superior Court order in favor of defendant, Chipsco, Inc. (defendant or Chipsco), granting Chipsco's motion to stay the Superior Court proceedings and directing the parties to proceed to arbitration of this dispute. Polytop is a manufacturer of molded dispensing closures for use on plastic squeeze bottles. Chipsco manufactures and sells injection molds. In January 1999, Chipsco presented to Polytop a quotation for a specific mold; three weeks later Polytop issued a purchase order for that item. The plaintiff ordered a second type of mold in August 1999 based upon an April 1, 1999 quote by defendant. The language contained in Chipsco's quotations and Polytop's responding purchase orders has given rise to this dispute.

Believing that both molds were delivered late and were of poor quality, Polytop brought this action in Superior Court, seeking damages as a result of Chipsco's alleged breach of contract. Chipsco, contending that the contract included an agreement to resolve contract disputes through arbitration, filed a motion to stay the proceedings and to refer the dispute to arbitration. According to Chipsco, each quotation contained an arbitration provision that, upon acceptance by Polytop, was conclusive on the issue of dispute resolution. Contained in Chipsco's quotation, under the heading "Terms and Conditions," was a provision requiring arbitration of all contract disputes. Polytop disagreed that this provision was a part of the contract between the parties because its purchase orders included the following:

> Please enter our order for the following subject to the terms and conditions below and attached hereto and made a part hereof. Any additional or different terms proposed by seller are rejected unless expressly assented to in writing by buyer's authorized agent.[2]

In his decision ordering a stay of the Superior Court proceedings and directing the parties to proceed to arbitration, the hearing justice concluded that the language in Polytop's purchase order that "[a]ny additional or different terms proposed by seller are rejected unless expressly assented to in writing by buyer's authorized agent[,]" applied to any terms or conditions the seller may seek to impose in the future. He concluded that the import of this language is controlled by G.L.1956 §6A-2-207(2) of the Rhode Island Uniform Commercial Code, which, between merchants, allows the additional terms to become part of the contract unless "(a) [t]he offer expressly limits acceptance to the terms of the offer [or] (b) [t]hey materially alter it[.]" Finding that Chipsco's offer did not limit acceptance to its terms nor did Polytop's acceptance materially alter the original terms of the contract, the trial justice concluded that arbitration of contract disputes was in fact agreed upon by the parties. He granted defendant's motion to stay the proceedings and ordered arbitration of this dispute.

On appeal, plaintiff argues that the trial justice erred in finding an agreement to arbitrate. Polytop asserts that it did not agree to arbitration with Chipsco and that its acceptance of Chipsco's offer amounted to a rejection of the arbitration provision in defendant's quotation. The plaintiff contends that, "[n]o one is under a duty to arbitrate unless with clear language he [or she] has

---

[2] Commonly (as illustrated by the example at the beginning of this section), the buyer's purchase order is the offer, and the seller's response is the purported acceptance. However, this case is different: The seller's quotation is the offer, and the buyer's purchase order is the acceptance. —EDS.

agreed to do so," *Bush v. Nationwide Mutual Insurance Co.*, 448 A.2d 782, 784 (R.I. 1982), and, by the general rejection clause in its purchase order, Polytop expressly rejected the arbitration provision and all other contradictory provisions contained in Chipsco's quotation.

[margin handwriting: Polytop expressly rejected arbitration]

The defendant argues that a finding that the parties agreed to submit their disputes to arbitration depends upon the contract that was formed by the exchange of quotations and purchase orders and whether a valid arbitration provision is contained in the contract. The defendant cites §6A-2-207 of the Rhode Island Uniform Commercial Code entitled, "Additional terms in acceptance or confirmation," as the controlling authority in this case. [The court quotes UCC 2-207.] . . .

It is the law in this jurisdiction that a person may waive his or her right to have the courts adjudicate a contract dispute, but "there can be no waiver in the absence of an agreement signifying [his or her] assent." *McCarthy v. Azure*, 22 F.3d 351, 355 (1st Cir. 1994). This Court previously has held that a finding that contracting parties have agreed to substitute arbitration for adjudication must rest on clear contract language as evidence of definite intent to do so. An examination of the documents that comprise the agreement of the parties must demonstrate evidence of mutual assent to arbitration.

[margin handwriting: there must be mutual assent to arbitration]

Under the common law "mirror image" rule, "an invoice from the seller containing terms materially different from those in the buyer's offer would be considered a mere counteroffer," and not an acceptance of the offer or the formation of a contract. *JOM, Inc. v. Adell Plastics, Inc.*, 193 F.3d 47, 53 (1st Cir. 1999) (per curiam). The Uniform Commercial Code, specifically U.C.C. §2-207, restricted application of this "mirror image" rule to certain limited circumstances in which the offer or acceptance was expressly conditioned upon acceptance of additional or different terms.

Before this Court, plaintiff argues that its acceptance of Chipsco's proposal expressly was made conditional by the provision in its purchase order requiring that any additional or different terms proposed by the seller would be rejected unless accepted in writing by its agent. . . . Polytop urges this Court to conclude that by expressly requiring seller's assent to any additional terms to its purchase order, it rejected the arbitration provision set forth in Chipsco's proposal. To support its argument that its acceptance was conditional, plaintiff cites *Commerce & Industry Insurance Co. v. Bayer Corp.*, 433 Mass. 388, 742 N.E.2d 567 (2001). That case presented the unique circumstance in which the defendant, Bayer Corporation (Bayer), sought the enforcement of an arbitration provision contained in the plaintiff's purchase order. The plaintiff, Malden Mills Industries Inc. (Malden Mills), had purchased bulk nylon fiber from Bayer that was alleged to have caused a catastrophic fire at Malden Mills's manufacturing facility. Malden Mills initiated purchase of the material from Bayer by a purchase order that included, on the reverse side, an arbitration provision and language providing that the purchase order represented the entire agreement of the parties notwithstanding any communication from seller and that the document cannot be modified except in writing and signed by plaintiff's representative. The defendant sent Malden Mills an invoice that indicated that Malden Mills's order was accepted but subject to the terms and conditions on the reverse side of Bayer's invoice, including a provision that acceptance of any order by plaintiff "'is expressly conditioned on [Malden Mills's] assent to any additional or conflicting terms contained herein.'" When the defendant sought to enforce the arbitration provision in plaintiff's purchase order, Malden Mills responded that an agreement to arbitrate was never reached by the parties. The Massachusetts Supreme Judicial Court agreed and determined that, pursuant to Mass. Gen. Laws Ann. ch. 106, §2-207(3), a contract arose from the parties' conduct and not in accordance with the provisions of §2-207(1). The Court concluded that Bayer's acceptance of Malden Mills's offer was expressly conditioned on Malden Mills's assent to its additional terms and Malden Mills never communicated its acceptance of any of the terms contained in Bayer's invoices. Further, Malden Mills specifically limited Bayer's acceptance to the terms of its purchase order and expressly provided that the terms contained in its offer could not be modified except in writing signed by an authorized representative. Thus, finding that no agreement was reached by the writings of the parties, the Court looked to the conduct of the parties and concluded a contract was formed under §2-207(3). In such an instance, the terms of the contract are determined exclusively by the language of subsection (3): "those terms on which the writings of the parties agree, together with any supplementary terms incorporated under any other provisions of [title 6A]."

The case before this Court is inapposite to the facts in *Commerce & Industry Insurance Co.* Polytop received an offer from Chipsco that included an arbitration provision and, although Polytop contends that it rejected the arbitration clause by including its own terms and conditions in its acceptance, Polytop failed, in accordance with §6A-2-207(1) to condition its acceptance on Chipsco's assent to the additional or different terms contained in its purchase order. Although Polytop's purchase order indicated that any *additional* terms proposed by the seller would be rejected unless expressly agreed to by the buyer, Polytop's acceptance was unconditional. Further, Polytop's acceptance was silent on the issue of dispute resolution and therefore did not materially alter the terms of the original proposal. *See* §6A-2-207(2)(b). We are of the opinion that by the exchange of quotations and purchase orders between the parties, a contract was formed pursuant to §6A-2-207(1). Polytop's acceptance of Chipsco's quotations, without expressly requiring that Chipsco accept its different or additional terms, amounted to the formation of a contract that included an arbitration provision. The additional or different terms in Polytop's purchase order did not materially alter the agreement and, because the parties are merchants, these terms became part of the contract.

Because we are satisfied that the writings of the parties led to the formation of a contract, we reject plaintiff's contention that the terms of the contract should be controlled by the provisions of §6A-2-207(3). We are satisfied that the writings exchanged by the parties, including Chipsco's quotations and Polytop's purchase orders, resulted in an enforceable contract and that resorting to an examination of the conduct of the parties to determine the existence of a contract and/or its terms is not necessary. Section 6A-2-207(3) is applicable only in situations in which no contract is formed by the exchange of offer and acceptance, clearly not the case before this Court.

disposition [Accordingly, for the reason stated herein, the plaintiff's appeal is denied and dismissed. The judgment is affirmed and the case is remanded to the Superior Court.

■ PROBLEM 6.1

Your client is a major supplier of plumbing parts and supplies. It receives and fills thousands of orders for goods every day through its website and by phone, mail, and e-mail. Its head office is located in Kansas. To avoid the expense and inconvenience of litigating in states all over the country, it wants to make sure that all litigation arising from disputes with its customers takes place in the courts of its home state. It therefore wishes all of its transactions to be subject to an enforceable forum selection clause in which its customers agree to the exclusive jurisdiction of the courts of Kansas. Can it accomplish this? How?

expressly state that filling the order is contingent on acceptance

Apply UCC 2-207 to resolve the following problems in light of the preceding explanatory text and cases.[3] Also consider how the problems would be resolved under common law. (In some of the questions you may not be able to provide a final answer without knowing the Article 2 default rule—the gap filler—that would be applicable. If so, it is enough for you to recognize that the term would have to be supplied by a gap filler, even if you do not know what the gap filler might be.)

■ PROBLEM 6.2

On May 1 Al Chemist, the owner of a pharmacy, sent a purchase order to Charlotte Anne's Chemical Concoctions, Inc., a manufacturer of pharmaceutical products. The purchase order was a printed form that looked as follows. In both Al's and Charlotte Anne's forms as represented

---

[3] As mentioned in Section B.2.c, the reference to different terms in UCC 2-207(1) and its omission from UCC 2-207(2) has caused interpretational difficulty. As a result, treatment of different terms is uncertain and varies from one jurisdiction to another. However, you should disregard this and not worry about it for the sake of resolving the problems. That is, simply treat any variation in the acknowledgment as if it is an additional term.

here, the printed portions are shown in roman type. The underlined italics represent terms written in the blanks in the forms.

PURCHASE ORDER
Al's Apothecary (Prop. Al Chemist) 100 Main St., Hometown, CA

To: *Charlotte Anne's Chemical Concoctions*
        500 Factory Blvd, Industria, PA
Date: *May 1, 2017*

Please supply the following goods, to be delivered to the above address by not later than *May 15, 2017*:
Description and price of goods: *1000 Carbolic Smoke Balls, item 2400 on your price list, at $5 per ball.*
Payment: *30 days after delivery, treated as cash.*

TERMS AND CONDITIONS
1. This order will lapse unless written acceptance is received by not later than five days of its date, as reflected above.
2. The time of delivery is of the essence of this contract.
3. Seller warrants that the goods supplied under this order are free of defects. — *Warranty*

[handwritten: excludes mailbox rule]

Charlotte Anne received the purchase order on May 3. On May 5 it responded by sending back the following form, which was received by Al on May 7: *[handwritten: after 5 days (not reasonable)]*

ACKNOWLEDGMENT
Charlotte Anne's Chemical Concoctions, Inc.,
500 Factory Blvd., Industria, PA

Order received from: *Al's Apothecary, 100 Main St., Hometown, CA*

Thank you for your order which we are pleased to accept as set out below.
Description of order: *1000 Carbolic Smoke Balls, item 2400 on our price list, at $5 per ball.*
Delivery date: *May 17, 2017.*
Payment terms: *C.O.D.*

Did a contract exist after Al received Charlotte Anne's response? *[handwritten: no.]*

[handwritten: Common law → varies delivery & payment (counter offer)]

[handwritten: materially altered the delivery date]

■ PROBLEM 6.3

Change the facts of Problem 6.2 as follows: Charlotte Anne's response was sent to Al on May 3 and received by him on May 4. It read as follows:

ACKNOWLEDGMENT
Charlotte Anne's Chemical Concoctions, Inc.,
500 Factory Blvd., Industria, PA

Order received from: _Al's Apothecary, 100 Main St., Hometown, CA_

Thank you for your order, which we are pleased to accept as set out below.
Description of order: _1000 Carbolic Smoke Balls, item 2400 on our price list, at $5 per ball._
Delivery date: _On or before May 15, 2017._
Payment terms: _Credit confirmed—30 days after delivery._

Terms of Sale.
We warrant that the goods supplied under this order are free of defects.

Note our return policy: Defective goods may be returned for exchange within 60 days of delivery. The Buyer's remedy is limited to the exchange of defective goods. No refunds will be given.

In light of these changed facts, answer the following questions:

(a) On May 12 Charlotte Anne notified Al that it would not deliver the smoke balls. Al bought 1,000 smoke balls from another manufacturer at $7 each and wishes to claim damages from Charlotte Anne. Did a contract come into existence between them? _Yes_

(b) Charlotte Anne did deliver the smoke balls on May 15. Over the next few weeks Al sold 200 smoke balls. By mid-June, 150 had been returned by customers as defective: The opening was blocked so that no powder came out when the ball was squeezed. On June 20 Al demanded that Charlotte Anne take back the defective smoke balls and refund the price, but it refused, claiming that Al had no right to a refund under the contract. Is Charlotte Anne correct? _Yes_

(c) Change the facts of question (b) as follows: Al was not a pharmacist. Instead he operated a dress factory in which he employed 200 workers. He had never bought any medical supplies for his staff before, but his production had been badly affected by a flu epidemic last year. He therefore ordered the balls to supply to his workers and their families to protect them from the flu next winter. He tested them in mid-June and found that 15 of them were defective. He demanded that Charlotte Anne take them back and refund their price, but the company refused. Would your answer be different from that in question (b)? ~~no~~ *yes.*

*not a merchant so new terms
don't get added*

PROBLEM 6.4

Al, the pharmacist, sent the same purchase order as in Problem 6.2 except that it contained the following additional standard term: "This purchase order may be accepted only on the terms set forth above. Any terms in the acceptance at variance with this purchase order will be ineffective and disregarded." Charlotte Anne sent an acknowledgment on May 3, received by Al on May 4. The acknowledgment complied exactly with all the terms Al had written into his purchase order. It had only one standardized term, which read, "Overdue accounts will be charged interest at 12% per annum." Do the parties have a contract? If so, is Charlotte Anne's standard provision part of the contract? *yes — no material alteration & no ~~conditioned~~ acceptance*

yes

PROBLEM 6.5

On May 1 Al Chemist, the owner of a pharmacy, sent an e-mail to Charlotte Anne's Chemical Concoctions, Inc., a manufacturer of pharmaceutical products. The body of the e-mail read as follows:

> Please supply 1,000 carbolic smoke balls, item 2400 on your price list, at $5.00 per ball. Delivery must be made by no later than May 8 (time is of the essence) and payment will be made on delivery.
> This offer will lapse unless accepted by May 5.

On May 2, Charlotte Anne sent an e-mail to Al in response. The body of the e-mail read as follows. (The term that begins with the words "Please note" is a standard term that Charlotte Anne inserts into all its e-mail order acknowledgments.)

> Thank you for your order, which will be shipped on May 5. Please allow 3 to 5 days for delivery.

Please note that any dispute or claim arising out of this sale will be settled by arbitration in accordance with the rules of the American Arbitration Association. Our acceptance of your order is conditional on your agreement to this term. Unless you advise us to the contrary before shipment, we will assume that you have no objection to this term.

(a) Al did not respond to Charlotte Anne's e-mail. Charlotte Anne shipped the goods on May 5, and they arrived on May 7. In the interim, Al had changed his mind about buying smoke balls, and he rejected the shipment. He claims that he is entitled to do so because he had no contract with Charlotte Anne. Is Al's assertion correct?

(b) Al did not respond to Charlotte Anne's e-mail. Charlotte Anne shipped the goods on May 5, and they arrived on May 7. Al accepted and paid for them. A few weeks later, a dispute arose between Al and Charlotte Anne about the quality of the smoke balls. Is Al obliged to arbitrate that dispute?

■ PROBLEM 6.6

On May 1 Al Chemist, the owner of a pharmacy, visited the website of Charlotte Anne's Chemical Concoctions, Inc., a manufacturer of pharmaceutical products. He selected 1,000 carbolic smoke balls priced at $5.00 each, which he placed in his electronic shopping cart. He then hit the "buy now" link on the web page, which brought up an electronic order form. He completed the form by entering all the required information, such as his name, e-mail address, delivery address, and credit card information. He then hit the "submit" link. A few minutes later, the website displayed the message "Thank you for your order which will be shipped immediately. Your confirmation code is GHJK445633."

About 15 minutes later, Al received the following e-mail from Charlotte Anne:

This is an automatically generated message. Do not reply to it. We confirm the following order: 1,000 carbolic smoke balls, price $5,000 for immediate delivery. Please note our dispute resolution policy: Any dispute or claim arising out of this sale will be settled by arbitration in accordance with the rules of the American Arbitration Association.

This was the first mention of dispute resolution or arbitration. Charlotte Anne's website made no reference to it at all. Do the parties have a contract? If so, is the arbitration term part of it?

STANDARD TERMS REVEALED AFTER GOODS OR SERVICES ARE ORDERED: "CASH NOW, TERMS LATER," "SHRINKWRAP" TERMS, AND "ROLLING CONTRACTS"

We introduce standard-form contracts in Chapter 3, where we focus on the "duty to read" standard terms and examine the scope and meaning of the "duty to read" those terms present in various forms, including printed writing, posted notices, packaging, and Internet notices. In the cases that we study in Chapter 3, the standard contract terms were made available to the party at the time of contracting, so the issue was whether the terms were presented in a way that gave the nondrafting party reasonable notice of them. If so, the nondrafting party usually has a "duty to read" the standard terms and is held to her manifested assent to them. However, it does not always happen that the standard terms are presented to the nondrafting party when the goods or services are ordered. Instead, the terms may only be conveyed to the nondrafting party at some later date.

For example, a customer buys a home entertainment system at an electronics store. The transaction at the store's checkout station is simple: The cashier scans the bar code on the box, the price is entered on the cash register, and the customer pays with her credit card and leaves the store with the goods. There is no discussion of any possible standard terms governing the sale, and no document containing such terms is given to the customer. When the customer gets home and opens the box, she finds some literature included with the entertainment system—a (rather skimpy and uninformative) manual, a booklet with pages of unintelligible blabber mandated by the FCC, and a one-page document headed "Standard Terms and Conditions." One of the standard terms is an arbitration provision. (Terms included with a product in sealed packaging are introduced in Chapter 3 and are commonly called "shrinkwrap" terms.) A dispute later arises with regard to the sale. The customer sues, and the seller seeks to dismiss the suit on the grounds that the customer agreed to arbitrate the dispute.

There are several possible ways of approaching the question of whether the customer assented to the arbitration provision. Courts disagree on which approach is appropriate under what circumstances. The results may vary widely, depending on which approach a court applies. Consider, for instance, the following three alternative approaches:

1. A court could find that the customer should reasonably have realized that the sale was subject to standard terms and therefore had a duty to find out what they were at the time of buying the goods. On this approach, the customer is held to the unknown term because she was derelict in her "duty to read."

2. Alternatively, a court could find, as the court found in *Lively v. IJAM*, that terms conveyed to the customer only after the time of purchase are not terms of the contract but are merely postcontractual proposals for different or additional terms. Under both traditional common law doctrine and UCC 2-207, these terms would not enter the contract unless the customer expressly assented to them.

3. Alternatively, a court could find that the postcontractual terms are an amendment to the contract, but that the customer agreed in the original contract to give the other party the power to make unilateral amendments to the contract by giving the customer notice of amendment. This alternative is discussed and rejected on the facts in *Schnabel v. Trilegiant Corporation*, below. It can only work if the original contract does give the party that right of unilateral amendment and the customer has adequate notice of both the original contract terms and the amendment.

Add a fact to the example: The one-page "Standard Terms and Conditions" included in the box containing the entertainment system ends with the following language in bold capitals: "IF YOU DO NOT AGREE TO THESE TERMS AND CONDITIONS, RETURN THIS PRODUCT TO THE PLACE OF PURCHASE WITHIN 30 DAYS OF PURCHASE FOR A FULL REFUND OF THE PRICE." This sentence suggests that maybe the contract was not concluded at the point of purchase but instead is only concluded after the customer has seen the shrinkwrap terms and has kept the goods for 30 days. A contract that is formed in this way over a period of time following the initial (or preliminary) manifestation of agreement is called a "rolling contract." In essence, a court may conclude that the customer's ability to reject the standard terms and return the goods delays contract formation until her right to return the goods has expired. The next case is a landmark in establishing and offering a justification for the rolling contract analysis.

PROCD, INC. v. ZEIDENBERG

86 F.3d 1447 (1996)
United States Court of Appeals, Seventh Circuit

EASTERBROOK, Circuit Judge.

Must buyers of computer software obey the terms of shrinkwrap licenses? The district court held not. . . . [It found that] they are not contracts because the licenses are inside the box rather than printed on the outside. . . . [W]e disagree with the district judge's conclusion. . . . Shrinkwrap licenses are enforceable unless their terms are objectionable on grounds applicable to contracts in general. . . . Because no one argues that the terms of the license at issue here are troublesome, we remand with instructions to enter judgment for the plaintiff.

[ProCD, the plaintiff, developed an electronic database called "Selectphone" that consisted of information compiled from over 3,000 telephone directories. The database included an application program that allowed the user to search the database. The database cost more than $10 million to compile and was expensive to keep current. Businesses could use the data for sophisticated searches for marketing purposes, but members of the general public (consumers) could also use it as a nationwide electronic phone directory. ProCD therefore sold the software both to business customers, who would have full use of the database, and to consumers, who would be restricted to using the database for the limited purpose of a phone book. The program was contained on boxed CD-ROM discs that could be purchased in retail stores. The price ProCD charged for full use of the program was much higher than that for the limited use offered to consumers. The software on the discs contained no technical barrier that would prevent a consumer buyer from using it for the higher-priced business purpose. Instead, ProCD imposed the restriction on the use of the consumer version by granting a limited license to use the program only for non-commercial purposes. Every box containing the consumer product stated that the software was subject to restrictions contained in the license enclosed in the box. The license was printed in a manual included in the box and was also encoded on the CD-ROM disks and appeared on the user's screen every time the software ran.

Matthew Zeidenberg bought the consumer package from a retail store in Madison, Wisconsin, but he ignored the license restriction. He formed a company that resold the information on the Internet for a price lower than that which ProCD charged its business customers. ProCD sued Zeidenberg, seeking an injunction against further dissemination of the data. The trial court refused an injunction on the grounds that the licenses were ineffectual because the license terms did not appear on the outside of the package containing the disks, and the buyer could not be bound by terms that were not disclosed at the time of purchase.]

... Following the district court, we treat the licenses as ordinary contracts accompanying the sale of products, and therefore as governed by the common law of contracts and the Uniform Commercial Code. ... Zeidenberg ... argue[s], and the district court held, that placing the package of software on the shelf is an "offer," which the customer "accepts" by paying the asking price and leaving the store with the goods. In Wisconsin, as elsewhere, a contract includes only the terms on which the parties have agreed. One cannot agree to hidden terms, the judge concluded. So far, so good—but one of the terms to which Zeidenberg agreed by purchasing the software is that the transaction was subject to a license. Zeidenberg's position therefore must be that the printed terms on the outside of a box are the parties' contract—except for printed terms that refer to or incorporate other terms. But why would Wisconsin fetter the parties' choice in this way? Vendors can put the entire terms of a contract on the outside of a box only by using microscopic type, removing other information that buyers might find more useful (such as what the software does, and on which computers it works), or both. The "Read Me" file included with most software, describing system requirements and potential incompatibilities, may be equivalent to ten pages of type; warranties and license restrictions take still more space. Notice on the outside, terms on the inside, and a right to return the software for a refund if the terms are unacceptable (a right that the license expressly extends), may be a means of doing business valuable to buyers and sellers alike. Restatement (2d) of Contracts §211 comment a (1981) ("Standardization of agreements serves many of the same functions as standardization of goods and services; both are essential to a system of mass production and distribution. Scarce and costly time and skill can be devoted to a class of transactions rather than the details of individual transactions."). Doubtless a state could forbid the use of standard contracts in the software business, but we do not think that Wisconsin has done so.

Transactions in which the exchange of money precedes the communication of detailed terms are common. Consider the purchase of insurance. The buyer goes to an agent, who explains the essentials (amount of coverage, number of years) and remits the premium to the home office, which sends back a policy. On the district judge's understanding, the terms of the policy are irrelevant because the insured paid before receiving them. Yet the device of payment, often with a "binder" (so that the insurance takes effect immediately even though the home office reserves the right to withdraw coverage later), in advance of the policy, serves buyers' interests by accelerating effectiveness and reducing transactions costs. Or consider the purchase of an airline ticket. The traveler calls the carrier or an agent, is quoted a price, reserves a seat, pays, and gets a ticket, in that order. The ticket contains elaborate terms, which the traveler can reject by canceling the reservation. To use the ticket is to accept the terms, even terms that in retrospect are disadvantageous. Just so with a ticket to a concert. The back of the ticket states that the patron promises not to record the concert; to attend is to agree. A theater that detects a violation will confiscate the tape and escort the violator to the exit. One could arrange things so that every concertgoer signs this promise before forking over the money, but that cumbersome way of doing things not only would lengthen queues and raise prices but also would scotch the sale of tickets by phone or electronic data service.

Consumer goods work the same way. Someone who wants to buy a radio set visits a store, pays, and walks out with a box. Inside the box is a leaflet containing some terms, the most important of which usually is the warranty, read for the first time in the comfort of home. By Zeidenberg's lights, the warranty in the box is irrelevant; every consumer gets the standard warranty implied by the UCC in the event the contract is silent; yet so far as we are aware no state disregards warranties furnished with consumer products. Drugs come with a list of ingredients on the outside and an elaborate package insert on the inside. The package insert describes drug interactions, contraindications, and other vital information—but, if Zeidenberg is right, the purchaser need not read the package insert, because it is not part of the contract.

Next consider the software industry itself. Only a minority of sales take place over the counter, where there are boxes to peruse. A customer may place an order by phone in response to a line item in a catalog or a review in a magazine. Much software is ordered over the Internet by purchasers who have never seen a box. Increasingly software arrives by wire. There is no box; there is only a stream of electrons, a collection of information that includes data, an application program, instructions, many limitations ("Megapixel 3.14159 cannot be used with BytePusher 2.718"), and the terms of sale. The user purchases a serial number, which activates the software's features. On Zeidenberg's arguments, these unboxed sales are unfettered by terms—so the seller has made a broad warranty and must pay consequential damages for any shortfalls in performance, two "promises" that if taken seriously would drive prices through the ceiling or return transactions to the horse-and-buggy age.

According to the district court, the UCC does not countenance the sequence of money now, terms later. . . . What then does the current version of the UCC have to say? We think that the place to start is §2-204(1): "A contract for sale of goods may be made in any manner sufficient to show agreement, including conduct by both parties which recognizes the existence of such a contract." A vendor, as master of the offer, may invite acceptance by conduct, and may propose limitations on the kind of conduct that constitutes acceptance. A buyer may accept by performing the acts the vendor proposes to treat as acceptance. And that is what happened. ProCD proposed a contract that a buyer would accept by using the software after having an opportunity to read the license at leisure. This Zeidenberg did. He had no choice, because the software splashed the license on the screen and would not let him proceed without indicating acceptance. So although the district judge was right to say that a contract can be, and often is, formed simply by paying the price and walking out of the store, the UCC permits contracts to be formed in other ways. ProCD proposed such a different way, and without protest Zeidenberg agreed. Ours is not a case in which a consumer opens a package to find an insert saying "you owe us an extra $10,000" and the seller files suit to collect. Any buyer finding such a demand can prevent formation of the contract by returning the package, as can any consumer who concludes that the terms of the license make the software worth less than the purchase price. Nothing in the UCC requires a seller to maximize the buyer's net gains.

. . . In the end, the terms of the license are conceptually identical to the contents of the package. Just as no court would dream of saying that Select-Phone (trademark) must contain 3,100 phone books rather than 3,000, or must have data no more than 30 days old, or must sell for $100 rather than $150—although any of these changes would be welcomed by the customer, if all other things were held constant—so, we believe, Wisconsin would not let the buyer pick and choose among terms. Terms of use are no less a part of "the product" than are the size of the database and the speed with which the software compiles listings. Competition among vendors, not judicial revision of a package's contents, is how consumers are protected in a market economy. ProCD has rivals, which may elect to compete by offering superior software, monthly updates, improved terms of use, lower price, or a better compromise among these elements. As we stressed above, adjusting terms in buyers' favor might help Matthew Zeidenberg today (he already has the software) but would lead to a response, such as a higher price, that might make consumers as a whole worse off. . . . [The court reverses the District Court judgment in favor of the buyer and remands with instructions to enter judgment for the seller.]

■ QUESTIONS

(1)   Unlike the Court of Appeals, the trial court did not see this as a "rolling contract." It held that the seller made the offer by placing the goods on the store shelf, which the buyer accepted by taking the goods to the checkout counter and paying for them. If the Court of Appeals had agreed with the trial court's view of when the offer and acceptance occurred, would it have upheld the trial court's disposition of the case?

(2)   Let's say that the shrinkwrap terms did not give the buyer any right to return the goods if he disagreed with the terms. How do you think the court would have resolved the case? How should it have resolved the case?

(3)   As you can see, *ProCD* does not simply involve a technical application of offer and acceptance rules. It has a definite policy rationale and a clear normative basis. What is Judge Easterbrook's philosophy on the law of contracts? What values does he emphasize or de-emphasize? In considering these questions, review the discussion on theoretical perspectives in Chapter 1, Section A.5.

(4)   Although the court treats the contract as a sale of the software from ProCD to Zeidenberg, the facts show that Zeidenberg never dealt directly with ProCD. He bought the software from a retail store. Does that not mean that his contract is with the store and not ProCD? If so, how does ProCD have a contract cause of action against him?

(5)   The court states that the license is governed by the common law of contracts and the UCC, and it cites UCC 2-204 in its analysis. As we note in Chapter 2, the applicability of UCC Article 2 to software licenses is uncertain and controversial. Does the court's holding depend on the application of UCC Article 2, or could it have reached the same result under common law?

ProCD is an influential case but also a controversial one. Many courts have distinguished or disagreed with it. One of the difficult points of distinction is whether to treat shrinkwrap terms as a rolling contract, as *ProCD* did, or, instead, to treat the shrinkwrap terms as mere postcontractual proposals for additional or different terms. That is, to qualify as a rolling contract, the circumstances must indicate that the parties did not intend offer and acceptance to be complete at the time of their initial interaction, so that the offer is made later by the drafter of the standard terms, and acceptance occurs only when the nondrafting party accepts those terms either expressly, or by failure to reject them. However, a situation in which terms are delivered after the initial interaction between the parties could be ambiguous. It could be that a rolling contract was not intended at all, but that a contract was formed by offer and acceptance at the time of that initial interaction. In such a case, there are two possibilities. The first is that although the terms were only delivered after the offer was accepted, they were in fact part of the contract, and the offeree had a duty to acquaint himself with them and should have known about them. The second possibility is that they were not part of the contract at all, so that the postcontractual delivery of the terms was merely a proposal by the offeror to modify the contract.

The court in *ProCD* found that Zeidenberg's right to reject the software after reading the terms delayed offer and acceptance so that the transaction was a rolling contract. However, it could have found, as the trial court did, that a contract was concluded at the time that Zeidenberg bought the software at the retail store. If so, the license restriction might still have been part of the contract if Zeidenberg had reason to know that standard terms existed and he had sufficient notice of them to be bound by them, despite his failure to determine what they were. However, if he did not have a duty to ascertain the pre-existing terms, the license restriction would have been a proposal for additional terms. Because the court treated the transaction as a sale of goods, these additional terms would have been handled under UCC 2-207. Under UCC 2-207(2), the license restriction likely would not have become part of the contract unless Zeidenberg affirmatively assented to it.

Judge Easterbrook's opinion, as we have edited it, makes no reference to UCC 2-207. However, in a passage that we omitted, he does allude to UCC 2-207 and concludes that UCC 2-207 did not apply to the transaction because only one form was used. This rationalization is unconvincing. The real reason why UCC 2-207 would not apply is because the court found a rolling contract, formed by Zeidenberg's acceptance of ProCD's shrinkwrap offer, which included the license restriction. In addition, there is nothing in UCC 2-207 that confines that section to situations in which both parties send competing forms. It is quite possible (and appears clearly contemplated by UCC 2-207(1)) that a single form with additional or different terms could be sent by one of the parties following an oral or informal agreement.

The next case deals with the question of whether the delivery of terms after the initial interaction between the parties might qualify the transaction as a rolling contract, or whether it should be analyzed under UCC 2-207.

DEFONTES v. DELL, INC.

984 A.2d 1061 (2009)
Rhode Island Supreme Court

WILLIAMS, Chief Justice (ret).

This litigation began on May 16, 2003, when Mary E. DeFontes, individually and on behalf of a class of similarly situated persons, brought suit against Dell, alleging that its collection of taxes from them on the purchase of Dell optional service contracts violated the [Rhode Island] Deceptive Trade Practices Act . . . [because the contracts] were not taxable within the State of Rhode Island. . . . Dell is an international computer hardware and software corporation . . . [whose subsidiaries sell] computers via the internet, mail-order catalogs, and other means to individual and business consumers. Dell ships these orders throughout all fifty states from warehouses located in Texas and Tennessee. As part of these purchases, Dell offers consumers an optional service contract for on-site repair of its products. . . . Parties opting to purchase a service contract are charged a "tax," which is either paid to the State of Rhode Island directly or collected by the third-party service provider and then remitted to the state. . . . [Dell] filed a motion to stay proceedings and compel arbitration, citing an arbitration provision within the parties' purported agreements.[4] The defendants argued that the arbitration provision was part of a "Terms and Conditions Agreement," which they contended plaintiffs had accepted by accepting delivery of the goods. Specifically, they averred that plaintiffs had three separate opportunities to review the terms and conditions agreement, to wit, by selecting a hyperlink on the Dell website, by reading the terms that were included in the acknowledgment/invoice that was sent to plaintiffs sometime after they placed their orders, or by reviewing the copy of the terms Dell included in the packaging of its computer products.

The hearing justice . . . found that although plaintiffs had three opportunities to review the terms, none was sufficient to give rise to a contractual obligation. First, he noted that plaintiffs could have reviewed the terms and conditions agreement had they clicked a hyperlink that appeared on Dell's website. The hearing justice found, however, that this link was "inconspicuously located at the bottom of the webpage" and insufficient to place customers on

---

[4] The arbitration clause . . . provided,

> ANY CLAIM, DISPUTE, OR CONTROVERSY (WHETHER IN CONTRACT, TORT, OR OTHERWISE, WHETHER PREEXISTING, PRESENT OR FUTURE, AND INCLUDING STATUTORY, COMMON LAW, INTENTIONAL TORT AND EQUITABLE CLAIMS) AGAINST DELL, its agents, employees, successors, assigns or affiliates . . . arising from or relating to this Agreement, its interpretation, or the breach, termination or validity thereof, the relationships which result from this Agreement (including, to the full extent permitted by applicable law, relationships with third parties who are not signatories to this Agreement), Dell's advertising, or any related purchase SHALL BE RESOLVED EXCLUSIVELY AND FINALLY BY BINDING ARBITRATION ADMINISTERED BY THE NATIONAL ARBITRATION FORUM (NAF) under its Code of Procedure then in effect. . . . The arbitration . . . will be limited solely to the dispute or controversy between Customer and Dell. . . . Any award of the arbitrator(s) shall be final and binding on each of the parties, and may be entered as a judgment in any court of competent jurisdiction.

notice of the terms and conditions. Nevertheless, the hearing justice noted that the terms and conditions agreement also appeared both in the acknowledgment that Dell sent to plaintiffs when they placed their orders and later within the packaging when the computers were delivered. The hearing justice noted that "courts generally recognize that shrinkwrap agreements,[5] paper agreements enclosed within the packaging of an item, are sufficient to put consumers on inquiry notice of the terms and conditions of a transaction." He also observed, however, that shrinkwrap agreements generally contain an express disclaimer that explains to consumers that they can reject the proposed terms and conditions by returning the product. The crucial test, according to the hearing justice, was "whether a reasonable person would have known that return of the product would serve as rejection of those terms." He looked to the introductory language of the terms and conditions agreement, which he quoted as follows:

> *PLEASE READ THIS DOCUMENT CAREFULLY! IT CONTAINS VERY IMPORTANT INFORMATION ABOUT YOUR RIGHTS AND OBLIGATIONS, AS WELL AS LIMITATIONS AND EXCLUSIONS THAT MAY APPLY TO YOU. THIS DOCUMENT CONTAINS A DISPUTE RESOLUTION CLAUSE.*
>
> This Agreement contains the terms and conditions that apply to purchases by Home, Home Office, and Small Business customers from the Dell entity named on the invoice ("Dell"). By accepting delivery of the computer systems, related products, and/or services and support, and/or other products described on that invoice. [*sic*] You ('Customer') agrees [*sic*] to be bound by and accepts [*sic*] these terms and conditions.... These terms and conditions are subject to change without prior written notice at any time, in Dell's sole discretion.

The hearing justice found that this language was insufficient to give a reasonable consumer notice of the method of rejection. He found that defendants' failure to include an express disclaimer meant that they could not prove that plaintiffs "knowingly consent[ed]" to the terms and conditions of the agreement. Accordingly, the hearing justice found that Plaintiffs could not be compelled to enter arbitration.... [The trial court denied the defendant's motion to compel arbitration, and the defendants appealed.]

[The court notes that the Federal Arbitration Act (FAA) is applicable and it requires the enforcement of privately negotiated arbitration agreements unless there are grounds in contract law to refuse to recognize the validity of the agreement.]... We therefore evaluate whether plaintiffs are bound by the terms and conditions agreement by resorting to a careful review of the provisions of the U.C.C. Under U.C.C. §2-204, contracts for the sale of goods may be formed "in any manner sufficient to show agreement, including conduct by both parties which recognizes the existence of such a contract." The U.C.C. creates

---

[5] A "shrinkwrap agreement" refers to the common commercial practice of including additional terms and conditions either on the outside of a package or within it when it is shipped to the consumer. Often these packages are covered in plastic or cellophane which must be breached to open.

the assumption that, unless circumstances unambiguously demonstrate otherwise, the buyer is the offeror and the seller is the offeree. *See Klocek v. Gateway, Inc.*, 104 F. Supp. 2d 1332, 1340 (D. Kan. 2000). [The court also quotes U.C.C. 2-206.] . . .

If contract formation occurred at the moment Dell's sales agents processed the customer's credit card payment and agreed to ship the goods, as plaintiffs argue, then any additional terms would necessarily be treated as "[a]dditional [t]erms in [a]cceptance or [c]onfirmation" under U.C.C. §2-207 or offers to modify the existing contract under U.C.C. §2-209. Yet, the modern trend seems to favor placing the power of acceptance in the hands of the buyer after he or she receives goods containing a standard form statement of additional terms and conditions, provided the buyer retains the power to "accept or return" the product.

The eminent Judge Frank Easterbrook has authored what are widely considered to be the two leading cases on so-called "shrinkwrap" agreements. In *ProCD, Inc. v. Zeidenberg*, 86 F.3d 1447, 1452-53 (7th Cir. 1996), the court challenged the traditional understanding of offer and acceptance in consumer transactions by holding that a buyer of software was bound by an agreement that was included within the packaging and later appeared when the buyer first used the software. The court first held that U.C.C. §2-207 was inapplicable because in cases involving only one form, the "battle-of-the-forms" provision was irrelevant. *ProCD, Inc.*, 86 F.3d at 1452. It then proceeded to evaluate the agreement under U.C.C. §2-204 and reasoned that "[a] vendor, as master of the offer, may invite acceptance by conduct, and may propose limitations on the kind of conduct that constitutes acceptance. A buyer may accept by performing the acts the vendor proposes to treat as acceptance." *ProCD, Inc.*, 86 F.3d at 1452. In *Hill v. Gateway 2000, Inc.*, 105 F.3d 1147, 1148-49 (7th Cir. 1997), the court expanded its earlier holding in *ProCD* beyond transactions involving software where the consumer is prompted to accept or decline the terms when he first uses the program. It determined that when a merchant delivers a product that includes additional terms and conditions, but expressly provides the consumer the right to either accept those terms or return the product for a refund within a reasonable time, a consumer who retains the goods beyond that period may be bound by the contract. *Id.* Judge Easterbrook explained, "Practical considerations support allowing vendors to enclose the full legal terms with their products. Cashiers cannot be expected to read legal documents to customers before ringing up sales. If the staff at the other end of the phone for direct-sales operations such as Gateway's had to read the four-page statement of terms before taking the buyer's credit card number, the droning voice would anesthetize rather than enlighten many potential buyers. Others would hang up in a rage over the waste of their time. And oral recitation would not avoid customers' assertions (whether true or feigned) that the clerk did not read term X to them, or that they did not remember or understand it."

The defendants argue that *ProCD* represents the majority view and we have found considerable support for their contention. . . . Moreover, as plaintiffs' counsel has initiated nationwide litigation, a number of sister jurisdictions have decided more or less the precise issue put before us in defendants' favor. For instance, in *Stenzel v. Dell, Inc.*, 870 A.2d 133 (Me. 2005), the Maine Supreme Judicial Court reviewed a similar terms and conditions agreement sent to Dell customers that included the language,

> By accepting delivery of the computer systems, related products, and/or services and support, and/or other products described on that invoice[, the customer] agrees to be bound by and accepts these terms and conditions. If for any reason Customer is not satisfied with a Dell-branded hardware system, Customer may return the system under the terms and conditions of Dell's Total Satisfaction Return Policy. . . .

The court held that by "accepting delivery of the computers, and then failing to exercise their right to return the computers as provided by the agreement, [the plaintiffs] expressly manifested their assent to be bound by the agreement. . . ."

Courts have not been universal in embracing the reasoning of *ProCD* and its progeny, however. In *Step-Saver Data Systems, Inc. v. Wyse Technology*, 939 F.2d 91, 98 (3d Cir. 1991), the court determined that when parties exchange the shipment of goods for remuneration the existence of a contract is not in doubt; rather, any dispute relates solely to the nature of its terms. After deciding that U.C.C. §2-207 applies to situations in which a party sends a confirmatory document that claims to establish additional terms of the contract, the court held that [the mere act of proceeding with the performance of the contract after receiving the different or additional terms is not sufficient to signify assent to those terms]. . . . The court therefore held that a licensing agreement affixed to the packaging constituted a proposal for additional terms that was not binding unless expressly agreed to by the purchaser; *see also Klocek*, 104 F. Supp. 2d at 1339, 1341 (finding buyer's "act of keeping the computer past five days was not sufficient to demonstrate that plaintiff expressly agreed to the Standard Terms" and criticizing the *Hill* court's summary dismissal of U.C.C. §2-207 by stating "nothing in its language precludes application in a case which involves only one form"); *Licitra v. Gateway, Inc.*, 189 Misc. 2d 721, 734 N.Y.S.2d 389, 396 (N.Y. Civ. Ct. 2001) (construing arbitration clause of a shrinkwrap agreement as a proposal for additional terms under U.C.C. §2-207 because it materially altered the existing agreement).

The Supreme Court of Oklahoma, which has also been drawn into this nationwide class-action suit against defendants, has rejected *Hill*'s reasoning as well. *See Rogers* [*v. Dell Computer Corp.*, 138 P.3d 826 (Okla. 2005)]. Although remanding the case to determine whether the arbitration provision was included in the parties' agreement, it noted,

> The plaintiffs' accepting the computers and not returning them is consistent with a contract being formed at the time that the orders were placed and cannot be construed as acquiescing in the "Terms and Conditions of Sale" document whether

included with the invoice or acknowledgment or with the computer packaging. If the contracts were formed at the time the orders were placed, *see* U.C.C. §2-206(1), the "Terms and Conditions of Sale" document, including the arbitration provision, would be an additional term of the contracts under section 2-207. The arbitration provision would not be part of the contracts but proposals to add it as a term to the contracts.

After reviewing the case law pertaining to so-called "shrinkwrap" agreements, we are satisfied that the *ProCD* line of cases is better reasoned and more consistent with contemporary consumer transactions. It is simply unreasonable to expect a seller to apprise a consumer of every term and condition at the moment he or she makes a purchase. A modern consumer neither expects nor desires to wade through such minutia, particularly when making a purchase over the phone, where full disclosure of the terms would border on the sadistic. Nor do we believe that, after placing a telephone order for a computer, a reasonable consumer would believe that he or she has entered into a fully consummated agreement. Rather, he or she is aware that with delivery comes a multitude of standard terms attendant to nearly every consumer transaction.

We therefore decline to adopt the minority view, as urged by plaintiffs, that a contract is fully formed when a buyer orders a product and the seller accepts payment and either ships or promises to ship. Instead, formation occurs when the consumer accepts the full terms after receiving a reasonable opportunity to refuse them. Yet in adopting the so-called "layered contracting"[6] theory of formation, we reiterate that the burden falls squarely on the seller to show that the buyer has accepted the seller's terms after delivery. Thus, the crucial question in this case is whether defendants reasonably invited acceptance by making clear in the terms and conditions agreement that (1) by accepting defendants' product the consumer was accepting the terms and conditions contained within and (2) the consumer could reject the terms and conditions by returning the product.

On the first question, defendants notified plaintiffs that "[b]y accepting delivery of the computer systems, related products, and/or services and support, and/or other products described on that invoice[,] You ('Customer') agrees to be bound by and accepts those terms and conditions." This language certainly informed plaintiffs that defendants intended to bind them to heretofore undisclosed terms and conditions, but it did not advise them of the period beyond which they will have indicated their assent to those terms. . . . [M]any of the courts that have enforced so-called "approve-or-return" agreements cite language informing the consumer of a specific period after which he or she will have accepted the terms. *See, e.g., Hill,* 105 F.3d at 1148 (terms govern if

---

[6] This phrase is taken from the Supreme Court of Washington and is meant to denote that "while some contracts are formed and their terms fully defined at a single point in time, many transactions involve a rolling or layered process." *M.A. Mortenson Co. v. Timberline Software Corp.,* 140 Wash. 2d 568, 998 P.2d 305, 313 n. 10 (2000) (quoting the Uniform Computer Information Transactions Act §208 cmt. 3 (Approved Official Draft)).

consumer retains beyond thirty days); *Brower*, 676 N.Y.S.2d at 570 ("By keeping your Gateway 2000 computer system beyond thirty (30) days after the date of delivery, you accept the Terms and Conditions.").

The more problematic issue, however, is whether plaintiffs were aware of their power to reject by returning the goods. . . . Many of the cases upholding shrinkwrap agreements cite explicit disclaimers advising consumers of their right to reject the terms. *See, e.g., ProCD, Inc. v. Zeidenberg*, 908 F. Supp. 640, 644 (W.D. Wis. 1996) ("If you do not agree to the terms of this License, promptly return all copies of the software, listings that may have been exported, the discs and the User Guide to the place where you obtained it."); *M.A. Mortenson Co.*, 998 P.2d at 308 ("IF YOU DO NOT AGREE TO THESE TERMS AND CONDITIONS, PROMPTLY RETURN . . . TO THE PLACE OF PURCHASE AND YOUR PURCHASE PRICE WILL BE REFUNDED"). . . . [The court concludes that the language in the contracts relating to rejection was confusing and ambiguous. It did not clearly convey to customers that they had the power to reject the terms and return the goods; nor did it adequately inform them of the method to be used to effect the rejection.] In reviewing the language of the terms and conditions agreement it cannot be said that it was reasonably apparent to the plaintiffs that they could reject the terms simply by returning the goods. We believe that too many inferential steps were required of the plaintiffs and too many of the relevant provisions were left ambiguous. We are not persuaded that a reasonably prudent offeree would understand that by keeping the Dell computer he or she was agreeing to be bound by the terms and conditions agreement and retained, for a specified time, the power to reject the terms by returning the product. . . . [We therefore] hold that the hearing justice properly denied the defendants' motion to compel arbitration on the ground that the plaintiffs did not agree to be bound by the terms and conditions agreement. . . . For the reasons set out above, the judgment of the Superior Court is affirmed. . . .

As Judge Easterbrook pointed out in *ProCD*, the problem of "cash now, terms later" is not confined to sales of goods and can arise in different contexts, such as the purchase of an insurance policy, the terms of which are delivered only after the insurance has been secured, or the purchase of airline or concert tickets that contain terms delivered only when the buyer receives the ticket. These transactions often are not intended to be rolling contracts. Contract formation is intended to occur at the point of sale of the policy or tickets, and the purchaser has no right to cancel the transaction by rejecting it after reading the terms. UCC 2-207 does not apply to these transactions because they are sales of services, not goods. They must therefore be resolved under principles of common law. Where a rolling contract is not intended, there are two possibilities: Either the terms in the policy or ticket were adequately noticed to the buyer at the time of contracting, so he is bound by them even if he did not take the trouble to find out what they were, or they were not adequately brought to his attention, so they should be treated as proposals to modify the contract, which will not become part of the contract unless specifically accepted by the buyer.

The next case and problem explore these alternatives.

SCHNABEL v. TRILEGIANT CORPORATION

697 F.3d 110 (2012)
United States Court of Appeals, Second Circuit

SACK, Circuit Judge.

[This is a class action in which the named plaintiffs claim that Trilegiant engaged in deceptive and unfair trade practices in violation of several state and federal statutes. The issue in this opinion is whether the suit should be dismissed on the grounds that the plaintiffs agreed to arbitrate disputes and waived the right to institute a class action. Trilegiant operates an online program called "Great Fun" that offers goods and services at a discount. The solicitation to join Trilegiant's program appears as a hyperlink on the websites of other retailers, and invites customers to click on the link to receive cash back on their purchases. Next to the link there is a button. On some websites it reads "see details" and on others "learn more." If a customer clicked on this button, Trilegiant's standard terms and conditions would appear. However, the customer only needs to click on the "cash back" hyperlink to enroll in the program and does not need to click on the "see details" or "learn more" button to proceed. Upon clicking on the "cash back" hyperlink, the customer is taken to an enrollment page in which he must enter personal information and create a password. The enrollment page contains a brief general description of some of the terms of the standard contract, including a statement that the first month's membership in the program is free, but that the customer will thereafter be charged a monthly membership fee of $14.99 until such time as he cancels his membership. At the end of this general description, the text states that by entering the personal information and password, and clicking a "yes" button, the purchaser acknowledges that he has read the standard terms and conditions. This brief description does not mention most of the other standard terms, including the arbitration provision, which can be accessed only by clicking on a link on the enrollment page, labeled "terms and conditions." After the customer has enrolled in the program, Trilegiant e-mails him a document headed "Great Fun Membership Terms and Conditions," which contains the standard terms.

The named plaintiffs enrolled in Trilegiant's program by clicking on the "cash back" button on merchants' websites after buying goods from those merchants. Apparently they thought that they were just getting a discount on the current purchase, and did not realize that they were enrolling in a discount program for which they would be paying a monthly membership fee. In fact, they did not even realize that the discount program was operated by a party other than the merchant from whom they had bought the goods. They had no idea of Trilegiant's standard terms because they did not click on any of the links that would have revealed the standard terms to them. They also claimed not to have received or read the subsequent e-mail from Trilegiant. It seems that they were not very attentive to their credit card bills either, because it took them some time to realize that they had been paying the $14.99 monthly membership fee. (One of the plaintiffs did not notice the debits for about two years and three months, and the other for about five months.) None of the named plaintiffs had ever taken advantage of discounts offered by the program, apart from the very first discount at the time of enrollment.

On discovering that they had inadvertently been paying membership fees to Trilegiant for a service that they did not want, they commenced this class action against Trilegiant, alleging that the manner in which it had set up its program, without making it clear that the program was operated by a third party and that monthly membership fees would be charged, was an unfair and deceptive trade practice. Trilegiant filed a motion to dismiss the suit on the grounds that the plaintiffs had consented to its standard terms, which included a provision compelling arbitration and waiving the customer's right to bring a class action.

The district court denied Trilegiant's motion to compel arbitration. It concluded that the parties had never agreed to arbitrate. The district court found that the contract was formed at the moment the plaintiffs entered their information into the online enrollment screen. The contract included the terms that were visible on the enrollment screen—the monthly charge in exchange for savings and the cancellation policy—but not the other standard terms, including the arbitration provision, that would only be revealed by clicking on the "terms and conditions" link.

The court begins its discussion by noting that the Federal Arbitration Act embodies a national policy favoring arbitration, but that the policy is intended to uphold the parties' agreement to arbitrate, not to impose arbitration on a party who did in fact not agree to it. The threshold question in a motion to compel arbitration is therefore whether the parties have in fact agreed to arbitrate, determined by their objective manifestations of intent.]

... Trilegiant ... asserts that the plaintiffs assented to the arbitration provision by enrolling in Great Fun, receiving the e-mailed terms, and then not cancelling their Great Fun memberships during the free trial period. As we explained at length in *Register.com, Inc. v. Verio, Inc.*, 356 F.3d 393 (2d Cir. 2004), the mere acceptance of a benefit—and we assume here that membership in Great Fun, without the use of any of its discounts, is a benefit in itself—may constitute assent, but only where the "offeree makes a decision to take the benefit with knowledge [actual or constructive] of the terms of the offer. ..." *Id.* at 403. As Professor Williston's treatise observes, "one who accepts the benefit of services rendered may be held to have impliedly made a promise to pay for them ... [if] the offeree ... knew or had reason to know that the party performing expected compensation." 2 Richard A. Lord, *Williston on Contracts* §6: 9 (4th ed. 1991).

Therefore, in cases such as this, where the purported assent is largely passive, the contract-formation question will often turn on whether a reasonably prudent offeree would be on notice of the term at issue. In other words, where there is no actual notice of the term, an offeree is still bound by the provision if he or she is on *inquiry* notice of the term and assents to it through the conduct that a reasonable person would understand to constitute assent. Inquiry notice is actual notice of circumstances sufficient to put a prudent man upon inquiry. In making this determination, the clarity and conspicuousness of the term is important. [The named plaintiffs] . . . assert that they were not on actual notice of the arbitration provision, and Trilegiant cannot point to any evidence in the record upon which a jury could rely to conclude otherwise. The questions we must address, then, are whether the plaintiffs were on inquiry notice of the arbitration provision through the e-mails sent after their enrollments and, if so, whether their conduct in enrolling in Great Fun, and then not cancelling their memberships before the free trial period expired, constituted an objective manifestation of their assent to the arbitration provision.

Trilegiant does not dispute (as, of course, it cannot) that the arbitration provision does not appear on the pages that either of the plaintiffs would have first encountered during his enrollment in Great Fun. It argues, however, that the plaintiffs were put on notice of the provision, and thus were in a position to assent to it both through the "terms and conditions" hyperlink on the enrollment form available before enrollment, and through the e-mail sent to each plaintiff after his enrollment. . . .

[The court agrees with the district court that the contract was entered into at the time that the plaintiffs enrolled in the program on the website. The accessibility of the arbitration provision from the link on the enrollment screen might have created a substantial question as to whether the arbitration provision was part of the contract entered into by the parties at that time, because the link to the terms and conditions was clearly apparent on the enrollment screen. It could therefore be argued that a person enrolling in the program had a duty to read the standard terms and would be bound by them, even if he failed to read them. However, Trilegiant failed to raise this argument in the district court and thereby forfeited it on appeal. The sole question on appeal is therefore whether the terms in the e-mail sent to the plaintiffs after enrollment were part of the contract.]

The issue preserved on appeal is . . . whether the plaintiffs were put on inquiry notice of the arbitration provision through the transmission of the terms by e-mail after the initial enrollment and then assented to this provision by failing to cancel their Great Fun memberships after the expiration of the free-trial period. . . . [I]ndeed there are cases—Trilegiant argues that this is one—where terms are effectively added to an agreement at the instance of the offeror subsequent to the establishment of a contractual relationship. The conventional chronology of contract-making has become unsettled over recent years by courts' increased acceptance of this so-called "terms-later" contracting. There are at least two analytical approaches available to Trilegiant to argue that despite the time sequence here and its divergence from the typical offer-with-all-terms-then-acceptance progression, the parties entered into a contract that included the arbitration provision e-mailed to each plaintiff after his enrollment.

First, Trilegiant might contend that the arbitration clause became effective after the plaintiffs received the terms-and-conditions e-mail and then assented to the offer by not cancelling their Great Fun memberships. This conception of the parties' dealing is similar to the theory undergirding conventional shrink-wrap-license cases. In shrinkwrap-license cases, the terms at issue are typically provided inside the packaging of consumer goods. Whether or not there is notice to the consumer on the outside of the packaging that terms await him or her on the inside, courts have found such licenses to become enforceable contracts upon the customer's purchase and receipt of the package and the failure to return the product after reading, or at least having a realistic opportunity to read, the terms and conditions of the contract included with the product. *See Hill v. Gateway 2000, Inc.*, 105 F.3d 1147, 1150 (7th Cir. 1997); *ProCD, Inc. v. Zeidenberg*, 86 F.3d 1447, 1448-49 (7th Cir. 1996). As we explained in *Register.com*, "in the shrinkwrap context, the consumer does not manifest assent to the shrinkwrap terms at the time of purchase; instead, the consumer manifests assent to the terms by later actions." 356 F.3d at 428. In this case the "later actions" would be not the failure to return goods but the failure to cancel the Great Fun membership after receipt of the e-mail.

Alternatively, the plaintiffs' initial enrollment in Great Fun may be seen, as the district court saw it, to be the formation of an agreement for each of them to pay a specified monthly fee in exchange for the membership benefits offered by Great Fun. The arbitration provision and other additional terms contained in the e-mail would then be proposed amendments to that existing contract. According to Trilegiant, the e-mailed terms would have been accepted by the plaintiffs' acts of continued payments of fees on their credit cards and mainte-nance of the opportunity to make use of Great Fun—or, put otherwise, their failure to cancel the service in a timely manner. . . . [Irrespective of which approach is taken, the court concludes that the terms e-mailed later, including the arbitration clause, were in any event never accepted by either plaintiff.]

A person can assent to terms even if he or she does not actually read them, but the offer must nonetheless make clear to a reasonable consumer both that terms are being presented and that they can be adopted through the conduct that the offeror alleges constituted assent. An offeree, regardless of apparent manifestation of his consent, is not bound by inconspicuous contractual provisions of which he is unaware, contained in a document whose contractual nature is not obvious. We do not think that an unsolicited e-mail from an online consumer business puts recipients on inquiry notice of the terms enclosed in that e-mail and those terms' relationship to a service in which the recipients had already enrolled, *and* that a failure to act affirmatively to cancel the membership will, alone, constitute assent.

Courts have recognized that in the modern commercial context, there are reasons to allow parties to contract without consideration of, and the possibility to negotiate, every term. But cases applying the "duty to read" principle to terms delivered after a contracting relationship has been initiated do not nullify the requirement that a consumer be on notice of the existence of a term before he or she can be legally held to have assented to it. "While new commerce on the Internet [and elsewhere] has exposed courts to many new situations, it has not fundamentally changed the principles of contract." *Register.com*, 356 F.3d at 403. What constitutes sufficient inquiry notice of a term not actually read by the offeree depends on various factors including, but not limited to, the conspicuousness of the term, the course of dealing between the parties, and industry practices. Ultimately, however, the touchstone of the analysis is whether reasonable people in the position of the parties would have known about the terms and the conduct that would be required to assent to them. Courts, including this one, have concluded as a matter of law in some circumstances that parties were on inquiry notice of the likely applicability of terms to their contractual relationship even when those terms were delivered after that relationship was initiated. These decisions appear to have in common the fact that in each such case, in light of the history of the parties' dealings with one another, reasonable people in the parties' positions would be on notice of the existence of the additional terms and the type of conduct that would constitute assent to them.

In *Register.com*, we considered whether a website development service provider, Verio, was on "legally enforceable notice" of contractual terms restricting Verio in making certain uses of information supplied by Register.com although the terms were submitted to Verio after it had already downloaded the information from Register.com. *Register.com*, 356 F.3d at 401. We concluded that Verio was on sufficient notice of the terms because it accessed the information "daily" and was repeatedly confronted with the same terms. Thus, even if the terms applying to any given download of information were transmitted *after* that download, because of the course of dealing between Verio and Register.com, there was a basis for "imputing . . . knowledge of the terms on which the [information] was offered" each time the download occurred. *Id.* at 402. . . . It is elementary that in such circumstances, a reasonable browser becomes aware of the existence of additional terms . . . even if he or she is not then familiar with their precise contours. . . .

Similarly in the shrinkwrap cases, when a purchaser opens the packaging for goods and discovers that they are covered by additional provisions, the reasonable purchaser will understand that unless the goods are returned, he or she takes them subject to those provisions. *See Hill*, 105 F.3d at 1150 ("Competent adults are bound by such documents, read or unread."). The late-arriving terms are necessarily included with the product—they are inside the shrinkwrap with the item being transferred. *See, e.g., M.A. Mortenson Co., Inc. v. Timberline Software Corp.*, 140 Wash. 2d 568, 575, 998 P.2d 305, 309 (2000) (noting that even though offeree had not actually read the shrink-wrapped terms, he had actually opened the packaging within which they were enclosed). The purchaser therefore cannot begin using the product until after he or she has been presented with the terms, whether or not the purchaser actually reads them.

The amendment cases cited by Trilegiant illustrate other ways in which parties may be put on notice of terms that arrive after a contract is formed—but all of these cases, too, are rooted, expressly or otherwise, in the reasonable expectations of the parties ... [because the original agreement gives one of the parties the right to make unilateral amendments to the contract after formation.] For example, in many of these cases the amendment is transmitted with a bill or billing statement concerning the offeree's continued use of the service. Even there, whether such notice would be effective in the absence of a statute specifically allowing transmission of new terms after enrollment, or a term in the original contract giving notice of the possibility of amendment, the conveyance of the amendment in such a manner, similar to the sending of the terms of a contract with the product in the shrinkwrap cases, may support a conclusion that a reasonable person would be on actual notice of the amendment's applicability to the contractual relationship.

In the case at bar, the plaintiffs were presented with the arbitration provision in an e-mail delivered to each of them after they had enrolled in Great Fun. Trilegiant asserts that the fact that we can assume that the e-mail was received by the plaintiffs is enough to support the conclusion that they were on inquiry notice of its terms. But that someone has received an e-mail does not without more establish that he or she should know that the terms disclosed in the e-mail relate to a service in which he or she had previously enrolled and that a failure affirmatively to opt out of the service amounts to assent to those terms. In this case unlike, for example, *Register.com,* there was no prior relationship between the parties that would have suggested that terms sent by e-mail after the initial enrollment were to become part of the contract. Nor would a reasonable person likely understand in some other way that disputes arising between him or her and Trilegiant were to be resolved by an alternative dispute resolution procedure. Thus, assuming as Trilegiant asserts that the plaintiffs received the e-mails in question, there was still no basis for imputing to the plaintiffs knowledge of the terms on which Great Fun was offered.

Unlike shrinkwrap agreements, moreover, the recipient of the terms in this case would not have been confronted with the existence of additional terms before being able to benefit from Great Fun. As noted, even if a purchaser of a shrink-wrapped product is not required to read the shrink-wrapped terms or affirmatively to acknowledge their existence before using the product in order to be bound by the terms, at least he or she necessarily learns of the existence of those terms upon opening the packaging—or, as is the case in many of the amendment cases cited by Trilegiant, during the course of maintaining and using the service to which the terms apply. By contrast, the arbitration provision here was both temporally and spatially decoupled from the plaintiffs' enrollment in and use of Great Fun; the term was delivered after initial enrollment and Great Fun members such as the plaintiffs would not be forced to confront the terms while enrolling in or using the service or maintaining their memberships. In this way, the transmission of the arbitration provision lacks a critical element of shrinkwrap contracting—the connection of the terms to the goods (in this case the services) to which they apply.

A reasonable person may understand that terms physically attached to a product may effect a change in the legal relationship between him or her and the offeror when the product is used. But a reasonable person would not be expected to connect an e-mail that the recipient may not actually see until long after enrolling in a service (if ever) with the contractual relationship he or she may have with the service provider, especially where the enrollment required as little effort as it did for the plaintiffs here. In this context the e-mail would not have raised a red flag vivid enough to cause a reasonable person to anticipate the imposition of a legally significant alteration to the terms and conditions of the relationship with Trilegiant.

To be sure, the "duty to read" rule combined with the "standardized form" contract makes it unlikely in many contexts that a consumer will actually read such a agreement beyond a quick scan, if that. But inasmuch as consumers are regularly and frequently confronted with non-negotiable contract terms, particularly when entering into transactions using the Internet, the presentation of these terms at a place and time that the consumer will associate with the initial purchase or enrollment, or the use of, the goods or services from which the recipient benefits at least indicates to the consumer that he or she is taking such goods or employing such services subject to additional terms and conditions that may one day affect him or her. Here, Trilegiant effectively obscured the details of the terms and conditions and the passive manner in which they could be accepted. The solicitation and enrollment pages . . . made joining Great Fun fast and simple and made it appear—falsely—that being a member imposed virtually no burdens on the consumer besides payment. . . .

A requirement that the plaintiffs expressly manifest assent to the arbitration provision together with such assent would likely have overcome the e-mail's defects in providing notice. Yet Trilegiant argues that the plaintiffs agreed to the provision through far more passive conduct—continuing to pay their monthly membership fees, which were automatically charged to the plaintiffs' credit cards, after receipt of the e-mails. It does not follow, however, from the fact that this conduct may, in other situations, be consistent with assent to a contractual term that there was indeed such assent here. In order to constitute acceptance, the failure to act affirmatively must carry a significance that reasonable people in the parties' positions would understand to be assent. A party cannot require an evidentiary trial before a trier of fact simply by asserting that the other party assented through a failure to respond to proffered contractual terms. There must be facts in the record to support a finding that the counterparty intended to accept the terms. Such acceptance need not be express, but where it is not, there must be evidence that the offeree knew or should have known of the terms and understood that acceptance of the benefit would be construed by the offeror as an agreement to be bound. That is not the case here.

The plaintiffs were never put on inquiry notice of the arbitration provision, and their continued credit-card payments, which were auto-debited from their credit cards, were too passive for any reasonable fact-finder to conclude that they manifested a subjective understanding of the existence of the arbitration and other e-mailed provisions and an intent to be bound by them in exchange for the continued benefits Great Fun offered. . . .

For the foregoing reasons, we affirm the order of the district court denying the defendants' motion to compel arbitration, and remand the case to that court for further proceedings.

■ QUESTIONS

(1) The court notes that Trilegiant failed to preserve on appeal the argument that the arbitration term was adequately noticed on the enrollment web-page, and therefore formed part of the original agreement. The court indicates that had this argument not been waived, it would have created a substantial question for resolution in the case. Based on what you have read about conspicuousness of terms, adequate notice, reasonable expectations, and the duty to read, how should this question have been resolved had it been preserved on appeal?

(2) Even if Trilegiant had waived that argument, should the fact that the terms were readily apparent on the enrollment website be relevant to the question of whether a reasonable consumer would have adequate notice of the terms contained in the e-mail?

(3) It sounds as if the plaintiffs were pretty oblivious when they enrolled in the program, and remained inattentive when they failed to notice the monthly membership fee debited to their credit cards over quite a long time. Do you agree with the court that their conduct was too passive to constitute a manifestation of assent to the standard terms?

■ PROBLEM 6.7

In *Casavant v. Norwegian Cruise Line,* 63 Mass. App. 785, 829 N.E.2d 1171 (2005) the Casavants booked a cruise from Boston to Bermuda. They booked their ticket through a travel agent in October, 2000, and the cruise was due to depart on September 16, 2001. They paid a deposit at the time of booking and paid the rest of the price of the cruise by July 18, 2001. Norwegian did not mail their cruise tickets to them, with the standard contract terms, until August 27, and they were received by the Casavants around September 3. The terms that accompanied the cruise tickets were set out on two pages of fine print. A box on the first page stated

"Acceptance of this Passenger Ticket Contract by Passenger shall constitute the agreement of Passenger to these Terms and Conditions." Clause 28 on the second page contained a forum selection provision, requiring all litigation under the contract to be conducted in the courts of Florida.

About a week after the Casavants received their tickets, and a few days before the cruise was to depart, the September 11 terrorist attacks occurred. The planes that were crashed into the World Trade Center originated from Boston's Logan Airport, whose security was run by the same organization that was responsible for harbor security. The Casavants, fearing the possibility of more terrorist attacks, decided that they did not wish to go on the cruise on September 16. They sought to reschedule it for a later date. Norwegian refused and the Casavants sued in a Massachusetts court. Norwegian filed a motion to dismiss the suit on the grounds that the Casavants had assented to Norwegian's standard forum selection clause.

The court refused to enforce the forum selection clause because Norwegian had not sent the standard terms to the Casavants until nearly a year after the booking, and only about 13 days before the departure date. The court held that the late delivery of the terms did not give the Casavants adequate and fair notice of the terms, so they could not bind the Casavants in the absence of some affirmative signification of acceptance.

The focus of the opinion is on the unfairness of sending the terms so late. There is no indication in the opinion that this was a rolling contract in which the Casavants had the right to reject the terms and cancel the cruise within a stated or reasonable time of receiving them. Nor does the court indicate whether it considered the terms proposals for addition to the contract.

Assume the following (fictional) facts:

(i) This was not a rolling contract. The clear intent was that a contract was formed when the Casavants booked the cruise. Once booked, the tickets were nonrefundable and the cruise date could not be changed.

(ii) At the time that they booked the cruise through the travel agent, the Casavants visited the agent's office. After they booked the cruise, the agent gave them a written booking confirmation that set out the date and itinerary of the cruise, the payment terms, a warning that the cruise was nonrefundable and a recommendation that the passengers take out travel insurance, and a statement that the cruise tickets and detailed information about the cruise would be delivered to the passengers closer to the date of the cruise.

(iii) The booking confirmation did not refer to Norwegian's standard contract terms. However, it did list Norwegian's website and encouraged the passengers to visit the website for more information. The Casavants did not visit the website. Had they done so, they would have found a prominent link to Norwegian's standard terms.

(iv) This was not the Casavants' first cruise. They had been on three cruises in the past: One on a Norwegian ship and the other two on other cruise lines.

Do you think that the standard terms should be viewed as incorporated into the contract at the time of formation, or are they better viewed as proposals for addition to the contract? If the latter, do you think that the Casavants accepted or rejected the proposed additional terms?

D THE UNIDROIT PRINCIPLES AND CISG PROVISIONS ON THE BATTLE OF THE FORMS

Both the UNIDROIT Principles and the CISG have provisions that deal with standard contract terms and the battle of the forms.

Article 2.1.11 of the UNIDROIT Principles sets out the general approach to a response that purports to modify an offer. If the new terms materially digress from the offer, the Principles treat the response as a counteroffer. However, a response with nonmaterial alterations qualifies as an acceptance unless the offeror objects to them. In the absence of objection, the modifications in the acceptance become part of the contract. Article 2.1.12 adopts a similar approach to additional or different terms in a confirmation. They become part of the contract unless they are material or the other party objects to them.

In addition to these general rules, Articles 2.1.19 to 2.1.21 of the UNIDROIT Principles have special rules relating to standard-form contracts. It is not entirely clear how these rules mesh with the general rules. Article 2.1.19(1) states that the usual rules of formation apply where one or both parties use standard terms, subject to the qualification that if the other party did not know of or reasonably expect the standard term, it is not enforceable unless that party expressly agreed to the term. Where the contract has a standard term that conflicts with a nonstandard term, the latter governs.

The solution to the battle of the forms in the UNIDROIT Principles resembles the approach of UCC 2-207(3) but is more general in its application. Article 2.1.22 provides that where both parties use standard terms and they reach agreement except on those terms, a contract is formed on the basis of the agreed terms as well as any standard terms that are essentially the same. (That is, the contract consists only of those terms, whether standard or nonstandard, about which the parties are in accord. One-sided standard terms fall away.) However, either party is able to reject the contract by clearly notifying the other, either in advance or without undue delay, that it does not intend to be bound by the contract.

CISG Article 19(1) sets out what is essentially a liberalized version of the "mirror image" rule. It treats a response to an offer as a rejection and a counteroffer, even if it purports to be an acceptance, if it contains additions, limitations, or other modifications. However, it qualifies this rule in Article 19(2) by providing that if the additional or different terms in the purported acceptance do not materially alter the offer, it qualifies as an acceptance unless the offeror objects to the discrepancy without delay. If the offeror fails to object, the modifications in the acceptance become terms of the contract. Article 19(2) only covers nonmaterial additional or different terms. Therefore, any material alteration of the terms of the offer in the response will render the response, even if it purports to be an acceptance, a counteroffer, and no contract will be formed. Article 19(3) provides some examples of what kinds of alteration would be material. The list includes terms relating to price, payment, quality or quantity, delivery, the extent of liability, and dispute resolution.

CHAPTER 7

Preliminary, Incomplete, and Indefinite Agreements

A   THE SCOPE OF THIS CHAPTER

Ideally, after parties have engaged in contract negotiations, they reach agreement on all the terms of the transaction and form a contract that fully and clearly expresses what they have agreed upon. However, human interaction often produces results that fall short of the ideal. Either during or at the end of the process of negotiation, the parties may form different impressions of their progress toward agreement—one may believe that they have reached the point of final agreement on a contract, while the other thinks that they have not. Even if they both think that they have made a contract, its terms may be so vague, imprecise, or unsettled that it is difficult to determine whether they really reached agreement at all or what they actually agreed. This chapter deals with several related issues that might arise where the parties dispute whether their discussions resulted in an enforceable contract.

B   PRELIMINARY AGREEMENTS

Sometimes, particularly where the transaction is complex, or it requires ongoing negotiation to resolve matters that arise only after the parties have begun to take action in relation to the transaction, the parties may enter into a preliminary agreement that does not deal comprehensively with all the issues that will or might arise as they move ahead with the transaction. Where the parties have reached such a preliminary agreement, it may not be clear what they intended its legal effect to be. There are three possibilities:

1. It could be that the parties intend their understanding to be purely preliminary and non-binding until such time as they have resolved all issues and entered into a final, binding contract. In this case, the preliminary understanding is merely an expression of the desire to work towards entering a contract, and it does not yet impose any legal obligations on either party.

2. It could be that, despite its preliminary nature, the parties do intend the preliminary agreement to be a binding contract. As we will see, where the preliminary agreement either makes it clear that the parties do not intend to be bound until a final formal contract is signed, or where there is still too much missing from the preliminary agreement, the presumption is that the preliminary agreement is not yet a contract.

3. It could be that the parties have not yet made a contract that binds them to their ultimate objective, but they have made a binding commitment to continue working with each other in good faith to try to reach that objective. If an agreement to negotiate in good faith exists, it does not mean that the parties will ultimately reach agreement. It means simply that they are both committed to make an honest and reasonable effort to try. It should be emphasized that in the usual case, there is no such obligation. In most situations, negotiations are not meant to bind either party. Each is free to terminate negotiations for any reason, and has no legal obligation to offer an explanation or justification for doing so. However, there are some circumstances in which the nature of the transaction and the relationship between the parties do indicate that the parties have expressly or impliedly agreed that neither of them will simply walk away from negotiations, and that they did intend to assume the duty to keep bargaining in good faith.

Of these, courts have viewed the third possibility with particular skepticism. If the parties articulate an agreement to negotiate in good faith in clear and express language, it is easier to accept that they really did intend to be bound to continue to negotiate in good faith. However, in most cases where this issue comes up, one of the parties claims that the duty was impliedly undertaken under the particular circumstances of the negotiations. Courts are generally wary about finding an obligation to continue negotiating in good faith. Such an obligation is commonly not contemplated in most negotiations, and too ready a recognition of it would place the risk on negotiating parties of being bound to a commitment before they have actually entered the contract. This could cast a pall on negotiations and inhibit the parties' discussions. Therefore, courts are only likely to find such an obligation where there are very strong indications that the parties intended it. The next case, *Brown v. Cara*, will give you an idea of what these indications might be.

1. Preliminary Agreements that Contemplate the Ultimate Execution of More Final Documents

BROWN v. CARA

420 F.3d 148 (2005)
United States Court of Appeals, Second Circuit

STRAUB, Circuit Judge.

[The plaintiffs are Jeffrey Brown and his corporation, Jeffrey M. Brown Associates, Inc. (JMB). The defendants are Charles Cara and his corporation, Tracto Equipment Corp. (Tracto). Brown is a construction contractor. Tracto owns property in Brooklyn (referred to by the court as the "Jay Street property")]. . . . In March 2000 the Jay Street Property was in use as a parking lot and was subject to zoning limitations that made it unsuitable for substantial commercial or residential development. At some time prior to March 2000, JMB and Cara together contemplated developing the Jay Street Property for commercial and residential use. The discussions that followed culminated in a two-page Memorandum of Understanding ("MOU"), signed by Brown for "Jeffrey M. Brown Associates, Inc., and his companies, entities, etc.," and by Cara for "Charles Cara and his companies, entities, etc.," on March 27, 2000, by which the parties agreed to "work together to develop, build, market and manage a new real estate venture planned for an existing site at 100 Jay Street in Brooklyn, NY" ("Jay Street Project" or the "Project").

The MOU, referring to prior meetings between the parties, sets forth a general working framework for the Project, including basic design parameters and provisions for the division and distribution of future proceeds. According to the stated terms, Cara is to "provide[ ] the property at no cost to the partnership (or whatever combined entity is formed in the future to develop the project)." Brown is to "provide[ ] his company and individual experience, lender relationships, architect/engineering relationships, legal relationships and governmental relationships to lead the development effort . . . [including] the rezoning process, conceptual design of the project, conceptual budgeting, arranging for possible financing avenues and helping to establish an effective marketing plan." The MOU sets forth Cara's responsibility for compensating a named consultant and Brown's responsibility to compensate another named consultant. It provides that "Brown will build the project with union labor, if needed," and establishes that "Cara will act in the capacity of an Owner's representative on the project." "Brown agrees to front the costs of development up to an amount not exceeding $175,000," and the parties agree to pursue jointly the provision of necessary financing. Finally, the MOU declares that "time is of the essence," and states the parties' intent to "enter into a formal contract shortly."

In a letter dated April 5, 2000, and addressed to Brown, Cara states his desire to negotiate final terms of the partnership, design, and project financing. None of the proposed terms were settled, however, allegedly because the parties agreed that the costs associated with the negotiations would be wasted if the Property was not suitably rezoned. Consistent with the terms outlined in the MOU, JMB commissioned the design of a multi-use, two-tower, building, which came to be known as the "Light Bridges at Jay Street." JMB subsequently sought, through a process of applications, publicity, community meetings, lobbying, and presentations to community boards, rezoning of the Property to allow construction of the Light Bridges Project. Cara was aware of these efforts and attended some of the meetings. In November and December 2001, the Project received the needed approvals.

Ready to move forward, the parties attempted to negotiate the necessary corporate, financing, construction, and operating agreements. Negotiations proceeded through 2002 and into 2003. During the spring of 2003, Cara requested from JMB a proposed construction management agreement. JMB complied, but Cara was not pleased with the terms described in that document. JMB claims that the wrong document was sent to Cara and that JMB so informed Cara at the time. However, Cara's displeasure and offense were so deep that he refused to continue with negotiations and ceased all communication and collaboration with JMB. . . . [In June 2003 JMB brought this diversity action to enforce the MOU. The trial court found that there was no enforceable contract and granted summary judgment in favor of Cara, dismissing the contract claim. On appeal, the court deals with two issues. First, it considers whether the MOU was a binding preliminary agreement to develop the property. It finds that it is not. Second it considers whether the MOU imposed on the parties the obligation to continue negotiations in good faith. It finds that it did.]

. . . The first question presented on appeal is whether the MOU is an enforceable preliminary agreement. The District Court found that it is not. We agree that the MOU does not bind the parties to complete the Jay Street Project but disagree insofar as the District Court found that the MOU does not bind the parties to negotiate in good faith open terms that must be settled in order for the development to proceed within the framework described by the MOU.

"Ordinarily, where the parties contemplate further negotiations and the execution of a formal instrument, a preliminary agreement does not create a binding contract." *Adjustrite Sys., Inc.* [*v. GAB Bus. Servs., Inc.*, 145 F.3d 543 (2d Cir. 1998)]. There is no dispute that this is the situation here. At the signing of the MOU, JMB and Cara knew that further negotiations would be required. The MOU itself contemplates a "formal contract" to be entered into in the future. Further, only days after the MOU was signed, Cara solicited JMB to enter negotiations toward the execution of significant and necessary agreements, demonstrating the parties' contemporary understanding that, though they had signed the MOU, further negotiations and formal agreements were necessary.

"In some circumstances, however, preliminary agreements can create binding obligations." *Adjustrite*, 145 F.3d at 548. The extent of the obligations created depend on the preliminary agreement in question, though, in general, "binding preliminary agreements fall into one of two categories." *Id*. These two types are most authoritatively described in *Teachers Ins. & Annuity Ass'n. v. Tribune Co.*, 670 F. Supp. 491 (S.D.N.Y. 1987), where Judge Leval, collecting the relevant New York law, describes "Type I" preliminary agreements as "complete," reflecting a meeting of the minds on "all the issues perceived to require negotiation." Because it is complete, a Type I preliminary agreement "binds both sides to their ultimate contractual objective." *Adjustrite*, 145 F.3d at 548. "Type II" preliminary agreements, by contrast, are "binding only to a certain degree," reflecting agreement "on certain major terms, but leav[ing] other terms open for further negotiation." *Id*. Type II agreements "do[ ] not commit the parties to their ultimate contractual objective but rather to the obligation to negotiate the open issues in good faith in an attempt to reach the . . . objective within the agreed framework." *Id*. (internal quotation marks and alteration omitted).

The District Court . . . found that the MOU is not a "Type I" preliminary agreement. We agree. The hallmark of a Type I agreement is that the parties have agreed to all necessary elements of the contract and are, therefore, bound to the ultimate objective despite the fact that a more formal or elaborate writing has yet to be produced. However, "[t]here is a strong presumption against finding binding obligation in agreements which include open terms, call for future approvals and expressly anticipate future preparation and execution of contract documents." *Arcadian Phosphates, Inc. v. Arcadian Corp.*, 884 F.2d 69, 73 (2d Cir. 1989) (quoting *Tribune*, 670 F. Supp. at 499); *see also Carmon v. Soleh Boneh Ltd.*, 206 A.D.2d 450, 614 N.Y.S.2d 555, 556 (1994) ("[W]here an agreement contains open terms, calls for future approval, and expressly anticipates future preparation and execution of contract documents, there is a strong presumption against finding a binding and enforceable obligation."). The category of Type I preliminary agreements is, then, limited to agreements that are "preliminary" in name only. *Adjustrite*, 145 F.3d at 548.

There are four factors relevant to determining whether a preliminary agreement is enforceable as to the ultimate contractual objective: (1) whether there is an expressed reservation of the right not to be bound in the absence of a writing; (2) whether there has been partial performance of the contract; (3) whether all of the terms of the alleged contract have been agreed upon; and (4) whether the agreement at issue is the type of contract that is usually committed to writing.

The first factor, which is frequently the most important, requires the Court to determine whether the language of the contract discloses an intention by the parties to be bound to the ultimate objective. This factor is frequently determined by explicit language of commitment or reservation. However, the "fact that [a] preliminary agreement contains no express reservation of the right not to be bound is not dispositive of whether it is binding [because] a reservation of right not to be bound presumes that there is some expression of commitment or agreement in the writing." *Williston on Contracts*, §4:8. Where there is no language that may be read to bind the parties to the ultimate goal, an explicit reservation would serve no purpose. There is no explicit reservation in the

MOU. Rather, the language is decidedly non-committal, suggesting, at most, a promise to "work together." As plaintiffs admit, all of the critical design, business, construction, and financing details were utterly contingent upon the rezoning. In comprehension of this uncertainty, the language of the MOU is scrupulously reserved. For example, rather than committing the parties "to develop, build, market, and manage the Light Bridges of Jay Street," the MOU only purports to "outline the terms under which [the parties] will *work together* to develop, build, market, and manage a new real estate venture" (emphasis added). The MOU goes on to foretell entrance "into a formal contract," and concludes by stating that the parties "agree to work together." Because the language is so non-committal, the absence of an expressed reservation is of little significance, particularly in view of the MOU's statement that a formal contract is forthcoming. Plaintiffs may argue that language more precise and strong was not suitable to the circumstances, given that all the final terms were contingent upon eventual rezoning. While true, this adds no weight to the claim that the MOU is a Type I agreement. To the contrary, it suggests that, given the circumstances, the most the parties could hope to achieve in the MOU was a commitment to negotiate in good faith additional terms, within the framework provided in the agreement, as conditions evolved.

There can be no serious dispute that the second factor weighs heavily in favor of plaintiffs. JMB expended significant time and energy to design the Project and to clear a number of political and regulatory hurdles. Cara was contemporaneously aware of this performance and, on some occasions at least, was present for presentations conducted by JMB before various boards and citizen groups. These efforts bore fruit and constitute significant partial performance by JMB, which was accepted by Cara and has resulted in significant benefits accruing to the Property.

The third factor, by contrast, falls in favor of defendants. No credible case can be made that the MOU documents a "complete agreement . . . on all the issues perceived to require negotiation." *Tribune*, 670 F. Supp. at 498. To the contrary, the MOU reaches almost *none* of the terms of the Light Bridges Project that require negotiation. For example, the MOU is silent on critical terms of design, financing, construction, compensation, corporate form, and ownership. The several-years-long process of negotiation that followed the rezoning is ample evidence that much is missing from the MOU. JMB argues that, given the circumstances, this level of detail was impossible to achieve when the MOU was signed. Assuming this to be true does not make the MOU a more binding contract, however. Moreover, we are not convinced that, had they so desired, the parties could not have negotiated a fully binding contract regardless of the unknown. Contracting parties faced with similar uncertainty routinely negotiate objective methodologies by which open terms are later to be determined. JMB may claim that such an exercise would have been pointless until the rezoning process was completed. Of course, that says no more than that JMB, rather than expending the resources necessary to achieve a fully-binding agreement, decided to assume the risk that the parties would not, in the end, be able to "work together."

The fourth factor also weighs in favor of defendants. New York courts have recognized that the "complexity and duration of [an] alleged agreement" is particularly significant in determining whether it must be reduced to formal writing in order to be fully enforceable. *See Warwick Assocs. v. FAI Ins. Ltd.*, 275 A.D.2d 653, 713 N.Y.S.2d 178 (2000). As contemplated by the parties, the Light Bridges is a project of enormous complexity that would likely span decades were it pursued to completion. All parties admit that the two-page MOU is not sufficient to the task of developing and managing the final Project. . . .

For these reasons, we agree with the District Court and hold that the MOU is not a binding Type I preliminary agreement. We affirm the judgment of the District Court to the extent that it is consistent with this holding.

[Although the court concludes that the memorandum of understanding was not a binding Type I preliminary agreement to develop the project, it goes on to consider whether it qualified as a Type II preliminary agreement that committed the parties to continue negotiating in good faith:] . . . In *Tribune*, Judge Leval identified two core, but often competing, policy concerns relevant to preliminary agreements. The first is to "avoid trapping parties in surprise contractual obligations that they never intended." The second is the "enforce[ment] and preserv[ation of] agreements that were intended as binding, despite a need for further documentation or further negotiation." The path between this Scylla and Charybdis is, of course, to enforce a preliminary agreement only to the extent that the parties intend it to be binding. In this regard, "giving legal recognition to [Type II agreements] serves a valuable function in the marketplace . . . permit[ting parties] to make plans in reliance upon their preliminary agreements and present market conditions . . . [without] expend[ing] enormous sums negotiating every detail of final contract documentation before knowing whether they have an agreement, and if so, on what terms." *Tribune*, 670 F. Supp. at 499. In our view, this is exactly what these parties did when they signed the MOU.

This flexibility comes with limitations, of course. While a Type I preliminary agreement is fully binding as to the final contractual goal, a Type II agreement "does not commit the parties to their ultimate contractual objective but rather to the obligation to negotiate the open issues in good faith in an attempt to reach the . . . objective within the agreed framework." *Adjustrite*, 145 F.3d at 548. "This obligation does not guarantee that the final contract will be concluded if both parties comport with their obligation, as good faith differences in the negotiation of the open issues may prevent a reaching of final contract." *Tribune*, 670 F. Supp. at 498. Whether the differences that have terminated the parties' working relationship in this case reflect good faith is a question for the District Court on remand.

The considerations relevant to whether a preliminary agreement is a binding Type II agreement are: (1) whether the intent to be bound is revealed by the language of the agreement; (2) the context of the negotiations; (3) the existence of open terms; (4) partial performance; and (5) the necessity of putting the agreement in final form, as indicated by the customary form of such transactions. While some of these factors are the same as those applied to determine whether a document is a Type I preliminary agreement, they "have a somewhat different significance where . . . the nature of the contract alleged is that it commits the parties in good faith to negotiate the open terms." *Tribune*, 670 F. Supp. at 499. More to the point, if the question posed is whether the parties have agreed to proceed within an open framework toward a contractual goal, leaving necessary terms for later negotiation, rather than whether the parties have agreed to achieve the ultimate contractual goal, then the language of the agreement, its contents and omissions, and the context in which it was negotiated and signed, may lead to different conclusions.

The essence of a Type II preliminary agreement is that it creates an "obligation to negotiate the open issues in good faith in an attempt to reach the [ultimate contractual objective] within the agreed framework." *Tribune*, 670 F. Supp. at 498; *see also Adjustrite*, 145 F.3d at 548. Measuring the MOU by the relevant factors in light of this limited contractual goal it is clear that it is a binding preliminary agreement to work toward the goal of developing the Jay Street Property within a defined framework, preserving for later negotiation in good faith business, design, financing, construction, and management terms necessary to achieve the ultimate goal of developing and exploiting the Jay Street Property.

As to the first factor, while the MOU does not disclose an intention by the parties to be bound to the ultimate goal of the contract, it clearly states the parties' agreement to "work together to develop, build, market, and manage [the Jay Street Property]" and to "work together in accordance with the terms and conditions outlined [in the MOU]." We cannot imagine more clear evidence of an intention to be bound to the MOU as a general framework in which the parties will proceed in good faith toward the goal of developing the Property while preserving for later negotiation the specific details of necessary business, design, construction, financing, and management terms.

The second factor also supports a finding that the MOU is a binding Type II agreement. As the parties agree, at the time the MOU was signed, the Jay Street Project was subject to numerous contingencies that had the potential to dramatically affect planning, execution, and management. It was in this context that the parties elected to negotiate a general framework within which they could proceed while preserving flexibility in the face of future uncertainty. While it was possible in the abstract to negotiate a more definitive contract, using determinative methodologies to be applied to open issues, the context of the negotiations did not require derivation of such algorithms if the parties opted instead for a more open arrangement. The MOU is evidence of such an arrangement, and, as a Type II agreement, is consistent with the context of the negotiations.

Turning to the third factor, where the existence of open terms creates a presumption against finding a binding contract as to the ultimate goal, *see Adjustrite*, 145 F.3d at 548, these same omissions may actually support finding a binding Type II agreement, *see Tribune*, 670 F. Supp. at 499. The MOU leaves open terms—critical to every aspect of the Jay Street Project, from design, to business structure, to ownership and management. However, these omissions do not warrant against finding the MOU enforceable as a Type II agreement. In view of indeterminate regulatory and market conditions, JMB and Cara simply elected to pursue rezoning first, leaving finalization of project design and execution for later negotiation within the framework described in the MOU.

Consistent with views expressed in our discussion of the MOU as a Type I agreement, we find that the fourth prong, partial performance, cuts strongly in favor of finding the MOU to be a Type II agreement. JMB provided extensive and valuable performance within the framework described by the MOU. Plaintiffs are entitled to demand defendants' good faith in negotiating remaining open terms.

Finally, while the requirement for a more formal future contract may be terminal to a Type I claim, Type II agreements, by definition, comprehend the necessity of future negotiations and contracts. Here, there can be little debate that creation of the holding corporation, construction, financing, and management of the Property, all required more formal and extensive contracts, both practically and as matters of customary form. The MOU clearly contemplated these future agreements, and, after rezoning, the parties expended considerable effort to negotiate some of these agreements.

... For these reasons we reverse the judgment of the District Court to the extent that it dismissed causes of action based on plaintiffs' claim that the MOU is a Type II preliminary agreement. We hold that the MOU is a Type II preliminary agreement binding the parties to negotiate in good faith terms necessary to pursue joint development of the Jay Street Property. We remand for further proceedings consistent with this holding.

■ QUESTIONS

(1) In its discussion of whether the MOU constitutes a Type I preliminary agreement, the court sets out a four-factor test. In dealing with the third factor, the court says "[W]e are not convinced that, had they so desired, the parties could not have negotiated a fully binding contract regardless of the unknown." In a transaction this complex, with so many variables and contingencies that would have to be dealt with as the transaction developed, is it realistic to think that the parties would have been able to make a binding contract at the time that they initiated the project? If so, how would they have provided for the uncertainties that lay ahead?

(2) Had the parties entered a binding Type I contract, JMB would have been able to claim expectation damages from Cara as a result of Cara's breach of contract. These damages would be calculated to place JMB in the position it would have been in had the contract been performed. In a complex development project, such as the one involved in this case, the expectation damages (if provable with reasonable certainty) could be quite high, and might include

profits lost by JMB as a result of the abandonment of the project. However, a Type II preliminary agreement only commits the parties to negotiate in good faith. Even if they do comply with that obligation, there is no guarantee that the good faith negotiations would ultimately result in a contract. How might this impact the remedy that a plaintiff could seek for a breach of an obligation to negotiate in good faith?

(3) In *Brown*, Cara abandoned the negotiations. Therefore it seems highly likely that, on remand, Brown will be able to show that Cara failed to honor his obligation to bargain in good faith. This suggests a possible danger of strategic behavior by a defendant who realizes that he might have a duty to bargain in good faith but no longer wishes to make a contract. What might this behavior be? What problems would it cause for the plaintiff?

In *Brown*, the court discussed two alternatives: That the preliminary agreement was either a "Type I" binding contract or a "Type II" agreement to negotiate in good faith. As the text at the beginning of this section indicates, there is a third possibility that is likely to be the result in most cases: That the preliminary agreement is nothing more than a non-binding indication of desire to enter into a contract in the future.

The *Brown* court adopts the *Tribune* factors to determine if the preliminary agreement qualifies as a "Type I" binding contract or a "Type II" agreement to negotiate in good faith. The factors taken into account in both inquiries are phrased a bit differently, but they boil down to substantially the same test, in which the following considerations are dominant: Does the language of the agreement indicate the parties' intent? Has there been partial performance? Are there any open terms that have not been settled? Is it customary for this type of agreement to be committed to writing? In the case of "Type II" agreements, the court also looks at the context of negotiations. As you might expect, if the parties have articulated the legal effect of the preliminary agreement, their expressed intent will be the dominant consideration, as the next case shows.

COCHRAN v. NORKUNAS

398 Md. 1, 919 A.2d 700 (2007)
Maryland Court of Appeals

RAKER, Judge.

This case arises out of the execution of a letter of intent for the purchase of property in Baltimore City between petitioners, Rebecca Cochran, et al., ("Buyers") and respondent Eileen W. Norkunas ("Seller"). We granted certiorari to consider . . . [whether] a negotiated letter of intent that contains all essential and material terms of a proposed contract to be entered, supported by consideration, and executed by all parties [is] an enforceable agreement under Maryland law. . . . We shall hold that because the parties did not intend to be bound, the letter of intent is unenforceable.

Eileen Norkunas is the owner of . . . [a home in Baltimore]. The petitioners, Robert and Hope Grove, and Robert and Rebecca Cochran, expressed their interest in purchasing the property. Assisted by a real estate agent, the Buyers drafted a handwritten letter of intent that spelled out key terms of an offer. . . . [The letter of intent also stated that a standard form Maryland Realtors contract would be delivered to seller within 48 hours.] The Buyers presented the letter of intent and a deposit check for $5,000 to Ms. Norkunas. The parties signed the letter of intent on March 7, 2004. The Seller accepted the check, but there is no evidence in the record that the check was ever deposited or negotiated by the Seller. Shortly after signing the letter of intent, Ms. Norkunas received a package of documents from the Buyers' real estate agent. The package included a cover letter [from the real estate agent as well as other documents, including the standard-form contract, filled in and signed by the buyers]. The contract incorporated the terms of the letter of intent, and it contained several additional provisions that were not included in the letter of intent. . . . After receiving the package of documents, the Seller read the contract and addenda. The Seller signed the contract and addenda on the majority of the signature lines, but . . . crossed out and did not sign [some of the provisions]. After reviewing the documents, the Seller did not return the documents to the Buyers or their agent, however. Nor did she otherwise communicate to the Buyers or their agent that she had accepted their offer. The Seller simply retained the signed documents.[1] After a week or so had passed, the Seller communicated to the Buyers that she was taking the property off the market. . . .

[The Buyers filed suit seeking specific performance of the letter of intent. The trial court found that the letter of intent was an enforceable contract and granted summary judgment to the Buyers. An intermediate court of appeals reversed, holding that the language of the letter of intent did not show that the parties had reached final agreement at the time that it was signed. The matter was then appealed to this court.]

A letter of intent is a form of a preliminary agreement. Letters of intent have led to "much misunderstanding, litigation and commercial chaos." 1 Joseph M. Perillo, *Corbin on Contracts* §1.16, p. 46 (Rev. ed. 1993). It is recognized that some letters of intent are signed with the belief that they are letters of commitment and, assuming this belief is shared by the parties, the letter is a memorial of a

---

[1] The fact that Ms. Norkunas signed the standard form contract only appeared during her deposition during discovery. On finding out about this during discovery, the Buyers amended their complaint to add an alternative basis for alleging a binding contract. They argued that even if the letter of intent did not constitute a contract, Ms. Norkunas accepted their subsequent offer by signing the standard form. However, because she never returned the signed acceptance or otherwise communicated with the Buyers after signing it, the court held that this was not an acceptance because it was never communicated to the offeror. The Buyers therefore lost on this alternative ground as well. We omit the court's analysis of this issue and focus on the Buyers' claim that the letter of intent bound the parties.—Eds.

contract. In other cases, the parties may not intend to be bound until a further writing is completed. . . . We must decide whether the negotiated letter of intent at issue in this case created an enforceable agreement under Maryland law. Petitioners assert that the letter of intent constitutes an enforceable contract because it was formed by offer and acceptance, supported by consideration, contained all definite and material terms, and was signed by the parties. Respondent replies that the letter of intent was not an enforceable contract because it was not intended, based on an objective review, to be the parties' final expression of their mutual assent. . . . It is universally accepted that a manifestation of mutual assent is an essential prerequisite to the creation or formation of a contract. Manifestation of mutual assent includes two issues: (1) intent to be bound, and (2) definiteness of terms. Failure of parties to agree on an essential term of a contract may indicate that the mutual assent required to make a contract is lacking. If the parties do not intend to be bound until a final agreement is executed, there is no contract. In the case *sub judice*, we assume *arguendo* that the letter of intent contained all essential material terms, and we need not address whether the letter of intent contained all the material terms essential to complete a contract, because it is clear that the parties did not intend to be bound by the letter of intent alone. . . . [The court articulates the *Tribune* factors discussed in *Brown.*] Each of the above-named factors may be relevant in determining whether a letter of intent is enforceable, but the most important factor is the language of the agreement.

We analyze the parties' intent to be bound according to the principles of Maryland contract law because petitioner asserts that a valid contract was formed. Maryland adheres to the principle of the objective interpretation of contracts. If the language of a contract is unambiguous, we give effect to its plain meaning and do not contemplate what the parties may have subjectively intended by certain terms at the time of formation. Thus, our search to determine the meaning of a contract is focused on the four corners of the agreement. Under the objective theory of contracts, we look at what a reasonably prudent person in the same position would have understood as to the meaning of the agreement. Ambiguity arises if, to a reasonable person, the language used is susceptible of more than one meaning or is of doubtful meaning. In addition, Maryland utilizes the following rule of construction when interpreting contracts: "A recognized rule of construction in ascertaining the true meaning of a contract is that the contract must be construed in its entirety and, if reasonably possible, effect must be given to each clause so that a court will not find an interpretation which casts out or disregards a meaningful part of the language of the writing unless no other course can be sensibly and reasonably followed." *Sagner v. Glenangus Farms*, 234 Md. 156, 167, 198 A.2d 277, 283 (1964).

We first review the language of the letter of intent to determine if the parties intended to be bound. The letter of intent is a one-page, handwritten document with essentially five paragraphs. The first paragraph states that the Buyers "offer to buy" the property for $162,000 with payment "by $5,000 check, this date and $157,000" not later than April 17, 2004. The second paragraph states that a "standard form Maryland Realtors Contract *will be delivered* to Seller within 48 hours" (emphasis added). The letter of intent also sets forth some financing details, specifically stating that "*[t]he contract will contain* a financing requirement for buyers, but buyers *will guarantee* closing and *not invoke* the financing contingency" (emphasis added). The Buyers also stated that "*[w]e will delete* the standard home inspection contingency" (emphasis added). Finally, the letter of intent states in the margin that, "Buyer to honor seller's leases." We conclude that a reasonable person would have understood the letter of intent to mean that a formal contract offer was to follow the letter of intent. Three of the paragraphs in the letter of intent make direct reference to the Maryland Realtors Contract and the terms that shall be included in that contract. The plain language of the letter of intent in this case is unambiguous and indicates clearly that the parties intended to finalize the property sale through a standard form Maryland Realtors Contract.

. . . In *Eastover Stores, Inc.*[*v. Minnix*, 219 Md. 658, 150 A.2d 884 (1959)], the owner of a shopping center contended that an enforceable contract was entered into when the contractors' bid was accepted, as opposed to when a formal written agreement was executed by the parties approximately one month later. We noted that parties who contemplated that their agreement would be reduced to a final writing before it would become binding were at liberty to withdraw from negotiations prior to when the final writing is signed. We then affirmed the lower court's determination that the contractors had not manifested their assent to final formation of the contract prior to when the agreement was finally executed by the contractors and delivered to the shopping center owner.

Similarly, in *Peoples Drug Stores v. Fenton Realty Group*, 191 Md. 489, 62 A.2d 273 (1948), we held that the parties did not intend to conclude their lease and building contract via correspondence letters, but were only settling the terms of a future agreement that they planned to enter after the particulars were completely reconciled. *Id.* at 495, 62 A.2d at 276. We summarized the relevant contract law as follows:

> It is familiar law that a valid contract may be entered into by letters. Where one party makes a definite offer by letter and the other party accepts the offer unconditionally on the same terms on which it was made, the letters constitute a binding contract. But, of course, the parties can make the completion of their contract depend upon the execution of a written instrument. The question whether the parties negotiating a contract intended to be bound by their oral agreement but contemplated a written instrument merely as evidence of their agreement, or whether they did not intend to bind themselves until a contract was prepared and signed by them, must be decided from the facts and circumstances in each particular case. If it appears that the terms of the contract are in all respects definitely understood and agreed upon, and there is nothing left for future settlement, and that a part of the understanding of the parties is that a written contract embodying these terms shall be executed by them to serve merely as evidence of their agreement, the mere fact that the parties understood that the contract

should be reduced to writing does not leave the transaction incomplete and without binding force. *If, on the other hand, it appears that the parties, although they agreed upon all the terms of the contract, intended to have them reduced to writing and signed before the bargain should be considered as complete, neither party will be bound until that is done, as long as the contract remains without any acts done under it on either side.* (Emphasis added.)

In *Peoples Drug Stores*, the offer and acceptance letters indicated that the final agreement was "subject to approval of the lease." We concluded that the parties intended to be bound by a final agreement that was carefully drawn and that the correspondence leading up to that agreement was not enforceable. In the case *sub judice*, the letter of intent states explicitly that a "standard form Maryland Realtors Contract will be delivered to Seller within 48 hours" and describes how certain terms of that contract will be construed. We conclude that the language in the letter of intent is indicative of an intent to memorialize the property sale through a final standard form contract, just as a final agreement was intended by the parties in *Eastover Stores, Inc.* and *Peoples Drug Stores*. Here, there is no question that the parties demonstrated an intent to use a Maryland Realtors Contract to formalize their agreement. Petitioner's assertion that the letter of intent is enforceable because it was formed by offer and acceptance, supported by consideration, satisfied the statute of frauds, and contained all definite and material terms is unpersuasive because there is no binding contract if the parties do not intend to be bound until a formal document is executed. . . . We hold that the letter of intent is the type of preliminary "agreement to agree" that has generally been held unenforceable in Maryland. . . .

■ PROBLEM 7.1

Hardy Bargainer, an entrepreneur, invited Cookie Tough to invest some money in a new venture that Hardy intended to launch. Cookie was interested in the proposition, and the parties met. Hardy explained the venture to Cookie in some detail and produced a detailed business strategy as well as figures and projections on expenses and earnings. Hardy's figures showed that he would need capital of at least $1 million to get the venture started. After spending several hours discussing the business plan and asking probing questions, Cookie was convinced that Hardy's plan was sound and that the venture was promising. She said that she was willing to invest $1 million in it. However, to protect her investment from bad management or poor decision-making, she required the power to monitor and exercise some control over the business. Hardy asked what kind of protections she had in mind, and Cookie replied, "Don't worry about that. My attorney has done several of these transactions for me before, and she has worked out a bunch of standard terms that do the job." Hardy seemed satisfied with this, and the parties proceeded to negotiate other matters, such as when and how the $1 million would be paid, what share of the business and profits Cookie would have, and what Hardy would have to pay Cookie if he later decided that he wished to buy out her share. They reached agreement on all these issues.

During the course of the meeting, as they reached agreement on a particular issue, Hardy wrote down the gist of what they had agreed to on a legal pad. At the conclusion of the meeting, Hardy wrote at the foot of this memorandum "Hardy Bargainer and Cookie Tough have agreed that Cookie will invest $1 million in Hardy's venture on the above terms. Cookie will instruct her attorney to draft a contract reflecting these terms as well as appropriate terms to protect her investment. The contract will be signed as soon as possible." They both then signed the memorandum.

Immediately after the meeting Cookie had second thoughts about the investment. She never instructed her attorney to draft a formal agreement. A couple of days after the meeting she called Hardy and told him that she had changed her mind and would not make the investment.

Hardy contends that Cookie has no right to change her mind—they had a deal at the end of their meeting, and the drafting and execution of the final agreement was merely intended to create a formal record. Cookie disagrees. She says that she would never agree to make an investment of $1 million without first having her attorney review the transaction and prepare a carefully drawn contract, properly executed by the parties. She claims that this is obviously why they provided for the execution of the formal agreement. They intended not to be bound until they agreed to its content and signed it. Who is correct? How can you tell?

2. Agreement to Agree: Deferred Contract

At the end of its opinion, the *Cochran* court described the letter of intent as an "agreement to agree" as distinct from an enforceable contract. This principle is often expressed by courts in distinguishing a contract—the final binding agreement between the parties—from a preliminary understanding or "agreement in principle" that parties may reach in the process of working toward a final agreement. As the preceding discussion in Section B.1 shows, the question of whether a manifestation of agreement qualifies as a final contract, or is merely an unenforceable "agreement to agree," is a matter of interpretation, which requires an examination of the language used by the parties in context. An important consideration in deciding whether a binding contract was formed is the extent to which the parties have settled all the terms, or at least the material terms, of their relationship.

In *Cochran* the court applies the principle that an "agreement to agree" is not a contract in the context of a letter of intent that did seem to settle all material terms, but which also expressed the intention that contract formation would not occur until the Maryland Realtors' standard contract was signed. In other cases, the principle comes up where parties have reached agreement on most terms of their proposed contractual relationship, but they have deferred agreement on an important aspect of it. For example, after negotiating for a while, Seller and Buyer enter into an agreement that Buyer will buy Seller's home. They agree on all aspects of the sale except for the price, on which they are several thousand dollars apart. They hope that over the course of further discussions they will be able to close the gap. They sign a document headed "Contract of Sale" in which they record that Seller has sold the house to Buyer. The "contract" sets out all the agreed terms of the sale, but provides that the price will be agreed upon by the parties in the future. As much as the parties would like to enter the transaction, this cannot be a contract, because the parties have not reached agreement on a material term. If a court finds this to be a contract, and comes up with some kind of reasonable price, it is, in essence, making an agreement for the parties.

This illustration is a clear example of an "agreement to agree." However, the circumstances may be more ambiguous. Sometimes a missing or apparently unresolved term may not really result from deferred agreement. It may be that the parties intended that the apparent gap or uncertainty in their agreement would be settled in some way that does not require further negotiation. Where the court is persuaded that the parties really did intend a contract despite the unresolved term, there may be a basis for the court to give content to that term and find a contract. The next case explores such a situation. (Note that the case is not concerned with the initial formation of a contract, but with a price escalation provision in an existing contract. However, the principle is the same where one deals with the question of whether a contract has been formed.)

ARBITRON, INC. v. TRALYN BROADCASTING, INC.

400 F.3d 130 (2005), aff'd without published opinion following remand, 328 Fed. Appx. 755 (2009)
United States Court of Appeals, Second Circuit

CALABRESI, Circuit Judge.

This breach of contract dispute raises the question of whether, under New York law, two parties entering into a licensing agreement for radio ratings and data may authorize one party to adjust the price of that data unilaterally at some point in the future. . . . [W]e conclude that the contract before us delegated, with unmistakable clarity, price-setting authority to a single party, and that New York law does not invalidate such contracts. We therefore vacate the district court's order of summary judgment and remand for reconsideration.

Plaintiff-appellant Arbitron, Inc. is a popular listener-demographics data provider for North American radio stations. Arbitron licenses its copyrighted listener data to regional AM and FM stations, which then use the demographic profiles of station listeners to attract advertisers. In 1997, Arbitron entered into one such license—a "Station License Agreement to Receive and Use Arbitron Radio Listening Estimates" with defendant Tralyn Broadcasting, Inc. The License Agreement permitted Tralyn's only radio station (WLUN-FM in the Gulfport, Mississippi area, later known as WLNF-FM) to use Arbitron listening data reports. Over its five-year term, the License Agreement charged Tralyn a monthly rate of $1,729.57 for the use of Arbitron's listening data reports by this single station.

Were this monthly license fee the only pricing portion of the License Agreement, this case would present an extremely simple contract dispute. But another clause of the agreement—which we shall call the "escalation clause"—provided that, were Tralyn or its successor to acquire additional radio stations in the same or adjacent regional markets, a new license fee would be charged. Upon acquiring such stations, Tralyn was required to notify Arbitron so that Arbitron could determine a new license fee, and, if necessary, approve the assignment of the licensing agreement to a new party in interest. Any new licensing fee would be set, according to the escalation clause, at Arbitron's discretion. . . . Thus, the escalation clause assumed that, as Tralyn acquired additional regional stations, it would share listener data among each of these stations, and, by allowing Arbitron to increase Tralyn's fees, the clause provided Arbitron with a mechanism to reflect this additional use. . . .

[In October 1999, Tralyn was purchased by JMD, Inc. (a codefendant), which controlled four other radio stations in the area. Tralyn assigned the license agreement to JMD, which took over its rights and duties under the agreement. In breach of the agreement, neither JMD nor Tralyn notified Arbitron that JMD operated five radio stations; instead, they continued to pay the fee for one station. Arbitron discovered this in June 2000, and it notified JMD that it was exercising its right to increase the monthly licensing fee, in essence, by multiplying the fee for one station by five and applying a volume discount. The revised monthly charge was $5,784.93. Arbitron sent JMD an invoice notifying it of a prospective payment increase and also claimed payment of the shortfall in fees from the time of JMD's acquisition of Tralyn in October 1999. JMD never paid these invoices and subsequently refused to pay anything at all. Arbitron therefore stopped sending JMD its listening data reports and filed this suit against Tralyn and JMD for breach of contract. It claimed $172,394.22, representing all moneys due under the agreement (plus interest) from June 1999 to the end of the contract's five-year term. The district court granted summary judgment for the defendants. It concluded that the escalation clause was unenforceably vague because the agreement contained no basis for determining the new rate to be paid Arbitron.]

The district court reasoned that

> [New York courts] have refused to enforce similarly uncertain agreements. For instance, where a permit failed to specify the amount of rent reduction in the event the landlord exercised an option to reclaim a portion of the premises, the court held that there "was not a sufficiently definite offer which could give rise to an enforceable agreement." *In Matter of Exp. Indus. and Terminal Corp.*, 93 N.Y.2d 584, 591, 693 N.Y.S.2d 857, 715 N.E.2d 1050 (1999). . . . Likewise, in *Joseph Martin, Jr., Delicatessen, Inc. v. Schumacher*, 52 N.Y.2d 105, 436 N.Y.S.2d 247, 417 N.E.2d 541 (1981), the court struck a renewal clause in a lease providing for future agreement on rent as overly vague. It would have "sufficed" for the "methodology for determining the rent . . . to be found within the four corners of the lease," but there must be some "objective, extrinsic event, condition or standard on which the amount was to depend."

In concluding that the escalation clause (but not the rest of the License Agreement) was void for vagueness, the district court emphasized the following passage from *Delicatessen*: "[B]efore the power of law can be invoked to enforce a promise, it must be sufficiently certain and specific so that what was promised can be ascertained. Otherwise, a court, in intervening would be imposing its own conception of what the parties should or might have undertaken, rather than confining itself to the implementation of a bargain to which they have mutually committed themselves. Thus, definitiveness as to material matters is of the very essence of contract law. Impenetrable vagueness and uncertainty will not do." . . .

The district court based its decision on three New York cases, each dealing with contracts for the sale or lease of real property. Upon review of these same cases, we conclude that the escalation clause is enforceable under the common law of New York. This is so because the clause before us is not an "agreement to agree," under which future negotiations between the parties must occur, but is instead an acknowledgment that, if certain conditions arise in the future, *no* new agreement is required before Arbitron may set new license terms. Such an agreement is not unenforceably vague under New York's common law.

The seminal New York precedent on unenforceably indefinite contracts is *Joseph Martin, Jr., Delicatessen, Inc.* There, the Court of Appeals was faced with an agreement between a landlord and a tenant to lease a commercial space for five years at a monthly rate beginning at $500 and escalating over five years to $650, with the option to renew the lease for another five-year term at a rent to be determined by the parties. At the close of the lease's five-year term, the landlord sought to increase the rent from $650 to $900 monthly. Surprised, the tenant employed an assessor, who appraised the market value of the premises at no more than $550 per month. The tenant sued for specific performance, seeking a new five-year lease at the fair market rate of $550. In resolving the case, the *Delicatessen* majority recognized that the U.C.C., as implemented by the New York legislature, counseled in favor of supplying missing price terms to save and enforce the agreement, and that the terms supplied by a court under the U.C.C. would correspond to a good's fair market value. Nevertheless, because the New York statute's terms made clear that leases or contracts for the sale of real property were not covered by the U.C.C., the Court of Appeals refused to enforce the agreement. It concluded that "it is rightfully well settled in the common law of contracts in this State that a mere agreement to agree, in which a material term is left for future negotiations, is unenforceable. This is especially true of the amount to be paid for the sale or lease of real property. The rule applies all the more, and not the less, when, as here, the extraordinary remedy of specific performance is sought."

In a separate opinion, Judge Meyer concurred in the judgment and opined that the U.C.C.'s principles might now be part of the common-law fabric of New York commercial law. . . . And for similar reasons, Judge Jasen dissented altogether. ("While I recognize that the traditional rule is that a provision for renewal of a lease must be 'certain' in order to render it binding and enforceable, in my view the better rule would be that if the tenant can establish its entitlement to renewal under the lease, the mere presence of a provision calling for renewal at 'rentals to be agreed upon' should not prevent judicial intervention to fix rent at a reasonable rate in order to avoid a forfeiture.")[2]

In *Cobble Hill Nursing Home v. Henry & Warren Corp.*, 74 N.Y.2d 475, 548 N.Y.S.2d 920, 548 N.E.2d 203 (1989), the Court of Appeals again faced the question of unspecified price terms. The contract in *Cobble Hill* gave the plaintiff a purchase option for a nursing home, but did not provide a specific price for the property. The agreement instead permitted plaintiff to buy the property "at a price determined by the Department [of Health] in accordance with the Public Health Law and all applicable rules and regulations of the Department." When the plaintiff exercised that option and attempted to buy the nursing home at the price set by the Department of Health, defendants refused to honor the option, citing a perceived discrepancy between the property's fair market value and the Department of Health's assessment. Plaintiff filed suit for breach of contract, seeking specific performance at the price set by the Department. Defendants claimed that the agreement was unenforceably vague because its four corners did not include a definite price term. Evaluating these arguments, the Court of Appeals emphasized that "[f]ew principles are better settled in the law of contracts than the requirement of definiteness," and that under New York law "[i]f an agreement is not reasonably certain in its material terms, there can be no

---

[2] We note that, despite its "seminal" status, *Delicatessen* is of limited precedential value in this case. The majority opinion emphasized that its conclusion was "especially true" in relation to the subject matter at hand (real property), and "all the more, and not the less" true for the requested remedy (specific performance). *See* 52 N.Y.2d at 109-10, 436 N.Y.S.2d 247, 417 N.E.2d 541. Those qualifications undermine *Delicatessen*'s applicability in contractual disputes related to the subject matter ("licenses" for listener data reports), and the requested remedy (monetary damages), before us.

legally enforceable contract." But it also noted that a price term is not necessarily indefinite because the agreement fails to specify a dollar figure, or leaves fixing the amount for the future, or contains no computational formula. "Where at the time of agreement the parties have manifested their intent to be bound, a price term may be sufficiently definite if the amount can be determined objectively without the need for new expressions by the parties; a method for reducing uncertainty to certainty might, for example, be found within the agreement or ascertained by reference to an extrinsic event, commercial practice or trade usage. A price so arrived at would have been the end product of agreement between the parties themselves." Applying that reasoning to the option contract, the Court concluded that, because it was "apparent from the agreement that these parties reposed discretion in the Department to make the price determination, limited only by the requirement that it apply provisions that were suitable, pertinent and appropriate for the task at hand, [and because the] terms of agreement and the appropriate remedy can be readily determined, and it is plain that the parties intended this to be a complete and binding contract, [there was] no legal justification for voiding this agreement."

Most recently, in *In Re Express Indus. & Terminal Corp.*, 93 N.Y.2d 584, 693 N.Y.S.2d 857, 715 N.E.2d 1050 (1999), the Court of Appeals refused to enforce a lease agreement whose material terms, including the price term, were simply left blank by the parties. A unanimous Court concluded that because the lease agreement's terms—including the date on which an option would expire, and the amount of rent reduction that would correspond to the exercise of that option—were represented by blank spaces, and because there was "no objective evidence that the parties [to the lease agreement] intended that [the lessor] be allowed to fill in these blanks with any reasonable terms [it] chose," the contract was not enforceable under New York law. But the Court also suggested that, in the face of sufficient evidence demonstrating that both parties intended to give one party the power to select "any reasonable terms [it] chose," a similar contract for the sale or lease of real property might be enforceable. . . . "[T]here are some instances where a party may agree to be bound to a contract even where a material term is left open, [but] there must be sufficient evidence that both parties intended that arrangement."

Upon review of *Delicatessen*, *Cobble Hill*, and *Express Industries*, we conclude that the License Agreement's escalation clause is indeed enforceable under the common law of New York. The escalation clause, unlike the promise to set a future rent rate collectively in *Delicatessen*, does not require the parties to reach an "agreement" on price at some point in the future. That is, the escalation clause is not an "agreement to agree." Instead, like the contract in *Cobble Hill*, it is a mechanism for objectively setting material terms in the future without further negotiations between both parties. It does so, moreover, with "sufficient evidence that both parties intended that [pricing] arrangement." *Express Indus.* The escalation clause clearly and unambiguously states that, in the event that Tralyn or its successors acquired new radio stations in the same (or an adjacent) geographic market, "Arbitron may redetermine its Gross Annual Rate for the Data, Reports and Services licensed hereunder . . . effective the first of the month following [the acquisition]." The escalation clause further provides, in unambiguous language, that Arbitron may exercise this power to "redetermine" the license fee "[n]otwithstanding Station's failure to notify Arbitron" that an acquisition had occurred.

The intent of the parties is manifest in the language of the agreement. Both Arbitron and Tralyn explicitly agreed that Arbitron was authorized to adjust the license fee in the event that Tralyn or its successors began to operate additional stations. This fact makes the instant case very different from those disputes in which courts are faced with "no objective evidence" of a shared intent to permit one party to set prices in the future. *See Express Industries.* And it in no way leads a court enforcing the contract to "impos[e] its own conception of what the parties should or might have undertaken." *Delicatessen.* Accordingly, we conclude that the district court erred in holding the License Agreement's escalation clause "impenetrably vague" under New York law.

In reaching this conclusion, we note that the cases discussed above are not the only New York precedents on the issue of missing contract terms. Under New York's implementation of the Uniform Commercial Code, there is a strong presumption that agreements are enforceable even if their price terms are not definite. N.Y. U.C.C. §2-305 provides that:

> (1) The parties if they so intend can conclude a contract for sale even though the price is not settled. In such a case the price is a reasonable price at the time for delivery if (a) nothing is said as to price; or (b) the price is left to be agreed by the parties and they fail to agree; or (c) the price is to be fixed in terms of some agreed market or other standard as set or recorded by a third person or agency and it is not so set or recorded.
>
> (2) A price to be fixed by the seller or by the buyer means a price for him to fix in good faith.

[Comment 1 to UCC 2-305] makes clear that "[t]his Article rejects in these instances the formula that 'an agreement to agree is unenforceable' . . . and rejects also defeating such agreements on the ground of 'indefiniteness.' Instead this Article recognizes the dominant intention of the parties to have the deal continue to be binding upon both."

It is not clear whether, under New York law, a license agreement of the sort at issue in this case constitutes a contract for the sale of goods, or is otherwise governed by the U.C.C.[3] We note, however, that were this section of New York's

---

[3] This ambiguity is not unique to New York. In many states, it is not clear whether "license" agreements—be they for the right to use software, or data such as Arbitron's, or other types of property—are contracts for the sale of "goods" and therefore within the U.C.C.'s purview. . . . Although courts have typically pondered the problem of "license" agreements in the software context, the same problem presents itself when analyzing a "license" for the use of Arbitron's listener data reports. Such a "license" could be understood, on the one hand, as an agreement for the sale of the physical embodiment of the data (i.e., the sale of the book in which the data is printed), or on the other hand, as a contract for data-reporting services (i.e., the temporary grant of a right to read, but not own, the book containing copyrighted material). This is, in many ways, the same difficulty

commercial code applied to the License Agreement, then the escalation clause would undoubtedly be a valid contract term under New York law; it would simply establish "[a] price to be fixed by the seller," and would be enforceable so long as that price was fixed "in good faith." But the applicability of the U.C.C. to the license agreement before [us] is not something we need to decide today.

Because we believe that the License Agreement's escalation clause is not inconsistent with New York law, we conclude that the district court erred in granting summary judgment to JMD. We therefore vacate the district court's order and remand the case for further proceedings. On remand, the district court may wish to consider whether Arbitron has exercised its authority under the escalation clause in "good faith" within the meaning of N.Y. U.C.C. §2-305 (which, as we have previously noted, may or may not apply to a "license" of this sort), or more generally, in a manner consistent with Arbitron's implied duty of fair dealing under New York law. *See, e.g., Carvel Corp. v. Diversified Mgmt. Group, Inc.*, 930 F.2d 228, 230 (2d Cir. 1991) ("Under New York law, every contract contains an implied covenant of good faith and fair dealing."). We express no opinion on either question.[4] . . .

■ PROBLEM 7.2

(a) After negotiating for a while, Mega Corporation and Leda Glorious enter into an agreement that Mega will employ Leda as its president. They agree on all aspects of the employment contract except for Leda's salary, on which they are several thousand dollars apart. Notwithstanding this difference, they both desire the transaction. They therefore sign a document headed "Contract of Employment" in which they record that Leda has agreed to assume the position of president of Mega. The "Contract of Employment" sets out all the agreed terms, but simply omits mention of Leda's salary. Do the parties have a contract? If so, what is Leda's salary?

(b) Change the facts of question (a) to the following extent: The "Contract of Employment" does not omit the salary. Instead it states that the parties agree to a "reasonable salary." Do the parties have a contract? If so, how is the salary to be determined?

(c) Would your analysis of or answer to question (a) or (b) be different if the subject matter of the transaction was not Mega's employment of Leda, but a sale of goods by Leda to Mega?

---

animating the software cases—are "license" agreements for software programs covenants covering the sale of the physical embodiment of the program (for example, in CD-ROM format), or are they instead contracts for programming services?

[4] On remand, JMD failed to show that Arbitron violated the implied covenant of good faith and fair dealing in setting the price escalation. The district court therefore granted judgment in favor of Arbitron (526 F. Supp. 2d 441 (S.D.N.Y. 2007)). This was affirmed by a summary order on appeal (328 Fed. Appx. 755 (2d Cir. 2009)).—Eds.

> ### ■ PROBLEM 7.3
>
> Mega Corporation is your client. It consults you before executing the "Contract of Employment" described in Problem 7.2. Mega tells you that the parties have agreed to a reasonable salary. Mega makes it clear that neither party is ready to commit to a specific salary because neither is sure what a reasonable salary is. Would you approve the "reasonable salary" term in the contract, or would you suggest that they change it? If it should be changed, what language would you recommend?

 ## THE PROBLEM OF INDEFINITENESS OR VAGUENESS IN AN AGREEMENT

In the course of discussing the enforceability of the escalation clause, *Arbitron* raises the issue of indefiniteness in an agreement. Sometimes, a court's decision that the parties have merely made an "agreement to agree" is based on the fact that they have completely omitted a term, or that they have expressly stated (as happened in the *Joseph Martin, Jr., Delicatessen* case, discussed in *Arbitron*) that they will agree in the future. However, sometimes a court reaches the conclusion that the parties' apparent agreement is an unenforceable "agreement to agree" because their language is too vague or unclear to establish the parameters of their agreement.

The problem of indefiniteness or vagueness is not confined to the narrow issue of whether parties have deferred agreement. Indefiniteness could be the result of deferred agreement, but it could be caused by other reasons—for example, the parties may have expressed themselves poorly or imprecisely, or they may have overlooked or glossed over some aspect of the transaction. In general, indefiniteness in terms proposed during contract negotiations could preclude formation of a contract where it is not possible to ascertain what the parties agreed to. Even where indefiniteness is not so severe as to preclude contract formation (or where the parties begin performance, thereby removing any doubt that they intended a contract), indefiniteness in contract terms can still be a problem. It could give rise to a dispute over the content of the performance obligations of a party.

Where it seems that the parties really did intend a contract, courts are reluctant to disappoint their expectations by finding their agreement too indefinite to enforce as a contract. Sometimes, the court is able to clarify and give content to indefinite terms through the process of interpretation and gap filling. However, this is not always possible, and in some cases the only conclusion the court can reach is that the indefiniteness of the terms indicates a failure of agreement. The next case and the problem that follows deal with the impact indefiniteness can have on the formation and performance of a contract and with the means that courts may use in some cases to cure the problem.

BAER v. CHASE

392 F.3d 609 (2004)
United States Court of Appeals, Third Circuit

GREENBERG, Circuit Judge.

This matter comes before this court on Robert V. Baer's ("Baer") appeal from an order of the district court entered February 20, 2004, granting summary judgment to the defendants, David Chase and DC Enterprises, Inc. (together called "Chase"). . . . This dispute centers on the creation and development of the well-known television series, *The Sopranos*. Through this action, Baer seeks compensation for what he perceives was his role in the creation and development of the popular and financially successful television series.

Chase, who originally was from New Jersey, but relocated to Los Angeles in 1971, is the creator, producer, writer and director of *The Sopranos*. Chase has numerous credits for other television productions as well. Before Chase met Baer, Chase had worked on a number of projects involving organized crime activities based in New Jersey, including a script for "a mob boss in therapy," a concept that, in part, would become the basis for *The Sopranos*. . . . [Chase and Baer had a mutual friend who knew Chase was looking for new writers and also knew that Baer, a former New Jersey prosecutor, wanted to pursue a career in writing, directing, and producing. The friend sent some of Baer's work to Chase, who liked it and suggested meeting with Baer. The mutual friend set up a lunch meeting between Baer and Chase in Los Angeles in June 1995. At the meeting, Baer described his experience as a prosecutor and suggested a film or television show about the New Jersey Mafia.]

In October 1995, Chase visited New Jersey for three days. During this "research visit" Baer arranged meetings for Chase with Detective Thomas Koczur, Detective Robert A. Jones, and Tony Spirito who provided Chase with information, material and personal stories about their experiences with organized crime. Koczur served as a tour guide and drove Chase and Baer to various locations in northern New Jersey. Koczur also arranged a lunch between Chase and Spirito. Spirito told true and sometimes personal stories involving loan sharking, a power struggle with two uncles involving a family business, and two individuals, Big Pussy and Little Pussy Russo. Chase also met with Jones, a detective with the Union County Prosecutor's office who had experience investigating organized crime. Baer does not dispute that virtually all of the ideas and locations that he "contributed" to Chase existed in the public record.

After returning to Los Angeles, Chase sent Baer a copy of a draft of a *Sopranos* screenplay that he had written, which was dated December 20, 1995. Baer asserts that after he read it he called Chase and made various comments with regard to it. Baer claims that the two spoke at least four times during the following year and that he sent a letter to Chase dated February 10, 1997, discussing the *Sopranos* script. . . . We accept Baer's allegations regarding his input into the *Sopranos* draft. . . . [Baer testified that the services that he performed for Chase took place mostly in 1995 but extended to 1997.]

Baer asserts that he and Chase orally agreed on three separate occasions that if the show became a success, Chase would "take care of" Baer, and "remunerate [Baer] in a manner commensurate to the true value of [his services]." According to Baer, he and Chase first made this oral agreement on the telephone during one of their first two or three conversations during the summer of 1995. The second occasion was on the telephone and occurred immediately prior to Chase's October 1995 visit to New Jersey. The third time the parties reached the agreement was in person when they met in New Jersey in October 1995. Baer claims that on each of these occasions the parties had the same conversation in which Chase offered to pay Baer, stating "you help me; I pay you." Baer always rejected Chase's offer, reasoning that Chase would be unable to pay him "for the true value of the services [Baer] was rendering." Each time Baer rejected Chase's offer he did so with a counter-offer, "that I would perform the services while assuming the risk that if the show failed [Chase] would owe me nothing. If, however, the show succeeded he would remunerate me in a manner commensurate to the true value of my services." Baer acknowledges that this counteroffer, which in these proceedings we treat as having become the parties' agreement, always was oral and did not include any fixed term of duration or price. There is no other evidence in the record of any other discussion between Baer and Chase regarding the terms of the contract. For purposes of the motion for summary judgment, Chase accepts Baer's version of the events as true and thus concedes there was an oral agreement to the extent that Baer sets it forth. Notwithstanding this agreement, insofar as we can ascertain, other than Baer's calls to Chase after he received the *Sopranos* script, the next time Baer heard anything from or about Chase was when he received a phone call from Detective Koczur telling him that Chase was in Elizabeth shooting *The Sopranos*. In fact, Chase has not paid Baer for his services. . . .

[In May 2002, Baer instituted suit against Chase alleging various causes of action including breach of contract. We include here only the breach of contract claim. Chase moved for summary judgment, asserting that the alleged contract was too vague, ambiguous, and lacking in essential terms to be enforced. The trial court agreed with Chase and granted summary judgment in his favor. The court of appeals affirms.]

The parties agree for purposes of the summary judgment motion that there was a contingent oral agreement providing for Chase to compensate Baer, depending on Chase's "success," in exchange for the aid Baer provided in the creation and production of *The Sopranos*. . . . A contract arises from offer and acceptance, and must be sufficiently definite so that the performance to be rendered by each party can be ascertained with reasonable certainty. . . . Therefore parties create an enforceable contract when they agree on its essential terms and manifest an intent that the terms bind them. If parties to an agreement do not agree on one or more essential terms of the purported agreement courts generally hold it to be unenforceable. New Jersey contract law focuses on the performance promised when analyzing an agreement to determine if it is too vague to be enforced. . . . A contract, therefore, is unenforceable for vagueness when its essential terms are too indefinite to allow a court to determine with reasonable certainty what each party has promised to do.

New Jersey law deems the price term, *i.e.*, the amount of compensation, an essential term of any contract. An agreement lacking definiteness of price, however, is not unenforceable if the parties specify a practicable method by which they can determine the amount. However, in the absence of an agreement as to the manner or method of determining compensation the purported agreement is invalid. Additionally, the duration of the contract is deemed an essential term and therefore any agreement must be sufficiently definitive to allow a court to determine the agreed upon length of the contractual relationship. . . . If possible, courts will . . . attach a sufficiently definite meaning to the terms of a bargain to make it enforceable . . . and in doing so may refer to commercial practice or other usage or custom. But the courts recognize that a contract is unenforceable for vagueness when its terms are too indefinite to allow a court to determine with reasonable certainty what each party has promised to do. . . .

A contract may be expressed in writing, or orally, or in acts, or partly in one of these ways and partly in others. There is a point, however, at which interpretation becomes alteration. In this case, even when all of the parties' verbal and non-verbal actions are aggregated and viewed most favorably to Baer, we cannot find a contract that is distinct and definitive enough to be enforceable. Nothing in the record indicates that the parties agreed on how, how much, where, or for what period Chase would compensate Baer. The parties did not discuss who would determine the "true value" of Baer's services, when the "true value" would be calculated, or what variables would go into such a calculation. There was no discussion or agreement as to the meaning of "success" of *The Sopranos*. There was no discussion how "profits" were to be defined. There was no contemplation of dates of commencement or termination of the contract. And again, nothing in Baer's or Chase's conduct, or the surrounding circumstances of the relationship, shed light on, or answers, any of these questions. The district court was correct . . . [in finding the contract to be] vague, indefinite and uncertain; no version of the alleged agreement contains sufficiently precise terms to constitute an enforceable contract. We therefore will affirm the district court's rejection of Baer's claim. . . .

■ QUESTIONS

   (1)   Would Baer have had more success if he had hired Big Pussy or Little Pussy, rather than a lawyer, to recover his contract claim?

   (2)   Do you agree with the court that the agreement is too indefinite for enforcement as a contract? Is there any basis on which the court could and

should have found enough content in the indefinite terms? Is there any argument or evidence that Baer's attorney should have offered to persuade the court to do that?

(3) In the *Arbitron* case, the court found that the escalation provision in the license agreement was not too vague. It could be reasonably interpreted to give Arbitron the discretion to fix the amount of the escalation in good faith. What, if anything, justifies the different approach in *Baer*?

■ PROBLEM 7.4

The questions in this problem are based on *B. Lewis Productions, Inc. v. Angelou*, not reported in F. Supp. 2d, 2005 WL 1138474 (S.D.N.Y. 2005).

The poet Maya Angelou entered into a collaboration with Butch Lewis, a promoter, for the purpose of having Lewis market Angelou's works to greeting card companies. In November 1994, Lewis and Angelou signed a "letter agreement" establishing what the letter called a "joint venture" between Angelou and Lewis's company, B. Lewis Productions (BLP). In terms of the letter, Angelou agreed to contribute "original literary works" to the venture, and BLP agreed to "seek to exploit the rights for publishing" them in "all media forms including, but not limited to greeting cards, stationery and calendars, etc." BLP would contribute all the capital to fund the venture, and Lewis would manage it. Gross revenue earned would first go to repay BLP's capital contribution and expenses, and the net profits would then be shared equally by BLP and Angelou. Lewis began to market Angelou's work and initiated negotiations for a license agreement with Hallmark, the greeting card company. Lewis secured a proposed agreement with Hallmark, but before Angelou accepted it, she and Lewis had a falling out, and their relationship ended. Angelou subsequently executed a contract with Hallmark on her own.

Lewis sued Angelou for breach of contract. Angelou defended the suit on the basis that the letter agreement was too indefinite and lacked essential terms, so that it did not qualify as a contract. She moved for summary judgment. The court denied her motion, finding that the agreement was clear enough to allow for its enforcement as a contract—although the court recognized that the agreement did not specify the nature and quantity of the literary works Angelou would contribute, when she would contribute them, and what was meant by "all media forms." The court said that this lack of detail did not preclude contract formation where the parties had set out a framework for future collaboration and contemplated that details as to the exact nature of the work would have to be worked out as they negotiated licensing agreements. The exact nature of Lewis's capital contribution and the distribution of income earned under the arrangement was not spelled out in the agreement, but the provision was clear enough to be subject to reasonable interpretation. The letter's failure to specify the duration of the relationship meant simply that it was terminable at will.

Finally, the court noted that there is a general obligation of good faith and fair dealing in every contract. This duty is particularly strong in an exclusive dealings agreement like this one, in which Lewis had the exclusive right to distribute Angelou's original work relating to greeting cards and similar products.[5] This general obligation of good faith further assists in filling the gaps in the express terms of the parties' agreement.

(a) In filling the gaps in a rather undetailed agreement, a court must balance two countervailing concerns: It does not wish to invalidate an agreement where the evidence indicates that the parties really intended to be bound, yet it does not wish to impose a contract on the parties where none was intended. In this case (at least for purposes of disposing of Angelou's motion for summary judgment), the court feels that there was an intent to form a contract, despite the vagueness of the letter's terms. From the facts summarized above, do you agree? What factors persuade you to agree or disagree?

(b) *B. Lewis Productions* inclined in the direction of finding a contract, but *Baer* reached the opposite result. Are the cases distinguishable? If so, what distinguishes them?

(c) It is apparent from *B. Lewis Productions* that parties may wish to enter into a binding contract that leaves some important aspects of their relationship open-ended and flexible. It is not always possible or desirable to try to tie up the parties' performance obligations in advance by drafting clear, rigid terms. This is especially true where the parties contemplate a long-term relationship where circumstances may change, later issues may need to be resolved, or later judgments may need to be made. Yet leaving matters open in this way could lead to a dispute about whether a contract was formed, and it is difficult to predict how a court may react to indefiniteness. What can be done at the drafting stage to minimize the risk that a court may later find that the parties failed to create a binding contract?

---

[5] In its discussion of the general obligation of good faith and fair dealing, the court discussed at length the famous case of *Wood v. Lucy, Lady Duff Gordon*, 222 N.Y. 88, 118 N.E. 214 (1917), which we study in Chapter 9. There are a number of parallels between *Wood* and *B. Lewis Productions*—in fact, in *B. Lewis Productions* the court characterized Angelou as "a Lady Duff Gordon for the modern age." Both cases involved contracts conferring on an agent the exclusive right to place the principal's creative work, and in both the principal violated the exclusive agency by placing her work on her own. In *Wood*, as in this case, the court recognized that the parties intended a contract and it cured a lack of specificity in the express terms by implying an obligation that derived from the principle of good faith and fair dealing.

D THE TORT OF INTERFERENCE WITH CONTRACT RELATIONS: LIABILITY FOR ENTICING A PARTY TO BREACH A CONTRACT OR A PRELIMINARY AGREEMENT

In *B. Lewis Productions, Inc. v. Angelou,* summarized in Problem 7.4, BLP also sued Hallmark Cards for tortious interference with contract. BLP claimed that although Hallmark was aware that BLP had the exclusive right to represent Angelou, it induced Angelou to breach her agreement with BLP by negotiating to enter into a licensing agreement with her directly. This is a claim in tort, not contract. It arises where a valid contract exists and a third party, knowing of the existence of the contract, intentionally and improperly procures or induces a breach of the contract. Hallmark moved for summary judgment on BLP's claim, but the court denied the motion: There was at least a material issue of fact as to whether BLP and Angelou had a valid contract. Hallmark clearly did know of the contract, and in fact had written notice of it by virtue of the letter signed by Angelou, affirming BLP's authority to act on her behalf. The court also found that there was a material issue of fact on the question of whether Hallmark intentionally brought about Angelou's breach of contract. After it had become aware of the rift between Angelou and Lewis, it made advances to her to negotiate a licensing agreement. There was at least enough evidence to create a factual question about whether Hallmark was conscious that Angelou might still be committed to BLP and about whether it engaged in strategies to help Angelou disentangle herself from that relationship.

The existence of a valid contract is one of the prerequisites for this tort action, so it usually cannot be brought where a third party induces one of the parties to break off negotiations that might have led to a contract. However, if the parties have made a binding preliminary agreement or have agreed to continue to negotiate in good faith, this preliminary commitment itself might qualify as protected contractual relationship. A third party might therefore incur tort liability if it intentionally causes one of the parties to abandon an enforceable agreement in principle or an agreement to conduct good-faith negotiations.

Texaco, Inc. v. Pennzoil Co., 729 S.W.2d 768 (Tex. App. 1987), is surely the most spectacular case of this kind. Pennzoil had been negotiating with the stockholders and the board of Getty Oil Company to acquire Getty Oil. The parties eventually reached an "agreement in principle" for Pennzoil's purchase of the shares in Getty Oil, subject to the execution of a definitive agreement. While the lawyers were working on the Pennzoil contract, Getty began negotiations to sell the shares to Texaco. Texaco offered a higher price, and Getty accepted the offer and renounced the Pennzoil deal. Pennzoil sued Texaco for tortious interference with its contractual right to acquire the Getty shares. The jury found that the "agreement in principle" was intended to be binding even though the formal contract had not yet been worked out.

It made a massive damages award to Pennzoil—$7.53 billion in compensatory damages and $3 billion in punitive damages. The Texas Court of Appeals upheld the award (but reduced the punitive damages to $1 billion). It found that even though Texaco may not have been sure that a binding contract had been entered between Pennzoil and Getty, it knew enough to realize that Pennzoil had contract rights. Although it was Getty and not Texaco that had initiated the discussions, Texaco pursued the acquisition of the shares aggressively and strategically. It thereby did intentionally induce Getty's breach of the "agreement in principle." (After losing this case, Texaco filed bankruptcy and used the bankruptcy process to settle the claim for far less than the amount of the judgment.)

CHAPTER 8

The Statute of Frauds

A | THE BASIC PRINCIPLE

Although parties often execute their agreements in writing for the purpose of precision, record-keeping, and proof, most contracts do not have to be in writing to be legally enforceable. That is, although it may be harder to prove the existence and exact terms of an oral contract, once they are established by testimony, a court will, in most transactions, enforce the contract. However, there are exceptions to this rule. Certain types of contracts are required by law to be in writing; if they are not, they cannot be enforced by legal action. The requirement of a writing for a specified group of contracts was originally enacted in a statute passed in England in 1677 known as An Act for the Prevention of Frauds and Perjuries, which came to be known by the shortened name, the statute of frauds. The purpose of the act was to ensure that a person could not falsely claim, on the basis of perjured oral evidence, that a contract covered by the act had been entered into.

The original statute of frauds became the model for similar statutes enacted in almost every American state (or, in a small minority of jurisdictions, was incorporated into the common law by judicial decision). Although the transactions covered by the old English statute were selected in response to conditions that existed in England in the seventeenth century, the coverage of the statute has been surprisingly durable. Modern versions of it cover substantially the same types of transactions as the original. There are some variations and additions, of course, and states have commonly enacted other statutes that require writing for a variety of additional types of transactions. For example, UCC

Some contracts can not be orally entered in-to

Article 2 has a statute of frauds for sales of goods, which was one of the categories of transaction covered by the original statute. However, other Articles of the UCC include writing requirements for transactions that were not encompassed within the original statute: For instance UCC Article 2A has a statute of frauds applicable to leases of goods in which the rent exceeds a specified amount, and UCC Article 9 has a statute of frauds for agreements granting a security interest in personal property. Despite additions to the original group of covered transactions, it remains true that the list of contracts that have to be in writing to be enforceable is relatively small and discrete.

[margin note: very small # of contracts that must be in writing]

As its name suggests, the goal of the statute of frauds is to act as a barrier to fraud. However, a rule barring the enforcement of oral contracts could just as easily be used to prevent the enforcement of a genuine oral contract by a dishonest person who later wishes to renege on it. Courts are sensitive to this potential for abuse and are therefore wary of applying the statute rigidly. As is shown throughout this chapter, they have developed a number of rules to keep the statute within reasonable bounds by making it harder for the statute to be used by those who seek to evade genuine oral contracts.

A defense based on the statute of frauds is often raised right at the beginning of a case by means of a motion to dismiss or an application for summary judgment. If the plaintiff loses at that stage, it is the end of her case based on the alleged oral contract. One of the benefits of the statute of frauds is that it allows for this kind of summary disposition at the outset of the case, saving the use of judicial resources and the costs of trial. If the plaintiff overcomes this early challenge based on the statute of frauds, the case will go to trial on the merits. The plaintiff's victory on the statute of frauds issue is just preliminary, however; she then has to go on to establish that a contract was entered into on the terms that she alleges, that the defendant breached it, and that the plaintiff suffered a harm for which she is entitled to relief.

[margin note: typically brought by a motion to dismiss or summary judgment]

B   THE REQUIREMENTS OF THE STATUTE

In essence, the statute of frauds has three requirements that must be satisfied to make the contract enforceable: a writing (or record), a signature, and sufficient content to evidence the contract. These requirements are reflected in Restatement, Second §131, which sets out the language that one might find in a typical statute applicable to contracts governed by the common law, and UCC 2-201, which applies to contracts for the sale of goods. (Because the statute of frauds is enacted as a statute in most states, the language of each state's statute may differ from that of the Restatement, Second. Nevertheless, we use the language of the Restatement, Second, as a representation of what a typical statute of frauds is likely to provide.)

[margin note: 1) writing 2) signature 3) sufficient content]

RESTATEMENT, SECOND §131. GENERAL REQUISITES OF A MEMORANDUM

Unless additional requirements are prescribed by the particular statute, a contract within the Statute of Frauds is enforceable if it is evidenced by any writing, signed by or on behalf of the party to be charged, which

(a) reasonably identifies the subject matter of the contract,

(b) is sufficient to indicate that a contract with respect thereto has been made between the parties or offered by the signer to the other party, and

(c) states with reasonable certainty the essential terms of the unperformed promises in the contract.

UCC 2-201 is set out in Section F. In essence, it requires that there must be a written memorial of the transaction, signed by the party against whom enforcement is sought, sufficient to indicate that the parties have made a contract of sale. UCC 2-201(1) states that the omission or incorrect statement of a term does not make the writing insufficient, but the contract is not enforceable beyond the quantity stated in the writing.

[handwritten margin note: Contract can't go beyond what is stated in writing]

1. Writing or Record

Traditionally, the agreement must be recorded in a writing—the inscription of words in a tangible medium. Modern law accepts that other forms of recording that may not have tangible existence, particularly electronic recording, qualify as writings. While Restatement, Second §131 and UCC 2-201 refer to a "writing,"[1] the concept of writing is expanded by statute and court decision to include electronic records. As mentioned in Chapter 4,[2] in 2000 Congress enacted the Electronic Signatures in Global and National Commerce Act (E-SIGN), 15 U.S.C. §7001-7031, which recognizes the validity of electronic records and electronic signatures. In addition, in 1999 NCCUSL (ULC)[3] promulgated the Uniform Electronic Transactions Act (UETA), a model state law that has similar provisions. If a state has enacted UETA (as 49 jurisdictions have done), E-SIGN defers to state law. UETA §7(a) and E-SIGN §7001(a)(1) both provide that a record or signature may not be denied legal effect or enforceability solely because it is in electronic form. Therefore, unless the context indicates otherwise, we use the words

[handwritten margin note: electronic records can count as writing]

---

[1] In the attempted 2003 revision of UCC Article 2, the drafters sought to update UCC 2-201 by substituting the word "record" for "writing," so as to expressly include electronically recorded information. Although the amendment was not enacted, it is not needed because electronic records are generally treated as writings, as explained in the text.

[2] See Section D of Chapter 4 for an introduction to these statutes.

[3] This organization is introduced in Section 1 of Chapter 2.

"writing" and "record" interchangeably to mean the same thing: They both include writing in tangible form and information stored in an electronic or other medium.

[margin note: typically not form specific]

[margin note: — adequately expresses the agreement]

The statute of frauds generally does not require a record to be in a particular form, provided that it adequately reflects the agreement and is signed by the party against whom enforcement is sought. The record need not be contained in a single document, and it could be pieced together from several related documents. Restatement, Second §132 reflects this by stating, "The memorandum may consist of several writings if one of the writings is signed and the writings in the circumstances clearly indicate that they relate to the same transaction." It is also not necessary that the record was deliberately made for the purpose of recording the contract. Restatement, Second §133 states that ". . . the Statute may be satisfied by a signed writing not made as a memorandum of contract." The comment to this section indicates that the purpose of the statute is evidentiary, so it does not matter whether the writing was intended to evidence the contract, or that it was sent to the other party. Even an internal memorandum or an informal letter to a third party could qualify. (UCC 2-201 does not contain expressly similar provisions, although its Official Comment does. Recall, also, that a court resolving an issue relating to a sale of goods can draw on common law principles if the court determines that they are not displaced by any provision of Article 2.)

2. Signature

[handwritten annotation: ↳ of the other party or an agent]

The record must be signed by the party against whom the contract is to be enforced. (The record can also be signed by the agent of the party to be charged, but most statutes require that the agent be authorized in a record to sign on behalf of the party.) Note that the record need not be signed by both parties, as long as the person who is denying the contract has signed it. The concept of "signature" is broad enough to cover more than a handwritten signature; it extends to various forms of authentication. Restatement, Second §134 defines "signature" to include "any symbol made or adopted with an intention, actual or apparent, to authenticate the writing as that of the signer." Comment a to the section says that "initials, thumbprint or an arbitrary code" will qualify; and the signature can be made by writing, printing, stamping, or other means. Also, where the record consists of more than one document, the signature need not appear on every document as long as the document on which it appears can be tied to the other records. UCC 1-201(b)(37) defines "signed," in terms similar to those used in Restatement, Second §134, to include "any symbol executed or adopted with present intention to adopt or accept a writing."

[margin note: ex. initials, thumb-print, code, etc.]

[margin note: by writing, printing, stamping, etc.]

Whenever we use the word "signature" in this chapter, we include electronic authentication. One of the principal purposes of UETA and E-SIGN is to give effect to signatures in electronic form. UETA §7 and E-SIGN §7001(a) both declare that a signature may not be denied legal effect merely because it is in electronic form. "Electronic signature" is defined in E-SIGN §7006(5) as "an electronic sound, symbol, or process, attached to or logically associated with a contract or other record and executed or adopted by a person with the intent to sign the record." The definition in UETA §2(8) is almost identical. Note that to qualify as a signature, the electronic symbol must be consciously made or adopted by the signatory. It is not enough that it is automatically generated by mechanical means. This does not mean that the mere fact that a signature is automated disqualifies it as a signature. For example, as discussed in Chapter 4, a party may program an electronic agent to form a contract without human intervention at the time of formation. If the party sets up the program to generate an electronic signature upon formation, this should satisfy the requirement that the signature was consciously made.

E-SIGN and UETA merely say that a signature cannot be denied validity because it is electronic. They do not suggest that an electronic signature cannot be challenged or invalidated for some other reason (for example, because it was forged, executed without authority, or coerced).

[handwritten: signatures can't be invalidated just because they're electronic]

3. Content

*[handwritten margin note: * record not required to be full & complete as long as its sufficient to prove a contract was entered into]*

Restatement, Second §131 does not require the record to be full and complete, provided that it has enough content to show that a contract was made, it identifies the subject matter, and sets out its material unperformed terms. (This formulation may be looser than the language of statutes enacted in some states, which require all material terms to be set out. Some state statutes even specify particular terms that must be included, such as the agreed price or the duration of certain contracts.) UCC 2-201 adopts a lenient standard for the content of the record with regard to all terms other than quantity. The record need not contain all the agreed terms and can even state some terms erroneously, provided that it is otherwise sufficient to indicate that the parties have made a contract for sale. However, this flexibility does not extend to the quantity term. If the quantity of goods sold cannot be ascertained from the record, it does not satisfy the statute. If it reflects a quantity less than actually agreed, the contract cannot be enforced beyond the quantity shown.

*[handwritten: * must have a quantity]*

C THE METHODOLOGY OF APPLYING THE STATUTE

There is a logical sequence to dealing with the statute of frauds. The analysis should ask three questions in the following order:

1. Is the contract subject to a statute of frauds? If the answer is no, the contract need not be in a record to be enforceable, and the analysis need proceed no further. If the answer is yes, the next question must be asked.

[handwritten margin note: yes? done no?]

2. Is there a signed record in a form sufficient to satisfy the statute? If the answer is yes, the contract is enforceable. If no, the contract is not enforceable unless the third question can be answered affirmatively.

3. Is there a recognized exception to the statute of frauds that will allow enforcement of this contract even though it is subject to the statute and there is no record sufficient to comply with it?

Both the common law and UCC Article 2 recognize that in some narrow and defined circumstances a contract may be enforceable even though it is generally subject to the recording requirement of the statute of frauds but does not comply. It must be emphasized that these exceptions are scarce and specific, so in most cases the answer to the third question is no. We discuss one exception recognized by the common law—the part performance exception—in Section E and a couple recognized by Article 2 in Section F. We discuss a further exception when we deal with promissory estoppel in Chapter 10.

[handwritten margin note: part performance exception]

D   AN OVERVIEW OF THE SIX TYPES OF CONTRACT COVERED BY THE TRADITIONAL STATUTE OF FRAUDS

The original statute of frauds covered six types of transactions.[4] In this section, we describe all six briefly, but in the remainder of the chapter, we focus on the three most common and important: contracts for the sale of land or the transfer of an interest in land (Section E.1); contracts that cannot be performed within a year from the time of their execution (Section E.2); and contracts for the sale of goods (Section F). In most states, the two types of contract discussed in Section E are still covered by the general statute, modeled on the original. Although sales of goods were one of the six categories included in the original statute, these contracts have been removed from the general statute and are now governed by UCC 2-201.

1. Contracts to Answer for the Debt or Obligation of Another

[handwritten margin note: surety – promises creditor $ for someone else's debt if default]

This provision covers suretyship contracts. A surety is a person who promises a creditor that he will pay a debt owed to the creditor by someone else (the

---

[4] As we note in Section A, while most state statutes still include many of these types of transactions, some states have added to or deleted from the list. A state may have deleted categories no longer considered appropriate, or may have added to the list of transactions that are required to be evidenced by a signed record. Therefore, this list of the original common law transactions subject to the statute of frauds is not definitive.

principal debtor) if the principal debtor fails to pay it. For example, Barry asks Larry for a loan. Barry has a rather shaky credit history, so Larry does not wish to rely solely on his ability to repay the loan. He therefore agrees to make the loan only if Barry can produce someone else who will back up Barry's repayment obligation by promising Larry to repay the loan if Barry defaults. Barry's friend Sally is willing to act as surety for the loan. Sally enters into a separate undertaking with Larry in which she commits to pay Larry if Barry does not. Barry, the principal debtor, is primarily liable on the loan and Sally is secondarily liable. Sally's undertaking to Larry is subject to the statute of frauds and it must be in a record and signed by her. The suretyship provision has a number of qualifications and complexities that we will not explore. The aim here is merely to introduce it and explain the type of transactions to which it applies.

2. Contracts of Executors or Administrators to Answer for the Duty of Their Decedents

estate who assumes liability for debt incurred before death

This provision covers a contract in which the executor or administrator of an estate assumes personal liability to a creditor of the decedent for a debt incurred by the decedent before his death. Normally, if there are not enough funds in the estate to pay the decedent's debts in full, the unpaid balance of those debts is uncollectible. The executor or administrator has no personal liability for them. By assuming personal liability, the executor or administrator undertakes to answer for the debt of another, so this provision is essentially a specialized application of the suretyship provision.

→ no personal liability assumed

3. Contracts Made upon Consideration of Marriage

prenup, postnup

A contract in consideration of marriage must be distinguished from a contract to marry. This provision does not apply to the prospective spouses' mutual promises to marry. Rather, it covers prenuptial contracts, motivated by the marriage, in which some property settlement or other financial arrangement is made relating to the marriage. The contract could be between the prospective spouses themselves or between the spouses and a third person, such as a parent.

4. Contracts for the Sale of Land or the Transfer of an Interest in Land

Restatement, Second §125 states, "A promise to transfer to any person any interest in land is within the Statute of Frauds." The statute applies not only to a contract to sell land but also to any other contract in which land or an interest in it is disposed of (such as the grant of a mortgage or an easement, or even a long-term lease). The inclusion of these types of transactions in the statute reflects the importance of land as a source of wealth at the time that the original statute was drafted. Land transactions are still important and often valuable. However, in the modern economy it is quite possible to find other transactions that are vastly more significant and involve a greater transfer of wealth. Nevertheless, many of those do not need to be evidenced by a record to be enforced. We examine this provision in Section E.1.

5. Contracts That Cannot Be Performed Within a Year of Execution

full performance is >1 year

Restatement, Second §130 provides "Where any promise in a contract cannot be fully performed within a year from the time the contract is made, all promises in the contract are within the Statute of Frauds. . . ." This provision is not confined to situations in which the performance of the contract will take more than a year. The actual period of the performance itself could be very short. The crucial question is whether there will be a gap of more than a year from the time the contract is made to the time that performance is completed. Note also that this is the only provision of the statute that is not concerned with the nature of the contract. It applies to any kind of contract, irrespective of its subject matter, if there will be a period of more than a year between execution and completed performance. We consider this provision in Section E.2.

6. Contracts for the Sale of Goods for the Price of $500 or More

As noted previously, the original statute covered contracts for the sale of goods, but this provision has now been incorporated into Article 2 and is covered by UCC 2-201, which is set out in Section F. UCC 2-201 applies to any contract for the sale of goods for the price of $500 or more. This dollar figure is the total contract price for all the goods bought under the contract. If the price is paid other than in cash, the value of the noncash price must be determined to decide whether the statute applies. The $500 threshold for UCC 2-201 is the original amount set when Article 2 was first promulgated more than 50 years ago, and the Official Text has never been adjusted to take account of inflation. This means that in most states, the statute of frauds now applies to transactions of much lower actual value than originally contemplated by the drafters of the UCC.[5]

---

[5] The proposed 2003 revision of Article 2 would have increased the amount to $5,000. A few states have enacted nonuniform amendments changing the threshold amount. See, e.g., Mich. Comp. Laws Ann. §440.2201 (setting the amount at $1,000).

■ PROBLEM 8.1

Look for a state of your choosing in which the general statute of frauds has been enacted in statutory form by the state legislature. Compare the types of contracts covered by that statute with the categories described here.

(a) Do any of the traditional categories appear to be missing?

(b) Does the statute that you found include any additional types of contracts?

(c) If there are any differences between the traditional categories and those covered by your statute, what might have motivated the state legislature to make those changes?

E CONTRACTS AT COMMON LAW: SALES AND TRANSFERS OF LAND AND CONTRACTS NOT PERFORMABLE WITHIN A YEAR OF EXECUTION

1. Sales and Transfers of Land

■ PROBLEM 8.2

Recall that in *Lucy v. Zehmer*, in Chapter 3, the contract for the sale of the farm was handwritten by Zehmer on the back of a blank guest check from his restaurant. The writing simply said, "We hereby agree to sell to W.O. Lucy the Ferguson Farm complete for $50,000, title satisfactory to the buyer." It was signed by both Mr. and Mrs. Zehmer.

 it was in writing

(a) Could Zehmer have made a tenable argument (in addition to denying that the parties intended to make a contract) that even if there was a contract, it would be unenforceable under the statute of frauds?

(b) Assume that Zehmer wished to proceed with the contract, but Lucy decided the next morning (before talking to his brother or his attorney) to renege on it. Would Lucy have been able to assert a defense based on the statute of frauds? *Lucy did not sign it*

(c) Suppose Zehmer wished to proceed with the contract. Initially, so did Lucy. On the day after Zehmer executed the writing on the guest check, Lucy wrote a note to his brother stating, "I have just bought the Ferguson farm from Zehmer for $50,000. Would you like to contribute half the price and be a co-owner with me? Let me know. W.O.L." The next day Lucy's brother declined his offer and Lucy had second thoughts. If Lucy now reneged on the contract, could he assert a defense based on the statute of frauds?

no — the writing (2nd) is signed

Although a sale of land must be evidenced by a signed record, in limited circumstances, the "part performance" doctrine may soften the impact of the statute of frauds. This doctrine, a judicially created exception to the statute of frauds, recognizes that part performance of an oral contract may provide enough proof of the contract's existence to justify enforcing it despite noncompliance with the statute. The rationale for the exception is that the conduct of the parties not only proves the contract but also demonstrates reliance on the contract that is worthy of protection. However, out of concern that that too liberal an exception would gut the statute, courts are quite begrudging in applying the part performance exception. Courts tend to be restrictive in their recognition of it. These are the commonly recognized requirements of and restrictions on the exception:

1. Because the exception derives from the court's equitable powers, many cases confine it to equitable suits for specific performance of an oral contract for the sale or transfer of land, and do not allow it in suits at law for damages. Other courts allow it in a suit for damages, but only in favor of the buyer, not the seller.

2. The exception is generally confined to the statute relating to the sale or transfer of land, and is not recognized with regard to other statutes, such as that applicable to contracts that cannot be performed within a year of execution.[6] (Note, however, that quite apart from this common law exception, Article 2 has its own version of the part performance exception, which is discussed in Section F.)

3. Because the principal rationale of the part performance exception is that the part performance serves as evidence that a contract was made, courts insist that the performance must in fact be persuasive evidence of the existence of an oral contract. Many courts therefore require that the performance must be attributable solely to the existence of an oral agreement, and that the conduct cannot be accounted for in any other way. That is, the conduct is not sufficient to satisfy the part performance exception if it is consistent with some explanation other than the existence of an oral contract.

4. Because the exception is equitable in nature, courts commonly require that the party seeking enforcement of the oral contract show equities in favor of

---

[6] We discuss the one-year provision of the statute of frauds more thoroughly in Section E.2. Several courts have refused to apply the part performance exception to enforce an alleged oral contract that cannot be performed within a year of its making. For example, the court refused to enforce an oral multiyear marketing agreement in *Coca-Cola Co. v. Babyback's International, Inc.*, 841 N.E.2d 557 (Ind. 2006). The court reasoned that, in contrast to a real estate contract, where part performance is likely evidence that the parties actually made the contract, initial performance of a multiyear contract is ambiguous and does not necessarily evidence a contract for an ongoing relationship. The court also made the general observation that exceptions to the statute should be sparingly recognized to ensure that the purpose of the statute is not undermined.

prove equities in favor of enforcement

enforcement, which usually requires justifiable reliance on the oral contract, and prejudice resulting from that reliance.[7]

5. If the court allows the exception, the party seeking enforcement of the oral contract may prove its terms by whatever evidence is available. However, the terms must be proved with some certainty, and the court will not enforce the oral contract if its terms were never fully settled or were too indefinite.

terms must be proven by enforcing party

COOKE v. GOETHALS

Not reported in P.3d, 157 Wash. App. 1067, 2010 WL 3639912 (2010)
Washington Court of Appeals

ARMSTRONG, Judge.

Steve and Dana Cooke sued Gilbert and Lena Goethals and the Goethalses' son Don, seeking specific performance of their oral agreement to buy property from the Goethalses. Alternatively, they sought damages for breach of contract and fraud. The Goethalses moved for summary judgment, arguing that the statute of frauds prevented the court from enforcing the Cookes' alleged oral agreement.

posture ← The trial court granted the Goethalses' motion, dismissing all of the Cookes' claims. Because issues of material fact exist as to whether the Cookes' evidence of part performance of the alleged oral agreement is sufficient to satisfy the statute of frauds, we reverse and remand. — *disposition*

The Cookes and the Goethalses were longtime friends. In May 2001, the Cookes talked with the Goethalses' son Don, a realtor, about buying property in the Lake Tapps area. The Cookes wanted property with an outbuilding suitable for building and storing a helicopter, as well as property large enough to build a home for Steve Cooke's mother. Don said that his parents had property they wanted to sell that might be suitable. The Cookes looked at the property, which was vacant except for a free-standing garage, and decided it would serve their purposes. The Goethalses offered to sell the property for $60,000. The Cookes agreed to the price but were unable to obtain financing until the Goethalses resolved a lot line adjustment issue. After the Goethalses assured the Cookes that the lot line adjustment would not be a problem, the parties agreed to a 30-year amortization of the purchase price to establish the Cookes' monthly payment. Don calculated that with an interest rate of six to seven percent, including taxes, the monthly payment would be $350. The parties further agreed to treat their arrangement like a sale on a real estate contract

---

[7] As we will see in Chapter 10, Section C.2, the reliance aspect of the part performance exception might give rise to an alternative argument for enforcement of the oral promise under the doctrine of promissory estoppel. We defer to Chapter 10 the discussion of the use of the doctrine of promissory estoppel to overcome noncompliance with the statute of frauds. For the present, it is just worth noting the link.

*terms, none
are written*

with a balloon payment in five years, after the Cookes obtained a loan. There was no written agreement reflecting any of these terms.

Steve Cooke attempted to resolve the lot line problem, but county officials said it was the Goethalses' responsibility. The Goethalses agreed to resolve it. The Cookes continued to make their monthly payments. They also removed garbage from the property and rebuilt the front of the garage, spending $6,000 to $7,000. In December 2007, a Federal Express truck accidentally ran into the garage, knocking out the power. The Goethalses offered suggestions to the Cookes about how to recover the cost of repairs but made no attempt to take care of the problem. In May 2008, the Cookes found loggers on the property clearing trees and confronted Don, who apologized and said that the trees should not have been cut down. . . .

*Cookes made
payments
for 7 years*

[Sometime in 2008, the Goethalses obtained the lot line adjustment. In October 2008 they reneged on their oral agreement to sell the property to the Cookes for $60,000 and served notice on the Cookes requiring them to leave the property. The Cookes had made monthly payments from May 2001 to December 2008. The Goethalses had paid the property taxes from the proceeds of these payments. The Cookes sued, seeking specific performance of the sales agreement or damages for breach of contract and fraud.] The Goethalses moved for summary judgment, arguing that no written sales agreement existed and that any oral agreement was barred by the statute of frauds. . . . [They claimed that because the Cookes could not afford to buy the property, they had simply rented it for $350 per month. The Cookes denied this, pointing out that their monthly checks contained a notation indicating that they were in payment of the "mortgage."] Todd Bohon, a longtime friend of the Cookes, stated that he heard the Cookes talking with the Goethalses in 2001 about their plans for the property and knew that the Cookes wanted to purchase it. He also heard the parties discussing the lot line issue that had to be resolved before Cooke could get financing. Bohon stated that the parties spoke specifically about why the Cookes were purchasing the property and talked of it as being the Cookes' property. "[T]here was absolutely no question, that the property was being sold to, and purchased by, Mr. Cooke[.]" Kevin Eliason, who works in the mortgage industry and knows both families, stated that the Cookes met with him in 2001 about obtaining financing to purchase property in Lake Tapps. Eliason walked the property with both Steve Cooke and Don and learned of Cooke's plans for the property as well as the lot line issue. Eliason added that he did "not ever see any copies of a purchase and sale agreement nor did [he] know of any price discussions or agreements." He also stated, however, that the Cookes were qualified to purchase the property at that time.

*G claimed the
Cookes to be
renters*

The trial court granted the Goethalses' motion for summary judgment and dismissed the Cookes' claims with prejudice. . . . The principal issue is whether the Cookes' claimed part performance of the oral agreement avoids a strict application of the statute of frauds and would allow the trial court to enforce the agreement. . . .

issue

The real estate statute of frauds provides that "[e]very conveyance of real estate, or any interest therein, and every contract creating or evidencing any encumbrance upon real estate, shall be by deed[.]" RCW 64.04.010. Every deed, in turn, "shall be in writing, signed by the party bound thereby, and acknowledged. . . ." RCW 64.04.020. The statute of frauds is intended to prevent fraud in contractual undertakings. More specifically, its purpose is to prevent fraud "arising from *uncertainty* inherent in oral contractual undertakings." *Miller v. McCamish*, 78 Wash. 2d 821, 829, 479 P.2d 919 (1971).

The Goethalses argue at the outset that the parties had only an agreement to agree, which is unenforceable as a matter of law without resort to the statute of frauds. *See Keystone Land & Dev. Co. v. Xerox Corp.*, 152 Wash. 2d 171, 176, 94 P.3d 945 (2004). The *Keystone* court explained that an agreement to agree is an agreement to do something that requires a further meeting of the minds, without which it would not be complete. *Keystone*, 152 Wash. 2d at 175, 94 P.3d 945. The Goethalses also cite the required elements of a contract and point out that few of these terms were discussed or agreed upon by the parties. *See Sea-Van Invs. Assocs. v. Hamilton*, 125 Wash. 2d 120, 128-29, 881 P.2d 1035 (1994) (holding that agreement did not escape the statute of frauds partly because it did not contain the 13 material terms of a real estate contract).[8] In *Keystone*, the parties began negotiations to enter into a purchase and sale agreement, but never agreed on how to proceed and no contract was formed. *Keystone*, 152 Wash. 2d at 179-80, 94 P.3d 945. The circumstances here are distinguishable. The Cookes argue that offer and acceptance occurred in 2001 and that no further agreement was contemplated or required. They concede that their agreement was oral but argue that it survives the statute of frauds under the part performance exception.

Courts have upheld oral agreements under the part performance exception to the statute of frauds without reference to the 13 material terms outlined in *Sea-Van. See, e.g., Pardee v. Jolly*, 163 Wash. 2d 558, 182 P.3d 967 (2008); *Powers v. Hastings*, 93 Wash. 2d 709, 612 P.2d 371 (1980); *Miller*, 78 Wash. 2d 821, 479 P.2d 919. Because the statute of frauds is intended to prevent fraud, courts will not apply it to protect or perpetrate a fraud. *Miller*, 78 Wash. 2d at 825-26, 479 P.2d 919. "[W]here one party to an oral contract for the sale of land has, in reliance on the contract, so far performed his part thereof that it would be a fraud upon him to allow the other party to repudiate the contract by invoking the statute of frauds, equity will regard the case as removed from the operation of the statute." *Richardson v. Taylor Land & Livestock Co.*, 25 Wash. 2d 518, 528, 171 P.2d 703 (1946) (quoting 49 Am. Jur. 725, *Statute of Frauds* §421). Consequently, an agreement to convey real property may be proved without a writing given sufficient part performance. *Miller*, 78 Wash. 2d at 826, 479 P.2d 919.

In determining whether there is sufficient part performance to "remove" an oral contract for the sale of real property from the operation of the statute of frauds, courts consider whether there has been delivery and assumption of

---

[8] Those terms are the time and manner of transferring title; the procedure for declaring forfeiture; allocation of risk with respect to damage or destruction; insurance provisions; responsibility for taxes, repairs, water and utilities; restrictions on capital improvements, liens, removal or replacement of personal property and types of use; time and place for monthly payments; and indemnification provisions. *Kruse v. Hemp*, 121 Wash. 2d 715, 722, 853 P.2d 1373 (1993).

[margin handwritten notes: assumption of possesion; payment/tender of consideration; permament & substantial emproument]

actual and exclusive possession; payment or tender of consideration; and the making of permanent, substantial, and valuable improvements in accordance with the contract. Although all three factors are not required, a strong case for applying the part performance doctrine exists where all three are established. Judicial relief may include specific performance or the recovery of legal damages if the property has been transferred to another purchaser.

Part performance removed an option to purchase property from the statute of frauds where the plaintiff maintained actual and exclusive possession of a residence for one year before seeking specific performance; where he paid $16,000 for the option; and where he made permanent, substantial, and valuable improvements to the residence at a cost exceeding $20,000. *Pardee*, 163 Wash. 2d at 564, 568, 182 P.3d 967. Another option contract escaped the statute of frauds where the plaintiffs had actual, exclusive possession of a farm pursuant to the parties' agreement; the initial payments of $1,000 per month increased to $1,500 after a year and substantially exceeded the defendants' bank payments on the property; the parties agreed that plaintiffs would pay taxes and insurance; and the plaintiffs spent $14,520 to improve the farm. *Powers*, 93 Wash. 2d at 717-18, 612 P.2d 371.

Part performance of an alleged oral agreement for the exchange of property was not established, however, where the plaintiff never possessed the property and made no improvements to it. *Richardson*, 25 Wash. 2d at 530-31, 171 P.2d 703. That the plaintiff paid for the livestock on the property was of no consequence as he sustained no loss on it. Furthermore, the court noted that paying the purchase price, in whole or in part, is not alone sufficient part performance to avoid the statute of frauds. *Richardson*, 25 Wash. 2d at 530, 171 P.2d 703; *see also Berg v. Ting*, 125 Wash. 2d 544, 558, 886 P.2d 564 (1995) (consideration alone is insufficient evidence of part performance).

The Cookes assert that they have satisfied all of the part performance factors. They point out initially that they had exclusive possession of the property for almost seven years. Although the Goethalses respond that the Cookes had possession only as tenants, the fact remains that they had sole possession. The Cookes argue that their possession as owners is shown by the Goethalses' reaction to the Federal Express incident, by the Goethalses' failure to draw up a lease agreement or increase the "rental" payments, and by the fact that the Cookes removed garbage from the property at their own expense. (The Cookes did not restore power to the garage after the Federal Express incident, however, nor did they repair the broken overhang to the garage entrance.)

As for consideration, the Goethalses assert that they continued to pay the property taxes while the Cookes possessed the property. The Cookes respond that they paid the consideration the Goethalses requested; that no down payment was required; that it was not their fault they could not obtain financing; that the property taxes were amortized into their monthly payment; and that there is no support for the Goethalses' claim that they could not afford to purchase the property. The Cookes add that they paid more than $42,000 in monthly payments.

The Goethalses also argue that the $2,000 the Cookes spent on the garage was minimal. The Cookes respond that they were barred from obtaining building permits until the property was in their name and that there was no structure other than the garage to improve. They also argue that the money they spent to modify the garage and clean up the property equaled approximately 10 percent of the purchase price.

holding When viewed in the light most favorable to the Cookes, we find that the facts show sufficient part performance to invoke the exception to the statute of frauds. Consequently, we reverse the trial court's summary dismissal of the Cookes' breach of contract claim. . . . Reversed and remanded.

■ QUESTIONS

(1) The court says that "paying the purchase price, in whole or in part, is not alone sufficient part performance to avoid the statute of frauds." This is a common approach. Why is this not sufficient?

(2) As mentioned in the text before this case, courts usually require that the conduct be attributable solely to the existence of an oral contract, and must not be consistent with any other explanation. Are you persuaded that the conduct of the Cookes after making the oral agreement is enough to justify enforcement of the oral contract that they allege?

(3) The court has reversed the trial court's summary judgment. Does this mean that the Cookes have won their suit? If not, what do they still have to do to prevail? *no, now the case moves forward to trial*

2. Contracts Not Performable Within One Year of Execution

The one-year rule states that a contract falls within the statute of frauds if it cannot, by its terms, be fully performed within a year from the time that the contract is made. Note that the rule does not apply only to long-term contracts that would take more than a year to perform. The one-year period relates not to the length of the performance but to the period between the making of the contract and the end of performance. It could therefore apply to a performance that lasts just a few minutes, if that performance will not occur within the year following the execution of the contract. For example, on August 1, at the beginning of the academic year, Student enters into a contract with Employer under which she will work for Employer as a paid intern from June 1 to August 31 of the following summer. Although the duration of the contract performance is only three months, the period between execution of the contract on August 1 of this year and the completion of its performance on August 31 of next year makes it a contract not performable within a year of the date it was made.

Many courts and commentators have criticized the one-year rule and have found it difficult to rationalize. Its purpose and effectiveness in achieving the aims of the statute of frauds is unclear, and if applied rigidly or technically, it could have arbitrary results and could prevent the enforcement of oral contracts that were genuinely entered into. Because most courts are skeptical of the value of the rule and are wary of the possibility of its use to defeat oral contracts that were actually made, they generally adopt a quite rigid test to decide if the contract cannot be performed within a year of its making. The question is not whether the contract performance might exceed that period, or even whether it is likely to, but whether the nature of the performance is such that it would actually be a breach of contract if the party completed the performance before the end of the one-year period. That is, by its terms, the contract must contemplate, as a contractual obligation, that the performance cannot be rendered in a period of less than one year of contract formation. In some contracts, this question is relatively easy to answer. For example, it is clear that in the internship illustration above, the parties expect the student to be on duty and available to work during the specified dates, and do not contemplate that she could accelerate her work schedule so as to complete her job a month early. Similarly, it would be clear that the contract would not fall within the one-year rule if the contract was executed on September 1, rather than August 1, and the work period was for the next July and August.

However, in some cases, it is not clear if there is a contractual requirement that the contract performance must be completed beyond a year of the contract's execution. In this area the case law is quite muddy, particularly because courts that do not like the one-year rule may go to great efforts to find that it does not apply. Therefore, if there is any possibility that the performance could be completed within the one-year period, courts tend to find that the contract does not fall within the statute, even if it is possible or even likely that the performance would in fact exceed that period.

Some examples illustrate this point: A contract for the construction of a building contemplates that the work will take 18 months to complete, so it is most unlikely that performance could end within a year after the contract is signed. However, if the contract does not forbid the contractor to accelerate its performance so that it completes the building before that time, a court will probably find that the contract is not subject to the statute of frauds even though the amount of work involved makes it unlikely that it would be physically possible for the work to be completed within a year. A contract between the owner of an apartment building and a pest control company, under which, for a period of 18 months, the pest control company would conduct monthly inspections of the building and eliminate vermin found, would be subject to the one-year rule. However, if the contract had a termination provision under which either party could cancel the contract on one month's notice, it would not be subject to the rule because performance could conceivably be completed within the year.

Many of the cases involving the one-year rule involve employment contracts. In many employment contracts, the parties do not specify the duration of the employment, so that the usual rule applies—the employment is at will and can be terminated by either party on notice. Even if the parties anticipate that the employment may be for a lengthy period, and even if it turns out that it lasts beyond a year, the at-will nature of the contract means that performance could have terminated within a year of the contract's execution, so the contract is not subject to the statute of frauds. However, matters become more complicated where the employment is for a stated period or until the happening of a stated event. The next case deals with such a situation.

MACKAY v. FOUR RIVERS PACKING CO.

145 Idaho 408, 179 P.3d 1064 (2008)
Idaho Supreme Court

JONES, Justice.

Stuart Mackay sued Four Rivers Packing Co. alleging the breach of an oral contract for long-term employment and claiming that Four Rivers terminated him . . . [in violation of that contract.] Four Rivers moved for summary judgment in district court, which the court granted. . . . Mackay appeals to this Court. We vacate the summary judgment order and remand.

Four Rivers operates an onion packing plant near Weiser, Idaho. Randy Smith, the general manager of Four Rivers, hired Stuart Mackay as a field man during the summer of 1999 to secure onion contracts from growers in the area. Four Rivers began experiencing financial difficulties in late 1999. All employees, including Mackay, were laid off at this time because one of the owners of Four Rivers filed suit to prevent the company from conducting business. When the lawsuit was resolved, Smith rehired Mackay as a field man. According to Mackay, Four Rivers offered him a long-term employment contract in March of 2000 to continue working as a field man up to the time of his retirement. Mackay claims he accepted the long-term offer of employment and advised Four Rivers that he may not retire for approximately ten years, at around age 62. Four Rivers denies extending such an offer to Mackay. According to Four Rivers, the owners informed Randy Smith in 2000 that they did not know whether the company would be in business the next fall due to continuing financial difficulties. In 2001, Mackay asked Four Rivers for a written contract of employment. He refused to sign the agreement that was prepared because it gave Four Rivers the right to terminate his employment at will. Subsequent efforts to arrive at a written employment agreement were unsuccessful.

In 2000, Mackay was diagnosed with Type II diabetes. . . . On March 7, 2003, Smith terminated Mackay's employment relationship without notice. According to Mackay, he did this because of Mackay's diabetes. . . . [Four Rivers denies that this was the reason for Mackay's termination.] Mackay filed a complaint on August 24, 2004, claiming Four Rivers breached his employment contract and discriminated against him in violation of the Idaho Human Rights Act (IHRA).

Four Rivers answered, alleging that Mackay was an "at will" employee. Further, it asserted an affirmative defense that a contract such as that claimed by Mackay is null, void, and unenforceable as violating Idaho Code §9-505 because the agreement could not be performed within one year of its making. Four Rivers moved for summary judgment in October 2006, and the district court granted its motion. The court concluded the alleged contract could not be performed by its terms within one year and would therefore be invalid in the state of Idaho. Thus, it granted summary judgment with regard to Mackay's breach of contract claim. . . . [The district court also granted summary judgment against Mackay on the discrimination claim. We omit the discussion of this cause of action.] Plaintiff subsequently filed a motion for reconsideration, which the district court denied, resulting in this appeal.

We are presented with the question . . . of whether the district court erred when it held the alleged oral contract between Mackay and Four Rivers fell within Idaho's Statute of Frauds. . . . The parties disagree regarding the proper application of Idaho's Statute of Frauds. According to Mackay, the longstanding rule in Idaho is that where an agreement depends upon a condition which may ripen within a year, even though it may not mature until much later, the agreement does not fall within the Statute. Since the alleged contract here contains a term that it will last until Mackay retires, and Mackay could have retired within the first year, the oral contract does not violate the Statute. Mackay argues this Court should construe the facts in his favor as the nonmoving party and determine that Four Rivers made a definite promise that he could work until retirement. Thus, summary judgment was inappropriate on the contract claim. Alternatively, if the Court concludes the contract was unclear as to its intended duration, summary judgment was inappropriate because the contract term must be determined by a jury.

Four Rivers denies entering into a long-term contract of employment, and further claims Mackay was at all times an "at will" employee. Four Rivers claims Mackay's allegations make it impossible to determine the term or duration of the alleged employment contract. Thus, the alleged contract fails for indefiniteness. Alternatively, Four Rivers claims the contract violates Idaho Code §9-505, relying on *Burton v. Atomic Workers Fed. Credit Union*, 119 Idaho 17, 803 P.2d 518 (1990). The employee in *Burton* claimed the employer breached an employment contract entitling her to work until she retired at age 65. According to Four Rivers, the contract in this case similarly falls within Idaho's Statute of Frauds. We consider that issue first.

Idaho's Statute of Frauds provision is found in Idaho Code §9-505. Section 9-505 provides that "an agreement that by its terms is not to be performed within a year from the making thereof" is invalid, unless the same or some note or memorandum thereof, be in writing and subscribed by the party charged, or by his agent. Evidence of such agreement cannot be received without the writing or secondary evidence of its contents. According to the Restatement (Second) of Contracts, courts construe this statute narrowly. Restatement (Second) of Contracts §130, cmt. a (1981). Under the prevailing interpretation, the enforceability of a contract under the one-year provision does not turn on the actual course of subsequent events, nor on the expectations of the parties as to the probabilities. Contracts of uncertain duration are simply excluded, and the provision covers only those contracts whose performance cannot possibly be completed within a year.

Leading treatises follow this general rule. It is well settled that the oral contracts invalidated by the Statute because they are not to be performed within a year include only those which *cannot* be performed within that period. 9 Samuel Williston, *A Treatise on the Law of Contracts* §24:3 (West 1999). A promise which is not likely to be performed within a year, and which in fact is not performed within a year, is not within the Statute, if at the time the contract is made there is a possibility in law and in fact that full performance such as the parties intended may be completed before the expiration of a year. The question is not what the probable, or expected, or actual, performance of the contract was, but whether the contract, according to the reasonable interpretation of its terms, required that it could not be performed within the year. Further, a promise which is performable at or until the happening of any specified contingency which may or may not occur within a year is not within the Statute.

Idaho cases are in accord. A contract which is capable of being performed and might have been fully performed and terminated within a year does not fall within the Statute. *Darknell v. Coeur D'Alene & St. Joe Transp. Co.*, 18 Idaho 61, 69, 108 P. 536, 539 (1910) (contract was to be terminated on sale of plaintiff's stock in the corporation, which sale might have taken place the following day or any day during the year). Where the termination of a contract is dependent upon the happening of a contingency which may occur within a year, although it may not happen until the expiration of a year, the contract is not within the Statute, since it may be performed within a year.

In this case, the district court applied the *Burton* decision and found that the alleged oral contract could not, by its terms, be completed within a year. In *Burton*, the plaintiff alleged there was an implied contract, which guaranteed her employment until she reached retirement, at age 65. Burton based this claim on evidence of oral representations, practices and procedures of the employer, and an employment manual prepared by the employer. The employer argued the claimed oral contract for employment "until age 65" violated the Statute of Frauds. This Court held that the alleged oral contract to employ Burton until age 65 could not by its terms have been performed within one year. Thus, the trial court should have instructed the jury on the employer's Statute of Frauds defense. This case differs. In this case, Mackay alleges the term of the contract is until retirement. Unlike the contract in *Burton*, which specified "until age 65," the alleged contract term in this case is indefinite. Thus, the district court erred when it held *Burton* applied to preclude enforcement of the contract alleged in this case.

Rather, this case falls under the general rule cited in numerous Idaho cases and in the Restatement (Second) of Contracts. For the purposes of summary judgment, we must take as true Mackay's allegation that the contract was to last

holding

"until retirement." Since Mackay could have retired within one year under the terms of the alleged contract, this contract is outside Idaho's Statute of Frauds provision. . . .

Four Rivers claims that, regardless of the Statute, Mackay's contract claim fails because he was an at will employee, subject to being terminated at any time. In Idaho, unless an employee is hired pursuant to a contract which specifies the duration of the employment, or limits the reasons for which the employee may be discharged, the employment is at the will of either party, and either party may terminate the relationship at any time for any reason (or no reason) without incurring liability. In this case, Mackay alleges the parties entered into a long-term contract for employment, which makes the default "at-will" rule inapplicable to this case. As the parties dispute whether the contract of employment was at will or whether it contained a provision regarding duration, the issue is not subject to determination on summary judgment.

whether or not the contract is at will is not a fact for summary judgement

Similarly, there is a disputed issue of fact as to whether the alleged contract contained a provision for its duration. Even if we did not take Mackay's contention as true, that the term of the contract is "until retirement," summary judgment would still be inappropriate because there are disputed issues of material fact as to the duration of the alleged contract. . . . [These] factual issues . . . should have been presented to a jury for determination. The district court erred when it granted summary judgment on Mackay's breach of contract claim. . . . We vacate the district court's order granting summary judgment against Mackay . . . and remand the case for further proceedings consistent with this opinion. . . .

summary judgement is not appropriate because there are questions on material facts

■ QUESTIONS

(1)   The court makes a point of distinguishing this case from *Burton v. Atomic Workers Fed. Credit Union* on the basis that in *Burton*, the contract specified that the employee would be employed until the age of 65. Presumably, both parties in *Burton* understood that she intended to retire at age 65. By contrast, although Mackay told Four Rivers that he anticipated working for approximately ten years, the alleged contract simply guaranteed his employment until he retired. What is the crucial distinction that the court finds between these cases? Do you agree that it is a meaningful distinction that justifies different results? Is it fair that Mr. Mackay is able to prove and enforce his oral contract, but Ms. Burton was not?

(2)   As in *Cooke*, the statute of frauds issue in *Mackay* is raised and disposed of in a motion for summary judgment. The case will therefore go to trial. What will Mackay have to prove at trial? Since he has no written record of what was agreed, what kind of evidence will he have to produce to persuade a factfinder of the terms of the contract? Based on the (albeit rather cursory) facts in the opinion, what difficulties do you anticipate he might have?

(3) A party may claim that he entered into an employment contract under which the employer agreed to employ him for life. Some courts, dealing with a an alleged oral contract on these terms have held that the contract is not subject to the one-year rule because it is conceivable that the contractual performance could have been completed within the year if the employee died before a year was up. Ms. Burton, who was allegedly promised employment until she reached the age of 65, could also have died within the first year of the contract. Why would the possibility of death not help Ms. Burton overcome the one-year rule? What makes her case different from that of the employee who was promised lifetime employment?

(4) Many opinions similar to *Mackay* take a narrow view of the one-year rule and decline to apply it if there is any credible argument that it does not apply. In Ms. Burton's case, however, the court was persuaded that the statute applied and covered her claim. Presumably both Ms. Burton and her employer had partially performed their obligations under the long-term contract. In Section E.1 we note that courts rarely allow part performance to overcome a defense based on the one-year rule. Given courts' general hostility to this provision, why do you think that they do not embrace the part performance exception in this context?

■ PROBLEM 8.3

Tucker v. Roman Catholic Diocese of Lafayette-In-Indiana, 837 N.E.2d 596 (Ind. App. 2005) involved an oral promise made by the Church to Ms. Tucker, who had been sexually abused by a church employee when she was a child. Many years later, as an adult, Ms. Tucker reported the abuse to the Church. She alleged that after reporting the abuse, she had made an oral contract with the Church under which she agreed not to sue the Church in exchange for the Church's promise to strip the abuser of his duties and to ensure that he would have no future contact with children at the parish. She sued the Church when it failed to honor its promise. The court dismissed her suit on several grounds. One of them was that the oral agreement was unenforceable under the one-year rule. The court reasoned that while the Church could have dismissed the abuser within a year, its promise to ensure that he had no contact with children at the parish had no time limit, and must necessarily impose a duty on the Church that extends beyond a year. The statute of frauds applied, and the alleged oral agreement was unenforceable.

Do you think this is the right decision? Could the court have found a basis for finding that this was a contract of indefinite duration, not subject to the one-year rule?

[handwritten margin notes: writing ✓ / signature ✓ / content ✓/✗ / ↳ reasonable minds can disagree]

■ PROBLEM 8.4

Noel Cowherd is a popular country and western singer. Because he is in great demand, he is booked up for months in advance. Patty Beef knew this and was anxious to have him perform at her "Grand Western Cookout" on July 4 next year. She therefore contacted Noel in June this year to engage his services. After some telephone negotiation, they met on June 30 this year. They agreed on the date of the performance, Noel's fee, the venue, and the program. Noel committed to perform at the cookout on July 4 next year.

On July 1 this year Patty sent an e-mail to Noel setting out the terms agreed to at their meeting and confirming their contract. On the same day she received a reply from Noel by e-mail. The reply included the message that Patty had sent to Noel with the following remark by Noel just above it: "Oops, on checking my calendar, I see that I have double-booked for July 4 next year. Sorry, I can't sing at your barbecue. Maybe some other time." This is all that Noel said in his reply. He did not include his name in the message, but it does appear in the copy of Patty's message. Noel's e-mail address (moo@yodeldedoo.com) is shown in the "From" line on the message.

Can Patty enforce the contract against Noel?

F │ THE STATUTE OF FRAUDS RELATING TO THE SALE OF GOODS

As mentioned previously, UCC 2-201 sets out the statute of frauds governing sales of goods.

UCC 2-201. FORMAL REQUIREMENTS; STATUTE OF FRAUDS

(1) Except as otherwise provided in this section a contract for the sale of goods for the price of $500 or more is not enforceable by way of action or defense unless there is some writing sufficient to indicate that a contract for sale has been made between the parties and signed by the party against whom enforcement is sought or by his authorized agent or broker. A writing is not insufficient because it omits or incorrectly states a term agreed upon but the contract is not enforceable under this paragraph beyond the quantity of goods shown in such writing.

, confirmation memo

(2) Between merchants if within a reasonable time a writing in confirmation of the contract and sufficient against the sender is received and the party receiving it has reason to know its contents, it satisfies the requirements of subsection (1) against such party unless written notice of objection to its contents is given within 10 days after it is received.

(3) A contract which does not satisfy the requirements of subsection (1) but which is valid in other respects is enforceable

(a) if the goods are to be specially manufactured for the buyer and are not suitable for sale to others in the ordinary course of the seller's business and the seller, before notice of repudiation is received and under circumstances which reasonably indicate that the goods are for the buyer, has made either a substantial beginning of their manufacture or commitments for their procurement; or

(b) if the party against whom enforcement is sought admits in his pleading, testimony or otherwise in court that a contract for sale was made, but the contract is not enforceable under this provision beyond the quantity of goods admitted; or — *judicial admission*

(c) with respect to goods for which payment has been made and accepted or which have been received and accepted. . . .

buyer accepts goods / seller accepts payment

INTERNATIONAL CASINGS GROUP, INC. v. PREMIUM STANDARD FARMS, INC.

358 F. Supp. 2d 863 (2005)
United States District Court, Western District of Missouri

LAUGHREY, District Judge.

[The issue in this case, involving a contract for the sale of all of the seller's output of hog casings, was whether an exchange of e-mails between the seller and the buyer satisfied the statute of frauds. The court considers this question in the context of a motion by ICG, the buyer, for a preliminary injunction restraining PSF, the seller, from selling the casings to a third party. In deciding whether to grant the preliminary injunction the court must decide whether the applicant has shown a likelihood of prevailing on the merits when the case goes to trial.]

. . . Because this dispute involves a contract for the sale of goods in excess of five hundred dollars, it must satisfy the Statute of Frauds . . . [which] has two requirements relevant to this dispute. The writing must evidence a contract for the sale of goods and it must be "signed," a word which includes any authentication which identifies the party to be charged. . . .

[Several writings and e-mail exchanges contained all the essential terms of the parties' agreement.] The fact that the terms of the agreement are contained

issue

① *writing must prove evidence of a contract for the sale of goods*
② *must be signed*

don't need to all be in one document

in separate documents does not prevent compliance with the Statute of Frauds. To satisfy the Statute of Frauds, the writing may comprise several writings that, in combination, supply the essential terms. . . .

The more difficult question is whether the writings which evidenced the sale of goods were signed. The answer depends on the definition of "signature" in the context of the UCC. The UCC's definition of "signed" includes "any symbol executed or adopted by a party with present intention to authenticate a writing." Mo. Rev. Stat. 400.1-201(39). The Comment to the UCC's definition states: "The inclusion of authentication in the definition of 'signed' is to make clear that as the term is used in this Act a complete signature is not necessary. Authentication may be printed, stamped or written; it may be by initials or by thumbprint. It may be on any part of the document and in appropriate cases may be found in a billhead or letterhead. No catalog of possible authentications can be complete

court to use common sense about a signature

and the court may use common sense and commercial experience in passing upon these matters."

Missouri has also adopted the Uniform Electronic Transactions Act ("UETA"). The UETA applies to Missouri's UCC provisions that govern the Statute of Frauds and the UETA defines an electronic signature as, "An electronic sound, symbol, or process attached to or logically associated with a record and executed or adopted by a person with the intent to sign the record." Mo. Rev. Stat. §432.205(8). Moreover, the UETA states, "If a law requires a signature, an electronic signature satisfies the law." Mo. Rev. Stat. §432.230(4). Hence,

e-signatures count as long as parties had the intention to authenticate

although [the parties'] . . . signatures were electronic, they satisfy the signature requirement of the UCC's Statute of Frauds, so long as each had the present intention to authenticate the document.

There is overwhelming evidence that [the parties'] . . . e-mails are authentic and that the information contained in them was intended by each to accurately reflect their communications with the other. Although they do not all contain a typed name at the bottom of the e-mails, each e-mail contains a header with the name of the sender. Given the testimony at the preliminary hearing, it is clear that [the parties] . . . by hitting the send button, intended to presently authen-

hitting send counts as authenticating

ticate and adopt the content of the e-mails as their own writing. This is enough to satisfy the UCC given the breadth of its definition of signature, as well as the UETA which specifically refers to a "process attached to or logically associated with a record."[9]

---

[9] The Court is aware that an e-mail can be fraudulently sent, indicating it is from one person when it is in fact from someone else. However, a contract written on paper can be forged. With e-mail, it can readily be determined whether the e-mail came from the computer of the reported sender or not, just as there are ways to determine whether a signature is forged. Therefore, the fact that the e-mail header with the name of the sender can be electronically "forged," should not render it an insufficient signature as a matter of law. Of course, this issue is irrelevant here because [the PSF representative] . . . has acknowledged under oath that he sent the e-mails.

Furthermore, the purpose of the UCC is to prevent fraud. In this case, there is no dispute about the content or authenticity of the parties' communications. Therefore, neither fraud nor perjury is a concern. Indeed, it would be contrary to the purpose of the UCC to permit a party to negotiate all the terms of an agreement, do so in a way which accurately records their negotiations and agreement, but then permit the party to escape responsibility for its promises because a piece of paper with a handwritten signature has not been produced. . . .

The Court's finding that an electronic signature in an e-mail satisfies the Statute of Frauds is supported by the developing case law. . . . Commentators have also suggested that an e-mail "signature" is sufficient to satisfy the Statute of Frauds provision in the UCC. . . .

PSF . . . argues that the Missouri and North Carolina UETA do not apply to [PSF's] . . . e-mails because the Acts require that the transactions are between "parties each of which has agreed to conduct transactions by electronic means." Mo. Rev. Stat. 432.220(2). In determining whether the parties have agreed, the Court may look to "context and surrounding circumstances, including the parties' conduct." *Id.* The Court has done so and concluded that a fact finder will probably infer from the objective evidence that the parties agreed to negotiate and eventually reach the terms of an agreement via electronic mail based on their ongoing e-mail negotiations during all of 2003 and the beginning of 2004. . . . Furthermore, in determining whether PSF agreed to "conduct transactions by electronic means," the Court looks to whether [its representative] . . . intended to authenticate the writing—not whether he subjectively intended to enter into a contract. In *Vess Beverages* [*Inc. v. Paddington Corp.*, 941 F.2d 651 (8th Cir. 1991)], the court rejected the argument that an individual authenticated his meeting notes when he created an attendance list for the meeting and included his own initials among the initials of the other attendees. The court stated, "the signature need not be legally effective assent to the contract, but the signer must sign with the intent to indicate that the document is his." The court further stated, "Lest there be any confusion, we emphasize that the standard is whether the party to be charged signed the writing with intention to authenticate *the writing.* Although one who signs a writing with intent to assent to its terms or to authenticate that an agreement exists fulfills the signature requirement in so doing, neither of these latter two types of intent is necessary to satisfy the Statute of Frauds." Thus, in determining whether [the PSF representative] . . . had the "present intention to authenticate" his . . . e-mails, the Court has considered whether [he] . . . intended to verify that the e-mails were his communications—not whether [his] . . . e-mails manifested a subjective intent to formalize in writing a binding contract. To find otherwise would undermine the objective theory of contracts which Missouri follows.

Accordingly, the Court finds that it is probable that ICG will prevail on the merits regarding the formation of a binding contract which satisfies the Statute of Frauds.

■ PROBLEM 8.5

Mens Sana, Inc., operates a number of counseling centers. It decided that it would be fitting to display a likeness of Sigmund Freud in each of its waiting rooms. Mens Sana discovered that Mike L. Angelo, a manufacturer of mass-produced sculptures, had once before made statues of Freud for a clinic in Austria, and it approached him to make 100 such statues for its waiting rooms. Mike told Mens Sana that he could make the statues for the centers but that the mold for the original statues had been destroyed some time ago, and he would have to make a new one specially for this order. Following some negotiation, the parties made an oral agreement on June 1 under which Mike agreed to make 100 statues of Freud, 18 inches in height and cast in a sturdy plastic. He would deliver them by the end of August. The price of the statues was $300 each. Mens Sana would pay a deposit of 10 percent within a week and would pay the balance of the price on delivery. Answer the following questions based on the above transaction:

(a) Mens Sana never paid the deposit. Instead, on June 7 it called Mike and told him that it no longer needed the statues and was canceling its order. When Mike protested that they had a contract, Mens Sana denied that a contract had been made. Mike had not yet taken any steps to begin making the statues. Can he enforce the oral contract against Mens Sana?

(b) Assume that the facts are as in question (a), except that Mike spent the whole day on June 5 making a mold to be used to produce the plastic casts. When Mens Sana seeks to cancel its order on June 7, can Mike enforce the oral contract?

(c) Assume that Mens Sana gave Mike a check for $3,000 at the conclusion of the meeting. The check was made payable to Mike, was signed by the president of Mens Sana, and contained on the memo line the words "Down payment for statues of Freud." Mike banked the check on June 1, and it cleared on June 3. By June 7, Mike had not yet taken any steps to begin making the statues. On that day, Mens Sana called Mike to cancel the order and denied that a contract had been made. To what extent (if at all) can Mike enforce the contract against Mens Sana?

(d) Disregard the facts of the previous questions and consider the following variation: On June 3 Mens Sana wrote a letter to Mike confirming their oral agreement. It stated all the terms to which they had agreed but incorrectly wrote the delivery date as September 1. No one at Mens Sana actually put a written signature on the letter, but the paper on which it was written had Mens Sana's logo printed at the top. Mike received the letter on June 5. He called Mens Sana on June 6 and denied making the contract. It is now June 15. Can Mens Sana enforce the contract against Mike?

We do not discuss at any length UCC 2-201(3)(b), the exception relating to admissions in pleadings, testimony, or otherwise in court. Neither *International Casings Group, Inc. v. Premium Standard Farms, Inc.* nor Problem 8.5 implicate this exception. This is a troublesome exception that raises difficult interpretation and policy issues. We leave it for courses on commercial law. It is worth noting, however, that while courts have been reluctant to recognize an exception under other statutes of frauds for admissions made in litigation, Article 2 does provide for such an exception. This means that a defendant who wishes to raise the defense of noncompliance with Article 2's statute of frauds must be very careful not to concede, whether in an affidavit, pleading, or otherwise in court, that a contract was made.

G   THE APPROACH OF THE CISG AND UNIDROIT PRINCIPLES TO THE STATUTE OF FRAUDS

As mentioned in the introduction to this chapter, our statute of frauds derives from an English statutory enactment of 1677. Although the statute has survived quite firmly in the United States (albeit with some loosening of its requirements), England has abolished its statute of frauds. It thereby moved closer to Civilian legal systems, which generally do not require a commercial contract to satisfy writing or recording formalities to be enforceable. The CISG and the UNIDROIT Principles reflect the Civilian and modern English approach.

England abolished the statute of frauds

CISG Article 11 states, "A contract of sale need not be concluded in or evidenced by writing and is not subject to any other requirement as to form. It may be proved by any means, including witnesses." However, this rule is qualified by Article 12, which declares Article 11 to be inapplicable where any party has its place of business in a contracting state (that is, a country) that has made a declaration that Article 11 does not apply. This means that if a signatory to the Convention has a statute of frauds relating to sales of goods in its domestic law, it may, in effect, opt out of Article 11. If it does so, that country's domestic law requiring a signed writing may apply to the transaction if international choice of law principles would lead to application of that country's law generally. The United States has not made the declaration, so Article 11 is not superseded merely because a party has its place of business in the United States. Therefore, a U.S. company would have to satisfy the statute of frauds in its domestic sales but generally would not have to do so in its international sales subject to the CISG.

states can opt out of Article 11

Article 1.2 of the UNIDROIT Principles follows the same approach to formalities as CISG Article 11. It states, "Nothing in these Principles requires a contract, statement or any other act to be made in or evidenced by a particular form. It may be proved by any means, including witnesses."

courts needed
to know what
situation gave
explicit
to the

CHAPTER 9

Consideration

A CONSIDERATION—THE BASIC DOCTRINE

1. Introduction to Consideration Doctrine

sort out those w/ legal consequences & those without

If not all promises are to carry the legal consequences of a contract, the law must have mechanisms to sort those that do from those that do not. As we have seen, offer, acceptance, and the other principles of contract formation addressed in earlier chapters play a role in deciding this question. We have hinted that consideration doctrine takes part, too. We now explore that doctrine.

As we begin, please recognize that consideration doctrine does not act in isolation. When we reach the end of our study, we will find that consideration, as strictly defined, is not always necessary; nor is it in itself sufficient to make a promise enforceable as a contract. Although many classical scholars gave consideration doctrine a starring role in their contracts jurisprudence, most scholars today acknowledge that consideration doctrine alone does not determine if an agreement carries legal consequences. There are other aspects of contract law, some of which we have studied and some of which we have yet to address, which help to perform this function. Likewise, there are other theories of recovery that may come to the aid of promisees when consideration doctrine disappoints them. There are even some instances where a party will be held to an obligation under a theory that resembles contract law, even though no promise was ever made and no consideration was present. The challenges for the law student are to understand when consideration alone attains the policy objectives of our legal system, when other doctrines and theories are needed to complete the job, and when important policies may remain unmet. To meet these challenges, it is helpful to understand where the concept of consideration came from and what its main outlines are.[1]

In its earliest iterations, the requirement of showing "consideration" may well have meant just that—in actions to enforce promises, the plaintiffs had to state the considerations that gave rise to the alleged promises. Without some sense of the circumstances under which the alleged promises were made, courts were unwilling or unable to use their powers to give them legal force. As to what factors were deemed adequate in the eyes of the law, early doctrine had little to say. Over time, however, the requirement of "consideration" grew to reflect the societal and legal contexts in which it arose. Courts used consideration as a concept to distinguish those promises that were both important from a societal point of view and capable of enforcement by the legal system of the times. Consideration, as a requisite for the enforcement of a promise, began to take on a decidedly commercial bent. Before the courts would trouble themselves with enforcing a purely executory promise, they would look to see if the promisor had in fact received something in exchange for the promise. In the commercial sphere, promises that were given in exchange for something were the norm, and it was primarily commerce that the courts sought to facilitate.

The exact outlines of consideration doctrine continued to develop over time, but the basic concept of exchange remains at its heart today. Before we explore what policies consideration doctrine might further, and how well it accomplishes the tasks set for it, we sketch the modern elements of the doctrine. Restatement, Second §17 tells us that consideration is a central component of a contract:

RESTATEMENT, SECOND §17. REQUIREMENT OF A BARGAIN

(1) Except as stated in Subsection (2), the formation of a contract requires a bargain in which there is a manifestation of mutual assent to the exchange and a consideration.

(2) Whether or not there is a bargain a contract may be formed under special rules applicable to formal contracts or under the rules stated in §§82-94.[2]

■   ■   ■

---

[1] Many scholars have detailed the history and development of consideration doctrine. Its roots date back centuries to the action of "assumpsit," the historical antecedent of the modern breach of contract lawsuit. (You may recall the brief discussion of the history of contract law, and in particular its origins in "assumpsit," included in Chapter 1.) A classic and thorough treatment of the early history of consideration doctrine is found in A.W.B. Simpson, *A History of the Common Law of Contract: The Rise of the Action of Assumpsit* 316-488 (Clarendon Press 1975). We present only the briefest glimpse of that history here and instead focus on its more recent evolution.

[2] You may find the language in Restatement, Second §17(2) a bit mysterious at this point. It is just one more reminder that the requirement of consideration is not absolute. The subsection references circumstances in which one of the usual requirements of a bargain, a manifestation of mutual assent or consideration, does not obtain. In those circumstances, many of which we study later, other doctrines such as promissory estoppel may step in to substitute for consideration.

Restatement, Second §71 goes on to explain what consideration is. The gist of this section is that, in order for a promise to be supported by consideration, the parties must bargain for a performance or a return promise. Of course, there is a great deal of texture and detail to this gist, which we explore in the rest of this chapter. But to get a sense for where we are going, here is the full text of §71:

RESTATEMENT, SECOND §71. THE REQUIREMENT OF EXCHANGE; TYPES OF EXCHANGE

(1) To constitute consideration, a performance or a return promise must be bargained for.

(2) A performance or return promise is bargained for if it is sought by the promisor in exchange for his promise and is given by the promisee in exchange for that promise.

(3) The performance may consist of

(a) an act other than a promise, or

(b) a forbearance, or

(c) the creation, modification, or destruction of a legal relation.

(4) The performance or return promise may be given to the promisor or to some other person. It may be given by the promisee or by some other person.

2. The "Benefit or Detriment" Test

Perhaps the clearest application of consideration doctrine is in the context of gifts. If the donor promises to make a gift with no strings attached but neglects or refuses to follow through, can the disappointed recipient sue in contract? The traditional answer to this question is no. <u>Any promise to make the gift is not supported by consideration.</u> There is no return performance or return promise at all. The promisee does not contribute anything (that is, as we will see, there is no "detriment to the promisee") and there is no exchange contemplated. That does not mean that the donor can always freely rescind gifts. Once a gift is made, or "delivered" or "executed" in the legal sense, it is effective. At that point, however, there is no executory promise for contract law to step in and enforce. Instead, any subsequent controversy is settled under the law of gifts.

In the next case, the plaintiff sought to enforce an executory promise to make what the court concludes was to be a gift. You will notice that the case, in addition to addressing consideration doctrine, also discusses the question of reliance. We study reliance as a basis for recovery in Chapter 10, when we discuss the theory of promissory estoppel. In the meantime, speculate about what policies underlie the enforcement (or nonenforcement) of promises in the context of cases such as this one, and how (or if) the requirement of consideration helps to further those policies.

no return promise

CONGREGATION KADIMAH
TORAS-MOSHE v. DeLEO

405 Mass. 365, 540 N.E.2d 691 (1989)
Massachusetts Supreme Judicial Court

LIACOS, Chief Justice.

Congregation Kadimah Toras-Moshe (Congregation), an Orthodox Jewish synagogue, commenced this action in the Superior Court to compel the administrator
of an estate (estate) to fulfill the oral promise of the decedent to give the
Congregation $25,000. The Superior Court transferred the case to the Boston
Municipal Court, which rendered summary judgment for the estate. The case
was then transferred back to the Superior Court, which also rendered summary
judgment for the estate and dismissed the Congregation's complaint. We granted
the Congregation's application for direct appellate review. We now affirm.

The facts are not contested. . . . [Saul Schwam, the decedent,] suffered a
prolonged illness, throughout which he was visited by the Congregation's
spiritual leader, Rabbi Abraham Halbfinger. During four or five of these visits,
and in the presence of witnesses, the decedent made an oral promise to give the
Congregation $25,000. The Congregation planned to use the $25,000 to transform a storage room in the synagogue into a library named after the decedent.
The oral promise was never reduced to writing. The decedent died intestate in
September, 1985. He had no children, but was survived by his wife.

The Congregation asserts that the decedent's oral promise is an enforceable
contract . . . because the promise is allegedly supported either by consideration
and bargain, or by reliance. We disagree.

The Superior Court judge determined that "[t]his was an oral gratuitous
pledge, with no indication as to how the money should be used, or what [the
Congregation] was required to do if anything in return for this promise." There
was no legal benefit to the promisor nor detriment to the promisee, and thus no
consideration. Furthermore, there is no evidence in the record that the Congregation's plans to name a library after the decedent induced him to make or to
renew his promise. Contrast *Allegheny College v. National Chautauqua County
Bank*, 246 N.Y. 369, 377-379, 159 N.E. 173 (1927) (subscriber's promise became
binding when charity implicitly promised to commemorate subscriber).

As to the lack of reliance, the judge stated that the Congregation's "allocation of $25,000 in its budget, for the purpose of renovating a storage room, is
insufficient to find reliance or an enforceable obligation." We agree. The inclusion of the promised $25,000 in the budget, by itself, merely reduced to writing
the Congregation's expectation that it would have additional funds. A hope or
expectation, even though well founded, is not equivalent to either legal detriment or reliance.

The Congregation cites several of our cases in which charitable subscriptions were enforced. These cases are distinguishable because they involved

written, as distinguished from oral, promises and also involved substantial consideration or reliance. . . . The promise to the Congregation is entirely unsupported by consideration or reliance. Furthermore, it is an oral promise sought to be enforced against an estate. To enforce such a promise would be against public policy.

Judgment affirmed.

■ QUESTIONS

detriment but not bargained for

(1) The court concludes that a hope or expectation is not equivalent to a legal detriment, and so the Congregation didn't provide consideration for Saul Schwam's promise. Suppose that before the estate refused to make good on the decedent's promise, the Congregation had not only planned to name a library after the decedent, but had also made a non-refundable $500 down payment on a plaque for the "Saul Schwam Memorial Library." Without more, would the Congregation have incurred a legal detriment, and if so, would that detriment constitute consideration for the decedent's promise?

(2) Many things may motivate individuals to make gifts. The donors may well feel that the gifts will be in their interests. At a minimum, it may please donors to know that their gifts will help others. So one might say that a donor often receives a benefit (psychic or otherwise) from promising to make a gift. The opinion suggests that the Superior Court found no legal benefit to the promisor in this case, and the Supreme Judicial Court doesn't question that holding. What do you think it means to say that there is no legal benefit to the promisor?

emotional Benefit ≠ legal Benefit

■ ■ ■

legal benefit or detriment

As the *DeLeo* case illustrates, if nothing is given or received in exchange for a promise, traditional contract doctrine refuses to enforce the promise on the grounds of lack of consideration. But what is it that has to be given in exchange for the promise? The *DeLeo* opinion recites a classic formulation of consideration doctrine—there was no legal benefit to the promisor nor detriment to the promisee, thus no consideration. This test had one of its most vivid expressions in the time-honored case of *Hamer v. Sidway*. As we will see, and as Restatement, Second §71 (set forth in Section A.1) illustrates, consideration doctrine has developed since the days of *Hamer*. Under the bargain theory of consideration, on which we focus in Section A.3, the crucial question is whether each party suffered a detriment in exchange for the detriment suffered by the other. Whether the promisor benefited from the detriment suffered by the promisee may be relevant to the question of whether the parties agreed to an exchange. So the definition of consideration cited in *Hamer*—that is, a benefit to the promisor or detriment to the promisee—is thus both incomplete and somewhat misleading under current case law. Nevertheless, the case remains important reading

[handwritten margin note: Benefit/detriment are terms of art]

for law students everywhere, as it so aptly illustrates that the words "benefit" and "detriment" are themselves terms of art and should not be taken at face value. Although *Hamer v. Sidway* was decided way back in 1891, it is still regularly cited by courts as a seminal consideration case.

HAMER v. SIDWAY

124 N.Y. 538, 27 N.E. 256 (1891)
New York Court of Appeals

. . . The plaintiff presented a claim to the executor of William E. Story, Sr., for $5,000 and interest from the 6th day of February, 1875. She acquired it through several mesne assignments from William E. Story, 2d.[3] The claim being rejected by the executor, this action was brought. It appears that William E. Story, Sr., was the uncle of William E. Story, 2d; that at the celebration of the golden wedding of Samuel Story and wife, father and mother of William E. Story, Sr., on the 20th day of March, 1869, in the presence of the family and invited guests, he promised his nephew that if he would refrain from drinking, using tobacco, swearing, and playing cards or billiards for money until he became 21 years of age, he would pay him the sum of $5,000. The nephew assented thereto, and fully performed the conditions inducing the promise. When the nephew arrived at the age of 21 years, and on the 31st day of January, 1875, he wrote to his uncle, informing him that he had performed his part of the agreement, and had thereby become entitled to the sum of $5,000. The uncle received the letter, and a few days later, and on the 6th day of February, he wrote and mailed to his nephew the following letter:

Buffalo, Feb. 6, 1875.
W. E. Story, Jr.—

Dear Nephew:
Your letter of the 31st ult. came to hand all right, saying that you had lived up to the promise made to me several years ago. I have no doubt but you have, for

---

[3] Notice that William E. Story, 2d, the nephew of William E. Story, Sr., and one of the protagonists in this drama, is not the plaintiff. It's hard to tell, exactly, who the plaintiff is, but she claims to be the successor to the nephew by virtue of one or more assignments. The lower court speculated that the alleged assignments were in fact manufactured as a device to get around a problem in the nephew's case. Apparently, the nephew and his father had gone into business, had gone bankrupt, and then were rescued by the uncle. In exchange, the nephew had signed a general release in favor of the uncle, which arguably was broad enough to cover the claim being made in this case. The plaintiff asserted (perhaps disingenuously) that the nephew assigned his claim to a third party before he signed the release, so the release had no effect on the continuing vitality of the claim. One can only wonder what the full story was, and why this report gave us only selected details. For the *Hamer v. Sidway* aficionados in the crowd, the lower court's opinion can be found at 11 N.Y.S. 182, 57 Hun. 229 (N.Y. Sup. Ct. 1890). We treat the modern law related to assignment of contract rights and obligations in Chapter 22. —Eds.

which you shall have five thousand dollars, as I promised you. I had the money in the bank the day you was twenty-one years old that I intend for you, and you shall have the money certain. Now, Willie, I do not intend to interfere with this money in any way till I think you are capable of taking care of it, and the sooner that time comes the better it will please me. I would hate very much to have you start out in some adventure that you thought all right and lose this money in one year. The first five thousand dollars that I got together cost me a heap of hard work. You would hardly believe me when I tell you that to obtain this I shoved a jack-plane many a day, butchered three or four years, then came to this city, and, after three months' perseverance, I obtained a situation in a grocery store. I opened this store early, closed late, slept in the fourth story of the building in a room 30 by 40 feet, and not a human being in the building but myself. All this I done to live as cheap as I could to save something. I don't want you to take up with this kind of fare. I was here in the cholera season of '49 and '52, and the deaths averaged 80 to 125 daily and plenty of smallpox. I wanted to go home, but Mr. Fisk, the gentleman I was working for, told me, if I left then, after it got healthy he probably would not want me. I stayed. All the money I have saved I know just how I got it. It did not come to me in any mysterious way, and the reason I speak of this is that money got in this way stops longer with a fellow that gets it with hard knocks than it does when he finds it. Willie, you are twenty-one, and you have many a thing to learn yet. This money you have earned much easier than I did, besides acquiring good habits at the same time, and you are quite welcome to the money. Hope you will make good use of it. I was ten long years getting this together after I was your age. Now, hoping this will be satisfactory, I stop. One thing more. Twenty-one years ago I bought you 15 sheep. These sheep were put out to double every four years, I kept track of them the first eight years. I have not heard much about them since. Your father and grandfather promised me that they would look after them till you were of age. Have they done so? I hope they have. By this time you have between five and six hundred sheep, worth a nice little income this spring, Willie, I have said much more than I expected to. Hope you can make out what I have written. Today is the seventeenth day that I have not been out of my room, and have had the doctor as many days. Am a little better today. Think I will get out next week. You need not mention to father, as he always worries about small matters.

Truly yours,
W. E. STORY.

P. S. You can consider this money on interest. *— he's going to hold the $ until he is capable of taking care of it*

The nephew received the letter, and thereafter consented that the money should remain with his uncle in accordance with the terms and conditions of the letter. The uncle died on the 29th day of January, 1887, without having paid over to his nephew any portion of the said $5,000 and interest.

PARKER, Judge.

The question which provoked the most discussion by counsel on this appeal, and which lies at the foundation of plaintiff's asserted right of recovery, is whether by virtue of a contract defendant's testator, William E. Story, became indebted to his nephew, William E. Story, 2d, on his twenty-first birthday in the sum of $5,000. The trial court found as a fact that "on the 20th day of March, 1869, . . . William E. Story agreed to and with William E. Story, 2d, that if he would refrain from drinking liquor, using tobacco, swearing, and playing cards or billiards for money until [he] should become twenty-one years of age, then he, the said William E. Story, would at that time pay him, the said William E. Story, 2d, the sum of $5,000 for such refraining, to which the said William E. Story, 2d, agreed," and that he "in all things fully performed his part of said agreement." The defendant contends that the contract was without consideration to support it, and therefore invalid. He asserts that the promisee, by refraining from the use of liquor and tobacco, was not harmed, but benefited; that that which he did was best for him to do, independently of his uncle's promise—and insists that it follows that, unless the promisor was benefited, the contract was without consideration—a contention which, if well founded, would seem to leave open for controversy in many cases whether that which the promisee did or omitted to do was in fact of such benefit to him as to leave no consideration to support the enforcement of the promisor's agreement. Such a rule could not be tolerated, and is without foundation in the law.

The exchequer chamber in 1875 defined "consideration" as follows: "A valuable consideration, in the sense of the law, may consist either in some right, interest, profit, or benefit accruing to the one party, or some forbearance, detriment, loss, or responsibility given, suffered, or undertaken by the other." Courts "will not ask whether the thing which forms the consideration does in fact benefit the promisee or a third party, or is of any substantial value to any one. It is enough that something is promised, done, forborne, or suffered by the party to whom the promise is made as consideration for the promise made to him." Anson, *Cont.* 63. "In general a waiver of any legal right at the request of another party is a sufficient consideration for a promise." Pars, *Cont.* 444. "Any damage, or suspension, or forbearance of a right will be sufficient to sustain a promise." 2 Kent, *Comm.* (12th Ed.) 465. Pollock in his work on *Contracts*, (page 166,) after citing the definition given by the exchequer chamber, already quoted, says: "The second branch of this judicial description is really the most important one. 'Consideration' means not so much that one party is profiting as that the other abandons some legal right in the present, or limits his legal freedom of action in the future, as an inducement for the promise of the first."

Now, applying this rule to the facts before us, the promisee used tobacco, occasionally drank liquor, and he had a legal right to do so. That right he abandoned for a period of years upon the strength of the promise of the testator that for such forbearance he would give him $5,000. We need not speculate on the effort which may have been required to give up the use of those stimulants. It is sufficient that he restricted his lawful freedom of action within certain

it is sufficient that he limited himself

prescribed limits upon the faith of his uncle's agreement, and now, having fully performed the conditions imposed, it is of no moment whether such performance actually proved a benefit to the promisor, and the court will not inquire into it; but, were it a proper subject of inquiry, we see nothing in this record that would permit a determination that the uncle was not benefited in a legal sense. . . .

The order appealed from should be reversed, and the judgment of the special term affirmed, with costs payable out of the estate. All concur.

disposition

■ QUESTIONS

(1) Reread Restatement, Second §71. Do you see where the Restatement, Second, articulates the equivalent of the benefit or detriment test?

(2) How does the test of the Restatement, Second, differ from that of *Hamer*? Are there any elements in the Restatement, Second, that are missing or not discussed in *Hamer*?

(3) In his letter, the uncle implies that young Willie had promised to mend his evil ways. Assume that he had in fact made such a promise, and assume further that instead of reforming, the nephew then proceeded to smoke, drink, and gamble to his heart's delight. Do you think the uncle could have successfully sought relief against him in contract?

3. The Bargain Theory of Consideration

Hamer speaks of "benefit" to the promisor or a "detriment" to the promisee. Although the Restatement, Second, refers instead to a "performance or return promise" serving as consideration for a promise, it remains common for courts to use the language of "benefit" or "detriment." Yet the subtleties of "benefit" and "detriment" do not end our study of consideration. Modern consideration doctrine requires further that the benefit or detriment serving as consideration be given in exchange for the promise to be enforced, or as the Restatement, Second, puts it, that it be "bargained for."

consideration must be bargained for ↓ *bargain theory*

The notion that a return promise or performance must be bargained for to constitute consideration has come to be known as the "bargain theory" of consideration. Some credit Oliver Wendell Holmes, Jr. with first articulating this theory. In the late 1800s, Holmes delivered a series of lectures at the Lowell Institute in Boston in which he attempted to describe systematically the entirety of the common law. In 1881 (about a decade before the decision in *Hamer v. Sidway*) he published a book based on these lectures, *The Common Law*. Holmes went on to serve as a justice on the U.S. Supreme Court (among other things), and is probably best remembered for his many, if sometimes controversial, opinions on matters of constitutional law. In *The Common Law*, Holmes discussed consideration at some length and noted:

It is said that any benefit conferred by the promisee on the promisor, or any detriment incurred by the promisee, may be a consideration. It is also thought that every consideration may be reduced to a case of the latter sort, using the word "detriment" in a somewhat broad sense. . . . It appears to me that it has not always been sufficiently borne in mind that the same thing may be a consideration or not, as it is dealt with by the parties. . . . In many cases a promisee may incur a detriment without thereby furnishing a consideration. The detriment may be nothing but a condition precedent to performance of the promise, as where a man promises another to pay him five hundred dollars if he breaks his leg. . . . This raises the question how a thing must be dealt with, in order to make it a consideration. It is said that consideration must not be confounded with motive. It is true that it must not be confounded with what may be the prevailing or chief motive in actual fact. A man may promise to paint a picture for five hundred dollars, while his chief motive may be a desire for fame. A consideration may be given and accepted, in fact, solely for the purpose of making a promise binding. But, nevertheless, it is the essence of a consideration, that, by the terms of the agreement, it is given and accepted as the motive or inducement of the promise. The root of the whole matter is the relation of reciprocal conventional inducement, each for the other, between consideration and promise.[4]

It's important to understand what "bargained for" means—and doesn't mean—in this context. Some courts suggest that the language or the circumstances must reveal that both parties intended an exchange. Courts do not require that the parties actually haggle over the terms of the bargain. Parties need not expressly state that the promise is given for the promisee's legal detriment or that the legal detriment is given in turn for the promise. If such negotiations are present, of course, it may be straightforward to establish that the parties intended an exchange. Courts are also willing to infer what the parties intended from the context of their dealings. As is so often the case in contract law, it is not the actual subjective intentions of the parties that are determinative, but rather what would be objectively reasonable to expect under the circumstances. As you read the following cases, try to articulate in your own words what it means to say that consideration for a promise must be "bargained for."

STEINBERG v. UNITED STATES

90 Fed.Cl. 435 (2009)
United States Court of Federal Claims

HEWITT, Chief Judge.

[Michael Steinberg filed a complaint against the United States, seeking to recover travel costs incurred during his trip to Washington, D.C. to attend

---

[4] Oliver Wendell Holmes, *The Common Law,* in *The Collected Works of Justice Holmes* vol. 2, 109, 264-265 (Sheldon M. Novick ed., U. Chi. Press 1995).

the 2009 presidential inauguration ceremonies. The plaintiff, acting *pro se*,[5] asserted that the government was in breach of contract when it refused him admittance to the festivities. The plaintiff's complaint was based in part on the theory of promissory estoppel, which we study in Chapter 10. The government moved to dismiss the complaint, arguing among other things that the court didn't have jurisdiction to hear the lawsuit. The United States Court of Federal Claims is a court of limited jurisdiction, and is primarily authorized to hear claims for money damages against the United States founded upon the Constitution, federal statutes, executive regulations, or contracts. As no constitutional, statutory, or regulatory claim was at issue here, the court would have the jurisdiction to hear Mr. Steinberg's complaint only if he sufficiently alleged breach of contract. The court concludes the complaint fails to allege the elements of a valid contract with the United States, in part due its failure to allege consideration.]

no consideration

no jurisdiction bc he couldn't prove breach of contract

holding

... The United States Congress established the Joint Congressional Committee on Inaugural Ceremonies (JCCIC) to coordinate and plan the inauguration of the President-elect. Congress appropriated funds to pay for the swearing-in ceremony and to staff events connected with the ceremony. ... After the election of President Obama, the JCCIC announced that it would distribute, to the general public, approximately 240,000 complimentary tickets to view the inauguration ceremonies. These tickets were available at no charge and interested parties could obtain tickets by contacting their Congressperson. Mr. Steinberg obtained two tickets from his Congressman for admission to the "Blue Section" of the reserved viewing area. After obtaining the tickets, Mr. Steinberg traveled to Washington, D.C. to attend the inauguration and incurred travel expenses.

given 2 complimentary tickets

Mr. Steinberg and his guest arrived at the designated "Blue Section" several hours before the inauguration ceremonies were scheduled to begin. They stood in line to enter into the designated "Blue Section," but were eventually refused admittance. Plaintiff asserts that he was never told by the JCCIC that there was a possibility that he and his guest might not be admitted into the designated viewing section.

no warning of limited capacity

Mr. Steinberg asserts that the JCCIC knew that many ticket holders would be unable to be admitted to the inauguration ceremonies and that the JCCIC had a contractual duty to advise him of this fact publicly before he incurred the expense of traveling to Washington. Plaintiff asserts that if the JCCIC had advised him that many ticket holders would not be admitted to the inauguration ceremonies, he could have made an educated decision whether to incur

π claim

---

[5] Litigants who act as their own lawyers are said to be acting *pro se*, that is, for themselves. Courts often extend the benefit of the doubt to *pro se* litigants, and the *Steinberg* court expressed a willingness to do so here. This was notwithstanding the fact that Mr. Steinberg himself was a lawyer. One senses the court was not entirely satisfied with his legal work, as in a footnote it quoted the U.S. Supreme Court as stating "Even a skilled lawyer who represents himself is at a disadvantage in contested litigation." *Kay v. Ehrler*, 499 U.S. 432, 437, 111 S. Ct. 1435, 113 L. Ed. 2d 486 (1991). "He is deprived of the judgment of an independent third party in framing the theory of the case . . . and in making sure that reason, rather than emotion, dictates the proper tactical response to unforeseen developments in the courtroom." *Id.*—Eds.

traveling expenses. Plaintiff asserts that the JCCIC breached a contractual duty it owed to him by failing to disclose known facts, which plaintiff detrimentally relied on and which defendant knew or should have known would be material to plaintiff in determining whether to incur travel expenses. . . .

To recover for a breach of contract, a party must allege and establish: (1) a valid contract between the parties, (2) an obligation or duty arising under the contract, (3) a breach of that duty, and (4) damages caused by the breach. To establish a valid contract with the government, a party must allege and establish: (1) mutuality of intent, (2) consideration, (3) lack of ambiguity in the offer and acceptance and (4) that the government official whose conduct the contractor relies upon has actual authority to bind the government in contract. *Anderson v. United States*, 344 F.3d 1343, 1353 (Fed. Cir. 2003). . . . "As a threshold condition for contract formation, there must be an objective manifestation of voluntary, mutual assent." *Anderson*, 344 F.3d at 1353 (citing Restatement §18 (1981)). To establish mutual intent to contract, a party must demonstrate the existence of an offer and acceptance of the offer by objective evidence. After an offer is made, there must be acceptance: "manifestation of assent to the terms thereof made by the offeree in a manner invited or required by the offer." Restatement §50(1). . . .

Valid contract formation also requires consideration. Id. §17(1). "[A]ny performance which is bargained for is consideration." Id. §72. "To constitute consideration, a performance or a return promise must be bargained for." Id. §71(1). "A performance or return promise is bargained for if it is sought by the promisor in exchange for his promise and is given by the promisee in exchange for that promise." Id. §71(2). . . .

Mr. Steinberg fails to assert that there was an objective manifestation of mutual assent on the part of the JCCIC or of any individual member of Congress sufficient to establish a meeting of the minds. See *Anderson*, 344 F.3d at 1353 (requiring mutuality of intent to establish a contract with the government). Mr. Steinberg alleges that he was owed "contractual duties" by the JCCIC and by defendant, but Mr. Steinberg fails to assert that there was a meeting of the minds or mutual intent on the part of the parties to enter into a contract. [The court's discussion of these issues is omitted. The court proceeds to discuss, had the government manifested a sufficient intent to be bound, whether any promise it made would be supported by consideration under the facts alleged in the complaint.] . . .

Mr. Steinberg asserts that "those persons offered tickets would have to personally pick up the tickets from his or her Congressperson's office." More specifically, in plaintiff's Motion, he asserts that "pick[ing] up the ticket in person was mandatory and thus acted as consideration in order to receive the ticket." In rendering a decision on a motion to dismiss, the court must presume that undisputed factual allegations in the complaint are true. Here, however, the factual allegation supporting plaintiff's claim that such "consideration" was required is contradicted by plaintiff himself. Even if a requirement of "pick[ing] up the ticket" in person could somehow be viewed as consideration, the

[handwritten margin notes:]
needed to prove breach
1) valid contract exists
2) obligation/duty arises
3) breach of that duty
4) damage caused by that breach

prove contract w/ govn't
1) mutuality of intent
2) consideration
3) lack of ambiguity in offer/acceptance
4) official who conduct established the contract had the authority to bind the gov'nt

π claim

π claim picking up the tickets was consideration

"mandatory" requirement on which Mr. Steinberg relies does not exist. Attached as an exhibit to the ... Complaint was an e-mail that Mr. Steinberg received from Cristin Datch, Staff Assistant to Congressman Bilirakis, which states that "if someone will be picking up tickets on your behalf, we must have his/her name and telephone number in order to verify his/her information when he/she arrives in our office. Therefore, if that is the case, please respond to this email with his/her contact information." Mr. Steinberg was not required to pick up his free ticket in person. Picking up the tickets in person could not serve as consideration necessary to establish a contract.

picking up the ticket is not consideration

Nor does the court find that Mr. Steinberg's traveling expenses constitute consideration. Plaintiff defines consideration as "a detriment to the promisee or a benefit to the promisor," and asserts that the cost of traveling to D.C. was a detriment to him and therefore constitutes consideration. A detriment to one party may serve as consideration, but only if such detriment is bargained for. See Restatement §72. Plaintiff fails to assert that his detriment, the cost of travel, was bargained for or sought by the government in any way.

not bargained for

Plaintiff also suggests that his attendance at the inauguration ceremonies is analogous to the activities of a plaintiff who participated in the promotion of a casino. ("The process was similar to a contest, with winners being selected.") (citing *Gottlieb v. Tropicana Hotel & Casino (Gottlieb)*, 109 F. Supp. 2d 324 (E.D. Pa. 2000)). In *Gottlieb*, the plaintiff was required to report information about her gambling habits to the casino and became "a part of the entertainment" at the casino. *Gottlieb*, 109 F. Supp. 2d at 329. The court in *Gottlieb* concluded that the casino "offered the promotion in order to generate patronage of and excitement within the casino." *Id.* at 330. The plaintiff in *Gottlieb* established bargained-for consideration and survived a motion for summary judgment. *Id.*

The court finds inapposite plaintiff's comparison of a presidential inauguration to a casino's business effort to attract customers in an attempt to turn a profit. Throngs of people traveled to Washington for the inauguration. Plaintiff notes that "[p]ersons who desired the tickets exceeded the number available." A message on plaintiff's tickets warned the holders to "arrive early due to large crowds." Unlike the proprietor of the casino in *Gottlieb*, the government did not bargain for Mr. Steinberg's attendance. The United States did not receive a bargained-for benefit from the spectators who attended the inauguration ceremonies.

Plaintiff asserts that "the JCCIC received an intangible benefit of promoting the Inauguration by means of the complimentary tickets offered through the various mediums." Plaintiff does not explain what such an intangible benefit might be. The government did not attempt to make money from the inauguration, nor did it need to attract participants as the casino in *Gottlieb* did. In determining whether there was consideration, the question is not whether one party received a benefit (tangible or otherwise), but whether the benefit was bargained for. See Restatement §71. If the benefit was not bargained for, and here it was not, it cannot constitute consideration necessary to support a contract. See *id.* §71(1). The government did not bargain for the attendance of plaintiff or others at the inauguration ceremonies. Because the inauguration

no profit made by the govt or this

issue →

is unlike the business in *Gottlieb*, the court finds that there was no bargained-for benefit, tangible or intangible, that could serve as consideration. . . .

[The court grants the government's motion to dismiss.]

■ QUESTION

If Mr. Steinberg had been required to pick up the tickets in person, could that have constituted consideration? Why or why not?

■ PROBLEM 9.1

In the *Gottlieb* case cited by the court, the plaintiff claimed she had won $1 million at the Tropicana Casino and Resort in Atlantic City, New Jersey, and that the casino had breached a contract with her when it refused to pay. Ms. Gottlieb had signed up for a free "Diamond Club" promotional program at the Casino. Diamond Club members received a card which they could swipe each time they played a game, and they received rewards based on their usage. Members were also entitled to one free spin at the "Million Dollar Wheel" each day. Ms. Gottlieb contended that one day she took advantage of her free spin and landed on the $1 million prize. Tropicana claimed she had won two free show tickets instead. When Ms. Gottlieb eventually sued the casino for the $1 million prize, the casino moved for summary judgment, arguing in part that participation in a free promotional contest cannot constitute sufficient consideration to support an enforceable contract. In denying the casino's motion for summary judgment, the court stated:

> Ms. Gottlieb had to go to the casino to participate in the promotion. She had to wait in line to spin the wheel. By presenting her Diamond Club card to the casino attendant and allowing it to be swiped into the casino's machine, she was permitting the casino to gather information about her gambling habits. Additionally, by participating in the game, she was a part of the entertainment that casinos, by their very nature, are designed to offer to all of those present. All of these detriments to Ms. Gottlieb were "the requested detriment[s] to the promisee induced by the promise" of Tropicana to offer her a chance to win $1 million. *Lucky Calendar* [*Co. v. Cohen*], 117 A.2d [107] at 495 [(1956)]. Tropicana's motives in offering the promotion were "in nowise altruistic." *Id.* at 496. It offered the promotion in order to generate patronage of and excitement within the casino. In short, Ms. Gottlieb provided adequate consideration to form a contract with Tropicana.

How does the court in *Steinberg v. United States* distinguish *Gottlieb*? Do you find the distinction persuasive? Why or why not?

Casino bargained for her business — get profit

One of the most troublesome issues in consideration doctrine is the distinction between consideration and a condition to a gift. In the quote set out before *Steinberg*, Justice Holmes gives the example of a man who promises another to pay him five hundred dollars if he breaks his leg. The implication is that this is simply a promise to make a gift, not supported by consideration. Absent more, this purely gratuitous promise would be unenforceable. We might all agree that breaking a bone is a detriment (whether legal or otherwise). Yet we would probably also agree that the detriment is not bargained for here. In the usual case, we would assume that the promisor is acting out of generosity, not out of any morbid desire to see the other party come to harm. Likewise, again in the usual case, we would assume that the promisee would not intentionally break his leg in order to take advantage of the promise. Since in the conventional case the detriment would not induce the promise and the promise would not induce the detriment, we would conclude that consideration for the promise was absent. As Holmes put it, there is no "relation of reciprocal conventional inducement, each for the other, between consideration and promise." Less clear cases abound, however, and some courts struggle to articulate the difference between an enforceable promise supported by consideration and a purely gratuitous promise subject to a condition.

The distinction between consideration that has been bargained for and a condition to a gratuitous promise is a central issue in the next case.

[handwritten margin note: you don't bargain to break your leg]

[handwritten note: promise w/ consideration   v.   gratuitous promise subject to conditions]

PENNSY SUPPLY, INC. v. AMERICAN ASH RECYCLING CORP.

2006 Pa. Super. 54, 895 A.2d 595 (2006)
Pennsylvania Superior Court

MELVIN, Judge.

Appellant, Pennsy Supply, Inc. ("Pennsy"), appeals from the grant of preliminary objections in the nature of a demurrer in favor of Appellee, American Ash Recycling Corp. of Pennsylvania ("American Ash"). We reverse and remand for further proceedings.

The trial court summarized the allegations of the complaint as follows:

> The instant case arises out of a construction project for Northern York High School (Project) owned by Northern York County School District (District) in York County, Pennsylvania. The District entered into a construction contract for the Project with a general contractor, Lobar, Inc. (Lobar). Lobar, in turn, subcontracted the paving of driveways and a parking lot to [Pennsy]. The contract between Lobar and the District included Project Specifications for paving work which required Lobar, through its subcontractor Pennsy, to use certain base aggregates. The Project Specifications permitted substitution of the aggregates with an alternate material known as Treated Ash Aggregate (TAA) or AggRite.

The Project Specifications included a "notice to bidders" of the availability of AggRite at no cost from [American Ash], a supplier of AggRite. The Project Specifications also included a letter to the Project architect from American Ash confirming the availability of a certain amount of free AggRite on a first come, first served basis.

Pennsy contacted American Ash and informed American Ash that it would require approximately 11,000 tons of AggRite for the Project. Pennsy subsequently picked up the AggRite from American Ash and used it for the paving work, in accordance with the Project Specifications.

Pennsy completed the paving work in December 2001. The pavement ultimately developed extensive cracking in February 2002. The District notified ... Lobar ... as to the defects and Lobar in turn directed Pennsy to remedy the defective work. Pennsy performed the remedial work during summer 2003 at no cost to the District.

The scope and cost of the remedial work included the removal and appropriate disposal of the AggRite, which is classified as a hazardous waste material by the Pennsylvania Department of Environmental Protection. Pennsy requested American Ash to arrange for the removal and disposal of the AggRite; however, American Ash did not do so. Pennsy provided notice to American Ash of its intention to recover costs.

Pennsy also alleged that the remedial work cost it $251,940.20 to perform and that it expended an additional $133,777.48 to dispose of the AggRite it removed.

On November 18, 2004, Pennsy filed a five-count complaint against American Ash alleging breach of contract (Count I); breach of implied warranty of merchantability (Count II); breach of express warranty of merchantability (Count III); breach of warranty of fitness for a particular purpose (Count IV); and promissory estoppel (Count V). American Ash filed demurrers to all five counts. Pennsy responded and also sought leave to amend should any demurrer be sustained. The trial court sustained the demurrers by order and opinion dated May 25, 2005 and dismissed the complaint. This appeal followed.

Pennsy raises three questions for our review:

1. Whether the trial court erred in not accepting as true ... [the] Complaint allegations that (a) [American Ash] promotes the use of its AggRite material, which is classified as hazardous waste, in order to avoid the high cost of disposing [of] the material itself; and (b) [American Ash] incurred a benefit from Pennsy's use of the material in the form of avoidance of the costs of said disposal sufficient to ground contract and warranty claims.
2. Whether Pennsy's relief of [American Ash's] legal obligation to dispose of a material classified as hazardous waste, such that [American Ash] avoided the costs of disposal thereof at a hazardous waste site, is sufficient consideration to ground contract and warranty claims.
3. Whether the trial court misconstrued the well-pled facts of the Complaint in dismissing Pennsy's promissory estoppel claim because Pennsy, according to the court, did not receive [American Ash's] product specifications until after the paving was completed, which was not pled and is not factual.

[The court states the applicable standard of review. When considering objections in the nature of a demurrer, which would result in dismissal of the complaint, all well-pleaded facts in the complaint are taken as true, and doubts are resolved in favor of a refusal to sustain the objections.] . . . In applying this standard to the instant appeal, we deem it easiest to order our discussion by count.

Count I raises a breach of contract claim. "A cause of action for breach of contract must be established by pleading (1) the existence of a contract, including its essential terms, (2) a breach of a duty imposed by the contract and (3) resultant damages." *Corestates Bank, N.A. v. Cutillo*, 723 A.2d 1053, 1058 (Pa. Super. 1999). While not every term of a contract must be stated in complete detail, every element must be specifically pleaded. Clarity is particularly important where an oral contract is alleged.

Instantly, the trial court determined that "any alleged agreement between the parties is unenforceable for lack of consideration." The trial court also stated "the facts as pleaded do not support an inference that disposal costs were part of any bargaining process *or* that American Ash offered the AggRite with an intent to avoid disposal costs." Thus, we understand the trial court to have dismissed Count I for two reasons related to the necessary element of consideration: one, the allegations of the Complaint established that Pennsy had received a conditional gift from American Ash, and, two, there were no allegations in the Complaint to show that American Ash's avoidance of disposal costs was part of any bargaining process between the parties.

It is axiomatic that consideration is "an essential element of an enforceable contract." *Stelmack v. Glen Alden Coal Co.*, 339 Pa. 410, 414-415, 14 A.2d 127, 128 (1940). *See also Weavertown Transport Leasing, Inc. v. Moran*, 834 A.2d 1169, 1172 (Pa. Super. 2003) (stating, "[a] contract is formed when the parties to it (1) reach a mutual understanding, (2) exchange consideration, and (3) delineate the terms of their bargain with sufficient clarity."). "Consideration consists of a benefit to the promisor or a detriment to the promisee." *Weavertown*, 834 A.2d at 1172 (citing *Stelmack*). "Consideration must actually be bargained for as the exchange for the promise." *Stelmack*, 339 Pa. at 414, 14 A.2d at 129.

It is not enough, however, that the promisee has suffered a legal detriment at the request of the promisor. The detriment incurred must be the "quid pro quo", or the "price" of the promise, and the inducement for which it was made. . . . If the promisor merely intends to make a gift to the promisee upon the performance of a condition, the promise is gratuitous and the satisfaction of the condition is not consideration for a contract. The distinction between such a conditional gift and a contract is well illustrated in *Williston on Contracts*, Rev. Ed., Vol. 1, Section 112, where it is said: "If a benevolent man says to a tramp,—'If you go around the corner to the clothing shop there, you may purchase an overcoat on my credit,' no reasonable person would understand that the short walk was requested as the consideration for the promise, but that in the event of the tramp going to the shop the promisor would make him a gift." *Weavertown*, 834 A.2d at 1172 (quoting *Stelmack*, 339 Pa. at 414, 14 A.2d at 128-29). . . .

The classic formula for the difficult concept of consideration was stated by Justice Oliver Wendell Holmes, Jr. as "the promise must induce the detriment and the detriment must induce the promise." John Edward Murray, Jr., *Murray on Contracts* §60 (3d. ed. 1990), at 227 (citing *Wisconsin & Michigan Ry. v. Powers*, 191 U.S. 379, 24 S. Ct. 107, 48 L. Ed. 229 (1903)). As explained by Professor Murray:

> If the promisor made the promise for the purpose of inducing the detriment, the detriment induced the promise. *If, however, the promisor made the promise with no particular interest in the detriment that the promisee had to suffer to take advantage of the promised gift or other benefit, the detriment was incidental or conditional to the promisee's receipt of the benefit.* Even though the promisee suffered a detriment induced by the promise, the purpose of the promisor was not to have the promisee suffer the detriment because she did not seek that detriment in exchange for her promise.

Id. §60.C, at 230 (emphasis added). This concept is also well summarized in American Jurisprudence:

> As to the distinction between consideration and a condition, it is often difficult to determine whether words of condition in a promise indicate a request for consideration or state a mere condition in a gratuitous promise. An aid, though not a conclusive test, in determining which construction of the promise is more reasonable is an inquiry into *whether the occurrence of the condition would benefit the promisor. If so, it is a fair inference that the occurrence was requested as consideration.* On the other hand, if the occurrence of the condition is no benefit to the promisor but is merely to enable the promisee to receive a gift, the occurrence of the event on which the promise is conditional, though brought about by the promisee in reliance on the promise, is not properly construed as consideration.

17A Am. Jur. 2d §104 (2004 & 2005 Supp.) (emphasis added). *See also* Restatement (Second) of Contracts §71 comment c (noting "the distinction between bargain and gift may be a fine one, depending on the motives manifested by the parties"); *Carlisle v. T & R Excavating, Inc.*, 123 Ohio App. 3d 277, 704 N.E.2d 39 (1997) (discussing the difference between consideration and a conditional gift and finding no consideration where promisor who promised to do excavating work for preschool being built by ex-wife would receive no benefit from wife's reimbursement of his material costs).

Upon review, we disagree with the trial court that the allegations of the Complaint show only that American Ash made a conditional gift of the AggRite to Pennsy. In paragraphs 8 and 9 of the Complaint, Pennsy alleged:

> American Ash actively promotes the use of AggRite as a building material to be used in base course of paved structures, and provides the material free of charge, in

an effort to have others dispose of the material and thereby avoid incurring the disposal costs itself. . . . American Ash provided the AggRite to Pennsy for use on the Project, which saved American Ash thousands of dollars in disposal costs it otherwise would have incurred.

Accepting these allegations as true and using the Holmesian formula for consideration, it is a fair interpretation of the Complaint that American Ash's promise to supply AggRite free of charge induced Pennsy to assume the detriment of collecting and taking title to the material, and critically, that it was this very detriment, whether assumed by Pennsy or some other successful bidder to the paving subcontract, which induced American Ash to make the promise to provide free AggRite for the project. Paragraphs 8-9 of the Complaint simply belie the notion that American Ash offered AggRite as a conditional gift to the successful bidder on the paving subcontract for which American Ash desired and expected nothing in return.

We turn now to whether consideration is lacking because Pennsy did not allege that American Ash's avoidance of disposal costs was part of any bargaining process between the parties. The Complaint does not allege that the parties discussed or even that Pennsy understood at the time it requested or accepted the AggRite that Pennsy's use of the AggRite would allow American Ash to avoid disposal costs. However, we do not believe such is necessary.

The bargain theory of consideration does not actually require that the parties bargain over the terms of the agreement. . . . According to Holmes, an influential advocate of the bargain theory, what is required [for consideration to exist] is that the promise and the consideration be in "the relation of reciprocal conventional inducement, each for the other." E. Allen Farnsworth, *Farnsworth on Contracts* §2.6 (1990) (citing O. Holmes, *The Common Law* 293-94 (1881)); *see also* Restatement (Second) of Contracts §71 (defining "bargained for" in terms of the Holmesian formula). Here, as explained above, the Complaint alleges facts which, if proven, would show the promise induced the detriment and the detriment induced the promise. This would be consideration. Accordingly, we reverse the dismissal of Count I.

Counts II, III and IV alleged breach of warranty claims under Article 2 of the Uniform Commercial Code ("UCC"). The trial court dismissed these counts as a group upon concluding the facts alleged failed to show a contract for the "sale of goods" as required to trigger application of UCC Article 2 . . . concluding, "the transaction as pleaded, by which American Ash gave Pennsy free AggRite, amounted to a conditional gift, not a contract of sale." . . . Again, we disagree that the allegations reveal a transaction that can only be characterized as a conditional gift. We turn now to whether the allegations otherwise trigger application of Article 2.

Article 2 applies to "transactions in goods." 13 Pa. C.S.A. §2102. AggRite is obviously a good. *See* 13 Pa. C.S.A. §2105 (defining "goods" as "all things (including specially manufactured goods) which are moveable at the time of identification to the contract."). Before the protections of the Article 2 warranties apply, "there must be a sale of goods." *Turney Media Fuel, Inc. v. Toll Bros., Inc.*, 725 A.2d 836, 840 (Pa. Super. 1999). . . .

"A sale [under Article 2] consists in the passing of title from the seller to the buyer for a price." 13 Pa. C.S.A. §2106 (parenthetical reference omitted). Section 2-304, entitled "Price payable in money, goods, realty or otherwise," provides in subsection (a) that as a general rule "[t]he price can be made payable in money or otherwise." 13 Pa. C.S.A. §2304. Pennsy argues that its acquisition of the AggRite whereby American Ash was relieved of disposal costs can constitute a price within the meaning of the "or otherwise" language in 13 Pa. C.S.A. §2304. We agree. The few courts to have interpreted the "or otherwise" language of a UCC provision like ours have concluded that it includes any consideration sufficient to ground a contract. *See Mortimer B. Burnside & Co. v. Havener Securities Corp.*, 25 A.D.2d 373, 269 N.Y.S.2d 724 (1966) (citing UCC §2-304 generally); *Wheeler v. Sunbelt Tool Co., Inc.*, 181 Ill. App. 3d 1088, 130 Ill. Dec. 863, 537 N.E.2d 1332 (applying Illinois version of UCC), appeal denied, 127 Ill. 2d 644, 136 Ill. Dec. 610, 545 N.E.2d 134 (1989); *see also* William D. Hawkland, 2 Uniform Commercial Code Series §2-304:3 (1998) (stating, "the entire thrust of section 2-304 seems to be toward making the scope of Article 2 as broad as possible, limited only by due concern for the laws governing the disposition of real property.") (footnote omitted). . . . [The court concludes that since Article 2 applies to the transaction at issue, Pennsy's complaint made sufficient allegations to support a claim for breach of warranty under Article 2.]

On these facts, we cannot say the law would clearly preclude recovery on Counts II, III and IV, and, accordingly, we reverse the grant of the demurrer to the extent dismissal of these counts was based on Pennsy's failure to allege a sale of goods. . . .

[The court's discussion of Count V, the claim for promissory estoppel, is omitted.]

■ QUESTIONS

(1) American Ash argues that it offered the AggRite as a conditional gift to bidders on the construction project. What would the consequences have been if it had proposed a conditional gift? How does the court distinguish a conditional gift from a bargained-for exchange?

(2) Suppose the facts of *Hamer v. Sidway* were to come before a modern court. Suppose further that the defendant argued that the requirement that the nephew refrain from his nefarious habits was merely a condition to the uncle's promise to make him a gift. In light of *Pennsy Supply* and the authorities discussed in the opinion, should the court find this argument persuasive?

(3) This case was decided, in part, under UCC Article 2. The UCC does not itself contain a definition of consideration, although (as we see in Chapter 11 and Chapter 13) it occasionally dispenses with the requirement of consideration in specific situations when common law would not. How is the court's discussion of consideration relevant to its conclusion that Counts II, III, and IV in the complaint were sufficient?

■ PROBLEM 9.2

Lara Lassie breeds collies. Her prize-winning collie recently gave birth to four puppies. Lara already signed contracts to sell three of the four puppies for $450 each. The fourth puppy, Lulu, was the runt of the litter, and remained unclaimed. One afternoon, Lara's neighbor Timmy Martin was admiring the puppies and expressed particular interest in Lulu. "I'd love to buy her," Timmy said, "but I just can't afford it right now." Lara responded, "You've been such a great neighbor and have done so many favors for me over the years that I wouldn't dream of charging you for her. I know you'd give her a good home. I'd be delighted if you'd take her. All I ask is that you agree to a few conditions. First, you'd need to wait ten weeks to get her, as she isn't ready to leave her mother yet. Second, while you wait to pick her up, you'll need to puppy-proof your home and make sure it is a safe place for Lulu to live. Finally, if you ever decide you can't keep her anymore, tell me and let me take her back, rather than giving her to someone else or taking her to a shelter." Timmy, overjoyed, thanked Lara for her generosity, shook Lara's hand, and said, "It's a deal."

Six weeks later, a potential purchaser offers to buy Lulu for $450. Lara would hate to disappoint Timmy, but she is short on cash. She is considering reneging on her promise to Timmy and accepting this offer instead. Does Lara have a contractual obligation to give Lulu to Timmy?

[handwritten margin notes: "not consid", "consideration", "what is Lara's benefit"]

4. The Elusive Purpose of Consideration Doctrine

Now that we have some sense of the broad outlines of consideration doctrine, it's time to pause and consider what policies, if any, explain this doctrine. As discussed in Section A.1, some of the reasons for consideration doctrine are historical. In part, consideration doctrine grew to allow the enforcement of commercial promises while not overburdening the court system with personal ones. This distinction does not explain all of the cases, however. For instance, *Hamer* involved a promise among family members. There might be other policies at play here.

As you may recall from Chapter 1, classical contract scholars concentrated on elaboration of legal rules. In doing so, they advocated clarity and predictability of rules rather than the furtherance of other social policies. To give just one illustration, in the entirety of the 1930s edition of his famous *Treatise on the*

Law of Contracts, classical scholar Williston reputedly never examined doctrines such as offer, acceptance, or consideration critically in light of the social interests they served, even though the treatise was nearly 8,000 pages long.[6] As legal philosophy evolved away from classicism, however, academics spilled countless bottles of ink on the question of what, if any, policies underlie the consideration requirement of contract law. Perhaps the most often quoted article on this subject is one Professor Fuller published in the Columbia Law Review in 1941.[7] In his article, Fuller argued that consideration doctrine serves both formal and substantive functions. Application of consideration doctrine could only be understood, Fuller argued, as a reflection of these various functions playing themselves out in particular contexts. The complexity of the doctrine lay in the fact that these functions may be at odds with each other, depending on the facts of the case. As a result, it is unreasonable and perhaps inappropriate to expect complete consistency in judicial results.

Professor Fuller suggested that formal requirements achieve policies beyond mere clarity and predictability. He argued, for instance, that formal requirements tend to ensure that evidentiary, cautionary, and channeling needs are met. If a court is to enforce a promise, it is helpful if the court can have some solid assurance that the promise was truly and seriously expressed. After all, life is full of misunderstandings, misinterpretations, and, unfortunately, lies. Formal requirements help ensure the promise was actually made and illuminate what it was (the evidentiary function of form). Further, individuals should not drift unknowingly into liability. If formal requirements are imposed, it is more likely that the individual will recognize that something serious is going on and act accordingly (the cautionary function of form). Finally, judicial resources are scarce, and the law should not force judges and juries to spend endless hours sorting the serious promises from those that are flippantly or unknowingly made. Accordingly, a formal requirement serves a purpose if it allows a court to easily separate the enforceable promises from those that should be ignored (the channeling function of form).

One can easily construct a legal system where formal requirements are designed to attain all of these objectives. A clear and predictable system is easy to construct. Imagine, for instance, a system that requires a promisor to write down every promise that the parties want to be enforceable. Suppose further that the parties must interweave multicolored ribbons into the writing and affix an elaborate wax seal at the end. And of course the promisor must sign the writing—in blood—obtained from the ritual sacrifice of a young chicken. . . . Surely if such a writing is produced in court, there can be little doubt that the promise was truly and seriously made. Somewhere along the line, the promisor (unless he is unusually trusting or dense) must have suspected that the promise

[6] Professor Fuller, whom we discuss next, leveled this charge at Williston in his review, Lon L. Fuller, *Williston on Contracts*, 18 N.C. L. Rev. 1, 9 (1939). We admit candidly that we have not verified the accuracy of Fuller's claim; nor do we plan to do so.
[7] Lon L. Fuller, *Consideration and Form*, 41 Colum. L. Rev. 799 (1941).

would have some consequences. And the judge should be able quickly to sort those writings that appear to satisfy the formal requirements from those that do not. But this legal system misses the point, doesn't it? Imagine, for instance, what the grocery store checkout line would look like. Contract law has a job to do, and at some point overzealous formalities can prevent that job from getting done.

What, then, is the job of contract law? This is a question that we have already discussed many times and will continue to discuss throughout the text. Professor Fuller posited a number of substantive purposes of contract law—including protecting the parties' private autonomy, protecting a party who may have relied to his or her detriment on the promise of another, and preventing unjust enrichment. Fuller then explored how consideration doctrine helps to preserve a balance between the formal functions described above and these substantive purposes. In pure, commercial exchanges, the kind that happen every day, he argued that the need for special formalities to protect promisors is weak. In light of the substantive benefits attained by enforcing such exchanges, the costs of requiring formalities in turn are large. Conversely, purely gratuitous promises among friends and family are more likely to be inspired by emotion, impetuosity, or influence, so formalistic requirements seem more in order. At the same time, the substantive reasons for legally enforcing such promises may be weaker. In the end, Fuller concluded that consideration doctrine is best understood and applied in light of the purposes it serves rather than in the niceties of its technical details.

In spite of the influence of Fuller's analysis, consensus on the purpose of consideration doctrine remains elusive. Some criticize the doctrine as an illogical accident of history and suggest that it neither normatively justifies nor accurately describes those promises that the courts choose to enforce. Proponents of the promise theory of contracts, for instance, have argued that a promise that is intentionally made is worthy of judicial enforcement, irrespective of the presence or absence of consideration.[8] Others urge us to understand consideration doctrine as an imperfect product of history, but one that continues to play a role in achieving valuable public policies. Consent theorists, for instance, have argued that the essential element that distinguishes enforceable promises from those that are not legally enforceable should be the manifestation of an intention to be bound.[9] Under this view, whether the party seeking to enforce the obligation was entitled to believe that the other party intended to be legally bound should be a factual inquiry, and the presence or

---

[8] A work that explored this theme in some detail was Charles Fried, *Contract as Promise: A Theory of Contractual Obligation* (Harvard U. Press 1981). Ultimately, Professor Fried argues that contract law is justified as it largely respects the moral obligation to keep a promise. More recent commentators have argued that contract law generally falls short of giving due respect to the moral obligations stemming from promises seriously made, and point to consideration doctrine as one of the culprits *See, e.g.,* Seana Valentine Shiffrin, *The Divergence of Contract and Promise,* 120 Harv. L. Rev. 708 (2007).

[9] One scholar who is closely identified with the consent theory of contract is Professor Barnett. *See, e.g.,* Randy E. Barnett, *A Consent Theory of Contract,* 86 Colum. L. Rev. 269 (1986).

absence of consideration is only one of many factors that may be relevant. The presence of consideration justifies a presumption that the parties manifested an intention to be bound, but the presumption should not be conclusive. Where consideration doctrine is confusing or inconsistent, perhaps it is because not all courts have felt free to recognize its limited role expressly. Instead, sometimes courts have stretched established doctrine to enforce obligations where the parties clearly manifested an intention to be bound (even though one party might have thought consideration, as usually conceived, was not present) or have resisted enforcement, doing some violence to doctrine in the process, where the requisite manifestation was missing (even though the technical requirements of consideration arguably were met). Critics and supporters alike agree that consideration doctrine is a limited and imperfect answer to the broader question of what promises the law should enforce.

The next case presents a slightly more detailed analysis of consideration than those we have encountered thus far. As you read this case, think about the policies the court is furthering in its decision. In your view, what policies support enforcement or nonenforcement of the promise in this case?

CARLISLE v. T&R EXCAVATING, INC.

123 Ohio App. 3d 277, 704 N.E.2d 39 (1997)
Ohio Court of Appeals

DICKINSON, Presiding Judge.

Defendant T&R Excavating Inc. has appealed from a judgment of the Medina County Common Pleas Court that awarded $35,790.75 in damages for breach of contract to plaintiffs Janis Carlisle, Wishing Well Preschool Inc., and Janis Carlisle, trustee, The Enrichment Center of Wishing Well, Inc. Defendant has argued that the trial court incorrectly found that there was a contract between the parties because their agreement lacked sufficient consideration. . . . This court reverses the judgment of the trial court because there was no consideration for the agreement between the parties and, therefore, no contract existed.

Defendant T&R Excavating, Inc. is solely owned and operated by Thomas Carlisle. Plaintiff Janis Carlisle is the owner and director of Wishing Well, Inc. and trustee of The Enrichment Center of Wishing Well, Inc., both of which were also plaintiffs in this action.

Ms. Carlisle and Mr. Carlisle married in 1988. According to Ms. Carlisle's trial testimony, shortly after they were married, she began doing all of the bookkeeping for T&R, including organizing and modernizing its bookkeeping system. Mr. Carlisle allegedly offered to pay her for her work, but she refused. He then allegedly stated to her that he would, instead, "do [her] work for [her] on [her] building." No testimony or other evidence was offered regarding when he made this offer to pay her or when he stated his intention to do work on her building.

During 1992, Ms. Carlisle decided to build a preschool and kindergarten facility. Mr. Carlisle helped her find a location for the preschool, and she purchased the land they selected. Following this, he helped her choose a general contractor for the construction of the preschool.

On September 25, 1992, T&R presented a "Proposal" to Ms. Carlisle in which it proposed the following:

> We hereby propose to do all of the excavation and site work at the above new Location. The total amount budgeted for this portion of the new building is $69,800.00. All labor, equipment costs, overhead and profit, necessary for the completion of this project, totalling $40,000.00 will be provided at no cost to Wishing Well Preschool, Inc. The $29,800.00 allotted for materials will be billed to Wishing Well Preschool, Inc. at T&R Excavating's cost.

On that same date, Ms. Carlisle signed an "Acceptance of Proposal," which was printed at the bottom of the "Proposal": "The above prices, specifications and conditions are satisfactory and are hereby accepted. You are authorized to do the work as specified. Payment will be made as outlined above."

During December 1992, Mr. Carlisle and Ms. Carlisle, in anticipation of a possible divorce, prepared a document in which they made provision for the division of certain property and agreed that neither would be responsible for supporting the other. Also included in that document was a paragraph regarding Ms. Carlisle's secretarial work and T&R's excavating work: "In repayment to Jan for her secretarial services and computer programming to T&R Excavating, Inc., Tom agrees to do all the excavating and site work for The Enrichment Center in a timely manner, as set forth in his proposal dated September, 1992. In this proposal, Wishing Well Preschool, Inc. agrees to pay Tom for the materials used at his cost."

On February 1, 1993, the general contractor prepared and presented to Mr. Carlisle a standardized American Institute of Architects document, signed by Ms. Carlisle, entitled "Abbreviated Form of Agreement Between Owner and Contractor." Some information specific to the preschool project was typed into the appropriate blank areas of the document, and the last several pages of the agreement consisted of printed contract language. The typed-in information included a description of the site work to be done, an estimate of $29,325.00 for materials, a plan for how payment was to be made, a start date of February 1, 1993, and a completion date of June 25, 1993. Also typed in were the following statements: "This contract is for material only. There is no charge for labor and equipment. The contract sum will be adjusted at the completion of this work to reflect the actual cost of materials installed." Mr. Carlisle never signed the document.

Sometime during early 1993, T&R began performing excavation and site work for the preschool. According to Mr. Carlisle's testimony at trial, Ms. Carlisle was no longer providing any bookkeeping or secretarial services to T&R after January 1993. They separated during March 1993, and T&R continued working on the project until it abandoned it in late May or early June 1993. By that time, Wishing Well Inc. had paid approximately $35,000 for materials used by T&R for excavation and site work. Ms. Carlisle hired other workers to finish the excavation and site work. The preschool opened for business on August 28, 1993, one week later than originally planned. Ms. Carlisle, individually and as trustee of The Enrichment Center, and Wishing Well Preschool sued T&R for breach of contract. They requested damages equal to the amount it cost to have others finish the excavation and site work, as well as the amount lost due to delays allegedly attributable to T&R's failure to work during certain periods prior to its final abandonment of the job. The trial court found that there was a contract for the excavation and site work and awarded plaintiffs $35,790.75 in damages for the cost of hiring others to finish that work after T&R left the project. . . . T&R timely appealed to this court.

. . . [T&R argues] that the trial court incorrectly found that there was a contract between the parties, because their agreement lacked sufficient consideration. . . . It has asserted that its offer to do the excavation and site work for the preschool was in the nature of a gift or a favor, and was not supported by any legally sufficient consideration. . . .

A contract consists of an offer, an acceptance, and consideration. Without consideration, there can be no contract. Under Ohio law, consideration consists of either a benefit to the promisor or a detriment to the promisee. To constitute consideration, the benefit or detriment must be "bargained for." Something is bargained for if it is sought by the promisor in exchange for his promise and is given by the promisee in exchange for that promise. The benefit or detriment does not need to be great. In fact, a benefit need not even be actual, as in the nature of a profit, or be as economically valuable as whatever the promisor promises in exchange for the benefit; it need only be something regarded by the promisor as beneficial enough to induce his promise. Generally, therefore, a court will not inquire into the adequacy of consideration once it is found to exist.

Whether there is consideration at all, however, is a proper question for a court. Gratuitous promises are not enforceable as contracts, because there is no consideration. A written gratuitous promise, even if it evidences an intent by the promisor to be bound, is not a contract. Likewise, conditional gratuitous promises, which require the promisee to do something before the promised act or omission will take place, are not enforceable as contracts. While it is true, therefore, that courts generally do not inquire into the adequacy of consideration once it is found to exist, it must be determined in a contract case whether any "consideration" was really bargained for. If it was not bargained for, it could not support a contract.

There is no evidence in the record of any benefit accruing to T&R or any detriment suffered by Ms. Carlisle due to their agreement that could constitute consideration for a contract. Statements made during trial regarding the parties' agreement failed to show that there was consideration for T&R's promise. Mr. Carlisle testified that he wanted to help Ms. Carlisle with the preschool and that they both agreed the preschool would be a good retirement benefit for them. The trial judge, at one point, stated his opinion that Mr. Carlisle made his promise because he was "a nice guy and wanted to help [Ms. Carlisle] out," that the consideration for his promise was the "relationship," and that they both hoped to benefit from the preschool.

A desire to help cannot be consideration for a contract; rather, it is merely a motive. Further, the possibility of sharing in the income from a spouse's business, which would be marital income, cannot be consideration for a contract because one is already entitled to share in marital income. No bargaining is necessary to obtain that which one already has. The decision to build the preschool to provide income later was more in the nature of a joint effort by Mr. Carlisle and Ms. Carlisle to obtain a single benefit together, than a bargained-for exchange. Finally, the relationship between Mr. Carlisle and Ms. Carlisle could not have been consideration for a contract.

Nor did Ms. Carlisle's testimony about her understanding of the parties' agreement demonstrate that there was consideration for a contract. Ms. Carlisle testified at trial that she understood the agreement to consist of T&R's promise to do excavation and site work for no charge, and her promise to "pay [T&R] back for the supplies." The promise of reimbursement for out-of-pocket costs, standing alone, was not a benefit or detriment supporting a contract. Money changed hands, but the reimbursement was not a bargained-for benefit to the promisor or detriment to the promisee. No reasonable interpretation of Ms. Carlisle's testimony could support a conclusion that T&R promised to provide the free services in order to induce her to promise to reimburse it for materials only. Rather, the testimony suggested that there was a gratuitous promise by T&R to provide free services on the condition that Ms. Carlisle agree to reimburse it for the cost of materials that would be used in providing those services.

Consideration was also not shown by Ms. Carlisle's testimony that Mr. Carlisle told her, after she refused payment for her bookkeeping services to T&R, that he would help her with her building. First, Ms. Carlisle did not argue that her secretarial services were consideration for T&R's promise. Second, there was no testimony or other evidence regarding when Mr. Carlisle made that statement or whether the two exchanged services in a bargain. Consequently, it may not be assumed that there was a contract on this basis. If Mr. Carlisle made the statement after Ms. Carlisle had done the work for T&R, her services were "past consideration" and could not support a contract. This is because past consideration cannot be a bargained-for benefit or detriment, since it has already occurred or accrued. If T&R was merely repaying Ms. Carlisle for past services, its promise to do the excavation and site work was not legally enforceable. Similarly, if Mr. Carlisle offered to help her with her building out of mere gratitude and she accepted it as such, that also precluded her services from being consideration.

The documents relied upon by the trial court for its finding that a contract existed also failed to show consideration for a contract. According to the proposal and acceptance signed by Mr. Carlisle and Ms. Carlisle during September

1992, T&R would provide services at no cost, and only materials would be billed to Wishing Well. Not one penny was to go into the pocket of T&R or Mr. Carlisle, nor was any other benefit to T&R apparent from the face of the proposal or any other evidence. This made the promise to reimburse for materials more likely to have been a condition for a gratuitous promise, rather than a detriment that would support a contract, because, once again, there was no reason for either party to understand the reimbursement promise as having induced T&R's promise.

Likewise, the "separation agreement" signed by Mr. Carlisle and Ms. Carlisle during December 1992 suggested a gratuitous promise by Mr. Carlisle. It described his promise to do the work as "repayment to Jan for her secretarial services and computer programming to T&R Excavating, Inc." The word "repayment" suggested that Ms. Carlisle's past services induced Mr. Carlisle's promise. As stated above, past consideration is not legally sufficient to support a contract.

Nor was that document itself an enforceable contract, even though one might argue that it showed a bargained-for exchange of certain property rights for excavation and site work. A married couple cannot make a contract that alters their legal relations, with the exception of a separation agreement that provides for support and property division if they immediately begin living in separate residences. See R.C. 310306. According to their testimony, Mr. Carlisle and Ms. Carlisle did not separate immediately after executing the agreement, but waited several months to do so. The agreement, therefore, could not operate as a valid separation agreement.

Finally, the American Institute of Architects document signed by Ms. Carlisle and presented by her to the trial court did not establish a contract. It contained the typed-in statements "This contract is for material only," "There is no charge for labor and equipment," and "The contract sum will be adjusted at the completion of this work to reflect the actual cost of materials installed." These statements, like Ms. Carlisle's trial testimony, indicated that her understanding of the agreement was that there was no contract for the excavating and site work services, and that she would merely reimburse T&R for the actual cost of materials used.

Contrary to plaintiffs' position, nothing in the record shows any reasonable possibility that T&R bargained away the free excavation and site work services in exchange for the "benefit" of collecting from Wishing Well the materials costs that T&R had to pay someone else. Nor does it show any possibility that Ms. Carlisle reasonably believed that her promise to reimburse induced the promise for free services. At the time of the agreement, therefore, there was no contract, and T&R cannot be held liable on that basis. Rather, the record establishes only a conditional gratuitous promise.

A discussion of conditional promises as distinguished from contracts is found in [3 Williston, *Contracts* (4th ed. 1992),] 348-352, Section 7:18. A requested performance attached to a gratuitous promise is a condition and not consideration, not because of the nature of the requested performance itself, but because of the reasonable understanding of the promisor and the promisee that the performance is requested as a condition of the promise and not as the price or exchange for the promise. Although there is no easy test for distinguishing between a condition and consideration, it is useful to ask whether the requested performance will benefit the promisor: if it will not, and if, in addition, it is obviously aimed at enabling the promisee to receive a benefit or gift, there is no consideration. This is true even though the promisee performs as requested in reliance on the promise.[10]

A condition for a promise, therefore, is different from consideration. Consideration induces the promise of the promisor, is bargained for, and results in a benefit to the promisor or a detriment to the promisee which is reasonably understood by the parties as the consideration for the promise. A condition for a promise, in contrast, does not induce the promise, is not bargained for, and is not reasonably understood as consideration. The evidence at trial showed that T&R's promise to provide the excavation and site work services for the preschool at no cost was a gratuitous promise, and T&R's promise to pay for any materials it used was, at most, merely a condition of T&R's promise to provide services. No benefit was to come to T&R; it could not reasonably be believed that T&R induced the promise of reimbursement as the price of its promise; and Ms. Carlisle's promise to pay for materials was for the purpose of enabling her to receive the benefit of free excavating and site work services.

. . . Ms. Carlisle failed to establish that there was consideration for T&R's promise to do free excavation and site work for the preschool, or that she relied to her detriment on the promise. [The court's discussion of reliance is omitted.] The promise, therefore, was not legally enforceable. T&R's assignment of error is sustained. The judgment of the trial court is reversed. Judgment reversed and cause remanded.

■ QUESTIONS

(1) What specific facts did the plaintiff point to in arguing that consideration was present? On what basis did the court reject each of these arguments?

(2) Suppose the parties had structured their agreement simply to provide for a lump-sum price of $30,000 for all labor and materials. Suppose further that at the time of the agreement, the parties anticipated that the cost of the materials to T&R would be approximately $30,000. Halfway through the project, T&R abandoned it. Would the result in the case have been the same?

---

[10] This Williston discussion uses an example of a rich man offering to a poor man that, if the poor man would go around the corner to a clothing store, the rich man would permit him to buy a coat on his credit. This is deemed a conditional gratuitous promise because, even though the poor man's walk to the store may be induced by, and taken in reliance on, the promise, it would be unreasonable for either man to understand the walk to the store as "consideration" or as the price of the promise. Rather, it would bring no benefit to the rich man, and would obviously be for the purpose of enabling the poor man to receive the gift of a coat.

(3)   Setting aside the niceties of consideration doctrine as explained by the court and instead viewing the result from a policy perspective, is this case well decided? What would Fuller's analysis suggest? How would promise theorists view the result in this case? What would consent theorists have to say? What do you think about the result, and why?

■ PROBLEM 9.3

Art Dent and Ima Dear were engaged to be married. As they planned their wedding, Art moved into Ima's house and paid off her mortgage. A few months after moving in together the couple started to fight. After a particularly bitter dispute Art packed up his things and moved out. The parties sought counseling to resolve their differences. Art indicated that he would be willing to give the relationship another try and move back into the home, but only if Ima agreed to convey a one-half interest in the home to him. Ima agreed, and the parties signed a written agreement to that effect. Art in fact moved back in, but after repeated requests Ima failed to convey any interest in the home to Art. Two weeks before the couple was scheduled to marry, Ima said the relationship was over and asked Art to leave the home. Art argues that Ima breached an enforceable contract to convey a half interest in the home to him and sues, seeking specific performance. Ima argues, among other things, that any promise she made to convey an interest in the home to Art lacks consideration. Assuming Ima made the promise as alleged, was it supported by consideration? Why or why not?

B   WHAT SUFFICES AS CONSIDERATION

DeLeo, the first case in this chapter, illustrates the clearest example of a promise that is not supported by consideration—a purely altruistic promise to make a gift. An elderly gentleman, approaching death, promised his attentive rabbi $25,000. Whether he was acting out of the kindness of his heart or out of hopes for a heavenly reward, as long as there were no strings attached to the promise, the parties did not bargain for an exchange. And where there is no exchange bargained for, there is no consideration. So a pure gift promise is not supported by consideration. What lies at the other end of the spectrum?

A fair and even commercial exchange is the prototype. Imagine, for instance, that Agricultural Conglomerate, Inc., thoughtfully and deliberately promises to sell 100,000 bushels of wheat to Flour Enterprises, Inc., for a set price. Flour

Enterprises, Inc., thoughtfully and deliberately agrees to pay the price in exchange for the wheat. The price to which the parties agree is the prevailing market price, and the exchange is to occur the next day. The next day comes and one of the parties reneges on its promise. It would be the foolhardy lawyer indeed who would argue that this transaction lacks consideration. Each party is promising to give up something concrete and real, and the clear inducement for each of their promises is the benefit of roughly equivalent value that they hope to receive in return. This is precisely the sort of commercial exchange that the consideration doctrine contemplates. Unless there is some unstated factor that raises concern under other principles of contract law, this is the kind of contract that courts routinely enforce.

In between these extremes lie a bevy of situations, many of which we will explore in the rest of this chapter. Yes, at first glance the parties seem to agree to some sort of exchange. Upon closer examination, however, the exchange is questionable. Perhaps the exchange is severely skewed to benefit one party over the other. Or perhaps in the heat of scrutiny the value of one of the promises evaporates. Although it may look like the parties had bargained for an exchange, in hindsight one party gave up a great deal more than it received. The disappointed party argues that consideration is lacking. These are the situations where the interstices of the consideration doctrine appear in all of their glory. We will explore three of those situations in this section. First, we will look at cases where one party argues that the consideration given by the other is inadequate. Next, we will examine situations where a party promises to do that which it is already legally obligated to do. Finally, we will see what happens when a party purports to give up a legal right as consideration, but in the end that right turns out to have been nonexistent or ill founded. In each of these three circumstances, it is the unequal nature of the resulting bargain that is at issue.

1. Adequacy of Consideration

We start with a bald statement, often asserted in the cases: It is not the job of the courts to review the adequacy of consideration. You may recall that the *Carlisle* court made this point. As long as the parties bargain for an exchange, the courts will not upset that exchange under the rubric of inadequate consideration—not even if one party gives up a kingdom for a "peppercorn." After all, the courts say, in our legal system we believe in the idea that parties should be free to contract. And freedom of contract carries with it the freedom to make a bad deal.

Sometimes, however, imprudent promises are procured through foul means. There are doctrines like fraud, duress, and unconscionability, all of which we address shortly, that help to protect victims of illegitimate conduct. Consideration doctrine occasionally also comes into play. Sometimes, when the exchange is particularly unbalanced or where the risk of untoward behavior is particularly acute, consideration doctrine swoops in to rescue the hapless aggrieved party. But sometimes it doesn't.

The challenge, then, is to understand the sphere in which consideration doctrine operates. This begins with an exploration of the technical content of the rules. The materials in this section are designed to help you in that exploration, but the task does not end there. It is very important to try to understand the rules in context. As history demonstrates, the rules of law in this area are by no means static or rigid. Where application of the doctrine leads to results that are unduly illogical or harsh, the legal rules in this area tend to evolve, or other legal theories arise to provide a remedy. As you study the materials to come, keep in mind the policy concerns that are operating in the background of the cases, and question whether consideration doctrine as formulated by the courts adequately addresses those concerns.

In the following case, the court refuses to examine the adequacy of the alleged consideration. What factors do you think most influenced the court? As a policy matter, do you agree with the result?

KESSLER v. NATIONAL PRESTO INDUSTRIES

Not reported in F. Supp., 1995 WL 871156 (1995)
United States District Court, Eastern District of Michigan

O'MEARA, District Judge.

On July 30, 1991, plaintiff Dawn Kessler was canning pickles with her friend Penny Kissinger, using a pressure cooker manufactured by defendant National Presto Industries. Plaintiff alleges that she let the steam escape and checked that the pressure gauge read "zero," before opening the lid. Unfortunately, the pan exploded, causing "numerous, severe and permanent burn injuries" to her body and face. On August 28, 1991, Plaintiff met with a representative of Ms. Kissinger's homeowner's insurance company. At that meeting she signed a document entitled "Release of All Claims" for the "valuable consideration" of $750.

On July 6, 1994, Plaintiff filed a products liability claim against National Presto Industries in Wayne County Circuit Court, alleging negligence (Count I), and breach of express and implied warranties (Count II). The defendant removed, on the basis of diversity jurisdiction, on July 22, 1994. On February 16, 1995, Defendant filed a motion for summary judgment asserting it is a third party beneficiary of the release Plaintiff signed, and therefore Plaintiff's claims against it are "improper." Plaintiff's response was filed March 13, 1995; and the reply on March 14, 1995. Oral argument on the motion was heard on May 25, 1995, and the motion taken under advisement. Having considered the motion and supporting and responsive briefs as well as the arguments made at the

[handwritten: → holding]

hearing, the court now grants Defendant's motion for summary judgment for the reasons stated below....

On August 28, 1995, Dawn Kessler signed a document provided to her by a representative of her friend's insurance company. The "Release of All Claims" states that for the "valuable consideration" of $750, Ms. Kessler:

> does hereby ... release, acquit and forever discharge Randall and Penny Kissinger and his, her, their, or its agents, servant, successors, heirs, executors, administrators and all other persons, corporations, firms, associations or partnerships of and from any and all claims, actions, causes of action, demands, rights, damages, costs, loss of service, expenses and compensation whatsoever, which the undersigned now has/have or which may hereafter accrue on account of or in any way growing out of any and all known and unknown, foreseen and unforseen [*sic*] bodily and personal injuries and property damage and the consequences thereof resulting or to result from the accident ... which occurred on or about the 30th day of July, 1991. ...

The agreement Ms. Kessler signed also provides, just above the signature line, that the "undersigned has read ... and fully understands" the release.

[handwritten in margin: presto would benefit from this release]

[The court first discusses whether National Presto Industries was entitled to the benefit of the release. Generally, only parties to contracts are entitled to enforce them. However, there is a narrow exception to this rule for third-party beneficiaries. A nonparty has the legal right to enforce a promise in a contract where the parties to the contract deliberately intend to confer a benefit on the nonparty and intend that the nonparty will have the legal right to enforce the benefit. National Presto Industries argues it is entitled to enforce the release as a third-party beneficiary. We address third-party beneficiaries and their rights in more detail in Chapter 22.] ... The document [Ms. Kessler] signed, and attested that she understood, is unambiguous. It is expressly broad enough to confer third party beneficiary rights ... [on] the manufacturer of the pressure cooker. By executing the release, Ms. Kessler gave her promise to "refrain from doing something directly to" a set of named and unnamed entities, the Kissingers and "all other persons, corporations." In signing the document, she relinquished her right to bring "any and all claims" she might have had resulting from the injuries she suffered in July 30, 1991 accident. As the manufacturer of the pressure cooker Ms. Kessler was using when she was injured, National Presto Industries belongs to that potential class of defendants entitled to release from liability by the terms of the agreement. *[handwritten: Presto was included in the class]*

[handwritten in margin: must deliberately intend the benefit to the third party]

[handwritten in margin: released her right to a claim]

Under Michigan law, because the agreement is unambiguous, the parties' subjective intent in executing the document is irrelevant to its interpretation. In her response brief, Plaintiff argues a less straightforward reading of the agreement, and asserts that she did not intend the release to apply to the defendant manufacturer. Although these arguments are emotionally compelling, they are unavailing, as they do not assert "concealment, duress, mistake, or similar irregularity" in the making of the contract. Therefore, the court may not reach beyond the terms of the agreement for its interpretation.

[handwritten in margin: won't look to subjective intent]

[handwritten: ↓ not present]

[handwritten margin note: contract is limited to the four corners]

[handwritten note at top: pTT claim]

Plaintiff also argues that $750 is insufficient consideration for her injuries, and states that she was unrepresented by counsel. Michigan follows the general rule of contract law that courts will not inquire into the adequacy of consideration in a contract, unless the consideration is so "grossly inadequate" as to shock the conscience of the court. *Moffit v. Sederlund*, 145 Mich. App. 1, 11 (1985). The Michigan Court of Appeals has defined "grossly inadequate consideration" as "an inequality so strong, gross and manifest that it must be impossible to state it to a man of common sense without producing an exclamation at the inequality of it." *Rose v. Lurvey*, 40 Mich. App. 231, 235-36 (1972). . . .

[handwritten margin note: must be so low to flag obvious deceit]

Although $750 may not be sufficient to cover Plaintiff's medical bills, it is not so grossly inadequate as to "shock the conscience of the court." Therefore, the court will neither inquire into the adequacy of the consideration nor contemplate rescission of the contract. *[handwritten: $750 is not too low]*

Plaintiff's argument that she was mistaken as to the contents, and therefore the ultimate reach of the release, is also unavailing. Under Michigan law, it is the plaintiff's burden to show why a release should be set aside; however a party to a contract "cannot seek to invalidate it on the basis that he or she did not read it or thought that its terms were different, absent a showing of fraud or mutual mistake." *Dombrowski v. City of Omer*, 199 Mich. App. 705, 710 (1993) (citations omitted). Ms. Kessler has not asserted fraud, duress, misrepresentation or any other conduct which would raise the validity of the signed release as an issue, rather Plaintiff states only that she did not understand the full consequences of the release. However, in signing the contract Ms. Kessler represented that she had read, and understood, the document before affixing her signature.

[handwritten margin note: you can't invalidate a contract bc you didn't read it or thought it meant something else]

Because Plaintiff has not met her burden, the court will not set aside the release she signed on August 28, 1991. . . . [The court grants summary judgment for the defendant.] *[handwritten: — holding TT did not meet burden for invalidation]*

■   ■   ■

Ms. Kessler challenged the adequacy of consideration in light of unfolding events. We can presume that her injuries turned out to be worse than she originally thought, and her medical expenses greater. Nonetheless, the court saw no reason why the promises she made in her release should not be enforced as written.

Sometimes, particularly in older cases, the courts will talk of consideration that is "grossly inadequate" or "so inadequate as to shock the conscience." (You might have noticed the *Kessler* court's discussion of this doctrine.) If a court finds the disparity of values in an exchange sufficiently offensive, it may invoke its equitable powers and decline to enforce what it sees as an indecent exchange of promises. However, this is an exceptional situation with strong elements of imposition and unfairness. For the most part, as the *Kessler* case shows, inadequacy of consideration alone does not void a contract. Where we discuss doctrines such as duress, fraud, unconscionability, public policy, illegality, and

[handwritten margin note: consideration must be inadequate in combo with something else]

mistake in Chapters 13, 14, and 17, you will see that inadequacy of consideration, combined with some other problem in the bargaining process or in the legitimacy of the transaction, can play a role in a court's decision to allow avoidance of a contract. In *Kessler*, the court alludes to these doctrines, but finds them inapplicable. For the most part, the law is as the case states it: Mere inadequacy of consideration will not void a contract. ✕

One rather curious limitation to this general rule arises when the exchange is manufactured for the specific purpose of making a promise enforceable. Imagine, for instance, that Saul Schwam, the elderly gentleman in the *DeLeo* case, decides while on his deathbed that he wants to promise his rabbi $25,000. Having spent some time in his youth studying contract law, Schwam knows that his promise will not be enforceable as a contract unless it is supported by consideration, so he says to his rabbi, "If you give me a plastic Hanukkah dreidel, I will promise to give you $25,000." The rabbi immediately hands over the dreidel. Is there consideration now? Under the cases we have just read, the answer would seem to be yes. (You may have noticed that Justice Holmes, in the passage quoted earlier in this chapter, expressed this view as well.) Inadequacy of consideration alone is not supposed to void a contract. Yet often, when faced with precisely such a question, courts will say that the token exchanged is "nominal" or a "sham," and as such not sufficient consideration. All appearances to the contrary, it strains credulity to believe that a de minimis item truly induces the return promise and therefore can hardly be said to have been "bargained for."

This result may seem to emphasize the niceties of the doctrine over some of the purposes it is thought to achieve. If Schwam genuinely wants his promise to be enforceable and if this desire is carefully thought out and thoroughly documented, many of the policies underlying the consideration doctrine seem to be satisfied. Yet, unless the promise somehow crosses that mysterious line between a gift transaction and an exchange transaction, conventional contract doctrine will consider it unenforceable. The policy that gift promises should not be enforced under contract law strains against the policy that parties should be free to make whatever legally binding promises they please. And for courts that worry about nominal or sham consideration, the policy against enforcing gift promises seems to win. If this result seems overly rigid to you, keep in mind that it is not universally accepted, and even where it is, legal theories such as promissory estoppel may provide some relief to the disappointed promisee.

[handwritten margin note: policy against enforcing promise of gifts]

2. Preexisting Duties *[handwritten note: bargained for promise of an obligation is sufficient consideration]*

A person who promises to take on a <u>new obligation suffers a "legal detriment."</u> If bargained for, the promise to take on that obligation can serve as consideration. As we have just seen, the relative size or value of that detriment, in light of what the promisor hopes to receive in exchange, is generally not a proper sphere of inquiry for the courts. But suppose a person merely promises to perform an obligation that he already owes. Is this promise a "legal detriment" that can serve as consideration? Traditional contract doctrine says no.

Consider the following example. A struggling restaurateur, Ed Coli, offers $10,000 to a health inspector to conduct a most careful and thorough inspection of his competitor's kitchen on her next scheduled visit to the competitor's premises. The health inspector, it seems, has a reputation for being rather sloppy and careless. When the time comes, however, she does conduct a thorough examination of the competing restaurant and uncovers several violations of applicable health regulations. A ream of health code citations ensue. When the health inspector seeks to enforce Ed's promise to pay $10,000 for her services, Ed reneges. His promise, he says, was unsupported by consideration. Presumably, the health inspector already had a duty to the public to inspect local restaurant kitchens carefully and thoroughly. Ed is merely asking her to perform an obligation that she already had. If so, what of legal significance did Ed get for his promise?

This is the question asked and answered by the preexisting duty rule. This rule is embedded in older contract cases but has been under attack as of late. The gist of the rule is that a preexisting legal duty cannot serve as consideration for a contract. Anything that is received in exchange for a promise to do what one is already obligated to do is a mere gratuity or, perhaps less kindly, a bribe. For those steeped in consideration doctrine, this rule may seem exactly right. At the time the health inspector made her promise, she already had a legal duty to perform. To promise performance once more or even to perform straight out is an empty act and no more than what she was obligated to do already. To allow her to collect for performance of such a duty smacks of corruption.

The Restatement, Second, formulates the preexisting duty rule as follows:

RESTATEMENT, SECOND §73. PERFORMANCE OF LEGAL DUTY

Performance of a legal duty owed to a promisor which is neither doubtful nor the subject of honest dispute is not consideration; but a similar performance is consideration if it differs from what was required by the duty in a way which reflects more than a pretense of bargain.

■　■　■

There is an air of extortion or illicit gain underlying many of the preexisting duty rule cases. Police officers demand rewards for catching criminals, criminals seek compensation for following the straight and narrow, and debtors exact indulgences for paying what they owe. A distaste for such sleaziness undoubtedly explains the origins of the rule.

The following case presents the preexisting duty rule in a slightly different context.

WHITE v. VILLAGE OF HOMEWOOD

256 Ill. App. 3d 354, 628 N.E.2d 616 (1993)
Illinois Appellate Court

HARTMAN, Justice.

Plaintiff, Angela White, appeals the dismissal of her negligence action as barred by an exculpatory agreement that she signed. The sole issue presented for review is whether the exculpatory agreement relieved defendants of liability.

Plaintiff's amended complaint against defendants arose from personal injuries she sustained in June 1990 while taking a physical agility test to become a firefighter/paramedic for the Homewood Fire Department. While traversing horizontal bars as part of the test, plaintiff fell and was injured. Count II of the amended complaint, the only count relevant to this appeal, alleged that defendants were negligent in administering the test.

Defendants moved to dismiss the negligence count . . . , asserting that the exculpatory agreement signed by plaintiff before taking the test released them from liability. The exculpatory agreement, attached as an exhibit, stated:

> **AGILITY TEST**
> *RELEASE OF ALL LIABILITIES*
> The undersigned, for good and valuable considerations, hereby releases, remises and discharges the Village of Homewood, a Municipal Corporation, its officers, servants, agents and employees of and from any and all claims, demands, and liabilities to me and on account of any and all injuries, losses and damages, to my person that shall have been caused, or may, at any time, arise as a result of a certain Fire Examination Agility Test conducted by the Board of Fire and Police Commissioners of said Village of Homewood, the intention hereof being to completely, absolutely, and finally release said Village of Homewood, and its officers, servants, agents and employees of and from any and all liability arising wholly or partially from the cause aforesaid.

Plaintiff filed a response in which she admitted signing the exculpatory agreement before taking the test, but stated she only did so to obtain employment. She maintained that the exculpatory agreement is unenforceable. The circuit court granted defendants' motion and dismissed with prejudice the ordinary negligence count. Plaintiff appeals.

Plaintiff contends that the exculpatory agreement is unenforceable because it lacks consideration and violates public policy. She seeks reinstatement of her ordinary negligence count.

Under certain circumstances exculpatory contracts may act as a total bar to a plaintiff's negligence claim. This is because public policy strongly favors the freedom to contract. To be efficacious in a court of law, however, a release must be based upon consideration. The same rules apply to an exculpatory agreement. Valuable consideration for a contract consists either of some right, interest, profit or benefit accruing to one party, or some forbearance, detriment, loss of responsibility given, suffered or undertaken by the other. The pre-existing duty rule provides that where a party does what it is already legally obligated to do, there is no consideration as there is no detriment. For example, where a guest was by statute entitled to use a hotel safe to store valuables, a promise by the guest to limit the liability of the hotel in exchange for using the safe is not supported by consideration because of the pre-existing duty rule. *Goncalves v. Regent International Hotels, Ltd.* (1983), 58 N.Y.2d 206, 460 N.Y.S.2d 750, 447 N.E.2d 693, 700.

Defendants maintain that, in consideration of the exculpatory agreement, they administered the physical agility test and allowed plaintiff to participate. Analysis reveals, however, that defendants gave no consideration for the exculpatory agreement. According to the Illinois Municipal Code, defendants were required by law to administer the physical agility test, and plaintiff had a legal right to participate. (65 ILCS 5/10-2.1-6 (West 1992).) Consideration cannot flow from an act performed pursuant to a pre-existing legal duty. As a result, the exculpatory agreement is unenforceable as a matter of law.

[handwritten margin note: already required to administer the test]

We reject defendants' claim that *Radloff v. Village of West Dundee* (1986), 140 Ill. App. 3d 338, 95 Ill. Dec. 135, 489 N.E.2d 356, controls this issue. There, plaintiff signed an exculpatory agreement before taking a physical aptitude test to become a village police officer. The release specifically stated that it was in "consideration of said Village arranging for the administration of said test." (*Radloff*, 140 Ill. App. 3d at 339, 95 Ill. Dec. 135, 489 N.E.2d 356.) While scaling a seven-foot barricade during the test, plaintiff injured herself. The circuit court dismissed plaintiff's cause of action, finding that the exculpatory agreement she signed relieved the village of liability. The appellate court affirmed, saying it was unpersuaded by the public policy arguments set forth by plaintiff. Defendants aver that the consideration contemplated by the release in *Radloff* is the same as the consideration contemplated in the instant case: administration of the physical agility test, and the benefit to plaintiff of participating therein. Defendants fail to note that the issue of lack of consideration never was raised in *Radloff*. Consequently, *Radloff* provides no precedent for the case *sub judice*.

[handwritten margin note: no precedent because they dont discuss consideration]

Defendants correctly point out that, generally, courts will not inquire into the sufficiency of consideration to support a contract between two parties. As long as the agreement is bargained for, and the amount of consideration is not so grossly inadequate as to shock the conscience of the court, the adequacy of the consideration will not be challenged. Here, however, adequacy is not the issue for absolutely no consideration flowed between the parties. Defendants' cited authority is irrelevant to the disposition of this case. . . .

[In the alternative, the plaintiff argued that it would be against public policy to enforce the exculpatory agreement. The court stated that exculpatory agreements are generally enforceable if supported by consideration, but under these particular circumstances it would be unconscionable and against public policy to hold the plaintiff to the terms of the release that she signed. We omit the court's discussion; however, we return to the defense of unconscionability in Chapter 13 and discuss public policy defenses in Chapter 14.]

For the reasons set forth above, we reverse the dismissal and remand to the circuit court with instructions to reinstate the ordinary negligence count of plaintiff's complaint. — *disposition*

■ QUESTIONS

↗ physical agility

(1)   What duty did the Village of Homewood have in this case? To whom was it owed? — *public interest*

(2)   Identify each element set out in the preexisting duty rule as formulated in Restatement, Second §73. Apply §73 to the facts of this case. Is the result the same?

(3)   In addition to arguing that the exculpatory agreement was not supported by consideration, Angela White also argued that enforcement of it would be contrary to public policy. In your view, what policies, if any, support enforcement of the exculpatory agreement in this case? What policies support invalidating it? Does consideration doctrine reflect any of the policies (for or against enforcement) you have identified?

open the police to big liability claims

(4)   Could the Village of Homewood have avoided the consideration problem in this case through more careful drafting of its release? Alternatively, would it have been effective to offer Angela White a small payment for her release?

they offer potential employment at the end   *yes ⊲*

■ PROBLEM 9.4

Darla Data works for a state public health agency. Her job responsibilities include providing data analysis and other support to biomedical researchers in the private sector. Darla promised that she would complete time-consuming data analysis for Cal Cure, a medical researcher seeking to find the causes and cures for a rare disease, so long as Cal agreed to list Darla as a co-author on any study he published as a result of the research. Cal agreed, and Darla in fact provided extensive research support to Cal. Although helpful, Cal did not consider her work to be particularly substantive. When he eventually published a paper based on the research, he decided not to credit Darla as a co-author. Darla sues Cal, alleging among other things breach of contract.

(a)   Cal asks the court to dismiss Darla's lawsuit, arguing that even if Darla's allegations were true, any promise he made to credit her as a co-author lacked consideration. Should Cal's argument prevail? Why or why not? *yes. darla was already contracted to do that kind of work*

(b)   Would it make any difference to your analysis if Darla worked not for a state agency, but instead for a private non-profit organization? *not really*

■ PROBLEM 9.5

Henry Hamer and Sara Sidway have been romantically involved for several years, although their relationship has been a stormy one. Sara periodically used cocaine and, when high, lost large sums of money playing video poker. Whenever this happened, Henry and Sara had a colossal fight, and Sara promised to mend her ways. After their latest fight, Henry told Sara that he was tired of her empty promises and felt he needed to give her an incentive to shape up. If she would remain clean and sober for nine months and would refrain from playing video poker during that entire period, at the end of the nine months he would buy her a Mercedes sports car like the one she had been admiring at a local dealership. Sara shook his hand and promised to do as he asked.

Nine months have passed, and Sara has neither used drugs nor gambled. Does Henry have a contractual obligation to buy her the Mercedes? Does it matter whether video poker is legal where Henry and Sara live?

[handwritten margin note: No, she had a preexisting duty to not use drugs]

[handwritten note: foreBearance in part]

Sometimes, the policies underlying the preexisting duty rule seem neither clear nor compelling. The preexisting duty rule is particularly controversial in the context of modification of contracts. We defer full discussion of contract modification until Chapter 13. A brief introduction to the source of the controversy, however, is useful at this point.

Alaska Packers' Association v. Domenico, 117 F. 99 (9th Cir. 1902), a classic from the early twentieth century, illustrates how the preexisting duty rule can threaten enforcement of a contract modification. Alaska Packers' Association owned a salmon cannery in Pyramid Harbor, Alaska, in which it had an investment of about $150,000. In March and April of 1900, it entered into contracts with a number of fishermen under which the fishermen agreed to be shipped to Alaska to work as sailors and fishermen for Alaska Packers' Association during the 1900 fishing season. As payment for their labor, the fishermen would receive a lump sum for the season (for some it was $50; for others, $60) plus two cents for every salmon they participated in catching.

The fishermen arrived in Pyramid Harbor in April. On May 19 they ceased work and threatened to return to San Francisco unless Alaska Packers' Association agreed to increase their lump sum payments to $100. At that stage of the short Alaskan salmon season, it would have been impossible to replace the fishermen with a new crew: After unsuccessfully resisting for a few days, the Association's superintendent in Pyramid Harbor acceded to their demands on May 22. The parties signed new contracts identical to the originals except for the increase in the lump sum wage.

When the fishermen returned to San Francisco at the end of the season, Alaska Packers' Association offered to pay them what was due under the original contract and refused to pay the increased amount agreed to by the superintendent. Some of the fishermen accepted this, but others sued. It was established at trial that the fishermen had not undertaken any new or extra obligation in exchange for the increase in their pay. The court held that the agreement to increase the wage was invalid because it lacked consideration.

We discuss contract modifications in more detail in Chapter 13, in which we observe that modern contract law recognizes the utility of contract modifications in some circumstances but not in others. Occasionally, agreements to modify a contract will be enforced even if they are not supported by separate consideration. In some jurisdictions, however, the preexisting duty rule retains its vitality. In such cases, without separate consideration, promises to modify a preexisting contract are largely unenforceable.

■ PROBLEM 9.6

In reaching its decision, the court in *Alaska Packers' Association* stated:

[The fishermen] agreed in writing, for certain stated compensation, to render their services to the appellant in remote waters where the season for conducting fishing operations is extremely short, and in which enterprise the appellant had a large amount of money invested; and, after having entered upon the discharge of their contract, and at a time when it was impossible for the appellant to secure other men in their places, the . . . [fishermen], without any valid cause, absolutely refused to continue the services they were under contract to perform unless the appellant would consent to pay them more money. Consent to such a demand, under such circumstances, if given, was, in our opinion, without consideration, for the reason that it was based solely upon the . . . [fishermen's] agreement to render the exact services, and none other, that they were already under contract to render. . . .

The court went on to quote the following language from an opinion in another case:

No astute reasoning can change the plain fact that the party who refuses to perform, and thereby coerces a promise from the other party to the contract to pay him an increased compensation for doing that which he is legally bound to do, takes an unjustifiable advantage of the necessities of the other party. Surely it would be a travesty on justice to hold that the party so making the promise for extra pay was estopped from asserting that the promise was without consideration. . . .

(a) It appears that the superintendent capitulated to the fishermen's demands and signed the modified contracts. It was the home office in San

Francisco that refused to honor the modified contracts at the end of the season. Do you think this fact could have played a role in the decision? If so, how and why?

(b) The above extracts from *Alaska Packers' Association* make it clear that the court was concerned with the extortionate nature of the modification. Assume that once the fishermen arrived in Pyramid Harbor, the superintendent (acting within the scope of his authority) learned that a competing salmon canning operation was offering its fishermen a lump sum payment of $100. The superintendent knew from experience that some fishermen, enticed by the higher pay, would jump ship and go to work for the competitor, although no one had yet threatened to do so. Even if most of the fishermen decided to stay on, the superintendent feared that morale would suffer. The superintendent decided it would be wise to offer the fishermen improved terms to foreclose any potential problems. The parties signed the same modified contracts described in the summary of the case. Upon the ship's return to San Francisco, Alaska Packers' Association refused to pay the increased amount to the fishermen. In light of the principles we have studied to date, would the case have turned out differently under these facts? Do you think it should have? Why or why not?

(c) Disregard the facts of part (b) and assume that the superintendent (again acting within the scope of his authority) did not wish to change the contracts, but did so because the fishermen refused to work unless he agreed to their terms. This time, however, one of the fishermen was a wily sea lawyer who knew something about consideration doctrine. On his advice, his shipmates included in the modified contract a new provision in which they promised not to spit on the deck of the boat for the remainder of the season. In light of the principles we have studied to date, would the case have turned out differently under these facts? Do you think it should have? Why or why not?

3. Agreements to Settle Disputed Claims or Defenses

Kessler, included in Section B.1, involved a settlement agreement. The insurer agreed to pay $750 to Ms. Kessler in exchange for her abandonment of all claims she had arising out of her injury. One issue in the case was whether $750 was adequate consideration for her release. The legal sufficiency of the consideration she provided—that is, the abandonment of her claims—was not in dispute. In this section, we examine under what circumstances abandonment of a claim or defense constitutes legally sufficient consideration.

under what situations is abandoning a legal right sufficient consideration?

ex. settlements

Disputing parties often decide that it is preferable to settle their differences, rather than expending time and energy pursuing a lawsuit. Settlement agreements are often enforceable as contracts. At first glance, this result seems to make perfect sense. The parties clearly seem to have bargained for an exchange. Both sides agree to forgo the litigation, and perhaps the parties exchange some promises to pay money or perform other actions. But when one factors in the preexisting duty rule and the policies it represents, the picture gets decidedly more complicated.

Suppose, for instance, that Deb Deadbeat owes $10,000 to her credit card company. Deb neglects to pay her monthly bill and ignores dunning phone calls. Ultimately, the credit card company sues her. Deb makes it an offer: If the credit card company drops its suit, Deb will pay it $1,000 in cold hard cash. Otherwise, she'll defend the suit to the utmost. Figuring $1,000 in hand is worth $10,000 in the bush, the credit card company agrees. It later comes to rue its promise and argues that the agreement is not enforceable. The company cites a lack of consideration. A strict extension of the preexisting duty rule would support this argument. Because Deb had a preexisting legal duty to pay the full $10,000, her promise to pay $1,000 was a legal nullity. Deb is using the threat of a frivolous defense to extract a forbearance from the credit card company.

Similar policy considerations come into play when one party makes a frivolous claim rather than a frivolous defense. Maybe Deb, disenchanted with her credit card troubles, decides to sue her college. It should have taught her more about money management, Deb asserts. Deb's lawsuit has no basis in fact or in law, and Deb knows that. Nevertheless, to preserve general alumni good will and to avoid wasting precious time in court, the college agrees to settle the suit with Deb for a modest sum. Should this settlement agreement be enforceable as a contract? No one has a preexisting legal duty here, yet Deb's promise to give up her claim against the college seems just as chimerical as her promise to give up her defense against the credit card company. Here, too, contract doctrine casts suspicion on Deb's promise. Forbearance in pursuing a patently invalid claim does not constitute good consideration, even if bargained for.

The difficult cases are the ones in the middle. Consider, for instance, if Deb's college roommate had borrowed Deb's credit card and had recklessly run up a balance of $10,000. Deb thinks that she shouldn't be responsible for the charges her roommate put on the card. The credit card company alleges that because she gave the card to her roommate, Deb implicitly authorized the charges and thus is liable. Nevertheless, Deb and her credit card company agree to settle the dispute for $1,000. In hindsight, it may be that one party could persuade a court that it was dead right on the law, and the other was dead wrong; yet at the time of the settlement, neither party knew with any certainty which way a court would go. Is Deb's promise to give up her defense enforceable? Is the credit card company's promise to give up its claim enforceable? Whether or not settlement of questionable claims or defenses can serve as consideration is a chronic area of dispute.

Restatement, Second §74 captures one view of when a settlement agreement is supported by consideration and when it is not:

RESTATEMENT, SECOND §74. SETTLEMENT OF CLAIMS

(1) Forbearance to assert or the surrender of a claim or defense which proves to be invalid is not consideration unless

(a) the claim or defense is in fact doubtful because of uncertainty as to the facts or the law, or

(b) the forbearing or surrendering party believes that the claim or defense may be fairly determined to be valid.

(2) The execution of a written instrument surrendering a claim or defense by one who is under no duty to execute it is consideration if the execution of the written instrument is bargained for even though he is not asserting the claim or defense and believes that no valid claim or defense exists.

■   ■   ■

Many interesting questions of interpretation are buried in §74. Some of these questions arise in the case of *Fiege v. Boehm.*

FIEGE v. BOEHM

210 Md. 352, 123 A.2d 316 (1956)
Maryland Court of Appeals

DELAPLAINE, Judge.

This suit was brought in the Superior Court of Baltimore City by Hilda Louise Boehm against Louis Gail Fiege to recover for breach of a contract to pay the expenses incident to the birth of his bastard child[11] and to provide for its support. . . .

Plaintiff, a typist, now over 35 years old, who has been employed by the Government in Washington and Baltimore for over thirteen years, testified in the Court below that she had never been married, but that at about midnight on January 21, 1951, defendant, after taking her to a moving picture theater on York Road and then to a restaurant, had sexual intercourse with her in his

---

[11] This phrase may sound jarring to the modern ear. At the time this case was decided, however, this was a conventional way to refer to a child born outside of marriage, as evidenced by the name of the paternity statute involved in the case. Because we feel the cultural milieu is an important factor to consider when reading the case, we have retained the original usage.—EDS.

automobile. She further testified that he agreed to pay all her medical and hospital expenses, to compensate her for loss of salary caused by the pregnancy and birth, and to pay her ten dollars per week for the support of the child upon condition that she would refrain from instituting bastardy proceedings against him. She further testified that between September 17, 1951, and May, 1953, defendant paid her a total of $480. [The plaintiff placed the child for adoption on July 13, 1954, and claimed that the amount accrued under the agreement through that date on account of expenses, lost salary, and support was $2,895.80. She demanded that the defendant pay her the remaining balance owing of $2,415.80, but he refused.] . . .

Defendant admitted that he had taken plaintiff to restaurants, had danced with her several times, had taken her to Washington, and had brought her home in the country; but he asserted that he had never had sexual intercourse with her. He also claimed that he did not enter into any agreement with her. He admitted, however, that he had paid her a total of $480. His father also testified that he stated "that he did not want his mother to know, and if it were just kept quiet, kept principally away from his mother and the public and the courts, that he would take care of it." Defendant further testified that in May, 1953, he went to see plaintiff's physician to make inquiry about blood tests to show the paternity of the child; and that those tests were made and they indicated that it was not possible that he could have been the child's father. He then stopped making payments. Plaintiff thereupon filed a charge of bastardy with the State's Attorney.

The testimony which was given in the Criminal Court by Dr. Milton Sachs, hematologist at the University Hospital, was read to the jury in the Superior Court. In recent years the blood-grouping test has been employed in criminology, in the selection of donors for blood transfusions, and as evidence in paternity cases. The Landsteiner blood-grouping test is based on the medical theory that the red corpuscles in human blood contain two affirmative agglutinating substances, and that every individual's blood falls into one of the four classes and remains the same throughout life. According to Mendel's law of inheritance, this blood individuality is an hereditary characteristic which passes from parent to child, and no agglutinating substance can appear in the blood of a child which is not present in the blood of one of its parents. The four Landsteiner blood groups, designated as AB, A, B, and O, into which human blood is divided on the basis of the compatibility of the corpuscles and serum with the corpuscles and serum of other persons, are characterized by different combinations of two agglutinogens in the red blood cells and two agglutinins in the serum. Dr. Sachs reported that Fiege's blood group was Type O, Miss Boehm's was Type B, and the infant's was Type A. He further testified that on the basis of these tests, Fiege could not have been the father of the child, as it is impossible for a mating of Type O and Type B to result in a child of Type A.

Although defendant was acquitted by the Criminal Court, the Superior Court overruled his [demurrer to plaintiff's pleadings in this lawsuit, as well as his] motion for a directed verdict [after the trial]. In the charge to the

π claims

jury the Court instructed them that defendant's acquittal in the Criminal Court was not binding upon them. The jury found a verdict in favor of plaintiff for $2,415.80, the full amount of her claim. Defendant filed a motion for judgment n.o.v. or a new trial. The Court overruled that motion also, and entered judgment on the verdict of the jury. Defendant appealed from that judgment.

posture

Defendant contends that, even if he did enter into the contract as alleged, it was not enforceable, because plaintiff's forbearance to prosecute was not based on a valid claim, and hence the contract was without consideration. He, therefore, asserts that the Court erred in overruling . . . [his motions].

It was originally held at common law that a child born out of wedlock is *filius nullius*, and a putative father is not under any legal liability to contribute to the support of his illegitimate child, and his promise to do so is unenforceable because it is based on purely a moral obligation. Some of the courts in this country have held that, in the absence of any statutory obligation on the father to aid in the support of his bastard child, his promise to the child's mother to pay her for its maintenance, resting solely on his natural affection for it and his moral obligation to provide for it, is a promise which the law cannot enforce because of lack of sufficient consideration. On the contrary, a few courts have stated that the natural affection of a father for his child and the moral obligation upon him to support it and to aid the woman he has wronged furnish sufficient consideration for his promise to the mother to pay for the support of the child to make the agreement enforceable at law.

fathers have no legal duty to support bastard children

However, where statutes are in force to compel the father of a bastard to contribute to its support, the courts have invariably held that a contract by the putative father with the mother of his bastard child to provide for the support of the child upon the agreement of the mother to refrain from invoking the bastardy statute against the father, or to abandon proceedings already commenced, is supported by sufficient consideration. In Maryland it is now provided by statute that whenever a person is found guilty of bastardy, the court shall issue an order directing such person . . . [to pay maintenance and support].

if she gives up her rights, that is sufficient consideration

Prosecutions for bastardy are treated in Maryland as criminal proceedings, but they are actually civil in purpose. While the prime object of the Maryland Bastardy Act is to protect the public from the burden of maintaining illegitimate children, it is so distinctly in the interest of the mother that she becomes the beneficiary of it. Accordingly a contract by the putative father of an illegitimate child to provide for its support upon condition that bastardy proceedings will not be instituted is a compromise of civil injuries resulting from a criminal act, and not a contract to compound a criminal prosecution, and if it is fair and reasonable, it is in accord with the Bastardy Act and the public policy of the State.

Of course, a contract of a putative father to provide for the support of his illegitimate child must be based, like any other contract, upon sufficient consideration. The early English law made no distinction in regard to the sufficiency of a claim which the claimant promised to forbear to prosecute, as the consideration of a promise, other than the broad distinction between good claims and bad claims. No promise to forbear to prosecute an unfounded claim was sufficient consideration. In the early part of the nineteenth century, an advance was made from the criterion of the early authorities when it was held that forbearance to prosecute a suit which had already been instituted was sufficient consideration, without inquiring whether the suit would have been successful or not.

In 1867 the Maryland Court of Appeals, in the opinion delivered by Judge Bartol in *Hartle v. Stahl*, 27 Md. 157, 172, held: (1) that forbearance to assert a claim before institution of suit, if not in fact a legal claim, is not of itself sufficient consideration to support a promise; but (2) that a compromise of a doubtful claim or a relinquishment of a pending suit is good consideration for a promise; and (3) that in order to support a compromise, it is sufficient that the parties entering into it thought at the time that there was a bona fide question between them, although it may eventually be found that there was in fact no such question.

We have thus adopted the rule that the surrender of, or forbearance to assert, an invalid claim by one who has not an honest and reasonable belief in its possible validity is not sufficient consideration for a contract. We combine the subjective requisite that the claim be bona fide with the objective requisite that it must have a reasonable basis of support. Accordingly a promise not to prosecute a claim which is not founded in good faith does not of itself give a right of action on an agreement to pay for refraining from so acting, because a release from mere annoyance and unfounded litigation does not furnish valuable consideration.

Professor Williston was not entirely certain whether the test of reasonableness is based upon the intelligence of the claimant himself, who may be an ignorant person with no knowledge of law and little sense as to facts; but he seemed inclined to favor the view that "the claim forborne must be neither absurd in fact from the standpoint of a reasonable man in the position of the claimant, nor obviously unfounded in law to one who has an elementary knowledge of legal principles." 1 *Williston on Contracts*, Rev. Ed., sec. 135. We agree that while stress is placed upon the honesty and good faith of the claimant, forbearance to prosecute a claim is insufficient consideration if the claim forborne is so lacking in foundation as to make its assertion incompatible with honesty and a reasonable degree of intelligence. Thus, if the mother of a bastard knows that there is no foundation, either in law or fact, for a charge against a certain man that he is the father of the child, but that man promises to pay her in order to prevent bastardy proceedings against him, the forbearance to institute proceedings is not sufficient consideration.

On the other hand, forbearance to sue for a lawful claim or demand is sufficient consideration for a promise to pay for the forbearance if the party forbearing had an honest intention to prosecute litigation which is not frivolous, vexatious, or unlawful, and which he believed to be well founded. Thus the promise of a woman who is expecting an illegitimate child that she will not institute bastardy proceedings against a certain man is sufficient consideration *she made that claim in good faith*

for his promise to pay for the child's support, even though it may not be certain whether the man is the father or whether the prosecution would be successful, if she makes the charge in good faith. The fact that a man accused of bastardy is forced to enter into a contract to pay for the support of his bastard child from fear of exposure and the shame that might be cast upon him as a result, as well as a sense of justice to render some compensation for the injury he inflicted upon the mother, does not lessen the merit of the contract, but greatly increases it. . . .

In the case at bar there was no proof of fraud or unfairness. Assuming that the hematologists were accurate in their laboratory tests and findings, nevertheless plaintiff gave testimony which indicated that she made the charge of bastardy against defendant in good faith. For these reasons the Court acted properly in overruling the demurrer to the amended declaration and the motion for a directed verdict.

Finally, in attacking the action of the Court in overruling the motion for judgment n.o.v. or a new trial, defendant made the additional complaint that there was error in the charge to the jury. As we have said, the Court instructed the jury that defendant's acquittal in the Criminal Court was not binding upon the jury in the case before them. Defendant urged strongly that he had been acquitted by the Criminal Court in consequence of scientific findings from blood tests. It is immaterial whether defendant was the father of the child or not. In the light of what we have said, we need not make any specific determination on this subject. . . .

As we have found no reversible error in the rulings and instructions of the trial Court, we will affirm the judgment entered on the verdict of the jury. Judgment affirmed, with costs. *disposition*

■ QUESTIONS

(1) What promise is at issue in this case, and what is the alleged consideration for that promise?

(2) At one point the court enunciates a two-pronged test for determining when forbearance in pursuing a claim can constitute consideration. First, the claim must be bona fide. Second, it must have a reasonable basis of support. What is the difference between these two prongs of analysis?

(3) Compare and contrast the court's analysis to Restatement, Second §74. Do you see any similarities? Any differences?

(4) The court states that it is immaterial whether the defendant was the father of the child. Is it immaterial whether the plaintiff and the defendant ever had sexual intercourse?

(5) The plaintiff said that she would not institute bastardy proceedings against the defendant. She proceeded to do precisely that. Why do you think this fact was not fatal to the plaintiff's case?

■ PROBLEM 9.7

Several years ago, Predatory Mortgage Co. provided Harry Homeowner with a $200,000 loan to help him purchase a house. To secure repayment of the loan, Predatory Mortgage Co. obtained a mortgage on the home, which entitled it to foreclose should Harry not pay as agreed. Unfortunately, Harry lost his job during a downturn in the economy and wasn't able to make his regular monthly payments. Real estate prices in the region had declined significantly by then, and the home was now worth substantially less than the amount left owing under the mortgage loan. Eventually, Predatory Mortgage Co. foreclosed on the home.

Under applicable real estate law, as long as Predatory Mortgage Co. properly complied with the requirements for conducting a proper foreclosure, it would be entitled to collect a deficiency from Harry. The deficiency would be equal to the difference between the amount owing under the mortgage loan and the price it received for the house in the foreclosure sale.

Shortly after the foreclosure, Predatory Mortgage Co. offered to forgive Harry's obligation to pay the deficiency, as long as Harry signed a written release surrendering any claims he might have for any irregularities in the foreclosure process. Without consulting an attorney, Harry signed the release form and returned it to Predatory Mortgage Co.

Harry recently saw a television exposé about lenders who have been sloppy in their foreclosure processes and learned that as a result homeowners had successfully challenged their lenders' attempts to collect deficiencies that would otherwise be owing. Some had even received significant damage awards against their lenders. He is in your law office, wondering whether it is worthwhile to investigate the foreclosure on his home and to seek remedies against Predatory Mortgage Co. in the event that it too failed to follow the proper procedures. What advice do you have for Harry? What additional information, if any, would you like to have?

C MUTUALITY AND ITS LIMITS

So far in this chapter we have seen that consideration doctrine focuses on whether the parties have a bargain that provides for an exchange. If a plaintiff seeks to enforce another party's promise as a contractual obligation, that plaintiff will have to demonstrate that it provided a return promise or performance. In the usual case, unless the plaintiff has put itself on the line, it will not be able to hold the other party contractually accountable. If the alleged contract is not binding on one party due to a lack of consideration, it will not be binding on the other party either. These concepts, that both parties to a contract must give something of legal value in order to get something in exchange, is broadly captured by the phrase "mutuality of obligation." If one of the parties has neither contributed nor promised to contribute anything that is meaningful in the eyes of the law, there cannot be said to be a contract. As such, the concept of mutuality of obligation follows from the principles of consideration as we have developed them so far. The phrase, however, is the source of substantial confusion and thus is worthy of some explanation.

1. Performance as Consideration

It is important to limit the requirement of mutuality to its proper sphere. Many courts assert that mutuality of obligation is a prerequisite to the existence of a contract. Others baldly state that either both parties are bound to a contract, or neither is bound. Such sweeping statements are overly broad. Applied literally, these requirements would void several types of contracts that courts routinely recognize.

Recall, for instance, that a return performance can serve as consideration for a promise. On several occasions, we have seen examples of contracts that are formed by one party actually performing the bargained-for consideration, rather than promising to do so. *Carlill v. Carbolic Smoke Ball Co.* is an example. There, Ms. Carlill didn't have an obligation to use the Carbolic Smoke Ball. She certainly didn't have an obligation to get influenza. In fact, she never obligated herself to do anything. Yet when she did use the smoke ball and became ill, the court found a contract in her favor. Her actions served as consideration for Carbolic Smoke Ball Co.'s promise to pay. Restatement, Second §71 states that a performance need not be an act; it may also consist of a forbearance. *Hamer v. Sidway* illustrates forbearance as consideration. In that case, the contract arguably wasn't formed, and the uncle had no obligation to pay, until the nephew had reached the age of 21 and had successfully refrained from his nefarious habits. Once the contract was formed, the nephew had no continuing obligations. There was no one point in time when both the uncle and the nephew were obligated to do anything. In either case, there was never a single point in time when both of the parties had promised to take some future action, yet still there was consideration. Consideration doctrine doesn't demand a return promise in all cases. Return performance, if bargained for, suffices. To put it another way, not all contracts require "mutuality of obligation."

The legal sufficiency of forbearance as consideration poses some conceptual challenges. For instance, courts have divided on the legal sufficiency of forbearance as consideration in the employment context. Absent agreement to the contrary, in many states employment is considered to be at will. This means that so long as the employer does not discriminate or otherwise act on a basis that is prohibited by law, it can fire an employee for any reason—or for no reason. (Likewise, again absent an applicable law or agreement to the contrary, an employee is free to quit his or her job at any time.) Sometimes employers require at will employees to assume obligations under threat of losing their positions if they refuse to agree. If the employees subsequently challenge the binding nature of such agreements, one question that may arise is the legal sufficiency of the consideration provided by the employer.

◼ PROBLEM 9.8

(a) Big Bank has decided to require its executive officers to sign agreements in which they agree not to work for any of Big Bank's direct competitors for a period of one year after their employment with Big Bank ceases.[12] Assume that Ed Executive is an employee at will. Under the circumstances described below, Big Bank discharges Ed after he signs a non-competition agreement. Ed immediately accepts a lower-paying position at Grand Bank, one of Big Bank's direct competitors. In each case, decide whether there is consideration for Ed's promise not to compete.

(i) When Big Bank first offers Ed Executive a job, it tells him that he must sign the non-competition agreement as a condition to taking the position. Ed signs the agreement and starts work the next day. One year later, Big Bank fires Ed.

(ii) Alternatively, assume Ed has been working as a teller at Big Bank for three years. Big Bank offers him a promotion to an executive position on the condition he sign the non-competition agreement. Ed signs the agreement and is promoted, but is fired one week later.

(iii) Alternatively, assume Ed has been working in an executive position at Big Bank for three years. Big Bank institutes a policy requiring all executive employees to sign non-competition agreements or else they will be terminated, effective immediately. Ed signs a non-competition agreement, but Big Bank fires him three years later. Was there consideration for Ed's promise not to compete? Based on principles we have studied to date, would it matter if Big Bank fired Ed a week after he signed the non-competition agreement? What if Big Bank fired him the day after he signed the agreement?

(b) Assume that in addition to requiring its executive employees to sign non-competition agreements, Big Bank decides to require them to sign agreements to submit any claims they may have against Big Bank to binding arbitration. Under each of the alternatives described in Part a of the Problem, Ed signs an arbitration agreement at the same time

---

[12] We return to non-competition agreements in Chapter 14.

he signs the non-competition agreement. After he is fired, Ed sues Big Bank for wrongful termination. Big Bank files a motion asking the court to dismiss the suit and order arbitration of the claim. Ed argues that there was no consideration for his promise to arbitrate disputes. Under each of the alternatives described in Part a, was there consideration for Ed's promise to arbitrate disputes? Why or why not?

2. Promises as Consideration

In general, there is no universal requirement that both parties be bound to the contract at the same time, to the same extent, or under the same circumstances. To say that the law always requires exact mutuality of obligation is, quite simply, incorrect. What, then, are courts doing when they invoke the concept of mutuality? Frequently, you will see discussions of mutuality when there is some question as to the legal significance of the undertaking of one of the parties to an alleged contract. Under principles we have already studied, if the parties are exchanging promises, each promise serves as consideration for the other only if both promises are meaningful in the eyes of the law. If either of the promises does not meet this standard, it cannot serve as consideration for the other, and there can be no contract. So when a court says that an alleged contract is not enforceable for lack of mutuality, it may really be concluding that one or both of the alleged promises is not legally sufficient consideration for the other.

An illusory promise is one that courts consider to have no legal significance for purposes of consideration doctrine. That is, although the promisor made a promise in positive terms, it has not really assumed any real legal detriment in doing so, and so has provided no consideration to the promisee. An example is a promise where the promisor retains complete discretion as to whether it will perform the promise. Say, for example, Dieter, your neighbor, has sold his house and is moving away. You have always admired his Great Dane. Dieter says to you, "I will give you my dog tomorrow, and you can pay me $1,000 for him next week if you feel like it." You say, "I agree," and plan to pick up the dog tomorrow. Dieter may have made a promise to you, but you have not made a promise to him. Your agreement to pay him $1,000 next week if you feel like it doesn't obligate you to do anything at all. His promise to give the dog to you is in fact gratuitous. As it is not supported by consideration, it would not be enforceable as a contractual obligation.

Although a promise that is completely discretionary is not a promise at all and therefore cannot serve as consideration, some level of discretion can be very helpful in commercial contexts. For this reason, courts sometimes stretch to find consideration where discretionary promises make commercial sense. If the promise seems seriously and reasonably made, and if the promisee appears to have genuinely bargained for the promise, the modern trend is to enforce it. Many courts do this not by ignoring consideration doctrine, but instead by implying an obligation to exercise one's discretion reasonably, in good faith, or otherwise in accordance with a similar standard. If, however, the circumstances suggest that the promisor wasn't acting seriously or didn't intend a real obligation, courts are less likely to find that a contract has been formed.

One frequently occurring example of a discretionary promise is one subject to a condition of satisfaction—that is, one of the party's promises is subject to the condition that he does not have to perform the promise unless he is satisfied with specified circumstances. Provided that the party's discretion is not absolute, the discretionary promise can qualify as consideration. Even if the agreement does not expressly include criteria by which satisfaction is to be measured, a court may imply an obligation to exercise the discretion in good faith, reasonably or in accordance with some similar standard. For example, in *Mattei v. Hopper*, 51 Cal. 2d 119, 330 P.2d 625 (1958), the California Supreme Court evaluated a clause in a real estate purchase agreement. The purchaser intended to erect a shopping center on the land, and the agreement conditioned the purchaser's obligation on acquisition of satisfactory leases. The seller refused to convey the property, and the purchaser sued. The seller argued, in part, that the satisfaction clause meant that there was no consideration for the seller's promise and hence no contract. In rejecting this argument, the court explained:

> While contracts making the duty of performance of one of the parties conditional upon his satisfaction would seem to give him wide latitude in avoiding any obligation and thus present serious consideration problems, such "satisfaction" clauses have been given effect. They have been divided into two primary categories and have been accorded different treatment on that basis. First, in those contracts where the condition calls for satisfaction as to commercial value or quality, operative fitness, or mechanical utility, dissatisfaction cannot be claimed arbitrarily, unreasonably, or capriciously, and the standard of a reasonable person is used in determining whether satisfaction has been received. . . . The second line of authorities dealing with "satisfaction" clauses . . . [are] those involving fancy, taste, or judgment. Where the question is one of judgment, the promisor's determination that he is not satisfied, when made in good faith, has been held to be a defense to an action on the contract. . . . Although these decisions do not expressly discuss the issues of mutuality of obligation or illusory promises, they necessarily imply that the promisor's duty to exercise his judgment in good faith is an adequate consideration to support the contract.

For the moment, our study of satisfaction clauses is limited to their treatment under consideration doctrine. It is important to note, however, that once a court is willing to imply an obligation to act reasonably, in good faith, or in accordance with some other standard, the court may be called upon to decide under what circumstances that standard has been met. Questions of what behavior is reasonable, or in good faith, permeate contract law. We have encountered questions like this on several occasions in earlier chapters. Similar issues came up in this chapter too, for instance in the challenge to the settlement Ms. Boehm reached with Mr. Fiege. We return to these matters again in later chapters and in particular address them in some detail in the context of contract interpretation in Chapter 15. For the time being, however, we simply draw your attention to the interpretive challenge and move on.

Sometimes, parties enter into elaborate agreements specifying the terms and conditions that will govern their relations yet nowhere expressly commit to do business with each other. They don't expressly reserve discretion over the nature of the performance required of them; rather, they make no express promises to perform at all. In these circumstances, courts have to decide whether the absence of any express promise to perform renders the agreements unenforceable for lack of consideration. The classic case of this sort is *Wood v. Lucy, Lady Duff-Gordon.*

This case is essential fare for law students not only because of Judge Cardozo's colorful language, but also because of the parties involved in the litigation. The defendant, Lady Duff-Gordon, was a character of some controversy. Famous for her diaphanous clothing designs, she became infamous through her participation in the Titanic disaster. Lady Duff-Gordon, with her husband, Sir Cosmo, were aboard the ill-fated ship but survived its encounter with the iceberg. Rumor has it that she and her husband bribed the ship's employees to allow their half-filled lifeboat to cast off. Apparently, the couple feared being swamped by desperate and drowning unfortunates. Yet, at the same time as their lifeboat drew away from the sinking ship, Lady Duff-Gordon was heard to lament to her maid the loss of lingerie. One can only wonder what role Lady Duff-Gordon's personality played in the *Wood* litigation. Irrespective of how she presented herself in court, the method of analysis used by Judge Cardozo in the resulting opinion remains vibrant and persuasive in today's contracts jurisprudence.

WOOD v. LUCY, LADY DUFF-GORDON

222 N.Y. 88, 118 N.E. 214 (1917)
New York Court of Appeals

CARDOZO, Judge.

The defendant styles herself "a creator of fashions." Her favor helps a sale. Manufacturers of dresses, millinery, and like articles are glad to pay for a certificate of her approval. The things which she designs, fabrics, parasols, and what not, have a new value in the public mind when issued in her name. She employed the plaintiff to help her to turn this vogue into money. He was to have the exclusive right, subject always to her approval, to place her indorsements on the designs of others. He was also to have the exclusive right to place her own designs on sale, or to license others to market them. In return she was to have one-half of "all profits and revenues" derived from any contracts he might make. The exclusive right was to last at least one year from April 1, 1915, and thereafter from year to year unless terminated by notice of 90 days. The plaintiff says that he kept the contract on his part, and that the defendant broke it. She placed her indorsement on fabrics, dresses, and millinery without his knowledge, and withheld the profits. He sues her for the damages, and the case comes here on demurrer.

The agreement of employment is signed by both parties. It has a wealth of recitals. The defendant insists, however, that it lacks the elements of a contract. She says that the plaintiff does not bind himself to anything. It is true that he does not promise in so many words that he will use reasonable efforts to place the defendant's indorsements and market her designs. We think, however, that such a promise is fairly to be implied. The law has outgrown its primitive stage of formalism when the precise word was the sovereign talisman, and every slip was fatal. It takes a broader view today. A promise may be lacking, and yet the whole writing may be "instinct with an obligation," imperfectly expressed (Scott, J. in *McCall v. Wright*, 133 App. Div. 62; *Moran v. Standard Oil Co.*, 211 N.Y. 187, 198). If that is so, there is a contract.

The implication of a promise here finds support in many circumstances. The defendant gave an exclusive privilege. She was to have no right for at least a year to place her own indorsements or market her own designs except through the agency of the plaintiff. The acceptance of the exclusive agency was an assumption of its duties. We are not to suppose that one party was to be placed at the mercy of the other. Many other terms of the agreement point the same way. We are told at the outset by way of recital that: "The said Otis F. Wood possesses a business organization adapted to the placing of such indorsements as the said Lucy, Lady Duff-Gordon, has approved."

The implication is that the plaintiff's business organization will be used for the purpose for which it is adapted. But the terms of the defendant's compensation are even more significant. Her sole compensation for the grant of an exclusive agency is to be one-half of all the profits resulting from the plaintiff's efforts. Unless he gave his efforts, she could never get anything. Without an implied promise, the transaction cannot have such business "efficacy, as both parties must have intended that at all events it should have." Bowen, L.J., in *The Moorcock*, 14 P. D. 64, 68. But the contract does not stop there. The plaintiff goes on to promise that he will account monthly for all moneys received by him, and that he will take out all such patents and copyrights and trade-marks as may in his judgment be necessary to protect the rights and articles affected by the agreement. It is true, of course, as the Appellate Division has said, that if he was under no duty to try to market designs or to place certificates of indorsement, his promise to account for profits or take out copyrights would be valueless. But in determining the intention of the parties the promise has a value. It helps to enforce the conclusion that the plaintiff had some duties. His promise to pay the defendant one-half of the profits and revenues resulting from the exclusive agency and to render accounts monthly was a promise to use reasonable efforts to bring profits and revenues into existence. For this conclusion the authorities are ample.

The judgment of the Appellate Division should be reversed, and the order of the Special Term affirmed, with costs in the Appellate Division and in this court.

▪ QUESTIONS

(1)   What factors persuaded the court to imply an obligation to use reasonable efforts in this case?

(2)   The court implies an obligation on Otis Wood to use reasonable efforts to perform his side of the bargain. Suppose Lady Duff-Gordon placed her indorsement on certain designs, but Otis Wood failed to market them to her satisfaction. Do you think Lady Duff-Gordon could have sued him successfully under a contract theory? How would the court determine the nature and extent of Otis Wood's obligations?

(3)   The court mentioned that Otis Wood's right to place Lady Duff-Gordon's indorsement on the designs of others was subject to her approval. Did this factor into the court's analysis, and if so, how? If not, should this factor have influenced the court's holding in the case?

 ## CONSIDERATION IN THE INTERNATIONAL CONTEXT

Consideration doctrine is a creature of common law legal systems. Although Civilian and other types of legal systems that do not follow the common law model have their own methods of distinguishing enforceable promises from unenforceable ones, consideration doctrine (as we know it) does not figure in their analysis. This is one arena where common law countries apply significantly different legal rules in their domestic transactions than other countries do.

In transnational commercial transactions, where the parties typically contemplate an exchange, consideration issues only occasionally arise. The CISG doesn't take an express position on whether a contract within its scope must be supported by consideration to be enforceable. Article 4 of the CISG, however, states that the Convention is not concerned with the validity of the contract. If a party believes a contract is not supported by consideration, it might argue that the lack of consideration goes to the "validity" of the contract under the domestic law otherwise applicable to it. As with UCC Article 2, however, there are a few specific situations where the CISG dispenses with any requirement of consideration where common law legal systems might otherwise require it. We will discuss some of these situations in Chapter 11, where we examine options and firm offers, and in Chapter 13, when we return to the enforceability of contract modifications.

The UNIDROIT Principles directly do away with the requirement of consideration. Article 3.1.2 of the UNIDROIT Principles states that a "contract is concluded, modified or terminated by the mere agreement of the parties, without any further requirement." The comments to this Article explain that in commercial dealings, a consideration requirement is of minimal practical importance because both parties almost always undertake obligations.

CHAPTER 10

Promissory Estoppel

not needed if there is consideration

A AN OVERVIEW OF PROMISSORY ESTOPPEL

Promissory estoppel is a theory that sometimes protects a promisee who has relied to his detriment on the promise, even though consideration or other elements of enforceability may not otherwise be present. As Chapter 9 indicates, consideration doctrine has positive and negative aspects: If consideration is present, a promise is presumptively enforceable, while a promise unsupported by consideration is not.[1] Promissory estoppel has its strongest expression where the lack of consideration threatens to make a promise unenforceable. If consideration is present, often there is no need to resort to the theory of promissory estoppel. As we have seen, however, even though a promise is arguably supported by consideration, conventional contract doctrine may still deem that promise unenforceable under a variety of circumstances. For instance, the promise may be so preliminary, incomplete, or indefinite that a court would conclude it does not qualify for enforcement as a contract. Or perhaps the promise is part of an oral agreement unenforceable under the statute of frauds. Sometimes in these circumstances courts allow some measure of recovery under a theory of promissory estoppel, even though conventional contract doctrine would not provide relief. In some contexts, the theory of promissory

---

[1] One author labels the negative aspects of consideration doctrine as its "gatekeeping function." *See* Mark B. Wessman, *Should We Fire the Gatekeeper? An Examination of the Doctrine of Consideration*, 48 U. Miami L. Rev. 45 (1993); Mark B. Wessman, *Retaining the Gatekeeper: Further Reflections on the Doctrine of Consideration*, 29 Loy. L.A. L. Rev. 713 (1996). This vivid image may help to put the function of consideration doctrine in context, as long as one realizes that consideration is not the only key to the enforcement gate and, at the same time, does not overcome all barriers to entry.

estoppel is well established; in others, it is more controversial. Over the course of the chapter, we explore its operation in a broad range of situations.

1. The Origins and Nature of Promissory Estoppel as a Theory of Recovery

for nonreciprocal promises

As we note above, the core application of promissory estoppel is in the realm of nonreciprocal promises, and that is where we begin our discussion. As Chapter 9 demonstrates, consideration doctrine operating in isolation protects those who make promises outside of the context of an exchange. A promisor who makes a gratuitous promise may be free to go back on her word without legal consequences. As a result, under consideration doctrine, policies that protect the promisor from liability win out over any competing policies that seek to favor the promisee. If people who receive gratuitous promises are disappointed when their would-be benefactors change their minds, consideration doctrine tells us, so be it. Perhaps it isn't contract law's function to protect the expectation of a windfall. Yet consideration doctrine does not tell the whole story.

law favors promisor

Not every promisee simply sits at home waiting for bounty to fall into his lap. Secure in his anticipated good fortune, he may forgo valuable opportunities or expend substantial efforts or money. Maybe his kindly benefactor even encourages him to take these actions. When the unhappy news of the promisor's change of mind reaches him, he is truly in a worse position than if the promise never had been made. He believes that his detrimental reliance should overcome any policies that militate against enforcement of the promise. It is precisely this sort of unfortunate who looks to promissory estoppel as his savior.

reliance is different than just disappointment

reliance leading to a disadvantage

The reliance of promisees has long been a concern of the courts. It may be that early courts applying the "benefit or detriment" test for consideration regularly enforced promises where reliance was shown.[2] After all, a promisee who has disadvantaged himself by relying on a promise has incurred a detriment. With the advent of the bargain theory of consideration, however, a detriment that the promisor did not bargain for could not (strictly speaking) constitute consideration. Courts applying the bargain theory of consideration struggled with these types of situations. Some courts, when faced with a plaintiff who had relied on a gratuitous promise, would stretch and contort consideration doctrine to find an enforceable contract. Others would stand by strict doctrine and, perhaps to their regret, refuse to enforce the promise. Over time, where there was justifiable reliance on a promise, courts began to hold promisors accountable even though the courts admitted that consideration as strictly

---

[2] One scholar states, for instance, "Promissory estoppel's ancient genealogy in equity and common law evidences that the doctrine is an ancient form of consideration predating the modern bargain theory of consideration by about five centuries." Eric Mills Holmes, *The Four Phases of Promissory Estoppel*, 20 Seattle U. L. Rev. 45, 52 (1996).

equitable estoppel

defined was absent. The basis on which they did so was not always entirely clear. But the general idea, that a promisor could be held accountable for a promise when the promisee justifiably relied on it, came to be known as promissory estoppel.

definition →

Promissory estoppel is related to the much older doctrine of equitable estoppel. Equitable estoppel, as its name suggests, is a theory used by courts to keep parties from benefiting from their own misstatements. If someone deliberately misstates (or conceals) a material fact to another, and, so deceived, the other proceeds to act to his detriment, courts may estop the party who made the misrepresentation from subsequently raising the true state of affairs. Traditionally, equitable estoppel only applied when the misstatements related to past or current facts. Promisors who subsequently renege have not necessarily engaged in this kind of misstatement: They may have simply changed their minds. As such, the theory of equitable estoppel is an awkward fit for those who rely to their detriment on promises rather than factual assertions. Nevertheless, some of the courts deciding these cases spoke in the language of estoppel—the promisor was "estopped" from arguing that there wasn't consideration when the promisee relied to his detriment.[3] The courts proceeded to enforce the promises as if consideration had been present.

In the 1920 edition of his treatise, Professor Williston described a number of these cases—cases where promises had been enforced, notwithstanding the lack of bargained-for consideration—and attempted to explain the themes that unified them.[4] You might recall from Chapter 1 that Professor Williston was a prominent classical scholar who strongly supported the logical articulation of legal rules. He was also the Reporter for the First Restatement of Contracts and was aided in that task by Professor Corbin, the staunch legal realist. Although the enterprise proved controversial, ultimately the drafters of the First Restatement of Contracts attempted to articulate a general theory of enforceability that could encompass these cases. The result of their efforts was the First Restatement of Contracts §90, which was included under the topic heading "Informal Contracts Without Assent or Consideration." The Restatement, Second, carries forward the theory (in a modified and more flexible version) in its own §90. Neither section speaks in terms of estoppel generally, and neither uses the phrase "promissory estoppel" specifically. Yet because of the theory's origins in equitable estoppel, it has become common to refer to it under the moniker of "promissory estoppel." Some argue that the name "promissory estoppel" is misleading because the modern doctrine is broader than its historical origins. Nevertheless, use of the name persists.

---

[3] As we will see, courts sometimes used (and still use) detrimental reliance as grounds for "estopping" the promisor from raising other challenges to the enforceability of a promise. For instance, promisors may be estopped from denying the enforceability of indefinite, incomplete, or preliminary promises; or from raising defenses based on the statute of frauds, the statute of limitations, or the parol evidence rule. Some of these themes come up later in this chapter. Discussion of the parol evidence rule is deferred until Chapter 16.
[4] Samuel Williston, _The Law of Contracts_, vol. 1, §139 (1st ed. 1920).

It is generally conceded that Restatement, Second §90 is one place where the drafters stated a view of what the law should be, rather than slavishly reporting the then current state of the law. Although the theory of promissory estoppel as reflected in Restatement, Second §90 is firmly entrenched in some of its details, we will see that in others it remains quite controversial. The elements of the theory, as well as how and under what circumstances it is applied, differ from jurisdiction to jurisdiction. Just so you have a sense of the discussion to come, however, here is Restatement, Second §90:

RESTATEMENT, SECOND §90. PROMISE REASONABLY INDUCING ACTION OR FORBEARANCE

(1) A promise which the promisor should reasonably expect to induce action or forbearance on the part of the promisee or a third person and which does induce such action or forbearance is binding if injustice can be avoided only by enforcement of the promise. The remedy granted for breach may be limited as justice requires.

only way to avoid harm is enforcement

(2) A charitable subscription or a marriage settlement is binding under Subsection (1) without proof that the promise induced action or forbearance.

■ PROBLEM 10.1

The early case of *Kirksey v. Kirksey*, 8 Ala. 131 (1845) illustrates as well as any the perceived injustices that led to the development of promissory estoppel. After his brother's death, Mr. Kirksey wrote the following letter to his sister-in-law:

> Dear sister Antillico—Much to my mortification, I heard, that brother Henry was dead, and one of his children. I know that your situation is one of grief, and difficulty. You had a bad chance before, but a great deal worse now. I should like to come and see you, but cannot with convenience at present. . . . I do not know whether you have a preference on the place you live on, or not. If you had, I would advise you to obtain your preference, and sell the land and quit the country, as I understand it is very unhealthy, and I know society is very bad. If you will come down and see me, I will let you have a place to raise your family, and I have more open land than I can tend; and on the account of your situation, and that of your family, I feel like I want you and the children to do well.

Mrs. Kirksey then abandoned her home and moved her family, and for two years enjoyed the comforts of her brother-in-law's house. She also cultivated land that he gave to her. For reasons that the court left to

not clear what is bargained for

-- no consideration

our imagination, the brother-in-law then moved her family to a rather less comfortable house in the woods and then required them to leave altogether.[5] When she sued the brother-in-law for breach of contract, the trial court ruled for Mrs. Kirksey. On appeal to the Alabama Supreme Court, the court's entire analysis read as follows:

> ORMOND, J. The inclination of my mind, is, that the loss and inconvenience, which the plaintiff sustained in breaking up, and moving to the defendant's, a distance of sixty miles, is a sufficient consideration to support the promise, to furnish her with a house, and land to cultivate, until she could raise her family. My brothers, however think, that the promise on the part of the defendant, was a mere gratuity, and that an action will not lie for its breach. The judgment of the Court below must therefore be reversed. . . .

(a) Viewed from a modern perspective, did Justice Ormond have the better view? To phrase it another way, in your opinion was there arguably consideration for the brother-in-law's promise? Even if there was consideration, is there anything else that might limit the enforceability of this promise under modern contract doctrine?

yes

she took action based on his promise

no time period of how long she could stay

(b) Assume you are a judge in a modern court which generally follows Restatement, Second §90. Facts similar to those of *Kirksey v. Kirksey*, as summarized above, come before your court. Should the plaintiff obtain relief under the doctrine of promissory estoppel? Why or why not? If so, what damages or other relief would you award and why?

reasonable reliance

2. The Theoretical Context of Promissory Estoppel and Why It Matters

alternative means of enforcing a contract

Legal scholars debate the precise status of promissory estoppel. Some argue that it is (or should be) a substitute for consideration—that is, an alternative means of determining if a promise is worthy of enforcement as a contract. Others argue that it is (or should be) an independent theory of recovery more akin to tort law or general equitable principles than to contract law. This debate is long-standing, and continues to the current day. This is not simply an academic exercise, fascinating to scholars alone; it potentially has profound real-world

---

[5] Those who can't bear this or other mysteries hidden in the facts of the case might find the following law review article to be of interest: William R. Casto & Val D. Ricks, *"Dear Sister Antillico . . .": The Story of* Kirksey v. Kirksey, 94 Geo. L.J. 321 (2006).

implications. If the elements of promissory estoppel merely substitute for consideration, once they are present a contract should be present. This means that all of the trappings that go along with a contract should be present as well. So if particular procedures apply to contract actions but not to others, as a baseline matter, they should apply to promissory estoppel actions. If certain defenses are available in contract actions but not in others, they should be available in promissory estoppel actions. Or if certain remedies lie in contract actions but not in others, they should lie in promissory estoppel actions. If, on the other hand, promissory estoppel is a separate theory of recovery related to but independent from contract, the trappings of contract law do not necessarily carry over, and rules from other areas of law might be more appropriate.

pe-seperate theory of recovery rather than a substitute

There is some evidence that Professor Williston, the classical contracts scholar and Reporter for the First Restatement referenced earlier, viewed justifiable reliance as a substitute for consideration, thus situating promissory estoppel firmly in the land of contract. Grant Gilmore, on the other hand, argued that promissory estoppel is essentially a tort-based theory.[6] Contract law is a vehicle for enforcing obligations that parties consensually assume. Tort law, broadly conceived, compensates victims for injuries that other parties inflict upon them. In Gilmore's view, by emphasizing the harm the promisee suffers, promissory estoppel is more a tort theory than a contract theory. Furthermore, he predicted in very colorful terms that tort law would ultimately swamp the bargain theory of consideration, thus leading (as the title of his book indicated) to the "death of contract."

thought camps of pe
1) theory of recovery as a tort
2) theory of recovery in line with contract
3) is neither tort or contract but its own theory entirely

Since the days of Gilmore, scholars have divided into three principal camps when it comes to describing the nature of promissory estoppel. The first group lines up with Gilmore, and concludes that promissory estoppel is more akin to tort than contract.[7] The second believes that the basis of promissory estoppel is promise or consent, and so promissory estoppel is best seen as a contract-based theory. Within this second group, there are sharp differences of opinion. Some of the authors argue that courts applying promissory estoppel in practice focus on the promises being made and pay little if any real attention to the promisees' reliance.[8] Other authors, while agreeing that promissory estoppel is a contract theory that depends on the existence of a promise, assert that the nature and extent of the promisees' reliance strongly shapes the way in which courts apply

---

[6] This was a central thesis of his famous book that we have alluded to previously, Grant Gilmore, *The Death of Contract* (Ronald K.L. Collins ed., 2d ed., Ohio St. U. Press 1995).

[7] One scholar who espoused this view was P.S. Atiyah, in *This Rise and Fall of Freedom of Contract* 777 (Clarendon Press 1979) (arguing that §90 "indicates a resurgence of reliance-based liability at the expense of consensual liability"). This theme was echoed and expanded in Michael B. Metzger & Michael J. Phillips, *The Emergence of Promissory Estoppel as an Independent Theory of Recovery*, 35 Rutgers L. Rev. 472 (1983).

[8] A few articles in this group include Daniel A. Farber & John H. Matheson, *Beyond Promissory Estoppel: Contract Law and the 'Invisible Handshake,'* 52 U. Chi. L. Rev. 903 (1985) (arguing that courts resort to promissory estoppel to enforce promises and invoke the promisees' alleged reliance as a mere formality to justify their holdings); Juliet P. Kostritsky, *A New Theory of Assent-Based Liability Emerging Under the Guise of Promissory Estoppel: An Explanation and Defense*, 33 Wayne L. Rev. 895 (1987) (positing that promissory estoppel is and should be about enforcing bargains, where there are "persuasive barriers to, or explanation for

the doctrine.[9] Scholars in the third group refuse to take sides in favor of contract or tort and instead argue that promissory estoppel spans contract and tort, that it lives in the never-never land between contract and tort, or that it is an equitable doctrine that inhabits a land all its own.[10] Just to further complicate the picture, some of these scholars attempt to describe what the law is, based on the results of reported decisions, while others focus on what the law should be.[11]

One's view of the theoretical status of promissory estoppel is important from a substantive point of view. The doctrinal emphasis of a given case may depend on the court's view of the nature of promissory estoppel as a theory of recovery. On the face of Restatement, Second §90, promissory estoppel appears to have a number of elements. The Restatement, Second, language does not specify how to weigh the various elements when some appear satisfied and others less so. If courts are most concerned with the intention of the promisor to be bound and see reliance merely as a substitute for consideration, they may weigh the nature of the promise more heavily in their analysis. If the promise is not as clear, definite, and specific as an offer, for instance, it might not lead to promissory estoppel liability even if there was substantial detrimental reliance. Conversely, if the promise is very strong, perhaps little in terms of reliance should substitute for consideration. If, on the other hand, courts are most concerned with the harm to the promisee, they may require less in terms of the promise and focus more on the nature and extent of the promisee's reliance in determining whether to allow relief.

Beyond coloring application of the doctrine itself, the theoretical status of promissory estoppel may decide a number of specific procedural, substantive, and remedial issues. For instance, a jury trial might be available in a contract lawsuit but not in a lawsuit brought in equity. One statute of limitations may apply to contract causes of action and another to tort causes of action. Expectation damages may be available in a contract lawsuit but not in a lawsuit of another sort.

---

the parties dispensing with . . . formalized contracting"); Edward Yorio & Steve Thel, *The Promissory Basis of Section 90*, 101 Yale L.J. 111 (1991) (arguing that like the rest of contract law, courts use promissory estoppel to decide what promises to enforce).

[9] For instance, Charles L. Knapp, in *Rescuing Reliance: The Perils of Promissory Estoppel*, 49 Hastings L.J. 1191 (1998), articulates this view. *See also* Marco J. Jimenez, *The Many Faces of Promissory Estoppel: An Empirical Analysis Under the Restatement (Second) of Contracts*, 57 UCLA L. Rev. 669 (2010) (stating "the data reveal that most judges require the existence of both promise and reliance before allowing a promissory estoppel claim to proceed").

[10] *See, e.g.*, Randy E. Barnett & Mary E. Becker, *Beyond Reliance: Promissory Estoppel, Contract Formalities, and Misrepresentations*, 15 Hofstra L. Rev. 443 (1987) (suggesting that liability based on promissory estoppel does not fit neatly either into contract or tort, but instead has elements of both); Eric Mills Holmes, *The Four Phases of Promissory Estoppel*, 20 Seattle U. L. Rev. 45, 48 (1996) (stating that "promissory estoppel is promissory estoppel—neither exclusively contract nor tort nor equity").

[11] At the risk of throwing you into the depths of existential despair, we mention in passing one scholar who argued that the entire framework of contract liability—whether it be based on neoclassical contract principles or tort law principles, consideration or promissory estoppel, promise or reliance—should be discarded. Instead, he argued that obligations flow from relationships, not discrete transactions, and advocated developing a contract law that explicitly focused on the extent to which those relationships should bear legal consequences. Jay M. Feinman, *The Last Promissory Estoppel Article*, 61 Fordham L. Rev. 303 (1992).

One context where the theoretical status of promissory estoppel can be determinative is where the plaintiff seeks to recover damages from a governmental entity. Under the doctrine of sovereign immunity, plaintiffs are not permitted to recover damages from the government (state or federal) unless the government has waived immunity. Generally, if the government enters into a contract, it is deemed to waive its immunity with respect to claims that might arise under that contract. If the plaintiff grounds its complaint in promissory estoppel, whether promissory estoppel sounds in contract or rather in tort or some other doctrinal category may determine if the suit can move forward. Recall, for instance, *Steinberg v. United States*, 90 Fed. Cl. 435 (2009), which we include in Chapter 9. In that case, Mr. Steinberg sought to recover damages from the United States when he was denied entry into President Obama's inaugural festivities. Mr. Steinberg originally claimed damages under a theory of promissory estoppel. The Federal Court of Claims concluded that its jurisdiction only extended to contracts that were either express or implied in fact, and not to claims on contracts "implied in law." The United States had waived sovereign immunity for liability under contracts it had entered through proper channels, but not for contract-like liability that might otherwise arise through application of general legal principles. The court stated that promissory estoppel would require the court to find a contract "implied in law," and accordingly concluded the court had no jurisdiction over any promissory estoppel claim Mr. Steinberg might raise. Although it would have had jurisdiction over a more conventional contract claim, as we saw in Chapter 9 the court concluded Mr. Steinberg hadn't alleged consideration for any promise the government might have made to him, so his contract claim failed as well.

In the following case, newspapers made promises of confidentiality to a source, but subsequently breached those promises after deciding that the identity of the source was itself newsworthy. The source sued, seeking damages for breach of the promise of confidentiality. In an earlier opinion, the Minnesota Supreme Court concluded that a contract cause of action would not lie. In this opinion, it reaches the opposite conclusion under the theory of promissory estoppel. As you read this case, think about this court's view of the theoretical context of promissory estoppel, and analyze how that view may have influenced the result.

COHEN v. COWLES MEDIA CO.

479 N.W.2d 387 (1992)
Minnesota Supreme Court

SIMONETT, Justice.

This case comes to us on remand from the United States Supreme Court. We previously held that plaintiff's verdict of $200,000 could not be sustained on a theory of breach of contract. On remand, we now conclude the verdict is

disposition

sustainable on the theory of promissory estoppel and affirm the jury's award of damages.

The facts are set out in *Cohen v. Cowles Media Co.*, 457 N.W.2d 199, 200-02 (Minn. 1990)[*Cohen I*], and will be only briefly restated here. On October 28, 1982, the Minneapolis Star and Tribune (now the Star Tribune) and the St. Paul Pioneer Press each published a story on the gubernatorial election campaign, reporting that Marlene Johnson, the DFL nominee for lieutenant governor, had been charged in 1969 for three counts of unlawful assembly and in 1970 had been convicted of shoplifting. Both newspapers revealed that Dan Cohen had supplied this information to them. The Star Tribune identified Cohen as a political associate of the Independent-Republican gubernatorial candidate and named the advertising firm where Cohen was employed.

Cohen then commenced this lawsuit against defendants Cowles Media Company, publisher of the Minneapolis Star Tribune, and Northwest Publications, Inc., publisher of the St. Paul Pioneer Press Dispatch. It was undisputed that Cohen had given the information about Marlene Johnson's arrests and conviction to a reporter for each of the newspapers in return for the reporters' promises that Cohen's identity be kept confidential. The newspapers' editors overruled these promises. The disparaging information about the candidate leaked in the closing days of the election campaign was such, decided the editors, that the identity of the source of the information was as important, as newsworthy, as the information itself. Put another way, the real news story was one of political intrigue, and the information about the particular candidate was only a part, an incomplete part, of that story. Moreover, not to reveal the source, felt the editors, would be misleading, as it would cast suspicion on others; and, in any event, it was likely only a matter of time before competing news media would uncover Cohen's identity. Finally, the Star Tribune had endorsed the Perpich-Johnson ticket in its opinion section, and thus to withhold Cohen's identity might be construed as an effort by the newspaper to protect its favored candidates. On the same day as the newspaper stories were published, Cohen was fired.

The case was submitted to the jury on theories of breach of contract and fraudulent misrepresentation. The jury found liability on both theories and awarded $200,000 compensatory damages against the two defendants, jointly and severally. The jury also awarded $250,000 punitive damages against each newspaper on the misrepresentation claim. The court of appeals set aside recovery on the basis of fraudulent misrepresentation (and with it the punitive damages award), but affirmed recovery of the compensatory damages on the basis of a breach of contract. *Cohen v. Cowles Media Co.*, 445 N.W.2d 248, 262 (Minn. App. 1989).

We affirmed denial of recovery for fraudulent misrepresentation but also held that there could be no recovery for breach of contract. While the newspapers may have had a moral and ethical commitment to keep their source anonymous, we said this was not a situation where the parties were thinking in terms of a legally binding contract. *Cohen I*, 457 N.W.2d at 203. "To impose a contract theory on this arrangement," we said, "puts an unwarranted legal rigidity on a special ethical relationship, precluding necessary consideration of factors underlying that ethical relationship." *Id.*

intentionally
*was there an^*
binding promise

The evidence at trial might be characterized as the pot calling the kettle black, with each side insinuating that the other's behavior was unethical or underhanded. We observed that when applying a contract analysis in this context "the focus was more on whether a binding promise was intended and breached, not so much on the contents of that promise or the nature of the information exchanged for the promise." *Id.* at 204. We concluded that a contract theory, which looks only to whether there was a promise and an acceptance, does not fit a situation where the essential concern is with the intrinsic nature of the overall transaction.

was enforcement
necessary to
prevent (injustice

We went on in *Cohen I* to consider enforcement of a confidentiality promise under the doctrine of promissory estoppel. Under this theory, the court would consider all aspects of the transaction's substance in determining whether enforcement was necessary to prevent an injustice. We found this approach, which differed from the neutral approach of the classic contract analysis, best fit the kind of confidential commitments that news media in newsgathering made. There was, however, a problem. To shed the neutrality of a contract analysis for an inquiry into the editorial process of deciding whether the identity of the news source was needed for a proper reporting of a news story constituted, we concluded, an impermissible intrusion into the newspaper's First Amendment free press rights. Consequently, we held plaintiff Cohen's verdict was not sustainable. 457 N.W.2d at 205.

promissory estoppel
does not implicate
the first ammendment

The United States Supreme Court granted certiorari and held that the doctrine of promissory estoppel does not implicate the First Amendment. The doctrine is one of general application, said the Court, and its employment to enforce confidentiality promises has only "incidental effects" on news gathering and reporting, so that the First Amendment is not offended. *Cohen v. Cowles Media Co.*, 501 U.S. 663, 111 S. Ct. 2513, 2518-19, 115 L. Ed. 2d 586 (1991). The Court refused to reinstate the jury verdict for $200,000 in compensatory damages, stating this was a matter for our consideration, and remanded the case.

issues

On remand, we must address four issues: (1) Does Cohen's failure to plead promissory estoppel bar him from pursuing that theory now; (2) does our state constitutional guarantee of a free press bar use of promissory estoppel to enforce promises of confidentiality; (3) does public policy bar Cohen from enforcing the newspapers' promises of confidentiality; and (4) if Cohen may proceed under promissory estoppel, should the case be remanded for retrial or should the jury's award of compensatory damages be reinstated?

Generally, litigants are bound on appeal by the theory or theories upon which the case was tried. Here, promissory estoppel was neither pled nor presented at the trial, and this court first raised the applicability of that theory during oral argument in *Cohen I*. See 457 N.W.2d at 204 n. 5. Nevertheless, this court considered promissory estoppel and held that the First Amendment barred recovery under that theory.

PE → variation on contract theory

The defendant newspapers argue it is too late for Cohen to proceed now under promissory estoppel, and this case should be at an end. We have, however, on rare occasions exercised our discretion to allow a party to proceed on a theory not raised at trial. See Minn. R. App. P. 103.04 (appellate courts "may review any . . . matter as the interest of justice may require."). Thus in *Christensen v. Minneapolis Mun. Employees Retirement Bd.*, 331 N.W.2d 740, 747 (Minn. 1983), we held that a public employee had a protectable interest in his pension based on a promissory estoppel theory, even though the plaintiff employee had raised only a contract theory at trial. Indeed, in *Cohen I* we relied on *Christensen*. 457 N.W.2d at 203. . . .

holding

We conclude it would be unfair not to allow Cohen to proceed under promissory estoppel. Throughout the litigation, the issue has been the legal enforceability of a promise of anonymity. Promissory estoppel is essentially a variation of contract theory, a theory on which plaintiff prevailed through the court of appeals. The evidence received at trial was as relevant to promissory estoppel as it was to contract, and the parties now have briefed the issue thoroughly. See *Babler v. Roelli*, 39 Wis. 2d 566, 572-73, 159 N.W.2d 694, 697 (1968) (plaintiff who raised only contract theory at trial allowed to proceed under promissory estoppel on appeal because facts plaintiff relied on to support the new theory were of record and defendant had opportunity to respond to those facts at trial). . . .

allowed Cohen to change the theory

What we have here is a novel legal issue of first impression where this court has adopted an approach closely akin to the theory on which the case was originally pled and tried; under these unique circumstances we conclude it is not unfair to the defendants to allow the case to be decided under principles of promissory estoppel.

The defendant newspapers next argue that in this case our own state constitution should be interpreted to provide broader free press protection than does the First Amendment. [The court concludes that neither the state constitution nor general principles of public policy bar enforcement of the newspapers' promise of confidentiality under a theory of promissory estoppel. Discussion of these issues is omitted.] . . .

nothing stops a promise of confidentiality from being enforced by promissory estoppel

What, then, should be the appropriate disposition of this case? We conclude a retrial is unnecessary. Under promissory estoppel, a promise which is expected to induce definite action by the promisee, and does induce the action, is binding if injustice can be avoided only by enforcing the promise. *Cohen I*, 457 N.W.2d at 204; Restatement (Second) of Contracts §90(1) (1981). First of all, the promise must be clear and definite. As a matter of law, such a promise was given here. *Cohen I*, 457 N.W.2d at 204 ("[W]e have, without dispute, the reporters' unambiguous promise to treat Cohen as an anonymous source"). Secondly, the promisor must have intended to induce reliance on the part of the promisee, and such reliance must have occurred to the promisee's detriment. Here again, these facts appear as a matter of law. In reliance on the promise of anonymity, Cohen turned over the court records and, when the promises to keep his name confidential were broken, he lost his job. *Id.*

① promise must be clear & definite

② must intend reliance & reliance causes detriment

↓ *promisee detriment*

3) does the promise need to be enforced to prevent injustice

do justice/prevent injustice

This leads to the third step in a promissory estoppel analysis: Must the promise be enforced to prevent an injustice? As the Wisconsin Supreme Court has held, this is a legal question for the court, as it involves a policy decision. *Hoffman v. Red Owl Stores, Inc.*, 26 Wis. 2d 683, 698, 133 N.W.2d 267, 275 (1965). . . . It is perhaps worth noting that the test is not whether the promise should be enforced to do justice, but whether enforcement is required to prevent an injustice. As has been observed elsewhere, it is easier to recognize an unjust result than a just one, particularly in a morally ambiguous situation. *Cf.* Edmond Cahn, *The Sense of Injustice* (1964). The newspapers argue it is unjust to be penalized for publishing the whole truth, but it is not clear this would result in an injustice in this case. For example, it would seem veiling Cohen's identity by publishing the source as someone close to the opposing gubernatorial ticket would have sufficed as a sufficient reporting of the "whole truth."

Cohen, on the other hand, argues that it would be unjust for the law to countenance, at least in this instance, the breaking of a promise. We agree that denying Cohen any recourse would be unjust. What is significant in this case is that the record shows the defendant newspapers themselves believed that they generally must keep promises of confidentiality given a news source. The reporters who actually gave the promises adamantly testified that their promises should have been honored. The editors who countermanded the promises conceded that never before or since have they reneged on a promise of confidentiality. A former Minneapolis Star managing editor testified that the newspapers had "hung Mr. Cohen out to dry because they didn't regard him very highly as a source." The Pioneer Press Dispatch editor stated nothing like this had happened in her 27 years in journalism. The Star Tribune's editor testified that protection of sources was "extremely important." Other experts, too, stressed the ethical importance, except on rare occasions, of keeping promises of confidentiality. It was this long-standing journalistic tradition that Cohen, who has worked in journalism, relied upon in asking for and receiving a promise of anonymity.

holding

Neither side in this case clearly holds the higher moral ground, but in view of the defendants' concurrence in the importance of honoring promises of confidentiality, and absent the showing of any compelling need in this case to break that promise, we conclude that the resultant harm to Cohen requires a remedy here to avoid an injustice. In short, defendants are liable in damages to plaintiff for their broken promise.

This leaves, then, the issue of damages. For promissory estoppel, "[t]he remedy granted for breach may be limited as justice requires." Restatement (Second) of Contracts §90(1) (1981). In this case the jury was instructed: A party is entitled to recover for a breach of contract only those damages which: (a) arise directly and naturally in the usual course of things from the breach itself; or (b) are the consequences of special circumstances known to or reasonably supposed to have been contemplated by the parties when the contract was made.

This instruction, we think, provided an appropriate damages remedy for the defendants' broken promise, whether considered under a breach of contract or a promissory estoppel theory. There was evidence to support the jury's award of $200,000, and we see no reason to remand this case for a new trial on damages alone.

Our prior reversal of the verdict having been vacated, we now affirm the court of appeals' decision, but on promissory estoppel grounds. We affirm, therefore, plaintiff's verdict and judgment for $200,000 compensatory damages.

Affirmed on remand on different grounds.

■ QUESTIONS

(1) In its previously published opinion, the Minnesota Supreme Court reversed the lower court's award of damages for breach of contract, concluding that there was no enforceable contract between the parties. As far as you can tell from the discussion in this opinion, why wasn't the newspapers' pledge of confidentiality enforceable as a contractual promise? In particular, was the absence of consideration the central issue?

(2) Does this court consider promissory estoppel to be a contract cause of action, a tort cause of action, or something else altogether? Does the theoretical status of promissory estoppel influence the court's analysis, and if so, how?

[handwritten: they allow recovery claims bc its under the originally argued theory]

(3) The court cites Restatement, Second §90. Were all of the elements of promissory estoppel, as formulated in Restatement, Second §90, discussed in this case? What, if anything, did the court have to say about what is required to establish each element? *[handwritten: not justice but prevent injustice]*

(4) Which elements of promissory estoppel were in dispute in this case? What facts seem to influence the court's decision that those elements were established sufficiently at trial? In particular, what factors, in your view, led the court to agree that injustice could be avoided only by enforcement of the promise?

(5) Setting aside the details of doctrine, in your opinion are there any reasons why a promise like this one should or should not be enforceable at law?

B USE OF PROMISSORY ESTOPPEL TO ENFORCE GRATUITOUS OR CHARITABLE PROMISES

Gratuitous promises, given in a personal or charitable context, are traditional fodder for consideration doctrine. You may recall from Chapter 9 that consideration doctrine is premised in part on the policy that gift promises are generally not enforceable as contracts. Perhaps they are improvidently made, so the promisor is in need of protection; perhaps they are of so little interest to a market economy that they are not worthy of judicial attention. Yet this view can be in tension with the very real consequences to the disappointed promisee.

Many early promissory estoppel cases were decided in the context of promises made among friends and family. Consider, for instance, the early case of *Ricketts v. Scothorn*, 57 Neb. 51, 77 N.W. 365 (1898). In this case, the Nebraska Supreme Court was willing to enforce a grandfather's gratuitous promise to his granddaughter. The elderly gentleman visited his granddaughter at work. He handed her a $2,000 promissory note and said "I have fixed out something that you have not got to work any more. None of my grandchildren work and you don't have to." The granddaughter kissed him, started to cry, and promptly quit her job, thereby sacrificing her luxurious salary of $10 a week. With the grandfather's consent she went back to work a little over a year later; however, the grandfather never repudiated the promissory note. He died before paying it off, and when his executor refused to pay the balance owing on the note, the granddaughter sued. The Nebraska Supreme Court concluded that the note was a gratuity and thus unsupported by consideration. However, given the charitable context of the grandfather's actions, "having intentionally influenced the plaintiff to alter her position for the worse on the faith of the note being paid when due, it would be grossly inequitable to permit the maker, or his executor, to resist payment on the ground that the promise was given without consideration." The court affirmed a judgment against the grandfather's estate.

Promissory estoppel remains a vibrant theory of recovery in the personal realm, as the following case suggests.

sugardaddy case

CONRAD v. FIELDS

Not reported in N.W.2d, 2007 WL 2106302 (2007)
Minnesota Court of Appeals

PETERSON, Judge.

holding

This appeal is from a judgment and an order denying post-trial motions. The judgment awarded respondent damages in the amount of the cost of her law-school tuition and books based on a determination that the elements of promissory estoppel were proved with respect to appellant's promise to pay for the tuition and books. We affirm the judgment. . . .

Appellant Walter R. Fields and respondent Marjorie Conrad met and became friends when they were neighbors in an apartment complex in the early 1990's. Appellant started his own business and became a financially successful businessman. Appellant built a $1.2 million house in the Kenwood neighborhood in Minneapolis and leased a Bentley automobile for more than $50,000 a year. Appellant is a philanthropic individual who has sometimes paid education costs for others.

In the fall of 2000, appellant suggested that respondent attend law school, and he offered to pay for her education. Respondent, who had recently paid off an $11,000 medical bill and still owed about $5,000 for undergraduate student loans, did not feel capable of paying for law school on her own. Appellant promised that he would pay tuition and other expenses associated with law school as they became due. Appellant quit her job at Qwest, where she had been earning $45,000 per year, to attend law school. Appellant admitted at trial that before respondent enrolled in law school, he agreed to pay her tuition.

Respondent testified that she enrolled in law school in the summer of 2001 as a result of appellant's "inducement and assurance to pay for [her] education." Appellant made two tuition payments, each in the amount of $1,949.75, in August and October 2001, but he stopped payment on the check for the second payment. At some point, appellant told respondent that his assets had been frozen due to an Internal Revenue Service audit and that payment of her education expenses would be delayed until he got the matter straightened out. In May 2004, appellant and respondent exchanged e-mail messages about respondent's difficulties in managing the debts that she had incurred for law school. In response to one of respondent's messages, appellant wrote, "to be clear and in writing, when you graduate law school and pas[s] your bar exam, I will pay your tuition." Later, appellant told respondent that he would not pay her expenses, and he threatened to get a restraining order against her if she continued attempting to communicate with him.

Respondent brought suit against appellant, alleging that in reliance on appellant's promise to pay her education expenses, she gave up the opportunity to earn income through full-time employment and enrolled in law school. The case was tried to the court, which awarded respondent damages in the amount of $87,314.63 under the doctrine of promissory estoppel. The district court denied appellant's motion for a new trial or amended findings. This appeal followed.

. . . "Promissory estoppel implies a contract in law where no contract exists in fact." *Deli v. Univ. of Minn.*, 578 N.W.2d 779, 781 (Minn. App. 1998), *review denied* (Minn. July 16, 1998). "A promise which the promisor should reasonably expect to induce action or forbearance on the part of the promisee or a third person and which does induce such action or forbearance is binding if injustice can be avoided only by enforcement of the promise." Restatement (Second) of Contracts §90(1) (1981).

The elements of a promissory estoppel claim are (1) a clear and definite promise, (2) the promisor intended to induce reliance by the promisee, and the promisee relied to the promisee's detriment, and (3) the promise must be enforced to prevent injustice. *Cohen v. Cowles Media Co.*, 479 N.W.2d 387, 391 (Minn. 1992). Judicial determinations of injustice involve a number of considerations, "including the reasonableness of a promisee's reliance." *Faimon v. Winona State Univ.*, 540 N.W.2d, 879, 883 (Minn. App. 1995), *review denied* (Minn. Feb. 9, 1996). . . .

Appellant argues that respondent did not plead or prove the elements of promissory estoppel. [The court concludes that the complaint was sufficient under the Minnesota rules of civil procedure to put appellant on notice of the promissory estoppel claim.] . . . At a pretrial deposition, respondent testified that negligence and breach of contract were the only two causes of action that she was pleading. Because promissory estoppel is described as a contract implied at law, respondent's deposition testimony can be interpreted to include a promissory estoppel claim.

In its legal analysis, the district court stated:

> The Court finds credible [respondent's] testimony that [appellant] encouraged her to go to law school, knowing that she would not be able to pay for it on her own. He knew that she was short on money, having helped her pay for food and other necessities. He knew that she was working at Qwest and would need to quit her job to go to law school. He offered to pay for the cost of her going to law school, knowing that she had debts from her undergraduate tuition. He made a payment on her law school tuition after she enrolled. [Respondent] knew that [appellant] was a wealthy philanthropist, and that he had offered to pay for the education of strangers he had met in chance encounters. She knew that he had the wealth to pay for her law school education. She knew that . . . he was established in society, older than she, not married, without children, an owner of a successful company, an owner of an expensive home, and a . . . [lessee] of an expensive car. Moreover, [appellant] was a friend who had performed many kindnesses for her already, and she trusted him. [Appellant's] promise in fact induced [respondent] to quit her job at Qwest and enroll in law school, which she had not otherwise planned to do. . . . [T]he circumstances support a finding that it would be unjust not to enforce the promise. Upon reliance on [appellant's] promise, [respondent] quit her job. She attended law school despite a serious health condition that might otherwise have deterred her from going.

holding These findings are sufficient to show that respondent proved the elements of promissory estoppel.

Appellant argues that because he advised respondent shortly after she enrolled in law school that he would not be paying her law school expenses as they came due, respondent could not have reasonably relied on his promise to pay her expenses to her detriment after he repudiated the promise. Appellant contends that the only injustice that resulted from his promise involved the *△ claim* original $5,000 in expenses that respondent incurred to enter law school. But appellant's statement that he would not pay the expenses as they came due did not make respondent's reliance unreasonable because appellant also told respondent that his financial problems were temporary and that he would pay her tuition when she graduated and passed the bar exam. This statement made it reasonable for respondent to continue to rely on appellant's promise *it was reasonable for her to rely* that he would pay her expenses.

In actions based on promissory estoppel, "[r]elief may be limited to damages measured by the promisee's reliance." *Dallum v. Farmers Union Cent. Exchange, Inc.*, 462 N.W.2d 608, 613 (Minn. App. 1990), *review denied* (Minn. Jan. 14, 1991). "In other words, relief may be limited to the party's out-of-pocket expenses

[handwritten: payment amount was reasonable]

made in reliance on the promise." *Id.* . . . [By this measure, the district court properly awarded respondent $87,314.63 (tuition plus books minus payment made by appellant).]

Appellant argues that respondent was obligated to mitigate her damages and she could have avoided all of her damages by dropping out of law school immediately after appellant refused to pay her tuition as it was incurred. But as we explained when addressing the reasonableness of respondent's reliance, appellant told respondent that his financial difficulties were temporary and that he would pay her expenses after graduation. Under these circumstances, respondent was not aware until after she graduated that she would suffer damages, and by the time she graduated, she had already paid for her tuition and books and had no opportunity to mitigate damages.

[handwritten: damages went until after graduation]

Appellant argues that because respondent received a valuable law degree, she did not suffer any real detriment by relying on his promise. But receiving a law degree was the expected and intended consequence of appellant's promise, and the essence of appellant's promise was that respondent would receive the law degree without the debt associated with attending law school. Although respondent benefited from attending law school, the debt that she incurred in reliance on appellant's promise is a detriment to her. . . .

■ QUESTIONS

(1) The court does not discuss whether consideration was present under these facts. Do you believe consideration was arguably present? Why or why not? *[handwritten: no. nothing was bargained for]*

(2) Does the theoretical status of promissory estoppel—be it a contract cause of action, tort cause of action, or something else altogether—matter in this case? If so, why?

(3) Like the *Cohen* court, this court cites Restatement, Second §90. Were all of the elements of promissory estoppel, as formulated in Restatement, Second §90, discussed in this case? What, if anything, did the court have to say about what is required to establish each element?

(4) The court concludes that it would be unjust not to enforce the promise in this case. It is sometimes said that justice (or its evil twin, injustice) is in the eye of the beholder. In your view, where does justice lie on these facts? Which factors, if any, favor enforcement of the promise, and which militate against it? *[handwritten: she was promised debt free graduation]*

[handwritten: promissory estoppel for charity]

Some of the early cases allowing enforcement of gratuitous promises in personal contexts analogized to charitable promises. A seminal case discussing promissory estoppel in the context of a charitable promise is *Allegheny College v. National Chautauqua County Bank of Jamestown*, 246 N.Y. 369, 159 N.E. 173 (1927). This case has inspired a spate of commentary in the legal literature, largely due to the inimitable linguistic and analytical style of its author, Judge Cardozo.[12] The case involved a charitable pledge of $5,000 that Mary Yates Johnston made to Allegheny College. The pledge was in writing, and recited that it was given in consideration of her "interest in Christian education" and in consideration of "others subscribing." It also stated that the proceeds of the pledge "shall either be added to the Endowment of the said Institution" or spent as instructed on the reverse side of the pledge, where it provided "In loving memory this gift shall be known as the Mary Yates Johnston memorial fund, the proceeds from which shall be used to educate students preparing for the ministry, either in the United States or in the Foreign Field. . . ." By its terms, the pledge was not payable until thirty days after her death. Nevertheless, she paid the college $1,000 about eighteen months after making the pledge, and the college set it aside to be used as a scholarship fund. About six months later, she repudiated the remainder of the pledge. Thirty days after her death, when her executor refused to pay the balance, Allegheny College sued.

[handwritten margin note: outline for how the money should be used]

Although Judge Cardozo discussed promissory estoppel at length in the opinion, he ultimately decided the case on consideration grounds. The moment that the college accepted Ms. Johnston's $1,000 payment, Cardozo held, it assumed an implicit obligation to perpetuate the donor's name in accordance with her wishes. This, he concluded, was sufficient consideration to support her promise. The dissent, written by Judge Kellogg, sharply disagreed, stating "The sum offered was termed a 'gift' by the offeror. I can see no reason why we should strain ourselves to make it, not a gift, but a trade."

[handwritten margin note: said there was enough for a contract]

Although the *Allegheny College* opinion is remarkable in its approach to consideration doctrine, of primary interest to us is Cardozo's dictum concerning promissory estoppel, included in Problem 10.2. It is interesting to speculate about why he discussed this alternate theory at such length. From the facts as he described them, it did not appear that the college relied on the pledge. The dictum may have been an instance of a masterful judge trying to nudge the common law towards its future without departing too rapidly from its past. Or perhaps it was the compromise a determined jurist made to overcome the strong dissent written by Judge Kellogg. Whatever the reason for its inclusion, the dictum is broadly cited and has proven to be very influential.

---

[12] Just a few of the many articles discussing this case include Curtis Bridgeman, *Allegheny College Revisted: Cardozo, Consideration, and Formalism in Context*, 39 U. Cal. Davis L. Rev. 149 (2005); Alfred S. Konefsky, *How to Read, or at Least Not Misread, Cardozo in the Allegheny College Case*, 36 Buff. L. Rev. 645 (1987); Leon S. Lipson, *The Allegheny College Case*, 23 Yale L. Rep. 8 (1977); Mike Townsend, *Cardozo's Allegheny College Opinion: A Case Study in Law as Art*, 33 Hous. L. Rev. 1103 (1996).

■ PROBLEM 10.2

In his *Allegheny College* opinion, Judge Cardozo described the evolution of consideration doctrine in the context of charitable subscriptions:

> The law of charitable subscriptions has been a prolific source of controversy in this state and elsewhere. We have held that a promise of that order is unenforceable like any other if made without consideration. On the other hand, though professing to apply to such subscriptions the general law of contract, we have found consideration present where the general law of contract, at least as then declared, would have said that it was absent.
>
> A classic form of statement identifies consideration with detriment to the promisee sustained by virtue of the promise. So compendious a formula is little more than a half truth. There is need of many a supplementary gloss before the outline can be so filled in as to depict the classic doctrine. "The promise and the consideration must purport to be the motive each for the other, in whole or at least in part. It is not enough that the promise induces the detriment or that the detriment induces the promise if the other half is wanting." *Wisconsin & Michigan R. Co. v. Powers*, 191 U.S. 379, 386, 24 S. Ct. 107, 108 (48 L. Ed. 229). . . . If A promises B to make him a gift, consideration may be lacking, though B has renounced other opportunities for betterment in the faith that the promise will be kept.
>
> The half truths of one generation tend at times to perpetuate themselves in the law as the whole truth of another, when constant repetition brings it about that qualifications, taken once for granted, are disregarded or forgotten. The doctrine of consideration has not escaped the common lot. As far back as 1881, Judge Holmes in his lectures on *The Common Law* (page 292), separated the detriment, which is merely a consequence of the promise from the detriment, which is in truth the motive or inducement, and yet added that the courts "have gone far in obliterating this distinction." The tendency toward effacement has not lessened with the years. On the contrary, there has grown up of recent days a doctrine that a substitute for consideration or an exception to its ordinary requirements can be found in what is styled "a promissory estoppel." Williston, *Contracts*, §§139, 116. Whether the exception has made its way in this state to such an extent as to permit us to say that the general law of consideration has been modified accordingly, we do not now attempt to say. Cases such as *Siegel v. Spear & Co.*, 234 N.Y. 479, 138 N.E. 414, 26 A.L.R. 1205, and *De Cicco v. Schweizer*, 221 N.Y. 431, 117 N.E. 807, L.R.A. 1918E, 1004, Ann. Cas. 1918C, 816, may be signposts on the road. Certain, at least, it is that we have adopted the doctrine of promissory estoppel as the equivalent of consideration in connection with our law of charitable subscriptions. So long as those decisions stand, the question is not merely whether the enforcement of a charitable subscription can be squared with the doctrine of consideration in all its ancient rigor. The question may also be whether it can be squared with doctrine of consideration as qualified by the doctrine of promissory estoppel.

We have said that the cases in this state have recognized this exception, if exception it is thought to be. Thus, in *Barnes v. Perine*, 12 N.Y. 18, the subscription was made without request, express or implied, that the church do anything on the faith of it. Later, the church did incur expense to the knowledge of the promisor, and in the reasonable belief that the promise would be kept. We held the promise binding, though consideration there was none except upon the theory of a promissory estoppel. [There are other cases where] . . . the moulds of consideration as fixed by the old doctrine were subjected to a like expansion. Very likely, conceptions of public policy have shaped, more or less subconsciously, the rulings thus made. Judges have been affected by the thought that "defenses of that character" are "breaches of faith towards the public, and especially towards those engaged in the same enterprise, and an unwarrantable disappointment of the reasonable expectations of those interested." W. F. Allen, J., in *Barnes v. Perine, supra* p. 24. . . . The result speaks for itself irrespective of the motive. Decisions which have stood so long, and which are supported by so many considerations of public policy and reason, will not be overruled to save the symmetry of a concept which itself came into our law, not so much from any reasoned conviction of its justice, as from historical accidents of practice and procedure. The concept survives as one of the distinctive features of our legal system. We have no thought to suggest that it is obsolete or on the way to be abandoned. As in the case of other concepts, however, the pressure of exceptions has led to irregularities of form.

not taking away consideration

It is in this background of precedent that we are to view the problem now before us. The background helps to an understanding of the implications inherent in subscription and acceptance. This is so though we may find in the end that without recourse to the innovation of promissory estoppel the transaction can be fitted within the mould of consideration as established by tradition. . . .

(a) Given the facts as summarized before the problem, do you believe Judge Cardozo "found consideration present where the general law of contract . . . would have said that it was absent," or rather fit the transaction "within the mould of consideration as established by tradition"?

(b) When Judge Cardozo says that the "half truths of one generation tend at times to perpetuate themselves in the law as the whole truth of another," what does he mean? What connection does he suggest between consideration doctrine and promissory estoppel?

(c) Here, as in the *DeLeo* case in Chapter 9, it was the estate of the promisor who was challenging the enforceability of the promise, rather than the promisor herself. Yet in *DeLeo*, Mr. Schwam passed to his reward without retracting his promise, while Mary Yates Johnston repudiated her promise before she died. In your view, is this difference important? If so, does it support the holdings in the two cases or challenge them?

A modern case that raises an issue similar to that of *Allegheny College* is next. When you read Restatement, Second §90, you may have noticed that §90(2) eliminates the requirement of reliance in the context of charitable subscriptions and marriage settlements. In the context of charitable subscriptions, this portion of §90 has gained limited acceptance. The analysis in the following case walks through the various theories for enforcing charitable subscriptions but ultimately stops short of the position suggested by §90(2).

limited acceptance

In re **MORTON SHOE COMPANY**

40 B.R. 948 (1984)
United States Bankruptcy Court, District of Massachusetts

GABRIEL, Bankruptcy Judge.

The Debtor's Objection to the Claim of Combined Jewish Philanthropies of Greater Boston ("CJP") came before the Court for hearing on March 21, 1984. The parties agreed to the relevant facts and submitted the case to me on oral argument and Memoranda of Law. Based upon the agreed-upon facts and a review of the Memoranda and applicable law, I find and rule as follows.

In 1979 and in 1980 Morton Shoe Company Inc. ("the debtor" or "Morton Shoe") pledged $10,000 per year to CJP during a campaign drive. In 1976, 1977 and 1978 Morton Shoe had made contributions in the same amount, all of which were paid. The 1979 and 1980 pledges totalling $20,000 remain unpaid. CJP has filed a proof of claim for $20,000 to which the debtor timely objected.

CJP solicits pledges by sending campaign workers to address potential corporate contributors at meetings convened for such a purpose. The solicitor describes the purpose and needs of the charity. A pledge card is executed by the subscriber. The card states that the subscription is in consideration of the pledges of others. After the pledge drive, CJP establishes an operating budget, determines the amount of and recipients of distributions, and hires personnel. In addition, based on the estimated amount of subscriptions, CJP borrows money from banks so that it can make immediate distributions to recipients before obtaining the actual pledge amount. The debtor objects to the claim of CJP, asserting that it is unenforceable for lack of consideration.

reliance
detriment
△ claim

Traditional legal principles require that consideration support a promise. Consideration is defined as "... a benefit to the maker of the promise, or a loss, trouble or inconvenience to, or a charge or obligation resting upon the party to whom the promise is made." *Cottage Street Methodist Episcopal Church v. Kendall*, 121 Mass. 528, 529-30 (1877).

The debtor objects to this claim asserting that the charitable pledge is unenforceable as it was a promise unsupported by consideration. The allowability of claims is to be determined under state law. Early Massachusetts decisions had ruled that "gratuitous or benevolent proposals prompted by charitable or religious motives ... will not require a performance." See, e.g., *Cottage Street*

pledge not supported by consideration

Methodist Church v. Kendall, 121 Mass. 528 (1877). The trend of judicial decisions during the [nineteenth] century, however, has been toward enforcement of charitable pledges as a means of encouraging philanthropy and of promoting religious, educational and social enterprises. Courts, including those of Massachusetts, have striven to find grounds for enforcing charitable subscriptions, not without engaging in difficult legal reasoning.

A review of the Massachusetts case law reveals two rationales the courts have employed to justify enforcement of charitable subscriptions. A series of decisions has found legal consideration in the traditional sense in the charity's agreement to appropriate funds in accordance with the terms of the subscription. [In] *Ladies Collegiate Institute v. French*, 82 Mass. 196 (1860), . . . the court enforced a charitable pledge to establish a college [on the ground that the promisee, by] . . . "accepting such a subscription . . . agrees on his part with the subscribers, that he will hold and appropriate the funds subscribed in conformity with the terms and the objects of the subscription. . . ." Similarly, in *Robinson v. Nutt*, 185 Mass. 345, 70 N.E. 198 (1908), the court enforced a promise to make a monthly contribution to a parish, which subscription was conditioned on the parish's raising the full amount by similar contributions. The court enforced the promise against the donor's estate [on the basis that the parish obtained additional pledges from others to make up the full amount required]. . . . A second rationale adopted by Massachusetts case law for enforcing charitable subscriptions does not attempt to discover consideration, but rather, enforces the pledge because of the charity's reliance on the promise, such as its expenditure of money, labor, and time in furtherance of obtaining the subscription. [In] *Farmington Academy v. Allen*, 14 Mass. 171 (1817) . . . the court utilized the pledgor's knowledge and the town's reliance to enforce the pledge, reasoning [that] ". . . he was an inhabitant of the town, and must have known of the erection of the building; and he actually advanced some part of the materials. . . . This was sufficient to justify the trustees in proceeding to incur expense, on the faith of the defendant's subscription." Similarly, in *Robinson v. Nutt*, 185 Mass. 345, 70 N.E. 198 (1908), the court also found that the church relied upon the promised pledge, in addition to finding legal consideration in the additional pledges of others. Based upon these principles, I believe it is firmly established Massachusetts law that an action to enforce a charitable subscription is enforceable based on a consideration or reliance theory.

As in Massachusetts, most courts have enforced charitable subscriptions by struggling to find reliance or consideration. It may be more expeditious and appropriate to eliminate the technical requirements and simply enforce pledges as a desirable social policy. In this vein, the Restatement of Contracts, Section 90, provides that a charitable subscription is enforceable without proof of reliance. Although the Restatement position is an improvement over the current need to satisfy the technical requirement, Massachusetts has not adopted this provision of the Restatement as law of this state, and it is necessary to apply current legal principles to the facts of the present case.

holding   Whether viewed in terms of consideration or reliance, the charitable subscriptions made by Morton Shoe to CJP are enforceable under Massachusetts law, and, therefore are allowable claims in bankruptcy. The pledge document executed by Morton Shoe clearly indicates that by accepting the subscription CJP agrees to apply the pledged amounts in accordance with the charitable purposes set forth in its charter. This is sufficient consideration to support the promise. Moreover, it is clear that CJP substantially relies on the amount of pledged subscriptions in developing operating budgets, in making commitments to beneficiaries, and in borrowing funds to make payments to recipients—all in reliance on the expected payment of outstanding pledges.

For these reasons, the claim of CJP in the amount of $20,000 is allowed.

■ QUESTIONS

(1)   The court concludes there was sufficient consideration to support the promise here. Based on the principles we studied in Chapter 9, do you agree with this conclusion? Why or why not? *the consideration was bargained*

(2)   You may recall that the *DeLeo* court in Chapter 9 declined to find Saul *for* Schwam's promise enforceable due to a lack of consideration. It concluded that the promise was not enforceable on a theory of promissory estoppel, either. What did the plaintiff suggest constituted reliance in that case? Did the Congregation's actions differ in any substantial way from CJP's actions here?

(3)   The *Morton Shoe* case was decided in the context of a bankruptcy proceeding. Do you think that the fact that the case arose in the context of bankruptcy proceedings made any difference in the result of the case? Should it have?

(4)   The *Morton Shoe* court, as a federal bankruptcy court applying Massachusetts law, felt unable to apply the rule of Restatement, Second §90(2). This *mass law still requires action* section would allow enforcement of a charitable subscription without proof of reliance, but the other elements of §90(1) would still have to be met. What policies support such a rule? What policies militate against it? Would you favor extending such a rule to all gratuitous promises? — *probably not*

(5)   Professor Baron has argued that consideration doctrine gives short shrift to the societal importance of gift promises and too quickly assumes that they are rare, suspect, and trivial.[13] Professor Eisenberg, on the other hand, has argued that the world of gift would be impoverished if purely donative promises were "folded into the hard-headed world of contract."[14] Which side of this debate do you favor, and why? Does the doctrine of promissory estoppel provide a better balance between legally enforceable and unenforceable gift promises than the doctrine of consideration acting alone?

---

[13] Jane B. Baron, *Gifts, Bargains, and Form*, 64 Ind. L.J. 155 (1989).

[14] Melvin Aron Eisenberg, *The World of Contract and the World of Gift*, 85 Cal. L. Rev. 821, 823 (1997).

C   PROMISSORY ESTOPPEL IN THE BROADER CONTEXT OF A BARGAIN

In the last section, we examine promissory estoppel in the context of promises with clear gratuitous overtones. Friends and family make promises out of love and affection. Philanthropists pledge to support colleges, museums, and other charitable fund drives. But in each case, the promisor's kindly impulses dissipate or are thwarted by subsequent events. The disappointed object of the charity sues, seeking to enforce the gift promise. The lawsuit bravely goes forward, in spite of the black letter rule that promises not supported by consideration are unenforceable. Sometimes, courts resist harsh application of the rule and allow enforcement of the promises. The holdings in these cases differ. Some find consideration by reading the doctrine broadly; others use a theory of promissory estoppel. Other courts admit to the possibility of recovery under a theory of promissory estoppel, but decline to allow it under the facts at hand. But it is fair to say that many courts are willing to relax the strict requirement of a "bargained for" exchange in personal and charitable contexts. The reliance of the donee can overcome any lack of a bargain.

If parties contemplate a bargain, as they often do in commercial relationships, the role of promissory estoppel as a theory of recovery is more controversial. Some of the early courts flatly refused to apply promissory estoppel in commercial contexts. In those cases where consideration was arguably lacking, some refused to allow reliance to serve as a substitute. The reasons were not always explicit, but some themes were common. One of the functions of consideration doctrine is to sort those promises that are seriously, thoughtfully, and knowingly made from those that are just casual statements of future intention. In the cold hard world of dollars and cents, promises are usually made in hopes of an exchange. Commercial promisors seldom intend to be bound unless exchanges are contemplated. If the promises are enforced, even though exchanges are not forthcoming, the promisors may be surprised to find themselves legally obligated. If promisees rely to their detriment on promises but the promisors do not bargain for that reliance, the promisees rely at their own risk. Given the prevalence of commercial motives in the business world and the rarity of charitable ones, any reliance on gratuitous promises in this context is almost by definition unreasonable. Promisees who want legal protection, so the argument goes, should enter into contracts supported by consideration.

As we have seen, lack of consideration is just one reason why a promise might not be enforceable under conventional contract doctrine. For instance, the parties may have agreed to a bargain, but the terms of that bargain may prove too indefinite to enforce as a contract. Alternatively, parties may have entered into an oral bargain yet failed to satisfy an applicable statute of frauds. Or the alleged bargain may suffer from any one of a number of other defects under conventional contract doctrine. If one of the parties reasonably relied to its detriment on the otherwise unenforceable bargain, it might argue that justice requires some measure of relief and that the theory of promissory estoppel should serve as a vehicle to provide that relief. Early courts were slow to accept arguments of this nature. The formalities of contract law serve a purpose, some courts concluded. Use of promissory estoppel to avoid those formalities would subvert the purposes they were designed to serve. Under this line of analysis, regardless of whether promises are supported by consideration, there is little room in the business world for the doctrine of promissory estoppel.

As noted in Section A, Grant Gilmore predicted that the burgeoning possibilities of reliance-based recovery would someday overwhelm the more traditional doctrine, thus leading in his words to the "death of contract." Some courts do apply promissory estoppel in commercial contexts, and allow relief where the circumstances are sufficiently compelling. Nonetheless, Gilmore's prediction has not come true. Commercial parties who raise promissory estoppel do not always win. Some studies suggest that promissory estoppel is of limited importance in commercial contexts, and traditional contract doctrine remains preeminent.[15] The precise conclusions of the studies vary, and in many respects they sharply disagree with each other. Yet on one point they seem unanimous: Promissory estoppel has not achieved the dominance that Grant Gilmore predicted.

■ PROBLEM 10.3

Assume there was a sharp downturn in the housing market, and the value of homes in many cities plunged. Many homeowners found the balances they owed on their mortgages were greater than the current values of their homes. Those who could not pay their mortgages were unable to sell their houses for an amount sufficient to cover their debts. To staunch the tide of foreclosures and to provide some relief to homeowners, some governmental agencies established programs that would help to pay down the debt of those homeowners who met certain qualifications. Eligible homeowners would receive payments sufficient to reduce the balances owing on

---

[15] To give you a sense of the scope of academic interest in this issue, we list here a few of the studies: Sidney W. DeLong, *The New Requirement of Enforcement Reliance in Commercial Promissory Estoppel: Section 90 as Catch-22*, 1997 Wis. L. Rev. 943; Robert A. Hillman, *Questioning the "New Consensus" on Promissory Estoppel: An Empirical and Theoretical Study*, 98 Colum. L. Rev. 580 (1998); Juliet P. Kostritsky, *The Rise and Fall of Promissory Estoppel or Is Promissory Estoppel Really as Unsuccessful as Scholars Say It Is: A New Look at the Data*, 37 Wake Forest L. Rev. 531 (2002); Phuong N. Pham, *The Waning of Promissory Estoppel*, 79 Cornell L. Rev. 1263 (1994). In contrast, one relatively recent author, after surveying more than 300 promissory estoppel cases decided after 1981, concluded, "Professor Gilmore, while certainly overstating his case, was more right than wrong." Marco J. Jimenez, *The Many Faces of Promissory Estoppel: An Empirical Analysis Under the Restatement (Second) of Contracts*, 57 UCLA L. Rev. 669, 689 (2010).

their mortgages to an amount less than the current market values of their homes.

Walt Worthy loses his job, but is able to find employment in a distant state. He is unable to sell his house for the amount of money he owes on it, and he doesn't know if he can afford to continue to make payments on the house until such time as the market improves. He schedules an appointment to discuss options with the banker who made him the loan to purchase his house. The banker tells him that Walt may well be eligible for his state's homeowner debt relief program, but only if he is at least three months behind in his mortgage payments. Walt expresses concern that the bank might foreclose on his house if he fails to make payments on time, and the banker tells him, "Don't worry; we know people are in a difficult situation right now. So long as you have applied for relief under the state debt relief program, we won't foreclose until the state has had time to process your application, and in any case not for at least a year or more." The banker doesn't put any of these statements in writing.

Relying on the banker's advice, Walt withholds three of his monthly mortgage payments and applies for relief under his state's debt relief program. Before the state can process his application, however, the bank sends Walt a notice of default, and threatens to foreclose on his house within thirty days unless he pays off his mortgage in full before that date—actions the bank would be entitled to take under the terms of the documents Walt signed when he first got the loan to purchase his house. Walt is unable to pay the mortgage in full, and the bank forecloses on his house. He subsequently receives notice that he would have qualified for the state's debt relief program, but since the bank has already foreclosed on his house, he is no longer eligible to receive a subsidy.

Walt sues the bank, alleging breach of contract and promissory estoppel. You are the judge deciding the case. Courts in your jurisdiction have expressed some willingness to apply Restatement, Second §90 in commercial contexts, but there is no binding precedent directly on point. Assuming the facts described above are established at trial, should Walt prevail under either theory? Why or why not?

1. Promissory Estoppel in Commercial Negotiations

Sometimes plaintiffs urge courts to use promissory estoppel to enforce promises made in the context of precontractual negotiations. For instance, suppose a defendant promises that a contract is forthcoming. The plaintiff, lulled into a sense of complacency by the assurances of the defendant, incurs huge expenditures in anticipation of an eventual contract. Yet, for reasons fair or foul, the expected contract never materializes. The plaintiff might try to argue that an informal contract had been reached, even though some of the terms remained open. We examine this type of argument in Chapter 7, where we discuss preliminary and incomplete agreements. A plaintiff in this situation faces real obstacles in making out its contracts case, particularly if the defendant has not yet manifested an intention to be bound or if the material terms have not yet been agreed. Yet if the defendant has, by its conduct, inexorably led the plaintiff down the primrose path, and the plaintiff has suffered thereby, promissory estoppel may provide some relief. Full enforcement of the contract that might have been may not be in order, but at least the plaintiff might be entitled to reimbursement of the expenses it suffered.

■ PROBLEM 10.4

Hoffman v. Red Owl Stores, Inc., 26 Wis. 2d 683, 133 N.W.2d 267 (1965), is a famous case invoking promissory estoppel in the context of precontractual negotiations. The Hoffmans owned a bakery, and sought to get into the grocery business. They contacted Red Owl, a supermarket chain, and asked about the possibility of obtaining a Red Owl franchise. The ensuing saga presents a poignant tale of a defendant luring a plaintiff into repeated missteps, all the while dangling the prospect of a contract just slightly out of reach.[16]

From the beginning, the Hoffmans emphasized that they had only $18,000 to invest in the venture, and Red Owl assured them that this amount would be sufficient. At the urging of Red Owl, the Hoffmans took multiple steps to prepare themselves. They bought a small grocery business to gain experience. After just a few months, upon assurances that "they would be in a new store by fall," they sold it at a loss. They put a deposit down on some land for the future grocery store site after being told that "everything was set." They sold their bakery business and building after the Red Owl representative told them that "everything is ready to go; get your money together and we are set." The Hoffmans moved their family to a new town in order to make themselves available to train in an

---

[16] The facts summarized here are based on the court's account. In a retrospective of the case, Professors Whitford and Macaulay suggest that the actual facts were even more egregious than those described by the court. Based on what they discovered from interviewing the plaintiff and scouring the trial and appellate record, the authors conclude that controversial as the case may be, in their view, justice was done. *See* William C. Whitford & Stewart Macaulay, Hoffman v. Red Owl Stores: *The Rest of the Story*, 61 Hastings L.J. 801 (2010). *Cf.* Robert E. Scott, Hoffman v. Red Owl Stores *and the Myth of Precontractual Reliance*, 68 Ohio St. L.J. 71 (2007) (calling *Hoffman* an "unfortunate" case and stating, "Putting aside for the moment the dubious accuracy of [the] holding as a matter of contract doctrine . . . *Hoffman* is an outlier; the case has not been followed in its own or other jurisdictions").

existing Red Owl store. After all of this disruption to their business and personal lives, the Hoffmans received unhappy news: Red Owl projected that the Hoffmans would have to come up with $24,100 rather than $18,000 in order to establish themselves in a Red Owl franchise. Two weeks after this projection, Red Owl's home office insisted that an additional $2,000 would be required for promotional purposes. And yet the Hoffmans didn't give up. Mr. Hoffman met with his father-in-law, who agreed to contribute $13,000 to the venture, as long as he could come in as a partner. Even this did not meet with Red Owl's approval. Instead, Red Owl prepared revised financial projections, which the Hoffmans interpreted to require a total cash outlay of $34,000, including an outright gift of $13,000 from the father-in-law.

More than two years after the Hoffmans first contacted Red Owl, they finally broke off negotiations, informing Red Owl that they simply could not go along with its latest proposal. Litigation ensued. Although the parties had by no means reached full agreement on the major points of the franchise agreement, the trial court and jury found Red Owl liable on a theory of promissory estoppel, and the Wisconsin Supreme Court (at least insofar as the theory of liability was concerned) affirmed.

(a)   Based on the summary above and our study of promissory estoppel to date, do you believe the elements of Restatement, Second §90 were met in this case? In particular, do you think it would be unjust not to enforce any promises made by Red Owl? Why or why not?

(b)   Assuming a court is willing to find liability on a theory of promissory estoppel in circumstances such as these, what relief should it allow the plaintiff?

(c)   In Chapter 7, we show that courts sometimes refuse to enforce "agreements to agree" or other agreements that are so indefinite that the court cannot determine what the parties intended their obligations to be. Does the Hoffman case suggest an alternative analysis?

Hoffman is a departure from the traditional view that a party is free to break off contract negotiations at any time for any reason. After the case was decided, some commentators wondered if it was a signal of a new, general duty in American jurisprudence to negotiate in good faith.[17] A few cases have taken

---

[17] For instance, Professor Summers once stated that should other courts follow the *Red Owl* holding, "it will no longer be possible for one party to scuttle contract negotiations with impunity when the other has been induced to rely to his detriment on the prospect that the negotiations will succeed." Robert S. Summers, *"Good Faith" in General Contract Law and the Sales Provisions of the Uniform Commercial Code*, 54 Va. L. Rev. 195, 225 (1968).

up the invitation of the *Hoffman* court to apply promissory estoppel in a precontractual setting. Yet it is fair to say that commentators who favored a broad-based expansion of the duty to negotiate in good faith have largely been disappointed. For instance, the *Garwood Packaging* case, coming up next, is much less generous in its application of promissory estoppel in the precontractual setting. Nevertheless, the analysis of *Hoffman* remains influential, even if its scope of application has not enlarged greatly since the original decision.

GARWOOD PACKAGING, INC. v. ALLEN & COMPANY, INC.

378 F.3d 698 (2004)
United States Court of Appeals, Seventh Circuit

POSNER, Circuit Judge.

This is a diversity suit, governed by Indiana law, in which substantial damages are sought on the basis of promissory estoppel. The suit pits Garwood Packaging, Inc., which created a packaging system designed to increase the shelf life of fresh meat, and its two principals, Garwood and McNamara, against Allen & Company (an investment company) and a vice-president of Allen named Martin. We shall refer to the plaintiffs collectively as "GPI" and the defendants collectively as "Allen." The district court granted summary judgment in favor of Allen and dismissed the suit. . . .

GPI had flopped in marketing its food-packaging system and by 1993 had run up debts of $3 million and was broke. It engaged Martin to help find investors. After an initial search turned up nothing, Martin told GPI that Allen (Martin's employer, remember) would consider investing $2 million of its own money in GPI if another investor could be found who would make a comparable investment. The presence of the other investor would reduce the risk to Allen not only by augmenting GPI's assets but also by validating Allen's judgment that GPI might be salvageable, because it would show that someone else was also willing to bet a substantial sum of money on GPI's salvation. To further reduce its risk Allen decided to off-load half its projected $2 million investment on other investors.

Martin located a company named Hobart Corporation that was prepared to manufacture $2 million worth of GPI packaging machines in return for equity in the company. Negotiations with Hobart proved arduous, however. There were two sticking points: the amount of equity that Hobart would receive and the obtaining of releases from GPI's creditors. Hobart may have been concerned that unless the creditors released GPI the company would fail and Hobart wouldn't be able to sell the packaging systems that it manufactured. Or it may have feared that the creditors would assert liens in the systems. All that is clear is that Hobart insisted on releases. They were also important to the other investors whom Allen wanted to bring into the deal, the ones who would contribute half of Allen's offered $2 million.

Martin told Garwood and McNamara (GPI's principals) that he would see that the deal went through "come hell or high water." Eventually, however, Allen decided not to invest, the deal collapsed, and GPI was forced to declare bankruptcy. The reason for Allen's change of heart was that the investors who it thought had agreed to put up half of "Allen's" $2 million had gotten cold feet. When Allen withdrew from the deal, no contract had been signed and no agreement had been reached on how much stock either Allen or Hobart would receive in exchange for their contributions to GPI. Nor had releases been obtained from the creditors.

GPI's principal claim on appeal, and the only one we need to discuss (the others fall with it), is that Martin's unequivocal promise to see the deal through to completion bound Allen by the doctrine of promissory estoppel, which makes a promise that induces reasonable reliance legally enforceable. Restatement (Second) of Contracts §90(1) (1981). If noncontractual promises were never enforced, reliance on their being enforceable would never be reasonable, so let us consider why the law might want to allow people to rely on promises that do not create actual contracts and whether the answer can help GPI.

The simplest answer to the "why" question is that the doctrine merely allows reliance to be substituted for consideration as the basis for making a promise enforceable. On this view promissory estoppel is really just a doctrine of contract law. The most persuasive reason for the requirement of consideration in the law of contracts is that in a system in which oral contracts are enforceable—and by juries, to boot—the requirement provides some evidence that there really *was* a promise that was intended to be relied on as a real commitment. *Gibson v. Neighborhood Health Clinics, Inc.*, 121 F.3d 1126, 1131 (7th Cir. 1997); . . . Lon L. Fuller, *Consideration and Form*, 41 Colum. L. Rev. 799, 799-801 (1941). Actual reliance, in the sense of a costly change of position that cannot be recouped if the reliance turns out to have been misplaced, is substitute evidence that there may well have been such a promise. The inference is especially plausible in a commercial setting, because most businesspeople would be reluctant to incur costs in reliance on a promise that they believed the promisor didn't consider himself legally bound to perform.

In other words, reasonable reliance is seen as nearly as good a reason for thinking there really was a promise as bargained-for reliance is. In many such cases, it is true, no promise was intended, or intended to be legally enforceable; in those cases the application of the doctrine penalizes the defendant for inducing the plaintiff to incur costs of reliance. The penalty is withheld if the reliance was unreasonable; for then the plaintiff's wound was self-inflicted—he should have known better than to rely.

A relevant though puzzling difference between breach of contract and promissory estoppel as grounds for legal relief is that while the promise relied on to trigger an estoppel must be definite in the sense of being clearly a promise and not just a statement of intentions, its terms need not be as clear as a contractual promise would have to be in order to be enforceable. Indiana may go furthest in this direction: "Even though there were insufficient terms for the enforcement of an express oral contract, and unfulfilled pre-existing conditions prohibiting recovery for breach of a written contract . . . we are not precluded from finding a promise under these circumstances. Indeed, it is precisely under such circumstances, where a promise is made but which is not enforceable as a 'contract,' that the doctrine of promissory estoppel is recognized." *First National Bank of Logansport v. Logan Mfg. Co.*, [577 N.E.2d 949, 955 (Ind. 1991)]. . . .

But even though the court is "not precluded from finding a promise" by its vagueness, *id.* at 955, the vaguer the alleged promise the less likely it is to be found to *be* a promise. And if it is *really* vague, the promisee would be imprudent to rely on it—he wouldn't know whether reliance was worthwhile. The broader principle, which the requirement that the promise be definite and at least minimally clear instantiates, is that the promisee's reliance must be reasonable; if it is not, then not only is he the gratuitous author of his own disappointment, but probably there wasn't really a promise, or at least a promise intended or likely to induce reliance. The "promise" would have been in the nature of a hope or possibly a prediction rather than a commitment to do something within the "promisor's" power to do ("I promise it will rain tomorrow"); and the "promisee" would, if sensible, understand this. He would rely or not as he chose but he would know that he would have to bear the cost of any disappointment.

We note, returning to the facts of this case, that there was costly reliance by GPI, which forewent other opportunities for salvation, and by Garwood and McNamara, who moved from Indiana to Ohio to be near Hobart's plant where they expected their food-packaging system to be manufactured, and who forgave their personal loans to GPI and incurred other costs as well. The reliance was on statements by Martin, of which "come hell or high water" was the high water mark but is by no means an isolated example. If GPI's evidence is credited, as it must be in the procedural posture of the case, Martin repeatedly confirmed to GPI that the deal would go through, that Allen's commitment to invest $2 million was unconditional, that the funding would be forthcoming, and so on; and these statements induced the plaintiffs to incur costs they would otherwise not have done.

But were these real promises, and likely to be understood as such? Those are two different questions. A person may say something that he intends as merely a prediction, or as a signal of his hopes or intentions, but that is reasonably understood as a promise, and if so, as we know (this is the penal or deterrent function of promissory estoppel), he is bound. But what is a reasonable, and indeed actual, understanding will often depend on the knowledge that the promisee brings to the table. McNamara, with whom Martin primarily dealt, is a former investment banker, not a rube. He knew that in putting together a deal to salvage a failing company there is many a slip 'twixt cup and lips [*sic*]. Unless blinded by optimism or desperation he *had* to know that Martin could not mean *literally* that the deal would go through "come hell or high water," since if Satan or a tsunami obliterated Ohio that would kill the deal. Even if

Allen had dug into its pockets for the full $2 million after the investors who it had hoped would put up half the amount defected, the deal might well not have gone through because of Hobart's demands and because of the creditors. GPI acknowledges that the Internal Revenue Service, one of its largest creditors, wouldn't give a release until paid in full. Some of GPI's other creditors also intended to fight rather than to accept a pittance in exchange for a release. Nothing is more common than for a deal to rescue a failing company to fall apart because all the creditors' consent to the deal cannot be obtained—that is one of the reasons for bankruptcy law. Again these were things of which McNamara was perfectly aware.

The problem, thus, is not that Martin's promises were indefinite, which they were not if GPI's evidence is credited, but that they could not have been reasonably understood by the persons to whom they were addressed (mainly McNamara, the financial partner in GPI) to *be* promises rather than expressions of optimism and determination. To move to Ohio, to forgive personal loans, to forgo other searches for possible investors, and so forth were in the nature of gambles on the part of GPI and its principals. They may have been reasonable gambles, in the sense that the prospects for a successful salvage operation were good enough that taking immediate, even if irrevocable, steps to facilitate and take advantage of the expected happy outcome was prudent. But we often reasonably rely on things that are not promises. A farmer plants his crops in the spring in reasonable reliance that spring will be followed by summer rather than by winter. There can be reasonable reliance on statements as well as on the regularities of nature, but if the statements are not reasonably understood as legally enforceable promises there can be no action for promissory estoppel.

Suppose McNamara thought that there was a 50 percent chance that the deal would go through and believed that reliance on that prospect would cost him $100,000, but also believed that by relying he could expect either to increase the likelihood that the deal would go through or to make more money if it did by being able to start production sooner and that in either event the expected benefit of reliance would exceed $100,000. Then his reliance would be reasonable even if not induced by enforceable promises. The numbers are arbitrary but the example apt. GPI and its principals relied, and may have relied reasonably, but they didn't rely on Martin's "promises" because those were not promises reasonably understood as such by so financially sophisticated a businessman as McNarama. So we see now that the essence of the doctrine of promissory estoppel is not that the plaintiff have reasonably relied on the defendant's promise, but that he have reasonably relied on its *being* a promise in the sense of a legal commitment, and not a mere prediction or aspiration or bit of puffery.

One last point. Ordinarily the question whether a plaintiff reasonably understood a statement to be a promise is a question of fact and so cannot be resolved in summary judgment proceedings. But if it is clear that the question can be answered in only one way, there is no occasion to submit the question to a jury. This, we believe, is such a case.

Affirmed.

■ QUESTION

Compare and contrast the actions of the defendants in *Hoffman* (as described in Problem 10.4) and *Garwood Packaging*. Do you see any material differences between the two cases? Are the differing judgments justified, and if so, why?

2. Promissory Estoppel and the Statute of Frauds

As we discuss in Chapter 8, oral contracts may exhibit the formal elements of offer, acceptance, and consideration yet may be unenforceable nevertheless if they fail to satisfy the statute of frauds. A disappointed plaintiff who has relied on such a contract may try to enforce it under a theory of promissory estoppel. Section 139(1) of the Restatement, Second, generally approves this tactic:

RESTATEMENT, SECOND §139. ENFORCEMENT BY VIRTUE OF ACTION IN RELIANCE

(1) A promise which the promisor should reasonably expect to induce action or forbearance on the part of the promisee or a third person and which does induce the action or forbearance is enforceable notwithstanding the Statute of Frauds if injustice can be avoided only by enforcement of the promise. The remedy granted for breach is to be limited as justice requires.

(2) In determining whether injustice can be avoided only by enforcement of the promise, the following circumstances are significant:

(a) the availability and adequacy of other remedies, particularly cancellation and restitution;

(b) the definite and substantial character of the action or forbearance in relation to the remedy sought;

(c) the extent to which the action or forbearance corroborates evidence of the making and terms of the promise, or the making and terms are otherwise established by clear and convincing evidence;

(d) the reasonableness of the action or forbearance;

(e) the extent to which the action or forbearance was foreseeable by the promisor.

■ QUESTIONS

(1) Compare the elements of Restatement, Second §139(1) with those of Restatement, Second §90. Do they differ in any significant way? Do they seek to achieve the same policies, or are different interests at stake?

(2) Restatement, Second §90 makes no attempt to define when injustice can be avoided only by enforcement of a promise. As you see, Restatement,

Second §139(2) takes a different approach. What, if anything, justifies this difference? Do you think it would have been helpful for the drafters to have included a list of significant factors in §90 as well? If so, what do you think those factors should have been?

———————

The majority in the next case allows the use of promissory estoppel to overcome the statute of frauds. A dissenting opinion disagrees. Generally, Restatement, Second §139 has received less than full acceptance in the courts, and in some jurisdictions it has been rejected outright. As you read this case, consider what you believe to be the best approach.

McINTOSH v. MURPHY

469 P.2d 177 (1970)
Hawaii Supreme Court

LEVINSON, Justice.

This case involves an oral employment contract which allegedly violates the provision of the Statute of Frauds requiring "any agreement that is not to be performed within one year from the making thereof" to be in writing in order to be enforceable. HRS §656-1(5). In this action the plaintiff-employee Dick McIntosh seeks to recover damages from his employer, George Murphy and Murphy Motors, Ltd., for the breach of an alleged one-year oral employment contract.

While the facts are in sharp conflict, it appears that defendant George Murphy was in southern California during March, 1964 interviewing prospective management personnel for his Chevrolet-Oldsmobile dealerships in Hawaii. He interviewed the plaintiff twice during that time. The position of sales manager for one of the dealerships was fully discussed but no contract was entered into. In April, 1964 the plaintiff received a call from the general manager of Murphy Motors informing him of possible employment within thirty days if he was still available. The plaintiff indicated his continued interest and informed the manager that he would be available. Later in April, the plaintiff sent Murphy a telegram to the effect that he would arrive in Honolulu on Sunday, April 26, 1964. Murphy then telephoned McIntosh on Saturday, April 25, 1964 to notify him that the job of assistant sales manager was open and work would begin on the following Monday, April 27, 1964. At that time McIntosh expressed surprise at the change in job title from sales manager to assistant sales manager but reconfirmed the fact that he was arriving in Honolulu the next day, Sunday. McIntosh arrived on Sunday, April 26, 1964 and began work on the following day, Monday, April 27, 1964.

As a consequence of his decision to work for Murphy, McIntosh moved some of his belongings from the mainland to Hawaii, sold other possessions, leased an apartment in Honolulu and obviously forwent any other employment opportunities. In short, the plaintiff did all those things which were incidental to changing one's residence permanently from Los Angeles to Honolulu, a distance of approximately 2200 miles. McIntosh continued working for Murphy until July 16, 1964, approximately two and one-half months, at which time he was discharged on the grounds that he was unable to close deals with prospective customers and could not train the salesmen.

At the conclusion of the trial, the defense moved for a directed verdict arguing that the oral employment agreement was in violation of the Statute of Frauds, there being no written memorandum or note thereof. The trial court ruled that as a matter of law the contract did not come within the Statute, reasoning that Murphy bargained for acceptance by the actual commencement of performance by McIntosh, so that McIntosh was not bound by a contract until he came to work on Monday, April 27, 1964. Therefore, assuming that the contract was for a year's employment, it was performable within a year exactly to the day and no writing was required for it to be enforceable. Alternatively, the court ruled that if the agreement was made final by the telephone call between the parties on Saturday, April 25, 1964, then that part of the weekend which remained would not be counted in calculating the year, thus taking the contract out of the Statute of Frauds. With commendable candor the trial judge gave as the motivating force for the decision his desire to avoid a mechanical and unjust application of the Statute.[18]

[After trial, the jury found that the contract was performable within a year and that the plaintiff was discharged without just cause. The jury returned a verdict for the plaintiff in the amount of $12,103.40. The defendant appealed on several grounds, none of which the Supreme Court found to have merit. Included here is the court's discussion of whether the plaintiff could maintain an action of the alleged oral one-year employment contract in light of the prohibition of the Statute of Frauds.]

... In determining whether a rule of law can be fashioned and applied to a situation where an oral contract admittedly violates a strict interpretation of the Statute of Frauds, it is necessary to review the Statute itself together with its historical and modern functions. The Statute of Frauds, which requires that certain contracts be in writing in order to be legally enforceable, had its inception in the days of Charles II of England. Hawaii's version of the Statute is found in HRS §656-1 and is substantially the same as the original English Statute of Frauds.

---

[18] THE COURT: You make the law look ridiculous, because one day is Sunday and the man does not work on Sunday; the other day is Saturday; he is up in Fresno. He can't work down there. And he is down here Sunday night and shows up for work on Monday. To me that is a contract within a year. I don't want to make the law look ridiculous, Mr. Clause, because it is one day later, one day too much, and that one day is a Sunday, and a non-working day.

The first English Statute was enacted almost 300 years ago to prevent "many fraudulent practices, which are commonly endeavored to be upheld by perjury and subornation of perjury." 29 Car. 2, c. 3 (1677). Certainly, there were compelling reasons in those days for such a law. At the time of enactment in England, the jury system was quite unreliable, rules of evidence were few, and the complaining party was disqualified as a witness so he could neither testify on direct-examination nor, more importantly, be cross-examined. The aforementioned structural and evidentiary limitations on our system of justice no longer exist.

Retention of the Statute today has nevertheless been justified on at least three grounds: (1) the Statute still serves an evidentiary function thereby lessening the danger of perjured testimony (the original rationale); (2) the requirement of a writing has a cautionary effect which causes reflection by the parties on the importance of the agreement; and (3) the writing is an easy way to distinguish enforceable contracts from those which are not, thus chanelling certain transactions into written form.[19]

In spite of whatever utility the Statute of Frauds may still have, its applicability has been drastically limited by judicial construction over the years in order to mitigate the harshness of a mechanical application. Furthermore, learned writers continue to disparage the Statute regarding it as "a statute for promoting fraud" and a "legal anachronism."[20]

Another method of judicial circumvention of the Statute of Frauds has grown out of the exercise of the equity powers of the courts. Such judicially imposed limitations or exceptions involved the traditional dispensing power of the equity courts to mitigate the "harsh" rule of law. When courts have enforced an oral contract in spite of the Statute, they have utilized the legal labels of "part performance" or "equitable estoppel" in granting relief. Both doctrines are said to be based on the concept of estoppel, which operates to avoid unconscionable injury.

Part performance has long been recognized in Hawaii as an equitable doctrine justifying the enforcement of an oral agreement for the conveyance of an interest in land where there has been substantial reliance by the party seeking to enforce the contract. *Perreira v. Perreira*, 50 Haw. 641, 447 P.2d 667 (1968) (agreement to grant life estate); *Vierra v. Shipman*, 26 Haw. 369 (1922) (agreement to devise land); *Yee Hop v. Young Sak Cho*, 25 Haw. 494 (1920) (oral lease of real property). Other courts have enforced oral contracts (including employment contracts) which failed to satisfy the section of the Statute making unenforceable an agreement not to be performed within a year of its making. This has occurred where the conduct of the parties gave rise to an estoppel to assert the Statute. *Oxley v. Ralston Purina Co.*, 349 F.2d 328 (6th Cir. 1965) (equitable

---

[19] Fuller, *Consideration and Form*, 41 Colum. L. Rev. 799, 800-03 (1941); *Note: Statute of Frauds—The Doctrine of Equitable Estoppel and the Statute of Frauds*, 66 Mich. L. Rev. 170 (1967).
[20] Burdick, *A Statute for Promoting Fraud*, 16 Colum. L. Rev. 273 (1916); Willis, *The Statute of Frauds—A Legal Anachronism*, 3 Ind. L.J. 427, 528 (1928).

estoppel); *Alaska Airlines, Inc. v. Stephenson*, 217 F.2d 295, 15 Alaska 272 (9th Cir. 1954) ("promissory estoppel"); *Seymour v. Oelrichs*, 156 Cal. 782, 106 P. 88 (1909) (equitable estoppel).

It is appropriate for modern courts to cast aside the raiments of conceptualism which cloak the true policies underlying the reasoning behind the many decisions enforcing contracts that violate the Statute of Frauds. There is certainly no need to resort to legal rubrics or meticulous legal formulas when better explanations are available. The policy behind enforcing an oral agreement which violated the Statute of Frauds, as a policy of avoiding unconscionable injury, was well set out by the California Supreme Court. In *Monarco v. Lo Greco*, 35 Cal. 2d 621, 623, 220 P.2d 737, 739 (1950), a case which involved an action to enforce an oral contract for the conveyance of land on the grounds of 20 years performance by the promisee, the court said:

> The doctrine of estoppel to assert the statute of frauds has been consistently applied by the courts of this state to prevent fraud that would result from refusal to enforce oral contracts in certain circumstances. Such fraud may inhere in the unconscionable injury that would result from denying enforcement of the contract after one party has been induced by the other seriously to change his position in reliance on the contract. . . .

See also *Seymour v. Oelrichs*, 156 Cal. 782, 106 P. 88 (1909) (an employment contract enforced).

In seeking to frame a workable test which is flexible enough to cover diverse factual situations and also provide some reviewable standards, we find very persuasive section 217A of the Second Restatement of Contracts.[21] That section specifically covers those situations where there has been reliance on an oral contract which falls within the Statute of Frauds. [The court quotes the language of the section.] . . .

We think that the approach taken in the Restatement is the proper method of giving the trial court the necessary latitude to relieve a party of the hardships of the Statute of Frauds. Other courts have used similar approaches in dealing with oral employment contracts upon which an employee had seriously relied. See *Alaska Airlines, Inc. v. Stephenson*, 217 F.2d 295 (9th Cir. 1954); *Seymour v. Oelrichs*, 156 Cal. 782, 106 P. 88 (1909). This is to be preferred over having the trial court bend over backwards to take the contract out of the Statute of Frauds. In the present case the trial court admitted just this inclination and forthrightly followed it.

There is no dispute that the action of the plaintiff in moving 2200 miles from Los Angeles to Hawaii was foreseeable by the defendant. In fact, it was required to perform his duties. Injustice can only be avoided by the enforcement of the

---

[21] Here the court is citing to an early draft of the Restatement, Second—that is, Tentative Draft No. 4, promulgated in 1969. The language of draft §217A is identical to the language that ultimately appeared in Restatement, Second §139, quoted at the beginning of this section.—EDS.

contract and the granting of money damages. No other remedy is adequate. The plaintiff found himself residing in Hawaii without a job.

It is also clear that a contract of some kind did exist. The plaintiff performed the contract for two and one-half months receiving $3,484.60 for his services. The exact length of the contract, whether terminable at will as urged by the defendant, or for a year from the time when the plaintiff started working, was up to the jury to decide.

In sum, the trial court might have found that enforcement of the contract was warranted by virtue of the plaintiff's reliance on the defendant's promise. Naturally, each case turns on its own facts. Certainly there is considerable discretion for a court to implement the true policy behind the Statute of Frauds, which is to prevent fraud or any other type of unconscionable injury. We therefore affirm the judgment of the trial court on the ground that the plaintiff's reliance was such that injustice could only be avoided by enforcement of the contract.

Affirmed.

ABE, Justice (dissenting).

The majority of the court has affirmed the judgment of the trial court; however, I respectfully dissent.

. . . Here on one hand the plaintiff claimed that he had a one-year employment contract; on the other hand, the defendant claimed that the plaintiff had not been hired for one year but on a trial basis for so long as his services were satisfactory. I believe the Statute of Frauds was enacted to avoid the consequences this court is forcing upon the defendant. In my opinion, the legislature enacted the Statute of Frauds to negate claims such as has been made by the plaintiff in this case. But this court holds that because the plaintiff in reliance of the one-year employment contract (alleged to have been entered into by the plaintiff, but denied by the defendant) has changed his position, "injustice could only be avoided by enforcement of the contract." Where is the sense of justice?

Now assuming that the defendant had agreed to hire the plaintiff under a one-year employment contract and the contract came within the Statute of Frauds, I cannot agree, as intimated by this court, that we should circumvent the Statute of Frauds by the exercise of the equity powers of courts. As to statutory law, the sole function of the judiciary is to interpret the statute and the judiciary should not usurp legislative power and enter into the legislative field. Thus, if the Statute of Frauds is too harsh as intimated by this court, and it brings about undue hardship, it is for the legislature to amend or repeal the statute and not for this court to legislate.

■ QUESTIONS

(1)   In this case, the majority applies promissory estoppel to overcome the operation of the statute of frauds. What hazards does the use of promissory estoppel in this context pose? Does the majority address those hazards, and if so, how?

(2) Where we discuss the statute of frauds in Chapter 8, we show that the part performance exception is sometimes recognized in the context of real estate transactions, but courts are generally hesitant to apply it in the context of contracts that cannot be performed within a year. What is the majority's view of the proper scope of the part performance exception to the statute of frauds?

(3) In Chapter 8, we also show that the statute of frauds is particularly controversial in the context of contracts that cannot be performed within a year and that courts tend to interpret the statute narrowly in that context. Do you believe the nature of the contract played a significant role here? For instance, do you believe that the majority's analysis would extend to an oral contract to sell land?

(4) Ultimately, which analysis do you find more persuasive, that of the majority, or that of the dissent?

▌ PROBLEM 10.5

Falter Enterprises was facing a major corporate restructuring. It sought a charismatic and well-respected leader to give it an air of stability during the tumultuous times to come. The board of directors identified Sally Slick, a rising corporate star, as its first choice for the position of chief executive officer. Falter offered Sally the position and a lavish salary to go along with it, as long as she would commit to a five-year employment contract. Falter explained its critical need to assure investors and employees that the new CEO was in it for the long haul. Without this assurance, the restructuring would be doomed.

After discussing in detail what the terms of her employment would be, Sally jumped at the opportunity. "I am completely on board. You can go ahead and announce that I am taking the post," Sally said. "Just send me a contract embodying the terms we've discussed, and I'll read it and sign it." That same afternoon, Falter issued a press release stating that Sally had assumed the position of chief executive officer. Falter's stock prices immediately went through the roof.

The next day, Falter provided Sally with a simple form contract, reflecting all of the terms to which the parties had orally agreed. Sally set it aside and neither read nor signed it. A few days later, Sally assumed the post of CEO without a signed contract, orally assuring the board that she would read and sign it as soon as she got a break in her schedule. On several occasions, Falter's board reminded her that they were still expecting a signed contract, and Sally repeatedly promised to attend to it as soon as she could. Three months into her employment, Sally resigned and took a more highly paid position at Rock Solid Industries. Falter's stock prices plunged.

Falter files suit, claiming Sally breached her five-year employment contract. Sally argues that there was no long-term employment contract yet, and even if there was, it was unenforceable because of the statute of frauds. You are the judicial clerk assigned to research the case. The lawyers have stipulated as to the facts listed above and have made cross-motions for summary judgment. In their briefs they cite a variety of precedents, some of which adopt Restatement, Second §139 and others of which decline to do so. None of the precedents are binding in your jurisdiction. Your judge has asked you to determine if Restatement, Second §139 is persuasive in the employment context, and if so, how it would apply to the facts of this case. What do you say? In the end, will you recommend that the court grant summary judgment and, if so, in favor of whom?

 ## D REMEDIES IN PROMISSORY ESTOPPEL ACTIONS

In this section, we focus on the remedies available to a plaintiff who makes out a promissory estoppel argument. We have hinted at this theme before. We start the chapter by acknowledging the existence of an academic debate: Is promissory estoppel a species of contract action, or is it an independent theory of liability? This debate is particularly relevant to the question of remedies. If promissory estoppel merely provides a substitute for consideration, a plaintiff should expect contract remedies. If, however, promissory estoppel is a completely independent theory of liability, the plaintiff has no reason to expect that the remedies will mirror those of a contract lawsuit. (Later in the text, we see that courts have flexibility to fashion remedies, even within the confines of a contract lawsuit.) Even if promissory estoppel is essentially a contract-based theory, that does not necessarily mean that it serves the same interests as consideration doctrine. Courts may exercise their discretion differently, depending on what they view the main emphasis of the two doctrines to be. You might recall that scholars disagree on this question too. They debate whether promissory estoppel is all about enforcing promises seriously made or whether it is aimed at compensating honest and reasonable reliance. Again, if promissory estoppel is more about enforcing promises, we might expect to see traditional contract relief. If instead it is about compensating injured plaintiffs, we might see a different measure of recovery, keyed more explicitly to the extent of the detriment the plaintiff suffered.

What we find is that the picture is a textured one. At times relief for promissory estoppel is almost indistinguishable from the remedies available in an analogous contract suit. At other times, the relief is quite different. Only closer examination will reveal the types of factors that tend to influence courts in providing remedies for promissory estoppel. To begin, it is helpful to survey the remedies typically available for breach of contract. We touch on these concepts from time to time throughout the book. Here we introduce them in more detail.

Suppose that Max contracts to sell Martha his doghouse for $100. Max inexplicably and inexcusably reneges on his side of the bargain. What type of relief might Martha seek? She might try to force Max to carry out his promise and deliver the doghouse. As we first note in Chapter 1, this type of relief, called "specific performance," is very much the exception rather than the rule in our legal system and is rarely available. Martha might instead seek to collect damages from Max. We have seen that generally, the goal of contract damages is to compensate Martha for the economic losses she suffered as a result of Max's breach. The amount of damages will vary depending on the circumstances. Typically, however, they are designed to give Martha the economic benefit of the bargain she had made with Max—or, to put it another way, to put her in the position she would have been in had Max gone through with the deal. These kinds of damages are called "expectation" damages.[22] When courts and commentators speak of "contract" remedies in the context of promissory estoppel cases, therefore, they are usually referring to expectation damages.

Restatement, Second §90 states that "the remedy granted for breach may be limited as justice requires." It is clear that judges who follow §90 have some discretion in fashioning remedies in promissory estoppel cases, even if the plaintiff establishes all of the elements of its case. How courts exercise that discretion, however, may depend on their view of the nature of promissory estoppel. The proper measure of damages is one issue in the case that follows.

TOUR COSTA RICA v. COUNTRY WALKERS, INC.

171 Vt. 116, 758 A.2d 795 (2000)
Vermont Supreme Court

SKOGLUND, Justice.

Defendants Country Walkers, Inc. (CW) and Robert Maynard (Maynard)[23] appeal from the superior court's denial of their ... motion for judgment as a

---

[22] In calculating the appropriate amount of damages, it has become customary to speak of three interests that the law might attempt to protect: Martha's "expectation interest," her "reliance interest," or her "restitution interest." This classic division stems from a two-part article written in the 1930s by Professor Fuller and his research assistant at the time, William Perdue: Lon L. Fuller & William R. Perdue, Jr., *The Reliance Interest in Contract Damages: 1*, 46 Yale L.J. 52 (1936); *The Reliance Interest in Contract Damages: 2*, 46 Yale L.J. 373 (1937). For the time being, our focus will be on what measure of damages is appropriate for promissory estoppel actions: expectation damages or reliance damages. We return to expectation, reliance, and restitution recoveries in contract actions later in the materials.
[23] CW and its owner, Maynard, are hereinafter referred to collectively as "defendant."

matter of law, following a jury verdict for plaintiff, Tour Costa Rica (TCR), on its promissory estoppel claim. The jury awarded plaintiff, a company that runs tours in Costa Rica, damages after finding that defendant had breached a promise of a two-year commitment to use TCR to develop, organize and operate Costa Rican walking tours for defendant during that period. We affirm.

Because this is an appeal from a denial of a motion for judgment as a matter of law, we view the evidence in the light most favorable to plaintiff. CW is a Vermont business, owned by Maynard and his wife, that sells guided tours at locations around the world. In 1994, Leigh Monahan, owner of TCR, contacted Maynard and offered to design, arrange and lead walking tours in Costa Rica for defendant. During negotiations, Monahan explained to Maynard that she had just incorporated the tour company and, because the company had limited resources, she could not afford to develop specialized tours for defendant unless she had a two-year commitment from CW to run its Costa Rican tours through TCR. In the summer of 1994, the parties entered into a verbal agreement under which plaintiff was to design, arrange and lead customized walking tours in Costa Rica for CW from 1995 through 1997. Pursuant to this agreement, Monahan designed a customized tour for CW, a task that included investigating and testing walking tours, investigating and booking hotels, making transportation arrangements, conducting research, checking medical facilities, writing and editing copy for CW's brochures and drafting itineraries for clients.

In March and April 1995, plaintiff conducted two walking tours for CW. Although other tours had been scheduled for 1995, both defendant and plaintiff canceled some for various reasons. Between the end of April and June of 1995, the parties discussed the details of, and scheduled the dates for, approximately eighteen walking tours for 1996 and 1997. Due to limited resources, plaintiff could not conduct tours for anyone else while working with defendant and, therefore, stopped advertising and promoting its business, did not pursue other business opportunities and, in fact, turned down other business during this period.

In August 1995, a few weeks before the next tour was to occur, defendant informed plaintiff that it would be using another company for all of its future tours in Costa Rica. When challenged by plaintiff with its promised commitment, Maynard responded: "If I did and I certainly may have promised you a two year commitment, I apologize for not honoring it." Notwithstanding this apology, defendant went on to operate tours in Costa Rica using a rival company. Plaintiff was forced to cancel transportation arrangements and hotel and restaurant reservations it had made on defendant's behalf. Due to the suddenness of the break with CW, plaintiff was left without tours to run during a prime tourist season, and without sufficient time to market any new tours of its own.

Plaintiff filed suit against defendant, alleging breach of contract, promissory estoppel, unjust enrichment, conversion, fraud, and breach of covenant of good faith and fair dealing. Plaintiff dismissed the conversion count at the beginning of trial. At the close of plaintiff's evidence, defendant moved for a directed verdict on the remaining counts. The court granted defendant's motion with respect to the fraud claim, but denied it with respect to the other claims. Defendant renewed its motion at the close of all the evidence, and the court denied it. At that time, defendant also requested a directed verdict with regard to damages, arguing that there was insufficient evidence to support a damage award. The court denied this motion, as well. Subsequently, the court presented the parties with its proposed jury instructions, which included the following: "As to the claims of breach of contract and promissory estoppel, plaintiff would be entitled to damages which would put it in the same position as if the contract or promise had been fulfilled by Country Walkers." The court then held a jury charge conference, during which both plaintiff and defendant objected to portions of the court's proposed instructions. Defendant, however, did not object to the above-quoted portion.

The case went to the jury, and the jury found for defendant on the breach of contract, unjust enrichment, and breach of covenant of good faith and fair dealing claims, but found for plaintiff on the promissory estoppel claim, and awarded expectation damages in the amount of $22,520.00. Defendant then filed a motion for judgment as a matter of law, alleging, as it had in its previous motions, that plaintiff had failed to prove promissory estoppel and that there was insufficient evidence to support the jury's damage award. Defendant also argued, for the first time, that, as a matter of law, expectation damages are not available in a promissory estoppel action. The court denied defendant's motion. This appeal followed. . . .

Defendant first argues that plaintiff failed to make out a prima facie case of promissory estoppel. [The court quotes the language of Restatement, Second §90.] . . . Defendant does not seriously dispute that there was a promise or that plaintiff did take action based on the promise. Rather, defendant argues that plaintiff's reliance was not reasonable or detrimental, and that this is not a case where injustice can be avoided only by enforcement of the promise. . . .

In determining whether a plaintiff reasonably relied on a defendant's promise, courts examine the totality of the circumstances. Here, plaintiff presented evidence that it relied on defendant's promise of a two-year exclusive commitment by (a) ceasing to advertise and promote the business, failing to pursue other business opportunities, and turning down other business; (b) making hotel and restaurant reservations and arranging for transportation for the tours it was to operate for CW; and (c) making purchases related to the tours it was to operate for CW. Plaintiff suggests that this reliance was reasonable because, in negotiations with Maynard, plaintiff made clear that it required a two-year commitment due to its limited resources, the time it would have to devote to develop specialized tours for CW, and the ongoing communication between the parties as to future dates and requirements for tours.

Defendant argues that plaintiff's reliance was not reasonable based solely on standard industry practice that permits the cancellation of tours upon thirty to sixty days' notice. While there was no dispute that tours could be canceled with appropriate notice, there was evidence that this industry practice did not apply to the parties' two-year commitment. Monahan testified that she and Maynard specifically agreed to the two-year time frame because she wanted a measure of security for her fledgling company. She further testified that it was her understanding, from negotiations with Maynard, that the two-year commitment was unaffected by the possibility that some scheduled tours might be canceled if, for example, too few people signed. . . .

Defendant next argues that plaintiff's reliance on defendant's promise was not detrimental. Defendant suggests that the only evidence of detriment offered by plaintiff was Monahan's testimony concerning expenses for a few minor equipment purchases. Plaintiff disagrees. . . . In reliance on a two-year commitment, plaintiff stopped soliciting business from other sources and declined other bookings, a substantial change in position for a fledgling tour business. [After defendant breached the agreement, plaintiff had no money to advertise or conduct other tours.] Further, plaintiff's reputation in Costa Rica's tourism industry was damaged [because it had to cancel two years' worth of reservations it had made on behalf of defendant.] . . . Accordingly, the jury could reasonably conclude that plaintiff's reliance on defendant's promise was detrimental.

Whether injustice can be avoided only by enforcement of the promise[24] is a question of law informed by several factors, including:

a. the availability and adequacy of other remedies, particularly cancellation and restitution;
b. the definite and substantial character of the action or forbearance in relation to the remedy sought;
c. the extent to which the action or forbearance corroborates evidence of the making and terms of the promise, or the making and terms are otherwise established by clear and convincing evidence;
d. the reasonableness of the action or forbearance; [and]
e. the extent to which the action or forbearance was foreseeable by the promisor.

Restatement (Second) of Contracts §139(2) (1981).

With regard to the availability and adequacy of other remedies, we have previously stated that, "[w]hile a full range of legal damages may be available, promissory estoppel plaintiffs are not necessarily entitled to them as of right." *Remes v. Nordic Group, Inc.*, 169 Vt. 37, 41, 726 A.2d 77, 79-80 (1999). Damages

---

[24] We do not literally apply the term "enforcement of the promise." To do so would mean the only remedy available in a promissory estoppel case is specific performance. We have never so held. *See Foote* [*v. Simmonds Precision Prods. Co.*], 158 Vt. [566,] 573-74, 613 A.2d [1277,] 1281 (stating promissory estoppel applies "if injustice can be avoided only by enforcement of the promise," concluding there was sufficient evidence for jury to make finding of promissory estoppel, and upholding jury's damage award in case where plaintiff had been wrongfully discharged); *cf. Remes v. Nordic Group, Inc.*, 169 Vt. 37, 41, 726 A.2d 77, 80 (1999) ("promissory estoppel damages should be discretely designed as corrective relief to rectify the wrong committed in a particular case").

available in a promissory estoppel action depend upon the circumstances of the case. While the jury in the instant case found no contract, an analysis of breach-of-contract remedies is relevant to the determination of whether injustice can be avoided only by enforcement of the promise. We do not, however, intend to suggest "that promissory estoppel damages are coextensive with full contractual remedies." *Id.* at 40, 726 A.2d at 79.

Expectation damages, which the jury awarded in this case, provide the plaintiff with an amount equal to the benefit of the parties' bargain. One potential component of expectation damages is loss of future profits. The purpose of expectation damages is to "put the non-breaching party in the same position it would have been [in] had the contract been fully performed." *McKinley Allsopp, Inc. v. Jetborne Int'l, Inc.*, No. 89 CIV. 1489 (PNL), 1990 WL 138959 at *8 (S.D.N.Y. Sept. 19, 1990). Restitution damages seek to compensate the plaintiff for any benefit it conferred upon the defendant as a result of the parties' contract. The purpose of restitution damages is to return the plaintiff to the position it held before the parties' contract. Reliance damages give the plaintiff any reasonably foreseeable costs incurred in reliance on the contract. As with restitution, the purpose of reliance damages is to return the plaintiff to the position it was in prior to the parties' contract.

Restitution damages are inapplicable in the instant case because there is no evidence that plaintiff conferred any benefit on defendant as a result of defendant's promise. Further, cancellation is inapplicable, as defendant had already breached its promise, and cancellation would provide no remedy for plaintiff. Reliance damages are also inappropriate because the majority of the harm plaintiff suffered was not expenditures it made in reliance on defendant's promise, but rather, lost profits from the tours it had scheduled with defendant, lost potential profits because it failed to pursue other business opportunities, and harm to its reputation. Therefore, an award of expectation damages is the only remedy that adequately compensates plaintiff for the harm it suffered.

As to the other factors considered, plaintiff's actions and inactions were of a definite and substantial character. These actions and inactions strongly corroborate both Monahan's and Maynard's testimony, as well as documentary evidence submitted by plaintiff, regarding the making and terms of the promise. As previously discussed, plaintiff's reliance on defendant's promise was reasonable, and plaintiff's actions and inactions were foreseeable by defendant. Defendant expected plaintiff to take specific actions on defendant's behalf and to design and conduct tours to defendant's specifications. Further, defendant was aware that plaintiff was a new company without a lot of capital, and that it was spending much of that capital preparing tours for defendant.

Taking the above factors into consideration, there was sufficient evidence to allow the jury to conclude that, in this case, injustice could be avoided only by enforcement of the promise through an award of monetary damages.

Next, defendant argues that, as a matter of law, expectation damages are not available in a promissory estoppel case. According to defendant, only reliance damages are available in such cases. Plaintiff, however, notes that, although defendant had the opportunity to object to the jury instructions and raise this argument earlier, it failed to raise the issue until its postjudgment motion for judgment as a matter of law. Consequently, plaintiff contends, defendant waived the right to appeal this issue. We agree....

As noted, in its instructions to the jury, the trial court stated that, if the jury found for plaintiff on the promissory estoppel claim, it could award expectation damages.[25] Prior to giving instructions to the jury, the court held a conference during which both plaintiff and defendant objected to portions of the proposed instructions. Defendant failed to object, however, either at the charge conference or after the court charged the jury, to the instruction that allowed the jury to award expectation damages. Thus, defendant waived the right to appeal this issue....

Finally, defendant argues that the evidence was insufficient to support the damage award. It contends that plaintiff was required, and failed, to prove what its actual expenses would have been for the tours that were canceled and that, because plaintiff did not produce evidence of its costs, the jury was forced to speculate in calculating the damage award.

On appeal from a jury's damage award, we view the evidence in the light most favorable to the prevailing party, excluding any modifying evidence, in order to determine whether the award was clearly erroneous.

Defendant first argues that the award was clearly erroneous because plaintiff was required to introduce evidence of what the actual expenses would have been for the canceled tours, but failed to do so, relying on *G & H Holding Co. v. Dutton*, 118 Vt. 406, 110 A.2d 724 (1955). According to defendant, because plaintiff had already arranged for transportation and reserved hotels and restaurants, costs for the tours were readily available.

Defendant misreads our holding in *Dutton*. That case does not stand for the proposition that, in all cases, plaintiffs must produce precise evidence of their actual expenses. In *Dutton*, we stated: "Where the character of the damages is such as to be capable of being estimated by a strict money standard, the plaintiff must give evidence thereof in dollars and cents." *Id.* at 411-12, 110 A.2d at 728. In explaining this rule, we subsequently stated: "This is not a rule demanding proof to the precise penny, as defendant would have it. . . . [I]t is merely distinguishing between those cases where damages can be measured in money and those cases which call for the trier of fact to translate inchoate qualities into dollar damages." *A. Brown, Inc. v. Vermont Justin Corp.*, 148 Vt. 192, 196, 531 A.2d 899, 902 (1987). Defendant has not cited, and we cannot find, any case that supports its contention that plaintiff was required to produce precise evidence of the expenses it would have incurred had the twelve tours gone forward.

---

[25] Specifically, the court stated: "As to the claims of breach of contract and promissory estoppel, Plaintiff would be entitled to damages which would put it in the same position as if the contract or promise had been fulfilled by Country Walkers."

Here, plaintiff presented evidence of its costs for the two trips that it conducted for defendant, and it presented evidence of how much it was to be paid for the twelve trips that were canceled when defendant breached the parties' agreement. Plaintiff requested $68,000 in damages, the approximate value of twelve tours, with fourteen participants per tour—the average number of participants that had been on the two tours that plaintiff conducted for defendant—minus the estimated costs associated with running those tours. The jury's award of $22,250 reflected the profit value of approximately twelve tours with ten participants per tour, the average number of participants that had participated in CW's Costa Rican tours after defendant breached the parties' agreement.

Moreover, as plaintiff notes, it could not provide precise data for the twelve canceled tours because, as Monahan testified, circumstances, and therefore prices, were subject to change at any time.

Defendant further argues that the documents plaintiff submitted to prove its damages were insufficient because they excluded some expenses, leaving the jury to speculate when calculating damages. Defendant had ample opportunity, however, to cross-examine, or present independent evidence, on this issue. As we noted in *Brown*, the fact that "the damage figures are approximations or estimates" is a reflection of the weight, not the sufficiency, of the evidence. *Id.* at 196-97, 531 A.2d at 902. The jury's damage award was not clearly erroneous.

Affirmed.

■ QUESTIONS

(1)   At the trial of this case, the jury found for the defendant on the contract claim, but for the plaintiff on the promissory estoppel claim. We don't know what instructions the trial court gave the jury as to the proper elements of a contract cause of action. Under the principles studied to date, do you think the facts described in this opinion should give rise to an enforceable contract, supported by consideration? Why or why not?

(2)   This case raised promissory estoppel in a commercial context. How does the court's discussion of promissory estoppel compare with similar cases we have seen earlier in the chapter? Do the facts of this case resemble any of the others we have read so far, and if so, which ones? Is the result in this case similar to those cases? To the extent the result in this case differs, do you think it is a matter of the court's approach to promissory estoppel as a source of liability, to differences in the underlying facts, or to other factors?

(3)   In this case, the court discusses the possible remedies of specific performance, expectation damages, reliance damages, restitution, and cancellation. What would each type of remedy mean under the facts of this case?

(4)   The defendant argued that expectation damages should never be available in a promissory estoppel cause of action. The court held that the defendant

waived the right to raise this argument on appeal, because it had failed to object to the instructions the trial court had given to the jury. Had the issue been properly before the court, do you think the case would have come out differently? Why or why not?

(5)   Glance back through the cases in this chapter. In each, can you determine what type of remedy the plaintiff sought? Do you see any hints as to what types of remedies the respective courts might allow in a promissory estoppel cause of action?

■ PROBLEM 10.6

For the last year, Sylvan Style has been negotiating to sell his designer shoe boutique to Maria Marcos. They have settled on a price, but many other features of the deal are still being debated. Sylvan has repeatedly assured Maria that they will come to terms. His boutique is his baby. He tells Maria that he is willing to give it to her for a steal because he trusts that she will carry it forward with the requisite panache and drama. Sylvan promises that the details will be ironed out in a week, or a month at the outside.

Anticipating a closing any day, Maria makes a trip to Italy for the fall shoe-buying season. She knows that if she waits to make her buying trip, she will lose any chance to stock the hottest new fashions until the next season. In Italy she orders (and pays for) truckloads of trendy Italian shoes. Further, she flies first class, stays in fancy hotels, and eats at gourmet restaurants. She thinks it important to make a "splash" as a new name in the shoe fashion industry.

Upon her return, Sylvan announces that he cannot bear to give up the boutique.

Maria sues Sylvan, arguing, among other things, breach of contract and promissory estoppel. She seeks the difference between the true value of the store and the bargain price that Sylvan had offered. Sylvan argues that Maria is entitled to no damages at all.

(a)   Do you think Maria should prevail on her contract claim? What about her promissory estoppel claim?

(b)   Assuming Maria is able to persuade you that Sylvan breached a contract between the parties, what damages would you award and why?

(c)   If instead Maria is able to persuade you of her promissory estoppel claim only, what damages would you award her and why?

CHAPTER 11

Options and Firm Offers

[handwritten margin note: you can revoke any offer not held by consideration]

[handwritten margin note: true even if there's a promise to remain open]

Our study of offer and acceptance revealed that offers are generally freely revocable until accepted. Under the classical view, this is true even if the offer by its terms is to remain open. Remember *Dickinson v. Dodds* from Chapter 5? There the court held that a written offer could be withdrawn at will notwithstanding the fact that it said "this offer to be left over until Friday." If the parties want to avoid this result, they can enter into an option contract in which the promise to keep the offer open is itself supported by consideration. But absent independent consideration, under the classical view any promise to keep an offer open is a legal nullity.

[handwritten margin note: promissory estoppel → recovery for when reliance on a contract is reasonable]

In this chapter, we study the various legal theories that serve to make an offer irrevocable. Many concepts in this chapter follow directly from materials presented in prior chapters. Yet a study of the limits on the revocability of offers provides an excellent opportunity to explore the development of doctrine and in particular to examine the interrelationships among offer and acceptance, consideration, and promissory estoppel. We begin with option contracts. A traditional option contract is created when an offeror, in exchange for consideration, promises to limit his power to revoke the offer. We find that courts have mitigated harsh outcomes by taking a more lenient approach to consideration doctrine in option contracts. We then consider the role that promissory estoppel plays in limiting an offeror's ability to revoke his offer. In some circumstances, if the offeree reasonably relies on an offer, courts require the offeror to keep the offer open long enough to allow the offeree to accept it. We proceed to a brief discussion of UCC 2-205, which requires neither consideration nor reliance to make certain offers irrevocable, as long as specific statutory requirements are met. We conclude with a glimpse of the treatment of irrevocable offers under the CISG and the UNIDROIT Principles, both of which liberally enforce statements of irrevocability in offers.

A   OPTION CONTRACTS

[handwritten margin note: purpose is to allow time to think about the offer]

The purpose of an option contract is to allow the offeree some time in which to decide whether to accept the offer. An option contract makes an offer firm—that is, it insulates the offer from the usual events that otherwise terminate the power of acceptance. The offeror obligates himself to keep the offer open. Any attempted revocation during the term of the option contract will be ineffective. Furthermore, if the offeree rejects the offer or makes a counteroffer, the original offer will remain in effect. Even if the offeror dies or loses legal capacity, the offer continues.

While the offer may be firm, the offeree makes no promise to ultimately accept it. This raises some danger that the offeree will speculate at the expense of the offeror. The offeror has no flexibility to change his mind, yet the offeree can wait and see how things develop before she makes her ultimate decision. For this reason, classical doctrine requires consideration before the offeror's promise to limit his power of revocation becomes enforceable. The consideration compensates the offeror for the risk he assumes when he commits to keeping the offer open. Anything that serves as consideration in a contract generally can serve as consideration in an option contract. The offeree can pay for the option, she can render some other performance, or she can promise to make a payment or render a performance. As long as her promise or return performance is bargained for, it will constitute sufficient consideration for the offeror's promise to keep his offer open.

[handwritten margin note: both parties must give something to leave an offer open]

*[handwritten margin note: consideration can be 1) payment 2) performance 3) promise to make payment/performance * must be bargained for]*

It is important to distinguish the option contract from the ultimate contract it contemplates. An example drawn from the business world illustrates this distinction. Suppose Ira Investor enters into an option contract with Commodities Co. Under the option, Ira has the right to buy 100 tons of pork bellies for $300,000 at any time before January 1 of a specified year. Ira pays $10 for this option. Under the option contract, Commodities Co. has the obligation to keep its offer to sell pork bellies open until the stated date. Ira has given consideration, his $10 payment, but he has no obligation to accept the offer or ultimately buy the pork bellies. If Ira decides to accept the offer, a second contract will come into being in which Ira has an obligation to pay $300,000, and Commodities Co. has an obligation to deliver 100 tons of pork bellies. The option contract is preliminary to, but distinct from, the contract to buy and sell pork bellies.

[handwritten margin note: acceptance results in a second contract]

Although courts look for consideration as one element of an option contract, they sometimes find consideration in this context when they wouldn't otherwise. In Chapter 9, we noted that courts tend to be suspicious of consideration that appears to have been manufactured for the sole purpose of making an otherwise unenforceable promise enforceable. The courts may refer to it as "nominal" or "sham" consideration and refuse to find a contract. With an option contract, however, the courts are much less likely to inquire whether a nominal payment induced the promise to keep the offer open. Likewise, some written

[handwritten margin note: not for option contracts]

Courts tend to be more lenient on option contracts

a contract can say there is consideration but there never was

contracts recite that consideration has been paid, when in fact it has not. In ordinary circumstances, a plaintiff challenging a contract may introduce evidence that the recited consideration was neither given nor expected. If so, the court may decline to enforce the alleged contract due to a lack of consid- *not enforced* eration. Here, too, the courts tend to be more lenient in the context of option contracts. In an option contract, a mere recital of consideration may be sufficient even if the consideration was never paid. Restatement, Second §87(1)(a) advocates this approach, and provides that an offer is binding as an option contract if it "is in writing and signed by the offeror, recites a purported consideration for the making of the offer, and proposes an exchange on fair terms within a reasonable time."

① *in writing*
② *signed by offeror*
③ *recites consideration*
④ *exchange of fair terms in a reasonable time*

What explains this slackening in consideration doctrine? Courts recognize that option contracts serve important commercial purposes. Option contracts allow offerees to plan, investigate, and deliberate without the fear that offers will be revoked before a decision to accept is made. Courts also acknowledge that option contracts often come at a stage where the parties are just beginning to bargain. Cumbersome consideration requirements at too early a stage may cause negotiations to crumble and foil consummation of the ultimate contract. The formalities of nominal consideration or written recitals of consideration may be sufficient to protect the offeror under these circumstances, given the limited obligation that the offeror assumes.

option contracts come early

■ PROBLEM 11.1

Sally Student just graduated from college, and is planning to go to law school next fall. She is trying to earn some money mowing lawns this summer, to help pay her law school tuition. Sally has been going door to door, trying to line up regular customers. She knocks at Louie Leisure's door, and tells him that she would be willing to mow his lawn every Monday morning for the next ten weeks, for a total charge of $1,000. Louie relishes the idea of having someone else mow his lawn, a job he dreads, but he also knows that he ought to ask his wife Louise before he commits to such a substantial expenditure. Louie tells Sally that he is very interested, and asks whether he could get back to her later that same afternoon. Under each of the factual variations below, decide whether Sally and Louie have a contract under the principles described above. If so, determine what their respective obligations are, if any.

just a promise, not enforceable

    (a) Sally replies, "Sure; just let me know before 5 P.M. or I may give the Monday morning slot to someone else." Louie agrees.

    (b) Sally replies instead, "Sure; I'll need $5 to hold the Monday morning slot for you. Be sure to let me know if you want it before 5 P.M. or I may give the slot to someone else." Louie agrees and hands her $5.

enforceable

[handwritten: valid consideration]

[handwritten: maybe a lenient court will say this is ok]

(c)   Instead of saying anything, Sally fills out a form and hands it to Louie. The form says, "In consideration of $5, Sally Student agrees to reserve her Monday morning mowing slot for Louie Leisure until 5 P.M." Both parties sign the form, but no money changes hands.

(d)   Before Sally could say anything, Louie continues, "I agree to take the Monday morning slot. I'll pay you $200 down by 5 P.M. today and the remainder after you have completed your tenth mowing job. The only hitch will be if my wife Louise objects, in which case I won't be able to go through with the deal." Sally replies, "Sounds great to me."

[handwritten: Counter offer and acceptance?]

B   PROMISSORY ESTOPPEL AND OFFERS

[handwritten: options may be impractical]

Parties do not always have the foresight to enter into an option contract. Sometimes option contracts are simply not practical. As we have seen, where there is no option contract, the general principle is that an offer may be freely revoked. However, free revocation of offers can cause hardship in some circumstances. Courts are not always unmindful of this hardship and have recognized exceptions to this general principle. We saw one example of this in Chapter 5, where we discussed Restatement, Second §45. As you may recall, §45 addresses situations where acceptance is through performance only but the performance cannot be accomplished instantaneously. In these types of situations, it seems particularly unfair to allow the offeror to snatch the offer away from the offeree just when she is on the brink of claiming her reward. The offeree cannot protect herself by simply promising to perform. A mere promise would not form a contract, because the offer looks only to actual performance as the sole means of acceptance. The requested performance takes time, and the offeree has no practical way to protect herself while she is performing. Restatement, Second §45 creates an option contract once the offeree begins (or tenders) the requested performance. Although the offeree has no obligation to complete

[handwritten: began performance no chance to revoke]

her performance, the offeror has lost the power to withdraw its offer. Restatement, Second §45 is not stated in terms of promissory estoppel or detrimental reliance, but a similar concern for the offeree motivates it.

We will examine analogous claims of hardship from the world of construction bidding and contracting. When a general contractor wants to bid on a construction contract, it often first solicits bids from subcontractors to perform discrete portions of the work. The general contractor then uses the information that it receives from potential subcontractors to submit its own bid for the overall project. If the general contractor is awarded the job, it is not unusual for a dispute to arise between the general contractor and a subcontractor with whom it had dealt earlier. Some of these disputes raise issues similar to, but different from, those presented by offers to enter into unilateral contracts. Since these cases arise perennially, they give us an unusual opportunity to see how the law has developed over time in the context of comparable disputes. We begin with perhaps the most famous of these disputes, that of *Drennan v. Star Paving Co.*

DRENNAN v. STAR PAVING CO.

51 Cal. 2d 409, 333 P.2d 757 (1958)
California Supreme Court

TRAYNOR, Justice.

Defendant appeals from a judgment for plaintiff in an action to recover damages caused by defendant's refusal to perform certain paving work according to a bid it submitted to plaintiff.

On July 28, 1955, plaintiff, a licensed general contractor, was preparing a bid on the "Monte Vista School Job" in the Lancaster school district. Bids had to be submitted before 8:00 P.M. Plaintiff testified that it was customary in that area for general contractors to receive the bids of subcontractors by telephone on the day set for bidding and to rely on them in computing their own bids. Thus on that day plaintiff's secretary, Mrs. Johnson, received by telephone between fifty and seventy-five subcontractors' bids for various parts of the school job. As each bid came in, she wrote it on a special form, which she brought into plaintiff's office. He then posted it on a master cost sheet setting forth the names and bids of all subcontractors. His own bid had to include the names of subcontractors who were to perform one-half of one per cent or more of the construction work, and he had also to provide a bidder's bond of ten per cent of his total bid of $317,385 as a guarantee that he would enter the contract if awarded the work.

Late in the afternoon, Mrs. Johnson had a telephone conversation with Kenneth R. Hoon, an estimator for defendant. He gave his name and telephone number and stated that he was bidding for defendant for the paving work at the Monte Vista School according to plans and specifications and that his bid was $7,131.60. At Mrs. Johnson's request he repeated his bid. Plaintiff listened to the bid over an extension telephone in his office and posted it on the master sheet after receiving the bid form from Mrs. Johnson. Defendant's was the lowest bid for the paving. Plaintiff computed his own bid accordingly and submitted it with the name of defendant as the subcontractor for the paving. When the bids were opened on July 28th, plaintiff's proved to be the lowest, and he was awarded the contract.

On his way to Los Angeles the next morning plaintiff stopped at defendant's office. The first person he met was defendant's construction engineer, Mr. Oppenheimer. Plaintiff testified: "I introduced myself and he immediately told me that they had made a mistake in their bid to me the night before, they couldn't do it for the price they had bid, and I told him I would expect him to carry through with their original bid because I had used it in compiling my bid and the job was being awarded them. And I would have to go and do the job according to my bid and I would expect them to do the same." Defendant refused to do the paving work for less than $15,000. Plaintiff testified that he "got figures from other people" and after trying for several months to get as low a bid as possible engaged L & H Paving Company, a firm in Lancaster, to do the work for $10,948.60.

[margin note: people who → actually did the paving]

The trial court found on substantial evidence that defendant made a definite offer to do the paving on the Monte Vista job according to the plans and specifications for $7,131.60, and that plaintiff relied on defendant's bid in computing his own bid for the school job and naming defendant therein as the subcontractor for the paving work. Accordingly, it entered judgment for plaintiff in the amount of $3,817.00 (the difference between defendant's bid and the cost of the paving to plaintiff) plus costs. Defendant contends that there was no enforceable contract between the parties on the ground that it made a revocable offer and revoked it before plaintiff communicated his acceptance to defendant.

[margin note: expectation damages △ claim]

There is no evidence that defendant offered to make its bid irrevocable in exchange for plaintiff's use of its figures in computing his bid. Nor is there evidence that would warrant interpreting plaintiff's use of defendant's bid as the acceptance thereof, binding plaintiff, on condition he received the main contract, to award the subcontract to defendant. In sum, there was neither an option supported by consideration nor a bilateral contract binding on both parties.

[margin note: no option contract or bilateral contract requiring it to stay open]

Plaintiff contends, however, that he relied to his detriment on defendant's offer and that defendant must therefore answer in damages for its refusal to perform. Thus the question is squarely presented: Did plaintiff's reliance make defendant's offer irrevocable? ... [The rule of the First Restatement of Contracts, §90] applies in this state. Defendant's offer constituted a promise to perform on such conditions as were stated expressly or by implication therein or annexed thereto by operation of law. Defendant had reason to expect that if its bid proved the lowest it would be used by plaintiff. It induced "action ... of a definite and substantial character on the part of the promisee."

[margin note: issue →]

Had defendant's bid expressly stated or clearly implied that it was revocable at any time before acceptance we would treat it accordingly. It was silent on revocation, however, and we must therefore determine whether there are conditions to the right of revocation imposed by law or reasonably inferable in fact. In the analogous problem of an offer for a unilateral contract, the theory is now obsolete that the offer is revocable at any time before complete performance. Thus section 45 of the [First] Restatement of Contracts provides: "If an offer for a unilateral contract is made, and part of the consideration requested in the offer is given or tendered by the offeree in response thereto, the offeror is bound by a contract, the duty of immediate performance of which is conditional on the full consideration being given or tendered within the time stated in the offer, or, if no time is stated therein, within a reasonable time."[1] In explanation,

---

[1] This language differs from that of Restatement, Second §45 but not in ways that need concern us here. —EDS.

comment b states that the "main offer includes as a subsidiary promise, necessarily implied, that if part of the requested performance is given, the offeror will not revoke his offer, and that if tender is made it will be accepted. Part performance or tender may thus furnish consideration for the subsidiary promise. Moreover, merely acting in justifiable reliance on an offer may in some cases serve as sufficient reason for making a promise binding (see §90)."

Whether implied in fact or law, the subsidiary promise serves to preclude the injustice that would result if the offer could be revoked after the offeree had acted in detrimental reliance thereon. Reasonable reliance resulting in a foreseeable prejudicial change in position affords a compelling basis also for implying a subsidiary promise not to revoke an offer for a bilateral contract.

The absence of consideration is not fatal to the enforcement of such a promise. It is true that in the case of unilateral contracts the Restatement finds consideration for the implied subsidiary promise in the part performance of the bargained-for exchange, but its reference to section 90 makes clear that consideration for such a promise is not always necessary. The very purpose of section 90 is to make a promise binding even though there was no consideration "in the sense of something that is bargained for and given in exchange." (See 1 Corbin, *Contracts* 634 et seq.) Reasonable reliance serves to hold the offeror in lieu of the consideration ordinarily required to make the offer binding. In a case involving similar facts the Supreme Court of South Dakota stated that "we believe that reason and justice demand that the doctrine (of section 90) be applied to the present facts. We cannot believe that by accepting this doctrine as controlling in the state of facts before us we will abolish the requirement of a consideration in contract cases, in any different sense than an ordinary estoppel abolishes some legal requirement in its application. We are of the opinion, therefore, that the defendants in executing the agreement (which was not supported by consideration) made a promise which they should have reasonably expected would induce the plaintiff to submit a bid based thereon to the Government, that such promise did induce this action, and that injustice can be avoided only by enforcement of the promise." *Northwestern Engineering Co. v. Ellerman*, 69 S.D. 397, 408, 10 N.W.2d 879, 884; . . . cf. *James Baird Co. v. Gimbel Bros.*, 2 Cir., 64 F.2d 344.

When plaintiff used defendant's offer in computing his own bid, he bound himself to perform in reliance on defendant's terms. Though defendant did not bargain for this use of its bid neither did defendant make it idly, indifferent to whether it would be used or not. On the contrary it is reasonable to suppose that defendant submitted its bid to obtain the subcontract. It was bound to realize the substantial possibility that its bid would be the lowest, and that it would be included by plaintiff in his bid. It was to its own interest that the contractor be awarded the general contract; the lower the subcontract bid, the lower the general contractor's bid was likely to be and the greater its chance of acceptance and hence the greater defendant's chance of getting the paving subcontract. Defendant had reason not only to expect plaintiff to rely on its bid but to want him to. Clearly defendant had a stake in plaintiff's reliance on its bid.

Given this interest and the fact that plaintiff is bound by his own bid, it is only fair that plaintiff should have at least an opportunity to accept defendant's bid after the general contract has been awarded to him.

It bears noting that a general contractor is not free to delay acceptance after he has been awarded the general contract in the hope of getting a better price. Nor can he reopen bargaining with the subcontractor and at the same time claim a continuing right to accept the original offer. In the present case plaintiff promptly informed defendant that plaintiff was being awarded the job and that the subcontract was being awarded to defendant.

Defendant contends, however, that its bid was the result of mistake and that it was therefore entitled to revoke it. It relies on the rescission cases of *M. F. Kemper Const. Co. v. City of Los Angeles*, 37 Cal. 2d 696, 235 P.2d 7, and *Brunzell Const. Co. v. G.J. Weisbrod, Inc.*, 134 Cal. App. 2d 278, 285 P.2d 989. In those cases, however, the bidder's mistake was known or should have been known to the offeree, and the offeree could be placed in status quo. Of course, if plaintiff had reason to believe that defendant's bid was in error, he could not justifiably rely on it, and section 90 would afford no basis for enforcing it. Plaintiff, however, had no reason to know that defendant had made a mistake in submitting its bid, since there was usually a variance of 160 per cent between the highest and lowest bids for paving in the desert around Lancaster. He committed himself to performing the main contract in reliance on defendant's figures. Under these circumstances defendant's mistake, far from relieving it of its obligation, constitutes an additional reason for enforcing it, for it misled plaintiff as to the cost of doing the paving. Even had it been clearly understood that defendant's offer was revocable until accepted, it would not necessarily follow that defendant had no duty to exercise reasonable care in preparing its bid. It presented its bid with knowledge of the substantial possibility that it would be used by plaintiff; it could foresee the harm that would ensue from an erroneous underestimate of the cost. Moreover, it was motivated by its own business interest. Whether or not these considerations alone would justify recovery for negligence had the case been tried on that theory, they are persuasive that defendant's mistake should not defeat recovery under the rule of section 90 of the Restatement of Contracts. As between the subcontractor who made the bid and the general contractor who reasonably relied on it, the loss resulting from the mistake should fall on the party who caused it. . . .

The judgment is affirmed.

■ QUESTIONS

(1)   In this case, is the bid by its terms revocable or irrevocable?

(2)   In *Drennan*, the parties could have insisted on an explicit option contract (supported by consideration) before they went forward. Yet they didn't. As it turns out, this type of dispute is relatively common. What practical advantages might there be to going forward without an explicit option contract, even in the face of legal uncertainty?

▪ PROBLEM 11.2

You may have noticed in *Drennan* that Justice Traynor noted in passing the case of *James Baird Co. v. Gimbel Bros*, 64 F.2d 344 (2d Cir. 1933). That case, decided approximately 25 years earlier, also involved a construction bidding dispute. As in *Drennan*, a subcontractor submitted a mistaken bid (this time for linoleum) at approximately half of what it should have charged. Also as in *Drennan*, the contractor in turn submitted a bid relying on the figures provided by the subcontractor. When the subcontractor informed the contractor of its error, the contractor formally accepted the subcontractor's bid, insisted on performance, and ultimately sued for breach of contract. The opinion in the case, written by Judge Learned Hand, took a decidedly different approach to the question of whether the subcontractor and contractor had entered a contract:

> Unless there are circumstances to take it out of the ordinary doctrine, since the offer was withdrawn before it was accepted, the acceptance was too late. To meet this the plaintiff argues as follows: It was a reasonable implication from the defendant's offer that it should be irrevocable in case the plaintiff acted upon it, that is to say, used the prices quoted in making its bid, thus putting itself in a position from which it could not withdraw without great loss. . . . The inevitable implication from all this was that when the [plaintiff] acted upon it, they accepted the offer and promised to pay for the linoleum, in case their bid were accepted.
>
> It was of course possible for the parties to make such a contract, and the question is merely as to what they meant; that is, what is to be imputed to the words they used. . . . However, it seems entirely clear that the contractors did not suppose that they accepted the offer merely by putting in their bids. If, for example, the successful one had repudiated the contract with the public authorities after it had been awarded to him, certainly the defendant could not have sued him for a breach. If he had become bankrupt, the defendant could not prove against his estate. It seems plain therefore that there was no contract between them. . . . The contractors had a ready escape from their difficulty by insisting upon a contract before they used the figures; and in commercial transactions it does not in the end promote justice to seek strained interpretations in aid of those who do not protect themselves.
>
> But the plaintiff says that even though no bilateral contract was made, the defendant should be held under the doctrine of "promissory estoppel." This is to be chiefly found in those cases where persons subscribe to a venture, usually charitable, and are held to their promises after it has been completed. It has been applied much more broadly, however, and has now been generalized in section 90, of the [First] Restatement of Contracts. We may arguendo accept it as it there reads, for it does not apply to the case at bar. Offers are ordinarily made in exchange for a consideration, either a counter-promise or some other act which the promisor wishes to secure.

In such cases they propose bargains; they presuppose that each promise or performance is an inducement to the other. But a man may make a promise without expecting an equivalent; a donative promise, conditional or absolute. The common law provided for such by sealed instruments, and it is unfortunate that these are no longer generally available. The doctrine of "promissory estoppel" is to avoid the harsh results of allowing the promisor in such a case to repudiate, when the promisee has acted in reliance upon the promise. But an offer for an exchange is not meant to become a promise until a consideration has been received, either a counter-promise or whatever else is stipulated. To extend it would be to hold the offeror regardless of the stipulated condition of his offer. In the case at bar the defendant offered to deliver the linoleum in exchange for the plaintiff's acceptance, not for its bid, which was a matter of indifference to it. That offer could become a promise to deliver only when the equivalent was received; that is, when the plaintiff promised to take and pay for it. There is no room in such a situation for the doctrine of "promissory estoppel."

Nor can the offer be regarded as of an option, giving the plaintiff the right seasonably to accept the linoleum at the quoted prices if its bid was accepted, but not binding it to take and pay, if it could get a better bargain elsewhere. There is not the least reason to suppose that the defendant meant to subject itself to such one-sided obligation. True, if so construed, the doctrine of "promissory estoppel" might apply, the plaintiff having acted in reliance upon it, though, so far as we have found, the decisions are otherwise. As to that, however, we need not declare ourselves.

Catalog the possible theories of recovery analyzed by Justice Traynor in *Drennan*, and compare those considered by Judge Hand in this excerpt from *Baird*. Where, precisely, do they differ?

In Section A, we note that the Restatement, Second, recommends a liberal approach to consideration doctrine in the context of option contracts. It also suggests that, under appropriate circumstances, an option contract can be created by reliance. Restatement, Second §87 provides in full as follows:

RESTATEMENT, SECOND §87. OPTION CONTRACT

(1) An offer is binding as an option contract if it

(a) is in writing and signed by the offeror, recites a purported consideration for the making of the offer, and proposes an exchange on fair terms within a reasonable time; or

(b) is made irrevocable by statute.

(2) An offer which the offeror should reasonably expect to induce action or forbearance of a substantial character on the part of the offeree before

acceptance and which does induce such action or forbearance is binding as an option contract to the extent necessary to avoid injustice.

■ QUESTION

consideration is not always necessary

How does Restatement, Second §87(2) differ from Restatement, Second §90? Is it consistent with the analysis in *Drennan*? Is it consistent with the portion of the analysis in *Baird* quoted in Problem 11.2?

C ■ FIRM OFFERS UNDER THE UCC

Where short-term offers to buy or sell goods are concerned, the drafters of the UCC decided to provide a clear method to make such offers irrevocable. Straightforward rules, they believed, would facilitate commerce and give effect to deliberate intentions of the parties. Especially where merchants were involved, the drafters saw no need to preserve the common law requirements of consideration or reliance. Read UCC 2-205, set out below, and then consider the following problems.

UCC 2-205. FIRM OFFERS

signed written terms of a promise to keep an option open is not revocable

An offer by a merchant to buy or sell goods in a signed writing which by its terms gives assurance that it will be held open is not revocable, for lack of consideration, during the time stated or if no time is stated for a reasonable time, but in no event may such period of irrevocability exceed three months; but any such term of assurance on a form supplied by the offeree must be separately signed by the offeror.

■ PROBLEM 11.3

Giant Co.'s drill press breaks down, and it seeks an immediate replacement. It faxes a signed purchase order on letterhead to one of its suppliers, Machinery Inc. The purchase order states in full "We hereby order one drill press, model XYZ, for immediate delivery at the address listed above. We will pay your list price of $50,000 in cash at delivery. We have been pleased with your service in the past, and commit to work with you if you are able to accommodate us. Advise ASAP if you are not be able to deliver within five business days, as we will need to seek another supplier." Immediately after faxing the purchase order, Giant Co. finds an equivalent drill press locally. It wonders if it can freely revoke its purchase order. Advise Giant Co.

promise to stay open

■ PROBLEM 11.4

Honor Guest caters wedding receptions, anniversary parties, and graduation ceremonies. Her practice is to sign contracts with her customers in which she commits to a fixed price for the affairs. Honor buys food, wine, and decorations and ties them all together into a glorious theme. When her customers first contact her, she puts together two or three proposals, each reflecting a different vision. She contacts her suppliers in advance and asks them to tell her how much it will cost to provide the various items she will need. She adds a profit margin for herself and comes up with a total price for each proposal. The customers then choose among the proposals. The entire process, from the day she starts gathering cost estimates to the day she enters into a formal contract with her customers, typically takes six to eight weeks. The <u>affairs themselves often do not happen until six months to a year later</u>.

Recently, several suppliers have refused to provide Honor needed items at the prices they had quoted, and she has suffered losses as a result. She is considering asking her suppliers to provide "firm" offers, rather than mere cost estimates.

sale of goods

firm offer

(a) Generally, Article 2 of the UCC applies to this situation, and UCC 2-205 is particularly relevant. Why? *> 3 months*

(b) Honor would like to prepare a form for her suppliers to fill out when they make a firm offer. She would like it to comply with UCC 2-205. Prepare a form for her to use. If you need further information, specify what it is.

(c) What advantages and disadvantages does UCC 2-205 present to Honor? Does she have any alternatives? *> 3 months   option contracts*

D   PROVISIONS IN THE UNIDROIT PRINCIPLES AND CISG ON THE REVOCABILITY OF OFFERS

Both the UNIDROIT Principles and the CISG allow offers to be irrevocable under certain circumstances. Generally, a party can make an offer irrevocable simply by saying so. Likewise, in some circumstances, reliance can make an offer irrevocable.

Article 2.1.4 of the UNIDROIT Principles states that an offer cannot be revoked if it indicates, whether by stating a fixed time for acceptance or otherwise, that it is irrevocable. This Article further states that an offer cannot be revoked if it was reasonable for the offeree to rely on the offer as being irrevocable and the offeree has acted in reliance on the offer. Article 16 of the CISG is to similar effect.

■ QUESTION

In the context of international transactions, the UNIDROIT Principles and the CISG liberally allow offers to be irrevocable. Do you favor retaining a consideration requirement for domestic option contracts? Why or why not? If you favor abolishing or further limiting the consideration requirement, under what circumstances would you suggest an offer should be deemed irrevocable?

Obligation Based on Unjust Enrichment and Material Benefit

 UNJUST ENRICHMENT

1. The Relationship Between Unjust Enrichment and Contract

Unlike contract or promissory estoppel, unjust enrichment is not based on a promise. Rather, it is a cause of action that arises where the claimant has conferred a benefit on the recipient under circumstances that make it unjust for the recipient to keep the benefit without paying for it. Sometimes the reason for conferring the benefit may have been a contractual relationship that terminated as a result of breach or for some other reason, but sometimes the circumstances under which the benefit was given may have nothing to do with contract at all. Therefore, although unjust enrichment has some relationship to contract, it is not a promissory theory of liability, and it is distinct from contract. It functions as a separate and independent cause of action.

For example, the owner of a house entered into a contract to sell it for $150,000. Before the closing date, the seller told the buyer that he refused to proceed with the sale. This is a breach of contract, which would entitle the buyer to expectation damages in contract. Expectation damages are measured by the buyer's loss of expectation as a result of the breach of the contract. For example, if the buyer would have to pay $160,000 to buy an equivalent house on the market, her loss of expectation is $10,000—the difference between what she expected to pay for the house and the higher price that she had to pay for the substitute. However, say that the buyer had made a down payment of $15,000 to the seller at the time of entering the contract. The seller then

403

breached the contract by refusing to proceed with the sale. The buyer can buy an equivalent house on the market for $145,000. In this case, the buyer has suffered no expectation damages because the price of a substitute is lower than the contract price. Nevertheless, she can still claim the return (restitution) of the $15,000 down payment. The purpose of this claim is to restore to the buyer a benefit that she conferred on the seller that it would be unfair for the seller to keep: Because the seller has breached the contract, there is no longer a justification for his keeping the down payment, and its retention would unjustly enrich him.

In the above example, the buyer's claim for restitution of the down payment under a theory of unjust enrichment arises in the context of a breach of contract. However, unjust enrichment is also available in situations in which a contract is unenforceable or the contract has a defect that allows one of the parties to set it aside (avoid it). For example, let's say that the contract for the sale of the house was unsigned by the seller so that it did not comply with the statute of frauds. Although the buyer could not enforce the contract,[1] if the seller reneges, the seller no longer has any right to the $15,000 down payment, and the buyer could recover the $15,000 under the theory of unjust enrichment. The same would be true if either party is able to set aside the contract on grounds such as fraud or duress (discussed in Chapter 13). Upon avoidance of the contract, the seller has no right to keep the down payment, and the buyer has a cause of action in unjust enrichment to get the down payment back.

Unjust enrichment may also serve as a remedy to restore a benefit that was conferred under circumstances that did not give rise to a contract. For example, suppose that a person collapses while walking down the street. He is rushed, unconscious, to the nearest hospital, where he is given emergency care. Although it cannot be said that he contracted for the care—he was unconscious and could not make a contract with the hospital—the principle of unjust enrichment would give the hospital a basis for claiming that he pay the cost of the medical services.

2. The Elements of Unjust Enrichment

The two elements of unjust enrichment are suggested by its name: One party must have been enriched by obtaining property, services, or some other economic benefit from the other; and the circumstances must be such that it would be unjust for the beneficiary to keep the benefit of that enrichment without paying or compensating the other party for the benefit. If the court finds that there has been unjust enrichment, the remedy granted is restitution, which may consist of an order for the return of the benefit itself (if it is tangible and the recipient still has it) or a money judgment for its value.

---

[1] The mere payment of the down payment would not be enough to satisfy the part performance exception to the statute of frauds, which is discussed in Chapter 8, Section E.

a. Injustice

It is not always unjust for a person to keep a benefit without payment. One of the reasons why this may not be unjust is because the benefit was intended to be gratuitous. For example, think back to the first case we studied in relation to the consideration doctrine: If, in the *DeLeo* case, the donor had given his donation of $25,000 to the congregation, rather than having just promised it, the gift would have been executed and would not be subject to invalidation because of a lack of consideration. Had that happened, there would be no injustice in allowing the congregation to keep the money without giving the donor a quid pro quo because he had intended it as a gift. For the same reason, you can wear that loud reindeer-and-snowflake-themed scarf given to you by your aunt last Christmas without worrying about her demanding that you reimburse her for its price. Indeed, even beyond gifts of nasty haberdashery, the usual assumption, in the absence of clear agreement to the contrary, is that services rendered by a family member or close friend are intended to be gratuitous. For example, in *Symons v. Heaton*, 316 P.3d 1171 (Wyo. 2014), Curtis Symons and Gary Plachek had been lifelong friends. Plachek was an alcoholic and was not able to care for himself properly, so during the last ten years of Plachek's life, Symons moved in with him, cared for him, and managed his affairs. After Plachek died, Symons claimed about $250,000 from his estate to compensate him for taking care of Plachek. Symons could not prove that the parties ever entered into an express or implied in fact contract under which he would be paid for his services. The court denied his unjust enrichment claim as well because he conferred the benefits on Plachek out of concern for him, and there was no indication that he expected payment for his acts of friendship.

Courts sometimes use the word "volunteer" to describe a person who confers a benefit with gratuitous intent. This word can be confusing because we usually assume that it means merely that a person acted with free will and without compulsion. Here it means more than that. In this context a "volunteer" also acts without intent to be compensated.

It is also not unjust for a person to retain a benefit that was imposed and cannot be returned; that is, the person who conferred the benefit had no justification for providing it without being asked, and the benefit cannot simply be given back. For example, Dusty Buggy's filthy car is parked outside her house. Without asking her, Soapy Bucket, her neighbor, goes out into the street and washes the car. Soapy should not be able to claim the value of that service because he had no business acting without Dusty's authorization. He should have contracted with her before doing the work. In the language often used by courts, Soapy is an "officious intermeddler," and the law should not encourage his meddling. The benefit has clearly been imposed without any choice on Dusty's part and because it is a service, it cannot be returned. Therefore, if Soapy was allowed to recover the value of washing the car, Dusty would be forced into paying for a service that she did not request and perhaps did not even want.

This case differs from the example of the hospital in which there was an emergency requiring immediate action and the recipient of the service was unconscious and unable to contract. In such a case, unless the circumstances indicate otherwise, it would be reasonable for the hospital to assume that the recipient would have wanted the care even though she could not ask for it. Therefore, the hospital is not intermeddling in providing it.

The equities change if the imposed benefit is property with tangible existence, which is returnable. For example, instead of cleaning Dusty's car, say that Soapy attached a cute license plate holder to it. If, on seeing the holder and reasonably understanding that it was not intended as a gift, Dusty decides to keep it instead of rejecting it, she has accepted the benefit. Her retention of the benefit when she could have returned it may cure Soapy's initial intermeddling, and may justify making her pay for it. If she does not want to pay for it, she should just ask Soapy to remove it. (Although the basis for making Dusty pay for the holder is used here to illustrate unjust enrichment, notice how closely the facts resemble an offer accepted by conduct where the offeree exercises ownership rights over the property. As we discuss below, the facts of a case may be ambiguous enough to make it arguable that the parties had an actual contract. If an actual contract can be established, it is not necessary to use the alternative theory of unjust enrichment.)

b. Enrichment—the Benefit

As noted above, the remedy for unjust enrichment is restitution, either by return of the benefit or a money judgment for its value. Where the benefit itself can be restored, such as in the case of the license plate holder, the court may order specific restitution of the item. However, often the actual benefit received cannot itself be returned. This may be because it has been consumed or lost, or because the benefit consisted of a service that is intangible (for example, the medical services provided by the hospital). In this case, restitution takes the form of a money judgment for the value of the benefit. A money judgment is also the necessary form of relief where the benefit is itself the payment of money (as in the example concerning the down payment for the house).

If restitution is based on the monetary value of the benefit, the court must determine its value. This is easy where the benefit is simply a money payment: Its value is self-evident. However, if the benefit is property that cannot be returned or is a service, it must be evaluated. Although other standards of evaluation are sometimes used in particular cases, the most common standard used is the market value of the goods or services. A Latin term is often used to describe this value: *quantum meruit* (as much as deserved) refers to the market value of services, and *quantum valebant* (as much as they are worth) is used to denote the market value of goods.

3. Terminology

The terminology used in this area often confuses students. We have already used some of the terms of art with which you should become familiar: "Unjust enrichment" refers to the theory of liability—the basis for giving relief; "restitution" refers to the remedy for unjust enrichment,[2] which can be measured by a market standard called "quantum meruit" or "quantum valebant."

Because of the historical roots of unjust enrichment, two other potentially confusing terms are often encountered. As we mention in dealing with the origins of contract law in Chapter 1, early common law was very rigid and operated on set writs or forms of action. When courts saw the need to develop new bases for relief, they adapted existing forms of action. There was no recognized claim for unjust enrichment, so courts fitted it into "assumpsit," the writ that had been established (also by interpolation) for contract. They did this by creating a legal fiction that the benefit had been contracted for. As a result, the unjust enrichment claim came to be known as "quasi-contract" or "contract implied in law." This signifies that it is not a real contract case but is merely treated as such for the procedural reason of fitting it into the existing contract form of action. As we have moved beyond the formalism of early law, we no longer need the legal fiction. Unjust enrichment has long been recognized as a distinct cause of action. However, the old terms have never disappeared, and courts frequently use them as alternative names for the basis of awarding restitutionary relief. It is important to note that even though they contain the word "contract," neither "quasi-contract" nor its synonym, "contract implied in law," refer to a real contract. A contract implied in law must be distinguished from one implied in fact, which is a real contract, created by conduct rather than by express agreement.

4. The Distinction Between Factually and Legally Implied Contracts

In some cases, it can be very difficult to distinguish between a contract implied in fact (a real contract implied by conduct) and a contract implied in law (the legal fiction of a quasi-contract designed to provide the basis for restitutionary relief on principles of unjust enrichment). This is because in some circumstances the conduct of the parties is ambiguous enough that it is hard to tell whether liability is based on actual agreement inferred from the parties' actions or on the need to provide restitution to prevent unjust enrichment. For example: A pipe in a home bursts, and the homeowner calls in a plumber to fix it. No mention is made of payment for the service either during the telephone call or

---

[2] However, be warned that the semantic distinction between "unjust enrichment" as the cause of action and "restitution" as the remedy is not always fastidiously observed. Courts sometimes use the word "restitution" to refer to the cause of action itself.

while the plumber is at the house, making the repairs. Based on common experience and a general expectation that plumbers do not repair pipes as a free service, we can readily infer from the parties' conduct that they intended a contract under which the plumber would be paid a customary or reasonable rate for his services. However, the plumber's claim for payment may seem to fit just as well under principles of unjust enrichment: Because the plumber was neither a volunteer (he did not intend to confer the benefit gratuitously) nor an intermeddler (he did not impose the service but responded to the homeowner's request), he would be entitled to restitution of the reasonable market value of his services.

Because the resolution of this example seems to be the same, whether we treat it as a contract implied in fact or a contract implied in law, there may not be a practical reason to struggle to characterize it as one or the other. However, sometimes it could make a difference. For example, the distinction between quasi-contract and contract implied in fact has legal consequences in the following three situations: The statute of limitations may be different for contract and unjust enrichment; the basis for determining the price to be paid for services may be different, because quasi-contract confines the price to market value, while some different amount (say, based on the service provider's customary charge) may be claimable in contract; and other damages, such as consequential damages, may be available in a claim on an actual contract but not in an unjust enrichment claim.

The close relationship and subtle distinction between actual contract implied in fact and quasi-contract are illustrated in the next two cases. In both, the courts make parallel arguments to address alternative contractual and unjust enrichment claims and reach the same result under the alternative theories.

MARTIN v. LITTLE, BROWN & CO.

304 Pa. Super. 424, 450 A.2d 984 (1981)
Pennsylvania Superior Court

WIEAND, Judge.

This appeal was taken from an order sustaining . . . a demurrer to appellant's pro se[3] complaint in assumpsit. The trial court held that a contract had not been made and that there could be no recovery on quantum meruit where appellant had volunteered information which enabled appellee, a publisher of books, to effect a recovery against a third person for copyright infringement. We agree and, accordingly, affirm.

---

[3] "Pro se" means that the appellant acted on his own behalf, without legal representation. Apparently (as revealed in a portion of the case that we omit), Martin was a law student putting his legal education to good use. —EDS.

The averments of the complaint disclose that on September 28, 1976, the appellant, James L. Martin, directed a letter to Bantam Books, Inc. in which he advised the addressee that portions of a paperback publication entitled "How to Buy Stocks" had been plagiarized by the authors of a later book entitled "Planning Your Financial Future." Appellant's letter offered to provide a copy of the book, in which appellant had highlighted the plagiarized passages, with marginal references to the pages and paragraphs of the book from which the passages had been copied. By letter dated October 21, 1976 and signed by Robin Paris, Editorial Assistant, the appellee, Little, Brown and Company, Inc., invited appellant to send his copy of "Planning Your Financial Future." This was done, and appellee acknowledged receipt thereof in writing. Thereafter, appellant made inquiries about appellee's investigation but received no response. Appellant was persistent, however, and upon learning that appellee had agreed with his assertions and was pursuing a claim of copyright infringement, he demanded compensation for his services. Appellee denied that it had contracted with appellant or was otherwise obligated to compensate appellant for his work or for his calling the infringement to the publisher's attention. Nevertheless, appellee offered an honorarium in the form of a check for two hundred dollars, which appellant retained but did not cash. Instead, he filed suit to recover one-third of the recovery effected by appellee.

These facts and all reasonable inferences therefrom have been admitted by appellee's demurrer. In determining whether they are sufficient to state a cause of action we are guided by the rule that a demurrer may be sustained only in clear cases, and all doubts must be resolved in favor of the sufficiency of the complaint.

The facts alleged in the complaint are insufficient to establish a contractual relationship between appellant and appellee. Appellant's initial letter did not expressly or by implication suggest a desire to negotiate. Neither did appellee's letter of October 21, 1976, which invited appellant to send his copy of the offending publication, constitute an offer to enter a unilateral contract. . . . Appellant's letter did not suggest that he intended to be paid, and appellee's response did not contain an offer to pay appellant if he forwarded his copy of the infringing work. In brief, payment to appellant was not discussed in any of the correspondence which preceded the forwarding of appellant's work to appellee.

"A contract, implied in fact, is an actual contract which arises where the parties agree upon the obligations to be incurred, but their intention, instead of being expressed in words, is inferred from their acts in the light of the surrounding circumstances." *Cameron v. Eynon*, 332 Pa. 529, 3 A.2d 423 (1939). . . . "Generally, there is an implication of a promise to pay for valuable services rendered with the knowledge and approval of the recipient, in the absence of a showing to the contrary. A promise to pay the reasonable value of the service is implied where one performs for another, with the other's knowledge, a useful service of a character that is usually charged for, and the latter expresses no dissent or avails himself of the service. A promise to pay for services can, however, only be implied when they are rendered in such circumstances as authorized the party performing to entertain a reasonable expectation of their payment by the party benefitted. The service or other benefit must not be given as a gratuity or without expectation of payment, and the person benefitted must do something from which his promise to pay may be fairly inferred." *Home Protection Building & Loan Association Case*, 143 Pa. Super. 96 at 98-99, 17 A.2d 755 at 756-57 (1941). When a person requests another to perform services, it is ordinarily inferred that he intends to pay for them, unless the circumstances indicate otherwise. Restatement, Restitution §107(2) (1937).[4] However, where the circumstances evidence that one's work effort has been voluntarily given to another, an intention to pay therefor cannot be inferred. In the instant case, the facts alleged in the complaint disclose a submission of information from appellant to appellee without any discussion pertaining to appellee's payment therefor. Clearly, there was no basis upon which to infer the existence of a unilateral contract.

Similarly, there is no factual premise to support a finding that appellee is entitled to recover in quasi-contract for the information supplied by appellant. Where one person has been unjustly enriched at the expense of another he or she must make restitution to the other. However, unjust enrichment is the key to an action for restitution. The vehicle for achieving restitution is a quasi-contract, or contract implied in law. "Unlike true contracts, quasi-contracts are not based on the apparent intention of the parties to undertake the performances in question, nor are they promises. They are obligations created by law for reasons of justice." *Schott v. Westinghouse Electric Corporation*, 436 Pa. 279, 290, 259 A.2d 443, 449 (1969), quoting Restatement (Second) of Contracts, §5, comment b. at 24. "Quasi-contracts may be found in the absence of any expression of assent by the party to be charged and may indeed be found in spite of the party's contrary intention." *Schott v. Westinghouse Electric Corporation, supra* at 290-91, 259 A.2d at 449. To sustain a claim of unjust enrichment, it must be shown by the facts pleaded that a person wrongly secured or passively received a benefit that it would be unconscionable to retain.

As a general rule, volunteers have no right to restitution. Appellant was a volunteer. It was he who made the unsolicited suggestion that he would be willing to submit to appellee his copy of "Planning Your Financial Future" with notations to show which portions had been purloined from "How to Buy Stocks." His offer to do so was not conditioned upon payment of any kind. He did not suggest, either expressly or by implication, that he expected to be paid for this information or for time spent in reducing the same to writing. Thus, the facts averred in the complaint establish that he was purely a volunteer

---

[4] Note that the restatement cited here is the Restatement of Restitution. As mentioned in Chapter 1, the American Law Institute has published restatements in several areas of the common law. —Eds.

and cannot properly be reimbursed for unjust enrichment.[5] . . . The claim was properly dismissed. Order affirmed.

■ ■ ■

Although it has nothing to do with the issue under consideration here, we cannot resist mentioning that Martin also asserted a claim against Little, Brown in tort for the intentional infliction of mental distress. He claimed that this distress was created when, in response to his threat to sue, Little, Brown's attorney made a return threat to counterclaim against him for abuse of process. The court dismissed the tort claim on the grounds that the threat was not improper. It noted that Martin, who himself initiated the litigation, should not complain if the target of his suit fought back.

■ QUESTIONS

(1) Martin was refused restitution because he was a volunteer. An alternative ground for denying recovery could have been that he was an officious intermeddler. Had he not been held to be a volunteer, would this ground have been a basis for dismissal on the facts of the case?

(2) The court indicates in footnote 5 that even if Martin had established grounds for restitution, he would not have been entitled to a percentage of the recovery. How would his restitutionary recovery have been determined? Can you think of any circumstances in which it would be proper to measure the amount of restitution as a percentage of the recovery?

■ PROBLEM 12.1

The court said that Martin was a volunteer because he never asked for nor suggested that he wanted payment. In the clearest case, a person can eliminate any question that he may be a volunteer by saying expressly that he

---

[5] The parties have not briefed and our decision makes it unnecessary that we consider the damages which appellant would otherwise be entitled to recover. It is clear, however, that such damages are measured by the reasonable value of services rendered and not by a percentage of the recovery achieved by appellee as a result of the copyright infringement first observed by appellant.

expects payment. However, the absence or presence of gratuitous intent can also be inferred from the circumstances.

Say that several publishers, concerned about plagiarism and other use of their materials, had advertised that they would pay a reward to anyone who furnished information to them about violations of their copyrights. Although it knew about these advertisements, Little, Brown had not itself so advertised, and it had no practice of rewarding reports of plagiarism. Martin had seen these advertisements offering rewards but had not paid attention to the names of the publishers that offered them. When Martin discovered the plagiarism of "How to Buy Stocks," he wrote to Little, Brown and received the reply as described in the case.

(a) Does this embellishment of the facts provide a stronger argument to Martin that Little, Brown's acceptance of his offer to send the marked-up copy of the book created a contract implied in fact?

(b) Alternatively, does it provide Martin with a stronger case for arguing that Little, Brown was unjustly enriched by taking the benefit without compensating him?

(c) In either case, if Martin's argument succeeds, how would the amount of his recovery be determined?

■ PROBLEM 12.2

Recall the example of the hospital that performed emergency services for the unconscious patient. Because the patient was unconscious at the time that the hospital rendered the services, there could be no contract implied in fact. However, because the hospital acted in an emergency, without a reasonable possibility of obtaining the patient's consent beforehand, it probably would not be treated as an intermeddler. In addition, because the hospital did not intend its services to be gratuitous, it probably is not a volunteer either. Therefore, provided that the medical services were of the level and nature that was necessary and appropriate to deal with the emergency, the hospital has a good prospect of obtaining restitution of the market value of the benefit conferred.

Assume that when the patient collapsed, a bystander came to his assistance. The bystander summoned a cab, lifted the unconscious patient into it, and rushed him to the hospital. Can the bystander claim reimbursement from the patient for the cab fare? How about reimbursement for his service of taking the patient to the hospital?

■ **PROBLEM 12.3**

In Chapter 7, Section C, we read *Baer v. Chase*, 392 F.3d 609 (3d Cir. 2004), in which Baer rendered services to Chase, the creator of *The Sopranos*, by describing his own experiences as a prosecutor, providing background information about organized crime in New Jersey, and introducing Chase to detectives and other notables such as Big Pussy and Little Pussy. Chase had undertaken that he would remunerate Baer for services rendered and would "take care of" him if the show became a success. Baer sued Chase when Chase failed to make any payment to him. Recall that the court upheld the trial court's award of summary judgment to Chase on the contract claim on the grounds that the undertaking was too vague to constitute a contract. Baer also claimed in the alternative on a theory of unjust enrichment; that is, he asserted that even if there was no actual contract, he was entitled to reimbursement for the value of his services. The court did not reach the merits of this claim because the focus was on whether it was barred by the statute of limitations (*Baer v. Chase*, 177 Fed. Appx. 261 (3d Cir. 2006)).

Do you think that Baer had grounds for relief for unjust enrichment? If so, how would you determine his quantum meruit recovery?

We now move from the restitutionary claim of an enterprising law student to that of an enterprising attorney.

FEINGOLD v. PUCELLO

439 Pa. Super. 509, 654 A.2d 1093 (1995)
Pennsylvania Superior Court

OLSZEWSKI, Judge.

On February 2, 1979, Barry Pucello was involved in a motor vehicle accident. One of Pucello's co-workers knew Allen Feingold, a personal injury attorney, and asked if he could give Feingold Pucello's name. Pucello agreed. Feingold called Pucello that very evening. Pucello explained that he wasn't feeling well, having just been in an accident, and would call back tomorrow. Feingold recommended a doctor he knew, and set up an appointment for Pucello. The next day, the two discussed the possibility of Feingold's representing Pucello. Pucello gave Feingold some basic information, but did not discuss fee arrangements. Feingold then went to work on the case. He inspected the accident site, took pictures, obtained the police report, and secured an admission of liability from the other driver. He had still never met with Pucello in person. Towards the end of February, Feingold mailed a formal contingency fee agreement to Pucello, which called for a 50/50 split of the recovery, after costs. Pucello balked at the high fee, and found other counsel. Pucello told Feingold he could keep any pictures, reports, and admissions; Feingold never forwarded the file. About a year later, Feingold sued Pucello in quantum meruit. . . . The trial court found that . . . the parties never even entered into an attorney-client relationship. The trial court thus found for Pucello, and Feingold appeals.

Feingold argues that Pucello orally agreed to have Feingold represent him, so he is entitled to be paid for the work he did even though Pucello never signed a written fee agreement. The trial court found that by working on the case without the agreement, Feingold proceeded at his own risk. Since there was never a meeting of the minds regarding representation, there was no contract and no obligation to reimburse for his work on the case. Feingold acknowledges the absence of an express contract, but argues that the circumstances imply a contract to support quantum meruit recovery. He contends that Pucello enjoyed the benefits of his efforts despite rejecting his work product: Feingold got Pucello a doctor's appointment, and once the tortfeasor admitted liability, he was unlikely to deny it later.

Quantum meruit is an equitable remedy. We therefore begin our analysis by noting that Feingold comes to this court with hands smudged by the ink which should have been used to sign his fee agreement. . . . [Under rules of professional conduct, attorneys are required to state their contingency fee in writing either before representing a client or within a reasonable time thereafter.]

Secondly, Feingold's proposed contingency fee of 50% of the recovery, after costs, is breathtakingly high. It struck the trial court as unethical. By pricing his services at the top end of the spectrum, Feingold should expect some prospective clients to balk. This makes stating the fee agreement up front all the more important. Contingency fee practice used to be badly abused by practitioners who would assure their injured clients not to worry—the case was in good hands. When the relationship had passed the point of no return and the client's reliance was entrenched, then the attorney mentioned what his hefty percentage of the take would be. The only way to counter this abuse was to require that attorneys state contingency fees up front and in writing. . . . We think Feingold's abject failure to comply with this rule precludes any equitable recovery.

Even without these equitable considerations, Feingold's claim still fails on its merits. In rejecting the proposed fee agreement, Pucello told Feingold to keep his work-product. Thus Feingold did not confer any tangible benefit on Pucello. Feingold argues that having admitted liability to Feingold, the tortfeasor was constrained from altering his story, which facilitated settlement. If so, then Feingold's claim would more properly lie against Pucello's attorney, who testified that he still could have won the case without Feingold's preliminary work. Thus, Pucello would have gotten his recovery either way; it is only Pucello's attorney whose job might have been facilitated by Feingold's services.

Feingold likens himself to the surgeon who may render emergency medical treatment first, and then ask for payment later. Pucello's claim had a two-year statute of limitation, and was for the sole purpose of obtaining money, not saving his life. Feingold could have held off working on the case long enough to properly commence the relationship by stating his contingency fee up front, and should have under our procedural and ethical rules. When Pucello learned of Feingold's exorbitant rates, he understandably balked and told Feingold to keep his file. Feingold's unclean hands and Pucello's rejection of his services clearly preclude any quantum meruit recovery. Order affirmed.

■ QUESTIONS

(1) Why did Feingold not have a cause of action in contract? Was it because, based on offer and acceptance principles, no contract was made, or because the rules of professional responsibility enact what amounts to a statute of frauds?

(2) (a) If Feingold had been able to establish a contract to represent the defendant, but there had been no express agreement on his fee, what basis would have been used to establish his recovery?

(b) If the court had found no contract but did find that there was enrichment and that it was unjust, what should the remedy have been? How does this compare to your answer to Question 2(a)?

(3) Could the plaintiff have established a claim that he should be entitled to relief under the doctrine of promissory estoppel for the period until the relationship was terminated? If this argument could be made, what would he recover?

(4) A concurring opinion in *Feingold* agreed with the result of the case on the "narrow basis" that Pucello received no benefit from Feingold—he had rejected any direct benefit by refusing to accept Feingold's files, and the indirect benefits asserted by Feingold were not sufficient to support restitution. Feingold claimed that he performed valuable services by arranging the physician's appointment on short notice and by obtaining the driver's written admission of liability, thus facilitating settlement of the case. However, the concurring judge held that arranging a physician's appointment is not a professional service requiring legal skill, and the claim that the admission facilitated settlement is speculative.

How does the concurrence differ from the majority? If the basis of the concurring judgment can be described as "narrow," in what way is the majority opinion wider?

(5) One of the cardinal maxims of equity is that "one who comes into equity must come with clean hands." Do you see reference to this doctrine in *Feingold*? What does it mean?

(6)   The court refers to quantum meruit[6] as an equitable remedy. Although courts do sometimes characterize the remedy as equitable (and therefore treat it as such), it is actually legal in derivation.[7] As we note in Section A.3, quasi-contract was developed in the courts of law. (There are equitable restitutionary remedies that were developed concurrently by the chancellor, but they relate to relief other than a monetary award.) Do you think that the result or reasoning of the opinion would have been different if the court had treated the case as legal rather than equitable? What bearing does Question 5 have on this question?

5. Volunteers and Intermeddlers

Because the words "volunteer" and "officious intermeddler" often cause confusion, it is worth restating what they mean in the context of unjust enrichment. A volunteer is a person who confers a benefit gratuitously. This could be because she has the deliberate intent to make a gift, or simply because she lacks the intent to be paid. By contrast, an officious intermeddler may fully intend to seek payment when she confers the benefit. The barrier to her recovery is not that she acted gratuitously, but that she imposed an unasked-for benefit on the recipient under circumstances that did not justify this imposition. (A person who confers a benefit without intent to be paid and in a meddlesome way could qualify as both a volunteer and an officious intermeddler, thereby providing justification on both grounds for refusing her relief.) In the next case, the court dismisses the plaintiff's claim for unjust enrichment. Was this because the plaintiff was a volunteer, an officious intermeddler, or both?

BIRCHWOOD LAND COMPANY, INC. v. KRIZAN

115 A.3d 1009 (2015)
Vermont Supreme Court

DOOLEY, Justice.

. . . The facts as alleged in Birchwood's amended complaint are as follows. In June 1982, Krizan purchased a vacant and landlocked parcel, currently described as 43 Tanglewood Drive, for $3000 from the Town of Essex. Because the deed to Krizan's parcel makes reference to a recorded plat, she acquired by

---

[6] Note that this is an example of the kind of loose talk that we mention in Section A.3. Quantum meruit is not, strictly speaking, the remedy but the basis for measuring the remedy, which is restitution. As we mentioned, courts do this often, but you as students trying to get the terminology straight should try not to.
[7] For an account of the legal derivation of quasi-contract, *see* Dan B. Dobbs, *Law of Remedies* 370, 383-391 (2d ed., West 1993).

law an implied access easement over the portion of the adjacent parcel depicted on the plat and now owned by Birchwood. This is the sole means of access to her property. Without frontage on a public road or access to utilities and other related infrastructure, Krizan's property was undevelopable. In the thirty years of ownership, she had made no effort to develop her property.

In December 2002, Birchwood purchased the land surrounding Krizan's parcel to the east, south, and west, including the fee simple ownership of the strip of land on which Krizan's access easement is located. In April 2005, Birchwood obtained approval from the Town to develop its property, including the construction and extension of Tanglewood Drive and the installation of water, sewer, and electrical lines, and other related infrastructure. The Krizan property was not included in the development approval. As part of its development, however, Birchwood extended road access and water and sewer line connections to Krizan's property. In July 2007, Birchwood completed the road and infrastructure improvements at a substantial expense.

After Birchwood completed the improvements, Krizan notified the Town of her intent to develop her property. The Town found that Krizan's lot is now developable because the lot is now located on a public road and is connected to the necessary infrastructure. Consequently, the Town increased the assessed value of Krizan's parcel from $10,800 to $92,700. The fair market value of Krizan's property, as determined by the sale price of a neighboring property, is no less than $117,000. Birchwood has calculated that Krizan's proportionate share of expenses for the construction and extension of Tanglewood Drive and related infrastructure, not including the $2,405 water and sewer connection cost, amounts to $50,100. Krizan initially expressed interest in reimbursing Birchwood for the cost of extending the sewer and water connections to her property but has refused to contribute to the road and other infrastructure improvements.

Birchwood filed a complaint against Krizan in the trial court, alleging that Krizan was unjustly enriched by the creation of the public road access to her lot and should be required to bear a proportionate cost of the construction. . . . In response, Krizan filed a motion to dismiss for failure to state a claim upon which relief can be granted. . . . [The trial court granted Krizan's motion to dismiss. The Supreme Court affirms.]

Birchwood claims that it is entitled to restitution from Krizan for the improvements it made to the road, utilities, and other related infrastructure because Krizan was unjustly enriched at Birchwood's expense. Birchwood argues that Krizan is a "free rider" who held onto her undeveloped property for thirty years awaiting the adjoining property owner to make the necessary improvements. . . . Krizan disputes that she . . . has any duty to contribute to Birchwood's improvements, which were voluntary, unrequested, and in Birchwood's self-interest. The trial court agreed with Krizan, finding no actionable claim for unjust enrichment.

Our case law recognizes claims of unjust enrichment, see, e.g., *Kellogg v. Shushereba*, 2013 VT 76, ¶ 22, 194 Vt. 446, 82 A.3d 1121 (stating that plaintiff is entitled to recovery from defendant for period defendant received benefit of living in plaintiff's home without paying for that benefit), but we have not yet ruled on the validity of a claim of unjust enrichment for unrequested benefits—that is, unrequested benefits voluntarily conferred upon the recipient by the claimant. See Restatement (Third) of Restitution & Unjust Enrichment §30 (2011) [hereinafter Restatement]. . . . Both parties rely, in part, on the Restatement in making their arguments.

Birchwood . . . [argues that] Krizan was unjustly enriched by the substantial increase in the value of her property as a consequence of Birchwood's improvements and therefore should be required to return to Birchwood some of that increase in value as a proportionate share of the improvement costs. . . .

Section 30 of the Restatement provides that a claim of unjust enrichment for benefits conferred on the recipient by the claimant's unrequested intervention is available only to the extent that "(a) liability in restitution replaces a money obligation or spares the recipient necessary expense; (b) the recipient obtains a benefit in money; or (c) relief may be granted to the claimant by specific restitution." Restitution for voluntarily conferred benefits rarely is granted, but is available in limited circumstances where it "may be achieved in a manner that avoids any forced exchange." Restatement §30 cmt. a. Potentially applicable here is subsection (a), which requires us to determine whether Krizan was under any obligation to pay for the improvements or, in other words, if Birchwood spared her a necessary expense. In applying this subsection, one consideration is that a claimant generally cannot compel the recipient to pay for benefits voluntarily conferred if, had the transaction been proposed as a contract, the recipient would have been able to reject it. *Id.* §30 cmt. b. For example, if adjacent property owners are under no obligation to make infrastructure improvements unless and until they develop their lots, a claimant who undertakes the improvements cannot recover in restitution from the benefitted recipient, even if the recipient's property value increased as a result of the improvements. *Id.* §30 cmt. b, illus. 4. That is the situation in this case.

The illustration above is based on *Ranquist v. Donahue,* 710 F. Supp. 1160 (N.D. Ill. 1989), which Birchwood cites in support of its argument that Krizan, as a "holdout owner" and "free rider," is under a duty to contribute to the improvements made by Birchwood. The facts of *Ranquist* are substantively similar to the facts in this case, and the court's analysis goes to the heart of the issue with which we are confronted. In *Ranquist,* the defendants purchased a single lot in a nine-lot subdivision, and the plaintiff subsequently bought the remaining eight lots. An agreement between the original developer and the municipality required lot owners to make certain improvements—including road, curb, sewer, and water main construction—before development of the subdivision. The plaintiff constructed the necessary improvements and demanded that the defendants pay their share of the cost. The defendants refused. The court held that if the defendants were not required to make the improvements until they developed their property, and could choose not to develop, they could not be held liable for a proportionate share of the cost of improvements. *Id.* at 1161. The court further held:

> [W]hat the defendants did with their property after the construction ended is irrelevant. . . . To be sure, the defendants' post-construction actions demonstrate that they derived a benefit from the construction, but the receipt of the benefits does not suffice to render a person liable. There must be some injustice in allowing him to keep them. The fact that the defendants made use of the improvements does not make their retention of the benefits unjust.

Id. at 1162 (citation omitted).

The plaintiff in *Ranquist* made the same arguments that Birchwood makes here. Specifically, the plaintiff argued there that, even if the defendants were under no obligation to make the improvements, they were still liable for restitution because they accepted the benefit by then developing their lot, which they otherwise would have been unable to do. As we noted above, the court squarely rejected the plaintiff's argument. The court also rejected the plaintiff's argument that the defendants' motives made their failure to share in the cost of improvements unjust because the defendants knew that the plaintiff would go forward with the construction even if they refused to participate. *Ranquist,* 710 F. Supp. at 1162. The court found the underlying motive of the defendants irrelevant. Looking at Birchwood's complaint, we find no allegations that either party was obligated to undertake the improvements irrespective of whether the lots were developed. . . . Thus, the rationale of *Ranquist,* now explicitly adopted by the Restatement, applies here.

As demonstrated by the foregoing discussion, Restatement §30 embraces the principle that incidental benefits—benefits conferred on the recipient by work that the claimant undertook for its own benefit—rarely are recoverable in restitution unless the benefits are a consequence of mistake, fraud, or compulsion. Restatement §30 cmt. b; see also *Dinosaur Dev., Inc. v. White,* 216 Cal. App. 3d 1310, 265 Cal. Rptr. 525, 530-31 (1989) (holding that plaintiff has no claim in restitution against defendant for expense of road improvements to road benefitting both parties' landlocked parcels because benefit was incidental to plaintiff's desire to improve its own property); *Major-Blakeney Corp. v. Jenkins,* 121 Cal. App. 2d 325, 263 P.2d 655, 664 (1953) (holding that plaintiff has no claim in restitution against defendant, adjoining landowner, for expense of off-site improvements benefitting both properties because "expenditures made and obligations paid were done exclusively in furtherance of plaintiff's own interest and to discharge commitments for which it alone was responsible").

Birchwood urges us to rely on the Restatement but argues that the unique facts of this case are so novel and extreme that §30 is inapplicable and that we should rely instead on the general policy of §1 that restitution can be ordered when a defendant is unjustly enriched. Birchwood argues that §30 applies when the benefit is *incidental* but not when the benefit is *substantial,* as alleged here. We disagree. Section 30 precisely fits the facts of this case, and the precedent on which it relies, *Ranquist v. Donahue,* is indistinguishable in substance. The terms incidental and substantial are not mutually exclusive, with the former requiring a conclusion that the enrichment is not unjust and the latter triggering a conclusion of unjust enrichment. The cases cited above, including *Ranquist,* demonstrate that a benefit can be both incidental and substantial.

Birchwood further urges that the purpose of the doctrine of unjust enrichment is to prevent benefits to a "free rider." Here, Birchwood has characterized Krizan as a free rider who unfairly held onto her property for thirty years waiting for someone else to pay for the improvements that would allow her to develop her lot. Under *Ranquist,* the characterization of the recipient as a "holdout owner" or "free rider" is of no consequence to the outcome. It is incident to the nature of property ownership that one owner's self-interested actions may benefit a neighboring owner, even though this may encourage free riding and discourage more industrious property owners from making improvements. . . .

We adopt Restatement §30 as the governing law for this case and conclude that Birchwood's unjust enrichment claim fails under §30. . . . We therefore conclude that the trial court did not err in . . . dismissing Birchwood's claim of unjust enrichment against Krizan. Affirmed.

■ PROBLEM 12.4

As treasurer of her neighborhood softball club, Emmy Bezzler was in control of its bank account. She was also a great authority on horse racing and had accumulated vast expertise in this field over many years of careful study. The big local race was coming up, and she had been researching it attentively. She came to the conclusion that a horse called Grand Larceny was sure to win. On the day before the race, she withdrew $2,000 from the softball club's bank account (this was almost all the money in the account) and bet it on Grand Larceny. The horse won, and Emmy was paid out $8,000. At the next meeting of the club's executive committee a few days later, she told the committee what she had done. She presented the club's president with her check for $2,000 as well as a complete set of new softball uniforms for the team, which she had bought with the winnings. The uniforms cost $1,500. She told the committee that she was keeping the remaining $4,500 as a reward for her skill and initiative.

The committee accepted the check and the uniforms. However, Emmy was shocked to find that the committee was not as grateful as she had expected. After taking the fruits of her efforts, they fired her and demanded the balance of $4,500. Is she entitled to keep the $4,500 or any other amount?

THE APPLICATION OF UNJUST ENRICHMENT PRINCIPLES TO PROMISES FOR PAST BENEFITS: THE "MORAL OBLIGATION" AND "MATERIAL BENEFIT" DOCTRINES

We have seen that unjust enrichment does not have a promissory basis. It focuses on whether it is fair to require the beneficiary to pay for the benefit conferred, and is not concerned with whether the beneficiary made any undertaking to pay for it. If the beneficiary promised to pay for the benefit before or at the time of receiving it, the promise would most likely qualify as a contract, so it could be enforced as such, without the need to apply principles of unjust enrichment. As a matter of logic and convenience, it would make sense to treat a promise made after the benefit was received in the same way as one made at the time it was conferred and to enforce the promise as a contract. After all, by making the promise, the beneficiary acknowledges receiving value and expresses the intention to pay for it. However, consideration doctrine stands in the way of this simple solution. A promise is enforceable as a contract only if it is given in exchange for a legal detriment. The exchange requirement means that a promise made in recognition of a prior detriment is not supported by consideration. (The prior detriment is sometimes inaccurately described as "past consideration"—a poor choice of language because it is not consideration at all.)

In a very narrow group of situations, courts have avoided the unfair results of strict application of the "past consideration" doctrine by recognizing an exception to it. This exception has come to be known as the "moral obligation" doctrine. (Like the term "past consideration," this is a poor choice of name and can lead to confusion. The doctrine is very limited in scope and should not be thought of as creating a general principle that a court will enforce a promise merely because it finds that the promisor has a moral obligation to perform what he promised.)

Most courts have recognized the doctrine only where a person makes a promise that is in effect a ratification of an existing but unenforceable or voidable legal obligation. The elements of the doctrine are best illustrated by one of the common examples of a situation in which courts have applied it—where the promisor promises to pay a debt that has become unenforceable because of the statute of limitations. Say that seven years ago, Creditor and Debtor entered into a contract under which Creditor performed services for Debtor for an agreed fee of $2,000. Debtor breached the contract by failing to pay Creditor. For some reason, Creditor never got around to instituting suit against Debtor to recover the debt. As a result, the six-year statute of limitations on the claim has run, and Creditor can no longer sue to enforce it. After the statute of limitations has run, Debtor makes a new promise to Creditor to pay the debt. Although Creditor gave no consideration in exchange for this new promise, the doctrine of "moral obligation" creates an exception to the "past consideration" rule and permits enforcement of the later promise.

In addition to cases in which the statute of limitations has run, courts have applied the doctrine to other situations in which a prior unenforceable or voidable obligation exists. For example, when a debtor becomes bankrupt, debts that he incurred prior to bankruptcy are discharged and cannot be enforced. However if, after bankruptcy, the debtor makes a new promise to pay the discharged debt, the promise may bind the debtor even though the creditor gave no new consideration for it.[8] Courts also apply the "moral obligation" doctrine to a minor's voidable contract where the minor ratifies the contract after becoming a major. As explained in Chapter 14, Section D, a contract entered into by a minor is generally voidable at his instance. However, the minor can fully validate the contract by affirming it after he reaches the age of majority. The other party to the contract is not required to give new consideration to make this ratification effective.

As these examples show, the generally accepted scope of the moral obligation doctrine is confined to cases in which the following elements are present: A person, acting without gratuitous intent, confers a benefit on another; the recipient should have paid for the benefit, and may even have had a legal obligation to pay for it, but did not, and therefore, his retention of the benefit without payment has unjustly enriched him; for some reason the person who conferred the benefit did not or could not sue to enforce the recipient's original obligation to pay; and at some later time, the recipient makes a new promise to pay for the benefit that could not otherwise be compelled by legal action.

It must be stressed again that most courts recognize the "moral obligation" doctrine sparingly and have confined it to situations in which a previously created legal obligation had become unenforceable or was voidable at the time that the later promise was made. However, Restatement, Second §86 has sought to widen the application of the doctrine to cover a broader range of promises in recognition of a prior benefit. Section 86 avoids use of the term "moral obligation" and instead describes its doctrine as "promise for benefit received." It has become known as the "material benefit" rule. Judging from the reported case law, few courts have been willing to follow the lead of the Restatement, Second, in expanding the scope of the doctrine. Restatement, Second §86 provides as follows:

RESTATEMENT, SECOND §86. PROMISE FOR BENEFIT RECEIVED

(1) A promise made in recognition of a benefit previously received by the promisor from the promisee is binding to the extent necessary to prevent injustice.

(2) A promise is not binding under Subsection (1)

---

[8] Although the "moral obligation" doctrine dispenses with new consideration to validate the promise, there are statutory barriers to the debtor's reaffirmation of a discharged debt. The Bankruptcy Code carefully regulates reaffirmations to ensure that they are not coerced and are in the debtor's best interests.

(a) if the promisee conferred the benefit as a gift or for other reasons the promisor has not been unjustly enriched; or

(b) to the extent that its value is disproportionate to the benefit.

———————

Section 86 was largely inspired by *Webb v. McGowin,* 27 Ala. App. 82, 168 So. 196 (Ala. App. 1935), *cert. denied,* 232 Ala. 374, 168 So. 199 (1936), a famous case decided in 1935, which still remains the leading case on the material benefit doctrine. Webb was employed by a lumber company. In August 1925, he was clearing the upper floor of a mill and was in the process of dropping a 75-pound block of wood from the upper floor to the ground below. Just as he was about to drop the block, he noticed that McGowin was standing on the ground in the path of the block. To prevent the block from crushing McGowin, Webb held onto it and fell with it, diverting its fall so that it missed McGowin. Webb was seriously disabled as a result of injuries he sustained in the fall. In gratitude for the brave and timely actions that saved him from death or terrible injury, and to compensate Webb for his disabling injury, McGowin promised to pay Webb $15 every two weeks for the rest of his life. McGowin honored this promise until he died in 1934, but his estate discontinued the payments.

Webb sued, and the court of appeals upheld the promise. It reasoned that by saving McGowin from death or grievous bodily harm, Webb had conferred a material benefit on him that morally bound McGowin to compensate Webb. McGowin's promise recognized this moral obligation. The court stressed that it was enforcing the promise not simply because of "mere moral obligation or conscientious duty" but because the moral obligation was connected to the promisor's receipt of a material benefit. Although the promise was not exchanged for the services, it was a ratification of the value of the prior services. The court considered that the strength of the promisor's moral obligation justified the legal fiction that the services were not rendered gratuitously and that they were rendered at McGowin's request. This presumption obviated the "past consideration" problem.

In denying certiorari, the Alabama Supreme Court expressly endorsed the reasoning of the court of appeals. The Supreme Court recognized that the moral obligation enforced in this case was founded on the promisor's duty to compensate for a material benefit that he had received, and was not simply based on some "supposed moral obligation . . . based upon some refined sense of ethical duty. . . ."

▪ QUESTIONS

(1) Why was it necessary in *Webb v. McGowin* to devise and apply the material benefit doctrine? Could the court not simply have reached the result by applying principles of unjust enrichment? In thinking about this question, consider whether Webb would have had any basis for recovery if McGowin had made no promise after Webb fell with the block.

(2) Like promissory estoppel, the material benefit rule is based on a promise. Could promissory estoppel have been used as a basis of enforcement in this case? If so, how would relief have been measured?

(3) As noted earlier, Restatement, Second §86 is inspired by *Webb v. McGowin*. Apply §86 to the facts of *Webb v. McGowin*. Is the analysis the same? Do you reach the same result?

■ PROBLEM 12.5

In *Dementas v. Estate of Tallas*, 764 P.2d 628 (Utah App. 1988), the court refused to recognize the moral obligation and material benefit doctrines. Tallas emigrated to the United States from Greece in 1914 and lived in Salt Lake City for nearly 70 years. During the last 14 years of his life, Tallas developed a close friendship with Dementas, who treated him like a father, had him at his house for dinner every week, and helped him with various routine chores such as picking up his mail, driving him to the doctor and the store, and assisting him in the management of his rental properties. The evidence showed that at the time he rendered these services, Dementas had no intention of charging Tallas for them. In December 1982, a couple of months before he died, Tallas executed a document in which he expressed his gratitude to Dementas, stated that he owed him $50,000 for his help over the years, and undertook to bequeath that amount to him in his will. (The services rendered were likely not worth anywhere near $50,000.) Tallas died without changing his will to include that bequest and Dementas sued his estate. The court declined to find a contract because the services rendered by Dementas preceded Tallas's promise and were therefore not consideration given in exchange for it. The court acknowledged that some courts might uphold the promise on the basis of the moral obligation doctrine, but that the Utah Supreme Court had declined to adopt the doctrine on the grounds that recognition of a moral obligation as a basis for enforcing a promise would severely erode the requirement of consideration.

(a) Would Dementas have had more success if he had sued on a theory of unjust enrichment? If so, how would his recovery have been measured?

(b) Would the result of the case have been different if the court had applied Restatement, Second §86?

(c) Say that Dementas established at trial that from the outset he and Tallas agreed that he would receive some compensation for his services, but they never discussed what that compensation would be. The promise made by Tallas just before he died (and gratefully acknowledged by Dementas at that time) fully reflected what Tallas considered the value of those services to be. However, the market value of the services was considerably less—they were worth $5,000. What is the impact of these changed facts on your answers to (a) and (b)?

voidable
contract puts
the power in
the parties
hands
↓
other party
cannot enforce
it

CHAPTER 13

Policing Contracts for Improper Bargaining

A   GENERAL INTRODUCTION TO THE DOCTRINES IN THIS CHAPTER

The doctrines considered in this chapter are regulatory in nature. They give the court the ability to police contracts by looking beyond the manifestation of assent. If the court finds that the apparent manifestation of one party's assent was induced by improper means, it may refuse to enforce the contract as a whole or some aspect of it. We see in Chapter 3 that assent is a crucial component of contract, but that assent is measured objectively by examining manifestations of assent rather than the actual state of mind of the parties. Although this principle is dominant in contract law, we caution in Chapter 3 that too rigid a focus on objective manifestations could lead to unfair results where one party's apparent assent is induced by the deceit, coercion, or unfair bargaining of the other. Each of the doctrines studied in this chapter is distinct, with its own elements and purpose. However, they have several points of connection, which makes it useful to think of them as a network of regulatory principles with distinct roles but also with common themes. Look for these interconnections. In some cases they will permit the application of more than one doctrine to the facts.

The remedial aspect of these doctrines is important. Here, again, you will find that although there are some variations between the doctrines, they do have a common remedial theme. As a general rule, where the court finds one of these doctrines applicable, the remedy is to allow the victim of the improper conduct to avoid the contract. An avoidable (or voidable) contract is not the same as a void contract. If a contract is void, it is not a contract at all but a legal nullity. Neither party can enforce it. However, if a contract is voidable, the aggrieved party can

allow the victim to avoid the contract

voidable contract puts the power in one partie's hands

↓

other party cannot enforce it

elect either to keep it in force or to exercise his right to rescind (avoid) it. The aggrieved party has the initiative to decide whether the contract will remain in effect. If he chooses to enforce it, the other party cannot resist on the basis that it is avoidable. However, if the aggrieved party elects to avoid the contract, the other party cannot enforce it. If a contract is avoided, the general rule (subject to exceptions in some cases) is that each party is entitled to restitution of any benefits conferred on the other under the contract up to the time of avoidance. Restitution is, of course, not based on the contract, but on unjust enrichment. A party entitled to avoid a contract may either sue affirmatively for avoidance or may use the right of avoidance defensively if sued by the other party.

remedy of avoidance & restitution

Although the remedy of avoidance and restitution is dominant in this area, it may not be the only remedy available. Other remedies (for example, enforcement of the contract with the excision of a particular term, or a claim for money damages) are possible and appropriate in certain cases. Our discussion pays attention to remedies, so you will have many opportunities to consider the commonality and distinctive aspects of the doctrines in this regard.

fraud & duress

The doctrines of fraud and duress are common law remedies, and UCC Article 2 has no provisions that codify these doctrines in relation to sales of goods. However, the doctrines do apply to sales of goods under UCC 1-103(b), which expressly includes them as common law doctrines applicable under Article 2.

B | FRAUDULENT MISREPRESENTATION

1. The General Principles and Elements of Fraud

fraud exists in contracts torts & criminal

Fraudulent misrepresentation crosses the borders between three different areas of law. The victim of the fraud has grounds to avoid the contract under principles of contract law. However, fraud is also a tort, which gives the victim the alternative remedy of seeking damages under tort law. In addition, fraud is a crime, which makes the perpetrator subject to criminal penalties. It is useful to bear this overlap in mind as you study the materials in this section.

1) material misrepresentation of fact
2) made w/ knowledge of its falsity
3) intent to induce a contract
4) success in inducing a contract

We begin this discussion of fraud by identifying its elements under contract law: A material misrepresentation of fact, made with knowledge of its falsity and intent to induce the contract, which does in fact justifiably induce the other party to enter the contract. These elements of fraud at common law apply in sales of goods as well. UCC Article 2 has no provisions dealing with fraud, so common law rules and principles govern under UCC 1-103(b).

a. A Misrepresentation of Fact

A misrepresentation is defined in Restatement, Second §159 as an assertion not in accordance with the facts. As this definition suggests, a misrepresentation centers on a fact and is a false representation that the fact is true. For example, the seller of a house with asbestos ceiling tiles makes a misrepresentation if she tells the prospective buyer that the house is asbestos-free. If the seller knows that this assertion is untrue and makes it deliberately to induce the buyer to buy the house, the misrepresentation is fraudulent. However, if the seller believes the assertion and does not know that the assertion is untrue, the misrepresentation may be negligent or innocent. We do not discuss negligent or innocent misrepresentation at any length but focus on fraudulent misrepresentation.

if unknown

A fraudulent misrepresentation may take the form of an express statement, such as the above statement about the asbestos ceilings. However, it could also be a deliberate concealment of a fact. For example, say that the seller of the house knows that its ceiling tiles contain asbestos. She realizes that this will discourage purchasers, so she conceals the ceiling tiles by plastering over them. This is as much an active falsehood as making an untrue statement, even though it is by conduct, not words. This is expressed in Restatement, Second §160:

active falsehood

RESTATEMENT, SECOND §160. WHEN ACTION IS EQUIVALENT TO AN ASSERTION (CONCEALMENT)

Action intended or known to be likely to prevent another from learning a fact is equivalent to an assertion that the fact does not exist. *— coverup*

passive conveyance ↓ silence

duty to provide info

There may also be fraud, although it is a less certain case, if the seller conveys a falsehood passively. For example, it might also constitute fraud for the seller to do nothing and keep silent on the question of asbestos, hoping that the buyer does not notice the problem. Because the ground of fraud here is failure to disclose, the seller's silence raises the question of whether she has a duty to provide the information. Although it is obvious that a party has a duty not to lie or actively conceal the truth, the question of whether she has a duty to come forward with information is more subtle. This is discussed in Section B.3.

✱ must be related to fact

The misrepresentation must relate to a fact. A mere expression of opinion or a prediction of the future generally does not qualify as fact. However, many opinions and predictions are based on fact. It is therefore possible for an opinion or prediction to be misrepresented where there is no factual basis for it. This is discussed in Section B.4.

A factual assertion—a representation that a fact exists—is likewise distinguishable from a contractual promise—a commitment to do something in the future. However, it could happen that a party deliberately and dishonestly misrepresents her future intention at the time of entering the contract. A court might treat this as a misrepresentation of a fact—that is, the promisor's current state of mind, so it could qualify as fraud. We deal with this type of misrepresentation in Section B.5. *misrepresentation of intent*

In most situations involving fraud in the formation of a contract, the misrepresentation was made by one of the parties (or her agent) to the other. While it is possible in some circumstances for a party to seek relief on the basis of a misrepresentation made by a person who is not a party to the contract, this is rare and the basis for relief is harder to establish.[1] We do not deal with this situation and the discussion here is confined to representations by a party or her agent.

b. *Knowledge of Falsity and Intent to Mislead (Scienter)*

If a misrepresentation is made with the knowledge that it is untrue and with an intent to mislead the other party, it is fraudulent. (The term "scienter" is sometimes used as shorthand for the two elements of knowledge of falsity and intent to mislead.) Knowledge of falsity certainly covers situations in which the maker of the misrepresentation knows that she is lying but could also include situations in which she is recklessly indifferent as to its truth. This is how Restatement, Second §162(1) defines fraud:

RESTATEMENT, SECOND §162. WHEN A MISREPRESENTATION IS FRAUDULENT . . .

(1) A misrepresentation is fraudulent if the maker intends his assertion to induce a party to manifest his assent and the maker
(a) knows or believes that the assertion is not in accord with the facts, or
(b) does not have the confidence that he states or implies in the truth of the assertion, or
(c) knows that he does not have the basis that he states or implies for the assertion.

c. *Materiality*

Restatement, Second §162(2) defines materiality as follows:

(2) A misrepresentation is material if it would be likely to induce a reasonable person to manifest his assent, or if the maker knows that it would be likely to induce the recipient to do so.

---

[1] Restatement, Second §164(2) allows avoidance of the contract on the grounds of the fraud of a nonparty if the victim was justified in relying on it, unless the other contracting party gave value or relied materially on the transaction in good faith and without reason to know of the misrepresentation. Therefore, if the other party was not complicit in the fraud, had no reason to know about it, and acted in reliance on the contract, the victim generally cannot seek avoidance of the contract. There is a certain type of fraud, often referred to as "fraud in the factum" which renders a contract void, even as against innocent third parties. We address this type of fraud in Section B.9.

Section 164 allows avoidance of a contract for misrepresentation either if the misrepresentation was fraudulent or negligent. Section 164(1) states, "If a party's manifestation of assent is induced by either a fraudulent or a material misrepresentation by the other party upon which the recipient is justified in relying, the contract is voidable by the recipient." As this language shows, Restatement, Second only recognizes materiality as an element of negligent misrepresentation but does not include it as an element of fraud. Section 162 reinforces this distinction by defining a fraudulent misrepresentation in §162(1) and materiality in §162(2).

Therefore, under the Restatement, Second formulation, a party seeking avoidance on grounds of fraudulent misrepresentation is not required to prove that the misrepresentation was material. Although some courts have adopted the approach of §164 and do not include materiality as an element of fraudulent misrepresentation, one must be careful in assuming that §164 accurately states the prevailing law on this question. Despite what §164 provides, materiality of the fraudulent misrepresentation is still required as an element of fraud by most courts. Even where a court says that it follows §164, it is quite common for the court to discuss materiality in its opinion anyway, thereby casting doubt that the court has really adopted the Restatement position of excluding materiality analysis in cases of fraud. In addition, the requirement of justifiable inducement suggests that despite what §164 says, the importance of the misrepresentation is likely to have some bearing on the question of whether it actually induced reliance and whether that reliance was justifiable.

d. Justifiable Inducement

fraud must induce reliance

It is not enough that one of the parties made a fraudulent misrepresentation. The victim of the fraud must also show that the misrepresentation induced her to enter the contract and that she was justified in relying on the misrepresentation. The causal relationship between the misrepresentation and the contract means that the victim would not have entered the contract, or would not have entered it on those terms, had she known the truth. This is why most courts evaluate the materiality of the misrepresentation despite the omission of this requirement in Restatement, Second §164—a misrepresentation as to an unimportant aspect of the contract is not likely to induce it, but inducement is relatively self-evident if the misrepresentation relates to a central aspect of the contract. In addition to showing actual inducement, the victim must show that she was justified in relying on the misrepresentation. Justifiable reliance mixes objective (reasonableness) and subjective elements to determine if the victim, given her personal attributes and circumstances, should have been taken in by the falsehood. If the victim should not have placed trust in the misrepresentation, or should have conducted her own inquiry into the facts, her unjustified reliance could deprive her of relief for fraud.

would not have entered in if they knew the truth

needs to relate to a central element

e. Remedy

voidable by the victimized party [handwritten]

Restatement, Second §164 states that a contract induced by a fraudulent misrepresentation by one of the parties is voidable by the other. The remedy of avoidance, identified in §164 is one of two possible remedies for fraudulent misrepresentation. It allows the victim of the misrepresentation to rescind the contract and to obtain restitution for any performance that has been rendered. The other remedy, damages, permits the victim to keep the contract in force and to sue for any loss in value of the performance as a result of the fraud. While the remedy of avoidance derives from contract law, the damages remedy arises from tort law. It is available to the victim of contractual fraud because fraud is a tort as well as the violation of the victim's rights under contract law. These alternative remedies are discussed more fully in Section B.8.

Can keep the contract and sue for damages [handwritten]

2. Affirmative Fraud

fraud by affirmative action & fraud by omission [handwritten]

Our first case illustrates an express fraudulent misrepresentation and allows us to consider the distinction between fraud by affirmative assertion and fraud by failure to disclose information. The case involves a claim in tort for the refund of child support and other expenses paid by a husband to his ex-wife under a divorce settlement agreement. However, while it is not, strictly speaking, a contracts case, it relates to a fraudulent misrepresentation that induced the settlement agreement and therefore illuminates the concept of fraud in a contractual setting while also showing the close connection between fraud and contract principles in this area.

HODGE v. CRAIG

382 S.W.3d 325 (2012)
Tennessee Supreme Court

KOCH, Jr., Justice.

. . . Chadwick Craig and Tina Marie Hodge met in a Future Farmers of America class at Mt. Pleasant High School. They were both sixteen years old and in the eleventh grade. Despite her youth, Ms. Hodge had already given birth to a daughter who was almost one year old when Ms. Hodge met Mr. Craig. Mr. Craig and Ms. Hodge dated on and off through the remainder of high school, although Ms. Hodge later characterized their relationship as "more on than . . . off." They were sexually intimate in this relationship. Ms. Hodge broke up with Mr. Craig for several weeks during early October 1991. During this hiatus, Ms. Hodge had sexual relations with Joey Hay. At one point Ms. Hodge believed that she was pregnant with Mr. Hay's child. However, after a negative pregnancy test, she told Mr. Hay that she was not pregnant. Ms. Hodge returned to Mr. Craig following her liaison with Mr. Hay, but she never told Mr. Craig that she had been intimate with Mr. Hay. Accordingly, by her own admission, Ms. Hodge had sexual relations with both Mr. Hay and Mr. Craig during the period when her son was conceived.

both could be the baby daddy

In early November 1991, Ms. Hodge told Mr. Craig that she believed she was pregnant. Mr. Craig suggested a pregnancy test and accompanied Ms. Hodge to her physician's office when the test was performed. After Ms. Hodge informed him that the test confirmed that she was pregnant, Mr. Craig, seeking reassurance, asked Ms. Hodge if she was sure that he was the child's father. Ms. Hodge responded that she was sure that he was the child's father and that the child could be no one else's. Based on these assurances, Mr. Craig proposed marriage to Ms. Hodge, and they were married on December 20, 1991. Ms. Hodge gave birth to a son named Kyle Chandler Craig on June 11, 1992.

proposed bc he believed he was the father

Mr. Craig raised Kyle believing him to be his biological son. He also adopted Ms. Hodge's daughter. In 1999, Mr. Craig had a vasectomy after he and Ms. Hodge decided that they did not desire more children. In October 2000, Mr. Craig took a job as an over-the-road truck driver to better support his family. Several weeks later, Ms. Hodge informed him that she was having an adulterous affair with Nicky Hodge who, at that time, was married to another woman. Ms. Hodge and Mr. Craig separated. In November 2000, Ms. Hodge filed a complaint in the Chancery Court for Maury County seeking a divorce on the ground of irreconcilable differences. The trial court entered a final divorce decree in February 2001 that incorporated the parties' marital dissolution agreement. The agreement provided that Mr. Craig and Ms. Hodge would have joint custody of the children and that Ms. Hodge would be the primary residential parent. Mr. Craig received visitation and was ordered to pay Ms. Hodge $250 per week in child support for both children and to provide medical insurance for the children.

joint custody

[Ms. Hodge remarried in 2002, and Mr. Craig remarried in 2003. Mr. Craig faithfully paid his child support and regularly traveled to Tennessee to visit Kyle and his adopted daughter. In 2005 Kyle began living with Mr. Craig and the child support order was changed. Mr. Craig had wanted another child with his new wife, but they decided not to try for a child because of the cost of having the vasectomy reversed, the likelihood that the procedure would be unsuccessful, and the fact that Mr. Craig already had a son to carry on the family name.]

. . . At some point during 2006 or 2007, Mr. Craig began to question whether he was Kyle's biological father. His doubts sprang from his belief that Kyle did not resemble him, comments made by others in the community, and an offhand comment made by Kyle following a visitation with Ms. Hodge. In February 2007, Mr. Craig surreptitiously obtained a DNA sample from Kyle while he was sleeping and submitted the sample for testing. The test confirmed that Mr. Craig was not Kyle's biological father. . . . [About a month later Mr. Craig told Ms. Hodge and Kyle about the test. Ms. Hodge reacted initially by saying that he was "crazy" and insisting on another test. However, she later conceded that

test confirmed he was not the dad

he was not Kyle's biological father and she told Kyle of this. Kyle reacted badly to the information. He moved back with Ms. Hodge and his relationship with Mr. Craig deteriorated. In April 2007, Ms. Hodge filed a pro se petition requesting custody of Kyle. After the parties acknowledged in open court that Mr. Craig was not Kyle's biological father, the trial court entered an order that returned Kyle to Ms. Hodge's custody and terminated Mr. Craig's child support obligation. In February 2008, Mr. Craig filed suit claiming that Ms. Hodge had intentionally or negligently misrepresented that he was Kyle's biological father. He sought $150,000 in compensatory damages and $150,000 in punitive damages. Ms. Hodge filed an answer in which she raised no affirmative defenses but denied that Mr. Craig asked Ms. Hodge in November 1991 to confirm that he was Kyle's father or that she ever had any reason to believe that Mr. Craig was not her child's father.]

Mr. Craig, Ms. Hodge, and Kyle testified at the bench trial on March 24, 2009. Mr. Craig testified that he would not have proposed to or married Ms. Hodge, that he would not have adopted Ms. Hodge's daughter, and that he would not have undergone a vasectomy had he known that there was a possibility that another man was Kyle's father. For her part, Ms. Hodge testified that she did not intend to mislead Mr. Craig about her son's parentage and that she believed at the time that Mr. Craig was her son's father. She also stated that she would not have married Mr. Craig had she known that he was not her son's father. Kyle testified that he was not interested in seeing Mr. Craig "at this moment."

In its order filed on April 3, 2009, the trial court observed that Ms. Hodge's "credibility . . . leaves much to be desired." The court also found that Ms. Hodge "knew that she and Joey Hay had sex and she knew there was a possibility that Joey Hay was the father of this unborn child." In addition, the court found that "[t]he fact that [Ms. Hodge] did not tell [Mr. Craig] about her sex with Joey Hay and allowed [Mr. Craig] to do the things he did after being told he was the father clearly shows her fraudulent intent to deceive [Mr. Craig] into thinking he was the father." Based on these factual findings, the trial court concluded that Ms. Hodge "purposely defrauded [Mr. Craig] into believing Kyle was his child, knowing she had sexual relations with Joey Hay at the time and a count on one's fingers would have revealed Joey Hay could be the father." As a result of Ms. Hodge's misrepresentation and failure to disclose a material fact, the trial court also concluded that she "practiced . . . fraud, misrepresentation and failure to disclose a material fact from December 20, 1991 when they married until their divorce February 9, 2001." . . .

[The trial court concluded that Ms. Hodge had committed fraud by intentionally misrepresenting to Mr. Craig that he was Kyle's father, and that Kyle could not have been fathered by anyone else. This finding was upheld by the Court of Appeals. The trial court awarded Mr. Craig damages of $25,244.44—a refund of the total child support, including medical expenses and insurance premiums that he had paid since Kyle's birth. It also awarded him damages for emotional distress and attorney's fees. The Court of Appeals reversed the damages award for child support, medical expenses, and insurance premiums on the grounds that the law prohibited a retroactive modification of an earlier child support order. It also reversed the $100,000 damage award for emotional distress on the grounds that noneconomic damages could not be awarded for a misrepresentation claim. Because it disallowed all the damages awards, it also reversed the award of attorney's fees. On appeal to the Supreme Court, Mr. Craig failed to raise the Court of Appeal's reversal of the emotional distress damages and attorney's fees, so his damages claim is confined to the refund of child support. The Supreme Court held that the Court of Appeals erred in finding that the award of compensatory damages for fraud constituted an impermissible retroactive modification of the child support order. We omit this portion of the opinion and include only the court's discussion of the fraud claim.]

The ancient common-law action for deceit provided the vehicle for persons to seek recovery from those who intend to deceive others for their own benefit. W. Page Keeton, *Prosser and Keeton on the Law of Torts* §105, at 727-28 (5th ed. 1984) ("Prosser & Keeton"). The basis for finding legal responsibility for deceit centered on the defendant's intent to deceive, mislead, or convey a false impression. Prosser & Keeton, §107, at 741. Throughout the centuries, the courts have had little difficulty finding the required intent to deceive when the evidence shows either that the defendant knows the statement is false or that the defendant made the statement "without any belief as to its truth, or with reckless disregard whether it be true or false." Prosser & Keeton, §107, at 741-42. When a victim of deceit sought restitution, the courts customarily considered the inequity of allowing the defendant to retain what he or she obtained from the plaintiff. However, in cases in which the deceit involved the transfer of something of value, the courts permitted the plaintiff to recover direct damages, along with special and consequential damages. Prosser & Keeton, §110, at 765-66.

Our current common-law claim for intentional misrepresentation is the successor to the common-law action for deceit. In fact, "intentional misrepresentation," "fraudulent misrepresentation," and "fraud" are different names for the same cause of action. In this opinion, we will refer to the cause of action as a claim for intentional misrepresentation, and, in order to avoid confusion, we suggest that this term should be used exclusively henceforth. To recover for intentional misrepresentation, a plaintiff must prove: (1) that the defendant made a representation of a present or past fact; (2) that the representation was false when it was made; (3) that the representation involved a material fact; (4) that the defendant either knew that the representation was false or did not believe it to be true or that the defendant made the representation recklessly without knowing whether it was true or false; (5) that the plaintiff did not know that the representation was false when made and was justified in relying on the truth of the representation; and (6) that the plaintiff sustained damages as a result of the representation.

Adopting the Restatement (Second) of Torts §549 (1977), this Court has held that the proper measure of damages for an intentional misrepresentation claim is:

> (1) The recipient of [an intentional] misrepresentation is entitled to recover as damages in an action of deceit against the maker the pecuniary loss to him of

which the misrepresentation is a legal cause, including (a) the difference between the value of what he has received in [the] transaction and its purchase price or other value given for it; and (b) pecuniary loss suffered otherwise as a consequence of the recipient's reliance upon the misrepresentation.

(2) The recipient of [an intentional] misrepresentation in a business transaction is also entitled to recover additional damages sufficient to give him the benefit of his contract with the maker, if these damages are proved with reasonable certainty.

The record in this case supports the conclusion of both the trial court and the Court of Appeals that Mr. Craig presented sufficient evidence to prove each of the elements of his intentional misrepresentation claim against Ms. Hodge. When Ms. Hodge discovered she was pregnant, she represented to Mr. Craig that he was the child's biological father and that no one else could be. This representation was false when it was made, and Ms. Hodge made this representation recklessly without knowing whether it was true or false. She knew that she had had sexual relations with Mr. Hay. Mr. Craig had no reason to know that Ms. Hodge's representation that he was the child's biological father was false, and he was justified in relying on the truth of Ms. Hodge's representation. Mr. Craig was damaged as a result of his belief that Ms. Hodge had told him the truth when she told him that he was the biological father of her child. Putting aside his decision to marry Ms. Hodge, Mr. Craig sustained monetary damages, not the least of which was his court-ordered obligation to pay child support and his payments for the child's medical expenses and insurance premiums following his divorce from Ms. Hodge.

The laudable goals of preserving intact families, promoting healthy relationships between parents and their children, and shielding children from their parents' vitriolic disagreements will not be advanced in this case by preventing Mr. Craig from pursuing his intentional misrepresentation claim against Ms. Hodge. The family unit here was already dissolved when Mr. Craig and Ms. Hodge divorced in 2001. The once healthy relationship between Mr. Craig and Kyle was extinguished in 2007. Providing stable financial support for Kyle is no longer a concern because the trial court relieved Mr. Craig of his obligation to support Kyle in 2005 and because Kyle turned eighteen in June 2010. . . . We affirm the determination of the Court of Appeals that Ms. Hodge intentionally misrepresented Kyle's paternity to Mr. Craig. . . . [W]e remand the case to the trial court with directions to amend its judgment to award Mr. Craig $25,244.44 in damages for the child support, medical expenses, and insurance premiums he paid following the divorce. . . .

■ QUESTIONS

(1)   Look at the various classifications of fraud in Restatement, Second, §162(1). How would you classify Ms. Hodge's assertion?

(2) As we noted earlier, although the Restatement, Second requires materiality only where the misrepresentation is non-fraudulent, many courts do not follow this approach. As you can see, *Hodge* is one such case. However, the court does not explain why the misrepresentation was material. Can you explain this? ~ *pregnancy was the central fact to this case*

(3) In our overview of remedies for fraud at the beginning of this section, we distinguished the contract remedy of rescission and restitution from the tort remedy of damages. Which remedy was granted in this case? (The answer to this question is not as obvious as it sounds.) *rescission & restitution*

(4) In an editor's note in the opinion, we mention that the trial court had awarded emotional distress damages to Mr. Craig, but that this was reversed by the Court of Appeals on the grounds that noneconomic damages could not be awarded for a misrepresentation claim. The Supreme Court did not consider this question because it had not been preserved on appeal. As we have noted periodically in discussing contracts damages, emotional distress damages are not usually allowed in contracts cases, but they are commonly available for *ED not recoverable in contracts cases* tortious injury. Had this question been before the Supreme Court, should it have reversed the Court of Appeals and upheld the trial court's award? Does your answer to Question 3 have any bearing on this?

(5) Ms. Hodge expressly told Mr. Craig, in answer to his question, that he was definitely Kyle's father and that no one else could be the father. How do you think this case would have been resolved if Mr. Craig had never asked that question and Ms. Hodge had never made that assertion expressly?

▇ PROBLEM 13.1

In *Sarvis v. Vermont State Colleges*, 172 Vt. 76, 772 A.2d 494 (Vt. 2001), Sarvis applied to be an adjunct professor at the Community College of Vermont (CCV). He submitted a resume stating that from 1984 to 1998 he was president and chairman of the board of CMI International, responsible for all operations and financial matters, and that since 1998 he had retired. He also stated that since 1998 he was an adjunct instructor in business at two other colleges. He said that he was "well equipped to teach" various business law and business ethics classes in which he had "the highest level of capability and interest." He particularly highlighted business ethics, which he said was "of particular concern" to him. The resume failed to mention that Sarvis had been convicted of bank fraud in 1995 and had been incarcerated from April 1995 to August 1998. The assertion that suggested that he was actively employed as president and chairman of CMI International during that period was therefore false. Sarvis discouraged CCV from contacting the other colleges, stating that it would be unfair to ask them for a reference because they did not know his work well. The real reason for discouraging contact was that the other colleges were aware of his criminal conviction.

After employing Sarvis, CCV learned of his criminal conviction and dismissed him. He sued CCV for wrongful dismissal. In its defense, CCV asserted that it was entitled to rescind the contract of employment on the grounds of his fraud. The court agreed. It held that Sarvis had misrepresented material facts by omitting the fact of his conviction and incarceration and asserting that he was actively working as president and chairman of the board of CMI International at the time that he was in jail. The court also found that his purpose in discouraging contact with the other colleges was to prevent that information being learned from that source.

(a) Fraud can take an affirmative form: an intentional lie or deliberate action to conceal a fact, intended to mislead the other party into entering the contract. It can also take a passive form, as the next section shows, where a party fails to disclose facts under circumstances in which he has a duty to do so. This case involves a deliberate lie. However, it also has elements of concealment and nondisclosure. Can you identify the falsehoods by commission and omission?

(b) Although the court indicates in its opinion that materiality is an element of fraud, it did not discuss why Sarvis's misrepresentation was material. Nor did it address the question of whether CCV was justified in relying on the resume at face value and making no other inquiries into Sarvis's background. Do you think that the misrepresentation was material? Why? Was CCV justified in relying on it? On balance, do you think that the court was correct to allow CCV to avoid any obligations it might otherwise have had under the employment contract?

3. Silence as Fraud: Fraudulent Nondisclosure and the Duty to Speak

Affirmative speech or conduct, in the form of a deliberate untrue statement or purposeful action to conceal a fact, presents a relatively clear case of fraud. It is more difficult to show fraud where the alleged deception consists of a failure to disclose information. As Restatement, Second §161 shows, silence is not tantamount to fraud in every situation. Sometimes a contracting party is entitled to keep information to himself.

RESTATEMENT, SECOND §161. WHEN NON-DISCLOSURE IS EQUIVALENT TO AN ASSERTION

A person's non-disclosure of a fact known to him is equivalent to an assertion that the fact does not exist in the following cases only:

(a) where he knows that disclosure of the fact is necessary to prevent some previous assertion from being a misrepresentation or from being fraudulent or material.

(b) where he knows that disclosure of the fact would correct a mistake of the other party as to a basic assumption on which that party is making the contract and if non-disclosure of the fact amounts to a failure to act in good faith and in accordance with reasonable standards of fair dealing.

(c) where he knows that disclosure of the fact would correct a mistake of the other party as to the contents or effect of a writing, evidencing or embodying an agreement in whole or in part.

(d) where the other person is entitled to know the fact because of a relation of trust and confidence between them.

KALOTI ENTERPRISES, INC. v. KELLOGG SALES COMPANY

283 Wis. 2d 555, 699 N.W.2d 205 (2005)
Wisconsin Supreme Court

ROGGENSACK, Justice.

On certification from the court of appeals, we review a decision of the circuit court for Waukesha County dismissing an amended complaint filed by petitioner, Kaloti Enterprises, Inc. (Kaloti), against respondents, Kellogg Sales Company (Kellogg) and Geraci & Associates, Inc. (Geraci), for failure to state a claim. [In summary, the question certified by the court of appeals is] . . . whether a duty to disclose facts arises between sophisticated parties to a commercial transaction where the parties have an established practice of doing business and the facts are material to a change in that practice of doing business. . . . Based solely on Kaloti's allegations, we conclude that Kellogg and Geraci had a duty of disclosure that they failed to satisfy, thereby providing a basis for Kaloti's intentional misrepresentation claim. . . . Therefore, we reverse the circuit court's dismissal of Kaloti's amended complaint, and we remand for further proceedings.

Kellogg is a wholly owned subsidiary corporation of Kellogg Company, Inc. Kaloti is a wholesaler of food products. Over several years, Kellogg and Kaloti entered into numerous transactions through Geraci, Kellogg's agent. In each transaction, Geraci approached Kaloti to sell Kellogg products. Geraci negotiated all elements of the transaction for Kellogg, including product specifics, price, delivery schedule, allowances, and terms of sale. Geraci accepted purchase orders from Kaloti and processed these orders, which were ultimately accepted by Kellogg. Following the negotiation of each contract, Kellogg "drop shipped" its product directly to Kaloti.... Kaloti then sold Kellogg's products. Kaloti alleges that, through a series of such transactions, a practice of doing business arose among Kaloti, Geraci and Kellogg, and that Geraci and Kellogg were aware that Kaloti bought Kellogg's products to resell them "as a 'secondary supplier' to large market stores."

Kellogg Company, Inc., acquired Keebler Foods Company (Keebler). As a result of that acquisition, Kellogg changed how it marketed NutriGrain and Rice Krispie Treat products. Instead of marketing these products through distributors or wholesalers such as Kaloti, Kellogg decided to sell them directly to the same large market stores to which Kaloti sold Kellogg's products. Kaloti did not know of Kellogg's decision to begin direct sales.

On May 14, 2001, after Geraci knew that Kellogg had changed to a direct-sales mode of marketing, Geraci solicited an order from Kaloti. The order was a $124,000 "quarterly promotion order," for NutriGrain and Rice Krispie Treats. Because of their past dealings with Kaloti, Geraci and Kellogg knew that it would take Kaloti three months to resell this order. Kaloti intended to market this order as it had in prior instances, as a secondary supplier to large stores, and it relied on that market being open. Further, in soliciting and accepting Kaloti's order, Geraci and Kellogg knew that Kellogg's change in marketing scheme would deny Kaloti the market it had used in the past to resell Kellogg's products.

Kellogg delivered the order to Kaloti on June 1, 2001, and Kaloti paid for it. On or about June 14, 2001, Kaloti's major and usual customers notified Kaloti that they would no longer purchase products from Kaloti because Kellogg was selling directly to them. On June 15, 2001, Geraci representative Michael Angele told Kaloti employee Mary Beth Welhouse that Geraci had not advised Kaloti of Kellogg's anticipated change in marketing strategy because of a confidentiality agreement between Kellogg and Geraci in respect to Kellogg's new marketing strategy. The same day, Kaloti notified Geraci and Kellogg that it was rescinding the May 14, 2001, purchase, advising them that it would not have placed the order or accepted the product if it had known that Kellogg had changed to a direct-sales mode of marketing. Kaloti attempted to return the product, but Kellogg has refused to accept delivery and has refused to reimburse Kaloti. Kaloti alleges that Geraci and Kellogg acted intentionally in concealing facts material to Kellogg's change in marketing strategy, which change caused Kaloti to be shut out of the market it had utilized in the past to resell Kellogg's products. Kaloti attempted to mitigate its damages and claims that, notwithstanding those efforts, it has lost $100,000 due to Kellogg's intentional misrepresentation.

We review a dismissal for failure to state a claim as a question of law, without deference to the circuit court's decision. In the present case, our inquiry begins with consideration of whether the amended complaint states an intentional misrepresentation claim, the determination of which turns on whether Geraci and Kellogg had a duty to disclose certain facts to Kaloti. Whether a duty exists is also a question of law that we review independently of the circuit court. . . .

There are three categories of common law misrepresentation: intentional, negligent, and strict liability misrepresentation. Kaloti's claim is for intentional misrepresentation, sometimes referred to as fraudulent misrepresentation, or common-law fraud. To state a claim for intentional misrepresentation, the following allegations must be made: (1) the defendant made a factual representation; (2) which was untrue; (3) the defendant either made the representation knowing it was untrue or made it recklessly without caring whether it was true or false; (4) the defendant made the representation with intent to defraud and to induce another to act upon it; and (5) the plaintiff believed the statement to be true and relied on it to his/her detriment. An intentional misrepresentation claim may arise either from a failure to disclose a material fact or from a statement of a material fact which is untrue. Here, Kaloti's intentional misrepresentation claim is based on the failure to disclose a material fact. However, "[a] person in a business deal must be under a duty to disclose a material fact before he can be charged with a failure to disclose." *Southard v. Occidental Life Ins. Co.*, 31 Wis. 2d 351, 359, 142 N.W.2d 844 (1966). When there is a duty to disclose a fact, the law has treated the failure to disclose that fact "as equivalent to a representation of the nonexistence of the fact." *Hennig v. Ahearn*, 230 Wis. 2d 149, 165, 601 N.W.2d 14 (Ct. App. 1999).

Whether Kellogg and Geraci had a duty to disclose is the only aspect of Kaloti's intentional misrepresentation claim that is at issue here. In particular, we are asked to determine whether Kellogg and Geraci had a duty to disclose a change in Kellogg's marketing strategy that largely closed the markets on which they knew Kaloti relied to sell Kellogg's products. In *Ollerman* [*v. O'Rourke Co.*, 94 Wis. 2d 17, 288 N.W.2d 95 (1980)], we decided that a duty to disclose had arisen in the course of a real estate transaction. We discussed at length the circumstances under which a duty to disclose a material fact may arise in business transactions. The usual rule is that there is no duty to disclose in an arm's-length transaction. However, courts have carved out a number of exceptions to that rule and have refused to apply the rule when to do so would work an injustice.[2]

Determining whether there is a legal duty and the scope of that duty presents questions of law that require courts to make policy determinations. The

---

[2] For example, we noted in *Ollerman* that courts have not applied the usual rule:

> where the seller actively conceals a defect or where [the seller] prevents investigation; where the seller has told a half-truth or has made an ambiguous statement if the seller's intent is to create a false impression and [the seller] does so; where there is a fiduciary relationship between the parties; or where the facts are peculiarly and exclusively within the knowledge of one party to the transaction and the other party is not in a position to discover the facts.

Ollerman, 94 Wis. 2d at 31, 288 N.W.2d 95.

Ollerman decision noted that, in making this determination, many factors interplay: the hand of history, our ideas of morals and justice, the convenience of administration of the rule, and our social ideas as to where the loss should fall. In the end the court will decide whether there is a duty on the basis of the mores of the community. As to the mores of the commercial world in particular, we further explained in *Ollerman*, "[T]he type of interest protected by the law of misrepresentation in business transactions is the interest in formulating business judgments without being misled by others—that is, an interest in not being cheated." *Id.* at 29-30, 288 N.W.2d 95.

We note that the Restatement (Second) of Torts §551 cmt. L (1977),[3] as well as several of the illustrations provided with it, have the following elements: (1) the non-disclosing party knew that the other party was not aware of the fact; (2) the mistaken party could not discover the fact by ordinary investigation or inspection, or he or she could not otherwise reasonably be expected to discover the fact; and (3) the mistaken party would not have entered into the transaction if he or she knew the fact.

The second element, that the mistaken party could not reasonably be expected to discover the fact, is particularly important to the present analysis. As we remarked in *Ollerman*, parties to a business transaction must "use their faculties and exercise ordinary business sense, and not call on the law to stand *in loco parentis* to protect them in their ordinary dealings with other business people." Further, "in a free market the diligent should not be deprived of the fruits of superior skill and knowledge lawfully acquired." *See also Market St. Assocs. Ltd. P'ship v. Frey*, 941 F.2d 588, 593-94. (7th Cir. 1991) (remarking that "the law contemplates that people frequently will take advantage of the ignorance of those with whom they contract, without thereby incurring liability").

However, it is another matter entirely when one party exclusively holds knowledge of facts material to the transaction that the other party has no means of acquiring. As we said in *Ollerman*, "where the [material] facts are peculiarly and exclusively within the knowledge of one party to the transaction and the other party is not in a position to discover the facts for himself [or herself]," disclosure is required. We similarly noted prominent legal commentator Dean Prosser's observation that courts have tended to find a duty to disclose in cases "*where the defendant has special knowledge or means of knowledge not open to the plaintiff* and is aware that the plaintiff is acting under a misapprehension as to facts which could be of importance to him, and would

---

[3] The comment provides this example:

> [A] seller who knows that his cattle are infected with tick fever or contagious abortion is not free to unload them on the buyer and take his money, when *he knows that the buyer is unaware of the fact, could not easily discover it, would not dream of entering into the bargain if he knew* and is relying upon the seller's good faith and common honesty to disclose any such fact if it is true.

Restatement (Second) of Torts §551 cmt. L (1977) (emphasis added).

probably affect his decision" (quoting William L. Prosser, *The Law of Torts* 697 (1971) (emphasis added)).

Drawing on the above-stated principles from our case law, we conclude that a party to a business transaction has a duty to disclose a fact where: (1) the fact is material to the transaction; (2) the party with knowledge of that fact knows that the other party is about to enter into the transaction under a mistake as to the fact; (3) the fact is peculiarly and exclusively within the knowledge of one party, and the mistaken party could not reasonably be expected to discover it; and (4) on account of the objective circumstances, the mistaken party would reasonably expect disclosure of the fact.

holding

In turning to application of this standard in the present case, . . . [w]e conclude that the allegations Kaloti made in its amended complaint . . . are sufficient, if proved at trial, to establish that Kellogg and Geraci each had a duty of disclosure. First, that Kellogg would be selling directly to the large stores in Kaloti's usual area of distribution is material, as Kaloti, a wholesaler and secondary supplier, bought products from Kellogg in order to resell them to these same large stores and would not have placed the May 14, 2001, order if it had known that Kellogg was going to sell directly. Second, Kellogg and Geraci knew that Kaloti was buying the products to resell them to these same stores, and that Kellogg's new mode of marketing would largely deny Kaloti its customary market. Third, while the Kellogg-Keebler merger may have been publicly announced, we infer from the confidentiality agreement between Kellogg and Geraci that the decision of Kellogg to engage in direct sales, rather than to sell through distributors or wholesalers, was not publicly announced. Accordingly, the fact that Kellogg had changed its mode of marketing was peculiarly and exclusively within Kellogg and Geraci's knowledge, and Kaloti could not reasonably be expected to have discovered this fact. Finally, because Kaloti had bought products from Kellogg for the purpose of acting as a secondary supplier for a number of years, it would be reasonable for Kaloti to expect that if Kellogg was going to sell these products directly to the same stores to which Kaloti customarily sold, Kellogg and its agent, Geraci, would advise Kaloti of this.

Kellogg and Geraci argue that they had no duty of disclosure to Kaloti because they were sophisticated, commercial entities engaged in an arm's-length transaction. As support for this proposition, they cite two federal court cases, *Guyer v. Cities Service Oil Co.*, 440 F. Supp. 630 (E.D. Wis. 1977) and *Badger Pharmacal, Inc. v. Colgate-Palmolive Co.*, 1 F.3d 621 (7th Cir. 1993). First, federal cases applying Wisconsin law provide persuasive, but not precedential, authority. In the 1977 *Guyer* decision, the district court concluded that the defendant oil company did not have a duty to disclose a change in marketing strategy to its gas station operators and lessees because there was no fiduciary relationship between the parties. *Guyer* was decided several years before our decision in *Ollerman* that recognized a broadening of Wisconsin law regarding the duty of disclosure and is therefore not persuasive. In *Badger Pharmacal*, the Seventh Circuit stated that "[w]hen two corporations, with the benefit of counsel, negotiate a commercial transaction at arms length, neither owes nor assumes a duty to disclose information to the other." This mischaracterizes Wisconsin law by speaking too broadly and by failing to recognize that there are exceptions to the traditional "no duty to disclose" rule. *See Ollerman*, 94 Wis. 2d at 29-42, 288 N.W.2d 95.

fails to recognize exceptions

Kellogg and Geraci further argue that an expansion of tort law will "wreak uncertainty on commercial arrangements that depend on order and certainty" and that, rather than rely on tort law, Kaloti should have acted diligently and negotiated contract terms to address the allocation of the risk at issue here. However, we are satisfied that our narrow holding in this case balances the general requirement that each party to a transaction must diligently protect its own self-interest, against the business community's interest in formulating business judgments without being intentionally misled by others.

Kellogg also argues that it had no duty of disclosure to Kaloti because the fact at issue did not satisfy the "basic fact" threshold,[4] as that term was proposed in the Restatement (Second) of Torts §551(2)(e), a standard that *Ollerman* drew upon. However, we declined in *Ollerman* to adopt the "basic fact" element of the Restatement standard, holding instead that it was the materiality of the fact that mattered. We similarly decline to adopt the "basic fact" versus "material fact" distinction and reaffirm that the relevant inquiry, as to that element of the standard articulated above, is whether the fact is material.

materiality of the fact matters

While we conclude that the allegations made in Kaloti's amended complaint are sufficient to state that Kellogg and Geraci had a duty of disclosure that they failed to meet, we note that Kaloti still must prove all the elements of the claim at trial, including whether the fact in question was material, whether Kellogg or Geraci knew Kaloti was mistaken as to this fact, whether Kaloti should reasonably have been expected to discover the fact, and whether Kaloti's reliance on Kellogg and Geraci's silence was justifiable. . . .

Based solely on Kaloti's allegations, we conclude that Kellogg and Geraci had a duty of disclosure that they failed to satisfy, thereby providing a basis for Kaloti's intentional misrepresentation claim. . . . Therefore we reverse the circuit court's decision to dismiss Kaloti's amended complaint and we remand for further proceedings. . . .

---

[4] Comment j to Restatement (Second) of Torts §551 discusses the distinction the Restatement position makes between facts that are basic and those that are material, stating in part: "A basic fact is a fact that is assumed by the parties as a basis for the transaction itself. It is a fact that goes to the basis, or essence, of the transaction, and is an important part of the substance of what is bargained for or dealt with. Other facts may serve as important and persuasive inducements to enter into the transaction, but not go to its essence. These facts may be material, but they are not basic."

■ PROBLEM 13.2

In re House of Drugs, Inc., 251 B.R. 206 (Bankr. D.N.J. 2000), involved a suit for damages for the failure of its business by House of Drugs, a bankrupt drugstore, against the lessor of retail premises in a shopping mall. The lessee claimed that the lessor had committed fraud by failing to disclose, at the time of entering the lease, that two of the largest tenants in the mall were about to go out of business. During the negotiations for the lease, the lessee did not ask the lessor whether any tenants were planning to leave the mall, and although the lessor knew that the major tenants were about to close down, it did not divulge this information. The lessee attributed the failure of its own business to the departure of the major tenants. Although the court acknowledged that an omission may constitute a material misrepresentation for the purpose of determining fraud, it did not decide whether the lessor's failure to disclose the information was fraudulent because even if it was, the element of reliance was missing. The lessee's officers had business education and experience, the lessee was represented by counsel, and the officers had conducted an independent investigation of the feasibility of operating their business in the mall. Their investigation included an assessment of traffic patterns in and the customer base of the mall, the lessee's officers were aware that one of the major tenants was in financial difficulty, and they assumed that there would be turnover of tenants in the mall. This information should have led them to inquire further about the financial stability of the large tenants.

(a) Would the lessee in *In re House of Drugs* have been better served by not conducting an investigation into the feasibility of doing business in the mall?

(b) As noted above, the court in *In re House of Drugs* resolved the case on the basis of the lessee's lack of reliance, so it did not reach the issue of whether the lessor's nondisclosure otherwise amounted to fraud. Decide this issue by applying the tests set out in *Kaloti Enterprises* and Restatement, Second §161. (Are the tests substantially the same?)

At common law (in the absence of any statute that provides otherwise), sales of real property are not subject to any implied warranty with regard to the condition and fitness of the property. Therefore, unless the seller agrees to provide a warranty, the buyer takes the property subject to any defects that may exist in the property. This principle is expressed in the Latin phrase, *caveat emptor*, or "let the buyer beware." However, the principle of *caveat emptor* is qualified by the seller's duty not to defraud the buyer, either by an affirmative false statement or by failing to disclose facts that the seller has a duty to disclose. Where the buyer claims fraud by nondisclosure, it can be difficult to decide if the seller had a duty to disclose in light of the buyer's responsibility to conduct adequate inquiry to protect his own interests.

MILLIKEN v. JACONO

60 A.3d 133 (2012)
Pennsylvania Superior Court

FORD ELLIOTT, President Judge Emeritus.

[On November 24, 2008, Janet Milliken, the buyer of a house, filed a Complaint against Kathleen and Joseph Jacono, the sellers of the house, and various real estate agents, alleging fraud regarding the sale of the property in that the defendants had failed to disclose that there had been a murder/suicide in the house. On February 11, 2006, the owner of the property prior to the Jaconos, Konstantinos Koumboulis, shot his wife and himself at that property. The Jaconos bought the property from the Koumboulis estate at an auction on September 23, 2006. The listing real estate agent made extensive inquiries and ascertained that under the state's Real Estate Seller Disclosure Law (RESDL), the murder/suicide was not treated as a material defect in the property, and therefore did not have to be disclosed. As a result, the seller's statutorily-required Property Disclosure Statement did not disclose the murder/suicide as a known material defect. However, the title report did show that the Jaconos had owned the property for only about seven months and had not lived in it. It showed that Koumboulis was the previous owner and last occupant, and that the property had been conveyed to the Jaconos by the Koumboulis estate. Had the plaintiff checked into the ownership history of the house, she could have discovered the murder/suicide. The plaintiff did not do so, and she bought the house. She did not become aware of the murder/suicide until three weeks after she moved into the property, sometime in September 2007. Upon discovering the house's history, the plaintiff sued the defendants, for rescission of the contract and the repayment of costs associated with the purchase of the property.

The trial court granted summary judgment in favor of the defendants. Two of the issues raised by the plaintiff on appeal were, first, whether failure to disclose the murder/suicide violated the RESDL because it constituted a "material defect" requiring disclosure, and second, whether the intentional nondisclosure of the murder/suicide constituted grounds for fraud. (We omit the other grounds raised by the plaintiff.)]

... We begin by noting that each of Buyer's claims on appeal relies, first, upon the existence of a material defect in the property and, second, upon the failure to reveal, or concealment of, that defect, or some deceptive conduct connected to that defect. In each instance, Buyer puts forward as the offending defect, certain psychological damage to the property occasioned by the murder/

holding

not a material defect

reputation is not considered

this expansion is too broad

suicide of Konstantinos and Georgia Koumboulis. Thus, if the murder/suicide cannot be considered a defect legally, or if the Sellers were under no legal obligation to reveal this alleged defect, there can be no liability predicated upon the failure to so inform. Today, we find that psychological damage to a property cannot be considered a material defect in the property which must be revealed by the seller to the buyer. Thus, each of Buyer's issues on appeal must fail. . . .

[The court first determines whether the RESDL requires the murder/suicide to be disclosed. The RESDL requires disclosure of "material defects," which it defines as "a problem with a residential real property or any portion of it that would have a significant adverse impact on the value of the property or that involves an unreasonable risk to people on the property. . . ." However, this general definition is then qualified by the prescribed content of the disclosure form, which has a detailed listing of the types of defects that must be disclosed. They all relate to the structural soundness of the property, hazardous conditions on the property, and potential legal impairments to ownership. There is no reference to matters that affect the reputation of the property or any kind of psychological damage to it. The court concludes that the legislature did not intend to include in the required disclosures matters that go to psychological damage, even if it could be argued that this might cause a diminution in the value of the property. The court notes that the exclusion of this type of damage makes sense because it would be very difficult to know what impact bad events would have on the value of property, whether this would diminish over time, and which kind of bad events should be included.]

The fact that a murder once occurred in a house falls into that category of homebuyer concerns best left to *caveat emptor*. If psychological defects must be disclosed then we are not far from requiring sellers to reveal that a next-door neighbor is loud and obnoxious, or on some days you can smell a nearby sewage plant, or that the house was built on an old Indian burial ground. Indeed, one could identify numerous psychological problems with any house. Sellers should only be required to reveal material defects with the actual physical structure of the house, with legal impairments on the property, and with hazardous materials located there. To allow consideration of possible psychological defects opens a myriad of disclosures that sellers will need to reveal, and starts a descent down a very slippery slope.

Moreover, an expansion of required seller disclosures from the physical to the psychological is a massive expansion in the character of disclosure. It requires the seller to warn not only of the physically quantifiable but also of utterly subjective defects. We find that such a change is one that can only reside with the Legislature. In sum, the RESDL does not require the disclosure of psychological defects such as the murder/suicide at issue here, and there was no liability under the RESDL for failing to disclose the matter. The trial court properly granted summary judgment.

Likewise, we find no liability . . . [for fraud]. In order to prove fraud the following elements must be shown: (1) a representation; (2) which is material to the transaction at hand; (3) made falsely, with knowledge of its falsity or recklessness as to whether it is true or false; (4) with the intent of misleading another into relying on it; (5) justifiable reliance on the misrepresentation; and (6) the resulting injury was proximately caused by the reliance.

non-material fact = no fraud

Sellers cannot be found liable for fraud because they did not conceal or fail to disclose a material defect in the property. As our analysis under the RESDL has revealed, Sellers were under no legal obligation to tell Buyer about the murder/suicide. On her part, Buyer argues that the murder/suicide was material because she would not have purchased it had she been aware of the murder/suicide. Buyer also argues that the matter is material because she had expert testimony that the murder/suicide diminished the value of the property.

In support, Buyer cites to *Reed v. King,* 145 Cal. App. 3d 261, 193 Cal. Rptr. 130 (1983), and *Van Camp v. Bradford,* 63 Ohio Misc. 2d 245, 623 N.E.2d 731 (Ohio Ct. of Common Pleas 1993), which relies directly on *Reed. Reed* involved the sale of a house in which a woman and her four children had been murdered 10 years earlier. *Van Camp* involved the sale of a house in which a rape had been committed within the last year, coupled with the fact that additional rapes had recently been committed in the neighborhood. In finding actionable fraud, *Reed* adopted a broad meaning of materiality:

> In general, a seller of real property has a duty to disclose "where the seller knows of facts *materially* affecting the value or desirability of the property which are known or accessible only to him and also knows that such facts are not known to, or within the reach of the diligent attention and observation of the buyer, the seller is under a duty to disclose them to the buyer." [Emphasis added; citations omitted.]

The problem with this analysis is one we alluded to during our discussion of the RESDL; it changes the measure of materiality from an objective to a subjective basis. Under *Reed,* not only must a seller inform a buyer about objective structural defects or objective legal impairments, but also wholly subjective problems that might have an impact on the buyer's decision. This would open the same slippery slope we addressed earlier, requiring sellers to recite a litany of potential psychological defects. We decline to adopt the view of materiality championed by *Reed.*

holding

While the murder/suicide may have been subjectively material to Buyer's decision, we hold that under common law fraud a seller of real estate is only liable for failing to reveal objective material defects. Psychological damage to real estate does not constitute a defect that the law is presently prepared to recognize as material. No action for fraud could be maintained on this basis and the trial court properly granted summary judgment. . . .

■ ■ ■

The decision of the Pennsylvania Superior Court (the intermediate court of appeals) was appealed to the Supreme Court of Pennsylvania, which affirmed the grant of summary judgment in favor of the defendants: *Milliken v. Jacono*, 103 A.3d 806 (Pa. 2014). The Supreme Court agreed that a psychological stigma attaching to property does not qualify as a material defect, either for purposes of the RESDL or for fraud. The court noted that the implications of recognizing non-disclosure of psychological stigma as fraud would be overwhelming as courts try to distinguish which genres of murder, suicide, or violence are sufficiently traumatizing as to rise to the level of materiality. "The occurrence of a tragic event inside a house does not affect the quality of the real estate, which is what seller disclosure duties are intended to address. We are not prepared to set a standard under which the visceral impact an event has on the populace serves to gauge whether its occurrence constitutes a material defect in property."

■ QUESTION

The Pennsylvania Superior Court says that if it required disclosure of psychological defects, such as the suicide-murder in this house, "we are not far from requiring sellers to reveal that a next-door neighbor is loud and obnoxious, or on some days you can smell a nearby sewage plant, or that the house was built on an old Indian burial ground." The Supreme Court makes the point of distinguishing psychological stigma from the physical quality of the real estate.

Do you think that these three other problems mentioned by the Superior Court are analogous to the problem in this case, or do they relate to the physical quality of the property? Do you agree that a seller should not have to reveal them?

■ PROBLEM 13.3

In *Milliken* the court's resolution of the fraud issue was strongly influenced by the existence of a statute setting out the seller's disclosure obligations. Such statutes have become common in many states with regard to sales of residential real property. The Pennsylvania RESDL applicable in *Milliken* had to be interpreted by the court to determine if it applied to "psychological defects." Some statutes are more express in excluding non-physical attributes of the property—typically arising out of some past event (such as suicide, murder, or death from AIDS) that creates a purely psychological stigma on the property. The policy of these statutes is to preclude rescission of a contract solely on the basis of prejudice deemed to be irrational.

Stambovsky v. Ackley, 572 N.Y.S.2d 672, 169 A.D.2d 254 (1991) is a much-loved case, primarily because of its supernatural facts and facetious opinion. It was decided before New York had any such statute, so the court had to determine whether the common law *caveat emptor* rule precluded the buyer's claim of fraud by nondisclosure.

Shortly after buying a house in the village of Nyack on the Hudson River, the buyer discovered that the house was widely reputed to be possessed by poltergeists. The seller was well aware of this reputation and had in fact encouraged and promoted it by reporting the apparitions to both the local press and *Reader's Digest* and including the house as a "riverfront Victorian (with ghost)" in a walking tour of Nyack. The buyer sought to rescind the sale, arguing that the house's haunted reputation greatly diminished its market value. The seller moved to dismiss the suit on the basis of *caveat emptor.* The trial court granted the motion to dismiss but the majority of the Appellate Division reversed, reinstating the action. The court held that while a buyer would have had the duty, under the *caveat emptor* rule, to inspect the premises and public records to ascertain physical and structural defects in the house, he could not be expected to inquire into or ascertain its haunted reputation. This was a condition created by the seller, was peculiarly within her knowledge, and was unlikely to be discovered by a prudent purchaser. The seller had created and perpetuated the public belief that the house was possessed and therefore, notwithstanding the *caveat emptor* rule, had a duty to the buyer to inform him of this condition.

A dissenting judge pointed out that the haunted reputation of the house was well publicized in both the local press and in *Reader's Digest.* The parties had dealt with each other at arm's length, were represented by counsel, and the contract specifically stated that neither party relied on any representation made by other. Under the *caveat emptor* rule, the buyer had the duty to ascertain the facts about the house and could not rely on the seller's failure to mention its haunted reputation.

Both the majority and the dissent balanced the buyer's duty to make reasonable inquiry against the seller's failure to disclose. The dissent suggests that the house's well-publicized haunted reputation was discoverable by reasonable inquiry. However, the majority concludes, in essence, that even though there was information available about the house's possession by poltergeists, a reasonable plaintiff would not even think to look into that. He would know to inspect the property for structural defects and to examine public records, but he could not be expected to contemplate or inquire into poltergeist infestation.

(a) The crucial distinction between these views is the expectation of what would be reasonable. Which is the correct view?

(b) How does one determine the character and nature of a reasonable buyer and what the scope of his inquiry should be?

(c) To what extent should prevailing cultural attitudes (such as a belief that ghosts or spirits are or are not imaginary) be relevant to this inquiry?

4. Misrepresentation of Fact, Opinion, or Prediction

Fraud is based on a misrepresentation of fact. As a general rule, one can say that a fact is distinguishable from a mere expression of opinion or a prediction. However, where an expression of opinion or a prediction has a factual basis, the expression of a false opinion or prediction could qualify as fraud. The challenge is to decide when a false opinion or prediction crosses the line into fraudulent factual assertion.

when it has a factual basis

RODI v. SOUTHERN NEW ENGLAND SCHOOL OF LAW

389 F.3d 5 (2004)
United States Court of Appeals, First Circuit

SELYA, Circuit Judge.

This is an appeal from a terse order dismissing a . . . complaint for failure to state a claim upon which relief might be granted. . . . We conclude that the complaint states one potentially actionable claim and another that is not beyond hope of repair. Consequently, we reverse the order of dismissal in part and remand for further proceedings.

desposition

. . . [W]e take the facts as they are alleged in the plaintiff's complaint. . . . In July of 1997, plaintiff-appellant Joseph Rodi, a would-be law student who resided in New Jersey, received a recruitment letter from Francis J. Larkin, dean of Southern New England School of Law (SNESL). The letter stated in pertinent part that the accreditation committee of the American Bar Association (ABA) had voted to recommend SNESL for "provisional accreditation," a status that would be granted upon ratification of the recommendation by two other ABA bodies. The letter also stated that SNESL was "highly confident" of receiving the needed ratifications and that the future of the school "has never been brighter." Because the plaintiff intended to take the New Jersey bar examination, the prospect of accreditation was critically important to him; New Jersey requires bar applicants to hold law degrees from ABA-accredited institutions.

needed the school to be accredited

Larkin's letter ended with a pitch for enrollment. The solicitation bore fruit; the plaintiff enrolled at SNESL that month. He received a catalogue from SNESL containing, inter alia, a statement (in the same type size and font as the surrounding text) to the effect that: "The Law School makes no representation to any applicant or student that it will be approved by the American Bar Association prior to the graduation of any matriculating student." The complaint alleges that, despite the cheery optimism of Larkin's letter, the dean knew full well that SNESL had identifiable deficiencies that would almost certainly preclude ABA accreditation.

not promising it will be accredited

Dean had knowledge the school couldn't be accredited

The ABA denied SNESL's application for accreditation in September of 1997. As a result, the plaintiff considered transferring to an accredited law school for his second year of study. Word of his ambivalence reached the dean's office. David M. Prentiss, who was then the acting dean, wrote to the plaintiff in order to "make sure" that he was "fully informed of the school's current status regarding ABA accreditation." That communique stated in substance that the school had improved the four areas found deficient by the ABA and that there should be "no cause for pessimism" about the school achieving accreditation before the plaintiff's forecasted graduation date.

encouraged him not to transfer

In reliance on these and other representations—all of which the complaint says were knowingly false—the plaintiff remained at SNESL. He came to regret the choice: according to the complaint, SNESL knew, but elected not to disclose, that the ABA was highly critical of SNESL; that any faint hope of attaining accreditation depended upon a complete overhaul of the faculty, administration, curriculum, and student body; and that the level of non-compliance made the prospect of SNESL's near-term accreditation remote. To compound this mendacity, the school frustrated students' attempts to learn about the true status of the accreditation pavane.

made it hard to find out the real status

In November of 1999—during the plaintiff's third year of legal studies—the ABA denied SNESL's renewed application for accreditation. SNESL failed to appeal to the ABA's House of Delegates as it previously had promised. Instead, the school cashiered half of its full-time faculty, thereby straying even further from ABA-mandated standards. The plaintiff completed his studies in June of 2000. SNESL remained unaccredited. Notwithstanding his diploma, the plaintiff has not been able to sit for the New Jersey bar examination.

wasn't allowed to sit for the bar

... On June 9, 2003, the plaintiff, acting pro se, sued the ... defendants [SNESL, Larkin, and Prentiss] in the United States District Court for the District of Massachusetts ... [on grounds of] diversity of citizenship and the existence of a controversy in the requisite amount. ... We confine our discussion to the two claims that the plaintiff presses on appeal: (i) that the defendants' statements constituted actionable fraud or misrepresentation, and (ii) that SNESL's actions violated a consumer protection statute. ... [The court's discussion of the second claim is omitted.] The defendants filed a timely motion to dismiss, positing that the complaint, for a variety of reasons, failed to state a claim upon which relief could be granted. As to the fraudulent misrepresentation count, the defendants asseverated that the "misrepresentations" were non-actionable statements of opinion ... [and that] the plaintiff's professed reliance on those statements was unreasonable. ... [The district court] entered a cryptic order, providing in its entirety that the motion to dismiss should be allowed. ...

The defendants advance a motley of potential defenses to the plaintiff's fraudulent misrepresentation claim. We address them sequentially. We start by testing the vitality of the claim as a whole. We will uphold a dismissal on this ground only if the plaintiff's factual averments hold out no hope of recovery on any theory adumbrated in his complaint. Our task is not to decide whether the plaintiff ultimately will prevail but, rather, whether he is entitled to undertake discovery in furtherance of the pleaded claim. In this process, the fact that the plaintiff filed the complaint pro se militates in favor of a liberal reading. Sitting in diversity, we look to the substantive law of the forum state (here, Massachusetts) to guide our analysis. Under Massachusetts law, a claim for misrepresentation entails a false statement of material fact made to induce the plaintiff to act and reasonably relied upon by him to his detriment. The plaintiff's claim passes this screen.

As to Larkin, the complaint, read liberally, alleges the following: (i) Larkin knew that the plaintiff was a New Jersey resident who wanted to practice law there; (ii) he also knew that the plaintiff could not sit for the New Jersey bar unless he graduated from an accredited law school; (iii) he sent a letter to the plaintiff in New Jersey stating that SNESL was "highly confident" of receiving accreditation, knowing that this statement was materially false because SNESL had substantial deficiencies that would make accreditation difficult if not impossible; and (iv) the plaintiff, relying on Larkin's letter, enrolled at SNESL, paid substantial sums for tuition, and invested three years of his life in mastering its curriculum. We think that these allegations, if proven, would make out a viable claim for fraudulent misrepresentation. *See Kerr v. Shurtleff*, 218 Mass. 167, 105 N.E. 871, 872 (1914) (holding that college committed fraudulent misrepresentation by falsely telling prospective student that it could "make [him] a D.M.D." when student enrolled and graduated but school lacked the authority to grant the degree).

A similar analysis applies to the plaintiff's fraudulent misrepresentation claim against Prentiss. Prentiss's statement that there was "no cause for pessimism" about the prospect of near-term accreditation is materially false if there was in fact cause for pessimism due to the extent of the school's known shortcomings. The plaintiff alleges that Prentiss knowingly made this false statement in order to induce him to remain enrolled at SNESL and that he (Rodi) took the bait and relied on it to his detriment.

As pleaded, SNESL is vicariously liable for these fraudulent misrepresentations. It is reasonable to infer from the allegations contained in the complaint that Larkin and Prentiss were high-ranking employees of SNESL acting within the scope of their employment. Consequently, their misrepresentations are attributable to SNESL on respondeat superior grounds. Accordingly, the complaint, on its face, states a claim for fraudulent misrepresentation against all three defendants.

The defendants' effort to short-circuit this claim is multifaceted. Their first counter is that the cited statements were, at most, statements of opinion. That is true, in a sense, but it does not get the defendants very far. A statement, though couched in terms of opinion, may constitute a statement of fact if it may reasonably be understood by the reader or listener as implying the existence of facts that justify the statement (or, at least, the non-existence of any facts incompatible with it). *See McEneaney v. Chestnut Hill Realty Corp.*, 38 Mass. App. Ct. 573, 650 N.E.2d 93, 96 (1995); *see also Restatement (Second) of Torts* §539 (1977) (explaining that "[a] statement of opinion as to facts not disclosed [may] be interpreted . . . as an implied statement that the facts known to the maker are not incompatible with his opinion"); *cf. Levinsky's, Inc. v. Wal-Mart Stores, Inc.,* 127 F.3d 122, 127 (1st Cir. 1997) ("A statement couched as an opinion that presents or implies the existence of facts which are capable of being proven true or false can be actionable."). Thus, it is an actionable misrepresentation for a corporation falsely to tell investors that a specific project is "a great success" that is "proceeding smoothly . . . and better than expected" in order to keep them from pulling the plug. *Stolzoff v. Waste Sys. Int'l, Inc.,* 58 Mass. App. Ct. 747, 792 N.E.2d 1031, 1036-37, 1042 (2003). Similarly, it is an actionable misrepresentation for a car dealer to tell a buyer that he "believes" a vehicle is in "good" condition when he knows that it has significant mechanical defects. *Briggs v. Carol Cars, Inc.,* 407 Mass. 391, 553 N.E.2d 930, 933 (1990).

[handwritten margin note: opinions that imply the existence of fact may be actionable]

The Restatement, favorably referenced in the Massachusetts cases, gives a stunningly appropriate example:

> [W]hen an auditor who is known to have examined the books of a corporation states that it is in sound financial condition, he may reasonably be understood to say that his examination has been sufficient to permit him to form an honest opinion and that what he has found justifies his conclusion. The opinion thus becomes in effect a short summary of those facts. When he is reasonably understood as conveying such a statement, he is subject to liability if he . . . has not found facts that justify the opinion, on the basis of his misrepresentation of the implied facts.

[handwritten margin note: opinion may become a short summary of fact]

Restatement (Second) of Torts §539, cmt. b. The parallel is apparent. The plaintiff's complaint alleges that the ABA has formulated certain objective criteria that inform its decisions about whether and when to accredit law schools. It also alleges that Larkin, knowing of these criteria, wrote a letter to the plaintiff implying that the school was reasonably capable of satisfying them. If Larkin did know of disqualifying and probably irremediable deficiencies (as the plaintiff has alleged), his statement that SNESL was "highly confident" of accreditation was actionably misleading. Prentiss's statement that there 'was "no cause for pessimism" about the fate of the school's renewed accreditation application is subject to much the same analysis.

To be sure, knowing falsity is much easier to allege than to prove. Here, however, the district court jettisoned the fraudulent misrepresentation count at the pleading stage. . . . [T]hat dismissal cannot rest on the "opinion" defense. . . .

[The court went on to deal with the argument by SNESL that a disclaimer in the law school's catalog precluded Rodi from relying justifiably on the assertions made by the deans. The court rejected this argument. We defer to Section B.6 a discussion of the impact of a contractual disclaimer on justifiable reliance.]

For the reasons elaborated above, we reverse the district court's order insofar as it dismisses the fraudulent misrepresentation count.

■   ■   ■

Following remand and discovery, the district court granted summary judgment to SNESL on the fraudulent misrepresentation claim on the grounds that even if the deans had made false statements of material fact, Rodi was not justified in relying on those misrepresentations. Rodi again appealed, and this time the court of appeals affirmed the judgment of district court, *Rodi v. New England School of Law*, 532 F.3d 11 (1st Cir. 2008). The court agreed with the district court that Rodi did not in fact act in reliance on the deans' statements—he was not induced by the statements to stay at SNESL. He had actually tried to transfer to other schools and remained at SNESL only because his attempts to transfer were unsuccessful. In addition, the court held that even if he had relied on the statements, that reliance was not justified. Rodi was aware of the difficulties SNESL was having in its accreditation efforts, and his interaction with the deans over time should have made him skeptical of relying on their predictions of success.

[handwritten margin note: didn't actually rely on the statement]

■ PROBLEM 13.4

As *Rodi* shows, some expressions of opinion or predictions of future events are sufficiently fact-based to qualify as representations of fact. However, other opinions are more properly seen as expressions of taste, viewpoint, or subjective judgment or belief. Where, say, a seller of goods extols the virtues of its product, it could be making a representation about the qualities of the product, or could simply be engaging in "puffery" or "seller's talk." It can be difficult to decide whether an opinion or prediction should be treated as a fact that induces justifiable reliance, or should be disregarded as hype. To make this determination, one must consider not only the apparent factual underpinnings of the opinion or prediction, but also the relationship of the parties. The basic inquiry is whether, under all the circumstances, the party to whom the opinion is expressed was justified in relying on it as a fact-based assertion. In some transactions (such as those involving the rendition of professional services) there could be heavy reliance on the honest opinion of a party, which is expected to be based on expert skill and judgment.

In light of this, consider whether fraudulent misrepresentations were made in the following situations. Assume in each case that the party to whom they were expressed believed them and was induced to enter the contract by them:

(a) The seller of a used sports utility vehicle decided to sell it because it had a dangerously high center of gravity, was disappointingly lacking in power, and guzzled gas. He told the buyer, "I love this car and hate to sell it. It's a great recreational vehicle, and its gas consumption will astound you." The written contract of sale says nothing about the qualities of the vehicle and states that it is sold "as is."

(b) In an advertisement, the seller of a house described it as a "charming Victorian." She does not believe that it is at all charming and knows that although it is Victorian in style, it was built in 1920 and is therefore not truly Victorian. The written contract does not contain this language and has a merger clause stating that no representations have been made, save for those contained in the writing.

(c) In convincing a customer to buy a painting, the owner of an art gallery said, "This painting is a major work of a brilliant young artist. His painting technique is unique and exquisite. He will go far." The gallery owner did in fact like the painting. However, the gallery owner is an ignoramus who knows nothing about art or the art market. He really has no clue about the technique or prospects of the artist.

(d) An attorney believes that his client has a poor case. Nevertheless, he has told the client that the case has strong merits and a good chance of success. The attorney therefore encourages the client to enter a contract engaging him to litigate the case.

(e) The seller of a loud plaid coat has persuaded his customer to buy it by telling him, "This is the latest thing in fashion. It looks great on you. The color is right for your skin tone, and you look slim in it." In fact, the design of the coat is not new—it is just that it is so flashy that it is rare to find anyone wearing it. Also, the seller thinks that the color accentuates the customer's pasty complexion and, because the customer is considerably overweight, the seller knows that nothing can make him look slim.

5. Misrepresentation of Intent

fraud is at the time of contracting

As we have seen, fraud involves a misrepresentation of fact at the time of contracting. Therefore, where a party breaches a contract after it has been entered, even if that breach is deliberate, there is seldom a basis for the victim to assert a claim for fraud. The proper relief is a remedy for breach of contract. However, it sometimes happens that the victim of the breach can show that the breaching party never intended to perform as promised. If the victim can prove that when the breacher entered the contract, she had already determined to breach it, this could constitute a fraudulent misrepresentation. Although the contractual promise is not a representation of fact, but an expression of future intent, it can qualify as a misrepresentation of the fact of the party's state of mind at the time of making the contract. This situation is quite rare and not easy to prove. Because the misrepresenting party will surely have been careful to conceal her true intentions, the fraudulent intent must usually be shown by circumstantial evidence.

Can't claim fraud once a contract is breached

it can be fraud if you enter a contract, intending to breach it

■ **PROBLEM 13.5**

Carey v. FedEx Ground Package System, Inc., 321 F. Supp. 2d 902 (S.D. Ohio 2004) is a case in which the court held that the plaintiff had alleged sufficient facts to proceed to trial on the question of whether there had been a fraudulent misrepresentation of intent. Carey had entered into negotiations with FedEx for the purpose of acquiring a FedEx route. Over a two-year period, FedEx gave him repeated specific and unambiguous assurances that he would receive a route. While it was holding out this expectation of a route, FedEx took advantage of Carey's services by employing him as a temporary driver. Carey never received the route. He sued FedEx on several theories, including fraud. The court denied FedEx's motion for summary judgment and held that Carey had made out a cause of action for fraud. The court said that although fraud generally cannot be predicated upon promises or representations relating to future action, a promise could be fraudulent where a party has no intention of keeping the promise when he makes it. In this case, a jury could find that when FedEx made the successive promises to give Carey a route, it had no intention of doing that, but was merely stringing him along so that he would continue to work for the company as a temporary driver.

(a) When the case goes to trial, what kind of evidence would Carey have to offer to prove fraudulent misrepresentation of intent?

(b) In *Kaloti Enterprises, Inc. v. Kellogg Sales Co.* (in Section B.3) the court found that Kellogg had committed fraud by nondisclosure. Do the facts of that case support a finding on the alternative ground of fraudulent misrepresentation of intent?

(c) In June, Employee entered into a one-year employment contract with Employer. Employer insisted on a one-year contract because employees are not very productive during the training period over the first three months on the job. At the time of contracting, Employee had already been accepted into graduate school for the fall semester. He intended to resign and enter the graduate program at the beginning of the semester on August 30. However, he did not tell Employer this because he knew that Employer would not have hired him for only 3 months. In mid-June Employer found out about Employee's plan to terminate the contract in August and can prove that Employee never intended to work for the year-long contract period. Can Employer dismiss Employee on grounds of fraud? Could Employer instead dismiss Employee on grounds of breach of contract? How does dismissal on grounds of fraud differ from dismissal on grounds of breach?

6. Justifiable Inducement and Contracting Out of Fraud

The issue of whether the plaintiff was justified in being induced by the affirmative misrepresentation or nondisclosure was raised in the discussion of the elements of fraud in Section B.1 and has arisen in many of the cases following. It is the focus of the next case, which also raises the question of whether a party can shield itself from liability for fraud by including a disclaimer in the contract. Courts often state that, as a matter of public policy, a party cannot contract out of fraud—that is, it cannot insulate itself from a claim of fraud by including a disclaimer of representations, a waiver, or some other provision in the contract that precludes the other party from asserting a claim of fraud.

The court dealt with this issue in a portion of the opinion in *Rodi v. New England School of Law* that we edited out of the case in Section B.4. The law school made the argument that a disclaimer in its catalog precluded justifiable reliance on any representation that may have been made by the deans. The catalog disclaimed any "representation to any applicant or student that [SNESL] will be approved by the American Bar Association prior to the graduation of any matriculating student." The court said that the disclaimer did not cover the representations of the deans. It simply stated that the school did not represent that it would be accredited by the time of any student's graduation, but the plaintiff's complaint alleged that the deans falsely implied that the school had the capacity to achieve near-term accreditation. The court said this was a meaningful distinction. "It is one thing for an actor to demur when asked to guarantee a third party's actions. It is quite another for an actor to mislead a person into believing that the actor itself possesses means and abilities fully within its control." The court went on to say that even if the disclaimer had covered the misrepresentations, it would not have been effective because a party may not contract out of fraud. The court left open the possibility that the presence of the disclaimer could have had an impact on the issue of whether Rodi relied justifiably on the representations of the deans, but said that this issue was not properly disposed of at the stage of a motion to dismiss. This qualification by the court indicates a qualification on the general assertion that a party cannot contract out of fraud. Justifiable reliance is an element of fraud and in some cases the fact that the victim of the fraud executed a contractual disclaimer or waiver could lead to the conclusion that the party was not justified in relying on misrepresentation or nondisclosure that is at odds with the disclaimer or waiver.

PSENICSKA v. TWENTIETH CENTURY FOX FILM CORP.

Not reported in F. Supp., 2008 WL 4185752 (2008), aff'd,
409 Fed. Appx 368 (2d Cir. 2009)
United States District Court, Southern District of New York

PRESKA, District Judge.

The above captioned actions[5] all arise from the film *BORAT—Cultural Learnings of America for Make Benefit Glorious Nation of Kazakhstan* ("*Borat*" or "the Movie"). In short, Plaintiffs all seek damages for the use of their images in the Movie, and Defendants[6] have moved to dismiss each complaint under Rule 12(b)(6) of the Federal Rules of Civil Procedure. For the reasons discussed more fully below, I conclude that each Plaintiff has executed a valid agreement releasing the claims he or she now attempts to litigate, and, consequently, Defendants' motions are hereby granted.

[handwritten: ← holding]

[handwritten margin note: π released their claims]

Released in theaters in 2006, *Borat* tells the story of a fictional Kazakh television personality, Borat, sent to the United States to report on American culture. . . . [T]he movie employs as its chief medium a brand of humor that appeals to the most childish and vulgar in its viewers. At its core, however, *Borat* attempts an ironic commentary of "modern" American culture, contrasting the backwardness of its protagonist with the social ills [that] afflict supposedly sophisticated society. The movie challenges its viewers to confront, not only the bizarre and offensive Borat character himself, but the equally bizarre and offensive reactions he elicits from "average" Americans.

Each Plaintiff in the above-captioned actions appeared in the Movie; the circumstances surrounding their appearances are described below. . . . Plaintiff Michael Psenicska ("Psenicska") has owned a driving school for 32 years, where he personally administers driving lessons. In May 2005, he was contacted by Defendant Schulman, who informed him that Defendant One America was producing a "documentary about the integration of foreign people into the American way of life." Psenicska was interested in participating in the Movie and agreed to meet the production crew in Washington, D.C. for filming on June 13, 2005. Before filming, Psenicska informed Schulman that he would need to leave by 5:00 P.M. to teach a driving class at 6:00 P.M. On the day of filming, however, Schulman and the production crew arrived 90 minutes late with $500 in cash for Psenicska, as well as papers "needed by the producers for the documentary." According to his Complaint, Psenicska was unaware that

---

[5] The case consolidates several similar suits by different plaintiffs.—EDS.

[6] In addition to Twentieth Century Fox, the plaintiffs sued Sacha Baron Cohen, the actor who played the Borat character in the movie, and Todd Schulman. The court's opinion does not indicate what Schulman's role was in producing the movie. However, it appears from news reports of the case that he was the "field coordinator" for the movie. As the opinion indicates, he was responsible for eliciting the plaintiffs' participation in the movie.—EDS.

didn't know he would have to sign anything

he would be asked to sign something and, consequently, failed to bring his reading glasses. Nevertheless, because he was rushed for time due to Schulman's late arrival, Psenicska signed the document, entitled the Standard Consent Agreement ("the Agreement"), without reading it, claiming to rely on previous conversations with Schulman. Psenicska was then shown to a driver-education car and instructed to follow a production van through a driving course. The ensuing events involved Defendant Cohen, as Borat ("Cohen/Borat"), driving irresponsibly and erratically while engaging in conversations with strangers and making derogatory and offensive remarks about sexual intercourse, Jews, women and African-Americans. Once taping ended, Psenicska approached a group of men he believed were producers of the Movie and accused them of setting him up, but elicited no response. Over the next several days, Psenicska attempted to contact Schulman to determine the intent of the film but again received no response and subsequently commenced his action on December 3, 2007.

Plaintiff Cindy Streit ("Streit") is the owner of an etiquette training business called ETS. In October 2005, she was contacted by Schulman and asked to provide etiquette training to a Belarus dignitary and arrange a dinner party with guests to be filmed for an educational documentary made for Belarus television. On October 24, 2005, Streit and Defendant . . . negotiated and signed a written contract for Streit's services. That same day, Schulman informed Streit that Cohen/Borat would not attend the etiquette training session but would attend the 6:00 P.M. dinner as previously arranged. Plaintiffs Sarah Moseley, Ben McKinnon, Michael Jared and Lynn Jared (collectively with Streit, the "Streit Plaintiffs") were among the guests attending the dinner party. Schulman and the film crew arrived at 6:30 P.M.; Cohen/Borat arrived approximately one hour later. Schulman did not present the Streit Plaintiffs with copies of the Agreement until immediately before Cohen's arrival. Though Schulman allegedly rushed them to review the Agreement, each of the Streit Plaintiffs signed and returned a copy. During the dinner, Cohen/Borat performed offensive acts and made sexist remarks before introducing the guests to an African-American woman who Cohen/Borat described as a prostitute. The Movie depicts that certain of the guests chose to leave at that point, whereupon Cohen/Borat made derogatory comments insinuating that the guests were racially intolerant. After the Movie's release, the Streit Plaintiffs commenced this action in the U.S. District Court for the Northern District of Alabama, and it was subsequently transferred to this Court on February 15, 2008.

Plaintiff Kathie Martin ("Martin") owns and operates the Etiquette Training School of Birmingham. In October 2005, Martin was contacted by Schulman to provide dining etiquette training to a foreign reporter whose travel experiences were being filmed by Springland Films for Belarus television. The etiquette class was scheduled to take place on October 23, 2005, at Martin's home. While awaiting the film crew, Schulman learned that Martin's husband, who was present at the house, was somewhat familiar with another character created by Cohen in connection with his television show, "Da Ali G Show." According to the Martin

Complaint, Schulman requested to reschedule the filming for the following day to avoid any chance Mr. Martin might recognize Cohen. At the rescheduled meeting, Martin was presented with $350 and the Agreement, described by Schulman as a "standard filming release form," which Martin signed and returned. Over the course of the etiquette class, Cohen/Borat allegedly repeatedly offended Martin by making sexist and anti-Semitic remarks, as well as by producing naked photographs of Cohen/Borat's supposed son. At the end of filming, the director apologized to Martin for the inappropriate photos, and Martin left the hotel. After hearing about Cohen's behavior, Mr. Martin identified the alleged foreign reporter as Cohen, and Martin made an unsuccessful attempt to contact Schulman. Thereafter, Martin commenced her action in this Court on February 22, 2008. . . .

[T]he Agreements signed by the various Plaintiffs herein are identical in all material respects. They set forth each Plaintiff's consent to appear in a "documentary-style . . . motion picture" intended "to reach a young adult audience by using entertaining content and formats." Each Agreement states that the relevant Plaintiff:

> specifically, but without limitation, waives, and agrees not to bring at any time in the future, any claims against the Producer, or against any of its assignees or licensees or anyone associated with the Film, that include assertions of (a) infringement of rights or publicity or misappropriation (such as any allegedly improper or unauthorized use of the Participant's name or likeness or image), . . . (d) intrusion (such as any allegedly offensive behavior or questioning or any invasion of privacy), . . . (m) prima facie tort, . . . [and] (n) fraud (such as any alleged deception or surprise about the Film or this consent agreement).

Furthermore, each Agreement includes a merger clause[7] which notes, among other things, that "the Participant acknowledges that in entering into [the Agreement], the Participant is not relying upon any promises or statements made by anyone about the nature of the Film or the identity of any other Participants or persons involved in the Film."

On a motion to dismiss, the court must accept as true all material facts alleged in the complaint and draw all reasonable inferences in the plaintiff's favor. . . . Each Agreement at issue in these actions contains an explicit waiver clause that on its face prevents Plaintiffs from bringing the above-captioned actions. To avoid their waivers, Plaintiffs argue that the Agreement—specifically, the term "documentary-style film" as it is used in Paragraph 4 of the Agreement—is ambiguous and cannot be enforced at this stage of the litigation. Further, Plaintiffs argue that the term "documentary-style film" does not

---

[7] A merger clause is a provision in a written agreement declaring that the writing contains all the terms agreed upon by the parties. The purpose is to preclude a party from claiming that the agreement is subject to terms that are not set out in the writing. We discuss merger clauses in Chapter 16 in relation to the parol evidence rule.—EDS.

describe *Borat* and, therefore, that they have not waived any right to bring claims against Defendants relating to *Borat*. . . . [The court holds that the term "documentary-style film" is not ambiguous—it means a movie that displays the characteristics of a film that provides a factual record or report. The court also finds that although the Borat film is not a documentary, it is a documentary-style film. The Borat character is fictional, but the story is told in the style of a true one, and includes interviews with real people and depicts real events.]

Nevertheless, each Plaintiff seeks to avoid the waiver clause in the Agreement by arguing that he or she was fraudulently induced to enter the Agreement. Specifically, each Plaintiff argues that Schulman's representations about the nature of the film and the identities of Schulman, Cohen and Springland Films were false and were meant to induce him or her to appear in the film. That line of argument is foreclosed to Plaintiffs here, however, because each waived his or her reliance on "any promises or statements made by anyone about the nature of the Film or the identity of any other Participants or persons involved in the Film." [In] *Danann Realty Corp. v. Harris*, 5 N.Y.2d 217, 320, 184 N.Y.S.2d 599, 601 (1959) . . . the New York Court of Appeals held that the defense of fraud in the inducement is foreclosed to a party who disclaims, in the contract itself, reliance on fraudulent statements allegedly made to induce him to enter into the contract. *See Danann* 5 N.Y.2d at 323.[8] As this Court recently observed, "specificity was the touchstone of the disclaimer in *Danann*: the purchaser in that case could not claim to have relied on the allegedly fraudulent representations when, in the contract, the purchaser stated that 'the Purchaser hereby expressly acknowledges that no such representations have been made.'" *UBS AG, Stamford Branch v. Healthsouth Corp.*, No. 07 Civ. 8490 (LAP), 2008 WL 2337846, at 5 (S.D.N.Y. June 6, 2008).

Here, each Plaintiff argues that the Agreement's merger clause is too general to preclude his or her defense of fraud in the inducement. The relevant merger clause, however, states that Plaintiff has not relied "upon any promises or statements made by anyone about the *nature of the Film* or the *identity* of any other Participants or persons involved in the Film." As in *Danann*, so too here: a Plaintiff may not claim to have relied on a statement upon which he or she has explicitly disclaimed reliance.

In the alternative, each Plaintiff argues that Defendants had a duty to disclose the nature of the film and the identities of those involved in the film. Each Plaintiff invokes the duty to disclose that arises when a "party possesses superior knowledge, not readily available to the other, and knows that the other is acting on the basis of mistaken knowledge," *Aaron Ferer & Sons, Ltd. v. Chase Manhattan Bank, N.A.*, 731 F.2d 112, 123 (2d Cir. 1984), and the principle

---

[8] To maintain a claim for fraud in the inducement, a party must show: (1) a material representation or omission of fact made by a defendant with knowledge of its falsity and intent to defraud; and (2) damages sustained as a result of a plaintiff's reasonable reliance on that representation. *See Crigger v. Fahnestock and Co., Inc.*, 443 F.3d 230, 234 (2d Cir. 2006).

that "an express disclaimer will not be given effect where the facts are peculiarly within the knowledge of the party invoking it," *Banque Arabe Et Internationale D'Investissement v. Maryland Nat. Bank*, 819 F. Supp. 1282, 1292 (S.D.N.Y. 1993). These Plaintiffs cannot avoid the consequences of their waivers, however, simply by restyling their allegations of misrepresentation as allegations of omission. Such would empower these Plaintiffs to avoid the clear wording of their own contracts in a manner I must decline to condone under well-settled New York law. In light of the above disposition, I do not reach Defendants' additional arguments.

For the reasons stated above, the Agreements in each of the above-captioned actions is unambiguous and, based on the language of those Agreements, these Plaintiffs may not now maintain a defense of fraud in the inducement. The Agreements are thus enforceable, and the provisions contained therein waiving Plaintiffs' respective rights to bring any and all claims against Defendants with respect to *Borat* prevent the instant actions. Therefore, Defendants' motion[s] to dismiss are all hereby granted. — *disposition*

■ QUESTIONS

(1) Is *Borat* a case of affirmative fraud, concealment, or nondisclosure?

(2) In many cases, the goal of the fraud is to gain an unfair economic advantage by deceiving the other party. The purpose of the alleged deception in this case seems to be different. What do you think it was? Do you think this had a bearing on the disposition of the case? *↳ make a movie*

(3) As noted above, courts often articulate the public policy that a party should not be allowed, by a contractual provision, to insulate itself from a claim of fraud. Why did that policy not help the plaintiffs in this case? *↓*

7. The Distinction Between Fraudulent and Negligent Misrepresentation

they couldn't find fraud w/ the merger clause

The essential difference between fraud and negligence lies in the state of mind of the party making the misrepresentation. A negligent misrepresentation is not deliberately false but is made carelessly: The party making the misrepresentation failed to exercise reasonable care in obtaining or communicating the information. As you can see if you look at the definition of "fraudulent misrepresentation" in Restatement, Second §162, fraud could be constituted by making statements without confidence in their truth or without the necessary information to support the assertion. Therefore, there is quite a thin dividing line between fraudulent and negligent sloppiness with the truth.

negligent is careless

Because negligent misrepresentation is less morally culpable than deliberate fraud, Restatement, Second §164 includes materiality as an element for

[handwritten: no materiality for fraud]

negligent misrepresentation, but not for fraud. Recall, however, that many courts require materiality as an element of fraud as well. So in many states, this element does not differ depending on whether the misrepresentation is fraudulent or negligent. However, courts do recognize other differences. For example, a limitation, disclaimer, or merger clause in the contract may not shield a party who has committed fraud. (The *Rodi* case expressed this principle.) However, these contractual provisions are usually effective where the misrepresentation is negligent. Some states restrict relief for negligent misrepresentation to cases in which a professional person has negligently supplied incorrect information for the guidance of others in commercial transactions. Other states confine relief for negligent misrepresentation to cases in which the misrepresentation leads to personal injury, and not merely economic loss.

[handwritten left margin: You may not waive fraud but you can shield an action against it]

[handwritten: × limits on negligent misrepresentation]

8. The Choice of Remedy for Fraud; Punitive Damages

As we noted in Section B.1.e, rescission (accompanied by restitution if there has been partial performance) and damages are the two most common alternative remedies for fraudulent misrepresentation. That is, the victim of fraud may choose either to terminate the contract completely and to recover anything paid or delivered under the contract on grounds of unjust enrichment, or to keep the contract in force and to claim damages for loss caused by the fraud. Commonly, this loss is measured as the difference in value between the actual worth of the performance and what it would have been worth as represented.

[handwritten left margin: actual worth v. what it would have been worth]

The cases in this section illustrate both principal forms of relief available to a victim of fraud. In some, the plaintiff sought rescission and in others the claim was for monetary compensation. Review the cases to identify which form of relief was being claimed in each of them.

Historically, the only contract remedy recognized for fraud was rescission and restitution. However, because fraud constitutes a deliberate tort as well as a basis for avoiding the contract, tort law could be used if the plaintiff wished to obtain damages instead of rescission. In most modern courts, the derivation of the alternative remedies is of little practical significance. Courts simply accept that fraud gives rise to relief in the form of either rescission or damages at the plaintiff's election. However, in some situations the choice of remedy may have an important impact beyond the immediate goal of restoring or compensating the plaintiff.

[handwritten left margin: Can use tort law to obtain damages]

The most dramatic consequence lies in the availability of punitive damages.[9] As we have mentioned before, punitive damages are not usually allowed in

---

[9] As noted in Question 4 following *Hodge v. Craig* in Section B.2, emotional distress damages are commonly available in tort, but not in contract. Therefore, choice of the tort or contract remedy could have an impact on the availability of emotional distress damages, as well.

punitive damages available when fraud is intentional

contracts cases. However, they are sometimes available where the defendant has committed an intentional tort, and <u>fraud is surely intentional.</u> This could mean that if the plaintiff sues for rescission, he may be deprived of punitive damages, but if he sues for compensatory damages, he may seek punitive damages too. This result is odd, considering that both remedies are based on the very same wrongful act.

Courts that recognize this incongruity decline to follow the contract-tort distinction. For example, in *Seaton v. Lawson Chevrolet-Mazda, Inc.*, 821 S.W.2d 137 (Tenn. 1991), the car dealer sold a new model "demonstrator" (driven about 6,500 miles by the dealer) without revealing to the customer that the car had been involved in a wreck and repaired. The customer sued for rescission for fraud. (As this was a sale of goods, the claim was based on UCC Article 2, not the common law. Article 2 does not have specific provisions relating to fraud—fraud remedies are governed by general principles of common law—but it does provide for a remedy akin to rescission and restitution.) The jury awarded the customer rescission and a refund of the price as well as punitive damages of $20,000. The intermediate appellate court reversed the punitive damages award on the ground that it is not available when the plaintiff sues for rescission. The Tennessee Supreme Court disagreed. It observed that where fraud is committed, the wanton and intentional tort is "inextricably mired with elements of contract," making the award of punitive damages appropriate and consistent with the general remedial policy of Article 2, which requires a nontechnical approach to remedies. Although the case deals specifically with the remedial provisions of Article 2, the underlying reasoning is just as applicable at common law.

UCC leaves fraud to be governed by common law

9. Fraud in the Inducement Distinguished from Fraud in the Factum

The fraudulent misrepresentations alleged in the cases in this section involve fraud used for the purpose of inducing agreement. That is, the misrepresentation relates to a fact that forms the basis of the agreement and <u>falsely gives the other party an incentive to enter into the contract.</u> This is the most common type of fraud, known as fraud in the inducement. However, it sometimes happens that the fraud concerns not a fact underlying the contract, but the very nature of the contract document itself—its character or essential terms. For example, while a busy lawyer is preparing for court, her law clerk enters her office and asks her to sign a document, which the clerk represents to be a letter of recommendation that the lawyer had previously agreed to sign. Without looking at the document, the lawyer signs it. In fact, it is not a letter of recommendation at all; it is a contract to employ the clerk as an associate for a handsome salary after he graduates. As she did not read the document before signing it, the lawyer had no idea that she had signed an employment contract. The clerk's <u>false representation of the nature of the document is called fraud in the</u>

fraud can be the nature of the contract

fraud of the nature of the contract

factum—it relates not to an underlying fact but to the document being executed.

The lawyer's justification in relying on the representation in light of her duty to read what she signed will play a central role in deciding if she should be allowed to escape her apparent manifestation of assent. As is generally true in fraud cases, the clerk's deceptive conduct will be balanced against the lawyer's failure to act reasonably in safeguarding her own interests. Courts, and Restatement, Second §163, recognize fraud of this kind and give relief for it provided that (in the words of §163) the person who was induced by the misrepresentation to manifest assent to the document "... neither knows nor has reasonable opportunity to know of the character or essential terms of the proposed contract...."

manifestation induced by fraud is not sufficient manifestation

Restatement, Second §163 follows traditional analysis by declaring that a manifestation induced by fraud in the factum is ineffective as a manifestation of assent. In effect, this treats fraud in the factum as rendering the apparent contract void, not merely voidable. Theoretically, because a void contract is a legal nullity, this could mean that the defrauded party does not have the option to keep the contract in force. For example, even if the lawyer-employer in the illustration above decides that she is happy with the employment contract despite the circumstances of its execution, she cannot enforce it against the clerk. The clerk could raise the defense that the contract is void. As between the parties themselves, a court is most unlikely to allow the clerk to raise a defense based on his own fraud, and the defense could be dismissed on grounds of estoppel or public policy. However, the distinction does become relevant with regard to certain types of commercial paper, such as a promissory note, in which the legal rights encompassed in the document can be transferred to a third party by endorsement (signature) and physical delivery of the document itself. (This type of transfer is known as "negotiation.") A person who takes a document by negotiation in good faith, for value, and without knowledge of defects, may take it free of claims of voidability, but will not be able to enforce it against the person whose execution of the document is void.

■ QUESTION

Look at the *Borat* case again. Could it be characterized as a case of fraud in the factum? If the plaintiffs had pursued it as a fraud in the factum case, do you think they would have had a better chance of success?

 DURESS

Like deception, coercion can undermine the free will of a party, giving rise to a false manifestation of assent. Coercion may consist of the application of actual force—for example, clutching the victim's throat and applying increasing pressure until he signs a contract. More commonly, coercion takes the form of a threat of adverse consequences. Duress, the compulsion of a manifestation of assent by force or threat, has long been recognized as a basis for avoiding a contract. However, the doctrine has developed and expanded over the years. Older common law confined the doctrine to cases in which apparent assent was induced by actual violence against, imprisonment of, threats of imprisonment of, or physical harm to the victim. It favored a rigorous objective test in which the harm threatened could not simply be economic, or even a mere beating, but death or maiming.

used to have strict application

It is now well established in modern law that duress may consist not only of a threat of physical violence to the other party (or someone the party cares about) but also of economic harm or loss—sometimes called "economic duress." It could even consist of a threat of harm to a significant interest that cannot be measured in economic terms. Some cases still make a distinction between traditional duress by threat of violence or bodily harm and economic duress. However, there is no longer a real need to distinguish traditional and economic duress because threats of an economic nature are unquestionably recognized in most jurisdictions as a basis for relief and are surely the much more common variety.

Restatement, Second §175(1) sets out a generally accepted formulation of the test for duress—apparent assent has been induced by an improper threat by the other party. Restatement, Second §175(2) deals with an improper threat by someone who is not a party to the contract. It has a rule equivalent to that for nonparty fraud, mentioned in Section B.1: The victim of duress may avoid a contract induced by the duress of a nonparty unless the other contracting party gave value or relied materially on the transaction in good faith and without reason to know of the duress.

assent is induced by improper threat

*nonparty fraud

The usual consequence of duress is that the contract is avoidable—the victim of the duress may elect to avoid the contract and claim restitution of the benefit of any performance rendered under the contract. However, where the duress is so powerful that it amounts to physical coercion, a court may declare the contract not merely avoidable but completely void.[10] Restatement, Second §174 recognizes this by stating that if conduct that appears to be a manifestation of assent is not intended as such by a party, and is "physically compelled by duress," the "conduct is not effective as a manifestation of assent." The comment to §174 makes it clear that physical compulsion is force so severe that the victim becomes "a mere mechanical instrument." The comment illustrates this by the example of the perpetrator who grasps the victim's hand and compels her by physical force to sign.

① *avoid the contract*
② *claim restitution*

not assent if its made under duress

Here's the general test for duress, as formulated by the Restatement, Second:

---

[10] This is analogous to the distinction described in Section B.9 between fraud in the factum, which renders the contract void, and fraud in the inducement, which makes it avoidable at the instance of the victim.

test for duress

RESTATEMENT, SECOND §175. WHEN DURESS BY THREAT MAKES A CONTRACT VOIDABLE

(1) If a party's manifestation of assent is induced by an improper threat by the other party that leaves the victim no reasonable alternative, the contract is voidable by the victim. . . .

★ no reasonable alternative

Section 176 expands on this by articulating the circumstances in which a threat is improper:

RESTATEMENT, SECOND §176. WHEN A THREAT IS IMPROPER

(1) A threat is improper if

(a) what is threatened is a crime or a tort, or the threat itself would be a crime or a tort if it resulted in obtaining property,

(b) what is threatened is a criminal prosecution,

(c) what is threatened is the use of civil process and the threat is made in bad faith, or

(d) the threat is a breach of the duty of good faith and fair dealing under a contract with the recipient.

(2) A threat is improper if the resulting exchange is not on fair terms, and

(a) the threatened act would harm the recipient and would not significantly benefit the party making the threat,

(b) the effectiveness of the threat in inducing the manifestation of assent is significantly increased by prior unfair dealing by the party making the threat, or

(c) what is threatened is otherwise a use of power for illegitimate ends.

———

It is very common for a party to experience some degree of compulsion in entering into a contract, particularly where that party has a strong need or desire for the benefits that the contract provides. This need or desire could make the party particularly vulnerable to hard bargaining by the other, and may make him feel compelled to agree to any undesirable terms that the other party demands. However, hard bargaining or unfair pressure may not rise to the level of duress. It is important to remember that an improper threat is a crucial element of duress, and mere market pressure or the other party's hard bargaining or insistence on self-serving terms is not enough to constitute duress.[11]

hard bargaining or unfair pressure is not duress

★ must have an improper threat

———

[11] Where the other party's hard bargaining amounts to unfair and oppressive conduct and the resulting contract is unfair and one-sided, relief may be available, even in the absence of duress, under the doctrine of unconscionability, which is discussed in Section F.

just economic pressure, not duress

■ PROBLEM 13.6

In *Quigley v. KPMG Peat Marwick, LLP*, 330 N.J. Super 252, 749 A.2d 405 (2000), the plaintiff, Joseph Quigley, was terminated from his position as senior manager with the defendant KPMG Peat Marwick, LLP, after 18 years of employment. He sued KPMG for damages for wrongful dismissal (including lost salary, bonuses, and pension benefits), claiming that he had been dismissed on account of his age, in violation of New Jersey's antidiscrimination statute. KPMG sought to dismiss his complaint and compel arbitration on the grounds that his employment contract required him to arbitrate the claim. He had signed the employment agreement in 1984 when he was promoted to senior manager, 12 years before he was fired. It required all claims and disputes arising out of the agreement to be settled by arbitration. Quigley claimed that he had agreed to the arbitration provision under duress because he needed the job and his supervisor had told him that if he did not sign the agreement as presented, he would not only lose the promotion, but would be dismissed. He signed the agreement under protest and took the unusual step of inserting the letters "U.D." (meant to signify that he was signing "under duress") between his first and last name in his signature.

The court rejected Quigley's duress argument. It said that "it is feasible to consider the threat of termination of employment for refusing to agree to arbitration oppressive or morally wrong." However, this did not amount to *not improper a unlawful force* duress because it was not improper or unlawful. KPMG had the right to fire Quigley, an at-will employee. Although Quigley's desire to keep his job placed KPMG in a superior bargaining position and allowed it to present the contract on a "take-it-or-leave-it" basis, this was not enough foundation for a claim of duress. The court also noted that Quigley signed the contract in consideration of promotion and received the benefit of continuing to work for KPMG for 12 years after signing the contract. The court did not regard the fact that Quigley had noted his protest by inserting the "U.D." in his signature—he manifested assent to the contract despite this cryptic insertion.

(a) The court said that it was feasible to consider the threat of dismissal to be oppressive or morally wrong but it was not improper or unlawful. Clearly, it was not unlawful if KPMG had the legal right to fire Quigley, but do you agree with the court that an oppressive and immoral threat should not be considered improper for purposes of duress? Why or why not? In answering this question, take note of the definition of an improper threat in Restatement, Second, §176.

(b) Had Quigley not been an at-will employee, but had a contract for a definite term which had not yet expired at the time of entering the arbitration agreement, the threat to dismiss him if he did not agree to the arbitration provision would have been a breach of contract and therefore illegal or improper.[12] The first element set out in Restatement, Second §175 thus would have been satisfied. However, Quigley would also have to satisfy the second element of inducement—that he had no reasonable alternative but to assent to the contract. Based on the facts as set out in the summary of the case, do you think he could establish this element?

■ PROBLEM 13.7

Anna Conda rents a house from Phoebe O'Phidio. Anna keeps a pet snake in a cage in the house. Although the snake is not venomous or harmful, it is large and evil-looking and could be mistaken for a deadly viper. Phoebe does not know that Anna has the snake. Anna is aware that Phoebe would be very upset if she did know because this is not only a violation of a clause in the lease that forbids pets on the premises, but also because Phoebe had mentioned to Anna that she suffers from ophidiophobia—an intense and irrational fear of snakes. Last week, Phoebe decided to move back into her house and gave Anna the required one month's notice to terminate the lease. Anna does not wish to leave the house. She asked Phoebe to come over to the house to discuss the termination notice and Phoebe obliged. After Phoebe came into the living room, Anna brought the caged snake into the room and locked the door. She told Phoebe that unless she agreed to withdraw the termination notice and give her a two-year lease, Anna would open the cage door and Phoebe could "negotiate further with my friend here." Phoebe had no idea if the snake was dangerous, and neither asked nor cared. She screamed, "I agree—just keep that cage door closed!" The parties immediately signed a lease that Anna had prepared, rescinding the termination notice, eliminating the no-pets clause, and granting Anna a two-year lease on the house at the rent that Anna was currently paying. Because residential rents had been rising, this rent is about 20 percent lower than what Phoebe could obtain on the market.

Immediately after she left the house and escaped the snake, Phoebe sought to rescind the new lease entered into with Anna. Is she able to argue that she entered into the lease under duress, as defined in Restatement, Second §§175 and 176?

---

[12] This is discussed more fully in Section D on duress in the modification of a contract.

The next case, *Germantown Manufacturing Co. v. Rawlinson,* involves a petition to open a confessed judgment. A brief explanation of this procedure may help you to understand the procedural posture of the case: Normally, if a creditor wishes to enforce a claim after the debtor fails to pay the debt on the due date, the creditor must commence suit and obtain judgment. If the debtor defends the suit, the creditor may have to go through the whole process of trial before getting its judgment. If the debtor does not defend the suit, the creditor can obtain judgment by default. Sometimes a creditor may seek to truncate this process by having the debtor sign a document (either at the time that the debt is incurred or after the debtor has defaulted) in which the debtor acknowledges owing the debt and appoints the creditor (or the creditor's attorney) as her agent to confess to the judgment on her behalf. This document is called a "confession of judgment" or a "warrant of attorney." It is, in effect, a waiver of the right to defend the suit and an authorization to the creditor to obtain judgment by default. Because this remedy can have harsh effects and can be abused by a creditor, the law provides the debtor with several safeguards.[13] One of these is the right to apply to court after the judgment for its opening (reversal) so the debtor can defend the case. To obtain this relief the debtor must show that she acted promptly in seeking to open the judgment and must produce evidence of a meritorious defense, such as would require submission of the issue to a jury. The question involved in *Germantown Manufacturing* is whether the debtor has sufficiently shown a meritorious defense to permit her to open the judgment and defend the suit.

Apart from covering the issue of duress, *Germantown Manufacturing* illustrates the point that improper bargaining may permit analysis under more than one policing doctrine.

GERMANTOWN MANUFACTURING CO. v. RAWLINSON

341 Pa. Super. 42, 491 A.2d 138 (1985)
Pennsylvania Superior Court

CAVANAUGH, Judge.

... Robert G. Rawlinson was employed by The Germantown Manufacturing Company in Marple Township as its assistant controller. Over a period of twenty-one months, Mr. Rawlinson embezzled $327,011.22 from the company. On Friday, May 21, 1982, the company discovered the misappropriation. Mr. Rawlinson admitted his wrongdoing to the company controller,

[13] With regard to some types of transactions, the law does more than provide these safeguards. A Federal Trade Commission regulation, 16 C.F.R. 444.2, declares it to be an unfair credit practice for a lender or seller to include a confession of judgment in a contract for the extension of consumer credit.

Mr. Harry Dinkel, and was fired. However, Mr. Rawlinson did not tell his wife about either the misappropriation of the company monies or the loss of his job until the following Monday, May 24, 1982. Sometime between Friday and Monday, Mrs. Joan Rawlinson, Robert's wife, answered a phone call for her husband from a Mr. Peter Kulaski who identified himself as an insurance adjuster. On Monday, May 24, 1982, she answered a second call for her husband from Mr. Kulaski. Sensing that something was amiss, she summoned her husband to the phone but stayed on an extension and overheard Mr. Kulaski say, "Have you told your wife yet?" At this, she hung up the phone, and when her husband had finished his conversation she demanded to know what was going on. Mr. Rawlinson told his wife that he had lost his job because he had taken about $20,000.00 from the company. He also asked his wife if she wanted a divorce. Mrs. Rawlinson testified that upon hearing all of this, her "whole world fell apart." She also testified that because she had suffered a miscarriage in late April, she was already tired and depressed when she learned of her husband's malefactions.

The following day, Tuesday, Mrs. Rawlinson spoke by phone with Mr. Kulaski, who was a representative of the company's insurer, and learned that he was coming to the house "to discuss documents." He did not tell her he would attempt to have her co-sign two judgment notes. Nor did he tell her the amount her husband had misappropriated. Mr. Kulaski arrived later that day and spent thirty to forty-five minutes with Mr. and Mrs. Rawlinson. Mrs. Rawlinson apparently succeeded in keeping her two young children from knowing the purpose of the meeting.

The purpose of the meeting, from Mr. Kulaski's perspective, was to have Mr. and Mrs. Rawlinson sign two judgment notes. The first note was for $160,000.00—the amount Mr. Rawlinson admitted having taken. The second was for "any and all amounts in excess of One hundred and sixty thousand dollars ($160,000) which are determined by Affidavit of the President of Germantown Manufacturing Company, which Affidavit, when presented with this Note, shall constitute sufficient proof of a sum certain for the purpose of the Confession of Judgment contained herein." Both notes authorized any attorney to confess judgment in favor of Germantown Manufacturing against the Rawlinsons. Mrs. Rawlinson was surprised to see her name on the documents. She asked Mr. Kulaski if she and her husband would need an attorney. Mr. Kulaski calmly stated that if the Rawlinsons dealt in good faith and continued to cooperate, there would be no need for an attorney. Kulaski also stated that his principal was not interested in a criminal prosecution as long as Mr. and Mrs. Rawlinson cooperated. Mrs. Rawlinson understood this to mean that if she signed the notes her husband would not go to jail.

Mrs. Rawlinson had never before seen a judgment note, and while she read them as best she could, she was crying for part of the time that she read them and believed that she was signing only one note for a total of $160,000.00. Mr. Kulaski told the Rawlinsons that since they had readily available assets totaling $160,000.00, the judgment was, in effect, already taken care of. She signed because she knew her husband had a check for $150,000.00 and the remaining $10,000.00 could be obtained without difficulty.... [Germantown Manufacturing thereafter calculated the amount owing on the second note as $212,113.21. It obtained judgment by confession on the first note for $160,000.00 and on the second for $212,113.21.] The first note has been satisfied. Mrs. Rawlinson's obligation as to it is not at issue. The only issue before us is whether the lower court abused its discretion in opening judgment on the *second* note.[14] ... [The court notes that a confession of judgment is a drastic remedy in which the debtor gives up her right to defend the creditor's claim. The law therefore insists on proof that the note was executed voluntarily and consciously. Where the debtor petitions the court to open a confessed judgment, the court's decision on whether to open the judgment and allow the case to go to a jury is within the court's equitable discretion. The petitioner must bring the petition promptly and must sufficiently demonstrate a meritorious defense. In deciding whether the defense is meritorious, the court must view the alleged facts in the light most favorable to the petitioner. The trial court's decision will not be reversed on appeal absent a clear and manifest abuse of discretion.]

In analyzing the judgment notes in question, we are to be guided by the rules which apply to other written contracts. The lower court found that appellee, Joan Rawlinson, presented ... [the meritorious defenses of fraud and duress], which permitted it to exercise its equitable discretion and open judgment.... [W]e affirm the judgment of the lower court....

[The court first addresses the defenses of fraud and misrepresentation and finds that the trial court did not abuse its discretion in finding sufficient evidence of these defenses to constitute a meritorious defense. Viewing the evidence in the light most favorable to Mrs. Rawlinson, Kulaski fraudulently misrepresented to her that her liability was only $160,000, whereas the second note made her liable for an unspecified further amount, which ultimately increased her debt to a total of over $372,000.00. Kulaski knew or should have known that he had deceived her. However, even if Kulaski did not deliberately make the misrepresentation with knowledge that it was untrue, it was still material in that it was likely to have induced a reasonable person to make the contract.] Mrs. Rawlinson testified that she would not have signed had she known the terms of the second note. Thus, the representation may be said to have induced her to sign....

[Although Mrs. Rawlinson did not raise it, and the trial court did not address it, there may also be a meritorious defense based on fraud in the factum.] A typical example of this involves a surreptitious substitution of one document for another, and the innocent party signing it without knowledge or a reasonable opportunity to know the character and essential terms of the substituted document. Here Mrs. Rawlinson believed she was signing one document with a maximum liability of $160,000. ...

---

[14] [T]his appeal concerns only the opening of the judgment as to Mrs. Joan Rawlinson, appellee. The judgment we render will have no effect on Mr. Robert Rawlinson's obligation.

contract is voidable

[We also agree with the trial court that] . . . appellee presented sufficient evidence of duress to constitute a meritorious defense and thus render the contract voidable. Pennsylvania appellate courts have given scant attention of late to this defense as applied to the situation now confronting us.[15] . . . [Restatement, Second §§175(1) and 176(l)(b) make it clear that it is improper to threaten criminal prosecution to induce an embezzler or his

Can't threaten criminal prosecution to induce assent

relative to undertake to repay. This is the improper use of the criminal process for private benefit. The threat is not made less improper merely because the prosecution would be well founded. In fact, the likelihood that it will result in imprisonment increases the coercive power of the threat.]

In the instant case, appellant took the unsolicited liberty of including Mrs. Rawlinson's name on the judgment notes and did not even tell her it was doing so until minutes before she was asked to sign them. Mrs. Rawlinson had already been in a weakened mental state as the result of a recent miscarriage, and was visibly upset during the meeting, having learned of her husband's malefactions. At the meeting, she was told that if she cooperated, she would have no need for legal counsel. She understood this to mean that if she signed the notes, her husband would not go to jail. She had no rea-

no reasonable alternative but to sign

sonable alternative but to sign. That Germantown Manufacturing was ready to carry out its threat is evidenced by . . . [a letter from Germantown's attorney to the attorney subsequently retained by Mrs. Rawlinson in which he gave notice that unless the efforts to attack the judgments were withdrawn, he would present the evidence of the embezzlement to the prosecutor].

Appellee's admission that Mr. Rawlinson actually took the funds does not harm and may even strengthen her defense of duress as "it may be easier to show that the threat actually induced assent in the case of guilt." Restatement (Second) of Contracts §176 comment c. Moreover, the fact that Mr. Kulaski did not threaten "imminent" arrest should be of no concern in the present analysis.

threat doesn't have to be imminent and can be implied

Nor should it matter if the threat of prosecution was not expressly stated. "[T]he bargain is just as illegal when the agreement is implied as when it is express." 6A A. Corbin, *Corbin on Contracts* §1421 (1962). It is an affront to our judicial sensibilities that one person's ability to seek another's prosecution can be bartered and sold the same as commodities in the market place. It is even more repugnant when the foul stench of oppression pervades the transaction.

It is clear beyond peradventure that the "choice" available to Mrs. Rawlinson exuded impermissible coercion. We note that appellee's status as spouse to the

---

[15] *Palatucci v. Woodland*, 166 Pa. Super. 315, 70 A.2d 674 (1950), the most recent case on point cited by appellant, bears a resemblance to the instant case. There, appellant, wife of a man who borrowed $1,600.00 from appellee, alleged that appellee threatened that if she did not sign a judgment note for $1,600.00, then he would have her husband arrested and prosecuted. The Superior Court . . . [held that the case did not present a meritorious defense of duress because the wife had the opportunity to consult counsel before executing the note.] . . . This differs from the instant case, where appellee's option of consulting counsel before executing the note was not a viable one, as such an action may have been deemed "noncompliance" by the appellant, thus resulting in the prosecution of Mr. Rawlinson, which appellee so dreaded.

alleged embezzler, though not argued as such by appellee, lends credence to our finding of duress in the instant case. Mrs. Rawlinson signed the documents presented her believing that her cooperation was necessary to keep her husband from going to jail. We dare not lend our judicial imprimatur to a transaction which holds the institution of the family in such lowly regard. . . . The only alternative for a reasonable party in the position of Mrs. Rawlinson was to refuse to sign and thus place an almost assuredly unbearable stress on her marriage and on the tranquility of the Rawlinson household. This is the epitome of duress. . . . For these reasons, we affirm the lower court's order opening the judgment.[16] *disposition*

■ QUESTIONS

(1) In dealing with the issue of fraud, the court identified two possible meritorious fraud defenses that Mrs. Rawlinson could raise: fraud in the inducement and fraud in the factum.

   (a) What fact was misrepresented? *nature of the debt*
   (b) Was the misrepresentation an affirmative statement or by nondisclosure? *nondisclosure*
   (c) Based on our discussion of fraud in Section B, do you agree with the court that these defenses are meritorious? *yes*

(2) The court also says that the misrepresentation was material in that it would have caused a reasonable person to make the contract. To support this, the court alludes to Mrs. Rawlinson's testimony that she would not have signed had she known the terms of the second note.

   (a) Do you think that the court adequately justifies this conclusion? *yes*
   (b) Did the court overlook something about the significance of this testimony? In thinking about this question, ask yourself if it was wise for Mrs. Rawlinson to make this assertion, and what impact it might have on her defense of duress. *undermines the duress in that her signature only came from misrepresentation*

(3) The court leaves us in no doubt about its feelings for Germantown Manufacturing and its agent, Mr. Kulaski ("... an affront to our judicial sensibilities ...," "... foul stench of oppression ...") and its sympathy for Mrs. Rawlinson, who had endured a miscarriage, followed by the discovery that her husband was a crook and a liar, and then an encounter with Mr. Kulaski and his judgment notes. Would it have made a difference to the court's analysis and resolution of the duress defense if Mrs. Rawlinson had not suffered a miscarriage in the prior month, she had a tough, self-reliant *She was viewed as less reasonable*

---

[16] The court continues its analysis by applying the doctrine of unconscionability, which it holds also would be a meritorious defense. The court's discussion of unconscionability is taken up in Section F.—EDS.

personality, and her husband had told her about his embezzlement and firing on Friday, May 21?

(4)   Assume that the facts are as set out in the case except that before she signed the note, Mrs. Rawlinson excused herself from the room and called her attorney. After she told her attorney of the circumstances and read the judgment note to him, the attorney explained what a confession of judgment was and said, "Well, you had better sign it; otherwise they will prosecute your husband. Courts hate those notes, so we will probably be able to get it nullified by challenging it if they try to collect on it." How do you think this might affect the outcome of the case? Do you think that the attorney's advice was good and helpful?

(5)   Is the court's concern about the policy of protecting the marriage relationship and the contract's impact on the Rawlinsons' marriage justified and relevant?

(6)   Say that it was not Mrs. Rawlinson but rather Mr. Rawlinson who was seeking to open the confessed judgment that he had signed so that he could raise the defense of duress. Could he show a meritorious defense of duress?

■ PROBLEM 13.8

Like *Germantown Manufacturing*, the well-known case of *Odorizzi v. Bloomfield School District*, 246 Cal. App. 2d 123, 54 Cal. Rptr. 533 (1966), involved excessive pressure exerted on a vulnerable party in his own home by aggressive conduct of the other party. Odorizzi was employed by the school district as an elementary school teacher. He was arrested on criminal charges for homosexual activity, which was illegal in California at the time. He was released on bail after having been arrested, questioned, and booked. He was distraught by the time that he returned to his apartment and was also exhausted because he had not slept for 40 hours. Shortly after he returned home, he received a visit from the principal of his school and the superintendent of the district. They claimed that they wished to help him and had his best interests at heart. They urged him to resign immediately, told him that he had no time to consult an attorney, and warned him that if he did not resign, he would be dismissed. Dismissal would attract publicity that would cause him public humiliation and would make it difficult for him to find another teaching job. Odorizzi signed a letter of resignation. He later sued to rescind it on the basis that the school officials had coerced him into signing it. The trial court dismissed his suit.

The court of appeals found that Odorizzi had sufficiently alleged a cause of action that entitled him to go to trial on the theory that the school district had used coercive and oppressive tactics that took advantage of his weakness and overbore his will.[17] In reaching its conclusion, the court identified the following factors as tending to demonstrate that the school district had used oppressive bargaining tactics: At a time that Odorizzi was exhausted and under severe emotional strain, the school district officials descended on him at home. The time and place of the discussion was inappropriate, they insisted that the question of his resignation be resolved at once, they painted an ugly picture of the consequences of delay, and they discouraged him from consulting an attorney or other advisor. The court noted that the school officials did not act improperly merely by suggesting Odorizzi's resignation and by threatening to institute proceedings to dismiss him if he did not resign. They had a legal right to do this. The problem was in the manner that they set about persuading him to resign.

no; no improper threat

(a) Would Odorizzi be entitled to relief for duress under Restatement, Second §§175 and 176?

(b) Assume that Odorizzi had the presence of mind to call an attorney while the school officials were in his apartment and before he signed the resignation. His attorney advised him not to resign and to demand that the officials leave his apartment immediately. Odorizzi tried this, but the officials refused to leave and continued to persuade him. He was just not strong-willed enough to resist, and he eventually signed the resignation contrary to his attorney's advice. What impact do these additional facts have on your answer to (a)?

D DURESS AND BAD FAITH IN RELATION TO CONTRACT MODIFICATION

1. The Interaction of Consideration and Duress Doctrines

Once the parties have made a contract, each is bound by it, and neither party has the right to change its terms on his own without the consent of the other

---

[17] The theory on which the court allowed the case to proceed to trial was not duress, but undue influence. This is because the California Civil Code has a very narrow definition of duress, which is limited to unlawful confinement of a person, his relatives, or property. Cal. Civ. Code §1569. (The definition is expanded somewhat by the separate ground of menace in §1570, which includes a threat of duress or of injury to person or property.) Because duress is so narrowly defined in California, the court upheld the dismissal of Odorizzi's claim of duress. However the court did allow him to proceed to trial on a theory of undue influence, defined broadly in Cal. Civ. Code §1575 to include coercive and oppressive persuasion which takes advantage of a person's weakness and overbears his will. As we will see in Section E, the scope of undue influence in California is wider than that under the Restatement, Second, which reflects the more conventional approach.

party. Any such unilateral attempt to do so would be a breach of the contract. However, it stands to reason that, in the same way that the parties together had the capacity to form the original contract, they are able, acting in concert, to make a subsequent agreement to amend that contract. The new agreement to modify the original contract is itself a contract and is fully subject to all the rules that govern the formation and validity of contracts. Although any rule of contract law may arise in relation to a contract to modify an existing contract (such as rules of offer and acceptance or the statute of frauds), two issues emerge most strongly. The first is the principle that a contract, whether it is the initial agreement between the parties or a later agreement to amend that initial agreement, needs consideration to be valid. The second is that an agreement, including one to amend an existing contract, can be avoided if it is induced by duress. These two principles can interact in a muddled way where contract modifications are at issue.

The preexisting duty rule is discussed in Chapter 9, Section B.2: If a person promises to perform something that she is already obliged to do, this is not consideration because the promisor suffers no detriment in merely promising to perform a legal duty that she already has. However, if the new promise contains any elements that go beyond the preexisting duty, consideration is present. The new elements may be quite trivial, because courts do not normally inquire into adequacy of consideration—unless, possibly, the added detriment is found to be nominal or a sham. The preexisting duty rule therefore does not create a problem where the agreement to modify an existing contract involves the undertaking of a new detriment by each of the parties. The exchange of the new detriments provides consideration for the agreement to modify the original contract. The parties may also be able to avoid the preexisting duty rule by making an agreement to terminate the existing contract (so that each gives consideration by abandoning the right to performance under the contract) and then entering into a new contract containing the terms as modified. However, where the parties agree to modify the terms of an existing contract in a way that affects the obligations of only one of them, a consideration problem may arise. As a planning matter, therefore, parties who seek to modify a contract should either terminate the contract and make a new one, or ensure that the performance obligations of each party are changed sufficiently to establish a bargained-for exchange at the time of modification.

Consideration doctrine can be a nuisance where it impedes the ability of the parties to enter a fairly bargained and consensual modification. For this reason, Article 2 has abolished it with regard to sales of goods, as discussed in Section D.3. However, in cases that do not involve the sale of goods, it can sometimes serve a useful function by giving the court grounds to refuse enforcement of a modification that was coerced or otherwise not fairly bargained. Of course, the doctrine can only fulfill this role if one of the parties failed to alter its performance obligations so as to incur additional detriment. *Alaska Packers' Association v. Domenico*, discussed in Section B.2 of Chapter 9, illustrates both the use of and drawbacks of consideration doctrine to police unfair contract modifications. Recall that a salmon cannery had entered into contracts with fishermen under which the fishermen agreed to work for the cannery in Alaska during the 1900 fishing season. After the fishermen arrived in Alaska, they refused to continue working unless the cannery increased their remuneration. The cannery's superintendent in Alaska agreed because it would have been impossible to replace the fishermen with a new crew within the short fishing season. At the end of the season, the cannery refused to pay the extra amount agreed to by its superintendent. The court held that the agreement to increase the fishermen's pay was unenforceable because the fishermen gave no new consideration to the cannery in exchange for it. Although the court relied on the preexisting duty rule to deny effect to the modification, the opinion made it clear that the court's real concern was that the fishermen coerced the modification from the cannery, which had no realistic choice but to accept their terms. As we point out in our discussion of this case in Chapter 9, the court would not have been able to use consideration doctrine to negate the modification had the fishermen undertaken even a modest new detriment in exchange for it.

Unless the parties have avoided the preexisting duty rule by providing for new consideration by both parties, or by terminating the contract and making a new one, consideration doctrine gets in the way of upholding a genuinely voluntary and fair modification of a contract. A court may try hard to find some new detriment on the part of the party whose obligations seem unaltered, but in many cases, there is simply no factual basis for doing that. However, where a modification is unfairly coerced, courts do have other theories on which to invalidate it. The next case applies the doctrine of economic duress to police a coerced modification. As mentioned in the introductory text to Section C, in modern law, duress encompasses not only threats of physical harm, but also threats of economic and other harm. Therefore, even though some courts may call the doctrine "economic duress," this is just a subcategory of duress, with the same elements to be proven.

CITY OF SCOTTSBLUFF v. WASTE CONNECTIONS OF NEBRASKA, INC.

282 Neb. 848, 809 N.W.2d 725 (2011)
Nebraska Supreme Court

CONNOLLY, Judge.

[The facts of this case are quite complex. We summarize and simplify the pertinent facts. In 1992, the City closed its landfill and entered into a contract with Waste Connections for the removal of its solid waste. The contract expired in 2005. After it ended, the City entered into a short-term contract with Waste Connections, which would expire in April 2008. Towards the end of this period, the City decided to look for a less expensive means of disposing of its waste, and it told Waste Connections that it would not renew the contract if it found a cheaper option. In July 2007, it did find a cheaper alternative by entering into an agreement with a neighboring town to use its landfill. However, the new waste disposal contract would not take effect immediately, but would only begin in July 2008. Waste Connections therefore agreed in July 2007 to continue hauling waste for the City under its short-term contract until the other disposal means became available. At the time of entering into the short-term contract, Waste Connections charged the City the agreed amount of $42.50 per ton. However, immediately after hearing that its short-term contract would not be renewed, Waste Connections unilaterally increased its rate to $60 per ton. This was a 41 percent increase in the price, and considerably more than it was charging its other customers. It claimed that it needed to increase the price to compensate for losing the City's waste haulage business. Although the court's opinion is not entirely clear on this point, it seems that Waste Connections at least made the implicit threat to cease hauling the City's waste unless the increased price was paid. The City objected to the price increase, but Waste Connections refused to reduce the price and the City paid it until the short-term contract ended in July 2008. The City then sued Waste Connections for refund of about $48,000—the total difference between $60 and $42.50 per ton that it had paid during the course of the short-term contract.

The trial court awarded this amount as restitution on the grounds that the contract did not give Waste Connections the right to raise the price unilaterally, the City had paid the additional price under protest and under circumstances in which it had no reasonable alternative but to pay it, and that Waste Connections was unjustly enriched by the amount paid in excess of $42.50 per ton. The trial court also rejected Waste Connections' arguments based on waiver and estoppel. Waste Connections argued that the City waived its right to pay the lower price by paying the $60 price or, alternatively, that because it paid the higher price it should be estopped from arguing it had never agreed to it. The court held that neither waiver nor estoppel applied because the City had made the payments involuntarily and under protest.

The Supreme Court considered several issues on appeal. We focus on its discussion of whether the City was bound by the $60 per ton price, which Waste Connections argued was a modification of the contract, accepted by the City in continuing to use its services and paying the $60 price.]

... The issue here involves Waste Connections' purported unilateral modification of its agreement with the City for temporary services by increasing its rate to $60 per ton. Normally, a plaintiff cannot recover money voluntarily paid under a claim of right to payment if the plaintiff knew of facts that would permit the plaintiff to dispute the claim and withhold payment. But exceptions exist if the plaintiff shows that its consent was imperfectly voluntary, or ineffective, for a legally recognized reason.

One of the exceptions to the voluntary payment rule is duress. If a plaintiff's overpayment to the defendant was induced by duress, the plaintiff can seek restitution to the extent that the defendant was unjustly enriched. The Restatement (Third) of Restitution and Unjust Enrichment [§35(1)] specifically includes restitution claims for performance in excess of contractual requirements that result in the recipient's unjust enrichment:

> (1) If one party to a contract demands from the other a performance that is not in fact due by the terms of their agreement, under circumstances making it reasonable to accede to the demand rather than to insist on an immediate test of the dispute obligation, the party on whom the demand is made may render such performance under protest or with reservation of rights, preserving a claim in restitution to recover the value of the benefit conferred in excess of the recipient's contractual entitlement.

[Restatement (Third) of Restitution and Unjust Enrichment, §14(1) states] "Duress is coercion that is wrongful as a matter of law." [Comment g to §14(1) states:]

> Lawful coercion becomes impermissible when employed to support a bad-faith demand: one that the party asserting it knows (or should know) to be unjustified. [Coercion does not include hard bargaining, but it can include circumstances in which] the stronger party exploits the other's vulnerability in a manner that passes the bounds of economic self-interest. Legitimate self-interest (and lawful coercion) encompasses the usual freedom to deal with another on one's own terms or not at all. So long as the stronger party is not responsible for the other's vulnerability, driving a hard bargain does not constitute duress. But the exploitation of a superior bargaining position will predictably be found wrongful when the stronger party seeks additional leverage by exploiting a vulnerability to which the weaker party (in dealing [with] the stronger) is not properly subject. . . . Threats to exercise what would normally be a legal right may constitute duress when employed to achieve an advantage unrelated to the interests that the legal right is supposed to protect.

Threatening to take advantage of business exigency to impose unjust demands is commonly referred to as "economic duress" or a "business compulsion." . . . Economic duress may be found in threats, or implied threats, to cut off a supply of goods or services when the performing party seeks to take advantage of the circumstances that would be created by its breach of an agreement. . . . To be voidable because of duress, an agreement must not only be obtained by means of pressure brought to bear, but the agreement itself must be unjust, unconscionable, or illegal. . . . Under the Restatement's principles, we believe that these economic duress rules apply to modifications of a contract also.

. . . Whether a plaintiff voluntarily or involuntarily made a payment under a claim of right is a question of fact. The [trial] court specifically found that the City was in a disadvantaged bargaining position because it had to dispose of 40 tons of solid waste each day. It specifically found that the City had no reasonable alternative immediately available for disposing of its waste except to pay Waste

Connections' $60-per-ton rate. This finding was not clearly wrong. We also note that the City could not have litigated its dispute with Waste Connections before paying for its services when it had no reasonable alternative for disposing of its waste. The issue is whether Waste Connections took advantage of the circumstances to impose unjust demands. . . . [T]here was evidence to support a finding that Waste Connections was exploiting the exigency that its denial of services would create by unjustifiably increasing its price only for the City. . . . Waste Connection's $60 rate represented a 41-percent price increase over the $42.50 rate that the City had agreed to pay. . . . It increased its price by this amount in the span of a month, immediately after it learned that the City would terminate the . . . [short-term] contract in a year, and it did not charge this price to any other customer using its services. . . . [Waste Connections admitted that the rate increase was an attempt to compensate it for losing the City's business, and to cover the cost of maintaining the size of its workforce as well as increased fuel costs.] But the [trial] court obviously did not find . . . [Waste Connections'] explanations credible. It found no economic justification for Waste Connections' charging the City $17.50 more per ton than it charged to smaller volume customers. . . . It concluded that Waste Connections' attempt to cover its anticipated losses [from the non-renewal of the City's contract] was not a valid justification for its price increase.

Under our standard of review, we cannot say that the court's findings were clearly wrong. Sufficient evidence supported its finding that the City was not voluntarily paying the $60-per-ton rate. The record showed that the City had no reasonable alternative and that Waste Connections took advantage of the circumstances that its denial of services would have created to unjustly enrich itself. Because the facts support a finding of economic duress, we conclude that the court did not err in determining that the City was entitled to restitution. . . .

[The court then addresses the amount of the trial court's restitution award, based on the difference between the $60 charged and paid and the originally-agreed rate of $42.50.] Waste Connections' later increase of its rate to $60 per ton was a unilateral modification of the contract, to which the City assented under economic duress and for which no new consideration existed. . . . We have held that the parties may orally modify the terms of a written executory (not fully performed) contract after its execution and before a breach has occurred, without any new consideration, *Pennfield Oil Co. v. Winstrom*, 272 Neb. 219, 720 N.W.2d 886 (2006).[18] But a modification of an existing contract that substantially changes the liability of the parties requires mutual assent.

---

[18] This passage suggests that in Nebraska, the modification of an executory contract may not be subject to the preexisting duty rule, and may not require new consideration. If this is so, lack of consideration would not be a basis for attacking the modification, which would be valid unless it could be avoided on grounds of duress, fraud, unconscionability, or some other policing doctrine. Like *City of Scottsbluff*, the *Pennfield Oil Co.* case (as well as earlier cases cited by the court in that case) merely states the principle in these broad terms without explanation or discussion.—EDS.

That assent may be express or implied. But a weaker party's assent to a unilateral contract modification, which is to that party's disadvantage, should obviously not be implied from its conduct when the weaker party has shown that its assent was obtained through economic duress.... We conclude that because the City did not voluntarily assent to the modification, it did not change the ... contract. That is, the City's contractual liability under the implied contract obligated it to pay $42.50 per ton for disposal services.

The measure of restitution is normally a defendant's unjust gain. When a party to a contract shows that because of duress, it agreed under protest to the other party's demands for overperformance of its obligation, it may seek restitution for the value of the benefit conferred in excess of the recipient's contractual entitlement. So the court correctly determined that the City was entitled to recover its involuntary payments that were over the City's contractual obligation to pay $42.50 per ton.... We affirm its restitution award for these overpayments. Because the City protested the charges under circumstances that showed it was reasonable for it to accede to Waste Connections' demand, the [trial] court properly rejected Waste Connections' waiver and estoppel claims....

■ PROBLEM 13.9

Austin Instrument, Inc. v. Loral Corp., 29 N.Y.2d 124, 324 N.Y.S.2d 22, 272 N.E.2d 533 (1971) is a well-known case in which the court refused to uphold a coerced modification because of economic duress. Loral had a $6 million contract with the Navy to produce radar sets. Timely delivery to the Navy was crucial, not only because of significant penalties for late delivery, but also because Loral relied heavily on the Navy for its business and could not afford to be perceived by the Navy as unreliable. Loral awarded a subcontract to Austin for the supply of precision gear components for the radar sets. Loral thereafter received a second contract from the Navy, on which Austin bid, but Loral declined its bid because it was not the lowest. According to Loral, Austin reacted to this by telling Loral that it would not deliver any components under the current contract unless Loral awarded it the subcontract for the second contract and agreed to a price increase for the gears to be supplied under the current contract. Loral approached ten other manufacturers in an attempt to find another gear supplier, but could not find anyone who could produce the gears in time. It therefore gave in to Austin's demands, telling it that because it could not find another supplier, it had no choice but to meet its conditions. Austin then delivered the gears, and Loral completed its Navy contract on time.

After the Navy contracts had been fully performed, Loral sued Austin for a refund of the additional amounts paid for the gears under the contract modification. The lower courts dismissed Loral's complaint on the ground that Loral had not shown that it could not have found the gears elsewhere in time to complete the Navy contract. The majority of the Court of Appeals reversed. It held that Loral had entered into the contract under economic duress. Austin had made a wrongful threat to breach the contract by withholding the gears unless Loral agreed to award the second subcontract to it and to pay an increased price under the current contract. This deprived Loral of its free will because it had no reasonable alternative but to accede to Austin's demands: Despite great effort, it could not obtain gears elsewhere in time and would have been forced into breaching the Navy contract, making it liable to the Navy for significant penalties, and jeopardizing its relationship with the Navy.

A dissenting justice, siding with the lower courts, questioned the majority's conclusions. The dissent considered that Loral had not adequately shown economic duress. Firstly, there was conflicting testimony on whether Austin actually had made a threat to withhold the gears, rather than just requesting a renegotiation of the price for legitimate reasons. Secondly, Loral had not clearly established that it had no reasonable alternative but to agree to the modification—there were other suppliers available but it did not contact them.

In both *Austin Instrument* and *City of Scottsbluff* the courts found that one of the parties made an improper threat to breach an existing contract and that the other party had no reasonable alternative but to agree to the modification. In *Austin Instrument*, in addition to questioning whether Loral had shown an improper threat, the dissenting justice agreed with the lower courts that Loral failed to prove that it had no reasonable alternative but to accede to Austin's demands. Even if an improper threat can be shown, the threatened party could have difficulty in persuading a court that the threat left it with no reasonable alternative but to agree to the modification. Based on these two cases and the previous cases in this section, what degree of hardship or dire consequences must a victim of a coerced modification show to meet the burden of proving no reasonable alternative? If you were representing Loral or the City of Scottsbluff, what facts would you look for to establish that they had no reasonable alternative but to agree to the modification?

2. Supervening Difficulties as a Basis for Upholding a Modification Without Consideration

As noted above, the preexisting duty rule creates a barrier to the enforcement of contract modifications without consideration, even where it is clear that the modification was fair and not coerced. However, there is one situation in which courts have widely recognized the validity of a modification without new consideration: Where events following the formation of contract create a difficulty not anticipated by the parties at the time of contracting, a fairly bargained modification of the contract to take account of that unforeseen difficulty is valid. This principle is known as the supervening difficulties exception to the preexisting duty rule. For the exception to apply, there are several requirements that must be satisfied:

1. A substantial and burdensome unanticipated difficulty in the performance of one of the parties must arise after the contract had been entered into.
2. The risk of that difficulty must not have been expressly or impliedly assumed in the contract by the party who suffers the burden and seeks the modification.
3. The difficulty must not have resulted from that party's error, oversight, or misjudgment.
4. The other party's agreement to the modification must be genuine and the modification must be fair and equitable in light of the unanticipated difficulty.
5. The party seeking the modification must have dealt honestly and fairly in requesting it, and must not be trying to take advantage of the necessities of the other in coercing the modification.

For example, an excavating company enters into a contract to excavate a building site for the owner. The excavator's price is based on the anticipated scope of the work, as determined by geological surveys of the site supplied by the owner. Unknown to both parties, there is an undetected solid mass of hard rock under the surface of the area of excavation, which requires considerably more work, including blasting with dynamite. Upon discovering this problem, the excavator does not threaten to abandon the job, but merely approaches the owner and asks for a reasonable increase in price to compensate for the extra work, equipment, and materials that will be needed. The owner understands that the request for a price increase is fair under the circumstances and agrees to the modification. It may seem, under these circumstances, that each party did give new consideration for the modification because the owner paid more and the excavator did additional work. However, if all the excavator is doing is performing its preexisting duty to complete the excavation, the extra work may not be new consideration at all. Nevertheless, because the modification is a good-faith recognition by both parties that an adjustment to the contract is called for, it is likely to be upheld under the supervening difficulties exception, even in the absence of new consideration.

3. Contract Modifications Under UCC Article 2

UCC Article 2 has no provisions governing duress (or, for that matter, fraud, undue influence, or capacity). Therefore, under UCC 1-103(b), the common law principles of these doctrines apply to sales of goods. However, in the matter of contract modification, UCC 2-209(1) departs from the common law by stating "an agreement modifying a contract within this Article needs no consideration to be binding."

Official Comment 1 to UCC 2-209[19] makes it clear that the purpose of the section is to get rid of the awkward effects of the preexisting duty rule by giving effect to "all necessary and desirable modifications ... without regard to the technicalities which at present hamper such adjustments." Although UCC 2-209 does not itself provide for any standard by which these "necessary and desirable" modifications are to be tested, Official Comment 2 expresses the principle that modifications must satisfy the UCC's general test of good faith. The Comment goes on to state: "The effective use of bad faith to escape performance on the original contract terms is barred, and the extortion of a 'modification' without legitimate commercial reason is ineffective as a violation of the duty of good faith."

"Good faith" is notoriously difficult to define. (The same is true, of course, of its evil nemesis, "bad faith.") The UCC does make an attempt to define "good faith," but the language is nonspecific. UCC 1-201(b)(20) defines good faith to mean "honesty in fact and the observance of reasonable commercial standards of fair dealing." This definition combines a subjective standard of actual honesty with an objective standard based on prevailing commercial mores.[20] Clearly, the concept of bad faith includes coerced modifications, but the concept includes more than duress, and may encompass modifications that, while not necessarily extracted by duress, fail to comply with broader standards of honesty and fair dealing.

■ PROBLEM 13.10

Otto Motive entered into a contract to buy a new car for $35,000. The dealer did not have the car in stock, so it had to order one from the manufacturer. Under the written and signed purchase agreement, the dealer undertook to have the car available for Otto to take delivery two weeks after the contract was signed. A few days after the contract was signed, and

---

[19] Recall from the introduction to the UCC in Chapter 2 that when the Code was drafted, the drafters included an official comment for each section. These comments are part of the model Code (called the "Official Text") but are not part of the actual statute as enacted by the state legislatures. Therefore the Official Comments, while highly influential, have the force only of persuasive authority.

[20] Prior to the revision of Article 1 in 2001, "good faith" was defined in Article 1 to include only "honesty in fact" and did not include the objective standard. A separate provision of Article 2 had an enhanced definition of good faith, applicable only to merchants, which included the objective standard. By adding the objective standard to the general definition in §1-201(b)(20), the 2001 revision of Article 1 eliminated the distinction between merchants and non-merchants in defining good faith. This change was controversial and many states declined to enact the revised definition of good faith when adopting the 2001 revision of Article 1.

before the dealer had placed the order for the car, the manufacturer raised the price charged to dealers for the car by $2,000. The dealer therefore had to pay the manufacturer $2,000 more to get the car. When Otto came to collect the car, the dealer told him of the price increase and said that it could not deliver the car to Otto for $35,000, but would require him to pay $37,000. Otto protested but the dealer persisted in its refusal to deliver the car unless Otto paid the increased price. Otto had already sold his old car and had no means of transportation. In addition, he really liked the car that he had bought and did not wish to go through the process of looking for a different car. He therefore agreed to the price increase and signed an amendment to the contract substituting the higher price. A few days after Otto received and paid for the car, he regretted agreeing to pay more for it and felt that he should have insisted on getting the car for the price originally agreed. He contacted the dealer and demanded a refund of the additional $2,000 that he had paid. Does the modification bind him under UCC 2-209? Would your answer be different under common law and, if so, how?

E   UNDUE INFLUENCE → *narrow*

when fraud or duress are not present

The doctrine of undue influence is quite narrow in the realm of contracts. It was developed by courts of equity to deal with situations in which neither fraud nor duress could be shown but where one of the parties had a strong influence over the other and abused that influence or dominance to induce the other party to enter into a disadvantageous contractual relationship. In short, the focus of the doctrine is on self-dealing by a person who has breached some duty of trust to the party with whom he has contracted. For example, say that two brothers, Cain and Abel, have lived together for many years. Cain has always been the dominant and economically sophisticated sibling and has generally taken care of Abel's affairs. Abel trusts Cain and readily takes his advice on all financial matters. One day, Cain persuades Abel to enter into a contract under which Abel sells Cain property for a price considerably lower than its market value. When Abel later discovers Cain's breach of faith, he seeks to avoid the contract. There has been no duress, because Cain made no threat to induce Abel to enter the contract. There might possibly be an argument for misrepresentation by nondisclosure, but it may be difficult to establish the elements of fraud. However, *relationship of trust* the relationship of trust between the parties may give Abel grounds for avoidance under the doctrine of undue influence.

Restatement, Second §177(2) provides that a person whose manifestation of assent is induced by undue influence may avoid the contract. Section 177(1) defines undue influence as "... unfair persuasion of a party who is under the

someone is dominant or you trust them

unless it is done in good faith & w/o reason to know of the undue influence

domination of the person exercising the persuasion or who by virtue of the relation between them is justified in assuming that the person will not act in a manner inconsistent with his welfare." Section 177(3) deals with undue influence by one who is not a party to the contract. The provision is to the same effect as §164(2) relating to fraud and §175(2) relating to duress: The victim can avoid a contract induced by the undue influence of a nonparty unless the other party to the contract in good faith, and without reason to know of the undue influence, gives value or relies materially on the transaction.

Because the doctrine of unconscionability (discussed in Section F) is broad enough to cover many situations that do not fit into the elements of misrepresentation or duress, but which involve unfair bargaining and unfair advantage-taking, there has not been an incentive, in modern law, to try to expand the doctrine of undue influence beyond its traditional boundaries. These are identified in the comment to §177 as involving transactions between people who have a relationship of particular trust, such as close family members, clergymen and parishioners, and physicians and patients.

1) family 2) clergy 3) doctor

F   UNCONSCIONABILITY

1. The Derivation and Meaning of "Unconscionability"

unconscionable ↓ something that is not right

In common usage, something is unconscionable if it is not in accordance with what is right. It offends the conscience because it is unreasonably excessive, unscrupulous, or egregious. "Unconscionable" is a strong expression of condemnation, connoting a moral judgment and a sense of outrage. Its legal meaning is not that different. When applied to a contract or a contract term, the word suggests that the transaction is so unfair that it would offend the conscience of the court to enforce it.

equity ↓ now a general doctrine

The practice of refusing to enforce an unconscionable contract arose in courts of equity under the general principle that equitable jurisdiction was aimed at providing justice in cases where strict legal doctrine did not afford relief. A court whose focus is on doing equity can hardly be expected to give relief to a party whose own conduct, in extracting an outrageously unfair contract, is itself inequitable. Because unconscionability is an equitable doctrine, it was initially confined to cases in which the relief sought was equitable (for example, where the plaintiff sought specific performance of a contract), and it would not be available where the relief claimed was legal (for example, where the plaintiff's claim was for damages). As the law has developed, the distinction between law and equity has become attenuated. Most modern courts are courts of both law and equity, and the distinctions between legal and equitable principles are in an advanced stage of deterioration. In the case of unconscionability, the trend toward recognizing the doctrine as universal, applicable

~~beyond equitable~~ suits to legal claims as well, was accelerated by its inclusion in UCC Article 2. By adopting unconscionability as a general policing doctrine, the drafters of the UCC abolished any notion that, at least in contracts for the sale of goods, it should be limited to cases that were equitable in nature. This trend was further reinforced by the Restatement, Second, which followed the example of Article 2 and declared unconscionability to be a doctrine of general application. Unconscionability doctrine is now firmly established as a general doctrine, applicable whether the suit is equitable or legal in nature. Although there may still be some modern courts that do not recognize unconscionability as a general doctrine of law, we have not encountered any contemporary decisions that have refused to apply the doctrine on the grounds that it is inapplicable in a suit at law. The unconscionability provisions of Article 2 and the Restatement, Second, are as follows:

UCC 2-302. UNCONSCIONABLE CONTRACT OR CLAUSE

(1) If the court as a matter of law finds the contract or any clause of the contract to have been unconscionable at the time it was made the court may refuse to enforce the contract, or it may enforce the remainder of the contract without the unconscionable clause, or it may so limit the application of any unconscionable clause as to avoid any unconscionable result.

(2) When it is claimed or appears to the court that the contract or any clause thereof may be unconscionable the parties shall be afforded a reasonable opportunity to present evidence as to its commercial setting, purpose and effect to aid the court in making the determination. *have the chance to prove a right meaning*

RESTATEMENT, SECOND §208. UNCONSCIONABLE CONTRACT OR TERM

If a contract or term thereof is unconscionable at the time the contract is made a court may refuse to enforce the contract, or may enforce the remainder of the contract without the unconscionable term, or may so limit the application of any unconscionable term as to avoid any unconscionable result. — *same remedy as UCC*

2. The Remedy Where a Contract or Term Is Found to Be Unconscionable

The cases that follow deal with the elements of unconscionability, but they also inevitably present issues about the appropriate relief for unconscionability. Where the court finds unconscionability, remedial issues are included in the opinion. However, even where the plaintiff does not succeed in persuading the court that the contract is unconscionable, we still get insight into the possible remedy by taking note of what relief the plaintiff has claimed. We draw your attention to remedies at the outset, and we will raise questions about relief as we proceed through this section, because it is important to remain conscious of the remedial aspects of the cases. As you study the cases, consider whether the availability of a flexible range of remedies may have affected the court's willingness to find a contract or term to be unconscionable.

The remedial flexibility of the doctrine is apparent from both UCC 2-302 and Restatement, Second §208. They both provide that upon finding unconscionability, the court may refuse to enforce the contract (the remedy of avoidance that we have seen in relation to the other doctrines in this chapter); or it may enforce the remainder of the contract without the unconscionable term (that is, it may sever the unconscionable aspect of the contract); or it may limit the application of the unconscionable term so as to avoid the unconscionable result (that is, it may, in effect, rewrite the contract to get rid of its unconscionable effect). By falling short of complete avoidance, the latter two remedies give the court the option of adjusting the contract terms rather than making the all-or-nothing decision to fully enforce or completely invalidate the contract. However, these remedies must be used cautiously because they have the potential of saddling the parties with an arrangement that deviates significantly from what they actually agreed. As we have often seen, courts do not see it as their role to make a contract for the parties, and in some cases, severance or revision of an unconscionable term would take the resulting transaction too far from what the parties bargained for.

3. The Elements of Unconscionability

Notice that the provisions of UCC 2-302 and Restatement, Second §208 are very similar. Both of them do little more than recognize the power of the court to refuse enforcement of an unconscionable contract in whole or in part. Also, both identify the court, rather than the jury, as the arbiter of unconscionability. (UCC 2-302 is particularly clear on this point, characterizing unconscionability as a matter of law.) There are two reasons why the determination of unconscionability is left to the judge. One is traditional: Unconscionability derives from equity, and courts of equity do not have juries. The other is practical: Because unconscionability is such a fluid doctrine, the determination of unconscionability is best left to the judge, who has the training to apply it more dispassionately.

Neither UCC 2-302 nor Restatement, Second §208 says what standards must be applied to decide if a contract is unconscionable. Official Comment 1 to UCC 2-302[21] provides some guidance in this issue by stating, "The basic test is

---

[21] As noted earlier, the Official Comments are part of the model code (the "Official Text") but are not part of the statute as enacted by state legislatures. While they are very influential, they are only persuasive authority.

whether, in the light of the general commercial background and the commercial needs of the particular trade or case, the clauses involved are so one-sided as to be unconscionable under the circumstances existing at the time of making the contract." It also says, "The principle is one of the prevention of oppression and unfair surprise . . . and not of disturbance of allocation of risks because of superior bargaining power." This is not exactly the most precise and lucid set of guidelines. The commentary to Restatement, Second §208 is conceptually similar, albeit somewhat fuller, but unconscionability by its nature defies precise definition. It relies on a discretionary judgment by the court, to be exercised in light of all the circumstances of the case.

In a famous early criticism of UCC 2-302,[22] Professor Leff said, "If reading [UCC 2-302] makes anything clear, it is that reading this section alone makes nothing clear about the meaning of 'unconscionable' except perhaps that it is pejorative." Neither does he find the vague abstractions of the Official Comment particularly useful in articulating the standards to be applied in deciding whether a contract or term is unconscionable. He concludes that UCC 2-302 does little more than encourage the court to react emotionally to the transaction. About 50 years have passed since Leff wrote his article in 1967, so courts have had considerable time to give concrete form to the abstractions of UCC 2-302 and Restatement, Second §208.

a. Procedural and Substantive Unconscionability.

In his article on unconscionability, Leff identified two components of unconscionability. His analysis has been immensely influential and has been widely adopted by courts. He saw unconscionability as having both a procedural and a substantive element. The procedural element (which he called "bargaining naughtiness") relates to the way in which the contract was formed. It focuses on unfair bargaining tactics, disparity of power leading to imposition, and other factors that made it possible for one party to take unfair advantage of the other. The substantive element relates to the terms of the resulting contract. It focuses on whether, as a result of behaving in a procedurally unconscionable way, one of the parties was able to impose an unfair contract or term on the other. In following this analysis, for a finding of unconscionability many courts require that both the procedural and substantive elements be satisfied at least to some degree. However, courts do balance the elements and may be satisfied with a very modest showing of one of them if the other is shown emphatically. Some courts have been willing to grant relief on a showing of just one of the elements if the bargaining behavior or the unfairness of the term is sufficiently egregious.

---

[22] Arthur A. Leff, *Unconscionability and the Code—The Emperor's New Clause,* 115 U. Pa. L. Rev. 485 (1967).

■ PROBLEM 13.11

In Section C we read the court's disposition of the fraud and duress issues in *Germantown Manufacturing Co. v. Rawlinson*, 341 Pa. Super. 42, 491 A.2d 138 (1985). Recall that Mrs. Rawlinson signed judgment notes in an effort to prevent the prosecution of her husband for embezzlement. The notes contained a confession of judgment, which the employer used to obtain a judgment against her on the one note that was not paid. The issue in the case was whether she had a meritorious defense to the note that would justify opening the confessed judgment. After finding that Mrs. Rawlinson had meritorious defenses based on fraud and duress, thereby entitling her to open the judgment, the court also found that unconscionability constituted a third alternative meritorious defense.

The court did not analyze unconscionability on the basis of the procedural and substantive elements, but instead quoted the well-known definition of "unconscionability" expressed in one of the early landmark cases, *Williams v. Walker-Thomas Furniture Co.*, 350 F.2d 445, 449 (D.C. Cir. 1965): "Unconscionability has generally been recognized to include an absence of meaningful choice on the part of one of the parties together with contract terms which are unreasonably favorable to the other party." Even though the transaction at issue was not a sale of goods, the court also found guidance on the meaning of unconscionability in Official Comment 1 to UCC 2-302, which looks at whether the contract or clause is too one-sided under all the circumstances, and whether there has been "oppression" and "unfair surprise." The concept of "unfair surprise" in the Official Comment denotes contractual terms that are not typically expected by the party who is being asked to agree to them. They often appear in the boilerplate of a printed form and are either not read or not understood. The court considered that the confession of judgment met this standard. It was a harsh term that surely surprised Mrs. Rawlinson unfairly: "She had never before seen a judgment note and was crying for part of the time when she read the documents presented to her, although she tried her best to read them. The lack of real choice inherent in the transaction may have counseled against any need to thoroughly read and understand what she was signing. Furthermore, neither the insurance agent nor her husband offered her any guidance as to the extent of the liability to which she was agreeing. In fact, she was misled as to her liability. . . ."

The court continued that even if Mrs. Rawlinson had been aware of and had fully understood the confession "in all of its star-chamber ramifications," she could not be held to have assented to it because the clause was adhesive—she had no choice but to sign it, because the performance under the contract was important to her economic or physical well-being, and she had no power to resist the terms dictated by the party with superior bargaining power.

(a) In addition to "unfair surprise," Official Comment 1 refers to "oppression." Was there also oppression in the *Germantown Manufacturing* case? Was the contract one-sided? If so, how does that affect the "unfair surprise" and "oppression" analysis?

(b) Although the court did not specifically use the procedural and substantive unconscionability analysis, do you think that the court would have reached the same conclusion had it used that analysis?

(c) Do you agree with the court that the confession of judgment was unconscionable?

(d) In *Germantown Manufacturing*, the court had already found sufficient allegations of the meritorious defenses of fraud and duress, so a finding of unconscionability was not needed to allow Mrs. Rawlinson to open the judgment. Contrast unconscionability to the defenses of fraud and duress. How does it differ, and what does it add to the collection of remedies available to a victim of unfair bargaining? After the judgment is set aside and the case goes to trial, what will be the drawbacks and advantages of each of the defenses, based on the facts set out in the opinion?

b. Contracts of Adhesion.

In *Germantown Manufacturing*, the court calls the confession of judgment that Mrs. Rawlinson signed "adhesive." This is a reference to a concept that was originally used in relation to insurance policies (which are a classic example of prepackaged form contracts) but has now become much more widely used to describe any contract in which one of the parties has enough bargaining power to be able to dictate the terms of the contract to the other on a take-it-or-leave-it basis, and the weaker party has no choice but to "adhere" to the terms. Although the term "contracts of adhesion" has been in use since the 1920s, Professor Kessler wrote the classic article about them in 1943.[23] He argued that traditional conceptions of contract law, based on individualized contracts between persons of roughly equivalent bargaining power, failed to take into account that a vast number of contracts were based on standard terms. (Of course, standard-term contracts have become even more

[handwritten: take it or leave it terms]

___

[23] Friedrich Kessler, *Contracts of Adhesion—Some Thoughts About Freedom of Contract*, 43 Colum. L. Rev. 629 (1943).

standard term contracts are so common now

commonplace since 1943 and now surely outnumber individualized contracts.) He noted the burgeoning use of standard form contracts in all areas of commerce and recognized their importance in day-to-day dealings. Standard-form contracts reduce transaction costs, allow for centralized decision making on the terms on which a large business will enter contracts, and can be drafted to control or avoid risks. However, he recognized that the advantages and efficiency of standard contracting have a dangerous side effect. Powerful corporations are able to impose their terms on weaker parties, who may have little or no choice but to accept the terms, either because the powerful party has dominance that amounts to a monopoly or because its competitors use the same terms. Kessler argued that unless contract law became more sensitive to this phenomenon, its rules could facilitate oppression and undermine freedom of contract.

powerful corps. can impose unfair terms on weaker parties

Kessler's insights, which have been the foundation of much of the modern discussion of the problem of adhesion, must be seen in perspective. Standard-form contracting is not evil in itself; in fact, it is indispensable. (Recall the discussion on this point in Chapter 3.) However, a powerful contractor who uses standard forms may have the ability and desire to impose a one-sided and unfair transaction on the parties with whom it contracts. If this happens, there may be grounds for using the doctrine of unconscionability to ameliorate the effects of that imposition. Looked at in this light, adhesion is so closely related to unconscionability that it is just one aspect of unconscionability. If a contract is described as "adhesive," this may signify that there may have been some degree of oppression in its formation. If, in addition, the contract has unfair terms, its adhesive nature may alone be enough (without any additional bargaining misbehavior) to supply the procedural element of unconscionability; that is, adhesion becomes unconscionable and is actionable if the abuse of bargaining dominance imposes unfair terms.

adhesive implies some level of oppression

Notwithstanding the association of adhesion and unconscionability, it should also be noted that the word "adhesion" tends to be used quite loosely today. A court may describe a contract as adhesive merely because it consists of nonnegotiable standard terms. The nature of the transaction and the availability of competing products on the market may mean that the person who adheres to the terms may not really lack meaningful choice and may not really be the victim of oppression. Therefore, it makes sense not to assume too readily that just because a contract is offered on nonnegotiable terms, it is adhesive and is by necessity unconscionable. To make a proper determination of whether a contract is unconscionable, one must evaluate the facts of the transaction and analyze both the bargaining conduct and the contract's substantive terms. It also needs to be stressed that while size and power often go hand in hand, this is not inevitably true. In a competitive market, even a small consumer may have considerable bargaining power. If she is adequately informed and assertive, she may use this leverage to resist adverse terms, or may simply obtain the goods or services elsewhere.

adhesion does not necessarily equate with "non negotiable"

*look at
① bargaining conduct
② substantive terms*

■ PROBLEM 13.12

Reexamine the facts of *Odorizzi* set out in Problem 13.8. Do they support a finding of procedural unconscionability? Do they support a finding of substantive unconscionability?

A portion of the next case, *Feldman v. Google, Inc.*, was included in Chapter 3, Section C.4 in relation to the duty to read standard clickwrap terms. You may recall that the court held that Feldman had manifested assent to Google's standard terms, including a forum selection clause, by clicking on an "I agree" box on its website. The court then went on to consider whether the forum selection clause was unconscionable. We include that portion of the opinion here. The two cases following *Feldman*, *Lhotka v. Geographic Expeditions, Inc.* and *Zuver v. Airtouch Communications, Inc.*, consider whether standard arbitration provisions are unconscionable. These days it seems almost inevitable that a standard agreement will contain an arbitration provision, a forum selection clause, or some other provision that limits or confines the nondrafting party's right to litigate a dispute that may arise under the contract. This trend is reflected in the large number of cases in which the validity of such provisions is challenged.

There is nothing inherently unconscionable in a provision that confines litigation to a particular jurisdiction or that requires disputes to be settled by arbitration. Forum selection provisions are generally upheld if reasonable and fairly bargained. Even greater deference is given to arbitration provisions because federal law[24] recognizes a general public policy in favor of arbitration. This policy is embodied in §2 of the Federal Arbitration Act, 9 U.S.C. §§1-16 (FAA), which states:

generally upheld if reasonable

> A written provision in any maritime transaction or a contract evidencing a transaction involving commerce to settle by arbitration a controversy thereafter arising out of such contract or transaction, or the refusal to perform the whole or any part thereof, or an agreement in writing to submit to arbitration an existing controversy arising out of such a contract, transaction, or refusal, shall be valid, irrevocable, and enforceable, save upon such grounds as exist at law or in equity for the revocation of any contract.

Section 2 makes it clear that even though arbitration agreements are favored, an agreement to arbitrate must qualify as a contract, and its validity

agreement to arbitrate must qualify as a contract

---

[24] Some states also have statutes that effectuate this public policy.

can be challenged[25] on any grounds applicable to contracts generally. The savings clause of §2 calls for the application of state law. This means that an agreement to arbitrate can be avoided, like any other contract, on the basis that it is unconscionable.

You will see, as you read these three cases, that they reach different results: *Feldman* upholds a forum selection clause, *Lhotka* avoids an arbitration provision as unconscionable, and *Zuver* finds an arbitration provision to be unconscionable only in part. Pay attention to the courts' reasoning and see if you can discern points of distinction that explain these different results.

FELDMAN v. GOOGLE, INC.

513 F. Supp. 2d 229 (2007)
United States District Court, Eastern District of Pennsylvania

GILES, District Judge.

. . . On or about January 2003, Plaintiff, a lawyer with his own law firm, Lawrence E. Feldman & Associates, purchased advertising from Defendant Google, Inc.'s "AdWords" Program, to attract potential clients who may have been harmed by drugs under scrutiny by the U.S. Food and Drug Administration. In the AdWords program, whenever an internet user searched on the internet search engine, Google.com, for keywords or "Adwords" purchased by Plaintiff, such as "Vioxx," "Bextra," and "Celebrex," Plaintiff's ad would appear. If the searcher clicked on Plaintiff's ad, Defendant would charge Plaintiff for each click made on the ad. This procedure is known as "pay per click" advertising. The price per keyword is determined by a bidding process, wherein the highest bidder for a

---

[25] The question of who decides whether an arbitration agreement is unconscionable is intriguing, complex, and beyond the sensible scope of a first-year contracts course. However, this is a matter that has received the attention of the U.S. Supreme Court in several cases, so it is of interest to sketch the principle briefly: Where the parties have entered into an agreement to arbitrate, but one of the parties (the plaintiff) disregards that agreement and initiates suit in court, the other party (the defendant) may move to dismiss or stay the suit and request the court to compel arbitration. The plaintiff may oppose the defendant's motion on the grounds that the arbitration provision is unconscionable. In some cases, the court itself will decide on the question of unconscionability. If it decides that the arbitration agreement is unconscionable, it will deny the motion and allow the litigation to proceed. If it finds that the arbitration agreement is not unconscionable, it will dismiss or stay the suit and compel arbitration. However, the U.S. Supreme Court has held, in a series of cases culminating in *Rent-A-Center, West, Inc. v. Jackson*, 130 S. Ct. 2772 (2010), that there are some circumstances in which the court must not itself decide the issue of unconscionability, but must refer that question to the arbitrator. This occurs where the arbitration agreement itself gives the arbitrator the exclusive authority to resolve disputes as to the validity of the contract. It could also occur where the claimed unconscionability relates not to the arbitration agreement itself, but to some other aspect of the contract or to the contract as a whole; that is, where a party challenges the contract as a whole, not simply the arbitration agreement, the challenge to the arbitration agreement is regarded as tangential. In this situation, the arbitration provision is, in effect, severed from the remainder of the contract and enforced, so that the arbitrator decides whether the agreement as a whole is unconscionable. In essence, the arbitrator gets to decide if the contract under which she is empowered to conduct the arbitration is valid.

keyword would have its ad placed at the top of the list of results from a Google.com search by an internet user. Plaintiff claims that he was the victim of "click fraud." Click fraud occurs when entities or persons, such as competitors or pranksters, without any interest in Plaintiff's services, click repeatedly on Plaintiff's ad, the result of which drives up his advertising cost and discourages him from advertising. Click fraud also may be referred to as "improper clicks" or, to coin a phrase, "trick clicks." Plaintiff alleges that twenty to thirty percent of all clicks for which he was charged were fraudulent. He claims that Google required him to pay for all clicks on his ads, including those which were fraudulent. Plaintiff does not contend that Google actually knew that there were fraudulent clicks, but alleges that click fraud can be tracked and prevented by computer programs, which can count the number of clicks originating from a single source and whether a sale results, and can be tracked by mechanisms on websites. Plaintiff alleges, therefore, that Google had the capacity to determine which clicks were fraudulent, but did nothing to prevent the click fraud, and did not adequately warn him about click fraud or investigate his complaints about click fraud. Plaintiff alleges that Google informed him that it did not keep records on an advertiser's account and click history for more than the most recent three months, and that Google disclaimed liability for clicks older than sixty days. . . . Plaintiff alleges Google charged him over $100,000 for AdWords from about January 2003 to December 31, 2005. Plaintiff seeks damages, disgorgement of any profits Defendant obtained as a result of any unlawful conduct, and restitution of money Plaintiff paid for fraudulent clicks.

This cross-summary judgment battle turns entirely on a forum selection clause in the AdWords online agreement. It is undisputed that the forum selection clause provides: "*The Agreement must be* construed as if both parties jointly wrote it, governed by California law except for its conflicts of laws principles and *adjudicated in Santa Clara County, California.*" Annie Hsu, an AdWords Associate for Google, Inc., testified by affidavit that the following procedures were in place at the time that Plaintiff activated his AdWords account in about January 2003. Although Plaintiff claims that the AdWords Agreement "was neither signed nor seen and negotiated by Feldman & Associates or anyone at his firm" and that he never "personally signed a contract with Google to litigate disputes in Santa Clara County, California," Plaintiff does not dispute that he followed the process outlined by Hsu.

It is undisputed that advertisers, including Plaintiff, were required to enter into an AdWords contract before placing any ads or incurring any charges. To open an AdWords account, an advertiser had to have gone through a series of steps in an online sign-up process. To activate the AdWords account, the advertiser had to have visited his account page, where he was shown the AdWords contract. Toward the top of the page displaying the AdWords contract, a notice in bold print appeared and stated, "**Carefully read the following terms and conditions**. If you agree with these terms, indicate your assent below." The terms and conditions were offered in a window, with a scroll bar that allowed the advertiser to scroll down and read the entire contract. The contract itself included the pre-amble and seven paragraphs, in twelve-point font. The contract's preamble, the first paragraph, and part of the second paragraph were clearly visible before scrolling down to read the rest of the contract. The preamble, visible at first impression, stated that consent to the terms listed in the Agreement constituted a binding agreement with Google. A link to a printer-friendly version of the contract was offered at the top of the contract window for the advertiser who would rather read the contract printed on paper or view it on a full-screen instead of scrolling down the window.

At the bottom of the webpage, viewable without scrolling down, was a box and the words, "**Yes**, I agree to the above terms and conditions." The advertiser had to have clicked on this box in order to proceed to the next step. If the advertiser did not click on "**Yes**, I agree . . ." and instead tried to click the "Continue" button at the bottom of the webpage, the advertiser would have been returned to the same page and could not advance to the next step. If the advertiser did not agree to the AdWords contract, he could not activate his account, place any ads, or incur any charges. Plaintiff had an account activated. He placed ads and charges were incurred. . . .

[The court first dealt with the question of whether Feldman bound himself to the clickwrap terms by clicking on the "Yes, I agree" button on the web page, even if he had not actually read the terms. As mentioned above, the court held that Feldman did make a binding manifestation of assent to those terms, including the forum selection clause. After resolving that question, the court went on to consider Feldman's argument that the forum selection clause was unconscionable.]

Plaintiff argues that the AdWords Agreement and in particular the forum selection clause are unconscionable. Unconscionability is a general defense to the enforcement of a contract or its specific terms. Unconscionability has procedural and substantive components. . . . The procedural component is satisfied by the existence of unequal bargaining positions and hidden terms. . . . The substantive component is satisfied by overly harsh or one-sided results that shock the conscience. . . . The party challenging the contractual provision has the burden to prove unconscionability.

Under California law, a contract or its terms may be procedurally unconscionable if it is an adhesion contract. A contract of adhesion is a form or standardized contract prepared by a party of superior bargaining power, to be signed by the party in the weaker position, who only has the opportunity to agree to the contract or reject it, without an opportunity to negotiate or bargain. The opportunity to negotiate by itself does not end the inquiry into procedural unconscionability. Courts consider factors such as the buyer's sophistication, the use of high-pressure tactics or external pressure to induce acceptance, and the availability of alternative sources of supply. Plaintiff argues the AdWords Agreement was a contract of adhesion because it was not negotiated at arms length and was offered on a "take it or leave it" basis, without an opportunity to bargain. Internet users had to agree to the terms in order to activate an AdWords account and purchase AdWords. Defendant counters that Plaintiff is a sophisticated purchaser, an attorney, who had full notice of the terms, who was capable of understanding them, and who assented to them. Plaintiff has not alleged high-pressure tactics or external pressure to accept the Agreement.

Defendant also argues that other internet providers offer similar advertising services, including MSN Search, AOL Search, Ask.com, Yahoo!, Excite, Infospace, and HotBot, and thus <u>Plaintiff could have chosen to take his business elsewhere.</u> Plaintiff counters that the availability of other internet service providers does not undercut the existence of an adhesion contract. Plaintiff also asserts that only Yahoo offers comparable advertising and that Yahoo's sign up system is similar to Google's. Plaintiff, however, has not offered any evidence in support of his assertion. As such, he has not met his affirmative burden on his summary judgment motion to make a sufficient showing that other online companies did not offer similar, competing advertising services, which lacked forum selection clauses. On this factor in the analysis, the agreement stands up as <u>not being procedurally unconscionable.</u> . . .

A contract is not necessarily one of adhesion simply because it is a form contract. Courts have recognized the prevalence and importance of standardized contracts in people's everyday lives. *ProCD, Inc. v. Zeidenberg*, 86 F.3d 1447, 1451 (7th Cir. 1996) (quoting Restatement (2d) of Contracts §211 cmt. a (1981)) ("Standardization of agreements serves many of the same functions as standardization of goods and services; both are essential to a system of mass production and distribution. Scarce and costly time and skill can be devoted to a class of transactions rather than the details of individual transactions."). Because Plaintiff was a sophisticated purchaser, <u>was not in any way pressured to agree to the AdWords Agreement</u>, was capable of understanding the Agreement's terms, consented to them, and could have rejected the Agreement with impunity, this court finds that the AdWords Agreement was not procedurally unconscionable.

Even if the AdWords Agreement were procedurally unconscionable, it is not substantively unconscionable. Under California law, a contract found to be procedurally unconscionable may still be enforceable if its substantive terms are reasonable. California courts focus on whether there was a lack of mutuality in contract formation and on the practical effects of the challenged provisions. Plaintiff argues that the <u>forum selection clause and other provisions lacked consideration and assent from the Plaintiff, and</u> therefore the Agreement was lacking a modicum of bilaterality. As the court has found that the AdWords Agreement provided reasonable notice of its terms, had mutual assent, and was in other respects a valid express contract, the court rejects this argument.

Plaintiff next argues that the AdWords Agreement contains several unilateral clauses, including the forum selection clause, which make it substantively unconscionable. He argues that the forum selection clause unreasonably favors Google because it requires billing disputes to be adjudicated in California. Plaintiff characterizes as unreasonable provisions disclaiming all warranties, limiting liabilities, and requiring that claims relating to charges be brought within sixty days of the charges. Plaintiff contends that the effect of these provisions, in

[handwritten margin note: ¶ claim-point was to discourage billing dispute]

combination with the forum selection clause, is to discourage meritorious litigation regarding billing disputes.

First, the court is not persuaded that the forum selection clause, or any other provision cited by Plaintiff, is unreasonable or shocks the conscience. As the United States Supreme Court has found, a forum selection clause in a standardized, non-negotiable contract may be permissible for several reasons, reasons which apply here. *See Carnival Cruise Lines, Inc. v. Shute*, 499 U.S. 585, 593-94, 111 S. Ct. 1522, 113 L. Ed. 2d 622 (1991). Just as a cruise line has a special interest in limiting fora because it could be subject to suit where its passengers come from many locales, Defendant has the same interest where its internet users are located across the United States and the world. *See id.* at 593, 111 S. Ct. 1522. Another

[handwritten margin note: internet users are everywhere]

benefit of such a forum selection clause is that it dispels confusion over where suits are to be brought, conserving both litigant and judicial resources. *Id.* at 593-94, 111 S. Ct. 1522. Finally, just as for the passengers in *Carnival Cruise Lines*, the benefits of such a forum selection clause may be passed to internet users in the form of reduced rates for services, because of savings enjoyed by internet service providers by limiting the fora for suit. *See id.* at 594, 111 S. Ct. 1522. Plaintiff's

[handwritten margin note: reject claim of discouraging suits]

argument that the terms discourage litigation of billing disputes thus is not persuasive, especially where Defendant's principal place of business is in California.

Further, the provision requiring that claims relating to charges be brought within sixty days of the charges is not unconscionable. Contractual limitations periods are valid and can be shorter than limitations periods prescribed by statute so long as the period for bringing claims is reasonable. California courts have upheld contractual limitations periods similar to the one here.... Finally, as to the other provisions, including those disclaiming all warranties and limiting liabilities, Plaintiff has not met his burden of persuasion as to unconscionability and does not present case law to support his position. No basis has been presented for the court to conclude that these commonplace terms are unreasonable. In addition, even if any of the provisions of the contract were unenforceable, these provisions could be modified or severed under the AdWords Agreement's severability clause. The court finds that neither the AdWords Agreement nor its terms, including the forum selection clause, are unconscionable, and that the AdWords Agreement and its forum selection clause are enforceable....

LHOTKA v. GEOGRAPHIC EXPEDITIONS, INC.

104 Cal. Rptr. 3d 844, 181 Cal. App. 4th 816 (2010)
California Court of Appeal

SIGGINS, Justice.

Geographic Expeditions, Inc. (GeoEx) appeals from an order denying its motion to compel arbitration of a wrongful death action brought by the survivors of one

posture
↑
*arbitration
clause was
unconscionable*

*wrongful
death*

*broad
waiver*

terms

*all or
nothing*

of its clients who died on a Mount Kilimanjaro hiking expedition. GeoEx contends the trial court erred when it ruled that the agreement to arbitrate contained in GeoEx's release form was unconscionable. Alternatively, GeoEx contends that if the court correctly concluded the arbitration clause was unconscionable, the court abused its discretion in striking the clause in its entirety rather than severing the objectionable provisions and enforcing the remainder. We find neither point is persuasive, and therefore affirm the order. *disposition*

Jason Lhotka was 37 years old when he died of an altitude-related illness while on a GeoEx expedition up Mount Kilimanjaro with his mother, plaintiff Sandra Menefee. GeoEx's limitation of liability and release form, which both Lhotka and Menefee signed as a requirement of participating in the expedition, provided that <u>each of them released GeoEx from all liability in connection with the trek and waived any claims for liability "to the maximum extent permitted by law."</u> The release also required that the parties would submit any disputes between themselves first to mediation and then to binding arbitration. It reads: "I understand that all Trip Applications are subject to acceptance by GeoEx in San Francisco, California, USA. I agree that in the unlikely event a dispute of any kind arises between me and GeoEx, the following conditions will apply: (a) the dispute will be submitted to a neutral third-party mediator in San Francisco, California, with both parties splitting equally the cost of such mediator. If the dispute cannot be resolved through mediation, then (b) the dispute will be submitted for binding arbitration to the American Arbitration Association in San Francisco, California; (c) the dispute will be governed by California law; and (d) the <u>maximum amount of recovery to which I will be entitled under any and all circumstances will be the sum of the land and air cost of my trip with GeoEx.</u> I agree that this is a fair and reasonable limitation on the damages, of any sort whatsoever, that I may suffer. I agree to fully indemnify GeoEx for all of its costs (including attorneys' fees) if I commence an action or claim against GeoEx based upon claims I have previously released or waived by signing this release." Menefee paid $16,831 for herself and Lhotka to go on the trip.

A letter from GeoEx president James Sano that accompanied the limitation of liability and release explained that the form was mandatory and that, on this point, "our lawyers, insurance carriers and medical consultants give us no discretion. A signed, <u>unmodified release form is required before any traveler may join one of our trips.</u> Ultimately, we believe that you should choose your travel company based on its track record, not what you are asked to sign. . . . My review of other travel companies' release forms suggests that our forms are not a whole lot different from theirs."

After her son's death, Menefee sued GeoEx for wrongful death and alleged various theories of liability including fraud, gross negligence and recklessness, and intentional infliction of emotional distress. GeoEx moved to compel arbitration. The trial court found the arbitration provision was unconscionable under *Armendariz v. Foundation Health Psychcare Services, Inc.* (2000) 24 Cal. 4th 83, 99 Cal. Rptr. 2d 745, 6 P.3d 669 (*Armendariz*), and on that basis denied the motion. It ruled: "The agreement at issue is both procedurally and

procedural →

substantive ←

substantively unconscionable. . . . The Sano letter establishes that the agreement was presented as a Take It Or Leave It proposition and was also represented to be consistent with industry practice. As a consequence[,] if the plaintiff and decedent wished to go on this trip, they could do so only on these terms. Unconscionability also permeates the substantive terms of the agreement to arbitrate. The problematic terms are the limitation on damages, the indemnity of GeoEx, the requirement that GeoEx costs and attorneys' fees be paid if suit is filed related to certain claims, splitting the costs of mediation, the absence of an agreement on the cost of arbitration and the lack of mutuality as to each of these terms. As a consequence, this is not a case where the court may strike a single clause and compel arbitration."

Can't seperate→
the contract
out & compel
arbitration

issue

This appeal timely followed. The questions posed here are: (1) whether the agreement to arbitrate is unconscionable and, therefore, unenforceable; and (2) if so, whether the court properly declined to enforce the entire arbitration clause rather than sever unconscionable provisions. We answer both questions in the affirmative. . . .

We turn first to GeoEx's contention that the court erred when it found the arbitration agreement unconscionable. Although the issue arises here in a relatively novel setting, the basic legal framework is well established. . . . [The court sets out the principles of unconscionability by a series of quotes from prior cases. We omit the quote marks and citations.] Unconscionability has generally been recognized to include an absence of meaningful choice on the part of one of the parties together with contract terms which are unreasonably favorable to the other party. Phrased another way, unconscionability has both a procedural and a substantive element. The procedural element requires oppression or surprise. Oppression occurs where a contract involves lack of negotiation and meaningful choice, surprise where the allegedly unconscionable provision is hidden within a prolix printed form. The substantive element concerns whether a contractual provision reallocates risks in an objectively unreasonable or unexpected manner. Under this approach, both the procedural and substantive elements must be met before a contract or term will be deemed unconscionable. Both, however, need not be present to the same degree. A sliding scale is applied so that the more substantively oppressive the contract term, the less evidence of procedural unconscionability is required to come to the conclusion that the term is unenforceable, and vice versa. This notion of a "sliding scale," as will be seen, figures centrally in the analysis of the agreement at issue here.

oppression:
lack of
negotiation
& meaningful
choice

substantive
↳ reallocates
risk in an
unreasonable/
unexpected
manner

★must meet
procedural &
substantive
elements

GeoEx argues the arbitration agreement involved neither the oppression nor surprise aspects of procedural unconscionability. GeoEx argues the agreement was not oppressive because plaintiffs made no showing of an "industry-wide requirement that travel clients must accept an agreement's terms without modification" and "they fail[ed] even to attempt to negotiate" with GeoEx. We disagree. GeoEx's argument cannot reasonably be squared with its own statements advising participants that they must sign an *unmodified* release form to participate in the expedition; that GeoEx's "lawyers, insurance carriers and medical consultants give [it] no discretion" on that point; and *that other travel companies were no different.* In other words, GeoEx led the plaintiffs to understand not only that its terms and conditions were non-negotiable, but that plaintiffs would encounter the same requirements with any other travel company. This is a sufficient basis for us to conclude the plaintiffs lacked bargaining power.

GeoEx also contends its terms were not oppressive, apparently as a matter of law, because Menefee and Lhotka could have simply decided not to trek up Mount Kilimanjaro. It argues that contracts for recreational activities can *never* be unconscionably oppressive because, unlike agreements for necessities such as medical care or employment, a consumer of recreational activities *always* has the option of foregoing the activity. The argument has some initial resonance, but on closer inspection we reject it as unsound. While the nonessential nature of recreational activities is a factor to be taken into account in assessing whether a contract is oppressive, it is not necessarily the dispositive factor. *Szetela v. Discover Bank* 97 Cal. App. 4th 1094, 118 Cal. Rptr. 2d 862 (2002) is informative. The defendant, a credit card company, argued the plaintiff could not establish procedural unconscionability because there were "market alternatives" to its product—i.e., the plaintiff had the option of taking his business to a different bank. The court disagreed, and held the customer's ability to walk away rather than sign the offending contract was not dispositive. "The availability of similar goods or services elsewhere may be relevant to whether the contract is one of adhesion, but even if the clause at issue here is not an adhesion contract, it can still be found unconscionable. Moreover, in a given case, a contract might be adhesive even if the weaker party could reject the terms and go elsewhere. Therefore, whether Szetela could have found another credit card issuer who would not have required his acceptance of a similar clause *is not the deciding factor.*" (Italics added.) The focus of procedural unconscionability in *Szetela*, rather, was on the manner in which the disputed clause was presented. Faced with the options of either closing his account or accepting the credit card company's "take it or leave it" terms, Szetela established the necessary element of procedural unconscionability despite the fact that he could have simply taken his business elsewhere.

The cases on which GeoEx relies do not hold otherwise. GeoEx relies on *Morris v. Redwood Empire Bancorp*, 128 Cal. App. 4th 1305 at 1320, 27 Cal. Rptr. 3d 797 (2005), for its statement that the "procedural element of unconscionability may be defeated . . . if the complaining party has a meaningful choice of reasonably available alternative sources of supply from which to obtain the desired goods and services free of the terms claimed to be unconscionable." "[M]ay be defeated," true—but not "must," in all cases and as a matter of law. *Morris* takes its premise from *Dean Witter Reynolds, Inc. v. Superior Court*, 211 Cal. App. 3d 758, 772, 259 Cal. Rptr. 789 (1989), in which Division Two of this court expressly declined to hold or suggest "that *any* showing of competition in the marketplace as to the desired goods and services defeats, as a matter of law, *any* claim of unconscionability." Indeed, *Morris* itself recognizes that some contracts may be oppressive despite the availability of market alternatives, albeit in the context of employment or medical care—i.e., contracts for "life's

[handwritten margin notes: "∏ lacked bargaining power"; "Δ claim ✓"; "not a dispositive factor"; "focus on the manner of presentation"]

necessities." Many of the other authorities cited by GeoEx are inapposite because they concern challenges to release of liability clauses under the rule that invalidates exculpatory provisions that affect the public interest. In this specific context, our courts consistently hold that recreation does not implicate the public interest, and therefore approve exculpatory provisions required for participation in recreational activities. But these cases do not focus on unconscionability, and they do not hold that contracts for recreational activities are immune from analysis for procedural unconscionability.

Here, certainly, plaintiffs could have chosen not to sign on with the expedition. That option, like any availability of market alternatives, is relevant to the existence, and degree, of oppression. But we must also consider the other circumstances surrounding the execution of the agreement. GeoEx presented its limitation of liability and release form as mandatory and unmodifiable, and essentially told plaintiffs that any other travel provider would impose the same terms. "Oppression arises from an inequality of bargaining power which results in no real negotiation and an absence of meaningful choice. . . ." (*Crippen v. Central Valley RV Outlet*, 124 Cal. App. 4th 1159, 1165, 22 Cal. Rptr. 3d 189 (2004) [finding no oppression where evidence showed no circumstances surrounding the execution of the agreement, so no showing of unequal bargaining power, lack of negotiation, or lack of meaningful choice].) Here, in contrast to *Crippen*, GeoEx presented its terms as both nonnegotiable and *no different than what plaintiffs would find with any other provider*. Under these circumstances, plaintiffs made a sufficient showing to establish at least a minimal level of oppression to justify a finding of procedural unconscionability.

With the "sliding scale" rule firmly in mind we address whether the substantive unconscionability of the GeoEx contract warrants the trial court's ruling. *Harper v. Ultimo*, 113 Cal. App. 4th 1402, 7 Cal. Rptr. 3d 418 (2003), is analogous. The Harpers hired a contractor to perform work on their property. The contractor allegedly broke a sewer pipe, causing concrete to infiltrate the plaintiffs' soil, plumbing and sewer and wreak havoc on their backyard drainage system. Unfortunately for the Harpers, the arbitration provision in the construction contract limited the remedies against their contractor to a refund, completion of work, costs of repair or any out-of-pocket loss or property damage—and then capped any compensation at $2,500 unless the parties agreed otherwise in writing. In the words of Justice Sills, substantive unconscionability was "so present that it is almost impossible to keep from tripping" over it. "Substantive unconscionability focuses on the one-sidedness or overly harsh effect of the contract term or clause. In the present case, the operative effect of the arbitration is even more one-sided against the customer than the clauses in any number of cases where the courts have found substantive unconscionability. . . . [T]he limitation of damages provision here is yet another version of a 'heads I win, tails you lose' arbitration clause that has met with uniform judicial opprobrium." (*Harper v. Ultimo, supra.*) The arbitration provision in the Harpers' contract did not allow even a theoretical possibility that they could be made whole, because there was no possibility of obtaining meaningful compensation unless the contractor agreed—which, not surprisingly, it did not.

The arbitration provision in GeoEx's release is similarly one-sided as that considered in *Harper*. It guaranteed that plaintiffs could not possibly obtain anything approaching full recompense for their harm by limiting any recovery they could obtain to the amount they paid GeoEx for their trip. In addition to a limit on their recovery, plaintiffs, residents of Colorado, were required to mediate and arbitrate in San Francisco,—all but guaranteeing both that GeoEx would never be out more than the amount plaintiffs had paid for their trip, and that any recovery plaintiffs might obtain would be devoured by the expense they incur in purs[u]ing their remedy. The release also required plaintiffs to indemnify GeoEx for its costs and attorney fees for defending any claims covered by the release of liability form. Notably, there is no reciprocal limitation on damages or indemnification obligations imposed on GeoEx. Rather than providing a neutral forum for dispute resolution, GeoEx's arbitration scheme provides a potent disincentive for an aggrieved client to pursue any claim, in any forum—and may well guarantee that GeoEx wins even if it loses. Absent reasonable justification for this arrangement—and none is apparent—we agree with the trial court that the arbitration clause is so one-sided as to be substantively unconscionable.

GeoEx argues that, even if the limitation of liability provision was unconscionable, the court abused its discretion when it refused to strike it and enforce the remainder of the arbitration clause. We disagree. Civil Code section 1670.5, subdivision (a) gives the trial court discretion to either refuse to enforce a contract it finds to be unconscionable, or to strike the unconscionable provision and enforce the remainder of the contract. It provides: "If the court as a matter of law finds the contract or any clause of the contract to have been unconscionable at the time it was made the court may refuse to enforce the contract, or it may enforce the remainder of the contract without the unconscionable clause, or it may so limit the application of any unconscionable clause as to avoid any unconscionable result." The trial court has discretion under this statute to refuse to enforce an entire agreement if the agreement is "permeated" by unconscionability. (*Armendariz, supra.*) An arbitration agreement can be considered permeated by unconscionability if it "contains more than one unlawful provision. . . . Such multiple defects indicate a systematic effort to impose arbitration . . . not simply as an alternative to litigation, but as an inferior forum that works to the [stronger party's] advantage." (*Armendariz, supra.*) "The overarching inquiry is whether 'the interests of justice . . . would be furthered' by severance." (*Armendariz, supra.*)

Here, the trial court identified multiple elements of the agreement that indicate GeoEx designed its arbitration clause "not simply as an alternative to litigation, but as an inferior forum" that would give it an advantage. In addition to limiting the plaintiffs' recovery, the agreement required them to indemnify GeoEx for its legal costs and fees if they pursued any claims covered by the release agreement. These one-sided burdens were compounded by the

[handwritten margin notes:]
recovery is too limited

making it too expensive to pursue a remedy

* no reciprocal limitations

Δ claim wanted to strike the unconscionable portion

trial court has discretion

requirements that plaintiffs pay half of any mediation fees and mediate and arbitrate in San Francisco, GeoEx's choice of venue, far from plaintiffs. It was within the court's discretion to conclude this agreement was so permeated by unconscionability that the interests of justice would not be furthered by severing the damages limitation clause and enforcing the remainder. The order denying GeoEx's motion to compel arbitration is affirmed.

disposition

ZUVER v. AIRTOUCH COMMUNICATIONS, INC.

153 Wash. 2d 293, 103 P.3d 753 (2004)
Washington Supreme Court

BRIDGE, Justice.

issue

This case requires us to consider the enforceability of a predispute arbitration agreement between an employer, Airtouch Communications, Inc. (Airtouch), and its employee, Therese R. Zuver. Zuver appeals a superior court order granting Airtouch's motion to compel arbitration and stay proceedings. She principally argues that the arbitration agreement is both procedurally and substantively unconscionable, and thus, this court should strike down the entire arbitration agreement. Conversely, Airtouch claims that the arbitration agreement is neither procedurally nor substantively unconscionable; however, in the event that we find any of the agreement's provisions substantively unconscionable, Airtouch asserts that the agreement's severability clause requires this court to sever the offending provisions and enforce the remainder. We hold that the provisions of the agreement pertaining to confidentiality and limitation of remedies are substantively unconscionable but agree with Airtouch that the agreement's severability clause requires us to sever these provisions and enforce the remainder of the agreement.

π claim

severability clause
↓
valid

On April 10, 1997, Airtouch offered Zuver employment as a sales support representative at the yearly salary of $21,000. As part of its offer of employment, Airtouch required that Zuver accept certain conditions. One of these conditions was that Zuver sign an agreement to arbitrate her disputes.

The arbitration agreement states in relevant part:

AGREEMENT FOR ARBITRATION
Any claim, controversy or dispute between you and . . . [Airtouch] unless otherwise covered by a collective bargaining agreement, whether sounding in contract, statute, tort, fraud, misrepresentation, discrimination or any other legal theory, including, but not limited to, disputes relating to the interpretation of this Attachment . . . whenever brought shall be resolved by arbitration. . . . You hereby waive and release all rights to recover punitive or exemplary damages in connection with any common law claims, including claims arising in tort or contract,

against . . . [Airtouch]. **By signing this Attachment, you voluntarily, knowingly, and intelligently waive any right you may otherwise have to seek remedies in court or other forums, including the right to a jury trial and the right to seek punitive damages on common law claims.** The Federal Arbitration Act, 9 U.S.C. §§1-16 ("FAA") shall govern the arbitrability of all claims, provided that they are enforceable under the Federal Arbitration Act. . . . Additionally, the substantive law of Colorado, only to the extent it is consistent with the terms stated in this Agreement for Arbitration, shall apply to any common law claims.

A single arbitrator engaged in the practice of law shall conduct the arbitration under the applicable rules and procedures of the American Arbitration Association ("AAA"). Any dispute that relates to your employment with . . . [Airtouch] or to the termination of your employment will be conducted under the AAA Employment Dispute Resolution Rules. . . . All arbitration proceedings, including settlements and awards, under the Agreement will be confidential. The parties shall share equally the hourly fees of the arbitrator. [Airtouch] . . . shall pay the expenses (including travel and lodging) of the arbitrator. The prevailing party in any arbitration may be entitled to receive reasonable attorney's fees. . . . If any party hereto files a judicial or administrative action asserting claims subject to this arbitration provision, and another party successfully stays such action and/or compels arbitration of such claims, the party filing said action shall pay the other party's costs and expenses incurred in seeking such stay and/or compelling arbitration, including reasonable attorney's fees.

SEVERABILITY AND SURVIVAL OF TERMS

In case any one or more of the provisions of this Attachment shall be found to be invalid, illegal or unenforceable in any respect, the validity, legality and enforceability of the remaining provisions contained in this Attachment will not be affected. . . . The provisions of this Attachment regarding trade secrets and confidential information and arbitration shall survive the termination of your employment by . . . [Airtouch].

Zuver signed the arbitration agreement on April 25, 1997. She claims that she was not offered an option to negotiate the terms of the agreement.

Zuver had been diagnosed with fibromyalgia in November 1996. After she accepted Airtouch's offer of employment, her condition worsened. As a result of her increasing fatigue and chronic pain, she requested accommodation from Airtouch in March 1999. Specifically, she requested that she be allowed to work part-time and to telecommute, working at home. Although Airtouch allegedly permitted other similarly situated employees to telecommute, it denied Zuver's request but permitted her to work part-time beginning in June 1999. Zuver began her part-time work schedule in June 1999, but by July 1999, she could no longer work even part-time because of her disability. Consequently, she went on medical leave until April 6, 2000, when Airtouch terminated her employment.

On June 3, 2002, Zuver filed a complaint in superior court alleging that Airtouch violated the Washington Law Against Discrimination (WLAD), chapter 49.60 RCW, by discriminating against her because of her disability and by failing to accommodate her disability. . . . [Airtouch denied her allegations and moved to compel arbitration.] On May 30, 2003, the superior court granted Airtouch's motion to compel arbitration and stayed further proceedings. . . . Zuver filed a motion for discretionary review to this court asserting that the arbitration agreement is unenforceable because it is both procedurally and substantively unconscionable. We granted review.

The Federal Arbitration Act (FAA), 9 U.S.C. §§1-16, applies to all employment contracts except for employment contracts of certain transportation workers. Section 2 of the FAA provides that written arbitration agreements "shall be valid, irrevocable, and enforceable, save upon such grounds as exist at law or in equity for the revocation of *any* contract." The United States Supreme Court has stated that "[s]ection 2 is a congressional declaration of a liberal federal policy favoring arbitration agreements, notwithstanding any state substantive or procedural policies to the contrary."[26] *Moses H. Cone Mem'l Hosp. v. Mercury Constr. Corp.*, 460 U.S. 1, 24, 103 S. Ct. 927, 74 L. Ed. 2d 765 (1983). . . . Both state and federal courts must enforce this body of substantive arbitrability law. Courts must indulge every presumption "in favor of arbitration, whether the problem at hand is the construction of the contract language itself or an allegation of waiver, delay, or a like defense to arbitrability." *Moses H. Cone Mem'l Hosp.*, 460 U.S. at 25, 103 S. Ct. 927.

Although federal and state courts presume arbitrability, "generally applicable contract defenses, such as fraud, duress, or unconscionability, may be applied to invalidate arbitration agreements without contravening §2." *Doctor's Assocs., Inc. v. Casarotto*, 517 U.S. 681, 687, 116 S. Ct. 1652, 134 L. Ed. 2d 902 (1996). However, courts may not refuse to enforce arbitration agreements under state laws that apply only to such agreements. We engage in de novo review of a trial court's decision to grant a motion to compel or deny arbitration. The party opposing arbitration bears the burden of showing that the agreement is not enforceable.

It is black letter law of contracts that the parties to a contract shall be bound by its terms. Zuver argues that she should be exempt from the terms of the contract with her employer here because it is both procedurally and substantively unconscionable. . . . In Washington, we have recognized two categories of unconscionability, substantive and procedural. Substantive unconscionability involves those cases where a clause or term in the contract is alleged to be one-sided or overly harsh. . . . Procedural unconscionability is the lack of meaningful choice, considering all the circumstances surrounding the transaction including the manner in which the contract was entered, whether each party had a reasonable opportunity to understand the terms of the contract, and whether the important terms were hidden in a maze of fine print. We have cautioned that these three factors [should] not be applied

---

[26] Washington State also has a strong public policy favoring arbitration of disputes. *Int'l Ass'n of Fire Fighters, Local 46 v. City of Everett*, 146 Wash. 2d 29, 51, 42 P.3d 1265 (2002).

mechanically without regard to whether in truth a meaningful choice existed.... [The court has not explicitly decided whether a party challenging a contract must show both substantive and procedural unconscionability, and it declines to decide that question in this case.]

As noted, to determine whether Zuver's and Airtouch's arbitration agreement is procedurally unconscionable we look to the ... circumstances surrounding their transaction to determine whether Zuver lacked meaningful choice.... First, Zuver asserts that the arbitration agreement is an adhesion contract, which she contends justifies a finding of procedural unconscionability. We have adopted the following factors to determine whether an adhesion contract exists: (1) whether the contract is a standard form printed contract, (2) whether it was prepared by one party and submitted to the other on a "take it or leave it" basis, and (3) whether there was no true equality of bargaining power between the parties. In *Yakima County (W. Valley) Fire Prot. Dist. No. 12 v. City of Yakima*, 122 Wash. 2d 371, 393, 858 P.2d 245 (1993) we noted that "to the extent that the characterization of a contract as an adhesion contract has any relevance to determining the *validity* of a contract, it is only in looking for procedural unconscionability." However, the fact that an agreement is an adhesion contract does not necessarily render it procedurally unconscionable.

Zuver's and Airtouch's arbitration agreement is an adhesion contract. First, all Airtouch employees received the standard form printed arbitration agreement. Airtouch informed Zuver that she must sign the agreement as a condition of its offer of employment, i.e., on a "take it or leave it basis." Presumably, Zuver could not negotiate the terms of the agreement with Airtouch. Thus, there was no true equality of bargaining power. Nonetheless, the fact that Zuver's and Airtouch's arbitration agreement is an adhesion contract does not end our inquiry. Zuver further asserts that the arbitration agreement is procedurally unconscionable because her unequal bargaining power precluded her from enjoying a meaningful opportunity to negotiate and choose the terms of the contract. Airtouch, however, argues that the mere presence of unequal bargaining power does not render the agreement procedurally unconscionable. Airtouch claims that it provided Zuver with a reasonable opportunity to consider the terms of the agreement and that its terms were fully disclosed. Thus, Airtouch reasons that Zuver had a meaningful choice to sign the agreement. We agree with Airtouch. Washington courts have long held that the fact that unequal bargaining power exists will not, standing alone, justify a finding of procedural unconscionability. Rather, the key inquiry for finding procedural unconscionability is whether Zuver lacked meaningful choice. As described in detail below, the facts here show that Zuver had a meaningful choice.

First, Airtouch sent Zuver a letter on April 10, 1997, explaining that it was extending her an offer of employment for a sales support representative position provided that she sign six documents, one of which was the arbitration agreement. Airtouch did not demand that Zuver return the agreement immediately. In fact, Zuver did not sign the agreement until April 25, 1997, 15 days after Airtouch first contacted her. She had ample opportunity to contact counsel or even Airtouch with any concerns or questions she might have had about the terms of the agreement. She did neither. Additionally, the important terms of the arbitration agreement were not hidden in a maze of fine print. Although Zuver received the agreement with five other attachments, the agreement was clearly labeled "**ARBITRATION AGREEMENT**," underlined, bolded, and in capital letters. Lastly, the agreement's terms were in normal typeface and font, and the agreement itself was only one page long. In the end, Zuver relies solely on her lack of bargaining power to assert that we should find the agreement procedurally unconscionable. This will not suffice. At minimum, an employee who asserts an arbitration agreement is procedurally unconscionable must show some evidence that the employer refused to respond to her questions or concerns, placed undue pressure on her to sign the agreement without providing her with a reasonable opportunity to consider its terms, and/or that the terms of the agreement were set forth in such a way that an average person could not understand them. Indeed, as the Fourth Circuit aptly reasoned, if a court found procedural unconscionability based solely on an employee's unequal bargaining power, that holding "could potentially apply to [invalidate] every contract of employment in our contemporary economy." *Adkins v. Labor Ready, Inc.*, 303 F.3d 496, 501 (4th Cir. 2002).

Next, Zuver argues that the arbitration agreement's fee-splitting, attorney fees, confidentiality, and remedies limitations provisions are substantively unconscionable. Airtouch, however, asserts that . . . none of the cited provisions are substantively unconscionable. Zuver claims that the fee-splitting provision in the arbitration agreement is substantively unconscionable because "[t]he arbitration process cannot generally require the employee to bear any *type* of expenses that the employee would not be required to bear if he or she was free to bring the action in court." *Armendariz v. Found. Health Psychcare Servs., Inc.*, 24 Cal. 4th 83, 110-11, 6 P.3d 669, 99 Cal. Rptr. 2d 745 (2000). Zuver contends that requiring her to split the arbitrator's fees would make the costs of her suit prohibitively expensive. Airtouch, on the other hand, argues that pursuant to the United States Supreme Court's decision in *Green Tree Financial Corp.* [*v. Randolph*], 531 U.S. 79, 121 S. Ct. 513 (2000), Zuver has failed to meet her burden to produce evidence showing that this fee-splitting provision makes arbitration prohibitively expensive. Airtouch also argues that, since it has offered to pay the arbitrator's fees in full, Zuver's argument is moot.

In *Green Tree Financial Corp.*, the United States Supreme Court considered an argument similar to Zuver's. 531 U.S. at 91-92, 121 S. Ct. 513. There the petitioner, Randolph, argued that an arbitration agreement's fee-splitting provision effectively denied her a forum to vindicate her discrimination claims. The Court acknowledged that arbitration fees could prohibit employees from bringing their discrimination claims but held that "where . . . a party seeks to invalidate an arbitration agreement on the ground that arbitration would be prohibitively expensive, that party bears the burden of showing the likelihood of incurring such costs." *Id.* at 92, 121 S. Ct. 513. Like Randolph, Zuver offers no specific information about the arbitration fees she will be required to share and why such fees would effectively prohibit her from bringing her claims. . . . [She must provide evidence of both the extent of the costs and of her particular circumstances to establish that she cannot afford the costs of arbitration, and that those costs would preclude her from vindicating her rights. She has failed to provide any such evidence here.] Moreover, even if Zuver had provided such evidence, Airtouch has offered to defray the cost of arbitration by paying arbitration fees. Thus, given the circumstances of this case, we conclude that Zuver's claim is moot.[27]

The arbitration agreement also provides that "[t]he prevailing party in any arbitration *may* be entitled to receive reasonable attorney's fees." Zuver argues that this provision is substantively unconscionable because it would dissuade individuals who have endured discrimination from pursuing their claims because an arbitrator might make them pay the employer's attorney fees if they failed to prevail. Zuver further asserts that in the event she does prevail, the arbitrator is not obligated to award her attorney fees as would be required under RCW 49.60.030(2) [which provides that the prevailing party *shall* recover attorney's fees.] Airtouch, however, argues that this court cannot assume that the arbitrator would fail to abide by RCW 49.60.030(2), and that nothing in the Arbitration Agreement reduces Zuver's right to recover attorney's fees if she were to prevail on the merits. . . . [That is, Zuver argues that the use of the word "may" rather than "shall" in the agreement violates Washington law because it gives the arbitrator impermissible discretion to award attorney's fees. The court holds that the case law interpreting the statute affords courts some discretion in deciding whether to award attorney's fees to a prevailing party, and there is no basis for concluding that an arbitrator would exercise discretion improperly so as to violate the statute as interpreted by the courts.] Consequently, we conclude that this attorney fees provision is not substantively unconscionable.

. . . [The arbitration agreement requires that "[a]ll arbitration proceedings, including settlements and awards, under the Agreement will be confidential."] Zuver asserts that the confidentiality provision unduly favors Airtouch and, thus, is substantively unconscionable. . . . [The basis of Zuver's argument is that Airtouch gains a considerable advantage in arbitration by means of this provision. While it has all the information about what occurred in other arbitrations on employment disputes, employees have no access to this information. This places employees at an unfair disadvantage and also violates public policy in favor of open proceedings.] Airtouch . . . argues that since confidentiality provisions are routinely included in arbitration agreements, such provisions cannot be substantively unconscionable. . . . Indeed, this court has acknowledged that

---

[27] Zuver also argues that we cannot consider Airtouch's offer to pay the arbitrator's fees now because we have stated that courts must consider the conscionability of an agreement at the time the parties entered into the contract. . . . [However, a] case by case approach . . . properly balances the important public policy favoring arbitration of disputes with the financial means of individual plaintiffs. Thus, we refuse to ignore Airtouch's offer to pay the arbitration fees.

arbitrations are often confidential. . . . Nonetheless, although courts have accepted confidentiality provisions in many agreements, it does not necessarily follow that *this* confidentiality provision is conscionable. . . . The effect of the provision here benefits only Airtouch. As written, the provision hampers an employee's ability to prove a pattern of discrimination or to take advantage of findings in past arbitrations. Moreover, keeping past findings secret undermines an employee's confidence in the fairness and honesty of the arbitration process and, thus, potentially discourages that employee from pursuing a valid discrimination claim. Therefore, we hold that this confidentiality provision is substantively unconscionable.

Zuver also argues that the agreement's provision stating, "[y]ou hereby waive and release all rights to recover punitive or exemplary damages in connection with any common law claims, including claims arising in tort or contract, against [Airtouch]" is substantively unconscionable because it applies only to her, i.e., the provision is unilateral . . . [and] fails to equally apply to Airtouch, e.g., Airtouch could still seek punitive or exemplary damages against her for claims based on disclosure of confidential information. . . . Airtouch contends that complete mutuality of remedies is not required in arbitration agreements. . . . Washington courts have long held that mutuality of obligation means both parties are bound to perform the contract's terms—not that both parties have identical requirements. Zuver, however, *does not* simply argue that the arbitration agreement here lacks mutuality. Rather, she contends that the *effect* of this provision is so one-sided and harsh that it is substantively unconscionable. We agree. Indeed, this provision appears to heavily favor Airtouch. It bars Zuver from collecting any punitive or exemplary damages for her common law claims but permits Airtouch to claim these damages for the only type of suit it would likely ever bring against Zuver, that is, for breach of her duty of non-disclosure of Airtouch's confidential information. The remedies limitation provision blatantly and excessively favors the employer in that it allows the employer alone access to a significant legal recourse. Consequently, we conclude that this provision is substantively unconscionable in these circumstances.

Zuver argues that the taint of the unconscionable provisions requires us to declare the entire arbitration agreement unenforceable despite its severability clause. Conversely, Airtouch argues that pursuant to the agreement's severability clause, we should simply strike any unconscionable provisions. We agree with Airtouch. Courts are generally loath to upset the terms of an agreement and strive to give effect to the intent of the parties. Consequently, when parties have agreed to a severability clause in an arbitration agreement, courts often strike the offending unconscionable provisions to preserve the contract's essential term of arbitration. Although some courts have declined to sever unconscionable provisions where those provisions pervade an agreement, here we are faced with only two unconscionable provisions. We can easily excise the confidentiality and remedies provisions but enforce the remainder. Indeed, the parties have explicitly expressed their intent for us to do so by agreeing to a severance clause. . . .

We reject Zuver's claims that the arbitration agreement is procedurally unconscionable and that the provisions pertaining to attorney fees are substantively unconscionable. We hold that Zuver's claim that the fee-splitting provision is substantively unconscionable is moot since Airtouch has agreed to pay the entire amount of the arbitrator's fees. However, we agree with Zuver that the confidentiality and remedies provisions of the agreement are substantively unconscionable. While we conclude that these two provisions are substantively unconscionable, pursuant to the severance clause in the parties' agreement, we now sever those provisions and affirm the trial court's order compelling arbitration.

■ QUESTIONS

(1)   The court says that it declines to decide whether both procedural and substantive unconscionability must be present to permit relief. Did the court really decline to decide this question?

(2)   In a partial dissent, one of the justices took issue with the majority's finding that the provision excluding punitive or exemplary damages was substantively unconscionable. The dissent noted that exculpatory clauses such as the one in this agreement are generally not against public policy. The dissent argued that by overturning the provision, the majority, in effect, has declared that an agreement must provide equal and equivalent rights to both parties. This violates the longstanding principle that as long as each party has given some consideration, the contract need not provide for mutuality of obligation. For substantive unconscionability to exist, the term at issue must be overly one-sided and harsh, not merely one-sided. The dissent expressed the concern that the majority had, in effect, eroded the usefulness of employment arbitration agreements by opening the door to claims of unconscionability whenever the parties' obligations are not exactly equivalent. Do you think that the dissent makes a persuasive argument?

(3)   In *Zuver* the court severed two unconscionable terms but otherwise enforced the arbitration provision.[28] However, in *Lhotka* the court refused to sever the limitation of liability provision and enforce the rest of the arbitration agreement. What distinguishing facts, if any, justify these different approaches?

---

[28] Although the court's decision to sever the terms in *Zuver* is reinforced by the existence of a severance provision in the agreement, Restatement, Second §208 (as well as UCC 2-302) makes it clear that a court has the discretion to sever an unconscionable term even in the absence of a provision in the contract that expressly allows for severance of invalid terms. Conversely, even where an agreement does contain a severance provision, a court may decline to sever an unconscionable term if it considers it inappropriate to do so.

■ PROBLEM 13.13

Zuver and *Lhotka* were concerned with the severance of substantively unconscionable terms. *Brower v. Gateway 2000, Inc.*, 246 A.D.2d 246, 676 N.Y.S.2d 569 (1998), illustrates the relief of adjusting substantively unconscionable terms so as to cure the unconscionable result.

Purchasers of Gateway computers sued for damages, alleging that Gateway had engaged in deceptive sales practices. Gateway moved to dismiss the suit on the grounds that an arbitration agreement was contained in its standard terms (included with the computer in the box shipped to buyers).[29] The arbitration agreement required all disputes to be settled by arbitration to be conducted in Chicago in accordance with the rules of the International Chamber of Commerce ("ICC").

The plaintiffs argued that the arbitration provision was unconscionable because the ICC, headquartered in France, was not a forum commonly used in consumer cases. It was difficult to access its rules or to communicate with it directly, and the cost of arbitrating before it was prohibitive. Its fees and costs (an advance fee of $4,000 was payable, of which $2,000 was a nonrefundable registration fee) greatly exceeded the value of a Gateway computer. In addition, a purchaser would have to incur the cost of traveling to Chicago to participate in the arbitration and would have to pay Gateway's legal fees if he lost.

The court found no procedural unconscionability. Although the contract was on standard terms, it was not adhesive or unfairly imposed. The customer did not lack meaningful choice and had ample time to review and reject the terms and the goods. However, the court did find the choice of the ICC as the arbitration forum to be substantively unconscionable. The complexity, and particularly the high cost of the ICC arbitration process, would deter consumers from invoking it.

The court observed that New York courts normally require that both procedural and substantive unconscionability be present but that severe enough substantive unconscionability can alone be grounds for relief. The court declined to invalidate the arbitration provision completely. Rather, it held that the ICC arbitration provision should be replaced by one that was more appropriate to the type and extent of dispute involved in these transactions. The court remanded the case to the trial court to allow for the substitution of a more suitable arbitration provision.

---

[29] Like *ProCD, Inc. v. Zeidenberg*, discussed in Chapter 6, Section C, the contracts here were "rolling contracts." The terms were included in the box, and the customer had 30 days to reject them by returning the computer. Thus, as in *ProCD*, the court found that the offer and acceptance did not occur when the goods were ordered. The standard terms in the box were the offer, which the buyer accepted by retaining the goods beyond 30 days.

(a) The court found neither adhesion nor procedural unconscionability in the manner in which the standard arbitration provision was contracted for. Do you agree? Do you think that the court would have changed the arbitration provision if it truly did not believe that there was no adhesion or procedural unconscionability? (Consider this same question in relation to *Zuver*.)

(b) One of the advantages of a flexible remedy is that the court has options other than avoidance if it finds unconscionability. Do you think that the court would have found unconscionability in *Brower* or *Zuver* if the inevitable consequence was total avoidance of the contract?

4. The Range of Unconscionability Doctrine

Unconscionability is a general doctrine of contract law, so a claim that a contract or term is unconscionable could be made in any contract, irrespective of its subject matter and the attributes of the parties. It is sometimes said that unconscionability is more commonly found in consumer transactions—that is, transactions in which goods or services are purchased by an individual for her personal, family, or household purposes. *Lhotka* and *Brower* involve consumer transactions, but *Germantown Manufacturing, Google,* and *Zuver* do not. Therefore, although it may be true that unconscionability doctrine is commonly associated with consumer transactions, the selection of cases in this chapter shows that it goes well beyond that range.

As the cases in this chapter suggest, claims of unconscionability are most commonly asserted against the larger or more dominant party by the smaller or more subservient party, such as a consumer, an employee, or some other individual who had no role in drafting the standard contract. This is to be expected because the problems of adhesion and abuse of bargaining power are most likely to be found where one party has the market power and legal sophistication to insist on a contract on its own self-serving terms. However, it is important to recognize that the doctrine is not confined to such situations. It could be invoked by a sophisticated business entity, or in a transaction in which the terms were specifically negotiated. Of course, the fact that the party claiming unconscionability has the sophistication and resources to resist the imposition of unfair terms, or has had the opportunity to negotiate the terms, makes it less likely that a court would find unconscionability.

■ PROBLEM 13.14

Mr. and Mrs. Mommenpopp are the sole shareholders and officers in a small corporation, Mommenpopp Enterprises, Inc. For the last 25 years, the corporation has owned and operated a convenience store in a strip mall. In January the mall was bought by Consolidated Realty Holdings, Inc., a large out-of-state corporation with extensive real estate holdings around the country. Mommenpopp Enterprises, Inc.'s lease of its premises was due to expire in July. In March Mrs. Mommenpopp, as president of the corporation, approached Consolidated's local representative to negotiate a renewal of the lease. During the negotiations, Consolidated's local representative made it clear that she had other tenants interested in the premises and did not much care if Mommenpopp Enterprises, Inc., renewed its lease. She insisted on a 50 percent increase in the rent. She would not agree to a renewal of the lease for a period of ten years, as Mrs. Mommenpopp requested, but was willing to renew the lease for only three years. She also insisted that the lease contain terms that had not been in the previous lease: First, Mr. and Mrs. Mommenpopp would have to give a personal guarantee for the rent owing by their corporation. Second, Consolidated would have the right to inspect the premises, books, and records on demand. Third, Consolidated would have the power to seize of all the lessee's assets in the event of a default in rent payments. Fourth, the store would have to be open during prescribed times on the weekend and holidays. Fifth, the lessee would have no right to terminate the lease or to sublet the premises. Mrs. Mommenpopp argued with Consolidated's representative for some time, but she would not budge on her demands.

After the meeting, Mr. and Mrs. Mommenpopp discussed the proposed lease renewal. They also looked around the neighborhood to see if there were any other premises that may be suitable for their store, but they found nothing. Although they were very unhappy with the terms, they did not see any alternative to entering the lease, so they reluctantly executed it on behalf of their corporation, Mommenpopp Enterprises, Inc. Six months later, some very desirable and considerably less expensive premises became available in another building in the neighborhood. Mommenpopp Enterprises, Inc., would like to terminate the lease with Consolidated and move to the other premises. May it avoid the lease on grounds of unconscionability?

5. Unconscionability and the Prohibition of Class Actions

Provisions in standard contracts barring class actions were introduced in Chapter 3, Section C.2. These provisions have become increasingly common, and are usually included in the arbitration provision, so their effect is both to compel arbitration and to preclude the customer from initiating a class action. We explain class actions again here with a focus on whether prohibition waiver of the right to bring a class action might be challenged as unconscionable.

Where there exists a large but ascertainable group of people who all have similar claims against a defendant, a representative group of named plaintiffs may commence a class action against the defendant, in which the named plaintiffs represent not only their own interests but also the interests of the whole class of similarly situated unnamed plaintiffs. In consumer transactions, the ability to bring a class action may be an important remedy, especially where the damages or other remedy for each individual plaintiff are too small to make individual litigation economically feasible. Corporations that do business with large numbers of individuals do not much like the idea of having to deal with class actions. One way for the corporation to avoid class actions is to include a term in its standard contract that prohibits the customer from initiating or participating in a class action. However, in some states, such a prohibition has been viewed as unconscionable as a matter of state contract law.

AT&T Mobility adopted such a device in its standard agreement for cell phone sales and service. Its standard contract provided not only that all disputes between the customer and AT&T must be arbitrated but also that any claims must be brought by the customer in an individual capacity and not as a member of a class. Notwithstanding this provision, some customers initiated a class action in federal court in California. Applying California case law, both the district court and the Ninth Circuit Court of Appeals found that the prohibition on classwide procedures in consumer transactions rendered the arbitration provision unconscionable. The basis for this decision was a holding by the California Supreme Court that a waiver of class action is unconscionable where the contract is a consumer contract of adhesion, disputes predictably will involve small amounts of damages, and the party with superior bargaining power has deliberately set up a scheme to cheat individual consumers out of their small claims. In *AT&T Mobility LLC v. Concepcion*, 131 S. Ct. 1740 (2011), the U.S. Supreme Court reversed. Justice Scalia, writing for the majority, held, in essence, that invalidation of the contractual bar on classwide proceedings violated the FAA because it interfered with arbitration. Arbitration is generally not suited to classwide resolution of disputes, and if classwide procedures were attempted, they would defeat the principal advantage of arbitration—its speed and informality. The majority held that the prohibition of class action waivers in consumer transactions would violate federal law by effectively barring arbitration in a broad range of disputes.

AN INTERNATIONAL PERSPECTIVE

The UNIDROIT Principles generally recognize doctrines equivalent to those discussed in this chapter, although the terminology is different and the elements are not set out in the same way. This brief note sketches the UNIDROIT Principles in very general terms to give you an idea of their approach.

The Principles recognize that a party may avoid a contract on several grounds that correspond to the common law doctrines of fraud, duress, undue influence, and unconscionability. Article 3.2.13 gives a court authority to grant avoidance of the contract in its entirety or, in appropriate circumstances, to confine avoidance to an offending term or terms. Articles 3.2.9 to 3.2.12 require a claim of avoidance to be made within a reasonable time, and the right to avoid may be lost if a party fails to seek avoidance in time or otherwise acts in a way that impliedly affirms the contract. (Although no similar time limits are articulated in the domestic American law that we have studied, undue delay in seeking avoidance could preclude the right to avoid under principles of estoppel, waiver, or implied ratification.)

Article 3.2.5 permits a party to avoid a contract for fraud, including the failure to disclose information that should have been disclosed under reasonable commercial standards of fair dealing. Article 3.2.6 allows a party to avoid a contract induced by an unjustified threat by the other party that, under the circumstances, is so "imminent and serious as to leave the first party no reasonable alternative." Article 3.2.6 defines a threat as unjustified if the threatened act or omission is wrongful in itself, or if it is wrongful to use it as a means of inducing the contract. Article 3.2.7 has a doctrine that is analogous to unconscionability (and also incorporates principles of undue influence). It allows a party to avoid a contract or term if, at the time of contracting, the contract or term unjustifiably gave the other party an "excessive advantage." The Article identifies several factors to be taken into account in deciding whether the advantage is excessive, including taking advantage of dependence, economic distress, or lack of bargaining capacity. A court is given the power to adapt the offending term to bring it into accord with reasonable commercial standards.

The CISG does not cover the doctrines discussed in this chapter. Article 4 states that the CISG is not concerned with the validity of a contract. Issues relating to avoidance for unfair bargaining are properly classified as questions going to the validity of the contract. Therefore, even in a transnational sales transaction, they are resolved under the domestic law otherwise governing the contract.

CHAPTER 14

Illegality, Violation of Public Policy, and Lack of Contractual Capacity

A INTRODUCTION

The policing doctrines discussed in Chapter 13 are intended to counter specific types of improper conduct in the contracting process. They share the fundamental basis of protecting one party against a manifestation of assent that was induced by improper means, whether it be dishonesty, an improper threat, abuse of power or trust, or oppressive bargaining. In allowing the victim of improper bargaining to avoid the contract or to seek one of the other remedies covered in Chapter 13, the court takes into account the competing public policies of freedom of contract and the protection of a party from dishonest or overbearing conduct. There are other situations in which a contract may be voidable, not because of the improper bargaining conduct of a party, but because the contract violates a rule of law or an important public policy, or has been entered into by a party who lacks the capacity to contract. To seek avoidance of the contract on the grounds of one of these defects, the party claiming rescission does not have to prove bargaining unfairness or oppressive terms. If, in addition to the problem of illegality, violation of public policy, or incapacity, one of the parties has engaged in improper bargaining, this fact is an additional relevant consideration in the resolution of the case, and the doctrines of fraud, duress, or unconscionability could furnish additional or alternative grounds for avoidance.

As intimated above, the common remedy under the doctrines in this chapter is avoidance of the contract. If the problem is lack of contractual capacity, the right of avoidance lies with the incapacitated party. In this respect, incapacity is akin to fraud, duress, undue influence, and unconscionability, in

519

which we have seen that it is only the victim, and not the perpetrator, who has the right to claim avoidance. The situation is different with illegality or a violation of public policy. Because these doctrines are not dependent on a showing that one of the parties was incapacitated or victimized, it could be either party who seeks avoidance of the contract. Although avoidance of the contract is based on the protection of the public interest, it is not "the public" (in the person of a public official or a group of concerned citizens) that sues to prevent enforcement of the contract. Rather, one of the parties raises the transaction's illegality or violation of public policy as a basis for avoidance. Typically, he does this not because he has suddenly repented or become public-spirited but because invalidation of the contract serves his own self-interest. (It is also possible that a court could raise illegality *sua sponte*, but this does not happen often.)

either party can seek avoidance

↳ *without formal prompting*

Section B deals with contracts that are illegal—the contract violates a statute or the common law. For example, a contract for the sale of a prohibited drug may be fully consensual, fairly bargained, and on fair terms. Nevertheless, if the seller breaches the contract by failing to deliver the drugs and the buyer sues for damages, a court would be most unlikely to enforce the contract. Similarly, if the seller delivered the drugs to the buyer, but the buyer did not pay for them, a court would not likely enforce the seller's claim for the payment of the price. (As we will see, the court may not even be willing to allow the seller restitution for the buyer's unjust enrichment—the illegality of the transaction may deprive the seller of all relief.) Of course, the sale of the prohibited drug is not merely illegal, but is also a criminal offense, so it is not hard to see why the court would refuse to enforce the contract (quite apart from any criminal sanctions that might be imposed in a prosecution for the crime). However, many illegal contracts are not crimes, but are merely a violation of the law that prohibits contracts of that kind. For example, a state statute may forbid the transfer of a liquor license and may void any such contract of transfer. Even though the parties have not committed a criminal offense in entering into the contract, the public interest in not allowing such a contract likewise most likely will result in non-enforcement.

won't even ← allow restitution

Section C deals with contracts that violate public policy. Although a contract may not be illegal, its nature or purpose may be so contrary to the public interest that a court concludes that it would violate an important public policy to enforce it. For example, it is not illegal for a contract to absolve a party from liability for its own negligence, but in some circumstances a court may find that such a disclaimer is so harmful to the public interest in holding a tortfeasor liable for its negligence that it violates public policy. Similarly, a noncompetition clause (a provision in an employment contract forbidding a resigning employee from working for a competitor of the employer for a stated period in a stated area) is not generally illegal, but if the provision goes beyond the protection of the employer's legitimate interests, it may violate important public policies that protect employees and enhance competition in the marketplace. The dividing line between illegal contracts and those that violate public policy can be quite

disclaimer of negligence may be injurious to the public

blurry. If courts invariably refuse to uphold particular contracts on the ground that they violate public policy, the judicial precedent could ultimately become firm enough to constitute a complete bar on that type of contract, making it, in effect, illegal. — *Can Become illegal through common law*

Although illegality and violation of public policy could lead to avoidance of the entire contract, it is possible that it is not the contract as a whole that is offensive, but only one of its terms. In that case, it is possible that the court will not avoid the contract in its entirety, but will refuse to enforce only the offending term. The decision to sever an offending term, rather than to avoid the contract as a whole, depends on several factors, including the seriousness of the violation of law or public policy, the nature of the contract, and the appropriateness of enforcing the contract without the term.

Can sever a contract

1) how serious is the violation

2) nature of contract

3) appropriateness of enforcing the remainder

Section D deals with contracts entered into by minors. The basic rule is that a minor usually is able to avoid her contractual commitments. The policy underlying the rule is that a minor needs protection from her own immaturity and the possibility of exploitation by others. However, this does not mean that the minor needs to prove immaturity or exploitation. Usually, the mere objective fact of minority is enough to permit avoidance. *is enough*

Section E covers contracts entered into by adults who suffer from a mental illness or defect that impairs their ability to form genuine contractual intent. In our discussions up to now, we have taken it for granted that both parties to the contract have the mental and legal power to create a contract. As a general matter, this is a fair assumption. Lack of contractual capacity is not an issue in most contracts, and the law presumes, in the absence of proof to the contrary, that all adults have the freedom and ability to enter binding contractual relationships. However, in modern law[1] this presumption can be overturned by a showing that at the time of contracting, a party to the contract suffered from some mental illness or defect that rendered her incapable of forming the requisite contractual intent.

D — minors
E. lack mental capacity

---

[1] We say "modern law" to draw attention to the fact that the law used to contain other restrictions on capacity based on gender or race. Until relatively recently, married women had no capacity to enter contracts. During the era of slavery, African Americans were property. Not only did they have no capacity to contract, but they were the very subject matter of contracts of sale. For an article that reviews the impact of contract doctrine on African Americans from the period of slavery through modern times, see Anthony R. Chase, *Race, Culture, and Contract Law: From the Cottonfield to the Courtroom*, 28 Conn. L. Rev. 1 (1995). Professor Chase argues that even after the abolition of slavery and the termination of legal incapacity, African Americans remained victims of the "neutral" principles of contract law that treated all contracting parties equally and failed to take into account the social and economic aftermath of slavery. The color-blind application of contract law perpetuated economic oppression by operating on the fiction that African Americans were truly free agents. He considers that we still suffer from the legacy of race insensitivity by failing to look past facially nondiscriminatory doctrine.

B   ILLEGALITY

A contract is illegal if it violates a statute or rule of common law. There is a broad and well-established common law doctrine, expressed in the Latin maxim *ex turpi causa non oritur actio* (no action arises out of an immoral act), that a court will not give relief to a plaintiff arising out of the plaintiff's illegal conduct. In its absolute form, this doctrine denies all relief to the wrongdoing plaintiff, so that he can neither enforce an illegal transaction nor seek any other relief, such as restitution of a benefit given to the other party in the course of the transaction. This is a general principle of law, not confined to contracts cases, but applicable elsewhere—for example, where a plaintiff is injured in the course of committing an illegal act and claims damages from the tortfeasor. In the area of contracts, the *ex turpi causa* principle applies where the plaintiff seeks relief arising out of an illegal contract.

The absolute bar of the *ex turpi causa* maxim is qualified by another well-established common law principle, reflected in the maxim *in pari delicto potior est conditio defendentis* (where the parties are in equal guilt, the position of the defendant is the stronger). This maxim suggests that the court will not completely bar the plaintiff's remedy, but will only refuse relief where the plaintiff was as or more guilty than the defendant in entering into the illegal transaction. On its face, the *in pari delicto* rule focuses on the relative guilt of the parties. However, in its application by courts, the rule is much more complex. Where the parties have entered into an illegal contract, the court does not merely ask whether the plaintiff (the party seeking to enforce the contract, or claiming some other remedy arising out of the defendant's breach) is equally or more guilty than the defendant. Although this is one of the considerations weighed by the court, the inquiry is much more far-ranging and involves a balancing of several factors in making the decision of whether the defendant can avoid the contract on grounds of illegality, thereby depriving the plaintiff of a remedy arising out of the defendant's breach.

The *in pari delicto* rule is treated as an equitable defense, so when the defendant raises it in response to the plaintiff's breach of contract claim, the court exercises considerable discretion in setting the balance. The factors that the court weighs, in addition to relative guilt, are the seriousness of the illegality, the purpose of the law that has been violated, the public interest in refusing or allowing a remedy, and the equities between the parties. The public interest is the most important consideration, and it encompasses many concerns: the reluctance of the court to aid a lawbreaker; the public policy of upholding the law that has been violated; the creation of a disincentive to future violations of the law; whether refusal of a remedy would further or hinder the purpose of the law that has been violated; and the impact of refusing or granting relief on the public good. In some cases, the court may also take into account the remedy sought—whether it is enforcement of the contract or restitution of benefits conferred on the defendant under the contract. A court may be more inclined to grant restitutionary relief because that does not involve the enforcement of the illegal contract.

An example illustrates the nature and scope of the court's balancing process: An employer enters into a contract to employ an undocumented alien who does not have a permit to work in the United States. The employee works for the employer for a month and then quits. The employer refuses to pay the employee the wages that he earned during that month and the employee sues to recover the wages. Both parties violated the law in entering into the contract—the employer was forbidden from hiring the worker and the worker was forbidden from working without a work permit. If both parties knew that they were acting illegally, it could be that they were *in pari delicto*. So, if relative guilt was the simple scope of the inquiry, the employee would be barred from claiming the wages due under the contract. However, there is much more to the balancing process, which may lead the court to conclude that the employer should not be able to raise the *in pari delicto* defense to resist paying the employee. The court may be influenced by several reasons. First, an undocumented alien's violation of the law forbidding him to work is not a heinous offense, but more the infringement of a regulatory statute. Second, because the employment contract has already been performed and the illegality is not ongoing, there is no public benefit in depriving the employee of his wages. Third, holding the employer accountable for paying the wages removes the benefit of getting free labor, thereby aiming the disincentive at employers, who may be more likely to respond to it because they are more sophisticated, less needy, and in a stronger bargaining position. Fourth, the equities favor allowing relief to the employee because otherwise the employer would be unjustly enriched by the free labor. If, despite these considerations, the court is still reluctant to enforce the contract, giving the employee restitutionary relief based on quantum meruit allows the court to permit a remedy based on unjust enrichment, rather than on enforcement of the illegal contract.

■ PROBLEM 14.1

Diversified Group, Inc. v. Sahn, 259 A.D.2d 47, 696 N.Y.S.2d 133 (1999), involved a sale of season tickets to Rangers and Knicks games at Madison Square Garden. Coleman & Co. held the subscription rights to the season tickets, which were explicitly nontransferable under Madison Square Garden regulations. Nevertheless, Coleman sold them to Mitchell Sahn in March 1997 for a price of $90,000 above the face value of the tickets. In July 1997, Sahn sold the rights to the tickets to James Haber for $140,000 above face value. This contract explicitly stated that the transfer of the subscription rights was prohibited, and if Madison Square Garden canceled the subscription or tickets, Haber would have no further rights against Sahn. In August 1997 Madison Square Garden discovered the sale of the rights and canceled the Coleman subscription. It refunded the face-value price of the tickets to Coleman, which was repaid to Haber. However, Sahn refused to repay Haber the $140,000 that Haber had paid above the face value, so Haber sued Sahn for rescission of the contract and refund of the $140,000. One of the grounds of the action was that the contract violated New York's anti-scalping law, which makes it illegal to resell tickets without a license to do so and to resell tickets at more than the established price of the tickets plus a modest premium.

Although the court found the contract to be illegal—a violation of the anti-scalping law—it refused to allow Sahn to assert the *in pari delicto* defense and granted Haber the remedy of rescission and a refund of the $140,000 paid. It identified the primary goal of the law as the deterrence of ticket speculation. The law reflects the policy of protecting the public against ticket resales at exorbitant prices by unscrupulous dealers for excessive profit. Although the court agreed with Sahn's argument that Haber was not an innocent victim, but a willing and equally guilty participant in the illegal transaction, it found that the statutory policy overrode the general equitable principles expressed in the maxim. The statute specifically provides for a private right of action to recover actual damages, so the legislature contemplated giving relief to purchasers of scalped tickets even though they can generally be assumed to know that ticket scalping is illegal.

Consider the factors used in the equitable balancing under the *in pari delicto* rule, as described in the text before this problem. Had the statute not provided for the private right of action, would it have been appropriate for the court to refuse relief to Haber under the *in pari delicto* rule?

[handwritten margin note: law is designed to protect the scalper]

■ PROBLEM 14.2

In *Diversified Group* the court's balancing process was made easier because the statute provided for a private right of action and made it clear that the restitutionary remedy was intended by the legislature. Not all statutes are that clear. If the statute is silent on the question of remedy, the court must consider the purpose and goal of the law to decide whether the *in pari delicto* rule should preclude a remedy. An important consideration is whether the violated law is designed to protect one of the contracting parties or is intended to effect a policy that goes beyond the protection of a party. For example, usury laws, which limit the rate of interest that may be charged, are primarily designed to protect borrowers. Therefore, if the suit in question involves the creditor's claim for enforcement of the usurious interest rate, even in the absence of a statutory provision on remedy, a court is likely to conclude that nonenforcement and restitution to the borrower of any excessive interest paid both serves the public good and protects the individual (the borrower in this contract) intended to be protected.

Say that the seller and buyer of liquor entered into a contract under which the buyer illegally bought the liquor without paying the taxes imposed by the state. The obvious purpose of this law is not to protect either the buyer or the seller, but to raise revenue for the state treasury. Both parties knew that they were violating the law by evading the tax. The buyer failed to pay for the liquor and the seller sued for the price. How should a court resolve the application of the *in pari delicto* rule in this suit?

parties are
= equal in
guilt

In the next case, the court must decide whether the *in pari delicto* rule bars a claim for payment against an attorney by a "runner" (a person who solicited clients for the attorney) where the employment of such a person by an attorney violates both the law and the legal profession's rules of professional responsibility. Because we make the distinction in this chapter between illegal contracts and contracts that violate public policy, there is some language in the court's opinion that you may find confusing: Even though the contract in this case qualifies as illegal, the court talks about contracts that are "illegal or against public policy," thereby apparently equating the two. This terminology is commonly used by courts, but is best understood to mean an illegal contract—one that violates a rule of law.

DANZIG v. DANZIG

79 Wash. App. 612, 904 P.2d 312 (1995)
Washington Court of Appeals

MUNSON, Judge.

... [Steven Danzig sued Jeffrey Danzig for breach of contract. In his complaint, Steven alleged that in January 1992, Jeffrey, an attorney, approached Steven, and offered to pay him one-third of any fee that Jeffrey received from every client Steven steered into Jeffrey's office. Steven was not an attorney.] Steven states he

send billable hours

accepted the offer and directed clients to Jeffrey. In each case, Jeffrey directed him to <u>submit a billing statement making it appear as though he was billing for</u> his time at an hourly rate. The total amount of the bill never deviated appreciably from one-third of the total fee. In each case, he was paid by Jeffrey. Steven maintains he directed a client to Jeffrey in March 1993; Jeffrey breached the agreement and refused to pay him. Steven states the one-third of the fee due him is about $89,000. The trial court found the alleged contract was illegal and unenforceable under Washington law and dismissed Steven's claim with prejudice. . . . Steven contends the trial court erred in granting Jeffrey's motion to dismiss [on the basis that Steven's] pleadings do not state a claim upon which relief may be granted. . . . [The court reversed. Steven did state a claim on which relief could be granted.]

posture

As a general rule, contracts which are illegal or against public policy will not be enforced by the courts. That rule, however, is subject to an exception where a court determines the parties are not in pari delicto, that is, they are not equally culpable. In those cases, a court may choose to enforce a contract despite the fact it is illegal or against public policy. "In pari delicto" is only a label, and the <u>decision to enforce a contract contrary to public policy requires more than just</u> <u>a weighing of fault and requires consideration of public policy.</u> As the court stated in *Tri-Q, Inc. v. Sta-Hi Corp.*, 63 Cal. 2d 199, 404 P.2d 486, 498, 45 Cal. Rptr. 878, 890 (1965): "Where, by applying the [general] rule, the public cannot be protected because the transaction has been completed, where no serious moral turpitude is involved, where the defendant is the one guilty of the greatest moral fault, and where to apply the rule will be to permit the defendant to be unjustly enriched at the expense of the plaintiff, the rule should not be applied."

public can't be protected because it is already done

Under the alleged contract, Steven was to serve as a "runner" who solicited clients for Jeffrey. Such a contract would be illegal, as to the lawyer, under RCW 9.12.010, Washington's barratry statute . . . [which makes it a misdemeanor for an attorney to solicit legal work personally or though another]. The alleged agreement is also in violation of RPC 7.2(c) which states a "lawyer shall not give anything of value to a person for recommending the lawyer's services. . . ." Agreements which violate the Rules of Professional Conduct are contrary to public policy. Although Jeffrey argues RCW 9.12.010 criminalizes Steven's conduct, we . . . disagree. . . . RCW 9.12.010 clearly only addresses the conduct of attorneys. Likewise, the Rules of Professional Conduct apply only to those admitted to practice law in the State of Washington. In both cases, <u>the prohibitions apply only to Jeffrey's conduct, not Steven's.</u>

violation of the rule is against public policy

Jeffrey argues that Steven's admission in his complaint that he submitted billing statements falsely detailing hours worked is evidence of moral fault. Jeffrey maintains a reasonable person should have deduced the alleged contract was improper. While Steven's statement may be evidence of moral fault on his part, he may yet be able to prove facts in support of his claim which entitle him to relief. . . . [He will not be denied relief if he can show that he was excusably ignorant of facts or of legislation of a minor character, especially if the legislation is of a local, specialized, or technical nature, and he reasonably could have assumed that the other party had knowledge of such matters.] Both RCW 9.12.010 and RPC 7.2(c) are specialized in that they address only the conduct of members of the legal profession. As an attorney, Jeffrey may be assumed to have knowledge of such matters.

Here, the conduct proscribed by RCW 9.12.010 and RPC 7.2(c) has already occurred. Refusing to enforce the sole remaining task under the alleged contract, payment of money, would not further protect the public. Jeffrey argues public policy would best be served by sending a message to potential runners that their efforts will not be rewarded. Knowing that disclosure of their unethical acts would almost certainly lead to disciplinary proceedings would serve a strong disincentive to attorneys considering an agreement like that at issue here. These issues cannot be resolved on a . . . [motion to dismiss]. Finally, Jeffrey argues he did virtually all the work resulting in the fee at issue. However, if Steven's allegations are true, Jeffrey would not have even had the client if not for Steven's efforts.

holding

Taken as true, the allegations in Steven's complaint state a claim upon which relief may be granted. The trial court erred in granting the . . . motion to dismiss. Whether Steven can support those allegations in further proceedings remains to be seen. . . . We reverse that portion of the trial court's order dismissing Steven's claim and remand for further proceedings. . . .

[A dissenting opinion in *Danzig* argued that the contract between Steven and Jeffrey should not be enforced because it is contrary to the statute, the Rules of Professional Conduct, and general public policy against the brokerage of lawyer services—all of which are aimed at the protection of the public rather than at the protection or punishment of either party to the contract. The dissent felt that the court should leave the parties as it found them. It reasoned that Steven was hardly blameless. He should be presumed to know that Jeffrey was acting illegally, and Steven's own acts in aiding and abetting that illegality should not be rewarded. In addition, Steven admitted completing time sheets for services he never performed. The dissent acknowledged that this conclusion has the ill effect of allowing an attorney to escape liability on the basis of his own violation of the law and professional ethics. However, the dissent felt that it is worse to allow the use of the courts to enforce such illegal contracts, thereby sanctioning the brokering of legal services. The dissent took consolation in the prospect that Jeffrey still has to answer, beyond this civil litigation, for his unprofessional and unlawful conduct.]

■ QUESTIONS

(1) The conflict between the majority and the dissent illustrates the dilemma facing a court in deciding how to deal with an illegal contract. Which do you think is the better argument, and why?

(2)   Steven won this battle, but he still has to establish his case at trial. Based on the majority opinion, what are the crucial facts that he will have to prove? On your reading of the allegations as set out in the opinion, how do you rate his prospects of success?

he was not bound by the rule

(3)   Compare the relief sought by the plaintiff, Haber, in *Diversified Group* with the relief sought by Steven in *Danzig*. How do the claims differ? Should this difference affect the balance that the court must strike in deciding whether to grant relief?

■ PROBLEM 14.3

Lars Enny was the president of Easymark Investments, Inc., which solicited funds from customers to invest in a share portfolio that it managed. About two years ago Lars began to operate a Ponzi scheme. He accepted funds from investors, but did not invest the funds as he was supposed to. He skimmed a significant portion of them for his own use and avoided detection of the scheme by paying out earlier investors from funds received from new investors. Easymark employed Aida A. Bettor as its auditor. Aida should have been able to discover Lars's fraud easily had she audited the company accounts properly, but she was grossly negligent and failed to do so. The Ponzi scheme was not sustainable and it collapsed about two years after it started because Lars could not generate enough new investment to cover the payments due to previous investors. As a result of Lars's fraud, Easymark was liable to the defrauded investors and had to liquidate a large portion of its assets to compensate them for their losses.

Easymark sued Aida for the damages it had suffered. This suit was based on Aida's malpractice, which was a breach of her contract to render competent professional services to Easymark. Aida defended the suit on the basis of the *in pari delicto* rule. She argued that Lars's deliberate fraud was much more culpable than her negligence in failing to detect it, so Lars's guilt exceeded hers. Because Lars was an agent of Easymark and committed his illegal actions in the course of his employment, principles of the law of agency imputed his guilt to Easymark, his principal.

The court agrees that Lars's guilt exceeded Aida's, and also holds that Aida is correct in arguing that Lars's illegal conduct is imputed to Easymark under principles of agency law. The court must now apply the equitable balancing under the *in pari delicto* rule to decide if Aida's *in pari delicto* defense should prevail. Conduct the balancing, consider the public interest and equities both in favor of and against allowing the defense, and decide the resolution that best serves the goals and purposes of the rule.

C   CONTRACTS IN VIOLATION OF PUBLIC POLICY

For purposes of analysis, we draw a clear distinction between a contract that is illegal—it offends a rule of statutory or common law—and one that violates public policy: it does not violate the law, but is so contrary to the public interest that the court concludes that it should not be enforced. Courts do not always articulate this distinction, and it is quite common to find opinions that refer an illegal contract as one that offends "law or public policy" (as noted in the introduction to the *Danzig* case, that case is an example of this usage). When courts use this language, they often mean an illegal contract. Also, the distinction between an illegal contract and one that offends public policy is a matter of degree, because if there is consistent judicial precedent for refusing to enforce a contract on grounds of public policy, at some point that precedent becomes so well established that it would be more correct to think of the contract having become illegal at common law. Nevertheless, we think that it helps understanding to make the distinction clear and to recognize that the process of analysis differs between these two categories. A significant difference is that the *in pari delicto* rule does not play a role where a contract is not illegal, but is unenforceable on public policy grounds. Because neither party has violated the law, there is no occasion to evaluate relative fault or to engage in the discretionary balancing discussed in Section B. Nonetheless, a court may engage in a similar balancing of interests in deciding whether a contract violates public policy in the first instance.

Although the preceding paragraph talks of the nonenforcement of a contract on public policy grounds, it often happens that it is not the contract as a whole that offends public policy, but just one term of that contract. Where that happens, the court may leave the contract in force, but just excise the term that violates public policy, provided the violation of public policy does not permeate the contract and severance does not significantly remake the contract. (These are the same considerations that a court takes into account in deciding whether to eliminate an unconscionable term in a contract.)

The decision to refuse to enforce a contract or contract term on policy grounds is more tenuous than a refusal to enforce an illegal contract, because there is no statute or rule of common law that invalidates the contract. If the contract was entered into voluntarily by both parties who desired the contract and neither was subjected to unfair bargaining, the public policy of freedom of contract pulls strongly in the direction of enforcement. Therefore, it is only when the public interest in not enforcing the contract is strong enough to outweigh upholding freedom of contract that a court will consider it appropriate to refuse enforcement by allowing avoidance of the contract as a whole or of an offending term. Of course, where there has been some bargaining unfairness or adhesion in the formation of the contract, the weight of the policy of freedom of

public policy violation v. illegal

typically just one term is offensive

public policy pulls for freedom of contract

contract is lessened, so that it may be easier to persuade the court to allow avoidance on policy grounds.

The next case could have been included in Section D on the contractual incapacity of a minor, because it involves the question of whether a parent can validly enter into a release of liability on behalf of a minor. However, we include it here because of the insight it provides on the courts' role in formulating general public policy in the context of resolving a particular contract dispute between parties to litigation. All members of the court agreed on the result of the case—that a parent cannot bind the minor to a waiver of liability for personal injury. However, the justices disagreed on the rationale for this decision and each delivered a separate concurring opinion. There is therefore no majority opinion of the court. We include here the opinion of Justice Young (referred to as the "lead opinion"), which addresses the concerns that courts must weigh when asked by a party to litigation to resolve a case on the basis of public policy that has not been incorporated into legislation.

WOODMAN v. KERA LLC

486 Mich. 228, 785 N.W.2d 1 (2010)
Michigan Supreme Court

YOUNG, Justice.

[Five-year-old Trent Woodman had his birthday party at Bounce Party, an indoor play area operated by Kera LLC. Before the party, Trent's father signed a waiver of liability on behalf of Trent, releasing Kera from any liability for personal injury. During the party, Trent jumped off a slide and broke his leg. His mother brought suit against Kera on his behalf, and Kera moved to dismiss the suit on the grounds that the suit was barred by the liability disclaimer. The court held that under clear principles of Michigan common law, firmly established more than a century before, a minor cannot be bound in contract by a parent or guardian. Although a parent can waive his own rights to sue for injury to his child, he has no authority to waive the child's rights. The court noted that the legislature had varied this common law rule in certain specific cases—for example, in medical malpractice cases. However, the rule still applied in areas in which the legislature had not abrogated it. The court then went on to address Kera's argument that the court should change the common law rule.]

△ claim →

... In this case, we are ... asked to alter a common law doctrine that has existed undisturbed for well over a century. There is no question that, if this Court were inclined to alter the common law, we would be *creating* public policy for this state. ... [T]his Court does not lightly exercise its authority to change the common law. Indeed, this Court has acknowledged the prudential principle that we must ... exercise caution and ... defer to the Legislature when called upon to make a new and potentially societally dislocating change to the common law. . . . Whether to alter the common law is a matter of prudence and, because we share this authority with the Legislature, I believe we must consider whether the prudent course is to take action where the Legislature has not.

issue →

This Court has recognized that the Legislature is the superior institution for creating the public policy of this state: "As a general rule, making social policy is a job for the Legislature, not the courts. See *In re Kurzyniec Estate*, 207 Mich. App. 531, 543, 526 N.W.2d 191 (1994). This is especially true when the determination or resolution requires placing a premium on one societal interest at the expense of another: 'The responsibility for drawing lines in a society as complex as ours—of identifying priorities, weighing the relevant considerations and choosing between competing alternatives—is the Legislature's, not the judiciary's.' *O'Donnell v. State Farm Mut. Automobile Ins. Co.*, 404 Mich. 524, 542, 273 N.W.2d 829 (1979)."

creating public policy should be reserved for legislature

The superiority of the Legislature to address matters of public policy is positively correlated with the complexity of the government's role in our society. During the nineteenth century, courts exercising their authority to alter the common law did so within the context of a simpler, agrarian economy. The legislatures of that era exercised a more limited regulatory role. In contrast, today's modern legislatures exercise robust regulation of all facets of our modern, internationalized economy and the rights and responsibilities of citizens. The need for a judiciary responsive to perceived public policy needs of the state has been correspondingly reduced by the development of the Legislature as a full-time institution and its pervasive statutory regulation of our increasingly complex society.

This case illustrates why this Court should frequently defer policy-based changes in the common law to the Legislature. When formulating public policy for this state, the Legislature possesses superior tools and means for gathering facts, data, and opinion and assessing the will of the public. The Legislature can hold hearings, gather the opinions of experts, procure studies, and generally provide a forum for all societal factions to present their competing views on a particular question of public policy. The judiciary, by contrast, is designed to accomplish the discrete task of resolving disputes, typically between two parties, each in pursuit of the party's own narrow interests. We are . . . limited to one set of facts in each lawsuit, which is shaped and limited by arguments from opposing counsel who seek to advance purely private interests. . . . We do not generally consider the views of nonparties on questions of policy, and we are limited to the record developed by the parties. The reality of our judicial institutional limitations is a significant liability in regard to our ability to make informed decisions when we are asked to create public policy by changing the common law.

legislature is in a better position to create public policy

This case demonstrates these institutional limitations. Defendant openly concedes that the principal impetus for seeking enforcement of parental pre-injury waivers is the protection that waivers afford its business in the face of the increasingly litigious nature of society. But for the perceived increased likelihood of a lawsuit and accompanying litigation costs, businesses such as defendant would not need parental preinjury waivers. Accordingly, in seeking to have its waiver enforced, defendant requires a modification of the common law rule and thus necessarily (but only impliedly) asserts that the societal benefits of enforcing the waiver—saving defendant litigation costs—outweigh the societal costs of abrogating the common law. Defendant, however, has not provided this Court with anything beyond mere conjecture that this is true.

This is a purely policy-driven matter with numerous costs, benefits, and trade-offs—none of which defendant has bothered to raise, much less explicate. Certainly, enforcing the common law would protect minors' contractual and property rights and presumably encourage greater care in preventing negligent injuries to children. These are, without question, admirable societal goals with significant societal benefits that have a long provenance in this state's jurisprudence. Changing the common law would arguably save litigation costs for businesses offering recreational activities for children and concomitantly promote the availability of a wide range of activities for children. These too are admirable societal goals. Of concern, however, are the potential hidden costs that might occur if the common law were changed. For example, if parental preinjury waivers were to be enforced, there would be a possibility that business owners will have diminished incentives to maintain their property appropriately, resulting in an increased number of injuries to children. Moreover, the enforcement of preinjury waivers might result in an increased burden on taxpayers for children whose parents waived their children's right to pursue a tort remedy but cannot afford their necessary medical care.

These are but two illustrations of possible unintended consequences that a change in the common law here might occasion. Undoubtedly, there are many others. How are we as jurists to determine whether enforcing or changing the common law rule will result in a net benefit to society? Here we would only be able to make an uneducated guess. . . . When engaging in such rank guesswork, the weight of common law authority that has existed for more than a century must be preferred. In accord with Hippocrates' admonition, maintaining the status quo has the significant benefit of doing no greater harm.

As stated previously, the Legislature is not similarly constrained to make policy on the basis of blind speculation. Thus, if changing the common law to permit a parent to bind his child to a preinjury waiver is deemed to result in a net societal benefit, the Legislature can determine that fact with reasonable assurance before subjecting the public to such a change. Illustratively, defendant's proffered rationale for a revision of what a majority of justices have concluded is the existing rule is the argument that a parent is presumed to act in his child's best interests and has a fundamental right to make decisions pertaining to the care, custody, and control of that minor child. That rationale, however, is not discretely limited to preinjury waivers. Under defendant's proffered analysis, a parent would be able to bind the child in *any* contract, no matter how detrimental to the child. Thus, defendant's rationale would arguably completely abrogate the common law prohibition of guardians contractually binding their minor wards. As explained, the common law rules regarding minors and limitations on those who would contract on their behalf exist solely for the protection of the minors. As unfortunate as it may be, a parent does not always act in his child's best interests. . . . [T]hose favoring the modification of the common law rule might reflexively respond to the fact that parents do not always act in the best interests of their children by adding a qualifier to the modification of the common law rule: a parental waiver is binding on the child only if the waiver is in the *"child's best interests."* However, this effort to avoid eviscerating the protection of children now recognized in the common law rule would undoubtedly create as many problems as it would resolve. Certainly, such an approach would create ancillary litigation over whether the parental waiver was in the child's best interests. While society might generally benefit from allowance of parental waivers for minor children, it could reasonably be asked: Is *any* preinjury waiver that is later asserted against a particular minor *ever* in the best interests of the *injured child*? The existing common law is well established, clear, and easy to apply and consistently protects children; it must be preferred over a chaotic, ad hoc alternative. . . .

[In a concurring opinion, another member of the court, Justice Markman, agreed with the judgment on the narrow ground that as a matter of contract interpretation, the language of the release did not actually waive the minor's claims but covered only the father's claims. Justice Markman took issue with Justice Young's reluctance to move away from the established rule invalidating parental liability waivers. The gist of the concurring opinion is: The common law constantly evolves to reflect prevailing public policy, and courts are in a good position to fine-tune legal rules to reflect current norms. Public policy has moved in the direction of increasing the legal autonomy of minors and recognizing the power of parents to make important decisions concerning the upbringing and welfare of their children. Both courts and the legislature have recognized a parent's authority to make important and life-altering decisions on behalf of a child in many different areas, such as medical care, abortion, marriage, and even tattoos and body piercings. It therefore makes little sense to be squeamish about allowing a parent to waive liability for injury on behalf of a child who participates in a recreational activity. Where a parent makes a knowing and voluntary waiver so that the child can engage in an activity, the court should not disturb the parent's decision by allowing the parent to later claim that the waiver is unenforceable. The refusal to enforce such waivers places a great risk on those who would provide recreational opportunities for children, and concern over potential liability must ultimately lead to a reduction in the opportunity for those activities.]

■ QUESTIONS

(1) In a common law system, courts frequently develop rules of law, which means that they just as often formulate public policy—legal rules always have a policy foundation. Indeed, Justice Young indicates that in the case of parental

waivers of liability, the Michigan Supreme Court developed the policy of non-enforcement many years ago. The court is asked in this case to overturn that policy. Why do you think Justice Young is so reluctant to change judicial policy in this case? Is it because, as suggested, the legislature is better equipped to perform that function, or do you detect some other reason for the adverse reaction to "creating public policy for this state"?

(2)   It is apparent from Justice Young's opinion and the summary of Justice Markman's opinion that there are many policy questions to be taken into account in deciding whether to enforce a waiver of liability. What are these various policies, and how do they interact with each other? How should a court resolve the policy question in light of all the countervailing considerations raised in the opinions?

———

One type of contractual provision that is commonly evaluated to assess its validity on grounds of public policy is a noncompetition provision. This is a provision in, say, an employment or partnership contract in which the employee or partner agrees not to engage in commercial activity in competition with the employer or partnership for a specified time, in a specified geographic area, following termination of the employment or partnership. Noncompetition provisions are also commonly found in contracts for the sale of a business, in terms of which the seller agrees not to open a competing business for a stated time and in a stated area after the sale. The competing public policies that are raised by noncompetition provisions are the policy of freedom of contract, which favors upholding a validly agreed noncompetition clause, and the policy in favor of protecting and sustaining competition in the marketplace. An unduly restrictive or unjustified noncompetition provision could frustrate this latter policy by restricting the party who made the commitment in her ability to work in her field, and by reducing the level of competitive commercial activity.

In evaluating the validity of a noncompetition clause, courts usually follow an approach known as the "rule of reason." A court applying the "rule of reason" will uphold a noncompetition clause to the extent that it is reasonable as to its duration, the geographic area that it covers, and the scope and extent of the activity that it restrains. In deciding this question, the court examines the totality of the circumstances, including the degree to which it is needed to protect the legitimate interests of the party in whose favor it operates, any undue hardship that it will impose on the restrained party, and the general public interest. (Of course, the court only applies the "rule of reason" if the noncompetition provision was freely bargained. If, for example, an unfairly rigorous noncompetition provision is included in a contract of adhesion, the court might find it to be unconscionable and refuse enforcement on that ground.)

When a court evaluates a noncompetition clause under the "rule of reason," it takes into account the nature of the relationship formed by the contract and covered by the clause. When the noncompetition provision is part of a contract for the sale of a business, a court is likely to give it the greatest degree of deference. Here, the clause is usually imposed to protect the goodwill of the business that the buyer has just bought and paid for. It is not difficult to see that the buyer of a business could lose a substantial basis of his bargain if, immediately after the sale, the seller opened a competing business in the same market.

Noncompetition clauses in partnership agreements are designed to protect the partnership business from competition from a partner who leaves the partnership to work on his own or with another firm. As a former owner of the business, the dissociating partner may be in a position to take customers, clients, staff, or partnership secrets with him, so a reasonable restraint on his ability to compete with the partnership could be justifiable. Noncompetition clauses in employment contracts are usually subject to the most careful scrutiny, and in some states they are not permitted at all. The employee may have little to take away from the business apart from his own skill. If so, a restraint on his ability to remain in the field, in the area of his choice, after leaving his employment does not really protect a legitimate property interest of the employer and may harm the employee by cutting down on his options to make a living. (A noncompetition clause must be distinguished from a more justifiable provision in a contract that forbids the employee to take property that belongs to the employer, such as customer lists and trade secrets.)

The next case shows how a court weighs the countervailing interests of the employer, the employee, and society in deciding on the validity of a noncompetition provision in an employment contract.

SYNCOM INDUSTRIES, INC. v. WOOD

155 N.H. 73, 920 A.2d 1178 (2007)
New Hampshire Supreme Court

BRODERICK, Chief Justice.

Defendants Eldon Wood and William Hogan, former employees of plaintiff Syncom Industries, Inc. ("Syncom" or "the company"), appeal an order entered after a bench trial in the Superior Court awarding Syncom injunctive relief, compensatory and enhanced damages and attorney's fees on its claims of breach of contract, breach of fiduciary duty, and loss of business reputation and goodwill. . . .

The following facts were found by the trial court or are otherwise supported by the record. Syncom provides cleaning and maintenance services for movie theaters. The company was established in 1995 by its current president and CEO, Matthew Sinopoli. Wood executed a "key employment contract" with Syncom in June 2001, and served as Syncom's vice-president of sales. Hogan executed a similar contract in September 2001, and served first as an area manager and later as a regional manager. Each contract was for a term of three years and included a section titled "extent of services" that contained the two restrictive covenants underlying Syncom's breach of contract claims:

> The [employee] ... agrees that for a period of three (3) years (36 months) after termination of his employment, whether with or without cause, the [employee] will not directly or indirectly, solicit business from any of the Company's customers located in any territory serviced by the Company while he was in the employment of the Company. The [employee] also agrees that during such period the [employee] will not become interested in or associated, directly or indirectly, as principal, agent or employee, with any person, firm or corporation which may solicit business from such customers. [The employee] shall not disclose the private affairs of the Company or any secrets or confidential information of the Company which he may learn while in the Company's employ.

... In late November or early December 2001, while they were still employed by Syncom, Wood and Hogan, along with at least one other Syncom employee, began plans to establish a new movie theater cleaning company, which they envisioned as a competitor to Syncom. On one occasion in December 2001, Wood, Hogan and another Syncom employee, Fabio Flores, met at a restaurant in Connecticut, during working hours, to discuss the establishment of Wood's new company. Also during that month, Wood negotiated with three of Syncom's customers, Regal Brandywine, Regal Burlington and Regal Cumberland, and lined them up as customers for himself upon his departure from Syncom and the establishment of his new company. In late December, Wood asked his father to loan him $30,000 to cover three weeks of payroll costs he expected to incur in the course of providing cleaning services to the three Regal theaters he had lined up as his future customers. On January 2, 2002, Wood's superiors at Syncom confronted him with their suspicions that he was planning to form a rival company. He denied it, but indicated that he would consider doing so, and threatened to breach the restrictive covenants in his employment contract.

After the January 2 meeting, Syncom's senior vice-president of operations, Carl DeSimone, sent Wood a memorandum noting that Wood "not only openly refused to deny, but ... cemented [his] participation in this offense [attempting to start his own competing business and trying to destroy Syncom] by telling the President of the company, in front of the Sr. Vice President, that [he, Wood] had approached [his] father for funding for [his] start-up company." For that offense, DeSimone informed Wood that he would be suspended without pay from January 14 through January 20, 2002. By letter dated January 14, 2002, Wood resigned from Syncom, citing the lack of commission payments and his suspension. Two days later, with the assistance of legal counsel, Wood filed articles of organization for Big E Theater Cleaning, LLC (Big E) with the Connecticut Secretary of State.

Within two weeks of Wood's resignation from Syncom, Big E began performing cleaning and maintenance at the three Regal theaters Wood had solicited for Big E while he was still employed by Syncom. By the end of February, Big E had also displaced Syncom at . . . [several other Regal theaters.] Within six weeks of his resignation, Wood secured as a Big E client an AMC theater complex in New York City (Empire 25) that he had previously spent six months soliciting for Syncom. Subsequently, Big E entered into cleaning contracts with six other Regal theaters . . . and displaced Syncom at four additional theaters. . . .

On February 11, 2002, Syncom terminated Hogan's employment. After Wood resigned but before Hogan was terminated, Hogan performed various tasks for Big E such as providing production rates and advising on budgetary matters. One day in early February, before he was terminated, Hogan went to Wood's home during working hours, carrying a stack of papers. At some point in late March or thereafter, several faxes from Hogan containing confidential Syncom information were recovered from Wood's trash. Those faxes were sent on various dates in March 2002. In May 2003, approximately fifteen months after Syncom terminated Hogan, Big E hired him.

In May 2002, Syncom brought a verified petition for declaratory judgment, permanent injunction and other relief against Wood, Hogan and Flores. Specifically, Syncom asked the court to: (1) declare that the defendants were bound by the restrictive covenants in their employment contracts; (2) determine that the defendants, through Big E, solicited business and contracted with theaters in violation of the restrictive covenants; (3) permanently enjoin the defendants from rendering any services to any current or former Syncom customers; (4) require the defendants to provide a complete accounting of their dealings with any current or former Syncom customers; and (5) award Syncom an amount equal to the profits the defendants earned as a result of violating the restrictive covenants. During trial, the court granted Syncom's motion to add a claim for breach of fiduciary duty, for which it sought compensatory and enhanced damages. . . . [Flores failed to defend the suit, and the trial court awarded a judgment against him by default.] Syncom's claims against Wood and Hogan were tried to the court. At trial, Wood argued, among other things, that the restrictive covenants were unenforceable as a matter of law because they were overly broad and otherwise unreasonable . . . [Wood also claimed that Syncom could not enforce the covenants because it had breached the employment contract. Discussion of that claim is omitted.] Hogan defended on similar grounds.

The trial court . . . ruled that Wood and Hogan breached both the restrictive covenants and their fiduciary duties to Syncom. Based upon those rulings, the trial court enjoined the defendants from rendering services to any current or former customer of Syncom for a period of eighteen months, starting on January 1, 2005, and awarded Syncom $1,145,700 in compensatory damages, $250,000 in enhanced compensatory damages and $100,000 in attorney's fees. . . .

Both defendants argue that the restrictive covenants are unenforceable as a matter of law. The covenants obligated the defendants, for a period of three years after leaving Syncom, not to "directly or indirectly, solicit business from any of the Company's customers located in any territory serviced by the Company while [they were] in the employment of the Company" or to become affiliated with a person or organization that solicited such business. The trial court rejected the defendants' arguments that the covenants were unreasonably broad and, consequently, unenforceable. We disagree.

The law does not look with favor upon contracts in restraint of trade or competition. Such contracts are narrowly construed. However, restrictive covenants are valid and enforceable if the restraint is reasonable, given the particular circumstances of the case. A covenant's reasonableness is a matter of law for this court to decide. To determine the reasonableness of a restrictive covenant ancillary to an employment contract, we employ a three-pronged test: first, whether the restriction is greater than necessary to protect the legitimate interests of the employer; second, whether the restriction imposes an undue hardship upon the employee; and third, whether the restriction is injurious to the public interest. If any of these questions is answered in the affirmative, the restriction is unreasonable and unenforceable. In determining whether a restrictive covenant is reasonable, the court will look only to the time when the contract was entered into.

The first step in determining the reasonableness of a given restraint is to identify the legitimate interests of the employer, and to determine whether the restraint is narrowly tailored to protect those interests. Legitimate interests of an employer that may be protected from competition include: the employer's trade secrets that have been communicated to the employee during the course of employment; confidential information communicated by the employer to the employee, but not involving trade secrets, such as information on a unique business method; an employee's special influence over the employer's customers, obtained during the course of employment; contacts developed during the employment; and the employer's development of goodwill and a positive image.

Wood argues that the restrictive covenants are unreasonable and thus unenforceable because they: (1) covered theaters that were not Syncom customers when he worked for the company; (2) included areas in which he never operated and theaters with which he never had contact; (3) prevented him from soliciting any theater in a chain with a theater served by Syncom; (4) covered both current and former Syncom customers; and (5) extended for too long. . . . Hogan argues that the covenants are unenforceable as to him because: (1) he did not have the type of job with Syncom that allowed him to appropriate the company's goodwill; (2) he worked for Syncom for too short a time to appropriate any of the company's goodwill; and (3) the covenants imposed an undue hardship upon him. Syncom argues, to the contrary, that the covenants reasonably restricted the defendants from doing business with Syncom customers with whom they had no direct contact because Syncom's unique business model provided the defendants with important inside information about all Syncom customers.

It is well established in our case law that when the legitimate interest an employer seeks to protect with a restrictive covenant is its goodwill with customers, a covenant that restricts a former employee from soliciting business from the employer's entire customer base sweeps too broadly. Because the restrictive covenants in this case extended to Syncom customers with which Wood and Hogan had no direct contact, they were broader than necessary for the purpose of advancing Syncom's legitimate interest in protecting its goodwill.

However, employers also have a legitimate interest in protecting information about their customers gained by employees during the course of their employment. To protect that interest, an employer may restrict a former employee from soliciting business from customers with which that employee had no direct contact, so long as the employee gained significant knowledge or understanding of those customers during the course of his or her employment. The restrictive covenants in this case are broader than necessary to protect Syncom's legitimate interest in information Wood and Hogan may have acquired about Syncom customers during the course of their employment. If that were the intent of the covenants, they could have been written to prohibit the defendants from soliciting business from Syncom customers about which they had gained information while employed by Syncom. But, as drafted, the covenants barred the defendants from soliciting "business from *any* of the Company's customers located in *any territory* serviced by the Company while [they were] in the employment of the Company." (Emphasis added.) It is difficult to imagine how the defendants, had they terminated their employment within several weeks of being hired, could have gained ... [protectable] inside information ... with regard to *all* of Syncom's customers in *all* of its territories. And, as the record demonstrates, Syncom hired Wood in part to gain the benefit of Wood's previous experience in the theater industry, which provided him with knowledge of Syncom customers independent of the knowledge he may have gained as a Syncom employee.

Moreover, while Syncom appears to argue, at least implicitly, that its "top-down" marketing strategy somehow created a situation in which all of the company's knowledge of its customers could be imputed to every employee, we do not accept that reasoning. ... [T]he legitimate interests an employer may protect with a restrictive covenant must be direct and concrete rather than attenuated and speculative. Here, because the restrictive covenants barred the defendants from soliciting all of Syncom's customers, rather than just those customers about which they had gained information while working for Syncom, and because that deficiency in the framing of the covenants is not cured by Syncom's invocation of its top-down marketing strategy, we conclude that the restrictive covenants are broader than necessary to protect Syncom's legitimate interest in its proprietary information.

As a matter of law, the two restrictive covenants at issue are unenforceable because they are unreasonably broad in their scope. Thus we hold that the trial court erred by ruling to the contrary. Accordingly, we reverse that ruling. That is not, however, the end of the matter. Courts have the power to reform overly broad restrictive covenants if the employer shows that it acted in good faith in the execution of the employment contract. . . . We express no opinion on whether the covenants should be reformed as to either or both of the defendants. Rather, as resolution of that issue will require factual determinations, it is for the trial court to consider on remand. Finally, as the defendants have challenged both the geographic and temporal scope of the restrictive covenants, and have properly preserved those challenges, both aspects of the covenants are open to possible reformation. . . .

■ QUESTIONS

(1) The court remanded the case to the trial court to determine if the covenants should be reformed. The court notes that the resolution of that question will require factual determinations. What facts need to be determined?

(2) Assume that the trial court finds that the employer did act in good faith in the execution of the employment contracts. Do you think that the covenants should be reformed? If so, what would you consider to be the reasonable scope of the covenants?

(3) What public policies does the court seek to protect in refusing to enforce the restrictive covenants as written? Do any public policies favor enforcing them?

■ PROBLEM 14.4

Although the "rule of reason" is generally applicable to noncompetition provisions, the law may invalidate such provisions completely in certain transactions. If so, the noncompetition agreement is ineffective as a matter of law—and is best seen as an illegal contract, rather than one that offends public policy. Therefore, no "rule of reason" analysis is applied. For example, California outlaws them in employment contracts. Further, the rules of professional responsibility in most states forbid attorneys from making such agreements. ABA Model Rule of Professional Conduct 5.6(a) prohibits partnership and employment agreements from restricting the right of a lawyer to practice after termination of the relationship. A similar provision, in the Illinois Code of Professional Responsibility, was at issue in *Stevens v. Rooks Pitts and Poust*, 289 Ill. App. 3d 991, 682 N.E.2d 1125 (1997). A law firm's partnership agreement provided that a departing partner would lose one-fifth of the payout of his partnership interest if, within a year of leaving the firm, the partner engaged in the practice of law in competition with the partnership in the Chicago metropolitan area. Stevens left the partnership and joined another Chicago law firm. Rooks Pitts and Poust paid him four-fifths of his share of the partnership but refused to pay him the remaining one-fifth on the strength of the noncompetition provision. The Illinois Appellate Court found the provision to be invalid under the Code of Professional Conduct. First, the court held that even though the provision did not absolutely bar the withdrawing partner from practicing in the Chicago area, the financial disincentive that it created discouraged competition and just as much violated the Code. The court recognized that the 'rule of reason' was appropriate in other cases, but it could not be applied to attorneys. In enacting the Code, the state supreme court had weighed attorneys' freedom of contract against the policy of protecting the public's right to choose legal counsel and had found the latter to predominate. Because the Code of Professional Conduct barred the noncompetition clause, the clause was in effect illegal (not merely a violation of public policy), so the court did apply the *in pari delicto* rule. It found that although the parties shared equal guilt in agreeing to the clause, the public interest was best served in giving Stevens relief. The court therefore severed the noncompetition clause from the partnership agreement and allowed Stevens to recover the balance of his payout.

Assume that Rooks Pitts and Poust was not a law firm but an accounting firm, and that noncompetition clauses are not proscribed by the rules of ethics governing the accounting profession. Would the clause satisfy the 'rule of reason'?

D INCAPACITY BASED ON MINORITY

1. General Principles

The basic general rule relating to a minor's contract is that it is avoidable at the instance of the minor. Because the contract is avoidable, not void, a minor who wishes to keep the contract may simply refrain from disaffirming it. However, the right to avoid the contract continues at least until the minor becomes a major, so even if the minor initially decides not to seek avoidance, she can change her mind.

The public policy basis of minority doctrine is the protection of minors who are deemed to be unable to act with maturity and rationality in their own

[handwritten: don't need to prove exploitation]

interests in entering the contract, making them vulnerable to exploitation. However, although exploitation is a concern, it is not an element that must be shown for avoidance—the policy of protecting the minor usually outweighs concern about protecting the other party's reliance interest, even if that party did not act unfairly or exploitatively. Therefore, with a few narrow exceptions, a minor can avoid her contract simply by showing that she was a minor at the time she made it. She does not need to show that the other party was guilty of improper bargaining or deliberate advantage-taking.

The age at which a person attains contractual capacity is typically fixed by statute. In most states it is 18, but the legislature might choose a different age. Until that age, the person is a minor. (Sometimes the old-fashioned term "infant" is used, which sounds odd in light of modern usage, especially since most of the "infants" involved in the cases are adolescents close to the age of majority.) The fundamental and longstanding approach to minors' contracts was set out in *Woodman v. Kera LLC*, which we presented in Section C for its discussion of public policy: As *Woodman* indicates (quite apart from the question of a parent's lack of capacity to bind the minor), the minor does not have the capacity to bind himself in contract, and may avoid a contractual commitment by disaffirming it.

[handwritten: can avoid a contract just by being a minor ↓ bright line test]

While there are some narrow exceptions to this rule recognized by common law or statute, the common law has traditionally been very solicitous of protecting minors from contractual liability, and this approach is very much in evidence in modern case law.

It is, of course, quite arbitrary to fix the transition from incompetence to capability at a defined birthday. This approach is convenient and relatively easy to administer, because an objective, mechanically ascertainable test is considerably simpler than a case-by-case evaluation of the subjective attributes of each individual minor. However, the test takes no account of the fact that minors who have reached adolescence are very different from children and may be quite as capable as an adult of making rational economic decisions. (As noted before, in many of the cases involving minors' contracts, the minor is close to the age of majority.) In addition, with the rapid rise of electronic commerce, minors surely constitute a significant segment of the market for online goods and services, and

[handwritten: minors are a considerable segment of the online market]

many of these minors probably have greater facility and experience with online purchasing than their parents. The greater participation of minors in the marketplace, and a changed perception of the contractual competence of adolescents may, over time, cause a shift in minority doctrine. To some extent, this has already begun to occur as legislatures carve out transaction-specific exceptions to the common law rule. Nevertheless, for the present, the law uses a bright-line objective test to determine the contractual capacity of minors.

2. Disaffirmance and Ratification

[handwritten: contract is voidable]

In most cases a minor's lack of contractual capacity makes the contract voidable, not void; that is, the minor may choose to avoid (or disaffirm) the contract

✶ contract is avoidable

on grounds of incapacity or to keep it in force. A minor may disaffirm the contract, expressly or by conduct, at any time before reaching majority or within a reasonable time after reaching majority. Once the contract is disaffirmed, it comes to an end, and the minor cannot change his mind and seek to enforce it. Because the law deems a minor to be too immature to make a binding decision relating to a contract before majority, it follows that he is given a reasonable time to disaffirm after he has gained the age of discretion, even if he never disaffirmed during his minority, or in fact actively affirmed or performed the contract during that period.

its over once disaffirmed

The choice to affirm or disaffirm the contract sounds like a good deal for the minor, but the advantage of the right of avoidance comes at a cost. The minor's ability to avoid the contract makes him an unreliable contracting party, and this could make the other party reluctant to contract with him.

In dealing with unconscionability in Chapter 13, Section F, we note that arbitration provisions in standard agreements have become increasingly common, so that many modern unconscionability cases involve challenges to such provisions. A similar trend can be found in cases involving the disaffirmance of minor's contracts.

FOSS v. CIRCUIT CITY STORES, INC.

477 F. Supp. 2d 230 (2007)
United States District Court, District of Maine

SINGAL, Chief Judge.

Before the Court are Defendant Circuit City Stores, Inc.'s Motions to Compel Arbitration and to Stay the Proceedings. Plaintiff Andrew Foss ("Foss") objects to Defendant's Motion on the grounds of infancy and unconscionability of the agreement to arbitrate. For the reasons stated below, Defendant's Motions to Compel Arbitration and to Stay the Proceedings are denied.

π claims dispositive

[At the time of this litigation, Circuit City Stores, Inc. ("Circuit City") was a national retailer of appliances and consumer electronics. (It has since gone out of business.)] . . . Circuit City has maintained an online application system. As an individual progresses through the application, he or she is required to provide information and consent to various agreements. The initial screen provides: "Before beginning the employment application, we will ask for your Social Security Number, contact information, consent to arbitration, and consent to perform a background check." At numerous times throughout the application, applicants are provided with opportunities to withdraw their application and exit the system. After consenting to proceed electronically, the applicant is presented with Circuit City's Dispute Resolution Agreement ("the Agreement"). The Agreement provides in pertinent part:

[B]oth Circuit City and I agree to settle any and all previously unasserted claims, disputes or controversies arising out of or relating to my application or candidacy for employment, employment and/or cessation of employment with Circuit City, exclusively by final and binding arbitration before a neutral Arbitrator. By way of example only, such claims include claims under federal, state and local statutory or common law, such as the Age Discrimination in Employment Act, Title VII of the Civil Rights Act of 1964, as amended, including the amendments of the Civil Rights Act of 1991, the Americans with Disabilities Act, the Family Medical Leave Act, the law of contract and law of tort. I understand that if I do file a lawsuit regarding a dispute arising out of or relating to my application or candidacy for employment, employment or cessation for employment, Circuit City may use this Agreement in support of its request to the court to dismiss the lawsuit and require me instead to use arbitration.

The applicant is then required to consent to the Agreement. When an applicant is less than eighteen years of age, the applicant is directed to obtain parental consent to the Agreement. Without parental consent, a person under eighteen is exited from the system. Throughout the application process, the applicant is given numerous opportunities to review and print a copy of the Agreement. Notably, an applicant must read and consent to the Agreement in order to be considered for employment.

On October 7, 2004, Foss applied for a non-management position with the Circuit City store in South Portland, Maine via the online application system. Foss was born on February 4, 1987 and thus was under eighteen at the time he applied for employment with Circuit City. As a result, when Foss reached the Agreement, he was directed to obtain a parent's consent. Foss's employment application reflects that the name "Sharon Foss" was entered and that this person consented to the Agreement. Sharon Foss is Andrew Foss's mother. Sharon Foss, however, has declared: "I never signed the Circuit City Dispute Resolution Agreement or gave my consent to Andrew to enter into the Agreement." Esten Foss, Andrew Foss's father, likewise maintains that he never signed or consented to the Agreement. Furthermore, through an affidavit, Foss states that neither parent signed or consented to the Agreement. On October 14, 2004, before Foss was actually hired by Circuit City, he was presented with and signed a hard copy of the Agreement. Notably, Circuit City did not require a parent's signature on this hard copy.

Foss began working for Circuit City in South Portland in October of 2004. Foss turned eighteen on February 4, 2005. In October 2005, Foss was transferred to the Circuit City in Keene, New Hampshire. While employed at the Keene Circuit City, Foss alleges that his supervisor created a hostile work environment. In December 2005, Foss provided two weeks' notice that he was going to terminate the employment. He was asked to stay for another week and was promised a transfer to the store in South Portland. Foss maintains that as a result of informing management of the hostile environment, including calling the Human Resources Department of Circuit City, he was terminated on December 15, 2005.

The reason provided to Foss for the termination was "improperly punching in." Foss alleges that this reason was a pretext and claims retaliation motivated his termination.

Foss filed this lawsuit on September 15, 2006 claiming a hostile work environment and retaliation in violation of Title VII of the Civil Rights Act of 1964, 42 U.S.C. §2000e, *et. seq.*, and the Civil Rights Act of 1991, 42 U.S.C. §1981(a). Circuit City has moved to compel arbitration and to stay the proceedings pursuant to sections 2 and 4 of the Federal Arbitration Act ("FAA"), 9 U.S.C. §§2 & 4 (2006).

[The court articulates the policy in favor of arbitration agreements, embodied in the FAA, and cites §2, which provides that a contract to settle disputes by arbitration ". . . shall be valid, irrevocable, and enforceable, save upon such grounds as exist at law or in equity for the revocation of any contract."] . . . In addition, section 4 provides a mechanism to compel arbitration by a party aggrieved by another party's refusal to arbitrate. Section 4 directs that "upon being satisfied that the making of the agreement for arbitration or the failure to comply therewith is not in issue, the court shall make an order directing the parties to proceed to arbitration in accordance with the terms of the agreement." Section 3 allows a court to stay the proceedings until the arbitration is complete.

Circuit City petitions the Court to compel arbitration pursuant to section 4 on the ground that the parties have agreed to arbitrate "any and all previously unasserted claims, disputes or controversies arising out of or relating to my application or candidacy for employment, employment and/or cessation of employment with Circuit City." Foss resists the motion to compel arbitration for two reasons. First, Foss asserts that because he was under eighteen when he signed the Agreement and he never ratified the Agreement in writing, no valid contract was ever formed. Second, Foss claims that even if there is a binding contract, the Agreement is unconscionable and therefore unenforceable. Because the Court finds the issue of infancy determinative, it does not reach the claim of unconscionability. At the threshold, the Court must determine whether the proper decision-maker for the claim of infancy is the court or the arbitrator. . . . [The court concludes that because a claim of infancy goes to the heart of the question of whether a binding arbitration agreement was ever formed, the claim is one that must be resolved by the court.[2]]

---

[2] In Chapter 13, footnote 25, we point out that where an arbitration clause is challenged as unconscionable, the question of whether the court or the arbitrator must decide the question of unconscionability is complex and beyond our scope. As this case indicates, the question may also come up where the challenge to an arbitration clause is based on minority. The court concludes that because a claim of minority is so central to the question of whether a contract (and thus the agreement to arbitrate) exists at all, it has to be classified as a "threshold matter" to be decided by the court itself. This case was decided before the U.S. Supreme Court decided *Rent-A-Center, West, Inc. v. Jackson*, 130 S. Ct. 2772 (2010), discussed in Chapter 13, footnote 25. It is not clear to us if the court's characterization of the infancy claim as a "threshold matter" is consistent with the Supreme Court's holding in *Rent-A-Center*. —EDS.

In determining whether a valid contract exists at all in a motion to compel arbitration, "state law, whether of legislative or judicial origin, is applicable *if* that law arose to govern issues concerning the validity, revocability, and enforceability of contracts generally." *Perry v. Thomas*, 482 U.S. 483, 492 n. 9, 107 S. Ct. 2520, 96 L. Ed. 2d 426 (1987). The Court thus looks to Maine law to determine whether the contract to arbitrate exists. The general law in Maine regarding the validity of a minor's contracts is clear: "No action shall be maintained on any contract made by a minor, unless he, or some person lawfully authorized, ratified it in writing after he arrived at the age of 18 years, except for necessaries or real estate of which he has received the title and retains the benefit." 33 M.R.S.A §52. Since at least 1832, Maine has recognized the "infancy doctrine" and the need to protect minors. As the Law Court stated in 1947: "These disabilities of the minor are really privileges which the law gives him, and which he may exercise for his own benefit. The object is to secure him in his youthful years from injuring himself by his own improvident acts." *Reed Bros., Inc. v. Giberson*, 143 Me. 4, 54 A.2d 535, 537 (1947). These same cases contain a warning to those who endeavor to contract with an infant: "Any person dealing with one who has not reached his majority, must do so at his peril." *Id.*

Circuit City acknowledges that Foss was less than eighteen years of age when he signed the agreement. Nonetheless, Circuit City maintains that the Agreement is valid because Foss ratified the contract after turning eighteen and Circuit City obtained the consent of Foss's parents. Ratification of a contract by a minor in Maine stands in contrast to ratification under the common law. Whereas under the common law and in some states, a minor can ratify a contract by actions or by a failure to disaffirm, Maine requires the ratification to be in writing. 33 M.R.A. §52. To be effective, ratification "should be voluntary, not obtained by circumvention, not under ignorance of the fact that he was entitled to claim the privilege." *Reed Bros.*, 54 A.2d at 538. In *Reed Bros.*, the Law Court declined to find ratification of a promissory note where an infant had joined in a mortgage, in which he acknowledged that the mortgage was subject to the promissory note. The Law Court stated that "[t]he ratification required by the statute must be something more than a recognition of the existence of the debt and the amount due thereon. It must be a deliberate written ratification." The ratification must also evidence a decision by the infant to be bound by the contract. *See id.* ("Ratification always resolves itself into a question of intention.").

Although Circuit City offers several forms of ratification, the Court finds each offer to be is insufficient. First, Circuit City maintains that Foss ratified the Agreement "[b]y completing and submitting daily time cards, upon which Circuit City relied and upon which Foss was paid. . . ." Mere completion and submission of a time card, is, at most, an acknowledgement of the time actually worked; it does not evidence intent by the infant to be bound by an independent agreement to arbitrate. If a mortgage that contained an acknowledgement of the promissory note in *Reed Bros.*, did not ratify the promissory note, the completion and submission of a time card cannot function to ratify an independent contract. In this situation, the Court is unable to state that punching and turning in a time card is a deliberate, voluntary and knowing written ratification of a separate agreement, which states "I agree to settle any and all previously unasserted claims . . . exclusively by final and binding arbitration."

Second, Circuit City claims that by continuing to work after turning eighteen, "Foss expressly consented to the Agreement." In Maine, action is insufficient for ratification absent a "deliberate written ratification." *See Lamkin & Foster v. Ledoux*, 101 Me. 581, 64 A. 1048, 1049 (1906) ("The defendant's conduct after coming of age may have shown a sufficient ratification at common law, but there was no ratification in writing, and hence the statute bars the action.").

Finally, Circuit City claims that Foss ratified the contract by filing this lawsuit, "as the Agreement was an integral part of Foss's employment arrangement upon which he is now suing." This proposition misconstrues the nature of the lawsuit. Foss is suing on statutory grounds independent of the Agreement, not upon any provision or action under the contract. Furthermore, other courts have found in similar cases that the filing of a lawsuit for sexual harassment is repudiation of the contract, not ratification.

Circuit City maintains that the Agreement is nonetheless enforceable because Circuit City obtained parental consent. As indicated previously, because Foss was under eighteen at the time he completed the online application for employment, he was required by the online application system to obtain parental consent. The name "Sharon Foss" appears in the application as having consented. In affidavits attached to Plaintiff's Opposition to Compel Arbitration, both Andrew Foss and Sharon Foss state that parental consent was not obtained or given to the Agreement. Furthermore, there is no claim that parental consent was provided when Foss signed the hard copy of the agreement on October 14.

The only conclusion the Court is left with is that Foss entered his mother's name without obtaining her consent. This misrepresentation, however, will not act as an estoppel to prevent Foss from asserting his infancy. *See Whitman v. Allen*, 123 Me. 1, 121 A. 160, 163-64 (1923) ("The only evidence of fraud is the false representation made by the plaintiff to the defendant that he was of age and had a right to trade. Such a false statement on the minor's part is held not to create an estoppel."). This immature and false representation is exactly why the law acts to protect the infant. As the Law Court stated in 1923: "It is simply the result of the improvidence of infancy which the law has always in mind." *Id.* at 163. The Court finds that without written ratification, the Agreement never came into existence between Foss and Circuit City.[3] Therefore, there is no agreement

_____

[3] The Court is aware of the hardship and difficulty this may place on those dealing with minors; nonetheless, given the strict adherence by the Law Court to the infancy doctrine, this Court is unwilling to strip the protections afforded the infant. *See Mellott v. Sullivan Ford Sales*, 236 A.2d 68, 74 (Me. 1967) ("We [the Law

to arbitrate the dispute, and the Motions to Compel Arbitration and Stay the Proceedings are denied.

■ QUESTIONS

(1)   As the court indicates, a minor who has not avoided a contract during his minority may ratify it upon becoming a major. Because Maine has a statute that requires a deliberate written ratification, Foss was held not to have ratified the contract by the conduct of submitting time cards, continuing to work for Circuit City, or commencing the lawsuit. The court indicates that this statutory requirement is stricter than the common law rule, under which a minor can ratify a contract by implication if he retains or continues to receive benefits under the contract after reaching majority or even if he simply fails to disaffirm the contract within a reasonable time after attaining majority.

Would Foss have ratified the contract by submitting time cards and continuing to work for Circuit City if the common law rule applied in this case?

(2)   Foss became a major when he turned 18 on February 4, 2005. He did not seek to disaffirm the arbitration agreement until he filed suit on September 15, 2006, about 19 months after attaining majority. Even in the absence of conduct from which ratification can be inferred, the common law recognizes that a minor may ratify a contract if he does not act to disaffirm it within a reasonable time after attaining majority. Should 19 months qualify as a reasonable time under the common law rule? What factors should be taken into account to determine if a delay in disaffirming is reasonable?

(3)   The court states that because it decides the case on the basis of infancy, it does not reach the question of whether the contract was unconscionable. Had the court reached this question, do you think that it should have found the contract unconscionable?

Given the high volume of Internet business done by teens and even pre-teens, one would expect lots of reported cases dealing with the disaffirmance of minors' Internet transactions. There are surprisingly few. The next case is one of them.

Court] feel that when social and economic changes require a further relaxation of common law limitations upon the contractual responsibility of minors, any modification of such a basic principle must come from the clearly expressed intentions of the Legislature.").

I.B. v. FACEBOOK, INC.

905 F. Supp. 2d 989 (2012)
United States District Court, Northern District of California

WILKEN, District Judge.

... Facebook operates the largest online social network in the world and provides a payment system, Facebook Credits, for users to make purchases within the Facebook website. Facebook permits minors to register on its website and use its service. In October 2011, Plaintiff I.B., a minor, asked his mother, Plaintiff Glynnis Bohannon, for permission to spend twenty dollars on his Facebook account using Bohannon's Wells Fargo Master Card, in exchange for twenty dollars in cash. I.B. purchased Facebook Credits from Facebook for use in "Ninja Saga." Subsequently, without any notice that his mother's credit card information had been stored by Facebook and the Facebook Credits system, or that his mother's credit card information was being used again after the initial twenty dollar purchase, I.B. made in-game purchases for which he thought he was spending virtual, in-game currency. As a result, Bohannon's credit card was charged repeatedly and without her consent, and the charges totaled several hundred dollars. Upon discovering the transactions, Bohannon tried to obtain a refund from Facebook by leaving a phone message at a phone number listed for Facebook but received no response.

In December 2011, Plaintiff J.W., a minor, began to make a series of charges via Facebook Credits using the debit card of his parents, Plaintiff Julie Wright and Steven Wright, which J.W. had taken from his parents without their permission. The total charges exceeded one thousand dollars. On or about February 8, 2012, after learning of these charges, Steven Wright submitted a complaint to Facebook as to the "20 debits directly to my bank account," noting that neither he nor his wife (the only authorized users of the debit card's account) had authorized any such charges, and requesting a refund.... [Facebook failed to refund these charges. The named plaintiffs therefore commenced a class action against Facebook on behalf of all Facebook users who were similarly charged as a result of the unauthorized credit card purchase of Facebook credits by minor children.] Facebook moves to dismiss the [complaint] ... for failure to state a claim and to strike the class allegations. Plaintiffs oppose the motions....

California Family Code section 6700 provides that ... "a minor may make a contract in the same manner as an adult, subject to the power of disaffirmance" provided by section 6710. California law permits a minor to disaffirm a contract during minority or within a reasonable time after reaching majority. Cal. Fam. Code §6710 ("Except as otherwise provided by statute, a contract of a minor may be disaffirmed by the minor before majority or within a reasonable time afterwards or, in case of the minor's death within that period, by the minor's heirs or personal representative"). California courts recognize that "sound policy considerations support this provision." *Berg v. Traylor,* 148 Cal. App. 4th 809, 818, 56

[handwritten margin note: public policy rationale]

Cal. Rptr. 3d 140 (2007). "The law shields minors from their lack of judgment and experience and under certain conditions vests in them the right to disaffirm their contracts. Although in many instances such disaffirmance may be a hardship upon those who deal with an infant, the right to avoid his contracts is conferred by law upon a minor for his protection against his own improvidence and the designs of others. It is the policy of the law to protect a minor against himself and his indiscretions and immaturity as well as against the machinations of other people and to discourage adults from contracting with an infant. Any loss occasioned by the disaffirmance of a minor's contract might have been avoided by declining to enter into the contract." *Id.* (quoting *Niemann v. Deverich*, 98 Cal. App. 2d 787, 793, 221 P.2d 178 (1950)).

[handwritten margin note: contract w/ minors at your own risk]

Simply stated, one who provides a minor with goods and services does so at her own risk. A contract (or conveyance) of a minor may be avoided by any act or declaration disclosing an unequivocal intent to repudiate its binding force and effect. Express notice to the other party is unnecessary. Disaffirmation by a minor rescinds the entire contract, rendering it a nullity. An action for disaffirmation is one in equity, governed in many respects by the rules relating to rescission of contracts, and the trial court is vested with a broad discretion to see that equity is done. Plaintiffs allege that minors have the right to disaffirm contracts such as those at issue here and that the Facebook Credit transactions are voidable pursuant to section 6710.

[handwritten margin note: Δ claim]

Facebook contends that minor Plaintiff I.B. cannot disaffirm his contract because he has already received the full benefit of the Facebook Credits that he purchased by using the Credits to make in-game purchases in "Ninja Saga." In support of its argument, Facebook relies on court decisions enforcing forum selection or other contract clauses against a minor. Facebook relies primarily on *E.K.D. v. Facebook, Inc.*, 885 F. Supp. 2d 894 (S.D. Ill.), where the plaintiffs challenged Facebook's practice of including its users' names and profile pictures in advertisements and alleged that users under the age of eighteen were legally incapable of consenting to commercialization of their identity. Granting Facebook's motion to transfer venue, the district court held that the minor plaintiffs could not disaffirm the forum selection clause in Facebook's Terms of Service. Relying on the principle that "minors, if they would disaffirm a contract, must disaffirm the entire contract, not just the irksome provisions," the court found that the plaintiffs "have used and continue to use facebook.com," and held that minors may not accept the benefits of a contract and then seek to disaffirm the contract "in an attempt to escape the consequences of a clause that does not suit them." The court determined that the forum selection clause was enforceable against the minor plaintiffs and granted Facebook's motion to transfer the action to the Northern District of California.

[handwritten margin note: disaffirm only a whole contract, not just parts]

Facebook contends that the ruling in *E.K.D.* on the enforceability of the forum selection clause is directly applicable here because minor Plaintiff I.B. has already accepted the benefits of the contract to purchase Facebook Credits, as demonstrated by his concession that he used the Credits to make "in-game purchases" in the Ninja Saga game. Although Plaintiffs do not allege what

Plaintiff J.W. did with the Credits that he purchased, Facebook infers that he also spent the Credits online and argues that allowing the minor Plaintiffs to disaffirm their contracts would result in an unfair windfall to the minor.

Under California law, a minor may disaffirm all obligations under a contract, *even for services previously rendered,* without restoring consideration or the value of services rendered to the other party. Explaining that "[o]ne deals with infants at his peril," the California Supreme Court has held, "Upon disaffirmance the minor is entitled to recover all benefits paid under the contract." *Burnand v. Irigoyen,* 30 Cal. 2d 861, 866, 186 P.2d 417 (1947) . . . [and is not required to restore any benefits received under the contract.] In support of its argument that the minor Plaintiffs may not disaffirm their contracts to purchase Facebook Credits, Facebook relies on authorities that declined to allow a minor to disaffirm a particular contract clause where the minor did not disaffirm the entire contract or continued to benefit from the contract. In *E.K.D.,* the minor challenged the enforceability of the forum selection clause contained in the Terms of Service but continued to use the Facebook networking website. In holding that the minor plaintiff could not continue using facebook.com and disaffirm the forum selection provision of the Terms of Service, the court cited a well-established maxim: "Minors must either accept or repudiate the entire contract, and they cannot retain the contract's fruits and at the same time deny its obligations." The court relied on decisions in the specific context of forum-selection clauses which declined to allow minors to accept the benefits but not the burdens of a contract. . . . [I]n *E.K.D.,* the court did not consider the question whether the minor plaintiffs stated a claim to disaffirm their contract to use Facebook's site. Rather, the *E.K.D.* court . . . relied on the fact that the minor plaintiffs continued to use the Facebook site to hold that the minors could not disaffirm the forum selection clause of the Terms of Service.

[In this case, unlike *E.K.D.,*] Facebook's motion to dismiss presents the question whether the minor Plaintiffs may disaffirm their contracts even after receiving the benefits of purchasing Facebook Credits. If all the allegations are accepted as true, the minor Plaintiffs allege a claim for declaratory relief that would disaffirm the entire contract, not just the irksome portions. Any unfair windfall that would be potentially gained by the minors might have been avoided by declining to enter into the contract. . . . [The court denies Facebook's motion to dismiss the claims by the minor plaintiffs to disaffirm their contracts.]

holding

■ QUESTION

I.B. v. Facebook states the principle that a minor cannot disaffirm only part of a contract—she cannot seek to avoid the parts of the contract that she does not like while keeping in force its beneficial aspects. Yet it looks like Andrew Foss did this. He sued for wrongful termination of his employment contract while seeking to avoid the arbitration provision that was part of that contract.

Is this not a situation in which he disaffirms a disadvantageous term of the contract while retaining his rights under the contract to sue for its breach? Do you find any explanation in the *Foss* opinion of why the court did not find this to be a problem?

3. Misrepresentation

In his online application, Foss misrepresented that his mother had consented to the employment agreement.[4] The court refused to estop Foss from disclaiming the contract on this ground, stating that the "immature and false representation is exactly why the law acts to protect the infant." Some but not all courts adopt this approach. Fraudulent misrepresentation is a tort, and liability for tort arises at an earlier age than contractual capacity. Therefore, some courts are more willing than the *Foss* court to entertain a claim for damages arising from the misrepresentation or even to enforce the contract by estopping the minor from asserting the right to disaffirm. However, even where a court is willing to hold the minor accountable for fraudulent misrepresentation, the major party must establish the elements of fraud.

TOPHEAVY STUDIOS, INC. v. DOE

Not Reported in S.W.3d, 2005 WL 1940159
Texas Court of Appeals

SMITH, Justice.

[The plaintiff was one of a group of 17-year-old girls who took part in a saucy spring break activity that was filmed and subsequently used in a video game called "The Guy Game." To participate in the filming, the girls were required to present proof that they were over 18 and to sign a release consenting to the use of the video footage. The plaintiff produced fake identification, showing that she was over 18, and she signed the release. Although there were apparent irregularities and inconsistencies in the identification card and release, Topheavy allowed the plaintiff to participate. About 18 months later, Topheavy released the video game. When the plaintiff discovered that it contained footage of her, she sued on several grounds, including invasion of privacy and misappropriation of her likeness. She sought a temporary injunction, restraining release of the game while the suit was pending. The trial court granted a temporary

---

[4] Recall from *Woodman* that in some states it is not clear if parental assent would even be effective in the absence of a statute validating it in a particular transaction.

injunction. Topheavy appealed, seeking release of the injunction on the ground that the plaintiff had executed the consent to the use of the video footage. The court refused to dissolve the injunction, holding that the trial court did not abuse its discretion in granting it, because there were issues of fact to be determined relating to the validity of the release.]

... In Texas, a contract between an adult and a minor is voidable at the option of the minor. A minor who fraudulently misrepresents her age to induce another to enter into a contract cannot void the contract. Therefore, a party seeking to prevent another party from voiding a contract on the basis of minority must establish that (1) the minor misrepresented her age, (2) the minor intended for the other party to rely on the misrepresentation, and (3) the party was injured as a result of its actual and justifiable reliance. . . . A party to an arm's length transaction must exercise ordinary care and reasonable diligence for the protection of his own interests, and a failure to do so is not excused by mere confidence in the honesty and integrity of the other party. . . . In this case, Doe did misrepresent her age, and Topheavy actually relied on that misrepresentation. However, if Topheavy's reliance was not justified, then there was no fraudulent misrepresentation, and Doe may void the contract. Jeff Spangenburg, Topheavy's Chief Executive Officer, testified that the company was aware of the possibility that minors would be present during the filming. Accordingly, numerous protocols were instituted to prevent a minor from taking part in the game. He testified further that Topheavy's concern regarding fake identification cards and driver's licenses prompted it to hire people to verify identification information at the contest and afterwards. According to Spangenburg, if there was any doubt regarding a contestant's age, Topheavy erred on the side of caution and did not use that contestant in the game.

Doe admits that she provided Topheavy with a fake identification card. However, [irregularities and inconsistencies in both the card and the signed release] . . . were suspicious. Nevertheless, Topheavy did not question or verify any of the information that Doe provided prior to using her image in the video game. Spangenburg testified that if he had known that the zip code Doe listed did not correspond with the city she listed on her release, or that the street she supposedly lived on did not exist, he would have been suspicious and would have attempted to verify her information. He explained that Doe's information was not verified because she did not look or act like she was as young as seventeen. . . .

4. Exceptions to a Minor's Lack of Capacity, Especially Contracts for Necessaries

Although a minor may avoid a contract at will, there are a number of specific exceptions to this general rule. Many of these exceptions have been created by

[handwritten margin note: exception where minors can be bound contract for necessaries]

statute, where the state legislature has determined that minors should be allowed to enter particular types of binding contracts. Apart from statutory exceptions, the common law recognizes a limited number of circumstances under which a minor may be bound by his contract or at least liable for the reasonable value of what he received under the contract. The most important common law exception relates to a contract for necessaries. The standard definition of "necessaries" covers goods or services essential for the minor's health and sustenance or reasonably necessary for the preservation or enjoyment of life, such as food, medical needs, clothes, or shelter. "Necessaries" is a broader term than "necessities," and it can go beyond goods or services essential to sustain life to include items that are not luxuries but are useful and appropriate, given the minor's reasonable standard of living. Because the definition is open ended and fact based, different courts may reach different conclusions over whether a particular item is a necessary, or the circumstances of one case may justify treating something as a necessary that would not be seen as such under different circumstances.

For example, in *Webster Street Partnership, Ltd. v. Sheridan*, 220 Neb. 9, 368 N.W.2d 439 (1985), the court held that minors who had entered into an apartment lease had not contracted for a necessary. Although one would normally think of shelter as quite a basic necessity of life (and courts include it along with food and clothing in the standard definition of necessaries), the court found that it was not a necessary under the circumstances of the case because the minors could have lived with their parents.

Courts express different views as to the effect of a contract for necessaries. Some treat the contract as fully enforceable against the minor. Others hold that where the contract is for necessaries, this still does not make the contract enforceable on its terms. The minor may still disaffirm the contract. However, the adult party has a claim against the minor in quasi-contract for the reasonable value of the goods or services.

[handwritten margin note: quasi contract —]

The issue of whether goods or services are necessaries is tied to the question of whether a minor is emancipated. A minor becomes emancipated when his parents' duty of support terminates. This may occur where the minor moves out of his parents' home and lives independently of them. However, some courts see emancipation more narrowly, and confine it to specific situations such as marriage or enlisting in the military. If a minor is not emancipated and is entitled to support from his parents, it is difficult for the other party to claim that goods or services furnished to the minor were necessaries. However, this does not mean that emancipation in itself creates contractual capacity in the minor for all purposes. Rather, it just makes it more likely that a contract entered into by a minor for appropriate goods or services will qualify as a contract for necessaries.

■ PROBLEM 14.5

As mentioned above, some courts enforce a minor's contract for necessaries. Other courts will not enforce the contract but will allow the adult party relief in quasi-contract for the market value of goods or services delivered to the minor under the contract.

Minnie Minor, a 17-year old high school student, lives with her parents. She was flabby and out of shape, so she decided to join a gym. She entered into a one-year contract with Necessary Fitness, Inc., under which she had daily access to Necessary's gym equipment and training facilities for an initiation fee of $100 and a monthly membership fee of $30. The contract states that the one-year membership cannot be cancelled, and that the member is not entitled to a refund of the initiation fee and is obliged to pay the monthly membership fee for the contract period, whether or not she uses the gym.

Minnie paid the initiation fee and her first month's membership fee and used the gym conscientiously every morning for two weeks. She then got bored with all that exercise and stopped going. She did not pay her second month's membership fee. When Necessary sent her a bill demanding payment, she cancelled her membership. Necessary claims that she is not entitled to do that and must pay the $30 each month for the rest of the year's membership period.

Necessary and other gyms allow non-members to buy a daily pass which allows them to use the gym's facilities for a day. Gyms charge between $5 and $10 for daily passes. Necessary's daily pass costs $10. It is well accepted that lack of physical exercise is detrimental to health and that exercising at a gym is an efficient way of getting beneficial physical activity.

(a) Does the gym membership qualify as a necessary?

(b) What are the legal consequences if it is a necessary? What are they if it is not?

5. Restitution on Disaffirmance

We see in Chapter 13 that restitution usually goes hand-in-hand with rescission, so that where a party avoids a contract on grounds of fraud or improper bargaining, each party has a cause of action in unjust enrichment for the return of any performance (or its value) that she rendered to the other under the contract. Where a minor's contract is not for a necessary and she disaffirms the contract, the approach to restitution is much more muddled and conflicting. All courts agree that the major party is required to restore to the minor any benefit he has received from the contract. They also agree that the minor is obliged to restore to the major party any property that she received under the contract and still possesses. For example, say that the minor buys a motorbike from a major for $3,000 and pays cash on delivery of the bike. The court finds the bike not to be a necessary and permits the minor to disaffirm the contract. The minor is entitled to restitution of the $3,000 that she paid, and the seller is entitled to return of the bike.

However, matters become more complicated if the minor no longer has the bike (say, because it was destroyed in an accident), or its value is greatly diminished (say, because it was damaged in an accident or has depreciated as a result of use and the passage of time). In such a situation, the traditional approach is to confine the minor's restitutionary obligation to the return of whatever contractual benefit she still retains at the time of disaffirmance. If the bike has been destroyed, the minor would owe nothing. If she still had the bike, she would be obliged to return it in its damaged or depreciated state, but would not be required to compensate the major for any loss in value. The rationale for confining the minor's liability to the return of what she still possesses is the policy of protecting a minor from improvident contracts and of discouraging adults from contracting with minors.

Under the traditional approach, the minor would also not be liable to pay the major party for services that the major has rendered that are, by their nature, intangible and incapable of being returned. For example, in *Webster Street Partnership*, cited in Section D.4 above, the court held that upon disaffirmance of the lease, the major party had to repay to the minors the entire amount of rent and the security deposit received under the lease. However, the minors had no obligation to pay anything to the lessor for the value of occupying the apartment up to the time of disaffirmance.

The traditional approach places the strongest emphasis on protecting the minor and allocates all the risk of contracting with a minor on the adult party. It does not hold the minor accountable for his conduct. This may be appropriate where the adult has taken advantage of the minor, but it is harder to justify where the contract was on fair terms and the minor received an economic benefit, such as the right to occupy an apartment, as in *Webster Street Partnership*, or the right to use the bike, as in our example. Some courts recognize this and are more inclined to hold the minor responsible for compensating the major party for the value of the benefit received. However, there is no clear and consistent trend away from the traditional rule. In addition, because a minor below the age of contractual capacity may be old enough to be liable in tort, a minor who commits fraud or who damages property negligently or willfully could incur tort liability, even if immune from restitutionary liability.

E INCAPACITY BASED ON MENTAL ILLNESS OR DEFECT

\ voidable by the incompetent party

As we have seen, the law presumes that a minor lacks contractual capacity. In most cases this presumption is, in effect, conclusive—the other party is not given the opportunity to rebut it by evidence that the minor was competent to enter a contract. By contrast, an adult is presumed to have contractual capacity. This presumption is rebuttable—a mentally incompetent party may overturn the presumption by evidence that establishes that she lacked contractual capacity at the time of entering the transaction. The burden of proving lack of capacity is on the person alleging it. The crucial time for measuring incapacity is the time of contracting. Of course, many mental disorders are long lasting or permanent, so that evidence of mental illness prior to or subsequent to that time may be relevant. However, the impairment must be shown to have existed at the time of contracting.

lacked mental capacity at the time of entering the contract

As in the case of a minor, the purpose of incapacity doctrine is the protection of a person who lacks the ability to act rationally in her own interests. Therefore, most courts treat incapacity as rendering the contract voidable by the incompetent party, not void, so if the incompetent party chooses not to avoid the contract, it is binding, and her incapacity cannot be raised as a defense by the other party. Sometimes the mentally incompetent person herself seeks to avoid the contract, but often the claim of avoidance is made by her personal representative, such as a court-appointed guardian or her estate. If a mentally incompetent person recovers capacity after making the contract, she can ratify it.

avoidance is made by a representative

The protection of a mentally incompetent person from exploitation is a principal goal of incapacity doctrine. As in the case of minors, a mentally incompetent person does not necessarily need to show that the contract is unfair or exploitive. However, the policy of protecting a mentally incompetent person is not as absolute as that applicable to minors, so that the need to protect the mentally incompetent party is more carefully weighed against the need to protect the other party's legitimate reliance. Therefore, the absence or presence of improper conduct by the other party is often weighed in the balance when a court decides whether to allow avoidance of the contract. That is, in deciding whether a contract should be avoided on grounds of mental incapacity, courts usually take into account not only the degree and seriousness of the mental incompetence but also whether the vulnerability of the incompetent party attracted exploitation by the other. The older test for mental incompetence is known as the "cognitive test": At the time of contracting, the party must have had such a severe mental illness that she was unable to understand the nature and consequences of the transaction. This strict test of incapacity was

cognitive test: unable to understand the nature and consequences of the transaction

consistent with the emphasis of classic contract law on a firm objective test and the security of transactions. As we have moved away from the rigidity of the classicists and have gained further understanding of mental illness, many courts have broadened the test to include cases in which the party may have understood the transaction, but the mental illness affected her ability to act rationally in relation the transaction. This is sometimes referred to as the "motivational test" or the "volitional test." The Restatement, Second, adopts the more modern view and recognizes both the cognitive and motivational tests. However, the Restatement, Second, still distinguishes cognitive disorders from motivational ones, as Restatement, Second §15 shows:

RESTATEMENT, SECOND §15. MENTAL ILLNESS OR DEFECT

(1) A person incurs only voidable contractual duties by entering into a transaction if by reason of mental illness or defect

(a) he is unable to understand in a reasonable manner the nature and consequences of the transaction, or

(b) he is unable to act in a reasonable manner in relation to the transaction and the other party has reason to know of his condition.

(2) Where the contract is made on fair terms and the other party is without knowledge of the mental illness or defect, the power of avoidance under subsection (1) terminates to the extent that the contract has been so performed in whole or in part or the circumstances have so changed that avoidance would be unjust. In such a case a court may grant relief as justice requires.

———

Because an adult is presumed competent and a minor is presumed incompetent, the state of mind and the reasonable expectations of the other party play a greater role in mental incapacity than they do when minority is an issue. At least in theory, a person who contracts with a minor is placed on inquiry by the minor's youthful appearance, but a person who contracts with an adult is not generally expected to wonder if the party is able to make contracts. Therefore, the other party's knowledge or reason to know of the mental defect (gained either by knowledge of the incompetent's background or by observation during the transaction) is relevant to the incompetent's right to avoid the contract, or to the remedy available if avoidance is allowed. As Restatement, Second §15 indicates, the other party's reliance interest weighs less heavily where the incompetent party suffers from a cognitive disorder, not only because of the more severe impact of the illness on capacity, but also because illness on this scale is presumed to be much more obvious.

Mental incompetence may take many forms deriving from illness, injury, old age, or substance abuse.[5] It is important to distinguish incompetence generated by these mental impairments from incompetence in business or personal affairs. Mental incompetence cannot be used as a basis for avoidance merely because a person manages her affairs poorly or has acted foolishly, recklessly, or with bad judgment. Her conduct must be attributable to a psychiatrically recognized condition. This means that expert testimony in the form of psychiatric diagnosis is usually necessary to establish the basis for avoidance.

IN RE SEMINOLE WALLS & CEILINGS CORP.

366 B.R. 206 (2007)[6]
United States Bankruptcy Court, Middle District of Florida

JENNEMANN, Bankruptcy Judge.

Joseph Jasgur is a very talented photographer who mingled with and photographed Hollywood celebrities starting in the 1940's. One celebrity he photographed was Norma Jean Mortenson, more popularly known as Marilyn Monroe. Jasgur apparently took her first professional photographs, including the only photo that suggests she had six toes on one foot. His collection, however, is much more extensive, includes many Hollywood celebrities from the 1940-1950's, and, by all accounts, is very impressive (the "Jasgur Collection"). . . . Unfortunately, Mr. Jasgur's marketing and business expertise does not equal his photographic ability. For decades, Jasgur has tried to capitalize on his work, to largely no avail. He has associated with many potential purchasers and marketers for his photographs. One of these potential purchasers, PITA Corporation, is intertwined with the debtor in this Chapter 7 bankruptcy case. . . .

[Some years before the bankruptcy, the collection of photographs was acquired by PITA, a subsidiary of the Seminole, the bankrupt company. The bankruptcy trustee claimed that the collection was an asset of the estate, but Jasgur disputed the trustee's claim and asserted that he had never given up ownership of the collection. To settle this dispute over the ownership of the photographs, the trustee and Jasgur entered into a settlement agreement in

---

[5] Alcohol or drugs may well induce contractual incompetence. However, courts tend to be warier of this form of mental incapacity, especially if the incapacitated party had some control over the decision to drink or take drugs. As a result, courts usually require a very debilitating degree of intoxication as a basis of avoidance (recall *Lucy v. Zehmer* in Chapter 3) and are unlikely to give relief unless it is clear that the other party exploited the alcohol or drug-induced incapacity.

[6] The opinion was affirmed in part and reversed in part by the district court, *In re Seminole Walls & Ceilings Corp.*, 388 B.R. 38 (M.D. Fla. 2008) and 412 B.R. 878 (M.D. Fla. 2008). However, the appeals concerned issues of bankruptcy law and were unrelated to the issue of mental incompetence. —EDS.

sell the collection & split proceeds

January 2005. The agreement was amended by mutual consent in March 2005. When he executed the agreement and its amendment, Jasgur was represented by counsel. In essence, the settlement agreement provided that the trustee would sell the collection and the parties would share the proceeds.

One of the issues in this complex bankruptcy case was whether the settlement agreement was enforceable against Jasgur. Jasgur, represented by a guardian at the time of this litigation, sought to avoid the agreement on several grounds, including the ground that he was mentally incompetent at the time that he executed it. (The court found that Jasgur had the right to rescind the settlement agreement on other grounds, so it did not have to pass on his claim of mental incompetence. However, it did discuss the merits of that claim.)]

π claim ——

Stanonik, Jasgur's guardian, asserts that Jasgur was not competent to sign the settlement agreement with the trustee on January 14, 2005, or to sign the amended version on March 21, 2005. There is no issue that Jasgur was declared mentally incompetent on August 10, 2005, that he is elderly, age 87 at the trial date, [that he had a mini-stroke shortly after signing the agreement,] or that he recently was diagnosed with some serious medical conditions. Jasgur was placed into a nursing facility after he broke his hip on December 2, 2005. During his stay, the treating physician, Dr. Son L. Chau, issued his diagnosis, dated January 23, 2006, that Jasgur suffered from "hypertension, hyperlipidemia, cardiomegaly, remote history of prostate [sic] cancer, *a stroke in March 2005*, and Alzheimer's Type dementia." (emphasis added). However, other than Dr. Chau's reference to a stroke in March 2005, there is no evidence or even implication that Jasgur was not competent to sign the Amended Settlement Agreement.

Of course, Dr. Chau was not treating Jasgur from January through March 2005, and his reference to a stroke was not based on personal knowledge. Moreover, the date of the alleged stroke appears incorrect. Rather, the evidence suggests that, on January 2, 2005, Jasgur was briefly admitted to Orlando Regional Hospital for a possible "small-mini-stroke." One of Jasgur's acquaintances, Terry Mogavero, took him to the hospital because, during a telephone conversation, Jasgur was having some difficulty speaking. Ms. Mogavero also drove Jasgur home after he was released from the hospital on January 5, 2005. Jasgur was given a prescription for some expensive medication and was asked to return for a check-up and further tests in two months. Certainly, Ms. Mogavero noticed a change in Jasgur's behavior after his hospital visit; however, Jasgur returned to his apartment, continued to live alone, and appeared to resume his old life.

Determining a person's current mental capacity is difficult; however, determining a person's capacity *retroactively* is nearly impossible. To avoid a contract by reason of incompetency, there must be a showing that the party seeking to do so lacked the mental capacity to enter into a contract at the time of the transaction. It is the capacity of the individual at the time of execution that is controlling and subsequent incapacity will not affect the contract. The burden of proof of incompetency is on the party alleging it by a preponderance of the evidence. Mere weakness of mind is insufficient to set aside an agreement if the person had sufficient intelligence to understand the transaction and act upon his own free will. Feebleness of body does not create a presumption of incompetence nor authorize a court to set aside a contract.

This is particularly true in a situation such as this where Jasgur never led a conventional life. Jasgur made odd business deals, lived in filth, never had any money, and was always searching for someone to whom he could tell a new story or yarn to about his glory days in Hollywood. He was always on the brink of success and lived in a dream world that his early pictures of Marilyn Monroe would someday bring him the riches he believed himself due. He never demonstrated the ability to handle the everyday stresses of life—getting his groceries, paying his bills, storing his work, or hiring people to help him. Jasgur had operated that way for 50 years, and nothing really changed after the possible ministroke in January 2005, except he may have been a little more forgetful. As Jasgur's former wife, Debra Van Neste, described her life with Jasgur: "It was constantly drama. He constantly got involved with people that were very unsavory. Anybody that would talk to him, would become his new manager. I constantly had to clean house of his mistakes. He picked up some guy, a crack head, once and decided that he was going to be his manager. . . . He was always looking for the next big thing and somebody to take care of him." No medical or testimonial evidence in the record establishes that Jasgur was any less competent on January 12, 2005, than he was one year earlier, or, for that matter, ten years earlier.

Moreover, those closest to Jasgur acted the same way with him both before and after the possible mini-stroke. Jasgur was represented by very capable counsel at the time he signed the two settlement documents in January and March 2005. The settlement was heavily negotiated over several months by the lawyers. Small details were revised and amended. The attorneys believed the settlement was fair, and by their own correspondence, indicated that Jasgur supported the agreement in late March 2005. If they had any contemporaneous belief that Jasgur could not understand the terms of the settlement, or if they thought he was not competent to sign the agreement, the Court is confident that counsel of this caliber would not have allowed Jasgur to sign the agreement. Rather than prevent Jasgur from going forward, they supported him.

At the time the settlement was executed, Jasgur and his lawyers had kept Stanonik apprised of the terms of the agreement. Stanonik actively participated in the negotiation of the agreement, offering specific comments to include in the final version. Most significantly, on January 4, 2005, around the time of Jasgur's alleged stroke, Stanonik confirmed that Jasgur was "ambulatory and lucid and at home." In the very same e-mail, Stanonik went on to offer various final suggestions to the terms of the settlement. Obviously, Stanonik, at almost the exact date the settlement was signed, believed Jasgur was competent to sign the agreement and believed the agreement was in his best interest.

In addition, the circumstances surrounding the execution of the settlement documents, both in January and March, also indicate that Jasgur was competent to sign the agreement. During this period, an acquaintance, Tom Endre, was very helpful to Jasgur. He visited Jasgur frequently, drove him to meetings, and ran errands for him. Endre also helped relay numerous messages and communications from Jasgur's attorneys to Jasgur about the settlement and was familiar with the terms of the settlement. He also witnessed Jasgur signing the original and amended settlement agreements. Uniquely, Endre was one of the few witnesses who had no financial involvement with Jasgur or his photographs and had nothing to gain or lose by his testimony. In January, the trustee's counsel gave Endre a copy of the final version of the proposed settlement agreement. Endre went to Jasgur's apartment, and then drove Jasgur to the office of a nearby notary. Jasgur signed the settlement agreement before the notary on January 14, 2005. None of those present, neither the notary nor Endre, expressed any concern that Jasgur was acting oddly or appeared confused. All testimony supports a conclusion that Jasgur knew what he was signing and understood his actions on January 14, 2005. The same is true when he executed the amended settlement agreement at the building where the trustee's lawyers work. None of the witnesses to the execution of Jasgur's signature, which again included Endre, expressed any concern about his mental capacity. Indeed, Endre's testimony was that Jasgur asked questions about the terms of the agreement, understood the settlement, and definitely understood he was signing a legal compromise.

holding

In summary, no credible medical evidence supports a finding of Jasgur's incapacity in January through March 2005. His lawyers and friends treated him the same before and after the possible mini-stroke, recognizing that Jasgur always was a somewhat difficult and odd fellow. Moreover, nothing surrounding the execution of the settlement documents indicates that he did not understand what he was signing. As such, the Court concludes that Jasgur was mentally competent at the time he signed the original settlement agreement on January 14, 2005, as well as when he signed the amended agreement on March 21, 2005. . . .

■ QUESTIONS

Is this court's standard for avoidance equivalent to that of Restatement, Second §15? If not, how does it differ?

FARNUM v. SILVANO

27 Mass. App. 536, 540 N.E.2d 202 (1989)
Massachusetts Appeals Court

KASS, Justice.

On the basis of a finding that Viola Farnum enjoyed a lucid interval when she conveyed her house to Joseph Silvano, III, for approximately half its market value, a Probate Court judge decided that Farnum had capacity to execute

posture

the deed. A different test measures competence to enter into a contract and we, therefore, reverse the judgment. *2 — disposition*

We take the facts from the trial judge's findings. . . . When she sold her real estate in South Yarmouth on July 14, 1986, Farnum was ninety years of age. The sale price was $64,900. At that time, the fair market value of the property was $115,000. Indeed, at the closing, the buyer, Silvano, obtained a mortgage loan from a bank of $65,000. Silvano, age twenty-four, knew Farnum from mowing her lawn and doing other landscape work. Farnum trusted him and had confidence in him. Before entering into the transaction, Silvano had been put on notice of the inadequacy of the price he was going to pay. He had been warned not to proceed by Farnum's nephew, Harry Gove, who is now Farnum's guardian and is pressing this action for rescission on her behalf.

well below fair market value

Farnum's mental competence had begun to fail seriously in 1983, three years before she delivered a deed to the South Yarmouth real estate. That failure manifested itself in aberrant conduct. She would lament not hearing from sisters who were dead. She would wonder where the people upstairs in her house had gone, but there was no upstairs to her house. She offered to sell the house to a neighbor for $35,000. (He declined, recognizing the property was worth much more.) She became abnormally forgetful. Frequently she locked herself out of her house and broke into it, rather than calling on a neighbor with whom she had left a key (on one occasion, she broke and entered through a basement window). She hid her cat to protect it from "the cops . . . looking for my cat." She would express a desire to return to Cape Cod although she was on Cape Cod. She easily became lost. Payment of her bills required the assistance of her sister and her nephew, who also balanced her checkbook.

There were several hospitalizations during the three-year period preceding the conveyance in 1986. On May 2, 1985, a brain scan examination disclosed organic brain disease. By January, 1987, some six months after the conveyance, Farnum was admitted to Cape Cod Hospital for treatment of dementia and seizure disorder. She was discharged to a nursing home.

In connection with drawing the deed and effecting the transfer of real estate, Farnum was represented by a lawyer selected and paid by Silvano. That lawyer, and a lawyer for the bank which was making a loan to Silvano, attended the closing at Farnum's house. At the closing Farnum was, as the trial judge expressed it, "aware of what was going on." She was cheerful, engaged in pleasantries, and made instant coffee for those present. After the transaction, however, Farnum insisted to others—her sister and nephew, for example—that she still owned the property. That may have been consistent with Farnum's ambivalence about giving up her home and going to a nursing home. It was not unusual, the judge concluded, for Farnum to be perfectly coherent and "two minutes later" be confused. When she signed the deed, "she was coherent or in a lucid interval."

she could be lucid when she signed

Acting during a lucid interval can be a basis for executing a will. "[A] person of pathologically unsound mind may possess testamentary capacity at any given time and lack it at all other *times.*" *Daly v. Hussey*, 275 Mass. 28, 29, 174 N.E. 916

[handwritten margin note: know the nature, consequences and quality of transaction]

(1931). Competence to enter into a contract presupposes something more than a transient surge of lucidity. It involves not merely comprehension of what is "going on," but an ability to comprehend the nature and quality of the transaction, together with an understanding of its significance and consequences. From a testator we ask awareness of the natural objects of bounty. The choice among those objects may be seen by others as arbitrary, but arbitrariness or capriciousness may be allowed a donor. In the act of entering into a contract there are reciprocal obligations, and it is appropriate, when mental incapacity, as here, is manifest, to require a baseline of reasonableness.

... [T]he synthesis of those principles now appear[s] in the Restatement (Second) of Contracts §15(1) (1981), which regards as voidable a transaction entered into with a person who, "by reason of mental illness or defect *[handwritten margin note: restatement]* (a) ... is unable to understand in a reasonable manner the nature and consequences of the transaction, or (b) ... is unable to act in a reasonable manner in relation to the transaction and the other party has reason to know of [the] condition." Applied to the case at hand, Farnum could be aware that she was selling her house to Silvano for much less than it was worth, while failing to understand the unreasonableness of doing so at a time when she faced serious cash demands for rent, home care, or nursing home charges. That difference between awareness of the surface of a transaction, i.e., that it was happening, *[handwritten margin note: need more than surface understanding]* and failure to comprehend the unreasonableness and consequences of the transaction by a mentally impaired person was recognized and discussed in an opinion for the court by Judge Breitel, in *Ortelere v. Teachers' Retirement Bd.*, 25 N.Y.2d 196, 202-206, 303 N.Y.S.2d 362, 250 N.E.2d 460 (1969). In the *Ortelere* case, a teacher who was enrolled in a retirement plan suffered a psychotic break. Her age was sixty and she also suffered from cerebral arteriosclerosis. While thus afflicted, Grace Ortelere changed her selection of benefit to choose the maximum retirement allowance payable during her lifetime with nothing payable after her death—this in the face of severely diminished life expectancy and her husband having given up his employment to care for her full time. The court observed that "her selection of a 'no option' retirement while under psychiatric care, ill with cerebral arteriosclerosis, aged 60, and with a family in which she had always manifested concern, was so unwise and foolhardy that a factfinder might conclude that it was explainable only as a product of psychosis." A major factor in the court's decision was that the retirement board "was, or should have been, fully aware of Mrs. Ortelere's condition."

On the basis of the trial judge's findings, we think Farnum did not possess the requisite contextual understanding. She suffered mental disease which had manifested itself in erratic and irrational conduct and was confirmed by diagnostic test. Her physician did not think she was competent to live alone. Relatively soon after the transaction, Farnum's mental deficits grew so grave that it became necessary to hospitalize her. The man to whom she sold her property for less than its value was not a member of her family or someone who had cared for her for long duration. Silvano's explanation that he gave Farnum the additional consideration of agreeing to let her stay in the house for some time after the closing is unpersuasive, as the purchase and sale agreement and the deed are silent about any such agreement. Farnum was not represented by a lawyer who knew her and considered her over-all interests as a primary concern. The mission of the lawyer secured by Silvano, and paid by him, was to effect the transaction. As we have observed, Farnum faced growing cash demands for her maintenance, and, in her circumstances, it was not rational to part with a major asset for a cut-rate price.

The decisive factor which we think makes Farnum's delivery of her deed to Silvano voidable was his awareness of Farnum's inability to act in a reasonable manner. See Restatement (Second) of Contracts §15(l)(b). Silvano knew or had reason to know of Farnum's impaired condition from her conduct, which at the times material caused concern to her relatives, her neighbors, and her physician. Silvano was aware that he was buying the house for about half its value. He had been specifically warned by Farnum's nephew about the unfairness of the transaction and Farnum's mental disability.

In view of our conclusion that Farnum lacked the capacity to enter into contractual arrangements for the sale of her house, we need not and do not consider the arguments of fraud, undue influence, and constructive trust which Farnum has advanced. Farnum is entitled to rescission of the conveyance. Silvano shall deliver a deed to the real estate in question to Farnum's guardian in his capacity as such, in return for the consideration paid by Silvano. The object of rescission is to arrive so far as possible at full restoration of the status quo before the transaction which is being cancelled. In achieving rescission, it is appropriate to give account to the value of possessing or the rental value of the real estate from July 14, 1986, to the date a revised judgment is entered. Consideration must be given to accounting for benefits which the claimant for rescission (i.e., Farnum) may have received, e.g., taxes paid on the real estate. Generally, consideration ought not to be given to any improvements in the property which Silvano may have made, because they were not requested by the plaintiff, or to Silvano's mortgage payments. When a defendant-buyer wrongly acquires real estate and rescission is ordered, it does not appear, on a review of the cases, that interest is generally required to be paid on the returned purchase price, although we do not hold that so to order would go beyond the discretion of a trial judge who is framing an order designed to effect a fair restoration of the status quo. The judgment is vacated, and the case is remanded to the Probate Court for the entry of a judgment of rescission consistent with this opinion.

■ QUESTIONS

(1)   Unlike Jasgur, Farnum was able to rescind the contract on grounds of mental incompetence. Are the different results explicable on the basis of factual differences between the cases? If so, what are the determinative distinguishable facts?

(2)   Although it is not clear how much Silvano knew about Farnum's mental condition, the sense of exploitation is strong. He was warned off the transaction by Farnum's nephew, and it is easy to infer that Silvano knew of Farnum's mental frailty before the sale. He surely knew that he was getting a great deal on the house. However, assume that he did not have a clue that there was anything wrong with Farnum, who was always pleasant and friendly when he came over to do the landscaping. One day she told him that she was moving into a nursing home and planned to sell the house for $100,000. Silvano offered her $90,000, and she accepted. Silvano had no contact with Farnum's nephew, and the sale closed. Would Farnum (represented by her nephew as guardian) be able to avoid the sale under these circumstances?

(3)   Should Farnum's incapacity be classified as cognitive or motivational? Does your answer to the previous question depend on how her incapacity is classified?

(4)   The court indicates that Farnum's lawyer was selected and paid by Silvano. Do you think that the lawyer, apparently representing both parties in this transaction, acted properly? Would it be possible for a lawyer to act properly under these circumstances?

■ PROBLEM 14.6

Farnum's nephew, who was appointed as her guardian at the time of suit, brought this action for rescission on her behalf. The opinion does not indicate how Farnum herself felt about the suit, or if she even had enough comprehension to form a view. Add the following embellishment to the facts of the case:

Although 90 years old and a longtime sufferer from dementia, Farnum was very fond of Silvano, who had taken care of her yard for the past ten years. He always took time to talk to her, was solicitous about her health, and often did little extra things to help her. Farnum was lonely. She had no friends left and was not very close to her only living relative, her nephew, who came to see her infrequently. In July 1986 she decided to get rid of her house and to move into an assisted-living establishment. She had enough money from savings and her pension to pay for this and to support herself, so she decided to offer the house to Silvano for half its value. She did this deliberately, realizing that the price was very low, but wishing to do something nice for her gardener and friend, who could afford to pay no more. Silvano accepted the offer, forming a contract.

When her nephew heard about this, he moved for a court order appointing him as Farnum's guardian. He established her incompetence by expert psychiatric evidence and was appointed. He instituted suit for rescission on Farnum's behalf against Silvano. The court ordered rescission based on psychiatric evidence similar to that set out in the opinion. Although mentally ill, Farnum knows what is going on, and she is very upset about the rescission. She really did want Silvano to have the house for half its value. Under these circumstances, has the incapacity doctrine protected her interests? If not, whose interests did it serve?

In *Farnum v. Silvano*, Farnum's right of avoidance was subject to Silvano's right of restitution. She had to restore Silvano to the status quo by refunding the price, adjusted as the court prescribed. What would have happened if she had spent all the proceeds of the sale on nursing care and living expenses and therefore was not able to return the price? In contrast to a minor, a major party who seeks avoidance of a contract on grounds of mental incapacity must generally restore the consideration that she received under the contract as a condition of avoidance. However, a court does have the equitable discretion to vary this rule where the other party knew or had reason to know of the incompetency, he acted in bad faith in taking advantage of the incompetent party, and the incompetent party is no longer able to make restitution. This was the resolution reached by the court in *Hauer v. Union State Bank of Wautoma*, 192 Wis. 2d 576, 532 N.W.2d 456 (Wis. App. 1995). Under an agreement with Ms. Hauer, the bank lent her $30,000, secured by shares that Ms. Hauer owned in a mutual fund. The bank knew that the purpose of the loan was to enable Ms. Hauer to invest the proceeds in the questionable business venture of another customer of the bank who was in financial difficulty. The bank had also been told by Ms. Hauer's stockbroker that she needed income from the mutual fund for living expenses and that she had suffered brain damage in an accident. The third party later became bankrupt and Ms. Hauer lost her investment. The court avoided the loan agreement on grounds of mental incompetence and granted restitution of the collateral to Ms. Hauer. However, it did not require her to make restitution of the loan amount to the bank because the bank had reason to suspect her mental disability and it violated its obligation of good faith in entering into the contract with her.

CHAPTER 15

Contract Interpretation and Construction

A | **THE CONTENT OF CONTRACTUAL OBLIGATIONS**

In this chapter, we focus on the methods courts use to discern and establish the content and meaning of a contract. What commitments, precisely, did the parties make to each other? Even if the parties admit they have a contract, they may disagree as to the nature and extent of their respective obligations. If the parties ask a court to resolve their dispute, the court often must choose among conflicting conceptions of what the contract requires. If the court is unable to do so in a manner that is reasonable or fair, it may decline to enforce the contract altogether.

We will see that themes developed earlier in the materials carry forward into this chapter. The intentions of the parties remain central to the inquiry. However, the objective theory of contracts demands that the court focus not on what the parties actually intended, or even what they actually understood their contracting partners to intend, but rather on what a reasonable party would have expected under the circumstances. Just as courts often look to surrounding circumstances to discern the reasonable expectations of the parties when they determine whether a contract has been formed, they often interpret the intended meaning of that contract in light of the context in which it was made, as well. Because this is to some extent a hypothetical inquiry, it adds a level of abstraction to the exercise that can be somewhat difficult to grasp.

There are other connections to materials we have already studied. Where relations between parties are informal, they may dispute whether those relations gave rise to a contract at all. As we saw in earlier chapters, even if the words and actions of the parties suggest a mutual intention to be bound, a court must also be persuaded that the parties have agreed to sufficiently definite terms before a contract will be deemed to exist. If the circumstances surrounding the parties' interactions are compelling enough, a court may find a reasonable basis for providing a remedy even in the absence of clearly articulated contract terms. If the court is unable to ascertain the terms of the parties' agreement at all, however, it will decline to enforce the agreement as a contract. Thus the question of whether a contract exists at all under these circumstances is directly related to the question of what the terms of that contract might be.

Even if both parties concede that a contract exists, they still may dispute what that contract obliges each of them to do. Often, the analysis of the scope and content of contractual obligations starts with an examination of the words the parties used in reaching agreement and the reasonable expectations such words might have engendered. The conduct of the parties may help to establish the outlines of their contractual relationship, as may other circumstances surrounding the transaction. Each party may have an interpretation that favors its own interests. To bolster its interpretation, each party may offer writings, testimony as to oral conversations and other actions, and other circumstantial evidence of contract meaning. As in all litigation, contract law must provide a mechanism for juggling various sources of evidence that are potentially unreliable or conflicting.

As we will see, if the parties sign a writing to memorialize the terms of their agreement, the words in that writing play a critical role in establishing the parties' respective obligations. In Chapter 16, we examine the parol evidence rule, which sometimes prohibits the consideration of evidence that would contradict or supplement a written agreement. But even the most explicit written terms, formally agreed by both parties, can appear vague, ambiguous, or uncertain in retrospect. To apply them, a court must still determine what they mean. Contextual evidence may provide some guidance as to what the parties might have intended when they used the words and phrases at issue.

The agreement of the parties, whether established by words, conduct, or other circumstances, may be incomplete. Sometimes parties may not have considered explicitly certain aspects of their relationship. As we have seen, if the missing terms go to the essence of the transaction, a court may conclude that the parties have not agreed to sufficiently definite terms to afford a reasonable basis for a remedy and may decline to enforce the contract altogether. However, in appropriate cases, courts may be willing to extrapolate from any explicit agreement and add terms the parties probably intended but did not clearly express. At other times, courts construe contracts to include certain terms, even though the words and conduct of the parties do not suggest that the parties intended or even considered such terms. To resolve the disputes before them, the courts invoke default rules of law to fill gaps in the parties' agreements.

The process of discerning the meaning reasonably intended by the parties to a contract is referred to as "interpretation." The process of determining the legal consequences of the parties' agreement is typically called "construction." An example may help to illustrate the concepts of interpretation and construction. You may recall the case of *Wood v. Lucy, Lady Duff-Gordon* from our study of consideration. In that case, the court found that an implied term of the contract required Mr. Wood to use his best efforts in marketing Lady Duff-Gordon's designs. Without some sort of obligation like this, the court concluded that the exclusive dealings contract would not have served any useful purpose to Lady Duff-Gordon. Left open in the case was precisely what efforts would have been required of Mr. Wood. If called upon to answer this question, the court might have scrutinized the dealings between the parties to determine whether there was any evidence of how extensive they intended their obligations to be. The search for the actual intent manifested by the parties—whether they expressed it clearly, they showed it through their conduct, or other circumstances pointed to it—would be the process of interpretation. If instead the court determined the parties' obligations by reference to background rules of law or by determining what was fair, just, or otherwise required by relevant public policies, the court would have engaged in the process of construction. Although interpretation and construction are closely related and perhaps are ultimately inseparable, we will introduce principles of contract interpretation first and will follow with principles of construction.

In unusual cases where a court cannot resolve the dispute over the meaning of a contract term by the processes of interpretation and construction, the court may invoke the doctrine of "misunderstanding." This doctrine applies where the parties manifested apparent assent to the same language but have materially different understandings of what the language means, and the court cannot use objective criteria to favor one party's understanding over the other's. In these situations a court may conclude that, despite appearances to the contrary, there is no contract to enforce. This doctrine has some connections to the materials in Chapter 7 on incomplete and indefinite agreements, but also has its own distinct flavor. We close the chapter with a discussion of this doctrine and the circumstances under which courts might apply it.

B INTERPRETATION

1. Sources of Contract Meaning

The Restatement, Second, and the UCC both take a highly contextual view of contract interpretation. Restatement, Second §202 states that "words and other conduct are interpreted in the light of all the circumstances. . . ." UCC 1-201 defines "agreement" broadly to mean "the bargain of the parties in fact, as found in their language or inferred from other circumstances . . ." and "contract" to mean "the total legal obligation that results from the parties' agreement. . . ." So we should expect courts to refer to the context of the transaction to interpret what obligations the parties intended to assume. However, the means of discovering this contextual evidence can be uncertain and contentious.

■ PROBLEM 15.1

Assume you represent Green Cheese Co., a company that produces "hormone free" organic cheese. Your client calls you to tell you about a problem it has been having with its distributor. For the last ten years, it has worked with Sustainable Supply Inc. to distribute its cheese to high-end grocery stores. Although the parties have never reduced the terms of their relationship to a written agreement, Green Cheese Co. delivers its entire production of cheese each month to Sustainable Supply Inc., along with an invoice for the cost of the cheese. Until recently, Sustainable Supply Inc. paid each of the invoices within thirty days of receipt. Last year, your client noticed that Sustainable Supply Inc. was getting slower in its payments, and soon over six months' worth of invoices remained unpaid. Although your client attempted to resolve the situation with Sustainable Supply Inc., it was unsuccessful. It recently started delivering its cheese to Reliable Distribution Co. instead.

Your client would like you to file suit against Sustainable Supply Inc. to recover the amount of its unpaid invoices. What facts do you think you would have to establish at trial to recover the sums your client seeks? How would you go about locating the evidence you might need in order to establish those facts?

■ PROBLEM 15.2

Assume you represent Sustainable Supply Inc. in the controversy described in Problem 15.1. Your client tells you that its practice has always been to pay Green Cheese Co.'s invoices as soon as it sells a given delivery of cheese to high-end grocery stores. Grocery stores have been placing fewer orders for the cheese over the last year, so it has taken Sustainable Supply Inc. longer and longer to pay Green Cheese Co. as a result. Sustainable Supply Inc. has heard through the grapevine that Green Cheese Co. has been selling its cheese to grocery stores through other channels, and it speculates that this may be one reason the grocery stores have reduced their orders of late.

Your client believes it has not breached its agreement with Green Cheese Co., and instead Green Cheese Co. has violated its understanding with your client by working with other distributors. What facts do you think you would have to establish at trial to make out your client's arguments? How would you go about locating the evidence you might need in order to establish those facts?

Once the parties present a broad range of evidence of what they meant (or reasonably understood each other to mean) when they entered a contract, a court may well discover that the evidence is in conflict. From these conflicting clues, a court (with appropriate help from a jury) must try to patch together a picture of the parties' agreement that is credible and coherent and allows for resolution of the dispute. One of the functions of contract law is to determine what types of clues are relevant and how conflicts among them are to be resolved. In the case of conflicting evidence, both the Restatement, Second, and the UCC give some guidance as to what evidence is likely to be the most probative of the parties' reasonable expectations. Consider for instance Restatement, Second §§202 and 203, set out below. Pay particular attention to the types of circumstances that the Restatement, Second, deems relevant to contract interpretation, and the hierarchy it establishes among conflicting indications of meaning.

RESTATEMENT, SECOND §202. RULES IN AID OF INTERPRETATION

(1) Words and other conduct are interpreted in the light of all the circumstances, and if the principal purpose of the parties is ascertainable it is given great weight.

(2) A writing is interpreted as a whole, and all writings that are part of the same transaction are interpreted together.

(3) Unless a different intention is manifested,

(a) where language has a generally prevailing meaning, it is interpreted in accordance with that meaning;

(b) technical terms and words of art are given their technical meaning when used in a transaction within their technical field.

(4) Where an agreement involves repeated occasions for performance by either party with knowledge of the nature of the performance and opportunity for objection to it by the other, any course of performance accepted or acquiesced in without objection is given great weight in the interpretation of the agreement.

(5) Wherever reasonable, the manifestations of intention of the parties to a promise or agreement are interpreted as consistent with each other and with any relevant course of performance, course of dealing, or usage of trade.

RESTATEMENT, SECOND §203. STANDARDS OF PREFERENCE IN INTERPRETATION

In the interpretation of a promise or agreement or a term thereof, the following standards of preference are generally applicable:

(a) an interpretation which gives a reasonable, lawful, and effective meaning to all the terms is preferred to an interpretation which leaves a part unreasonable, unlawful, or of no effect;

(b) express terms are given greater weight than course of performance, course of dealing, and usage of trade, course of performance is given greater weight than course of dealing or usage of trade, and course of dealing is given greater weight than usage of trade;

(c) specific terms and exact terms are given greater weight than general language;

(d) separately negotiated or added terms are given greater weight than standardized terms or other terms not separately negotiated.

Of note are three concepts introduced by Restatement, Second §§202 and 203: course of performance, course of dealing, and usage of trade. The UCC also uses these concepts and expands upon them. The following UCC section explains these concepts in some detail. Notice that the UCC establishes a hierarchy similar to that of the Restatement, Second:

UCC 1-303. COURSE OF PERFORMANCE, COURSE OF DEALING, AND USAGE OF TRADE

(a) A "course of performance" is a sequence of conduct between the parties to a particular transaction that exists if:

(1) the agreement of the parties with respect to the transaction involves repeated occasions for performance by a party; and

(2) the other party, with knowledge of the nature of the performance and opportunity for objection to it, accepts the performance or acquiesces in it without objection.

(b) A "course of dealing" is a sequence of conduct concerning previous transactions between the parties to a particular transaction that is fairly to be regarded as establishing a common basis of understanding for interpreting their expressions and other conduct.

(c) A "usage of trade" is any practice or method of dealing having such regularity of observance in a place, vocation, or trade as to justify an expectation that it will be observed with respect to the transaction in question. The existence and scope of such a usage must be proved as facts. If it is established that such a usage is embodied in a trade code or similar record, the interpretation of the record is a question of law.

(d) A course of performance or course of dealing between the parties or usage of trade in the vocation or trade in which they are engaged or of which they are or should be aware is relevant in ascertaining the meaning of the parties' agreement, may give particular meaning to specific terms of the agreement, and may supplement or qualify the terms of the agreement. A usage of trade applicable in the place in which part of the performance under the agreement is to occur may be so utilized as to that part of the performance.

(e) Except as otherwise provided in subsection (f), the express terms of an agreement and any applicable course of performance, course of dealing, or usage of trade must be construed whenever reasonable as consistent with each other. If such a construction is unreasonable:

(1) express terms prevail over course of performance, course of dealing, and usage of trade;

(2) course of performance prevails over course of dealing and usage of trade; and

(3) course of dealing prevails over usage of trade.

(f) Subject to Section 2-209 and Section 2A-208, a course of performance is relevant to show a waiver or modification of any term inconsistent with the course of performance.

(g) Evidence of a relevant usage of trade offered by one party is not admissible unless that party has given the other party notice that the court finds sufficient to prevent unfair surprise to the other party.

The next case describes a 20-year relationship that proceeded largely on the basis of a handshake. When the relationship broke down, the parties disputed one of the central terms of that relationship—that is, what payment was due for the services provided by one of the parties. In reviewing an award of summary judgment for the defendant, the court surveys a broad array of circumstances that the parties put forward to establish the terms of their agreement. As you read this case, try to isolate the various types of circumstances the court discusses. Assuming evidence of each of them was presented at trial, judge for yourself how probative you think that evidence should be in determining the reasonable expectations of the parties.

TERRY BARR SALES AGENCY, INC. v. ALL-LOCK COMPANY, INC.

96 F.3d 174 (1996)
United States Court of Appeals, Sixth Circuit

MARTIN, Circuit Judge.

Terry Barr Sales Agency appeals the district court's award of summary judgment in favor of All-Lock Company on its breach of contract claim. Believing that the oral agreement between the parties did not include a commitment by All-Lock to pay commissions to Terry Barr Sales after the termination of the parties' agency agreement, the district court awarded summary judgment in favor of All-Lock from the bench after a hearing. Because genuine issues of material fact exist as to whether All-Lock is bound to pay commissions to Terry Barr Sales after termination of the parties' relationship, we reverse.

Terry Barr Sales is a sales representative company based in Detroit. All-Lock is a corporation engaged in the manufacture of locks and latches for automobiles with its corporate headquarters in New Jersey and its main manufacturing plant in Alabama. Terry Barr, the president of Terry Barr Sales, and Ron Hermann, the president of All-Lock, entered into an oral agency agreement in 1973. Under the agreement, Terry Barr Sales made sales to, and/or obtained orders from, automobile manufacturers for the purchase of All-Lock's locks and latches for use in new automobiles. In exchange for this service, Terry Barr Sales, which in effect is a manufacturer's representative, received a commission on sales to these "original equipment" customers, which included Ford, General Motors, and Chrysler.

The commission rate for new business was three and one-half percent of total sales. In addition, at the time the parties entered into the agreement, All-Lock had some pre-existing sales that it previously had serviced in-house. Terry Barr Sales agreed to service this "inherited" business at a two percent commission rate. Over the years, the parties' relationship proved mutually financially beneficial. Terry Barr Sales received significant commissions for sales made to "original equipment" customers, and All-Lock's sales to those customers increased dramatically. By 1992, Terry Barr Sales had obtained purchase orders for All-Lock to supply locks and latches for the entire General Motors "Saturn" automobile line.

Sometime after this, and for no explained reason in the record, All-Lock decided to terminate Terry Barr Sales as its manufacturer's sales representative. In March of 1994, Ron Hermann met with Terry Barr at an airport hotel in Detroit and informed him that All-Lock was terminating Terry Barr Sales on the "latch" product line. All-Lock was, however, retaining Terry Barr Sales on its lock and switch accounts. Terry Barr's deposition testimony reveals that the parties' dispute concerning commissions began at that meeting in Detroit. When Hermann informed Barr that All-Lock was terminating Terry Barr Sales on the latch product line, Barr indicated his belief that Terry Barr Sales was due commissions on continuing orders for the "life of the part."[1] Hermann, however, responded that All-Lock was willing to pay commissions only for ninety days after termination of the agency relationship. Soon thereafter, Mike Smith, the vice-president at Terry Barr Sales, sent a letter to All-Lock which stated that:

> At this time we must request that All-Lock abide by the standards of our industry regarding the relationship between manufacturers and their representatives and

---

[1] "Life of the part" commissions are apparently a fairly common practice in the manufacturer's representative business. As we explained in *Kingsley Assoc., Inc. v. Moll PlastiCrafters, Inc.*, 65 F.3d 498, 502 n. 5 (6th Cir. 1995), sales representatives commonly insist on "life of the part" provisions in agency contracts "because the sales representative must invest a great deal of time, effort, and money in securing an initial sale." However, after an initial sale is made, "the buyer may continue to use the part in the manufacture of its automobiles for many years." *Id.*

pay us life of the part commissions on current business, as well as life of the part commissions on all programs we started that are sourced to All-Lock within 12 months of termination.

The parties dispute the import of this letter. Terry Barr Sales claims it was simply a reaffirmation of its position that it was due commissions on all sales procured by Terry Barr Sales for the "life of the part." All-Lock claims that Terry Barr Sales threatened to refuse to work on the lock and switch accounts it retained, and that this letter is evidence of Terry Barr Sales attempt to force All-Lock into a new agreement providing for "life of the part" commissions. In any event, the parties communicated back and forth over the next few months, with settlement negotiations eventually grinding to a halt. Terry Barr Sales then filed the instant lawsuit.

Terry Barr Sales filed suit against All-Lock on May 6, 1994 in the district court, asserting claims for its commissions based on breach of contract, unjust enrichment, and promissory estoppel theories. Terry Barr Sales also sought relief pursuant to Section 2961 of Michigan's Revised Judicature Act, Mich. Comp. Laws §600.2961, which allows for the recovery of treble damages for the intentional failure to pay commissions. Perhaps as a defensive maneuver in reaction to Terry Barr Sales' complaint, All-Lock subsequently filed suit against Terry Barr Sales in New Jersey, alleging that Terry Barr Sales breached the parties' oral agreement by performing poorly. The cases were consolidated in the Eastern District of Michigan.

After the parties conducted limited discovery, they filed cross motions for summary judgment on Terry Barr Sales' complaint. After a hearing on the motions, the district court awarded summary judgment from the bench in favor of All-Lock. The court found that a contract existed between the parties. The court then orally dismissed Terry Barr Sales' claims based on [unjust enrichment, promissory estoppel and statutory grounds.] . . . The court then dismissed Terry Barr Sales' claim that the parties' oral agreement included an obligation to pay commissions after termination of the agency relationship. . . . We review the district court's award of summary judgment de novo. Summary judgment is appropriate where there exists no genuine issue of material fact and the moving party is entitled to summary judgment as a matter of law. . . .

Before turning to the merits, we believe it appropriate to express our strong disapproval of the district court's decision to award summary judgment in favor of All-Lock without providing this Court with a written explanation of its reasoning. Instead, the district court simply entered judgment "for the reasons stated on the record in open Court on May 8, 1995." A written explanation of the district court's reasoning would have been extremely helpful for review in this case. This is particularly true where, as here, a district court awards summary judgment notwithstanding the parties' conflicting assertions of contractual intent, apparently rejecting contrary evidence introduced by the plaintiff in awarding summary judgment for the defendant. It is beyond dispute that, when confronted with a motion for summary judgment, the district court cannot make credibility determinations, weigh the evidence, or draw inferences from the facts. All evidence presented by the non-moving party is to be taken as true. When the non-moving party appears to have proffered evidence in support of its position and the district court yet awards summary judgment against the non-moving party, our review of the district court's conclusion that no genuine issue of material fact remains is difficult, if not impossible, without a clear, written explanation by the district court judge explaining his or her reasons for awarding summary judgment. With this said, we turn to the merits.

All-Lock's summary judgment motion required the district court to determine whether a genuine issue of material fact existed as to whether the parties intended post-termination commissions to be a term included in their original agreement. A court's primary responsibility in interpreting a contract is to "effectuate the intent of the parties, if ascertainable." *Ford Motor Co. v. Northbrook Ins. Co.*, 838 F.2d 829, 832 (6th Cir. 1988) (quoting *William C. Roney & Co. v. Federal Ins. Co.*, 674 F.2d 587, 590 (6th Cir. 1982)). In contract actions, summary judgment may be appropriate when the documents and/or evidence underlying the contract are undisputed and there is no question as to intent. Normally, however, disputed issues of contractual intent are considered to be factual issues which preclude an award of summary judgment.

Here, for the purposes of summary judgment, the parties do not dispute that a contract existed. However, they vigorously dispute whether post-termination commissions were included as a term of the original agreement. The prevailing rule in Michigan, as stated by the state's supreme court is that, "where an express [oral] contract is entered into between the parties, but they differ as to the terms thereof, and there is evidence tending to support the claim of each of them, it is for the jury to determine what the terms of the contract were. . . ." *Biagini v. Mocnik*, 369 Mich. 657, 120 N.W.2d 827, 828 (1963) (quoting *Geistert v. Scheffler*, 316 Mich. 325, 25 N.W.2d 241, 242 (1946)). In addition, the rule in Michigan governing disputed post-termination commissions is set forth in the seminal case of *Reed v. Kurdziel*, 352 Mich. 287, 89 N.W.2d 479, 482-83 (1958):

> The relationship between agent or broker and principal being a contractual one, it is immediately apparent that whether an agent or broker employed to sell personalty on commission is entitled to commissions on sales made or consummated by his principal or by another agent depends upon the intention of the parties and the interpretation of the contract of employment, and that, as in other cases involving interpretation, all the circumstances must be considered.

The court then further explained:

> It would appear that underlying all the decisions is the basic principle of fair dealing, preventing a principal from unfairly taking the benefit of the agent's or broker's services without compensation and imposing upon the principal, regardless of the type of agency or contract, liability to the agent or broker for commissions for sales upon which the agent or broker was the procuring cause, notwithstanding the sales

may have been consummated by the principal himself or some other agent. In Michigan, as well as in most jurisdictions, the agent is entitled to recover his commission whether or not be [sic] has personally concluded and completed the sale, it being sufficient if his efforts were the procuring cause of the sale. In Michigan the rule goes further to provide if the authority of the agent has been canceled by the principal, the agent would nevertheless be permitted to recover the commission if the agent was the procuring cause.

Here, the parties dispute whether they intended for post-termination commissions to be a term of their oral agreement. Nothing in the record indicates that the parties discussed this issue when Hermann and Barr formed the oral contract at their initial meeting in 1973. Hermann testified at his deposition that Terry Barr Sales was to receive a commission on "all sales to original equipment customers." However, Hermann also stated somewhat opaquely that it was his understanding that "when you work you were paid." All-Lock points to this statement as evidence that the parties did not intend for post-termination commissions to be a part of their agreement. Terry Barr testified as to the terms of the parties' agreement that:

> [I]t certainly was not all that involved. Ron's thing was we didn't need an agreement, a handshake was good enough. I mean, he's been saying that for years and years and I—that's fine with me. It was based upon the circumstances, it was—I would get a commission on parts, that I would take over some commission on parts that were already existing and new parts and I'd get a commission on the parts.

Barr also stated that the parties did not discuss the issue of post-termination commissions. All-Lock claims that this shows that post-termination commissions were not part of the original deal.

All-Lock also claims that the parties' course of performance establishes that post-termination commissions were not included in the agreement. Michigan law provides that the parties' practical interpretation of their contract, and their course of conduct under that contract, are entitled to great weight in interpreting ambiguous provisions of the contract. *Ford Motor Co.*, 838 F.2d at 832; *Detroit Greyhound Employees Federal Credit Union v. Aetna Life Ins. Co.*, 381 Mich. 683, 167 N.W.2d 274, 275-76 (1969). Focusing on several situations in which Terry Barr Sales did not request post-termination commissions after accounts were canceled, All-Lock claims that this establishes that the parties never contemplated the payment of these commissions. However, much of the force of this argument is reduced by Terry Barr Sales' explanation of the situations. In two of the situations in which Terry Barr Sales did not demand post-termination commissions, valued employees and close friends of Terry Barr sought to split off from Terry Barr Sales and work independently, with Terry Barr's blessing. Terry Barr actually set up one former employee in an office across the hall from Terry Barr Sales. In addition, Terry Barr allowed the employees to take one account each from the All-Lock line with them. While it is true that each former employee received the commissions for those accounts, they did so with Terry Barr's approval. All-Lock did not cause Terry Barr Sales to lose these accounts. In fact, All-Lock continued to send the commission checks to Terry Barr Sales, and the checks were then forwarded to the former employees by Terry Barr Sales.

The other canceled accounts that allegedly establish that the parties did not contemplate post-termination commissions were actually for products produced by General Automotive Specialty, All-Lock's parent company, and apparently the sales and commissions for those lines were insignificant. Terry Barr gave deposition testimony that the amount of commissions that would have been received on those accounts did not warrant the effort involved in attempting to obtain them. Taking the evidence in a light most favorable to Terry Barr Sales, Terry Barr's explanation of the circumstances involved when these accounts were canceled further supports our conclusion that a genuine issue of material fact remains suitable for trial in this case.

All-Lock also points to the fact that Terry Barr Sales received commissions on inherited business at the inception of the contract. This fact, according to All-Lock shows that the parties could not have contemplated post-termination commissions. Under its theory of the case, the agent that was the "procuring cause" of those accounts should have gotten the commissions on those deals. All-Lock argues that the fact that Terry Barr Sales received commissions on those inherited accounts indicates that Terry Barr Sales knew it would not receive post-termination commissions. This argument is not conclusive either. All-Lock does not dispute that the inherited accounts had previously been handled in-house, which refutes the notion that some other agent had been the procuring cause of the sales. Further, Terry Barr received a reduced two percent commission in exchange for taking over the servicing of these accounts, as opposed to the three and one-half percent commission it received on new business. This difference in the amount of commissions received by Terry Barr Sales between inherited and new business at the inception of the contract undermines All-Lock's claim that Terry Barr Sales' acceptance of inherited business establishes that the parties did not contemplate post-termination commissions to be a term of their agreement.

In support of its claim that post-terminations commissions were part of the deal, Terry Barr Sales points to Terry Barr's statements when Hermann terminated the agreement. Barr's deposition testimony stated:

> When Ron Hermann met me at the airport in Detroit here to tell me that he was terminating us and he asked me at that time, I told Ron life of the part. He told me 90 days, and I said something not very complimentary about it and I said Ron, life of the part. I don't know the exact sentence structure, but that's what he heard.

Terry Barr Sales also relies on the letter sent soon thereafter by Mike Smith, which asked All-Lock to "abide by the standards of our industry" and pay life of the part commissions as an indication that the parties believed that post-termination commissions were part of the original agreement. All-Lock, on the other hand, characterizes this letter as an attempt to renegotiate the original agreement to include "life of the part" commissions. We, of course, need not decide this issue. We simply note that the probative weight and effect of this letter is yet another disputed issue rendering this case unsuitable for summary judgment.

Finally, each party points to various other pieces of evidence in support of its claim, alternatively characterizing each piece as either supporting or refuting the notion that post-termination commissions were included as a term in their original agreement. As is usually the case, obstructing a quick resolution of the issue is the parties' tendency to take snippets of testimony out of context, refer to small portions of documents that, when read alone, seem to support their positions, and generally to construct a story out of the facts that borders on falsity. Nevertheless, whatever the ultimate outcome, this case is particularly ill-suited for resolution at the summary judgment stage. Whether post-termination commissions were or were not part of the parties' original intent, Terry Barr Sales certainly has introduced evidence to create a genuine issue of material fact. Only by viewing the facts in a light favorable to All-Lock could the district court conclude that summary judgment was appropriate. Accordingly, we will reverse the district court's award of summary judgment in favor of All-Lock, and remand for further proceedings. . . .

■ QUESTIONS

(1) Suppose that at trial, neither party introduced any evidence of interactions between the parties other than those surveyed here. In the absence of additional evidence, do you think the circumstances described here would be sufficient to support a finding that the parties' reasonable expectations included the payment of "life of the part" commissions? Why or why not?

(2) Of the circumstances surveyed by the court, which of them consist of words allegedly exchanged by the parties? Were those words exchanged before the contract was entered, contemporaneously with its formation, or after formation? How does timing affect the credibility or evidentiary weight of these communications?

(3) Do any of the circumstances surveyed by the court allege the existence of relevant course of dealing, course of performance, or usage of trade? How persuasive, if true, do you find these allegations?

(4) Terry Barr Sales claimed (and the court seemed to acknowledge) that "life of the part" commissions are a common feature of relationships among manufacturers and their sales representatives. If true, this may constitute some evidence of the existence of a relevant usage of trade. The existence and scope of usages of trade are often subject to significant dispute. Professor Bernstein researched the efforts of a number of closely knit industries, including

the hay, grain, and feed and textiles and silk industries, to codify their trade practices in writing.[2] She found that in many cases sharp disagreement about industry practices existed, and often the parties were unable to agree on a generally applicable standard. As a result, she concluded that the incorporation of usages of trade as a matter of course into contract obligations was problematic. From your own experience, can you think of a practice that you think constitutes a usage of trade? If so, how definite and widespread is it? In your view, how definite and widespread should such a usage be before a court consults it as a source of contract meaning?

2. Interpretation of Written Agreements

As the materials in Section B.1 suggest, parties do not always express their contractual intentions in writing, and when they do, they may do so in a casual or incomplete way. This approach may be in accord with commercial norms and may preserve cordial relations among the parties at the outset. If, however, the parties subsequently dispute the existence or terms of the contract between them, any resulting litigation may prove highly fact-specific and incapable of cheap or easy resolution. To diminish the possibility of disputes about the existence or terms of their contract, the parties may elect to memorialize their agreement in a writing adopted by both. The law affords a special status to written expressions of agreement, as we explain in Chapter 16. (As Chapter 16 shows, sometimes, to determine the scope of the parties' intended obligations, courts rely exclusively on the written memorials, and bar altogether evidence of agreements that are not reflected in the writing.) But even relatively formal written agreements can pose interpretive problems for a court. Both parties may agree that the written agreement expresses their intentions but may dispute what specific words or phrases in the agreement mean.

When faced with such an interpretive dispute, most courts consider the unambiguous language of the agreement to be conclusive of the parties' reasonable expectations. If the language is unambiguous on a certain matter, no further evidence of the meaning of the parties' agreement as to that matter is necessary or appropriate. However, if the language is ambiguous—that is, reasonably susceptible to more than one meaning—the fact-finder (the jury, or in the absence of a jury, the judge) may consult contextual evidence to guide its interpretation of the written agreement. So interpretation of a written agreement involves, at least in theory, two stages.[3] In the first stage, the judge

---

[2] Lisa Bernstein, *The Questionable Empirical Basis of Article 2's Incorporation Strategy: A Preliminary Study*, 66 U. Chi. L. Rev. 710 (1999).

[3] We say in theory here, because not all courts are as surgical in their division as we suggest. There is significant diversity in how courts approach contract interpretation issues, as we will see in the cases and discussion that follow. Nevertheless, as a generalization, the description is accurate in most jurisdictions under many if not all circumstances, and thus provides a useful framework for analysis.

decides whether the writing is unambiguous, and if it is, the judge interprets the parties' agreement to consist of the unambiguous meaning expressed in the writing. If the writing is ambiguous, the court progresses to the second stage: the jury (or the judge, as the case may be) determines which of the possible meanings is the most reasonable in context.

Courts are in disagreement as to the proper way to approach the first stage of this analysis—that is, the determination of whether the language of the writing is unambiguous. Traditionally, courts adopted a "plain meaning" approach to this question. In determining whether the language is unambiguous, a court following the plain meaning approach would attempt to discern the usual sense of the words used in the writing, as understood by a reasonable person. The judge might consult dictionaries, his or her own intuitions, or general rules and standards of interpretation, but generally, if the meaning of the writing appeared clear and unambiguous on its face, that's where the inquiry would end. The facts and circumstances surrounding the transaction were not to inform the decision at all. Further, interpreting the meaning of words in a written agreement was generally considered to be a "lawyerly" task—one best left to the judge rather than to the jury. Unless the writing was ambiguous on its face, whether the language adequately captured the actual intentions of the parties (as demonstrated by evidence other than the writing itself) was irrelevant.

As legal realism began to influence classical contract theory, some courts began to take a more textured and open approach to the initial determination of ambiguity. If contract law is all about effectuating the intentions of the parties, and if credible evidence suggests that the parties may have used words to express something other than their conventional meanings, some courts concluded that the plain meaning approach might do violence to the parties' expectations. These courts reasoned that further inquiry into the facts and circumstances surrounding the transaction might be appropriate to discern the parties' actual intentions when they used certain words or phrases. As a consequence of this line of thought, courts in some states rejected the pure plain meaning approach and allowed judges to consider circumstances outside the written agreement to determine whether the written agreement was ambiguous or unambiguous, even if the language of the agreement at first glance appeared to be clear. This approach, sometimes called the "contextual" approach to contract interpretation, has become the dominant approach in some jurisdictions, while the plain meaning approach persists at least to some degree in others.

The "contextual" approach rests on the intuition that ambiguities in an agreement may become apparent only when the language is read in context. Relevant contextual evidence, sometimes called "extrinsic" or "parol" evidence, might be drawn from a course of dealing between the parties, relevant usages of trade, or a course of performance under the written agreement in question. Relevant contextual evidence might also consist of oral or written communications before the written agreement was adopted by the parties or discussions surrounding the execution of the written agreement itself. Although the ultimate credibility of this evidence might be up to the fact-finder to decide, if a "contextual" court is persuaded that there is at least a question of fact as to what the parties intended the words of their agreement to mean, the court will consider the language to be ambiguous even if it appears clear on its face.

In recent years, some scholars have questioned the desirability of a contextual approach to the initial determination of ambiguity.[4] Because these scholars advocate a widespread return to the plain meaning approach of classical contract law, they are often called "neoformalists." The neoformalists have suggested that the contextual approach undermines the very certainty and predictability written agreements are designed to achieve. Even if the plain meaning approach may do violence to the actual intentions of the parties in individual cases, these scholars argue, the contextual approach has the potential to do the same. As any fact-based interpretation may require reconstruction of past circumstances based on incomplete and disputed evidence, the contextual approach does not necessarily guarantee that the litigation will reveal the "true" agreement of the parties. Further, the contextual approach has the added disadvantage of allowing extended factual inquiry, which may add to the expense and duration of the litigation. Sophisticated parties might prefer a system that allows for clear and easy resolution of disputes. In business disputes in particular, these scholars argue, the plain meaning approach should prevail.

Whether a court applies a pure plain meaning approach or a more contextual one, it is typically up to the judge to decide whether a given word or phrase in a written agreement is unambiguous. Because early cases tended to apply the plain meaning approach, courts determined whether a particular word or phrase was unambiguous without resorting to factual evidence. As a result, whether a writing was unambiguous was not considered a factual issue, and therefore it was appropriate for the judge to resolve it. Only if the judge considered the writing to be ambiguous was the jury involved in determining the reasonable expectations of the parties under the circumstances. It is thus sometimes said that interpretation of an unambiguous writing is a question of law, whereas interpretation of an ambiguous one is a question of fact. This distinction generally survives, even in jurisdictions that allow judges to consult extrinsic factual evidence in the initial determination of whether a writing is unambiguous.

As you read the next case, catalog the various techniques the court uses to determine what the written agreement requires. Which rely on the style or content of the writing itself? To what extent is the court willing to consult facts extrinsic to the writing?

---

[4] A seminal article in this vein is Alan Schwartz & Robert E. Scott, *Contract Theory and the Limits of Contract Law*, 113 Yale L.J. 541 (2003). This article has inspired a spate of academic commentary, both in disagreement with the authors' theories and in support.

RIGHT FIELD ROOFTOPS, LLC v. CHICAGO BASEBALL HOLDINGS, LLC

87 F. Supp. 3d 874 (2015)
United States District Court, Northern District of Illinois

KENDALL, District Judge.

A few things are inevitable when it comes to spring baseball at Wrigley Field: the ivy won't be green, the weather won't be warm, there will be many who say, "This is the year," and there will be a battle between the Chicago Cubs and the rooftop businesses that surround Wrigley Field. This spring is no different. The decades-old battle began back in the late 1990s and came to a head in 2002 when the Cubs sued certain Rooftop owners for misappropriating the Cubs' property rights by selling tickets to patrons to watch Cubs games from the Rooftops. Rather than having a judge resolve that matter on the law at that time, the parties opted to settle their differences. On January 27, 2004, the Cubs (who were then owned by the Chicago Tribune) entered into an agreement (the "License Agreement") that permitted the Rooftops to continue their business of wining and dining fans on the rooftops of various buildings surrounding Wrigley Field while viewing, albeit at a significant distance, the baseball game being played within the Friendly Confines. The License Agreement in its simplest terms required the Rooftops to give the Cubs 17% of their profits and in return, the Cubs agreed not to erect any barricades that would block the long-distance viewing of the game from across the street. There was, however, one clause within the License Agreement that permitted the Cubs to have an "expansion" of Wrigley Field if that expansion was approved by a "governmental authority." Therein, lies the rub. The Cubs, under the new ownership of the Ricketts family, are working to make THIS year the year, and in doing so, have received a government-issued permit to update the Friendly Confines with electronic signs and video boards that will entirely block the views of the field from the Rooftop clients. The Rooftops have cried foul and want the signs down, or they assert they will be put out of business entirely. The Cubs instead claim that their move is fair and within the expected understanding of the parties when they entered into the License Agreement eleven years ago. . . . [The Rooftops also argue that the Cubs have engaged in anti-competitive practices in violation of the antitrust laws.]

The ultimate dispute hinges on both contract and antitrust claims. Because the Court finds that the Cubs did not breach the 2004 License Agreement and . . . [that there has been no violation of the antitrust laws], the Court denies the Rooftops' Motion for Preliminary Injunction primarily because the Rooftops have no likelihood of success on the merits. . . . [We include only the Court's discussion of the proper interpretation of the 2004 License Agreement and omit discussion of the other claims.]

On January 20, 2015, Plaintiffs . . . brought a nine-count Complaint against Defendants, Chicago Cubs Baseball Club, LLC, Wrigley Field Holdings, LLC,

Chicago Baseball Holdings, LLC, and Thomas Ricketts, alleging a host of claims stemming from the Cubs' intention to install a "jumbotron" video board and billboard signage over the right field bleachers at Wrigley Field. The Rooftops sit on Sheffield Street in Chicago, Illinois, directly across the street from Wrigley Field. They sell tickets to patrons wishing to watch Cubs baseball games and other events, like concerts, occurring in Wrigley Field. The Rooftops contend that the construction will deprive them of their business. . . . [The Plaintiffs sought a temporary restraining order and a preliminary injunction enjoining the Cubs from installing the video board and any other signage. In a prior proceeding, the Court denied the Plaintiffs' motion for a temporary restraining order, a short-term pre-trial remedy often referred to as a "TRO." A TRO is only occasionally available during the pendency of the lawsuit, and among other things, the party seeking it must demonstrate a strong likelihood of ultimate success in the lawsuit, which the Court concluded the Plaintiffs had not yet established. In this opinion, the Court considers (and denies) the Plaintiffs' motion for a preliminary injunction, concluding that the Plaintiffs still had not established a likelihood of success on the merits of its claim. For purposes of the preliminary injunction, the facts (as presented in filings which comprise over 1,500 pages) are largely undisputed.]

The Rooftops control two buildings and businesses that sell tickets to view Cubs baseball games and other events taking place within Wrigley Field. . . . Since Wrigley Field's construction in 1914, spectators on the roofs of the buildings across the street on Sheffield enjoyed a view into Wrigley Field. Starting in the 1980s, owners of the buildings began to turn their roofs into grandstands for spectators and in 1998, the City of Chicago enacted an ordinance formally allowing the rooftop businesses to operate for profit. By 2002, there were eleven rooftop businesses operating for profit by selling tickets to patrons who wanted to watch Cubs games and other events from the roofs. The City designated Wrigley Field as a landmark on February 11, 2004, adopting the prepared Landmark Designation Report and limiting future alterations to Wrigley Field. Throughout the City's landmark process beginning in 2000, the Cubs expressed an intention to expand the Wrigley Field bleachers which they did in 2005.

Before the beginning of the 2002 Major League Baseball season, the Cubs installed a large green windscreen above the outfield bleachers. The windscreen negatively impacted views from the rooftop businesses across Sheffield. The Cubs proceeded to file suit against a number of the rooftop businesses on December 16, 2002, claiming that the rooftop businesses were misappropriating the Cubs' property by charging admission fees to watch Cubs games from the roofs. Before the start of the 2004 baseball season, the parties to the 2002 litigation reached a settlement leading to a contract (the "License Agreement") in which the rooftop businesses agreed to pay the Cubs a royalty of seventeen percent of their gross revenues in exchange for views into Wrigley Field until December 31, 2023. The License Agreement contains a number of provisions establishing protocol for the expansion of Wrigley Field, its potential effect on any rooftop business, and consequences:

6. Wrigley Field bleacher expansion.

    6.1 If the Cubs expand the Wrigley Field bleacher seating and such expansion so impairs the view from any Rooftop into Wrigley Field such that the Rooftop's business is no longer viable unless it increases the height of its available seating, then such Rooftop may in its discretion elect to undertake construction to raise the height of its seating to allow views into Wrigley Field and the Cubs shall reimburse the Rooftop for 17% of the actual cost of such construction.

    6.2 If the Cubs expand the Wrigley Field bleacher seating and such expansion so impairs the View from any Rooftop into Wrigley Field such that the Rooftop's business is no longer viable even if it were to increase its available seating to the maximum height permitted by law, and if such bleacher expansion is completed within eight years from the Effective Date, then if such Rooftop elects to cease operations . . . the Cubs shall reimburse that Rooftop for 50% of the royalties paid by that Rooftop to the Cubs. . . .

    6.4 If the Cubs expand the Wrigley Field bleacher seating and such expansion impairs the view from any Rooftop into Wrigley Field such that the Rooftop's Gross Revenue in the year of expansion is more than 10% below the average Gross Revenue for that Rooftop in the two years prior to expansion . . . then the affected Rooftop can seek a reduction in the Royalty rate for all subsequent years of the Term. . . .

    6.5 Nothing in this Agreement limits the Cubs' right to seek approval of the right to expand Wrigley Field or the Rooftops' right to oppose any request for expansion of Wrigley Field.

    6.6 The Cubs shall not erect windscreens or other barriers to obstruct the views of the Rooftops, provided however that temporary items such as banners, flags, and decorations for special occasions, shall not be considered as having been erected to obstruct views of the Rooftops. Any expansion of Wrigley Field approved by governmental authorities shall not be a violation of this Agreement, including this section.

The Cubs added approximately 1,790 seats to the bleachers of Wrigley Field after the 2005 baseball season.

The integral time period for the instant lawsuit is from 2009 onward. In the Fall of 2009, the Ricketts family and controlled entities purchased 95% of the Cubs and acquired Wrigley Field from the Tribune Company, subject to the preexisting Rooftop License Agreement. Soon after, the Cubs began to acquire ownership interests in a number of the rooftop businesses. The Cubs unsuccessfully attempted to purchase all of the rooftop businesses before beginning any construction. In early 2010, the Cubs announced plans to install a "Toyota" billboard in left field, which Ricketts said "[would not] affect any rooftops."

In late 2011 and early 2012, the Cubs began to lobby the City for approval of a number of Wrigley Field renovations, including bleacher seating expansion, an outfield sign package, and two video boards. On April 15, 2013, the Cubs announced the renovation plan would include a 6,000 square foot video board in left field and a 1,000 square foot billboard in right field. The Cubs released an illustration of the intended construction on May 28, 2013 to all the rooftop business owners and the illustration showed that the rooftop businesses would be largely blocked by the construction.[5] After many meetings and public hearings over the course of two years, where a number of rooftop businesses appeared and objected to the proposed construction, the Chicago Plan Commission, City Council, and Commission on Chicago Landmarks approved the Cubs' plan, including the construction of the bleachers, video boards, and billboards. The City approved the Cubs final plan to construct a total of eight outfield signs above the bleachers, including a video board in both left and right field. . . . As it currently stands, the Cubs are placing the right field video board directly in front of the Rooftops, while the Cubs-owned rooftop businesses are left unobstructed.

. . . As the Court stated in its opinion denying the Rooftops' motion for TRO, "it may be possible that with further briefing and analysis under the preliminary injunction hearing . . . one interpretation of that contract will prevail." Such is the case. Armed with the License Agreement, briefs, and arguments from the parties, the Court concludes that the Rooftops have not established a likelihood of success on the merits on their breach of contract claims. . . .

Because the parties entered into a twenty-year License Agreement and there are eight years left under that agreement, the Rooftops allege that the Cubs have breached the License Agreement because once the video board in right field goes up this Spring, the Cubs will have erected a barrier that they promised they would not for at least the duration of the License Agreement.[6] . . . The issue, therefore, is whether the Cubs have a contractual duty not to erect the video board that will block the Rooftops view into Wrigley Field.

Subsection 6.6 of the License Agreement provides that "any expansion of Wrigley field approved by governmental authorities shall not be a violation of this Agreement." The Rooftops concede that the proposed video board has been approved by a governmental authority, namely the Landmark Commission. Therefore, the Rooftops' position hinges on whether or not the video board constitutes "any expansion" for which governmental approval is a bulwark against breach.

The "cardinal rule" of contract construction is to give effect to the intent of the parties to the contract. The Court "must initially look to the language of [the] contract alone, as the language, given its plain and ordinary meaning, is the best indication of the parties' intent." *Gallagher v. Lenart*, 226 Ill. 2d 208, 314 Ill. Dec. 133, 874 N.E.2d 43, 58 (2007). "[B]ecause words derive their meaning from the context in which they are used, a contract must be construed as a whole, viewing each part in light of the others." *Id.* Only if the contractual language is

---

[5] A July 2014 rendering similarly showed that the signage approved for right field would substantially block the Rooftops.

[6] The Plaintiffs' claim is one of anticipatory repudiation, that is, a manifestation by one party to a contract of an intent not to perform its contractual duty when the time comes. If a plaintiff successfully makes out a claim for anticipatory repudiation, generally it is entitled to immediate remedies for breach, even though the time for performance had not yet arrived and so no failure to perform had yet occurred. We study anticipatory repudiation in Chapter 19.—EDS.

ambiguous may the Court look outside the contract to determine the parties' intent. Language is ambiguous if it is susceptible to more than one meaning.

Reading Section 6 as a whole, as the Court must, the Court concludes that "any" means "every or all." See, e.g., *Owens v. McDermott, Will & Emery*, 316 Ill. App. 3d 340, 249 Ill. Dec. 303, 736 N.E.2d 145, 154 (2000) (defining any). "Expansion," as confirmed by the word's plain meaning and its context within the License Agreement, means any change to Wrigley Field that adds volume or mass, including the addition of components unrelated to seating capacity. Section 6 confirms this definition. That Section 6 of the License Agreement is titled "Wrigley Field bleacher expansion" does not limit the phrase "any expansion" in Subsection 6.6 to projects that add seating capacity to the bleachers. In fact, by modifying "expansion" with the word "any," it actually distinguishes it as a different form of expansion. The Court must not attempt to divine the intent of the parties "from detached portions of [the] contract or from any clause or provision standing by itself." *Gallagher*, 314 Ill. Dec. 133, 874 N.E.2d at 58. When read as a whole, Section 6 contemplates forms of "Wrigley Field bleacher expansion" that add neither square footage nor seating capacity to the stadium. Subsection 6.1, for example, provides for reimbursement "[i]f the Cubs expand the Wrigley Field bleacher seating. . . ." Subsection 6.5 allows the Cubs to seek and the Rooftops to oppose "the right to expand Wrigley Field." Subsection 6.6 provides the circumstances under which the Cubs may "not erect windscreens or other barriers." If Section 6 were limited only to expansions that increased seating capacity, the variations in subject matter of each of the subsections would be unnecessary and illogical. Subsection 6.1 would not need to specify that it applied to seating expansions. The Section 6.6 provision related to windscreens would not belong in Section 6 at all because it plainly has nothing to do with seating capacity or area. Thus, while the four corners of the License Agreement limit the definition of expansion to expansion in the bleacher area of Wrigley Field, the term encompasses expansions that do not add seating capacity to the stadium.

The Court may also look to dictionary definitions to determine the plain and ordinary meaning of the term "expansion." The Oxford English Dictionary defines "expansion" as "the action or process of causing something to occupy or contain a larger space, or of acquiring greater volume or capacity[.]" This definition, as well as the dictionary definitions provided by both parties, is consistent with the Court's construction described above. Expansions above the outfield wall, such as windscreens, barriers, and video boards, cause Wrigley Field to occupy a larger space and add to the volume of the stadium.

The final clause of Section 6.6 further confirms the Cubs' construction. Again, the relevant sentence as a whole reads: "Any expansion of Wrigley Field approved by governmental authorities shall not be a violation of this Agreement, including this section." The preceding sentences of Subsection 6.6 discuss "windscreens or other barriers." Windscreens and barriers, needless to say, are not bleachers and do not increase the seating capacity or bleacher area of Wrigley Field. If "any expansion" were limited to construction projects that increased Wrigley Field's seating capacity, or even structural expansions, it would be unnecessary to specify that windscreens and other barriers were subject to the governmental approval exception. The Rooftops' construction, therefore, renders the final clause of Subsection 6.6 mere surplusage. See *Land of Lincoln Goodwill Indus., Inc. v. PNC Fin. Servs. Grp., Inc.*, 762 F.3d 673, 678 (7th Cir. 2014) (rules of contract interpretation include "goal of giving meaning to all provisions of the contract and avoiding an interpretation that renders any provision or term surplusage").

At oral argument, the Rooftops for the first time asked the Court to read ambiguity into the word "any expansion." The Rooftops argue that the Court should consider extrinsic evidence of intent in order to define the term "expansion." The Court declines to read ambiguity into a clause where there is none. See *In re Airadigm Comms., Inc.*, 616 F.3d 642, 664 (7th Cir. 2010) ("We will not bend the language of a contract to create an ambiguity where none exists[.]") (quoting *Chicago Bd. of Options Exch. v. Conn. Gen. Life Ins. Co.*, 713 F.2d 254, 258 (7th Cir. 1983)). When read together with the balance of the License Agreement's language, the meaning of "any expansion" in Subsection 6.6 is clear and unambiguous.

Extrinsic evidence, though, confirms that the Court's construction does not lead to an absurd result. The Rooftops argue that the Court's construction of "any expansion" would give the Cubs "carte blanche to obstruct the Rooftop Businesses' views into Wrigley Field merely by obtaining . . . a finding from the Landmark Commission that a proposed sign did not violate Wrigley Field's Landmark status." The Rooftops are correct that with Landmark Commission approval, the Court's construction provides great leeway to the Cubs to expand the bleacher area at Wrigley Field.

Before this dispute, the Rooftops, experienced business and real estate owners, were most likely comforted by the landmark status that had been imposed on Wrigley Field which limited future alterations without governmental approval. Even if they can somehow assert now that the governmental process was not as onerous as they had anticipated, such an understanding does not give reason to read ambiguity into the License Agreement. Nor have the Rooftops introduced any evidence that they were tricked or fooled into the License Agreement; nor could they, having spent years litigating the matter and finally entering into the Agreement after long negotiations monitored by a federal magistrate judge. Certainly, the Landmark Designation Report cited to "the varying height of the bleachers" and the "views of the surrounding townhouses" as important criteria that rendered Wrigley Field worthy of Landmark status back in 2004. Again, a savvy business owner would think that the video board proposed here clearly alters those features, and therefore might assume that no expansion would be approved. Bottom line, they were wrong. The Landmarks Commission approved the Cubs' proposed construction. Indeed, Subsection 6.5 of the License Agreement reserves for both the Cubs and the Rooftops the ability to advocate to governmental authorities for or against the propriety of expansion. The parties contemplated the uphill battle that the Cubs faced in obtaining approval from the Landmark Commission and, with the "any expansion" language of Subsection 6.6, delegated substantial control of Wrigley Field to governmental authorities. Though the Rooftops may now wish that the License Agreement provided them greater power over the height of Wrigley Field's outfield walls, "no court can rewrite a contract to provide a better bargain to suit one of the parties." *Owens*, 249 Ill. Dec. 303, 736 N.E.2d at 149; see also *S. Fin. Group, LLC v. McFarland State Bank*, 763 F.3d 735, 743 (7th Cir. 2014) ("Except in the most extraordinary circumstances, [courts] hold sophisticated parties to the terms of their bargain."). The Court therefore concludes that the Rooftops have not demonstrated a likelihood of success on the merits on their contract claim to warrant injunctive relief. . . .

■ QUESTIONS

(1) What interpretation of the clause at issue do the Plaintiffs advance in this case and why? Under the contract language, what would the result be if the court had accepted the Plaintiffs' proffered meaning?

(2) This opinion can be seen as an example of the plain meaning approach to contract interpretation. Where, precisely, does the court articulate what the plain meaning approach requires and why?

(3) At one point the court tells us that the Rooftops urged the court to consult extrinsic evidence to define the term "expansion." The court refuses to do so, stating that it declines to read ambiguity into a clause where there is none. Speculate about what evidence the Rooftops might have wanted to put before the court. Assuming the Rooftops had been able to locate evidence to bolster their interpretation of the License Agreement, in your view would it be better policy for a court to consider it, or to ignore it altogether?

■ PROBLEM 15.3

The court in the *Right Field Rooftops* case ultimately sides with the Defendants' interpretation of the clause at issue. Nonetheless, the Plaintiffs argued that the clause was ambiguous, based on the language used, the placement of that language, and possibly other factors. How would you redraft the language of the License Agreement to express unambiguously the interpretation favored by the Plaintiffs? Alternatively, how would you change the language to make it even clearer that the clause should be interpreted as the Defendants suggest?

As we noted previously, some courts have rejected use of the plain meaning approach to determine if a written agreement is unambiguous. Justice Traynor's discussion in the following case is one of the most famous opinions to have done so.

PACIFIC GAS & ELECTRIC CO. v. G.W. THOMAS DRAYAGE & RIGGING CO.

69 Cal. 2d 33, 442 P.2d 641, 69 Cal. Rptr. 561 (1968)
California Supreme Court

TRAYNOR, Chief Justice.

Defendant appeals from a judgment for plaintiff in an action for damages for injury to property under an indemnity clause of a contract.

In 1960 defendant entered into a contract with plaintiff to furnish the labor and equipment necessary to remove and replace the upper metal cover of plaintiff's steam turbine. Defendant agreed to perform the work "at (its) own risk and expense" and to "indemnify" plaintiff "against all loss, damage, expense and liability resulting from . . . injury to property, arising out of or in any way connected with the performance of this contract." Defendant also agreed to procure not less than $50,000 insurance to cover liability for injury to property. Plaintiff was to be an additional named insured, but the policy was to contain a cross-liability clause extending the coverage to plaintiff's property.

During the work the cover fell and injured the exposed rotor of the turbine. Plaintiff brought this action to recover $25,144.51, the amount it subsequently spent on repairs. During the trial it dismissed a count based on negligence and thereafter secured judgment on the theory that the indemnity provision covered injury to all property regardless of ownership.

Defendant offered to prove by admissions of plaintiff's agents, by defendant's conduct under similar contracts entered into with plaintiff, and by other proof that in the indemnity clause the parties meant to cover injury to property of third parties only and not to plaintiff's property. Although the trial court observed that the language used was "the classic language for a third party indemnity provision" and that "one could very easily conclude that . . . its whole intendment is to indemnify third parties," it nevertheless held that the "plain language" of the agreement also required defendant to indemnify plaintiff for injuries to plaintiff's property. Having determined that the contract had a plain meaning, the court refused to admit any extrinsic evidence that would contradict its interpretation.

When a court interprets a contract on this basis, it determines the meaning of the instrument in accordance with the ". . . extrinsic evidence of the judge's own linguistic education and experience." (3 *Corbin on Contracts* (1960 ed.) (1964 Supp. §579, p. 225, fn. 56).) The exclusion of testimony that might contradict the linguistic background of the judge reflects a judicial belief in the possibility of perfect verbal expression. (9 *Wigmore on Evidence* (3d ed. 1940) §2461, p. 187.) This belief is a remnant of a primitive faith in the inherent potency and inherent meaning of words.

The test of admissibility of extrinsic evidence to explain the meaning of a written instrument is not whether it appears to the court to be plain and unambiguous on its face, but whether the offered evidence is relevant to prove a meaning to which the language of the instrument is reasonably susceptible. A rule that would limit the determination of the meaning of a written instrument to its four-corners merely because it seems to the court to be clear and unambiguous, would either deny the relevance of the intention of the parties or presuppose a degree of verbal precision and stability our language has not attained.

Some courts have expressed the opinion that contractual obligations are created by the mere use of certain words, whether or not there was any intention to incur such obligations.[7] Under this view, contractual obligations flow, not from the intention of the parties but from the fact that they used certain magic words. Evidence of the parties' intention therefore becomes irrelevant. In this state, however, the intention of the parties as expressed in the contract is the source of contractual rights and duties. A court must ascertain and give effect to this intention by determining what the parties meant by the words they used. Accordingly, the exclusion of relevant, extrinsic evidence to explain the meaning of a written instrument could be justified only if it were feasible to determine the meaning the parties gave to the words from the instrument alone.

If words had absolute and constant referents, it might be possible to discover contractual intention in the words themselves and in the manner in which they were arranged. Words, however, do not have absolute and constant referents. "A word is a symbol of thought but has no arbitrary and fixed meaning like a symbol of algebra or chemistry...." (*Pearson v. State Social Welfare Board* (1960), 54 Cal. 2d 184, 195, 5 Cal. Rptr. 553, 559, 353 P.2d 33, 39.) The meaning of particular words or groups of words varies with the "... verbal context and surrounding circumstances and purposes in view of the linguistic education and experience of their users and their hearers or readers (not excluding judges).... A word has no meaning apart from these factors; much less does it have an objective meaning, one true meaning." (Corbin, *The Interpretation of Words and the Parol Evidence Rule* (1965), 50 Cornell L.Q. 161, 187.) Accordingly, the meaning of a writing ... can only be found by interpretation in the light of all the circumstances that reveal the sense in which the writer used the words. The exclusion of parol evidence regarding such circumstances merely because

---

[7] "A contract has, strictly speaking, nothing to do with the personal, or individual, intent of the parties. A contract is an obligation attached by the mere force of law to certain acts of the parties, usually words, which ordinarily accompany and represent a known intent." (*Hotchkiss v. National City Bank of New York* (S.D.N.Y. 1911), 200 F. 287, 293. ...)

the words do not appear ambiguous to the reader can easily lead to the attribution to a written instrument of a meaning that was never intended.

Although extrinsic evidence is not admissible to add to, detract from, or vary the terms of a written contract,[8] these terms must first be determined before it can be decided whether or not extrinsic evidence is being offered for a prohibited purpose. The fact that the terms of an instrument appear clear to a judge does not preclude the possibility that the parties chose the language of the instrument to express different terms. That possibility is not limited to contracts whose terms have acquired a particular meaning by trade usage,[9] but exists whenever the parties' understanding of the words used may have differed from the judge's understanding.

Accordingly rational interpretation requires at least a preliminary consideration of all credible evidence offered to prove the intention of the parties. Such evidence includes testimony as to the "circumstances surrounding the making of the agreement . . . including the object, nature and subject matter of the writing . . ." so that the court can "place itself in the same situation in which the parties found themselves at the time of contracting." (*Universal Sales Corp. v. Cal. Press Mfg. Co.*, 20 Cal. 2d 751, 761, 128 P.2d 665, 671.) If the court decides, after considering this evidence, that the language of a contract, in the light of all the circumstances, is "fairly susceptible of either one of the two interpretations contended for . . . ," extrinsic evidence relevant to prove either of such meanings is admissible.

In the present case the court erroneously refused to consider extrinsic evidence offered to show that the indemnity clause in the contract was not intended to cover injuries to plaintiff's property. Although that evidence was not necessary to show that the indemnity clause was reasonably susceptible of the meaning contended for by defendant, it was nevertheless relevant and admissible on that issue. Moreover, since that clause was reasonably susceptible of that meaning, the offered evidence was also admissible to prove that the clause had that meaning and did not cover injuries to plaintiff's property. Accordingly, the judgment must be reversed. . . .

■ QUESTIONS

(1) *Pacific Gas & Electric Co.*, like the *Right Field Rooftops* case, confronts the issue of whether a clause contained in a written agreement is unambiguous.

---

[8] Justice Traynor is referring to the parol evidence rule here. We study the parol evidence rule in Chapter 16.—EDS.

[9] The court cites cases in which extrinsic evidence of trade usage or custom has been admitted to show that "the term 'United Kingdom' in a motion picture distribution contract included Ireland . . . ; that the word 'ton' in a lease meant a long ton or 2,240 pounds and not the statutory ton of 2,000 pounds . . . ; that the word 'stubble' in a lease included not only stumps left in the ground but everything 'left on the ground after the harvest time' . . . ; that the term 'north' in a contract dividing mining claims indicated a boundary line running along the 'magnetic and not the true meridian'; . . . and that a form contract for purchase and sale was actually an agency contract. . . ."—EDS.

Is the approach suggested by Justice Traynor similar to the approach used in the *Right Field Rooftops* case? Do you see any differences?

(2) What specific circumstances, if any, does Justice Traynor suggest might reveal the reasonable meaning of the language used by the parties in their agreement?

(3) Two decades after the California Supreme Court decided *Pacific Gas*, the Ninth Circuit Court of Appeals was called upon to apply California law to a contract dispute. Writing for the court, Judge Kozinski stated: "Under *Pacific Gas*, it matters not how clearly a contract is written, ... nor how carefully it is negotiated, nor how squarely it addresses the issue before the court: the contract cannot be rendered impervious to attack by parol evidence."[10] Do you agree with this characterization of the reasoning in *Pacific Gas*? Why or why not?

WHITE CITY SHOPPING CENTER v. PR RESTAURANTS, LLC

Not Reported in N.E.2d, 21 Mass. L. Rptr. 565 (2006)
Massachusetts Superior Court, Worcester County

LOCKE, Justice.

... [PR Restaurants, LLC ("PR") operates a chain of café-style "Panera Bread" restaurants. The restaurants primarily serve sandwiches, soup and coffee. One of the restaurants is located in White City Shopping Center ("White City"). In its lease with White City, PR negotiated an exclusivity clause which read, in part, as follows:

> Landlord agrees not to enter into a lease, occupancy agreement or license affecting space in the Shopping Center or consent to an amendment to an existing lease permitting use ... for a bakery or restaurant reasonably expected to have annual sales of sandwiches greater than ten percent (10%) of its total sales or primarily for the sale of high quality coffees or teas, such as, but not limited to, Starbucks, Tea-Luxe, Pete's [sic] Coffee and Tea, and Finagle a Bagle. ... The foregoing shall not apply to (i) the use of the existing, vacant free-standing building in the Shopping Center for a Dunkin Donuts-type business, or for a business serving near-Eastern food and related products, (ii) restaurants primarily for sit-down table service, (iii) a Jewish delicatessen or (iv) a KFC restaurant operating in a new building following the demolition of the existing, freestanding building. No new building shall violate the no-build provision of this Lease.

---

[10] *Trident Center v. Connecticut General Life Insurance Co.*, 847 F.2d 564, 569 (9th Cir. 1988).

The language was subsequently amended to add the following provisions:

> The foregoing restriction shall also apply (without limitation) to a Dunkin Donuts location and to a Jewish-style delicatessen within the Shopping Center, but shall not apply to (i) use of the existing, freestanding building in the Shopping Center partially occupied by Strawberries and recently expanded for a business serving near-eastern food and related products, (ii) restaurants for primarily for sit down table service or (iii) a Papa Gino's restaurant (provided the same continues to operate with substantially the same categories of menu items as now apply to its stores and franchisees generally).

[Sometime after the amendment, White City entered negotiations with Chair 5 Restaurants ("Chair 5"), which sought to open a Qdoba franchise in the shopping center. Qdoba restaurants are Mexican-style establishments that sell such items as burritos, quesadillas, and tacos. PR objected that the establishment of a Qdoba franchise in the shopping center would violate the exclusivity clause in its lease with White City. Ultimately, it sought a preliminary injunction to restrain White City from going forward with the proposed lease with Qdoba.

In its consideration of the motion for a preliminary injunction, the court interpreted the meaning of the exclusivity clause and, in particular, the meaning of the term "sandwiches." The court noted that the lease didn't contain any definition of "sandwiches" or of "near-Eastern" food. It also stated that during lease negotiations, PR and White City did not discuss the definition of "sandwiches" or the type of food products they intended the term to cover. Furthermore, the court reported that the parties never indicated, specified, or agreed that the term "sandwiches" included tacos, burritos, and quesadillas.] . . .

Under the well-established test of *Packaging Industries Group v. Cheney*, 380 Mass. 609, 617, 405 N.E.2d 106 (1980), a preliminary injunction is warranted only when the moving party establishes both a likelihood of success on the merits of the claim, and a substantial risk of irreparable harm in the absence of an injunction. Once these factors are established, the Court must balance them against the harm that an injunction will inflict on the opposing party, and must also consider the impact on the public interest.

To demonstrate a likelihood of success on the merits, PR must establish as a reasonable interpretation that the Mexican-style food products which Qdoba sells fall within the Lease's restrictions. Absent an explicit and broad definition of "sandwiches" in the Lease itself, PR has not shown a likelihood of success to establish a right to injunctive relief under relevant contract principles.

The interpretation of a contract is question of law for the court. A contract is construed to be given reasonable effect to each of its provisions. "The object of the court is to construe the contract as a whole in a reasonable and practical way, consistent with its language, background and purpose." *USM Corp. v. Arthur D. Little Systems, Inc.*, 28 Mass. App. Ct. 108, 166, 546 N.E.2d 888 (1989). The starting point must be the actual words chosen by the parties to express their agreement. If the words of the contract are plain and free from ambiguity, they must be construed in accordance with their ordinary and usual sense.

Given that the term "sandwiches" is not ambiguous and the Lease does not provide a definition of it, this court applies the ordinary meaning of the word.[11] The New Webster Third International Dictionary describes a "sandwich" as "two thin pieces of bread, usually buttered, with a thin layer (as of meat, cheese, or savory mixture) spread between them." Under this definition and as dictated by common sense, this court finds that the term "sandwich" is not commonly understood to include burritos, tacos, and quesadillas, which are typically made with a single tortilla and stuffed with a choice filling of meat, rice, and beans. As such, there is no viable legal basis for barring White City from leasing to Chair 5.[12] Further, PR has not proffered any evidence that the parties intended the term "sandwiches" to include burritos, tacos, and quesadillas. As the drafter of the exclusivity clause, PR did not include a definition of "sandwiches" in the lease nor communicate clearly to White City during lease negotiations that it intended to treat burritos, tacos, quesadillas, and sandwiches the same. Another factor weighing against PR's favor is that it was aware that Mexican-style restaurants near the Shopping Center existed which sold burritos, tacos, and quesadillas prior to the execution of the Lease yet, PR made no attempt to define, discuss, and clarify the parties' understanding of the term "sandwiches." Accordingly, based on the record before the court, PR has not shown a likelihood of success on the merits. . . .

[The motion for a preliminary injunction is denied.]

■ QUESTIONS

(1) In your view, did this court take a plain meaning or a contextual approach to contract interpretation? Why?

(2) Using a plain meaning approach, can you think of any arguments not addressed in this opinion that would support a conclusion that the term "sandwiches" is ambiguous? Alternatively, can you think of any arguments using a contextual approach that would support such a conclusion?

---

[11] The parties have submitted numerous dictionary definitions for the term "sandwich," as well as expert affidavits.

[12] Further, PR's reliance on *Sabritas* [*SA. v. United States*, 998 F. Supp. 1123, 22 C.I.T. 59 (Ct. Int'l Trade 1998)] is misplaced. PR argues that a flour tortilla qualifies as "bread" and a food product with bread and a filling is a sandwich. In *Sabritas*, the International Trade Court applied the commercial meaning, rather than the ordinary meaning of bread, to corn tacos shells for purposes of levying tariffs. Here, the commercial meaning of "bread" is inapposite where it is the ordinary meaning that is relevant when interpreting an unambiguous contractual term such as "sandwiches."

■ PROBLEM 15.4

Suppose PR Restaurants, LLC ("PR") engages you to represent it in lease negotiations with Olde Town Shopping Center ("Olde Town"). PR tells you it would like to operate a Panera Bread restaurant on the premises, but this time it wants to have an exclusivity clause in the lease that would "stand up in court." PR has asked you to draft some language to present to Olde Town for inclusion in the lease. PR wants to appear reasonable in the negotiations, so asks you to come up with language that will adequately protect its interests while not being overly broad.

(a) What questions might you ask your client before you attempted to draft the requested language?

(b) Assume your client is engaged in other matters and is not available to answer your questions at the moment. Instead, it has suggested you just take your best stab at coming up with some language, with the idea that it can be refined before the lease is signed. Draft an exclusivity clause to launch negotiations with Olde Town.

3. Interpretation of Standard Contracts

In previous chapters, we discuss contract formation where one of the parties provides standard terms for the transaction. Often, the cases involve mass-market transactions in which sellers sell products, services, or intellectual property rights to the purchasers. These cases explore the tension created by the objective theory of contracts and, in particular, whether nondrafting parties should be deemed to assent to the terms of writings that purport to evidence their contract, regardless of whether they read and understand those terms. In some of the cases, the standard terms were revealed or made available before money changed hands. In those cases, courts generally give effect to the standard terms and do not refer to the individual circumstances of the purchaser in doing so. Occasionally, courts subject the term in controversy to special scrutiny and enforce it only if its import was reasonably brought home to purchasers generally. If the standard terms were revealed only after the purchaser paid for the product, service, or intellectual property rights, the cases are in disagreement as to whether the standard terms should become a part of the contract. Generally, it is not the content or the meaning of the terms that is at issue but, rather, whether they should be deemed a part of the parties' agreement at all. The questions addressed by these cases, however, are closely tied to questions of interpretation.

Even with standard contracts, if the content of the parties' obligations is at issue, courts generally start with the language of the standard terms. Yet most courts acknowledge that in mass-market transactions, it is seldom practical for purchasers to read standard terms before assenting to contracts. Even a very diligent purchaser who reads the terms may not understand them, or may not appreciate their full consequences. Very reasonable people may enter into such transactions with little awareness of what the content or meaning of the standard terms might be. Given that the party who supplies the terms is entering into repeated transactions, however, it has a strong incentive to take the time to draft the terms carefully to reflect its own business expectations and protect its own interests. For these reasons, some courts see standard contracts as inherently one-sided, and are particularly loath to tie themselves to a close and isolated reading of the words of a disputed standard term. But how far a court is willing to stray from unambiguous standard terms is a matter of substantial dispute.

Imagine a situation where one party imposes a detailed and lengthy agreement on the other in a take-it-or-leave-it fashion. What weight should be given to the words found in the back pages of that agreement? If an ambiguity is found, some courts interpret those ambiguities strictly against the drafter, without any further inquiry into the reasonableness of that interpretation. This principle traces back to the ancient maxim *verba fortius accipiuntur contra proferentum*, which roughly translated means that words should be taken most strongly against the party who uses them. Other courts use the *contra proferentum* principle as a tie-breaker: Between a reasonable interpretation advanced by the drafter and one advanced by the other party, the reasonable interpretation of the other party should prevail. Sometimes, however, the words themselves, when taken in isolation, seem perfectly clear and unambiguous; yet in the context of the broader dealings between the parties, they may bear little relationship to what one party seemed to be offering and what the other reasonably thought she was accepting. Some courts reluctantly enforce language that seems clear and unambiguous, even though it may come as a surprise to those who have not read it carefully or have failed to appreciate fully its consequences. Occasionally, however, a court will take an approach similar to that found in the next case.

ATWATER CREAMERY CO. v. WESTERN NATIONAL MUTUAL INSURANCE CO.

366 N.W.2d 271 (1985)
Minnesota Supreme Court

WAHL, Justice.

Atwater Creamery Company (Atwater) sought a declaratory judgment against its insurer, Western National Mutual Insurance Company (Western), seeking coverage for losses sustained during a burglary of the creamery's storage building. . . . The trial court . . . dismissed the jury for lack of disputed issues of fact and ordered judgment in favor of the insurer, concluding that the burglary insurance policy in effect defined burglary so as to exclude coverage of this burglary. [The central issue on appeal is whether the reasonable expectations of the insured as to coverage govern to defeat the literal language of the policy.] We . . . reverse as to the policy coverage.

Atwater does business as a creamery and as a supplier of farm chemicals in Atwater, Minnesota. . . . [One weekend, chemicals worth approximately $15,587.40 were stolen from a facility that Atwater called its "Soil Center." Some of the doors to this facility were secured by deadbolts, some by padlocks, and others by large hasps held tight by turnbuckles. On the Monday after the event in question, the deadbolts were still locked, but the padlocks were missing, and the turnbuckles were loosened. The local police, the sheriff's department, and the state Bureau of Criminal Investigation all looked into the matter and determined that Atwater's employees had not been involved in the burglary. Although they were suspicious of certain nonlocal individuals unconnected with the creamery, the law enforcement agencies did not apprehend anyone or charge anyone with the crime. Atwater was insured against burglary by Western up to a ceiling of $20,000. The insurance policy contained an "evidence of forcible entry" requirement in its definition of "burglary." The state criminal statute defining "burglary" contained no such requirement.] The creamery had recovered small amounts under this policy for two separate burglaries prior to the events in this case. . . .

Atwater filed a claim with Western under the burglary policy. Western denied coverage because there were no visible marks of physical damage to the exterior at the point of entrance or to the interior at the point of exit, as required by the definition of burglary in the policy. The creamery then brought suit against Western for the $15,587.40 loss, $7,500 in other directly related business losses and costs, disbursements and reasonable attorney fees.

Charles H. Strehlow, the owner of the Strehlow Insurance Agency in Willmar, Minnesota, and Western's agent, testified that he is certain he mentioned the evidence-of-forcible-entry requirement to Poe [the plant manager at the Soil Center] and members of the Atwater Board of Directors but was unable to say when the discussion occurred. Poe and the board members examined do not remember any such discussion. None of the board members had read the policy, which is kept in the safe at the main plant, and Poe had not read it in its entirety. He stated that he started to read it but gave up because he could not understand it. . . .

The burglary definition in the policy reads: "The felonious abstraction of insured property (1) from within the premises by a person making felonious entry therein by actual force and violence, of which force and violence there are visible marks made by tools, explosives, electricity or chemicals upon, or physical damage to, the exterior of the premises at the place of such entry, or . . . (3) from within the premises by a person making felonious exit therefrom by actual force and violence as evidenced by visible marks made by tools, explosives, electricity or chemicals upon, or physical damage to, the interior of the premises at the place of such exit." . . .

The definition of burglary in this policy is one used generally in burglary insurance. Courts have construed it in different ways. It has been held ambiguous and construed in favor of coverage in the absence of visible marks of forceable entry or exit. . . . We reject this analysis because we view the definition in the policy as clear and precise. It is not ambiguous.

In determining the intent of the parties to the insurance contract, courts have looked to the purpose of the visible-marks-of-forcible-entry requirement. These purposes are two: to protect insurance companies from fraud by way of "inside jobs" and to encourage insureds to reasonably secure the premises. As long as the theft involved clearly neither an inside job nor the result of a lack of secured premises, some courts have simply held that the definition does not apply. . . .

In the instant case, there is no dispute as to whether Atwater is attempting to defraud Western or whether the Soil Center was properly secured. The trial court found that the premises were secured before the robbery and that the law enforcement investigators had determined that it was not an "inside job." To enforce the burglary definition literally against the creamery will in no way effectuate either purpose behind the restrictive definition. We are uncomfortable, however, with this analysis given the right of an insurer to limit the risk against which it will indemnify insureds.

At least three state courts have held that the definition merely provides for one form of evidence which may be used to prove a burglary and that, consequently, other evidence of a burglary will suffice to provide coverage. . . . [However, the] Nebraska Supreme Court recently rejected this argument in *Cochran v. MFA Mutual Insurance Co.*, 201 Neb. 631, 271 N.W.2d 331 (1978). The *Cochran* court held that the definition is not a rule of evidence but is a limit on liability, is unambiguous and is applied literally to the facts of the case at hand. We, too, reject this view of the definition as merely a form of evidence. The policy attempts to comprehensively define burglaries that are covered by it. In essence, this approach ignores the policy definition altogether and substitutes the court's or the [criminal] statute's definition of burglary. This we decline to do. . . .

Some courts and commentators have recognized that the burglary definition at issue in this case constitutes a rather hidden exclusion from coverage. Exclusions in insurance contracts are read narrowly against the insurer. Running through the many court opinions refusing to literally enforce this burglary definition is the concept that the definition is surprisingly restrictive, that no one purchasing something called burglary insurance would expect coverage to exclude skilled burglaries that leave no visible marks of forcible entry or exit. Professor Robert E. Keeton, in analyzing these and other insurance cases where the results often do not follow from the rules stated, found there to be two general principles underlying many decisions. These principles are the reasonable expectations of the insured and the unconscionability of the clause itself or as applied to the facts of a specific case. Keeton, *Insurance Law Rights at Variance with Policy Provisions*, 83 Harv. L. Rev. 961 (1970). Keeton's article and subsequent book, *Basic Text on Insurance Law* (1971), have had significant impact on the construction of insurance contracts.

The doctrine of protecting the reasonable expectations of the insured is closely related to the doctrine of contracts of adhesion. Where there is unequal bargaining power between the parties so that one party controls all of the terms and offers the contract on a take-it-or-leave-it basis, the contract will be strictly construed against the party who drafted it. Most courts recognize the great disparity in bargaining power between insurance companies and those who seek insurance. Further, they recognize that, in the majority of cases, a lay person lacks the necessary skills to read and understand insurance policies, which are typically long, set out in very small type and written from a legalistic or insurance expert's perspective. Finally, courts recognize that people purchase insurance relying on others, the agent or company, to provide a policy that meets their needs. The result of the lack of insurance expertise on the part of insureds and the recognized marketing techniques of insurance companies is that "the objectively reasonable expectations of applicants and intended beneficiaries regarding the terms of insurance contracts will be honored even though painstaking study of the policy provisions would have negated those expectations." Keeton, 83 Harv. L. Rev. at 967.

The traditional approach to construction of insurance contracts is to require some kind of ambiguity in the policy before applying the doctrine of reasonable expectations. Several courts, however, have adopted Keeton's view that ambiguity ought not be a condition precedent to the application of the reasonable-expectations doctrine.

As of 1980, approximately ten states had adopted the newer rule of reasonable expectations regardless of ambiguity. Other states, such as Missouri and North Dakota, have joined the ten since then.[13] Most courts recognize that insureds seldom see the policy until the premium is paid, and even if they try to read it, they do not comprehend it. Few courts require insureds to have minutely examined the policy before relying on the terms they expect it to have and for which they have paid.

The burglary definition is a classic example of a policy provision that should be, and has been, interpreted according to the reasonable expectations of the insured. *C&J Fertilizer, Inc. v. Allied Mutual Insurance Co.*, 227 N.W.2d 169 (Iowa 1975) involved a burglary definition almost exactly like the one in the instant case as well as a burglary very similar to the Atwater burglary. The court applied

---

[13] We spare you the court's list of cases that apply the reasonable expectations doctrine, even in the absence of an ambiguity in the policy language. After citing a number of cases, however, the court did admit that two courts originally taking this approach had since overruled their precedents. Apparently, those two courts regretted their prior decisions because they arguably relieved the insured of responsibility to read the policy in question. —Eds.

the reasonable-expectations-regardless-of-ambiguity doctrine, noting that "the most plaintiff might have reasonably anticipated was a policy requirement of visual evidence (abundant here) indicating the burglary was an 'outside' not an 'inside' job. The exclusion in issue, masking as a definition, makes insurer's obligation to pay turn on the skill of the burglar, not on the event the parties bargained for: a bona fide third party burglary resulting in loss of plaintiff's chemicals and equipment." *Id.* at 177. The burglary in *C&J Fertilizer* left no visible marks on the exterior of the building, but an interior door was damaged. In the instant case, the facts are very similar except that there was no damage to the interior doors; their padlocks were simply gone. In *C&J Fertilizer*, the police concluded that an "outside" burglary had occurred. The same is true here.

Atwater had a burglary policy with Western for more than 30 years. The creamery relied on Charles Strehlow to procure for it insurance suitable for its needs. There is some factual dispute as to whether Strehlow ever told Poe about the "exclusion," as Strehlow called it. Even if he had said that there was a visible-marks-of-forcible-entry requirement, Poe could reasonably have thought that it meant that there must be clear evidence of a burglary. There are, of course, fidelity bonds which cover employee theft. The creamery had such a policy covering director and manager theft. The fidelity company, however, does not undertake to insure against the risk of third-party burglaries. A business that requests and purchases burglary insurance reasonably is seeking coverage for loss from third-party burglaries whether a break-in is accomplished by an inept burglar or by a highly skilled burglar. Two other burglaries had occurred at the Soil Center, for which Atwater had received insurance proceeds under the policy. Poe and the board of the creamery could reasonably have expected the burglary policy to cover this burglary where the police, as well as the trial court, found that it was an "outside job."

The reasonable-expectations doctrine gives the court a standard by which to construe insurance contracts without having to rely on arbitrary rules which do not reflect real-life situations and without having to bend and stretch those rules to do justice in individual cases. As Professor Keeton points out, ambiguity in the language of the contract is not irrelevant under this standard but becomes a factor in determining the reasonable expectations of the insured, along with such factors as whether the insured was told of important, but obscure, conditions or exclusions and whether the particular provision in the contract at issue is an item known by the public generally. The doctrine does not automatically remove from the insured a responsibility to read the policy. It does, however, recognize that in certain instances, such as where major exclusions are hidden in the definitions section, the insured should be held only to reasonable knowledge of the literal terms and conditions. The insured may show what actual expectations he or she had, but the factfinder should determine whether those expectations were reasonable under the circumstances. . . .

In our view, the reasonable-expectations doctrine does not automatically mandate either pro-insurer or pro-insured results. It does place a burden on insurance companies to communicate coverage and exclusions of policies accurately and clearly. It does require that expectations of coverage by the insured be reasonable under the circumstances. Neither of those requirements seems overly burdensome. Properly used, the doctrine will result in coverage in some cases and in no coverage in others.

We hold that where the technical definition of burglary in a burglary insurance policy is, in effect, an exclusion from coverage, it will not be interpreted so as to defeat the reasonable expectations of the purchaser of the policy. Under the facts and circumstances of this case, Atwater reasonably expected that its burglary insurance policy with Western would cover the burglary that occurred. Our holding requires reversal as to policy coverage. . . .

SIMONETT, Justice (concurring specially).

I would not apply the reasonable expectations test in the absence of ambiguity in the policy; but because I believe such ambiguity exists, I concur in the majority opinion to reverse.

■ QUESTIONS

(1) The majority suggests that the policy language is unambiguous, while the concurrence concludes that it is ambiguous. What do you think, and why?

(2) How does the court reach the conclusion that the insured had a reasonable expectation of coverage in this case? Do you see any evidence of course of performance, course of dealing, or usage of trade? What other circumstances are persuasive to the court?

(3) If the insurance company wished to avoid a repeat of this case in the future, how should it change its policy language or practices?

(4) This court is very accommodating to the insured, respecting its reasonable expectations even in the face of what it deems to be unambiguous policy language to the contrary. As you may have sensed from the opinion, this approach is controversial even in the insurance context. It is rarely applied outside of the insurance context. What special considerations, if any, make insurance policies different from other types of standard contracts? Do you consider the court's approach justified, even though Atwater is presumably a sophisticated commercial party, fully capable of hiring an attorney to help it understand the insurance policy if need be? Do you favor expanding this approach to other types of standard contracts? Why or why not?

■ PROBLEM 15.5

Dotty Toread bought a new computer for her home and wanted to upgrade to a higher-speed Internet connection. She visited the website of Lightning

Internet Services, Inc., and ordered "lightning Internet service" for her home. The website promised her service would be "up and running, and lightning fast" by the next day. In fact, activating the service involved a period of lengthy delays. Once the service was activated, Dotty experienced continual problems accessing the Internet, and when the service was operable, it was as slow as molasses. Dotty repeatedly called Lightning's customer service department. Every time she called, she spent hours on hold, and when she finally spoke to a customer service representative, she was never able to get her problems resolved. After spending hundreds of dollars in monthly charges and countless frustrating hours, Dotty canceled her service a year after she had signed up for it.

In conversations with her neighbors, Dotty found that everyone who ordered Internet service from Lightning experienced similar frustrations. They all bemoaned the time, money, and effort they wasted trying to resolve issues with the Internet service provider. Angry and demanding justice, Dotty and her neighbors filed a class action lawsuit against Lightning, alleging, among other things, breach of contract.

Lightning argues that every customer who signs up for "lightning Internet service" online must accept the terms of an "Internet service agreement" by clicking on a button that says "I accept" in a scroll box on their computer monitors. Although only a small portion of the agreement appears in the scroll box at any one time, customers can scroll through the entire agreement if they so desire before clicking on the "I accept" button. In fact, Lightning points out, there is a conspicuous statement at the top of the agreement that says "PLEASE READ THE FOLLOWING AGREEMENT CAREFULLY." The agreement, if printed out, would occupy 14 pages of small print. The final clause of the agreement states "You and Lightning Internet Services, Inc. consent to the exclusive personal jurisdiction of and venue in a court of competent jurisdiction located in Fairfax County, Virginia." Neither Dotty nor any of her neighbors remember clicking on the "I accept" button, although they concede they might have done so.

The class action was not filed in Virginia but rather in Dotty's home state. Further, Virginia was one of only two states at the time that did not allow a class action procedure for this type of lawsuit. Dotty argues that a consumer would not reasonably expect a clause in a contract of this sort limiting litigation to a distant court. Even if a forum selection clause would be unobjectionable in the usual case, Dotty argues, one that deprived the consumer of the generally available remedy of a class-action lawsuit would not be within a consumer's reasonable expectations. Accordingly, she argues that the contract should not be interpreted to include the forum selection clause. Lightning Internet Services, Inc., responds that the clause is completely reasonable from its point of view, because its corporate headquarters are located in Virginia.

(a) Lightning Internet Services, Inc., files a motion to dismiss, arguing that the unambiguous language of each of the relevant contracts requires any lawsuit to be filed in Fairfax County, Virginia. If you were the court, how would you resolve this motion to dismiss? Why?

(b) Assume, for whatever reason, you deny the motion to dismiss. Lightning Internet Services, Inc., now argues that resolution of these disputes by class action is not appropriate and requests that the court decline to certify the class. Assume that under the relevant rules of civil procedure, for a court to allow litigation to proceed as a class action (that is, certify a class), the plaintiffs must prove that they have issues of law and fact in common and that the common issues predominate over the individual ones. If the language of the contracts is ambiguous, Lightning Internet Services, Inc., argues, interpreting that language would require the court to inquire into the circumstances surrounding the execution of each of the individual contracts, thus making resolution by class action inappropriate. Would you be willing to allow this lawsuit to go forward as a class action in your court? Why or why not?

CONSTRUCTION OF CONTRACT OBLIGATIONS

If you are searching for the meaning of contract terms, you should start your search with the words of any written agreement, but you may well need to inquire into the circumstances surrounding the agreement as well. This is the lesson underlying much of this chapter so far. Sometimes, the search yields insufficient clues. Perhaps the parties simply didn't consider a particular issue and thus did not provide for it. Perhaps the parties discussed the issue but were unable to resolve it. Perhaps the evidence is contradictory, and there is no reliable way to resolve the conflict. In these cases, a court is often called upon to go beyond the intent that the parties actually manifested in the agreement in question. Instead, it may resolve the dispute with reference to more general principles of law. What the exact content of these principles are, or perhaps should be, has been a subject of much judicial and academic interest. Sometimes courts try to provide a term that the parties would have intended had they thought about the issue, or perhaps that they should have intended. As the analysis moves away from the facts of what happened toward what could have or should have happened, questions of public policy increasingly come into play.

The methods and considerations that courts use to determine the full legal obligations that result from the parties' agreement constitute the process of construction. This process is not very far removed from that of contract interpretation. Like interpretation, construction is generally couched in terms of the parties' probable intent. Frequently courts state that they have no wish to interpret or construe contracts so as to override or contradict clearly expressed intentions of the parties. Often the role of contract construction is to supplement the manifested intent of the parties, because the agreed-upon terms and the implications of the parties' conduct simply do not settle the dispute at hand. Yet, where considerations of fairness or public policy are particularly strong, some courts construe contracts so as to contradict or constrain the operation of fairly clear contractual language. Here, as in many places in contract law, courts seek to balance the parties' freedom to contract as they see fit with other important public policies.

As you read the cases, you will see that courts often use the words "interpret" and "construe" interchangeably, which can be confusing. Perhaps it is best to think of interpretation and construction as two ends of a continuum. Pure interpretation focuses on discerning the actual intent manifested by the parties. Pure construction supplies contractual content based on public policies or general principles of law. Most of the hard cases (and therefore most of the interesting cases) lie somewhere in between. In this section, we will explore in more detail how courts go about interpreting or construing the exact nature and extent of the parties' obligations in the absence of definitive contract language or other circumstances evidencing intent. We start by discussing specific gap fillers and will proceed to more general notions of good faith and fair dealing. As we do so, pay attention to where you think courts are persuaded by what they think the parties probably intended, and where you think they are influenced by more general considerations of public policy.

1. Gap Fillers

In Chapter 7, we see that if parties fail to settle on the essential outlines of their agreement, a court may conclude that the agreement fails for indefiniteness and cannot be enforced as a contract. If the intention to be bound is clear and most of the material terms are ascertainable, however, a court may seek to fill out any gaps in the parties' agreement. By supplying a term that seems reasonable under the circumstances, the court avoids frustrating the parties' expectation of contract formation. Yet the court arguably imposes obligations on the parties that they did not discuss and may not have contemplated. If a court feels that there is no reasonable basis for supplying a contract term necessary for resolution of a dispute, it is likely to refuse to enforce the contract altogether.

The Restatement, Second, generally endorses the gap-filling function of courts:

RESTATEMENT, SECOND §204. SUPPLYING AN OMITTED ESSENTIAL TERM

When the parties to a bargain sufficiently defined to be a contract have not agreed with respect to a term which is essential to a determination of their rights and duties, a term which is reasonable in the circumstances is supplied by the court.

There are certain fact patterns that have come up so frequently over the years that the law recognizes standard presumptions that can be used to fill out the parties' intent. Because of their function, these standard presumptions are often referred to as "gap fillers." Some of them have been developed by common law courts; others are found in statutes like the UCC. In the usual case, gap fillers are used when there truly is a gap in the parties' expression of intent. Such a gap filler will not be used if the parties have explicitly agreed to a different contract term, or the circumstances indicate that they reasonably intended something else. Occasionally, applicable law requires a particularly strong showing that the parties intended a different agreement from that suggested by the gap filler.[14] Yet, as long as that showing is present, the parties are for the most part free to set their agreement however they wish.

Article 2 of the UCC nicely illustrates how a statute can provide standard presumptions to fill gaps in the parties' agreement. You may recall that UCC 2-204 provides that even if one or more terms are left open, a contract for the sale of goods will not fail for indefiniteness "if the parties have intended to make a contract and there is a reasonably certain basis for giving an appropriate remedy." To aid the court in fashioning an appropriate remedy, the UCC provides a series of standard terms that can be used to fill gaps in the parties' agreement. As long as the parties had the intention to be bound, Article 2 will supply among other things a price, a method of payment, and a method of delivery if the parties failed to do so.

Consider, for instance, the following gap-filling provision:

UCC 2-311. OPTIONS AND COOPERATION RESPECTING PERFORMANCE

(1) An agreement for sale which is otherwise sufficiently definite (subsection (3) of Section 2-204) to be a contract is not made invalid by the fact that it leaves particulars of performance to be specified by one of the parties. Any such specification must be made in good faith and within limits set by commercial reasonableness.

----

[14] For instance, as we have alluded to from time to time, UCC Article 2 implies a warranty of merchantability if the seller is a merchant with respect to goods of that kind. It is possible for the seller to disclaim the implied warranty of merchantability, but to do so, the seller must follow specific statutory requirements set out in UCC 2-316. The details of the implied warranty of merchantability, and the requirements for disclaiming it, are beyond the scope of these materials, and are left to further study in a course on sales.

(2) Unless otherwise agreed specifications relating to assortment of the goods are at the buyer's option and . . . specifications or arrangements relating to shipment are at the seller's option. . . .

FAMILY SNACKS OF NORTH CAROLINA, INC. v. PREPARED PRODUCTS CO.

295 F.3d 864 (2002)
United States Court of Appeals, Eighth Circuit

BEAM, Circuit Judge.

Prepared Products Company, Inc. ("Prepco") appeals the decision of the district court granting summary judgment in favor of Family Snacks of North Carolina, Inc. ("Family Snacks"). We affirm the district court. . . .

This action arises out of a supply agreement entered into by Family Snacks and Prepco on February 17, 1998. Pursuant to the agreement, Prepco agreed to buy $10 million worth of private label canister nut products and kettle chip products from Family Snacks during the first year of the contract, beginning on July 1, 1998. These products were to be produced at a snack processing facility in North Carolina previously owned by Prepco and sold to Family Snacks in February 1998. In fact, the purchase price of the North Carolina facility was based upon an agreement between Family Snacks and Prepco that Prepco would reduce the purchase price of the facility and would recoup the difference through the implementation of a low-cost manufacturing arrangement with Family Snacks. This compact is outlined in the supply agreement, facilitating Prepco's plan to market to mass merchandisers under their private labels.

Under the supply agreement, Family Snacks would sell the products to Prepco on a "cost plus" basis, designed to yield a purchase price lower than the market price for wholesale snack foods. Thomas Lehmer, Prepco's CEO, personally guaranteed the full and timely payment and performance of all of Prepco's obligations under the contract. Further, the agreement contained a formula for calculating the price of the products. The charges were to be calculated through a formula based upon the manufacturing costs of the particular product, plus a fifteen percent profit margin. The manufacturing costs were to be determined using factors outlined in the formula, which was attached as Exhibit A. In addition, the manufacturing costs included a fixed overhead expense of twenty-nine cents per pound of product.

It is undisputed that during the first year of the supply agreement, Prepco bought nothing from Family Snacks. As a result, Family Snacks filed this suit for breach of contract seeking to collect $1.5 million in liquidated damages. In response to the lawsuit, Prepco claims that the supply agreement is not an enforceable contract because it is illusory. Prepco further argues that Family

Snacks hindered Prepco's performance under the contract by failing to provide necessary pricing information, thereby limiting Prepco's ability to solicit orders, and by refusing to acknowledge that Prepco's purchase of any product other than kettle chips and canister nuts would reduce its minimum purchase obligations under the agreement.

The district court entered judgment in favor of Family Snacks on its motion for summary judgment, concluding that under the Uniform Commercial Code and general principles of usage of trade, it was reasonable to require Prepco to first identify the products it wished to buy. The court held that Prepco breached its duty in this regard. As a result, the district court concluded that Family Snacks established its claim for breach of contract as a matter of law. As to Prepco's affirmative defense of hindrance, the district court held that because Prepco was required to act first, and failed to do so, the record did not support a finding that Family Snacks interfered with Prepco's obligation to purchase products. . . .

Under Missouri law, "summary judgment is appropriate [in a contract case] where the language of the contract is clear and unambiguous such that 'the meaning of the portion of the contract in issue is so apparent that it may be determined from the four corners of the document.'" *Missouri Consol. Health Care Plan v. BlueCross BlueShield of Mo.*, 985 S.W.2d 903, 908 (Mo. Ct. App. 1999) (citation omitted) (quoting *MECO Sys., Inc. v. Dancing Bear Entertainment, Inc.*, 948 S.W.2d 185, 191 (Mo. Ct. App. 1997)).

To prevail in its claim against Prepco, Family Snacks must establish (1) the making and existence of a valid and enforceable contract between the parties; (2) Family Snacks' rights and Prepco's obligations under the contract; (3) a breach; and (4) resulting damages. Prepco argues that Family Snacks failed to establish that the supply agreement is an enforceable contract, the first element of the breach of contract claim. Prepco bases this argument [in part on the allegation that because no price term is specified, the contract is fatally uncertain.] . . .

Section 3 of the supply agreement, which provides for the price of the product, states in part that "[t]he prices for the Products sold to [Prepco] pursuant to this Agreement shall be as is set forth in Exhibit A attached hereto (the 'Manufacturing Costs') plus an amount equal to the 'Profit Margin.'" The supply agreement then defines "profit margin" in greater detail. Prepco argues that no prices are set forth in Exhibit A and that Family Snacks attempted to reserve for itself the unilateral ability to set whatever price it wished. We disagree.

The supply agreement in this case embodies a sophisticated and highly detailed "cost plus" pricing formula. This hardly renders the supply agreement unenforceable. Although the process is tedious, the product price is certainly ascertainable. As long as the parties agreed to a process by which price was to be determined and as long as the price could be ascertained at the time of performance, the price requirement for a valid and enforceable contract was satisfied. The supply agreement is valid because it specifies a standard that would establish the consideration after the product was manufactured.

Therefore, it represents a valid and enforceable contract, satisfying the first element required in this breach of contract claim.

Prepco next argues that Family Snacks failed to establish the true nature of the parties' respective obligations under the supply agreement as required under the second element of the breach of contract claim. Prepco claims the existence of an implied condition—that Family Snacks was first required to supply basic pricing information for the products it already manufactured before Prepco could obtain orders from its customers and place an order with Family Snacks. According to Prepco, Family Snacks' failure to provide pricing information hindered, and therefore excused, Prepco's performance under the supply agreement.

The crux of the disagreement between the parties is a dispute over which party had the initial obligation to provide information relevant to establishing prices for products under the agreed upon formula. Stated another way, did the contract contain an implied condition that Family Snacks had to first provide a product and price list to Prepco in order to demand Prepco's performance? Or was it Prepco's initial obligation to provide Family Snacks with the necessary ordering information so that Family Snacks could then quote Prepco a price for products? This issue is not answered by the language in the supply agreement. Thus, the parties apparently had no expectations regarding this situation and we must now supply the missing term. *See* Restatement (Second) of Contracts §204.

We agree with the district court that as between the two parties, the supply agreement required Prepco to first provide Family Snacks with the description and quantity of product Prepco wished to buy before Family Snacks was obligated to give a price for the same. In order to reach this result, we, like the district court, find Section 400.2-204 of the Missouri Code instructive. "Even though one or more terms are left open a contract for sale does not fail for indefiniteness if the parties have intended to make a contract and there is a reasonably certain basis for giving an appropriate remedy." Mo. Rev. Stat. §400.2-204(3). In this case it is clear the parties intended to make a contract. The supply agreement was negotiated in juxtaposition with the pending purchase agreement regarding Prepco's sale of the North Carolina facility to Family Snacks. In fact, the purchase price for the facility, agreed upon by the parties in the purchase agreement, reflected a price reduction, which was to be recouped by Prepco through the implementation of a low-cost manufacturing arrangement. . . . Consequently, this contract does not now fail for indefiniteness due to lack of agreement on the issue now before the court.

Because we find that the supply agreement does not fail for indefiniteness, it is incumbent upon the court to supply the omitted term now at issue. In a case such as this, where the four corners of the supply agreement fail to provide for the dispute at hand, the court must fill the gap. *See* Restatement (Second) of Contracts §204. We find Missouri Statute §400.2-311 instructive at this stage. "Unless otherwise agreed[,] specifications relating to assortment of the goods are at the buyer's option. . . . " Mo. Rev. Stat. §400.2-311(2). The comment to section 400.2-311(2) states:

Options as to assortment of goods ... are specifically reserved to the buyer ... under subsection (2) where no other arrangement has been made. This section rejects the test which mechanically and without regard to usage or the purpose of the option gave the option to the party "first under a duty to move" and applies instead a standard commercial interpretation to these circumstances.

Mo. Rev. Stat. §400.2-311 cmt. 2. Accordingly, section 400.2-311 places the responsibility upon Prepco to identify the products it wished to buy. Prepco's obligation is further evidenced by the pricing formula for all products sold to Prepco, which calculates charges based upon current costs of ingredients and manufacturing costs. This pricing mechanism only makes sense if these factors are applied to products ordered by Prepco in specific quantities on specific dates, whether currently manufactured products or special order products. . . .

The supply agreement is a valid and enforceable contract that clarified the rights and obligations of the respective parties. Prepco was obligated to select and purchase $10 million worth of products in the first year and yet undisputably failed to do so. Thus, the breach requirement is satisfied. Further, the parties contracted for damages in the supply agreement. Family Snacks therefore established its claim for breach of contract as a matter of law. . . .

For the reasons set forth above, we affirm the district court.

■ QUESTIONS

(1)   Prepco argued that the agreement between the parties was insufficiently definite to be enforceable as a contract. The court disagreed. What factors did the court consider in reaching its decision?

(2)   According to the court, what gap did the parties leave in their agreement? Why was it necessary for the court to supply a term to fill that gap? What factors did the court consider in choosing the appropriate gap filler?

Courts in resolving disputes like the one in the *Family Snacks* case are often aided by established rules of law or, in the case of sales of goods, the relevant provisions of the UCC. Sometimes, however, a relevant gap filler is not readily apparent from applicable law. The court itself must decide how, or if, to fill the gap.

The question of what content (if any) the law should provide to fill gaps in contracts is an interesting and controversial one. Some commentators continue to focus on the parties and give great weight to the need to preserve their autonomy. For instance, Professor Barnett, who, you may recall, advocates a consent theory of contract, has suggested that gaps in a parties' specific agreement should be filled by reference to conventional or common-sense understanding in the community to which the parties belong, if any such understanding exists.[15] Although the parties themselves may not have explicitly or implicitly considered the point at issue, their entering the contract implies at least a tacit assent to commonly understood norms. Any other term supplied by a default rule of law would impose the state's choice upon private actors under the guise of contract law, a result that Barnett considers to challenge the basic autonomy of the parties.

Other authors look beyond the specific dispute and individual actors at issue and take a decidedly economic approach. Under this view, the function of gap fillers (or default rules of law) is to promote efficiency in contract law. How, precisely, that might best be accomplished is itself a question of some complexity. If most reasonable parties would negotiate a certain type of contract provision, perhaps the law should choose that provision as its default rule. That way, only those parties who wish to avoid the default rule would need to go into the matter in any detail in their contract, and everyone else would save the costs of fully developing this aspect of their agreement.[16] On the other hand, perhaps one of the parties has secret information, or there are other reasons why, all other things being equal, the parties will not bargain freely and openly even if it would cause them no additional time or expense to do so. It may be that the law can establish a default rule that is so disadvantageous that the parties are forced to negotiate and thereby reveal their secret information or overcome whatever other barrier stands in their way. The threat of the default rule encourages the parties to do what it takes to reach a more efficient result.[17] Although the writers who take an economic approach may differ in their concept of an ideal default rule, they seek to achieve a common policy in the interests of society as a whole: economic efficiency.

Some commentators move beyond efficiency and focus on broader societal or community goals. Professor Macneil[18] has noted that parties seldom attempt to specify all of their respective obligations to each other. Instead, they agree on the basics and plan to adjust as events develop. Their willingness to rely on their relationship rather than the specifics of any written agreement that they might sign and file away (perhaps unread) depends on an underlying belief that the

---

[15] *See* Randy E. Barnett, *The Sound of Silence: Default Rules and Contractual Consent*, 78 Va. L. Rev. 821 (1992).

[16] An essay that discusses this line of analysis in some detail, and also criticizes it, is Robert E. Scott, *The Case for Formalism in Relational Contract*, 94 Nw. U. L. Rev. 847 (2000).

[17] Leading articles advocating this type of approach are Ian Ayres & Robert Gertner, *Filling Gaps in Incomplete Contracts: An Economic Theory of Default Rules*, 99 Yale L.J. 87 (1989); *Strategic Contractual Inefficiency and the Optimal Choice of Legal Rules*, 101 Yale L.J. 729 (1992).

[18] Ian Macneil is one of the leading proponents of the relational theory of contract. His body of work is large and often complex. We can only sketch a few of his views here and do not purport to do them justice. Some of his writings on relational contracts can be found in Ian R. Macneil, *The New Social Contract* (Yale U. Press 1980); *Values in Contract: Internal and External*, 78 Nw. U. L. Rev. 340 (1983); *Efficient Breach of Contract: Circles in the Sky*, 68 Va. L. Rev. 947 (1982); *Economic Analysis of Contractual Relations: Its Shortfalls and the Need for a "Rich Classificatory Apparatus,"* 75 Nw. U. L. Rev. 1018 (1981); *Contracts: Adjustment of Long-Term Economic Relations Under Classical, Neoclassical and Relational Contract Law*, 72 Nw. U. L. Rev. 854 (1978); *Restatement (Second) of Contracts and Presentation*, 60 Va. L. Rev. 589 (1974); and *The Many Futures of Contracts*, 47 S. Cal. L. Rev. 691 (1974).

parties will continue to depend on and work with each other. The law has a role to play in reinforcing this type of belief in society. In view of what he agrees to be the relational nature of contracting, Professor Feinman rejects the power of economic theory to come up with useful gap fillers or default rules in the abstract. Instead, he advocates that judges consult "norms, insights, arguments and rules of thumb," taking due account of the relationship between the parties, in order to attain justice in a particular case.[19]

■ QUESTION

If you were in charge of developing default rules of law for filling contractual gaps, what approach (if any) would you favor, and why?

2. The Example of Exclusive Dealings and Output and Requirement Contracts

You might have noticed that UCC 2-311, which we include in Section C.1, provides a standard by which to measure the discretion the agreement gives to the parties. It states that if an agreement leaves particulars of performance to be specified by one of the parties, "[a]ny such specification must be made in good faith and within limits set by commercial reasonableness." We have seen several contexts in which one of the parties, whether expressly or by implication, reserves some discretion over its own performance. In Chapter 9, for instance, we discuss conditions of satisfaction, and note that courts often imply or construe an obligation to act reasonably, in good faith or in accordance with some other standard in determining satisfaction. Likewise, in our discussion of *Wood v. Lucy, Lady Duff-Gordon* in Chapter 9, we saw how courts sometimes imply or construe an obligation to use best efforts when the parties agree to deal exclusively with each other. Both at common law and under the UCC, courts regularly impose limitations of this sort on the discretion conferred on one of the parties under the agreement. Until now, we have largely deferred the question of what good faith, commercial reasonableness, or best efforts might require in any given situation. As we have seen, reasonableness, good faith, and best efforts are notoriously slippery concepts, and what precise behavior violates them may be difficult to categorize.

In this section, we return to exclusive dealings contracts, and introduce two closely allied situations—those of output and requirements contracts. In an output contract, the buyer agrees to purchase whatever goods the seller produces. In a requirements contract, the seller agrees to provide whatever goods

---

[19] *See, e.g.,* Jay M. Feinman, *Relational Contract and Default Rules,* 3 S. Cal. Interdisciplinary L.J. 43 (1993).

the buyer requires to satisfy its needs. In either case, one party is to some degree at the mercy of the other. The quantity of goods being sold seems to lie solely within the discretion of one of the parties. When market conditions make the terms of the agreement disadvantageous, a wily businessperson might elect to have his output or requirements (as the case may be) shrink to zero. And when the market makes the terms favorable, the business might inflate the quantity to the detriment of its trading partner. The degree to which standards of reasonableness, good faith, or best efforts are deemed to restrain the parties' discretion may prove to be a matter of significant commercial import.

Read UCC 2-306 and see what it has to say about output, requirements, and exclusive dealing contracts, and then consider the problems that follow.

UCC 2-306. OUTPUT, REQUIREMENTS AND EXCLUSIVE DEALINGS

(1) A term which measures the quantity by the output of the seller or the requirements of the buyer means such actual output or requirements as may occur in good faith, except that no quantity unreasonably disproportionate to any stated estimate or in the absence of a stated estimate to any normal or otherwise comparable prior output or requirements may be tendered or demanded.

(2) A lawful agreement by either the seller or the buyer for exclusive dealing in the kind of goods concerned imposes unless otherwise agreed an obligation by the seller to use best efforts to supply the goods and by the buyer to use best efforts to promote their sale.

■ PROBLEM 15.6

Science Education Co. offers private after-school science education opportunities to high school students throughout the Northeast. The students engage in various laboratory experiments and projects and often break significant quantities of test tubes, beakers, and other scientific glassware in the process. Science Education Co. decides it needs to find a reliable and cost-effective source for its scientific glassware, so it contacts Laboratory Supply, Inc., a scientific glassware manufacturer. Science Education Co. and Laboratory Supply, Inc., sign an agreement which states in relevant part:

> Science Education Co. agrees to purchase its requirements of scientific glassware from Laboratory Supply, Inc. Science Education Co. shall purchase, and Laboratory Supply, Inc., shall sell, such quantities of glassware as Science Education Co. shall order from time to time. In consideration for entering into this agreement, Science Education Co. shall be entitled to the discount

prices listed on the attached schedule. This agreement shall remain in full force and effect for six months.

Attached to the agreement is a schedule listing the various types of scientific glassware that Laboratory Supply, Inc., manufactures, along with a price per unit for each of type of item. Is this an output contract, a requirements contract, an exclusive dealings contract, or none of the above? What specific obligations, if any, does UCC 2-306 impose upon the parties?

■ PROBLEM 15.7

Once a court subjects a party to a duty of reasonableness, good faith, or best efforts, it may be necessary to determine what such a duty demands under the circumstances at hand. The case of *Indiana-American Water Co. v. Town of Seelyville*, 698 N.E.2d 1255 (Ind. App. 1998), is illustrative. The Town of Seelyville entered into a 25-year contract to obtain its water from the Indiana-American Water Company. The relevant part of the contract provided that "Company agrees to sell to the Town, and Town agrees to purchase from Company, . . . such quantities of water as the Town may hereafter from time to time need. . . ." The contract limited the quantity of water that the town could purchase to 1 million gallons of water a day.

Fourteen years after the contract was entered, the town announced plans to develop a well field of its own. The water company sued, seeking a declaratory judgment that the town would breach the contract if it proceeded to create its own water supply. Any other interpretation, the water company argued, would render the contract unenforceable, as the town's purported obligation to satisfy its needs through the water company would be illusory. The trial court denied the requested declaratory judgment, and the Indiana Court of Appeals affirmed.

In reaching its holding, the court of appeals noted that the town had an obligation to act in good faith under UCC 2-306, and this obligation was sufficient to render the contract enforceable. However, development of its own water supply would not breach the contract terms or the town's duty of good faith. The court reasoned:

> The most common problem arising out of a requirements contract is the situation where the price of the commodity is advantageous to the buyer, who then demands a quantity unreasonably in excess of his needs in

order to resell the excess at a profit, placing himself in competition with the seller. The provision in §2-306(1) forbidding the "demand" by a buyer under a requirements contract to a "quantity unreasonably disproportionate to any stated estimate" applies only to this type of situation where the buyer requests more, as opposed to less, of the commodity in question. *Empire Gas [Corporation v. American Bakeries Co.,]* 840 F.2d [1333] at 1337-38. . . . The *Empire Gas* court noted that there was no indication that the drafters of the UCC were equally, if at all, concerned about the case, such as the one at bar, where the buyer takes less than his estimated requirements, provided, of course, that he does not buy from anyone else. 840 F.2d at 1338.

Generally, the buyer in a requirements contract governed by UCC §2-306(1) is required merely to exercise good faith in determining his requirements and the seller assumes the risk of all good faith variations in the buyer's requirements even to the extent of a determination to liquidate or discontinue the business. However, the buyer is not free, on any whim, to quit buying from the seller. How exigent the buyer's change of circumstances must be to allow him to scale down his requirements is a difficult question. The seller assumes the risk of a change in the buyer's business that results in a substantial reduction in the buyer's needs, but the buyer assumes the risk of a less urgent change in circumstances. The essential ingredient of the buyer's good faith under such circumstances is that he not merely have had second thoughts about the terms of the contract and want to get out of it. However, if the buyer has a legitimate business reason for eliminating its requirements, as opposed to a desire to avoid its contract, the buyer acts in good faith. . . .

In the present case, Town had acquired a well field many years before the execution of the contract under scrutiny. Town's decision to develop its preexisting well field constitutes a legitimate, long-term business decision, and not merely a desire to avoid the terms of its contract with Water Company. Therefore, based on the above, we cannot conclude that Water Company carried its burden of overcoming the negative judgment in this case by demonstrating that the evidence leads unerringly to the conclusion that Town's development of its pre-existing well field to reduce its need to purchase water from Water Company constitutes bad faith. . . .

(a) Under the court's analysis, construct a specific scenario in which the town would not be acting in good faith. How does your example differ from the situation at hand? Is there any way the town could have preserved its right to act in the way you suggest, and if so, how? Ultimately, can the parties by their agreement limit or eliminate altogether the obligation to act in good faith?

(b) Suppose in the agreement the town had reserved the right to obtain its water from anyone. What would the legal consequences of this provision be?

3. The General Obligations of Good Faith and Fair Dealing

As the materials in the previous section indicate, the UCC tells courts to construe parties' obligations under output and requirements contracts in light of a good faith standard. As we have seen, this approach is not unique to the UCC or to output and requirements contracts. Rather, the obligation to perform contractual obligations in good faith is a general one that applies to all contracts—not just to those that are unclear or incomplete. This idea, that the parties must perform their obligations in good faith, has been enshrined in Restatement, Second §205 and also in UCC 1-304.

RESTATEMENT, SECOND §205. DUTY OF GOOD FAITH AND FAIR DEALING

Every contract imposes upon each party a duty of good faith and fair dealing in its performance and its enforcement.

UCC 1-304. OBLIGATION OF GOOD FAITH

Every contract or duty within [the Uniform Commercial Code] imposes an obligation of good faith in its performance and enforcement.

To say, however, that there is a general obligation of good faith in the performance and enforcement of contracts is not to give courts completely free hands to settle disputes in accordance with their own abstract notions of fairness. Rather, courts struggle to determine what good faith requires in light of the particular agreement of the parties. One issue that continues to trouble the courts is the extent to which the parties can rely on the express provisions of their agreements.

If an agreement explicitly gives one party the ability to take an action, can that party stand on its express contractual authority, or must it consider its power to be constrained by general notions of good faith or fair dealing? This is the question explored in the next case, which involves a termination clause in a contract. We include both the majority opinion and the dissent, as they take decidedly different approaches to interpretation and construction of the contract in question. As you read the case, try to discern the exact extent of the parties' obligations under each judge's reasoning. What, in the view of the respective opinions, would constitute a lack of good faith under the circumstances presented?

UNITED AIRLINES, INC. v. GOOD TASTE, INC.

982 P.2d 1259 (1999)
Alaska Supreme Court

BRYNER, Justice.

United Airlines terminated a catering contract with Saucy Sisters Catering[20] in Anchorage. Saucy Sisters sued, claiming fraud, breach of contract, and breach of the implied covenant of good faith and fair dealing. The trial court dismissed the breach of contract claim but allowed the other claims to be tried. A jury, finding no fraud but a breach of the implied covenant, awarded Saucy Sisters damages. We hold that under Illinois law, which the parties agree governs, the contract could be terminated at will, and the implied covenant did not require United to have a legitimate business reason for termination. We therefore remand for entry of judgment for United. . . .

[The facts, as summarized by the trial court and quoted in the opinion, were as follows:] In 1987, United contacted Saucy Sisters' President and invited her to bid on United's in-flight catering contract. Shortly after United's invitation, Saucy Sisters entered into discussions/negotiations with United regarding the particulars of the catering contract and the obligations of the parties. On March 14, 1988, United awarded Saucy Sisters the catering contract. As a result of being awarded the contract, and in order to meet United's operation requirements for contracting caterers, Saucy Sisters expanded its operation extensively, spending roughly one million dollars in the process. A "Catering Agreement" ("Agreement") was signed by the parties and was performed for approximately one year. On May 18, 1989, United gave Saucy Sisters a ninety (90) day notice of termination by which it notified Saucy Sisters that its performance under the Agreement would terminate as of August 15, 1989. The Agreement was terminated August 15, 1989.

United's ninety day termination notice was in accordance with a no-cause termination provision found in the Catering Agreement. The provision states: "Term: The term of this Agreement shall commence on May 1, 1988, and shall continue for a period of 3 years(s); provided, however, either party may terminate this Agreement upon ninety (90) days' prior written notice."

The facts surrounding this termination provision are at the center of this dispute. In its version of the facts, Saucy Sisters alleges that Roger Groth, United's contracting representative, assured Saucy Sisters that United had never used the ninety day termination provision in the past and that the provision existed only to provide United with an "out" in the event United chose not to fly to

---

[20] Good Taste, Inc., the plaintiff in this lawsuit, did business under the name "Saucy Sisters Catering." Because we particularly enjoy the alliteration, in the text we refer to the plaintiff as Saucy Sisters. We note that the court does as well.—Eds.

Anchorage in the future. Saucy Sisters claims it would not have undertaken such a massive and expensive expansion effort at the risk of a no-cause, ninety day termination notice but for Roger Groth's allegedly fraudulent representations regarding the restrictions on the termination provision. United fails to dispute these facts anywhere in the record, but stated during oral argument that Roger Groth would testify that he never made such statements regarding the termination provision. . . .

Here, the meaning of the disputed termination clause is clear and unambiguous on its face when its words are given "their plain, ordinary, popular, and natural meaning." This provision clearly fixes the Agreement's term at three years, but allows each party to end it earlier by doing nothing more than giving the other party ninety days' notice. As the superior court aptly noted, such termination clauses are hardly uncommon: Anyone familiar with real world business practices would instantly recognize this provision as a no-cause termination provision that is often used to limit an otherwise definite term. No-cause termination clauses like the one considered here are widely used, and this one in particular would not cause anyone to second-guess its clear and unambiguous terms. . . . [B]ecause United undisputedly abided by the literal terms of the provision—terminating the Agreement upon ninety days' written notice to Saucy Sisters—the trial court properly concluded that no genuine issue of material fact existed and that United was entitled to summary judgment on Saucy Sisters' breach of contract claim.

United asserts that Illinois law does not permit an implied covenant of good faith and fair dealing to supplant the clear language of a contract allowing termination without cause. According to United, because the disputed Agreement clearly and unambiguously allowed either party to terminate upon ninety days' notice and did not require good cause for termination, the trial court erred in finding the implied covenant applicable and in denying United summary judgment on this claim.[21]

Saucy Sisters responds that the ninety-day termination clause gave both parties broad discretion to terminate their agreement. In such situations, Saucy Sisters argues, Illinois law applies the implied covenant of good faith and fair dealing as a limit on the permissible bounds of contractual discretion. Thus, in Saucy Sisters' view, the implied covenant applied in this case, and the trial court properly allowed this claim to go to the jury. . . .

The covenant of good faith and fair dealing is well accepted in Illinois, and its broad contours are firmly established: the covenant is implied in every contract. The implied covenant guides the construction of contracts without creating independent duties for the contracting parties. Its implied terms

---

[21] A word here about the court's analysis is in order. You may be confused by the court's implication that this is something other than a breach of contract claim. Don't be. Both breach of the termination clause and breach of the implied duty of good faith are breach of contract claims. Some violations of good faith may give rise to an action in tort (as in the case of intentional fraud), but the court here is interested primarily in contractual obligations. We suspect any implication in the court's analysis to the contrary is unintended.—Eds.

cannot modify the express terms of the contract. The covenant operates to define the intent of contracting parties when a contract is ambiguous or when it vests the parties with broad discretion as to its performance. In cases involving unambiguous contracts that vest broad discretion in one of the parties, the covenant operates by constraining that party to exercise its discretion reasonably and fairly: "not arbitrarily, capriciously, or in a manner inconsistent with the reasonable expectation of the parties."

Of course, a contractual no-cause termination clause may accurately be characterized as vesting the parties with broad discretion as to the termination of their contract; for this reason, it might be plausible to argue in the case of a no-cause termination clause that the implied covenant requires the parties to terminate reasonably—that is, for some legitimate reason. This is essentially the view that Saucy Sisters advocated at trial. And in denying United's pretrial motion for summary judgment on the implied covenant claim, the court adopted Saucy Sisters' theory: "Although the implied covenant of good faith and fair dealing does not create an enforceable legal duty to be nice or to behave decently in a general way, it may require both United and Saucy Sisters to exercise the discretion afforded to them by the termination clause in a manner consistent with the reasonable expectation of both parties."

Saucy Sisters thereafter relied on this theory at trial. It expressly argued to the jury that even if United made no misrepresentations concerning the ninety-day no-cause termination clause, the implied covenant prevented it from violating Saucy Sisters' reasonable expectation that the agreement would be terminated only for a legitimate business reason. . . . Saucy Sisters invoked the same theme in opposing United's motions for judgment notwithstanding the verdict and a new trial on the implied covenant claim. . . . Applying this view of the law to the facts here, Saucy Sisters insisted that the jury's verdict on the implied covenant claim should be upheld because "reasonable jurors could have found that [Saucy Sisters] performed the contract properly, that any problems in performance were caused by United, and that United terminated the contract without any legitimate business reason whatsoever."

But as far as we can determine, Illinois courts have never held the implied covenant to require good cause or a legitimate business reason for terminating a contract with an express no-cause termination provision. To the contrary, Illinois courts seem to have recognized consistently that . . . terminable-at-will contracts are generally held to permit termination for any reason, good cause or not, or for no cause at all. . . . The courts have likewise recognized that applying the implied covenant to limit the terms of a no-cause termination provision would be "incongruous" with this general rule and might "eviscerate the at will doctrine altogether." [The court's citations are omitted.]

To be sure, some Illinois precedent hints that the implied covenant might apply in particular at-will termination situations. In *Hentze v. Unverfehrt* [237 Ill. App. 3d 606, 607 N.E.2d 536 (1992)], the Illinois Court of Appeals, finding bad faith conduct that amounted to "opportunistic advantage-taking," held the implied covenant applicable when a company terminated an at-will dealership contract and engaged in a variety of other bad-faith tactics specifically aimed at driving one of two competing dealers out of business. Saucy Sisters relies heavily on *Hentze*. It asserts that, as interpreted in *Hentze*, "The covenant of good faith and fair dealing requires, at a minimum, a proper motive to exercise the power [of termination without cause]." Because, in Saucy Sisters' view, the evidence at trial supported the conclusion that United ended its catering contract to seek a more lucrative arrangement with a competing caterer (Marriott), Saucy Sisters asserts that United's action, under *Hentze*'s approach, amounted to impermissible advantage-taking: "[A] party engages in opportunistic advantage-taking in Illinois when exercising the reserved power to terminate unreasonably and with an improper motive[.]"

But Saucy Sisters reads *Hentze* too broadly. The *Hentze* court took pains to acknowledge that, under the settled Illinois rule, the defendant company, DECO, "had the right to terminate the [dealership] contract for no reason at all." *Id.* at 540. So too, the *Hentze* court emphasized that, "had DECO merely . . . sent Hentze a termination letter . . . , we would be hard-pressed to find any absence of good faith." *Id.* The court thus made clear that its invocation of the implied covenant rested not on DECO's termination of the contract without, as Saucy Sisters puts it, "a proper motive to exercise the power," but rather on DECO's deliberate efforts to drive Hentze out of business by using other "tactics . . . [that] went far beyond the intendments of any at-will clause." *Id.* In short, the opportunistic advantage-taking described in *Hentze* was considerably more than an absence of the "legitimate business reason" that Saucy Sisters insists is a necessary ingredient for a valid at-will termination under Illinois law; it was instead a subjectively improper purpose—the malicious goal of driving Hentze out of business—combined with a variety of objectively unfair tactics designed to achieve that goal.

Stripped of its implied covenant trappings, Saucy Sisters' broad reading of *Hentze*—its contention that United could not act arbitrarily or capriciously, but instead was required to have a legitimate business reason for termination—amounts to a claim that United could terminate the catering contract only for cause. But, as we have seen, this claim cannot be countenanced under Illinois law. The settled rule in Illinois remains that a contract expressly terminable at will may be ended for any reason or no reason at all. *Hentze* does indicate that Illinois law might provide a measure of protection against a termination specifically motivated by bad faith and accompanied by unfair tactics. But Saucy Sisters neither alleged nor proved "opportunistic advantage-taking" of this kind. To the contrary, Saucy Sisters' complaint alleged no ulterior motive or subjective bad faith on United's part for terminating the contract, and its evidence at trial suggested only that United might have ended the contract in order to strike a better bargain with Marriott, not—as United claimed—because of Saucy Sisters' poor performance.

United's alleged desire for a more advantageous arrangement with Marriott certainly might not amount to "good cause" for terminating Saucy Sisters' contract, and from Saucy Sisters' perspective termination for this reason might even amount to arbitrary or capricious conduct, carried out for no legitimate business reason. But under Illinois law, the goal of achieving higher profits from a lower-bidding supplier is not itself inherently impermissible and does not amount to opportunistic advantage-taking; neither does reliance on an express at-will termination clause to attain this goal evince subjective bad faith or amount to an objectively unfair tactic....

In sum, we conclude that the trial court was mistaken in ruling that the implied covenant of good faith and fair dealing might "require both United and Saucy Sisters to exercise the discretion afforded to them by the termination clause in a manner consistent with the reasonable expectation of both parties." Under Illinois law, Saucy Sisters could not reasonably expect something other than what it expressly bargained for: a contract expressly terminable for any cause or no-cause upon ninety days' notice. Because we conclude that the court erred in submitting Saucy Sisters' implied covenant claim to the jury, we reverse the judgment against United. Our disposition makes it unnecessary to consider any other arguments raised on appeal or cross-appeal.

We affirm the trial court's order granting United summary judgment on Saucy Sisters' breach of contract claim, but reverse its order denying United summary judgment on the implied covenant claim. Accordingly, we vacate the judgment and remand for entry of judgment in favor of United.

MATTHEWS, Chief Justice, dissenting.

While I agree with the majority that Illinois law "favors the provisions of an express no-cause contract over potentially conflicting demands of the implied covenant [of good faith and fair dealing]," that type of contract is not at issue in this case. If this contract creates a right to terminate for no cause, the right exists because of a legal inference, not because that right is explicitly stated. I believe that a different legal inference should be drawn: that either party could terminate the contract for no cause if the reason for termination was consistent with the parties' reasonable expectations.

This reading is consistent with the implied covenant of good faith and fair dealing as expressed in section 205 of the Restatement (Second) of Contracts.... According to the Restatement, good faith enforcement "emphasizes faithfulness to an agreed common purpose and consistency with the justified expectations of the other party." One type of violation recognized by the Restatement is the "abuse of a power ... to terminate the contract." As authority for this comment the Restatement draws on various types of cases, including those involving franchise terminations.

The covenant of good faith and fair dealing was discussed in *Dayan v. McDonald's Corp.* [125 Ill. App. 3d 972], a franchise termination case involving Illinois law. The court reviewed its understanding of Illinois law regarding the covenant in terms materially indistinguishable from the Restatement: "As the above authorities demonstrate, the doctrine of good faith performance imposes a limitation on the exercise of discretion vested in one of the parties to a contract. In describing the nature of that limitation the courts of this state have held that a party vested with contractual discretion must exercise that discretion reasonably and with proper motive, and may not do so arbitrarily, capriciously, or in a manner inconsistent with the reasonable expectations of the parties."

Dayan confirms my view that the termination clause in the present case—since it does not state that the contract may be canceled without cause—should be construed to incorporate the covenant. . . . The parties in this case could have agreed on a termination provision which expressly stated that cancellation could be on any basis whatsoever, reasonable or unreasonable, just as they could have adopted a termination provision which required cause. They did neither. Instead, they left the provision open to differing interpretations. It is therefore logical to infer that the parties intended to operate in an atmosphere of good faith and fair dealing, and that the covenant applies. . . .

While it would be sufficient to end the analysis here, the following observations concerning the covenant's application to the facts of this case seem worth making. Determining the reasonable expectations of contracting parties is not necessarily an easy task. Contract language must be considered along with the parties' discussions and the purposes of the contract. And it may be useful to ask what the parties would have done had they considered the precise issue when the contract was formed. . . . Both parties knew that Saucy Sisters must undergo expensive renovations in order to serve United. Saucy Sisters claims a cost of $600,000. We might ask what the parties would have done had Saucy Sisters asked United whether United could terminate the contract either soon after start up or at any time during the three-year term solely because a competitor offered better terms. I think the answer would have been that United would forego [*sic*] that power. Had United asserted the right to terminate to get better terms, there likely would have been no contract. Saucy Sisters would probably not have spent what for it was a small fortune had United overtly reserved the right to make a better deal during the three-year period.

Most cases invoking the obligation to perform in good faith can be synthesized using the following principle: a party performs in bad faith by using discretion in performance for reasons outside the justified expectations of the parties arising from their agreement. Distinguishing allowed from disallowed reasons—opportunities forgone from opportunities preserved on entering a contract—will often be easy. But the distinction will be difficult in some cases. Specific disallowed reasons may be inferred from the express contract terms in light of the ordinary course of business and customary practice, in accordance with the usual principles of contract interpretation. It is not hard to infer from a fixed contract price, for example, that the parties have forgone opportunities to take advantage of market price fluctuations.

Thus, in my view, early termination by United motivated by a desire to contract with a competitor on better terms would have contradicted the justified expectations of Saucy Sisters.

In light of the foregoing, I believe that summary judgment in favor of United was therefore correctly denied. Whether particular conduct qualifies as good faith is a question of law for the court. But whether United in fact acted with an impermissible motive was properly a question for the jury. No question has been raised as to whether the jury was correctly instructed. I would therefore affirm the judgment on the question of liability.

■ QUESTIONS

(1) Compare the *Saucy Sisters* majority opinion with that of the dissent. What do they interpret the express or implied provisions of the contract to be? Do they agree that those provisions are qualified by an obligation of good faith? If so, how do they differ in their conceptions of what constitutes good faith? Do they weigh any public policies in interpreting and/or construing the contract?

(2) In the eyes of the dissent, could United have protected itself against a charge that it failed to act in good faith by drafting its agreement differently? Why, do you suppose, it drafted the agreement the way it did? To avoid future litigation of this sort, would you recommend that it change its standard contract language?

(3) Saucy Sisters alleged that Roger Groth made certain statements to it during contract negotiations. United disputed those allegations. Suppose you represented Saucy Sisters at the time the contract was entered and you were present when Roger Groth made the statements alleged in the case. What changes would you have requested to the contract language? If United Airlines had refused to make the changes that you requested, what advice would you have given to your client?

(4) Take a quick look back at Chapter 13. Any number of the doctrines studied in that chapter make reference to the concept of good faith. To name just a few, you may recall that good faith is relevant in determining whether failure to disclose a fact constitutes a misrepresentation or whether certain threats are improper and thus may give rise to a claim of duress. These doctrines represent limited exceptions to the notion that there is no general duty of good faith in the negotiation of a contract. Restatement, Second §205 and UCC 1-304 speak only of good faith in the performance or enforcement of a contract, not in its negotiation or formation. Why is requiring good faith in the initial negotiation of a contract different from requiring it in the contract's performance or enforcement? Do you think implying a general duty of good faith in contract negotiations is a good idea?

THE DOCTRINE OF MISUNDERSTANDING AND ITS RELATION TO CONTRACT INTERPRETATION AND CONSTRUCTION

As the materials in this chapter amply indicate, words are often susceptible to more than one meaning. A gardener's flourishing "green plant" may be a businessperson's environmentally conscious industrial facility. Whenever parties use language to capture their contractual expectations, there is a possibility that they will attach different meanings to the terms they use. Yet we have seen that it is the words and actions of the parties viewed in context that supply the content of the contract, not their internal subjective thoughts. Courts may conclude that the contract imposes obligations that are at odds with what one (or even both) of the parties argue they understood at the time the contract was entered. This result is thoroughly familiar to us by this stage of our study; contracts do not rest on what the parties subjectively understood at the time the contract was entered, but rather on what a court concludes would be reasonable to expect under the circumstances. The fact that the parties may have misunderstood each other's intentions generally does not prevent the formation of a contract. Once a contract is found, courts typically can employ the usual techniques of contract interpretation and construction to determine whose understanding should prevail and what the requirements of the ultimate contract should be.

On rare occasions, however, the parties use the same words but mean materially different things, and when a dispute arises courts are unable to resolve the differing interpretations in a manner that is reasonable or fair. The court concludes that there is no basis on which to prefer one party's interpretation over the other's and there is no standard by which an appropriate term can be supplied by the court. Where a misunderstanding of this nature exists, a court may conclude that any manifestation of mutual assent is illusory, and no contract has been formed. Courts and scholars often refer to these cases as resulting from "misunderstanding" or sometimes "complete misunderstanding."

The classic case in this area is that of the ship *Peerless*, or perhaps better said, the ships *Peerless*.[22] In that case, *Raffles v. Wichelhaus*, 2 Hurl. 906, 159 Eng. Rep. 375 (Exch. Div. 1864), the plaintiff agreed to sell some cotton arriving from Bombay on the ship *Peerless*. The defendant agreed to buy some cotton arriving from Bombay on the ship *Peerless*. As it turned out, there were at least two ships *Peerless* roaming the high seas: one slated to leave Bombay in October, the other in December. In a plunging cotton market, the defendant refused to accept the cotton that arrived by the later ship *Peerless*, arguing that he had meant the earlier ship when he had agreed to make his purchase. In a report that is notoriously difficult to read and interpret, the court held for the defendant. The court seemed to be persuaded by the argument that where the plaintiff meant one ship and the defendant another, there could be no meeting of the minds and thus no contract. Although the language of the *Peerless* case is rooted in an earlier era of contract doctrine, the general principle that it has come to

---

[22] The history of the *Peerless* case is discussed in detail in A.W. Brian Simpson, *Contracts for Cotton to Arrive: The Case of the Two Ships Peerless*, 11 Cardozo L. Rev. 287 (1989). Grant Gilmore also gave a riotous account of the case in his *The Death of Contract* 39-47 (Ronald K.L. Collins ed., 2d ed., Ohio St. U. Press 1995), although Gilmore's rendition is reputed to be stronger on rhetorical effect than historical accuracy. Gilmore, we understand, told a marvelous story and was sometimes willing to spin a few facts for the sake of the tale.

materially different meaning to important contract terms

represent lives on. Where parties attach materially different meanings to important contract terms, and neither knows nor has reason to know of the misunderstanding, no contract results.

rare occurrence

Modern cases and commentary consider the prospect of "complete misunderstanding," but actual reported cases that find it to have occurred are few and far between. More often, the interpretation advanced by one party is held to be better than the other. Sometimes, this is because one interpretation is more in line with the context of the transaction, and so is objectively more reasonable than the other. Alternatively, one party may prevail because the other is in some sense at fault for the misunderstanding. This would be the case, for instance, if

knowledge ya are using terms in different ways

the party held to be at fault knew or had reason to know that the parties were using terms in different ways but took no steps to clear up the misunderstanding. But occasionally complete misunderstandings do arise that lead a court to conclude that the parties did not form a contract.

What follows is a more recent misunderstanding case. (Notice that the court cites the *Peerless* case, even though it was decided more than a century earlier.) As you read the facts, think about whether either party knew or had any reason to know what the other party was thinking. Was one party more responsible for the misunderstanding than the other?

KONIC INTERNATIONAL CORP. v. SPOKANE COMPUTER SERVICES, INC.

109 Idaho 527, 708 P.2d 932 (1985)
Idaho Court of Appeals

WALTERS, Chief Judge.

Konic International Corporation sued Spokane Computer Services, Inc., to collect the price of an electrical device allegedly sold by Konic to Spokane Computer. The suit was tried before a magistrate sitting without a jury. The

posture

magistrate entered judgment for Spokane Computer, concluding there was no contract between the parties because of lack of apparent authority of an employee of Spokane Computer to purchase the device from Konic. The district court, on appeal, upheld the magistrate's judgment. On further appeal by Konic, we also affirm the magistrate's judgment but base our result on reasoning different from that of the lower court.

The magistrate found the following facts. David Young, an employee of Spokane Computer, was instructed by his employer to investigate the possibility of purchasing a surge protector, a device which protects computers from damaging surges of electrical current. Young's investigation turned up several units priced from $50 to $200, none of which, however, were appropriate for his employer's needs. Young then contacted Konic. After discussing Spokane

Computer's needs with a Konic engineer, Young was referred to one of Konic's salesmen. Later, after deciding on a certain unit, Young inquired as to the price of the selected item. The salesman responded, "fifty-six twenty." The salesman meant $5,620. Young in turn thought $56.20.

The salesman for Konic asked about Young's authority to order the equipment and was told that Young would have to get approval from one of his superiors. Young in turn prepared a purchase order for $56.20 and had it approved by the appropriate authority. Young telephoned the order and purchase order number to Konic, who then shipped the equipment to Spokane Computer. However, because of internal processing procedures of both parties the discrepancy in prices was not discovered immediately. Spokane Computer received the surge protector and installed it in its office. The receipt and installation of the equipment occurred while the president of Spokane Computer was on vacation. Although the president's father, who was also chairman of the board of Spokane Computer, knew of the installation, he only inquired as to what the item was and who had ordered it. The president came back from vacation the day after the surge protector had been installed and placed in operation and was told of the purchase. He immediately ordered that power to the equipment be turned off because he realized that the equipment contained parts which alone were worth more than $56 in value. Although the president then told Young to verify the price of the surge protector, Young failed to do so. Two weeks later, when Spokane Computer was processing its purchase order and Konic's invoice, the discrepancy between the amount on the invoice and the amount on the purchase order was discovered. The president of Spokane Computer then contacted Konic, told Konic that Young had no authority to order such equipment, that Spokane Computer did not want the equipment, and that Konic should remove it. Konic responded that Spokane Computer now owned the equipment and if the equipment was not paid for, Konic would sue for the price. Spokane Computer refused to pay and this litigation ensued.

Following trial, the magistrate found that Young had no actual, implied, or apparent authority to enter into the transaction and, therefore, Spokane Computer did not owe Konic for the equipment. In reaching its decision, the magistrate also noted that when Spokane Computer acquired full knowledge of the facts, it took prompt action to disaffirm Young's purchase. We agree with the magistrate's result. However, rather than base our decision on the agency principle of apparent authority, as did the trial court, we believe that more basic principles of contract are determinative in this case. . . .

Basically what is involved here is a failure of communication between the parties. A similar failure to communicate arose over 100 years ago in the celebrated case of *Raffles v. Wichelhaus*, 2 Hurl. 906, 159 Eng. Rep. 375 (1864), which has become better known as the case of the good ship "Peerless". . . . The *Peerless* rule later was incorporated into section 71 of the Restatement of Contracts and has now evolved into section 20 of Restatement (Second) of Contracts (1981).

Section 20 states in part: "(1) There is no manifestation of mutual assent to an exchange if the parties attach materially different meanings to their manifestations and (a) neither knows or has reason to know the meaning attached by the other." Comment (c) to section 20 further explains that "even though the parties manifest mutual assent to the same words of agreement, there may be no contract because of a material difference of understanding as to the terms of the exchange."

One commentator on the *Peerless* case, maintaining that the doctrine should be cautiously applied, indicates three principles about the case doctrine that are generally in agreement: (1) the doctrine applies only when the parties have different understandings of their expression of agreement; (2) the doctrine does not apply when one party's understanding, because of that party's fault, is less reasonable than the other party's understanding; and (3) parol evidence is admissible to establish the facts necessary to apply the rule. Young, *Equivocation in the Making of Agreements*, 64 Colum. L. Rev. 619 (1964).

The second principle indicates that the doctrine may be applicable to this case because, arguably, both parties' understandings were reasonable. Also, as pointed out by the district court, both parties were equally at fault in contributing to the resulting problems. The third principle is not relevant to the present case.

The first principle is not only directly applicable to the present case, but also corresponds to reasoning used in *Snoderly v. Bower*, 30 Idaho 484, 166 P. 265 (1917), citing the *Peerless* case. In *Snoderly* the court dealt with two parties who had contracted to grow hay. The parties had agreed that, after the hay was harvested and stacked, the hay would "be measured according to government rule." Unfortunately, there were several government rules in use in the vicinity for measuring hay. The court determined that "there was no meeting of the minds of the parties on the question as to what constituted the 'government rule' when the contract was entered into, and that provision in the contract would therefore be void." 30 Idaho at 488, 166 P. at 266, citing *Peerless*. *Snoderly* is somewhat different from the present case because in *Snoderly* both parties apparently wished to keep the benefits of their contract. Our Supreme Court therefore remanded for a determination of the reasonable value of services rendered. In the present case, Spokane Computer did not wish to retain the benefits of Konic's equipment as evidenced by the president's instruction that power to the equipment be turned off immediately and his demand on Konic to remove the equipment.

In the present case, both parties attributed different meanings to the same term, "fifty-six twenty." Thus, there was no meeting of the minds of the parties. With a hundred fold difference in the two prices, obviously price was a material term. Because the "fifty-six twenty" designation was a material term expressed in an ambiguous form to which two meanings were obviously applied, we conclude that no contract between the parties was ever formed. Accordingly, we do not reach the issue of whether Young had authority to order the equipment....

The decision of the district court is affirmed....

■ QUESTIONS

research meant his mistake was reasonable

(1)   The court indicates that Young investigated surge protectors before contacting Konic. In your view, is the investigation relevant to the result in this case? Would it matter if at the time Young contacted Konic, Konic's surge protector was by far the most expensive one on the market and Konic was aware of that fact? – *knowledge of potential mistake*

(2)   The magistrate concluded that there was no contract, because Young did not have the apparent, implied, or actual authority to bind Spokane. The court of appeals does not rest its decision on this analysis. In your view, would the analysis have proceeded differently if the president of Spokane had been the person communicating with Konic when the misunderstanding arose, rather than Young? – *not for appeals based on misunderstanding*

still would find no contract

(3)   Suppose Spokane elected to keep the surge protector. What price would they have to pay, and why?

→ more experience / knowledge

■ PROBLEM 15.8

Some misunderstandings have the potential to achieve folkloric status.[23] In 2001, the manager of a Hooters restaurant in Florida informed his staff that the chain was sponsoring a contest. Whoever sold the most beer during the month of April would be entered into a drawing; the winner of the drawing would win a new Toyota. In May, the manager informed waitress Jodee Berry that she had won the contest, and she was escorted to the parking lot, blindfolded. There her prize was revealed—a toy "Yoda." (Movie aficionados will recognize Yoda as the ancient Jedi master from the Star Wars series.) Berry, who had been expecting a new car, quit her job and sued her former employer. The lawsuit settled out of court. Had the lawsuit not settled, could the employer have persuasively argued, relying on a theory of misunderstanding, that no contract resulted under these facts? Why or why not?

---

[23] Professor Rowley discusses this case and some of the legal issues it raises in Keith A. Rowley, *You Asked For It, You Got It . . . Toy Yoda: Practical Jokes, Prizes, and Contract Law*, 3 Nev. L.J. 526 (2003).

CHAPTER 16

The Parol Evidence Rule

A   INTRODUCTION TO THE PAROL EVIDENCE RULE

Chapter 15 emphasizes the role of contextual evidence in the interpretation of contracts. Even when the parties reduce their agreement to a signed writing, the circumstances surrounding a contract can reveal the meaning of ambiguous contract terms. Evidence extrinsic to a writing—be it from negotiations, a usage of trade, a course of dealing, or a course of performance—can clarify what the parties contemplated by language contained in the written memorial of their agreement. However, as useful as this extrinsic evidence may be in guiding the court to the proper meaning of contract language, recourse to it has its hazards. Sometimes, the proffered evidence suggests an interpretation that is not readily apparent from the writing. In more extreme cases, the extrinsic evidence is difficult to reconcile with the language included in the written agreement. If the extrinsic evidence is inaccurate or unreliable and the writing alone reflects the reasonable expectations of the parties, reference to extrinsic evidence defeats rather than effectuates their intentions. Further, extensive fact-based arguments over contract terms complicate and protract litigation. In light of these concerns, as we discuss in Chapter 15, principles of contract interpretation generally give weight to the plain meaning of written terms and sometimes exclude evidence of meaning not drawn from the written agreement itself. The parol evidence rule reinforces and extends the preference given to written terms.

Although there are commonalities between interpretation of a written agreement and application of the parol evidence rule, the two are conceptually

gives preference to written terms

distinct. Through the process of interpretation, a judge (or a jury, as the case may be) decides the meaning of the terms included in a written agreement. Suppose, for instance, that Molto Agitato is planning to stage a concert. He enters into a signed, written agreement with Musical Rental Co. under which Musical agrees to rent a "bass" to Molto for one evening at the price of $600. If a dispute arose and one of the parties argued that the subject matter of the contract was a male singer with a deep voice, and the other argued that it was a musical instrument, the court hearing the dispute would need to interpret the meaning of the word "bass." If the judge determined that the word was unambiguous (whether based on its plain meaning as revealed by an examination of the writing as a whole or based on broader consideration of the context of the transaction), that meaning would prevail. Otherwise, it would be for the fact-finder to determine the reasonable meaning of the word based on all available contextual evidence.[1] Likewise, if the parties conceded that rental of a musical instrument was agreed but disputed whether it was to be an electric or an acoustic bass, the court would engage in the same process of interpretation to determine the meaning reasonably intended by the parties. In either case, the court would be establishing the meaning of the terms contained in the written agreement.

The parol evidence rule, instead, is relevant when one of the parties argues that the "true" expectations of the parties either contradict or supplement the written terms. Where a party seeks to contradict the terms of a written agreement, the parol evidence rule has its strongest expression. So if Molto argued that the parties' actual intentions were to rent a piano rather than a bass, the parol evidence rule might prevent Molto from introducing evidence to support his allegations. (Note that this is very similar to an analysis under contract interpretation principles: If Molto argues that the term "bass" means "piano," absent unusual circumstances that are difficult to imagine, a court would probably conclude that he has proffered a meaning to which the term "bass" is not reasonably susceptible, and thus evidence of his meaning should be kept from the trier of fact.)

Not only is it problematic to contradict a written agreement under the parol evidence rule; in some circumstances it may be difficult to supplement it as well. So, for instance, if one of the parties argued that Musical was to provide sheet music along with the bass, even though the written agreement was silent on that point, the parol evidence rule might prevent consideration of evidence of the existence or terms of that side agreement. As we will see, the parol evidence rule allows supplementation of writings in a broader range of circumstances than it allows contradiction of them; however, in many instances neither supplementation nor contradiction is permitted.

[1] As noted in Chapter 15, if there was no objective basis on which to decide between the differing interpretations, the court might invoke the doctrine of "misunderstanding" and refuse to enforce a contract at all. For purposes of this example, we assume the dispute can be resolved by the usual processes of interpretation.

no clear test for explanatory v. supplement

Even though the principles of contract interpretation are conceptually distinct from the parol evidence rule, a court often must determine what a written agreement means before it can decide if evidence contradicts or supplements the written terms. Further, it can be difficult to distinguish evidence that is offered to explain the terms of a writing from evidence that attempts to supplement it or contradict it. For instance, suppose Molto alleges that before he signed the rental agreement with Musical, Musical orally agreed to rent him the "Blue Bass," a rare antique instrument that Musical had recently purchased from a famous musician. Musical denies that this conversation ever took place and delivers a serviceable but undistinguished modern bass. Molto protests and ultimately files suit, alleging breach of contract. Assuming the written agreement is silent as to the precise bass to be rented, if Molto seeks to introduce testimony to support his allegations, what is the nature of that evidence? One could say that it goes to the reasonable expectations of the parties as to the meaning of the term "bass" at the time the contract was entered, and thus principles of contract interpretation should apply. Alternatively, one might argue that the testimony seeks to establish an agreement that is not reflected in the writing—that is, it seeks to supplement the writing—and therefore the parol evidence rule should control. Clear tests to recognize explanatory evidence (or, alternatively, supplemental or contradictory evidence) remain elusive. Accordingly, interpretation questions are often intertwined with parol evidence rule issues, and you will often see courts speaking of the two in the same breath.

difference in explaining v. supplement + contradict

parole evidence would stop this

The parol evidence rule is based on the assumption that when parties record their agreement in writing, they often intend the writing to incorporate the final and complete version of what they agreed and to supersede terms that they may have discussed or even agreed to in prior or contemporaneous negotiations. Any evidence of the parties' expectations that is not reflected in the written agreement, often referred to as "parol" or "extrinsic" evidence, may be suspect. Although courts and commentators articulate the parol evidence rule in different ways, its broad outlines are fairly simple to state. When the parties adopt a writing as a final statement of the terms of their agreement, the terms of that agreement may not be contradicted by parol evidence relating to matters that occurred prior to the writing or contemporaneously with the writing. When the parties intend their writing not only to be final but also to be comprehensive, then the terms of that agreement may not be supplemented by prior or contemporaneous parol evidence either.

final writing holds the final meaning

Parol evidence may come from various sources. "Parol" is an old form of the French "parole," meaning "word" or "speech." In common usage, it typically connotes the spoken word. However, its legal meaning is broader than this. The parol evidence rule covers not only evidence of oral interactions but also certain kinds of written evidence that is extrinsic to the written memorial of the agreement. When a written agreement exists, the parol evidence rule limits a party's ability to offer extrinsic evidence to supplement or contradict the written memorial, be the evidence written or oral. Since the parol evidence rule speaks

covers oral agreements + extra writings

look to parties intentions at the time they adopted the writing

to the parties' intentions at the time they adopted their written memorial, it doesn't apply to agreements the parties reach after adopting the writing. Instead, it largely applies to evidence of the parties' expectations that arose prior to or contemporaneously with the written agreement.

There is one subtlety regarding contemporaneous written evidence that bears mention. Sometimes parties adopt a series of writings to comprehensively memorialize the terms of their agreement. So whether contemporaneous supplementary evidence is subject to exclusion under the parol evidence rule may depend on whether that evidence is oral or written. For instance, when parties close a complex commercial transaction, they often sign a series of documents, each of which addresses a different aspect of their deal. Even if the documents do not so provide, it is understood that the terms of each document supplement the terms of the others. In effect, in these circumstances, at least insofar as contemporaneous evidence is concerned, a court is likely to treat the documents as one for purposes of the parol evidence rule; that is, contemporaneous oral evidence may not be introduced to supplement the terms of the documents taken as a whole, but the parol evidence rule will not bar using one of the documents to supplement the terms of the others. Accordingly, courts sometimes say that the parol evidence rule bars consideration of prior agreements altogether but bars contemporaneous agreements only if they are oral. For our present purposes, you need only note this subtlety and move on.

bars prior & bars contemporaneous oral ✸✸

To summarize, as long as the evidence in question is within the parol evidence rule's scope, the degree to which courts exclude that evidence depends on the nature of the writing and the purpose for which the evidence is being provided. Of these, it is the nature of the writing that causes the most conceptual difficulty. In a situation where the parties are disputing the scope and content of their agreement, they may also dispute the degree to which the parties intended a writing to be the authoritative and complete statement of their agreement. As in other areas of contract law, it is often not the actual intentions of the parties that control but rather their reasonable intentions as determined by the court. Common law courts use the term "integrated" to refer to a writing that expresses the final agreement of the parties as to the matters discussed in that writing. To the extent an integrated writing is reasonably intended not only to be final but to be comprehensive as well, it is "fully integrated." If it is not reasonably intended to be comprehensive, it is at most "partially integrated."[2] Accordingly, we spend much of the chapter exploring the processes and standards courts use to decide the degree to which a writing is integrated. At the outset a simple illustration may help to set the scene.

need to know the nature of the writings

fully v. partially

Suppose Wendy Wood constructs custom-built cabinets and bookshelves. Ben Book is interested in installing some new bookshelves in his bookstore. Ben

---

[2] As we will see, the UCC's version of the parol evidence rule uses different terminology to categorize writings, but the categories are roughly analogous to the common law concepts. We discuss the UCC's version of the parol evidence rule in Section B.3.

writes, signs, and sends a letter to Wendy, in which he states, "As we have discussed previously, I might be interested in having you build and install $50,000 worth of bookshelves for me. Contact me if you are interested in the job." The parties then meet to discuss terms, and Wendy ultimately builds and installs bookshelves for Ben. If a dispute subsequently arises about how much Ben agreed to pay, it's possible that Ben's letter might be relevant to that dispute.[3] But common experience would suggest that the letter would not be entitled to much weight; it itself references prior conversations without disclosing or superseding their content, it is by its terms preliminary, and it is unilateral because it comes from Ben alone. In short, there is no reason to believe that it reflects the agreement the parties ultimately reached. This writing is not integrated at all; the parties would not only be allowed to introduce evidence extrinsic to the writing to establish the price to which they agreed, but we would expect them to do so. The parol evidence rule, in short, would have no application.

Suppose, instead, that after they met to discuss terms, Ben sent Wendy a letter that stated in full as follows: "I am delighted that you have agreed to construct the bookshelves for me on the terms we discussed and agreed earlier today. I just wanted to confirm that you will be able to complete the work for $50,000. Please sign in the space provided below to confirm that you will complete the job for $50,000." Wendy signed the letter in the space provided and returned it to Ben. If a dispute subsequently arose about how much Ben agreed to pay, Wendy would not be able to introduce evidence of conversations that predated the letter in which Ben agreed to pay $55,000. In context, it is reasonable to assume that this writing, signed by both parties, superseded any previous conversations (if in fact the conversations even took place, which itself is likely to be a subject of disagreement). If, however, the dispute concerned when Wendy was supposed to start the job, or what wood she would be using, or who would be responsible for paying for the wood, then the result would be different. On these matters the writing was silent, and we would expect a court to allow the parties to rely on extrinsic evidence to prove up those aspects of their agreement. Since the letter was so thin and addressed so few aspects of the relationship between the parties, it is reasonable to suppose that it was not intended to be comprehensive. The writing is partially integrated; that is, while it cannot be contradicted by prior or contemporaneous parol evidence, it could be supplemented.

writing is partially integrated so it is supplemental

---

[3] As this transaction involves both goods and services, it might be governed by UCC Article 2. For our purposes, we will assume that the common law would apply. As an aside, if UCC Article 2 did apply to the transaction, the UCC's statute of frauds would be implicated. Although both the statute of frauds and the parol evidence rule emphasize the importance of writings, recognize their functions and requirements are quite distinct. Nevertheless, the curious may question whether the UCC's statute of frauds could ever be satisfied if Ben doesn't sign anything that specifies a quantity term. Even if there is no signed writing that satisfies the statute, some other exception may apply. For instance, if Wendy completes construction and installation of the bookshelves and Ben accepts them, the parties' performance would satisfy the statute under UCC 2-201(3)(c).

Imagine instead that Ben, along with his team of lawyers, met with Wendy and her team of lawyers every morning for a period of weeks. They negotiated at length the language and content of a 30-page written agreement, which they ultimately signed at a formal closing ceremony. The written agreement included extensive specifications of the work to be done, an elaborate construction and payment schedule, representations and warranties as to the solvency and experience of the parties, covenants to comply with applicable laws and construction standards (among other things), a list of events that would constitute a default under the agreement, and procedures for exercising remedies in the event a default occurred. In the many pages of boilerplate at the end of the agreement, there was a clause that said, "This Agreement represents the entire agreement between the parties and supersedes all prior negotiations, representations or agreements, whether written, oral, or arising from other circumstances." A dispute subsequently arose, and one of the parties attempted to prove that the writing didn't represent the parties' "real" agreement at the time. That party attempted to introduce parol evidence that either contradicted the written terms or else addressed a matter not discussed at all in the written agreement. It is likely that a court would deem this agreement to be fully integrated and would not allow consideration of prior or contemporaneous parol evidence, regardless of whether it was being offered to contradict the writing or merely supplement it.

As is so often the case, the disputes that give rise to reported decisions are seldom as clear-cut as these simple examples. In the next section, we introduce the processes courts use and the factors they consider in applying the parol evidence rule.

B APPLICATION OF THE PAROL EVIDENCE RULE

Although the parol evidence rule is relatively easy to state, real difficulties arise in trying to apply it. The difficulties emerge at each stage of the analysis. Whether a writing is integrated, and if so, whether it is "partially integrated" or "fully integrated" are questions of some subtlety, and their answers are elusive. The degree to which the parol evidence itself should be considered in determining the nature of the writing has proven to be a particularly contentious issue. Likewise, whether a party is offering parol evidence merely to explain a writing, thereby invoking principles of contract interpretation, or rather to contradict or supplement the writing, thus implicating the parol evidence rule instead, can itself be a matter of some controversy.

is the evidence explaining?
✕ issue with the nature of the writing!

It is important to recognize that the complexity in applying the parol evidence rule arises from the fact that it has a potential for both good and harm. The rule serves the cause of fairness by acting as a barrier to a party who tries to claim that the contract included a term that was in fact never agreed to, but it can defeat the cause of fairness by excluding evidence of something that was truly agreed. Likewise, literal enforcement of writings may increase the certainty, efficiency, and predictability of litigation, while recourse to parol evidence may have the opposite effect. These competing considerations cause some courts to apply the parol evidence rule quite gingerly, as they try to walk the narrow line between too harsh and too liberal an application of the rule. (As we discuss in Chapter 15, these concerns animate the law's treatment of interpretation of written agreements as well. They are also similar to those raised in connection with the statute of frauds, where most courts try to balance the use of the statute so that it blocks dishonest claims of oral agreement and allows for efficient settlement of disputes, but does not aid a person who seeks to deny the existence of a genuine oral agreement.) In the end, the courts' delicate balancing act has shaped a doctrine that is complex, subtle, and occasionally incoherent.

The process of dealing with parol evidence at common law typically has two stages, much as the process of interpreting a written agreement often has two stages.[4] As we discuss in Chapter 15, when interpreting a written agreement, it is the function of the judge to determine whether the language contained in the written agreement is ambiguous. Depending on the jurisdiction, the judge may or may not consider evidence extrinsic to the writing in making this initial determination. The fact-finder hears extrinsic evidence of meaning only if the court finds the written agreement to be ambiguous.

judge decides the ambiguity — *goes to fact finder*

Likewise, when one of the parties tenders parol evidence that arguably contradicts or supplements a written agreement, it is the function of the judge to determine whether the parol evidence rule bars consideration of that evidence. As the discussion in Section A suggests, this determination rests both on the level of integration of the writing (that is, whether it is fully integrated, partially integrated, or not integrated at all) and on the purpose for which the parol evidence is being offered (that is, to contradict or merely to supplement the writing). Again, jurisdictions differ in the degree to which judges may consider evidence extrinsic to the writing (including the parol evidence at issue) in making these initial determinations. If the judge finds that the parol evidence rule bars the evidence at issue, the fact-finder does not consider it. If the judge finds that the parol evidence rule does not bar the evidence at issue, the fact-finder hears it and weighs its credibility much as it does with regard to any factual issue.

The impact of allowing or excluding parol evidence will depend on how central it is to the claim or defense of the party who seeks to rely on it. If the judge decides that the fact-finder may consider the parol evidence, this is only a provisional victory for the party seeking to rely on it. The party tendering the evidence still has to persuade the fact-finder that the evidence is credible and the parties agreed to the alleged term. If the judge concludes that the parol

---

[4] Again, courts do not always observe the division we describe here. Nor do they necessarily approach the issues in this order; parol evidence issues can arise in many guises and at many stages of a lawsuit. We provide only a general overview of the usual approach here.

evidence rule bars consideration of the evidence, its exclusion may result in the collapse of the claim or defense; however, if arguments relying on the excluded evidence are merely corroborative or supplementary of other arguments, the claim or defense may still prevail, albeit in a possibly weaker state.

The law could have simply left it to the fact-finder to decide if the parties truly agreed to the alleged term, despite its absence from (or contradiction with) the writing. However, this approach has been disfavored for two reasons. First, if the parol evidence is not relevant to any determination of the reasonable expectations of the parties, its exclusion may result in reducing the length and cost of the litigation. This is particularly true where a claim or defense depends on the parol evidence. If a judge evaluates the evidence and bars consideration of it at an early stage of the case—for example, upon a motion for dismissal or summary judgment—the judge might dispose of the case without trial. Second, even when the parol evidence is not critical to the continued viability of a case, the rule serves as a control over the jury. An important premise of the parol evidence rule is that a judge needs to guide and control the jury's decision-making process. If the parol evidence is unreliable, misleading, or perjured, the jury who hears it risks making an inappropriate decision. The judge, through application of the parol evidence rule, screens the jury from such evidence. As noted previously, there are strong parallels among the concerns described here and those that animate the similarly bifurcated treatment of the interpretation of written agreements.

1. The Evolution of the Parol Evidence Rule

As mentioned in the last section, the judge first must decide whether the parol evidence rule bars the fact-finder's consideration of the evidence at issue. This typically requires the judge to consider the degree to which the writing is integrated, as well as the purpose for which the parol evidence is offered. Both aspects can raise challenging and difficult issues, but it is the determination of the degree of integration that has caused the most controversy among courts and commentators. The issue of whether a writing is integrated at all does not come up that often. However, the methods courts use to distinguish fully integrated writings from partially integrated ones have attracted significant debate. The analyses used by judges to make this distinction have evolved over time and remain inconsistent from jurisdiction to jurisdiction, and even within some jurisdictions.

In the older cases, but even in many recent ones, you may find courts limiting themselves to the "four corners" of a document when they try to decide if that document represents a fully integrated writing. There is a close conceptual connection between the "plain meaning" approach to interpretation, discussed in Chapter 15, and the "four corners" approach to the parol evidence rule. Although courts sometimes use the phrases "plain meaning" and "four corners" interchangeably, the two approaches are at least in theory distinct. "Plain meaning" interpretation is a method used to determine the meaning of the actual words used by the parties. Sometimes courts who take this approach invoke the phrase "four corners" as well, for instance by stating something like "only if language is ambiguous may a court look outside the four corners of a written agreement to determine the parties' intent." In contrast, when used in connection with the parol evidence rule, the phrase "four corners" relates not to the determination of ambiguity, but rather to the question of the degree to which the writing at issue integrates the parties' agreement.

is it part of the four corners

Under a "four corners" approach to the parol evidence rule, the judge determines whether the writing was intended to be a comprehensive statement of the parties' agreement on the basis of the appearance of the writing itself. The judge pays little attention to the specific circumstances of the parties or the credibility of the proffered parol evidence. If the writing appears to be complete on its face, it is supposed to be treated as complete—that is, it is fully integrated. In these instances, parol evidence is not admissible to contradict or supplement the writing.

This "four corners" approach to determining the completeness of the writing, much like the "plain meaning" approach to ambiguity, emphasizes the logical and objective resolution of disputes in accordance with formal rules. If courts treated agreements that appeared to be complete as if they were complete and if courts interpreted words consistently in accordance with their plain meaning, in theory greater clarity and predictability would result. If parties wanted a different outcome, they would be encouraged to put their full agreements in writing and, if necessary, use different words.

The strict "four corners" approach to the parol evidence rule strains to account for situations where the parties may have entered into a parol agreement entirely unrelated to the subject matter of an integrated writing. Suppose, for instance, that Terra Firma entered into a written agreement with Louise Landscaper, in which Terra agreed to purchase a parcel of real estate from Louise. Suppose further that a "four corners" court would consider the writing to be complete on its face. Under what circumstances should the parol evidence rule bar allegations that during the course of negotiating the purchase of the real estate, Louise also agreed to mow Terra's lawn? Although the writing may completely memorialize the parties' understandings regarding the real estate transaction, they may have viewed the lawn mowing transaction as unrelated. It might not have occurred to the parties (in fact, they might have considered it bizarre) to include the terms of the lawn mowing agreement in their written memorial. Even the early cases admitted the possibility that separate parol agreements could be enforceable, yet they struggled to distinguish completely independent parol agreements, which should be enforced, from those that sought to supplement a facially complete writing, which presumably should not be enforced.

The classic case of *Mitchill v. Lath*, 247 N.Y. 377, 160 N.E. 646 (1928), wrestled with this distinction. In *Mitchill v. Lath*, a buyer of real estate alleged that the seller had promised to remove an unsightly icehouse from an adjoining piece of property. The written agreement signed by the parties was silent on this issue. Judge Andrews, writing for the majority, held that the writing appeared to be complete on its face and excluded the proffered evidence. Nowhere did he

Credibility
of parole evidence
was irrelevant

express any doubt as to the buyer's veracity—the credibility of the parol evidence was simply irrelevant to his deliberations. The dissent, written by Judge Lehman, questioned how the issue of the parties' intentions could be settled through an examination of the writing alone, stating:

> [T]he question we must decide is whether or not, assuming an agreement was made for the removal of an unsightly ice house from one parcel of land as an inducement for the purchase of another parcel, the parties would ordinarily or naturally be expected to embody the agreement for the removal of the ice house from one parcel in the written agreement to convey the other parcel. Exclusion of proof of the oral agreement on the ground that it varies the contract embodied in the writing may be based only upon a finding or presumption that the written contract was intended to cover the oral negotiations for the removal of the ice house which lead up to the contract of purchase and sale. To determine what the writing was intended to cover "the document alone will not suffice. What it was intended to cover cannot be known till we know what there was to cover. The question being whether certain subjects of negotiation were intended to be covered, we must compare the writing and the negotiations before we can determine whether they were in fact covered." (*Wigmore on Evidence* [2d ed.], section 2430.)

Williston found both the strict "four corners" approach and the case law on collateral agreements prevailing at the time to be unsatisfactory. Instead, he advocated applying a test much like the one enunciated by Judge Lehman and quoted above. The First Restatement of Contracts, for which Williston was the reporter, incorporated this approach. If the parties would "naturally" make a parol agreement yet not reflect it in the written agreement, the parol evidence should be admitted. In modern parlance, the written agreement would be partially integrated with respect to that parol evidence. Conversely, if parties who made such a parol agreement would "naturally" demand that it be included in the written agreement, evidence of its making should be excluded; that is, the written agreement should be deemed fully integrated. As to how a court determined what was "natural" and what was not, Williston forcefully argued that the analysis of the parties' intentions should remain objective. Rather than seeking to uncover what the parties in fact intended by reference to the credibility of the parol evidence or extensive investigation into the parties' individual circumstances, a court should seek to determine whether reasonable parties would normally demand that the agreement, if made, be reflected in the writing. Although this represented a departure from strict application of a "four corners" approach, it was a modest departure, and the focus remained on what the judge believed objectively reasonable parties would do, rather than on the actual intentions or circumstances of the litigants at hand.

what is
natural?

Over time, the First Restatement's version of the "four corners" test, along with its cousin, the "plain meaning" rule of contract interpretation, began to further erode under pressure from the legal realists. Many continued to argue the futility of judging the scope of an agreement on its face or of interpreting words in isolation. Further, critics bemoaned the potential of the four corners

interpretation

and plain meaning rules to frustrate the actual expectations of the parties. Corbin was a particularly prominent advocate for a more contextual parol evidence rule, one that placed the actual intentions manifested by the parties at the center of the analysis. In fact, Corbin was not a big fan of the parol evidence rule generally. He once remarked that "it would have been far better had no such rule ever been stated."[5]

Ultimately, largely because of the influence of Corbin, Llewellyn, and other legal realists, both the Restatement, Second, and the UCC adopted a parol evidence rule that was much more liberal than that demanded by the classical courts and scholars. Nevertheless, remnants of the four corners approach are still alive in many jurisdictions, and some scholars have noted its resurrection in others.[6]

The next case is decided by the Supreme Court of California. Justice Traynor authored the majority opinion in this case, as he did in the *Pacific Gas & Electric* case in Chapter 15. The two cases were decided within a few months of each other. *Pacific Gas & Electric* is one of the most notorious expositions of the contextual or "soft" approach to contract interpretation; this case is equally famous, and serves as an early example of the contextual or "soft" approach to the parol evidence rule.

MASTERSON v. SINE

68 Cal. 2d 222, 436 P.2d 561, 65 Cal. Rptr. 545 (1968)
California Supreme Court

TRAYNOR, Chief Justice.

Dallas Masterson and his wife Rebecca owned a ranch as tenants in common. On February 25, 1958, they conveyed it to Medora and Lu Sine by a grant deed "Reserving unto the Grantors herein an option to purchase the above described property on or before February 25, 1968" for the "same consideration as being

---

[5] 3 Arthur Linton Corbin, *Corbin on Contracts* §582, at 455 (2d ed. 1960).

[6] Professor Mooney, for instance, stated:

> [R]ecent decisions . . . reflect a far more conceptualist "four-corners, plain-meaning" mindset. Seeking once again the chimera of certainty, judges in the last dozen or so years have repeatedly reversed jury interpretations with which they disagreed, declaring such matters to be solely questions of law.

Ralph J. Mooney, *The New Conceptualism in Contract Law*, 74 Or. L. Rev. 1131, 1160 (1995). Professor Posner, referring to a four corners approach to the parol evidence rule as "hard-PER" and a contextual one as "soft-PER," elaborated:

> [W]ithin a single jurisdiction, the parol evidence rule may vary considerably over time. In Pennsylvania, for example, hard-PER prevailed from the 1920s to the 1950s, confusion that gradually resolved itself into soft-PER prevailed from the late 1950s through the 1970s, and hard-PER has made a comeback in the late 1980s and 1990s. In California, hard-PER prevailed until the 1960s and soft-PER thereafter. In contrast, Virginia has maintained hard-PER fairly consistently during the last century, with only minor variations. In virtually every jurisdiction, one finds irreconcilable cases, frequent changes in doctrine, confusion, and cries of despair.

Eric A. Posner, *The Parol Evidence Rule, the Plain Meaning Rule, and the Principles of Contractual Interpretation*, 146 U. Pa. L. Rev. 533, 539 (1998).

paid heretofore plus their depreciation value of any improvements Grantees may add to the property from and after two and a half years from this date." Medora is Dallas' sister and Lu's wife. Since the conveyance Dallas has been adjudged bankrupt. His trustee in bankruptcy and Rebecca brought this declaratory relief action to establish their right to enforce the option.

The case was tried without a jury. Over defendants' objection the trial court admitted extrinsic evidence that by "the same consideration as being paid heretofore" both the grantors and the grantees meant the sum of $50,000 and by "depreciation value of any improvements" they meant the depreciation value of improvements to be computed by deducting from the total amount of any capital expenditures made by defendants grantees the amount of depreciation allowable to them under United States income tax regulations as of the time of the exercise of the option. The court also determined that the parol evidence rule precluded admission of extrinsic evidence offered by defendants to show that the parties wanted the property kept in the Masterson family and that the option was therefore personal to the grantors and could not be exercised by the trustee in bankruptcy.

The court entered judgment for plaintiffs, declaring their right to exercise the option, specifying in some detail how it could be exercised, and reserving jurisdiction to supervise the manner of its exercise and to determine the amount that plaintiffs will be required to pay defendants for their capital expenditures if plaintiffs decide to exercise the option.

Defendants appeal. They contend that the option provision is too uncertain to be enforced and that extrinsic evidence as to its meaning should not have been admitted. The trial court properly refused to frustrate the obviously declared intention of the grantors to reserve an option to repurchase by an overly meticulous insistence on completeness and clarity of written expression. It properly admitted extrinsic evidence to explain the language of the deed to the end that the consideration for the option would appear with sufficient certainty to permit specific enforcement. The trial court erred, however, in excluding the extrinsic evidence that the option was personal to the grantors and therefore nonassignable.

When the parties to a written contract have agreed to it as an "integration"—a complete and final embodiment of the terms of an agreement—parol evidence cannot be used to add to or vary its terms. When only part of the agreement is integrated, the same rule applies to that part, but parol evidence may be used to prove elements of the agreement not reduced to writing.

The crucial issue in determining whether there has been an integration is whether the parties intended their writing to serve as the exclusive embodiment of their agreement. The instrument itself may help to resolve that issue. It may state, for example, that "there are no previous understandings or agreements not contained in the writing" and thus express the parties' "intention to nullify antecedent understandings or agreements" (See 3 Corbin, *Contracts* (1960) §578, p. 411.) Any such collateral agreement itself must be examined, however, to determine whether the parties intended the subjects of negotiation it deals with to be included in, excluded from, or otherwise affected by the writing.

Circumstances at the time of the writing may also aid in the determination of such integration.

California cases have stated that whether there was an integration is to be determined solely from the face of the instrument, and that the question for the court is whether it "appears to be a complete . . . agreement. . . ." Neither of these strict formulations of the rule, however, has been consistently applied. The requirement that the writing must appear incomplete on its face has been repudiated in many cases where parol evidence was admitted "to prove the existence of a separate oral agreement as to any matter on which the document is silent and which is not inconsistent with its terms"—even though the instrument appeared to state a complete agreement. Even under the rule that the writing alone is to be consulted, it was found necessary to examine the alleged collateral agreement before concluding that proof of it was precluded by the writing alone. It is therefore evident that "The conception of a writing as wholly and intrinsically self-determinative of the parties' intent to make it a sole memorial of one or seven or twenty-seven subjects of negotiation is an impossible one." (9 Wigmore, *Evidence* (3d ed. 1940) §2431, p. 103.) For example, a promissory note given by a debtor to his creditor may integrate all their present contractual rights and obligations, or it may be only a minor part of an underlying executory contract that would never be discovered by examining the face of the note.

In formulating the rule governing parol evidence, several policies must be accommodated. One policy is based on the assumption that written evidence is more accurate than human memory. This policy, however, can be adequately served by excluding parol evidence of agreements that directly contradict the writing. Another policy is based on the fear that fraud or unintentional invention by witnesses interested in the outcome of the litigation will mislead the finder of facts. McCormick has suggested that the party urging the spoken as against the written word is most often the economic underdog, threatened by severe hardship if the writing is enforced. In his view the parol evidence rule arose to allow the court to control the tendency of the jury to find through sympathy and without a dispassionate assessment of the probability of fraud or faulty memory that the parties made an oral agreement collateral to the written contract, or that preliminary tentative agreements were not abandoned when omitted from the writing. (See McCormick, *Evidence* (1954) §210.) He recognizes, however, that if this theory were adopted in disregard of all other considerations, it would lead to the exclusion of testimony concerning oral agreements whenever there is a writing and thereby often defeat the true intent of the parties. (See McCormick, *op. cit supra*, §216, p. 441.)

Evidence of oral collateral agreements should be excluded only when the fact-finder is likely to be misled. The rule must therefore be based on the credibility of the evidence. One such standard, adopted by section 240(1)(b) of the Restatement of Contracts, permits proof of a collateral agreement if it "is such an agreement as might naturally be made as a separate agreement by parties situated as were the parties to the written contract." The draftsmen of the Uniform Commercial Code would exclude the evidence in still fewer instances:

a fortiori → used to express a conclusion which there is strong evidence for a different conclusion

if the factrare the kind that would normally be included, they must be kept from the trier of fact

If the additional terms are such that, if agreed upon, they would certainly have been included in the document in the view of the court, then evidence of their alleged making must be kept from the trier of fact." (Com. 3, §2-202.)[7]

The option clause in the deed in the present case does not explicitly provide that it contains the complete agreement, and the deed is silent on the question of assignability. Moreover, the difficulty of accommodating the formalized structure of a deed to the insertion of collateral agreements makes it less likely that all the terms of such an agreement were included. The statement of the reservation of the option might well have been placed in the recorded deed solely to preserve the grantors' rights against any possible future purchasers and this function could well be served without any mention of the parties' agreement that the option was personal. There is nothing in the record to indicate that the parties to this family transaction, through experience in land transactions or otherwise, had any warning of the disadvantages of failing to put the whole agreement in the deed. This case is one, therefore, in which it can be said that a collateral agreement such as that alleged "might naturally be made as a separate agreement." A fortiori, the case is not one in which the parties "would certainly" have included the collateral agreement in the deed.

It is contended, however, that an option agreement is ordinarily presumed to be assignable if it contains no provisions forbidding its transfer or indicating that its performance involves elements personal to the parties. The fact that there is a written memorandum, however, does not necessarily preclude parol evidence rebutting a term that the law would otherwise presume. . . . Of course a statute may preclude parol evidence to rebut a statutory presumption. Here, however, there is no such statute. In the absence of a controlling statute the parties may provide that a contract right or duty is nontransferable. Moreover, even when there is no explicit agreement—written or oral—that contractual duties shall be personal, courts will effectuate presumed intent to that effect if the circumstances indicate that performance by substituted person would be different from that contracted for.

writing does not automatically mean parole evidence is barred

holding

In the present case defendants offered evidence that the parties agreed that the option was not assignable in order to keep the property in the Masterson family. The trial court erred in excluding that evidence.

The judgment is reversed.

disposition

---

[7] Corbin suggests that, even in situations where the court concludes that it would not have been natural for the parties to make the alleged collateral oral agreement, parol evidence of such an agreement should nevertheless be permitted if the court is convinced that the unnatural actually happened in the case being adjudicated. (3 Corbin, *Contracts*, §485, pp. 478, 480.) This suggestion may be based on a belief that judges are not likely to be misled by their sympathies. If the court believes that the parties intended a collateral agreement to be effective, there is no reason to keep the evidence from the jury.

BURKE, Justice, dissenting.

I dissent. The majority opinion: (1) Undermines the parol evidence rule as we have known it in this state since at least 1872 by declaring that parol evidence should have been admitted by the trial court to show that a written option, absolute and unrestricted in form, was intended to be limited and nonassignable; (2) Renders suspect instruments of conveyance absolute on their face; (3) Materially lessens the reliance which may be placed upon written instruments affecting the title to real estate; and (4) Opens the door, albeit unintentionally, to a new technique for the defrauding of creditors.

The opinion permits defendants to establish by parol testimony that their grant to their brother (and brother-in-law) of a written option, absolute in terms, was nevertheless agreed to be nonassignable by the grantee (now a bankrupt), and that therefore the right to exercise it did not pass, by operation of the bankruptcy laws, to the trustee for the benefit of the grantee's creditors.

And how was this to be shown? By the proffered testimony of the bankrupt optionee himself! Thereby one of his assets (the option to purchase defendants' California ranch) would be withheld from the trustee in bankruptcy and from the bankrupt's creditors. Understandably the trial court, as required by the parol evidence rule, did not allow the bankrupt by parol to so contradict the unqualified language of the written option.

The court properly admitted parol evidence to explain the intended meaning of the "same consideration" and "depreciation value" phrases of the written option to purchase defendants' land, as the intended meaning of those phrases was not clear. However, there was nothing ambiguous about the granting language of the option and not the slightest suggestion in the document that the option was to be nonassignable. Thus, to permit such words of limitation to be added by parol is to contradict the absolute nature of the grant, and to directly violate the parol evidence rule. Just as it is unnecessary to state in a deed to "lot X" that the house located thereon goes with the land, it is likewise unnecessary to add to "I grant an option to Jones" the words "and his assigns" for the option to be assignable. . . .

At the outset the majority in the present case reiterate that the rule against contradicting or varying the terms of a writing remains applicable when only part of the agreement is contained in the writing, and parol evidence is used to prove elements of the agreement not reduced to writing. But having restated this established rule, the majority opinion inexplicably proceeds to subvert it. . . . The meaning of this rule (and the application of it found in the cases) is that if the asserted unwritten elements of the agreement would contradict, add to, detract from, vary or be inconsistent with the written agreement, then such elements may not be shown by parol evidence.

The contract of sale and purchase of the ranch property here involved was carried out through a title company upon written escrow instructions executed by the respective parties after various preliminary negotiations. The deed to defendant grantees, in which the grantors expressly reserved an option to repurchase the property within a ten-year period and upon a specified consideration, was issued and delivered in consummation of the contract. In neither the written escrow instructions nor the deed containing the option is there any language even suggesting that the option was agreed or intended by the parties to be personal to the grantors, and so nonassignable. . . . But the majority hold that . . . [the testimony of Dallas Masterson, the bankrupt holder of the option,] should have been admitted, thereby permitting defendant optionors to limit, detract from and contradict the plain and unrestricted terms of the written option in clear violation of the parol evidence rule and to open the door to the perpetration of fraud.

Options are property, and are widely used in the sale and purchase of real and personal property. One of the basic incidents of property ownership is the right of the owner to sell or transfer it. . . . The right of an optionee to transfer his option to purchase property is accordingly one of the basic rights which accompanies the option unless limited under the language of the option itself. To allow an optionor to resort to parol evidence to support his assertion that the written option is not transferable is to authorize him to limit the option by attempting to restrict and reclaim rights with which he has already parted. A clearer violation of two substantive and basic rules of law—the parol evidence rule and the right of free transferability of property—would be difficult to conceive. . . .

[D]espite the law which until the advent of the present majority opinion has been firmly and clearly established in California and relied upon by attorneys and courts alike, that parol evidence may not be employed to vary or contradict the terms of a written instrument, the majority now announce that such evidence "should be excluded only when the fact finder is likely to be misled," and that "The rule must therefore be based on the credibility of the evidence." But was it not, inter alia, to avoid misleading the fact finder, and to further the introduction of only the evidence which is most likely to be credible (the written document), that the Legislature adopted the parol evidence rule as a part of the substantive law of this state?

Next, in an effort to implement this newly promulgated "credibility" test, the majority opinion offers a choice of two "standards": one, a "certainty" standard, quoted from the Uniform Commercial Code, and the other a "natural" standard found in the Restatement of Contracts, and concludes that at least for purposes of the present case the "natural" viewpoint should prevail. This new rule, not hitherto recognized in California, provides that proof of a claimed collateral oral agreement is admissible if it is such an agreement as might naturally have been made a separate agreement by the parties under the particular circumstances. I submit that this approach opens the door to uncertainty and confusion. Who can know what its limits are? Certainly I do not. For example, in its application to this case who could be expected to divine as "natural" a separate oral agreement between the parties that the assignment, absolute and unrestricted on its face, was intended by the parties to be limited to the Masterson family? . . . [A]s loose as the new rule is, one judge might deem it natural and another judge unnatural. And in each instance the ultimate decision would have to be made ("naturally") on a case-by-case basis by the appellate courts. . . .

I would hold that the trial court ruled correctly on the proffered parol evidence, and would affirm the judgment.

■ QUESTIONS

(1) According to Justice Traynor, how does one determine if a writing is fully integrated, partially integrated, or perhaps not integrated at all? Does Justice Burke differ from Justice Traynor on this point and, if so, how? What are the consequences of this classification?

(2) Again, according to Justice Traynor, what was the nature of the writing in this case, and what factors did he take into account in reaching this decision? Did Justice Burke disagree with Justice Traynor on this point?

(3) The principal issue in this case is the assignability of the option. In offering parol evidence that the parties agreed that the option would not be assignable, did the plaintiff seek to contradict, supplement, or explain the writing? Do Justice Traynor and Justice Burke have a difference of opinion here?

(4) What policies does Justice Traynor serve through his decision? What policies does Justice Burke find compelling? Between the two, whose argument do you find more persuasive?

(5) Although the two justices have decidedly different approaches to the parol evidence rule, both agree that the trial court properly admitted parol evidence as to what the agreed option exercise price was. Why? What was the plaintiff's purpose in offering this evidence?

(6) Did the defendants necessarily win this case and preclude exercise of the option by Dallas Masterson's bankruptcy trustee?

2. Contemporary Approaches to the Parol Evidence Rule

Two relatively recent cases follow. In one, parol evidence is excluded, while in the other it is allowed. Are the varying results justified by the facts alone, or do the courts seem to take different approaches to the parol evidence rule itself?

MYSKINA v. CONDÉ NAST PUBLICATIONS, INC.

386 F. Supp. 2d 409 (2005)
United States District Court, Southern District of New York

MUKASEY, District Judge.

In this diversity action, plaintiff Anastasia Myskina sues defendants . . . [Condé Nast Publications, Inc. and its magazine Gentleman's Quarterly (collectively

only looking to breach of contract claim

referred to as "Condé Nast"), Mark Seliger, and Mark Seliger Studio (collectively referred to as "Seliger")] for violations of Sections 50 and 51 of New York Civil Rights Law, misappropriation, unjust enrichment, negligence, and breach of contract. [The court's discussion of the breach of contract claim is below; its discussion of the other claims is omitted.] The claims arise out of the alleged unauthorized dissemination of photographs taken of Myskina by defendants in connection with the October 2002 "Sports" issue of GQ, and publication of these photographs in the July/August 2004 issue of the Russian magazine Medved.

posture

Defendants move to dismiss the complaint pursuant to Fed. R. Civ. P. 12(b)(6) or alternatively, for summary judgment pursuant to Fed. R. Civ. P. 56. Because the parties have submitted affidavits and other exhibits, defendants' motion will be treated as one for summary judgment. For the reasons set forth below, defendants' motion is granted.

Myskina, a Russian citizen, is the 2004 French Open champion who at the time of the filing of this complaint was ranked fourth among female professional tennis players worldwide. She was 20 years old at the time that the photographs at issue were taken. Condé Nast is a New York publishing company; GQ is one of its publications. Seliger, who owns Seliger Studio, is a professional photographer who resides in New York.

In July 2002, Condé Nast editor Beth Altschull contacted International Sports Advisors—a publicity agency that represented Myskina at the time—to inquire whether Myskina would be interested in being photographed in the nude by Seliger for the cover and interior of GQ's 2002 "Sports" issue as part of a pictorial and profile of female tennis players. Myskina expressed interest, and her agent instructed Kenneth Gantman, a 23-year-old administrative assistant at International Sports Advisors, to set up the appointment and accompany Myskina to the photoshoot. Altschull and Gantman spoke on several occasions before the date of the photoshoot to agree on a convenient date and time for Myskina to come to New York and participate in the photoshoot.

On July 16, 2002, Myskina arrived at the photoshoot with Gantman and Jens Gerpach, who was her coach and then-boyfriend. Gantman claims that it was only at the photoshoot—and not during previous conversations with Altschull—that Altschull explained that the cover photograph of Myskina would depict her as "Lady Godiva"—lying nude on the back of a horse. It is not clear from Altschull's affidavit whether she claims that this information was communicated before the date of the photoshoot. In any event, Myskina expressed concern about being photographed in the nude. According to Myskina and Gantman, Altschull explained that Myskina would wear nude-colored underpants and have long hair taped to her body to cover her breasts and that, except for the Lady Godiva photographs to be published in the GQ issue, the photographs taken during the photoshoot would not be published anywhere. Myskina claims that only after this assurance did she agree to be photographed.

π claims

Before shooting began, Altschull presented Gantman with Condé Nast's standard release form ("Release") for models appearing in Condé Nast publications and informed him that absent his objection, she would ask Myskina to sign it. The Release, which is printed on Condé Nast letterhead, provides that the signatory model "hereby irrevocably consent[s] to the use of [her] name and the pictures taken of [her] on [a specified date] by [Condé Nast], . . . and others it may authorize, for editorial purposes." The Release does not contain a merger clause. Myskina's signature appears on the Release. *no merger*

Myskina claims that Gantman was neither an agent nor a publicist at International Sports Advisors and did not represent himself as such to Altschull, anyone at GQ, or anyone at the studio where the photoshoot took place. Defendants claim that Gantman voiced no objection to the Release or to Myskina's signing it. In addition to denying that he was ever presented with the Release, Gantman claims that he neither discussed the Release with Myskina nor observed her signing it. Myskina does not recall signing or discussing a Release with Condé Nast. Moreover, Myskina claims that she could not have understood the terms of the Release because at the time she was not fluent in English and "would not have signed [the Release] had it been explained to her that [it] would or might authorize GQ and Mark Seliger to publish, sell or disseminate her photographs from [the photoshoot] beyond publication of the Lady Godiva photograph for the 2002 'Sports Issue' of GQ."

Myskina claims that she was photographed topless in blue jeans after Seliger finished with the Lady Godiva photographs and that these had "nothing to do with the 'Lady Godiva' concept." She recalls that Seliger asked her whether he could take these topless photographs "for himself" so long as they were already in the studio. She "told him he could only take these photographs if these photographs would not be published anywhere," to which he "understood and agreed."

only take the extra pictures if they won't go anywhere

Condé Nast eventually published Myskina's profile and a "Lady Godiva" photograph from the photoshoot, which appeared on both the issue's cover and in a two-page spread inside the issue. Myskina was not paid in connection with the publication of her photograph in GQ.

[Seliger's contract with Condé Nast allowed him to exploit for editorial purposes all photographs taken on assignment after expiration of an "exclusivity period" in favor of the publisher. After the exclusivity period expired for the Myksina photographs, Seliger] . . . licensed five of the July 16, 2002 photoshoot images to Medved. In July 2004, these photographs appeared in the July/August 2004 issue of Medved, and soon after on Medved's website. One of the photographs was published on the issue's cover, and the other four appeared inside. Three, including the cover shot, depict frontal nudity and two appear to be versions of the Lady Godiva photograph that appeared in the October 2002 GQ issue.

Meanwhile, Medved had approached Myskina after her French Open win about an interview and photography session. She "told them that [she] couldn't do it." However, it appears that she granted the interview but not the photoshoot. Medved represented to her that it would use an "on the court" action photograph of her by a Russian sports photographer. The Medved article, entitled "Nastya Myskina: The Champion's Private Life," included a biography of Myskina and excerpts from the interview, which covered her thoughts on her

said they would use "on the court" photos

Medved published the nude photos

French Open win, press reports of her romantic life, and life on the professional tennis tour. According to Myskina, Medved never notified her that it had acquired and intended to publish photographs taken of her by Seliger during the July 16, 2002 photoshoot. Myskina claims that the publication of the photographs in Medved "are highly embarrassing and have caused [her] great emotional distress and economic harm and injury to her reputation." She also claims that Seliger has sold the same photographs to other parties.

π claim

Myskina filed the instant complaint on August 5, 2004. She sues for compensatory and exemplary damages as well as injunctive relief restraining the sale and dissemination of the photographs at issue. . . . Myskina contends that the Release was not "knowingly or intelligently signed, that she could not in any event understand its meaning," and that regardless, "defendants agreed with . . . Myskina to limit publication to [the] 'Lady Godiva' photograph" in the October 2002 issue of GQ. Myskina claims also that she never discussed the Release with Altschull or Gantman and that she does not recall signing the Release. However, she admits that the signature that appears on the Release is hers and does not otherwise deny that she actually signed the Release. Regardless, in order to raise a genuine issue of material fact as to whether she actually signed the Release, it is not enough for Myskina simply to aver, in conclusory fashion, that she does not recall signing the Release.

According to Myskina, Altschull assured her and Gantman "that the only photographs of [her] that would ever be published would be the Lady Godiva photographs in the October 2002 sports issue of GQ." Gantman states the same. Myskina claims also that the other photographs that appeared in Medved were taken after the Lady Godiva photographs, and only upon Seliger's request to "take [them] for himself since [they] were already in the photo studio." "He indicated that he understood and agreed" with Myskina's condition that these photographs could not be published anywhere. None of these understanding[s] and agreements were put in writing.

claims misunderstanding of the release are unfounded – failure to read

Absent allegations of fraud, duress, or some other wrongdoing, Myskina's claimed misunderstanding of the Release's terms does not excuse her from being bound on the contract. Nor can she avoid her obligations under the Release because of her purported failure to read its contents, or because of a language barrier. *See Holcomb v. TWR Express, Inc.,* 11 A.D.3d 513, 782 N.Y.S.2d 840 (2d Dep't 2004) ("A person who is illiterate in the English language is not automatically excused from complying with the terms of a contract simply because he or she could not read it.").

As for the oral agreement that Myskina claims limited her consent to publication only of the GQ photographs, the parol evidence rule bars the admission of any prior or contemporaneous negotiations or agreements offered to contradict or modify the terms of a written agreement. Even where an agreement is not completely integrated—meaning that the writing was intended by the parties to be a final and complete expression of all the terms agreed upon—parol evidence may be admitted only to complete the agreement or to resolve some ambiguity therein, and not to vary or contradict its contents. . . .

parole evidence may only come in to complete agreements or resolve ambiguity.

Absent a merger clause or language that explicitly states that the written agreement is integrated, the issue of whether the writing is an integrated agreement is determined "by reading the writing in the light of surrounding circumstances, and by determining whether or not the agreement was one which the parties would ordinarily be expected to embody in the writing." *Wilson-Gray v. Jay Feinberg, Ltd.*, No. 90-0001, 1990 WL 209635, at *2 (S.D.N.Y. Dec. 17, 1990) (quoting *Braten v. Bankers Trust Co.*, 60 N.Y.2d 155, 162, 468 N.Y.S.2d 861, 864, 456 N.E.2d 802 (1983)) (internal quotation marks and citation omitted).

Several factors indicate that the Release is an integrated agreement as to which photographs Myskina authorized the defendants to use for editorial purposes. The Release does not mention the alleged oral agreement—or any other agreement outside the Release, for that matter—that would limit Myskina's consent to the GQ photographs. Further, it addresses a straightforward transaction and plainly sets forth that Myskina consented to defendants' use of all photographs taken on July 16, 2002. Although the Release does not contain an explicit merger or integration clause, its language ("I, the undersigned, hereby irrevocably consent. . . .") indicates an intention to treat the issue of consent comprehensively and to be bound only by the terms of the Release.

Moreover, the purported oral agreement contemplates a condition fundamental to Myskina's consent, such that it hardly would have been omitted by the parties. Also, however unwise it may have been to bring only an administrative assistant from the publicity firm to the photoshoot, there appears to be no dispute that Myskina was still represented by the firm throughout the process. Under these circumstances, the Release constitutes a fully integrated contract as to Myskina's consent.

The purported oral agreement contradicts the plain language of the Release. Under the alleged oral agreement, Myskina consented only to the publication of the photographs in the October 2002 issue of GQ. By contrast, under the Release, Myskina expressly consented to the "use . . . for editorial purposes" by defendants of all photographs taken of her on July 16, 2002. Hence, the Release and the oral agreement are inconsistent in that the Release does not single out or otherwise limit which photographs taken during the July 16, 2002 photoshoot could be used for editorial purposes. Hence, the oral agreement is not admissible.

Although the Release is plainly integrated, evidence of an extrinsic oral agreement to limit Myskina's consent nevertheless could be considered if it satisfies three conditions: "(1) the agreement must in form be a collateral one; (2) it must not contradict express or implied provisions of the written contract; (3) it must be one that parties would not ordinarily be expected to embody in the writing. . . . It must not be so clearly connected with the principal transaction as to be part and parcel of it." *Namad v. Salomon*, 147 A.D.2d 385, 387, 537 N.Y.S.2d 807 (quoting *Mitchill v. Lath*, 247 N.Y. 377, 381, 160 N.E. 646, 647 (1928)). However, the alleged oral agreement in this case fails to satisfy any of the three conditions. It is not "collateral," but central to the parties' agreement as to Myskina's consent. It contradicts directly the plain language of the Release. Finally, its central provision—restriction of publication—was Myskina's main, if

[handwritten margin note: failure to include in the written contract bars proof of its existence]

not only condition of participating in the photoshoot, and is a matter that the parties would have been expected to memorialize in writing. Hence, "[f]ailure to include it in the written contract bars proof of its existence." *Gulf Int'l Bank B.S.C., New York Branch v. Othman*, No. 93-3161, 1994 WL 116015, at *6 (S.D.N.Y. Mar. 28, 1994) (citing *Mitchill*, 247 N.Y. at 380, 160 N.E. 646). . . .

Myskina alleges that because Condé Nast "agreed with [her] that a photograph selected from the Photoshoot for the GQ October 2002 issue would be the only photographs that would be published, . . . Condé Nast . . . materially breached [the] Agreement by failing to prevent photographs from the Photoshoot to be published in other publications, including Medved." As discussed above, the Release defeats such a claim. . . .

[handwritten margin note: both claims fail]

In a footnote in her opposition brief, Myskina requests leave to amend her complaint to add a breach of contract claim against Seliger based on the same purported oral agreement underlying her breach of contract claim against Condé Nast—that none of the photographs taken during the photoshoot would be published except in the October 2002 GQ issue. Here, the proposed additional claim against Seliger fails for the same reasons that the breach of contract claim against Condé Nast fails. Defendants have established that the Release is a fully integrated agreement that sets forth Myskina's consent to defendants' use for editorial purposes of all photographs taken of her during the July 16, 2002 photoshoot. The oral representations relied on by Myskina in her proposed claim—which are no different from the ones relied on in her other claims—directly contradict the plain language of the Release. Accordingly, Myskina's request to amend her complaint is denied.

[handwritten margin note: her oral arguments directly contradict written]

For the reasons set forth above, defendants' motion for summary judgment is granted.

■ QUESTIONS

(1)   The *Myskina* case is decided under New York law. In your view, assuming this case is representative, does New York apply a "four corners" approach to the parol evidence rule or a more contextual one?

(2)   The *Myskina* court concluded that the release she signed barred consideration of extrinsic evidence. Was the release fully integrated or partially integrated? What factors did the court consider in characterizing it as such?

(3)   What, precisely, did Myskina offer as parol evidence? Through offering the evidence, did she seek to contradict, supplement, or explain the writing at issue?

(4)   Apparently, Myskina did not include a breach of contract claim against Seliger in her complaint. The court suggests that such a claim would have been unsuccessful in any case. Do you agree with the court that the breach of contract claim against Seliger should fail for the same reasons the breach of contract claim against Condé Nast should fail?

(5)   The court alludes to situations where evidence barred by the parol evidence rule should nevertheless be admissible. What are those circumstances?

LOPEZ v. REYNOSO

129 Wash. App. 165, 118 P.3d 398 (2005)
Washington Court of Appeals

SCHULTHEIS, Judge.

Parol evidence is generally admissible to construe a written contract and to determine the intent of the parties. However, parol evidence cannot add to, modify, or contradict the terms of a fully integrated contract.

Stephany Lopez bought a used car from Ramon Reynoso (doing business as Triple R Auto Sales) pursuant to an installment sales contract. When Ms. Lopez did not make all the payments listed in her amortization schedule, Mr. Reynoso repossessed the car. Ms. Lopez sued for replevin and additional recovery. She moved to exclude parol evidence offered by Mr. Reynoso to show that a $2,000 payment by Ms. Lopez on the day of the sale or one day later was deducted from the sale price listed on the contract. She contends the $2,000 was actually an additional payment that reduced her obligation under the contract. The trial court allowed the parol evidence and entered judgment for Mr. Reynoso.

On appeal, Ms. Lopez contends the trial court erred in admitting parol evidence that contradicted terms in the integrated contract.... We conclude that the trial court was justified in examining extrinsic evidence to determine whether the contract was the final expression of the parties' agreement.... [We affirm.]

Mr. Reynoso began selling used cars as Triple R Auto Sales in May 2000. His family had known Ms. Lopez for several years. In late May 2000, Ms. Lopez visited Triple R and asked the price of a 1994 Ford Explorer. Mr. Reynoso was out of town, but an employee called him and learned that the asking price was $8,500. Ms. Lopez tried to negotiate a lower price with the employee, but he asked her to return when Mr. Reynoso could talk with her.

Two days later, on June 2, Ms. Lopez purchased the Explorer from Mr. Reynoso. According to her, the parties agreed to a sale price of $6,500 with $500 down and interest at three percent. She claims she gave Mr. Reynoso $500 down in cash but never received a receipt for the payment. Mr. Reynoso claims he agreed to lower the sale price to $8,000 if Ms. Lopez agreed to pay $2,000 down. He asserts Ms. Lopez's boyfriend, Fernando Ortega, gave him $1,800 on June 2, when the agreement was executed, and Ms. Lopez brought in the additional $200 the next day. The receipt for the $1,800 payment is undated and numbered 3100; the receipt for the $200 payment is dated June 3, 2000 and numbered 3112.

Mr. Reynoso insists Ms. Lopez did not want the sales contract to show that the couple had paid $2,000 down. He was not sure why Ms. Lopez wanted the contract to state the sale price was $6,500 with a down payment of $500, but because the payments would be the same, he agreed to write it the way he says Ms. Lopez wanted it. At trial, Mr. Reynoso's daughter, a childhood friend of Ms. Lopez, testified that she witnessed the execution of the contract and that

Ms. Lopez had the idea to write the contract with a price reduced by $2,000 because she did not want Mr. Ortega's name to be on the title to the car.

The terms of the contract, as drafted by the Triple R accountant on June 2, state that the price of the vehicle is $6,500, the tax and license fee are over $500, and the down payment is $500, for a total price of $6,533. Language at the bottom of the purchase order form states: "This order cancels and supercedes any prior agreement and as of the date herein comprises the complete and exclusive statement of the terms of this agreement." After Ms. Lopez signed the agreement, the accountant compiled an amortization schedule for $250 monthly payments and gave a copy to Ms. Lopez. This schedule indicates that Ms. Lopez's last payment was due in September 2002. If, as Mr. Reynoso contends, the actual price of the Explorer was $8,000, reduced to $6,000 by the $2,000 down payment, the tax and fee would have been the same and the total obligation would still have been $6,533.

According to Mr. Reynoso, Ms. Lopez was often late with payments and did not make her December 2001 payment. When she appeared at his office in January 2002 with a $250 payment, he refused it, claiming she owed him for two months. Ms. Lopez contends she asserted at that time that her $2,000 payment was made after the sale agreement and lowered her obligation by another $2,000, which would be paid in full by the December 2001 payment. Mr. Reynoso says Ms. Lopez did not claim she had paid the full amount with the December payment. Ms. Lopez again offered to pay $250 in February 2002 and Mr. Reynoso again rejected the payment. He repossessed the Explorer in March 2002. Later that month, Ms. Lopez hired Molly Earhart to prepare an amortization schedule based on a purchase price of $7,033 (the sale price plus tax and license), a down payment of $500, and a post-sale payment of $2,000. According to this new amortization schedule, Ms. Lopez's final payment should have been only $145 in January 2002.

Ms. Lopez filed a complaint against Mr. Reynoso, his wife, Triple R, and the bonding company on April 11, 2002. She requested return of the Explorer, treble damages, and attorney fees for breach of the contract and violations of chapter 46.70 RCW (proscribing unfair motor vehicle business practices) and chapter 19.86 RCW (Washington's Consumer Protection Act). In September 2002 she moved for an order in limine to exclude parol evidence and for judgment on the pleadings.[8] The motions were denied after a hearing. After a bench trial in September 2003, the court entered judgment for the defendants. . . . [Ms. Lopez filed a timely appeal.]

Ms. Lopez . . . challenges the trial court's consideration of evidence extrinsic to the written contract. She contends the trial court used this evidence to contradict or vary the express, unambiguous terms of the integrated contract. We review the trial court's findings of fact regarding the admissibility of parol

---

[8] A motion in limine is a pretrial motion that requests the court prevent the introduction of potentially irrelevant, prejudicial, or otherwise inadmissible evidence at trial. —Eds.

evidence for substantial evidence. The evidence is viewed in the light most favorable to the prevailing party, and we defer to the trier of fact on issues of witness credibility.

view in the light most favorable to the prevailing party

In Washington, "[t]he touchstone of contract interpretation is the parties' intent." *Tanner Elec. Coop. v. Puget Sound Power & Light*, 128 Wash. 2d 656, 674, 911 P.2d 1301 (1996). This intent may be discerned from the language of the agreement as well as from viewing the objective of the contract, the circumstances around its making, the subsequent conduct of the parties, and the reasonableness of their respective interpretations. Under the parol evidence rule, "prior or contemporaneous negotiations and agreements are said to merge into the final, written contract," *Emrich v. Connell*, 105 Wash. 2d 551, 556, 716 P.2d 863 (1986), and evidence is not admissible to add to, modify, or contradict the terms of the integrated agreement. But the parol evidence rule is only applied to writings intended as the final expression of the terms of the agreement. Extrinsic evidence may be used to ascertain the intent of the parties, to properly construe the writing, and to determine whether the writing is actually intended to be the final expression of the agreement. Washington's codification of the use of parol or extrinsic evidence under the Uniform Commercial Code mirrors the common law. . . . [The court quotes UCC 2-202].[9] *CL & UCC are mirrored*

evidence can't add, modify or contradict

Generally people have the right to make their agreements entirely oral, entirely in writing, or partly oral and partly in writing. With a written contract, "it is the court's duty to ascertain from all relevant, extrinsic evidence, either oral or written, whether the entire agreement has been incorporated in the writing or not. That is a question of fact." *Barber* [*v. Rochester*, 52 Wash. 2d 691,] 698, 328 P.2d 711 [(1958)]. If the writing is a complete integration, any terms and agreements that are not contained in it are disregarded. If it is not intended to be the complete expression of the parties' intent—in other words, if it is only partially integrated—the writing may be supplemented or replaced by consistent terms or agreements shown by a preponderance of the evidence.

rule ✗

The Lopez-Reynoso written agreement executed on June 2, 2000 stated that the cash price of the vehicle was $6,500, the down payment was $500, and Ms. Lopez would make 26 payments of $250 and a final payment of $264.87. The sales contract included an integration clause that stated that the writing comprised the complete and exclusive statement of the terms. When Mr. Reynoso responded that the writing was an incomplete expression of the entire negotiations and agreements of the parties, the trial court was obligated to consider any extrinsic evidence to determine whether the agreement was fully integrated, and if not, what other terms consistent with the written agreement were operative.

needed evidence to decide if its integrated

---

[9] We discuss UCC 2-202 in Section B.3. Although the sale of the car is a transaction in goods, the court's analysis doesn't draw any distinctions between the UCC's approach to the parol evidence rule and the common law approach prevailing in Washington. Accordingly, we include this case as a broader example of contemporary approaches to the parol evidence rule and postpone discussion of the UCC's version of the parol evidence rule until Section B.3.—Eds.

After considering the parties' inconsistent recitations of the events leading up to the sale, the testimony of witnesses, and evidence of customary retail business practices, the trial court found Mr. Reynoso's explanation more credible and reasonable and implicitly concluded that the written agreement was only partially integrated. These findings are supported by substantial evidence. For instance, Mr. Reynoso testified that he invested almost $6,000 in the Explorer, suggesting that a sale price of $6,500 was not believable. The trial court also found it unrealistic that a used car dealer financing a sale himself would accept a down payment of less than 10 percent. We defer to the trial court's firsthand determination of the witnesses' credibility.

Assuming that the written sale agreement was only partially integrated and that the parties had orally agreed to additional terms, we address the remaining question: whether the purported oral agreement contradicts any valid terms of the written contract. Evidence that the parties agreed to reduce the sale price by the $2,000 down payment is not inconsistent with the actual terms of repayment included in the contract and the amortization schedule. The reduced price of $6,000 does contradict the written terms of a $6,500 sale price and a $500 down payment, but the result is the same: a contract price of $6,000 for a vehicle originally priced at $8,500. Ultimately, the extrinsic evidence of prior negotiations reveals terms that do not contradict the written terms of the vehicle's price and the number of payments Ms. Lopez owed.

Ms. Lopez notes that the integration clause at the bottom of Mr. Reynoso's "vehicle purchase order" explicitly provides that the written agreement is fully integrated. The relevant statements on this standard form are as follows:

> Purchaser agrees that (1) this order includes all the terms and conditions on both the face and the reverse side of, together with any attachments herein referred to. (2) This order cancels and supercedes any prior agreement and as of the date herein comprises the complete and exclusive statement of the terms of this agreement relating to the subject matters covered hereby.

Although an integration clause is a strong indication that the parties intended complete integration of a written agreement, a boilerplate clause will not be given effect if it appears that the provision is factually false. Parol evidence is admissible to show whether language denying the existence of any other agreement is controlling. When material extrinsic evidence shows that outside agreements were relied upon, those parol agreements should be given effect rather than allowing boilerplate "to vitiate the manifest understanding of the parties." *Lyall* [*v. DeYoung*, 42 Wash. App. 252, 58, 711 P.2d 356 (1985)]. . . .

The integration language here is in a boilerplate clause attached to the vehicle purchase order form. The trial court's decision to ignore the integration clause is supported by substantial evidence that the parties based the sales contract on an outside agreement to lower the sale price by the $2,000 down payment. . . .

In summary, the trial court's examination of extrinsic evidence to determine whether the parties intended the written contract to be the final expression of their terms was (proper.) Its conclusion that Mr. Reynoso's explanation of the negotiations was more credible is supported by a preponderance of the evidence and by the trial court's inherent authority to determine the credibility of the witnesses. Sufficient evidence supports the trial court's findings of fact, which in turn support its conclusion that the $2,000 down payment reduced the sale price to $6,000, and that Mr. Reynoso lawfully repossessed the Explorer after Ms. Lopez defaulted on the monthly payments due in January, February, and March 2002. Because Mr. Reynoso's repossession was lawful, he did not violate chapter 46.70 RCW or chapter 19.86 RCW. Dismissal of Ms. Lopez's complaint and judgment for Mr. Reynoso were therefore justified. . . .

SWEENEY, Acting Chief Judge (dissenting).

I respectfully dissent. Parol evidence tending to contradict the terms of a written contract should <u>not,</u> in the face of oral testimony corresponding with the unambiguous language in the contract, be <u>allowed to nullify the language of the instrument.</u> If the parol evidence rule does not apply to these facts, it is meaningless.

> *this is a classic case where parole evidence should apply*

   The parties do not dispute the facts. Stephany Lopez bought a car from Ramon Reynoso pursuant to an unambiguous, integrated, written contract. The contract states the price as $6,500. Ms. Lopez began missing payments, and Mr. Reynoso repossessed the car. In response to Ms. Lopez's action for replevin, Mr. Reynoso repudiated the plain terms of the written contract and successfully enforced an alleged oral agreement that the price was really $2,000 higher than the written contract price. The trial court erred in admitting parol evidence directly contradicting the terms of the written contract.

   The contract Mr. Reynoso now repudiates was his contract. He drafted it. He was responsible for it. Mr. Reynoso included in his contract an ironclad integration clause. . . . This language may be "boilerplate." But, again, it is Mr. Reynoso's boilerplate. Ms. Lopez did not change the language or add anything to this contract as a result of her discussions with the seller. And while the absence of such a clause suggests that the agreement or purchase order was not the complete agreement of the parties, the inclusion of an integration clause suggests just the opposite.

   Moreover, even under [a rule which] admits parol evidence to determine the intent of the parties, parol evidence is not admissible to contradict or vary the terms of a fully integrated contract. <u>This contract was fully integrated.</u> And according to its clear language the parties intended it to be. Once it is established that an agreement is completely integrated, parol evidence offered to contradict or vary its terms should be (rejected.) A central element of any contract is the price. Here, the price is stated as $6,500. The price Mr. Reynoso claims, $8,000, certainly contradicts or varies the terms of this written agreement.

> *since it was fully integrated nothing should be left in*

   I would, then, enforce the contract as written. If parties to an integrated written contract have a secret handshake agreement to contrary terms, it is the written agreement the courts will enforce.

■ QUESTIONS

[handwritten margin note: four corners — NY v. contextual WA]

(1)   While the *Myskina* case is decided under New York law, the *Lopez* case is decided under Washington law. How would you compare the *Lopez* majority's general approach to the parol evidence rule to the approach reflected in *Myskina*? How would you characterize the dissent's general approach?

(2)   The *Lopez* majority affirmed the trial court's recourse to parol evidence, while the dissent would reverse the trial court's decision. According to the majority, was the agreement fully integrated or partially integrated? What factors did the majority consider in characterizing it at such? Did the dissent quarrel with this conclusion, and if so, why?

[handwritten margin note: the merger clause was boiler plate so it looked at the intentions of the parties]

(3)   What, precisely, did Mr. Reynoso offer as parol evidence? Through offering the evidence, did he seek to contradict, supplement, or explain the writing at issue? Are the majority and the dissent in agreement on this issue?

(4)   Because the parol evidence rule is in large part made necessary by the use of a jury system in civil trials, one might think that it falls away when the case is tried by the judge without a jury. However, neither *Masterson v. Sine* nor *Lopez* involved jury trials, yet both implicated the parol evidence rule. What role does the parol evidence rule play when the judge also serves as fact-finder? What hints do you pick up from *Lopez* about Washington's approach to the division of labor between the judge and the fact-finder in the context of parol evidence disputes generally? Does it differ from the typical approach discussed in the introduction to Section B, and if so, how?

[handwritten margin note: oral agreements]

[handwritten margin note: parole evidence shouldn't even be presented to the fact finder]

———

The *Myskina* opinion and the *Lopez* majority and dissenting opinions all discuss the effect of the absence or presence of a "merger" clause in the writing at issue. The release in *Myskina* did not include an explicit merger clause, while the agreement in *Lopez* did. A few additional words about merger clauses may be helpful to put these discussions in context.

As we have seen, under the parol evidence rule, the effect that a writing has on the admissibility of extrinsic evidence depends on how definitive the parties intend the writing to be. Some parties add specific language to their writings to address this issue. It is very common for parties to include a clause that states that a written memorial not only supersedes prior agreements, but also contains the entire agreement of the parties. These clauses, sometimes called "merger" clauses but also often called "integration" clauses, differ in their wording, but their objective is the same: to invoke the strongest possible protection available under the parol evidence rule. In the event of a dispute, the drafter hopes that a merger or integration clause will establish that the writing is fully integrated. This would result in the exclusion of as much extrinsic evidence as possible, thereby encouraging the court to resolve the dispute on the basis of the writing alone and potentially foreshortening litigation.

Courts often conclude that a writing is fully integrated simply because it includes a merger or integration clause. This is particularly true in jurisdictions that take a "four corners" approach to the parol evidence rule, but even courts that take a more contextual approach tend to give great weight to such clauses. The parties' failure to include a merger or integration clause, however, does not necessarily mean that they did not intend the writing to fully integrate their agreement. The release in the *Myskina* case did not contain a merger or integration clause, for instance. But the absence of a merger or integration clause is one factor a court may consider in deciding the nature and effect of the writing.

In the power of merger and integration clauses also lies their danger. A sophisticated and powerful party in charge of drafting an agreement may include language that strongly favors its interests and even contradicts explicit understandings of the parties. These provisions may go unnoticed or, if noticed, unchallenged by the less sophisticated or less powerful contracting partner. The hazards are not limited to the unsophisticated, however. A complex commercial contract may take weeks or even months to draft, negotiate, and revise. Often, the lawyers spend many late hours in the nights leading up to a closing putting the polishing touches on contractual language. Occasionally, surprises come up at the closing table, and the parties scurry to find a last-minute accommodation to prevent the transaction from collapsing. Woe to the lawyer, not to mention the client, who in the rush to completion fails to reflect these understandings adequately in the written agreement.

Because of the potential of merger and integration clauses to defeat legitimate expectations, courts do not always give them conclusive effect. In extreme cases, avoidance doctrines related to bargaining misbehavior or the like may allow some relief. Absent the circumstances giving rise to relief under such doctrines, courts only occasionally conclude that the merger or integration clause did not adequately reflect the intentions of both parties, and therefore should not be given effect. *Lopez*, for instance, is an example of this. In the usual case, however, the plaintiff who seeks to introduce parol evidence to contradict or supplement a written agreement containing a merger or integration clause faces a losing battle.

PROBLEM 16.1

Tallmadge Brothers, Inc. v. Iroquois Gas Transmission System, 252 Conn. 479, 746 A.2d 1277 (2000), illustrates the level of deference courts often give to merger or integration clauses. In *Tallmadge Brothers*, the owners of a natural gas pipeline entered into written settlement agreements with some operators of a shellfishery to resolve disputes regarding the owner's construction of an underwater pipeline. The operators of the shellfishery subsequently sued, claiming among other things that the owner of the pipeline had violated the terms of the settlement agreements by conducting construction operations in a broader area than allegedly agreed.

One of the issues involved in the litigation was whether, in light of the merger clauses included in the parties' written agreements, the trial court erred in allowing the consideration of parol evidence to support the alleged expectations of the parties. In concluding that the consideration of parol evidence was improper, the Connecticut Supreme Court reasoned:

> Although the question of what weight should be given to a merger clause has prompted a number of differing views,[10] much of this disagreement has occurred in the context of unequal bargaining power between the parties, fraud, duress, or contracts in contravention of public policy. The general rule of contract law remains that "a [merger] clause . . . is likely to conclude the issue [of] whether the agreement is completely integrated." 2 Restatement (Second), Contracts §216, comment (e) (1981).
>
> None of the concerns that might call the merger clauses into question is present in this case. . . . [T]he parties here possessed relatively equal bargaining power, and they executed the settlement agreements only after a lengthy drafting process during which they had received the advice of counsel. We conclude, therefore, that the parties' insertion of the merger clauses into the settlement agreements is conclusive evidence of their intent to create fully integrated contracts, and that the trial court's subsequent consideration of extrinsic evidence was improper.

The majority in the *Lopez* case allowed consideration of parol evidence notwithstanding the presence of a merger clause in the written agreement. As suggested by the excerpt from the *Tallmadge Brothers* case, this is an exceptional result, typically justified only under compelling circumstances. The dissent in *Lopez* strongly challenged this holding. Under the circumstances described in *Lopez*, who do you think has the better side of the argument—the majority or the dissent? Why?

■ PROBLEM 16.2

Recall the *Saucy Sisters* case in Chapter 15. United could have advanced the argument that the parol evidence rule precluded consideration of evidence that the termination agreement could only be exercised for cause.

(a) Is it possible to determine from the facts given whether the agreement was fully integrated, partially integrated, or not integrated at all?

---

[10] For example, some jurisdictions have held that the insertion of a merger clause into a contract constitutes conclusive evidence that the parties intended their agreement to be integrated. Other jurisdictions, however, have held that the existence of a merger clause is merely presumptive evidence of the parties' intent.

> What facts should the judge have considered in deciding this question? Specifically, should the judge have considered Groth's alleged statement about the circumstances under which United would exercise its rights under the termination clause?
>
> (b) Assume that Saucy Sisters sought to introduce Groth's alleged statement as evidence that the parties agreed that the termination clause could only be exercised for cause. Does this evidence seek to explain the written agreement, supplement it, or contradict it? What consequences flow from this characterization?

3. Application of the Parol Evidence Rule Under the UCC → *contextual approach*

As we note on several occasions, Article 2 of the UCC strongly reflects Karl Llewellyn's legal realist philosophy. We have seen how the definition of "agreement" emphasizes context, resting as it does on the bargain of the parties "in fact." Llewellyn may well have been content had Article 2 omitted a parol evidence rule altogether and allowed consideration of parol evidence in all cases. If in fact he advocated this view, he was not successful: Article 2 does contain a parol evidence rule, in UCC 2-202. However, UCC 2-202 takes a decidedly contextual approach to the admissibility of parol evidence to supplement the terms of a written agreement.

In its broad outlines, this iteration of the parol evidence rule is very similar to the "soft" or contextual approach described previously. Application of the UCC's parol evidence rule is not an abstract exercise done on the basis of an isolated examination of the four corners of the written agreement. Instead, at every step of the analysis, the decision-maker is invited to examine the words in light of the commercial context within which they were used. The UCC parol evidence rule still operates to exclude reliance on parol evidence in certain circumstances, but the exclusions are likely to reflect the intentions actually manifested by the parties, as discerned in light of the surrounding circumstances, rather than a formal reading of the words contained in a document.

exclude things when the parties meant for then to be excluded

To work your way through Problem 16.3, refresh your memory of UCC 1-303, which relates to course of performance, course of dealing, and usage of trade, and is found in Chapter 15. Also read UCC 2-202 and its associated Official Comment. As you read UCC 2-202, take note of any portions of the statutory language or the Official Comment that relate to interpretation of a written agreement. Also identify what parts of the statute embody the concept of an integration and where the analogue of "fully integrated" agreements is distinguished from "partially integrated" agreements. Throughout, look for ways, if any, in which the treatment of parol evidence is more liberal than you might have come to expect at common law.

UCC 2-202. FINAL WRITTEN EXPRESSION: PAROL OR EXTRINSIC EVIDENCE

Terms with respect to which the confirmatory memoranda of the parties agree or which are otherwise set forth in a writing intended by the parties as a final expression of their agreement with respect to such terms as are included therein may not be contradicted by evidence of any prior agreement or of a contemporaneous oral agreement but may be explained or supplemented

exceptions

(a) by course of performance, course of dealing, or usage of trade (Section 1-303), and *course of performance*

(b) by evidence of consistent additional terms unless the court finds the writing to have been intended also as a complete and exclusive statement of the terms of the agreement. *consistent additional terms*

Official Comment

1. This section definitely rejects:

not all matters should be assumed as final

(a) Any assumption that because a writing has been worked out which is final on some matters, it is to be taken as including all the matters agreed upon;

words can have commercial meaning

(b) The premise that the language used has the meaning attributable to such language by rules of construction existing in the law rather than the meaning which arises out of the commercial context in which it was used; and

(c) The requirement that a condition precedent to the admissibility of the type of evidence specified in paragraph (a) is an original determination by the court that the language used is ambiguous.

goal is finding the true understanding

2. Paragraph (a) makes admissible evidence of course of dealing, usage of trade and course of performance to explain or supplement the terms of any writing stating the agreement of the parties in order that the true understanding of the parties as to the agreement may be reached. Such writings are to be read on the assumption that the course of prior dealings between the parties and the usages of trade were taken for granted when the document was phrased. Unless carefully negated they have become an element of the meaning of the words used. Similarly, the course of actual performance by the parties is considered the best indication of what they intended the writing to mean.

oral →

3. Under paragraph (b) consistent additional terms, not reduced to writing, may be proved unless the court finds that the writing was intended by both parties as a complete and exclusive statement of all the terms. If the

additional terms are such that, if agreed upon, they would certainly have been included in the document in the view of the court, then evidence of their alleged making must be kept from the trier of fact.

■ PROBLEM 16.3

Ella Eldon, a housepainter, orally agreed to purchase 1,000 gallons of paint from Dolores Devine, a manufacturer of designer house paints. After the parties entered into the oral agreement, each sent the other a signed, written confirmation form, confirming the quantity, price, description, and delivery date for the paint. Although the forms agreed in these particulars, they each contained standard printed terms on the back that differed in some minor respects from each other.

(a) Ella received a shipment of the paint, and tested a sample on a patch of drywall. She found the texture of the paint to be unsatisfactory for her purposes, and sought to return it. Dolores claimed that there was nothing wrong with the paint, and refused to take it back. Neither of the forms discussed what the rights and remedies of the parties would be if Ella was dissatisfied with the properties of the paint. Under each of the alternatives below, determine if Ella should be entitled to introduce the proffered evidence to prove a right to return the paint:

(i) Ella testifies that she discussed the importance of the paint's texture in her initial discussions with Dolores, and Dolores orally agreed to allow her to return any paint should the texture not prove satisfactory for her purposes.

(ii) Alternatively, Ella offers a letter from Dolores, dated prior to either of the confirmation forms, in which Dolores promised to allow Ella to return any paint should the texture not prove satisfactory for her purposes.

(iii) Alternatively, Ella testifies that she has purchased paint from Dolores on many previous occasions. Twice, when the texture of the paint proved unsatisfactory, Dolores allowed her to return it without complaint.

(iv) Alternatively, the president of a major paint manufacturer testifies that the texture of paint is often difficult to ascertain until the paint has been delivered and tested. As a result, most manufacturers allow customers to return paint if they find the texture to be unsatisfactory for their purposes.

(b) Alternatively, suppose the paint was to be delivered in three separate shipments. Ella received the first lot, tested it, and found it satisfactory. She received the second lot, tested it, and found it unsatisfactory for her purposes. When she sought to return it, Dolores accepted it without complaint and refunded Ella's purchase price. Ella then received the third lot, tested it, and again found it unsatisfactory. This time, when she sought to return the shipment, Dolores claimed there was nothing wrong with the paint, and refused to take it back. Ella seeks to prove a right to return the third shipment based on this chain of events. Should she be allowed to do so? *Course of performance*

(c) Suppose that after the parties entered into the oral agreement, only Dolores sent a confirmation. Her confirmation was as described above, except that one of the standard terms printed on the confirmation form stated, "This confirmation constitutes the final, complete, and exclusive statement of the terms of our agreement." Dolores asked Ella to sign the confirmation and return a copy of it to her; Ella did so. Ella did not send a confirmation of her own. Would this change your answers to (a) or (b)? If so, how and why?

a i & ii
merger clause wont allow the oral or written evidence

sometimes the UCC is followed in contextual common law

UCC 2-202 is remarkable in its amenable approach to evidence of usage of trade, course of dealing, and course of performance. Some common law courts, under contextual approaches to contract interpretation and the parol evidence rule, follow suit. The controversial case of *Nanakuli Paving & Rock Co. v. Shell Oil Co.*, 664 F.2d 772 (9th Cir. 1981), illustrates how far one court, under the auspices of UCC 2-202, was willing to depart from the "plain meaning" and "four corners" rules. In this case, Nanakuli Paving & Rock Co. was a paving contractor in Hawaii. Nanakuli wanted to grow its business, and Shell Oil Co. wanted to expand its share of the asphalt business in Hawaii. Nanakuli and Shell entered into two written, long-term supply contracts for asphalt, under which Nanakuli committed to purchase its asphalt requirements from Shell, and Shell agreed to charge its "posted price at time of delivery." The agreements contained merger clauses. About ten years into the relationship, in response to the OPEC oil embargo, Shell nearly doubled its posted price for asphalt. Nanakuli claimed that it was entitled to the lower price until such time as it had fulfilled its existing paving contracts. Shell's obligation to "price protect" it, Nanakuli claimed, stemmed from Shell's past practice and from a more general usage in the asphalt trade. Shell, which was then under new management, refused, and litigation ensued.

When the case ultimately found its way to the Ninth Circuit, the court upheld a jury verdict in favor of Nanakuli, which depended, in part, on testimony and other evidence regarding usages of trade and the course of performance between the parties. Taking into account the context of the relationship, the court concluded that the alleged practice of price protection did not conflict with the express price term in the contracts. Even if the price protection clauses appeared unambiguous, the court held no initial finding of ambiguity was required before the fact-finder could hear evidence of a trade usage or course of performance that ascribed a different meaning to the terms in question. Further, as the alleged practice did not conflict with the written agreements, the evidence was admissible to supplement the terms of the agreements, notwithstanding merger clauses contained in the agreements. The court concluded that the merger clauses alone were not conclusive evidence that the parties intended the writings to be complete and exclusive statements of the terms of their agreements. Even if the writings were intended to be complete and exclusive statements of the terms of the agreements, under UCC 2-202(a) usage of trade and course of performance evidence would still be admissible to supplement the writings. Finally, the court held that there was sufficient evidence in the record to support "price protection" as a course of performance or usage of trade. *Nanakuli* inspired heated academic commentary and remains controversial to this day.[11]

[handwritten margin note: no need for initial ambiguity for evidence of trade usage]

[handwritten note: × merger clauses are not dispositive]

C   THE SCOPE OF THE PAROL EVIDENCE RULE

The parol evidence rule rests on the assumption that the writing reflects a valid contract. Suppose your contracts professor, in a moment of whimsy, handed out blank contract forms, ordered all of the students to pair up, and demanded that you all sign on the dotted lines. In the interests of humoring her and curious as to where this was going to lead, you all complied. Should these written and signed documents somehow feature prominently in a subsequent lawsuit, where you are the defendant, surely you would be permitted to prove the circumstances of your signature to negate the requisite manifestation of intent. No one in the room thought that anyone else was making a serious commitment. In analogous situations, courts have held that the parol evidence rule would not stand as a bar to your argument, no matter how fully integrated the written agreement appeared to be. Generally speaking, extrinsic evidence that would successfully demonstrate that an alleged contract is either void or voidable is admissible, even in the face of the parol evidence rule. Consider, for instance, the following problem:

---

[11] *See, e.g.,* Jody S. Kraus & Robert E. Scott, *Contract Design and the Structure of Contractual Intent,* 84 N.Y.U. L. Rev. 1023, 1081 (2009) (suggesting that *Nanakuli* improperly substitutes the court's conception of the parties' contractual ends for the contractual means expressly agreed); and Douglas K. Newell, *Will Kindness Kill Contract?,* 24 Hofstra L. Rev. 455 (1995) (discussing specifically the court's approach to good faith issues).

■ PROBLEM 16.4

Design Co. designs precision electronic parts. Air Inc. manufactures components for military aircraft. Design Co. and Air Inc. sign a 20-page written agreement, in which Design Co. agrees to design certain avionics for Air Inc., and Air Inc. agrees to pay for the designs upon completion. The written agreement contains extensive representations, warranties and covenants and specifies in detail the circumstances under which either party will be deemed in breach, but does not speak directly to any of the matters specified below. The agreement also contains a merger clause. A dispute arises between the parties, and Air Inc. seeks to introduce the evidence to support the claims it makes in the respective parts of the problem. Design Co. argues that the parol evidence rule bars consideration of the evidence at issue. In each instance, assuming Air Inc. has evidence to support its claims, should the court allow the fact-finder to hear that evidence? Why or why not?

(a) Air Inc. claims that Design Co. threatened to inform the government that there were safety issues with Air Inc.'s products unless Air Inc. signed the written agreement, which contains terms that are highly unfavorable to Air Inc. Even false rumors of safety problems could ruin the reputation of manufacturers in this industry. Even though Air Inc. didn't believe its products were unsafe, it felt it had no alternative but to agree to Design Co.'s demands. Air Inc. offers this evidence to support its claim to avoid the contract on grounds of duress.

(b) Instead, assume that at the time Design Co. and Air Inc. signed the written agreement, Air Inc. was bidding for a major government contract but did not yet know if its bid would be successful. Air Inc. argues that it only needed the designs from Design Co. should it be the successful bidder on the government contract, and that Design Co. knew that. The parties decided to go ahead and finalize the terms of their written agreement, but orally agreed that the written agreement wouldn't go into effect unless Air Inc. obtained the government contract. As it turned out, Air Inc. was not the low bidder on the government contract, and it now offers the evidence to claim that a condition to the effectiveness of the contract was not satisfied.

In some situations, evidence tending to show that an alleged contract is voidable also may be relevant to the question of what the parties' expectations were when they signed a written memorial of the alleged contract. In these situations, it can be difficult to determine whether and to what extent the parol evidence applies. One context where courts have struggled with the appropriate scope of the parol evidence rule is where a party seeks to introduce evidence that a writing was induced through fraud or a material misrepresentation. In Chapter 13 we discuss how misrepresentations in some cases can render a contract voidable or even void. As Chapter 13 demonstrates, misrepresentation generally makes a contract voidable only if it is fraudulent or material, if it induces the other party's manifestation of assent, and if the other party is justified in relying on it. Where a writing is not in accord with the alleged negotiations of the parties, the party seeking to introduce evidence of the negotiations might allege that the conflict is due to a misrepresentation made by the other party.

Sometimes the exact basis of the alleged misrepresentation is unclear, but a few examples serve to illustrate. Suppose Ned wants to introduce evidence of prior negotiations. Perhaps he argues that the other party, Sue, misrepresented the content or effect of the writing. An example might be if Ned and Sue had exchanged several drafts of the proposed contract but right before Ned signed, Sue (unbeknownst to him) revised a provision in the middle of the document. He didn't notice the change, and Sue assured him that the document he was signing was identical to the last draft he reviewed.[12] Or perhaps Ned alleges that Sue made a false representation of fact some time during the course of negotiations, but the contract they signed says no representations were made, or if made, they were merged into the written agreement. Possibly Sue even made a promise to Ned that she didn't intend to keep at the time she made it. You may remember that some courts would consider this to be a misrepresentation, even though it is a promise rather than a strict statement of fact. When Ned ultimately looks at the signed contract, it is suspiciously silent on the point at issue or perhaps even states that no such promise was made.

Some courts categorically state that the parol evidence rule does not apply to evidence introduced to prove misrepresentation or fraud. Yet if courts routinely consider evidence of misrepresentation, particularly if courts routinely allow juries to hear such evidence, the exception for misrepresentation would have the potential to swallow the parol evidence rule. So attempts to introduce parol evidence to prove misrepresentation can be subject to special scrutiny. Sometimes, this scrutiny arises under the guise of the misrepresentation analysis itself. For instance, some courts might question whether Ned justifiably relied on Sue's misrepresentation if he had a clear writing in front of him that at a minimum did not reflect the misrepresentation and perhaps even contained a merger clause or an express provision that denied the existence of any representations beyond the terms of the writing.

The facts of some of the cases denying relief are quite egregious; consider, for instance, the case of *Cole v. Cates*, 113 Ga. App. 540, 149 S.E.2d 165 (Ga. App.

---

[12] Yes, such things do happen. For instance, consider the facts of *Hennig v. Ahearn*, 230 Wis. 2d 149, 601 N.W.2d 14 (Wis. App. 1999), where the court found fraud from the fact that one party presented a draft to the other knowing that the other party thought it contained terms different from those actually included.

1966). In *Cole*, the defendant was an 85-year old man who suffered from numerous health complaints. He was blind in one eye and could only read with the use of glasses and a magnifying glass, and even then with some difficulty. According to the defendant's allegations, he was considering selling some real estate and invited a longtime friend who was a real estate broker to come talk to him about the prospects of selling his property. The broker gave him an agreement to sign, telling him it was a listing agreement. When he said he would go get his glasses to read it more closely, the broker reiterated that it was only listing agreement to enable the broker to advertise the property and obtain some bids and that it would not obligate him to sell his property. As the broker was a trusted friend, the defendant signed the agreement without reading it. As it turned out, the agreement was in fact a contract to sell his property. When the defendant subsequently refused to sell, the broker sued him for payment of the commission he would have earned from the sale. The defendant claimed that the agreement should be avoidable on the basis of fraud or misrepresentation; however, the trial court dismissed his claim on summary judgment.

Upholding the summary judgment, the court of appeals stated:

> The often announced rule that one having the capacity and opportunity to read a written contract and who signs it, not under any emergency, and whose signature is not obtained by any trick or artifice of the other party, but solely on the representations of the other party as to its contents, cannot afterwards set up fraud in the procurement of the signature of the instrument, is but another statement of the rule that one cannot claim to be defrauded by the false representations of another, where, by the exercise of ordinary diligence, such person could have discovered the falsity of the representations before acting thereon.

Concluding that the defendant's reliance on the broker was unjustified as a matter of law, the court affirmed the decision of the trial court.

An alternative analysis relies not on principles of misrepresentation but rather on the parol evidence rule. Returning to the example of Ned and Sue, some courts might deny relief on the theory that Ned should not be allowed to make a misrepresentation argument as a device to avoid application of the parol evidence rule. In effect, Ned is seeking to introduce evidence that conflicts with an integrated agreement or, if the agreement is deemed to be fully integrated, either supplements or contradicts it. For instance, consider *Bank of America National Trust & Savings Association v. Lamb Finance Co.*, 3 Cal. Rptr. 877, 880 (Cal. Dist. App. 1960), in which the court stated, "[I]f, to induce one to enter into an agreement, a party makes an independent promise without intention of performing it, this separate false promise constitutes fraud which may be proven to nullify the main agreement; but if the false promise relates to the matter covered by the main agreement and contradicts or varies the terms thereof, any evidence of the false promise directly violates the parol evidence rule and is inadmissible."

If Sue's behavior is unsavory or reckless, and if Ned suffered significant prejudice, it may stick in the judicial craw to allow Sue to escape the consequences of her misdeeds. Under the parol evidence rule, courts have a difficult task in drawing the lines between what extrinsic evidence of misrepresentation should not carry any weight at all, what evidence the judge alone should evaluate, and what evidence the jury should appropriately hear.

The following case involves an attempt to introduce terms that are at variance with a writing that appears to be complete on its face. As you read the case, try to discern the analytical basis for the arguments that the parties raise and the court addresses. Are the parties arguing that the writing was not integrated? That the proffered term does not contradict the writing? Or that notwithstanding the parol evidence rule, the court should consider evidence of fraud or misrepresentation? Or are they making different arguments altogether?

SOUND TECHNIQUES, INC. v. HOFFMAN
50 Mass. App. 425, 737 N.E.2d 920 (2000)
Massachusetts Appeals Court

PERRETTA, Justice.

In *Bates v. Southgate*, 308 Mass. 170, 182, 31 N.E.2d 551 (1941), the court held that "contracts or clauses attempting to protect a party against the consequences of his own fraud are against public policy and void where fraud inducing the contract is shown. . . ." This appeal brings before us the question whether *Bates* applies with equal force when a party enters into a contract containing such a clause, commonly referred to as a merger clause, an integration clause, or an exculpatory clause, in reliance upon a negligent rather than deliberate misrepresentation. In this case, the lessee, Sound Techniques, Inc. (Sound), brought an action against the lessor, Barry Hoffman, alleging that, prior to the execution of the lease, Hoffman (through his real estate agent) made certain false representations concerning the expected noise level at the leased premises. The jury rejected Sound's claims for breach of contract and deceit but awarded damages on the count for negligent misrepresentation. On Hoffman's appeal, we conclude that the merger clause set out in the lease was enforceable and precluded Sound from recovering damages on the basis of its allegations of a negligent misrepresentation. We reverse the judgment.

There was evidence to show that in 1989, Sound, the operator of a professional sound recording studio, was seeking to lease commercial space in Boston. Michael McGloin, an employee of Hoffman's leasing agent, showed James Anderson, Sound's president, vacant space on the second floor of a building owned by Hoffman and located at 1260 Boylston Street. The first floor of the building was occupied by Boston Ramrod (Ramrod), a bar owned by Saturday Afternoon, Inc. McGloin showed the premises to Anderson several times. On all these occasions, Anderson made it clear that Sound was seeking space for purposes of building a state-of-the-art recording studio. Noticing that Ramrod was doing expansion work, Anderson asked McGloin about the extent of the planned expansion. McGloin told Anderson that he need not worry and that Ramrod was expanding its dining area in which only background music would be provided. He assured Anderson that the space in question would accommodate Sound's needs.

At the time of the signing of the lease, October 10, 1989, Sound was represented by counsel who had assisted in the lease negotiations and had reviewed the terms of the lease prior to its execution. The lease was conditioned upon Sound successfully completing an acoustical inspection of the premises before October 13, 1989. Prior to the signing of the lease, no one from Sound had walked through Ramrod on a weekend night to determine the noise level. Sound's acoustical engineer conducted a brief visual inspection of Ramrod during a weekday afternoon and concluded that the second-floor space was suitable for Sound's purposes. Although Sound's studio operates around the clock, seven days a week, the engineer did not visit the Ramrod late at night or during the weekend, did not measure the ambient sound level, and did not talk with anyone at Ramrod about the operation of its sound system.

Soon after relocating to the premises in issue, Sound began to experience problems with noise coming from Ramrod, and Sound discovered that, contrary to McGloin's representations, Ramrod's expansion went beyond providing background music in the dining area. Rather, Ramrod had upgraded its sound system and had expanded its premises to include a dance floor. There were times, Sound claimed, when the whole building throbbed; sessions in its recording studio were disrupted and Sound was losing business. Sound then brought an action against Hoffman, claiming breach of contract, deceit, and negligent misrepresentation and alleging that McGloin's statements to Anderson regarding the limited nature of Ramrod's expansion plans induced it to enter into the lease. Although the jury found in Hoffman's favor on Sound's claims of breach of contract and deceit, they found in Sound's favor on its claim for negligent misrepresentation.

But for Anderson's testimony relating McGloin's statements concerning Ramrod's expansion plans, Sound could not have sustained its burden of proof on its claim for negligent misrepresentation. The question before us is whether Anderson's testimony was inadmissible by reason of the clause in the lease entitled "Waiver by landlord; representations," which, in pertinent part, reads: "Tenant acknowledges that Tenant has not been influenced to enter into this transaction nor has Tenant relied upon any warranties or representations not set forth in this instrument." . . .

"The rule that written agreements may not be varied or added to by parol evidence of antecedent or contemporaneous negotiations is not one merely of evidence, but is a rule of substantive law." *Goldenberg v. Taglino*, 218 Mass. 357, 359, 105 N.E. 883 [1914]. Before that rule comes into operation, however, the court must be sure that it has before it a written contract intended by the parties as a statement of their complete agreement. Sound does not contend that the merger clause is ambiguous in its terms or that it was itself obtained by fraud. Moreover, there is nothing in the record appendix that suggests that the lease was other than a fully integrated contract.

Whether we refer to the clause in question as a merger clause, an integration clause, or an exculpatory clause, the settled rule of law is that a contracting party cannot rely upon such a clause as protection against claims based upon fraud or deceit. This established rule is an exception to the basic principles concerning the freedom to contract and is grounded upon public policy concerns. . . .

Although it is the established policy of this Commonwealth to refuse to enforce a merger clause for purposes of protecting a party from liability on account of his fraud and deceit, the instant case does not concern fraud and deceit. . . . Rather, the judgment in Sound's favor rests solely upon the jury's finding of a negligent misrepresentation.[13] The question whether public policy concerns also preclude recovery on account of negligently made statements shown to be false is a question of law spoken to but left undecided by this court in *Sheehy v. Lipton Indus.*, 24 Mass. App. Ct. at 193 n. 5, 507 N.E.2d 781. There we stated: "We believe, although we do not decide, that the rule in *Bates v. Southgate*, 308 Mass. [at 182], 31 N.E.2d 551, would apply to a misrepresentation that was determined to be negligent rather than intentional or reckless." . . . Hoffman's appeal puts the question squarely before us.

In considering this issue, as it pertains to commercial transactions, courts of other jurisdictions have reached opposite conclusions. Those that ignore the merger clause do so, essentially, on the basis that the parol evidence rule applies only to contract claims and has no relevance to a plaintiff's tort action. On the other side of the issue, in those jurisdictions where recovery has been denied, the courts have taken the view that, in the absence of a deliberate wrongdoing, the terms of the contract control.

Sound argues that, based upon the dictum in *Sheehy* . . . , we should adopt the reasoning of the court set out in *Formento v. Encanto Bus. Park* [154 Ariz. 495, 744 P.2d 22 (Ct. App. 1987)], and conclude that the parol evidence rule and merger clauses do not preclude an action for negligent misrepresentation. The *Formento* decision is based upon two grounds: (1) because the harm done to the party relying upon the misrepresentation is the same irrespective of whether the misrepresentation was intentionally or negligently made, there is no rational basis for distinguishing between fraud and negligent misrepresentation, and (2) the parol evidence rule has no application in actions based upon tort claims. We think *Formento* lacking in persuasive force for the following reasons.

In concluding that there is no practical difference between fraud and negligent misrepresentations, *Formento* proceeds on the basis that because both

---

[13] Hoffman readily concedes that the merger clause would not have relieved it of liability had the jury found that McGloin's statements concerning the expected noise level to the Boston Ramrod were intentional misrepresentations.

categories of claim stand on the same policy ground, that is, the promotion of honesty and fair dealing in business relationships, the fraud exception to the parol evidence rule should have equal force in a claim based upon a negligent misrepresentation. As authority for its reasoning, *Formento* relies upon *Hill v. Jones*, 151 Ariz. 81, 84-86, 725 P.2d 1115 (Ct. App. 1986), a case involving a seller's failure to disclose to the buyer termite damage known to the seller of a residence. In that case, the court states, at 84: "Although the law of contracts supports the finality of transactions, over the years courts have recognized that under certain limited circumstances it is unjust to strictly enforce the policy favoring finality. . . . There is also a judicial policy promoting honesty and fair dealing in business relationships. This policy is expressed in the law of fraudulent and negligent misrepresentations. Where a misrepresentation is fraudulent or where a negligent misrepresentation is one of material fact, the policy of finality rightly gives way to the policy of promoting honest dealings between the parties."

We decline to follow *Formento* and *Hill* because they fail to acknowledge and to take into account the significance of the intent of the misrepresenting party. To ignore a merger clause and allow recovery for a negligent misrepresentation does little to promote honesty and fair dealing in business relationships. An individual who makes negligent misrepresentations has honest intentions but has failed to exercise due care. . . . As we read *Bates v. Southgate*, 308 Mass. at 182, 31 N.E.2d 551, it is intentional misconduct that justifies judicial intrusion upon contractual relationships in order to prevent the wrongdoer from securing contractual benefits for which he had not bargained. As stated in *Isler v. Texas Oil & Gas Corp.*, 749 F.2d [22, 23-24]:

> In tort, the legislatures and the courts have set the parameters of social policy and imposed them on individual members of society without their consent. The social policy in the field of contract has been left to the parties themselves to determine, with judicial and legislative intervention tolerated only in the most extreme cases. Where there has been intervention, it has been by the application of well established contract doctrines, most of which focus on threats to the integrity of the bargaining process itself, such as fraud or extreme imbalance in bargaining power.

There is nothing in the evidence before us that shows or even suggests that the integrity of the bargaining process was tainted by illegality, fraud, duress, unconscionability, or any other invalidating cause. The lease was not a contract of adhesion. . . . Nothing suggests that the bargaining powers of the parties were unequal. Indeed, the evidence showed that Sound was represented by counsel throughout the negotiation process and its acceptance of the lease was conditioned upon an inspection by an acoustical engineer that was in fact conducted. Based upon the evidence presented and the public policy of this Commonwealth, there is no reasonable basis for ignoring the plain language of the merger clause, in which Sound agreed that it was entering into the contract free from influence by or in reliance upon any representations other than those set out in the contract.

On the pleadings and evidence presented, we think mistaken the notion that the parol evidence rule has no application in this tort action.... We are not prepared to ignore our general policy of upholding freedom to contract by allowing Sound to avoid a contractual disclaimer that it agreed to, uninfluenced by any fraud or other egregious or intentional misbehavior on Hoffman's part.[14]

The defendant's motion for judgment notwithstanding the verdict should have been allowed. The judgment in Sound's favor is reversed, and judgment is to enter for the defendant.

■ PROBLEM 16.5

One of the policies underlying the parol evidence rule is that it shields the jury, which is likely to be more sympathetic to the economic underdog, from emotive and unreliable evidence. Some are concerned with the distribution of power in our society and prefer a rule that advantages the less powerful party on the grounds that such a rule would help to level an inherently skewed playing field. In this vein, consider the following arguments:

(a) A textually based, "hard" parol evidence rule favors the rich and powerful, because they are the parties most likely to prepare the contract and have lawyers during the contract negotiation and drafting process. As a result, the written agreement is more likely to reflect their interests.

(b) A contextually based, "soft" parol evidence rule favors the rich and powerful, because they are the parties most likely to be able to afford to conduct the extensive factual inquiry such an approach requires and to suffer the consequent delays and litigation expenses. Since the written contract is always subject to question, in the event of a dispute the rich and powerful party can extract settlement from the other through threat of extended litigation.

Do you find either (or both) of these arguments persuasive? In the end, what approach to the parol evidence rule do you favor, and why? Do you think application of the rule should depend on the relative bargaining positions of the parties or on whether they were represented by counsel?

---

[14] Our holding is based upon the circumstances of the case. We expressly leave for another day those situations involving, among others, consumers, a gross disparity in the bargaining positions of the parties, or unconscionable contract clauses.

CONTRACT INTERPRETATION AND PAROL EVIDENCE UNDER THE UNIDROIT PRINCIPLES AND THE CISG

Under the UNIDROIT Principles, all circumstances surrounding the transaction are relevant to discern the intention of the parties, and to interpret statements and other conduct of the parties. In particular, Article 4.3 allows resort to preliminary negotiations between the parties, practices that the parties have established between themselves, the conduct of the parties subsequent to the conclusion of the contract, the nature and purpose of the contract, the meaning commonly given to terms and expressions in the trade concerned, and usages.

Article 8 of the CISG is to similar effect and provides that, in interpreting the statements and other conduct of parties to an international sales contract, "due consideration is to be given to all relevant circumstances of the case including the negotiations, any practices which the parties have established between themselves, usages and any subsequent conduct of the parties."

Accordingly, the factual context of the transaction is highly relevant in interpreting the parties' contract in an international transaction governed by either the UNIDROIT Principles or the CISG. Further, neither the UNIDROIT Principles nor the CISG contain a parol evidence rule. Should the parties wish to exclude evidence extrinsic to their written agreement, they may be able to achieve the effect of the parol evidence rule through use of a well-drafted and mutually agreed merger or integration clause.

■ **PROBLEM 16.6**

As noted in Problem 16.5, one of the policies underlying the parol evidence rule is that it shields the jury from potentially emotive and unreliable evidence. In explaining the varied approaches to parol evidence in different countries, a CISG Advisory Council Opinion[15] noted:

> The civil law generally does not have jury trials in civil cases and civilian jurisdictions usually do not place limits on the kind of evidence admissible to prove contracts between merchants. Though the French Civil Code, for example, incorporates a version of the Parol Evidence Rule for ordinary contracts, all forms of proof are generally available against merchants. In German law, no Parol Evidence Rule exists for either civil or commercial contracts, though German law presumes that a contractual writing is accurate and

---

[15] CISG-AC Opinion no. 3, *Parol Evidence Rule, Plain Meaning Rule, Contractual Merger Clause and the CISG*, 23 October 2004.

complete. This is also the case in other laws, e.g., Japanese law and Scandinavian law. . . .

The Opinion continued:

> There were several practical reasons for not including a Parol Evidence Rule in the CISG. First, most of the world's legal systems admit all relevant evidence in contract litigation. Secondly, the Parol Evidence Rule, especially as it operates in the United States, is characterized by great variation and extreme complexity. It has also been the subject of constant criticism.

On balance, do you think our system of civil juries justifies retention of the parol evidence rule for contracts governed by domestic law, or do you think the parol evidence rule should be abolished altogether in the United States? Why?

CHAPTER 17

Mistake and Excuse Due to Changed Circumstances

This chapter features doctrines that are interrelated. In limited circumstances, the doctrine of mistake and the various doctrines that allow excuse for changed circumstances may relieve a party from its contractual obligations if circumstances make it inappropriate to hold the party to its apparent agreement. Each of the doctrines, however, has a distinct role to play.

Mistake relates to the parties' beliefs about the factual circumstances underlying the contract. One or both of the parties are operating under a misapprehension of fact when they enter a contract. Although the parties share a common understanding of the terms of their contract, the complaining party alleges that he would not have concluded the contract but for the mistaken belief. If the complaining party provides a sufficiently compelling case, relief from the contract may be available under the doctrine of mistake. Although he manifested assent to the contract, the court is unwilling to hold him to his bargain. The actual benefits and burdens of the contract differ so radically from the complaining party's original expectations that it seems inappropriate to enforce the contract. Mistake, as it focuses on the circumstances surrounding contract formation, has much in common with the doctrines in Chapter 13 that allow relief when improper bargaining induces a contract. However, although improper bargaining may underlie a mistake, that is not necessarily the case. Both parties may be innocently mistaken as to the fact at issue, or one party may be mistaken and the other simply ignorant of or indifferent to the underlying facts.

The doctrine of mistake focuses on facts in existence when the parties enter the contract. Of course, new facts may occur after the date of the contract. Occasionally, something happens after the parties form the contract that radically alters the nature or effect of the agreed performance. Perhaps a change in conditions causes a promised performance to be impossible, or at least highly impractical. Or maybe circumstances change such that a party's reason for entering the contract disappears. The risk the disadvantaged party assumed when she agreed to the contract, she argues, does not fairly encompass performance under the circumstances at hand. The disappointed party may seek to be excused from her burdensome or pointless contractual obligations. Excuse due to changed circumstances may be available under one of two closely related doctrines: impracticability (sometimes called impossibility) or frustration of purpose.

We start by examining mistake and from there proceed to excuse for changed circumstances. What we find is that although relief is sometimes available under these doctrines, in most cases parties are required to bear the consequences of burdensome contracts. The aggrieved party may find the requirement of performance to be harsh, but relief often would be equally harsh to the other party. Relief is especially unlikely to be available if the aggrieved party was responsible for the situation or explicitly or implicitly assumed the risk of the resulting burden. In each case, the precise calculus for when relief should be available is somewhat uncertain. Although courts and commentators have developed a number of tests to distinguish those situations that merit relief from those that do not, application of the tests often requires a delicate balancing of interests.

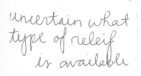

uncertain what type of relief is available

A MISTAKE

Suppose two parties agree on the terms of a contract. In reaching that agreement one or both of them are operating under an assumption that a certain state of affairs exists. At some later point, it becomes clear that the assumed state of affairs in fact does not exist and did not exist at the time the parties concluded the contract. This makes the contract less desirable for one of the parties. Had he only known, the aggrieved party argues, he wouldn't have entered into the contract in the first place. In some cases, the law will provide relief to the adversely affected party under the doctrine of mistake, but it is important to understand the limitations of this doctrine.

Every ill-advised contract does not give rise to an argument of mistake. Just because a contract may look like a bad idea in retrospect does not mean that relief will be available. One of the functions of contract law is to allocate the risks of bad events. If the party who is disappointed by a bargain is always free to seek relief from its strictures, the value of the bargain to the other party disappears. Accordingly, the doctrine of mistake seeks to strike a balance between the party who is adversely affected by the mistake and the party who would be adversely affected if the court were to grant relief from the contract.

Mistake is a well-established doctrine, and common law courts have long recognized mistake as equitable grounds for providing relief. Yet courts and commentators have struggled to articulate precisely when relief for mistake will be available. An examination of the authorities reveals three general themes. The first concerns the nature of the mistake. The mistake must relate to a fact that was in existence at the time of the contract. It cannot be a mistake in judgment or a mistaken prediction as to future events. The second theme focuses on the seriousness of the mistake. The mistake must relate to something that is central to the contract, rather than a minor or peripheral matter, and it must have a significant effect on the benefits the mistaken party receives or the burdens he undertakes under the contract. The third theme is perhaps the most difficult to delineate and grasp. For relief to be available in cases of mistake, it must be unfair or otherwise inappropriate to allocate the risk of the mistake to the aggrieved party. We will draw out these elements of the doctrine as reflected in some of the modern cases and the Restatement, Second.

Courts and commentators often divide mistakes into mutual mistakes and unilateral mistakes. Although the two categories are theoretically distinct, they are best understood as different points along a continuum. A mutual mistake only arises when both parties have a mistaken belief of fact. Unilateral mistakes can also give rise to relief in some circumstances, but typically only where enforcement of the contract would lead to palpable injustice.

1. Mutual Mistake

We begin with mutual mistake. Two famous old cases illustrate the difficulty in distinguishing those cases where relief is not available from those cases where relief will be granted. In *Wood v. Boynton*, 64 Wis. 265, 25 N.W. 42 (1885), Ms. Wood sold a stone to Mr. Boynton, a jeweler, for $1. Ms. Wood informed Mr. Boynton that she had been told that it might be a topaz, and he responded he wasn't sure but thought it probably was. When it later became clear that the stone was in fact an uncut diamond worth over $700, Ms. Wood sought to rescind the sale. The trial court concluded that both parties were in fact ignorant of the nature of the stone at the time of the sale but did not allow the rescission. On appeal, the Wisconsin Supreme Court affirmed the trial court, saying that there was no mistake as to the identity of the thing sold. Rather, at most there was a mistaken belief as to its probable value. In contrast, in the venerable case of *Sherwood v. Walker*, 66 Mich. 568, 33 N.W. 919 (1887), the plaintiff Sherwood contracted to buy a cow for $80 from the defendant Hiram Walker (of whiskey fame). Both parties were under the impression that the cow, Rose 2d of Aberlone, was barren and unable to breed. When the time for performance came, the seller refused to deliver Rose to the buyer. Rose, it seemed, was pregnant. Being a breeder, rather than barren, she was worth at least $750. The Michigan Supreme Court held rescission might be available under facts such as these, where the mistake or misapprehension of the parties went to the whole substance of the agreement, even though there was no mistake as to the identity of the creature.

Generations of law students, lawyers, and judges have sought to distinguish the facts of *Wood v. Boynton* from those of *Sherwood v. Walker*. The tests articulated in the two cases prove unhelpful and indeterminate. In §152, the drafters of the Restatement, Second, attempted to outline an analysis that would reflect reported decisions yet prove more functional to apply in practice:

RESTATEMENT, SECOND §152. WHEN MISTAKE OF BOTH PARTIES MAKES A CONTRACT VOIDABLE

(1) Where a mistake of both parties at the time a contract was made as to a basic assumption on which the contract was made has a material effect on the agreed exchange of performances, the contract is voidable by the adversely affected party unless he bears the risk of the mistake under the rule stated in §154.

(2) In determining whether the mistake has a material effect on the agreed exchange of performances, account is taken of any relief by way of reformation, restitution, or otherwise.

Section 152(1) refers to Restatement, Second §154:

RESTATEMENT, SECOND §154. WHEN A PARTY BEARS THE RISK OF A MISTAKE

A party bears the risk of a mistake when
(a) the risk is allocated to him by agreement of the parties, or
(b) he is aware, at the time the contract is made, that he has only limited knowledge with respect to the facts to which the mistake relates but treats his limited knowledge as sufficient, or
(c) the risk is allocated to him by the court on the ground that it is reasonable in the circumstances to do so.

■ PROBLEM 17.1

As an initial exercise, try to reconcile *Wood v. Boynton* and *Sherwood v. Walker* under the standards of Restatement, Second §§152 and 154. Do you find the tests contained in these sections helpful? Do you think the elements they enunciate adequately distinguish those cases where relief should be available from those where the contract should stand as agreed?

A recent case, in which the court declines to allow avoidance of a stock sale transaction on the basis of mutual mistake, follows.

SCI MINNESOTA FUNERAL SERVICES, INC. v. WASHBURN-McREAVY FUNERAL CORPORATION

795 N.W.2d 855 (2011)
Minnesota Supreme Court

GILDEA, Chief Justice.

The case arises from a stock sale transaction, and we are asked to decide whether appellants are entitled to reformation or rescission of the transaction because two vacant lots were transferred in the stock sale. Appellant SCI Minnesota Funeral Services, Inc. (SCI) sold Crystal Lake Cemetery Association (Crystal Lake) to appellant Corinthian Enterprises, LLC (Corinthian) in a stock sale agreement. Corinthian subsequently sold and assigned Crystal Lake to respondent Washburn-McReavy Funeral Corporation (Washburn) in a share purchase agreement. SCI and Corinthian brought this action contending the parties did not intend to include the vacant lots in the sale of Crystal Lake, and they sought equitable relief to remedy this claimed mistake. The district court held that SCI and Corinthian were not entitled to reformation or rescission based on mutual mistake, and the court of appeals affirmed. Because we conclude that neither rescission nor reformation is available, we affirm.[1]

The parties do not dispute the facts that are material to the disposition of this case. In 2005, the parent company of SCI placed several cemeteries and funeral homes on the market. Corinthian purchased some of these cemeteries and funeral homes. Crystal Lake was one of the businesses offered for sale by SCI and purchased by Corinthian. Crystal Lake was comprised of three cemeteries in Minnesota—Crystal Lake Cemetery/Crematory in Minneapolis (Crystal Lake Cemetery), Dawn Valley Funeral Home/Memorial Park in Bloomington (Dawn Valley), and Glen Haven Memorial Gardens in Crystal (Glen Haven).

Although no one involved in the transaction was aware of it, Crystal Lake's assets also included the two vacant lots at issue here. One lot is located in Colorado and one lot is located in Burnsville. SCI either acquired or purchased the vacant lots for Crystal Lake several years prior to the Crystal Lake sale. A former employee of SCI testified that SCI purchased the Colorado land in

---

[1] As the court indicates, the appellants seek either rescission or reformation. Rescission is equivalent to avoidance of the contract. If the court allows reformation, it in effect modifies the contract to alleviate the consequences of a mutual mistake. Apart from a brief reference to reformation at the end of the opinion, we have omitted the court's discussion of the reformation remedy and instead focus on the court's discussion of the merits of the mistake claim and the remedy of rescission. We deal with reformation in Section A.3.—EDS.

the late 1990s for tax purposes "as part of a like-kind exchange," and it acquired the Burnsville land when it "had been carved out of the asset sale of another cemetery property years ago." SCI continued to pay property taxes on the Colorado lot after the 2005 sale of Crystal Lake. The parties agree that the value of the two lots is approximately $2 million.

SCI and Corinthian agreed from the beginning of negotiations that they would structure the sale of Crystal Lake as a stock transaction based on their conclusion that Minnesota law prohibits the acquisition of cemeteries for profit.[2] But SCI and Corinthian also agreed that they would classify the sale of Crystal Lake as an asset transaction for tax purposes. The parties agree that the subject matter of the stock sale agreement is the stock of Crystal Lake.

On July 20, 2005, SCI and Corinthian reduced their agreement to writing and entered into a stock sale agreement. In the agreement, SCI agreed to sell all of its shares of Crystal Lake to Corinthian. The purchase price of the stock was $1 million. The stock sale agreement listed the three cemeteries—Crystal Lake Cemetery, Dawn Valley, and Glen Haven—but it did not specifically mention the vacant lots. The agreement did provide, however, for the removal of some of Crystal Lake's assets and operations. The agreement provided that SCI "shall and may cause to be removed" from the Crystal Lake sale all assets owned by Crystal Lake that are "not utilized in or related to the operation of the Business in its present form."

Also on July 20, 2005, Corinthian entered into a share purchase agreement with Washburn in which Corinthian agreed to sell its outstanding shares of stock in Crystal Lake to Washburn for $1 million. In this agreement, Corinthian assigned everything it received from SCI under the stock sale agreement to Washburn. The share purchase agreement listed the three cemeteries—Crystal Lake Cemetery, Dawn Valley, and Glen Haven—as transferring to Washburn.[3]

There was no language in either the stock sale agreement or the share purchase agreement that expressly excluded or included the vacant lots from the sale or that limited the sale of Crystal Lake's shares to the three cemeteries owned by Crystal Lake. The parties do not dispute the fact that they intended neither to include nor to exclude the vacant lots from either the stock sale agreement or the share purchase agreement. The parties contend they had no such intention because they did not know about the existence of the vacant lots. But appellants do not dispute that under the terms of the agreements, SCI could have removed the vacant lots from the assets of Crystal Lake prior to the transaction because the lots were not utilized in the operation of the cemetery business.

[2] Minnesota Statutes §306.88, subd. 1 (2010), provides in relevant part that "[a] lodge, order, or association of a purely religious, charitable, or benevolent description, may acquire the cemetery property of the cemetery association by gift or purchase and maintain and enlarge it if it . . . does not operate for purposes of profit."
[3] In the share purchase agreement, Corinthian also assigned any rights it had in the stock purchase agreement to Washburn. As a result and as appellants note in their brief, "Washburn stepped into the shoes of Corinthian as it relates to SCI."

The record is unclear about when SCI first learned that the Crystal Lake sale included the vacant lots. Washburn first became aware sometime in 2007 or 2008 that it owned the Colorado lot. This occurred when the chief executive officer of Washburn received a phone call from a potential purchaser inquiring about the Colorado property and when Washburn's chief financial officer received a phone call from SCI requesting a quit claim deed for the property. Washburn did not become aware that it was the owner of the Burnsville lot until this lawsuit was commenced.

SCI and Corinthian sued Washburn and requested several forms of equitable relief from the district court, including reformation of both agreements (the stock sale agreement and the share purchase agreement), and rescission. The parties each moved for summary judgment. The district court granted Washburn's motion for summary judgment and denied appellants' motion for summary judgment. The court held that it could not reform the agreements because the evidence did not satisfy the elements required for reformation. As for rescission, the court considered only the equitable remedy of rescission based on mutual mistake. The court, relying on *Costello v. Sykes*, 143 Minn. 109, 172 N.W. 907 (1919), held that appellants were not entitled to rescission based on mutual mistake because a stock sale transfers all assets and liabilities unless specifically excluded. Because the subject matter of the contract was 100% of SCI's stock in Crystal Lake, the court reasoned that "the parties all knew that a stock transaction would transfer everything that was not specifically excluded," and therefore there was no mutual mistake. Finally, the court dismissed SCI's unjust enrichment claim as a matter of law.[4]

SCI and Corinthian appealed and a divided court of appeals affirmed. . . . We granted appellants' petition for review.

. . . Rescission is an equitable remedy. In general, "a court may order an agreement rescinded if both parties were mistaken with respect to facts material to the agreement." *Gartner v. Eikill*, 319 N.W.2d 397, 398 (Minn. 1982). Appellants argue that rescission is allowed on two grounds—mutual mistake and the absence of mutual assent. We address each argument in turn.

Appellants first argue that they are entitled to rescission based on mutual mistake. The district court relied on *Costello v. Sykes*, 143 Minn. 109, 172 N.W. 907 (1919), and held that appellants were not entitled to rescission. Appellants contend that *Costello* does not apply to this case because the subject matter of the agreements was the three cemeteries and not shares of Crystal Lake stock. Specifically, appellants argue that because the parties agreed to treat the stock sale as an asset transaction for tax purposes, this treatment provides evidence that the subject matter of the sale was the cemeteries and not the stock. Appellants also contend that because of the vast difference between what the parties actually transferred—three cemeteries and two vacant lots (valued at $3

---

[4] Only SCI sought relief for unjust enrichment. Because SCI did not raise its unjust enrichment claim on appeal, we do not discuss this claim further.

million)—and what the parties intended to transfer—three cemeteries (valued at $1 million)—we should not apply *Costello*. Alternatively, appellants contend that we should overturn *Costello*. We agree with the district court that *Costello* controls and we decline to overrule *Costello*.

In *Costello*, the plaintiff purchased 10 shares of stock in the Calhoun State Bank from the defendant shareholders. At the time of the purchase, the parties to the transaction believed that the bank was capitalized, that its assets and liabilities were known, and that "the surplus and profits" stated in the books were accurate. The parties were mistaken in all respects. Specifically, the parties to the sale were "mutually mistaken as to the assets of the bank, the actual value and the book value of its stock, and the amount of its surplus and undivided profits." The parties were mistaken because employees of the bank, who had misappropriated bank funds, altered the bank's records to conceal their actions. Based on the mistakes, the plaintiff sued for rescission of the contract.

The question presented in the case was "whether the mistake alleged is of such a character as to give rise to a right to rescind." [143 Minn.] at 111, 172 N.W. at 908. We held that it was not. Specifically, we concluded that a sale of corporate stock may not be "rescinded merely because both parties were mistaken about the nature or extent of the assets or liabilities of the corporation" as long as the "means of information are open alike to both and there is no concealment of facts or imposition." *Id.* at 114, 172 N.W. at 909. We reached this conclusion because the subject matter of the contract was the stock of the bank, and the purchaser received the shares of stock that he intended to buy. Under these circumstances, where the purchaser's complaint was only about the value of the shares, and "[i]n the absence of fraud or inequitable conduct," rescission was not an available remedy.

Costello bars rescission in this case. *Costello*, like this case, involved the sale of stock. The parties' intent, as reflected in their written agreement, was to transfer all of SCI's stock in Crystal Lake to Corinthian and then to Washburn. Even if there was a mistake as to the value of the transaction, as appellants contend, under *Costello* we do not look behind the form of the transaction when the mistake is one of value. As we said in *Costello*, "[a] mistake relating merely to the attributes, quality, or value of the subject of a sale does not warrant rescission." 143 Minn. at 111, 172 N.W. at 908. We hold that under the rule of *Costello*, appellants are not entitled to rescission.

If we conclude, as we have, that *Costello* bars the rescission claim, appellants urge us to overrule *Costello*. Based on the principle of stare decisis, "[w]e are 'extremely reluctant to overrule our precedent . . .' and 'require a compelling reason' to do so." *Zutz v. Nelson*, 788 N.W.2d 58, 63 (Minn. 2010) (quoting *State v. Martin*, 773 N.W.2d 89, 98 (Minn. 2009)). Appellants contend that we should overrule *Costello* because under *Costello*, there could never be rescission in a stock sale transaction. We do not read *Costello* so broadly.

Contrary to appellants' argument, in *Costello* itself, we suggested situations where rescission might be possible even in a stock sale. We noted that rescission might be possible when the parties are mistaken about the actual existence or identity of the stock. For example, rescission might be available if the parties believe they are selling and purchasing shares of stock in Company X and instead, they are selling and purchasing shares of Company Y. We also noted that courts might grant rescission in the context of the sale of stock when there has been dishonesty by one of the parties. *Costello* therefore should not be read to bar rescission in all stock sale transactions, even though it operates to bar rescission in this case.

Appellants also rely on *Clayburg v. Whitt*, 171 N.W.2d 623 (Iowa 1969), a decision from the Iowa Supreme Court, in arguing that we should overrule *Costello*. In *Clayburg*, the court rejected "the proposition that the existence or non-existence of corporate assets is immaterial." 171 N.W.2d at 626. The court reasoned that under the facts of the case, "[b]oth buyers and sellers were concerned with the underlying assets and liabilities of [a] closely held family corporation and they considered the financial structure of the corporation in striking a bargain." *Id.* Given that the corporation's assets and liabilities were material to the agreement, the court held that simply because the transaction was structured as a stock sale should not preclude rescission. . . . "Under the circumstances present in this case we hold it was proper for the court to look beyond the form of the asset transferred (corporate stock) to the substance of the transfer (corporate assets and liabilities) in deciding whether there was a mutual mistake such as would justify refusing enforcement or rescission of the contract." [*Id.*]

Appellants contend that *Clayburg* supports their argument that we should look beyond the form of the transfer—a stock transaction—and look to the substance of the transfer—three cemeteries—to determine whether appellants are entitled to rescission because the parties considered Crystal Lake's assets and liabilities when negotiating the agreement. . . . The *Clayburg* court adopted a rule different from our rule in *Costello* that rescission is not available in the stock sale context when the parties are mistaken about the extent of the assets of the corporation. But the analysis in *Clayburg* does not establish that the reasoning in *Costello* is unsound. *Clayburg* therefore does not provide a basis upon which we should depart from our precedent. In sum, appellants have not presented any compelling reason for us to depart from our established precedent. Under that precedent, we hold that rescission does not apply in this case.

Rather than rely on *Costello*, appellants urge that we apply the analysis from the Restatement (Second) of Contracts §152 to assess the rescission claim. See Restatement (Second) of Contracts §152 (1981) (explaining that "[w]here a mistake of both parties at the time a contract was made as to a basic assumption on which the contract was made has a material effect on the agreed exchange of performances, the contract is voidable by the adversely affected party unless he bears the risk of the mistake under the rule stated in §154"). . . . Even if we were to apply the basic-assumption test of section 152, the rescission claim would still fail. Under section 152, rescission is not available if the party "bears the risk of the mistake." Restatement (Second) of Contracts §152. As discussed more fully below, because SCI had the opportunity to exclude property that was not utilized in the operation of Crystal Lakes' cemetery business, SCI bore the risk of any mistake here, and rescission is therefore not appropriate even assuming there had been a mutual mistake for purposes of assessing rescission under section 152. See Restatement (Second) Contracts §154 cmt. B (1981) (stating that a party may "agree, by appropriate language or other manifestations, to perform in spite of mistake that would otherwise justify his avoidance").

As an alternative to their mutual mistake argument, appellants argue that they are entitled to rescission due to a lack of mutual assent. Specifically, appellants contend there was no mutual assent between the parties when forming the stock sale agreement because there was only a "meeting of the minds" to sell, purchase, and transfer the cemeteries and not the vacant lots. The formation of sales contracts requires mutual assent among the parties involved in the transaction. Mutual assent entails a "meeting of the minds concerning [a contract's] essential elements." *Minneapolis Cablesystems v. City of Minneapolis*, 299 N.W.2d 121, 122 (Minn. 1980); see also *Black's Law Dictionary* 132 (9th ed. 2009) (defining mutual assent as an "[a]greement by both parties to a contract . . . in the form of offer and acceptance"). Whether mutual assent exists is tested under an objective standard. When viewed under an objective standard, there was mutual assent to sell the Crystal Lake stock. The stock sale agreement clearly stated that "[SCI] does hereby agree to sell, transfer, assign and deliver . . . all of the issued and outstanding shares of capital stock of [Crystal Lake] which are owned by [SCI]." In the context of a stock sale agreement, the law presumes that all assets and liabilities transfer with the stock. *Cf. Specialized Tours, Inc. v. Hagen*, 392 N.W.2d 520, 536 (Minn. 1986) ("When a business is sold through a stock transfer, the buyer assumes not only the assets of the corporation, but also the liabilities."). When the undisputed evidence is examined under an objective standard, it establishes that mutual assent existed to sell the Crystal Lake stock, which included the vacant lots as part of the assets. We therefore hold that appellants are not entitled to rescission for lack of mutual assent. . . .

[Further,] the undisputed evidence establishes that appellants cannot prove that the stock sale agreement failed to express the true intentions of the parties because of a mutual mistake. We therefore hold that appellants are not entitled to reformation. [The court's discussion of reformation is omitted.]

Affirmed.

■ QUESTIONS

(1)   The court quotes the *Gartner* case for the proposition that a contract may be rescinded (that is, avoided) if both parties were mistaken as to facts material to the agreement. According to SCI and Corinthian, what were the facts at issue? Is there any dispute as to whether the parties were mistaken as to those facts? In your view, were the facts at issue material? Why or why not?

(2)   The court cites and follows the *Costello* case to conclude that the mistake here was one of value, not of fact. On what basis does the court make this distinction? Is it important that this was a sale of stock, and if so, why do you think that is? What would, in this context, constitute a mistake of fact?

(3) How does *SCI* compare to *Wood v. Boynton* and *Sherwood v. Walker*? Which of those two older cases seems more in accord with the rationale and result in *SCI*?

(4) As an alternative ground for its holding, the court analyzes Restatement, Second §152, and concludes that even under the Restatement, Second, test, the contract is not avoidable because SCI bore the risk of the mistake. The court doesn't discuss how the other elements of the Restatement, Second, test would apply to these facts. What are those elements, and do you think they were satisfied here? Why or why not?

(5) In its analysis of Restatement, Second §152, the court points to the clause that allows SCI to exclude properties from the sale. Why does this clause suggest that SCI bore the risk of the mistake at issue? Had the contract not contained this clause, who in your view would have borne the risk of the mistake?

(6) As an alternate argument, SCI and Corinthian argue that there was no contract for lack of mutual assent. What is the nature of this argument? Are you surprised that it didn't prevail? If not, why, do you think, did they consider this argument worth raising?

■ PROBLEM 17.2

For many years, Jethro lived in a small cabin in the hills. One of his friends, Jed, told him that he would like to buy the cabin and associated land and use it for hunting. Jethro decided to sell his land to Jed and move to the city. Jed paid him $20,000, and the transaction was completed with few formalities. A few weeks later, Jed was hunting on the land with his faithful dog, Duke. He attempted to shoot a possum but missed. Crude oil gushed out of the ground.

Jethro subsequently hears about this event. He is amazed—he never knew there was oil on the land. He also hears that an oil company has offered Jed $25 million for the land. Jethro seeks to avoid his sales contract with Jed, alleging mutual mistake. Should Jethro prevail? Why or why not?

---

a. Mistake of Current Fact as Distinguished from Other Mistaken Judgments, Assumptions, or Beliefs

In our study of fraud in Chapter 13, we saw how subtle the distinction can be between a fact and something that is not a fact (say, for instance, a judgment). Similar issues arise here, because the doctrine of mutual mistake only applies if the mistake relates to facts in existence at the time of the contract. Opinions and judgments, as well as facts that arise after the contract is entered into, are not appropriate grounds for relief under mistake doctrine. Sometimes the mistake of fact is quite clear. Assume, for instance, that Sara agrees to sublet Mark's apartment for $5 per square foot per month. Both parties believe the apartment to be 1,000 square feet in area. In fact, the apartment contains 1,400 square feet. The size of the apartment is arguably a fact. Both parties, believing the apartment to be smaller than it was, were mistaken as to this fact. If the other elements of mutual mistake are met, there may be grounds for voiding the contract. Less clear cases abound, however.

Suppose again that Sara agrees to sublet Mark's apartment. Both parties believe the neighborhood to be unfashionable and generally undesirable, and they set the rent accordingly. The day after the parties sign the sublease, they discover that an influential lifestyle blog just the previous week had rated the neighborhood as the hottest up-and-coming area in the city. In the weeks after the contract is signed, movie stars, sports figures, and assorted young professionals begin to move into the neighborhood in droves. Prevailing rents skyrocket. Mark files suit and seeks to avoid the contract on the basis of mutual mistake.

Most courts would deny relief to Mark. Their analyses may differ, but many would say that there was no mistake in this case as to a current fact. The desirability of the neighborhood at the time the contract was entered was a judgment call. The influx of fashionable tenants and the associated explosion in the rental market were future events, which Mark failed to predict. Changing market conditions were precisely the sort of risk that the parties intended to allocate by the contract, and relief should not be available to reallocate that risk.

Mark would counter that the blog post was a fact in existence at the time the contract was entered into, and neither party was aware of its existence. Had they known of the blog post, Mark would have charged a higher rent, and Sara would have agreed to pay it. Serious as Mark may consider his ignorance of the blog post to be, the court may perceive this to be so wrapped up in his mistake of judgment that it does not qualify as a mistake of fact at all. Other courts might follow the lead of the *SCI Minnesota Funeral Services* case and conclude that even if a mistake of fact was made, Mark bore the risk of the mistake. The result is the same: Mark loses the argument.

Sometimes a party seeks to avoid a contract because at the time the contract was entered, neither party appreciated the legal consequences of the agreement. Once those consequences become clear, one of the parties finds the contract to be much less advantageous than it had assumed, and it argues the contract should be avoided as a result. Suppose, for instance, that Sara and Mark go forward with the sublease, believing on advice of an accountant that the transaction will not have any tax ramifications. Under current tax law, however, the transaction as they have structured it will impose significant income tax liability on Mark. When this comes to Mark's attention, he seeks to avoid the sublease, and relies on the doctrine of mistake. In this instance, the mistake of the parties consists of ignorance of a law that will impose consequences on their behavior. There exists some difference of opinion as to whether a "law" can also be a "fact" for purposes of the mistake doctrine. Some cases refuse to characterize an error as to the current state of the law as a "mistake in fact." Instead, they reason that parties are presumed to know the law, and thus failure to verify the state of the law is a mistake in judgment, not in fact. If they attempted to verify the law but received bad advice, any remedy is against the advisor, not avoidance of the contract. Some modern cases considering the issue disagree with this conclusion, and acknowledge that the existence of a law can be a fact.

■ PROBLEM 17.3

Mattson v. Rachetto, 1999 S.D. 51, 591 N.W.2d 814 (1999), illustrates one case where a court allowed relief for mistake of law. Jon Mattson and Jerry Rachetto were law partners, and Jon Mattson was married to Jerry Rachetto's sister. When Jerry Rachetto graduated from law school and went to work for Jon Mattson, the Mattsons deeded a tract of land on the Mattsons' family farm to the Rachettos free of charge. The Rachettos built a house on it, and made it their home. About ten years later, the Rachettos approached the Mattsons and asked to purchase an adjoining tract (also part of the Mattsons' family farm) to serve as a buffer between their home and a new subdivision that was going in nearby. The Mattsons agreed to sell them the buffer tract at a bargain price, but insisted that the Rachettos lease the tract back to them to allow them to cultivate hay and graze livestock on the property. The Rachettos were amenable to this requirement, and the parties consummated the transaction. In spite of the fact that both Jon Mattson and Jerry Rachetto were lawyers, no one realized that the lease was void under a state statute invalidating long-term agricultural leases. After 12 years had passed, Jerry Rachetto discovered the law invalidating the agricultural lease. He erected an electric fence around the property, thus preventing the Mattsons from cultivating hay or grazing their livestock. The Mattsons attempted to settle the dispute, but the Rachettos (who had since built a golf green and tee box on the property) refused.

The Mattsons took the matter to court, and asked that the sale-leaseback transaction be rescinded for mutual mistake. The Rachettos argued rescission was not appropriate. Alternatively, they argued, if rescission was appropriate, only the lease should be rescinded, not the transaction as a whole. The South Dakota Supreme Court ultimately heard the dispute. The court held that the parties had contracted under a "mutual misapprehension of the law," and rescinded not only the lease, but the underlying sale of the buffer tract as well.

(a) The *Mattson* court treated the parties' ignorance of the law as a mistake of fact. As noted above, some courts consider mistakes of law to be mistakes of judgment, not fact. What would the result have been if the court had considered the parties' ignorance of the law as a mistake of judgment in this case? In particular, would the Mattsons be legally entitled to continue to cultivate hay and graze livestock on the property?

(b) Apply the elements of Restatement, Second §§152 and 154 to the facts summarized here. Assuming mistake of law may be characterized as one of fact generally, are the other elements of the Restatement, Second tests satisfied here? In particular, who do you think bore the risk of this particular mistake and why?

■ PROBLEM 17.4

E. Lee Mosynary regularly served as a temporary foster parent for children who were at risk. Although the need for foster parents was great, Lee had a small home and could rarely take in more than one or two children at a time. He inherited a large sum of money and decided to use it to purchase a larger house where he could operate a group home for 15 to 20 children at a time.

Ed Elderly owned a mansion that he hoped to sell so he could retire to sunnier climes. The high-end real estate market, however, was very slow. In the nearly three years the mansion had been on the market, Ed had observed little interest in it and had received no offers at all. So when Ed saw a news report about Lee and his efforts to open a group home for foster children, Ed contacted Lee directly and offered to sell Lee his mansion.

Lee was very interested in Ed's offer, so he called the state's Department of Child and Family Services to verify that the mansion would be a suitable location for a group home. The state employee (who knew nothing about zoning law) confirmed that the mansion would be a suitable location for a group home, as it was undoubtedly zoned for residential use. Lee asked the state employee if there was anything else he should verify before going forward with the transaction, and the state employee said no.

Lee verified with Ed and the local county clerk that the mansion was in fact zoned for residential use. Lee and Ed then signed a contract in which Lee agreed to purchase the mansion for $2.5 million in one month's time. Lee paid Ed a down payment of $25,000. The contract allowed Lee to inspect the property for structural defects before being obligated to close but otherwise contained no financing or other contingencies.

Before the transaction could close, Lee learned that local zoning laws do not permit group homes of this sort to operate in areas zoned for residential use. Lee seeks to avoid enforcement of the contract on the basis of mutual mistake. Should Lee prevail? Why or why not?

b. When a Party Bears the Risk of a Mistake

One of the important functions of contract law is to allow parties to allocate risks of unknown or uncertain events. The doctrine of mistake, if applied too broadly, has the potential to upset the expectations of the parties and undercut the risk allocation function of contracts generally. As a result, if the language of a contract clearly and expressly allocates risk of the mistake at issue to one of the parties, a court will refuse to allow avoidance of the contract. As we have seen, if the language of the contract is unclear or if the contract doesn't address the matter at all, courts examine whether under the circumstances it is appropriate to allocate the risk of the mistake to the aggrieved party. If so, a court will refuse to avoid the contract. If not, relief under mistake doctrine may be available. In the *SCI Minnesota Funeral Services* case, the court concluded, among other things, that SCI and Corinthian bore the risk of the mistake at issue. In this section, we examine more closely the types of circumstances courts consider when they explore who bore the risk of a particular mistake. The next two cases address this issue, and like *SCI Minnesota Funeral Services*, both refuse to grant relief. Both also refer to Restatement, Second §154, included in the introduction to Section A.1. As you read the cases, identify precisely what factors persuaded the courts.

ESTATE OF NELSON v. RICE

198 Ariz. 563, 12 P.3d 238 (2000)
Arizona Court of Appeals

ESPINOSA, Chief Judge.

Plaintiff/appellant, the Estate of Martha Nelson, through its copersonal representatives Edward Franz and Kenneth Newman, appeals from a summary judgment in favor of defendants/appellees Carl and Anne Rice in the Estate's action seeking rescission or reformation of the sale of two paintings to the Rices. The Estate argues that these remedies are required because the sale was based upon a mutual mistake. . . . We affirm.

. . . After Martha Nelson died in February 1996, Newman and Franz, the copersonal representatives of her estate, employed Judith McKenzie-Larson to appraise the Estate's personal property in preparation for an estate sale. McKenzie-Larson told them that she did not appraise fine art and that, if she saw any, they would need to hire an additional appraiser. McKenzie-Larson did not report finding any fine art, and relying on her silence and her appraisal, Newman and Franz priced and sold the Estate's personal property.

Responding to a newspaper advertisement, Carl Rice attended the public estate sale and paid the asking price of $60 for two oil paintings. Although Carl had bought and sold some art, he was not an educated purchaser, had never made more than $55 on any single piece, and had bought many pieces that had "turned out to be frauds, forgeries or . . . to have been [created] by less popular artists." He assumed the paintings were not originals given their price and the fact that the Estate was managed by professionals, but was attracted to the subject matter of one of the paintings and the frame of the other. At home, he compared the signatures on the paintings to those in a book of artists' signatures, noticing they "appeared to be similar" to that of Martin Johnson Heade. As they had done in the past, the Rices sent pictures of the paintings to Christie's in New York, hoping they might be Heade's work. Christie's authenticated the paintings, *Magnolia Blossoms on Blue Velvet* and *Cherokee Roses*, as paintings by Heade and offered to sell them on consignment. Christie's subsequently sold the paintings at auction for $1,072,000. After subtracting the buyer's premium and the commission, the Rices realized $911,780 from the sale.

Newman and Franz learned about the sale in February 1997 and thereafter sued McKenzie-Larson on behalf of the Estate, believing she was entirely responsible for the Estate's loss. The following November, they settled the lawsuit because McKenzie-Larson had no assets with which to pay damages. During 1997, the Rices paid income taxes of $337,000 on the profit from the sale of the paintings, purchased a home, created a family trust, and spent some of the funds on living expenses.

The Estate sued the Rices in late January 1998, alleging the sale contract should be rescinded or reformed on grounds of mutual mistake. . . . In its subsequent motion for summary judgment, the Estate argued the parties were not aware the transaction had involved fine art, believing instead that the items exchanged were "relatively valueless, wall decorations." In their opposition and cross-motion, the Rices argued the Estate bore the risk of mistake. . . . The trial court concluded that, although the parties had been mistaken about the value of the paintings, the Estate bore the risk of that mistake. . . . Accordingly, the court denied the Estate's motion for summary judgment and granted the Rices' cross-motion. . . .

The Estate . . . argues that it established a mutual mistake sufficient to permit the reformation or rescission of the sale of the paintings to the Rices. A party seeking to rescind a contract on the basis of mutual mistake must show by clear and convincing evidence that the agreement should be set aside. A contract may be rescinded on the ground of a mutual mistake as to a "basic assumption on which both parties made the contract." *Renner v. Kehl,* 150 Ariz. 94, 97, 722 P.2d 262, 265 (1986), *quoting* Restatement (Second) of

Contracts §152 cmt. b (1979). Furthermore, the parties' mutual mistake must have had "such a material effect on the agreed exchange of performances as to upset the very bases of the contract." *Id., quoting* Restatement §152 cmt. a. However, the mistake must not be one on which the party seeking relief bears the risk under the rules stated in §154(b) of the Restatement.

In concluding that the Estate was not entitled to rescind the sale, the trial court found that, although a mistake had existed as to the value of the paintings, the Estate bore the risk of that mistake under §154(b) of the Restatement, citing the example in comment a. Section 154(b) states that a party bears the risk of mistake when "he is aware, at the time the contract is made, that he has only limited knowledge with respect to the facts to which the mistake relates but treats his limited knowledge as sufficient." In explaining that provision, the Washington Supreme Court stated, "In such a situation there is no mistake. Instead, there is <u>an awareness of uncertainty</u> or conscious ignorance of the future." *Bennett v. Shinoda Floral, Inc.,* 108 Wash. 2d 386, 739 P.2d 648, 653-54 (1987).

The Estate contends neither party bore the risk of mistake, arguing that §154 and comment a are not applicable to these facts. In the example in comment a, the risk of mistake is allocated to the seller when the buyer discovers valuable mineral deposits on property priced and purchased as farmland. Even were we to accept the Estate's argument that this example is not analogous, comment c clearly applies here and states:

> *Conscious ignorance.* Even though the mistaken party did not agree to bear the risk, he may have been aware when he made the contract that his knowledge with respect to the facts to which the mistake relates was limited. If he was not only so aware that his knowledge was limited but <u>undertook to perform in the face of that awareness</u>, he bears the risk of the mistake. It is sometimes said in such a situation that, in a sense, there was not mistake but "conscious ignorance."

Through its personal representatives, the Estate hired two appraisers, McKenzie-Larson and an Indian art expert, to evaluate the Estate's collection of Indian art and artifacts. McKenzie-Larson specifically told Newman that she did not appraise fine art. In his deposition, Newman testified that he had not been concerned that McKenzie-Larson had no expertise in fine art, believing the Estate contained nothing of "significant value" except the house and the Indian art collection. Despite the knowledge that the Estate contained framed art other than the Indian art, and that McKenzie-Larson was not qualified to appraise fine art, the personal representatives relied on her to notify them of any fine art or whether a fine arts appraiser was needed. Because McKenzie-Larson did not say they needed an additional appraiser, Newman and Franz did not hire anyone qualified to appraise fine art. <u>By relying on the opinion of someone who was admittedly unqualified to appraise fine art to determine its existence, the personal representatives consciously ignored the possibility that the Estate's assets might include fine art</u>, thus assuming that risk. . . . Accordingly, the trial court correctly found that the Estate bore the risk of mistake as to the paintings' value.

The Estate asserts that the facts here are similar to those in *Renner*, in which real estate buyers sued to rescind a contract for acreage upon which they wished to commercially grow jojoba after discovering the water supply was inadequate for that purpose. The supreme court concluded that the buyers could rescind the contract based upon mutual mistake because both the buyers and the sellers had believed there was an adequate water supply, a basic assumption underlying formation of the contract. The parties' failure to thoroughly investigate the water supply did not preclude rescission when "the risk of mistake was not allocated among the parties." 150 Ariz., at 97 n. 2, 722 P.2d at 265 n. 2. The Estate's reliance on *Renner* is unavailing because, as stated above, the Estate bore the risk of mistake based on its own conscious ignorance.

[margin note: didn't need to allocate the risk because they already bore it]

Furthermore, under Restatement §154(c), the court may allocate the risk of mistake to one party "on the ground that it is reasonable in the circumstances to do so." In making this determination, "the court will consider the purposes of the parties and will have recourse to its own general knowledge of human behavior in bargain transactions." Restatement §154 cmt. d. Here, the Estate had had ample opportunity to discover what it was selling and failed to do so; instead, it ignored the possibility that the paintings were valuable and attempted to take action only after learning of their worth as a result of the efforts of the Rices. Under these circumstances, the Estate was a victim of its own folly and it was reasonable for the court to allocate to it the burden of its mistake. . . .

[margin note: holding]

Affirmed. — *[margin note: disposition]*

CHERRY v. McCALL

138 S.W.3d 35 (2004)
Texas Court of Appeals

ANGELINI, Justice.

Appellants Robert and Maria Cherry b[r]ought a declaratory judgment action against Brian and Rebekah McCall. The McCalls moved for summary judgment, and the trial court granted the motion. The Cherrys appeal the judgment. . . . We affirm the judgment of the trial court.

The Cherrys bought a home from the McCalls. After the Cherrys bought the home, they discovered a walled-in room in the basement. The room was filled with trash, including rusty plumbing fixtures, bathtubs, sinks, commodes, boards, pipes, rocks, and used building materials. The trash was damp and contaminated with mold. The Cherrys brought a declaratory judgment action, seeking declaration that (1) the McCalls breached the contract; and (2) the walled-in room constitutes a mutual mistake justifying rescission. The McCalls answered by general denial. The McCalls also asserted the "as is" provision of the contract as an affirmative defense and counterclaimed for attorney fees. . . . [The trial court granted summary judgment in favor of the McCalls, and awarded the McCalls $30,000 in attorneys' fees. The Cherrys appealed.]

The Cherrys allege that the McCalls breached the contract by "delivering [b]uyers a mold contaminated home, with a number of hidden rooms, containing defective plumbing and electricity." Therefore, to be entitled to a declaratory judgment that the McCalls breached the contract, the Cherrys had to prove that the contract required the McCalls to deliver buyers a home without these defects. Here, however, the Cherrys contracted to accept the property "in its present condition," or "as is." Thus, the Cherrys have taken "the entire risk as to the quality of the [property] and the resulting loss." *Mid Continent Aircraft Corp. v. Curry County Spraying Serv., Inc.*, 572 S.W.2d 308, 313 (Tex. 1978).

The Cherrys argue, however, that the "as is" clause is unenforceable under the "totality of the circumstances" test set out by *Prudential Insurance Co. of America v. Jefferson Associates*, 896 S.W.2d 156, 161 (Tex. 1995). In that case, the court held:

> *get out of "as-is"*
>
> . . . A buyer is not bound by an agreement to purchase something "as is" that he is induced to make because of a fraudulent representation or concealment of information by the seller. . . . Also, a buyer is not bound by an "as is" agreement if he is entitled to inspect the condition of what is being sold but is impaired by the seller's conduct. A seller cannot obstruct an inspection for defects in his property and still insist that the buyer take it "as is." In circumstances such as these an "as is" agreement does not bar recovery against the seller.
>
> We also recognize that other aspects of a transaction may make an "as is" agreement unenforceable. The nature of the transaction and the totality of the circumstances surrounding the agreement must be considered. Where the "as is" clause is an important part of the basis of the bargain, not an incidental or "boilerplate" provision, and is entered into by parties of relatively equal bargaining position, a buyer's affirmation and agreement that he is not relying on representations by the seller should be given effect.

Prudential, 896 S.W.2d at 162. The Cherrys do not allege that the McCalls fraudulently induced them to buy the house or concealed knowledge about the hidden room. Nor do they allege that they were prevented from making their own inspection. Rather, they argue that their lack of sophistication, the fact that the "as is" provision was not negotiated but a standard boiler-plate provision, the high price the Cherrys paid for the property, and the fact that the defect was hidden are all factors indicating that the "as is" clause is unenforceable under the "totality of the circumstances."

We disagree. While there is some evidence indicating that Mrs. Cherry, who had never handled the details of purchasing a home on her own before, was less sophisticated than the McCalls, who owned rental properties, there is no evidence that the Cherrys and the McCalls entered into the contract from unequal bargaining positions or that the transaction was not made at arm's length. Additionally, there is no evidence to support the Cherrys' argument that the "as is" provision was not freely negotiated. In fact, Mrs. Cherry confirmed in her deposition testimony that she "agreed to purchase the property in its current condition" and that she "accepted the risk" that the property might be deficient. . . . Because the Cherrys contracted to accept the property "as is," they cannot, as a matter of law, prevail on their breach of contract claim.

In order to be entitled to a declaratory judgment that the contract was made under a mutual mistake, the Cherrys had to prove: (1) a mistake of fact, (2) held mutually by the parties, (3) which materially affects the agreed-upon exchange. *de Monet v. PERA*, 877 S.W.2d 352, 357 (Tex. App.—Dallas 1994, no writ). Under section 154 of the Restatement, however, a party bears the risk of mistake when the risk is allocated to him by agreement or when he knowingly treats his limited knowledge of the facts surrounding the mistake as sufficient. *Monet*, 877 S.W.2d at 359 (citing Restatement (Second) of Contracts §154(a) & (b) (1981)). Here, the risk of mistake was allocated to the Cherrys by agreement when they contracted to accept property "in its current condition." Accordingly, their claim of mutual mistake fails as a matter of law.

The Cherrys argue, however, that the contract itself is invalid because a mutual mistake prevented the "meeting of the minds" necessary to the formation of a valid contract. *See Monet*, 877 S.W.2d at 357 ("When mutual mistake is alleged, the task of the court is not to interpret the language contained in the contract, but to determine whether the contract itself is valid."). We disagree. As discussed above, Mrs. Cherry confirmed in her deposition testimony that she "agreed to purchase the property in its current condition" and that she "accepted the risk" that the property might be deficient. Thus, the evidence confirms that a meeting of the minds *did* take place, i.e., though neither party knew of the hidden room when it entered into the agreement, both parties agreed to place the risk of any unknown defects on the Cherrys.

Because the McCalls proved as a matter of law that the Cherrys are not entitled to a declaratory judgment on either breach of contract or mutual mistake, we hold that the trial court did not err in granting . . . summary judgment in favor of the McCalls. . . .

[W]e affirm the judgment of the trial court.

■ QUESTIONS

Apparently, the McCalls did not know of the hidden room or its fusty contents. Would it have made any difference to the result had they had discovered the room themselves but simply said nothing about it? What if they had not only known of the room but had walled it off themselves in hopes that the Cherrys would not discover it? Are any other avoidance doctrines arguably relevant under these circumstances?

2. Unilateral Mistake

In the previous section, we consider mistakes that are shared by the parties. In this section, we address situations where the mistake relates more to one party than to the other. Under the formulation found in the Restatement, Second, a mutual mistake requires, among other things, that parties share the mistake of fact, the mistaken fact be a basic assumption on which the contract was made, and the mistake have a material effect on the agreed exchange of performances. The mutuality of the mistake is key: The mistake, in essence, must be fundamental to both parties. They both must share it, they both must have assumed it to have been true, and the effect of the mistake on the balance of the exchange must be material. Even if the mistake is material to both parties, relief will be available only if the court determines that the complaining party did not bear the risk of the mistake.

The elements of unilateral mistake, as set out in the Restatement, Second §153, bear a striking resemblance to those of mutual mistake. While they relax the requirements of shared mistake, they also focus on materiality and risk allocation. But as in many mutual mistake cases, while one party argues that the mistake has defeated its expectations under the contract, the other argues avoidance of the contract would defeat its own legitimate expectations of enforcement. Under unilateral mistake doctrine, because one party is more mistaken than the other or the mistake is more material to one party than it is to the other, courts require a particularly strong showing of inequity in order to avoid the contract. Contrast the elements as summarized below:

Mutual Mistake

- The mistake relates to facts in existence at the time of the contract
- The mistake is shared by both parties
- The mistake relates to a basic assumption on which the contract was made
- The mistake has a material effect on the agreed exchange of performances

- The complaining party did not bear the risk of the mistake

Unilateral Mistake

- The mistake relates to facts in existence at the time of the contract
- The mistake may be by one party only
- The mistake relates to a basic assumption on which the mistaken party made the contract
- The mistake has a material effect on the agreed exchange of performances that is adverse to the mistaken party
- The mistaken party did not bear the risk of the mistake
- Either (a) the effect of the mistake is such that enforcement of the contract would be unconscionable or (b) the other party had reason to know of the mistake or his fault caused the mistake

The concept of a mistake that is essentially one-sided requires some explanation. In some circumstances, one party has a mistaken belief of fact, while the other knows the true state of affairs. This is the clearest example of unilateral mistake. To protect the noncomplaining party's reasonable expectations, relief will be available only if enforcement of the contract would lead to palpable injustice. In other circumstances, both parties may share the same mistaken belief of fact, but the mistake really isn't particularly relevant to the noncomplaining party's intentions or purposes when it enters the contract. Even though the mistake is shared, and therefore "mutual" in the ordinary sense, it is not mutual in the legal sense. The mistake may relate to a basic assumption for the complaining party only, or materially affect the performance of the complaining party only. The noncomplaining party, though mistaken, is relatively indifferent to the true state of affairs. The erroneous fact was not one that had a bearing on that party's determination to enter the contract on the agreed terms. If analyzed under the doctrine of mutual mistake as formulated by Restatement, Second §152, no relief would be available to the complaining party under these circumstances. The mistake is not material to both parties, and the noncomplaining party may have a strong and legitimate interest in seeing the contract go forward. If a court instead applies the doctrine of unilateral mistake, a strong showing that the equities favor relief would be required, but if such showing can be made, relief may be available.

Whether one labels a case of mistake as mutual or unilateral ultimately may make little difference, because the elements are functionally so similar. Under either doctrine, courts are likely to balance the noncomplaining party's legitimate expectations under the contract against the inequity of enforcing the contract against the complaining party. The more the noncomplaining party can be said to have legitimate expectations flowing from the contract, the less likely it is that relief will be available.

BERT ALLEN TOYOTA, INC. v. GRASZ

909 So. 2d 763 (2005)
Mississippi Court of Appeals

CHANDLER, Judge.

[Horst Grasz reached an agreement with Bert Allen Toyota to buy a specially ordered 2003 Toyota Tacoma, and he made a $500 down payment. When he went to pick up the truck, the dealership argued that its computer had made a computational error, and Grasz owed an additional $2,000 beyond the balance he thought was still owing.] ... Grasz refused to pay the higher price and filed a complaint in the Harrison County Chancery Court. The chancellor entered judgment in favor of Grasz ... [and] granted Grasz's request for specific performance.... Bert Allen Toyota appeals....

During the spring of 2003, Horst Grasz wanted to purchase a 2003 Toyota Tacoma pickup truck. He visited Bert Allen Toyota on several occasions in an effort to negotiate a purchase. Throughout the negotiations process, Grasz made it clear that he intended to pay cash for the truck and was unwilling to spend more than $15,000 for his purchase. Everyone at Bert Allen Toyota knew that Grasz was a tough negotiator.

Kevin Gabbert is a sales manager for Bert Allen Toyota and had been working in that capacity for eight years. As the sales manager, it is Gabbert's responsibility to approve all sales, including checking the math on the paperwork submitted to him for approval. On April 2, 2003, Gabbert offered to sell Grasz a 2003 Tacoma for $16,951,[5] less a rebate of $1000, plus tax and title. He entered the numbers into a computer, which generated a four-page document which listed all the specifications for the truck as requested by Grasz, as well as the price of the vehicle. . . . A mathematical error occurred because the computer miscalculated the numbers. If the computer had correctly added the numbers, the final price would have been $17,017.50. Both Gabbert and Grasz testified that they never manually calculated the numbers on the computer generated contract.

The cash price of $16,951, the rebate of $1,000, and the amount of $15,017.50 marked "amount financed" were highlighted in yellow and given to Grasz for review. The offer to sell the truck was quoted as "$16,951.00 less a rebate of $1,000.00 plus tax and title." The document listed the agreement as "Deal Number 15031" and "Contract Date 04/02/03." In four separate places, the document listed the selling price as $15,017.50. This amount was listed in the areas marked "payment," "total financed," "total of payments," and "unpaid balance." Gabbert circled the price as $15,017.50 and hand wrote the word "everything" directly below the sum of $15,017.50.

Grasz attempted to write a check for the amount of $15,017.50 immediately. Gabbert explained that the truck had to be ordered and built to Grasz's contract specifications. Gabbert instead requested a $500 deposit, which Grasz paid with a credit card. Gabbert wrote at the bottom of the agreement, "14,517.50 due @ delivery." The computer-generated documents were given to Grasz. Gabbert testified that he believed he had performed something miraculous for negotiating a deal with Grasz. Everyone at Bert Allen Toyota celebrated for having closed the deal.

Approximately four or five weeks later, the truck arrived from Toyota Motor Corporation to Bert Allen Toyota. Gabbert prepared the final paperwork, at which time he claimed to have discovered an error in the original purchase price. Gabbert testified that this was the first time he had seen the error and the first time he had checked the math of the computer, even though he had knowledge that the computer had miscalculated the sales price on two separate occasions. Gabbert notified Grasz of the mistake and told him that the actual purchase price was $17,017.50. Grasz was advised that if he did not accept, the

[5] $16,951 is $300 over the dealer cost.

dealership would sell the vehicle to someone else. Grasz refused and demanded the original due on delivery price of $14,517.50.

The next day, a Saturday, Grasz presented a check in the amount of $14,517.50 to the dealership and demanded the truck. A representative of the dealership took the check but refused to deliver the truck. On Monday, Grasz returned to the dealership and demanded the truck. Gabbert demanded an additional $2,000. Grasz refused, and Gabbert returned Grasz's check. [Bert] Allen Toyota credited Grasz's credit card with his $500 deposit. Bert Allen Toyota eventually sold the truck to someone else.

Grasz filed a lawsuit in the Harrison County Chancery Court seeking specific performance. The chancellor found that the parties had entered into a clear and unambiguous contract. Furthermore, the chancellor found that the parties treated the written agreement as a contract and behaved in accordance with having reached a contract; that there was a meeting of the minds as to all essential elements of the contract, including a definite selling price; and that there was an unqualified offer by Allen Toyota and an unqualified acceptance by Grasz. The chancellor found that the mathematical error did not "create an unconscionable advantage in favor of Grasz resulting in an intolerable injustice thereby allowing for rescission of the contract." The court granted Grasz's request for specific performance and ordered Bert Allen Toyota to supply an unused 2003 Toyota Tacoma.

Allen Toyota argues that the testimony of Grasz himself established that the price of the truck was $16,951.00, less a rebate of $1,000, plus fees and taxes. As a result, argues Allen Toyota, the unpaid balance listed on the purchase information sheet was not an offer but a miscalculation. In addition, Gabbert reaffirmed the offer by highlighting the cash price of $16,951.00 and the rebate of $1,000.00. Grasz acknowledges that there was an arithmetic error, but he contends that he was interested only in the bottom line and did not notice the error. Grasz testified that he thought he was purchasing a 2003 Toyota Tacoma for the bottom line price amount of $15,017.50, while Gabbert believed he was selling the vehicle for $16,951, less a rebate, plus tax and title. . . .

A mutual mistake is defined as "[a] mistake that is shared and relied on by both parties to a contract." *Black's Law Dictionary* (8th ed. 2004). Bert Allen Toyota contends that there was a mutual mistake between the two parties, claiming that both parties believed that the offer was $16,951, less the rebate, plus tax and title. Grasz claims that he cared only about the bottom line.

Bert Allen Toyota claims that a mutual mistake existed because both parties relied upon the dealership's computer to calculate the fees and taxes on the truck and to add these figures to the offered cash price of $16,951, less the $1,000 rebate. Bert Allen asserts that both parties were incorrect, and that a mutual mistake took place because both parties were wrong for failing to double-check the computer's arithmetic. However, Bert Allen Toyota does not claim that Grasz was responsible for the computational error. Moreover, as recognized by the chancellor, "[t]here's just so many things that go into the marketing of a car that is creative marketing that I think that the customer looks at the bottom line." This Court finds that Bert Allen Toyota failed to prove mutual mistake. . . . Therefore, we affirm on this issue.

The chancellor found that the computational error was a unilateral mistake on the part of Bert Allen Toyota. The remedy for unilateral mistake is rescission. However, rescission on the grounds of unilateral mistake is inappropriate unless a four-part test is met. First, the mistake was of so fundamental a character that the minds of the parties have not, in fact, met. Second, there was no gross negligence on the part of the plaintiff. Third, no intervening rights have accrued. Fourth, the parties may still be placed in *status quo.* In addition, "as a general proposition, equity will not act to rescind a contract where the mistake was induced by the negligence of the party seeking rescission." *Turner v. Terry,* 799 So.2d 25, 36 (¶36) (Miss. 2001).

Because there are no Mississippi cases concerning rescission of a contract based exclusively on a computational error, Bert Allen Toyota relies on judicial precedent from other jurisdictions. One case upon which Bert Allen Toyota relies is *S.T.S. Transport Service, Inc. v. Volvo White Truck Corp.*, 766 F.2d 1089 (7th Cir. 1985). "In the typical case of this sort [where a party is mistaken as to the price], a seller or contractor will miscalculate in adding up a list of items. Under the appropriate circumstances courts will now recognize a right to avoidance of this sort of mistake." *Id.* at 1092. Under Illinois law, where there is a mistake as to price, "[t]he mistake must . . . have occurred despite the exercise of reasonable care." *Id.* at 1093. Mississippi law, like Illinois law, will not allow rescission of a contract if, in the exercise of reasonable care, an error would have been detected. *Hunt v. Davis*, 208 Miss. 710, 725, 45 So. 2d 350 (1950). In *S.T.S.*, the Seventh Circuit affirmed the district court and allowed rescission of the contract because the computational error, once made, would not have been easily detected. *S.T.S.*, 766 F.2d at 1093. In the present case, the chancellor specifically found that Gabbert failed to use reasonable care. This finding was supported by the evidence, given Gabbert's knowledge of the cost of the vehicle, the profit margin for the dealership, and the fact that Gabbert manually subtracted the $500 down payment from the asking price of $15,017.50. . . .

[The court concluded that the contract was enforceable as written, and affirmed the chancellor's finding that it could not be rescinded on grounds of mutual or unilateral mistake. The court questioned whether specific performance was the appropriate remedy under the facts, and remanded the case for further findings on this issue.]

■ PROBLEM 17.5

Suppose the facts were as described in the *Grasz* case, except the computer erroneously listed the sales price as $1,501.75. This amount was listed in the areas marked "payment," "total financed," "total of payments," and "unpaid balance," but Gabbert neither circled the amount nor subtracted out the amount of Grasz's down payment. Instead, he simply gave the documents to Grasz to sign without looking at them. Grasz, knowing an incredibly good deal when he saw one, signed the documents immediately, and tendered a check for the full amount. Gabbert told him to hold on to his check, as the truck still needed to be ordered, and requested a $500 down payment instead. The down payment was charged to Grasz's credit card. Grasz now seeks to purchase the truck for the balance of $1,001.75.

(a) Should these facts affect the reasoning or result in the case? Why or why not?

(b) Suppose Grasz admitted in a deposition that he knew, at the time he signed the contract, that the computer had made a computational error and that's why the contract reflected such a low price. Would that affect your analysis in Part (a) of the problem, and if so, how?

■ PROBLEM 17.6

Remember the case of *Drennan v. Star Paving Co.*, which you read in Chapter 11. We studied this case in the context of the revocability of offers. The case also provided a nice example of a unilateral mistake, and of a court's reluctance to grant relief for that mistake. The facts in the case involved a subcontractor who submitted a bid of $7,131.60 to do some paving work and subsequently attempted to withdraw the bid as being too low. Justice Traynor, writing for the California Supreme Court, ultimately held that Drennan's reliance on the bid made it irrevocable. Star Paving argued in part that its bid was the result of mistake, and it was therefore entitled to revoke it. The court denied relief on this basis, stating:

> Defendant contends, however, that its bid was the result of mistake and that it was therefore entitled to revoke it. It relies on the rescission cases of *M. F. Kemper Const. Co. v. City of Los Angeles*, 37 Cal. 2d 696, 235 P.2d 7, and *Brunzell Const. Co. v. G.J. Weisbrod, Inc.*, 134 Cal. App. 2d 278, 285 P.2d 989. In those cases, however, the bidder's mistake was known or should have been known to the offeree, and the offeree could be placed in status quo. Of course, if plaintiff had reason to believe that defendant's bid was in error, he could not justifiably rely on it, and section 90 would afford no basis for enforcing it. Plaintiff, however, had no reason to know that defendant had made a mistake in submitting its bid, since there was usually a variance of 160 per cent between the highest and lowest bids for paving in the desert around Lancaster. He committed himself to performing the main contract in reliance on defendant's figures. Under these circumstances defendant's mistake, far

from relieving it of its obligation, constitutes an additional reason for enforcing it, for it misled plaintiff as to the cost of doing the paving. Even had it been clearly understood that defendant's offer was revocable until accepted, it would not necessarily follow that defendant had no duty to exercise reasonable care in preparing its bid. It presented its bid with knowledge of the substantial possibility that it would be used by plaintiff; it could foresee the harm that would ensue from an erroneous underestimate of the cost. Moreover, it was motivated by its own business interest. Whether or not these considerations alone would justify recovery for negligence had the case been tried on that theory, they are persuasive that defendant's mistake should not defeat recovery under the rule of section 90 of the Restatement of Contracts. As between the subcontractor who made the bid and the general contractor who reasonably relied on it, the loss resulting from the mistake should fall on the party who caused it.

In *Drennan*, the calculation of the bid was in the hands of Star Paving, so it is fair to say that Star Paving was the only party who was mistaken. Drennan didn't make any assumptions about the facts underlying the bid; it simply accepted Star Paving's figure and used it in computing its own bid. In the face of Drennan's reasonable reliance on Star Paving's mistake, the court concluded that the loss should fall on the mistaken party. Where only one party is mistaken, it will take a strong showing of unconscionability or unfairness to relieve that party of the consequences of its own mistaken actions.

In light of this discussion, under what specific circumstances might Star Paving have been able to avoid its bid on the grounds of unilateral mistake?

3. Mistake in Expression and Reformation

In the cases we have read, we have already seen some hints as to the scope of relief available for mistake. Some courts are rather strict: The only relief for mistake is rescission, and rescission is available only when the contract is purely executory—or, at a minimum, when the parties can be restored to the status quo. Rescission is essentially the same thing as avoiding the contract. It means that the transaction is unwound: The parties gain relief from their contractual obligations, but they disgorge the benefits received to date from the contract as well. The Restatement, Second, and a few recent cases take a broader view toward relief and contemplate a wider array of remedies. The Restatement, Second, suggests that courts grant relief as justice may require, including in a proper case protecting the parties' reliance interests or even adjusting or reforming the terms of the contract. As the doctrine of mistake is rooted in equity, it is not surprising to see a certain level of flexibility in a court's ability to fashion a remedy. Nevertheless, courts have been rather slow to pick up the invitation to craft remedies as justice may require in cases of mistake.

With this background, a short note concerning reformation of written contracts is in order. You may recall that as an alternative to their request for rescission, the plaintiffs in the *SCI Minnesota Funeral Services* case in Section A.1 sought the remedy of reformation. In effect, the plaintiffs were arguing that the written agreement didn't reflect the "true" agreement of the parties. As the court concluded there was no actionable mutual mistake, it declined to reform the contract. In contrast, there are instances where the writing itself is clearly in error. Consider, for instance, the following example.[6] Shipping Co. is entering into a complex transaction with Careful Insurance Co. Under the terms of the deal, Shipping Co. is to pay Careful Insurance Co. $92,885,000. The lawyers are putting the finishing touches on the documents necessary to evidence the deal. A member of the word processing staff omits three zeros from the amount Shipping Co. is to pay—listing it as $92,885—and the typographical error is subsequently copied into dozens and dozens of contract documents. Teams of lawyers review the drafts, but no one catches the error. In fact, the error does not come to light until the documents are signed and the deal is closed. This type of error is often called a "mistake in expression." The final documents, signed by both parties, do not express what the parties actually intended. If both parties admit that an error was made and are amenable, the document can typically be amended by mutual agreement. But there may be some disagreement, honest or otherwise, about whether an error was made.

A party seeking to establish an error in expression over the objection of the other party to the contract should be able to obtain relief if she can persuade the court that an error in expression was in fact made. However, it is not always easy to distinguish a pure mistake in expression (as illustrated by the preceding example) from an erroneous term in a contract caused by an underlying mistake as to a fact external to the writing. If a true error in expression can be established, often the relief requested is not avoidance of the contract but instead reformation to reflect the terms to which the parties actually agreed. This is one

---

[6] Lest you think this example is purely whimsical, you should know that it is based on the facts of an actual transaction between United States Lines (USL) and Prudential Insurance Co. USL negotiated to restructure $92,885,000 in debt it owed to Prudential Insurance Co. As part of the restructure, Prudential received a mortgage on one of USL's ships. In the mortgage document, the outstanding balance of USL's debt was listed as $92,885.00 rather than the correct amount of $92,885,000.00. This typographical error carried over into several other documents. The mistake was not uncovered until USL subsequently filed bankruptcy. Although no one disputed that the parties actually intended the amount of the debt to be $92,885,000.00, the intervening bankruptcy complicated matters. Prudential had to defend against (and ultimately settle) challenges to the enforceability of its mortgage in bankruptcy. Prudential reportedly lost approximately $31 million litigating and settling its claim in USL's bankruptcy. *See* Andrew Kull, *Zero-Based Morality: The Case of the $31-Million Typo*, Business Law Today, July/August 1992, at p. 11. To recover some of its losses, Prudential ultimately sued several prominent law firms for malpractice. *See Prudential Insurance Co. of America v. Dewey, Ballantine, Bushby, Palmer & Wood*, 80 N.Y.2d 377, 605 N.E.2d 318, 590 N.Y.S.2d 831 (1992).

context in which courts routinely allow reformation rather than insisting on rescission.

Reformation is not limited to cases where there has been a mistake in expression. Sometimes, courts will reform a contract to adjust the parties' obligations under circumstances where there has been a mistake in fact. In these circumstances, courts are crafting obligations for the parties that their agreement did not contemplate. You may recall analogous issues from our study of unconscionability doctrine in Chapter 13: When a court finds a contract or one of its clauses to be unconscionable, the court may decline to enforce the contract, may sever the unconscionable clause, or may limit the application of an unconscionable clause to avoid any unconscionable result. This approach gives the court a great deal of flexibility but may do violence to the reasonable expectations of the parties. Under mistake doctrine, the hazards of upsetting the parties' reasonable expectations are arguably even more acute, because the doctrine does not require identifiable wrongdoing by either of the parties. As a result, courts tend to be cautious about resorting to the remedy of reformation to adjust for a mistake of fact unless the circumstances are particularly clear.

B EXCUSE DUE TO CHANGED CIRCUMSTANCES

A common theme connects mistake and the doctrines to which we now turn. In each, one of the parties claims that the contract should not be enforced according to its terms. The actual performance of the contract is significantly different from what the party originally expected. As we see in the previous section, the doctrine of mistake applies to errors of fact made at the time of contracting. By contrast, the doctrines of impracticability and frustration of purpose look to events subsequent to contract formation. Developments have so changed the environment in which performance is to take place and are so contrary to the assumptions made at the time of contracting that the very premises of the contract have been overturned. Where a party asserts that its contract performance has become impracticable or where it argues that its purpose in performing the contract has been frustrated, it is saying that a profound change of circumstances has defeated its legitimate expectations under the contract. As a result, it seeks excuse from performing as originally promised. It asks the court to avoid the contract altogether or to adjust the performances required under the contract to take account of the changed circumstances.

As with the doctrine of mistake, the crucial issues to be evaluated in deciding whether a contractual performance has become impracticable or its purpose frustrated are materiality and risk allocation. Relief is only available if the supervening change in circumstances imposes a severe and unwarranted burden on the party seeking relief and it is not appropriate to place the risk of the change on that party. The process of determining risk allocation also resembles that used in an analysis under mistake doctrine. The court must interpret the

determine how it allocates risk if none, court decides where to place it

contract to determine if it expressly or impliedly allocates the risk. If it does not, the court must decide where to place the risk under all of the circumstances of the case.

The doctrine of impracticability is more central in contemporary law than that of frustration of purpose. In fact, one could argue that the modern concept of impracticability has become broad enough to encompass most circumstances of frustration of purpose as well. Many frustration cases can be analyzed under the doctrine of impracticability, with indistinguishable results. The common law still recognizes the doctrine of frustration of purpose, and cases still draw the distinction between impracticability and frustration, so it is important to consider both. We begin with impracticability.

1. Impracticability

In its earlier form, the common law did not recognize changed circumstances as a basis for excusing the performance of a contract. A party was committed to its promise even if subsequent events made performance of that promise pointless, burdensome, or even impossible. A classic case in this regard is *Paradine v. Jane*, 82 Eng. Rep. 897 (King's Bench 1647). Prince Rupert, a German prince, occupied territory and ejected a tenant from his land. The tenant sought relief from his obligation to pay rent. The court questioned why relief should be available, even under an argument of impossibility; after all, there was nothing to prevent the tenant from paying rent. If he wanted to protect himself from the contingency of military occupation, he should have done so in his contract. Dicta in the case revealed the full extent of the court's hostility toward claims of excuse:

> When the party by his own contract creates a duty or charge upon himself, he is bound to make it good, if he may, notwithstanding any accident by inevitable necessity, because he might have provided against it by his contract. And therefore if the lessee covenant to repair a house, though it be burnt by lightning, or thrown down by enemies, yet he ought to repair it.

The case credited with changing this approach is a mid-nineteenth-century English case, *Taylor v. Caldwell*, 122 Eng. Rep. 309 (King's Bench 1863). A music hall hired under a contract burned down before the time for performance. The express terms of the contract made no provision excusing the owner from his obligation to furnish the hall under these circumstances. However, the court held that it was an implied term of the contract that the hall would still be in existence at the time performance was due. Its destruction, not caused by the fault of the owner, made the contract objectively impossible to perform and defeated this basic assumption of the contract. (Note, however, that presumably it still would have been possible for the owner to pay damages to the other party, the relief the other party sought in the lawsuit.) Since the owner's performance was objectively impossible, he was excused from his obligation to provide the hall and, significantly, to pay damages for his failure to do so. In this early form, the doctrine—known as "impossibility of performance"—required not merely that the supervening event caused the performance to become unfairly burdensome or difficult, but that it made performance objectively impossible. A reasonable person in the position of the party claiming excuse would have to be incapable of performing it.

In the years since *Taylor*, the doctrine has broadened. It is no longer necessary that the performance become objectively impossible. It is enough that the change in circumstances so drastically increase the burden on the party claiming relief that performance can fairly be regarded as impracticable. To reflect this expansion of the doctrine, it is common to refer to it as "impracticability" or "commercial impracticability" but some courts still use the more restrictive label of "impossibility."

The Restatement, Second, captures the general outlines of the doctrine as follows:

commercial impracticability

RESTATEMENT, SECOND §261. DISCHARGE BY SUPERVENING IMPRACTICABILITY

Where, after a contract is made, a party's performance is made impracticable without his fault by the occurrence of an event the non-occurrence of which was a basic assumption on which the contract was made, his duty to render that performance is discharged, unless the language or the circumstances indicate the contrary.

CNA INTERNATIONAL REINSURANCE CO. v. PHOENIX

678 So. 2d 378 (1996)
Florida District Court of Appeal

JOANOS, Judge.

In these consolidated appeals from final orders granting appellee's motions to dismiss, appellants raise two issues: (1) whether the defense of impossibility of performance due to death applies when the impossibility is, allegedly, the fault of the person obligated to perform the personal services contract, and (2) whether the trial court erred in ruling that the effective dates of the policies of insurance involved here were in November, 1993, after the widely publicized death in question. [Discussion of the second issue is omitted.] We affirm in part and reverse in part.

The case arises from the unfortunate death of the young actor, River Phoenix, originally of Gainesville, Florida, apparently due to an overdose of illegal drugs, before completion of two films, "Dark Blood" and "Interview With the Vampire," in which he had contracted to appear. As a result of the death, the "Dark Blood" project was totally abandoned. "Interview With the Vampire" was completed with another actor replacing Phoenix. CNA and American Casualty, which are both members of the CNA group of insurance companies, had written entertainment package insurance policies covering various aspects of the two productions. After paying the policy holders, CNA and American Casualty became subrogated to the claims the insureds had against the estate.[7]

CNA attempted to state a cause of action for breach of contract against Phoenix's estate, based on an "actor loanout agreement," between Jude Nile, a corporation owned and run by Phoenix and his mother, Arlyn Phoenix, and Scala Productions[, the production company for "Dark Blood."] The agreement, signed by Phoenix, allegedly included a general obligation not to do anything which would deprive the parties to the agreement of its benefits. CNA further alleged that by deliberately taking illegal drugs in quantities in excess of those necessary to kill a human being, Phoenix deprived the parties of his services and breached his obligation. American Casualty also couched its complaint for declaratory judgment in terms of breach of contract based on an actor loanout agreement between Jude Nile and Geffen Pictures, which gave Geffen the right to loan Phoenix to Time Warner. . . .

The estate moved to dismiss both complaints, contending there could be no cause of action for breach of contract because the personal services contracts were rendered impossible to perform due to the death. . . . After hearings, the trial court granted the motions to dismiss with prejudice.

On appeal, CNA and American Casualty contend that the defense of impossibility of performance does not apply in this case because that doctrine requires that the impossibility be fortuitous and unavoidable, and that it occur through no fault of either party. They contend that because the death occurred from an intentional, massive overdose of illegal drugs, that this is not a situation in which neither party was at fault. The trial court very clearly ruled that even if the death was a suicide (there is no indication in the record that it was) or the result of an intentional, self-inflicted act, the doctrine of impossibility of performance applied.

Appellants have candidly conceded that no case authorities exist in support of their position concerning fault in a case of impossibility due to death. Appellants ask this court to find support for their theory in the following language of the Restatement of Contracts 2d §§261 and 262:

> §261 Where, after a contract is made, a party's performance is made impracticable without his fault by the occurrence of an event the non-occurrence of which was a basic assumption on which the contract was made, his duty to render that

---

[7] CNA paid out over $5.7 million under its policy. American Casualty had not yet paid all claims, and sought a declaratory judgment on the coverage issue. It had paid out $15,000 of approximately $400,000 in claims.

performance is discharged, unless the language or the circumstances indicate the contrary.

§262 If the existence of a particular person is necessary for the performance of a duty, his death or such incapacity as makes performance impracticable is an event the nonoccurrence of which was a basic assumption on which the contract was made.

Appellants contend the Restatement dictates that impossibility of performance due to the destruction of one's own health is not the sort of conduct that will excuse performance, citing *Handicapped Children's Education Board v. Lukaszewski*, 112 Wis. 2d 197, 332 N.W.2d 774 (Wis. 1983), and that the same reasoning should apply in a case of self-induced death. Appellants also suggest a policy basis for the ruling they advocate, arguing that in a society dealing with increasing problems created by illegal drug abuse, such conduct should not excuse the performance of the contract.

At oral argument of this case, it became apparent that any attempt to discern fault in a death case such as this one, or in a similar case, perhaps involving the use of tobacco or alcohol would create another case by case and hard to interpret rule of law. Being mindful that there are already too many of these in existence, we are not persuaded by the facts or the arguments presented to depart from the clear and unambiguous rule that death renders a personal services contract impossible to perform. See 17A Am. Jur. 2d "Contracts" §688 (1991). In such contracts, "there is an implied condition that death shall dissolve the contract." *Id.* With this implied condition in mind, we believe the parties to the agreements could have provided specifically for the contingency of loss due to the use of illegal drugs, as they provided for other hazardous or life threatening contingencies.[8] We affirm the trial court's ruling that the doctrine of impossibility of performance applies in this case. . . .

■ QUESTIONS

(1) The court quotes Restatement, Second §§261 and 262. In its reasoning, does the court adopt or reject these sections as providing an appropriate rule of law? In particular, what elements of the sections are at issue in this case, and how does the court resolve each issue?

---

[8] For example, the actor loanout agreement pertaining to "Interview With the Vampire" provided:

> From the date two (2) weeks before the scheduled start date of principal photography until the completion of all services required of Employee hereunder, Employee will not ride in any aircraft other than as a passenger on a scheduled flight of a United States or other major international air carrier maintaining regularly published schedules, or engage in any ultrahazardous activity without Producer's written consent in each case.

The entertainment package policies contained exclusions based on similar activities.

(2) The court does not discuss risk allocation in so many words, yet it must have decided that the policyholders bore the risk of the actor's untimely death. In your view, was it appropriate to place the risk there? Why or why not?

(3) What role, if any, did the provision in the actor loanout agreement quoted in footnote 8 play in this case? Why isn't the use of illegal drugs in the quantities alleged an "ultrahazardous activity," or is the answer to that question irrelevant to the holding in the case?

(4) CNA and American Casualty did not contract directly with River Phoenix or his company, Jude Nile. Instead, they are able to bring this cause of action because they are subrogated to the rights of their policyholders. So there are two classes of contracts potentially relevant to this dispute: the insurance contracts among the insurers and their policyholders, and the underlying contracts between the movie production companies and River Phoenix or his company. If the insurance companies wanted to avoid results such as the result in this case, what specific language could they insert in their insurance policies to accomplish that goal? If you represented the insurance companies, would you recommend that they consider such language? Why or why not?

———

Among other things, the *CNA International Reinsurance Co.* case quotes Restatement, Second §261. Modern common law cases where impossibility or impracticability are at issue often cite this section, and frequently adopt its elements to structure their analyses. The equivalent rule applicable to a sale of goods is UCC 2-615(a). Although there are differences in the wording of these two provisions, their concept and elements are substantially the same.

UCC 2-615. EXCUSE BY FAILURE OF PRESUPPOSED CONDITIONS

Except so far as a seller may have assumed a greater obligation . . .

(a) Delay in delivery or non-delivery in whole or in part by a seller . . . is not a breach of his duty under a contract for sale if performance as agreed has been made impracticable by the occurrence of a contingency the non-occurrence of which was a basic assumption on which the contract was made or by compliance in good faith with any applicable foreign or domestic governmental regulation or order whether or not it later proves to be invalid. . . .

———

Consider the following case involving a transaction in goods.

CLARK v. WALLACE COUNTY COOPERATIVE EQUITY EXCHANGE

26 Kan. App. 2d 463, 986 P.2d 391 (1999)
Kansas Court of Appeals

LEWIS, Presiding Judge.

Ray C. Clark is a farmer. The Wallace County Cooperative Equity Exchange (Coop) operates, among other things, a grain elevator through which it buys and sells grain. In January 1995, Clark and Coop entered into a written agreement in which Clark agreed to sell Coop 4,000 bushels of corn to be delivered after the crop was harvested. At the time the contract was made, there may have been corn planted somewhere in Kansas, but it would have been far short of maturity. In September 1995, there was a freeze in the area, which severely damaged the corn crop. As a result of this freeze, Clark raised only 2,207.41 bushels of corn, which he delivered to Coop. Clark then maintained he was excused from delivering the remaining 1,392.59 bushels (after an allowed 10% reduction) because of the freeze. Coop insisted he was not excused and held the cost of the shortage out of the grain sale by Clark to Coop. This action was brought by Clark to recover the $1,622.97 that Coop withheld from his grain sale.

First, we note that these are rather common agreements used in the grain business. Anyone involved in this sort of an agreement realizes that one of the big risks is that the farmer may not be able to grow sufficient grain to deliver the required number of bushels. Clark seeks to be excused from his obligation to deliver because his crop was damaged by the weather. We suspect that if we adopted his reasoning, we would put an end to trading grain in this manner throughout the entire state of Kansas. It would have the effect of taking all the risk away from the farmer and placing the entire risk of loss on the grain elevators and, in fact, creating a potential situation where grain elevators could be bankrupted in the event of a large area crop loss. . . .

[The court quotes Kansas's version of UCC 2-615, K.S.A. 84-2-615.] The first element which must be established to apply the statute . . . is that performance must be impracticable. We addressed the issue of impracticability in *Sunflower Electric Coop., Inc. v. Tomlinson Oil Co.*, 7 Kan. App. 2d 131, 638 P.2d 963 (1981), *rev. denied*, 231 Kan. 802 (1982). In that case, we indicated there was a difference between subjective and objective impracticability. This difference can be illustrated by an individual who says "I cannot do it" versus a statement to the effect that "the thing cannot be done." Only objective impracticability may relieve a party of his or her contractual obligation. In this case, there was no objective impracticability since the corn was not identified to be from specific land. The thing Clark had to do in this case was deliver 4,000 bushels of corn to the elevator. He could have done this. This is shown by the fact that

Coop was able to cover the shortage on the instant contract by acquiring corn from another source. The fact is, Clark did not want to deliver the grain, but he had the ability to do so by purchasing grain to replace the grain he did not raise.

The Kansas comments to K.S.A. 84-2-615 state: "A seller ... will not be excused under this section if (1) the non-occurrence of the contingency was the seller's fault; (2) the seller had reason to know of the impracticability (i.e., the contingency was foreseeable); or (3) the seller assumed the risk of the contingency." We do not deem it difficult to conclude that farmers in Kansas can foresee late September freezes which will reduce their corn yields. It has happened a number of times. If we were to excuse Clark from his obligation to deliver on the agreement, we would allow a farmer to enter into a forward grain contract on unspecified land, gamble on the extent of his supply, being aware of the fact that he may not raise sufficient grain, and then escape with impunity when his grain crop proves inadequate.

In addition, official UCC comments (5) and (9) to K.S.A, 84-2-615 refer to the concept of identifying the source of supply of the crop to be sold. As we pointed out above, the contract before this court did not identify a particular source of supply or a particular area where the corn was to be grown.

We hold that Clark's performance on the grain sales agreement in question was not excused by the provisions of K.S.A. 84-2-615. Affirmed.

■ QUESTIONS

(1) In *Clark*, the court said that it did not "deem it difficult to conclude" that a farmer can foresee that a late freeze will reduce crop yields. Why is this so easy to foresee and what is the impact of this foresight? Is it easier for a farmer to foresee this possibility than it is for a movie production company to foresee that an actor might die of a drug overdose? Can you explain the differing results in *Clark* and *CNA International*?

(2) Explain in your own words what the *Clark* court means when it distinguishes subjective and objective impracticability. Was it subjectively or objectively impracticable for River Phoenix to refrain from using drugs? Alternatively, was it subjectively or objectively impracticable for the estate of River Phoenix to pay damages for his failure to perform the terms of his contract? Would it have been subjectively or objectively impracticable for Clark to deliver 4,000 bushels of corn to the elevator, had the contract stated that the grain was to come from his own field?

(3) Does the distinction between subjective and objective impracticability manifest itself in the elements of Restatement, Second §261 or UCC 2-615(a)? If so, how?

ALL POINTS CAPITAL CORP. v. BOYD BROTHERS, INC.

Slip Copy, 2011 WL 2790170 (2011)
United States District Court, Northern District of Florida

SMOAK, District Judge.

Before me are Plaintiff's Motion for Summary Judgment and Incorporated Memorandum of Law and Defendants' Response in Opposition and Request for Continuance.

Beginning on July 7, 2006, Defendants entered into a series of installment promissory notes with RCA Capital Corp, the predecessor in interest to Plaintiff. On October 1, 2007, Defendants executed a cross-collateral and cross-default agreement on the promissory notes. Defendants have purportedly defaulted on these agreements.[9]

Defendants seek continuance pursuant to Fed. R. Civ. P. 56(f) so that they may conduct further investigation to support their defenses. However, for the majority of their defenses, any further discovery would be unnecessary because those defenses fail as a matter of law. . . . [The defendants raise a number of affirmative defenses; we omit the court's discussion of unrelated defenses.]

Defendants claim in their . . . affirmative defense that the defense of commercial impracticability due to the BP oil spill excuses their nonperformance.[10] They assert that a significant portion of their customers are located on the Gulf coast and were devastated by the oil spill. As a result, Defendants' printing business was severely impacted.

The doctrine of commercial impracticability provides that "where, after a contract is made, a party's performance is made impracticable without his fault by the occurrence of an event the non-occurrence of which was a basic assumption on which the contract was made, his duty to render that performance is discharged, unless the language or the circumstances indicate the contrary." *Seitz v. Mark-O-Lite Sign Contractors*, 210 N.J. Super. 646, 65, 510 A.2d 319, 322 (Law Div. 1986) [citing Restatement, Second §261]. "The continuation of existing market conditions and of the financial situation of the parties are ordinarily not such [basic] assumptions, so that mere market shifts or financial inability do not usually effect discharge under the rule." [Restatement, Second §261, cmt. b.]

Here, [defendants'] business may have been affected by the oil spill. However, the oil spill was but one of numerous factors that made up the general market conditions along the Gulf coast which the parties did not contemplate during their agreement. In all likelihood, the parties also did not consider a host of other factors which, subsequent to their agreement, would affect their

---

[9] The promissory notes at issue are governed by the laws of New Jersey.

[10] The court is referring to the catastrophic spill that occurred in 2010 after the explosion and sinking of the *Deepwater Horizon* oil rig. BP had operated the *Deepwater Horizon* in the Gulf of Mexico.—Eds.

business: the impending decline in the real estate market; the collapse of Wall Street firms and the subsequent tightening of credit; the rising cost of petroleum; a surge in commodity prices; multiple rounds of quantitative easing. Performance cannot be simply discharged for all unforeseen conditions that affect one's business. Otherwise, every fisherman, hotel worker, and palm-reader along Bourbon Street could forgo their mortgage payment, cancel their cell phone contract, and defer their credit card bills in the wake of the oil spill. This is obviously not a correct interpretation of the law. Rather, there must be a more direct connection to warrant the defense of commercial impracticability. Two examples in the Restatement are instructive.

> Several months after the nationalization of the Suez Canal, during the international crisis resulting from its seizure, A contracts to carry a cargo of B's wheat on A's ship from Galveston, Texas to Bandar Shapur, Iran for a flat rate. The contract does not specify the route, but the voyage would normally be through the Straits of Gibraltar and the Suez Canal, a distance of 10,000 miles. A month later, and several days after the ship has left Galveston, the Suez Canal is closed by an outbreak of hostilities, so that the only route to Bandar Shapur is the longer 13,000 mile voyage around the Cape of Good Hope. A refuses to complete the voyage unless B pays additional compensation. A's duty to carry B's cargo is not discharged, and A is liable to B for breach of contract.
>
> The Suez Canal is closed while A's ship is in the Canal, preventing the completion of the voyage. A's duty to carry B's cargo is discharged, and A is not liable to B for breach of contract.

[Restatement, Second §261, illustrations 9 & 10.]

Here, the oil spill did not prevent Defendants from doing their printing business. Rather, it made their printing business more difficult and less profitable. Under these circumstances, they are not excused from performance. . . . [The] affirmative defense is dismissed because the doctrine of commercial impracticability does not excuse performance.

■ PROBLEM 17.7

Connie Doe was an investment banker who worked on Wall Street. In early 2008, she signed a purchase contract in which she agreed to pay $2,500,000 for a luxury condominium in a new high-rise building then under construction. She provided a down payment of $500,000 at signing, and agreed to pay the balance once the building was complete and the living units were ready for occupancy. She planned to use a combination of savings, her salary and bonuses, and a modest bank loan to complete the purchase. Shortly after she entered into the contract, the country experienced a financial crisis now considered by many economists to be one of the worst since the Great Depression of the 1930s. Due to its losses, Connie's employer filed bankruptcy and she lost her job. Further, most lenders severely curtailed their mortgage lending activity, and residential loan applications were routinely denied. Although Connie still had substantial savings, she thought she might need to rely on them to pay her basic living expenses. She felt certain that it might take some time to find a new job, and was quite sure she wouldn't be able to obtain a bank loan of any kind until she did.

In light of these events, once the high rise was complete, Connie refused to complete the purchase of the luxury condominium as agreed, and sought the return of her down payment. She argued that her performance had been rendered impracticable, and sought relief on that basis. Do you think Connie should obtain relief? If so, what would the nature of that relief be?

■ PROBLEM 17.8

In a law review article,[11] Professor Silber argues that in the aftermath of hurricanes, oil spills, and other disasters, consumers suffer particular hardship. Disasters, he argues, lead to job losses, property loss, and dislocation, and consumers are often unable to pay their financial obligations as a result. While businesses can and do protect themselves from the risks of disasters through insurance and contractual allocations of risk, consumers are less likely to do so. So consumers may remain obligated to pay car loans when cars are submerged in water and may remain liable on mortgages or leases even though their homes are uninhabitable. Further, during any period when payment of debts is delayed, consumers may rack up significant interest charges and late fees. Because Professor Silber concludes impracticability doctrine is unlikely to excuse consumers from paying or delaying their financial obligations in the aftermath of a disaster, he recommends that federal law mandate that all consumer credit contracts include a clause that excuses consumers under an enumerated list of catastrophic conditions. Do you think Professor Silber's suggestion would be good policy? Why or why not?

---

[11] Norman I. Silber, *Debts, Disasters, and Delinquencies: A Case for Placing a Mandatory Force Majeure Provision into Consumer Credit Agreements*, 34 N.Y.U. Rev. L. & Soc. Change 760 (2010).

■ PROBLEM 17.9

You represent Timely Builders. Timely has been negotiating a contract with Mammoth Manufacturing, Inc., under which Timely would renovate Mammoth's plant to add some much-needed manufacturing facilities. This is a big contract for Timely; it doesn't want to be held responsible to perform if "something unexpected comes up." Timely has asked you to draft a clause in the construction contract, relieving it of responsibility for events beyond its control. (This kind of clause is sometimes called a "force majeure" clause.) Without consulting outside sources, attempt to draft such a clause, and then answer the following questions.

(a) If the clause, as you have drafted it, is included in the contract, would it pose any risks to Timely? If so, why?

(b) Do you anticipate that the clause, as you have drafted it, would be acceptable to Mammoth? If not, what revisions might it request? Should those revisions be acceptable to your client in your view?

2. Frustration of Purpose

Like impossibility, the defense of frustration of purpose was not available at early common law. The case that formulated the doctrine of frustration of purpose in English law was *Krell v. Henry*, 2 K.B. 740 (1903). Krell owned a flat on Pall Mall, London, which overlooked the route to be taken by the coronation procession of King Edward VII, to take place on June 26 and 27, 1902. About ten days before the coronation, Henry noticed a sign in the window of the flat offering it for use to view the procession. He responded to the notice and on June 20 he entered into a contract with Krell for the use of the flat on the days in question, and paid a deposit. After the contract was made, the coronation was postponed because the king became ill. The court had to decide whether Henry was liable for the remainder of the price of the rooms even though the purpose for which they were hired had fallen away. It could not simply apply the precedent of *Taylor v. Caldwell* because the contract had not become impossible to perform. The rooms had not been destroyed, and Henry could still have taken occupancy on June 26 and 27. The court therefore had to extend the doctrine established by *Taylor* beyond the limits set in that case. It held that performance would also be excused where a change in circumstances following the contract defeated the mutually understood purpose of the contract. The assumption must be fundamental to the contract, and must be shared. It could not be merely the private purpose of one of the parties.

[handwritten margin note: must be mutual purpose]

Restatement, Second §265 reflects the doctrine of frustration of purpose. As you can see, its wording bears a striking resemblance to that of Restatement, Second §261. It states:

RESTATEMENT, SECOND §265. DISCHARGE BY SUPERVENING FRUSTRATION

Where, after a contract is made, a party's principal purpose is substantially frustrated without his fault by the occurrence of an event the non-occurrence of which was a basic assumption on which the contract was made, his remaining duties to render performance are discharged, unless the language or the circumstances indicate the contrary.

The UCC doesn't contain an analogous provision for frustration of purpose. In the rare case where the buyer of goods, rather than the seller, seeks excuse for supervening circumstances, UCC 2-615(a) will not by its terms apply, as it addresses only sellers. Possibly the common law doctrine of impracticability or frustration of purpose could provide some solace to the buyer, provided a court allowed it to supplement the terms of the UCC by virtue of UCC 1-103(b).

[handwritten margin note: x UCC doesn't have this / only applies to sellers]

The next case gives you the opportunity to consider whether, as suggested earlier, impracticability and frustration of purpose really do amount to the same thing in modern law or if they continue to operate in separate spheres. The case also encourages you, once again, to think about how courts should allocate the risk of a supervening occurrence. What would it have taken for this court to allow excuse on the basis of impracticability? Or, alternatively, what would have amounted to frustration of purpose?

LINDNER v. MEADOW GOLD DAIRIES INC.

515 F. Supp. 2d 1154 (2007)
United States District Court, District of Hawaii

SEABRIGHT, District Judge.

Plaintiff Jeffrey Lindner ("Lindner") and Third-Party Defendant Southern Food Group, L.P. ("SFG") have moved for partial summary judgment as to Lindner's claim for liquidated damages. . . . Lindner argues that the plain language of the Lease entitles him to a lump sum liquidated damages cash payment. The court agrees and rejects SFG's arguments that performance under the Lease was frustrated. . . .

Lindner is the fee simple owner of real property leased to Meadow Gold Dairies, Inc. ("Meadow Gold") under a 1988 Lease ("Lease"). On May 28, 1997 [sic—this should be 1998], Meadow Gold exercised its renewal options, extending the Lease until September 30, 2013. A few months later, Meadow Gold assigned its interests and obligations under the Lease to SFG.[12]

Meadow Gold leased the land, located on the island of Kauai, to operate a dairy farm ("Moloa'a Dairy Farm"). The downstream parcel was originally occupied by the Papa'a Bay Ranch, a working ranch. On January 15, 1998, a little over four months before Meadow Gold exercised its right to a fifteen-year renewal of the Lease, the downstream parcel was sold to Mandalay Properties Hawai'i, Inc. ("Mandalay") and developed into the "Tara Plantation," a 15,000 square foot, 6 bedroom, 8.5 bath, two-living room home with two separate 4,000 square foot guest bungalows, a spring-fed swimming pool, and an on-site yoga studio.[13] The Tara Plantation was originally developed as one of the personal homes of Peter Guber ("Guber"), principal of Mandalay and current chairman and owner of film production company Mandalay Entertainment.

The relationship between neighbors Guber and Meadow Gold quickly soured. In an April 1999 meeting with representatives of SFG, Guber stated that he planned to spend millions of dollars developing Tara Plantation and that the Moloa'a Dairy Farm (then still in operation upstream) "was a good farm, but in a bad location." Michael Koenig ("Koenig"), the Vice President of Operations of SFG, understood these statements to mean that the dairy farming operations were too close to Guber's property. During the meeting, Guber allegedly emphasized his contacts with environmental organizations and national media outlets.

. . . [Guber and Mandalay grew increasingly vehement in their complaints about Meadow Gold's operations. They complained of raw sewage from the operations and contamination of downstream land and water. They filed a complaint regarding manure on the Moloa'a Dairy Farm with the Hawaii Department of Health. They provided notice that Mandalay intended to file a "citizen's lawsuit" against Meadow Gold under the Clean Water Act, and asserted that they would seek the maximum civil penalty of $25,000 per day per violation of that Act.] Following receipt of Mandalay's intent to sue letter, SFG contacted the Hawaii Department of Health (which administers the Clean Water Act in Hawaii) to inquire whether Meadow Gold was required to [take the measures suggested by Mandalay.] . . . The Hawaii Department of Health was not able to give SFG a firm opinion on the matter.

Shortly thereafter, Meadow Gold announced the closure of the Moloa'a Dairy Farm, explaining in a press release that "the decision to close the farm was driven by the realities of market and regulatory forces that have changed over the years." Meadow Gold terminated the Lease effective December 31, 2000,

---

[12] The court does not clarify the relationship between Meadow Gold and SFG, except to explain (later in the opinion) that Meadow Gold remains obligated on the lease after the assignment. As the court at times refers to Meadow Gold and SFG interchangeably, we suggest you assume that just as both remain obligated on the lease after the assignment; if one is excused, both are. —EDS.

[13] The Tara Plantation was recently listed for sale at 46.5 million dollars.

almost thirteen years early. In several letters to Lindner, SFG requested that Lindner waive the liquidated damages provision contained in the Lease. The liquidated damages provision provides [in relevant part]:

> Lessee may terminate this Lease prior to the expiration of the term upon giving written notice to Lessor of its intent to terminate six (6) months prior to the effective date of such termination, together with a lump sum cash payment representing the present value (capitalized at the then prevailing Bank of Hawaii prime rate charged to its most responsible commercial customers) of the minimum rent due for the remainder of the term of the Lease, but not more than the present value of five (5) years of rent. . . . The foregoing payment shall constitute liquidated damages and not a penalty since the damages to be suffered by Lessor would be difficult to determine if Lessee were to terminate the Lease. . . .

Meadow Gold remained responsible for the payment of liquidated damages notwithstanding its assignment of the Lease to SFG. See Lease Art. IV §9 ("In the event of an assignment . . . Lessee shall not be released from any liability or obligations under the Lease, Lessor reserving all of its rights and remedies against Lessee hereunder."). Neither Meadow Gold nor SFG paid Lindner a lump sum liquidated damages cash payment. . . .

"Absent an ambiguity, contract terms should be interpreted according to their plain, ordinary, and accepted sense in common speech." *Found. Int'l, Inc. v. E.T. Ige Const., Inc.*, 102 Hawai'i 487, 495, 78 P.3d 23, 31 (2003). To determine whether an ambiguity exists, the court "should look no further than the four corners of the document," and examine "whether or not particular words or phrases in themselves be uncertain or doubtful in meaning." *Id.* at 496-97, 78 P.3d at 32-33. "A contract term or phrase is ambiguous only if it is capable of being reasonably understood in more than one way." *Wittig v. Allianz, A.G.*, 112 Hawai'i 195, 201, 145 P.3d 738, 745 (2006).

The language of the liquidated damages provision of the Lease is clear and unambiguous. In the event of Lessee's early termination of the Lease . . . Article I §2 requires the Lessee to pay Lessor "a lump sum cash payment representing the present value . . . of the minimum rent due for the remainder of the term of the Lease, but not more than the present value of five (5) years of rent." Because the Lease was terminated a little under thirteen years early, Lindner is due a lump sum cash payment of the present value of five years of rent.

SFG does not contest the reasonableness or validity of the liquidated damages provision itself.[14] Instead, . . . SFG argues that the purpose of the Lease was frustrated and, as such, it should be excused from performance and not liable for liquidated damages for its early termination. Because the only permissible use of the land under the terms of the Lease was the operation of a dairy farm and related pasture use, SFG argues that the Lease was frustrated

---

[14] We discuss limitations on the enforceability of clauses that provide for liquidated damages in Chapter 21.—Eds.

when the downstream parcel was sold to Mandalay and Guber. As Glenn Muranaka, the General Manager of SFG explains,

> The claims alleged by Mandalay . . . , the legal uncertainty and potential litigation costs with respect to those claims, the costs and burdens of regulations, particularly environmental regulations as interpreted by Mandalay, placed on relatively small, locally based dairy operations and related pasture uses such as the Moloa'a Dairy, the realities of the market, and in the 1999-2000 time period the changing character of the area surrounding the Moloa'a Dairy's operation from traditional farming and pasture uses to high end subdivisions engineered to accommodate "gentlemen farmer estates," and Tara Plantation converged to substantially undermine and frustrate the principal purpose of the Lease which was operating a dairy farm and rendered the transaction senseless. . . . The basic assumptions upon which the parties entered into the Lease on October 1, 1988 did not contemplate the occurrences of the radical changes to the use of the lands that comprised Papa'a Bay Ranch, a claim by the owner of Tara Plantation that the pastures of Moloa'a Dairy . . . [were regulated under the Clean Water Act], and the other developments . . . that frustrated a continuing commercial dairy operation on the Premises.

SFG's Mot. for Partial Summ. J., Muranaka Decl. ¶¶6, 10.

Excuse by frustration of purpose of contract[15] requires the following: (1) the purpose that was frustrated was a principal purpose of the contracting party; (2) the frustration was substantial or severe; and (3) the event causing the frustration was not foreseeable to the parties when they entered the Lease. See Restatement (Second) of Contracts §265 cmt. a ("First, the purpose that is frustrated must have been a principal purpose of that party in making the contract. . . . Second, the frustration must be substantial. It is not enough that the transaction has become less profitable for the affected party or even that he will sustain a loss. The frustration must be so severe that it is not fairly to be regarded as within the risks that he assumed under the contract. Third, the non-occurrence of the frustrating event must have been a basic assumption on which the contract was made."). The court finds that SFG has failed to satisfy the second and third elements.

SFG alleges that Mandalay and Guber's litigiousness and the potentially applicable environmental laws and regulations imposed severe and substantial hardships, making the operation of the Moloa'a Dairy Farm commercially impracticable. As SFG wrote in a September 22, 2000 letter to Lindner,

---

[15] Although it sometimes refers to performance being "impractical," SFG claims excuse by frustration of purpose of contract, not excuse by impossibility or commercial impracticability. The two doctrines are similar and the same facts may give rise to both theories. Compare Restatement (Second) of Contracts §261 (discussing the doctrine of impossibility or impracticability . . .) with *id.* §265 (discussing frustration of purpose . . .).

Meadow Gold believes that the core fact is that this property cannot be practically used for a commercial dairy operation because of changes in the law arising from amendments to the Clean Water Act[16] and by the interpretation of those amendments and related rules and regulations by neighbors to the farm. As one neighbor stated, "it's a good farm, but in a bad location." Hence, the very purpose of the . . . lease has been frustrated and made impractical of performance.

A lease is the conveyance of a property interest. As the Lessee, Meadow Gold held an estate in land, and found itself facing increasing costs and hardships associated with its tenancy, including complying with environmental laws in the operation of its dairy farm operations. These, however, are the hallmarks of the risks of a business, not excuses for breach of contract. While compliance with the Clean Water Act and other environmental laws may have made Meadow Gold's performance more expensive or even unprofitable, it does not severely or substantially frustrate the purpose of the Lease. See *Corbin on Contracts* §77.4 ("To justify a discharge, the lessee must show that the frustration of purpose is severe. Inconvenience, unprofitability, and unexpected income reductions or cost increases will usually not suffice."). As SFG itself admits in its briefing, "[i]t is not enough that the transaction has become less profitable for the affected party or even that [Meadow Gold] will sustain a loss." SFG's Mot. for Partial Summ. J. 20 (quoting Restatement (Second) of Contracts §265 cmt. a). Instead, as SFG also admits, "[t]he frustration must be so severe that it is not fairly to be regarded as within the risks that he assumed under the contract." *Id.* A threatened lawsuit and the costs of bringing the Moloa'a Dairy farm into compliance with federal law are not sufficiently severe to excuse Meadow Gold's performance. Meadow Gold could have continued to operate the Moloa'a Dairy Farm on the leased premises so long as it complied with the Clean Water Act.[17] Nothing in the record shows that doing so would have imposed severe economic hardship upon Meadow Gold.[18] More importantly, compliance with the Clean Water Act is required wherever Meadow Gold locates its dairy farming operations and regardless of whether its downstream neighbor is litigious. Meadow Gold's decision to terminate the Lease—rather than incur the expenses of complying with federal law—may indeed have been fiscally prudent, but it does not provide a legal basis excusing Meadow Gold from its contractual obligations.

---

[16] SFG did not clarify what specific changes or amendments to the applicable laws made performance impractical.

[17] The present case is thus distinguished from cases where newly-passed zoning regulations outlaw commercial activity which is the sole subject of the contract.

[18] SFG has not provided evidence as to the costs likely to be incurred to bring the premises in compliance with the Clean Water Act. The court is thus unable to conclude, based on this record, that the expenses of compliance would be so excessive, extreme, or unreasonable as to result in sufficiently severe or substantial hardship or commercial impracticability. More to the point, Meadow Gold has failed to demonstrate that the compliance costs arose after its renewal of the Lease. Legal compliance expenses that existed prior to signing of a Lease—even if not undertaken—cannot excuse a subsequent failure to perform when lawsuits are threatened.

Nor was the event causing the alleged frustration unforeseeable to the parties at the time Meadow Gold entered into the contract and renewed it. First, the obligation to comply with environmental standards was a stated and known obligation. Indeed, the Lease explicitly required Meadow Gold to comply with all present and future laws, statutes, ordinances, rules, and regulations, including those concerning water pollution, hazardous wastes and environmental contamination . . . SFG argues that, at the time of renewing the lease, Meadow Gold could not have foreseen that the Papa'a Bay Ranch would be converted to a 46.5 million dollar home for a film production magnate. Such an argument misses the point entirely: Meadow Gold was required to comply with federal environmental standards irrespective of whether its downstream neighbors were likely to protest. It was the compliance cost (and perhaps a changing dairy market in Hawaii), not a new downstream neighbor, which ultimately forced Meadow Gold to abandon the Moloa'a Dairy Farm operations.

Even if the court were to accept SFG's argument that the acquisition of the land by Mandalay and Guber was in and of itself the causal event, the court would reject SFG's frustration argument on the grounds that Meadow Gold entered into the fifteen year renewal of the Lease four months after the downstream land parcel formerly occupied by Papa'a Bay Ranch was sold to Mandalay and Guber to be developed into the Tara Plantation.

Second, the Clean Water Act was adopted in 1948, with various amendments occurring thereafter. Meadow Gold and SFG were thus subject to—and presumptively aware of—the provisions of the Clean Water Act from the commencement of their tenure on the land. Indeed, Meadow Gold appeared to be aware of its obligations under the Clean Water Act as it commissioned a waste management plan . . . as early as 1989. SFG does not point to any amendments adopted after Meadow Gold's renewal of the Lease which were unforeseeable and which frustrated its performance. . . .

For the foregoing reasons, the court grants the Plaintiff's Motion for Partial Summary Judgment and denies the Third-Party Defendant's Motion for Partial Summary Judgment as to liquidated damages. . . .

■ QUESTIONS

(1) The court describes the defense raised by Meadow Gold and SFG as one of frustration, not commercial impracticability. On what basis does it make this distinction? Of what relevance, if any, is the restriction in the lease that the property be used only for the operation of a dairy farm and associated pasture?

(2) At least at the stage of this litigation, it had not been established conclusively that either Meadow Gold or SFG had, in fact, violated environmental laws. Would it matter if Meadow Gold and SFG had been advised that they had a good chance of defeating the claims of Guber and Mandalay but only if they were to pursue lengthy and expensive litigation?

(3)   SFG argues that the requirements of the Clean Water Act had become more stringent, thus rendering full compliance impracticable. The court was not satisfied with SFG's evidence on this point. Suppose Meadow Gold or SFG had proven that the Clean Water Act had been amended after the lease was renewed to impose new, costly obligations on dairy operations such as the Moloa'a Dairy Farm. Would the excuse of commercial impracticability be available under those circumstances? What about the excuse of frustration of purpose?

CHAPTER 18

Conditions and Promises

A   AN OVERVIEW OF THE COMPONENTS OF A CONTRACT: CONDITIONS AND PROMISES

A promise is a commitment to act or refrain from acting in a specific way in the future. The fundamental role of promises in contracts is thoroughly familiar by now. We have seen that a relationship does not qualify as a contract unless at least one party has made a promise to be performed in the future. More commonly, not one but both parties make promises, thereby creating a bilateral contract. Although the promise as a basic element of contract has been featured regularly in our discussions, there has been little reference so far to conditions. However, conditions are also important and very common components of contracts and have in fact been present in most, if not all, of the contracts that we have encountered up to now. In this chapter, we identify conditions and explain what they are, what role they play in a contract, and how they interrelate with promises to structure the relationship between the parties.

"Condition" is defined in Restatement, Second §224 as "an event, not certain to occur, which must occur ... before performance under a contract becomes due." That is, when making the contract, the parties agree that the obligation to render a particular performance (or set of performances) is contingent on the happening of a specified uncertain event. Although the definition of "condition" describes it as an event, the "event" need not be an affirmative happening; it could also be a non-happening. That is, a performance could be conditional either on the stated uncertain event occurring or on it not occurring.

The following example begins our discussion of breaking down a contract into promises and conditions. Amber Ayle plans to open a pub. Bud Brewster owns a small apartment building that has vacant retail space on the ground floor, which would be suitable for Amber's pub. On June 1, Amber enters into a written contract with Bud, under which Amber leases the retail premises from Bud for a period of five years, commencing on August 1, for the purpose of operating the pub. The lease includes the following terms:

1. Bud will deliver possession of the premises to Amber on September 1 and will allow Amber to occupy and conduct business on the premises for the term of this lease.
2. Amber will pay monthly rent of $15,000 for the premises, payable in advance on the fifteenth day of each month, commencing on August 15.
3. At the time of executing this lease, the parties have not ascertained the permissible retail uses of the premises under current zoning regulations. This lease will be of no force or effect if the current zoning of the property does not allow the operation of a pub on the premises.
4. Amber has submitted an application for a liquor license. This lease is contingent on Amber's pending application for a liquor license being approved by the state liquor board by not later than July 30.
5. Amber may renew this lease for a further period of five years on the same terms set out in this agreement, save that the monthly rent will increase to $16,500. To exercise this option to renew, Amber must give written notice of intent to renew to Bud no later than March 31 of the final year of the initial lease period.
6. At the termination of this lease, Amber will vacate the premises and redeliver them to Bud in the same condition as at the beginning of the lease term.

We now analyze this lease to identify terms that are promises and terms that are conditions, to explain the reasons why the parties chose to structure the agreement in the way that they did, and to outline the legal consequences of that choice.

1. Identification of Promises and Conditions

Two central express promises are exchanged in this contract: Bud promises to give Amber occupation of the premises for the period of the lease, beginning on September 1, and Amber promises to pay rent and to return the premises in good condition at the end of the lease term. (We classify these as express promises because, even though the word "promise" is not used, they are stated undertakings by the parties, expressed in the agreement.) The parties' obligations to perform these promises are subject to several conditions; that is, their promises are contingent on the occurrence of a number of uncertain events. Two of these conditions are expressly stated in the lease to be conditions: Clause 3 states that the lease will be of no force or effect if the current zoning of the property does not allow a pub to be operated on the premises, and Clause 4 makes the lease contingent on the grant of a liquor license to Amber. If either of these conditions is not satisfied, the lease does not go into effect, so that

Amber is not obliged to perform her promise to pay rent, and Bud is not obliged to furnish the premises to Amber.

In addition to these two express conditions, there are two other conditions, not expressly stated as such but easily inferred from the intent of the parties, as set out in the language of the lease: From the way the parties have structured the sequence of performances, we can see that Bud's obligation to give possession of the premises to Amber on September 1 is conditional on Amber paying the September rent on August 15; that is, we can readily infer that the parties intend that Bud would not be obliged to hand over the premises to Amber on September 1 if she failed to honor her commitment to pay the rent on August 15. Similarly, if Bud fails to give Amber occupation of the premises in September, Amber would not be obliged to make her advance payment of the October rent on September 15; that is, her obligation to pay rent for the next month is conditional on Bud performing his obligation to allow her to occupy the premises this month. This situation, in which the fulfillment of each party's promised performance is a condition of the other party's performance, persists during the entire period of the lease, culminating in the performance of Amber's final promise to vacate the premises and return them in good condition to Bud.[1] The rendition of performance by each party is an uncertain future event because it is not inevitable that Amber will pay the rent or that Bud will allow Amber to continue in occupation of the premises.

Finally, Amber's renewal option in Clause 5 also contains a condition. Bud's obligation to allow the extension of the lease for an additional five years is conditional on Amber's giving timely written notice of intent to exercise her renewal right. This provision does not actually say that the continuation of the lease for the renewal period is "conditional on" or "subject to" Amber's timely delivery of the written notice. However, the words "to exercise this option to renew" make it clear that timely written notice of intent to renew is a condition. Arguably, this language makes the condition express, but even if not, it is readily inferred. If the condition of timely notice is satisfied, both parties become bound for a further five-year period, and their conditional obligations, as described in the previous paragraph, continue during that period.

2. The Requirement of Uncertainty in Relation to Future Events and Past Events

The requirement of uncertainty is a matter of common sense. If an event is certain to occur, there is little purpose in making a promise conditional on it. The element of uncertainty means, in most cases, that the event

---

[1] This example assumes that there is no contrary rule in a state's landlord-tenant law that may require the payment of rent, even where the landlord fails to comply with his obligations to the tenant, or that may preclude eviction of a tenant who has not paid rent.

contemplated must be one that will occur in the future because an event that has already occurred cannot usually qualify as uncertain. However, it is not an invariable rule that the event must lie in the future. Sometimes even though an event has occurred, the parties may not know, at the time of executing the contract, if it happened. A condition based on a past event may serve a useful purpose where the parties themselves are unsure about whether it occurred and cannot readily ascertain that information at the time of contracting. If they wish to enter the contract before they have the information rather than risk losing the deal while they wait until they acquire the knowledge, they can make the performance under the contract conditional on the event's currently unknown outcome. This is illustrated by the condition relating to the zoning of the property in Clause 3. The zoning of the property has already been determined by the local authority, so it is an existing state of affairs. Because the parties do not know the zoning of the property at the time of executing the lease, they have used the device of making the proper zoning a condition so that they can enter the contract in ignorance of the zoning, with a means of escaping it if subsequent inquiry reveals that the established zoning precludes the operation of a pub.[2] The other conditions in the lease relate to future uncertain events. It is not settled at the time of the contract if the liquor license will be granted, if the parties will honor their commitments to perform, or if Amber will decide to give a notice of renewal.

3. What Purposes Do the Parties Seek to Achieve in Including Conditions in the Contract?

Parties do not include conditions in a contract just for the fun of it. Each condition has a particular purpose. One of the best ways to avoid being confused about conditions is to make sure that one understands the different purposes of conditions and the various reasons why parties choose to include them in a contract. As you work through this chapter, you will encounter many different situations in which conditions are included in a contract, either expressly or impliedly. In each case, make sure you understand why the parties made the term a condition and what purpose it serves in the transaction. Let's begin this inquiry by identifying the various purposes of the conditions in the lease between Amber and Bud.

The conditions in Clauses 3 and 4 serve the role of escape clauses—they allow one or both of the parties to escape the contract if the condition is not

---

[2] Distinguish this from a situation in which the parties know that the current zoning does not permit the operation of a pub but they make the lease conditional on a successful application to change the zoning to allow a pub to operate on the premises. This condition would relate to a future uncertain event—the local authority's approval of the rezoning.

fulfilled. These conditions relating to the zoning and the liquor licenses were no doubt included on Amber's initiative because she does not want to be stuck with a five-year lease of premises if government regulation precludes her from operating a pub.

The conditions relating to the parties' performances, which we have found to exist as a matter of interpretation or construction, serve the purpose of sequencing the performances. The parties could have provided, for example, that Amber must pay the full five years' rent in advance or that the full five years' rent is only payable at the end of the lease term. However, a provision like this would put all the risk of default on one or other of the parties. Therefore, they have broken up the performances into stages to ameliorate the unacceptable credit risk that would otherwise have to be borne by one of them. They have decided that Amber must go first in making advance payment of rent for each month, thereby giving Bud some protection from default, but Amber is also protected because her obligation to pay in future months is contingent on Bud continuing to allow her the use and occupation of the premises.

The parties have agreed that Amber has the right to extend the lease for an additional five years if she so desires. Bud is protected by the condition that Amber must give written notice by not later than March 31 of the final year of the initial lease period. The written notice will provide Bud with documentary evidence of the extension and ensures that he will know in good time whether or not he may seek a new tenant.

4. The Sequencing of Performance: Conditions Precedent and Concurrent Conditions

Where a condition must be satisfied before the performance subject to that condition will become due, the condition is described as a "condition precedent." All the conditions in the lease are conditions precedent. Both conditions in Clauses 3 and 4 are conditions precedent to the parties' obligations under the lease—each must be satisfied before the parties are required to perform. Amber's rent payment on August 15 is a condition precedent to Bud's obligation to deliver the premises to her on September 1, and his delivery of the premises is a condition precedent to Amber's payment of the October rent on September 15, and so on for every succeeding month. Finally, Amber's timely written notice of renewal is a condition precedent to the renewal of the lease for an additional five-year term. A condition precedent must be distinguished from concurrent conditions, which are essentially a set of promises that are dependent on each other and must be performed simultaneously. There are no concurrent conditions in the lease. However, say that instead of providing that Amber pay the first month's rent on August 15, the lease provided that it would be paid on September 1, at the same time that Bud delivered the premises to Amber.

Because those two performances will occur concurrently, and because each party's performance is a condition of the other's, the payment of the first month's rent and the delivery of the premises would be concurrent conditions. Problem 18.3 provides another example of concurrent conditions.

5. The Arcane and Confusing Distinction Between Conditions Precedent and Conditions Subsequent

The distinction between conditions precedent and concurrent conditions is important because it goes to the very structure of the contract and relates to the order in which performance obligations arise under the contract. Apart from this, there is a considerably less important but potentially much more confusing distinction between conditions precedent and subsequent. This is a finicky distinction that you will not encounter in this book, apart from this brief note, but may read about elsewhere. Our purpose here is to describe the distinction and to explain why it does not much matter in the context of contract law.

The common confusion experienced by students when they hear of conditions subsequent is to think of them as part of a trilogy: A condition precedent must occur before performance, and a concurrent condition must be satisfied together with performance, so it seems to follow that a condition subsequent must somehow come after performance. This is not true. A condition subsequent does not describe a third order of performances; it is really just the same, for sequencing purposes, as a condition precedent.

As we have seen, a condition precedent is an event that must occur *before a contractual duty becomes due.* For example, in the lease, the grant of a liquor license to Amber must occur for the parties' duties under the lease to arise. However, the common law, particularly in older cases, makes a subtle distinction: If the parties wrote their agreement a little differently so that the lease was stated to come into effect immediately but would terminate if Amber did not get the liquor license, the condition would be described as subsequent; that is, a condition precedent gives rise to a duty, while a condition subsequent *discharges a duty that is already in existence.* Another example will show how much this distinction could depend on a slight change in wording. If a contract for the sale of land says "Buyer's duty to pay the purchase price is conditional upon a building permit being issued by the county," the condition is precedent. But if it says "Buyer's duty to pay the purchase price is excused if a building permit is not issued by the county," it is subsequent. As you can see, a person drafting a contract can simply avoid any issue of whether a condition is subsequent by making sure that the event is described as a condition of the duty rather than as a means of terminating it. However, contract drafters are not always that careful about observing these niceties.

Fortunately, for most purposes, little turns on this elusive distinction. Whether the condition is characterized as precedent or subsequent, the ultimate effect of its nonoccurrence is the same: The contingent promise need not be performed. The principal difference between conditions precedent and subsequent lies in the allocation of the burden of proof. The occurrence of a condition precedent must be proved as an element of the claim by the party alleging a breach, while a condition subsequent must be proved as a basis for excuse by the party denying a breach. Therefore, unless the fact of the occurrence of the condition is in dispute and equivocal, so that the party with the burden of proof will lose the case, the distinction does not matter.

The distinction does not come up often in modern contracts cases, probably in part because most cases do not turn on close questions of burden of proof and in part because courts tend to follow the preference indicated in Restatement, Second §227. Section 227 states a clear preference for interpreting conditions as precedent where any doubt exists as to the intent of the parties. (The Restatement, Second, does not even use the term "condition subsequent," but it does acknowledge the concept in §230, which deals with events "that terminate a duty.")

6. An Introduction to the Distinction Between Express Conditions and Construed or Implied Conditions

In our initial discussion of the lease at the beginning of this section, we intimate that a condition may be expressly stated as such in an agreement. We indicate that the conditions in Clauses 3 and 4 are express conditions because the language of the lease so denominates them in express terms: Clause 3 does this by saying the lease will be of no force or effect if the current zoning does not allow for the operation of a pub, and Clause 4 expresses that the grant of a liquor license is a condition by saying that the lease is contingent on it. However, even where a provision in a contract is not expressly labeled as a condition in the agreement, it could be inferred, as a matter of interpretation or construction, that the parties intended or reasonably must have intended it to be a condition. For example, even though the lease did not call it a condition, we readily infer that Amber's payment of rent is a condition precedent to Bud's obligation to deliver the premises and that his furnishing of the premises is a condition precedent to Amber's payment of the next month's rent.

The distinction between express conditions and implied or construed conditions is a source of some confusion to many students when they first encounter it. For some purposes, it does not matter to the final disposition of the case whether a condition is express. After all, once a condition is found to exist, its ultimate legal effect is the same whether it is stated expressly to be a condition or is found to be one by implication or construction. However, the distinction does have one significant consequence: If the parties have expressed a condition, a court will give great weight to their expressed intention and will strictly enforce the condition, requiring exact compliance with its requirements.

For example, in *Oppenheimer & Co. v. Oppenheim, Appel, Dixon & Co.*, 86 N.Y.2d 685, 660 N.E.2d 415, 636 N.Y.S.2d 734 (1995), Oppenheimer and Co., the tenant of office premises (the sublessor), entered into an agreement with Oppenheim, Appel, Dixon & Co. (the sublessee) under which the sublessor agreed to sublease the premises to the sublessee. The sublease was subject to the express condition that on or before February 25, 1987, the sublessor would deliver to the sublessee the prime landlord's written consent to the installation of communications equipment on the premises. The sublease stated that if the sublessee did not receive the written consent by the specified date, the sublease would be "null and void and of no further force and effect." The sublessor did get the prime landlord's consent to the work in time, and the sublessor's attorney informed the sublessee of this by telephone on February 25. However, the written consent was not delivered to the sublessee by the deadline. The sublessee immediately notified the sublessor that it did not intend to go forward with the sublease, which it contended was "invalid" because of the sublessor's failure to deliver the written consent on time. The sublessor sued the sublessee for breach of contract, arguing that it had substantially complied with the condition.

The court dismissed the sublessor's claim. It found that the language of the sublease unambiguously established the timely delivery of the prime landlord's written consent as a condition. Because the condition was express, it must be exactly and strictly complied with, and there was no justification for requiring the sublessee to accept anything short of full and precise compliance. The court reasoned, in essence, that where it construes an unexpressed condition, it can grant some leeway for substantial compliance. But where the parties have themselves expressly stated an event to be a condition, they must be taken to intend that nothing less than the exact terms of the condition must be satisfied. Although this strict reading of the language of the agreement may seem unduly technical or harsh, under principles of freedom of contract, a court cannot interpret a contract to avoid such results if the contract unmistakably expresses the intent to treat an event as a condition.

Of course, even where a condition is express, there could be a question of interpretation as to whether the happening of the event did in fact constitute exact compliance with the express condition. In *Oppenheimer & Co.* there was no basis for interpreting the late notice to comply with the terms of the condition, because the agreement specified that written notice had to be received by a specified date. However, say that the contract had provided that the sublessor must "notify" the sublessee in writing by a specified date, and the sublessor had mailed the notice before the specified date, but it was received only after that date. The court could interpret the word "notify" to mean "mailed," not "received," so that the condition was in fact exactly satisfied. A court may try particularly hard to interpret an unclear term in a condition to find compliance where nonfulfillment of the condition would have an unfair or harsh result.

It is usually easy to identify a condition as express because the language used by the parties articulates the intention that a particular performance is subject to the stated contingency. Commonly the parties do this by using language such as we see in Clauses 3 and 4 of the lease. Note, however, that for a condition to be express, it is not enough that the term is express. The intent to make it a condition also must be articulated. For example, in the lease, Amber's promise to pay rent and Bud's promise to deliver the premises are both express promises, but they are not express conditions because the parties did not expressly spell out the intention that they are conditions. However, as we note in Section A.1, the parties' intent that they be conditions is readily inferred, either through the process of interpretation or construction.

We have been using the words "implied" and "construed" conditions interchangeably to distinguish express conditions from those arising by inference. Recall, as discussed in Chapter 15, that there is a difference between implication (interpretation) and construction. In essence, a condition is implied in fact where it is not expressly stated but can be inferred as a matter of evidence from the language in context. A condition is construed (or implied in law) where there is not enough evidence to draw a factual inference, but either a rule of law recognizes a condition under the circumstances or the court concludes as a matter of law that it is reasonable and fair, given the nature of the relationship and the usual expectations in this type of contract, to find that a condition exists. In most cases, the boundary between factual inference and legal construction is hard to draw because courts seldom construe something as a condition in the absence of any factual basis to justify the construction. Furthermore, the practical difference is inconsequential—in both cases the end result is that a condition is found to exist. Thus, the primary purpose of the distinction goes more to the rationale for finding the condition to exist—to what extent it is based on actual evidence of intent and to what extent it is based on interpolation by the court, motivated by considerations of reasonableness, fairness, or policy. The important point is that even where the contract does not say in so many words that a term is a condition, courts may find, based on the nature and purpose of the contract, that it was intended to be a condition or that the parties, acting fairly and reasonably, must be taken to have intended it as such. We focus on the process of implying or construing conditions and the impact of the distinctions between those conditions and express conditions in Section C.

■ QUESTION

In Section A.3 we stress that parties include conditions in a contract to achieve a particular purpose. What might the purpose have been in *Oppenheimer & Co.*?

■ PROBLEM 18.1

In the lease between Amber and Bud, Amber has the right to renew the lease for a further five-year term. Clause 5 of the lease states that to exercise this right of renewal, Amber must give written notice to Bud no later than on March 31 of the final year of the initial lease period. We note in Section A.1 that the requirement of timely written notice of renewal is arguably clear enough to qualify as an express condition, or even if not, it is readily implied. During the final year of the initial period of the lease, Amber decided to exercise her right of renewal. Will any of the following forms of notice satisfy the condition in Clause 5 of the lease?

(a) Amber hand-delivered a written notice of renewal to Bud at 8 A.M. on April 1.

(b) At 6 P.M. on March 31, Amber sent an e-mail to Bud, notifying him of her intent to renew the lease. The e-mail message was delivered to Bud's inbox immediately, but his office closed at 5 P.M., so he did not see the e-mail until the morning of April 1.

(c) At noon on March 31, Amber called Bud and told him that she intended to exercise her right of renewal. Later that day, she mailed a written notice of renewal to Bud, which he received on April 2.

7. Pure Promises, Pure Conditions, and Terms that are Both Conditions and Promises (Promissory Conditions)

It has been implicit in much of our discussion up to now, and will become even clearer when we deal with breach of contract later, that if a party fails to perform a promise, she breaches the contract. The breach gives the other party the right to claim damages or other appropriate remedies for breach. As we have just seen, the nonfulfillment of a condition excuses the performance that was contingent on the condition.

Where a term is a pure condition—that is, it is only a condition, and neither party makes any promise that it will be fulfilled—the nonfulfillment of the condition excuses the performance that was contingent on it. Because no promise of fulfillment was made, neither party breaches as a result of the non-fulfillment, and the nonperformance of the obligation contingent on the condition is not a breach of contract. For example, neither party to the lease promised expressly or impliedly that the conditions in Clauses 3 and 4 would be satisfied: Neither Amber nor Bud gave an assurance that the zoning of the premises permitted the operation of a pub, and Amber did not promise that her liquor license application would be granted. Indeed, as we have noted above, the parties included these conditions in the lease because they did not want to be bound to the lease if either of these conditions was not satisfied. Therefore, if either of these conditions is not satisfied, Amber will not be obliged to pay the first month's rent on August 15, and Bud, in turn, will not be obliged to deliver the premises to her on September 1. The nonfulfillment of either of these conditions excuses the parties from their obligations under the lease, so that failure to perform is not a breach of contract. Similarly, if, at the end of the term of the lease, Amber does not give Bud notice of renewal, this condition precedent to the extension of the lease is not fulfilled. Again, Amber did not promise to give the notice, and it seems clear, on a reasonable interpretation of their intent, that the parties meant Amber to retain the discretion to exercise the renewal if she so wishes. If she does not exercise it, the lease terminates at the end of the initial five-year period.

However, not all conditions are pure. In fact, it is very common for parties to promise, either expressly or impliedly, that a condition will be fulfilled. For example, we have identified Amber's payment of rent as a condition precedent to Bud's obligation to deliver the premises and Bud's giving Amber possession of the premises as a condition precedent to her obligation to pay the next month's rent. Clearly, these are not pure conditions—each of the parties is promising that they will be fulfilled. Where a term in a contract is both a promise and a condition, it is called a "promissory condition." If a promissory condition is not fulfilled, the consequences of both a failure of a condition and a breach of contract follow; that is, the person responsible for fulfilling the condition will be liable for damages or some other remedy, and the other party is relieved of the obligation to render the performance contingent on the condition. Therefore, if the conditions in Clauses 3 and 4 are satisfied, but Amber fails to pay the rent on August 15, Bud is not obliged to deliver possession of the premises to her on September 1, and he can claim from Amber any damages that he suffers as a result of her breach of the lease.

Although many promises in a contract are also conditions (that is, promissory conditions), there could be a promise in a contract that is not a condition of any further performance. An unconditional promise is called a "pure promise." The only pure promise in the lease is Amber's promise, in Clause 6, to vacate the premises and redeliver them to Bud in the same condition as at the beginning of the lease term. This is a pure promise because it is not an event that must occur before some performance under the contract becomes due—there is no subsequent duty of performance by Bud that is contingent on Amber's performance of this promise.

8. Interpretation to Determine if a Term is a Condition or Merely a Timing Provision

Where parties use express language, making it clear that a particular event is a condition, a promise, or a promissory condition, it is usually quite easy to glean what they intended. However, parties are often not that clear, and the nature of the provision must be decided by interpretation or construction.

■ PROBLEM 18.2

In *Koch v. Construction Technology, Inc.*, 924 S.W.2d 68 (Tenn. 1996), the prime contractor (CTI) entered into a subcontract with Koch under which he would paint a structure erected by the prime contractor for the property owner. The subcontract contained a payment provision that read, "Partial payments subject to all applicable provisions of the Contract shall be made when and as payments are received by the Contractor."

Koch completed his work, but CTI only paid him part of the contract price. CTI refused to pay the balance because it had not been paid by the owner in full. CTI argued that the "pay when paid" term in the subcontract made the owner's payment a condition precedent to CTI's obligation to pay Koch. Koch sued CTI for the balance of the contract price. The lower courts held that the owner's payment to the prime contractor was a condition precedent to its obligation to pay Koch. The Supreme Court disagreed. It reversed and awarded Koch the balance due to him under the contract. The court noted that the overwhelming majority of courts have interpreted a "pay when paid" clause as not being a condition, which would release the general contractor from paying the subcontractor in the event that the owner fails to pay. Rather, they have treated it simply as a provision that fixes the timing of the payment; that is, although the general contractor's obligation to pay the subcontractor does not become due until the general contractor has been paid by the owner, the general contractor is not excused from paying the subcontractor if the owner fails to pay at all. The reasoning behind this interpretation is that the general contractor has dealt with owner and must be taken to have assumed the risk that the owner will not be able to pay. The subcontractor has no contractual relationship with the owner, so a simple "pay when paid" provision in the subcontract cannot reasonably be interpreted to shift the credit risk of the owner's nonpayment onto the subcontractor. If the parties intend the subcontractor to assume this risk, the subcontract should contain an express condition that clearly shows this to be the parties' intention.

(a) If CTI really did want to make its obligation to pay Koch conditional on its receipt of payment from the owner, how should it have drafted the payment provision?

(b) If Koch does not intend payment to him to be subject to the owner paying the general contractor, and he does not want to have to litigate the issue if this comes up again in another contract, how should he draft the payment provision?

(c) If CTI's payment by the owner had been a condition of CTI's payment of Koch, would it have been a promissory or pure condition? Would it have been precedent or concurrent?

■ PROBLEM 18.3

This problem, based on a simple sale of real estate, is an exercise to allow you to apply the principles outlined in this section.

Seller owns a house occupied by Tenant, whose lease expires on September 30. Under the terms of the lease, Tenant has the option to purchase the property, provided that he exercises the option by September 1. On August 15, Seller enters into a contract with Buyer under which Buyer agrees to buy the house from Seller for $400,000. The following terms are included in the contract:

1. It is understood that the current tenant of the property has an option to purchase it, exercisable on or before September 1. This contract is conditional upon the present tenant not validly exercising his option to purchase the property.
2. Buyer shall make a down payment of $40,000, to be paid into escrow[3] on or before September 5.
3. This sale will be closed in escrow. Closing documents shall be executed, and the balance of the purchase price deposited in escrow by October 15 or as soon thereafter as financing documents can be prepared and marketable title delivered.
4. Seller shall vacate the property and deliver physical possession of it to the buyer within five days of closing.

(a) Identify any pure conditions, pure promises, and promissory conditions contained in this agreement. With regard to conditions, articulate what the uncertain event is and what performance is contingent on the happening of that event.

(b) Determine which conditions are express and which are construed or implied.

(c) Which conditions are precedent? Which are concurrent?

(d) Identify the role that each condition and promise plays in the contract, and consider why the parties may have chosen to structure the contract as they have done.

---

[3] For those who are not familiar with this term, "escrow" means that the title documents and purchase price are delivered to an independent third party who holds them until each party has performed. When the title transfer documents are complete and executed and the price has been received by the escrow agent, the agent pays the seller and registers the transfer of title to the buyer.

B A PROMISE TO TAKE ACTION TO TRY TO SATISFY A CONDITION

We have seen that some conditions are pure in that neither party makes any promise that the condition will be fulfilled. (For example, we identified the conditions in Clauses 3 and 4 of the lease agreement between Amber and Bud as pure conditions.) Other conditions are promissory, in that one of the parties promises that the condition will be fulfilled. (For example, we classified the conditions that Amber pay rent and Bud deliver the premises to her as promissory conditions.) There is a third category that lies between these two, in which the condition is not fully promissory, in that a party does not promise that it will be fulfilled, but it is not a pure condition either, because a party promises to take some action to try to get it fulfilled. The promise to try to bring the condition about might be expressed—the contract might specify the action to be taken, or it might more generally oblige the party to make reasonable or good-faith efforts to attempt to secure the fulfillment of the condition. However, even where the contract does not state a promise expressly, it might be inferred by interpretation or construction.

For example, the lease entered into by Amber and Bud stated that the parties' duty of performance was conditional on the approval of Amber's pending application for a liquor license by not later than July 30. We identified this as an escape clause for Amber's benefit so that she would not be bound to a lease if she could not get a license to operate the pub. We characterized the condition as pure because Amber had already submitted the application, and all that remained was the decision of the licensing authority, which was beyond her control. However, say that Amber had not yet applied for the license, and the lease provided: "This lease is contingent on Amber being granted a liquor license by the state liquor board by not later than July 30." There would be no prospect of Amber getting the license unless she submitted an application and pursued the application process properly, so in the absence of a promise to make reasonable or good-faith efforts to obtain the license, Amber could prevent the condition from being fulfilled simply by failing to try to get the license. For this reason, the lease should contain a promise, either stated expressly or inferred as a matter of interpreting the parties' reasonable intent, that Amber must make the application and pursue it conscientiously. If the promise is expressed, the contract might specify precisely what Amber needs to do, or it could just state in general terms that she will make reasonable or good-faith efforts to submit and pursue the application. If the promise is not expressed, or if specific action is not specified, the court would have to determine what action would be needed to satisfy the reasonable or good-faith efforts. The condition of obtaining the license is not promissory in that Amber does not promise that she will get the license. However, there is an ancillary promise of reasonable or good-faith efforts that is attached to the condition.

■ PROBLEM 18.4

Where it is unclear from the language of the contract whether a term is a pure condition, a promissory condition, or a condition subject to an ancillary promise of reasonable or good-faith efforts, the extent of a party's control over an event can be a helpful indication of the parties' intent. However, it is important to understand that the extent of a party's ability to control the outcome of an event is just a factor from which intent can be inferred. It is not dispositive and could be outweighed by the language of the contract. Consider the interaction of the control factor and the contractual language in deciding whether the following terms in a contract for the sale of a home for $400,000 are pure conditions, promissory conditions, or conditions subject to an ancillary promise of reasonable or good-faith efforts.

(a) Buyer will make a down payment of $40,000 into escrow on or before September 5. Seller's duties under this contract are contingent on Buyer's timely payment of the down payment.

(b) An inspection of the premises has revealed that the wooden deck attached to the house is rotting and unstable. By not later than October 10, Seller will have the rotten deck removed and have a new deck built of the same type, style, and dimensions. If Seller fails to perform this work, buyer will be entitled to a reduction of $10,000 in the price of the house.

(c) Buyer will not be obliged to proceed with this purchase and will be entitled to a refund of the down payment if Buyer is unable, by not later than October 15, to obtain a loan of $350,000 on market terms and at the prevailing interest rate, to be secured by a first mortgage on the property.

■ PROBLEM 18.5

Emmy Nester owns a home that has become much too big for her since her children grew up and moved out. One day, she dropped into the sales office of Upscale Downsizers, Inc., the owner-developer of a new and fashionable condominium tower. An Upscale sales representative took Emmy up to a ritzy but compact condominium on the thirty-fifth floor of the tower. She fell in love with it and could not wait to buy it. However, she could not afford to buy the condo until she sold her house, which she had not yet put on the market. The Upscale representative suggested that she buy the condominium contingent upon her selling the house. Emmy had been following home prices in her neighborhood and believed that her house was worth between $500,000 and $550,000. The parties therefore entered into a contract under which Emmy purchased the condominium. The contract contained a provision stating, "Buyer's obligation to proceed with this sale is conditional upon her selling her existing home for not less than $500,000 within 60 days of signing this agreement." This is all that the contract said about the contingency.

The day after executing this contract, Emmy employed a real estate agent to find a buyer for the house. The agent said he would try, but he thought that Emmy was asking too much for it. In the two weeks after the house was listed, the real estate agent brought three offers to Emmy. One was for $450,000, one for $460,000, and one for $475,000. Emmy rejected all of them. Emmy received no further offers in the next three weeks. About five weeks after Emmy placed her home on the market (that is, about 35 days after she signed the contract to buy the condominium), a house in Emmy's street, similar to her house in size and condition, sold for $445,000. Emmy was discouraged, and she concluded that she would never be able to sell her house for the amount that she had expected. She therefore took it off the market. At the expiry of the 60-day period, Emmy notified Upscale that she had not been able to sell her house for $500,000. On being informed of Emmy's efforts to sell the house, Upscale claims that she did not try hard enough and has breached the contract. Is Upscale correct?

SUBSTANTIAL COMPLIANCE WITH CONSTRUED (OR IMPLIED) CONDITIONS

As mentioned in Section A, a condition is express if the parties use language in the contract (such as "on condition that," "contingent upon," "provided that," "subject to," or equivalent words) that makes it clear that the stated event is intended to be a condition. Further, we saw that just because a term is express does not mean that it is an express condition. For a term to qualify as an express condition, its language must state that an event is intended to be a condition. For example, the following language in a contract to sell a home is both an express promise and an express condition: "The buyer undertakes to make a down payment of $10,000 within a week of the execution of this agreement. The seller's obligations under this contract are conditional upon the buyer making the down payment." The clarity of the language leaves no doubt that this provision not only contains the buyer's express promise to pay but also expressly makes that payment a condition of the seller's performance. Not only the event (making the down payment) but its conditional nature is articulated. However, suppose that the contract said only, "The buyer undertakes to make a down payment of $10,000 within a week of the execution of this agreement." Here the promise is still express, but it is not expressed as a condition. To decide if it is to operate as a condition, the court will have to use interpretation or construction[4] to determine the intended or reasonably apparent meaning of the term within the context of the contract and its surrounding circumstances; that is, even where a term is not expressed as a condition, the parties could actually have intended it to be a condition, or it could be reasonable or fair to treat it as a condition. The term "constructive condition of exchange" is sometimes used to describe the situation in which the court construes one party's promise to be a condition of the promise of the other.

As discussed in Section A, where the parties clearly and unambiguously express a condition, the doctrine is that the court should strictly enforce it to give effect to the parties' manifested intent and should not find that approximate or substantial satisfaction is good enough. However, if the term is not expressly stated as a condition, so that the court has to interpret or construe it as such, the court has much more flexibility. It may interpret or construe the content and terms of the condition in a way that allows it to find that the condition has in fact been satisfied, or it may use its discretion to find that the condition can be satisfied by substantial compliance. *Jacob & Youngs, Inc. v. Kent* is probably the most famous case on the subject of constructive conditions of exchange. We set out the case here for its treatment of construed conditions and return to it in Chapter 19 in relation to the doctrine of substantial performance.

JACOB & YOUNGS, INC. v. KENT

230 N.Y. 239, 129 N.E. 889 (1921)
New York Court of Appeals

CARDOZO, Judge.

The plaintiff built a country residence for the defendant at a cost of upwards of $77,000, and now sues to recover a balance of $3,483.46, remaining unpaid. The work of construction ceased in June, 1914, and the defendant then began to occupy the dwelling. There was no complaint of defective performance until March, 1915. One of the specifications for the plumbing work provides that "All wrought-iron pipe must be well galvanized, lap welded pipe of the grade

---

[4] As noted previously in this chapter, interpretation and construction are closely related but distinct processes. If the parties' intent to create a condition is ascertainable from an interpretation of the language of the agreement in context, the condition is properly described as "implied." However, even where the evidence is not clear enough to give rise to this factual implication, a court may conclude that the parties must reasonably or fairly be taken to have intended the term to be a condition. As the court moves beyond the evidence to decide the meaning of a term based on reasonableness or fairness, it crosses the blurry line from interpretation to construction.

known as 'standard pipe' of Reading manufacture." The defendant learned in March, 1915, that some of the pipe, instead of being made in Reading, was the product of other factories. The plaintiff was accordingly directed by the architect to do the work anew. The plumbing was then encased within the walls except in a few places where it had to be exposed. Obedience to the order meant more than the substitution of other pipe. It meant the demolition at great expense of substantial parts of the completed structure. The plaintiff left the work untouched, and asked for a certificate that the final payment was due. Refusal of the certificate was followed by this suit.

The evidence sustains a finding that the omission of the prescribed brand of pipe was neither fraudulent nor willful. It was the result of the oversight and inattention of the plaintiff's subcontractor. Reading pipe is distinguished from Cohoes pipe and other brands only by the name of the manufacturer stamped upon it at intervals of between six and seven feet. Even the defendant's architect, though he inspected the pipe upon arrival, failed to notice the discrepancy. The plaintiff tried to show that the brands installed, though made by other manufacturers, were the same in quality, in appearance, in market value, and in cost as the brand stated in the contract—that they were, indeed, the same thing, though manufactured in another place. The evidence was excluded, and a verdict directed for the defendant. The Appellate Division reversed, and granted a new trial.

We think the evidence, if admitted, would have supplied some basis for the inference that the defect was insignificant in its relation to the project. The courts never say that one who makes a contract fills the measure of his duty by less than full performance. They do say, however, that an omission, both trivial and innocent, will sometimes be atoned for by allowance of the resulting damage, and will not always be the breach of a condition to be followed by a forfeiture. The distinction is akin to that between dependent and independent promises, or between promises and conditions. Some promises are so plainly independent that they can never by fair construction be conditions of one another. Others are so plainly dependent that they must always be conditions. Others, though dependent and thus conditions when there is departure in point of substance, will be viewed as independent and collateral when the departure is insignificant. Considerations partly of justice and partly of presumable intention are to tell us whether this or that promise shall be placed in one class or in another. The simple and the uniform will call for different remedies from the multifarious and the intricate. The margin of departure within the range of normal expectation upon a sale of common chattels will vary from the margin to be expected upon a contract for the construction of a mansion or a "skyscraper." There will be harshness sometimes and oppression in the implication of a condition when the thing upon which labor has been expended is incapable of surrender because united to the land, and equity and reason in the implication of a like condition when the subject-matter, if defective, is in shape to be returned. From the conclusion that promises may not be treated as dependent to the extent of their uttermost minutiae without a sacrifice of justice, the progress is a short one to the conclusion that they may not be so treated without a perversion of intention. Intention not otherwise revealed may be presumed to hold in contemplation the reasonable and probable. If something else is in view, it must not be left to implication. There will be no assumption of a purpose to visit venial faults with oppressive retribution.

Those who think more of symmetry and logic in the development of legal rules than of practical adaptation to the attainment of a just result will be troubled by a classification where the lines of division are so wavering and blurred. Something, doubtless, may be said on the score of consistency and certainty in favor of a stricter standard. The courts have balanced such considerations against those of equity and fairness, and found the latter to be the weightier. The decisions in this state commit us to the liberal view, which is making its way, nowadays, in jurisdictions slow to welcome it. Where the line is to be drawn between the important and the trivial cannot be settled by a formula. "In the nature of the case precise boundaries are impossible." 2 *Williston on Contracts*, §841. The same omission may take on one aspect or another according to its setting. Substitution of equivalents may not have the same significance in fields of art on the one side and in those of mere utility on the other. Nowhere will change be tolerated, however, if it is so dominant or pervasive as in any real or substantial measure to frustrate the purpose of the contract. There is no general license to install whatever, in the builder's judgment, may be regarded as "just as good." The question is one of degree, to be answered, if there is doubt, by the triers of the facts, and, if the inferences are certain, by the judges of the law. We must weigh the purpose to be served, the desire to be gratified, the excuse for deviation from the letter, the cruelty of enforced adherence. Then only can we tell whether literal fulfillment is to be implied by law as a condition. This is not to say that the parties are not free by apt and certain words to effectuate a purpose that performance of every term shall be a condition of recovery. That question is not here. This is merely to say that the law will be slow to impute the purpose, in the silence of the parties, where the significance of the default is grievously out of proportion to the oppression of the forfeiture. The willful transgressor must accept the penalty of his transgression. For him there is no occasion to mitigate the rigor of implied conditions. The transgressor whose default is unintentional and trivial may hope for mercy if he will offer atonement for his wrong.

In the circumstances of this case, we think the measure of the allowance is not the cost of replacement, which would be great, but the difference in value, which would be either nominal or nothing. Some of the exposed sections might perhaps have been replaced at moderate expense. The defendant did not limit his demand to them, but treated the plumbing as a unit to be corrected from cellar to roof. In point of fact, the plaintiff never reached the stage at which evidence of the extent of the allowance became necessary. The trial court had excluded evidence that the defect was unsubstantial, and in view of that ruling there was no occasion for the plaintiff to go farther with an offer of proof. We think, however, that the offer, if it had been made, would not of necessity have been defective because directed to difference in value. It is true that in most cases the cost of replacement is the measure. The owner is entitled to the money which will permit him to complete, unless the cost of completion is grossly and unfairly out of proportion to the good to be attained. When that is true, the measure is the difference in value. Specifications call, let us say, for a foundation built of granite quarried in Vermont. On the completion of the building, the owner learns that through the blunder of a subcontractor part of the foundation has been built of granite of the same quality quarried in New Hampshire. The measure of allowance is not the cost of reconstruction. "There may be omissions of that which could not afterwards be supplied exactly as called for by the contract without taking down the building to its foundations, and at the same time the omission may not affect the value of the building for use or otherwise, except so slightly as to be hardly appreciable." *Handy v. Bliss,* 204 Mass. 513, 519, 90 N.E. 864, 134 Am. St. Rep. 673. The rule that gives a remedy in cases of substantial performance with compensation for defects of trivial or inappreciable importance has been developed by the courts as an instrument of justice. The measure of the allowance must be shaped to the same end.

The order should be affirmed, and judgment absolute directed in favor of the plaintiff upon the stipulation, with costs in all courts.

McLAUGHLIN, Judge, dissenting.

I dissent. The plaintiff did not perform its contract. Its failure to do so was either intentional or due to gross neglect which, under the uncontradicted facts, amounted to the same thing, nor did it make any proof of the cost of compliance, where compliance was possible. Under its contract it obligated itself to use in the plumbing only pipe (between 2,000 and 2,500 feet) made by the Reading Manufacturing Company. The first pipe delivered was about 1,000 feet and the plaintiff's superintendent then called the attention of the foreman of the subcontractor, who was doing the plumbing, to the fact that the specifications annexed to the contract required all pipe used in the plumbing to be of the Reading Manufacturing Company. They then examined it for the purpose of ascertaining whether this delivery was of that manufacture and found it was. Thereafter, as pipe was required in the progress of the work, the foreman of the subcontractor would leave word at its shop that he wanted a specified number of feet of pipe, without in any way indicating of what manufacture. Pipe would thereafter be delivered and installed in the building, without any examination whatever. Indeed, no examination, so far as appears, was made by the plaintiff, the subcontractor, defendant's architect, or any one else, of any of the pipe except the first delivery, until after the building had been completed. Plaintiff's architect then refused to give the certificate of completion, upon which the final payment depended, because all of the pipe used in the plumbing was not of the kind called for by the contract. After such refusal, the subcontractor removed the covering or insulation from about 900 feet of pipe which was exposed in the basement, cellar, and attic, and all but 70 feet was found to have been manufactured, not by the Reading Company, but by other manufacturers, some by the Cohoes Rolling Mill Company, some by the National Steelworks, some by the South Chester Tubing Company, and some which bore no manufacturer's mark at all. The balance of the pipe had been so installed in the building that an inspection of it could not be had without demolishing, in part at least, the building itself.

I am of the opinion the trial court was right in directing a verdict for the defendant. The plaintiff agreed that all the pipe used should be of the Reading Manufacturing Company. Only about two-fifths of it, so far as appears, was of that kind. If more were used, then the burden of proving that fact was upon the plaintiff, which it could easily have done, since it knew where the pipe was obtained. The question of substantial performance of a contract of the character of the one under consideration depends in no small degree upon the good faith of the contractor. If the plaintiff had intended to, and had, complied with the terms of the contract except as to minor omissions, due to inadvertence, then he might be allowed to recover the contract price, less the amount necessary to fully compensate the defendant for damages caused by such omissions. But that is not this case. It installed between 2,000 and 2,500 feet of pipe, of which only 1,000 feet at most complied with the contract. No explanation was given why pipe called for by the contract was not used, nor that any effort made to show what it would cost to remove the pipe of other manufacturers and install that of the Reading Manufacturing Company. The defendant had a right to contract for what he wanted. He had a right before making payment to get what the contract called for. It is no answer to this suggestion to say that the pipe put in was just as good as that made by the Reading Manufacturing Company, or that the difference in value between such pipe and the pipe made by the Reading Manufacturing Company would be either "nominal or nothing." Defendant contracted for pipe made by the Reading Manufacturing Company. What his reason was for requiring this kind of pipe is of no importance. He wanted that and was entitled to it. It may have been a mere whim on his part, but even so, he had a right to this kind of pipe, regardless of whether some other kind, according to the opinion of the contractor or experts, would have been "just as good, better, or done just as well." He agreed to pay only upon condition that the pipe installed were made by that company and he ought not to be compelled to pay unless that condition be performed. The rule, therefore, of substantial performance, with damages for unsubstantial omissions, has no application.

What was said by this court in *Smith v. Brady* [17 NY 173] is quite applicable here: "I suppose it will be conceded that every one has a right to build his house, his cottage or his store after such a model and in such style as shall best accord with his notions of utility or be most agreeable to his fancy. The specifications of the contract become the law between the parties until voluntarily changed.... [T]he builder has no right to substitute his own judgment or that of others. Having departed from the agreement, if performance has not been waived by the other party, the law will not allow him to allege that he has made as good a building as the one he engaged to erect. He can demand payment only upon and according to the terms of his contract, and if the conditions on which payment is due have not been performed, then the right to demand it does not exist. To hold a different doctrine would be simply to make another contract, and would be giving to parties an encouragement to violate their engagements, which the just policy of the law does not permit."

I am of the opinion the trial court did not err in ruling on the admission of evidence or in directing a verdict for the defendant. For the foregoing reasons I think the judgment of the Appellate Division should be reversed and the judgment of the Trial Term affirmed.

■ ■ ■

Judge Cardozo classifies sets of promises into three categories: promises that are so plainly independent that they can never be conditions of each other, promises that are so plainly dependent that they must always be conditions, and promises that are dependent in matters of substance but independent with regard to insignificant departures. It is difficult to understand what he means without some background about the concept of dependence. Modern law largely takes it for granted that there is a relationship of dependence between most promises exchanged under a contract. Unless a promise is so trivial as to be inconsequential, or the parties expressly declare it to be independent (which would be unusual), it is hard to think of a current example of a "plainly independent" promise. However, earlier common law (about four centuries ago) treated most promises as independent. Assume that parties entered into a contract for the sale of a horse for £5, payment to be cash on delivery (C.O.D.). If the seller failed to show up and deliver the horse, he could still sue the buyer for the £5. Because the law treated the promises as independent, the buyer could not raise as a defense the fact that the seller had not delivered the horse. He would be liable on his promise to pay the £5 and would have to maintain a separate action for delivery of the horse. The absurdity of this result is quite apparent today.

It was only in 1773, in the case of *Kingston v. Preston*, 99 Eng. Rep. 437 (King's Bench 1773), that Lord Mansfield, the great English jurist, established the principle that promises in a contract could be construed as dependent—that is, as conditions of each other. On this basis, even though the parties to the sale of the horse did not expressly state that the buyer's obligation to pay for the horse was dependent on the seller delivering it, the nature of the contract and the reasonable expectations of the parties allow the court to construe the promises as dependent—that is, as conditions of each other. Because of the C.O.D. term, they are concurrent conditions. Therefore, if the seller does not deliver the horse, the condition to the buyer's promise to pay the £5 is not satisfied.

■ QUESTIONS

(1)   Which of the statements below correctly describes Judge Cardozo's view?

(a)   The owner's promise to pay is independent of the builder's promise to build the house.

(b)   The owner's promise to pay is dependent on the builder's promise to build the house.

(c)   The owner's promise to pay is dependent on the builder's promise to build the house but only as regards matters of substance, not as regards insignificant departures.

(2)   Translate the third paragraph of Judge Cardozo's opinion into language that you can understand, eliminating the concept of dependent and independent promises but retaining the sense and substance of what he said.

(3)   Judge McLaughlin strongly disagrees with the majority. What is the essence of his disagreement? Does he consider that the owner's promise to pay was dependent on the builder's promise to install Reading pipe?

(4)   Do you think that Judge Cardozo would have reached a different conclusion if the builder had used absolutely no Reading pipe at all but had used only Cohoes pipe?

(5)   Judge Cardozo says that the wrong pipe was used because of a subcontractor's oversight. What if, after half the house was built, the builder realized that the wrong pipe had been bought and delivered to the site; nevertheless, he concluded that there was no difference in quality between Reading pipe and the pipe that had been delivered, so he decided not to make an issue of it with the subcontractor, who continued to install the wrong pipe? Would this have made a difference to the result of the case?

(6)   The promise to use Reading pipe was part of a lengthy list of specifications relating to the materials to be used in the house. Do you think that Judge Cardozo would have reached a different conclusion if, instead, the language "All wrought-iron pipe must be well galvanized, lap-welded pipe of the grade known as 'standard pipe' of Reading manufacture" was included as a self-standing clause in the agreement?

■ PROBLEM 18.6

In the example above of the sale of the horse, the buyer had to pay the £5 upon delivery of the horse. These promises of delivery and payment are surely to be treated as dependent in modern law and are therefore constructive concurrent conditions of each other. It is not possible to have the same arrangement in a building contract, because the performance of the promise to pay can be rendered instantaneously, while performance of the promise to build the house must take some time. The parties therefore have a few options: The building contract could provide that the owner pays the full contract price in advance, before the builder begins work; or, conversely, the contract could provide that the owner pay the price at the completion of the building work; or (most likely) the contract could break up the performance of the parties into stages.

(a) Say that the parties elect either the first or the second options—that is, the contract expressly provides that the owner must pay in advance or arrear of the work. However, the contract uses no expressly conditional language. What is the relationship between the promises by both parties?

(b) Say that the building contract follows the third option. The contract is executed on July 1. It provides that the owner must make an initial down payment of 10 percent by July 8. The builder must complete excavation of the foundations by July 30. The owner must pay another 5 percent of the price on July 31. The builder must lay the foundation by August 30. The owner must pay a further 5 percent of the price on September 1. The rest of the construction work and payments are alternated in this way until the building work is complete and only 5 percent of the price remains unpaid. The builder promises to finish the house on December 1, and the owner promises to pay the 5 percent balance on January 5. Assume that no express language of condition is used in the contract. What is the relationship among the various promises made by both parties?

 # **D** CONDITIONS OF SATISFACTION

A condition of satisfaction is a form of escape clause that allows a party to escape its obligations under the contract if that party is not satisfied with the other party's performance or some other specified state of affairs. It is used where a party's desire for the contract is dependent on her being satisfied with the outcome of some uncertain event. For example, a lender's agreement to make a loan to a borrower may be made conditional on the lender's satisfaction with the borrower's credit rating, as shown on a credit report to be obtained, or a buyer's promise to take delivery of and pay for a painting commissioned by the buyer may be conditional on her being satisfied with the finished product.

A condition of satisfaction may be dependent on the satisfaction of the party herself (that is, she will make the judgment), but it could also be made dependent on some third party acting on her behalf. For example, a buyer's promise to purchase a home may be subject to her architect being satisfied, on inspection of the building, that it is structurally sound.[5]

We encountered conditions of this kind when we dealt with promises in connection with consideration doctrine in Chapter 9. If a party retains unlimited discretion to decide whether to perform, she really has made no commitment, and her apparent promise is an illusion. It therefore does not constitute a legal detriment. In the first example above, the lender's promise to make the loan if it is satisfied with the credit report would be illusory if its judgment of the credit report could not be questioned and was completely within its discretion. However, the promise would not be illusory if the lender agreed, either expressly or impliedly, that its determination of satisfaction would be based on a measurable standard. It would then suffer the legal detriment of binding itself to that standard, so that it could not act on a whim and would have to justify its lack of satisfaction. Courts assume that parties do not normally intend promises to be illusory, and that they expect that the exercise of discretion to be subject to some control. Therefore, even if the contract does not set out a standard for determining dissatisfaction, courts readily infer that the parties intended this judgment to be subject to some measurable standard.

Where the contract itself does not specify the standard to be used, courts generally favor an objective standard—the party's dissatisfaction must be reasonable. However, in some contracts, where the object is to cater to the particular tastes and desires of the party, a court may be inclined to a subjective standard—the party's dissatisfaction must be genuine and honest. In the above examples, subjective good faith might be the most appropriate standard to determine if the buyer of the painting was genuinely dissatisfied with it, but the lender's dissatisfaction with the credit report or the architect's dissatisfaction with the structural soundness of the building are more appropriately decided on an objective reasonableness standard. (As is usually so, it is hard to draw a bright line between the subjective and objective standards because it is difficult for a party to show honest dissatisfaction where there is no rational basis for it.)

---

[5] As the first paragraph in *Jacob & Youngs* indicates, final payment to the contractor in that case was conditional on an architect's certificate, which was refused. The court did not discuss the nonfulfillment of this condition or explain why it held in favor of the contractor despite the nonfulfillment. We can surmise, however, that because the court found that the failure to use Reading pipe was a trivial departure from the contract, there was no justifiable basis for the architect's dissatisfaction, and the condition should therefore be deemed fulfilled.

■ PROBLEM 18.7

Buyer bought some land with the intention of developing it for a shopping center if such a project appeared feasible. Because Buyer did not want the land if it could not be developed economically as a shopping center, the parties included a provision in the contract stating that the contract was "subject to Buyer obtaining leases satisfactory to him." After making a conscientious effort to solicit prospective tenants, Buyer concluded that he was not able to obtain enough lease commitments of the quality and kind that he desired. He therefore notified Seller that he would not proceed with the sale because the condition of satisfaction had not been fulfilled.[6] Seller objected and ultimately sued Buyer for breach of contract, claiming that Buyer had in fact found satisfactory lease commitments and had improperly asserted a lack of satisfaction.

At trial, the evidence established that Buyer had found enough prospective tenants to fill about 60 percent of the proposed shopping center. The prospective tenants were diverse; they were willing to pay rent at market rates; and they were willing to commit to five-year leases. Although some tenants were new stores with no credit history, at least half were established multistore chains with a good record of earnings. Two shopping center developers called by Seller as witnesses testified that they considered the prospective tenants to be entirely satisfactory. They also testified that most developers would be very pleased and encouraged if they were able to pre-lease 60 percent of an unbuilt shopping center to tenants of this quality.

Buyer's testimony revealed that he is very cautious and risk-averse. He feels that it is unduly risky to proceed with construction without lease commitments for at least 80 percent of the space in the center. Also, he has concerns about the financial viability of several of the new businesses that he found, and at least two of the established retailers had lately had weak profits. Buyer does not like the mix of tenants because there would be too many boring everyday stores such as a pharmacy, dry cleaner, hairdresser, and vitamin store, and not enough interesting boutiques and specialty stores.

Should Buyer's dissatisfaction be measured by an objective or subjective standard? To what extent would the analysis and result be different under these standards?

---

[6] The facts of this problem are based on *Mattei v. Hopper*, 51 Cal. 2d 119, 330 P.2d 625 (1958), summarized in the text note on promises as consideration in Chapter 9. In the actual case, it was the buyer who wanted to proceed with the sale, but the seller reneged and argued that the contract was invalid for lack of consideration because the condition of satisfaction made the buyer's promise illusory. The court disagreed, holding that a subjective good-faith or objective reasonableness standard could be readily implied to curtail the buyer's discretion and avoid the illusory promise problem.

■ PROBLEM 18.8

Ecstatic Estates, an expensive resort, hired Happy Snapper, a photographer, to produce a set of photographs of the resort, to be used by Ecstatic for promotional purposes on its website and on lavish glossy brochures. Ecstatic made it clear that it wished for photographs that would be enticing to prospective guests and would capture the elegant and luxurious character of the resort. Upon Ecstatic's insistence, Happy agreed to a term in the contract that stated, "Ecstatic Estates will not be obliged to accept or pay for the photographs unless it considers, in its sound and sole judgment, that the photographs present the image of its resort that it seeks to portray."

Happy took a set of very good, high quality, and accurate photographs of the resort but Ecstatic rejected them. Although Ecstatic conceded that the photographs were technically of high quality and accurately portrayed the features of the property, it felt that they were indistinguishable from the glossy photos used by many other resorts, failed to capture the special Ecstatic ambiance, had the overall effect of being quite boring, and were unlikely to capture the attention and interest of a public that that was already overexposed to well-produced but otherwise unexceptional promotional literature.

(a) Should a subjective or objective test be used to decide whether the condition of satisfaction has been fulfilled?

(b) If the correct standard is subjective, should Ecstatic be entitled to refuse to accept and pay for the photographs? What if the standard is objective?

THE USE OF CONDITIONS TO PROVIDE FOR ALTERNATIVE PERFORMANCES

The conditions discussed so far have all had the effect of excusing the contingent performance entirely. In many cases, because that performance was itself a condition of the other party's performance, the nonfulfillment of the condition leads to termination of the contract as a whole. However, a condition need not have this effect. Instead, it could be used as a channeling device: The parties need not provide that a party's obligation to perform is dependent in its entirety on the condition being satisfied. They could use a condition to structure the contract so that if the condition is satisfied, the party renders one performance, and if it is not satisfied, the party must render another.

> ### ■ PROBLEM 18.9
>
> Alternative Performances Corp., Inc. (APC), an independent movie studio, entered into a contract with Bess Seller, a best-selling author. Under the contract, APC bought the rights to make a movie of Bess's popular romantic novel *The Conditional Promise: A Saga of Hope and Betrayal* for $2 million. The contract stated that APC would pay Bess the $2 million immediately upon execution of the contract. The contract made it clear that APC had no obligation to produce the movie, or if it did make the movie, had no obligation to release it. However, the contract provided that if APC did produce and release the movie, it would pay Bess, in addition to the initial $2 million, 1 percent of the net profits earned from the release.
>
> Analyze this contract by identifying each condition and explaining its function.

 THE USE OF CONDITIONS TO SEQUENCE PERFORMANCES WHERE THE PERFORMANCE OF THE PARTIES WILL NOT BE INSTANTANEOUS AND SIMULTANEOUS

Many of the principles applicable in this section have been discussed previously in this chapter. It may be helpful to begin by restating them:

1. If a condition has to be satisfied before a promised performance becomes due, it is a condition precedent. Some conditions are pure—that is, they have no promissory content. Others have a promise of best efforts or of the exercise of good faith or reasonableness associated with them. Yet others are fully promissory, in that one of the parties promises, expressly or by implication, that she will make the condition happen.

2. Many promises are conditions precedent as well. For example, a contract for the sale of a car provides that the seller promises to deliver the car to the buyer on Monday, and the buyer promises to pay the agreed price of the car on the following Friday. The contract may go on to state that the buyer's obligation to pay on Friday is conditional on the seller's delivery of the car on Monday. If the contract says this, the delivery of the car is not only a promise; it has also expressly been made a condition precedent to the buyer's performance. It is an express promissory condition, and the parties have made it clear that the condition must be satisfied before the buyer's obligation to pay for the car arises.

3. Even if the contract did not expressly make the delivery of the car a condition of payment, it could be interpreted as or construed to be a condition. A court would have little trouble in interpreting or construing delivery as a promissory condition precedent. This seems to flow quite obviously from the fact that the parties have provided in the contract for the performance of their promises to be sequenced so that the seller must go first. It is reasonable to suppose that the buyer would not have to pay for the car if the seller failed to deliver it. Stated in the language of dependent promises, it is a reasonable inference that the buyer's promise was dependent on the seller's prior performance.

4. The parties need not have structured the contract this way. They could have provided that the buyer pay on Monday and the seller deliver the car on the next Friday, in which case payment would be a promissory condition precedent to delivery. As in the immediately preceding example, the parties could have made the payment an express condition, but if they did not, it would be so implied or construed. Alternatively, the contract could have stated that the seller and buyer would meet on Monday and that the seller would deliver the car to the buyer in exchange for the buyer's payment of the price in cash. Here each performance undertaken in these dependent promises would be a condition of the other. (Again, the agreement might state this expressly, but if not the condition would be readily implied or construed.) However, in this cash on delivery (C.O.D.) transaction, the promised performances are to be rendered simultaneously so neither promise would be a condition precedent to the other. Where promises are dependent on each other (that is, each is a promissory condition of the other) and they have to be performed at the same time, they are called "concurrent conditions."

As this summary and examples show, the use of promissory conditions to structure the sequence of performance is commonplace and allows the parties to set up the contract in a way that allocates or distributes the risk of who goes first. Therefore, if delivery is a condition precedent to payment, the seller becomes the creditor of the debtor for five days and runs the risk that she will not be paid for the car. If payment is made a condition precedent of delivery, the risk shifts to the buyer. If the promises are made concurrent conditions, neither party assumes the risk of performing and not receiving the exchange performance. Parties could devise all kinds of permutations of this sequence depending on how they would like to arrange the transaction. For example, the contract could provide that the buyer must make a down payment on Monday; the seller must deliver possession of the car on Wednesday; and the parties must meet on Friday, when the balance of the price is to be paid in exchange for the title documents for the car. Here we have sequential promissory conditions followed by a set of concurrent promissory conditions.

Where one or both performances cannot be completed instantaneously, there is even a stronger incentive for the parties to spread the risk of nonperformance by breaking up performances and providing a sequence for performing components of each. This type of sequencing is illustrated in Problem 18.6, involving the contract in which the owner had to make periodic payments to the builder at specified stages of construction.

We said above that if the parties provide for a sequence of performances but do not expressly state that an earlier performance is a condition precedent to a later one or that simultaneous performances are concurrent conditions of each other, the court will fill this gap by implication or construction. What happens if the parties simply set out the promised performances, but make no provision for sequencing? (For example, suppose that the car sale contract simply says that the seller promises to deliver the car and the buyer promises to pay the price, but the contract does not specify if either performance must go first or if they are to be simultaneous.)

As a general rule, if a contract is silent on the sequence of performance, a court is likely to construe the performances as concurrent if they can be performed instantaneously and simultaneously. (That is, with instantaneous performances, the default rule is to assume that the parties intended a C.O.D. transaction.) Restatement, Second §234(1) adopts this position. The rule that instantaneous performances must be concurrent is also reflected in UCC 2-511(1), which states, "Unless otherwise agreed tender of payment is a condition to the seller's duty to tender and complete any delivery," and UCC 2-307, which states, "Unless otherwise agreed all goods called for by a contract for sale must be tendered in a single delivery and payment is due only on such tender. . . ."

However, if one of the performances is capable of instantaneous completion (such as the payment of money) and the other will take time (such as the construction of a house), the usual rule is that the longer performance is construed as a condition precedent to the instantaneous one. This is reflected in Restatement, Second §234(2), which provides that ". . . where the performance of only one party . . . requires a period of time, his performance is due at an earlier time than that of the other party, unless the language or the circumstances indicate the contrary." The default rule therefore places the full credit risk on the party with the noninstantaneous performance. Unless he is willing to assume the risk of performing on credit, the party with the noninstantaneous performance can avoid the default rule by specifying a sequence of performances in the contract.

It should also be noted (as discussed more fully in Chapter 19) that because the conditions are promises as well as conditions, the failure of a condition may both excuse the contingent performance and give rise to a claim for breach of contract. For example, in the contract where the seller promises to deliver the car on Monday and the buyer promises to pay on the next Friday, if the seller fails to deliver the car, the buyer not only would be relieved of any obligation to pay but may also be able to claim damages from the seller for breaching the contract.

■ PROBLEM 18.10

On June 1, Brooke Bubbling bought a marble and stainless steel fountain from Watery Wonders, Inc., for $10,000. The contract states that Watery Wonders will deliver the fountain to Brooke's home on June 5. The contract has no term stating when Brooke must pay the price of the fountain.

On June 2 Brooke entered into a contract with Lovely Landscapes, Inc., for installation of the fountain. The contract states that Lovely will excavate the site where the fountain will be placed, will perform the necessary plumbing and electrical work, and will complete the installation by paving and planting around the fountain. The installation work is to begin on June 7 and must be completed by June 20. The contract price is $7,000, but the contract does not state when the price is to be paid.

(a) On June 5 Watery Wonders delivered the fountain. Before offloading the fountain, its driver told Brooke that he had been instructed to collect payment of the $10,000 price in cash or by cashier's check. Brooke replied that she had neither cash nor a cashier's check available at present, but would pay for the fountain by mailing a personal check at the end of the month. Would the driver be justified in refusing to complete the delivery?

(b) Brooke resolved her dispute with Watery Wonders over payment of the price and the fountain was offloaded at her home on June 5. On June 7, Lovely Landscapes arrived to begin the work on the installation. Its foreman insisted on being paid the $7,000 installation fee in cash or by cashier's check before he began work. Brooke refused and said she would pay the price upon completion of the installation. Who is right?

■ PROBLEM 18.11

Wishing to avoid the dispute described in Problem 18.10, Lovely Landscapes includes the following term in the next contract that it enters for the installation of a fountain:

> The customer will pay 10 percent of the installation fee to Lovely Landscapes upon signing the contract. The customer will pay a further 40 percent of the installation fee when Lovely Landscape's workers arrive at the premises to begin installing the fountain, and will pay the balance when the work has been completed to the customer's satisfaction. All payments will be in cash or by cashier's check.

Identify and describe the conditions and promises in this contract term and explain their functions.

EXCUSE OF CONDITIONS

As discussed in Section A.6, courts usually enforce express conditions strictly. The rationale is that a court's primary function is to enforce what the parties agreed, so when the parties have provided expressly that a specified event must occur before a performance becomes due, the court should not normally interfere with the parties' clear intentions. However, this rule, like most, is not absolute and unbending. As with other contract terms, an express condition is subject to the court's power to police contracts for fraud, duress, and other bargaining impropriety. Even in the absence of any defense of this kind, there are circumstances in which it is not appropriate to insist on strict enforcement of a condition. In this section, we look at four situations in which courts have felt justified in excusing a condition, even though it was legitimately and expressly agreed to by the parties. The focus here is on express conditions because the rule that express conditions must be strictly enforced most commonly gives rise to a need to find a basis for excusing the condition. While the grounds for excuse are potentially available to overcome implied or construed conditions, they are less likely to be needed because the court has more flexibility in interpreting or construing the content of the unstated condition to dispose of any harsh or unfair effect.

Three of the grounds for excuse—waiver, estoppel, and obstructive or uncooperative conduct—arise from post-formation words or actions of the party for whose benefit the condition was included in the contract. The basis for excuse here is that the party's behavior forfeits his right to hold the other party to the condition. The fourth—unfair forfeiture—is a more general ground, based on the court's discretionary power to do justice between the parties. Because it involves the exercise of judicial discretion to disregard what the parties have provided in their agreement, it is more controversial. Courts that recognize it use it sparingly.

1. Waiver and Estoppel

Although waiver and estoppel are distinct doctrines, it is very easy to confuse them. They arise from approximately the same conduct, they have the same end result, they are often referred to in the same breath, and the courts are not always careful to keep the distinction clear. The basic point of both doctrines is that after the contract has been entered, the party who is the beneficiary of the condition manifests the intention, reasonably interpreted from words or conduct, that he will not require the condition to be satisfied as a prerequisite to his performance; that is, he can be reasonably understood to have abandoned the condition, so that his duty to perform has become unconditional. Although these are the similarities between waiver and estoppel, these two bases of excuse have differences that distinguish them.

a. Waiver

A waiver is a knowing and voluntary abandonment of a right. It may be made expressly or by implication from words or conduct. Waivers can come up in two different situations. In the first, the waiver is asserted by the party who has the right to claim nonfulfillment of the condition. Although he can rely on nonfulfillment to escape the contract, he wishes the transaction to proceed despite the nonfulfillment. In the second situation, the party who is protected by the condition (Party A) seeks to assert that it has not been fulfilled, but the other party (Party B) claims that Party A cannot rely on the condition because he has waived it. The context is important because it affects the principles applicable to the waiver. The following example illustrates the use of waiver in these two situations:

Developer plans to construct an office tower on a city block that currently contains two smaller buildings owned by different owners. Developer needs to buy both properties for the planned development of the new full-block office tower. He negotiates a contract with the owner of Property A, but has not yet been able to get the owner of Property B to agree to sell. He therefore enters into a contract with Owner A to buy Property A, subject to the condition that within 30 days he is able to secure the purchase of Property B. Although he tries very persistently over the next 30 days, Developer is unable to persuade Owner B to sell.

If despite this, Developer decides that he still wishes to buy Property A, he may simply waive the condition, making the purchase of Property A unconditional. Provided that the condition was included solely for the benefit of Developer, and its waiver has no adverse impact on the contractual rights of Owner A, Owner A cannot object to the waiver and must perform. This is an example of the first situation, in which the party who is the beneficiary of the condition chooses to abandon the protection of the condition because he wants to proceed with the transaction despite nonfulfillment of the condition.

By contrast, in the second situation, the party benefitting from the condition does not want to give it up, but the other party to the contract claims that he waived it by his words or conduct, and cannot assert its nonfulfillment. For example, an insurance policy states that to be reimbursed for any loss covered by the policy, the insured must submit a claim to the insurer within 10 days of the loss. The insured submits a claim 12 days after the loss. The insurer does not reject the claim when it receives it but accepts and processes it. A short while later, the insurer rejects the claim as having been filed beyond the 10-day period. The insurer's conduct in accepting the late claim with knowledge that it was filed late could be interpreted to indicate the intent to relinquish the condition—that is, the insurer may have waived the condition by its conduct.

Where a claim of waiver is raised against the party protected by the condition (the insurer), consideration doctrine imposes a restriction on the validity of a waiver. Unlike a modification, which is a bilateral agreement with consideration,[7] a waiver is a one-sided relinquishment of a right for no consideration. Therefore, the non-waiving party may raise waiver by the other only if the waived right is a nonmaterial or ancillary part of the contract. If the right is a material part of the exchange, it can only be abandoned by a modification contract under which consideration is given for relinquishing it. In short, a party claiming that the other party waived a condition must show not only that the waiver was knowing and voluntary, but also that the right waived was nonmaterial. In the example of the insurer's waiver by conduct of the 10-day filing condition, the question would be whether the timeliness of notice of loss was a material term of the insurance policy. As always, the determination of materiality must be resolved by interpretation in context.

■ PROBLEM 18.12

As in the first example above, Developer plans to construct an office tower on a city block that currently contains two smaller properties owned by Owners A and B. Developer needs to buy both properties for the development of the entire block, but has only been able to enter into a contract of sale with Owner A. This contract contains a condition that allows Developer to escape the contract if he cannot secure the purchase of Property B within 30 days. Although he tried very persistently for several days, Developer was unable to persuade Owner B to sell. By the tenth day after executing the contract, Owner B made it clear that he would not even consider selling his property and threatened to obtain a restraining order if Developer even tried to approach him again. Notwithstanding this insurmountable setback, Developer continued to pursue city approval of his development plan during the subsequent 20 days, paying fees and submitting documents required for the approval process. Developer also sent surveyors and engineers to Property A to obtain accurate measurements and to gather data needed for planning and construction. In the end, Developer decided to scrap the project and on the 31st day after the contract was executed, Developer informed Owner A that the condition had not been satisfied and he was withdrawing from the transaction. Owner A claims that Developer cannot invoke the nonfulfillment of the condition because he waived it by conduct.

Has Developer waived the condition by conduct?

---

[7] Recall that consideration is generally required to validate a modification contract at common law, but it is not required by UCC 2-209 to modify a contract for the sale of goods.

b. *Estoppel*

Estoppel operates in this context where the beneficiary of a condition indicates by words or conduct that he will perform the contingent promise despite non-fulfillment of the condition. As is true generally with estoppel, the party to be estopped must have known or had reason to know that his words or conduct were likely to have been relied on by the other party, and they must in fact have been relied on by that party to her detriment. (If the beneficiary of the condition promises to perform despite nonfulfillment of the condition, promissory estoppel, rather than equitable estoppel, may be the more appropriate doctrine.)

The behavior that gives rise to a waiver is often exactly the same as that creating grounds for estoppel, which is one of the reasons why the doctrines are so easily confused. However, the difference between them lies in the elements that must be satisfied to hold the actor accountable for that behavior. Unlike estoppel, waiver does not require justifiable reliance and detriment. Unlike waiver, estoppel is not confined to nonmaterial changes in the contract, and the behavior need not meet the same standards of a knowing and voluntary abandonment of a right—a party may be estopped on the basis of careless action not deliberately intended to give up a right. Therefore, if the words or conduct abandon a nonmaterial condition, waiver can be used. However, if the condition is material, it can be excused only if estoppel can be established by showing conduct of the party to be estopped that is justifiably relied on by the other party to her detriment.

■ PROBLEM 18.13

As in Problem 18.12, Developer's contract with Owner A contains a condition that allows Developer to escape the contract if he cannot secure the purchase of Property B within 30 days. It became unquestionably clear ten days after the contract was executed that Developer would never be able to get Owner B to change his adamant refusal to sell, yet Developer continued to pursue city approval of his development plan during the subsequent 20 days, paying fees and submitting documents required for the approval process. Developer also sent surveyors and engineers to Property A to obtain accurate measurements and to gather data needed for planning and construction. The question to be asked in relation to estoppel is not whether this constitutes a voluntary abandonment of a nonmaterial right, but whether Developer's actions manifested the intention not to assert the condition, and whether Owner A justifiably relied upon that manifested intent.

(a) Assume that the condition is a material term of the contract to buy Property A. Do these facts support a claim of estoppel by Owner A?

(b) Would your answer change if, on the 25th day after the contract was executed, Owner A, believing as a result of Developer's continuing actions, that this transaction would proceed despite the nonfulfillment of the condition, rejected an offer by a third party to buy Property A?

■ PROBLEM 18.14

Mercedes-Benz Credit Corp. v. Morgan, 312 Ark. 225, 850 S.W.2d 297 (1993) involved the repossession of a Porsche following the default of Morgan, the buyer, who bought the Porsche on credit in 1990. Mercedes-Benz Credit Corporation (MBCC) financed the purchase and had a security interest in the car, which gave MBCC the right to take possession of the car if Morgan defaulted on his payments. Under the car loan agreement, Morgan was obliged to pay 48 monthly installments of $253.37 beginning on March 1, 1990. Morgan made monthly payments over the next 14 months, but all except one were late. Some payments were a few days late, and some were as much as a full month late. MBCC periodically contacted Morgan about his late payments, but it always accepted the late payments and never told him that it intended in the future to strictly enforce its rights under the contract. Finally, in March 1991, MBCC exercised its right to repossess the car. After the car was repossessed, Morgan sued MBCC for conversion. The jury awarded damages to Morgan, and the verdict was affirmed by the Arkansas Supreme Court.

The court acknowledged that Morgan had defaulted in his payments and that MBCC would have had the right under the agreement to repossess the car. However, because it had repeatedly accepted late payments, MBCC had waived its right to repossess merely because a payment was overdue. MBCC could at any time have retracted its waiver and reinstated its right to repossess for late payment, but to do so, it had to give Morgan notice that he would have to comply strictly with the payment terms in future. Because it never gave such notice, its repossession was wrongful and a conversion.

(a) What is the condition in issue here, and what promise is contingent on its occurrence?

(b) The court recognized that although MBCC could not have enforced the condition insofar as it related to past defaults, it could have reinstated its rights by notice (that is, retracted its waiver) with regard to future installments. Why should that be allowed? Why is a waiver, once made, not binding forever?

(c) The case was decided on the basis of waiver. Would the facts support excusing the condition on grounds of estoppel?

2. Obstructive or Uncooperative Conduct

We have already seen that a party can promise that a condition will be satisfied (a promissory condition) or may at least commit to exercising good faith or reasonable efforts to bring it about (such as in a financing contingency or a condition of satisfaction). Even if there is no promise to make a condition occur, or to try to make it happen, most contracts will likely contain an undertaking not to do anything to obstruct or hinder its occurrence. This may be stated expressly in the contract, but more likely it will be implicit as part of the general obligation of good faith and fair dealing. For example, think about the condition that was part of the contract in Problem 18.3, involving the sale of a house: "It is understood that the current tenant of the property has an option to purchase it, exercisable on or before September 1. This contract is conditional upon the present tenant not validly exercising his option to purchase the property." Clearly, the seller is not promising that the tenant will not exercise the option; nor is he promising to use best efforts to dissuade him from exercising it. However, we might infer from the purpose of the condition that the seller makes an implied promise not to actively bribe or put pressure on the tenant to exercise the option.

Of course, while it may be appropriate in most contracts to imply a promise not to impede fulfillment of a condition, this is not true in all contracts. It may be clear from the language or circumstances of a contract that the parties did not intend such a promise to be made. For example, a contract for the sale of a business recites that the seller would prefer that his daughter take over the business and makes the sale conditional on the daughter declining to do so. We can reasonably infer here that the parties contemplate that the owner has the right to try to prevent the fulfillment of the condition by persuading his daughter to take over the business.

Where a promisor prevents fulfillment of a condition in breach of the duty not to hinder or impede its occurrence, the proper response is to excuse the condition, making the promise unconditional. If the promisor then fails to perform, he is in breach of the contract.

SULLIVAN v. BULLOCK

124 Idaho 738, 864 P.2d 184 (1993)
Idaho Court of Appeals

WALTERS, Chief Judge.

The issue at trial in this action was whether it was the homeowner or the contractor who breached a written contract to remodel several rooms in a home. The jury returned a special verdict finding that although the contractor had not substantially performed under the contract, he had been prevented from doing so by the homeowner. The jury awarded . . . damages to the contractor . . . [for breach of contract.] The homeowner filed a motion for judgment n.o.v. or for a new trial, which was denied. The homeowner appeals the judgment and denial of her motion. She contends that the jury's verdict is contrary to the law and the evidence presented. . . . We affirm the denial of the motions in so far as the decision below holds that the homeowner prevented the contractor's complete performance. However, we reverse and remand the decision to the extent it approved an erroneous measure of damages in favor of the contractor. . . .

The evidence presented at trial established that in April 1991, Cora Sullivan hired Dallas Bullock, doing business as New Home Development, to remodel her kitchen, hallway, utility room, bathroom and sewing room, for a total price of $6,780. The written contract set out the major aspects of the project but lacked detail. No design sketches were agreed to by the parties. Less than detailed communications between Mrs. Sullivan and Mr. Bullock resulted in misunderstandings regarding exactly what the final product would look like. Eventually the contract was breached in several respects. The work was not begun or completed by the dates set out in the contract. Mrs. Sullivan, however, assented to the delays. Evidence was presented that the work performed by Mr. Bullock and the subcontractors he hired was sometimes below the industry standard for the area, not as Mrs. Sullivan had requested, and was not performed to her satisfaction. . . . However, evidence was presented that during the time the work was being performed, Mrs. Sullivan did not clearly convey to Mr. Bullock her dissatisfaction and he continued with the perception that the project was progressing with approval. . . .

For a period while construction was progressing, Mrs. Sullivan did not live at the home. Eventually, however, she moved in while the remodeling continued. At one time, Mrs. Sullivan told Mr. Bullock that she would not be at home on a certain day and, feeling protective of her personal belongings, she did not want the workmen there while she was gone. Unfortunately and unbeknownst to Mr. Bullock, one of the workmen entered the home through a window to complete some work while Mrs. Sullivan was gone. This so upset Mrs. Sullivan that she angrily confronted Mr. Bullock and told him that neither he nor his workmen were to ever set foot in her house again. Further requests by Mr. Bullock and others to enter the home and continue the project were refused by Mrs. Sullivan. On July 1, 1991, Mr. Bullock submitted a "final" bill to Mrs. Sullivan for $2,956.40, purportedly for work completed, but also representing the contract balance for the completed project.

In October 1991, Mrs. Sullivan filed a complaint in the district court, asserting that Mr. Bullock's workmanship was grossly defective and that he had been unresponsive to requests to improve his product. The complaint sought damages . . . [based on the cost of completely redoing the work, plus the return of what Mrs. Sullivan had already paid Mr. Bullock]. Mr. Bullock answered Mrs. Sullivan's complaint and filed a counterclaim. He alleged that his work was satisfactory that any unsatisfactory work could be fixed, but that Mrs. Sullivan had prohibited him from finishing the project or fixing defects.

He stated that Mrs. Sullivan had paid $5,906 and he requested $2,956.40 in damages for the work he had performed. He also asserted a claim against Mrs. Sullivan, seeking damages for slander.

The trial addressed the breach of contract claim. The counterclaim alleging slander was voluntarily dismissed. The jury returned a special verdict finding that Mr. Bullock had not substantially performed under the contract, but that he had been prevented or substantially hindered from performing by Mrs. Sullivan. The jury awarded him $2,956.40. . . . Mrs. Sullivan moved for judgment n.o.v. or new trial. Her motion was denied. She appeals the judgment and the denial of her motion. . . .

First, we examine the jury's finding that Mrs. Sullivan prevented or hindered Mr. Bullock's performance. Implied in every contract is a condition to cooperate. "In any case where the plaintiff's performance requires the cooperation of the defendant, . . . the defendant, by necessary implication, promises to give this cooperation and if he fails to do so, he is immediately liable although his only express promise is to pay money at a future day. Indeed, there is generally in a contract subject to either an express or an implied condition an implied promise not to prevent or hinder performance of the condition. Such prevention, if the condition could otherwise have been performed, is, therefore, an immediate breach of contract, and if of sufficiently serious character, damages for the loss of the entire contract may be recovered." 11 Williston, *Contracts* §1316 (3rd ed. 1968). In construction contracts, the duty to cooperate encompasses allowing access to the premises to enable the contractor to perform the work. . . .

To excuse a party's nonperformance, however, the conduct of the party preventing performance must be "wrongful" and "in excess of their legal rights." 17A C.J.S. *Contracts* §468. Other authorities have stated that the conduct of the party preventing performance must be outside what was permitted in the contract and "unjustified," or outside the reasonable contemplation of the parties when the contract was executed. . . .

Here, the trial court's instructions to the jury properly reflected . . . the law. . . . The jury returned a verdict stating that Mr. Bullock had not substantially performed but that Mrs. Sullivan had unreasonably prevented his performance. There was substantial evidence from which the jury could conclude that Mr. Bullock's failure was to be excused by Mrs. Sullivan's act of denying access to her home. True, an employee did enter Mrs. Sullivan's home when he was not supposed to. However, when Mrs. Sullivan denied any further access to her home [based purely on the employee's improper entry, and not on Mr. Bullock's failure to perform the work properly,] she acted in a manner that was outside the contemplation of the contract. . . . [T]he evidence supports the verdict. . . .

3. Unfair Forfeiture

In Section A.6 we discuss the general principle that courts generally enforce an express condition strictly and require exact compliance with its terms. We explain that the reason for this approach is that where parties have spelled out a condition expressly, courts do not consider it appropriate to interfere with the parties' expressed intent by finding that something short of exact compliance constitutes satisfaction of the condition. Although courts are reluctant to disregard the clear and express terms of a contract, they also do not like to aid a party who tries to use a technicality to evade its obligations. We have seen that courts can sometimes accommodate both these concerns by interpreting the language of the contract to avoid an unfair result, or by using doctrines such as waiver or estoppel. However, where neither the language of the contract nor the facts permit such a resolution, the use of equitable discretion may be the only way to avoid an unfair result by excusing technical noncompliance with a condition. There are occasionally situations in which a court may exercise its equity power to excuse the condition or exact compliance with the condition, but the courts use this equitable power sparingly. As the next case shows, it can be difficult to balance the need to prevent unfair forfeiture against the need to enforce the clear terms of the contract.

UNITED PROPERTIES LIMITED v. WALGREEN PROPERTIES, INC.

134 N.M. 725, 82 P.3d 535 (2003)
New Mexico Court of Appeals

PICKARD, Judge.

In this case, we are presented with an issue related to commercial leases: will a late notice to the landlord of intent to renew the lease for another term be given effect when the lateness of the notice is due to the tenant's own negligence? We hold that the late notice was ineffective in the circumstances of this case. Consequently, we reverse.

This case concerns commercial property ... [owned by Walgreens (Landlord) and leased to United Properties Limited (Tenant)]. [T]he rental payments on the lease were $44,640 per year, the term of the lease was due to expire on December 31, 1999, and there were three additional five-year terms remaining. Tenant spent over $1.272 million on capital improvements to the property. These capital improvements included remodeling to adapt the property to Tenant's use, landscaping, and bringing the existing facilities up to code, as well as enhancing the existing buildings with additional fixtures. Ultimately, Tenant subleased various portions of the property to ... [other businesses which collectively pay a total annual rent of $263,500 to Tenant. If Tenant wished to renew the lease for an additional five-year term, it was required to give written notice of its intent to extend by September 30, 1999. Tenant simply forgot to give the notice.] On November 8, 1999, Landlord notified Tenant that the date for giving written notice of intent to renew had passed. ... [The next day, Tenant attempted to exercise the option to renew by sending written notice to Landlord, but Landlord refused to renew the lease on the grounds that the notice was late.]

On December 2, 1999, while the lease was still in effect, Tenant filed an action for injunctive and declaratory relief, acknowledging that it failed to send a timely notice and asking that the district court exercise its equitable powers to order Landlord . . . to extend the lease for another five-year term. . . . [B]oth sides filed motions for summary judgment. Tenant argued that strictly enforcing the three-month notice requirement of the lease would be inequitable and result in a forfeiture. Landlord . . . argued that under New Mexico law the district court was required to strictly enforce the terms of the option to renew the lease. . . . [The district court granted the relief requested by Tenant, and Landlord appealed.]

The precise issues raised by this case have been the subject of numerous appellate decisions from across the country. At one end of the spectrum are cases that hold that "[e]quity will not relieve a lessee of the consequences of his failure to give written notice of renewal of the lease within the time required by the provisions of the lease when the failure resulted from the negligence of the lessee unaccompanied by fraud, mistake, accident or surprise and unaffected by the conduct of the lessor." *Ahmed v. Scott*, 65 Ohio App. 2d 271, 418 N.E.2d 406, 411 (1979). At the other end of the spectrum are cases that hold that "in cases of mere neglect in fulfilling a condition precedent of a lease, [even if the cases] do not fall within accident or mistake, equity will relieve when the delay has been slight, the loss to the lessor small, and when not to grant relief would result in such hardship to the tenant as to make it unconscionable to enforce literally the condition precedent of the lease." *F.B. Fountain Co. v. Stein*, 97 Conn. 619, 118 A. 47, 50 (1922).

At oral argument, both parties characterized the differences in the cases as reflecting a true split of authority. Although some cases have held that one view or another is the "majority" rule or the "modern" rule, we believe that such characterizations are not particularly helpful. For example, the court in *Trollen v. City of Wabasha*, 287 N.W.2d 645, 647 (Minn. 1979) characterized the *Fountain* rule as the "modern" rule. Yet, the latest two jurisdictions to weigh in on this issue after canvassing the authorities on both sides have squarely sided with the traditional rule favoring definiteness of contracts. Thus, instead of characterizing the cases, we perceive that our task in this case is to decide which view best reflects the law and its policy underpinnings in New Mexico. For the reasons that follow, we conclude that the view that favors the definiteness of contracts is the view most consistent with New Mexico law. . . . [The court recites the basic principle that where parties freely enter a contract, they are bound and the court must enforce what they have agreed. There is a strong public interest in protecting the parties' contractual expectations.] Thus, we decide this case against a long-standing backdrop of New Mexico law enforcing contractual obligations as they are written. . . . [T]here is nothing to construe in this case. . . . [T]he lease agreement here was clear as can be, and there is no contention that it is ambiguous. . . . We similarly note that there is no contention that the terms of the lease themselves were unconscionable.

Landlord argues that New Mexico law holds that an option must be exercised strictly according to its terms and that the failure to exercise an option does not result in a forfeiture. Indeed, this Court and our Supreme Court have held that when the parties enter into an option contract for the purchase of land, the option must be exercised according to the terms of the contract. . . . [T]he person holding the option to purchase has no legal rights in the land unless and until the option is exercised according to its terms. Thus, by definition, the failure to exercise an option does not result in a forfeiture. We recognize that this case could be viewed differently . . . [because Tenant has spent about $1.2 million to adapt the property to its purposes and Landlord gave Tenant the right to renew the arrangement for several successive periods.] Nonetheless, the fact remains that the option was required to be exercised in a certain way according to the lease agreement signed by the parties. Other cases in the lease-renewal situation have held that there is no forfeiture calling for equitable intervention in circumstances where a lessee has simply neglected to give timely notice, even when there is a large difference between the rent the lessee pays and the rent that could be demanded or when the lessee has expended considerable sums of money on improvements.

The way the option was required to be exercised in this case was by "send[ing] notice thereof to Landlord at least three months prior to the expiration" of the then term of the lease. When option or other contracts contain specific time limitations, time is of the essence. Further, the exercise of an option in the manner spelled out in the contract is a condition precedent to enforcing the option. . . .

Tenant relies most heavily on *Car-X Serv. Sys., Inc. v. Kidd-Heller*, 927 F.2d 511, 514-17 (10th Cir. 1991), and *J.N.A. Realty Corp. v. Cross Bay Chelsea, Inc.*, 42 N.Y.2d 392, 397 N.Y.S.2d 958, 366 N.E.2d 1313, 1317 (1977), both of which relied on the value of improvements made by the tenant and a balancing of the harms visited upon either the landlord or the tenant. Landlord, in turn, relies on the dissent in *J.N.A. Realty Corp.*, 397 N.Y.S.2d 958, 366 N.E.2d at 1321-22. Landlord expresses concern for the "instability and uncertainty" that it contends would ensue if we adopted the rule allowing equity to intervene. Landlord suggests that the rule adopted by the district court would, in the words of Chief Judge Breitel, "allow for *ad hoc* dispensations in particular cases without [the] reliable rule so essential to commercial enterprise." *Id.* at 1321 (Breitel, C.J., dissenting). Landlord also points to another concern expressed in the dissent: allowing relief in these circumstances would allow a tenant, "under the guise of sheer inadvertence, [to] gamble with a fluctuating market, at the expense of his landlord, by delaying his decision beyond the time fixed in the agreement." *Id.* We are most persuaded by the concern of instability and uncertainty. We think that the concern about gambling with the market could easily be remedied by adoption of a rule that excluded such intentional acts from its scope. We do not perceive that adoption of the rule relied on by the district court is certain enough to provide the necessary stability and predictability for commercial transactions. A few examples will demonstrate. The *Fountain* rule contains three basic elements: (1) that the delay in giving notice be slight, (2) that the loss to the landlord be small, and (3) that the loss to the tenant be so large that it would be unconscionable to enforce the notice provision. . . . [The court concludes that these elements are too uncertain. Courts that have applied them have had very different ideas of how long a delay should qualify as "slight," and in deciding the severity of the respective losses of the landlord and tenant.] Moreover, we believe that adoption of the *Fountain* rule would allow courts to change the basic nature of the parties' agreements, contrary to what they have bargained for at arm's length. . . . We consider the practical effect of Tenant's argument in circumstances like those provided for in the lease in this case. Toward the end of the current lease term, a landlord will wonder whether a tenant will renew. The three-month notice provision is designed to allow the landlord sufficient time to seek other tenants. . . . We will not use equitable principles to save a party from the circumstances it created. . . . [U]nder the circumstances of this case in which the notice was quite late when measured against the notice period provided in the lease and when the reason for the late notice is simple neglect, a court may not relieve a party of the bargain it made and must enforce the lease as it was written. Accordingly, the trial court erred in awarding summary judgment to Tenant. The judgment of the district court is reversed.

CASTILLO, Judge (dissenting).

While I agree with the majority that our task in this case is to decide which line of cases best reflect the law and policy of New Mexico, I respectfully dissent. I believe that equity should be allowed to intervene because this case involves a possible forfeiture. The majority opinion decides as a matter of law that equity cannot be considered in cases where a tenant forgets to timely send a notice of lease renewal. This holding is based on three points: (1) courts may not rewrite obligations that the parties bargain for themselves; (2) in the absence of well-defined equitable exceptions, equity should not intervene; and (3) instability and uncertainty would ensue if we adopted the *Fountain* rule. There is New Mexico law to support these general propositions, but not in cases such as this where forfeiture is a possible result. New Mexico law is clear: equity abhors forfeiture. As early as 1922 our Supreme Court, in recognizing the harshness of forfeiture, held that equity could intervene to relieve a tenant of commercial property from "forfeiting" the lease simply because the tenant was late in paying one month's rent. . . .

   The Restatement uses the term forfeiture to mean the denial of compensation to an obligee because of the non-occurrence of a condition after the obligee has relied substantially on the expectation of the bargained-for exchange, either by preparation or performance. [Restatement (Second) of Contracts §227 cmt. b

(1981)]. "When it is said that courts do not favor forfeitures, the meaning is that they do not like to see a party to a contract getting something for nothing." 3A Arthur Linton Corbin, *Corbin on Contracts* §748, at 465 (1960). ... [T]his case deals with a notice to renew a long term lease on premises developed at substantial cost to Tenant. In this case, Landlord will receive a fully developed piece of property having paid little or nothing for the development. While we recognize that Tenant has received rents in excess of what is paid to Landlord, the difference is used to recoup the investment. If the lease is terminated now, Landlord is entitled to that rental income, or it may re-let the premises at a higher rate, all without having any substantial investment in the development of the property. This is "getting something for nothing," and is exactly the type of situation that requires at least the consideration of equity. ...

I disagree that application of the factors in *Fountain* or its progeny will introduce excessive instability or insecurity into commercial transactions. This type of arrangement or series of transactions has become increasingly common as a method of developing commercial property. The holding in *Fountain* is more consistent with commercial realities and will provide increased stability for those who wish to develop commercial property, with no unexpected losses to the owners of the land on which the development takes place. Normally, when leased premises have been developed and are sub-let, landlords expect the lease to be renewed. In those cases, the failure to tender a timely notice is unexpected and in some cases a surprise. It may also result in a windfall for the landlord. ... It is clear from the record that the district court did in fact consider all the equities as set out in *Fountain* before granting relief and that the equities were heavily in favor of Tenant in this case. First, it was undisputed that Tenant did not intentionally fail to give timely notice. Second, while the notice of a desire to extend the lease was not given in a timely fashion, it was still given, and indeed suit was filed, before that term of the lease expired. ... Third, the district court considered the substantial hardship to Tenant which in this case is tantamount to forfeiture. ... Fourth, the district court considered the extent to which Landlord's interests would be prejudiced by granting the requested relief. In the district court, it was undisputed that Landlord had not changed its position in reliance on the failure to give timely notice. Indeed, the only prejudice to its interests that Landlord could point to was the fact that it would continue to receive rent at a rate set in the 1960s and substantially below what the market would bear today. This, however, is the result of the rental rate and the number of extensions allowed under the lease and has nothing to do with the timeliness or untimeliness of the notice of intent to renew for an additional term. Lastly, the district court also considered the interests of possible third parties. It was undisputed below that Landlord had not looked for or found a new tenant, nor had Landlord listed the property for sale, so its interests did not implicate those of any third parties or owner whose interests had to be considered. On the other hand, it was equally undisputed that the interests of the Subtenants would also have been significantly harmed if relief was not granted. In short, this was a case in which the equities favored giving relief.

In summary, I believe New Mexico law should allow the exercise of equitable powers and require a Landlord to treat as timely an untimely notice of intent to extend a long term lease for another term of years if, as is true here, the delay in giving notice is not willful or deliberate, the length of the delay is relatively short, the notice of intent to extend is given before the term of the lease expires, and the hardship to the tenant in denying relief clearly outweighs any hardship that will be incurred by the landlord if relief is granted. For the above reasons, I respectfully dissent.

CHAPTER 19

Material Breach, Substantial Performance, and Anticipatory Repudiation

 ## A THE DISTINCTION BETWEEN MATERIAL AND NONMATERIAL BREACH

1. Material Breach

As Chapter 18 shows, if a condition is not fulfilled (and there are no grounds for excusing it), the performance contingent on it need not be rendered. We have also seen that if a promise is broken, the promisee has a claim for breach. If the term is a promissory condition—both a promise and a condition—then its non-fulfillment results in both of these consequences: The breach of the promissory condition entitles the other party both to decline her performance and to claim breach. The combination of these consequences is very common because most promises exchanged by the parties are interpreted or construed as dependent, even if not expressly stated to be conditions of each other. Therefore, the breach by one party of his promise to perform before or concurrently with the performance of the other will, in most cases, be not only a breach of promise, but also the nonoccurrence of a condition.

For example, Matt Arial entered into a contract with Perfect Paving & Patio Co. for the construction of a tile patio at the entrance to his house. The contract provided that Perfect would prepare the surface and build a 15- by 20-foot patio, using "Prairie Gold" quarry tile selected by Matt. The price of the job (materials and labor) was $10,000. The contract specified that Perfect would begin work on April 1 and would complete it by not later than April 20. Payment in full was due on April 25. Even if the contract uses no express language of condition, the specified sequence of performance leads to the inference that Matt's obligation to pay is conditional on Perfect's completion of the patio. If, on April 1, Perfect reneges on the contract and refuses to show up and do the work, this is both a breach of its promise and nonfulfillment of the condition precedent to Matt's promise to pay. Matt may terminate the contract and find another contractor to build the patio. If that contractor charges more than $10,000 for the patio, Matt may recover the difference from Perfect as expectation damages.

Where a breach is so serious that it allows the other party to decline his performance, terminate the contract, and sue for full expectation damages, it is called a material and total breach. Where the breach is not of this gravity, it is called a partial breach, and the performance of the breaching party, even though it falls short of what is required by the contract, is called substantial performance.

2. Substantial Performance

To illustrate the difference between material breach and substantial performance, change the facts of the example as follows: Perfect does build the patio within the time specified in the contract but uses the wrong color tile—it installs "Desert Dusk" tile instead of "Prairie Gold." The workmanship is excellent and the quality of the tile is the same as that ordered. The two colors are almost indistinguishable—the tile installed is a bit lighter and has a slightly redder tone than the one ordered. Perfect refuses to fix the problem. This is undoubtedly a breach of contract because the tile used is not what was called for in the contract. It is not clear, however, if this is a material breach. We need more information to decide whether the color specification is an important enough term of the contract to make the deviation from the contract a material breach.

The stakes in deciding whether this is a material breach can be high. If the breach is material, Matt would be entitled to reject Perfect's performance, refuse payment, and terminate the contract. He would then be entitled to claim the cost of hiring another contractor to remove the patio tile and to lay the correct tile. Not only would Perfect earn nothing for its work, but it would also be liable to Matt for the difference between the contract price of $10,000 and the extra cost that Matt would have to pay the second contractor to demolish and rebuild the patio. However, if the breach is not material, Matt cannot terminate the contract and refuse to pay anything to Perfect. As we learn from *Jacob & Youngs, Inc. v. Kent* in Chapter 18, Section C, where the breaching party has substantially performed, it is entitled to payment of the contract price, which is offset against the damages suffered by the other party as a result of the nonmaterial breach. These damages are normally the cost of rectifying the deficiency in performance. However, if that cost is excessive and disproportionate, the owner could be confined to a lesser amount of damages, such as the reduction in the market value of the performance.[1] (We explore the issue of proper relief for substantial performance in Section B.)

In *Jacob & Youngs*, Judge Cardozo did not explain why he found the builder's breach to be trivial. Judge McLauglin, in dissent, disagreed that the breach was minor. It is important to remember, despite Judge Cardozo's seemingly facile conclusion on this issue, that materiality is a factual question, not simply a matter of assumption. Restatement, Second §241 offers some guidance on the factors to be considered in deciding whether a breach is material:

RESTATEMENT, SECOND §241. CIRCUMSTANCES SIGNIFICANT IN DETERMINING WHETHER A FAILURE IS MATERIAL

In determining whether a failure to render or to offer performance is material, the following circumstances are significant:

(a) the extent to which the injured party will be deprived of the benefit which he reasonably expected;

(b) the extent to which the injured party can be adequately compensated for the part of that benefit of which he will be deprived;

(c) the extent to which the party failing to perform or to offer to perform will suffer forfeiture;

(d) the likelihood that the party failing to perform or to offer to perform will cure his failure, taking account of all the circumstances including any reasonable assurances;

(e) the extent to which the behavior of the party failing to perform or to offer to perform comports with standards of good faith and fair dealing.

■ PROBLEM 19.1

In the example above, involving the laying of the incorrect tile, we said that we would need more information to know whether Perfect's use of the wrong tile was a material breach. Considering the factors listed in Restatement, Second §241, list the information you would need to decide if the breach was material.

---

[1] In Chapter 18, we study *Jacob & Youngs* in relation to constructive conditions of exchange, but the case is essentially about substantial performance. Recall that Judge Cardozo found the specification of Reading pipe to be an independent promise because he considered the builder's breach in failing to use Reading pipe to be both trivial and inadvertent. In *Jacob & Youngs* the owner was not claiming damages but sought only to avoid paying the balance due to the builder.

■ PROBLEM 19.2

As in the above example, Matt Arial entered into a contract with Perfect Paving & Patio Co. for the construction of a 15- by 20-foot "Prairie Gold" tile patio at the entrance to his house. The price of the job (materials and labor) was $10,000 and the contract specified that Perfect would begin work on April 1 and would complete it by not later than April 20. Payment in full was due on April 25. Taking into account the factors listed in Restatement, Second §241, consider whether there has been material breach or substantial performance in the following situations. If you do not have enough information to answer the questions, consider what additional facts you would need to resolve them.

(a) On the morning of April 1, Perfect called Matt and told him that it would not be able to begin work on that day because it had fallen behind schedule. Perfect assured Matt that it would begin work on April 3 and should still complete it by April 20. Assuming that Perfect will in fact begin work on April 3, is this delay a material breach?

(b) Perfect began work on April 1. However, it did not complete the work by April 20. At that date Perfect had laid most of the tile, but still had to finish the tiling and the grouting. The remaining work would take another week. Matt is obsessive about punctuality and has trouble dealing with delay. He confronted Perfect's foreman about its failure to complete the patio on time and a heated exchange followed, which resulted in Matt firing Perfect and ordering its workers off his property. Did Perfect commit a material breach? Did Matt?

3. Total and Partial Breach and the Concept of Cure

We have distinguished material and total breach from partial breach and substantial performance. However, there is another aspect of this distinction. A breach may be material, so that if it persists, the deficient performance will not qualify as substantial. However, it still may not be total in that it can be cured. Stated differently, sometimes a party can avoid committing a total and material breach by rectifying even a serious defect in performance before the problem gets to the point of becoming a total breach. For example, say that Perfect began the patio on time and completed it by April 15. However, it incorrectly installed "Desert Dusk" tile instead of "Prairie Gold." Assume that the tile selection was a material term of the contract so that installation of the wrong tile was a material breach. Matt would be entitled to reject Perfect's performance and to refuse payment. However, although the breach is material, it is not yet a total breach because Perfect has until April 20 to complete the job. If it concedes the breach, it may be willing to remedy it by removing the "Desert Dusk" tile and replacing it with "Prairie Gold." If Perfect offers to cure the breach, Matt may be required to give it the opportunity to do so. This means that he cannot terminate the contract for total breach on April 15 but must wait to see whether Perfect eliminates the material breach by cure within the proper time.

The proper time for cure depends on the terms of the contract. If the completion date for the patio is a material term of the contract, Perfect must complete cure by April 20. If it fails to do that, the delay in completion will itself be a material breach. However, if the completion date is not material, Perfect may have a reasonable period beyond April 20 to cure; that is, by redoing the patio, Perfect eliminates the material breach of using the wrong tile, and if its delay in completing performance is nonmaterial, it has turned its material breach into substantial performance.

RAYMOND WEIL, S.A. v. THERON

585 F. Supp. 2d 473 (2008)
United States District Court, Southern District of New York

McMAHON, District Judge.

Plaintiff Raymond Weil, S.A. filed this suit against defendants Charlize Theron and Denver & Delilah Films, Inc. seeking damages for alleged breaches of an endorsement contract and for fraud. Before this Court are the parties' cross motions for summary judgment. Raymond Weil moves for judgment in its favor on its claim for breach of contract. Theron and Denver & Delilah Films move for summary judgment dismissing all the claims asserted against them. . . .

Raymond Weil ("RW") is a Swiss corporation, with its general place of business in Geneva, Switzerland. It manufactures and sells high-end luxury watches in countries around the globe. Charlize Theron ("Theron") is an Oscar-winning actress and entertainer. Denver and Delilah Films ("DDF") is a California corporation owned and operated by Theron. It acts as both a film production company and a so-called "loan-out" corporation. A loan-out corporation enters into agreements whereby Theron (the "Artist") renders services of various kinds to third-parties (*i.e.* is "loaned out" to them).

On or about May 17, 2005, Raymond Weil entered into an agreement (the "Agreement") with DDF, whereby RW agreed to pay to DDF three million dollars in exchange for the use of Theron's image in a world-wide print media advertising campaign for Raymond Weil's "Shine" watch collection. For our purposes, the relevant provisions of the Agreement are as follows:

Paragraph 8. Exclusivity
As of the signing of this Agreement, Artist [Theron] commits not to wear publicly any other watches other than RW watches during the Term. Additionally, Artist

hereby agrees that during the Term she shall not endorse or advertise watches or jewelry for any other person, entity or company. . . .

Notwithstanding the foregoing, RW acknowledges and agrees that Artist is permitted to wear jewelry of her choice in public and to awards shows during the Term.

Additionally, Artist may be asked to wear non-RW watches as part of her performance in a feature film and/or television show and that such action by Artist shall not be deemed a breach by Artist, provided however, no merchandising or commercial tie-in campaign shall be allowed in connection with non-RW watches utilizing her name, voice and/or likeness in connection with such film or television show that is released and/or broadcast during the Term.

This contract does not prevent RW for [sic] using other artists or celebrities to endorse its products. However, RW agrees that Artist shall be the sole female artist to endorse RW during the Term in Europe and the United States.

In the event of a breach of the Agreement by either party, the Agreement provides that:

No party shall have the right to terminate this Agreement or sue for breach of this Agreement until it gives written notice of the alleged breach to the other party and a period of five (5) business days . . . to cure the breach and such period elapses without such cure, unless the breach is of such a nature that it cannot be cured. In that case, termination or suit may proceed immediately.

The term of Agreement ran from . . . [October 2005 through December 31, 2006.] RW sued Theron and DDF (collectively, "Defendants") on February 5, 2007, well after the Agreement had expired by its terms. It alleged that Theron had breached the agreement on several occasions during its term. . . . RW sought to recover all sums previously paid to Theron under the Agreement, as well as all monies expended by RW for the Shine watch advertising campaign, all monies paid to Defendants by competing manufacturers to promote their products, and such other damages as may appropriately be awarded in a case of this nature. Defendants filed an answer denying the allegations in the complaint. . . .

[RW alleges several breaches of the agreement. Two are pertinent here, and the others are omitted. One of the breaches involves the use of Theron's image by Montblanc to advertise its jewelry, and the other involves Theron's wearing of a Dior watch to a press conference at a film festival.]

Montblanc sells luxury goods, primarily writing instruments, but also watches, leather goods and, more recently, women's jewelry. In the fall of 2006, Montblanc launched a line of silver jewelry. . . . [Theron agreed to be photographed wearing Montblanc jewelry. Montblanc created a 14 foot poster with an image of Theron with a Montblanc necklace draped over her forearm, and used the poster at the 2006 Salon International de La Haute Horlogerie (SIHH), a prestigious watch and jewelry trade show and exhibition. The poster was displayed in Montblanc's booth at the show from about April 3 to 5, 2006.]

According to Montblanc, the image was only displayed inside the booth, such that it was not visible to visitors passing by and was exposed only in one key entrance area. Nonetheless, the poster was up and people at the SIHH undoubtedly saw it. After the poster had been on display for about two or three days, RW notified DDF that defendants were in breach of paragraph 8 of the Agreement. DDF immediately mobilized its lawyers, who persuaded Montblanc to take the poster down. The poster was removed sometime between fourteen and thirty-six hours later—within the five day cure period provided for in the Agreement. As far as the court knows, RW made no effort to terminate the Agreement once the poster was removed.

On March 14, 2006, Theron attended a screening of East of Havana, a documentary film Ms. Theron produced through DDF, at the South by Southwest Film Festival ("SXSW"), an annual, regional film festival held in Austin, Texas. Theron, together with the producers of other films featured at the festival, participated in a panel discussion before an audience that included members of the public and professional photographers. Theron wore a Christian Dior ("Dior") watch to the press conference—a decision she now calls "regrettable."

Theron is one of the world's most beautiful women—she has even been named "The Sexiest Woman Alive" by Esquire Magazine—and many photographs were taken of her during the press conference. Some of those photographs showed Theron wearing the Dior watch, and some of those photos were posted to a website called "Wireimage"—essentially a clearing house for professional photographers. When someone sees an image on Wireimage that he wants to use, he downloads it and pays a fee, which is split between the photographer and the proprietors of Wireimage. Once a photographer has uploaded an image to Wireimage, she does not control, or necessarily even know, who will subsequently use the image or how. The celebrity depicted apparently knows even less.

One of several third parties to download the image of Theron wearing the Dior watch was LVMH Watch and Jewelry USA, another maker of luxury goods and the owner of Dior watches. LVMH submitted the image to Tourneau LLC "Tourneau," a prominent retailer and manufacturer of high end watches. Tourneau is among the leading retailers of almost every brand of watch it carries based upon annual volume. Tourneau carries both RW and Dior watches in its inventory. Tourneau publishes an in-store annual called the *Tourneau Times*, which is mailed to about one hundred thousand, high-spending Tourneau customers and is made available free of charge in Tourneau retail locations. The October 2006 *Tourneau Times* ran a photograph taken at the SXSW Festival depicting Theron wearing the Christian Dior watch on her wrist. The photograph of Theron in the Dior watch appeared on page fifteen of the publication in the "Star Watch" section, over a caption that reads, "Charlize Theron wears Dior." RW became aware of the image of Theron in the *Tourneau Times* in November of 2006. . . .

The display of the poster of Theron holding the Montblanc necklace at the SIHH, a prestigious watch and jewelry trade show, constituted a breach of the Agreement between RW, Theron and DDF. While the parties dispute exactly what Theron knew about the final image used in the poster, it is clear from the record that Theron loaned her image to a purpose that was forbidden under the Agreement—to promote and advertise Montblanc silver jewelry. . . . However, the Agreement permitted a breaching party to cure within five days and the breach—the public display of the poster with Theron's image and the necklace at an event promoting Montblanc products—was, in fact, remediated within five days after RW notified DDF of the breach. Therefore, RW's claim for breach of contract on this score must be dismissed. . . . The point of drafting a contract with a cure period provision is to allow the parties, in the event of breach, to correct their course and maintain the promises in their contract. "The concept of cure is grounded in the belief that protecting expectations while avoiding waste is, or should be, a primary goal of contract damages. The basis for the cure concept stems from the notion that our remedial system encourages parties to enter contracts by giving damages based on the benefit of the bargain for disappointed expectations, than rather than trying to deter contract breaches through compulsion or punishment." William H. Lawrence, *Cure after Breach of Contract Under the Restatement (Second) of Contracts: An Analytical Comparison with the Commercial Code*, 70 Minn. L. Rev. 713, 727 (1986).

RW argues that the cure provision is irrelevant, because the breach was of the incurable variety. It notes that the people who saw the poster while it was hanging cannot "un-see it." RW misidentifies the breach. It is not the act of viewing the poster by third parties that constitutes the breach—third parties are not bound by the Agreement and so cannot breach it. It is, rather, Theron's participation in Montblanc's advertising campaign . . . that breaches the contract. That breach is perfectly curable, as demonstrated by the fact that the breach was cured: the poster was taken down. This satisfied RW at the time; Bernheim, the company's CEO, testified at his deposition that he considered the removal of the Montblanc poster to be an adequate cure of the breach. In view of Bernheim's admission, it is difficult to see why RW persists in arguing that Theron's breach is actionable. It is not.

Defendants' cross motion for summary judgment dismissing the breach of contract claim insofar as it is predicated on the Montblanc incident is granted. RW's motion for summary judgment on this issue is denied.

By wearing a Christian Dior watch at a film festival, Theron breached her covenant not to "wear publicly any other watches other than RW." Theron recognizes as much, calling her decision to wear the watch "regrettable." It was more than "regrettable;" it was a clear breach of the Agreement. Defendants' contention that Theron only wore the Dior watch for "about one hour of the fifteen month contract term" is an obvious effort to render the breach immaterial. But clearly it was not: Theron was photographed wearing the watch; the photographs ended up on the Internet, where they were sold to a competitor of RW, which made sure that they were used to promote its products. Since the essence of the contract is Theron's agreeing to represent RW exclusively during the term of the Agreement, a breach, however fleeting, that resulted in the use of Theron's image in connection with another manufacturer's watch cannot be deemed immaterial.

Theron cannot hide behind the fact that she had no control over what the photographers did with the pictures they took at the panel discussion, or of the use that customers of the web site made of photographs they purchased. Her breach was wearing the watch. Subsequent uses over which she had no control are relevant, not to the issue of breach, but to the issue of damages. Moreover, it was foreseeable to Theron—a famous movie star—that photographs of her would be made available for purchase and that they might appear in publications. Her lack of involvement in what happened with the pictures does not mean she is not culpable for any damage they caused to RW.

Therefore, RW's motion for partial summary judgment on the issue of liability for breach is granted to the extent of the claim arising out of the Dior watch incident and its subsequent use, and Defendants' motion for summary judgment on that claim on the issue of actual breach is denied. . . .

■ QUESTIONS

(1)   The court finds that Theron breached the contract by participating in the Montblanc promotion but that the breach was cured. The court does not say whether this was a material breach. Based on the information set out in the opinion and the guidelines articulated in Restatement, Second §241, do you think the breach was material? Why?

(2)   The court finds that the breach was cured even though the consequences of the breach (the fact that the poster had been seen) cannot be undone. Do you agree with the court that it is possible to cure a breach by ceasing the action that constitutes the breach, even though that action has already caused harm? If so, does the plaintiff have any recourse for that harm?

(3)   The contract contained a cure provision. Would the court have treated the Montblanc breach in the same way if the contract made no provision for cure?

(4)   In relation to the Dior breach, the court says, "a breach, however fleeting, that resulted in the use of Theron's image in connection with another manufacturer's watch cannot be deemed immaterial." The court does not explain why. Do you agree with the court? Why or why not?

(5)   Theron took the Dior watch off after wearing it for about an hour. Why was that not a cure of her breach?

(6)   The court said that the subsequent use of the Dior pictures by third parties is relevant not to breach but to damages. What does this mean? What damages do you think RW might be able to establish?

(7)   Say that before she went to the supermarket one afternoon, Theron took her favorite Dior watch out of her jewelry box and put it on her arm. She

wore the watch while shopping for an hour at the supermarket. During this shopping excursion, she wore dark glasses and a baseball cap so that no one recognized her. There is no evidence that anyone at the supermarket noticed the watch either, except for an employee of Raymond Weil, who happened to be shopping at the same supermarket and immediately reported this sighting to the Raymond Weil legal department. Would Theron's conduct be a material breach of the contract?

■ PROBLEM 19.3

Ali Mentary owns a restaurant. The mechanism for extracting smoke from the kitchen broke, resulting in the discharge of smoke into the dining area. Ali had to close the restaurant until the extractor mechanism could be fixed. She called Fanny Fixit, an electrician, to repair the extractor, telling her that the job had to be done urgently so that she could reopen the restaurant that evening. Fanny came to the restaurant immediately. After inspecting the mechanism, she agreed to fix the extractor by 5 P.M. on that day for a price of $500. Fanny completed the repair by late afternoon, but she did not fix the mechanism properly. When she turned it on to test it, it emitted a shower of sparks and blew the electrical breakers. Ali was horrified. Fanny assured her that she could resolve the problem by returning the next morning to work further on the mechanism. However, Ali had lost faith in her. Ali fired Fanny and refused to pay her for the work. The next morning Ali brought in another electrician who fixed the mechanism in a couple of hours.

Fanny is upset. She says Ali should have given her a chance to complete the repair. Is she right?

 THE CONSEQUENCES OF SUBSTANTIAL PERFORMANCE

1. The Usual Measure of Relief for Substantial Performance

As noted previously, substantial performance is nevertheless a breach and gives rise to a claim of damages for the deficient performance. However, the relief available against a party who substantially performs can be very different from that against a party who commits a material and total breach. In both cases, because a breach has occurred the victim of the breach is entitled to damages to compensate for the loss caused by the breach—to be placed in the position she would have been in had the breach not occurred. Where the breach is failure to complete the contractual performance as promised, a common form of damages for both material breach and substantial performance is the cost of completing the performance so that it complies with the contract. The most important difference between total, material breach and substantial performance is that a total and material breach allows the victim of the breach to withhold her own performance and terminate the contract. The victim has no such right of termination if there has been substantial performance.

In Section A, we include an example involving Matt Arial and his tiling project. Consider this similar, but slightly more complex example. Suppose Ali Mentary, the restaurateur in Problem 19.3, entered into a contract with Jack Hammer under which Jack undertook to renovate the interior of her restaurant for $200,000. One of the items included in the renovation was laying new tile on the floor. The contract specifications called for the tile color to be "Prairie Gold." Ali was to pay the contract price on completion of the work. Jack began the job by laying the tiles. He erroneously installed "Desert Dusk" tiles instead of the "Prairie Gold" tiles called for by the contract.

As we have seen, if this is a material and total breach, Ali can terminate the contract, dismiss Jack, and hire another builder to complete the renovation. This means that Jack loses the job and any profit that he would have made from the work that he would have done. Jack will be liable for any damages caused by the breach, which will typically be measured as the difference between the contract price of $200,000 and what Ali has to pay the substitute contractor to complete the job. (This amount would include whatever it costs to remove and replace the wrong floor tiles, which will involve demolishing Jack's work and re-laying the correct tile, as well as any higher amount that the substitute contractor may charge for the rest of the work covered by the contract.) Jack cannot claim under the contract for the work and materials that he has supplied, because a party who materially breaches a contract loses the right to enforce it. (The material breach results in nonfulfillment of the condition precedent to the unperformed obligations of the other party.) As discussed further in Section B.3, under some circumstances Jack may have a restitutionary claim for the value of what he has furnished under principles of unjust enrichment—provided that Ali did in fact receive any actual value from the portion of the performance that Jack completed. Any restitutionary claim that Jack has would be set off against Ali's damages. If Jack's incorrect tilework can be fixed only by demolishing it and retiling the floor, Jack would have given no value to Ali, so he would have no restitutionary claim.

By contrast, say that the use of the wrong tile is found not to be a material breach but substantial performance. Ali would still be entitled to the benefit of her bargain, so she can still recover the cost of rectifying the incorrect tile work. However, she would not be entitled to terminate the contract and hire another contractor to complete the renovation. Jack would be entitled to complete the job and to earn the $200,000 contract price, less an offset of the cost of rectifying the defective tilework.

2. Relief for Substantial Performance Where the Cost to Rectify the Defective Performance Is Disproportionately High

Although damages for substantial performance are usually the cost of rectifying the deficiency in performance, it could sometimes happen that this cost is so high that a court balks at awarding it and looks for an alternative measure of relief. *Jacob & Youngs, Inc. v. Kent* is the classic illustration. Judge Cardozo articulated the principle that it is not appropriate to award the cost of rectifying the nonconformity in performance where the breach is neither material nor willful, and the cost of remedying the defect in performance is grossly out of proportion to the harm caused by the breach. In such a case, Judge Cardozo found it to be more appropriate to confine damages to the amount by which the defective work had reduced the market value of the product of the performance—the house. In that case, the breach apparently caused no reduction in market value. Although *Jacob & Youngs* establishes the principle that it may, in some circumstances, be fair to take into account the disproportionate cost of rectifying the defect, one should not assume that courts will invariably apply this rule. In some cases, cost of rectification is the proper remedy even if the defect has little or no impact on the market value of the product of the performance. That is, the presumption is that the plaintiff is entitled to the benefit of the bargain, so that the cost of remedying the defect is the usual measure of damages for substantial performance. However, in some cases, where this measure of damages would impose an unfair forfeiture on the defendant and effectively overcompensate the plaintiff, the court may look to diminution in market value as an alternative means of determining the plaintiff's loss. The next case explains this principle. It cites and discusses *Jacob & Youngs* but concludes that the cost of rectifying the breach is the proper measure of damages under the circumstances. What distinguishes this case from *Jacob & Youngs*?

LANDIS v. WILLIAM FANNIN BUILDERS, INC.

193 Ohio App. 3d 318, 951 N.E.2d 1078 (2011)
Ohio Court of Appeals

KLATT, Judge.

Defendant-appellant, William Fannin Builders, Inc. ("Fannin Builders"), appeals from a judgment of the Franklin County Court of Common Pleas in favor of plaintiffs-appellees, Steve Landis and Nancy Weidman. . . . For the following reasons, we affirm.

In 2004, Landis and his wife, Weidman, decided to build a custom home on land that Landis owned in Pleasantville, Ohio. After interviewing three builders, they chose Fannin Builders to construct their home. On May 4, 2004, appellees signed a contract with Fannin Builders, in which Fannin Builders agreed to construct appellees' home in accordance with the plans and specifications attached to the contract for $356,750. The specifications for appellees' home called for T1-11 exterior siding covered with two coats of stain in a color of appellees' choice. T1-11 siding is a plywood siding with one-inch-deep vertical grooves spaced 11 inches apart. Appellees chose T1-11 siding for their home because it provided a more natural, rustic look than other types of siding. Before signing the construction contract, appellees sought, and received, assurances from Fannin Builders that it had experience with installing and staining T1-11 siding. . . . When the time came to apply the stain to the exterior siding, Fannin Builders provided appellees with a brochure . . . [which] depicted stains in over 30 colors, each available in two different pigment levels: semitransparent (lightly pigmented) or semisolid (extra pigment). Appellees chose a semitransparent stain in a green color, which Cabot, the stain manufacturer, named "allagash." Landis communicated his and his wife's choice to Fannin Builders in a September 2, 2004 e-mail. . . .

[The siding was stained with the allagash semitransparent stain, but some of the siding turned out a noticeably darker hue than the other batch, giving the house a striped or patchwork appearance. Weidman noticed this, but Fannin assured her that a second coat of stain would blend the two shades so that they would match. The second coat of stain had not yet been applied when the house was otherwise complete and the closing occurred in January 2005. The application of the second coat was further delayed until spring 2005 because it was not advisable to apply it during the cold weather. When the second coat was applied, it did not improve the patchwork appearance of the house. Appellees and Fannin Builders discussed various ways in which to fix the patchwork appearance. In spring 2005, appellees allowed Fannin Builders to remove siding from the back of the garage in order to try stain matching. The attempt was unsuccessful in producing a uniform color. In June 2005 the parties agreed that the siding would be replaced. However, when it was delivered, it was unacceptable because the stain had come out as a yellowish color rather than green. They therefore decided not to install the replacement siding, and tried again to fix the color of the siding on the house, but the parties agreed that the result looked horrible. The best solution that Fannin could come up with was to use the solid allagash stain, which would cover the patchwork appearance. Appellees were unhappy with that solution because the solid stain would mask the wood grain and would not have the natural appearance that they wanted. Nevertheless, they allowed Fannin to test it on a sheet of siding. Appellees did not like either the color or the opacity of the solid stain.

The parties continued to discuss potential solutions over the next 18 months, but could not reach agreement. Appellees filed a complaint against Fannin Builders with the Professional Standards Committee of the Building Industry Association of Central Ohio ("BIA") which concluded that the color variance in the siding did not comply with professional standards in the residential construction industry. Ultimately, in April 2007, appellees filed suit against Fannin Builders which counterclaimed for payment of $3,908.98 allegedly still owing for the construction of the house.

At a bench trial, Appellees adduced expert testimony that the color variance of the stain on the siding does not meet industry standards and that correction of the patchwork appearance would require complete removal and replacement of the siding. The trial court found in favor of Appellees on their breach of contract claim and awarded them damages of $66,906.24—the cost of replacing the siding—offset against Fannin's counterclaim of $3,908.98 still owing under the contract, resulting in a net award to Appellees of $62,997.26. Fannin appealed, contending that the trial court erred, *inter alia*, by concluding that Fannin breached the contract and by assessing damages based on the cost of replacing the siding rather than on the diminished value of the house.]

The trial court . . . held that Fannin Builders had breached the construction contract because it had failed to provide Appellees siding with a uniform shade of oil-based Cabot semi-transparent stain, . . . [creating] a patchwork appearance of the siding. . . . Contracts for the future construction of a residence include a duty, implied by law, that the builder must perform its work in a workmanlike manner. This implied duty requires a construction professional to act reasonably and to exercise that degree of care which a member of the construction trade in good standing in that community would exercise under the same or similar circumstances. In determining whether a builder has breached its implied duty to perform in a workmanlike manner, a fact-finder must assess whether the builder used proper materials and workmanlike skill and judgment.

In the case at bar, the parties do not dispute that the evidence establishes that Fannin Builders fell below local industry standards in constructing a house with siding of such disparate color. Fannin admitted that the siding is unacceptable under industry standards. The BIA report states that the color variance in the siding "does not comply with professional standard's [sic] in the residential construction industry." Finally, appellees' expert witness testified that the patchwork appearance of the siding does not meet industry standards. Given this evidence, we conclude that the trial court did not err in finding that Fannin Builders' failure to provide siding in a uniform color amounted to a breach of contract. Because the siding does not conform to industry standards, Fannin Builders breached its implied duty to perform in a workmanlike manner. . . .

Fannin Builders argues that the trial court erred in awarding appellees damages based on the cost to replace the mismatched siding instead of the difference in the market value of the house as contracted for and as received. We disagree. Generally, the appropriate measure of damages in an action for a breach of a construction contract is the cost to repair the deficient work, that is, the cost of placing the building in the condition contemplated by the parties at the time they entered into the contract. Some Ohio courts subscribe to an exception to this general measure of damages. Although never adopted by this court, various other Ohio appellate courts have applied the economic-waste rule to determine damages for the breach of a construction contract. Under the economic-waste rule, if repair of a construction defect will involve unreasonable economic waste, damages are measured by the difference between the market value that the structure contracted for would have had and that of the imperfect structure received by the plaintiff. Economic waste arises when the total cost to remedy a construction defect is grossly disproportionate to the good to be attained.

The seminal case of *Jacob & Youngs, Inc. v. Kent* (1921), 230 N.Y. 239, 129 N.E. 889, best articulates the economic-waste rule. In that case, a contract for the construction of a house required the use of plumbing pipe manufactured in Reading. A subcontractor's oversight led to the installation of plumbing pipe manufactured in Cohoes, not Reading. Although Cohoes pipe equaled Reading pipe in quality, the homeowner demanded that the builder tear out the Cohoes pipe and replace it with Reading pipe. To tear out the pipe, the builder would have had to demolish substantial parts of the completed structure. When the builder refused to replace the Cohoes pipe with Reading pipe, the plaintiff sued. The court held that given the circumstances: "[T]he measure of the allowance is not the cost of replacement, which would be great, but the difference in value, which would be either nominal or nothing. . . . The owner is entitled to the money which will permit him to complete, unless the cost of completion is grossly and unfairly out of proportion to the good to be attained. When that is true, the measure is the difference in value."

The economic-waste rule emanates from courts' disinclination to award windfalls. Sometimes, the owner of a defective structure receives sufficient value from the builder's work that he or she will decide not to fix the defect, and instead, will pocket any damages awarded based on the cost of repairs. The likelihood of this outcome increases in situations such as those presented in *Kent,* where the wrong pipe was commensurate to the contracted-for pipe in both quality and functionality. In such situations, the injured party is unjustly enriched because he or she receives work of approximately equal value to the contracted-for work and, in addition, money damages based on the cost of repair. Restatement of the Law 2d, Contracts (1981), Section 348, Comment c (if "the cost to remedy the defects will be clearly disproportionate to the probable loss in value to the injured party," then "[d]amages based on the cost to remedy the defects would . . . give the injured party a recovery greatly in excess of the loss in value to him and result in a substantial windfall").

Similar concerns about unjust enrichment underlie the rule establishing the measure of damages for temporary injury to real property. In *Ohio Collieries v. Cocke* (1923), 107 Ohio St. 238, 248-249, 140 N.E. 356, the Supreme Court of Ohio held that if wrongful injury to real property can be repaired, then "[T]he measure of damages is the reasonable cost of restoration, plus reasonable compensation for the loss of the use of the property between the time of the injury and the restoration, unless such cost of restoration exceeds the difference in the market value of the property before and after the injury, in which case the difference in market value becomes the measure." Like the economic-waste rule, this rule seeks to preclude the injured party from receiving a monetary windfall. In the case of temporary injury to real property, the injured party achieves this windfall by choosing to sell the property rather than restore it, resulting in a profit to the extent that the restoration costs exceed the diminution in market value.

Recently, in *Martin v. Design Constr. Servs., Inc.,* 121 Ohio St. 3d 66, 2009 Ohio 1, 902 N.E.2d 10, the Supreme Court of Ohio limited the rule enunciated in *Ohio Collieries.* The court recognized the relevance of evidence regarding the diminution in market value of injured property in setting a damage award. However, the court abjured *Ohio Collieries'* automatic limitation of damages to the loss of market value when the cost of restoration exceeded that loss. In the place of the *Ohio Collieries* rule, the court imposed a reasonableness test. While diminution in market value remains a consideration, "the essential inquiry is whether the damages sought are reasonable."

The economic-waste rule and the rule expressed in *Ohio Collieries* developed in different contexts. The economic-waste rule restricts the damages recoverable for breach of contract. The rule governing imposition of damages for the temporary injury to real property originated from, and is generally applied to, tort cases. Nevertheless, we conclude that the reasonableness test announced in *Martin* precludes a strict application of the economic-waste rule. The fundamental rule of the law of damages is that the injured party shall have compensation for all of the injuries sustained. Thus, in both contract and tort actions, the appropriate measure of damages is that which will make the injured party whole. Consequently, both the economic-waste rule and the rule governing temporary injury to real property share the same objective. Moreover, as we explained above, both rules emerged from a desire to prevent the injured party from receiving a windfall. Given the rules' identical purpose and origin, we conclude that the economic-waste rule, like the *Ohio Collieries* rule, must cede in favor of the reasonableness test.

Therefore, in a case involving a breach of a construction contract where the breaching party seeks to limit damages to the diminution in value, a fact-finder must determine whether under the facts of that case, it is more reasonable to award damages based on the cost of the remedy or based on the diminution in value. Although a fact-finder may consider whether the cost of the remedy grossly exceeds the difference in the value of the structure with and without the defect, that consideration will not necessarily control the amount of the damage award. Since the goal of any damage award is to make a party whole, a fact-finder must determine which measure of damage best accomplishes that goal without exceeding the bounds of reasonableness.

Here, the trial court awarded Appellees the cost to replace the siding because it determined that damages based on loss of market value could not fully compensate Appellees. Because the purpose of the contract was the construction of a custom-built home with the aesthetics Appellees desired, Fannin Builders' failure to achieve those aesthetics warranted an award of damages that would allow Appellees to correct the defect. We find the trial court's decision to award Appellees the cost of replacement, rather than the loss of market value, reasonable in this case. As appellees testified, they contracted for the construction of a custom-built home. Appellees decided to build such a home because they wanted a particular house design and the ability to choose any material and finish they liked. Appellees explained to Fannin Builders that they wanted their house to have a natural, rustic look and that to achieve this look, they wanted T1-11 exterior siding stained with a semitransparent stain. Although the contract did not designate any particular stain opacity, Fannin conceded in his trial testimony that under the contract, Fannin Builders was obligated to apply stain with the opacity that appellees chose. Indisputably, appellees chose a semitransparent stain. Because appellees placed such importance on the natural appearance of their home, they repeatedly rebuffed Fannin Builders' suggestion that they accept a solid stain. Appellees hired Fannin Builders to construct their "dream home," in which they planned to live many years. Consequently, appellees vigorously opposed Fannin Builders' attempts to get them to compromise on their desire to have T1-11 siding with a semitransparent stain.

According to [the] . . . expert witness, the market value of appellees' home is $8,500 less than it would be if it was stained a uniform color. The expert witness arrived at this valuation because the cost to apply two coats of solid stain to the siding is $8,500. Under the economic waste rule, appellees' damages might have amounted to only $8,500, as opposed to the $66,906.24 necessary to replace the siding. We, however, concur with the trial court that $8,500 could not fully compensate appellees. Given that appellees contracted for a custom home and that appellees place a high value on the rustic look, the cost to achieve the rustic look is the only reasonable measure of damages. Thus, the trial court did not err in awarding appellees damages based on the cost to replace the siding. . . . Because the trial court's award of damages is both reasonable and supported by competent, credible evidence, we conclude that the trial court did not err in setting appellees' damages at $62,997.26. . . . Judgment affirmed.

■ PROBLEM 19.4

As in *Jacob & Youngs*, the contract in *Landis* had been fully performed, so there was no question of whether the plaintiff had the right to terminate it for total and material breach—the only issue is the plaintiff's remedy for the shortfall in performance. Although the court hints that the breach was likely material, it does not actually discuss whether it was. It focuses simply on the question of the proper measure of damages and considers whether the normal measure of damages should be reduced on grounds of unfair forfeiture or "economic waste." The unfair forfeiture doctrine is most commonly used where there has been substantial performance, but because the doctrine is equity-based, a court does have the discretion to apply it even where a breach is material. This is why (given that there is no issue of terminating the contract) it was not necessary for the court to decide the question of whether or not the breach was material.

Change the facts of the case as follows: The dispute about the unsightly patchwork siding came to a head during the course of construction, before the house had been fully built. The owners insisted that the builder remove and replace all the siding, but the builder refused, proposing that the problem be rectified by using the opaque stain. The parties could not resolve this dispute, so the owners fired the builder and refused to allow it to complete the rest of the construction project. The owners would have been justified in doing this if the failure to provide properly stained siding was a material breach of the contract.

Do you think this was a material breach? Why or why not?

3. The Recovery of the Breaching Party: Unjust Enrichment or Recovery Under the Contract

As noted previously, if a party materially and totally breaches the contract, he cannot recover any damages under the contract. A material breacher has no right to enforce the contract that he has violated. If the breacher has partially performed before his material breach he may be allowed to recover the value of his performance under principles of unjust enrichment. Such a claim is not assured. Some courts will not even allow restitution in favor of a material breacher. (This absolute bar is more commonly found in older cases and is not much favored by modern courts.) Others may permit the restitutionary claim if justice requires it—for example, where the nonbreaching party has clearly been unjustly enriched, and the breach was not egregious. Even if restitution is allowed, the remedy in favor of a material breacher could be limited by measuring the benefit in a more restrictive way than usual: The breacher is not unqualifiedly entitled to receive the market value of the performance (quantum meruit) but is likely to get only the actual economic enrichment of the other party. Furthermore, if the value placed on the performance in the contract is less than its market value, the restitutionary claim may be limited by the contract value. In addition, any restitutionary recovery by the breacher is offset against any damages to which the other party is entitled as a result of the breach.

By contrast, as we have seen, if the breach is not material and the breacher has rendered substantial performance, the breacher can enforce the contract and is entitled to the full contract price less any allowance to the other party for rectifying the defect or, in a proper case, for compensating for the loss in value of the performance. It is not hard to see why the stakes could be very high in deciding whether or not a breach is material.

Even where a breach is material, the contract may be structured in a way that allows the breacher to argue that it can be divided into self-contained units, so that a breach relating to some of the units is isolated and confined to those units and does not affect other aspects of the contract. This argument can only be made where it is consistent with the apparent intent of the parties, as revealed in the structure of the contract; that is, the interpretation of the contract as divisible is justified only if the reasonable expectations of the parties would not be defeated by breaking down the contract into independent, self-standing components.

Carrig v. Gilbert-Varker Corp., 314 Mass. 351, 50 N.E.2d 59 (1943), is one of the best-known cases on this subject. It demonstrates the kind of circumstances that may lead a court to conclude that a contract is divisible, and shows why divisibility might matter. The developer of a subdivision contracted with a builder for the construction of 35 houses. After building 20 of the houses, the builder repudiated the contract and refused to build the remaining 15 houses. The 20 houses that had been built had been constructed properly in compliance with contract specifications.

The court awarded the developer expectation damages for the additional cost it incurred in having the remaining 15 houses built by someone else. The question was whether the builder could offset against those damages the contract price due to it for the 20 houses that had been built. If it could, it would be paid in full at the contract price for the performance it had rendered, less the developer's damages. If not, it would still have to pay damages to the developer but would recover, at best, the quantum meruit value of its labor and materials. (In *Carrig* the stakes were even higher than this because the jurisdiction followed the rule that denied a material breacher restitutionary recovery.)

The builder's failure to complete the 15 houses was a material breach. This meant the builder would recover nothing on the contract unless that portion of the contract that it had completed could be severed from the portion that it had breached. The court held that the contract was divisible. It stated that divisibility of a contract depends on the parties' intent, as revealed by the language and structure of the contract, its purpose, and the circumstances of its execution and performance. The court found this contract to be divisible because it treated the houses as distinct units. The contract included plans and specifications indicating which house was to be built on each lot. It allocated a portion of the price and the construction financing to each house, and it provided for separate completion schedules and payment schedules for each of them. When completed, each house was a self-contained economic unit that could be sold to a customer.

The next case reaches the opposite conclusion from *Carrig* with regard to the divisibility of a contract.

MENORAH CHAPELS AT MILLBURN v. NEEDLE

386 N.J. Super. 100, 899 A.2d 316 (2006)
New Jersey Superior Court, Appellate Division

PAYNE, Judge Appellate Division.

In this appeal, we consider the nature of damages that can be recovered as the result of the failure by a funeral home that caters to members of the Jewish faith to ensure that orthodox ritual requirements are met when the rituals have been requested by a member of the deceased's family.

On the Friday that his father-in-law died, defendant Emanuel Needle arranged with plaintiff Menorah Chapels of Millburn, promoted as a "Jewish Funeral Chapel," to provide funeral and related services. Because of the Sabbath, commencing at sundown on Friday, the funeral could not be conducted until Sunday, February 21, 1999. Decedent was an orthodox Jew. Menorah Chapels does not contest that it is customary in the orthodox Jewish faith that watchers or shomerim conduct a continuous vigil or shmeerah over the body of the deceased until the time of the funeral. A General Price List for Menorah Chapels, effective June 1, 1998, provided:

> The special Orthodox ritual requirements of Tahara [ritual washing] and Watcher [shomer] will be carried out whether decedent is a man or woman by qualified persons in a religiously satisfactory manner upon request, and can be verified if desired. The Tahara will be provided along with a muslin shroud at no additional cost.
>
> A "Shomer Shabbos" [Sabbath] watcher is also available for a small additional charge if requested.

A "Removal, Embalming and Preparation Release Form" pertaining to the deceased and dated February 19, 1999 specified "shrouds & shmeerah." Additionally, the "Statement of Goods and Services Selected" that was executed by Needle on Sunday February 21, 1999 discloses that he requested, and Menorah Chapel agreed to provide, shomerim to conduct the shmeerah. The Statement discloses that six shifts would be necessary to properly conduct the shmeerah, at a cost of $900.

Menorah Chapel subcontracted the provision of shomerim to a burial society. However, allegedly because of the Sabbath, the society did not provide the requested services, and in fact only three of the six shifts of shomerim appeared, commencing on Saturday evening after the Sabbath had ended. Neither Needle nor any of his family members was informed of the failure to provide the full contracted-for services until shortly before the funeral service was to commence and after the body had been left alone in a fashion contrary to orthodox Jewish custom and belief.

In October 1999, the Chapel brought a collection action against Needle in the Special Civil Part, demanding the full cost of its funeral services, subject to a $390 discount as the result of the absence of three shifts of shomerim. Needle entered a general denial of the allegations of the complaint and filed a counterclaim in which he alleged that the failure to provide the required shomerim constituted negligence and breach of warranty resulting in emotional distress to the family. Although breach of contract was not specifically alleged, it can be fairly inferred from Needle's breach of warranty claim and from the general denials contained in defendant's answer. [Menorah sought summary judgment on the counterclaim. The trial court granted the motion, dismissed Needle's counterclaim, and granted judgment in favor of Menorah on its complaint. Needle appeals. The court first addresses Needle's argument that the dispute involved matters of a religious nature which should not be heard by a secular court but should be referred to a Jewish religious court. He contended that by adjudicating the dispute, the court would entangle itself in religious matters, thereby violating the separation of church and state under the First Amendment. The court agrees with the trial court that the case simply involves contract rights, which are secular in character and do not implicate religious doctrine.] . . .

Although the services at issue may be required under the tenets of the orthodox Jewish faith, the dispute does not concern the manner in which they were performed, but solely whether they were performed at all—a nondoctrinal matter. We note additionally that in his counterclaim Needle does not allege damage to the deceased as the result of the absence of the shomerim, but only emotional distress to surviving family members, a form of consequential damages that is customarily available in civil proceedings. We thus reject any argument that the court should have abstained from consideration either of the complaint itself or the counterclaim.

The [trial] judge found the contract underlying this dispute to have been divisible in nature, and as a result permitted recovery by Menorah Chapel for the goods and services provided, subtracting only the cost of the shomerim. Needle argues that this determination was erroneous. We agree. A party may not repudiate one part of a nondivisible contract and claim the benefit of the residue, because to do so "would amount to unjust enrichment and would bind the parties 'to a contract which they did not contemplate.'" *County of Morris v. Fauver*, 153 N.J. 80, 97, 707 A.2d 958 (1998) (quoting 17A *Am. Jur. 2d, Contracts* §548 (2d ed. 1991)). "Only where a contract is severable into different transactions may one of those separate transactions be avoided." *Ibid.* "A contract is said to be entire when the consideration moving from the promisor is conditioned upon the complete performance by the promissee of his promise. On the other hand, a contract is said to be divisible when performance is divided in two or more parts with a definite apportionment of the total consideration to each part." *Integrity Flooring, Inc. v. Zandon Corp., Inc.*, 130 N.J.L. 244, 247, 32 A.2d 507 (Sup. 1943). A determination whether a contract is divisible or entire depends upon the intent of the parties as gathered from the agreement itself and the surrounding circumstances. The Supreme Court has framed the determination of the parties' intent in the following terms:

> Would the agreement have been made were the parties not under the impression that it would be performed in its entirety? We recognize that the intentions of the parties may not be easily gleaned. Hence, we also encourage the . . . court to determine whether it is fair to the parties to deem the agreement severable.

[*Bonnco Petrol, Inc. v. Epstein*, 115 N.J. 599, 613, 560 A.2d 655 (1989).]

Menorah Chapel argues that its contract with Needle was severable because its services were independently priced . . . in the Statement of Funeral Goods and Services Selected that was executed by Needle. [However, providers of funeral services are obliged by statute and regulation to give customers a written, itemized price list at the time that the contract is made. The list is intended to protect customers by ensuring that they have detailed information on the cost of all services.] . . .

The itemization thus cannot be reasonably construed as dispositive evidence of a severable contract. "The mere fact that there is a contract rate of payment per unit of performance to be rendered by the plaintiff, is not sufficient to make the contract divisible." 12 *Corbin on Contracts* §1111 at 41 (1964). As Corbin points out, when viewed in context, neither party may have been willing to accept part performance at the rate specified in lieu of performance of the entire contract. This principle is discussed in the *Restatement (Second) of Contracts* §240, which provides for an analysis of a contract to determine whether it can be divided into corresponding pairs of part performance by one contracting party and payment by the other. Even when such apportionment is possible, however, the *Restatement* requires that a court look to the parties' intent to determine whether the value to the injured party of what he received is equivalent to its stated price or whether that value is materially diminished by the part performance.[2] *Id.* cmt. e.

We find no evidential support for the . . . [trial] judge's conclusion in the context of the provision of funeral services in this case that the undertaking by Menorah Chapel to provide enumerated goods and services was severable, so that, for instance, its failure to transfer the remains of the decedent to the funeral home, to embalm if requested, to supply the coffin ordered by the family of the decedent, or to render any other goods or services material to the undertaking could be cured by a simple deduction of the price of that service from the total contract amount. Such an intent clearly was not manifested by the parties at the time that the contract for services was executed, and cannot reasonably be inferred in the circumstances presented.

---

[2] For instance, an installment contract for the monthly delivery of specified goods might be divisible, whereas a contract for the delivery of a machine and attachments specific to the machine might not if the attachments are not otherwise available.

We leave to a jury to determine whether the full provision of shomerim constituted a material condition of the contract. If a jury finds that Menorah Chapel committed a material breach of its contract with Needle, the Chapel may nonetheless be entitled to recovery of the value of its remaining services on a *quantum meruit* basis. However, its damages cannot be measured solely by reference to the unit price of the goods and services actually provided. "Fairness requires that a party, having received only a fraction of the performance that he expected under a contract, not be asked to pay an identical fraction of the price that he originally promised on the expectation of full performance, unless it appears that the performance that he actually received is worth to him roughly that same fraction of what full performance would have been worth to him." *Restatement (Second) of Contracts*, §240 cmt. e. . . .

[The court goes on to consider whether the trial court was correct in dismissing Needle's counterclaim for damages. Needle suffered no financial loss as a result of the breach, so his claim was purely for emotional distress damages. The court recognizes that emotional distress damages are not ordinarily claimable for breach of contract. However, such damages may be awarded where the very basis of the contract is to furnish services that are designed to bring comfort to a party or to alleviate his emotional distress. A contract for funeral services has been recognized by many courts as being a contract of this kind. It is therefore highly likely that at the time of contracting, the parties reasonably contemplated that emotional distress would be a natural result of a breach by the provider of the funeral services and should be compensable. The court reverses the trial court's dismissal of the counterclaim and remands for trial.]

■ QUESTIONS

(1) Can you reconcile *Menorah Chapels* with *Carrig*? If so, what is the crucial difference in the contracts that makes one divisible and the other not?

(2) Based on the guidance offered to the trial court by the court of appeals in *Menorah Chapels*, what do you think, in general terms, will be the most likely remedial outcome if the case goes to trial?

(3) We have seen a divisibility case before this. In connection with our study of the doctrine of mistake in Chapter 17, we introduced *Mattson v. Rachetto* in Problem 17.3. In that case the buyers purchased land subject to a right of leaseback in favor of the sellers. At the time the contract was entered, the parties did not realize that the leaseback was invalid, and the issue in the case was whether the parties' mutual mistake of law gave the seller grounds for avoiding the contract. In an attempt to save the sale from avoidance, the buyer argued that the sale portion of a contract was divisible from the invalid leaseback. The court disagreed. What is the crucial distinction between *Carrig* and *Mattson* that makes the contract divisible in *Carrig* but indivisible in *Mattson*?

BREACH AND SUBSTANTIAL PERFORMANCE UNDER UCC ARTICLE 2: THE PERFECT TENDER RULE

1. Perfect Tender Under Article 2

The seller's principal obligation under a contract for the sale of goods is to tender delivery of the goods at the time and place provided in the contract. Upon delivery, the buyer has the right to inspect the goods. If the tender of delivery conforms to the contract, she must accept them and pay for them in the manner and at the time specified in the contract. If the seller breaches the contract by making a nonconforming delivery (which may include delivering goods that are defective or otherwise not in accordance with the contract specifications, or delivering them late, or at the wrong place, or incorrectly packaged), the common law rules discussed in the last section would call for an inquiry into the significance of the breach. If it is material and incurable, the buyer would be able to reject the goods, refuse payment, and claim total breach. However, if the breach is minor, the buyer would be confined to the remedy for substantial performance.

However, the drafters of the Code decided not to adopt the common law rule in Article 2. Instead they retained a different rule that had been part of sales law for some time. This rule, known as the "perfect tender rule" is set out in UCC 2-601:

UCC 2-601. BUYER'S RIGHTS ON IMPROPER DELIVERY

... [U]nless otherwise agreed, ... if the goods or the tender of delivery fail in any respect to conform to the contract, the buyer may
> (a) reject the whole; or
> (b) accept the whole; or
> (c) accept any commercial unit or units and reject the rest.

■ PROBLEM 19.5

On August 1, Vanity Versifier entered into a contract with Self Publishing Printers, Inc. (SPP), under which SPP agreed to print 100 copies of Vanity's book of poetry for the price of $1,500. The contract specified the type of paper, the binding, the printing font, and the layout. It also stated that the books were to be delivered to Vanity by September 1. Vanity does not intend to use the books for commercial purposes. She plans to give copies to friends and family as Christmas presents.

This contract probably qualifies as a sale of goods because Vanity is buying the tangible end product of SPP's manufacturing process. However, it is conceivable that a court could apply the predominant purpose test and find that services were the predominant purpose of the contract. Therefore, the following questions ask you to apply both UCC Article 2 and the common law.

(a) The books were printed on the wrong paper (it was off-white instead of pure white, as specified in the contract) and in the wrong font. The overall quality and appearance of the books is satisfactory by trade standards, but the books do not have the look that Vanity wanted. Does Vanity have the right to reject the books under UCC Article 2? Would she have the right to reject them under common law?

(b) The books were printed exactly as specified in the contract. However, SPP did not deliver them to Vanity until September 3. Does Vanity have the right to reject the books under UCC Article 2? Would she have the right to reject them under common law?

(c) Would your answer to question (b) change if the contract had stated "Time of delivery is of the essence of this contract"?

2. Limitations on the Perfect Tender Rule

The perfect tender rule can cause hardship to a seller where the nonconformity is minor and readily curable. Article 2 has some qualifications to the rule that ameliorate the harshness of its application in some circumstances. We leave details of these qualifications to the course on sales and just highlight them here. The two most important limitations on the perfect tender rule are the seller's right to cure under UCC 2-508 and the use of a substantial performance standard in UCC 2-612, where the contract calls for delivery of the goods in installments.

a. Cure

In Section A we mention the general common law principle that a breaching party may have the right to cure a partial breach. If the breacher has the right to cure (which depends on many factors, including the nature of the breach and the party's ability to rectify it within the proper time), the victim of the breach cannot immediately declare total breach. It must give the breacher the opportunity to accomplish the cure, and can only treat the breach as total if the breacher fails to cure effectively and in time.

At common law, the right to cure a breach plays its most important role where the breach would be material if left uncured. However, under Article 2, the right to cure takes on wider significance because UCC 2-601 does not permit a seller to claim that a nonconforming tender constitutes substantial performance. The seller's right to cure is provided for in UCC 2-508. In essence, UCC 2-508 makes a distinction between the seller's cure rights before and after the time for performance has expired.

UCC 2-508(1) applies if the seller tenders the goods and the buyer rejects them before the agreed date for delivery. At this stage, the seller has a broader right to cure by substituting a conforming tender before the expiry of the agreed time for delivery. The seller must have acted in good faith in making the nonconforming tender. It must give the buyer timely notice of its intent to cure and must pay the expenses of curing and compensate the buyer for any loss caused by the breach. If the seller acted in good faith and takes these steps, the buyer is obliged to accept the cure and proceed with its own performance.

If the seller seeks to cure a nonconforming tender after the agreed time for delivery has passed, UCC 2-508(2) applies. In addition to the requirements of subsection (1), this subsection also requires the cure to be appropriate and timely under the circumstances; that is, because the contractual delivery date has passed, a seller that wishes to cure must show that the cure will give the buyer its contractual expectations notwithstanding the delay in completing proper performance.

■ PROBLEM 19.6

Consider an issue of cure relating to the contract described in Problem 19.5, under which SPP undertook to print 100 copies of Vanity Versifier's poetry book. The contract specified the type of paper, the binding, the printing font, and the layout, and required delivery of the books to Vanity by September 1. As before, Vanity does not intend to use the books for commercial purposes but will give them to friends and family as Christmas presents.

(a) SPP delivered the books to Vanity on August 25. They were printed on the wrong paper and in the wrong font. If Vanity rejects the books upon delivery on August 25, does SPP have the right to cure the breach? If so, what must it do, and what must it show to accomplish an effective cure?

(b) Say that SPP did not deliver the defective books on August 25. Instead it delivered them early in the morning on September 2. Vanity rejected the books on delivery. Does SPP have a right to cure? If so, what must it do, and what must it show to accomplish an effective cure?

b. Contracts That Call for Delivery in Installments

Where a contract qualifies as an "installment contract," UCC 2-612 does not follow the perfect tender rule but instead adopts a substantial performance doctrine. "Installment contract" is defined in UCC 2-612 as "one which requires or authorizes the delivery of goods in separate lots to be separately accepted. . . ."

If the contract is an installment contract, UCC 2-612(2) allows the buyer to reject any nonconforming installment of goods only if the nonconformity "substantially impairs the value of that installment and cannot be cured. . . ." For example, say that the buyer, a retail store, bought 50 boxes of glasses from the seller, to be delivered in five equal batches of ten boxes at different dates over a two-month period. When the first batch is delivered on the first date, the buyer inspects the glasses and finds that some of them have flaws. Under the perfect tender rule, the buyer could have rejected the tender of this installment. However, under UCC 2-612(2) the buyer can reject this installment only if the nonconformity substantially impairs the value of the installment to the buyer and it cannot be cured. This is, in essence, a substantial performance standard. If the nonconformity is not material, or it can be cured, the buyer must accept the delivery. If the seller then cures the delivery, the buyer's only claim is for compensation for any losses resulting from the originally noncompliant tender. If the seller fails to cure, and the breach becomes material, the buyer can then reject the goods. If the uncured breach is not material, the buyer has the right to a price reduction for the flawed glasses.

UCC 2-612(3) deals with the situation in which a buyer who receives a non-conforming tender in one installment wishes to use that nonconformity as the basis for terminating the contract in its entirety. Here too, the section imposes a substantial performance standard. It provides that if the "nonconformity or default with respect to one or more installments substantially impairs the value of the whole contract," the buyer can treat the breach in an installment as a breach of the whole contract. Say, in the preceding example, the seller delivered the first batch of glasses. On inspecting them, the buyer finds that they are all flawed. This likely would qualify as a material defect that substantially impairs the value of that installment to the buyer, entitling it to reject the installment under UCC 2-612(2). However, the buyer cannot use the nonconformity to cancel the entire contract unless it can also show that the problems with this installment are so severe and far-reaching that they affect the value of the entire contract. To establish this, the buyer would have to go beyond showing that the installment was materially nonconforming. It would also have to demonstrate that problems in that installment defeat its reasonable expectations for the whole contract.

D | ANTICIPATORY REPUDIATION AND PROSPECTIVE NONPERFORMANCE

1. Anticipatory Repudiation

Because a performance promised in a contract is not due until the time for performance arrives, a party cannot breach that promise before its due date. For example, on March 1 the owner of a home contracts with a builder to replace a broken door for $1,000. The contract provides that the owner will make a down payment of $250 to the builder by no later than March 7, the builder will do the work on March 10, and the owner will pay the balance of the price by March 12. Because the builder's obligation to replace the door is not due until March 10, it is self-evident that she has no obligation to perform before that date. However, it sometimes happens that before the date for performance, the party who has promised a performance makes it clear by words or conduct that she will not perform when the time for performance falls due. For example, if the builder calls the homeowner on March 3 and tells him that she is too busy and will not replace the door, she, in effect, notifies him in advance of her intent to breach the contract by not performing when the time for her performance falls due. This advance notification of breach is called an "anticipatory repudiation." Sometimes a repudiation occurs, as in the above example, before either party's performance is due under the contract. However, it could also occur after one or both parties have begun performance and one of them makes it clear that she will not perform an obligation that is due some time later in the performance period. For example, we would also call it a repudiation if the builder notified the owner of her intent not to replace the door on March 8, after the owner had made the down payment but before the builder's time for performance fell due, or if the builder walked off the job halfway through the installation, stating that she would not return.

The concept of anticipatory repudiation was not recognized in older common law, which meant that even though the builder made it clear on March 3 that she would not perform by replacing the door on March 10, the owner could do nothing in response to this information. The owner would still have to make the down payment on March 7 and would have to wait until the builder failed to show up on March 10 before he could declare a breach. The inconvenience and inefficiency of such a system is obvious, and courts began to recognize this in the nineteenth century. The case credited with firmly establishing the doctrine of anticipatory repudiation in common law is *Hochster v. De La Tour*, 118 Eng. Rep. 922 (Q.B. 1853). In April 1852, the parties made a contract under which Hochster was to serve as De La Tour's courier for a three-month European tour, commencing on June 1, 1852. On May 11 De La Tour wrote to Hochster that he had changed his mind and would not use his services. Hochster sued immediately and was met with the argument by De La Tour that the action was premature—there could be no breach until June 1. The court disagreed and held that where a party utterly renounces the contract by a clear declaration of intent not to perform or by an act that makes it impossible for him to perform, a cause of action for its breach arises immediately. The court noted that in the absence of such a rule, the plaintiff, despite knowledge that the defendant will breach when the time comes to perform, would have to continue preparations for and hold himself available to render his own performance. In the interim, he would not be able to commit to a contract with someone else as a substitute or to take other action to mitigate his losses. It concluded that it was more rational, fairer to the plaintiff, and more likely to prevent or reduce loss to allow the plaintiff to declare a breach and to seek relief immediately. The recognition of this principle is now firmly established and unquestioned.

The requirement of material breach applies to repudiations as it does to breaches. Therefore, to be treated as a repudiation, giving rise to the right to declare advance breach of contract, the indication of intent not to perform must relate to a material term of the contract. In both the *Hochster* case and in the example involving the builder's notification of intent not to perform, the materiality of the breach is self-evident because in both situations, the repudiating party expressed the intent of not performing at all. However, it could happen that one of the parties does not indicate in advance that she will not perform at all but rather states that she will not perform exactly as promised. For example, the builder may not have told the owner that she would not replace the door but may have said that she was running behind on another project and could not get to the job until March 12. This is an advance statement that the contract will be breached by late performance, and it is therefore a repudiation of the builder's contractual promise. However, it is not clear if a two-day delay in performance is material. If it is not, the owner cannot react to the repudiation by withholding his own performance, canceling the contract, and suing for expectation damages based on total breach.

UCC Article 2 follows the same approach in relation to repudiation. Even though UCC 2-601 adopts the perfect tender rule with regard to breach by nonconforming delivery, Article 2's provision relating to repudiation (UCC 2-610 quoted below) requires a prospective breach to be material. Therefore, whether one applied either the common law or Article 2, an advance notification, such as the builder's notification that she would breach by not performing until March 12, can only be acted on as a repudiation if a two-day delay in performance would qualify as a total breach.

The contemporary doctrine of repudiation is set out, in similar terms, in Restatement, Second §§250 and 253, and UCC 2-610.

RESTATEMENT, SECOND §250. WHEN A STATEMENT OR AN ACT IS A REPUDIATION

A repudiation is

    (a) a statement by the obligor to the obligee indicating that the obligor will commit a breach that would of itself give the obligee a claim for damages for total breach . . . , or

(b) a voluntary affirmative act which renders the obligor unable or apparently unable to perform without such a breach.

RESTATEMENT, SECOND §253. EFFECT OF A REPUDIATION AS A BREACH AND ON OTHER PARTY'S DUTIES

(1) Where an obligor repudiates a duty before he has committed a breach by non-performance and before he has received all of the agreed exchange for it,[3] his repudiation alone gives rise to a claim for damages for total breach.

(2) Where performances are to be exchanged under an exchange of promises, one party's repudiation of a duty to render performance discharges the other party's remaining duties to render performance.

UCC 2-610. ANTICIPATORY REPUDIATION

When either party repudiates the contract with respect to a performance not yet due the loss of which will substantially impair the value of the contract to the other, the aggrieved party may

(a) for a commercially reasonable time await performance by the repudiating party; or

(b) resort to any remedy for breach (Section 2-703 or Section 2-711), even though he has notified the repudiating party that he would await the latter's performance and has urged retraction; and

(c) in either case suspend his own performance or proceed in accordance with the provisions of this Article on the seller's right to identify goods to the contract notwithstanding breach or to salvage unfinished goods (Section 2-704).

———

As noted above, the right of the victim of a repudiation to act on it immediately is no longer subject to question under most circumstances. The difficult issue in contemporary law usually involves the more subtle question of what constitutes a material repudiation, especially where the apparent intent not to perform is gleaned from an unclear statement or conduct. This presents a hazard to a party who, believing that the other has repudiated, declares an advance breach and cancels the contract. If she was wrong in her interpretation of the words or conduct, she may herself have repudiated the contract by cancelling it.

———

[3] The language "before he has received all of the agreed exchange for it" reflects a rule, followed by some courts, that if the victim of a repudiation has fully performed before the repudiation he does not get an immediate right to sue for total breach. The rule is odd and has no principled justification.—EDS.

WHOLESALE SAND & GRAVEL, INC. v. DECKER

630 A.2d 710 (1993)
Maine Supreme Judicial Court

ROBERTS, Justice.

Wholesale Sand & Gravel, Inc., appeals from a judgment entered in the Superior Court . . . in favor of James Decker on its claim for the breach of their contract. On appeal, Wholesale contends that the court erred in holding that its conduct constituted an anticipatory repudiation of the contract. . . . Finding no error, we affirm the judgment.

On June 13, 1989, James Decker and Wholesale Sand & Gravel, Inc., entered into a contract whereby Wholesale agreed to perform earth work, including the installation of a gravel driveway, on Decker's property in Bowdoin. The contract contained no provision specifying a completion date for the work. Indeed, the only time reference made in the contract was that payment was to be made within 90 days. Although Carl Goodenow, Wholesale's president, believed the company had 90 days within which to complete the work, he told Decker that the driveway portion of the work would be completed within one week. Wholesale began work on the driveway on the weekend after the contract was executed and immediately experienced difficulty because of the wetness of the ground. In fact, Wholesale's bulldozer became stuck in the mud and had to be removed with a backhoe. Wholesale returned to the site the following weekend, when it attempted to stabilize the driveway site by hauling out mud and hauling in gravel. Because the ground was too wet to allow Wholesale to perform the work without substantially exceeding the contract price, Goodenow decided to wait for the ground to dry out before proceeding further.

On July 12, 1989, Decker contacted Goodenow concerning the lack of activity at the site and his urgent need to have the driveway completed. Goodenow responded that he would "get right on it." On July 19, Decker telephoned Goodenow to inquire again about the lack of activity and gave him one week in which to finish the driveway. Again, Goodenow said that he would "get right on it." On July 28, Decker called Goodenow for the purpose of terminating the contract. When Goodenow stated that he would be at the site the next day, Decker decided to give him one more chance. Goodenow, however, did not appear at the site and Decker subsequently terminated the contract. At that point, Goodenow believed Wholesale still had 45 days to complete the job. Decker, however, hired another contractor to finish the driveway and complete the excavation work.

Wholesale commenced this action against Decker by a complaint seeking damages for a breach of their contract. After a jury-waived trial, the court entered a judgment in favor of Decker. Although it found that a reasonable time for the completion of performance was 60 days, the court concluded that Wholesale's conduct constituted an anticipatory repudiation of the contract, permitting Decker to terminate the contract during the 60-day period. This timely appeal followed.

An anticipatory repudiation of a contract is "a definite and unequivocal manifestation of intention on the part of the repudiator that he will not render the promised performance when the time fixed for it in the contract arrives." 4 Corbin, *Corbin on Contracts* §973 (1951); Restatement (Second) of Contracts §250 (1979). The manifestation of an intention to repudiate a contract may be made and communicated by either words or conduct. The words or conduct evidencing such refusal or inability to perform, however, must be definite, unequivocal, and absolute. Wholesale contends that the court erred in concluding that its conduct constituted an anticipatory repudiation of the contract. We disagree. After its second weekend of work at the site, Wholesale removed its equipment and did not return. Moreover, on two occasions Goodenow, responding to Decker's inquiries about the progress of the job, promised to get right to work but did not do so. Indeed, when confronted by the fact that Wholesale would be fired if he did not appear at the job site the following day, Goodenow promised that he would be at the site but did not appear. On this record it was reasonable for Decker to conclude that Wholesale would never complete its performance under the contract. We conclude therefore that the court properly found that Wholesale, through its conduct, manifested an unequivocal and definite inability or unwillingness to perform within a reasonable time. Judgment affirmed.

WATHEN, Chief Justice, dissenting.

I must respectfully dissent. In my judgment both this Court and the Superior Court misapply the doctrine of anticipatory repudiation. The record is devoid of any words or conduct on the part of plaintiff that distinctly, unequivocally, and absolutely evidence a refusal or inability to perform. There was a disagreement between the parties as to how much time was allowed for performance, but it is clear that plaintiff expected to perform the contract as soon as circumstances permitted. The Superior Court found a repudiation of the contract even though the 60 days it found available for performance had not passed. I would vacate the judgment.

■ PROBLEM 19.7

In *Wholesale Sand & Gravel* the majority of the court held that Wholesale had repudiated the contract by its conduct, but the dissent disagreed. In light of these contending views, do you think that a repudiation occurred in each of the situations described below? (If you cannot answer any question on the facts provided, list what additional facts you would need to know.)

(a) On March 31, Roy Pudiator entered into a contract with Mo Bile under which Roy agreed to sell his camper to Mo for $25,000. The contract provided that Mo would pay a deposit of $2,500 on April 10, Roy would deliver the camper and its title papers on April 15, and Mo would pay the balance of the price on April 30.

On April 5 it belatedly occurred to Roy that because he was giving Mo a couple of weeks' credit for the balance of the price, he should check Mo's creditworthiness. He obtained a credit report that showed that there were several unsatisfied judgments against Mo and that Mo was delinquent in his payments on three credit cards. Roy called Mo on April 6 and told him that he would not deliver the camper to Mo unless Mo paid the full price of $25,000 in advance of the delivery date. Has Roy repudiated?

(b) The contract is the same as in Question (a). Mo did not pay the deposit to Roy on April 10. When he arrived at Roy's home with $2,500 cash in hand early on the morning of April 11, Roy refused to accept the payment because it was late and told Mo that the contract was terminated. Did Roy repudiate the contract?

(c) The contract is the same as in Question (a). On April 2 one of Roy's creditors obtained a default judgment against him. On April 5 the sheriff, acting pursuant to a writ of execution issued on behalf of that creditor, seized the camper. The camper will shortly be sold by the sheriff at an execution sale, advertised to take place on April 14. On April 7, Mo heard about the levy and pending sale. Has Roy repudiated the contract?

2. Retraction of Repudiation

Because a repudiation occurs before the date due for the performance, the repudiating party may be able to repent and nullify the repudiation by withdrawing it and reaffirming his intent to honor the contract. Restatement, Second §256(1) provides that "... a statement ... constituting a repudiation ... is nullified by a retraction of the statement if notification of the retraction comes to the attention of the injured party before he materially changes his position in reliance on the repudiation or indicates to the other party that he considers the repudiation to be final." If the repudiation was by conduct that rendered the repudiator unable to perform, §256(2) treats it as retracted if, to the knowledge of the injured party, the event constituting the repudiation ceases to exist before he materially changes his position in reliance on the repudiation or indicates to the repudiator that he considers the repudiation to be final.

UCC 2-611 sets out these principles in similar terms. UCC 2-611(1) allows the repudiating party to retract before his next performance is due unless the other party has "since the repudiation cancelled or materially changed his position or otherwise indicated that he considers the repudiation final." UCC 2-611(2) provides that the retraction can be by any method that clearly indicates to the other party that the repudiator intends to perform. UCC 2-611(3) states that the retraction reinstates the repudiator's rights under the contract.

3. Prospective Inability to Perform

RESTATEMENT, SECOND §251. WHEN A FAILURE TO GIVE ASSURANCE MAY BE TREATED AS A REPUDIATION

(1) Where reasonable grounds arise to believe that the obligor will commit a breach by non-performance that would of itself give the obligee a claim for damages for total breach . . . the obligee may demand adequate assurance of due performance and may, if reasonable, suspend any performance for which he has not already received the agreed exchange until he receives such assurance.

(2) The obligee may treat as a repudiation the obligor's failure to provide within a reasonable time such assurance of due performance as is adequate in the circumstances of the particular case.

The rule in Restatement, Second §251 is based on UCC 2-609, which is worded a little differently but is substantially to the same effect. UCC 2-609 reads as follows:

UCC 2-609. RIGHT TO ADEQUATE ASSURANCE OF PERFORMANCE

(1) A contract for sale imposes an obligation on each party that the other's expectation of receiving due performance will not be impaired. When reasonable grounds for insecurity arise with respect to the performance of either party the other may in writing demand adequate assurance of due performance and until he receives such assurance may if commercially reasonable suspend any performance for which he has not already received the agreed return. . . .

(4) After receipt of a justified demand failure to provide within a reasonable time not exceeding thirty days such assurance of due performance as is adequate under the circumstances of the particular case is a repudiation of the contract.

The purpose of these sections is to allow the obligee to respond to circumstances that fall short of an outright repudiation but that create reasonable apprehension that the obligor will breach when the time for performance falls due. Therefore, although the obligee has no certain grounds to declare a repudiation—there has been no clear statement of intent not to perform or any voluntary conduct making the obligor's future performance impossible—the obligee has reasonable cause for concern. Something said or done by the obligor or some change in circumstances suggests that there may be trouble in getting the promised performance when it becomes due. These sections give the obligee the power to take precautionary action. She may suspend her own performance and make a reasonable demand of the obligor to provide an appropriate and adequate assurance that the obligor's performance will be forthcoming. If she makes this demand and the demand is justifiable both in its motivation and its scope, the obligor must respond by giving the reasonable assurance. If he does not, the failure to do so becomes a repudiation.

Although the ability to demand adequate assurance of performance may allow the obligee to relieve the uncertainty in some situations involving insecurity short of actual repudiation, it presents a number of difficult questions for both parties. If the obligee makes an unwarranted demand and suspends performance, she may herself have repudiated the contract. This means that she has two concerns. First, she must decide if the circumstances warrant making the demand. Second, if she concludes that they do, she must decide what should be demanded. If she asks for too little, any assurance she gets may be insufficient to protect her, but if she asks for too much, the obligor will be within his rights in refusing to meet the demand, and the demand plus any suspension of performance may make the obligee into the repudiator or breacher. The obligor is also at risk. When the demand is made, he must decide how to react to it. If the demand is reasonable and he refuses to accede to it, the prospective inability to perform will have solidified into a repudiation. The following problems explore the operation of Restatement, Second §251 and UCC 2-609.

■ PROBLEM 19.8

On August 1, Seller and Buyer entered into a contract under which Buyer agreed to buy Seller's home for $500,000. The contract provided that the transaction would close on September 20. At the time of executing the agreement, buyer paid a down payment of $50,000 into escrow. The contract made no mention of Buyer's means of financing the purchase, and it had no financing contingency. However, Seller knew that Buyer planned to obtain a loan, secured by a mortgage on the property, for the remaining $450,000. On August 25, Seller's real estate agent told him that Buyer had applied for loans from two different banks and that both applications had been declined. The real estate agent had also discovered that the reason for denial of the applications was that Buyer has a poor credit history. Seller is concerned that Buyer will not be able to obtain the financing necessary to buy the house and that he will be unable to close, thereby breaching the contract. If this is so, Seller would prefer to put the house back on the market immediately, rather than wait until September 20.

(a) Does Seller have the right to declare that Buyer has repudiated the contract?

(b) If not, does he have grounds to demand an assurance of performance?

(c) If he is entitled to an assurance of performance, what demand would be both adequate and legally permissible?

■ PROBLEM 19.9

Look back at Question (c) of Problem 19.7: On March 31, Roy Pudiator sold his camper to Mo Bile for $25,000. The contract provided that Mo would pay a deposit of $2,500 on April 10, Roy would deliver the camper and its title papers on April 15, and Mo would pay the balance of the price on April 30. On April 2 one of Roy's creditors obtained a default judgment against him. On April 5 the sheriff, acting pursuant to a writ of execution issued on behalf of that creditor, seized the camper. It is due to be sold by the sheriff at an execution sale, scheduled for April 14.[4]

Under state law, where goods are seized in execution, the judgment debtor (that is, Roy) has the right to redeem the seized goods from the sheriff before the execution sale takes place by paying the amount of the debt owed to the creditor. Assume that on April 6, Mo heard of the execution sale. Mo consulted his attorney, who decided that these facts were not enough to amount to a repudiation. However, she felt that they did provide Mo with grounds for demanding an assurance of performance. On the advice of his attorney, Mo wrote a letter to Roy, hand-delivered to him on April 6, in which Mo stated:

> I am aware that the camper that you sold me was levied upon by the sheriff yesterday and is scheduled to be sold in execution on April 14. Please deliver to me, in writing, by not later than April 9, an assurance that you intend to proceed with the sale to me, and furnish proof to me that you have the means to redeem the camper from the sheriff before our agreed delivery date of April 15. If I do not receive an adequate response from you by April 9, I will treat your failure to provide such assurance as a repudiation of our contract.

---

[4] Problem 19.7 asks if the sheriff's levy on the camper would constitute a repudiation of the contract by Roy.

On April 7, Roy delivered a written response to Mo in which he stated, "I have received your insulting and rude demand. Yes, I still intend to sell the camper to you. I will get it back from the sheriff before I am due to deliver it to you on April 15, so don't worry about that. How I do that is my business, and I don't have to prove anything to you. I expect your down payment, as agreed, by April 10."

Was Mo entitled to make his demand? How should he react to Roy's response?

CHAPTER 20

Introduction to Contract Damages and the "Benefit of the Bargain"

THE GOAL AND FUNDAMENTAL PRINCIPLES OF CONTRACT DAMAGES

In previous chapters, you have encountered contract remedies in many of their forms. This is how it should be; in almost every contract lawsuit a desire to obtain remedies from the court motivates the plaintiff. It is time now to pull many of these familiar themes together. In this chapter, we focus on contract damages and, in particular, explore the notion that contract damages provide the aggrieved party with the "benefit of the bargain." In Chapter 21, we expand our discussion of remedies beyond standard contract damages. There we consider noneconomic and noncompensatory damages, agreed remedies, and alternate remedies.

We begin with a note on perspective. Contract law is profoundly shaped by the notion that, ultimately, a disappointed party may seek relief in court. That is not to say that all or even a significant portion of disappointed contracting parties do so. Many business people will tell you that litigation is the remedy of last resort. When problems arise in ongoing commercial relationships, it is usually preferable to work through the problems informally and reach a resolution satisfactory to all parties. Even under the best of circumstances, litigation tends to get nasty. Although a court battle may settle a particular dispute, parties are often left with no desire to see their courtroom adversaries again, much less work with them cooperatively. Where an ongoing relationship has value, negotiating a means to settle a dispute out of court is an attractive alternative.

Even if there is no ongoing relationship to preserve, litigation is an unsettling prospect. For clients, litigation can be time-consuming, expensive, and emotionally devastating. The end results are uncertain. One can seldom predict with complete confidence who will prevail at trial and whether the court will grant a satisfactory remedy. Enforcement problems further complicate the client's prospects. In the case of money damages, even if they are sufficient in amount, they may be difficult to collect from the losing party. Because of these hazards and uncertainties, many people who cannot resolve their disputes easily outside of court simply absorb their losses and move on. Others anticipate the problems of litigation and in their original contract provide for alternative means of dispute resolution, such as mediation or arbitration.

In the end, however, courts stand ready to enforce contractual obligations. The presence of the courts and the remedial powers they exercise influence the behavior of parties at all stages of contractual relationships. Even where parties arbitrate or mediate a dispute, the remedial principles of contract law underlie its resolution. As a result, it is important to understand all dimensions of contract remedies, whether or not one ever plans to invoke them in court.

A court has several tools available to accomplish the remedial purposes of contract law. In the unusual case, the court may actually order the breaching party to perform. As we have noted, in our system of jurisprudence specific performance is an exceptional remedy; it is not available as a matter of right. Likewise, a court may on occasion enjoin one party from taking some action that might damage or impair the contractual rights of the other. Again, injunctions that prohibit breach are an exceptional remedy; they are not routinely available. Alternatively, in some instances a court may rescind a contract and order restitution. In Chapter 21, we discuss specific performance, injunctions, and rescission in more detail and examine further the situations in which each might be available. The workhorse remedy for breach of contract, however, is money damages. Once a court determines that a defendant has unjustifiably breached a contract, the court typically awards damages in an amount calculated to mirror the plaintiff's compensable losses. If the losing party does not pay the judgment voluntarily, in many cases its assets will be subject to seizure and sale.

1. The Distinctions Among the Expectation, Reliance, and Restitution Interests

It is not an easy task to determine the proper amount of damages in any given case. Conventionally, contract damages seek to make the aggrieved party whole. In general, their object is not to deter, punish, or exact revenge. In concept, a damage award will make the aggrieved party as well off as if the contract had been performed but no better off. This is the expectation measure of damages: the measure that gives the aggrieved party the "benefit of the bargain." It is important to recognize that this approach is neither universally applied nor perfectly realized. As we will see, the primacy of expectation damages as a contract remedy is a subject of some controversy. Even where courts seek to protect the aggrieved party's expectation interest, it is widely conceded that damages do not and cannot realize this goal with perfect accuracy. Nevertheless, expectation damages are the quintessential contract remedy, and they serve as the centerpiece of our study.

To better understand the nature of the expectation interest, it is helpful to review some related concepts introduced earlier in the text—the reliance interest and the restitution interest.[1] The Restatement, Second, states that the purposes of contract remedies are as follows:

RESTATEMENT, SECOND §344. PURPOSES OF REMEDIES

Judicial remedies under the rules stated in this Restatement serve to protect one or more of the following interests of a promisee:

(a) his "expectation interest," which is his interest in having the benefit of his bargain by being put in as good a position as he would have been in had the contract been performed,

(b) his "reliance interest," which is his interest in being reimbursed for loss caused by reliance on the contract by being put in as good a position as he would have been in had the contract not been made, or

(c) his "restitution interest," which is his interest in having restored to him any benefit that he has conferred on the other party.

———

Although Restatement, Second §344 separates the expectation interest, the reliance interest, and the restitution interest, it is important to understand that depending on the circumstances, reliance or even restitution costs may constitute components of the expectation interest. As the three interests overlap, it is important not to double-count and overcompensate the aggrieved party. We mention this to alert you to the potential for confusion; you will encounter specific examples to illustrate this point as the chapter continues.

■ PROBLEM 20.1

As an introduction to the distinctions among the expectation interest, the reliance interest and the restitution interest, consider the following facts as

———

[1] As you may recall from Chapter 10, where we also discuss this way of categorizing contractual interests, these concepts trace back to a two-part article written in the 1930s by Lon Fuller and William Perdue. We return to the theories of Fuller and Perdue in the next section.

described in *World of Boxing, LLC v. King*, 634 Fed. Appx. 1 (2d Cir. 2015).[2] Promoter Don King and his company, Don King Productions, Inc. (collectively "King"), entered into a contract with Vladimir Hrunov and Andrey Ryabinskiy, who do business as World of Boxing, LLC (collectively "World of Boxing"). Under the contract, King committed to produce boxer Guillermo Jones for a bout scheduled on a specific date, and to ensure that the boxer was in compliance with the rules of the World Boxing Association. For his services, King received one payment when the contract was signed, and was entitled to receive another after the bout took place. As it turns out, the boxer was unable to compete because he tested positive for a banned substance; the bout was called off, and World of Boxing made no further payments to King. Instead, it sued, seeking damages for breach of contract. Assume you represented World of Boxing in the litigation.

(a) Suppose your client claimed damages to protect its expectation interest in the contract with King. If you were to speculate, what sorts of damages might such a claim encompass? What difficulties do you anticipate you would face in trying to establish those damages to the court's satisfaction?

(b) Suppose instead your client claimed damages to protect its reliance interest in the contract with King. How would these damages differ from the expectation damages you identified in Question (a)?

(c) Suppose instead your client sought to protect its restitution interest. What, precisely, might that entail?

■ PROBLEM 20.2

Mildred and Morton Amour are about to celebrate their 50th wedding anniversary. They plan a huge celebration of this milestone, and they contract with Jacques LeChef to cater the affair for $20,000. When the Amours sign the contract, they give Jacques a 15 percent deposit of $3,500. Shortly thereafter, the Amours have some gold-embossed invitations printed, stating that the affair will be catered by Jacques. The invitations cost $2,000.

Jacques receives an offer to cater a celebrity wedding on the same day as the Amours' party. Preferring the exposure he would receive at the wedding, Jacques repudiates his contract with the Amours. The Amours

---

[2] Federal decisions and orders that are not selected for publication in the official Federal Reporter may be issued in the Federal Appendix. Decisions by summary order and included in the Federal Appendix do not have precedential value.

scurry to make alternate arrangements. They contract with Paulette Gourmande, another chef of Jacques's stature, to cater the party. Paulette charges $26,000 for her services. The Amours also reprint the invitations, this time naming Paulette as the caterer. The replacement invitations cost the same as before—that is, $2,000. On the appointed day, all of their friends and family attend, and the celebration is a huge success.

The Amours file suit in small claims court to obtain remedies for Jacques' breach.

(a) If the court compensated the Amours for their lost expectation, how much would they recover?

(b) If the court compensated the Amours for their reliance, how much would they recover?

(c) If the court instead awarded restitution to the Amours, how much would they recover?

Hawkins v. McGee introduces the "benefit of the bargain" and contract damages generally. Generations of law students have paled in horror at this the classic case, more commonly known in law school circles as the "hairy hand" case. If you are a movie buff, perhaps you remember Professor Kingsfield in *The Paper Chase*, who in the opening scene grilled the hapless protagonist on the facts of the case.

The opinion is spare in its facts and procedural history. As the opinion notes, Dr. Edward R. B. McGee performed experimental skin graft surgery on George Hawkins's palm. The surgery was not successful, and Hawkins sued McGee in assumpsit (that is, in modern parlance, breach of contract) and negligence. Although the opinion does not detail Hawkins's claims, the opinion in subsequent litigation between Dr. McGee and his insurer does.[3] It notes that Hawkins alleged that after the surgery, the new tissue grafted onto his hand developed a matted and unsightly growth to such a degree that the growth restricted the motion of the hand and rendered it useless. The negligence action was dismissed as a matter of law; however, the jury granted a verdict for the plaintiff on the assumpsit cause of action. The defendant moved for a judgment notwithstanding the verdict on the grounds that it was contrary to the law and the evidence, and that the damages awarded by the jury were excessive. Although the trial court held that the verdict was supported by the law and the evidence, it concluded that the damages were excessive and set aside the verdict. The plaintiff appealed.

---

[3] See *McGee v. U.S. Fidelity & Guaranty Co.*, 53 F.2d 953 (1st Cir. 1931).

HAWKINS v. McGEE

84 N.H. 114, 146 A. 641 (1929)
New Hampshire Supreme Court

BRANCH, Justice.

The operation in question consisted in the removal of a considerable quantity of scar tissue from the palm of the plaintiff's right hand and the grafting of skin taken from the plaintiff's chest in place thereof. The scar tissue was the result of a severe burn caused by contact with an electric wire, which the plaintiff received about nine years before the time of the transactions here involved. There was evidence to the effect that before the operation was performed the plaintiff and his father went to the defendant's office, and that the defendant, in answer to the question, "How long will the boy be in the hospital?" replied, "Three or four days, not over four; then the boy can go home and it will be just a few days when he will go back to work with a good hand." Clearly this and other testimony to the same effect would not justify a finding that the doctor contracted to complete the hospital treatment in three or four days or that the plaintiff would be able to go back to work within a few days thereafter. The above statements could only be construed as expressions of opinion or predictions as to the probable duration of the treatment and plaintiff's resulting disability, and the fact that these estimates were exceeded would impose no contractual liability upon the defendant. The only substantial basis for the plaintiff's claim is the testimony that the defendant also said before the operation was decided upon, "I will guarantee to make the hand a hundred per cent perfect hand or a hundred per cent good hand." The plaintiff was present when these words were alleged to have been spoken, and, if they are to be taken at their face value, it seems obvious that proof of their utterance would establish the giving of a warranty in accordance with his contention.

The defendant argues, however, that, even if these words were uttered by him, no reasonable man would understand that they were used with the intention of entering "into any contractual relation whatever," and that they could reasonably be understood only "as his expression in strong language that he believed and expected that as a result of the operation he would give the plaintiff a very good hand." It may be conceded, as the defendant contends, that, before the question of the making of a contract should be submitted to a jury, there is a preliminary question of law for the trial court to pass upon, i.e. "whether the words could possibly have the meaning imputed to them by the party who founds his case upon a certain interpretation," but it cannot be held that the trial court decided this question erroneously in the present case.

It is unnecessary to determine at this time whether the argument of the defendant, based upon "common knowledge of the uncertainty which attends all surgical operations," and the improbability that a surgeon would ever contract to make a damaged part of the human body "one hundred per cent perfect," would, in the absence of countervailing considerations, be regarded as conclusive, for there were other factors in the present case which tended to support the contention of the plaintiff. There was evidence that the defendant repeatedly solicited from the plaintiff's father the opportunity to perform this operation, and the theory was advanced by plaintiff's counsel in cross-examination of defendant that he sought an opportunity to "experiment on skin grafting," in which he had had little previous experience. If the jury accepted this part of plaintiff's contention, there would be a reasonable basis for the further conclusion that, if defendant spoke the words attributed to him, he did so with the intention that they should be accepted at their face value, as an inducement for the granting of consent to the operation by the plaintiff and his father, and there was ample evidence that they were so accepted by them. The question of the making of the alleged contract was properly submitted to the jury.

The substance of the charge to the jury on the question of damages appears in the following quotation: "If you find the plaintiff entitled to anything, he is entitled to recover for what pain and suffering he has been made to endure and for what injury he has sustained over and above what injury he had before." To this instruction the defendant seasonably excepted. By it, the jury was permitted to consider two elements of damage: (1) Pain and suffering due to the operation; and (2) positive ill effects of the operation upon the plaintiff's hand. Authority for any specific rule of damages in cases of this kind seems to be lacking, but, when tested by general principle and by analogy, it appears that the foregoing instruction was erroneous.

"By 'damages,' as that term is used in the law of contracts, is intended compensation for a breach, measured in the terms of the contract." *Davis v. New England Cotton Yarn Co.*, 77 N.H. 403, 404, 92 A. 732, 733. The purpose of the law is "to put the plaintiff in as good a position as he would have been in had the defendant kept his contract." 3 Williston Cont. §1338. The measure of recovery "is based upon what the defendant should have given the plaintiff, not what the plaintiff has given the defendant or otherwise expended." 3 Williston Cont. §1341. "The only losses that can be said fairly to come within the terms of a contract are such as the parties must have had in mind when the contract was made, or such as they either knew or ought to have known would probably result from a failure to comply with its terms." *Davis v. New England Cotton Yarn Co.*, 77 N.H. 403, 404, 92 A. 732, 733, *Hurd v. Dunsmore*, 63 N.H. 171.

The present case is closely analogous to one in which a machine is built for a certain purpose and warranted to do certain work. In such cases, the usual rule of damages for breach of warranty in the sale of chattels is applied, and it is held that the measure of damages is the difference between the value of the machine, if it had corresponded with the warranty and its actual value, together with such incidental losses as the parties knew, or ought to have known, would probably result from a failure to comply with its terms.

The rule thus applied is well settled in this state. "As a general rule, the measure of the vendee's damages is the difference between the value of the goods as they would have been if the warranty as to quality had been true, and the actual value at the time of the sale, including gains prevented and losses sustained, and such other damages as could be reasonably anticipated by the parties as likely to be caused by the vendor's failure to keep his agreement, and could not by reasonable care on the part of the vendee have been avoided." *Union Bank v. Blanchard*, 65 N.H. 21, 23, 18 A. 90, 91.

We therefore conclude that the true measure of the plaintiff's damage in the present case is the difference between the value to him of a perfect hand or a good hand, such as the jury found the defendant promised him, and the value of his hand in its present condition, including any incidental consequences fairly within the contemplation of the parties when they made their contract. Damages not thus limited, although naturally resulting, are not to be given.

The extent of the plaintiff's suffering does not measure this difference in value. The pain necessarily incident to a serious surgical operation was a part of the contribution which the plaintiff was willing to make to his joint undertaking with the defendant to produce a good hand. It was a legal detriment suffered by him which constituted a part of the consideration given by him for the contract.[4] It represented a part of the price which he was willing to pay for a good hand, but it furnished no test of the value of a good hand or the difference between the value of the hand which the defendant promised and the one which resulted from the operation.

It was also erroneous and misleading to submit to the jury as a separate element of damage any change for the worse in the condition of the plaintiff's hand resulting from the operation, although this error was probably more prejudicial to the plaintiff than to the defendant. Any such ill effect of the operation would be included under the true rule of damages set forth above, but damages might properly be assessed for the defendant's failure to improve the condition of the hand, even if there were no evidence that its condition was made worse as a result of the operation.

It must be assumed that the trial court, in setting aside the verdict, undertook to apply the same rule of damages which he had previously given to the jury, and, since this rule was erroneous, it is unnecessary for us to consider whether there was any evidence to justify his finding that all damages awarded by the jury above $500 were excessive. . . .

[The court orders a new trial.]

---

[4] This statement bears further explanation, as conventionally it would appear to be an incorrect statement under consideration doctrine. Although undergoing an operation and suffering the attendant pain is undoubtedly a legal detriment, in the usual case it would not be bargained for and thus could not constitute consideration. Although a doctor's promise to cure might induce a patient to undergo an operation, in the usual case we wouldn't expect a doctor to be induced to cure a patient in order to see the patient suffer. Here, however, as the court alludes to the fact that Dr. McGee may have had a particular interest in persuading George Hawkins to undergo this experimental surgery, one could argue that the patient's willingness to undergo the surgery (and suffer the attendant pain) did induce the doctor's promise to cure and vice versa. —Eds.

■ QUESTIONS

(1) *Hawkins v. McGee* is perhaps the most famous expectation damages case of all time. How, precisely, does the court articulate the expectation measure of damages?

(2) Recall that on many occasions in prior chapters where cases have raised damages, we have seen that the extra cost of obtaining a substitute performance provides a common measure of damages. Are the damages in *Hawkins v. McGee* substitutionary? If not, how do they differ from substitutionary damages, and why is the measurement different in this case?

(3) Do you see any discussion of what we would now call the reliance measure of damages? What about restitution?

(4) Courts worry about subjecting breaching parties to unexpected and potentially unlimited liability. As a result, courts limit the injured party's expectation recovery through application of a number of different legal doctrines. As we discuss in Section D, to recover contract damages, the injured party must establish them with reasonable certainty, show that they were within the reasonable contemplation of the parties at the time the contract was entered, and overcome any objection that they reasonably should have been avoided. Do you see any traces of any of these limitations in *Hawkins v. McGee*? Based on what you know of the facts, do you think any of these limitations might pose an obstacle to Hawkins's recovery? In particular, what evidence do you think Hawkins might introduce to establish his damages with reasonable certainty?

(5) In a contracts cause of action, damages for pain and suffering or emotional distress typically are not available. As we discuss in Chapter 21, an exception is often available where the breach causes bodily harm. Yet in *Hawkins v. McGee*, the court holds that damages for the plaintiff's pain and suffering from the operation are not proper components of his recovery. Why not?

■ PROBLEM 20.3

Sullivan v. O'Connor, 363 Mass. 579, 296 N.E.2d 183 (1973), another law school classic, was an updated version of *Hawkins v. McGee*. In a very similar situation to that of *Hawkins v. McGee*, the Massachusetts Supreme Judicial Court concluded that the reliance measure of damages was appropriate as a matter of policy. In *Sullivan*, the plaintiff was a professional entertainer. Her nose had been straight but long and prominent. She alleged that the defendant, a surgeon, had promised to enhance her beauty and improve her appearance through plastic surgery. He planned two operations to make her nose shorter and less prominent. The surgeries were not successful—the plaintiff underwent one additional, corrective surgery, but the end result was a nose that had a concave line halfway down, after which it became bulbous. Her postsurgery nose was asymmetrical and, according to the plaintiff, anything but pleasing. Ultimately, the plaintiff sued the surgeon for negligence and for breach of contract. The surgeon was found not to have been negligent, but the plaintiff was awarded damages for breach of contract.

At issue on appeal were the judge's instructions to the jury on contract damages. The Massachusetts Supreme Judicial Court noted:

> It is not hard to see why the courts should be unenthusiastic or skeptical about the contract theory [of recovery in a lawsuit by a patient against her doctor]. Considering the uncertainties of medical science and the variations in the physical and psychological conditions of individual patients, doctors can seldom in good faith promise specific results. Therefore it is unlikely that physicians of even average integrity will in fact make such promises. Statements of opinion by the physician with some optimistic coloring are a different thing, and may indeed have therapeutic value. But patients may transform such statements into firm promises in their own minds, especially when they have been disappointed in the event, and testify in that sense to sympathetic juries. If actions for breach of promise can be readily maintained, doctors, so it is said, will be frightened into practicing "defensive medicine." On the other hand, if these actions were outlawed, leaving only the possibility of suits for malpractice, there is fear that the public might be exposed to the enticements of charlatans, and confidence in the profession might ultimately be shaken. The law has taken the middle of the road position of allowing actions based on alleged contract, but insisting on clear proof. Instructions to the jury may well stress this requirement and point to tests of truth, such as the complexity or difficulty of an operation as bearing on the probability that a given result was promised.

The court then proceeded to discuss the proper measure of damages, should breach of contract be found. Citing *Hawkins v. McGee*, the court observed that some cases treated a physician's promise like an ordinary commercial promise and allowed "expectancy" damages as a matter of course. Alternatively, the patient could elect to rescind the contract and recover the fee paid to the doctor as "restitution" damages. Other cases, the court suggested, while not distinctly repudiating the analysis in *Hawkins v. McGee*, applied an intermediate measure:

> This measure is expressed in somewhat variant ways, but the substance is that the plaintiff is to recover any expenditures made by him and for other detriment (usually not specifically described in the opinions) following proximately and foreseeably upon the defendant's failure to carry out his promise. This, be it noted, is not a "restitution" measure, for it is not limited to restoration of the benefit conferred on the defendant (the fee paid) but includes other expenditures, for example, amounts paid for medicine and nurses; so

also it would seem according to its logic to take in damages for any worsening of the plaintiff's condition due to the breach. Nor is it an "expectancy" measure, for it does not appear to contemplate recovery of the whole difference in value between the condition as promised and the condition actually resulting from the treatment. Rather the tendency of the formulation is to put the plaintiff back in the position he occupied just before the parties entered upon the agreement, to compensate him for the detriments he suffered in reliance upon the agreement.

The court concluded that in circumstances where an agreement of this sort should be enforced at all, recovery limited to restitution seemed too meager, while expectancy recovery may well be excessive. The court instead favored applying a reliance measure to facts such as those presented. (The court did not ultimately decide whether the plaintiff could have received full expectation damages or whether to limit her recovery to reliance damages, because the plaintiff did not press for full expectation damages on appeal.)

(a) Based on this summary of the *Sullivan* case, catalog the damages the plaintiff would claim under an expectancy measure of recovery, a reliance measure of recovery, and a restitution measure of recovery. Where, precisely, do the differences among the measures lie?

(b) The *Sullivan* case discussed policy concerns in some detail and indicated that the nature of the contract at issue had some bearing on the appropriate measure of damages. Do you agree that damages should be available for breach of contract under these circumstances? If so, what measure of damages do you believe is most appropriate from a policy point of view?

2. Theoretical Perspectives on "Benefit of the Bargain" Damages

The idea that an aggrieved party should receive damages to compensate him for a breach of contract is a longstanding feature of the Anglo-American system. As Justice Oliver Wendell Holmes once famously said in this regard, "The duty to keep a contract at common law means a prediction that you must pay damages if you do not keep it—and nothing else."[5] Expectation damages seek to compensate the aggrieved party for the benefit he would have received from the bargain, measured in economic terms. Sometimes, especially when the plaintiff's motives are not entirely economic, this measure seems inadequate to capture

---

[5] Oliver Wendell Holmes, *The Path of the Law*, 10 Harv. L. Rev. 457, 462 (1897).

his broader disappointment and losses. In those circumstances the plaintiff may question why our legal system focuses on compensating the party aggrieved by a breach of contract, rather than deterring or punishing the person in breach. Apart from the distinction between compensation and deterrence or punishment, the common law system draws a sharp distinction between monetary compensation and specific performance. Certainly it would be possible to have a legal system that sought to compel parties to carry out their contracts. Many civil law systems, for instance, pay homage to the maxim *pacta sunt servanda*—commitments must be honored—and declare that the principal goal of contract law is to encourage performance.

While plaintiffs may argue that expectation damages are insufficient, defendants may argue expectation damages provide a windfall to the plaintiff. Especially where the plaintiff has not incurred any out-of-pocket costs or otherwise relied on the contract and the defendant breaches due to circumstances beyond her control, the defendant may question why she is obligated to compensate the plaintiff at all.

The optimal structure of contract remedies has inspired lively academic debate, and scholars remain in sharp disagreement. Earlier in the chapter we allude to the famous two-part article by Fuller and Perdue in which they separate the objectives of contract law into protecting the expectation interest, the reliance interest, and the restitution interest.[6] (As noted in the previous section, this categorization is now reflected in Restatement, Second §344.) The article went beyond simply presenting the by now familiar classification scheme. The authors argued against an inflexible view of contract damages.

It may be helpful to put the authors' arguments into historical context. At the time the article was written, specific performance was an exceptional remedy, perhaps even more so than it is today. Under some circumstances, an aggrieved party could request that a contract be rescinded and thus receive restitution, but this was often not sufficient to compensate the aggrieved party for its losses. (As we discuss in Chapter 21, the remedy of rescission remains an option for many plaintiffs but still proves less than satisfactory in the usual case.) Typically, then as now an aggrieved plaintiff would seek to enforce the contract by seeking damages. The prevailing view at the time was that such a lawsuit could have two possible outcomes: The defendant breached the contract and owed expectation damages, or the defendant didn't breach the contract and owed no damages at all. Fuller and Perdue argued that the prevailing view did not capture the actual decisions of courts and was not defensible from the perspective of policy. They argued that in reality, courts often awarded reliance damages instead of expectation damages. As a normative matter, they defended this result. The expectation interest, they noted, is "treated as a mere corollary of

---

[6] The articles in question are Lon L. Fuller & William R. Perdue, Jr., *The Reliance Interest in Contract Damages: 1*, 46 Yale L.J. 52 (1936); and Lon L. Fuller & William R. Perdue, Jr., *The Reliance Interest in Contract Damages: 2*, 46 Yale L.J. 373 (1937).

a more fundamental principle, that the purpose of granting damages is to make 'compensation' for injury. Yet in this case we 'compensate' the plaintiff by giving him something he never had. This seems on the face of things a queer kind of 'compensation.'"[7] Further, they argued, "the promisee who has actually relied on the promise . . . certainly presents a more pressing case for relief than the promisee who merely demands satisfaction for his disappointment in not getting what was promised him."[8] Nevertheless, they justified the expectation interest as a convenient proxy for the reliance interest, as true reliance on a contract in many instances may be difficult to prove and quantify.

Ever since, scholars have been debating the primacy of the expectation measure of contract damages.[9] Some scholars argue that specific performance should be the norm. Others argue that expectation damages are too meager and that instead, damages should in some cases be measured by the "disgorgement interest"; that is, the breaching party should be obligated to disgorge the benefits it receives upon breach. Yet others follow the lead of Fuller and Purdue and support the expectation interest as the conventional measure of contract damages, either because it is appropriate in its own right or because it is the most straightforward to predict and administer and, in the usual case, adequately attends to the interests most worthy of protection. Still others argue that the expectation measure of damages is too generous and that damages in the usual case should be calculated on the basis of the reliance interest instead.

In recent decades, a number of scholars have sought to explain and justify the primacy of the expectation measure of damages by reference to economic theory. The central concept that has emerged from this theory is that of "efficient breach."[10] The theory of efficient breach rests on the view that the central purpose of contract law is to facilitate the transfer of resources from less to more valuable uses. Although details of the theory remain subject to debate, we sketch its outlines here.

The exchange of goods and services is generally a good thing, because those who value them more are willing to pay to obtain them from those who value them less. The law has little role to play where the exchanges are simultaneous. Where one or both of the parties promise to perform in the future, however, one function of contract law is to help make those promises reliable so as to encourage parties to commit to exchanges in the first place.

One way to fulfill this function would be to allow the parties to compel performance of promises through legal means. This approach, however, presents its own problems. The performing party may have decided to breach

---

[7] 46 Yale L.J. at 52.

[8] 46 Yale L.J. at 56. Fuller and Perdue gave even heavier weight to the restitution interest, stating "The 'restitution interest,' involving a combination of unjust impoverishment with unjust gain, presents the strongest case for relief." *Id.* Again, we discuss restitution more thoroughly in Chapter 21.

[9] We allude to one aspect of this debate in Chapter 10 in our discussion of promissory estoppel.

[10] One of the best-known proponents of this theory is Judge Posner, whose judicial opinions we have encountered on a number of occasions. *See, e.g.,* Richard A. Posner, *Economic Analysis of Law* 95-102 (9th ed., Aspen 2014); Richard A. Posner, *Let Us Never Blame a Contract Breaker*, 107 Mich. L. Rev. 1349 (2009).

because it found someone else who valued the performance even more than the original contracting partner. To compel performance in this instance might not further the economic goal of contract law; it might frustrate it.

An economically preferable system would be one that would admit to the possibility of "efficient breach." In other words, the legal system could structure remedies such that breach would be permitted without penalty, as long as the nonbreaching party receives adequate compensation. In this way, a party could rationally choose to breach a contract if, taking into account the damages it would have to pay to the nonbreaching party, it would be profitable to do so. If its potential liability for damages was greater than any benefit to be gained from breaching the contract, presumably the party would elect to perform the contract instead. Promisors would have an incentive to direct their efforts to the most valued use. Promisees could continue to rely on contractual promises, because should breach occur they would nevertheless be entitled to the "benefit of their bargain." A legal system structured in this way would allow for efficient results, and society as a whole would be better off.

Substantial academic controversy surrounds the theory of efficient breach. As a normative matter, some scholars question whether efficient breach should be encouraged.[11] After surveying the case law, one student author concluded, as a descriptive matter, the theory fails to capture the interstices of contract doctrine.[12] Yet others argue that, regardless of the normative or doctrinal position one takes, the practical consequences of the theory as it operates in the real world are not efficient breach and full compensation but rather inefficient breach and opportunism.[13]

In its simplest form, as we have summarized it here, efficient breach theory is at best an approximation of what contract law can accomplish. It assumes that beneficial exchanges will go forward, because parties will deem

---

[11] See, e.g., Patricia H. Marschall, *Willfulness: A Crucial Factor in Choosing Remedies for Breach of Contract*, 24 Ariz. L. Rev. 733 (1982); Seana Shiffrin, *Could Breach of Contract Be Immoral?*, 107 Mich. L. Rev. 1551 (2009); and Dawinder S. Sidhu, *A Crisis of Confidence and Legal Theory: Why the Economic Downturn Should Help Signal the End of the Doctrine of Efficient Breach*, 24 Geo. J. Legal Ethics 357 (2011). Some authors examine whether the theory of efficient breach might be acceptable in legal systems other than ours, and conclude that significant societal and cultural factors suggest it should not. *See, e.g.*, Ronald J. Scalise, Jr., *Why No "Efficient Breach" in the Civil Law?: A Comparative Assessment of the Doctrine of Efficient Breach of Contract*, 55 Am. J. Comp. L. 721 (2007); Ni Zhu, *A Case Study of Legal Transplant: The Possibility of Efficient Breach in China*, 36 Geo. J. Int'l L. 1145 (2005).

[12] Craig Warkol, Note, *Resolving the Paradox Between Legal Theory and Legal Fact: The Judicial Rejection of the Theory of Efficient Breach*, 20 Cardozo L. Rev. 321 (1998).

[13] Professor Macaulay, for instance, wrote ". . . when relational concerns do not matter, many large corporations and their law firms do not efficiently breach. They do not seek to buy their way out of contracts for anything like the other party's expectation damages. They just breach, at best offer an insulting token settlement, and practice scorched earth litigation tactics, taken out of that unpublished but very real text, *Discovery Abuse for Fun and Profit*." Stewart Macaulay, *Relational Contracts Floating on a Sea of Custom? Thoughts About the Ideas of Ian Macneil and Lisa Bernstein*, 94 Nw. U. L. Rev. 775, 782 (2000). *See also* Richard R.W. Brooks, *The Efficient Performance Hypothesis*, 116 Yale L.J. 568 (2006) (agreeing that contract law should not require that an inefficient contract be performed, yet questioning why the breaching party gets to retain gains obtained upon breach).

compensation an adequate substitute for performance. As noted in the introductory paragraphs to this section, not all parties judge the value of their contracts in objective monetary terms. Those who enter into contracts for reasons other than profit may prefer contract performance to compensation and may not find the prospect of compensation alone sufficient assurance. Furthermore, the theory of efficient breach posits that the legal system is available to all aggrieved parties and that courts accurately measure and award full compensation for their losses. This is demonstrably not the case. As we will see, there are significant limitations on a plaintiff's ability to collect damages. Some losses are not capable of adequate proof; others are not compensable. Significantly even a successful plaintiff often cannot recover attorneys' fees and other costs of litigation. Nevertheless, the "benefit of the bargain" norm permeates contracts jurisprudence, regardless of whether theory justifies it or courts fully achieve it in practice.

B THE "BENEFIT OF THE BARGAIN" AT COMMON LAW

1. Components of Expectation Damages

We are now ready to turn to the expectation measure of contract damages and to explore its operation in more detail. The loss to the plaintiff of the value of the contract is the quintessential component of expectation damages. Often, you will see courts refer to this component of damages as "direct" or "general" damages—damages to compensate for the loss of the value that would have come directly from the contract itself. Where there is a complete lack of performance, this amounts to the value of the entire contract from the plaintiff's point of view. (If the breach excused the plaintiff's own performance, the expenses the plaintiff saved by not having to perform must be taken into account.) Sometimes the defendant has partially performed but then breaches—either by not completing the performance or by performing in a deficient manner. (*Hawkins v. McGee* and *Sullivan v. O'Connor* are both examples of this.) In those cases, the "direct" damages would consist of the difference in value between what the plaintiff expected to get from the contract and what the plaintiff actually received.

When a defendant breaches a contract, however, the plaintiff often suffers losses in addition to the mere loss of the value of the contract. Courts sometimes characterize these losses as "indirect" or "special" losses, and often separate them further into "consequential" and "incidental" losses. The plaintiff may suffer consequential losses if the defendant's performance was essential to some aspect of the plaintiff's business and the breach caused the plaintiff to forego potentially profitable opportunities that it could have pursued had the defendant performed. In addition to compensating for gains that were prevented, consequential damages are also available where the plaintiff suffers some harm, loss, or injury (whether economic or personal) that would have been averted or would not have arisen had the defendant performed the contract. Thus, lost profits in other transactions and injuries that are caused by the breach are sometimes compensable consequential damages. "Incidental" losses generally refer to the plaintiff's costs of coping with the breach, such as the costs of inspecting the defective performance or the costs of arranging substitute performance.

In practice, it can be difficult to distinguish among direct, consequential, and incidental losses. In many situations, as long as double-counting is avoided, the characterization of the losses does not matter, because they can be recovered in any case. But, as we will see, recovery of direct, consequential, and incidental damages is subject to significant limitations, and the limitations may differ depending on the characterization of the loss.

The classification of a particular loss may determine whether the loss is compensable at all. For instance, in *Mitsui O.S.K. Lines, Ltd. v. Consolidated Rail Corp.*, 327 N.J. Super. 343, 743 A.2d 362 (2000), a New Jersey appeals court faced the question of whether certain losses were consequential or incidental. The plaintiff had shipped some cargo by train, and the train derailed. In the aftermath of the derailment, the plaintiff spent $42,382 to have experts inspect and survey the damaged cargo. Conrail, the rail company at issue, paid the plaintiff for the damage to the cargo but refused to reimburse the plaintiff for the survey and inspection costs. Conrail claimed that these expenses were consequential damages and thus could not be recovered because a clause in the shipping contract barred recovery of consequential damages. The clause was silent on the subject of incidental damages. The court concluded that, although such clauses were generally enforceable (a subject we address in Chapter 21), the damages were incidental and thus not barred by the clause.

As the *Mitsui* case indicates, the choice of appropriate terminology may be a subject of heated debate. As you read the cases and materials to come, be alert to situations in which the distinctions among direct, consequential, and incidental damages arise, and try to discern which damages fall into each category.

2. Introduction to Measurement of the Expectation Interest

Just as there are many different types of contracts, there are myriad ways in which those contracts can be breached. Courts take a broad range of factors into account when they compare the plaintiff's actual situation to the situation he would have been in had the contract gone forward. As a result, it is difficult to state a single formula that fully and accurately captures the diverse analyses that courts use. Nevertheless, any measurement of the plaintiff's expectation interest must tally up the losses he suffered and offset any gains or savings he realized as a result of the breach. The Restatement, Second, puts it this way:

RESTATEMENT, SECOND §347. MEASURE OF DAMAGES IN GENERAL

Subject to the limitations stated in §§350-53, the injured party has a right to damages based on his expectation interest as measured by

(a) the loss in the value to him of the other party's performance caused by its failure or deficiency, plus

(b) any other loss, including incidental or consequential loss, caused by the breach, less

(c) any cost or other loss that he has avoided by not having to perform.

A few examples may help to illustrate the measurement of expectation damages along the lines suggested in Restatement, Second §347. Imagine that Ed Expectation runs a business out of his home. In March, he enters into a contract with Anna Accountant, in which Anna agrees to prepare Ed's annual income tax return for a flat fee of $1,000. Ed agrees to pay her fee once the return is finished. The parties agree that Ed will file the return with the IRS, and will pay any expenses of filing. Shortly after entering the contract, Anna gets unexpectedly busy, and concludes she will not have time to prepare Ed's return after all. She contacts Ed, and informs him that she must breach their contract.

Suppose Ed decides to prepare his income tax return himself. He spends an hour or two on it, and sends it in to the IRS on time. It would have been possible to line up another accountant to do the work for the same flat fee Anna would have charged, but Ed is angry about Anna's breach, and no longer wants to deal with an accountant at all. In this case, Ed probably has suffered no compensable expectation losses. Although he has lost the value of Anna's performance, he has also been excused of his obligation to pay her. The fact that another accountant would have charged approximately the same flat fee suggests that his contract with Anna was not an unusually advantageous one, so there is no direct loss attributable to Anna's failure to perform. Ed has lost a few hours of his time, but unless he can demonstrate that there are economic consequences directly attributable to this loss, typically Ed would not be able to recover for it. Likewise, damages will not be available for the emotional distress he may have suffered on Anna's breach absent unusual circumstances.[14] So this example does not posit any incidental or consequential losses. Likewise, other than the price that he no longer has to pay, Ed doesn't avoid any costs by not having to perform under this example.

---

[14] We return to this limitation in Chapter 21.

This general formulation, that Ed's expectation interest is measured by his direct loss, plus his incidental and consequential losses, less any avoided costs, applies in a broad range of circumstances. Suppose Anna refused to perform because she concluded that she had agreed to a price that was too low. She hadn't raised her rates for many years, and repudiated when she learned that all other accountants in the area charge $2,000 to prepare a return like Ed's. Upon Anna's breach, Ed hires another accountant to prepare his return, but because of the late date, is told that the work cannot be finished before the April 15 filing deadline. The new accountant does, in fact, charge him $2,000, but this charge includes filing the return electronically with the IRS as soon as it is completed. Even with electronic filing, the return is late, and Ed has to pay interest and penalties to the IRS. In this case, Ed would have expectation damages. His expectation losses would consist of:

- the difference between the $2,000 he paid the new accountant and the $1,000 he had agreed to pay Anna (his direct loss)
- plus any costs he may have incurred in locating the new accountant, along with the penalties and interest he has to pay to the IRS (his incidental and consequential losses)
- less any cost Ed would have incurred in filing the return had Anna performed as agreed, say the cost of a stamp or any cost of electronic filing (his avoided costs).

Ed's direct loss is clear when he enters into a substitute transaction. Even in the absence of a substitute transaction, however, Ed may suffer a direct loss. Again, assume Anna breached the contract because she concluded that she undercharged Ed. Ed tries to find another accountant to complete his return but cannot afford to pay the going rate—that is, $2,000. Ed decides to complete the return himself, and manages to file it before the April 15 deadline. Even though Ed did not enter into a substitute transaction, he has still lost the value of the unusually advantageous contract he had with Anna. Accordingly, his expectation damages include the difference between the going rate for this kind of service—that is, $2,000—and the $1,000 he had agreed to pay Anna. (We assume, as before, that his lost time is not compensable.) Because he managed to file the return on time, he doesn't have incidental or consequential losses. However, he hasn't saved any costs due to Anna's breach, because unlike the previous example, he still had to incur any costs associated with filing the return. So his expectation losses would equal $1,000.

In all of the preceding examples, Anna has failed to perform altogether. The general formulation for expectation losses holds, even when Anna partially performs. Suppose Anna starts the job, but for whatever reason is unable to finish it, and so materially breaches the contract with Ed. After her breach, Ed finds another accountant who is able to complete the return and file it on time. The other accountant would have charged Ed $2,000 to do the entire job, but since Anna had already done some of the preliminary computations, the accountant only charges Ed $1,500. Assume Ed suffers no incidental or consequential losses, but neither does he avoid any costs by dealing with the new accountant. In this case, Anna's partial performance has some value. But since his contract with Anna was unusually favorable, Ed still has expectation damages due to her breach. Had Anna completed the job, he would have paid her $1,000. Since she didn't complete the job, and thus materially breached the contract, he need not pay her, but he pays the other accountant $1,500 to finish her work. In sum, he pays $500 more than he expected to, and that is the measure of his expectation losses in this example.

As you can see, the calculation of expectation damages is highly fact-specific. Initially, we concentrate on the portion of the formulation that reflects direct losses—that is, the loss in value of the other party's performance. We turn to a more detailed treatment of consequential and incidental losses later in the chapter.

HUBBELL HOMES v. KEY

786 N.W.2d 519 (table), 2010 WL 2077173 (2010)
Iowa Court of Appeals

POTTERFIELD, Judge.

Hubbell Homes (Hubbell) is in the business of building and selling single-family houses and townhomes. In 2006, Hubbell began negotiating with Billy Michael Key (Mike) and Donna Elizabeth Powers Key for the sale of a new home in Norwalk, where Mike's employer had reassigned him. Mike's employer offered to pay a monthly rental housing allowance for one year as a reassignment benefit. Accordingly, the parties negotiated a Purchase Agreement for $376,900 with a delayed closing date of October 2, 2007, to allow the Keys to take advantage of this benefit. The parties also signed a Dwelling Unit Rental Agreement (Rental Agreement), for rental of the home by the Keys from October 2, 2006, through September 30, 2007. The Rental Agreement provided that the Keys would have the option to purchase the home for $376,900. The Rental Agreement also contained a "put" option that reserved for Hubbell the right to require the Keys to close on the purchase of the home for $376,900 at the end of the term of the lease.

In July 2007, Mike's position was eliminated, and he became unemployed. On August 6, 2007, Hubbell notified the Keys of its intent to exercise its option to force the sale of the property to them. Under the terms of the Rental Agreement, this required the Keys to close on the property at the end of the lease term on September 30, 2007. However, on September 28, 2007, the parties negotiated a First Modification of Dwelling Unit Rental Agreement (Amended Rental Agreement). The modification extended the term of the Rental Agreement for a three-month period ending December 31, 2007. The Keys offered to go forward with their purchase of the house at the original purchase price if Hubbell agreed to sell on contract or with Hubbell's financing. Hubbell rejected the offer, the sale did not take place, and the Keys moved out in early January 2008. Hubbell listed the house for sale at the contract price of $376,900.

About six months later, in the summer of 2008, Hubbell accepted an offer to buy the house for $350,000. However, the offer was contingent on the sale of the prospective buyer's current residence, a contingency which did not occur. The sale was never completed, and the house remained on the market at the time of trial at a reduced listing price.

Hubbell filed a petition against the Keys on March 26, 2008, seeking compensatory damages, consequential damages, and attorney fees. At the trial to the court, Hubbell first sought general damages of $36,137.50 in lost profits, calculated as the difference between the contract price and the costs Hubbell had incurred to build the house. Hubbell chose to request this calculation of general damages rather than the difference between the contract price and market value, although the house had not sold at the time of trial.

Second, Hubbell sought consequential or incidental damages for . . . [repairs made to the house, utility payments, loan interest and legal fees. It also] sought reimbursement for additional commission it would have to pay an outside realtor to sell the home, asserting that Hubbell's inside marketing agents only sell new homes. . . . [All told, Hubbell claimed consequential and incidental damages totaling $70,494.58.]

The Keys asserted defenses of frustration of purpose and unconscionability. They also contended they had an independent action for misrepresentation.[15] The district court concluded there was no factual basis upon which the Keys could be granted relief on their defenses of frustration of purpose or unconscionability. Regarding Hubbell's claim for general damages, the district court determined the fair market value of the house at the time of the breach was $350,000, relying on Hubbell's acceptance of the contingent offer as an indication of fair market value. The district court therefore awarded Hubbell damages in the amount of $26,900, the difference between the $350,000 value and the contract price. The court also awarded Hubbell . . . [some, but not all, of the consequential and incidental damages it claimed.]

Hubbell appeals, arguing the district court erred in calculating general damages. Hubbell asserts the district court should have awarded lost profits instead of the difference between fair market value and contract price. Hubbell also argues the district court erred in declining to award all of its requested consequential [and incidental] damages. . . .

The Keys cross-appeal, arguing the district court erred in failing to grant relief on their defense of frustration of purpose. [The court affirms the district court's conclusion that the Keys did not establish the defense of frustration of

---

[15] This claim appears to be based on problems relating to an open ditch and pooling water in the backyard of the house. It is not at issue on appeal.

purpose. We omit discussion of this issue.] The Keys also argue that the district court erred in determining a fair market value of the house when Hubbell failed to meet its burden of proof on that issue or, in the alternative, that the fair market value of the house was $376,900, the contract price at which the Keys offered to buy the house on contract following the expiration of the lease. Finally, the Keys argue the district court erred by awarding Hubbell [certain consequential and incidental damages.]

. . . Hubbell recognizes that Iowa case law establishes, "In real estate contract actions, general damages are measured by the difference between the contract price and the fair market value of the real estate on the date of the breach." *Macal v. Stinson*, 468 N.W.2d 34, 35 (Iowa 1991). However, Hubbell contends this measure of damages is inadequate because it would not put Hubbell in the position it would have occupied had the contract been performed. "The ultimate purpose behind the allowance of damages is to place the injured party in the position he or she would have occupied if the contract had been performed." *Id.* at 36. Hubbell asserts that lost profits is the correct measure of damages when it is evident that market value does not fully compensate the non-breaching party.

The general rule on lost profits is as follows:

> [P]rofits which would have been realized had the contract been performed are recoverable if their loss was within the contemplation of the defaulting party at the time the contract was made, and the profits can be proved with reasonable certainty.

Employee Benefits Plus, Inc. v. Des Moines Gen. Hosp., 535 N.W.2d 149, 156 (Iowa Ct. App. 1995). If it is speculative and uncertain whether damages have been sustained, recovery is denied. If uncertainty lies only in the amount of damages, recovery may be had if there is a reasonable basis in the evidence from which the amount can be inferred or approximated.

Hubbell presented evidence that the actual cost to build the home as of January 1, 2008, was $340,762.50. Pursuant to the Purchase Agreement, the Keys were to purchase the house at a price of $376,900. The difference represents the profits Hubbell would have realized if the Keys had performed under the contract. However, the profits actually must be lost to qualify as damages, and any amount lost depends on the price at which the house eventually sells.

Hubbell argues on appeal that it should be awarded the full difference between the contract price and the cost to build without reference to the price at which the home may eventually sell. Since it filed its petition and proceeded to trial before the house was sold, Hubbell was not able to prove the amount of its lost profits beyond its conjecture that it would have lost every possible profit dollar. Hubbell did not prove that a future sale of the home would result in a loss of all of the profits it anticipated to receive from the sale of the home to the Keys. We must deny recovery of lost profits because it is speculative and uncertain whether and in what amount these damages will be sustained. . . .

For these reasons, we conclude that the proper measure of general damages in this case is the difference between the fair market value of the home and the contract price. See *Gordon v. Pfab*, 246 N.W.2d 283, 288 (Iowa 1976) (holding the measure of general damages for breach of a land contract is the difference between market value at the date of breach and the contract price). Hubbell contends there was no market value for this home following the Keys' inability to purchase it. Despite Hubbell's contentions to the contrary, we determine the record reflects there was a market (although a depressed one) for homes during this period.

The Keys contend the district court erred by determining a fair market value for the home when Hubbell failed to meet its burden of proving fair market value. We acknowledge the district court's findings that "neither party gave evidence of the fair market value of the residence at the time of the breach." However, we find that the record contains substantial evidence to support the district court's determination of fair market value.

In the summer of 2008, Hubbell accepted a $350,000 contingent offer on the home. Though this sale was never completed because the contingency never occurred, the offer and acceptance to sell the home at this price is evidence of the market value of the home. Iowa courts "take a broad view in determining the sufficiency of evidence of damages." *Westway Trading Corp. v. River Terminal Corp.*, 314 N.W.2d 398, 403 (Iowa 1982). We agree with the district court that Hubbell's sale of the home in the summer of 2008 "can be considered as an indication of fair market value." This proposition is supported by numerous cases from other jurisdictions. See, e.g., *Kemp v. Gannett*, 50 Ill. App. 3d 429, 8 Ill. Dec. 726, 365 N.E.2d 1112 (Ill. App. Ct. 1977) (resale price nearly a year later); *Gilmartin Bros., Inc. v. Kern*, 916 S.W.2d 324 (Mo. Ct. App. 1995) (resale price six months after breach); *Roesch v. Bray*, 46 Ohio App. 3d 49, 545 N.E.2d 1301 (Ohio Ct. App. 1988) (resale price a year later). We therefore find the district court did not err in determining a fair market value for the house.

[The court's discussion of consequential and incidental damages is omitted.] . . . We affirm the district court's judgment and award in its entirety except that we find the Keys are responsible for the interest and utility expenses paid by Hubbell from January 1, 2008, through March 31, 2008. We remand for the district court to calculate these expenses and amend its judgment in a manner consistent with this opinion.

■ QUESTIONS

(1)   Hubbell sought damages based on lost profits—that is, the difference between what it cost to build the house and what the Keys had agreed to pay for it. The court held that this measure of damages was not appropriate in these circumstances. If the court had allowed damages based on this measure, would they have represented direct damages, consequential damages, or incidental damages?

(2) Do you agree that the lost profits measure is not appropriate in this case? Why or why not?

■ PROBLEM 20.4

One of the defendants' arguments in *Hubbell Homes v. Key* was that the plaintiff presented insufficient evidence of the market value of the house at the time of the breach. The court concludes that the $350,000 price agreed in the summer of 2008 can be considered as an indication of fair market value, even though the breach occurred several months before that. Often appraisers determine fair market value by examining comparable sales data. Suppose evidence had been introduced of numerous sales of comparable houses in the area on the date of breach, and all of them had sold for more than $376,900. What, in your view, would be an appropriate measure of damages under those circumstances? Would your answer differ if the plaintiff Hubbell had not only agreed to sell the house in the summer of 2008 for $350,000 but in fact had actually sold it for that price?

3. Measurement of the Expectation Interest When Neither Party Performs

Suppose a party breaches a contract by failing to perform altogether. The other party in turn refuses to perform its obligations under the contract, as it is entitled to do. But it also sues, seeking expectation damages for the other party's breach. In these circumstances, to determine whether the plaintiff suffered direct losses, the court must examine whether the defendant's performance would have had any economic value to the plaintiff. To measure this economic value, courts typically refer to one of three measures. As in *Hubbell Homes v. Key*, courts sometimes look to the market value of the promised performance and compare it to the terms of the contract at issue. If the plaintiff enters into a substitute transaction, a court may compare the terms of that transaction to the terms of the breached contract. In the *Hubbell* case, the plaintiff had not yet sold the house by the time the suit came to trial. Accordingly, measurement of the contract damages with reference to an actual substitute transaction was not an option for the court. Occasionally, if the facts merit it, a court will conclude that a measurement based on market value or a substitute transaction will not adequately protect the plaintiff's expectation interest. In these circumstances, courts may refer instead to the profit the plaintiff would have gained under the contract—that is, the difference between what the plaintiff would have received under the contract and what it would have cost the plaintiff to perform had the contract gone forward. This is the measurement requested, but rejected, in *Hubbell*. We address each of these measures in turn.

a. Measurement by Reference to Market Value

When a court uses a market value measure, it determines a party's direct losses by comparing the contract price to the market value of the performance promised under the contract. As the *Hubbell* case hints, this measure can involve difficult problems of proof, as it is in some sense hypothetical. A market measure seeks to compensate the plaintiff for the economic value it would have received had the defendant performed the contract. If the plaintiff neither seeks nor obtains the equivalent of contract performance elsewhere, however, the market value may bear no relation to out-of-pocket losses the plaintiff suffered. Even if this is so, the plaintiff is usually entitled to use the market value as the basis of calculating the loss of economic value due to the breach.

Generally, the contract price is easy to ascertain. Likewise, sometimes the party who seeks to recover damages can provide readily available and reliable evidence of that market value. In other cases, the task of establishing either the contract price or the market value can itself be one of significant complexity. Consider, for instance, the following case:

TURNER BROADCASTING SYSTEM, INC. v. McDAVID

303 Ga. App. 593, 693 S.E.2d 873 (2010)
Georgia Court of Appeals

BERNES, Judge.

This case involves Turner Broadcasting System, Inc.'s ("Turner") alleged breach of an oral agreement to sell the Atlanta Hawks and Atlanta Thrashers sports teams and the operating rights to Philips Arena to appellee David McDavid. Following a jury trial, a $281 million verdict was entered in favor of McDavid on his breach of contract claim. Turner filed a motion for judgment notwithstanding the verdict ("j.n.o.v."), or in the alternative, for a new trial, which the trial court denied. Turner appeals, contending that (1) the evidence failed to show (a) that the parties intended to be bound in the absence of an executed written agreement or (b) that the parties reached agreement on all material terms of the sale; (2) the evidence failed to show that the basketball and hockey leagues would have approved the sale; (3) the trial court erred in failing to give its requested jury charge on league approval; and (4) the damages were speculative, excessive, and decidedly against the weight of the evidence. We discern no error and affirm.

. . . [T]he evidence at trial showed that Turner is the former owner of the Hawks and the Thrashers, with operating rights to Philips Arena (the "assets"). In October 2002, Turner publicly announced its interest in selling the assets as part of a "deleveraging program" to reduce its mounting debts. In November 2002, McDavid expressed an interest in buying the assets and entered into negotiations with Turner. [The parties executed a "Letter of Intent," outlining proposed terms and establishing a 45-day exclusive negotiation period. After it expired, the parties continued to negotiate.] . . . When McDavid inquired about extending the Letter of Intent, Turner's principal negotiator told him, "Don't worry about it. We're very, very close to a deal. You're our guy." [The parties continued to negotiate, and in particular tried to resolve some tax issues. Turner proposed a resolution to the tax issue. McDavid's advisors stated that he would agree to Turner's proposal on the condition that it would resolve all remaining issues and finalize the deal.] . . . Turner's CEO, Phil Kent, agreed and announced, "we have a deal."

The parties subsequently exchanged multiple drafts of the purchase agreement and its exhibits. During the legal drafting process, the parties' counsel identified additional "open issues" for the written agreements. . . . Turner [ultimately] drafted an internal memo to its employees and planned for a press conference to publicly announce the deal with McDavid. In August 2003, Turner consulted with McDavid and his advisor on team management decisions, including the hiring of a general manager and a head coach for the Hawks. Turner also obtained McDavid's approval before hiring a trainer, assistants, and scouts.

On or about August 16, 2003, as the drafting process continued, Turner's executive and principal negotiator, James McCaffrey, approached McDavid about a simplified restructure for the transaction, assuring him that the restructure would "not change the deal," that the "deal was done," and that "they were ready to close on the deal that [they] made on July 30th." McDavid agreed to the simplified restructure, and the attorneys circulated revised draft agreements that reflected the restructured terms.

On August 19, 2003, the corporate board of directors of Time Warner, Turner's parent company, approved the sale of the assets to McDavid based upon the restructured terms. However, two of the board members, Ted Turner and Steve Case, opposed the deal, concerned that the assets had been undervalued and had resulted in a "fire sale."

On the day after the Turner board of directors meeting, Ted Turner's son-in-law, Rutherford Seydel, and the son of a member of the Hawks' board of directors, Michael Gearon, Jr., approached Turner about purchasing the assets on behalf of their corporation, Atlanta Spirit, LLC. While Turner continued to exchange drafts of the purchase agreement with appellees, it also began negotiations with Atlanta Spirit.

On or about September 12, 2003, McDavid and Turner verbally reached a final agreement on each of the alleged open items for the written agreement and Turner's principal negotiator announced, "[t]he deal is done. Let's get documents we can sign and we'll meet in Atlanta for a press conference and a closing [early next week]." But later that same day, Turner's principal negotiator and its in-house counsel signed an agreement for the sale of the assets to Atlanta Spirit.

On September 15, 2003, as McDavid was preparing to travel to Atlanta for the closing and a press conference to announce the sale, he received a phone call informing him that Turner was "going in another direction" and had sold the assets to Atlanta Spirit. McDavid and his advisors, who had spent months finalizing the McDavid deal, were "stunned," "shocked," "disappointed," and felt "completely broadsided."

McDavid filed suit against Turner, alleging claims of breach of an oral contract to sell the assets, promissory estoppel, fraud, and breach of a confidentiality agreement. [We omit discussion of the claims other than breach of contract.] Turner denied the existence of any binding agreement, arguing that the parties had not executed a final written purchase agreement and had continued to negotiate the material terms of the transaction. Following an eight-week trial, the jury returned a verdict in favor of McDavid on the breach of oral contract claim and awarded $281 million in damages. Judgment was entered accordingly.

Turner first argues that the trial court erred in denying its motion for j.n.o.v. or for a new trial on the breach of oral contract claim. Turner contends that the uncontroverted evidence established that the parties manifested an intent to be bound only in writing, and that the parties never reached agreement on all material terms of the sale. We disagree. The evidence on the issue of contract formation was highly controverted and presented genuine issues of fact for the jury's resolution. Because there was evidence supporting the jury's verdict, we must affirm. . . .

[The existence and terms of the contract were hotly contested. However, the court concluded that there was sufficient evidence to support the jury's conclusion that the parties intended to be bound in the absence of an executed written agreement. Further, there was also sufficient evidence to support the jury's conclusion that the parties reached agreement on all material terms of the sale. In particular, the court pointed to testimony, board memos and other evidence that supported the conclusion that the deal structure was as McDavid alleged it to be.] McDavid was to obtain an 85% ownership interest in the assets for a purchase price of approximately $215 million, representing the total enterprise value. McDavid agreed to accept liabilities, including deferred player compensation, capital accounts, and $140 million of arena area debt for his acquisition of arena rights. Turner was to contribute $104 million in support payments to offset operating losses during the transition. . . . [Turner was also to obtain the release of a lien on the Hawks' assets that served as collateral for some bonds that had been issued to the public to finance the construction of the arena. The court described other contributions that each party agreed to make, according to the evidence available to the jury.]

Spirit's counsel testified that he assumed Turner was using documents from the McDavid deal for their transaction since the terms were already very detailed and the drafts were complete. Material terms of the Atlanta Spirit deal, including . . . the percentage of ownership interest and purchase price value [among others] were the same or substantially similar to those reached in the McDavid deal. While McDavid spent eight to ten months negotiating the terms of his deal, Atlanta Spirit obtained the same deal within a matter of weeks. . . .

Turner argues that the $281 million judgment entered upon the verdict must be reversed since the jury's damages award was speculative, excessive, and decidedly against the weight of the evidence. Generally, the jury's award cannot be successfully attacked so as to warrant a new trial unless it is so flagrantly excessive or inadequate, in light of the evidence, as to create a clear implication of bias, prejudice or gross mistake on the part of the jurors. Even though the evidence is such as to authorize a greater or lesser award than that actually made, the appellate court will not disturb it unless it is so flagrant as to shock the conscience. Moreover, the trial court's approval of the verdict creates a presumption of correctness that will not be disturbed absent compelling evidence. . . .

The jury was instructed that the proper measure of damages in this case was "the difference between the contract price and the fair market value of the [assets] at the time the contract was breached." The trial court further defined fair market value as "the price that [the asset] will bring when it is offered for sale by one who desires but is not obliged to sell it and is bought by one who wishes to buy but is not under a necessity to do so." The parties raise no challenge to the propriety of the trial court's instructions in this regard.

The fair market value of the assets was a highly contested issue, and both parties presented experts who gave valuation opinions. Turner's expert, Donald Erickson, was an experienced business appraiser. Erickson opined that the fair market value was $255 million based upon 100% ownership of the assets, and that the contract price offered by McDavid was the determinative fair market value. Erickson's valuation was based upon the assumption of normal market conditions in which Turner was a willing seller, not under any compulsion, and in which McDavid was a knowledgeable buyer.

McDavid's experts were Roger Brinner, Ph.D., a renowned economist with experience in business valuations, and Robert Lieb, a consultant who specialized in sports economics. Dr. Brinner opined that the value of the assets was $516 million for 100% ownership interest,[16] based upon a market approach method used to value the teams and an income approach method to value the arena. Dr. Brinner's opinion was based upon his finding that the contract price was low

---

[16] The court explains in a footnote that according to Dr. Brinner, the Hawks' value was $294 million, the Thrashers' value was $116 million, and the arena rights value was $106 million. Dr. Brinner's valuation did not include the value of certain assets associated with the arena. According to Lieb, inclusion of these assets would have raised Dr. Brinner's valuation to $656 million. —EDS.

compared to comparable team assets and acquisition deals in the market. Lieb opined that the value of the assets was approximately $647 million for 100% ownership interest. . . . Lieb also opined that McDavid's contract price was "amazingly low" based upon market comparables and did not reflect the fair market value of the assets. In addition to the expert's opinions, there was evidence that Forbes, a valuation source, had valued the team assets at $340 million, excluding the arena value and debt. There was also evidence that Turner had internally valued the assets at $400 million.

Moreover, there was additional evidence that the actual contract price offered by McDavid and paid by Atlanta Spirit was not the fair market value of the assets. Significantly, board members of Turner's parent company had expressed concern that the assets had been undervalued and resulted in a "fire sale." There was other evidence showing that the teams had sustained financial losses, which impacted Turner's stock earnings and caused Turner to want to sell the assets and remove them from their financial records.[17] Internal e-mails exchanged between Turner executives indicated that they were facing "a lot of pressure . . . to get a deal done." Turner executives had also stated that they "knew that given the losses this would be a difficult sale" and that "getting full value for these teams [was] not possible." Based upon these circumstances, the jury was authorized to find that Turner was selling the assets at a price below fair market value to draw potential buyers and to promote a quick sale. Under these circumstances indicating that the contract price was below fair market value, the contract price did not conclusively establish the value of the assets.

As argued by McDavid, under Lieb's valuation, damages could be calculated at $335 million.[18] McDavid further argued that under the Forbes value, adjusted to include the . . . [value of the arena assets], damages could be calculated at $283 million.[19] Because the jury's $281 million verdict was within the range of the evidence, no basis for reversal has been shown.

We recognize that damages for breach of contract claims are compensatory awards designed to give the injured party the benefit of his bargain. In this case, Turner makes a compelling argument that the damages award seems disproportionate to the extent that it awarded McDavid more than he would have paid for the assets if the contract had not been breached. Nevertheless, Turner does not dispute that the measure of damages required the jury to determine the fair market value of the assets at the time of the breach. The trial evidence conflicted significantly as to whether the fair market value of the assets exceeded or

---

[17] McDavid and his advisors thought that the teams could be made profitable. McDavid had previously purchased a professional basketball team for $125 million and sold it for $280 million four years later.

[18] Lieb's total value of $647 million, adjusted to the 85% ownership interest, presented a fair market value of $549.95 million. Calculating the difference between the $215 million contact price and the $549.95 million fair market value yielded a damages estimation of $334.95 million.

[19] The Forbes total value of $586 million, adjusted to the 85% ownership interest, presented a fair market value of $498.1 million. Calculating the difference between the $215 million contract price and the $498.1 million fair market value yielded a damages estimation of $283.1 million.

was equivalent to the contract price, thereby presenting a question of fact for the jury's resolution in rendering its damages award. "Our role is not to enter the jury box. The jury made its award in its enlightened conscience and based upon the evidence [presented]. Thus, as the trial court declined to disturb the jury's verdict, we likewise decline to find error." *Gold Kist* [*v. Base Mfg.*, 289 Ga. App. 690] at 694(1), 658 S.E.2d 228 [(2008)].

Judgment affirmed.

■ QUESTIONS

(1)   For purposes of calculating McDavid's expectation damages, the court indicated that the contract price he agreed to pay for the assets was $215 million. In a portion of the opinion we omit here, the court states that some of contributions Turner agreed to make had the effect of reducing the purchase price to $96 million in accordance with the simplified structure of the deal. What factors complicate the determination of the contract price in this case?

(2)   The court surveys the evidence of market value presented at trial. When all is said and done, in your view, how reliable does that evidence seem to be? Is the answer to this question related to your answer to Question (1) above, and if so, how?

(3)   McDavid and Turner had an informal, oral understanding that McDavid would purchase the Atlanta Hawks, the Atlanta Thrashers, and the operating rights to Philips Arena for a "fire sale" price. Before the parties could sign a formal written contract to memorialize the terms of their deal, Turner agreed to sell the assets to the Atlanta Spirit on approximately the same terms. Nevertheless, McDavid is awarded $281 million in damages for breach of contract. In your view, does this result represent an unjustified windfall to McDavid or good policy? Why?

b. Measurement by Reference to a Substitute Transaction

Sometimes, the plaintiff obtains a replacement for the defaulted performance. If the replacement is less advantageous than the contract performance would have been, a comparison between the two can serve as a measure of the direct losses the plaintiff has suffered because of the breach. Sometimes, the defendant questions whether the substitute transaction was an appropriate replacement for the defaulted contract performance, and argues that it should not serve as the basis for calculating the plaintiff's expectation losses.

In the following case, a disappointed employer seeks and hires a replacement employee. Here, the court is willing to measure the employer's expectation damages based on the difference between the salary it has agreed to pay to the substitute employee and the salary it had contracted to pay the defendant. The court discards the defendant's argument that the substitute employee's increased salary is not an appropriate reference point for gauging damages.

HANDICAPPED CHILDREN'S EDUCATION BD. v. LUKASZEWSKI

112 Wis. 2d 197, 332 N.W.2d 774 (1983)
Wisconsin Supreme Court

CALLOW, Justice.

In January of 1978 the Handicapped Children's Education Board (the Board) hired Elaine Lukaszewski to serve as a speech and language therapist for the spring term. Lukaszewski was assigned to the Lightfoot School in Sheboygan Falls, which was approximately 45 miles from her home in Mequon. Rather than move, she commuted to work each day. During the 1978 spring term, the Board offered Lukaszewski a contract to continue in her present position at Lightfoot School for the 1978-79 school year. The contract called for an annual salary of $10,760. Lukaszewski accepted.

In August of 1978, prior to the beginning of the school year, Lukaszewski was offered a position by the Wee Care Day Care Center, which was located not far from her home in Mequon. The job paid an annual salary of $13,000. After deciding to accept this offer, Lukaszewski notified Thomas Morrelle, the Board's director of special education, that she intended to resign from her position at the Lightfoot School. Morrelle told her to submit a letter of resignation for consideration by the Board. She did so, and the matter was discussed at a meeting of the Board on August 21, 1978. The Board refused to release Lukaszewski from her contract. On August 24, 1978, the Board's attorney sent a letter to Lukaszewski directing her to return to work. The attorney sent a second letter to the Wee Care Day Care Center stating that the Board would take legal action if the Center interfered with Lukaszewski's performance of her contractual obligations at the Lightfoot School. A copy of this letter was sent to the Department of Public Instruction.

Lukaszewski left the Wee Care Day Care Center and returned to Lightfoot School for the 1978 fall term. She resented the actions of the Board, however, and retained misgivings about her job. On September 8, 1978, she discussed her feelings with Morrelle. After this meeting Lukaszewski felt quite upset about the situation. She called her doctor to make an appointment for that afternoon and subsequently left the school. Dr. Ashok Chatterjee examined Lukaszewski and found her blood pressure to be high. Lukaszewski asked Dr. Chatterjee to write a letter explaining his medical findings and the advice he had given her. In a letter dated September 11, 1978, Dr. Chatterjee indicated that Lukaszewski had a hypertension problem dating back to 1976. He reported that on the day he examined Lukaszewski she appeared agitated, nervous, and had blood pressure readings up to 180/100. It was his opinion that, although she took hypotensive drugs, her medical condition would not improve unless the situation which caused the problem was removed. He further opined that it would be dangerous for her to drive long distances in her agitated state. Lukaszewski did not return to work after leaving on September 8, 1978. She submitted a letter of resignation dated September 13, 1978, in which she wrote: "I enclose a copy of the doctor's statement concerning my health. On the basis of it, I must resign. I am unwilling to jeopardize my health and I am also unwilling to become involved in an accident. For these reasons, I tender my resignation."

A short time later Lukaszewski reapplied for and obtained employment at the Wee Care Day Care Center. After Lukaszewski left, the Board immediately began looking for a replacement. Only one qualified person applied for the position. Although this applicant had less of an educational background than Lukaszewski, she had more teaching experience. Under the salary schedule agreed upon by the Board and the teachers' union, this applicant would have to be paid $1,026.64 more per year than Lukaszewski. Having no alternative, the Board hired the applicant at the higher salary.

In December of 1978 the Board initiated an action against Lukaszewski for breach of contract. The Board alleged that, as a result of the breach, it suffered damage in the amount of the additional compensation it was required to pay Lukaszewski's replacement for the 1978-79 school year ($1,026.64). A trial was held before the court. The trial court ruled that Lukaszewski had breached her contract and awarded the Board $1,249.14 in damages ($1,026.64 for breach of contract and $222.50 for costs).

Lukaszewski appealed. The court of appeals affirmed the circuit court's determination that Lukaszewski breached her contract. However, the appellate court reversed the circuit court's damage award, reasoning that, although the Board had to pay more for Lukaszewski's replacement, by its own standards it obtained a proportionately more valuable teacher. Therefore, the court of appeals held that the Board suffered no damage from the breach. We granted the Board's petition for review.

There are two issues presented on this review: (1) whether Lukaszewski breached her employment contract with the Board; and (2) if she did breach her contract, whether the Board suffered recoverable damages therefrom. It is undisputed that Lukaszewski resigned before her contract with the Board expired. The only question is whether her resignation was somehow justified. Lukaszewski argues that, because she resigned for health reasons, the trial court erred in finding a breach of contract. According to Lukaszewski, the uncontroverted evidence at trial established that her employment with the Board endangered her health. Therefore, her failure to fulfill her obligation under the employment contract was excused.

We recognize that under certain conditions illness or health dangers may excuse nonperformance of a contract. This court held long ago that "where the act to be performed is one which the promisor alone is competent to do, the obligation is discharged if he is prevented by sickness or death from performing it." *Jennings v. Lyons*, 39 Wis. 553, 557 (1876). See also Restatement (Second) of Contracts sec. 262 (1981). Even assuming this rule applies to Lukaszewski's failure to perform, we are not convinced that the trial court erred in finding a breach of contract.

A health danger will not excuse nonperformance of a contractual obligation when the danger is caused by the nonperforming party.[20] Nor will a health condition or danger which was foreseeable when the contract was entered into justify its breach. It would be fundamentally unfair to allow a breaching party to escape liability because of a health danger which by his or her own fault has precluded performance.

In the instant case the trial court expressly found that the danger to Lukaszewski's health was self-induced. Lukaszewski testified that it was stressful for her to return to the Lightfoot School in the fall of 1978 because she did not want to work there and because she resented the Board's actions to compel her to do so. Citing this testimony, the court concluded: "The Court finds that the defendant's medical excuse was a result of the stress condition she had created by an attempted repudiation of her contract, and was not the product of any unsubstantiated, so-called, harassment [sic] by the plaintiff's board." Lukaszewski further complained about the hazard of driving 45 miles to and from Sheboygan Falls each day. She alone, however, caused this commute by choosing to live in Mequon. The trial court pointed out in its decision from the bench that she could have eliminated this problem by simply moving to Sheboygan Falls. Thus the court clearly found that any health danger associated with performance of the employment contract was the fault of Lukaszewski, not the Board. This factual finding alone is enough to invalidate the medical excuse for Lukaszewski's breach. . . . Accordingly, we affirm that portion of the court of appeals' decision which affirmed the circuit court's determination that Lukaszewski breached her employment contract.

. . . This court has long held that an employer may recover damages from an employee who has failed to perform an employment contract. Damages in breach of contract cases are ordinarily measured by the expectations of the parties. The nonbreaching party is entitled to full compensation for the loss of his or her bargain—that is, losses necessarily flowing from the breach which are proven to a reasonable certainty and were within contemplation of the parties when the contract was made. Thus damages for breach of an employment contract include the cost of obtaining other services equivalent to that promised but not performed, plus any foreseeable consequential damages.

In the instant case it is undisputed that, as a result of the breach, the Board hired a replacement at a salary exceeding what it had agreed to pay Lukaszewski. There is no question that this additional cost ($1,026.64) necessarily flowed from the breach and was within the contemplation of the parties when the contract was made. Lukaszewski argues and the court of appeals held, however, that the Board was not damaged by this expense. The amount a teacher is paid is determined by a salary schedule agreed upon by the teachers'

---

[20] You may recall that the insurers in *CNA International Reinsurance Co. v. Phoenix* in Chapter 17 cited *Lukaszewski* for this proposition, arguing River Phoenix's death was due to his own fault and thus should not excuse his nonperformance. The *CNA International* court rejected the argument under the facts of that case. —Eds.

union and the Board. The more education and experience a teacher has the greater her salary will be. Presumably, then, the amount of compensation a teacher receives reflects her value to the Board. Lukaszewski argues that the Board suffered no net loss because, while it had to pay more for the replacement, it received the services of a proportionately more valuable teacher. Accordingly, she maintains that the Board is not entitled to damages because an award would place it in a better position than if the contract had been performed.

We disagree. Lukaszewski and the court of appeals improperly focus on the objective value of the services the Board received rather than that for which it had bargained. Damages for breach of contract are measured by the expectations of the parties. The Board expected to receive the services of a speech therapist with Lukaszewski's education and experience at the salary agreed upon. It neither expected nor wanted a more experienced therapist who had to be paid an additional $1,026.64 per year. Lukaszewski's breach forced the Board to hire the replacement and, in turn, to pay a higher salary. Therefore, the Board lost the benefit of its bargain. Any additional value the Board may have received from the replacement's greater experience was imposed upon it and thus cannot be characterized as a benefit. We conclude that the Board suffered damages for the loss of its bargain in the amount of additional compensation it was required to pay Lukaszewski's replacement.

This is not to say that an employer who is injured by an employee's breach of contract is free to hire the most qualified and expensive replacement and then recover the difference between the salary paid and the contract salary. An injured party must take all reasonable steps to mitigate damages. Therefore, the employer must attempt to obtain equivalent services at the lowest possible cost. In the instant case the Board acted reasonably in hiring Lukaszewski's replacement even though she commanded a higher salary. Upon Lukaszewski's breach, the Board immediately took steps to locate a replacement. Only one qualified person applied for the position. Having no alternative, the Board hired this applicant. Thus the Board properly mitigated its damages by hiring the least expensive, qualified replacement available, we hold that the Board is entitled to have the benefit of its bargain restored. Therefore, we reverse that portion of the court of appeals' decision which reversed the trial court's damage award. The decision of the court of appeals is affirmed in part and reversed in part.

■ QUESTIONS

(1) Given the court's opinion, was Lukaszewski's breach an efficient one?

(2) Why does Lukaszewski argue that the substitute employee's salary is not an appropriate reference point for gauging damages? How does the court address this argument?

(3) What limitations does the court acknowledge on a plaintiff's ability to recover expectation damages? How do the limitations play out under the facts of this case?

(4) Lukaszewski apparently went to work for a few days, and only left her job on September 8. The court does not tell us whether she was paid for the days that she worked. Assume that she was not. Should this fact be relevant to the Board's damage determination, and if so, how?

(5) Suppose Lukaszewski had not resigned but instead had been fired, in breach of her contract. She took the job at the Wee Care Day Care Center at the salary mentioned. Would she be entitled to damages for the Board's breach?

■ **PROBLEM 20.5**

In May Dulcie Tones entered into a contract with Mary Time in which she agreed to play the piano in the bar of Mary's seaside hotel, Maritime Motor Lodge, in the seaside town of Four Seas. Under their contract, Dulcie promised to work on weekends from 8 P.M. to 2 A.M. and weeknights from 6 P.M. until 11 P.M. The employment was to last during the summer season from July 1 to September 30, and Dulcie was to be paid $2,000 per month. On June 20 Dulcie was offered the opportunity to accompany a well-known singer, beginning on July 1. Dulcie accepted this offer and repudiated her contract with Mary. Mary immediately sought a substitute pianist. At that late date, the only person she could find was a retired concert pianist who lived in a distant inland city. He was willing to come out of retirement for the summer but only if Mary would pay his airfare to Four Seas ($500), his accommodations ($1,000 a month), and his fee of $3,000 per month. Mary reluctantly hired the retired pianist on the terms that he demanded. He worked for the months of July, August, and September and was paid the fee and expenses as agreed. What claim, if any, does Mary have against Dulcie?

---

c. Measurement by Reference to Lost Profits

In *Hubbell Homes v. Key* and *Turner Broadcasting, Inc. v. McDavid*, the courts sought to uncover the market value of the lost contract performance. In *Lukaszewski*, the court measured the value of the lost contract performance by referring to the cost of a substitute performance. In some situations, a court will conclude that neither the market value measure nor the substitute measure of the plaintiff's loss adequately compensates the plaintiff. Instead, the court concludes that the plaintiff should receive the profit it would have earned under the contract at issue.

Return to the example of Ed Expectation and Anna Accountant. As before, Ed runs a business out of his home. In March, he enters into a contract with

Anna, in which Anna agrees to prepare Ed's income tax return for a flat fee of $1,000. (Assume this amount would represent pure profit to Anna; other than her time, she would have no expenses. Assume further that this is the going rate for services of this kind.) Ed agrees to pay the fee once the tax return is finished. Before Anna has started work, Ed decides he would prefer to prepare his tax return himself, and calls up Anna to renege on the contract. Suppose that on such short notice, Anna is not able to replace Ed's business. She spends the hours she would have dedicated to Ed's tax return organizing her desk and washing out her coffee cup. The hours that she otherwise would have spent in gainful employment cannot be recaptured. The court would be likely to award her the full $1,000 Ed had agreed to pay her, as she has lost the opportunity to earn the profit represented by the contract. Although she doesn't have to perform the work, and thus has in some sense saved effort due to the breach, time she spends not working does not provide her with any economic benefit and thus is ignored for purposes of the profit calculation.

Of course, we know from *Hubbell Homes v. Key* that the lost profits measure of damages is not always available. Suppose that upon Ed's breach, Anna immediately starts work on another client's tax return and receives $1,000 for doing the job. Under these circumstances, the substitute measure would yield no damages. (The market measure wouldn't yield any damages either, as we are assuming $1,000 is the going rate for services of this kind.) So one might think that lost profits is not an appropriate measure of her damages in this circumstance. Yet Anna might argue had Ed not breached, she would have prepared both returns and earned $2,000. Unless Anna was fully booked, she could have completed both Ed's return and that of the other client. If a court is persuaded by her argument, it would consider Anna to have "lost volume"—had there been no breach, she would have earned the profit from two transactions. If Anna has lost volume due to Ed's breach, it would be appropriate to award her the profits she would have received from Ed's business. If, however, Anna was fully booked, and Ed's breach enabled her to take on a client that she wouldn't otherwise have been able to serve, the lost profits measure of damages would not be available. To award her lost profits without recognition of the additional profits she was able to earn due to the breach would overcompensate her. She was able to replace Ed's lost business and as a result suffered no damages.

■ PROBLEM 20.6

Had Hubbell Homes been a lost volume seller, presumably it could have recovered the profit it lost when the Keys breached their obligation to purchase the home. Articulate why Hubbell Homes was not a lost volume seller. Can you describe a situation where it might qualify as one?

In Section B.1, we introduce the distinctions among direct damages, consequential damages, and incidental damages. Lost profits can be a particular source of confusion, because depending on the circumstances, they can either be direct damages or consequential damages. It is important to keep the two categories of lost profits straight. In our example, Anna's lost profits are a direct loss, because they represent the loss of the economic value of the contract itself. Suppose instead that Anna agreed to prepare Ed's tax return because he was very well regarded in the small business community, and she thought if she did a particularly nice job and word got out, she would garner additional clients. Because Ed breached the contract, Anna lost the expected exposure and claims she lost future business as a result. If she seeks to recover the profits she would have made in the future, she would be claiming consequential damages. Because the alleged profits would have come from potential contracts with other members of the business community, not from the contract with Ed, their loss cannot constitute a direct loss. As we will see, recovery of lost profits as consequential damages is subject to significant limitations (particularly, in this case, the limitation that damages must be proved with reasonable certainty), and Anna would have a difficult time persuading a court to award them.

4. Measurement of the Expectation Interest When the Breaching Party Performs in Part

In Section B.3, we assume that the breaching party had not rendered any performance at the time it breached the contract. Sometimes a party begins to perform but either does not complete performance or performs in an unsatisfactory manner. Recall that under the Restatement, Second, formulation of direct damages in §347, the plaintiff is to receive "the loss in the value to him of the other party's performance caused by its failure or deficiency. . . ." To the extent the deficient performance has value to the plaintiff, that value should be taken into account in determining damages for breach. In some situations, valuation of deficient performance presents difficult challenges to the courts.

Deficient performance may constitute a material and total breach, or it may constitute substantial performance and only a partial breach, depending on the circumstances. As you recall from our study of conditions and breach, material and total breach excuses the nonbreaching party from her own performance and also allows her to seek damages. In contrast, if the breaching party has substantially performed, the nonbreaching party must also perform, but she may have a claim for damages due to the incomplete or deficient performance. In either case, to properly calculate her direct losses, the court must measure the difference in value (if any) between what she expected and what she received under the contract. If her performance was itself excused by the breach, appropriate adjustments must be made to reflect any savings she realized as a result.

Construction cases illustrate the difficulties inherent in this calculation. Imagine that Nick, a homeowner, contracts to have his kitchen remodeled for $60,000. He chooses a quaint country kitchen design. Nora (the contractor) arrives, tears out the existing fixtures, and installs sleek aluminum appliances, black lacquered cupboards, and marble counters. Nick is aghast at the horrible mishap. He demands that Nora tear out the modern monstrosities and install the old world charm for which he had contracted. Nora refuses, telling him it would cost $85,000 to redo the job. Furthermore, she tells him, modern kitchens are all the rage these days, and her actions have actually enhanced the value of his home. If we take Nora's statements as true, has she breached the contract? Certainly. Has she materially and totally breached the contract? Probably. Has Nick suffered any direct losses due to the breach? That depends.

In a number of the cases we have read so far, courts have suggested that the usual measure of damages in construction cases is the cost of completion or repair. If this measure of damages applies, the loss in the value to Nick of the contractor's performance caused by the breach is the cost of converting a sleek kitchen to a country one. If, however, his damages are measured by the diminution in the market value of his home, a different result obtains. The first damage measure would yield substantial damages, the second possibly none.

If this controversy seems familiar to you, there is a reason. Perhaps you remember the *Jacob & Youngs, Inc. v. Kent* case in Chapter 18, and the contrasting case in Chapter 19, *Landis v. William Fannin Builders, Inc.* A brief refresher should remind you of the details. In *Jacob & Youngs*, Kent contracted to have a country residence built using Reading pipe. Instead, much of the plumbing consisted of pipes made by other factories. When Kent refused to pay the balance due on the contract, Jacob & Youngs sued him. Kent argued that Jacob & Youngs had breached the contract and that he should be relieved of his obligation to pay. The court disagreed but acknowledged that he should be entitled to an offset in the amount of damages he was owed. Although the usual measure of damages would be the cost of completion or repair, if such a measure would be "grossly and unfairly out of proportion to the good to be attained," the court held that the better measure would be the difference in value between a house with Reading pipe and a house with other brands of pipe (which was presumably nothing).

In *Landis* too, the plaintiffs complained of various discrepancies between the house that they had contracted for and the house they received. The plaintiffs had chosen a type of siding with a natural, rustic appeal, as well as a semitransparent green stain to enhance that appeal. Instead, the house as completed had a striped, patchwork appearance that the builders attempted to remedy without success. An expert testified that the mottled stain reduced the market value of the home by $8,500, and the defendant argued that damages should be limited to that amount. The trial court awarded damages based on the cost to replace the siding, which amounted to nearly $67,000. On appeal, the court concluded that the fact-finder must determine which measure of damage best accomplishes the goal of making a party whole without exceeding the bounds of reasonableness. Because the plaintiffs contracted to receive a custom-built home with certain aesthetics, an award based on the diminution in market value of the home would not fully compensate the plaintiffs. Further, it did not exceed the bounds of reasonableness under the circumstances to measure damages by the full cost of redoing the siding.

The *Jacob & Youngs* and *Landis* courts articulated similar legal rules, but reached opposite results on the facts before them. The challenge, of course, is distinguishing those cases where the cost of completion would work an unfair forfeiture (the test applied by *Jacob & Youngs*) or would exceed the bounds of reasonableness (the test enunciated in *Landis*) from those cases where it would do neither. There is no unanimity among the courts as to how to make these determinations, and courts consult a variety of factors. The extent of the waste may be critical, particularly when destruction of quality work would be required. The willfulness of the breach may also be relevant, as courts are more likely to allow disproportionate cost of completion damages when the breach is deliberate than when it is inadvertent. The desires and motivations of the nonbreaching party may also factor in, as courts may limit damages to diminution of market value where the interests at stake seem primarily pecuniary rather than personal. Often, the decisions rest on some combination of these factors.

■ PROBLEM 20.7

A case that has engendered substantial academic and judicial controversy is that of *Peevyhouse v. Garland Coal & Mining Co.*, 1962 Okla. 267, 382 P.2d 109 (1962).[21] Willie and Lucille Peevyhouse leased farmland to the Garland Coal Company. The Peevyhouses agreed to let Garland strip-mine for coal as long as it performed remedial work at the end of the five-year lease term. Garland mined the coal, but it didn't do the remedial work. The Peevyhouses sued, claiming damages in the amount of $25,000. This was the approximate amount necessary to restore the land to the condition promised by Garland. At trial, Garland did not dispute liability but argued that its damages should be limited to the diminution in the value of the Peevyhouse's farm due to its breach. It introduced evidence that the failure

---

[21] The reasoning in the *Peevyhouse* case has attracted commentary from many quarters. Professor Maute provided a fascinating yet troubling account of the *Peevyhouse* litigation itself in Judith L. Maute, Peevyhouse v. Garland Coal & Mining Co. *Revisited: The Ballad of Willie and Lucille*, 89 Nw. U. L. Rev. 1341 (1995). She performed extensive investigations into the background of the case and concluded that the facts reported by the court were grossly inaccurate and the case wrongly decided. She suggested that the Peevyhouses' limited resources, and a certain lack of skill, knowledge, and effort exhibited by their lawyer, contributed to the result. Judicial bias may have played a role as well. In the end, she concluded that the *Peevyhouse* case may teach us as much about the lawyering process and the capacities of our legal system as it does about legal theory and doctrine.

to restore the land had only reduced the market value of the farm by $300. The jury found damages in the amount of $5,000, although there was evidence in the record that this amount would exceed the value of the farm even had the remedial work been done. The Oklahoma Supreme Court affirmed judgment in favor of the Peevyhouses but reduced the amount of damages to $300 (all of which, apparently, went to pay for the costs of litigation). In so holding, the court stated:

> We therefore hold that where, in a coal mining lease, lessee agrees to perform certain remedial work on the premises concerned at the end of the lease period, and thereafter the contract is fully performed by both parties except that the remedial work is not done, the measure of damages in an action by lessor against lessee for damages for breach of contract is ordinarily the reasonable cost of performance of the work; however, where the contract provision breached was merely incidental to the main purpose in view, and where the economic benefit which would result to lessor by full performance of the work is grossly disproportionate to the cost of performance, the damages which lessor may recover are limited to the diminution in value resulting to the premises because of the non-performance. . . . Under the most liberal view of the evidence herein, the diminution in value resulting to the premises because of nonperformance of the remedial work was $300.00.

Based on this sketch, is *Peevyhouse* consistent with *Jacob & Youngs, Inc. v. Kent*? With *Landis v. William Fannin Builders, Inc.*? As a matter of policy, do you think *Peevyhouse* represents good or bad law, and why?

■ PROBLEM 20.8

As mentioned in Problem 20.5, Mary Time's hotel, Maritime Motor Lodge, is located in Four Seas. The town is a popular beach resort. Mary has owned and operated the hotel for ten years. It has 100 rooms as well as a reception area and pool deck. Mary wanted to add cabanas and a bar on the pool deck and also wanted to remodel the small and dingy reception area. She entered into a contract with I. Bungle Construction, Inc., under which Bungle agreed to do the work for $500,000.

Bungle began work as scheduled. Bungle started with the reception area, and did a nice job on the remodel. The construction continued to proceed smoothly until Bungle misread the plans and built the bar and the cabanas on the wrong side of the pool deck. As installed, the bar and the cabanas blocked the view of the ocean from the hotel. The bar and cabanas themselves, however, were beautiful. To rectify the error, the structures would have to be torn down and rebuilt, adding substantial cost to the project and likely delaying its completion. Bungle refused to bear the cost of demolishing and rebuilding the structures, and Mary declared a material and total breach and terminated the contract. At the time of termination, Mary had made progress payments totaling $300,000 to Bungle for work completed to that stage.

Mary immediately sought another contractor to complete the job. She obtained bids from several builders for completion of the project, including the demolition and rebuilding of the cabanas and bar. The lowest bid that she received was for $150,000, and the highest was for $450,000. Mary decided not to take the lowest bid because she had doubts about the bidder's reliability. She entered into a contract with Reliable Construction Co., Inc., the builder who submitted the second-lowest bid of $350,000. Reliable completed the project on time and to Mary's satisfaction.

What damages, if any, can Mary claim from I. Bungle?

"BENEFIT OF THE BARGAIN" DAMAGES UNDER THE UCC

In light of our study to date, many of the remedial themes in Article 2 of the UCC will seem familiar. The central precept of UCC remedies is that the aggrieved party is to receive compensation for its lost expectation. UCC 1-305(a) makes clear this emphasis on the expectation interest:

UCC 1-305(a). REMEDIES TO BE LIBERALLY ADMINISTERED

The remedies provided by [the Uniform Commercial Code] must be liberally administered to the end that the aggrieved party may be put in as good a position as if the other party had fully performed but neither consequential or special damages nor penal damages may be had except as specifically provided in [the Uniform Commercial Code] or by other rule of law. . . .

———————

As we will see, the UCC generally measures the expectation interest by either comparing the contract price and the terms of a substitute transaction or the contract price and market value, much as do many common law damage formulations. Furthermore, where the breaching party performs deficiently, the UCC, like common law, looks at the difference in value between the performance that was rendered and the performance that was promised. Study of the UCC formulations is useful in part because it provides a chance to review and refine one's understanding of contract damages in general. Although the UCC remedies bear striking resemblance to common law remedies, there are differences in detail and tone. As you read these materials, note the commonalities, but be alert for differences as well. We start by examining damages available to a buyer of goods when the seller breaches the contract. We then examine an aggrieved seller's damages.

1. Buyer's Damages Under the UCC

The remedies that Article 2 provides to buyers reflect the diversity of situations that give rise to them. Imagine that Jack Doe Equipment contracts to sell 100 lawnmowers to Chuck's Hardware Store. There are a number of ways in which Jack Doe might breach the contract, and several actions Chuck might take in response. Breaches can be grouped into situations where Jack Doe ultimately fails to supply Chuck with the goods and situations where Jack Doe supplies the goods but its performance is deficient in some way.

    Consider first the case of nonperformance. Jack Doe might repudiate the contract—that is, it might refuse to deliver the lawnmowers at all. Perhaps Jack Doe does this because it has found a more profitable outlet for the lawnmowers; perhaps it is unable to perform due to market conditions or some unfortunate event in its own business operations. Alternatively, Jack Doe might tender delivery of the goods, but Chuck may claim they do not conform to the contract. Say, for instance, that Jack Doe tenders push lawnmowers, but the contract called for riding mowers. If this nonconformity is unacceptable, Chuck may reject the goods. In other circumstances, Jack Doe may provide lawnmowers that appear to conform to the contract, and initially Chuck may accept them, but after some time it becomes clear that the mowers have some sort of defect. Chuck may revoke his acceptance of the lawnmowers and return them to Jack Doe.[22] All of these situations are treated in a similar fashion under the UCC—Chuck has lost the entire value that the contract held for him. To make Chuck whole, it will be necessary to determine what the value of the contract is to him. If Jack Doe is the only acceptable supplier of the type of lawnmower Chuck requires, Chuck may argue that specific performance is the only way to make him whole. As we see in Chapter 21, in the context of the sale of goods, this would be the exceptional case rather than the norm. More typically, Chuck would elect either to do

---

[22] We generally leave the details of revocation of acceptance to an advanced course in commercial law. Suffice it to say that a disappointed buyer who has accepted goods does not always have the option to revoke acceptance. The relevant code section, UCC 2-608, among other things, restricts revocation of acceptance to situations where the nonconformity of the goods is substantial. The section also imposes certain procedural requirements before a buyer can avail itself of the opportunity to revoke. Once acceptance of goods is effectively revoked, the situation is treated as if the buyer had rejected the goods on delivery.

without lawnmowers or to seek some sort of substitute in the market. In either case, damages may be available if the contract price was less than prices prevailing at a later date.

When the seller repudiates or fails to deliver or the buyer rightfully rejects or revokes acceptance of the goods, the contract is wholly executory: The seller has not performed, but the buyer does not have to pay either. (If the buyer has already made payment, it is entitled to reimbursement.) In contrast, sometimes the buyer accepts the goods even though they don't conform to the contract. Say, for instance, Jack Doe provides a cheaper model of lawnmower than that provided in the contract. Chuck may be willing to live with the cheaper model as long as there is an appropriate reduction in the price. Alternatively, the non-conformity may not be immediately obvious, and when it becomes obvious, it may be impractical or impermissible to revoke acceptance of the goods. Maybe lawnmowers delivered in the spring don't operate in colder weather, and Chuck doesn't realize this until his customers start bringing them in for repair late in the fall season. At that point, it may be too late for Chuck to revoke acceptance, even if that is his preference. In either of these situations, Chuck receives some value under the contract; it just isn't the value promised. As a result, when the seller performs but its performance is deficient, Article 2 looks to the difference in value between that which was promised and that which was provided as the appropriate measure of direct damages.

With that introduction, we are ready to explore the buyer's damages in more detail.

a. The Buyer's Damages When the Seller Repudiates or Fails to Deliver or When the Buyer Rightfully Rejects or Revokes Acceptance of the Goods

When the seller fails to perform, the buyer may make a substitute purchase. If the substitute purchase is more expensive than the contract price, the buyer can often recover the difference from the breaching seller. UCC 2-712 details this remedy, the remedy of "cover." As you read UCC 2-712, pay particular attention to the restrictions placed on the buyer, and speculate about their purpose.

UCC 2-712. "COVER"; BUYER'S PROCUREMENT OF SUBSTITUTE GOODS

(1) After a breach . . . the buyer may "cover" by making in good faith and without unreasonable delay any reasonable purchase of or contract to purchase goods in substitution for those due from the seller.

(2) The buyer may recover from the seller as damages the difference between the cost of cover and the contract price together with any incidental or consequential damages as hereinafter defined (Section 2-715), but less expenses saved in consequence of the seller's breach.

(3) Failure of the buyer to effect cover within this section does not bar him from any other remedy.

_____

The Official Comment to this section stresses that resort to cover is not mandatory; the buyer is free to choose between cover and a market measure of damages established by UCC 2-713. The Official Comment to UCC 2-713 clarifies that the market measure of damages only applies when and to the extent that the buyer has not covered in accordance with the terms of UCC 2-712. If the buyer does cover, its damages will be measured by UCC 2-712, but if it is unable to cover or if it chooses not to cover, UCC 2-713 will supply the relevant measure of damages:

UCC 2-713. BUYER'S DAMAGES FOR NON-DELIVERY OR REPUDIATION

(1) Subject to the provisions of this Article with respect to proof of market price (Section 2-723), the measure of damages for non-delivery or repudiation by the seller is the difference between the market price at the time when the buyer learned of the breach and the contract price together with any incidental and consequential damages provided in this Article (Section 2-715), but less expenses saved in consequence of the seller's breach.

(2) Market price is to be determined as of the place for tender or, in cases of rejection after arrival or revocation of acceptance, as of the place of arrival.

_____

The interaction of these two UCC sections poses some questions of interpretation. A buyer may enter into a particularly favorable substitute transaction and find that the cover measure of damages actually yields a smaller award than the market measure. In these circumstances, the buyer may argue that it should be able to keep the fruits of its diligence, and that the breaching seller should not be able to limit its recovery by reference to the substitute transaction. The breaching seller may respond that the cover measure of damages more accurately captures the actual damages to the buyer and, in line with the goal of giving the aggrieved party the benefit of its bargain but no more, the market measure of damages should not apply. As noted above, the Official Comment to UCC 2-713 sides with the seller in this debate. Alternatively, the buyer may proffer proof of a particularly expensive substitute transaction, and the seller may seek to limit the buyer's damages to the market measure. In such cases, the parties are likely to argue about whether the buyer was acting in good faith, whether the substitute transaction was entered into without unreasonable delay, and whether the substitute transaction was reasonable. Sometimes the parties contest whether the buyer covered at all.

CHRONISTER OIL CO. v. UNOCAL REFINING AND MARKETING

34 F.3d 462 (1994)
United States Court of Appeals, Seventh Circuit

POSNER, Chief Judge.

Chronister Oil Company brought this diversity suit for breach of contract against Union Oil Company (Unocal), to which Chronister had agreed to sell 25,000 barrels of gasoline. Unocal counterclaimed, charging that it was Chronister, not Unocal, that had broken their contract. The case is governed by the Uniform Commercial Code as interpreted by the Illinois courts; and the magistrate judge, to whom the case was assigned for trial by consent of the parties, held after a bench trial that Chronister had broken the contract, and he awarded damages of $26,000 to Unocal, precipitating this appeal. . . .

[Chronister was an oil trader. It contracted to provide 25,000 barrels of gasoline to a pipeline for shipment to Unocal. The contract price was 60.4 cents a gallon. The parties used terminology known in the trade to schedule delivery for some time around the first five days of March. To satisfy the contract, Chronister arranged through another oil trader to have Enron deliver the gasoline. Enron made the delivery on March 5, but the pipeline owner refused to take the gasoline because it contained too much water. When Unocal learned of the facts the next day, it demanded assurances from Chronister. Chronister (after consultation with Enron) offered to arrange delivery of replacement oil but said that the delivery would be delayed at least until the middle of March. Unocal refused the offer and within hours diverted gasoline that it already owned to satisfy its needs. The gasoline was in transit to storage at the time Unocal diverted it. Meanwhile, Chronister went ahead and contracted to purchase substitute gasoline from Enron for delayed delivery and, in the face of Unocal's continuing refusals to accept it, sold it at 55.3 cents a gallon to another user. The court affirmed the magistrate's ruling that Chronister was in breach.]

We move to the issue of damages. . . . Unocal had, back in February, promised to pay Chronister 60.4 cents a gallon. By the first week of March the price of gasoline for delivery to the Colonial Pipeline had fallen. On March 6, Chronister sold 25,000 barrels to Aectra at 55.3 cents a gallon, and it is not argued that Chronister could have gotten a higher price. Uncontradicted evidence revealed that there had been a similar sale at a similar price on March 2. Had Unocal gone out in the market and covered by buying 25,000 barrels on March 6 or 7 it would have paid somewhere in the neighborhood of 55 cents a gallon and thus would have saved 5 cents a gallon as a result of Chronister's breach. It makes no difference that instead of buying the gasoline on the open market it took it from inventory. As a matter of fact, because of an impending change in pressure by Colonial Pipeline that would make Unocal's inventory, stored mainly in a 300,000 barrel storage facility in Baton Rouge, shortly unshippable, Unocal had a strong interest in drawing down its inventory. The breach was a godsend. At argument Unocal's counsel candidly acknowledged that Unocal was made better off as a result of the breach and that this was evident not only by the time of trial, and hence early enough to figure in the calculation of damages, but within fifteen days after Chronister's breach.

Nevertheless, argues Unocal, it was entitled by UCC §2-712 to cover by obtaining a substitute for the lost 25,000 barrels, even from itself, and to obtain as damages the difference between the cover price, which it deems to be 63.14 cents a gallon, the average cost of the inventory from which it obtained the substitute supply of gasoline, and the contract price of 60.4 cents. This is a misreading of section 2-712.... Section 2-712 defines cover as purchasing or making a contract to purchase a substitute good. Unocal did not purchase any gasoline to take the place of the lost 25,000 barrels. It decided not to purchase a substitute good but instead to use a good that it already owned. You can't "purchase," whether in ordinary language or UCC speak (see §1-201(32)),[23] what you already own. The purpose of the cover provision is not to allow buyers to obtain damages when they have not been hurt, but to provide a market measure of the hurt. Taking a good out of your inventory and selling it is not a purchase in a market. There is no purchase price to use as a ready index of the harm that the buyer incurred by the seller's breach.

Two cases from other jurisdictions have shoehorned this kind of "self-cover" into section 2-712.... They had no need to do this violence to the text. Section 2-712 is not the only buyer's remedy that the UCC authorizes. The very next section allows the buyer to obtain damages measured by the difference between market price and contract price. If a reasonable response for the buyer to the breach would be to make the product itself, then the difference between the market price of that product and the contract price would be an appropriate measure of the harm from the breach. That is what ... [these other cases] hold; they merely cite the wrong section.

Unocal's response in diverting gasoline in transit to storage was reasonable; the only question, upon which its damages if any turn, is what that cost it. What it had paid for the gasoline—even less, the average price that it had paid for all the gasoline that it had not yet sold (the average cost of its inventory, in other words)—was not the cost of diverting the gasoline from storage to sale. At least it was not cost in a sense relative to damages. The object of an award of damages, as we have already noted, is to put the victim in the same place that he would have been in had the breach or other wrong of which he complains not occurred. It is to compensate him for a loss that he would have

[23] Judge Posner is referring to the UCC's definition of "purchase," which was contained in §1-201(32) at the time of the case but is now found in §1-201(b)(29). —EDS.

avoided had the violation not occurred. The concept of loss that underlies the computation of legal damages thus resembles the economist's concept of "opportunity cost": the opportunity one gives up by engaging in some activity is the cost of that activity. We must ask what Unocal gave up as a consequence of the breach, and whether it was something of value.

By diverting the gasoline in order to protect itself against Chronister's breach of contract, Unocal gave up the opportunity either to sell the gasoline on the market (in order to lighten its inventory), which we know would have yielded it substantially less than the average cost of its inventory because the market price was much lower than that cost, or to have a larger—an unnecessarily and, it would soon prove, unusably larger—inventory. Neither course of action would have yielded value equal to Unocal's average cost of inventory or equal to the contract price. The first point shows that the average cost of inventory was the wrong figure to use in estimating Unocal's damages, and the second point shows that it had no damages. The 25,000 barrels it diverted to its dealers cost it less—was worth less—than the 25,000 barrels that Chronister failed to deliver to it as promised. Sellers usually break their contracts in a rising market, where they can get more for the product by selling to someone other than the buyer with whom they signed the contract. Here a seller in a declining market broke a contract that he desperately wanted to perform, conferring a windfall gain on the buyer—which the latter would like as it were to double with the help of the courts.

The judgment of the district court is affirmed insofar as it determined that Chronister broke its contract with Unocal. But it is reversed with respect to damages and remanded with directions to enter judgment for Unocal for nominal damages (to which for reasons we do not understand every victim of a breach of contract, unlike a tort victim, is entitled) only.

■ PROBLEM 20.9

In the *Chronister* case, the average cost of the alleged cover (63.14 cents per gallon) exceeded both the contract price (60.4 cents per gallon) and the market price (55.3 cents per gallon). Suppose that Chronister had breached the contract because the price of gasoline had gone through the roof and was at the time of the breach three dollars per gallon. Instead of purchasing replacement gasoline, Unocal used gasoline from its inventory (at an average cost of 63.14 cents). Within a few months, the gasoline market settled down, and Unocal was able to replenish its inventory at the price of 55.3 cents per gallon. According to Judge Posner's reasoning, what would the measure of Unocal's damages be? Do you agree or disagree with this result, and why?

b. The Buyer's Damages upon Acceptance of Deficient Performance

The previous materials detail the buyer's damages when the buyer does not receive or ultimately accept the goods. We now turn to a buyer who accepts goods, notwithstanding the fact that the seller's performance does not conform to the contract. By accepting nonconforming performance, the buyer doesn't waive its rights to complain of the nonconformity. Assuming the buyer gives timely notice of the deficiency to the seller, the buyer can claim damages to compensate it for the seller's breach. The applicable Code section, UCC 2-714, gives a court substantial leeway to determine the appropriate measure of damages under these circumstances:

UCC 2-714. BUYER'S DAMAGES FOR BREACH IN REGARD TO ACCEPTED GOODS

(1) Where the buyer has accepted goods and given notification (subsection (3) of Section 2-607) he may recover as damages for any non-conformity of tender the loss resulting in the ordinary course of events from the seller's breach as determined in any manner which is reasonable.

(2) The measure of damages for breach of warranty is the difference at the time and place of acceptance between the value of the goods accepted and the value they would have had if they had been as warranted, unless special circumstances show proximate damages of a different amount.

(3) In a proper case any incidental and consequential damages under the next section may also be recovered.

2. Seller's Damages Under the UCC

When it becomes clear that a buyer is not going to perform its obligations under a contract, the UCC allows the seller to take a number of actions to protect its interests. Like the buyer's damages, the seller's damages under the UCC depend on the nature of the breach and the actions that the seller takes in response to the breach. You will see that there are striking parallels between a seller's damages and a buyer's damages.

a. The Seller's Action for the Price

Sometimes the buyer accepts conforming goods but simply refuses to pay for them. If so, the seller is entitled to the contract price. It has fully performed its side of the bargain, and all that remains to be done is to receive payment. A court that enforces the buyer's obligation to pay for goods that it has received and accepted is not really awarding damages for the buyer's breach; rather, the court is enforcing the buyer's obligation under the contract. In this sense, the seller's action for the price is akin to an action for specific performance. Since the seller asks for payment of a debt rather than performance of a nonmonetary obligation, however, it escapes many of the challenges posed by other specific performance actions. We defer consideration of these challenges for now. (We return to them in Chapter 21.) Instead, we focus here on those situations in which an action for the price is generally not available: when the buyer repudiates the contract or wrongfully rejects or revokes acceptance of the goods.[24]

b. The Seller's Damages When the Buyer Repudiates or Wrongfully Rejects the Goods

Sometimes the buyer repudiates before the seller performs, or the buyer fails to accept the goods when the seller tenders them. In either case, the seller doesn't have to provide the goods to the buyer, and the UCC damages formulations take this into account. In the usual case, the seller is not entitled to the full contract price as direct damages but rather the contract price less the value of the goods. This value can be measured in one of two ways—either by the price received by the seller in a substitute sale (this is the seller's equivalent of the buyer's cover) or by the market value of the goods. Sometimes these damage formulations are arguably inadequate to compensate the seller for its lost expectation. In those cases, the UCC looks to the profit the seller would have made on the contract with the buyer in computing the seller's damages.

UCC 2-706 contains the seller's remedy that is analogous to the buyer's remedy of cover. The seller enters into a substitute transaction, and its lost expectation is determined with reference to the substitute transaction. To arrive at direct damages, the resale price is deducted from the contract price. UCC 2-708(1) allows the seller to measure its damages with reference to the market value of the goods instead. Here, the market price is deducted from the contract price to arrive at direct damages. Unique to seller's remedies is UCC 2-708(2), which allows a seller to receive lost profits if the measure provided in UCC 2-706 or UCC 2-708(1) is inadequate to compensate the seller for its lost expectation.[25] Although UCC 2-706 and 2-708(1) largely mirror the analogous remedies for buyers, the treatment of consequential damages in the seller's remedies merits further exploration, as does the lost profits measure of damages.

---

[24] For the curious, the seller's action for the price is described in UCC 2-709. There are some circumstances where the seller may be able to collect the price for the goods, even though the buyer has not accepted them. These circumstances are limited to situations where the goods are for all practical purposes worthless in the seller's hands or where they have been destroyed. These subtleties are reserved for a course in commercial law.

[25] These lost profits constitute direct losses to the seller rather than consequential losses. Do not confuse them with the lost profits that establish a nonbreaching buyer's claim to consequential damages.

We start by reading the statutory language for the seller's various damage calculations. We then return to consequential damages and consider the degree to which sellers can claim them. We close with a discussion of the lost profits measure contained in UCC 2-708(2).

UCC 2-706. SELLER'S RESALE INCLUDING CONTRACT FOR RESALE

(1) Under the conditions stated in Section 2-703 on seller's remedies,[26] the seller may resell the goods concerned or the undelivered balance thereof. Where the resale is made in good faith and in a commercially reasonable manner the seller may recover the difference between the resale price and the contract price together with any incidental damages allowed under the provisions of this Article (Section 2-710), but less expenses saved in consequence of the buyer's breach. . . .

UCC 2-708. SELLER'S DAMAGES FOR NON-ACCEPTANCE OR REPUDIATION

(1) Subject to subsection (2) and to the provisions of this Article with respect to proof of market price (Section 2-723), the measure of damages for non-acceptance or repudiation by the buyer is the difference between the market price at the time and place for tender and the unpaid contract price together with any incidental damages provided in this Article (Section 2-710), but less expenses saved in consequence of the buyer's breach.

(2) If the measure of damages provided in subsection (1) is inadequate to put the seller in as good a position as performance would have done then the measure of damages is the profit (including reasonable overhead) which the seller would have made from full performance by the buyer, together with any incidental damages provided in this Article (Section 2-710), due allowance for costs reasonably incurred and due credit for payments or proceeds of resale.

As you recall, the buyer's damage calculations allow recovery of consequential and incidental damages. As you read the seller's damage calculations, you may have noticed that they allow recovery of incidental damages but omit any mention of consequential damages. The original reason for this omission is somewhat of a mystery. It may be that the drafters didn't include consequential damages in the seller's damage calculations because a seller so rarely incurs them. In spite of this omission, a few courts have held that sellers may recover

---

[26] UCC 2-703 refers to situations where the buyer "wrongfully rejects or revokes acceptance of goods or fails to make a payment due on or before delivery or repudiates with respect to a part or the whole."

consequential damages in those rare cases where they do arise. Other courts have reached the opposite result, relying on the language in UCC 1-305(a) that states "neither consequential or special damages nor penal damages may be had except as specifically provided in [the Uniform Commercial Code] or by other rule of law."

The lost profits measure of damages contained in UCC 2-708(2) should be familiar. As we see in Section B, at common law, courts sometimes award lost profits when reference to market value or a substitute transaction would not adequately compensate the plaintiff. As with the common law lost profits measure, the challenge is to determine when it is appropriate to apply UCC 2-708(2), and when it is not. Courts resort to this measure in a number of different situations. For instance, they routinely apply it if the seller is a lost volume seller.

We introduce the basic concept of a "lost volume" plaintiff in Section B. In the context of a sale of goods, the basic concept is quite straightforward. Consider, for instance, a seller who is in the business of selling the type of goods involved and has more goods available for sale than customers. If a buyer breaches a contract with the seller, neither the market measure of damages nor the resale measure of damages fully captures the harm to the seller. The market price may be the same as the contract price. Furthermore, the seller may be able to resell the goods to another buyer at the contract price. Yet, if the buyer had completed the contract, the seller might have been able to make two profitable sales, not just one. By breaching the contract, the buyer has deprived the seller of sales volume—and the profit that comes from one additional sale. If the market has not changed since the date the contract was entered, or if the substitute transaction is on the same terms as the breached contract, neither the market nor the resale measure of damages would yield any award at all.

In cases like this, the seller may argue that the profit it had hoped to make from the contract is a more accurate measure of its lost expectation than either the difference between the contract price and the market price or the difference between the contract price and the resale price. Although scholars have cast some doubt on the economics underlying this analysis,[27] the UCC and the cases interpreting it typically agree. It is not necessarily a simple task, however, to persuade a court that a seller qualifies as a lost volume seller and that it lost demonstrable profits upon the buyer's breach. Further, if the seller demonstrates that profits were in fact lost, the resulting damage calculations can be exceedingly complex.

Under UCC 2-708(2), a lost volume seller is entitled to recover the profit it would have made from the transaction, including its reasonable overhead. This

---

[27] The central critique is that this argument ignores the fact that the buyer, had it taken the goods but not wanted them, might have become a competitor of the seller. Even if the contract had gone forward, the seller might have lost sales volume due to the buyer's resale of the goods in the market. *See, e.g.*, Charles J. Goetz & Robert E. Scott, *Measuring Sellers' Damages: The Lost-Profits Puzzle*, 31 Stan. L. Rev. 323 (1979).

calculation merits further discussion. Suppose a buyer contracts to buy ten specially manufactured lathes from Machine Co., but then unjustifiably repudiates the contract. Suppose further that Machine Co. has sufficient capacity to manufacture many more lathes than it has orders. Machine Co. probably qualifies as a lost volume seller. To determine the damages the buyer owes Machine Co., one would have to know what Machine Co.'s cost would have been to perform under the contract had the buyer not breached. It presumably would have had to purchase parts, it might have had to retool its machines, and it might have had to hire additional workers to complete the manufacture. All of these costs, costs that it does not have to incur because it does not have to perform under the contract, must be deducted from the contract price to arrive at the profit figure. Courts refer to these costs as "direct" or "variable" costs—that is, these are costs that relate directly to the contract at issue and vary depending on the extent to which Machine Co. performs its side of the bargain. Machine Co. incurs other costs in operating its business—for instance, it pays its president a salary, it pays rent for its manufacturing facility, and it pays for heat and lighting. Courts refer to these costs as "fixed" costs or "overhead." Machine Co. will have to pay these costs whether or not it performs the contract with the buyer. To put it another way, these costs are not saved as a result of the breach. Accordingly, although accounting measures may deduct a portion of these costs from the seller's gross profit to arrive at a figure for the net profit it earns per lathe, the UCC damage formulations do not. Machine Co. is entitled to the contract price less its direct costs, with no deduction for the overhead otherwise attributable to the defaulted contract.

One further fact regarding the lost profits measure bears mention. You may have noticed that the final phrase of UCC 2-708(2) suggests that the lost profits damage calculation should give "due allowance for costs reasonably incurred and due credit for payments or proceeds of resale." This phrase has caused confusion, but when one limits it to its proper sphere, it makes sense. For instance, consider the admonition that the seller receive due allowance for costs reasonably incurred. These are sums the seller has already spent; it won't be able to save them by not performing. So if Machine Co. has already retooled its machines to produce lathes for the buyer when it learns of the buyer's breach, those costs will be sunk costs; there will be no way to recapture them unless Machine Co. can collect them from the buyer as part of its damages. Suppose instead Machine Co. has already started to manufacture the lathes. It has undoubtedly incurred some costs to purchase the parts and to begin manufacture. Machine Co. should receive due allowance for these costs as well. But if Machine Co. is able to repurpose the parts or resell the half-completed lathes, the proceeds it receives from mitigating its damages should be credited against the damages the buyer would otherwise have to pay. To put it another way, the buyer should receive due credit for proceeds of resale. All of this makes sense. What doesn't make sense is if the buyer receives credit for the proceeds of resale when a seller sells completed goods to another customer in the ordinary course of business—such an interpretation would effectively transform the lost profits measure of damages into something like the resale measure of damages. That is precisely the result the lost profits measure is designed to avoid—it only applies if the market and resale measures of damages are not adequate to compensate the seller. It is broadly conceded that this final phrase of UCC 2-708(2) should not be interpreted to allow this result but instead only authorizes a court to make adjustments around the margins to ensure that it doesn't under- or overcompensate the seller.

■ PROBLEM 20.10

Willie Walker owns a steel-bodied guitar from the 1930s, which he inherited from his blueswoman grandmother, Wichita Wanda Walker. Willie does not play the guitar himself, so he decides to sell it to someone who can put it to good use. Bessie Jones, a struggling musician, tells Willie that she would love to buy it, but she will need to save up to be able to afford his $7,500 asking price. Willie and Bessie sign a written contract to sell the guitar for $7,500 in ten months. After ten months have passed, Bessie tells Willie that she has become a software engineer and no longer has any interest in music. She refuses to take delivery of the guitar or to pay Willie anything.

(a) Upon Bessie's breach, Willie notifies her that he intends to sell the guitar on a popular Internet auction site. He lists the guitar on the site, and receives hundreds of bids. The highest bid for the guitar is $4,500, and Willie sells it for that price. What damages, if any, does Bessie owe to Willie? Is there any additional information you would want to have to answer this question, and if so, what would it be?

(b) Suppose instead that upon Bessie's breach, Willie decides to get the guitar appraised. The appraiser tells him that guitars of that vintage and in that condition are worth approximately $10,500. Willie decides to keep the guitar. What damages, if any, does Bessie owe to Willie? What if the appraiser said the guitar was worth approximately $3,500? Is there any additional information you would want to have to answer these questions, and if so, what would it be?

■ PROBLEM 20.11

Merry Music sells band instruments to aspiring musicians. Tony Deff visits Merry's store, and admires a beginner violin. He enters a contract with Merry to purchase it for $250 when he gets paid at the end of the month. Merry sets the violin aside. Before Tony picks up the violin or pays for it, he decides to take up water polo instead of music, and repudiates the contract. Upon Tony's unjustifiable breach, Merry puts the violin back on the shelves of her store, and sells it to another customer for $250. What damages, if any, does Tony owe to Merry? Is there any additional information you would want to have to answer this question, and if so, what would it be?

D LIMITATIONS ON RECOVERY OF "THE BENEFIT OF THE BARGAIN"

reasonable certainty
foreseeability
mitigation

Although the purpose of expectation damages is to place the plaintiff in the position she would have occupied had the contract been carried out, as prior materials have hinted, there are significant limitations on the plaintiff's ability to recover full expectation damages. In particular, three important principles operate to limit a plaintiff's potential recovery: the reasonable certainty principle, the foreseeability principle, and the mitigation principle. Each seeks to balance the risk of undercompensating the plaintiff against the risk of imposing excessive liability on the defendant. The plaintiff's claims are sometimes dubious, and skepticism about the alleged losses underlies the limitations. In other circumstances, the plaintiff appears to have suffered real losses, but holding the defendant fully accountable is deemed counterproductive or unfair as a matter of policy. We examine each of the three limitations in turn.

1. Reasonable Certainty of Damages

When a party to a contract is disappointed by breach, it is up to that party to prove the fact and amount of damages suffered. As we have seen repeatedly, courts focus on economic losses measured from an objective point of view, rather than on personal or eccentric losses as seen from a purely subjective point of view. Although the plaintiff's circumstances are taken into account, the plaintiff must prove that it suffered economic damage due to the breach, and it must prove the extent of those damages to the court's satisfaction. The plaintiff may encounter problems of proof with direct or incidental damages; however, consequential damages tend to present the greatest challenge.

Early American cases tended to require that damages be proven with a high degree of certainty. This was somewhat true in the case of direct and incidental damages, but was particularly true in the case of consequential damages. When

direct and incidental damages
consequential damages

consequential damages arise due to injury to persons or property, the fact of the damage is usually quite clear, and the amount is often fairly ascertainable. If consequential damages consist of <u>lost profits</u> or <u>other opportunities</u> forgone as a result of the breach, however, both the fact of the loss and the extent of the loss may be controversial. A requirement <u>that such damages be proven with a high degree of certainty may well defeat their recovery.</u>

must prove damages w/ a high degree of certainty

As case law developed, courts began to give the disappointed plaintiff significantly more leeway in proving damages. It is often said that a plaintiff must prove damages with reasonable certainty, not absolute certainty. A court may be willing to indulge in inferences, particularly when it is convinced that the defendant has breached the contract knowingly or willfully. Some courts have held that the fact of the damages must be proven with reasonable certainty, but the amount of those damages need not be established with precision. Other courts remain stringent and require a relatively high degree of certainty both as to the fact and as to the amount of the damages. What is clear, however, is that if damages are entirely speculative and uncertain, the plaintiff will not be able to recover.

Courts are particularly skeptical of unsubstantiated claims for loss of goodwill, business reputation, or future profits. This is especially true where the enterprise at issue is new. In the context of an ongoing business, there is at least evidence of past performance from which a court can extrapolate future losses. With a new, unproven business, it is anyone's guess as to whether, and under what circumstances, the business would have succeeded. Some courts have established a hard and fast rule that, with a new business, any losses of this nature are so speculative and uncertain that <u>they cannot be recovered as a matter of law.</u> In the following case, the court admits to the possibility that a new enterprise might be able to recover lost profits, subject to the usual requirement that the lost profits be established with reasonable certainty. Ultimately, as is often true with new enterprises, the requisite level of certainty proves elusive.

good will/ reputation/ future profit

↓

as a matter of law, new companies can't recover

RANCHO PESCADO, INC. v. NORTHWESTERN MUTUAL LIFE INSURANCE CO.

140 Ariz. 174, 680 P.2d 1235 (1984)
Arizona Court of Appeals

GREER, Judge.

The main issues we determine in this appeal are whether the trial court erred by: 1) denying appellee's application to compel arbitration and, 2) reducing the jury's award of damages to appellant from $2,500,000 to $101,510, by denying the damages awarded for loss of future profits. [We omit discussion of the first issue.] . . .

In 1971, James Jones (Jones) the president of appellant Rancho Pescado, Inc. (Rancho Pescado), became interested in and began studying the business of commercial catfish farming. He and his wife soon decided to enter the business for themselves. Jones read a great deal of literature on the subject and visited many experts in the field throughout the country. He eventually decided that the Gila Bend Canal in Gila Bend, Arizona, would be an ideal location to raise catfish. Jones contemplated using the existing water in the canals in which to raise the catfish, using an intricate system of screens to separate the fish and control algae problems.

The Gila Bend Canal was owned by appellee Northwestern Mutual Life Insurance Company (Northwestern) and used to deliver underground water to a large ranch operated by a wholly owned subsidiary of Northwestern, Painted Rock Development Company (Painted Rock). Jones explained his idea to Painted Rock in December, 1979 [*sic*—this should be 1971], and made a proposal to conduct a pilot program to determine the feasibility of raising catfish in the canal. After conducting a brief experimental program with mixed results, Jones submitted a license agreement to Painted Rock for approval. That proposal, as well as subsequent ones, was rejected by Painted Rock for various reasons. Negotiations broke off between the parties in 1972, but began again in July, 1973. Finally, in December, 1973, a license agreement, granting Rancho Pescado the exclusive right to raise fish in a five mile portion of the canal for a period of five years, was entered into between Northwestern and Rancho Pescado.

Jones spent much of the first half of 1974 raising money to finance his operation and solving an algae problem in the canal. Jones stocked the first delivery of catfish fingerlings in the canal in August, 1974. On the day before Thanksgiving, 1974, Jones was notified by Painted Rock's water development supervisor that the water flow in the canal would be shut off, as usual, for the holidays. Jones complained and the water was eventually turned back on. Northwestern concluded that continued flow of water through the canal when not needed for Painted Rock's ranch operations, such as during the Thanksgiving and Christmas holidays, constituted a serious interference with Painted Rock's ranching operation. As such, on December 10, 1974, Northwestern notified Rancho Pescado by letter that it was terminating the license agreement for cause because Rancho Pescado's demand for continuous flow of water interfered with the ranching operations in violation of paragraph two of the license agreement. Northwestern concluded the letter by advising Rancho Pescado that it had until April 1, 1975 to remove its property.

On January 6, 1975, Rancho Pescado filed a complaint for damages, including loss of future profits, against Northwestern, alleging that Northwestern had breached the license agreement. . . . [Northwestern filed a motion to compel arbitration, which the court denied. After trial, the jury returned a verdict against Northwestern in the amount of $2,500,000. Northwestern filed a motion for a new trial and a motion for judgment notwithstanding the verdict.] The court granted Northwestern's motion for judgment notwithstanding the verdict and reduced the amount of damages to $101,510, plus attorney's fees. The reduction in damage award represents the amount of damages awarded for loss of future profits. Rancho Pescado appealed the court's judgment notwithstanding the verdict. . . .

The thrust of Rancho Pescado's argument on appeal is that the court erred by eliminating the jury's award of damages for loss of future profits and thereby reducing the overall damage award from $2,500,000 to $101,510. Rancho Pescado contends the jury's award of damages for anticipated future profits was soundly supported by the evidence. Northwestern contends that Arizona has adopted a per se rule which prohibits an award of damages for loss of future profits to a new business. Northwestern further contends that even if a per se rule is not used, Rancho Pescado failed to sustain its burden of proving loss of future profits with reasonable certainty. . . .

Until recently, the majority rule in this country prohibited a jury's verdict of damages for lost profits of a new business. *See, e.g., Fredonia Broadcasting Corp. v. RCA Corp.*, 569 F.2d 251 (5th Cir. 1978), *cert. denied*, 439 U.S. 859, 99 S. Ct. 177, 58 L. Ed. 2d 167 (1978); *Mullen v. Brantley*, 213 Va. 765, 195 S.E.2d 696 (1973); . . . *see generally* Dunn, *Recovery of Damages for Lost Profits 2nd* §4.1 (1981). These cases were generally decided on the basis that loss of profits from a new business was merely speculative and incapable of being ascertained with the requisite degree of certainty. Such reasoning is supported by the generally accepted rule of contract law that damages are not recoverable unless they are reasonably certain.

Recent cases have eroded the once generally accepted rule against awarding damages for lost profits to a new business. The modern trend is to allow recovery for such lost profits if they can be proven with reasonable certainty. *See, e.g., Chung v. Kaonohi Center Co.*, 62 Hawaii 594, 618 P.2d 283 (1980); *Vickers v. Wichita State University, Wichita*, 213 Kan. 614, 518 P.2d 512 (1974). . . . In *Chung*, the Hawaii Supreme Court reasoned that, "it would be grossly unfair to deny a plaintiff meaningful recovery for lack of a sufficient 'track record' where the plaintiff has been prevented from establishing such a record by defendant's actions." 618 P.2d at 291. And, in *Vickers*, the Kansas Supreme Court noted that to preclude recovery "as a matter of law merely because a business is newly established would encourage those contracting with such a business to breach their contracts." 213 Kan. at 620, 518 P.2d at 517. The reasoning of these cases is highly persuasive.

This court has had two occasions to discuss the new business loss of profit rule. In *Earle M. Jorgensen Co. v. Tesmer Manufacturing Co.*, 10 Ariz. App. 445, 459 P.2d 533 (1969), we approved the modern view allowing recovery "where evidence is available to furnish a reasonably certain factual basis for computation of probable losses . . . even where a new business is involved." *Id.* at 450, 459 P.2d at 538. The per se rule seemingly re-emerged in *China Doll Restaurant, Inc. v. Schweiger*, 119 Ariz. 315, 580 P.2d 776 (App. 1978), in which this Court affirmed a summary judgment denying recovery for lost profits in a new business. We decline to follow *China Doll*, however, because the previous decision in *Earle M. Jorgensen v. Tesmer Manufacturing Co.*, was neither cited by counsel nor considered by the court in reaching its conclusion. We believe it would be patently unfair to deny damages to a business where they have been proved with reasonable certainty merely because the business venture was newly established.

Thus, the issue becomes whether the evidence introduced by Rancho Pescado, when considered in a light most favorable to upholding the jury verdict, established a reasonably certain factual basis for computation of lost profits. With reference to the evidence concerning lost profits, the principle is well established that once the fact of damages has been shown, the amount of damages may be established with proof of a lesser degree of certainty than required to establish the fact of damages. *Earle M. Jorgensen Co. v. Tesmer Manufacturing Co., supra.* However, there still must be a reasonable basis in the evidence for the trier of fact to fix computation when a dollar loss is claimed. The evidence required to prove loss of future profits depends on the individual circumstances of each case. While absolute certainty is not required, the court or jury must be guided by some rational standard in making an award.

In determining whether a plaintiff has met its burden of proof, courts have considered the profit history from a similar business operated by the plaintiff at a different location, and the profit history from the business in question if it was successfully operated by someone else before the plaintiff took over. Neither method was available for use in the instant case. However, as is the case with an established business, reasonable certainty may be provided when the plaintiff devises some reasonable method of computing his net loss.

In the instant case, Rancho Pescado had the burden of proving with reasonable certainty the fact that it could raise catfish in the canal and that it could thereafter market them at a profit as well as proving with reasonable certainty how much profit it would have realized. On appeal, Rancho Pescado maintains it has met its burden on all accounts with uncontroverted evidence that it could successfully raise and market fifteen million pounds of channel catfish per year at a profit of twenty-five to thirty cents per pound. Our review of the record, however, places Rancho Pescado's evidence in a different light.

Initially, we note that various experts testified that catfish farming is an extremely risky business, even for experienced farmers. According to the United States Department of Agriculture estimates, the failure rate is approximately ninety-five percent. Of the five percent who succeed in fish farming, most are already experienced aquacultural farmers.

The record also shows that instead of the pond method used by ninety-five percent of all fish farmers, Rancho Pescado utilized a raceway system for raising its fish. Rancho Pescado points to the feasibility studies conducted by Jones which, it claims, shows it would have overcome the high failure rate in fish farming. The record, however, shows that Jones' pilot program was inadequate in a number of important respects, including its accuracy in predicting the system[']s effect on disease propagation, control and mortality rate; growth rate of the fish; conversion ratio of feed to flesh; and stocking density. These factors were all considered important factors by various experts in predicting Rancho Pescado's success or failure.

In a similar vein, there was evidence that another expert believed additional development work had to be completed before Rancho Pescado could successfully raise fish in the canal. Specifically, Dr. Lawler was concerned about the downstream fish living in the waste products flowing from the fish upstream.

As mentioned above, Rancho Pescado also had the burden of proving with reasonable certainty that it could market the fish it raised. Evidence on this point was based upon oral conversations and a letter from the president of Frosty Fish, a California fish distributor, which indicated it was willing to purchase Rancho Pescado's entire production of catfish, f.o.b. Rancho Pescado's operation at the Gila Bend canal. Initially, we note that the number of fish Rancho Pescado intended to produce and sell was an inordinately high number of catfish each year. For instance, its projection of eight million pounds of catfish per year would be approximately 11.42 percent of the entire crop of catfish harvested nationwide in 1977. Leo Ray, the most successful catfish farmer in the country, had previously succeeded in raising and selling only four hundred thousand pounds of fish in his best year, utilizing conventional methods at a facility designed and used solely for the purpose of raising fish.

It is not reasonably certain from the record that Frosty Fish would have actually been able to market all of Rancho Pescado's production. For instance, Frank Mateljan, Frosty Fish's president, testified that Frosty Fish typically distributed only one thousand pounds of catfish per week, an amount far below that which Rancho Pescado contemplated producing. Mateljan also testified that he was not very close to the catfish market and had trouble selling catfish. When asked how he intended to distribute such a large quantity of catfish, he responded that he intended to sell a portion of it fresh, a portion of it frozen, and can the remainder. However, he admitted that he had never sold any canned catfish and had never heard of anyone who had. Most importantly, Mateljan testified that Frosty Fish was adjudicated bankrupt in 1976.

In conclusion, we view the evidence as a whole as amounting to nothing more than conjecture and speculation. The picture which emerges is one of an intelligent and enterprising individual who had an ambitious idea to take advantage of existing waterways to raise and sell catfish. However, the evidence is insufficient to prove that he would have succeeded in this highly risky industry. Although he had apparently done quite a bit of research into the catfish industry in general, his experiments on behalf of Rancho Pescado were woefully inadequate. Perhaps most damaging to Rancho Pescado's case is the lack of any conclusive evidence that it could have successfully marketed such large quantities of catfish. It is well settled that conjecture or speculation cannot provide the basis for an award of damages. The evidence must make an approximately accurate estimate possible. We are of the opinion that the jury did not have sufficient evidence to make a rational judgment as to the fact that Rancho

Pescado would have been successful and if so as to the amount of lost future profits. Thus, the trial court properly granted Northwestern's motion for judgment notwithstanding the verdict. . . .

Accordingly, the judgment of the trial court is hereby affirmed.

■ ■ ■

It can be difficult to establish expectation damages with reasonable certainty, especially where consequential damages like lost profits are at issue. In the worst case, operation of the reasonable certainty principle may demolish a plaintiff's claim to expectation damages. In some circumstances, the aggrieved party can recover the costs that she incurred in reasonable reliance on the contract, even if she cannot recover her full expectation damages. Typically, the party will not have expended more in reliance on the contract than she expected to gain, so reliance damages are usually smaller in amount than full expectation damages would be.

The ability to recover reliance damages is subject to the same limitations as damages generally. They too must be established with reasonable certainty. As we explore in Section D.2, they must have been such as to be within the reasonable contemplation of the parties at the time of contracting, and if the damages were reasonably avoidable (as we discuss in Section D.3), they cannot be recovered. These limitations tend not to be as powerful in the context of reliance damages as they are elsewhere, although they still have some room to operate.

As you read the next case, focus on the particular damages that the plaintiff claims. What makes expectation damages difficult to establish? Why don't the claimed reliance damages fall prey to the same difficulties?

HOLLYWOOD FANTASY CORP. v. GABOR

151 F.3d 203 (1998)
United States Court of Appeals, Fifth Circuit

ROSENTHAL, District Judge.

Appellee Hollywood Fantasy Corporation was briefly in the business of providing "fantasy vacation" packages that would allow participants to "make a movie" with a Hollywood personality and imagine themselves movie stars, for one week, for a fee. In May 1991, Hollywood Fantasy planned to offer its second fantasy vacation package, in San Antonio, Texas. Hollywood Fantasy arranged to have Zsa Zsa Gabor as one of two celebrities at the event. Two weeks before the fantasy vacation event, Ms. Gabor cancelled her appearance. A short time later,

Hollywood Fantasy cancelled the vacation event, to which it had sold only two tickets. A short time after that, Hollywood Fantasy went out of business.

Hollywood Fantasy sued Ms. Gabor for breach of contract and fraud. [A default judgment of $3 million, entered after Ms. Gabor failed to appear at docket call, was vacated, and a new trial was ordered.] After the trial judge found that Ms. Gabor and Hollywood Fantasy had reached a contract, the jury found that Ms. Gabor had breached that contract. The jury awarded Hollywood Fantasy $100,000 for the breach, as well as $100,000 for fraud. The district court set aside the jury's fraud verdict for lack of evidence and entered judgment in favor of Hollywood Fantasy for $100,000 on the breach of contract claim, plus attorneys' fees and post-judgment interest. Ms. Gabor appealed. We affirm the district court's judgment as to liability; reverse the district court's damages award; and render judgment for a lesser amount of damages.

Leonard Saffir created Hollywood Fantasy and served as its chief executive officer. The company Mr. Saffir created charged each vacation "client" $7,500 for a week of "pampering," instruction on making movies, rehearsals, and a "starring" role in a short videotaped film with a "nationally known" television or movie star. Mr. Saffir hoped that "bloopers" and "outtakes" from the videotapes would ultimately become the basis for a television series. A new venture, Hollywood Fantasy had conducted only one vacation event before the package scheduled to take place in San Antonio in May 1991. The first event, held in Palm Springs, California, had received some media coverage, but had lost money.

This case began with a letter Hollywood Fantasy sent Zsa Zsa Gabor dated March 4, 1991. The letter opened with the following language: "This will confirm our agreement whereby Hollywood Fantasy Corporation (HFC) will employ you under the following terms and conditions: . . . ." The letter set out the terms and conditions of Ms. Gabor's appearance in fourteen numbered paragraphs. The terms and conditions specified the dates of employment; the hours of work; the duties required; the payment; and certain perquisites to be provided. The letter stated that Ms. Gabor was to be employed from May 2-4, 1991, in San Antonio, Texas; was to be "on call" from after breakfast until before dinner each day; was to act in videotaped "movie" scenes with the clients, using scripts and direction provided by Hollywood Fantasy, and was to join the clients for lunch and dinner; was to allow Hollywood Fantasy to use her name and photograph for publicity; and was to provide media interviews "as appropriate" during her stay in San Antonio. Hollywood Fantasy was to pay Ms. Gabor a $10,000 appearance fee and $1,000 for miscellaneous expenses. Hollywood Fantasy would also provide Ms. Gabor two first-class round-trip plane fares from Los Angeles; transportation to the Los Angeles airport and in San Antonio; hair and makeup services; meals; hotel expenses, excluding long distance telephone calls; and a hotel suite with "two bath rooms if available."

Ms. Gabor made three handwritten changes to this letter before signing and returning it to Mr. Saffir. She inserted the word "one" into the sentence stating that she would make herself available for media interviews; inserted the words "two bedroom" above the sentence describing the hotel suite that was to be provided in San Antonio; and added the words "wardrobe to be supplied by Neiman Marcus" to the paragraph outlining the perquisites.

The last paragraph of the terms and conditions provided an "out clause": "[Hollywood Fantasy] agrees that if a significant acting opportunity in a film comes up [Gabor] will have the right to cancel [her] appearance in San Antonio by advising [Hollywood Fantasy] in writing by April 15, 1991." The final paragraph of the letter stated: "Please sign a copy of this agreement and fax it to me . . . as soon as possible so we can proceed." Ms. Gabor signed the letter in a signature blank above the words "Agreed and accepted" and sent it back to Leonard Saffir, who had already signed as the chief executive officer for Hollywood Fantasy.

On April 10, Ms. Gabor and Mr. Saffir talked by telephone. The parties differ as to the substance of that conversation. Mr. Saffir asserts that they discussed the changes Ms. Gabor had made and "everything was agreed." Ms. Gabor asserts that Mr. Saffir acted as if the original offer had been accepted. The parties agree that Ms. Gabor sent Mr. Saffir a telegram dated April 15, 1991, stating: "In accordance with the contract that exists between us the purpose of this telegram is to inform you that I must terminate it because I am due to be involved in preproduction and a promotion film for a motion picture I am contracted to do. The name of the film is Queen of Justice produced by Metro Films of Los Angeles. . . . I am very sorry to cause you any discomfort but will be happy to try to help in supplying you with a replacement and hopefully we'll be able to do something together in the very near future."

Hollywood Fantasy unsuccessfully attempted to replace Ms. Gabor for the San Antonio event. The San Antonio event was cancelled; the two ticket purchasers received their money back; Hollywood Fantasy went out of business; and this litigation began. . . . [The court concludes that the parties did reach a contract and that the jury was justified in finding that Ms. Gabor breached it. Although the contract allowed Ms. Gabor to cancel if a "significant acting opportunity" came up, the court concluded that no such opportunity was present here. Although she appeared in one movie and claimed she had committed to do promotional work for another, her appearance in the first was a 14-second cameo during the credits of *The Naked Gun $2\frac{1}{2}$: The Smell of Fear*, she did no preproduction work for the second, and in fact the second movie was never made. The court's discussion of damages follows.]

At trial, Ms. Gabor moved for judgment as a matter of law that there was insufficient evidence to support the jury's award of $100,000 for breach of contract. The district court denied Ms. Gabor's motion. Ms. Gabor renews her objection here. . . .

"It is a general rule that the victim of a breach of contract should be restored to the position he would have been in had the contract been performed." *Mistletoe Express Serv. of Okla. City, Okla. v. Locke*, 762 S.W.2d 637, 638 (Tex. App. 1988). "However, an injured party may, if he so chooses, ignore the element of profits and recover as damages his expenditures in reliance." *Nelson v. Data*

Terminal Sys., Inc., 762 S.W.2d 744, 748 (Tex. App. 1988) (citing Restatement (Second) of Contracts §§347, 349).

The $100,000 damages award cannot be supported as the recovery of lost profits. Mr. Saffir testified that Hollywood Fantasy lost $250,000 in profits from future fantasy vacation events and at least $1,000,000 in future profits from the creation of a television series based on "bloopers" and "outtakes" from the videotapes of clients "acting" with Hollywood personalities. Although . . . recovery of lost profits does not require that the loss be susceptible to exact calculation, . . . lost profits must be proved with "reasonable certainty." *Texas Instruments, Inc. v. Teletron Energy Management, Inc.*, 877 S.W.2d 276, 279 (Tex. 1994). . . .

Leonard Saffir's testimony that Hollywood Fantasy lost $250,000 in future profits was based on his estimate that Hollywood Fantasy would make a $25,000 profit from each of ten future events. Hollywood Fantasy was a new venture. It had put on one event, in which nine people participated, and in which it had lost money. Two weeks before the San Antonio event, only two people had bought tickets for the event. Hollywood Fantasy had no commitments to, or arrangements for, specific future events. "Profits which are largely speculative, as from an activity dependent on uncertain or changing market conditions, or on chancy business opportunities, . . . or on the success of a new and unproven enterprise, cannot be recovered." *Texas Instruments*, 877 S.W.2d at 279. "The mere hope for success of an untried enterprise, even when that hope is realistic, is not enough for recovery of lost profits." *Id.* In *Texas Instruments*, the Texas Supreme Court made it clear that the relevant "enterprise" in the lost profits inquiry is "not the business entity, but the activity which is alleged to have been damaged." There was no evidence at trial that the "movie fantasy vacation" enterprise promoted by Hollywood Fantasy had been a successful enterprise in any context. There was no evidence that the Hollywood Fantasy management had ever been involved in any prior fantasy vacation enterprise, let alone a successful one. . . .

In *Texas Instruments*, the Texas Supreme Court stated that even a new enterprise may attempt to recover lost profits when there are "firmer reasons" to "expect [the] business to yield a profit." There was no evidence at trial that Hollywood Fantasy had "firm" reasons to expect a profit. Nine participants attended the Palm Springs event; not all of those participants paid the full $7,500 price of admission and only "some" of the Hollywood Fantasy employees were paid for their work. As of April 15, 1991, two weeks before the San Antonio event, only two tickets had been sold. Mr. Saffir's testimony that he still expected twenty participants was based on the optimistic but unsupported assertion that people generally "don't send in their money right away."

Hollywood Fantasy's claim for loss of television revenue is even more speculative. Mr. Saffir admitted that he had not sold a television pilot, let alone a series, based on the fantasy vacation videotapes. Mr. Saffir testified that the actors appearing in the videotapes could have unilaterally declined to permit Hollywood Fantasy to use the tapes in a television pilot. Mr. Saffir testified that unidentified producers and others were enthusiastic about the "concept" of such a television series, but he had difficulty even estimating what the profits from a series might be. No "objective facts, figures, or data" substantiated the estimate of lost profits. Hollywood Fantasy's claims for lost profits also fail because there was no evidence of how Hollywood Fantasy estimated the profits or what data it used to do so.

Mr. Saffir also testified that Hollywood Fantasy lost $200,000 in "goodwill." Under Texas law, the loss of goodwill or business reputation is not recoverable in a breach of contract action.

Hollywood Fantasy also seeks to support the damages awarded as based on evidence of lost investment in the corporation. Mr. Saffir testified that Hollywood Fantasy lost $200,000 that had been invested in the corporation. Under Texas law, . . . actual damages may be recovered when loss is the natural, probable, and foreseeable consequence of the defendant's conduct. . . . The record must contain evidence that permits the jury . . . to assess with reasonable certainty the . . . causation of the damage by the breach or interference relative to other factors. . . . It is pure speculation that but for Ms. Gabor's breach, Hollywood Fantasy would not have gone out of business. Hollywood Fantasy had lost money on the Palm Springs event despite the fact that it had not charged the full fee to several participants and had not paid all of its employees. Hollywood Fantasy had sold only two tickets to the San Antonio event. Hollywood Fantasy is not entitled to an award of damages representing a return of $200,000 invested in the corporation.

Although Hollywood Fantasy did not present evidence to base an award of compensatory damages on either lost profits or lost investment, it did present sufficient evidence as to certain out-of-pocket expenses to justify their recovery. Mr. Saffir testified that Hollywood Fantasy incurred the following out-of-pocket expenses for the San Antonio event: (1) $8,500 in printing costs for color brochures and press releases; (2) $12,000 in marketing costs for mailings and advertising; (3) $22,000 in personnel and miscellaneous expenses, including air fares, staff accommodations, script-writing costs, telephone calls, and logo t-shirts; (4) $9,000 in travel expenses for Mr. Saffir and members of the Hollywood Fantasy "staff," including Margo Mayor, Hollywood Fantasy's president; and (5) $6,000 in expenses relating to preparations to film the San Antonio event for a possible television pilot. These expenses total $57,500.[28]

. . . [Ms. Gabor objects that the evidence was insufficient to establish these expenses, because Fantasy relied on testimony alone and did not produce any documents at trial. The court finds her objection unpersuasive.] Ms. Gabor presented no evidence controverting Mr. Saffir's testimony as to Hollywood Fantasy's lost out-of-pocket expenses for the San Antonio event. Mr. Saffir's testimony as to Hollywood Fantasy's out-of-pocket expenses is sufficient to support an award of $57,500 for breach of contract, but not to support an

---

[28] The general rule is that the non-breaching party may only recover out-of-pocket expenses incurred after the contract was formed. Saffir's testimony does not make it clear whether each of these expenses were incurred after Ms. Gabor returned the March 4, 1991 letter. However, Ms. Gabor does not challenge the jury's award on this ground.

award of $100,000.[29] The award of $100,000 is reversed in part on the basis that the evidence disclosed in the record does not support compensatory damages beyond $57,500. . . .

We affirm the district court's judgment with respect to Ms. Gabor's liability for breach of contract. We reverse the district court's award of $100,000 for breach of contract and render judgment in the amount of $57,500. . . .

■ QUESTIONS

(1)   The court suggests in a footnote that expenses incurred prior to formation of the contract would not be recoverable. Why should this be so?

(2)   The court also states that Hollywood Fantasy cannot recover the ticket prices it refunded when the event was cancelled. Why not?

(3)   In your view, were the out-of-pocket expenses costs incurred in "reasonable reliance" on the contract? If you had represented Ms. Gabor in this case, what arguments might you have raised?

2. Foreseeability of Damages

a. Introduction to the Principle of Hadley v. Baxendale

We turn from the requirement that the claimant establish damages with reasonable certainty and examine the second major limitation on the recovery of contract damages: the foreseeability principle. Even today, courts cite the classic English case of *Hadley v. Baxendale* for the proposition that damages, to be recoverable, must be foreseeable at the time the contract is entered. This proposition, although simply stated, is subtle and complex in its interpretation. Lawyers, judges, and commentators have been arguing about the precise meaning of *Hadley v. Baxendale* ever since it was decided a century and a half ago.[30] Although its contours remain subject to debate, the principle of

---

[29] Hollywood Fantasy cannot recover the $15,000 it refunded to the two individuals who had bought tickets to the San Antonio event before it was cancelled. The ticket price refund was not an out-of-pocket expense. Hollywood Fantasy presented no testimony as to what portion, if any, of this amount it would have kept as profit had the event gone forward with Ms. Gabor's participation.

[30] *Hadley v. Baxendale* is one of those cases that have attained almost mythical status among contracts cognoscenti. Grant Gilmore referred to it as "a fixed star in the jurisprudential firmament." *The Death of Contract* 92 (Ronald K.L. Collins ed., 2d ed., Ohio St. U. Press 1995). That is not to say that debate over the scope of the principle it has come to represent or its purpose has settled. Entire law review articles—many of them recent and influential—are dedicated to fresh exploration of *Hadley* and its progeny. A sampling includes Barry E. Adler, *The Questionable Ascent of* Hadley v. Baxendale, 51 Stan. L. Rev. 1547 (1999); Richard Danzig, Hadley v. Baxendale: *A Study in the Industrialization of the Law*, 4 J. Leg. Stud. 249 (1975); Thomas A. Diamond & Howard Foss, *Consequential Damages for Commercial Loss: An Alternative to* Hadley v Baxendale, 63 Fordham L. Rev. 665 (1994); Melvin Aron Eisenberg, *The Principle of* Hadley v. Baxendale, 80 Cal. L. Rev. 563 (1992); and George S. Geis, *Empirically Assessing* Hadley v. Baxendale, 32 Fla. St. U. L. Rev. 897 (2005). In the

foreseeability stemming from this case is firmly entrenched in American contracts jurisprudence.

We do not want to deprive you of the treat enjoyed by countless law students. So here it is: *Hadley v. Baxendale.*

HADLEY v. BAXENDALE

9 Ex. 341, 156 Eng. Rep. 145 (1854)
Court of Exchequer Chamber

. . . At the trial before Crompton, J., at the last Gloucester Assizes, it appeared that the plaintiffs carried on an extensive business as millers at Gloucester; and that, on the 11th of May, their mill was stopped by a breakage of the crank shaft by which the mill was worked. The steam-engine was manufactured by Messrs. Joyce & Co., the engineers, at Greenwich, and it became necessary to send the shaft as a pattern for a new one to Greenwich. The fracture was discovered on the 12th, and on the 13th the plaintiffs sent one of their servants to the office of the defendants, who are the well-known carriers trading under the name of Pickford & Co., for the purpose of having the shaft carried to Greenwich. The plaintiffs' servant told the clerk that the mill was stopped, and that the shaft must be sent immediately; and in answer to the inquiry when the shaft would be taken, the answer was, that if it was sent up by twelve o'clock any day, it would be delivered at Greenwich on the following day. On the following day the shaft was taken by the defendants, before noon, for the purpose of being conveyed to Greenwich, and the sum of £2/4s. was paid for its carriage the whole distance; at the same time the defendants' clerk was told that a special entry, if required, should be made to hasten its delivery. The delivery of the shaft at Greenwich was delayed by some neglect; and the consequence was, that the plaintiffs did not receive the new shaft for several days after they would otherwise have done, and the working of their mill was thereby delayed, and they thereby lost the profits they would otherwise have received.

On the part of the defendants, it was objected that these damages were too remote, and that the defendants were not liable with respect to them. The learned Judge left the case generally to the jury, who found a verdict with £25. damages beyond the amount paid into Court. . . .

---

summer of 2004, an academic conference was held in Gloucester, England, the city where the flour mill featured in the famous case still stands. In celebration of the case and its 150th anniversary, the Texas Wesleyan Law Review published a series of articles from the conference, *Symposium: The Common Law of Contracts as a World Force in Two Ages of Revolution: A Conference Celebrating the 150th Anniversary of* Hadley v. Baxendale, 11 Tex. Wesleyan L. Rev. 225 *et seq.* (2005).

ALDERSON, Baron.

We think that there ought to be a new trial in this case; but, in so doing, we deem it to be expedient and necessary to state explicitly the rule which the Judge, at the next trial, ought, in our opinion, to direct the jury to be governed by when they estimate the damages. It is, indeed, of the last importance that we should do this; for, if the jury are left without any definite rule to guide them, it will, in such cases as these, manifestly lead to the greatest injustice. . . .

Now we think the proper rule in such a case as the present is this: Where two other parties have made a contract which one of them has broken, the damages which the other party ought to receive in respect of such breach of contract should be such as may fairly and reasonably be considered either arising naturally, i.e., according to the usual course of things, from such breach of contract itself, or such as may reasonably be supposed to have been in the contemplation of both parties, at the time they made the contract, as the probable result of the breach of it. Now, if the special circumstances under which the contract was actually made were communicated by the plaintiffs to the defendants, and thus known to both parties, the damages resulting from the breach of such a contract, which they would reasonably contemplate, would be the amount of injury which would ordinarily follow from a breach of contract under these special circumstances so known and communicated. But, on the other hand, if these special circumstances were wholly unknown to the party breaking the contract, he, at the most, could only be supposed to have had in his contemplation the amount of injury which would arise generally, and in the great multitude of cases not affected by any special circumstances, from such a breach of contract. For, had the special circumstances been known, the parties might have specially provided for the breach of contract by special terms as to the damages in that case; and of this advantage it would be very unjust to deprive them. Now the above principles are those by which we think the jury ought to be guided in estimating the damages arising out of any breach of contract. . . .

Now, in the present case, if we are to apply the principles above laid down, we find that the only circumstances here communicated by the plaintiffs to the defendants at the time the contract was made, were, that the article to be carried was the broken shaft of a mill, and that the plaintiffs were the millers of that mill. But how do these circumstances shew reasonably that the profits of the mill must be stopped by an unreasonable delay in the delivery of the broken shaft by the carrier to the third person? Suppose the plaintiffs had another shaft in their possession put up or putting up at the time, and that they only wished to send back the broken shaft to the engineer who made it; it is clear that this would be quite consistent with the above circumstances, and yet the unreasonable delay in the delivery would have no effect upon the intermediate profits of the mill. Or, again, suppose that, at the time of the delivery to the carrier, the machinery of the mill had been in other respects defective, then, also, the same results would follow. Here it is true that the shaft was actually sent back to serve as a model for a new one, and that the want of a new one was the only cause of the stoppage of the mill, and that the loss of profits really arose from not sending down the new shaft in proper time, and that this arose from the delay in delivering the broken one to serve as a model. But it is obvious that, in the great multitude of cases of millers sending off broken shafts to third persons by a carrier under ordinary circumstances, such consequences would not, in all probability, have occurred; and these special circumstances were here never communicated by the plaintiffs to the defendants. It follows, therefore, that the loss of profits here cannot reasonably be considered such a consequence of the breach of contract as could have been fairly and reasonably contemplated by both the parties when they made this contract. For such loss would neither have flowed naturally from the breach of this contract in the great multitude of such cases occurring under ordinary circumstances, nor were the special circumstances, which, perhaps, would have made it a reasonable and natural consequence of such breach of contract, communicated to or known by the defendants. The Judge ought, therefore, to have told the jury, that, upon the facts then before them, they ought not to take the loss of profits into consideration at all in estimating the damages. There must therefore be a new trial in this case. . . .

■ PROBLEM 20.12

In a subsequent case, *Victoria Laundry (Windsor), Ltd. v. Newman Industries, Ltd*, 2 K.B. 528, 537 (Eng. C.A.) (1949), Lord Justice Asquith remarked on an inconsistency in *Hadley v. Baxendale* that you too may have noticed. In particular, he speculated that the headnote, which described the facts, must have been incorrect insofar as it stated that the plaintiff's servant told the defendant's clerk that the mill was stopped. Justice Asquith noted "If the Court of Exchequer had accepted these facts as established, the court must . . . have held the damage claimed was recoverable. . . ." Why is this particular fact so important? Do you agree that, given the court's reasoning, the case necessarily should have come out differently if the facts were as portrayed in the headnote?

Modern courts continue to quote the reasoning in *Hadley v. Baxendale*. It is rare to see a case that raises the issue of foreseeability of damages that doesn't make reference to this case in some way. Yet the reasoning of the case leaves many questions unanswered. The task of this section is to pose those questions and to explore how different courts have answered them.

The analysis in *Hadley* seems to allow recovery of two types of damages: those that arise naturally according to the usual course of things and those that were in the reasonable contemplation of the parties. *Hadley* limits damages when they meet neither test. Generally, direct and incidental damages survive scrutiny under *Hadley*. In rare cases, where changes in market conditions are sudden, unexpected, and disastrous, courts may occasionally invoke the principle to limit hugely disproportionate direct damage awards.[31] Absent these kinds of extreme circumstances, principles of foreseeability seldom come into play when determining what direct damages a breacher may owe. Likewise, as long as they are reasonable, foreseeability seldom limits the recovery of incidental damages. Perhaps courts feel that everyone should anticipate that if they breach a contract, they might be responsible for the direct and incidental damages caused by their breach.

Consider, for instance, a plumber who contracts to fix a homeowner's kitchen faucet for a fixed price. The homeowner pays the plumber for the work. The plumber, instead of fixing the faucet, leaves it in the same broken state in which he found it. The homeowner seeks to hold the plumber responsible. The usual measure of direct damages would be the cost of completion or repair. If the homeowner paid another plumber to diagnose the problem in the original work and it was reasonable to do so under the circumstances, that expense too would typically be compensable as incidental damages. These expenses are so closely tied to the original promise of the plumber that it is fair to say that they are the type of damages that arise naturally, according to the usual course of things, from the plumber's breach of contract. Likewise, because the damages are so natural and usual, when the contract was entered, the parties should have been contemplating them.

The same cannot always be said of consequential damages. This is the arena where *Hadley v. Baxendale* plays its most prominent role. Consider, for instance, if the plumber not only fails to repair the faucet, but in fact ruins it. The damage to the faucet itself is a direct consequence of the breach. Surely it should be compensable. But consider if water leaking from the ruined faucet damages the kitchen floor. Is the plumber responsible for that loss? Or suppose that the homeowner stores an original copy of the Magna Carta in a metal box below the kitchen sink, and water from the ruined faucet leaks, thus destroying the immensely valuable historical document. Is this loss chargeable to the plumber? Or perhaps the homeowner is a budding chef. Unbeknownst to the plumber, she had invited Gordon Ramsay to her kitchen in hopes of gaining the famous chef's endorsement. Chef Ramsay comes but storms out in disgust at the sight of the ruined faucet. The homeowner's hopes of a promising career in food service are dashed. Again, should the plumber be held responsible?

---

[31] The doctrine of impracticability, which we discuss in Chapter 17, also may provide some relief under these circumstances. You may recall that this doctrine too contains a component akin to foreseeability.

As the loss becomes more and more remote from the ordinary consequences of breach, the foreseeability principle increasingly comes into play. It is in elaborating the principle that the courts have faced their greatest challenge. Although the rule is often referred to as requiring foreseeability of damages, it does not rest on foreseeability alone, at least in the literal sense of the word. The rule in operation has many different aspects, and courts differ in their interpretations of each aspect. It is fair to say that there is no one accepted approach to the rule of *Hadley v. Baxendale.*

As noted above, if a loss stems from general requirements, the foreseeability principle does not limit compensation in the usual case. If, however, the loss flows from special or particular requirements, those requirements must have been brought home to the breaching party at the time of the contract. In many jurisdictions, if the breaching party is or should be aware of special or particular requirements at the time of the contract, the foreseeability principle is satisfied. Assuming the nonbreaching party can avoid other limitations on recovery (such as the reasonable certainty principle and the mitigation principle, which we discuss shortly), its prospects of compensation are good. A few courts take a more stringent view and apply the limitations of the foreseeability principle more broadly.

Justice Holmes, in an early U.S. Supreme Court case citing *Hadley v. Baxendale*, described what, in his view, it means to say that certain consequences were within the reasonable contemplation of the parties. He wrote that recovery

> . . . depends on what liability the defendant fairly may be supposed to have assumed consciously, or to have warranted the plaintiff reasonably to suppose that it assumed, when the contract was made. . . . The knowledge must be brought home to the party sought to be charged, under such circumstances that he must know that the person he contracts with reasonably believes that he accepts the contract with the special condition attached to it. . . . It may be said with safety that mere notice to a seller of some interest or probable action of the buyer is not enough necessarily and as matter of law to charge the seller with special damage on that account if he fails to deliver the goods.[32]

This idea, that the special circumstances must be brought home to the defendant to such a degree that he fairly may be supposed to have assumed the risk associated with those circumstances, has come to be known as the "tacit agreement" approach to *Hadley v. Baxendale.* Although it appears in older cases, modern cases tend to reject it. As we discuss in Section D.3.b, UCC Article 2 has incorporated a test akin to that of *Hadley v. Baxendale* in UCC 2-715. Official Comment 2 to UCC 2-715 notes, however, that the "tacit agreement' test for the recovery of consequential damages is rejected." Generally, both at common law and under the UCC, if the defendant merely knows or has reason to know of the

---

[32] *Globe Refining Co. v. Landa Cotton Oil Co.,* 190 U.S. 540, 544, 23 S. Ct. 754, 755 (1903).

special requirements, that is sufficient to charge him with responsibility for consequences that may flow from those circumstances in the event of breach.

McNAUGHTON v. CHARLESTON CHARTER SCHOOL FOR MATH AND SCIENCE, INC.

411 S.C. 249 (2015)
South Carolina Supreme Court

TOAL, Chief Justice.

. . . In late 2008, Cynthia McNaughton, who was in her early to mid 50's at the time, was accepted into the South Carolina Department of Education's Program of Alternative Certification for Educators (PACE program), which enables individuals who earned a college degree—but did not complete a traditional teacher preparation program—to become certified South Carolina public school teachers.[33] Before beginning the PACE program, McNaughton worked as a graphic designer and previously taught art and theater design in Florida for seven years. When McNaughton began the PACE program, she hoped to make teaching her "exit career," and to work as a certified teacher for eleven or twelve years, at which point she planned to retire.

In August 2010, Appellant's principal (the principal) hired McNaughton to teach 6th, 7th, and 8th grade art, along with the yearbook class. When she was hired, Appellant knew that McNaughton was participating in the PACE program, and that her completion of the program was contingent upon her fulfillment of further requirements, including the completion of an induction teaching year. McNaughton signed an employment agreement, which stated that McNaughton "agree[d] to be a full-time teacher at Charleston Charter School for Math and Science for the school year 2010-2011." The employment agreement further stated that it was "contingent on funding and enrollment". . . . A "Wage Payment Notice" indicated that Appellant would pay McNaughton a yearly salary of $34,040.

McNaughton received positive feedback from her students and their parents. According to the principal, McNaughton was a talented art teacher, especially when it came to designing cross-curricular lessons. Neither the principal nor any other faculty member experienced any problems with McNaughton's performance as a teacher, and McNaughton was never disciplined for any

---

[33] PACE is an intensive, selective program, and typically takes three years to complete after acceptance into the program. Individuals in the PACE program teach for a year as an "induction teacher," as well as complete other courses and requirements. If someone completing the PACE program stops the program (i.e., loses her teaching job) before completing the program, she "may be allowed to reapply" and possibly start the program over from the beginning.

matter. However, on December 1, 2010—in the middle of the school year—the principal informed McNaughton that Appellant was terminating her employment. The principal told McNaughton that Appellant needed to use the funds designated for McNaughton's salary to hire and pay a new math teacher because some of the students had performed poorly on a recent math achievement test. McNaughton was surprised to learn of her termination and immediately became concerned that she would be unable to find another job as an induction teacher, especially in the middle of the school year. . . .

The principal wrote McNaughton a letter of reference to assist with McNaughton's job search. However, McNaughton was only able to find a job teaching two days a week, which did not grant her enough teaching hours to remain in the PACE program. McNaughton applied for jobs in graphic design as well as entry level jobs, but was unsuccessful. McNaughton also applied for and received unemployment benefits.

McNaughton testified that as a result of losing her job, she was forced to purchase COBRA health insurance for $250 per month (until she could no longer afford it and discontinued it), withdraw the available funds from her state retirement fund, and defer her student loans (which resulted in $2,500 additional interest). In addition, McNaughton testified that she was unable to refinance her home, and that her bank foreclosed upon her mortgage.

McNaughton filed a complaint against Appellant, alleging . . . [among other things breach of contract. We omit discussion of her other claims.] In her complaint, McNaughton requested actual and special damages, costs, and attorney's fees. . . .

[After trial, the] jury returned a verdict in favor of McNaughton on her breach of contract claim, finding $20,623 in actual damages and $74,112 in special damages.[34] . . . [Appellant moved for a judgment notwithstanding the verdict and a new trial, and both motions were denied. The trial court also awarded attorneys' fees pursuant to the provisions of a South Carolina statute allowing litigants who sue public entities to recover attorneys' fees under certain circumstances. Appellant appealed to the court of appeals, and the case was certified to this court, the South Carolina Supreme Court, for resolution. The court held there was sufficient evidence to support the conclusion that Appellant breached McNaughton's employment contract because there was funding actually available for her position at the time of her termination. The court also affirmed the award of attorneys' fees under the South Carolina

---

[34] In her closing argument, McNaughton's attorney argued that McNaughton suffered damages of $17,000 in lost wages for the second semester of the 2010-2011 school year and $1,000, which would have been contributed to her retirement account if she had continued working for the remainder of the school year. The attorney also pointed out to the jury that as a result of her termination, McNaughton paid for COBRA health insurance after she lost her health insurance, and her home was foreclosed upon. In addition, the attorney argued that McNaughton had suffered career damages. She pointed out that McNaughton could have earned approximately $408,000 over the twelve years she planned to teach as a certified teacher, while she would have earned approximately $192,000 at a minimum wage job—a difference of $216,000.

statute. We omit discussion of these issues, and include only the court's discussion of the Appellant's challenge to the damage award.]

Special damages, also known as consequential damages, are actual damages. Unlike general damages, which must necessarily result from the wrongful act upon which liability is based and are implied by the law, special damages are damages for losses that are the natural and proximate—but not the necessary—result of the injury, and may be recovered only when sufficiently stated and claimed. Therefore, where a plaintiff seeks special damages in addition to general damages, he must plead and prove the special damages to avoid surprise.

If the plaintiff's proof is speculative, uncertain, or otherwise insufficient to permit calculation of his special damages, his claim should be denied. However, special damages "occasioned by breach of contract *may* be recovered when such damages may reasonably be supposed to have been within the contemplation of the parties at the time the contract was made." *Stern & Stern Assocs. v. Timmons*, 310 S.C. 250, 252, 423 S.E.2d 124, 126 (1992) (emphasis added) (quoting *Goodwin v. Hilton Head Co.*, 273 S.C. 758, 761, 259 S.E.2d 611, 613 (1979)). Although "the defendant need not foresee the exactly dollar amount of the injury, the defendant must know or have reason to know the special circumstance so as to be able to judge the degree of probability that damage will result...." *Id.* (quoting 5 Arthur Linton Corbin, *Corbin on Contracts* §1014 (1964)).

In other words, special damages may be recovered in a contract action if "the defendant had notice of the circumstances from which they might reasonably be expected to result at the time the parties entered into the contract, as the effect of allowing such damages would be to add to the terms of the contract another element of damages, not contemplated by the parties." *Moore v. Atl. Coast Line R.R. Co.*, 85 S.C. 19, 19, 67 S.E. 11, 12 (1910); see also *Timmons*, 310 S.C. at 251, 423 S.E.2d at 125 ("The party claiming special damages must show that the defendant was clearly warned of the probable existence of unusual circumstances or that because of the defendant's own education, training, or information, the defendant had 'reason to foresee the probable existence of such circumstances.'" (quoting 5 Arthur Linton Corbin, *Corbin on Contracts* §1011 (1964))).

A trial judge has considerable discretion in determining the amount of actual damages. Based on this discretion afforded to trial judges, review on appeal is limited to the correction of errors of law. Accordingly, this Court's task in reviewing a damages award is not to weigh the evidence, but to decide if any evidence exists to support the damages award.

Appellant first argues that the trial court erred in allowing special damages because under *Shivers v. John H. Harland Co.*, 310 S.C. 217, 423 S.E.2d 105 (1992), McNaughton was limited to recovering damages for the term of her contract—her unpaid salary for the remainder of the 2010-2011 school year. In *Shivers*, we examined whether an employee's recovery for wrongful breach of an employment contract was limited to the amount of pay and other benefits he would have received during the notice period provided for in his contract.[35]

Ultimately, we concluded that the trial court was correct in limiting the employee's damages to the amount of pay and benefits he would have received during the notice period because those damages placed him in as good a position as he would have been had the employer performed the contract. In coming to this conclusion, we outlined the purpose of contractual damages:

> When an employee[ ] is wrongfully discharged under a contract for a definite term, the measure of damages generally is the wages for the unexpired portion of the term. This measure of damages allows an employee to receive the benefit of the bargain by putting him in as good a position as he would have been had the contract been performed.

Id. at 220, 423 S.E.2d at 107 (internal citations omitted).

Notwithstanding this statement on contract damages, *Shivers* addressed a narrow issue involving a notice provision, and therefore does not limit McNaughton's recovery to the portion of her salary she would have received from December 2010 until the end of the 2010-2011 school year. Accordingly, we hold that McNaughton was entitled to recover the loss she actually suffered as a result of the breach of her employment agreement.

Appellant further argues that special damages were never contemplated because there is no evidence that Appellant would have employed McNaughton for more than one school year. We disagree, and find this argument irrelevant to the issue at hand because McNaughton did not contend that she is entitled to damages based on the extension of her employment agreement beyond one year. Instead, in arguing that she is entitled to special damages, she relies on her status as an induction teacher in the PACE program when she was terminated, and the fact that she planned to teach as a certified teacher in South Carolina for eleven to twelve years. Based upon the principal's testimony and the record, there is no doubt that at the time the parties entered into the employment agreement, Appellant was aware of McNaughton's involvement in the PACE program, and thus was "clearly warned" of the repercussions of McNaughton losing her job as an induction teacher. See *Timmons*, 310 S.C. at 252, 423 S.E.2d at 126.

Moreover, McNaughton presented evidence of her status in the PACE program, her inability to become a certified teacher through the PACE program after her employment was terminated, and the other financial consequences she suffered. Had Appellant not terminated McNaughton's employment, she most

---

[35] There, the employee's employment contract required at least fifteen days written notice of either party's termination of the contract. *Shivers*, 310 S.C. at 219, 423 S.E.2d at 106. The employer discharged the employee for cause under another provision of the contract without notice, and a jury found the discharge for cause was wrongful. The employer moved to limit the employee's damages as a matter of law to the amount of pay he would have received under the fifteen day notice provision.

likely would have completed the PACE program and become a certified teacher. The damages McNaughton suffered as a result of the special circumstance of losing her position in the PACE program after Appellant terminated her was clearly within the contemplation of Appellant, as required by *Timmons*.[36]

Accordingly, we find that McNaughton presented evidence to support the jury's special damages award, and that the trial court did not err in charging and allowing the jury to award McNaughton special damages for her breach of contract claim. . . .

[The court also affirms the award of attorneys' fees under the South Carolina statute.]

PLEICONES, Justice, concurring in part and dissenting in part.

I concur in part and dissent in part. I conclude that there is some slight evidence to support the trial court's denial of appellant's motions for directed verdict and JNOV on McNaughton's breach of contract claim, and therefore concur in the majority's affirmance of this issue. I dissent from those portions of the opinion which uphold the special damages award and the attorneys' fee award.

In order to recover special damages in this breach of contract suit, McNaughton was required to prove that appellant

> [w]as clearly warned of the probable existence of unusual circumstances or that because of the [appellant's] own education, training, or information, the [appellant] had "reason to foresee the probable existence of such circumstances."

Stern & Stern Assoc. v. Timmons, 310 S.C. 250, 423 S.E.2d 124 (1992). In my opinion, appellant's status as an induction teacher in the PACE program pursuant to a one-year contract was not sufficient to render appellant liable for McNaughton's losses beyond her lost salary and benefits for the school year 2010-2011. E.g., *Shivers v. John H. Harland Co., Inc.*, 310 S.C. 217, 423 S.E.2d 105 (1992) (proper measure of damages in breach of employment case). There is simply no evidence that McNaughton met the requirements of *Timmons*, and the rank speculation concerning her potential had she successfully completed the PACE program is not a substitute for such proof. . . .

---

[36] The dissent cites *Timmons*, apparently for the proposition that special damages are not appropriate here. The dissent's view is at odds with *Timmons*, however, as *Timmons* permitted a special damages award for the same reason we allow them here—because the record indicates that Appellant was aware of the damages that would be occasioned by a breach of contract. See 310 S.C. at 253, 423 S.E.2d at 126 (finding special damages appropriate because the "record below indicates that [the defendant] was aware of the need for fill dirt and aware of the probable damage that would result from a time delay prior to her signing the contract").

■ QUESTIONS

(1) As summarized in a footnote in the opinion, McNaughton's attorney described the damages she suffered when she lost her job. The losses the attorney detailed far exceeded the damages the jury awarded. Assuming McNaughton introduced credible evidence to support the attorney's allegations, should all of her losses have been compensable? Why or why not?

(2) The court explains the difference between general damages and special damages. Looking again at the attorney's description of McNaughton's losses, which of them would constitute general damages under the court's formulation? Which would be special damages? Does the characterization matter, and if so, why?

(3) Is this court taking a "tacit agreement" approach to the rule of *Hadley v. Baxendale*? How can you tell? Does its approach matter, and if so, why?

(4) Where does Justice Pleicones differ with the majority? Does he challenge whether the damages at issue were within the contemplation of the parties, or is he critiquing the majority's holding on some other basis?

■ PROBLEM 20.13

On November 30, Lacy's Department Store entered into a contract with Peerless Printing Co., under which Peerless would design, print, and deliver advertising flyers for Lacy's annual Christmas Sale for a total payment of $80,000. Before the parties signed the contract, Lacy's told Peerless that it must have the flyers in hand by Friday, December 15, or else there would not be time to send them to potential customers in advance of the sale. (This contract is a mixed contract involving both goods and services. You may assume that it is predominantly a contract for services, and the common law would apply to resolve any dispute.)

Peerless designed and printed beautiful brochures on an expedited basis and completed them on December 12. Peerless contracted with Timely Transport Co. to have them delivered to Lacy's on or before December 15 for a shipping charge of $1,000. At the time Peerless contracted with Timely, it told Timely that the shipment was "hot," which in the trade was understood to mean that it was time sensitive.

Timely's truck was delayed by minor weather conditions and traffic. It did not arrive in Lacy's city until the morning of Saturday, December 16. As there was no one available to accept deliveries over the weekend, Timely's driver delivered the container with the flyers to Timely's warehouse in the city where Lacy's was located. Timely left a voicemail message on

Peerless's phone notifying it that the delivery had been late and that Peerless should contact Timely to arrange alternate delivery.

Unfortunately, Peerless's office was closed from Monday, December 19 through January 2 for its annual holiday break. Peerless did not receive Timely's voicemail message until the morning of January 2. Peerless immediately arranged for Timely to deliver the flyers to Lacy's, but Lacy's refused to accept them.

(a) Lacy's typically earns 75 percent of its annual net profits in the ten days before Christmas. Due to insufficient advertising, Lacy's Christmas sale was a tepid affair, and its profits were down by $1 million from prior years. Lacy's refuses to pay Peerless for the flyers and further seeks $1 million in damages for the business it lost. Must Lacy's pay for the brochures? Should Lacy's be able to recover damages for its lost profits? Why or why not?

(b) Assume Lacy's is able to persuade a court that it need not pay for the brochures. Should Peerless be able to recover the $80,000 price from Timely Transport?

(c) Assume Lacy's is able to persuade a court that Peerless owes it damages for its lost profits. Should Peerless be able to recover the amount of those damages from Timely Transport?

(d) Do any of the answers to (a) through (c) depend on whether the applicable jurisdiction accepts the "tacit agreement" interpretation of *Hadley v. Baxendale*?

3. The Mitigation Principle

Often the extent of the plaintiff's damage depends on the actions (or inactions) she takes in response to the breach. If she acts quickly and decisively, she can often avoid many of the negative consequences of breach. If she fails to respond to the breach, damages can mount. Contract law places a burden on the non-breaching party to reduce the negative consequences of breach. The cases often refer to this principle as "the duty to mitigate damages." It is important to understand how this principle operates, however. Strictly speaking, it is inaccurate to refer to the principle as a "duty." The nonbreaching party doesn't have a duty to avoid the consequences of breach—she is not liable for her failure to do so. She is free to sit still and do nothing in response to the breach if that is her choice. Yet her ability to collect damages from the breaching party depends on her own reasonable efforts. If she doesn't make any effort, damages will not be available for the consequences she could have avoided by appropriate action.

The mitigation principle, like the reasonable certainty principle and the foreseeability principle, exists in some tension with the general compensation goal of contract damages. The nonbreaching party appears to be damaged by the breach but yet cannot recover the full measure of those damages from the breacher. Upon closer scrutiny, the mitigation principle is consistent with many of the policies underlying contract remedies. Think about it, for instance, in light of the theory of efficient breach. Under this theory, the goal of contract law is to encourage transactions that increase the collective net benefits of contractual relationships. If a contracting party is better off if he doesn't perform—for instance, if he can get a better deal elsewhere, even taking into account the damages he might have to pay under the breached contract—under efficient breach theory he should be free to do so. If the other party behaves wastefully in the face of the breach, and the breaching party is nonetheless required to pay damages, the net benefits of the contractual relationships decrease. The mitigation principle discourages such wasteful behavior.

discourages wasteful behavior

Consider a famous case from the 1920s, *Rockingham County v. Luten Bridge Co.*, 35 F.2d 301 (4th Cir. 1929). Amid great political controversy, the commissioners of Rockingham County, North Carolina, entered into a contract with Luten Bridge Company. Luten was to build a bridge to connect two stretches of new highway planned by the county. Almost immediately after the county awarded the contract, political squabbling broke out. One commissioner resigned and then attempted to rescind his resignation. Two others refused to attend future meetings. The remaining commissioners unanimously voted to call off the bridge contract and the highway project. The board of commissioners notified Luten that the project was off and that any further work done on the bridge would be done at Luten's own risk. At the same time, one of the members of the board allegedly insisted privately that Luten proceed with the construction. The board found out about these private urgings and publicly repudiated them. Luten had started work on the bridge at this point, but had not progressed very far. In spite of the repeated notices of repudiation that it subsequently received from the board, Luten finished the bridge and sued the county for payment.

In the end, the court held that <u>Luten had no right to "pile up damages by proceeding with the erection of a useless bridge."</u> Yes, the county had entered into a contract. Yes, the county had breached that contract. But no, Luten could not simply close its eyes to the facts, build a bridge going from nowhere to nowhere in the middle of a forest, and expect to be paid the full contract price. The proper measure of damages was an amount sufficient to compensate Luten for the costs it incurred <u>prior to the county's repudiation</u>, plus the profit it would have received from the contract had there been no breach. Beyond that, the cost of completing the bridge rested with Luten Bridge Company.

damages are just enough to make them whole

a. Reasonable Efforts to Mitigate Damages

The mitigation principle is typically raised as an affirmative defense by the breaching party. It is up to the breaching party to prove that the nonbreaching party failed to mitigate damages. All that is required is reasonable efforts; extraordinary efforts are not necessary. Not surprisingly, substantial controversy surrounds the question of what constitute reasonable efforts.

DeROSIER v. UTILITY SYSTEMS OF AMERICA, INC.

780 N.W.2d 1 (2010)
Minnesota Court of Appeals

MINGE, Judge.

Appellant contractor challenges the district court award of actual and consequential damages for breach of an oral contract. We affirm in part and reverse in part.

Respondent Chad DeRosier purchased undeveloped hillside property in Duluth with plans to construct a house. The property sloped steeply down from the street, requiring substantial fill. Because appellant Utility Systems of America, Inc. (USA) was excavating at a nearby road construction project, DeRosier approached USA's foreman in July 2004, explained his need for fill, and proposed that USA dump fill material on his property. The foreman agreed on condition that DeRosier obtain the proper permits. USA did not charge DeRosier because the arrangement allowed USA to avoid the cost of hauling and disposing of the excavated material at a more distant location. There was no written contract.

In late August 2004, DeRosier obtained a city permit allowing for the deposit of 1,500 cubic yards of fill, gave the USA foreman a copy of the permit, and left for a ten-day vacation. When DeRosier returned from vacation, his entire property was covered with fill. The estimated quantity was 6,500 cubic yards (or around 5,000 cubic yards above the permitted amount). The contractor who DeRosier originally retained to construct his house determined that he could not build until the excess fill was removed, estimated that the cost of removal would be at least $20,000, and withdrew as builder.

DeRosier complained to USA that its mistake in dumping excess material delayed construction, explained that he faced substantial removal costs, and demanded corrective action. USA denied liability, claiming that DeRosier failed to (1) provide a copy of the city permit; (2) advise it of the limit on fill; or (3) perform city-required compaction. A letter from DeRosier's counsel repeated the complaints and demanded that USA remove the extra fill under threat of lawsuit. USA responded by again denying responsibility but offering to remove the excess fill for $9,500, which it claimed were its costs. DeRosier refused to pay USA and hired G & T Construction to remove the excess fill.

DeRosier sued USA, requesting damages of $46,629 for the cost of removing the excess fill and for added expenses in constructing the foundation of the house. Following trial, the district court concluded that USA breached a contract to deposit 1,500 cubic yards of fill. It ordered USA to pay general damages of $22,829[37] and consequential damages of $8,000. USA appeals. . . .

USA challenges the district court's damage award on several fronts. . . . The first issue raised by USA is whether the district court erred in awarding consequential damages to DeRosier for delayed construction. USA argues that consequential damages were not alleged in the complaint, disclosed in discovery, or supported by any specific evidence presented at trial. . . . Minnesota pleading rules generally require only "a short and plain statement of the claim" and "a demand for judgment for the relief sought." Minn. R. Civ. P. 8.01. The rules, however, specify that "special damage[s] . . . shall be specifically stated." Minn. R. Civ. P. 9.07. In discussing damages incident to the Uniform Commercial Code, the supreme court stated: "[A]lthough remedies are to be liberally administered, the burden of pleading and proving consequential loss still remains on the buyer [alleging the damage]." *Bemidji Sales Barn, Inc. v. Chatfield*, 312 Minn. 11, 15, 250 N.W.2d 185, 188 (1977). To understand the phrase "consequential loss" or "consequential damages" and the issue before us, we must recognize the difference between general and special damages. Special damages require specific pleading but general damages do not. General damages, as opposed to special damages, "naturally and necessarily result from the act complained of." *Indep. Brewing Ass'n v. Burt*, 109 Minn. 323, 327, 123 N.W. 932, 934 (1909). Minnesota courts have stated, "[t]he term 'consequential damages' usually . . . refers to those items of damages which, because of particular circumstances, are to be distinguished from 'general' damages." *B.F. Goodrich Co. v. Mesabi Tire Co.*, 430 N.W.2d 180, 184 (Minn. 1988). Consequential damages are commonly called special damages. Special damages are the natural, but not the necessary, result of a breach. Although special or consequential damages flow naturally from the breach, they are not recoverable unless they are reasonably foreseeable to the parties at the time of the breach.

At the outset of trial, USA's counsel pointed out that there was no claim for delay damages in the pleadings or discovery. Perhaps most significantly, no evidence of monetary loss caused by delay was introduced at trial. Although the district court observed that DeRosier's attorney specifically mentioned delay in his pre-litigation demand, that did not constitute evidence of such damages. . . . Because consequential (or delay) damages were not pleaded and not supported by any evidence in the record, we conclude that the district court

---

[37] The district court appears to have under-calculated the general damages by $30. The general damage amount was based on $21,629 in removal costs (as testified by Johnson) plus $1,230 for the cost of trucks rented to haul excess fill. These amounts add up to $22,859, or $30 more than the $22,829 awarded as general damages. This miscalculation was first made by DeRosier in his proposed findings, was adopted by the district court, and is not challenged by DeRosier. We therefore accept the consequential damage award as specified in paragraph 20 of the district court's January 8, 2009 Findings of Fact, Conclusions of Law, Order for Judgment, and Judgment.

erred in awarding DeRosier $8,000 as consequential damages for delay in construction and we reverse that portion of the judgment.

The second issue raised by USA is whether the record contains sufficient evidence to support the award of general damages. The plaintiff must establish a reasonable basis for approximating a loss. Damages cannot be "speculative, remote, or conjectural." *Leoni v. Bemis Co.*, 255 N.W.2d 824, 826 (Minn. 1977). . . .

DeRosier's primary witness regarding the cost of removal was G & T owner Dan Johnson, who testified by deposition. USA claims that Johnson provided vague, guesswork testimony. We note that the record includes Johnson's invoices referencing work undertaken and machinery used to remove the fill. Johnson referred to these invoices and testified regarding various handwritten notes and calculations that appear on added pages of the exhibit. Although Johnson's testimony and notes contain ambiguities when considered separately, taken together they provide substantial, understandable detail. Johnson admitted that his measurements were not exact. However, based on his experience and the recorded invoices, Johnson provided details regarding the amount of fill hauled away, the items of equipment used, the time it took, and the equipment and labor expense. With this context, we conclude the evaluation of Johnson's deposition was a credibility determination for the district court. . . .

USA also argues that the district court's damage award includes various costs that are DeRosier's responsibility. These allegedly extra costs include excavation at the site that was necessary for the construction, removal of vegetation, and compaction of the fill. USA does not clearly identify any specific portion of Johnson's testimony or exhibits that involve work for such tasks or was otherwise unrelated to removal of excess fill deposited by USA. In fact, the record indicates that G & T's total charges for excavating and moving fill, sod, and other materials at the property was $29,189. Of this amount $7,560 was deducted as unrelated to excess-fill removal. The damage award only accounted for the cost of G & T's removal work plus the renting of additional trucking services for hauling the excess fill. We also note that the original contractor estimated the removal cost would exceed $20,000 when he first evaluated the situation.

Based on the record and the deference we afford the fact finder, we conclude the district court had a sufficient basis for calculating and did not abuse its discretion in granting $22,829 in general damages.

The third issue is whether DeRosier had a duty to mitigate damages that was breached by his failure to accept USA's offer to remove excess fill for $9,500. USA claims that, even if the actual-damage award was supported by the evidence, recoverable damages are limited to its $9,500 offer.[38] DeRosier responds that he was not obligated to do business with USA after its breach and that such an arrangement would have jeopardized his ability to sue by acting as a form of settlement.

---

[38] It is unclear whether $9,500 was akin to a settlement offer or only represented USA's minimal marginal costs. There is no claim that $9,500 would be the fair market charge for the work, even for work done by USA.

We first note that if USA had merely offered to cure, DeRosier would have been obliged to accept to mitigate damages. An implied right to cure exists in situations where cure is possible. Upon receiving proper notice, a party that defectively performs may cure if done within a reasonable time and there is adequate assurance of performance. . . .

Here, DeRosier notified USA of the defective performance, requesting that the excess fill be removed under threat of lawsuit. USA, however, only offered to fix the fill problem on condition that DeRosier make further payments. A breaching party may not insist that the damaged party pay additional compensation to correct work for which the breacher had already been fully paid to perform. Although USA had not received monetary payment for its work, it had benefited from its agreement with DeRosier and the absence of a monetary payment is not a material distinction. We conclude that because USA did not attempt to cure, but rather proposed a new contract with new consideration, USA waived its right to cure.

Nevertheless, DeRosier may still have had an obligation to enter into that new contract if such a step was a reasonable way to mitigate damages. Acceptance of USA's offer would have saved DeRosier over $13,000. The issue, then, is whether rejection of that offer was unreasonable.

Outside of employment situations, one reported Minnesota court decision has considered whether it is unreasonable to reject a breaching party's subsequent offer that would mitigate damages. *Coxe v. Anoka Waterworks Elec. Light & Power Co.*, 87 Minn. 56, 91 N.W. 265 (1902). In *Coxe*, the supreme court held that a buyer who contracted to purchase goods on credit did not have to accept an offer of the same goods for a cheaper cash price. *Id.* at 57-58, 91 N.W. at 265-66. The court reasoned that imposing the new contract as a mitigation requirement would "entirely abrogate[ ] the contract as made by the parties, and force[ ] upon them another and wholly different one, made by the court." *Id.* at 58, 91 N.W. at 266. The rationale of *Coxe* would not require such agreements to mitigate, especially where the new contract would supplant the old one without preserving a right to enforce the original agreement.

Other states have faced the issue and have held that the nonbreaching party can recover its full damages despite refusing the breacher's new offer that would have minimized the loss. See *Zanker Dev. Co. v. Cogito Sys., Inc.*, 215 Cal. App. 3d 1377, 1382, 264 Cal. Rptr. 76 (1989) (holding that landlord need not mitigate damages by reletting to tenant that repudiated lease); *Stanley Manly Boys' Clothes, Inc. v. Hickey*, 113 Tex. 482, 259 S.W. 160, 162 (1925) (stating that no one "should be required to contract a second time with one who has without cause breached a prior contract with him"); *City Nat'l Bank v. Wells*, 181 W. Va. 763, 384 S.E.2d 374, 384 (1989) ("[T]he plaintiff here justifiably revoked his acceptance of the defective truck and had no obligation to afford the defendant yet another opportunity to repair it").

We conclude that when one party to the contract defectively performs and subsequently offers to correct the breach through a new contract, the nonbreaching party may generally decline the offer and still recover its full damages.

Special circumstances may rebut the reasonableness of the rejection and call for exceptions to this rule. The facts before us support DeRosier's decision: (1) the $9,500 payment demanded was substantial; (2) DeRosier was not unreasonable in believing that acceptance could constitute an accord and satisfaction;[39] (3) other hauling services were readily available; and (4) DeRosier's relationship with USA was strained as USA was blaming DeRosier.

On this record, we conclude that DeRosier did not have an obligation to accept USA's $9,500 offer and that DeRosier is entitled to the costs he incurred in using others to remove the excess fill.

Although the district court erred in awarding DeRosier $8,000 in consequential damages, the district court did not abuse its discretion in awarding DeRosier general damages. DeRosier did not unreasonably reject USA's $9,500 offer, and therefore did not improperly fail to mitigate his general damages. We modify the judgment to the amount of the award for general damages: $22,829.

Affirmed in part and reversed in part.

■ ■ ■

The court indicates that the *Coxe* case is the only relevant reported decision in Minnesota outside the employment context, but does not explain whether (or how) cases in the employment context might differ. This issue arises in *Parker v. Twentieth Century-Fox Film Corp.*, 3 Cal. 3d 176, 474 P.2d 689 (1970), a contracts classic.[40] In *Parker*, the plaintiff was to play the female lead in a movie called "Bloomer Girl." The studio decided not to produce the movie, and offered instead a leading role in another film tentatively titled "Big Country, Big Man." The plaintiff decided not to accept the role, and instead sued for breach of the original contract. The studio defended by claiming that the plaintiff had failed to mitigate damages by turning down the role in "Big Country, Big Man." The trial court granted summary judgment for the plaintiff, awarding her recovery of the agreed compensation under the contract, and the studio appealed. The California Supreme Court affirmed and stated in part:

> In the present case defendant has raised no issue of *reasonableness of efforts* by plaintiff to obtain other employment; the sole issue is whether plaintiff's refusal of defendant's substitute offer of "Big Country" may be used in mitigation. Nor, if the "Big Country" offer was of employment different or inferior when compared

---

[39] "Accord and satisfaction acts to discharge a contract or a cause of action. It is itself an executed contract, and it may be expressed or implied from circumstances which clearly and unequivocally indicate the intention of the parties." *Roaderick v. Lull Eng'g Co.*, 296 Minn. 385, 389, 208 N.W.2d 761, 764 (1973). Although it is not evident that USA intended the new offer to constitute accord and satisfaction, DeRosier claims he feared that a new agreement might constitute a waiver of his rights under his original contract. That risk is material when considering the reasonableness of his rejection of USA's offer.

[40] The plaintiff's full name at the time of the case was Shirley MacLaine Parker. Perhaps this fact gives you some insight into why this case came to be a contracts classic.

with the original "Bloomer Girl" employment, is there an issue as to whether or not plaintiff acted reasonably in refusing the substitute offer. Despite defendant's arguments to the contrary, no case cited or which our research has discovered holds or suggests that reasonableness is an element of a wrongfully discharged employee's option to reject, or fail to seek, different or inferior employment lest the possible earning therefrom be charged against him in mitigation of damages.

The court concluded that the "Big Country" lead would have been different and inferior to that in "Bloomer Girl." "Bloomer Girl" was to be a musical, produced in Los Angeles, while "Big Country" was to be a western, produced in Australia. Further, the "Big Country" offer impaired some of the director and screenplay approval rights present in the "Bloomer Girl" contract.

■ PROBLEM 20.14

Parker involved a situation where the plaintiff failed to accept a substitute for the breached contract. The opposite situation, where the aggrieved party obtains alternative work, may also lead to controversy. Consider, for instance, a case decided by the Arkansas Court of Appeals. In *Marshall School District v. Hill*, 56 Ark. App. 134, 939 S.W.2d 319 (1997), Ron Hill challenged the amount of damages awarded to him in a breach of contract action. Hill had been the football coach and a teacher in the Marshall School District. When his contract expired, the district elected not to renew it. In the superintendent's opinion, "the football program had deteriorated to an unacceptable level." The district failed to follow the proper nonrenewal procedures, however, and Hill successfully sued on a breach of contract theory. In calculating damages, the trial court started with the salary he would have earned in the three school years preceding suit, which amounted to $93,234, and then subtracted the earnings he made in other employment during that same period. Among other jobs, Hill worked for a short period of time in a shirt factory and earned $10,317 for his labors. Hill challenged the damage award, claiming that the trial court should not have taken his earnings from other jobs into account. The appeals court affirmed the trial court's calculation.

(a) Suppose instead Hill established that he had found it demeaning to work in a shirt factory, given his illustrious past as a football coach and teacher, and that is why he quit when he did. Should Hill's award still be reduced by the $10,317 that he earned in the shirt factory?

(b) Alternatively, could the district successfully argue that his award should be reduced even further on the grounds that by quitting the shirt factory job, Hill had failed to mitigate damages?

b. Mitigation of Damages Under the UCC

The mitigation principle permeates UCC remedies. Article 2 doesn't explicitly set out the mitigation principle anywhere. (It comes the closest to doing so in the context of consequential damages, as we see shortly.) Nevertheless, the policies underlying it animate many of the UCC damage calculations. The formulae for deriving direct damages upon breach are a vivid illustration. Although the UCC affords the nonbreaching party a great deal of latitude in choosing its response to a breach, it seldom fully compensates for unreasonable actions (or inactions).

Suppose a caterer contracts to purchase three cases of vintage wine from a winery. If the winery breaches the contract and refuses to deliver the wine, the caterer has a choice. It can purchase substitute wine elsewhere, or it can do nothing. If it covers, it has avoided some of the negative consequences of breach, such as the inability to provide wine at catered events. The cover price may in fact be greater than the market price at the time the seller was supposed to perform, because it took some additional time to arrange cover, or the buyer did not get the best price on the market. The damage calculations still allow the buyer to recover the full difference between the cover price and the contract price, but only if the cover was effected in good faith without any unreasonable delay and in a reasonable fashion. The buyer, of course, has no duty to cover, but if it doesn't, its damages will be limited to the difference between the market price and the contract price.

The UCC's respect for the mitigation principle is nowhere more apparent than in the context of incidental and consequential damages. Expenses of mitigation can usually be recovered as incidental damages, but they must be reasonable. Further, through mitigation, the nonbreaching party can often avoid consequential damages altogether. If the nonbreaching party fails to take reasonable steps to avoid consequential damages, the UCC will prohibit their recovery. Taken together, these rules encourage reasonable mitigation. As we note in Section C.2.b, the UCC damage calculations do not expressly allow a seller to recover consequential damages. Those courts who imply a right to recover consequential damages in appropriate cases are likely to require reasonable efforts to mitigate those losses as well.

With that background, read UCC 2-710 and 2-715, and then analyze the problems that follow.

UCC 2-710. SELLER'S INCIDENTAL DAMAGES

Incidental damages to an aggrieved seller include any commercially reasonable charges, expenses or commissions incurred in stopping delivery, in the transportation, care and custody of goods after the buyer's breach, in connection with return or resale of the goods or otherwise resulting from the breach.

UCC 2-715. BUYER'S INCIDENTAL AND CONSEQUENTIAL DAMAGES

(1) Incidental damages resulting from the seller's breach include expenses reasonably incurred in inspection, receipt, transportation and care and custody of goods rightfully rejected, any commercially reasonable charges, expenses or commissions in connection with effecting cover and any other reasonable expense incident to the delay or other breach.

(2) Consequential damages resulting from the seller's breach include

(a) any loss resulting from general or particular requirements and needs of which the seller at the time of contracting had reason to know and which could not reasonably be prevented by cover or otherwise; and

(b) injury to person or property proximately resulting from any breach of warranty.

■ PROBLEM 20.15

In Section D.2, we note that UCC 2-715 alludes to the foreseeability principle of *Hadley v. Baxendale*. What specific language accomplishes this? Why do you think the language appears in UCC 2-715, but not in UCC 2-710 or the UCC damage formulations generally?

■ PROBLEM 20.16

Vintner Winery entered into a written contract to provide 100 bottles of wine to Wonderful Weddings. The total contract price was $3,000. At the time of the contract, Wonderful told Vintner that it planned to use the wine at a posh society wedding reception. One week before the wedding, Vintner discovered the wine was out of stock. Vintner immediately informed Wonderful that it would not be able to deliver the wine as agreed. Consider the following alternative scenarios, and determine what damages, if any, Wonderful can recover from Vintner for breach of contract.

(a) Upon Vintner's repudiation, Wonderful flew to Paris, bought 100 bottles of equivalent wine from a French wine boutique, and chartered a jet to fly the bottles of wine back to the United States. The price of the wine was quite reasonable; Wonderful was able to purchase it for the French equivalent of $3,000. The cost of Wonderful's plane ticket and the freight charges on the chartered jet, however, amounted to $15,000.

(b) Wonderful decided to serve coffee at the society wedding and hoped that no one would notice the lack of wine. The society couple noticed and rightfully reduced Wonderful's fee. Wonderful lost $10,000 in profits as a result.

(c) Upon Vintner's repudiation, Wonderful immediately started searching around for replacement wine and wasn't able to find any of the quantity and quality called for by the catering contract. Wonderful located one winery that had some appropriate wine for sale, but it was charging $10,000 for the wine, and Wonderful simply couldn't afford it. When Wonderful called up the society couple to explain the problem, the couple began to argue. A huge blowup ensued, and the wedding was canceled. Wonderful lost the $20,000 in profits it planned to make from the reception.

CHAPTER 21

Contract Remedies in the Broader Context

In Chapter 20, we explore in depth the quintessential contract remedy: the award of contract damages. These materials should have convinced you that it can be a subtle and complex undertaking to predict what damages will be available upon breach of contract. The general principle, that <u>an injured party should be compensated for the breach</u>, is simple to state but is often uncertain and imperfect in its application.

In this chapter, we expand our study of contract damages and place them in the broader context of contract remedies generally. We begin with a closer examination of the compensatory nature of contract damages. As Chapter 20 illustrates, contract damages conventionally aim at restoring the aggrieved party to the economic position it would have occupied had the contract been performed as agreed. Generally, neither noneconomic damages (such as those for emotional distress) nor punitive damages are available for breach. There are some exceptions to these limitations, however, and we explore them in more detail in Section A.

emotional distress & punitive

Some parties wish to specify or limit in advance the remedies that will be available to them. Those parties may include clauses in their contract that describe the nature and extent of remedies available for its breach. We will find that courts sometimes implement the remedies to which the parties have agreed; at other times they do not. The tension between freedom of contract and the remedial goals of contract law pervades the topic of agreed remedies. In Section B, we explore agreed remedies and, in particular, consider whether, and to what extent, courts give them effect and allow them to supplant general principles of contract damages.

liquidated damages

Although contract damages are the dominant remedy in our legal system, they are not necessarily the only remedy available upon breach. Some parties may seek to enforce the contract not through the collection of money damages but rather through specific performance. We have alluded to the circumstances under which specific performance might be available since we first introduced this remedy in Chapter 1; it is now time to elaborate those circumstances in more detail. We address situations in which a court might compel performance or restrain breach in Section C. Alternatively, the aggrieved party may elect not to enforce the contract but instead to rescind it and seek restitution. Restitution is familiar by now, as it is a common remedy upon avoidance of a contract due to bargaining misbehavior, misunderstanding, or mistake. Likewise, some measure of restitution may be available if a contract is illegal, implicates public policy concerns, or involves a party who lacked full legal capacity. You may also recognize restitution as the remedy for unjust enrichment in situations where the parties have not entered into a contract. We return to restitution in Section D and examine it as an alternate remedy upon breach of contract.

avoidance or return of ill-gotten gains

A NONECONOMIC AND NONCOMPENSATORY DAMAGES

As we have discussed, an emphasis on economic consequences permeates contract law. Although contracts do not operate exclusively in the commercial realm, economic concerns shape almost all aspects of contract doctrine. The dominance of economic considerations, sometimes to the exclusion of other compelling ethical and social policies, finds especially strong expression in the law of contract damages. Although the principal goal of contract damages is to fully compensate the aggrieved party, we have seen how compensation is almost always viewed in economic rather than personal terms.

* almost always viewed in economic over personal terms

Despite this general approach, an aggrieved party may pursue noneconomic or noncompensatory damages, particularly in an egregious case. Some plaintiffs claim compensation for pain, suffering, or emotional distress; others advocate punitive damages. Generally these plaintiffs are unsuccessful in their quests. Every once in a while, in narrow circumstances, courts grant them the relief they seek. In this section our task is to explore these narrow exceptions and to consider the policies underlying them. At the outset, however, it is important to stress the exceptional nature of our inquiry. In the overwhelming majority of contract cases, neither emotional disturbance damages nor punitive awards are available.

1. Damages for Pain, Suffering, and Emotional Distress

Under the theory of efficient breach, contracts present a choice to the parties bound by their strictures. One can either perform or pay damages. As long as the law stands ready to give the nonbreaching party the "benefit of the bargain," the theory holds that contract rules should be neutral as between the two alternatives. We have seen a number of ways in which the law of contract damages imperfectly achieves this compensation principle. First, the costs of litigation itself generally are not compensable. Second, damages are recoverable only if they can be established with reasonable certainty, they were foreseeable, and they were not reasonably avoidable. On several occasions, we have touched upon yet another limitation to the nonbreaching party's ability to attain the full benefit of the bargain: Generally, contract damages do not look to compensate the nonbreaching party for any emotional disturbance he may have suffered as a consequence of the breach. We now fill in the outlines of this limitation.

Contract breaches can and do lead to annoyance, emotional upset, and distress. To fully place the nonbreaching party in the position he would have occupied had the contract been performed as agreed, one might argue that compensation for the emotional distress flowing from the breach would be necessary. Nevertheless, the prospect that plaintiffs might manufacture claims of emotional distress troubles courts. Courts also worry about imposing unexpected, potentially unlimited, and ultimately unjustifiable liability on those who fail to perform ordinary contract obligations. Except in unusual cases, compensation for these types of claims is simply not the province of contract law. If some other area of law provides relief, the proper course of action is to seek remedies there. If not, so be it. Life carries with it many incompensable harms. The consequences of this view can be stark. Consider, for instance, the case of *Erlich v. Menezes.*

ERLICH v. MENEZES

21 Cal. 4th 543, 981 P.2d 978 (1999)
California Supreme Court

BROWN, Justice.

We granted review in this case to determine whether emotional distress damages are recoverable for the negligent breach of a contract to construct a house. A jury awarded the homeowners the full cost necessary to repair their home as well as damages for emotional distress caused by the contractor's negligent performance. Since the contractor's negligence directly caused only economic injury and property damage, and breached no duty independent of the contract, we conclude the homeowners may not recover damages for emotional distress based upon breach of a contract to build a house.

Both parties agree with the facts as ascertained by the Court of Appeal.[1] Barry and Sandra Erlich contracted with John Menezes, a licensed general contractor, to build a "dreamhouse" on their ocean-view lot. The Erlichs moved into their house in December 1990. In February 1991, the rains came. The house leaked from every conceivable location. Walls were saturated in [an upstairs bedroom], two bedrooms downstairs, and the pool room. Nearly every window in the house leaked. The living room filled with three inches of standing water. In several locations water "poured in . . . streams" from the ceilings and walls. The ceiling in the garage became so saturated . . . the plaster liquified and fell in chunks to the floor.

Menezes's attempts to stop the leaks proved ineffectual. Caulking placed around the windows melted, ran down [the] windows and stained them and ran across the driveway and ran down the house [until it] . . . looked like someone threw balloons with paint in them at the house. Despite several repair efforts, which included using sledgehammers and jackhammers to cut holes in the exterior walls and ceilings, application of new waterproofing materials on portions of the roof and exterior walls, and more caulk, the house continued to leak—from the windows, from the roofs, and water seeped between the floors. Fluorescent light fixtures in the garage filled with water and had to be removed.

The Erlichs eventually had their home inspected by another general contractor and a structural engineer. In addition to confirming defects in the roof, exterior stucco, windows and waterproofing, the inspection revealed serious errors in the construction of the home's structural components. None of the 20 shear, or load-bearing walls specified in the plans were properly installed. The three turrets on the roof were inadequately connected to the roof beams and, as a result, had begun to collapse. Other connections in the roof framing were also improperly constructed. Three decks were in danger of "catastrophic collapse" because they had been finished with mortar and ceramic tile, rather than with the light-weight roofing material originally specified. Finally, the foundation of the main beam for the two-story living room was poured by digging a shallow hole, dumping in "two sacks of dry concrete mix, putting some water in the hole and mixing it up with a shovel." This foundation, required to carry a load of 12,000 pounds, could only support about 2,000. The beam is settling and the surrounding concrete is cracking. According to the Erlichs' expert, problems were major and pervasive, concerning everything "related to a window or waterproofing, everywhere that there was something related to framing," stucco, or the walking deck.

---

[1] In its summary of the facts, the court salts in numerous quotes from the Court of Appeal's description (the opinion of the Court of Appeal appears at 71 Cal. Rptr. 2d 137 (1998)). To reduce distraction, we have edited out quotation marks without further indication.—EDS.

Both of the Erlichs testified that they suffered emotional distress as a result of the defective condition of the house and Menezes's invasive and unsuccessful repair attempts. Barry Erlich testified he felt "absolutely sick" and had to be "carted away in an ambulance" when he learned the full extent of the structural problems. He has a permanent heart condition, known as superventricular tachyarrhythmia, attributable, in part, to excessive stress. Although the condition can be controlled with medication, it has forced him to resign his positions as athletic director, department head and track coach. Sandra Erlich feared the house would collapse in an earthquake and feared for her daughter's safety. Stickers were placed on her bedroom windows, and alarms and emergency lights installed so rescue crews would find her room first in an emergency.

Plaintiffs sought recovery on several theories, including breach of contract, fraud, negligent misrepresentation, and negligent construction. Both the breach of contract claim and the negligence claim alleged numerous construction defects.

Menezes prevailed on the fraud and negligent misrepresentation claims. The jury found he breached his contract with the Erlichs by negligently constructing their home and awarded $406,700 as the cost of repairs. Each spouse was awarded $50,000 for emotional distress, and Barry Erlich received an additional $50,000 for physical pain and suffering and $15,000 for lost earnings.

By a two-to-one majority, the Court of Appeal affirmed the judgment, including the emotional distress award. The majority noted the breach of a contractual duty may support an action in tort. The jury found Menezes was negligent. Since his negligence exposed the Erlichs to "intolerable living conditions and a constant, justifiable fear about the safety of their home," the majority decided the Erlichs were properly compensated for their emotional distress. The dissent pointed out that no reported California case has upheld an award of emotional distress damages based upon simple breach of a contract to build a house. Since Menezes's negligence directly caused only economic injury and property damage, the Erlichs were not entitled to recover damages for their emotional distress. We granted review to resolve the question. . . .

[The court first analyzes the case under a tort theory. It concludes that tort law does not support recovery of emotional distress damages under these facts. A claim for breach of contract alone does not give rise to damages in tort, even if that breach is negligent; tort damages are permitted in contract cases only when there has been a violation of a duty completely independent of the contract, or where the breach is both intentional and intended to harm. The court concludes that none of these factors was present in this case. Even if such factors had been present, the court says, the facts would not support an award of tort damages for emotional distress. Tort damages for emotional distress are not available where the plaintiff suffers only property damage or economic loss.] Here, the . . . [alleged tort]—the negligent construction of the Erlichs' house—did not cause physical injury. No one was hit by a falling beam. Although the Erlichs state they feared the house was structurally unsafe and might collapse in an earthquake, they lived in it for five years. The only physical injury alleged is

Barry Erlich's heart disease, which flowed from the emotional distress and not directly from the negligent construction.

The Erlichs may have hoped to build their dream home and live happily ever after, but there is a reason that tag line belongs only in fairy tales. Building a house may turn out to be a stress-free project; it is much more likely to be the stuff of urban legends—the cause of bankruptcy, marital dissolution, hypertension and fleeting fantasies ranging from homicide to suicide. As Justice Yegan noted below, "No reasonable homeowner can embark on a building project with certainty that the project will be completed to perfection. Indeed, errors are so likely to occur that few if any homeowners would be justified in resting their peace of mind on [its] timely or correct completion. . . ." [Although there may be a connection] . . . between the service sought and the aggravation and distress resulting from incompetence, . . . the emotional suffering still derives from an inherently economic concern.

Having concluded tort damages are not available, we finally consider whether damages for emotional distress should be included as consequential or special damages in a contract claim. Contract damages are generally limited to those within the contemplation of the parties when the contract was entered into or at least reasonably foreseeable by them at the time; consequential damages beyond the expectations of the parties are not recoverable. This limitation on available damages serves to encourage contractual relations and commercial activity by enabling parties to estimate in advance the financial risks of their enterprise. . . . (*Applied Equipment* [*Corp. v. Litton Saudi Arabia Ltd.* (1994) 7 Cal. 4th 503 at p. 515, 28 Cal. Rptr. 2d 475, 869 P.2d 454]).

"[W]hen two parties make a contract, they agree upon the rules and regulations which will govern their relationship; the risks inherent in the agreement and the likelihood of its breach. The parties to the contract in essence create a mini-universe for themselves, in which each voluntarily chooses his contracting partner, each trusts the other's willingness to keep his word and honor his commitments, and in which they define their respective obligations, rewards and risks. Under such a scenario, it is appropriate to enforce only such obligations as each party voluntarily assumed, and to give him only such benefits as he expected to receive; this is the function of contract law" (*Applied Equipment, supra*, 7 Cal. 4th at p. 517, 28 Cal. Rptr. 2d 475, 869 P.2d 454).

Accordingly, damages for mental suffering and emotional distress are generally not recoverable in an action for breach of an ordinary commercial contract in California. "Recovery for emotional disturbance will be excluded unless the breach also caused bodily harm or the contract or the breach is of such a kind that serious emotional disturbance was a particularly likely result." (Rest. 2d Contracts, §353.) The Restatement specifically notes the breach of a contract to build a home is not "particularly likely" to result in "serious emotional disturbance."

Cases permitting recovery for emotional distress typically involve mental anguish stemming from more personal undertakings the traumatic results of which were unavoidable. . . . Cases from other jurisdictions have formulated a similar rule, barring recovery of emotional distress damages for breach of contract except in cases involving contracts in which emotional concerns are the essence of the contract. (*See, e.g., Hancock v. Northcutt* (Alaska 1991) 808 P.2d 251, 258 ["contracts pertaining to one's dwelling are not among those contracts which, if breached, are particularly likely to result in serious emotional disturbance;" typical damages for breach of house construction contracts can appropriately be calculated in terms of monetary loss]; *McMeakin v. Roofing & Sheet Metal Supply* (Okla. Ct. App. 1990) 807 P.2d 288 [affirming order granting summary judgment in favor of defendant roofing company after it negligently stacked too many brick tiles on roof, causing roof to collapse and completely destroy home, leading to plaintiff's heart attack one month later]; . . . *Creger v. Robertson* (La. Ct. App. 1989) 542 So. 2d 1090 [reversing award for emotional distress damages caused by foul odor emanating from a faulty foundation, preventing plaintiff from entertaining guests in her residence]; *Groh v. Broadland Builders, Inc.* (Mich. Ct. App. 1982) 120 Mich. App. 214, 327 N.W.2d 443 [reversing order denying motion to strike allegations of mental anguish in case involving malfunctioning septic tank system, and noting adequacy of monetary damages to compensate for pecuniary loss of "having to do the job over," as distinguished from cases allowing recovery because situation could never be adequately corrected].)

Plaintiffs argue strenuously that a broader notion of damages is appropriate when the contract is for the construction of a home. Amici curiae urge us to permit emotional distress damages in cases of negligent construction of a personal residence when the negligent construction causes gross interference with the normal use and habitability of the residence. Such a rule would make the financial risks of construction agreements difficult to predict. Contract damages must be clearly ascertainable in both nature and origin. (Civ. Code, §3301.) A contracting party cannot be required to assume limitless responsibility for all consequences of a breach and must be advised of any special harm that might result in order to determine whether or not to accept the risk of contracting.

Moreover, adding an emotional distress component to recovery for construction defects could increase the already prohibitively high cost of housing in California, affect the availability of insurance for builders, and greatly diminish the supply of affordable housing. The potential for such broad-ranging economic consequences—costs likely to be paid by the public generally—means the task of fashioning appropriate limits on the availability of emotional distress claims should be left to the Legislature.

Permitting damages for emotional distress on the theory that certain contracts carry a lot of emotional freight provides no useful guidance. Courts have carved out a narrow range of exceptions to the general rule of exclusion where emotional tranquility is the contract's essence. Refusal to broaden the bases for recovery reflects a fundamental policy choice. A rule which focuses not on the risks contracting parties voluntarily assume but on one party's reaction to inadequate performance, cannot provide any principled limit on liability. . . .

The available damages for defective construction are limited to the cost of repairing the home, including lost use or relocation expenses, or the diminution in value. The Erlichs received more than $400,000 in traditional contract damages to correct the defects in their home. While their distress was undoubtedly real and serious, we conclude the balance of policy considerations—the potential for significant increases in liability in amounts disproportionate to culpability, the court's inability to formulate appropriate limits on the availability of claims, and the magnitude of the impact on stability and predictability in commercial affairs—counsel against expanding contract damages to include mental distress claims in negligent construction cases.

The judgment of the Court of Appeal is reversed and the matter is remanded for further proceedings consistent with this opinion.

■ ■ ■

The court in *Erlich* states that emotional distress damages are sometimes available for breach of contract, but not under the facts before it. As the opinion suggests, a number of narrow exceptions have been carved out of the general prohibition on emotional distress damages, although the outlines of these exceptions and their acceptability differ from jurisdiction to jurisdiction. Many exceptions relate to the nature of the breach; others relate to the nature of the contract. We discuss these two categories in turn.

Common exceptions relate to the nature of the breach. If the breach is such as to cause bodily harm, many states will allow emotional distress damages. Further, if the breach is such that the facts establish an independent tort for which these types of damages are available under tort law, courts are likely to allow such damages in a contract cause of action as well. It is important to understand, as the *Erlich* court recognizes, that tort law does not automatically allow recovery of these types of damages either, but it tends to be much more generous in that regard than general principles of contract law.

Courts that adopt a more liberal approach to emotional distress damages sometimes allow these damages in cases of willful, wanton, or malicious breach quite separate from any analysis of whether the actions of the breaching party qualify independently as a tort. For example, in *Lutz Farms v. Asgrow Seed Co.*, 948 F.2d 638 (10th Cir. 1991), the court applied this rule to affirm the recovery of emotional distress damages to two brothers who were forced into bankruptcy when their onion crop failed. The onion growers sued the supplier of the onion seed. At trial, the brothers argued that in a calculated and considered effort to rush the onion seed to market, the supplier failed to test adequately the genetic quality of the seed. The brothers introduced evidence to support their claims. The court held that there was evidence of a willful and wanton breach adequate to support an award of damages for emotional distress. Whether the breach itself amounts to a tort or is merely tort-like in nature, the intentions of the breaching party are likely to be highly relevant to the recovery of emotional disturbance damages.

Where the nature of the contract itself makes emotional distress a particularly likely result of breach, some courts allow recovery of damages for that distress. This approach is not universal. Notice, for instance, that the *Erlich* court conceded that emotional distress is a likely result of breach of a contract to construct a home, yet still it refused to allow recovery of emotional distress damages. In most jurisdictions, courts sharply circumscribe the types of contracts that merit recovery of emotional distress damages as a matter of course, and typically allow such damages only where emotional well-being or security is itself one of the objects of the contract.

A paradigmatic example is a contract to perform funereal or mortuary services. The cases relying on this exception are long-standing and often present memorable, if grisly, facts. Many of them involve mishandled corpses or funereal disasters. For example, in *Ross v. Forest Lawn Memorial Park*, 153 Cal. App. 3d 988, 203 Cal. Rptr. 468 (1984), Francine Ross was allowed to pursue emotional disturbance damages when she alleged that a cemetery breached its contract to provide a funeral and burial for her 17-year-old daughter Kristie. Ms. Ross specified that the ceremonies be kept private. Because her daughter had been a punk rocker, Ms. Ross feared in particular that the services would be disrupted by her daughter's musical cohort and asked that they be excluded. Instead:

> Many punk rockers attended both the funeral services in the chapel and the gravesite burial services. Neither their appearance nor comportment was in accord with traditional, solemn funeral ceremonies. Some were in white face makeup and black lipstick. Hair colors ranged from blues and greens to pinks and oranges. Some were dressed in leather and chains and twirled baton-like weapons, while yet another wore a dress decorated with live rats. The uninvited guests were drinking and using cocaine, and were physically and verbally abusive to family members and their guests. A disturbance ensued and grew to the point that police had to be called to restore order. . . .

Faced with allegations of these facts in Ms. Ross's pleadings, the California Court of Appeal held that it was an error for the trial court to dismiss her lawsuit on the pleadings.

There is no unanimity among the jurisdictions as to what specific types of contracts justify the award of emotional disturbance damages. Contracts having something to do with death, communication of the fact of death, or treatment of dead bodies are commonly among them.[2] At one time, breaches of contracts to marry were often seen as deserving of emotional disturbance damages, but such contracts have been made unenforceable by statute in many states. The *Lane v. Kindercare Learning Centers, Inc.* case that comes next extends this reasoning to a day care contract. As you read this case, pay particular attention to the analogous types of contracts mentioned by the court.

---

[2] We will spare you the further tales of premature cremations, botched autopsies, bloated corpses, and missing body parts that pepper the case reports. Suffice it to say that some jurisdictions limit their view of contracts that by their nature are likely to lead to emotional distress to these very narrow categories.

LANE v. KINDERCARE LEARNING CENTERS, INC.

231 Mich. App. 689, 588 N.W.2d 715 (1998)
Michigan Court of Appeals

PER CURIAM.

... Plaintiff enrolled her eighteen-month-old daughter in day care with defendant. On December 9, 1992, plaintiff dropped off her daughter at defendant's facility at lunch time. Plaintiff's daughter had been prescribed medication, and plaintiff filled out an authorization form granting defendant's employees permission to administer the medication to her daughter that day. Just after 5:00 P.M. on December 9, 1992, one of defendant's employees placed the child, who had fallen asleep, in a crib in the infant room. At approximately 6:00 P.M., defendant's employees locked the doors of the facility and went home for the day, apparently unaware that plaintiff's daughter was still sleeping in the crib. Shortly thereafter, plaintiff returned to the facility to pick up her daughter and found the facility locked and unlit. Plaintiff called 911. A police officer who responded to the call looked through a window of the facility, with the aid of a flashlight, and saw the child sleeping in the crib. Another officer then broke a window and retrieved the child from the building. The child was upset after the incident, but was not physically harmed. When plaintiff went into the facility to retrieve her daughter's belongings, she apparently found the medication authorization form and observed that it had not been initialed to indicate that the child had been given the medication. Plaintiff alleged that she suffered emotional distress as a result of the incident.

Plaintiff filed a complaint against defendant, alleging breach of contract, statutory, regulatory, and internal policy violations, negligence, and gross negligence, and seeking exemplary damages. Defendant moved for summary disposition of plaintiff's claims. ... After a hearing, the trial court granted summary disposition of plaintiff's claims. ... Plaintiff first argues that the trial court erred in granting summary disposition of her breach of contract claim ... on the ground that plaintiff failed to allege compensable emotional distress. We agree.

This Court reviews a trial court's grant of summary disposition de novo. ...

The recovery of damages for the breach of a contract is limited to those damages that are a natural result of the breach or those that are contemplated by the parties at the time the contract was made. *Kewin v. Massachusetts Mut. Life. Ins. Co.*, 409 Mich. 401, 414; 295 N.W.2d 50 (1980); *Hadley v. Baxendale*, 9 Exch. 341; 156 Eng. Rep. 145 (1854). Therefore, it is generally held that damages for emotional distress cannot be recovered for the breach of a commercial contract. However, our Supreme Court has recognized that damages for emotional distress may be recovered for the breach of a contract in cases that do not involve commercial or pecuniary contracts, but involve contracts of a personal nature. [In] *Stewart v. Rudner*, 349 Mich. 459, 469; 84 N.W.2d 816 (1957), [o]ur Supreme Court explained:

increase power or wealth

> When we have a contract concerned not with trade and commerce but with life and death, not with profit but with elements of personality, not with pecuniary aggrandizement but with matters of mental concern and solicitude, then a breach of duty with respect to such contracts will inevitably and necessarily result in mental anguish, pain and suffering. In such cases the parties may reasonably be said to have contracted <u>with reference to the payment</u> of damages therefor in event of breach. Far from being outside the contemplation of the parties they are an integral and inseparable part of it.

emotional damages are an inseperable part of personal contract

examples

Examples of personal contracts include a contract to perform a cesarean section; a contract for the care and burial of a dead body; a contract to care for the plaintiff's elderly mother and to notify the plaintiff in the event of the mother's illness; and a promise to marry.[3]

We believe that a contract to care for one's child is a matter of "mental concern and solicitude," rather than "pecuniary aggrandizement." *Stewart, supra* at 471. Therefore, like the contract to care for the plaintiff's elderly mother in *Avery* [*v. Arnold Home, Inc.*, 17 Mich. App. 240, 169 N.W.2d 135 (1969)], the contract involved in the <u>instant case was personal in nature, rather than</u> commercial. At the time the contract was executed, it was foreseeable that a breach of the contract would result in mental distress damages to plaintiff, which would extend beyond the mere "annoyance and vexation" that normally accompanies the breach of a contract. *Kewin, supra* at 417. <u>Such damages are clearly within the contemplation of the parties to such a contract.</u>

foreseeable that breach will result in mental stress

The trial court granted summary disposition of plaintiff's breach of contract claim ... on the ground that plaintiff failed to plead that she suffered a definite and objective physical injury as a result of her emotional distress. However, damages may be awarded for emotional distress caused by a breach of a personal contract <u>even where the emotional distress does not result in a physical injury.</u> We therefore conclude that the trial court erred in granting summary disposition of plaintiff's breach of contract claim. . . .

holding

emotional distress does not need to manifest in physical harm for recovery

■ QUESTIONS

(1) Does the court address whether Ms. Lane's damages were reasonably foreseeable? In your view, is this test alone sufficient to determine if emotional disturbance damages should be available, or is special treatment merited?

yes

---

[3] Contracts that have been held to be commercial, rather than personal, include a no-fault automobile insurance contract, a disability insurance contract, a hospitalization insurance contract, and a contract for the construction of a house.

(2)   On remand, how would Ms. Lane establish her emotional disturbance damages? Does the court speak to whether she will need to establish them with reasonable certainty?

■ PROBLEM 21.1

In the text preceding the *Lane* case, we note that either the nature of the contract or the nature of the breach may allow for recovery of emotional distress damages. In *Lane*, do you think the court is persuaded by the nature of the contract alone, or is it also looking to the nature of the breach? Consider the following two possibilities:

(a) Suppose Ms. Lane had specified that her daughter was to have an hour-long nap, and instead Kindercare allowed her to sleep for two hours. Assume further, for reasons that are not entirely clear, that this caused Ms. Lane enormous and real emotional distress. Under the court's reasoning, should she be able to recover emotional disturbance damages? Would it matter if she had told the day care center how important it was that her daughter not be allowed to oversleep?

(b) Assume instead that the reason Ms. Lane used a day care center was because of her employment, and the day care center knew this. One morning, as she sought to drop off her daughter on the way to work, the day care center refused to take the child for no good reason. As a result, Ms. Lane had to miss a day of work and spent the whole day arranging alternative day care, suffering untold anguish and distress in the process. Under the court's reasoning, might she be able to recover emotional disturbance damages?

---

punish breacher, deter others

↑

courts don't favor → **2. Punitive Damages** = *exemplary damages*

Plaintiffs who argue for emotional disturbance damages often seek punitive damages as well. Although there is commonality in the ways courts treat emotional disturbance damages and punitive damages, it is important to appreciate the differences. Unlike emotional disturbance damages, which seek to compensate the plaintiff for harm caused by the breach, punitive damages are intended to punish the breacher and deter others from following the breacher's example. Because of their deterrent effect, these damages are also called "exemplary" damages—that is, damages that are intended to make an example of the evil defendant. Because they are aimed at punishment and deterrence rather than compensation, punitive damages are at heart inconsistent with the general policies underlying contract damages. We have seen that contract damages, *main goal of damages*

however imperfectly applied, ultimately seek to make the plaintiff whole. Further, assuming this can be done, the theory of efficient breach holds that the law should condone certain breaches, not deter them.

Courts do not favor punitive damages in a contract cause of action. While courts are generally hostile to emotional disturbance damages, at least such damages have at base a compensation goal, while punitive damages do not. They may have the incidental effect of compensating the plaintiff for losses that are not otherwise compensable, such as attorneys' fees, but that is not their objective.

The Restatement, Second, addresses punitive damages as follows:

RESTATEMENT, SECOND §355. PUNITIVE DAMAGES

Punitive damages are not recoverable for a breach of contract unless the conduct constituting the breach is also a tort for which punitive damages are recoverable.

You may recall that UCC 1-305(a) takes a similar approach, stating "... neither consequential or special damages nor penal damages may be had except as specifically provided in [the Uniform Commercial Code] or by other rule of law."

must specifically allow for punitive damages

Both provisions rely principally on tort or other rules outside of contract law to justify the award of punitive (or penal) damages. Just as with emotional disturbance damages, punitive damages are not automatically available every time the defendant commits a tort. The plaintiff not only must establish that the breach of contract amounted to a tort, but that it amounted to the type of tort that may carry punitive damages. The standards vary from state to state and from tort to tort, but generally a tort can justify punitive damages if it is willful, wanton, reckless, or malicious. There is the occasional court that will allow punitive damages for a particularly egregious breach of contract, even if that breach does not amount to a separate tort, but such courts are in the minority.

What types of contract breaches are also likely to establish an independent tort such that when they are sufficiently willful, wanton, reckless, or malicious, they could potentially attract an award of punitive damages? Clearly, a defendant who breaches a contract and in doing so inflicts a personal injury is likely to have committed a tort as well as a breach of contract. If the defendant acts with the requisite degree of willfulness, punitive damages may be available to the plaintiff. Beyond the context of willful physical harm, however, the examples are not so clear. Some courts allow recovery of punitive damages where the breach of contract is accompanied by significant willful fraud. Others view punitive damages favorably when the breach of contract also constitutes a severe breach of fiduciary duty or of some other special relationship. Of particular note in this regard are the insurance cases.

ex. insurance
breach of
contract

When insurance companies willfully deny claims without reasonable basis to do so, some courts allow punitive damages. In doing this, the courts reason that the insurance companies have a special relationship with their insureds that makes a willful and unreasonable breach of contract an act of bad faith. As we have seen, every contract has an implied obligation of good faith in its performance. A breach of this obligation in the insurance context may constitute an independent tort. In effect, the courts have created a tort specifically tailored to these circumstances—bad-faith denial of an insurance claim. These cases are remarkable in part because it is the breach of contract itself (refusal to pay) which constitutes the central element of the tort—not some separate or independent action associated with the breach.

> ### ■ PROBLEM 21.2
>
> The materials in this section suggest that plaintiffs in breach of contract actions can collect emotional distress or punitive damages only in limited circumstances. Plaintiffs are likely to have more success with these types of claims if they can also establish the elements of an independent tort. If they can establish claims under tort law, why don't they simply sue in tort? Can you imagine any circumstances under which the existence of a parallel contract cause of action could be important to them?

B   AGREED REMEDIES

It is helpful to start our discussion by imagining what the parties might hope to accomplish through an agreed remedy. Sometimes a party may be dissatisfied with the general compensation goal of contract remedies. Instead, that party may wish to compel, or at least strongly encourage, performance. One way to do this is to include a penalty for breach in the contract. If the penalty is sufficiently severe, where it has the option the party who owes performance may think long and hard before breaching the contract. It is a long-standing common law rule that contract penalties are unenforceable as against public policy. Here the principal remedial goal of contract law, compensation, wins out over the policy favoring freedom of contract. It is important to recognize that contract law need not be structured this way. In fact, many civil law jurisdictions allow contract penalties as a matter of course. Nevertheless, in the common law there remains a very strong hostility toward agreed remedies that are intended to act as penalties.

contract
penalties
are against
public policy

Agreed remedies may have aims beyond compelling performance. Sometimes parties seek to simplify and clarify remedies in advance rather than leaving them to the uncertain and contentious processes of litigation. One way to do this is to specify in the contract what the damages for breach will be. This kind of contract clause is called a "liquidated damages clause," because it liquidates (or makes certain) the damages that are available to the aggrieved party. There are many legitimate, nonpenal reasons why parties might want to liquidate damages in a contract. As we have seen, there are significant difficulties associated with collecting damages that cannot be established with reasonable certainty or that are not within the reasonable contemplation of the parties. By including a liquidated damages clause, parties may be able to agree to a dollar value in advance that is likely to approximate the damages they will suffer upon breach. This relieves the aggrieved party of the necessity of establishing those damages with reasonable certainty yet also puts the breaching party on notice of the extent of its potential liability. Furthermore, by establishing liability in advance, liquidated damages clauses may facilitate negotiated settlement of disputes rather than costly and uncertain litigation. At the same time, clauses that establish liquidated damages at too high a level may have the effect, and sometimes even the disguised intention, of deterring or penalizing breach. For this reason, courts tend to scrutinize them carefully and sometimes refuse to enforce them.

liquidated damages

Instead of penalizing breach or liquidating damages, the parties may seek to limit the remedies available for breach. Parties do this in myriad ways. One method is to put a cap on the damages available for breach. Clauses that set liquidated damages at too low a level, or as some courts say, "underliquidate" damages, may have the effect of limiting remedies. This effect may be intended or unintended. Another way to limit remedies is to specify that the breaching party will not be responsible for specified categories of damages. For instance, the parties may state that certain payments are nonrefundable or that consequential damages are not recoverable. Contractual limitations on remedy are very common.

cap too low
↓
under liquidate

Yet another device is to modify or restrict the types of remedies that are available or establish procedures for exercising remedies. For instance, a contract might say that if a buyer is dissatisfied with goods purchased under a contract, the buyer's sole remedy is the repair or replacement of defective parts rather than the collection of damages. Alternatively, the parties may state that should breach occur, the aggrieved party must give notice of the breach within a certain period of time or else be barred from any remedy. There are innumerable variations on this theme. In commercial transactions the parties may engage in hotly contested negotiations before settling on the ultimate parameters of a clause modifying or restricting the types of remedies available for breach. As a general rule, courts are often willing to enforce contractual limitations or modifications of remedy. Courts do tend to balk, however, if the parties have uneven bargaining power, especially if the agreement leaves the aggrieved party without a reasonable modicum of remedy for breach.

time limit

→ when courts won't enforce

We start by examining the methods that courts use to distinguish between unenforceable contract penalties and enforceable liquidated damages clauses. Because the conflicting policies are so acute in this area, it is difficult to draw a bright line between penalties and liquidated damages. Nevertheless, a relatively broadly accepted test has been developed to make the distinction. We study its outlines here and then proceed to examine contractual modifications and limitations of remedy, in particular modifications and limitations of remedy under the UCC.

1. Policing Liquidated Damages Clauses

The Restatement, Second, and the UCC state, in similar terms, the tests courts frequently use to police liquidated damages clauses:

RESTATEMENT, SECOND §356. LIQUIDATED DAMAGES AND PENALTIES

(1) Damages for breach by either party may be liquidated in the agreement but only at an amount that is reasonable in the light of the anticipated or actual loss caused by the breach and the difficulties of proof of loss. A term fixing unreasonably large liquidated damages is unenforceable on grounds of public policy as a penalty. . . .

public policy doesn't like penalties

UCC 2-718. LIQUIDATION OR LIMITATION OF DAMAGES; DEPOSITS

(1) Damages for breach by either party may be liquidated in the agreement but only at an amount which is reasonable in the light of the anticipated or actual harm caused by the breach, the difficulties of proof of loss, and the inconvenience or nonfeasibility of otherwise obtaining an adequate remedy. A term fixing unreasonably large liquidated damages is void as a penalty.

These provisions both require the amount of damages specified to be reasonable. Reasonableness is a highly fact-specific inquiry, but the provisions give some guidance as to what factors should be taken into account. The factors are related, but they deserve separate attention.

Restatement, Second §356 and UCC 2-718(1) both require that the damages be reasonable in light of the anticipated or actual harm caused by the breach. Older cases required liquidated damages to be reasonable in light of the anticipated harm caused by the breach. It was a forward-looking test: At the time of the contract, did the parties choose a liquidated damages formula that was likely to result in a figure that would approximate the harm due to the breach? If the parties chose a formula or figure that would yield damages far in excess of

test for reasonableness

any anticipated harm, there was reason to believe that the parties intended the clause to operate as a penalty rather than as a good-faith estimate of damages. The inquiry was somewhat paradoxical, however, because courts looked to the difficulties of proving loss as well. Damages that are difficult to prove may also be difficult to anticipate, thus making application of this older test problematic.

Over time, courts began to look to the actual damages suffered by the non-breaching party as a relevant factor under the "anticipated harm" test. In hindsight, courts reasoned, the actual damages might cast light on what the anticipated damages might have been at the time the contract was entered. As the actual damages were often concrete, they avoided some of the problems of measurement inherent in establishing anticipated damages. But courts continued to try to ascertain the damages the parties anticipated at the time of the contract, and at least formally, the liquidated damages needed to be reasonable in light of those anticipated damages. Two distinct types of fact patterns arose.

actual damages are greater

In the first type of fact pattern, the actual damages turned out to be much greater than the parties had anticipated at the time they entered the contract. Given what they knew at the time of the contract, it was likely that they anticipated that damages would be relatively small. Nevertheless, perhaps to encourage performance, they included a liquidated damages clause in their agreement that set recovery at a very high level, maybe even unreasonably high in light of the anticipated damages. For whatever reason—perhaps because of a sudden change in market conditions or other circumstances that the parties had not anticipated—the liquidated damages clause turned out to approximate the actual damages quite well. Under these circumstances, the liquidated damages clause was in consonance with the compensation policies underlying contract law. Even if the liquidated damages differed somewhat from the actual damages, the policy of freedom of contract weighed in to favor enforcement of the liquidated damages clause instead of awarding the exact amount of damages that could be established. As a result, when the UCC drafters were formulating UCC 2-718(1), they allowed the reasonableness of the liquidated damages to be measured either by the anticipated harm or by the actual harm caused by the breach. The Restatement, Second, followed suit. It is important to note that this test is an alternative one. If the liquidated damages are reasonable in light of either the anticipated harm or the actual harm, they should survive scrutiny under this test.

viewed in light of anticipated or actual harm

actual harm is ✓ small

The second type of fact pattern arose in cases where the actual harm turned out to be very small, even though the anticipated harm might have been large. When the liquidated damages were reasonable in light of the anticipated harm but not the actual harm, the liquidated damages clause could operate as a penalty, even though that was not the parties' intention when they entered the contract. The UCC and Restatement, Second, formulations suggest that the liquidated damages clauses should nevertheless be enforceable. Although many courts enforce liquidated damages clauses even when the liquidated damages substantially exceed the actual damages in the case, some courts refuse to do so when the actual damages appear to be nonexistent. In spite of the policy favoring the parties' freedom to set their own reasonable terms, the penal effect

✗ must have some actual harm

of such a clause on the breacher and the resulting windfall to the nonbreaching party are more than some courts are willing to swallow.

If there is a trend, it is probably toward enforcing liquidated damages clauses among sophisticated parties. The case that follows reflects this trend. The majority concludes at the summary judgment stage that the liquidated damages clause at issue is enforceable as written, while the dissent concludes genuine issues of material fact remain. As you read the case, think about which policy you consider to be more compelling in this context: the policy that favors freedom of contract, or the remedial principle that limits recovery to compensation. Then consider the problems that follow.

KENT STATE UNIVERSITY v. FORD

26 N.E.3d 868 (2015)
Ohio Court of Appeals

GRENDELL, Judge.

Defendant-appellant, Gene A. Ford, appeals from the judgments of the Portage County Court of Common Pleas, granting summary judgment in favor of plaintiff-appellee, Kent State University, on its claim for breach of contract, and awarding damages against Ford in the amount of $1.2 million. The issues to be determined in this case are whether a contract with a liquidated damages clause is unenforceable when it requires a breaching university coach to pay his salary for each year remaining under the contract, when there is limited evidence of actual damages, and whether damages in such a case can include only the salary of a replacement coach. For the following reasons, we affirm the decision of the lower court.

On April 26, 2011, Kent State filed a Complaint against Ford and Bradley University, asserting that Ford, the former head coach of the men's basketball team at Kent State, breached his contract by terminating his employment with Kent State four years before the contract's expiration and commencing employment with Bradley University.... [The complaint alleged breach of contract and breach of fiduciary duty by Ford, and tortious interference with a contract against Bradley University. All claims but the breach of contract claim were ultimately dismissed.]

In April of 2008, Ford and Kent State executed an Employment Contract, employing Ford as Kent State's head men's basketball coach for a period of four years, with an option for a fifth year. The Contract included his salary, supplemental salary, and various incentives based on performance. It also contained the following provision:

GENE A. FORD recognizes that his promise to work for the UNIVERSITY for the entire term of this four (4) year Contract is of the essence of this Contract with the

UNIVERSITY. GENE A. FORD also recognizes that the UNIVERSITY is making a highly valuable investment in his continued employment by entering into this Contract and its investment would be lost were he to resign or otherwise terminate his employment with the UNIVERSITY prior to the expiration of this Contract. Accordingly, he will pay to the UNIVERSITY as liquidated damages an amount equal to his base and supplemental salary, multiplied by the number of years (or portion(s) thereof) remaining on the Contract.

Further, the contract provided that if Ford terminated his employment prior to the contract's expiration, "and is employed or performing services for a person or institution other than the UNIVERSITY," he "shall pay . . . an amount equal to the balance of the then-current total annual salary due for the remaining amount of the term of this Contract."

In April 2010, Ford and Kent State renegotiated and executed a new Employment Contract, lasting for a term of five years, which increased his salary and supplemental salary by a total of $100,000, for a total salary of $300,000. This contract contained the same liquidated damages provision as above, changing only the number of years under the contract.

Joel Nielsen, the Kent State athletic director, testified that in early 2011, he received a phone call from Ford's agent, requesting permission for Ford to speak to other schools regarding employment. Nielsen granted such permission following the conclusion of the basketball season. On March 26, 2011, Ford made Nielsen aware of his conversations with Bradley University and expressed his possible interest in taking a coaching position there. At that time, Nielsen reminded Ford of the liquidated damages provision in the Contract. Soon thereafter, Ford accepted the position at Bradley University, at an annual salary of $700,000. Nielsen hired Coach Robert Senderoff in early April 2011 to replace Ford.

Nielsen testified that the liquidated damages clause was included to protect the University by providing coaching continuity, which aids in recruiting players. Nielsen did not know of any players who left the program or of any specific recruits that may have decided not to attend Kent State because of Ford's departure, although he believed it would impact some potential future recruits. Nielsen explained the cost associated with conducting a coaching search to replace Ford, including time and travel for interviews. He outlined as potential damages the "loss of investment" in Ford, including "equity" built up with fans and donors. He conceded that, when coaches left in the past, the team continued to perform well.

Thomas Kleinlein, Kent State's executive associate athletic director, testified that Ford had difficulty deciding whether to go to Bradley, and was concerned about having to pay the liquidated damages clause. Regarding potential damages resulting from Ford's departure, season ticket sales and advance ticket sales were "behind." Kleinlein also noted that there are often large "staff transitional costs" when a head coach leaves.

Dr. Lester Lefton, president of Kent State University, testified that liquidated damages "make up some of the differences" from the loss in ticket sales, advertising, recruiting and "having to start all over again" when a coach leaves prematurely. He believed that such damages "deter" individuals from leaving early. Dr. Lefton explained that when a coach leaves prior to the expiration of the contract, "the program suffers, recruiting suffers, ticket sales suffer, alumni and fan support suffers, [and] donations suffer." He testified that the liquidated damages clause contained in Ford's contract was similar to those currently used for head basketball and football coaches at Kent State and it was consistent with past policy.

Dr. Lefton opined that, at the time the second contract was signed by Ford, he "fully understood what liquidated damages were because he was trying to have them removed." He believed, from conversations with presidents from other universities, that they included similar liquidated damages clauses in their contracts.

Liang Kennedy, Kent State's athletic director until June of 2010, offered Ford his first head coaching contract at Kent State in April 2008. Kennedy asserted that the liquidated damages clause protects the coach and the institution's investment in the coach and the program. At the time the second contract was negotiated, Ford wanted the liquidated damages clause to be changed and asked for a "graduated reduction," i.e., the damages would decrease as the contract became closer to expiring. Ford eventually agreed to accept the liquidated damages clause as it had been previously and signed the new contract.

Kennedy testified that the base salary was used as the foundation to determine the amount of liquidated damages. He noted that if Ford left, consequences to the program would include decreased revenue, fundraising, and community outreach, which they "established . . . would cost about a year's salary per year." He explained that Kent State did not do a "financial analysis" prior to establishing the liquidated damages clause in Ford's contract.

Regarding damages that occurred after Ford's departure, Kennedy noted that he was disappointed with the results of a recent basketball outing. Kennedy explained that the goodwill of the program and the community outreach would suffer without Ford, since Ford was able to achieve high levels of attendance at community events. He also pointed to the loss of an effective director of basketball operations.

Ford filed a Motion for Summary Judgment . . . [arguing] that Kent State suffered no damages as a result of his departure. He asserted that the liquidated damages clause was defective, since its objective was "punitive deterrence of breach," and the amount was disproportionate to any anticipated or actual damages. . . . [Kent State also filed a motion for summary judgment, arguing] that the liquidated damages clause was valid and enforceable against Ford. . . . The court [granted summary judgment for Kent State, concluding] that Ford breached his employment contract and that the liquidated damages provision was enforceable. . . . [It awarded Kent State the damages specified in the contract. Ford appealed.]

Ford argues that the liquidated damages clause in his employment contract was an unenforceable penalty and does not comply with the factors contained in *Samson Sales, Inc. v. Honeywell, Inc.*, 12 Ohio St.3d 27, 465 N.E.2d 392 (1984). Liquidated damages are an "agreed upon amount of money to be paid in lieu of actual damages in the event of a breach of contract." (citation omitted.) "Liquidated damages . . . which are consistent with the principle of compensation . . . are permitted." *Cleveland Constr., Inc. v. Gatlin Plumbing & Heating, Inc.*, 2000 WL 973358, 2 (July 14, 2000).

When a party challenges a liquidated damages provision, the court must "step back and examine it in light of what the parties knew at the time the contract was formed and in light of an estimate of the actual damages caused by the breach." *Lake Ridge Academy v. Carney*, 66 Ohio St.3d 376, 382, 613 N.E.2d 183 (1993); *Village Station Assocs. v. Geauga Co.*, 84 Ohio App.3d 448, 451, 616 N.E.2d 1201 (11th Dist.1992) ("liquidated damages must have some relation to actual damages").

In *Samson*, the Supreme Court of Ohio set forth the test for determining whether a liquidated damages provision should be upheld:

> Where the parties have agreed on the amount of damages, ascertained by estimation and adjustment, and have expressed this agreement in clear and unambiguous terms, the amount so fixed should be treated as liquidated damages and not as a penalty, if the damages would be (1) uncertain as to amount and difficult of proof, and if (2) the contract as a whole is not so manifestly unconscionable, unreasonable, and disproportionate in amount as to justify the conclusion that it does not express the true intention of the parties, and if (3) the contract is consistent with the conclusion that it was the intention of the parties that damages in the amount stated should follow the breach thereof.

12 Ohio St.3d 27, 465 N.E.2d 392, at the syllabus.

The application of *Samson* to the facts of this case supports a conclusion that the liquidated damages provision was properly enforced by the lower court. The parties agreed on an amount of damages, stated in clear terms in Ford's second employment contract. Regarding the first factor, the difficulty of ascertaining the damages resulting from Ford's breach, it is apparent that such damages were difficult, if not impossible, to determine. Based on the testimony presented, the departure of a university's head basketball coach may result in a decrease in ticket sales, impact the ability to successfully recruit players and community support for the team, and require a search for both a new coach and additional coaching staff. Many of these damages cannot be easily measured or proven. This is especially true given the nature of how such factors may change over the course of different coaches' tenures with a sports program or team.

A similar conclusion regarding the difficulty of ascertaining damages from a university coach's breach was reached in *Vanderbilt Univ. v. DiNardo*, 174 F.3d 751 (6th Cir. 1999), one of the few cases related to liquidated damages in a university coaching scenario. The *DiNardo* Court cited the district court's opinion, which found that damages from losing a head football coach are uncertain and "[i]t is impossible to estimate how the loss of a head football coach will affect alumni relations, public support, football ticket sales, contributions, etc. . . . [T]o require a precise formula for calculating damages resulting from the breach of contract by a college head football coach would be tantamount to barring the parties from stipulating to liquidated damages evidence in advance." *Id.* at 756. The Court held that the university's head football coach was hired "for a unique and specialized position," with the parties understanding that damages could not be easily ascertained if a breach occurred, especially given that the provision was reciprocal and was the result of negotiations by both parties, which is the case in the present matter as well. *Id.* at 757.

Ford argues that his duty was to coach the team and the only damages that would result from his breach were from hiring a replacement coach, damages which are easily measurable. The court in *DiNardo* rejected this exact argument, holding that "[t]he potential damage to [Vanderbilt] extends far beyond the cost of merely hiring a new head football coach." *Id.* at 756. As he notes in his brief, Ford also had supplemental duties, such as fundraising and marketing. The contractual requirement that he perform these duties when requested represents the inherent importance and value in a basketball coach participating in activities benefitting the basketball program. Factors such as the potential loss of recruits and revenue that could result if a coach's early departure impacted the team's results are directly tied to his duties as a coach.

In this case, the contract stated that the liquidated damages clause was based on Kent State's "investment in [Ford's] continued employment." This is similar to *DiNardo*, where language was included regarding the importance of the "long-term commitment" and stability of the program. *Id.* at 756. The desire for Ford's continued employment, the renegotiation of his contract prior to its expiration, and Kennedy's statements to Ford that the contract would be renegotiated within a few years, made it clear that Kent State desired Ford to have long-term employment, which was necessary to establish the stability in the program that would benefit recruitment, retention of assistant coaching staff, and community participation and involvement. The breach of the contract impacted all of these areas. . . .

In the second factor, we must evaluate whether the contract was unconscionable and disproportionate in amount, such that it does not express the parties' intent. Ford argues that the liquidated damages provision is unenforceable because it is disproportionate to the foreseeable possible damage. He asserts that Kent State failed to estimate its damages prior to including the liquidated damages clause and instead chose an arbitrary amount.

As an initial matter, we note that there appears to be nothing unconscionable about the liquidated damages clause. "A contract is unconscionable if it did not result 'from real bargaining between parties who had freedom of choice and understanding and ability to negotiate in a meaningful fashion.'" (Citations omitted.) *Lake Ridge*, 66 Ohio St. 3d at 383, 613 N.E.2d 183. Ford was not an unsophisticated party and testimony indicated that he had consulted with an attorney and/or agent prior to signing the second employment contract. There is no evidence to show that he did not make an informed choice, especially given that he clearly negotiated in an attempt to remove the liquidated damages clause.

Regarding the alleged unreasonableness of the damages, Ford takes issue with the fact that actual damages were not proven by Kent State. In cases involving a valid liquidated damages clause, however, "the party seeking such damages need not prove that actual damages resulted from a breach." (Citation omitted.) While some evidence of the value of the actual damages helps to determine the reasonableness of the liquidated damages, based on the record, we find that the damages were reasonable. Even if the damages to Kent State were based solely on hiring a replacement coach, finding a coach of a similar skill and experience level as Ford, which was gained based partially on the investment of Kent State in his development, would have an increased cost. This is evident from the fact that Ford was able to more than double his yearly salary when hired by Bradley University. The salary Ford earned at Bradley shows the loss of market value in coaching experienced by Kent State, $400,000 per year, for four years. Although this may not have been known at the time the contract was executed, it could have been anticipated, and was presumably why Kent State wanted to renegotiate the contract and establish a new five-year coaching term. As noted above, there was also an asserted decrease in ticket sales, costs associated with the trip for the coaching search, and additional potential sums that may be expended.

Regarding Ford's contention that the liquidated damages contained in his employment contract were not properly estimated beforehand, as required under the *Samson* test, but were merely an arbitrary number, it has been noted by several courts that estimation by exacting standards cannot be achieved in every scenario. See *DiNardo*, 174 F.3d at 755-757 (allowing salary to be used for liquidated damages since future damages were unquantifiable). . . . Kennedy also testified that the base salary was used for the liquidated damages, based on considerations such as potential fundraising and revenue losses, and a review of the industry standard, resulting in the conclusion that it would cost about a year's salary to cover damages.

In the third factor, the court is to consider whether the contract is consistent with the fact that the parties intended that the damages follow the breach. The provision itself in this case is not ambiguous and it is clear that it would apply if the contract was breached by either party. Testimony was presented that such clauses, although they differ from contract to contract, are common for university coaches. Nothing indicated that the clause did not represent the parties' intent, especially given that testimony demonstrated Ford was aware of the provision and even attempted to change it during negotiations prior to signing the second contract.

Finally, Ford argues that the liquidated damages clause is unenforceable because it acted as a penalty to punish him for breaking his promise. "Whether the subject provision constitutes an illegal penalty provision or a liquidated damages provision depends on the facts and circumstances of each case."

Brunswick Ltd. Partnership v. Feudo, 171 Ohio App. 3d 369 [(2007)]. . . . As discussed extensively above, there was justification for seeking liquidated damages to compensate for Kent State's losses, and, thus, there was a valid compensatory purpose for including the clause. While there was some testimony the clause would deter Ford from leaving, this would be true of liquidated damages clauses in almost every contract, since an award of damages deters a breach. It appears that at least some losses were contemplated prior to the inclusion of this provision in the contract. Given all of the circumstances and facts in this case, and the consideration of the factors above, we cannot find that the liquidated damages clause was a penalty. . . .

CANNON, Presiding Judge, dissenting.

. . . [The dissent quotes the same passage from *Samson* included in the majority opinion.] A challenge to a stipulated damages provision requires the court to "step back and examine it in light of what the parties knew at the time the contract was formed *and* in light of an estimate of the actual damages caused by the breach. If the provision was reasonable at the time of formation and it bears a reasonable (not necessarily exact) relation to actual damages, the provision will be enforced." *Lake Ridge Academy v. Carney*, 66 Ohio St. 3d 376, 382, 613 N.E.2d 183 (1993), citing 3 Restatement of the Law 2d, Contracts, Section 356(1), at 157 (1981) (emphasis added).

Here, the formula utilized in the Contract does not, with any reasonable clarity, demonstrate an approximation of anticipated, actualized damages; rather, it rotely requires the breaching party to pay the sum of the salary remaining to be paid on the Contract, irrespective of any other variables germane to a damages calculation. This formula neither suggests any reasonable estimate of Kent State's probable losses nor describes in any way the specific areas of damage to be included in the estimate.

The formula utilized in the Contract, i.e., the number of years left on the Contract multiplied by Ford's yearly salary, produces a higher valuation of damages if the Contract is breached in the early years of the Contract rather than the last. Yet, such a disparity in valuation bears no reasonable relationship to the actual damages sustained. It is apparent the damages incurred by Kent State are essentially the same if the Contract is breached at any point during the Contract term. This formula may be the appropriate measure of damages if Kent State breached the Contract, as Ford's salary and the duration of the Contract is fixed. But to suggest the same measure of damages is appropriate in the event of a breach by Ford is absurd; there is no way the potential measure of damage to both parties would be remotely the same. When viewing the evidence submitted in a light most favorable to Ford, this lends itself to the suggestion that it was meant to penalize Ford, not compensate Kent State.

Further, it is difficult to assess the actual damages that might be sustained by Kent State in the event of a breach by Ford. In construing the evidence in a light most favorable to Ford, a question of fact remains as to whether the parties intended Section 7 of the Contract to be a "reasonable estimate" of damages. Unlike *Vanderbilt Univ. v. DiNardo*, 174 F.3d 751, 757 (6th Cir. 1999), where the liquidated damages were "in line with Vanderbilt's estimate of its actual damages," Kent State provided evidence of only minimal damages (less than $2,000) that were actually incurred as a result of Ford breaching the Contract and accepting the coaching position at Bradley University. Additionally, although Kent State asserted the possibility of various consequential losses, inter alia, adverse effects on alumni relations, decreased ticket sales, and loss of public support, Kent State failed to support this contention with any evidentiary material that such losses transpired, or how the potential losses in these areas could have approached the significant stipulated damages figure. More significantly, it appears that all parties are in agreement that no attempt was ever made by Kent State to conduct an assessment of what the losses might be, or what items of damages should be included in the assessment, prior to inclusion of the clause in the Contract.

The trial court and the majority herein cite to Kent State's contention that it lost a coach whose value increased by $400,000 since the signing of the Contract. However, assessment of damages in a liquidated damages case must be based on recoverable damages for breach. See *Lake Ridge*, supra, at 383, 613 N.E.2d 183. It is hard to imagine a circumstance under which the increase in the value of the coach would be a measure of damages in a breach of contract case, and it should not be considered a factor in assessing whether the stipulated liquidated damages clause is reasonable.

. . . In this case, without stipulations, submission of evidence to a fact finder, and an assessment of the credibility of the relevant evidence, I believe it is impossible to determine whether the stipulated damages clause is reasonable and proportionate. . . . [There remain genuine issues of material fact to be litigated.] For the foregoing reasons, I respectfully dissent from the opinion of the majority.

■ PROBLEM 21.3

Model Inc. is a fashion model management company. Ronna Runway and Model Inc. signed a contract under which Ronna agreed to perform modeling work exclusively for Model Inc.'s clients for a period of one year. In exchange for Model Inc.'s services, Model Inc. was entitled to a commission equal to 10 percent of "any and all gross monies or other consideration received" as a result of any modeling work Ronna did during the term of the contract. The contract provided that the clients would remit all payments to Model Inc., which would in turn deduct its commissions and pay over the balance to Ronna on a quarterly basis.

Ronna performed modeling work for Model Inc.'s clients for a period of 11 months, then began working with a different management agency in breach of the parties' contract. When Model Inc. learned of the breach it terminated the contract, as it was entitled to do. It also refused to turn over any payments it had received from clients for work Ronna had done in the months leading up to the termination. In retaining these funds, Model Inc. pointed to a clause in the contract that stated "Runway hereby agrees that in the event she breaches this Contract or otherwise refuses to fulfill her obligations hereunder, Model Inc. may, at its sole election, retain as liquidated damages all funds then held or subsequently received by Model Inc. on Runway's behalf."

Ronna argues that this clause is unenforceable as a penalty, and claims Model Inc. is only entitled to retain any commissions or other actual damages it can prove it is owed. Model Inc. asserts that the clause is instead a valid liquidated damages clause, and it should be entitled to retain the full amount of the funds in its possession without necessity of proof of damages. In your view, who has the better argument and why?

■ PROBLEM 21.4

Steve Social contracted with Betty Builder to remodel his home. He hoped to have the work completed in time for the busy round of entertainment he planned for the holiday season. The contract provided that all work was to be completed by December 1. Betty worked conscientiously and regularly at the remodeling job and was at the house every day. However, she worked more slowly than she had planned, and it took her an extra thirty days to complete the project. The contract contained the following clause:

> The parties record that time is of the essence in this contract. If Builder does not complete the work on time Owner will suffer damages that are difficult to forecast. The parties therefore agree that if Builder fails to finish the work by the completion date, she will pay Owner $200 for every day that completion is delayed beyond that date. The parties agree that this is not a penalty but a reasonable estimate of the probable harm that Owner will suffer as a result of the delay.

Consider the following alternatives:

(a) As it turned out, Steve was so busy attending affairs at other people's houses that he didn't have time to plan any of his own. In fact, he was invited to go skiing with friends and spent December 15 through January 1 in Aspen. Steve can't show that he actually suffered any harm, beyond slight inconvenience, as a result of the delay in completion. Nevertheless, he argues that Betty agreed to the clause without any pressure or unfair bargaining on Steve's part, and he is therefore entitled to damages of

$6,000. Is Steve correct? Are there any other facts you would want to know before you make your final determination?

(b) Contrary to the facts in (a), Steve planned a big holiday gala for December 15. When it became clear that his house would still be in a state of chaos on that date, he booked a hotel ballroom for the affair. He had to pay $2,000 rental for the ballroom, but otherwise the holiday gala went off without a hitch. Steve argues that Betty owes him $6,000 in damages. Is Steve correct? Are there any other facts you would want to know before you make your final determination?

(c) As in (b), Steve planned a big holiday gala for December 15 and booked a hotel ballroom when Betty's breach became clear. This time, however, the rental for the hall was $8,000, which was reasonable in light of prevailing market conditions. Steve argues that at a minimum he should be able to recover the $8,000 he paid for the hotel rental. In light of the difficulty of proving other losses attendant to the delay, he argues he should be entitled to collect the $6,000 provided for in the contract as well. Betty argues that she owes him nothing and in any event no more than $6,000. Who has the better side of this argument? Are there any other facts you would want to know before you make your final determination?

2. Contractual Limitations on and Modifications of Remedy

The previous subsection addressed clauses that fix damages at levels the breaching party is unwilling to pay. Sometimes the opposite result obtains. If the liquidated damages specified by the contract are low in comparison to the actual damages suffered by the nonbreaching party, the nonbreaching party may ask the court to ignore the parties' agreement.

WEDNER v. FIDELITY SECURITY SYSTEMS, INC.

228 Pa. Super. 67, 307 A.2d 429 (1973)
Pennsylvania Superior Court

WATKINS, Judge.

This is an appeal from the judgment of the Court of Common Pleas of Allegheny County entered after a nonjury trial on a burglar alarm system contract, in the amount of $312.00 in favor of Charles Wedner, doing business as Wedner Furs, the appellant, and against Fidelity Security Systems, Inc., the appellee.

This action involved a contract for a burglar alarm system. There was a burglary involving the loss of $46,180.00 in furs. It was first tried by Judge Silvestri without a jury and a nonsuit resulted. The nonsuit was removed and a new trial granted. It was then tried by Judge McLean without a jury and although he found the contract had been negligently breached, the appellant was only entitled to liquidated damages in the amount of $312.00 by the terms of the contract. Exceptions were filed and the Court En Banc by a majority vote dismissed the exceptions. This appeal followed.

The appellant suffered a loss of $46,180.00 due to the appellee's wrongful failure to perform under a burglary protection service contract, but because of a contract provision he was allowed recovery of only $312.00. The contract provided that the appellee, FEPS, was not to be liable for any loss or damages to the goods of the appellant and then continued: "If there shall, notwithstanding the above provisions, at any time arise any liability on the part of FEPS by virtue of this agreement, whether due to the negligence of FEPS or otherwise, such liability is and shall be limited to a sum equal in amount to the yearly service charge hereunder, which sum shall be paid and received by the Subscriber as liquidated damages." The appellant contends that this is an unreasonable forecast of the probable damages resulting from a breach of the contract.

The court below treated the matter as one of liquidated damages and said: "In his decision the trial judge pointed out, and the parties agree, that there is a well settled general principle that courts will not give effect to a provision in a contract which is a penalty, but will give effect to a provision in a contract which is deemed a liquidated damages provision. The trial judge further noted that deciding which is which can be difficult. In the absence of any Pennsylvania cases making the determination in the context of a contract for burglary alarm protection, the trial judge determined that the instant provision was one for liquidated damages, rather than a penalty, on the reasoning and analysis of *A. G. Schepps v. American District Telegraph Company of Texas*, 286 S.W.2d 684 (Texas Court of Appeals) (1956). . . ." However, although he ably supported his judgment on the theory of liquidated damages, he did not have to decide the matter on the premise alone.

Much reliance is placed upon the Restatement of Contracts §339,[4] but the appellant disregards Comment g, which provides: "An agreement limiting the amount of damages recoverable for breach is not an agreement to pay either liquidated damages or a penalty. Except in the case of certain public service contracts, the contracting parties can by agreement limit their liability in damages to a specified amount, either at the time of making their principal

---

[4] Restatement of Contracts §339 is the predecessor to Restatement, Second §356 on liquidated damages and penalties, discussed in Section B.1.—EDS.

contract, or subsequently thereto. Such a contract does not purport to make an estimate of the harm caused by a breach; nor is its purpose to operate in terrorem to induce performance." It can hardly be contended that the words "liability is and shall be limited" to the yearly service charge of $312 are anything but a limitation of liability and not really a liquidated damage clause. Surely, if the loss to the customer was $150, the expressed mutual assent was that recovery should be $150 and not $312.

The fact that the words "liquidated damages" were used in the contract has little bearing on the nature of the provision. It is well settled that in determining whether a particular clause calls for liquidated damages or for a penalty, the name given to the clause by the parties "is but of slight weight, and the controlling elements are the intention of the parties and the special circumstances of the case." *Laughlin v. Baltatden, Inc.*, 191 Pa. Superior Ct. 611, 617, 159 A.2d 26, 29 (1960). The same principle applies here. Nor can it be argued that the use of these words automatically creates an ambiguity to be resolved against the appellee as the drafter of the instrument. The meaning of the words is clear—the fixed limit of liability was $312. We are, therefore, not dealing with a liquidated damage problem.

The real question is whether any reason exists why the limitation on liability should not be given effect. There is no doubt as to its legality as between ordinary business men. "The *validity* of a contractual provision which exculpates a person from liability for his own acts of negligence is well settled if the contract is between persons relating entirely to their own private affairs." *Dilks v. Flohr Chevrolet*, 411 Pa. 425, 433, 192 A.2d 682, 687 (1963). That was the common law rule and is illustrated by *Bechtold v. Murray Ohio Mfg. Co.*, 321 Pa. 423, 428-9, 184 A. 49, 51 (1936), where the court stated: "It is not suggested that the transaction is affected by fraud or mistake. The parties agree that they said what they meant. Both parties and their counsel participated in stating the terms of the contract. The seller says that it has performed but, if it has not done so in the respect complained of, the buyer has agreed that he shall have no right to recover damages." In accord is the Restatement of Contracts §§574, 575. It is also the rule with respect to the sale of goods under the Uniform Commercial Code, 12A P.S. §2-719(3), which provides: "Consequential damages may be limited or excluded unless the limitation or exclusion is unconscionable. Limitation of consequential damages for injury to the person in the case of consumer goods is prima facie unconscionable but limitation of damages where the loss is commercial is not."

The common law exception as to public utilities, *Turek v. Pennsylvania R.R. Co.*, 361 Pa. 512, 64 A.2d 779 (1949), has been expanded to some extent by *Thomas v. First Nat. Bank of Scranton*, 376 Pa. 181, 185-6, 101 A.2d 910, 912 (1954), where the court concluded: "Banks, like common carriers, utility companies, etc., perform an important public service. The United States Government and the Commonwealth respectively stipulate how banks under their respective jurisdictions shall be incorporated and organized. All banks are examined and supervised by government or state officers with extreme particularity. The

United States insures deposits in banks up to a stipulated amount. If a person desires to deposit money in a bank, necessarily, he is relegated to a governmental or state regulated banking institution. The situation of a depositor is quite analogous to that of a passenger on a public carrier who is required to accept such means of transportation and to purchase a ticket in the nature of a contract. This Court has consistently decided that it is against public policy to permit a common carrier to limit its liability for its own negligence."

In this case, however, we have a private arrangement between two firms without the attendant state regulation that exists with banks and public utilities. The appellant had a choice as to how to protect his property, and whether or not he should obtain insurance. Although protection against burglary is becoming increasingly important, we believe that it has not yet reached the level of necessity comparable to that of banking and other public services.

Nor do we consider this a case of an unconscionable provision, assuming that unconscionability is applicable by adoption of the prevailing rule with respect to the sale of goods. Even under the foregoing reference to the Uniform Commercial Code the limitation of liability under the facts of the case is prima facie conscionable. Furthermore, there is this significant fact pointed out in the opinion of the trial judge: "In our case both plaintiff and defendant are experienced, established business persons. Additionally, plaintiff had for some 20 years prior to the instant contract had a similar type protection with similar type clause, with a competitor of defendant." Thus in this respect the case is comparable to *K & C, Inc. v. Westinghouse Elec. Corp.*, 437 Pa. 303, 308, 263 A.2d 390, 393 (1970), where the court concluded that "it is clear that the exclusion was not unconscionable here, where the buyer was hardly the sheep keeping company with wolves that it would have us believe."

I would affirm the judgment of the court below.

■ QUESTIONS

(1)   Why did the court determine that this was a limitation on damages rather than a liquidated damages clause?

(2)   What test does the court use to evaluate the enforceability of a contractual limitation on damages? How does this differ from the standards used to scrutinize liquidated damages? Can you think of any policy reasons to justify the difference in treatment?

———————

The UCC contains special provisions on contractual modification or limitation of remedy. Although they generally validate contractual remedy modifications and limitations, in some circumstances they do subject them to a close level of scrutiny. Read the following UCC section, and try to abstract any presumptions or restrictions that the UCC establishes with regard to remedy modifications or limitations. Then consider the problem that follows.

UCC 2-719. CONTRACTUAL MODIFICATION OR LIMITATION OF REMEDY

(1) Subject to the provisions of subsections (2) and (3) of this section and of the preceding section on liquidation and limitation of damages,

(a) the agreement may provide for remedies in addition to or in substitution for those provided in this Article and may limit or alter the measure of damages recoverable under this Article, as by limiting the buyer's remedies to return of the goods and repayment of the price or to repair and replacement of non-conforming goods or parts; and

(b) resort to a remedy as provided is optional unless the remedy is expressly agreed to be exclusive, in which case it is the sole remedy.

(2) Where circumstances cause an exclusive or limited remedy to fail of its essential purpose, remedy may be had as provided in this Act.

(3) Consequential damages may be limited or excluded unless the limitation or exclusion is unconscionable. Limitation of consequential damages for injury to the person in the case of consumer goods is prima facie unconscionable but limitation of damages where the loss is commercial is not.

■ PROBLEM 21.5

Mercedes Bends purchased a used car from Limon Used Cars. The purchase contract specified that the car came with a limited 90-day warranty, which covered most of the operating parts of the vehicle. The contract also contained the following clause, set out in conspicuous type and separately initialed by Mercedes:

> Buyer acknowledges and agrees that Buyer's remedy for breach of warranty shall be repair or replacement of defective parts. Under no circumstances shall Seller be responsible for damages, and in particular Seller shall bear no responsibility for consequential or incidental damages.

From the day Mercedes drove the car off the lot, the car had problems. First the trim fell off. Limon fixed it under the terms of the warranty. Then the bumper fell off. Again, Limon fixed it under the terms of the warranty. The driver's side door fell off, and Limon fixed it under the terms of the warranty. On the 89th day after Mercedes purchased the car, the steering wheel fell off, and Mercedes careened into a tree. Mercedes broke a leg and a set of antique crystal vases that she was taking to her elderly Aunt Bee. The car itself was so severely damaged that it could not be driven.

The day after the accident, Mercedes had the wreck towed to Limon's lot. She demanded that Limon give her her money back for the car and reimburse her for her medical expenses, the loss of the use of her leg, and the value of Aunt Bee's crystal vases. Limon offered to replace the car's steering wheel but argued that it had no further responsibilities under its contract with Mercedes. Applying UCC 2-719, what, if anything, does Limon owe Mercedes, and why?[5]

 SPECIFIC PERFORMANCE AND INJUNCTIONS

1. The Common Law's Preference for Damages

Chapter 20 is concerned principally with money damages. In that chapter, the central question is the amount of damages necessary or appropriate to compensate a party aggrieved by a breach of contract. There we explore expectation damages and reliance damages and the subtleties involved in measuring and recovering them. Since damages (particularly expectation damages) compensate the aggrieved party for the other party's failure to perform, they are often called "substitutional" remedies. Damages substitute for that which was contracted for—namely, performance. From time to time, the materials and the cases allude to an alternative type of remedy—that which gives the plaintiff the specific thing for which she contracted. Rather than awarding damages in substitution for performance, the court orders the defendant to perform. It is now time to return to this type of remedy, the remedy of specific performance.

In Chapter 1, we explain the historical roots of the preference for damages over specific performance. In the Anglo-American legal tradition, specific performance has its roots as an equitable remedy. Generally, courts of law operated within rigid legal rules and procedures and were limited in the types of remedies available. When relief was available, it typically consisted of damages. Courts of equity grew up to do justice in particular cases and to provide an alternative when the remedy at law was inadequate. As a result, specific performance was available in a court of equity only upon a showing that damages would be inadequate to compensate the plaintiff. Furthermore, even upon such a showing, the court of equity had to be convinced that it would be a sound exercise of its discretion to issue a decree for specific performance. Over time, a pattern began

---

[5] For purposes of this problem, you may ignore the fact that there are consumer regulations at the federal and state levels that may be relevant to Mercedes's predicament. Should you encounter a like fact problem in practice, of course, you ignore such regulations at your peril (and your client's, as well).

to develop that illuminated circumstances where justice or equity favored granting this type of relief.

Today, most courts of general jurisdiction in the United States exercise both legal and equitable powers. Nevertheless, specific performance still retains its character as an equitable remedy. As a result, specific performance continues to be an exceptional remedy—that is, it is available only if damages would be inadequate to compensate the plaintiff. Furthermore, even if damages would be inadequate, courts retain the discretion to deny specific performance should the circumstances so merit. If the court orders specific performance, however, the plaintiff has obtained an unusually powerful remedy. While a judgment for damages may make the defendant's assets subject to seizure and sale, the contempt power of the court is available to enforce a specific performance decree. Failure to observe the court's order may lead to fines and even imprisonment.

To say that history has had a role in shaping the availability of specific performance is not to justify our legal system's preference for damages. Not all legal systems are structured this way. Civilian legal systems, for instance, tend to see performance as the ideal and damages as a second-best alternative. American legal scholars have long been engaged in a lively debate over the desirability of preferring damages to a specific performance remedy. Some argue that damages lead to a better legal system, because they accommodate efficient breach.[6] If specific performance were the norm rather than the exception, those who could increase societal wealth by breaching rather than performing contracts would be prevented from doing so. Others argue that damages may promote more inefficient outcomes than specific performance.[7] Damages lead to efficient outcomes only if they truly compensate the nonbreaching party for its losses. For all sorts of reasons, many of which we have studied, money damages do a less than perfect job of compensation. Specific performance as a normal remedy, this second group of scholars argues, would be preferable. The party who could profit from breach but who faced the likelihood of being ordered to perform would have an incentive to negotiate a suitable settlement with the other party. That settlement would be more likely to compensate the nonbreaching party fully than the imprecise and uncertain damages measure chosen by a court of law. Other scholars argue for the primacy of specific performance not on efficiency grounds but on moral grounds.[8] Some of these scholars reject the theory of efficient breach outright. Instead, they argue that moral considerations should determine the availability of specific performance.

---

[6] An early exposition of this argument is found in Anthony T. Kronman, *Specific Performance*, 45 U. Chi. L. Rev. 351 (1978).

[7] This argument is often attributed to Professor Schwartz and an early article he published in the Yale Law Journal. *See* Alan Schwartz, *The Case for Specific Performance*, 89 Yale L.J. 271 (1979).

[8] One example is Peter Linzer, *On the Amorality of Contract Remedies—Efficiency, Equity, and the Second Restatement*, 81 Colum. L. Rev. 111 (1981).

One possible effect of the scholarly debate is that specific performance is now available in a somewhat broader range of cases than might have been the case previously.[9] Sometimes courts refer directly to the academic literature. Other times they follow or are influenced by the Restatement, Second, or the UCC, both of which exhibit a more relaxed approach to specific performance than that reflected by the earlier cases. In spite of this trend, specific performance remains an exceptional remedy that must be justified by the plaintiff, rather than an ordinary remedy that is available as a matter of course.

As a threshold question, one must ask whether damages would be inadequate to compensate the plaintiff. We will start by examining this question. If the answer is no, equitable relief is not appropriate. If the answer is yes, the second step in the analysis is to determine what factors a court is likely to weigh in deciding whether to order specific performance. As you read the cases in this section, be on the lookout for these two themes. See if you can draw out any general principles, or whether you conclude, as one famous critic put it, that the conscience of equity is measured by the length of the chancellor's foot.[10]

2. Inadequacy of Damages

Restatement, Second §359(1) states that "specific performance or an injunction will not be ordered if damages would be adequate to protect the expectation interest of the injured party." The concept of "adequate damages" conceals much subtlety and ambiguity. Sometimes courts deem damages inadequate due to the difficulty of obtaining a substitute for the promised performance. At other times they focus on the obstacles to recovery or to an accurate measurement of damages. If the performance promised under the contract is unique, no amount of damages will allow the plaintiff to obtain a replacement on the open market. Under these circumstances, courts may be willing to order specific performance. Even if the performance is in some sense unique, however, courts may deny

---

[9] Douglas Laycock, in *The Death of the Irreparable Injury Rule*, 103 Harv. L. Rev. 687, 691 (1990), goes so far as to say that in practice, "our law embodies a preference for specific relief if the plaintiff wants it." Not all scholars go this far.

[10] This refers to a stinging condemnation of equity advanced by Lord Selden:

> Equity is a rougish thing, for Law we have a measure, know what to trust to, Equity is according to the Conscience of him that is Chancellor, and as that is larger or narrower, so is equity. 'Tis all one as if they should make the Standard for the measure, we call a Chancellors Foot, what an uncertain measure would this be? One Chancellor has a long Foot, another a short Foot, a third and indifferent Foot. 'Tis the same thing in the Chancellors conscience.

John Selden, *Table-Talk* 46 (Edward Arber ed., first published in 1689; reprinted by Albert Saifer, Philadelphia 1972). Courts and commentators have seized the image, and repeat it regularly. The catchphrase a "chancellor's foot" when applied to a rule, standard, or law, has come to signify one that allows the decision maker unbridled and undisciplined discretion. *See, e.g., Amchem Products, Inc. v. Windsor*, 521 U.S. 591, 621, 117 S. Ct. 2231, 2248, 138 L. Ed. 2d 689, 711 (1997) (in reviewing the requirements for class certification under Rule 23 of the Federal Rules of Civil Procedure, Justice Ginsberg wrote, "[T]he standards set for the protection of absent class members serve to inhibit appraisals of the chancellor's foot kind—class certifications dependent upon the court's gestalt judgment or overarching impression of the settlement's fairness").

specific performance if they are confident that the plaintiff's harm is an economic one that can be accurately measured and compensated. A few examples might help to explore these concepts.

Traditionally, damages are routinely considered inadequate if a seller breaches a contract to sell real estate. Each piece of real estate, being unique in location and attributes, is in a sense irreplaceable. Money, even if it approximates the monetary value of the purchaser's expectation, will not enable the purchaser to obtain an exact substitute for the lost parcel. Imagine if you spent months finding your dream home. If the seller backed out of a contract to sell it to you, you would find compensation equal to the difference between the market price and the contract price to be cold comfort. Intuition suggests that damages are not adequate to protect the purchaser's expectation, because the purchaser's expectation is tied to the particular piece of real estate rather than solely some objective measure of its market value. Given the active and fluid real estate market in this country, this view of real estate may ring less true today than it did in earlier times. When the chancellor of equity was first called upon to order specific performance, for instance, the importance of a particular piece of real estate as an asset and as a symbol of societal status was paramount. Nevertheless, unless the equities strongly weigh in the other direction, specific performance will typically still be available to enforce a contract to purchase land.

In contrast to real estate, contracts to sell goods are generally not specifically enforceable. The older common law view was that specific performance was available only for truly unique goods, such as works of art or heirlooms. All other goods, presumably, were fungible and readily available in the market. Damages would be adequate to enable a disappointed purchaser to obtain an adequate substitute. This standard has been relaxed somewhat under the UCC, but specific performance remains an unusual remedy in the context of goods. UCC 2-716(1) states "specific performance may be decreed where the goods are unique or in other proper circumstances." Although the statute itself gives no further guidance as to what circumstances might be proper ones for a decree of specific performance, the Official Comment to the section suggests that the drafters intended a more liberal attitude toward specific performance than some courts had previously shown. In particular, inability of the disappointed buyer to cover is one indication that specific performance might be appropriate.

These examples suggest that if the plaintiff were unable to procure a suitable substitute for the promised performance, a court may deem damages inadequate to compensate the plaintiff. A similar analysis obtains in other contexts, such as sales of intangibles, service contracts, and other types of contracts not specifically mentioned here. Courts look at the contracts on a case-by-case basis to answer the question of fact: Would payment of damages be adequate?

Rather than looking to the nature of the promised performance, in some situations courts examine the nature of the negative consequences that would flow from failure to perform. For instance, we have seen that plaintiffs will have difficulty recovering damages that cannot be established with reasonable certainty. If a court is convinced that damages such as lost profits would be a credible result of nonperformance but it is unable to gauge them with reasonable certainty, specific performance may be appropriate.

In the *Van Wagner* case, the court was unwilling to force specific performance, even though real estate was involved. What factors influenced the court in its decision?

VAN WAGNER ADVERTISING CORP. v. S & M ENTERPRISES

67 N.Y.2d 186, 492 N.E.2d 756, 501 N.Y.S.2d 628 (1986)
New York Court of Appeals

KAYE, Judge.

. . . By agreement dated December 16, 1981, Barbara Michaels leased to plaintiff, Van Wagner Advertising, for an initial period of three years plus option periods totaling seven additional years space on the eastern exterior wall of a building on East 36th Street in Manhattan. Van Wagner was in the business of erecting and leasing billboards, and the parties anticipated that Van Wagner would erect a sign on the leased space, which faced an exit ramp of the Mid-town Tunnel and was therefore visible to vehicles entering Manhattan from that tunnel.

In early 1982 Van Wagner erected an illuminated sign and leased it to Asch Advertising, Inc. for a three-year period commencing March 1, 1982. However, by agreement dated January 22, 1982, Michaels sold the building to defendant S&M Enterprises. Michaels informed Van Wagner of the sale in early August 1982, and on August 19, 1982 S&M sent Van Wagner a letter purporting to cancel the lease as of October 18. . . . Van Wagner abandoned the space under protest and in November 1982 commenced this action for declarations that the purported cancellation was ineffective and the lease still in existence, and for specific performance and damages.

. . . At a nonjury trial, both parties introduced parol evidence, in the form of testimony about negotiations, to explain the meaning of [the cancellation provisions in the lease]. Additionally, one of S&M's two partners testified without contradiction that, having already acquired other real estate on the block, S&M purchased the subject building in 1982 for the ultimate purpose of demolishing existing buildings and constructing a mixed residential-commercial development. The project is to begin upon expiration of a lease of the subject building in 1987, if not sooner.

. . . Trial Term declared the lease "valid and subsisting" and found that the "demised space is unique as to location for the particular advertising purpose intended by Van Wagner and Michaels, the original parties to the Lease." However, the court declined to order specific performance in light of its finding that Van Wagner "has an adequate remedy at law for damages." Moreover, the court noted that specific performance "would be inequitable in that its effect would be disproportionate in its harm to the defendant and its assistance to plaintiff." Concluding that "[the] value of the unique qualities of the demised space has been fixed by the contract Van Wagner has with its advertising client, Asch for the period of the contract," the court awarded Van Wagner the lost revenues on the Asch sublease for the period through trial, without prejudice to a new action by Van Wagner for subsequent damages if S&M did not permit Van Wagner to reoccupy the space. On Van Wagner's motion to resettle the judgment to provide for specific performance, the court adhered to its judgment. On cross appeals the Appellate Division affirmed, without opinion. We granted both parties leave to appeal. . . .

[After reviewing the record, the court refused to overturn the trial court's finding that S&M's cancellation of Van Wagner's lease constituted a breach of contract.] Given defendant's unexcused failure to perform its contract, we next turn to a consideration of remedy for the breach: Van Wagner seeks specific performance of the contract, S&M urges that money damages are adequate but that the amount of the award was improper.

Whether or not to award specific performance is a decision that rests in the sound discretion of the trial court, and here that discretion was not abused. Considering first the nature of the transaction, specific performance has been imposed as the remedy for breach of contracts for the sale of real property, but the contract here is to lease rather than sell an interest in real property. While specific performance is available, in appropriate circumstances, for breach of a commercial or residential lease, specific performance of real property leases is not in this State awarded as a matter of course.

Van Wagner argues that specific performance must be granted in light of the trial court's finding that the "demised space is unique as to location for the particular advertising purpose intended." The word "uniqueness" is not, however, a magic door to specific performance. A distinction must be drawn between physical difference and economic interchangeability. The trial court found that the leased property is physically unique, but so is every parcel of real property and so are many consumer goods. Putting aside contracts for the sale of real property, where specific performance has traditionally been the remedy for breach, uniqueness in the sense of physical difference does not itself dictate the propriety of equitable relief.

By the same token, at some level all property may be interchangeable with money. Economic theory is concerned with the degree to which consumers are willing to substitute the use of one good for another (see, Kronman, *Specific Performance*, 45 U. Chi. L. Rev. 351, 359), the underlying assumption being that "every good has substitutes, even if only very poor ones," and that "all goods are ultimately commensurable." Such a view, however, could strip all meaning from uniqueness, for if all goods are ultimately exchangeable for a price, then all goods may be valued. Even a rare manuscript has an economic substitute in that there is a price for which any purchaser would likely agree to give up a right to buy it, but a court would in all probability order specific performance of such a contract on the ground that the subject matter of the contract is unique.

The point at which breach of a contract will be redressable by specific performance thus must lie not in any inherent physical uniqueness of the property but instead in the uncertainty of valuing it: "What matters, in measuring money damages, is the volume, refinement, and reliability of the available information about substitutes for the subject matter of the breached contract. When the relevant information is thin and unreliable, there is a substantial risk that an award of money damages will either exceed or fall short of the promisee's actual loss. Of course this risk can always be reduced—but only at great cost when reliable information is difficult to obtain. Conversely, when there is a great deal of consumer behavior generating abundant and highly dependable information about substitutes, the risk of error in measuring the promisee's loss may be reduced at much smaller cost. In asserting that the subject matter of a particular contract is unique and has no established market value, a court is really saying that it cannot obtain, at reasonable cost, enough information about substitutes to permit it to calculate an award of money damages without imposing an unacceptably high risk of undercompensation on the injured promisee. Conceived in this way, the uniqueness test seems economically sound." (45 U. Chi. L. Rev., at 362.) This principle is reflected in the case law, and is essentially the position of the Restatement (Second) of Contracts, which lists "the difficulty of proving damages with reasonable certainty" as the first factor affecting adequacy of damages (Restatement [Second] of Contracts §360[a]). Thus, the fact that the subject of the contract may be "unique as to location for the particular advertising purpose intended" by the parties does not entitle a plaintiff to the remedy of specific performance.

Here, the trial court correctly concluded that the value of the "unique qualities" of the demised space could be fixed with reasonable certainty and without imposing an unacceptably high risk of undercompensating the injured tenant. Both parties complain: Van Wagner asserts that while lost revenues on the Asch contract may be adequate compensation, that contract expired February 28, 1985, its lease with S&M continues until 1992, and the value of the demised space cannot reasonably be fixed for the balance of the term. S&M urges that future rents and continuing damages are necessarily conjectural, both during and after the Asch contract, and that Van Wagner's damages must be limited to 60 days [because the lease permitted cancellation on 60 days' prior notice under certain circumstances.] . . . Both parties' contentions were properly rejected.

First, it is hardly novel in the law for damages to be projected into the future. Particularly where the value of commercial billboard space can be readily determined by comparisons with similar uses—Van Wagner itself has more than 400 leases—the value of this property between 1985 and 1992 cannot be regarded as speculative. Second, S&M having successfully resisted specific performance on the ground that there is an adequate remedy at law, cannot at the same time be heard to contend that damages beyond 60 days must be denied because they are conjectural. If damages for breach of this lease are indeed conjectural, and cannot be calculated with reasonable certainty, then S&M should be compelled to perform its contractual obligation by restoring Van Wagner to the premises. Moreover, the contingencies to which S&M points do not, as a practical matter, render the calculation of damages speculative. While S&M could terminate the Van Wagner lease in the event of a sale of the building, this building has been sold only once in 40 years; S&M paid several million dollars, and purchased the building in connection with its plan for major development of the block. The theoretical termination right of a future tenant of the existing building also must be viewed in light of these circumstances. If any uncertainty is generated by the two contingencies, then the benefit of that doubt must go to Van Wagner and not the contract violator. Neither contingency allegedly affecting Van Wagner's continued contractual right to the space for the balance of the lease term is within its own control; on the contrary, both are in the interest of S&M. Thus, neither the need to project into the future nor the contingencies allegedly affecting the length of Van Wagner's term render inadequate the remedy of damages for S&M's breach of its lease with Van Wagner.

The trial court, additionally, correctly concluded that specific performance should be denied on the ground that such relief "would be inequitable in that its effect would be disproportionate in its harm to defendant and its assistance to plaintiff." It is well settled that the imposition of an equitable remedy must not itself work an inequity, and that specific performance should not be an undue hardship. This conclusion is "not within the absolute discretion of the Supreme Court" (*McClure v. Leaycraft*, 183 NY 36, 42). Here, however, there was no abuse of discretion; the finding that specific performance would disproportionately harm S&M and benefit Van Wagner has been affirmed by the Appellate Division and has support in the proof regarding S&M's projected development of the property. . . .

■ QUESTIONS

(1) This court distinguishes a leasehold interest in real estate from an ownership interest. Do you find the distinction persuasive? Why or why not?

(2) According to this court, how does one determine whether damages are an adequate remedy for a breach of contract? How does the court decide that damages are adequate here? Are you persuaded by its reasoning?

(3) What equities favor damages, rather than specific performance, in this case? Do any equities favor specific performance?

(4) Consider if Van Wagner itself were using the space for advertising, rather than subleasing it to an agency. If Van Wagner had argued that it would be deprived of incalculable profits as a result of losing the unique advertising location, would you expect it to have had more success in its quest for specific performance?

■ PROBLEM 21.6

Some years ago, a new owner of the Seattle Supersonics (an NBA basketball team) threatened to move the team to Oklahoma City. The owner initiated an arbitration proceeding, seeking a declaratory ruling that the team's stadium lease would not be specifically enforceable against the team. The city of Seattle, which was the landlord under the team's stadium lease, in turn filed suit to bar arbitration of the claim and instead to obtain a declaratory judgment that the lease was subject to specific performance. In its pleadings, the city of Seattle pointed to a clause in the stadium lease that maintained that the obligations of the parties under the lease were unique, and that the lease "may be specifically enforced by either party." The controversy settled before the issue of specific performance could be decided. Had this matter gone to trial, do you think the court would have allowed specific performance? Why or why not?

■ PROBLEM 21.7

Fred Farmer entered into a contract with Agro Corp., under which he agreed to buy an acre of land for $250,000. The land is a tract on a flat, featureless plain, and it has no attributes that would distinguish it from any other acre of land in the vicinity. Shortly after the contract was entered, Agro Corp. repudiated it by refusing to transfer the land. There are several lots of the same size in the region that are available on the market. The asking price of the lots is between $260,000 and $280,000.

(a) Fred Farmer is stubborn. He wants the piece of land that he contracted to buy, not some other lot. May he compel Agro Corp. to sell it?

(b) Would your answer change if Agro Corp. had already contracted to sell the land to another buyer? What if Agro Corp. had actually completed the sale to another buyer?

(c) Suppose instead that it is Fred Farmer who repudiated the contract, not Agro Corp. Around the same time as his repudiation, similar lots had sold for $200,000 to $220,000. May Agro Corp. compel him to purchase the tract as agreed?

■ **PROBLEM 21.8**

Fred Farmer entered into a contract with Agro Corp. under which he agreed to buy a used combine for $250,000. Fred gave Agro Corp. a $50,000 down payment. Shortly after the contract was entered, Agro Corp. repudiated and refused to sell Fred the combine. Furthermore, it informed Fred that due to cash flow problems, it wouldn't be able to refund his deposit right away. There were several other used combines available on the market, all of which varied in type, condition, and price from the combine Fred had contracted to buy from Agro Corp. The asking price of the cheapest was $225,000; the most expensive was $600,000. Absent the return of his deposit, Fred couldn't afford to buy any of the substitutes. Without a combine, Fred may be unable to harvest his wheat crop. Although wheat prices fluctuate wildly, Fred's losses are likely to be substantial. May Fred compel Agro Corp. to sell him the used combine as agreed?

3. The Discretionary Nature of the Remedy

In some circumstances, courts refuse to decree specific performance even if damages are potentially an inadequate remedy for breach. If the equities do not favor it, a court often declines to issue a decree of specific performance. The discretion to grant or refuse specific performance is not unbridled, however, and courts have developed a number of tests to determine whether a decree of specific performance is appropriate. An attentive reader will notice a number of colorful maxims recurring in the cases: "Equity follows the law"; "He who seeks equity must do equity"; Equity aids only those with "clean hands"; "Equity aids the vigilant." You will certainly discover others.

The cases are by their nature fact-specific, and the maxims are too broad to explain all of the results. Some generalizations, however, are useful. Because the idea underlying equitable remedies is to do justice where it otherwise would be denied, courts guard against using their powers to unfairly burden a defendant or third parties, to advantage a plaintiff unfairly, or to embroil the court in matters in which, as a matter of policy, it feels it should not be involved. As the *Van Wagner* case illustrates, in those instances where performance would cause excessive hardship or loss for the defendant, courts may deny specific relief even where the plaintiff is innocent of any misbehavior.

Where the plaintiff misbehaves, specific performance is typically denied. Consider, for instance, if the plaintiff engaged in shady bargaining practices in order to obtain a favorable contract. Perhaps there was some behavior akin to but slightly shy of misrepresentation, fraud, duress, undue influence, or the like, or maybe what the plaintiff received under the contract was grossly disproportionate to what it gave up. Although the contract may still be enforceable at law in any of these situations (assuming damages could be established), a court may nevertheless decline to enforce it through equity. If damages would truly be inadequate, denial of equitable relief may amount in practice to denial of a remedy altogether.

The propriety of judicial involvement may also be a determinative factor. If both parties are tainted or the transaction is unseemly or bordering on the illegal, the court may not wish to sully its own hands and may deny equitable relief. Even where the conduct of the parties is not untoward, a court may judge that it should not exercise its equitable powers where a decree would be particularly costly or difficult to fashion or administer. For example, courts regularly refuse to specifically enforce long-term construction contracts on the theory that ordering and overseeing the construction process would be an unsuitable use of judicial resources.

CAMPBELL v. CARR

361 S.C. 258, 603 S.E.2d 625 (2004)
South Carolina Court of Appeals

ANDERSON, Judge.

Martha M. Carr and Ruth Riley Glover appeal the master-in-equity's ruling of specific performance. We reverse.

In 1996, Carr, a resident of New York, inherited from her mother a 108-acre tract of unimproved land. In 1998, Carr contacted the Campbells, who had leased the property for thirty years, about selling the property to them. Carr had telephone discussions with Betty Campbell. Carr asked Betty Campbell "how much the property went for." Betty Campbell told her the Tax Assessor's agricultural assessed value of the property was $54,000. On August 6, 1998, Carr and Raymond Campbell entered into a written contract for $54,000, which averaged $500 an acre. Raymond Campbell paid an earnest money deposit of $1000. Carr did not attend the closing because she felt the sales price was unfair. Carr returned the earnest money, but it was refused and returned to her. On February 9, 1999, Carr conveyed an undivided one-half interest in the property to her cousin, Ruth Riley Glover.

In 1998, the Richland County Tax Assessor had computed the fair market value of the property at $103,700. [The agricultural assessed value was used for computing property taxes for so long as the land was used for agricultural purposes. It was significantly less than the assessed fair market value, which is the value that would be used for computing property taxes if the land was not used for agricultural purposes.] Raymond Campbell admitted he had probably seen the Tax Assessor's fair market value of the property . . . [and that his wife had told Carr only the agricultural assessed value.] The opinion expressed in the lender's Collateral I.D. Report was that the property would have sold for twenty-five percent to forty percent higher than the Tax Assessor's fair market value in 1998. This would give the property an expected sell-value of $129,625 to $145,180. Boston McClain, who was qualified by the trial court as an expert real estate appraiser, found that the property had a fair market value of $162,000, or $1500 an acre, when the contract was executed.

Prior to entering into the contract, Carr had only seen the property once when she was a child: "I had seen it as a child, and it was a long time ago. My parents drove down to South Carolina." Carr was diagnosed as having schizophrenia and depression in 1986. She has been on Haldol and Cogentin for her mental illnesses since 1986. At the time she entered into the contract, she was taking ten milligrams of Haldol and five milligrams of Cogentin. She has been hospitalized five or six times for depression and schizophrenia.

Schizophrenia is a psychotic disorder, which is characterized by disturbances in perception, inferential thinking, language and communication, behavioral monitoring, affect, fluency and productivity of thought and speech, hedonic capacity, volition and drive, and affection. *Diagnostic and Statistical Manual of Mental Disorders: DSM-IV* 274 (4th ed. 1994). The symptoms of schizophrenia are delusions, hallucinations, and grossly disorganized or catatonic behavior. *Id.* at 275. "Disorganized thinking ("formal thought disorder," "loosening of associations") has been argued by some (Bleuler, in particular) to be the single most important feature of Schizophrenia." *Id.* at 276. Depression is characterized by altered mood in which there is a loss of interest in all usually pleasurable outlets. *Taber's Cyclopedic Medical Dictionary* 478 (16th ed. 1989). Some of the symptoms of depression are: loss of interest or pleasure in usual activities, feelings of worthlessness, self-reproach, or excessive or inappropriate guilt, and complaints of or evidence of diminished ability to think or concentrate. *Id.*

Raymond Campbell brought this action against Martha Carr and Ruth Riley Glover seeking specific performance of a land contract entered into between Campbell and Carr. The master-in-equity tried the case without a jury and ordered specific performance of the contract.

An action for specific performance is one in equity. . . . "Specific performance should be granted only if there is no adequate remedy at law and specific enforcement of the contract is equitable between the parties." *Ingram v. Kasey's Assocs.*, 340 S.C. 98, 105, 531 S.E.2d 287, 291 (2000). Equity will not decree specific performance unless the contract is fair, just, and equitable. . . . "In order to compel specific performance, a court of equity must find: (1) there is clear evidence of a valid agreement; (2) the agreement had been partly carried into execution on one side with the approbation of the other; and (3) the party who comes to compel performance has performed his or her part, or has been and remains able and willing to perform his or her part of the contract." *Ingram*, 340 S.C. at 106, 531 S.E.2d at 291. "Mere inadequacy of consideration is not a ground for refusing the remedy of specific performance; in order to be a defense, the inadequacy must either be accompanied by other inequitable incidents, or must be so gross as to show fraud." *Id.*

When the accompanying incidents are inequitable and show bad faith, such as concealment, misrepresentations, undue advantage, oppression on the part of the one who obtains the benefit, or ignorance, weakness of mind, sickness, old age, incapacity, pecuniary necessities, and the like, on the part of the other, these circumstances, combined with inadequacy of price, may easily induce a court to grant relief, defensive or affirmative. When a grossly inadequate consideration is combined with weakness of mind on the part of the seller, a denial of specific performance is warranted. The inadequacy of price is determined at the date the contract was entered. The rule as to inadequacy of price as a basis for a denial of specific performance was early stated in the leading case of *Gasque v. Small*, (1848) 2 Strob. Eq. (21 S.C. Eq.) 72, 80, in these words: "The inadequacy must not be measured by grains, but it ought to be palpably disproportioned to the real and market value of the property, so as to constitute a hard, unreasonable, and unconscionable contract; but it is not necessary that it should be so gross as to excite an exclamation or to indicate imposition, oppression or fraud, for this would be sufficient ground not only for refusing a specific performance but for rescinding the contract."

The consideration stated in the contract between Carr and the Campbells was inadequate. The $54,000 sales price in the contract was significantly below the appraised value of $162,000, the Collateral I.D. report's expected sell value of $129,625 to $145,180, and the Richland County Tax Assessor's fair market value of $103,700. This inadequate consideration combined with Carr's weakness of mind, due to her schizophrenia and depression, makes it inequitable to order specific performance.... [T]he Campbells, as the prospective purchasers, had greater knowledge of the real estate value of the land, having leased the land for thirty years for personal hunting and farming purposes, compared with Carr, who lived in New York, had not visited the property since she was a child, and had no knowledge of the fair market value of the property....

We find the contract price of $54,000 is inadequate consideration for the 108-acre tract of land. The inadequacy of consideration in addition to Carr's mental illnesses, make it inequitable to order specific performance.

Accordingly, the decision of the master-in-equity is reversed.

■ QUESTIONS

(1) In light of the court's holding that specific performance is an inappropriate remedy, should the Campbells have been entitled to damages instead? If not, why not? If so, how would those damages have been measured?

(2) The court doesn't tell us whether the Campbells knew of Carr's schizophrenia or depression. Is the state of their knowledge about her condition relevant?

■ PROBLEM 21.9

Change the facts of *Campbell v. Carr* as follows. Suppose Carr had not suffered from schizophrenia or depression. Instead, she lived a healthy, busy, and prosperous life working as a lawyer in a Wall Street law firm. She didn't plan to return to South Carolina and had been interested in selling the land ever since she inherited it in 1996. In over two years, she had never found the time to list the property or otherwise arrange for its sale. One day, she decided to contact the Campbells to see whether they would be interested in buying it, since they already leased the property and their familiarity with it would simplify the transaction. Otherwise, the facts remained the same. Should this change in facts affect the result in the case?

4. Injunctive Relief as an Alternative to Specific Performance

At this point, a quick note about terminology is in order. The remedy of specific performance is a form of injunctive relief. When the court orders a breaching party to do something, it issues an injunction. If the injunction calls for positive action, it is sometimes referred to as a "mandatory" injunction. If instead the court commands that a certain action be avoided, this is called a "prohibitory" injunction. It is sometimes said that mandatory injunctions are more threatening than prohibitory injunctions. Further, courts occasionally state that mandatory injunctions will involve the courts more deeply in fashioning a decree and supervising its compliance. For these reasons, courts tend to be more conservative in granting mandatory injunctions than prohibitory injunctions. Where a mandatory injunction is not appropriate, sometimes a prohibitory injunction may be crafted that serves a similar but more circumscribed role.

Consider, for instance, a case where personal services are at issue. There is a strong line of authority that says a contract to perform personal services should not be specifically enforced in the usual case. The rationale for this rule lies not in the adequacy of damages but rather in the unfairness and difficulties of ordering performance. Where the party being ordered to perform is an individual, a court may be influenced by the bar against involuntary servitude contained in the Thirteenth Amendment of the U.S. Constitution. Whether the constitutional bar is directly applicable or not, the policies underlying it find strong expression in the cases. Forced labor smacks of unfair advantage to the employer and an unfair burden to the employee. Furthermore, courts perceive real difficulties in compelling and monitoring a continuing relationship under these circumstances.

Possibly, in a case such as this one, the plaintiff might seek an injunction against actions that are inconsistent with the contract. Such an injunction might fall short of forcing full performance of the contract, but it might also prevent the defendant from taking full advantage of the breach. Prohibitory injunctions may be particularly useful where the contract explicitly calls for a forbearance, rather than a performance alone. There is a raft of cases that allow injunctive relief against entertainers and sports figures, for instance, who unjustifiably "jump" exclusive contracts. One of the most famous, *Lumley v. Wagner*, 42 Eng. Rep. 687 (Ch. 1852), involved Johanna Wagner, an operatic diva who contracted to sing exclusively at Lumley's theatre in London. Before her three-month contract was complete, however, she perfidiously made arrangements to sing at the competing Covent Garden. In ordering her to abstain from singing at Covent Garden, the chancellor wrote: "It is true that I have not the means of compelling her to sing, but she has no cause of complaint if I compel her to abstain from the commission of an act which she has bound herself not to do, and thus possibly cause her to fulfil her engagement." Clearly Lumley, and perhaps the chancellor, hoped to cause her to perform, even if that result was not directly within the chancellor's equitable powers. Critics might say that such an injunction attempts to accomplish through the back door what the court hesitates to do through the front door. Proponents might counter that Wagner's performance for a competitor would likely harm the theatre, and in the absence of readily ascertainable or demonstrable damages, such an injunction might at least have salutary effect of encouraging the parties to reach a satisfactory settlement.

In many respects, the standards for obtaining an injunction against actions inconsistent with the contract resemble those for specific performance of the contract itself. Generally, it is necessary to show that damages would be an inadequate remedy for breach. Furthermore, granting an injunction is generally within the equitable discretion of the court. But to the extent a mandatory injunction would enmesh the court in supervision of a personal services contract while a prohibitory injunction would not, the equities may be somewhat easier to establish. Nevertheless, even prohibitory injunctions remain extraordinary remedies, and they are not available as a matter of right.

A common context in which plaintiffs request prohibitory injunctions is where former employees breach noncompetition clauses in their employment contracts. In these cases, courts weigh not only the equities between the employer and the employee, but broader concerns of public policy as well. In Section C of Chapter 14, we discuss some of the varying approaches courts take to noncompetition agreements. Some courts refuse to enforce noncompetition agreements altogether, as being in violation of public policy. The usual approach, however, is to follow a "rule of reason," and to uphold a noncompetition clause to the extent that it is reasonable as to its duration, the geographic area that it covers, and the scope and extent of the activity that it restrains.

In the case that follows, the court enforces the terms of a noncompetition agreement by granting an injunction, prohibiting the defendant from violating its terms.

SYSTEMS AND SOFTWARE, INC. v. BARNES

178 Vt. 389, 886 A.2d 762 (2005)
Vermont Supreme Court

REIBER, Chief Justice.

Defendant Randy Barnes appeals the superior court's order enjoining him from working for Utility Solutions, Inc. or any other direct competitor of his former employer, plaintiff Systems and Software, Inc., for a six-month period pursuant to the noncompetition agreement that he signed when he began working for plaintiff. He argues that the trial court should not have enforced the agreement because (1) plaintiff did not have a legitimate protectable interest; (2) the agreement contains unnecessary restrictions and imposes an undue hardship on him; (3) in any event, he did not violate the agreement; and (4) even if he did, plaintiff should be estopped from enforcing it. We affirm.

Plaintiff, a Vermont corporation located in Colchester, Vermont, is engaged in the business of designing, developing, selling, and servicing software that allows utility providers to organize data regarding customer information, billing, work management, asset management, and finance and accounting. In August 2002, plaintiff hired defendant as an at-will employee to become a regional vice-president of sales. At the time he commenced work for plaintiff, defendant signed a noncompetition agreement that, among other things, prohibited him—during his employment and for six months thereafter—from becoming associated with any business that competes with plaintiff. In April 2004, defendant voluntarily left his position with plaintiff and started a partnership with his wife called Spirit Technologies Consulting Group. Spirit Technologies' only customer was Utility Solutions, Inc., which, like plaintiff, services municipalities and utilities nationwide with respect to customer-information-systems software.

On April 27, 2004, plaintiff filed a complaint and a request for injunctive relief that sought enforcement of the parties' noncompetition agreement. A hearing was held in June 2004, and on July 22, 2004, the superior court granted plaintiff an injunction. In its final judgment order dated August 6, 2004, the court enjoined defendant from working as a consultant or otherwise with Utility Solutions or any other direct competitor of plaintiff. Defendant appeals from that judgment. Pursuant to a provision of the parties' noncompetition agreement, the six-month noncompetition period will not begin until a final nonappealable judgment is rendered.

Like many other courts, this Court has adopted a position with respect to enforcement of noncompetition agreements similar to that set forth in §188(1) of the Restatement (Second) of Contracts (1981), which provides that a restrictive covenant "is unreasonably in restraint of trade if (a) the restraint is greater than is needed to protect the promisee's legitimate interest, or (b) the promisee's need is outweighed by the hardship to the promisor and the likely injury to the public." . . . We have stated that "we will proceed with caution" when asked to enforce covenants against competitive employment because such restraints run counter to public policy favoring the right of individuals to engage in the commercial activity of their choice. *Roy's Orthopedic, Inc. v. Lavigne*, 142 Vt. 347, 350, 454 A.2d 1242, 1244 (1982). Nonetheless, we will enforce such agreements "unless the agreement is found to be contrary to public policy, unnecessary for protection of the employer, or unnecessarily restrictive of the rights of the employee, with due regard being given to the subject matter of the contract and the circumstances and conditions under which it is to be performed." *Vt. Elec. Supply Co. v. Andrus*, 132 Vt. 195, 198, 315 A.2d 456, 458 (1974).

Here, in arguing that the trial court erred by enforcing the parties' agreement, defendant first asserts that the agreement does not safeguard a legitimate interest of the employer because it was not needed to protect trade secrets or confidential customer information. This argument fails because it is based on a faulty premise—that noncompetition agreements may be enforced to protect only trade secrets or confidential customer information. Most jurisdictions do not limit the scope of noncompetition agreements to trade secrets or confidential customer information, which are often protected by other law even in the absence of such agreements. . . . Indeed, the recent draft of the third restatement on employment law expressly states that noncompetition agreements may protect legitimate employer interests such as customer relationships and employee-specific goodwill that are "significantly broader" than proprietary information such as trade secrets and confidential customer information. Restatement (Third) of Employment Law §6.05 cmt. b ("[Section] 6.05 sometimes allows an employer contractually to prevent all competition by a former employee, even competition that does not make use of the employer's proprietary information").

It is not necessary in this case to establish the range of employer interests, beyond trade secrets and confidential customer information, that may be protected through noncompetition agreements. Here, the trial court found that plaintiff had a legitimate protectable interest, and the evidence supports the court's finding. The trial court found that during his employment with plaintiff, defendant had acquired inside knowledge about the strengths and weaknesses of plaintiff's products—knowledge that he could use to compete against plaintiff. As the court pointed out, both plaintiff and United Solutions, defendant's only client, served a small market of customers; thus, the loss of even a single contract could deprive plaintiff of revenue for many years, especially considering the need for service and software updates. Given these circumstances, we find no basis for overturning the trial court's conclusion that plaintiff had a legitimate protectable interest.

Defendant argues, however, that even assuming the parties' agreement protects a legitimate interest, the agreement is more restrictive than necessary to protect that interest. He contends that less drastic solutions were available to the trial court to fashion a more reasonable restraint on his employment. For example, he suggests that the court could have simply prohibited him from soliciting plaintiff's current customers, or, at a minimum, prohibited him from dealing with noncooperative utilities, given that plaintiff has not dealt with cooperatives for nearly twenty years. According to defendant, a complete ban on competition is not only unduly restrictive, but it effectively prevents him from working in his field of expertise for six months, thereby imposing a hardship that far outweighs any potential harm to plaintiff.

We do not find these arguments persuasive, particularly in the context of this case, which does not present any of the hallmarks of an unequal bargaining relationship between employer and employee. Defendant is a sophisticated consultant, who accepted employment with plaintiff after working for one of plaintiff's competitors. At the time he was hired, plaintiff informed defendant that a condition of his employment was that he sign a covenant not to compete. Defendant signed the agreement, which explicitly provided that prohibiting him from competing with plaintiff for a six-month period following the parties' separation would not prevent defendant from earning a living. Defendant now claims hardship based on nothing more than a bald statement that he will be unable to work for six months if the agreement is enforced. We find no error in the court's decision not to invalidate the contract based on this unsupported claim.

Nor do we find error based on the superior court's refusal to rewrite the agreement to make it more favorable to defendant. Although a restraint on competition is easier to justify "if the restraint is limited to the taking of his former employer's customers as contrasted with competition in general," Restatement (Second) of Contracts §188 cmt. g, employers "may seek to protect the good will of the business with [either] a general covenant not to compete or with a specific prohibition on contact with customers," [G. Giesel, *Corbin on Contracts* §80.16, at 141 (rev. ed. 2003)].

"Determining which restraints are reasonable has not been an exact science." *Id.* §80.6, at 68. The reasonableness of the restrictions "will vary by industry and will depend highly on the nature of the interest justifying the restrictive covenant." Restatement (Third) of Employment Law §6.05 cmt. c. Generally, courts will uphold a contractual ban on an employee's post-employment competition if it would be difficult for an employer to determine when an employee is soliciting its customers. *Id.* §§6.05 cmt. c, 6.06 cmt. c ("Because it is essentially impossible to monitor an employee's 'use' of goodwill, this interest will support a complete ban on competition as long as it is reasonably limited temporally and geographically").

Here, the evidence demonstrates that plaintiff hired defendant to be a regional vice-president of sales and provided him access not only to existing customers but also to information concerning the strengths and weaknesses of plaintiff's products, the individual needs of the customers he served, and the prices paid by those customers for plaintiff's products and services. The superior court found that in the course of his employment with plaintiff, defendant acquired knowledge of plaintiff's software designs, customer base, marketing strategy, business practices, and other sensitive information revealing the strengths and weaknesses of plaintiff's software products. Because of the nature of plaintiff's business, which often involves customers initiating competitive bidding for contracts, it would be extremely difficult to monitor whether defendant was using the goodwill and knowledge he acquired while working for plaintiff to gain a competitive edge against plaintiff. Thus, the evidence supports the court's findings and conclusions, which, in turn, support its decision to enforce the agreement to the extent that defendant is prohibited for a six-month period from working for Utility Solutions or any other direct competitor of plaintiff.

Defendant also claims that he has not competed with plaintiff or violated the covenant not to compete, but the evidence supports the court's findings to the contrary. The only customer of defendant's consulting firm was Utility Solutions, which directly competed against plaintiff for at least two different contracts. Further, shortly after defendant left plaintiff's employ, he represented Utility Solutions at a trade fair in a booth near plaintiff's booth and identified himself as Utility Solution's sales director. Moreover, the superior court found "not credible" defendant's claim that he was hired by Utility Solutions exclusively to market a new software product for two of the company's existing cooperative clients. Under these circumstances, the superior court's injunction was reasonable.

We find unavailing defendant's reliance on *Concord Orthopaedics Professional Ass'n v. Forbes*, 142 N.H. 440, 702 A.2d 1273 (1997), for the proposition that the superior court was required to narrow the parties' agreement to restrict defendant from soliciting only plaintiff's current customers. In *Forbes*, a doctor left the employ of a physician's group and then sued his former employer, claiming that a covenant banning him from competing with the group within a twenty-five-mile radius of its business was unenforceable. The court upheld the agreement with respect to patients the doctor had treated while working for the group, but determined that the group lacked any legitimate interest in preventing the doctor from competing for new patients in the area. The instant case is distinguishable because, while working for plaintiff, defendant acquired specific information concerning plaintiff's customers, products, and services that could allow him to gain an advantage in competing against plaintiff for new clients. That was not the situation in *Forbes*.

Finally, we find no merit to defendant's argument that plaintiff should be equitably estopped from seeking enforcement of the noncompetition agreement. In support of this argument, defendant contends that he accepted employment with plaintiff and signed the agreement based on plaintiff's false representations that (1) its software products were suitable for cooperative electric and gas utilities; and (2) it would not seek to enforce the covenant not to compete unless defendant went to work for a major competitor of plaintiff. The trial court specifically found that defendant's testimony regarding these alleged representations was not credible. The court found that plaintiff did not mislead defendant about the capability of its products before he signed the noncompetition agreement and did not suggest to defendant that it would selectively enforce the agreement. Thus, the court properly rejected defendant's equitable estoppel claim.

Affirmed.

■ QUESTIONS

(1) What is the alleged breach in this case? In particular, did Barnes breach his contract by leaving the employ of Systems and Software, Inc.?

(2) In this case, is there any difference between specifically enforcing the contract and issuing the injunction at issue here?

(3) What factors did the court weigh in determining that an injunction was appropriate in this case? Do you think the court reached the proper balance among the various interests at stake?

■ PROBLEM 21.10

You have just been hired as general counsel for Sweatshop Software Co. Bright college graduates are eager to come work for Sweatshop. They are attracted by Sweatshop's excellent training program and lavish salaries. After a few years of working in the trenches, however, they tend to find the demanding hours and constant pressure oppressive, and leave the firm for less rigorous working environments. To make leaving the firm a less attractive option, management has suggested instituting a policy requiring all new employees to sign noncompetition agreements. The agreements would prohibit the employees from taking a position with a competing software company for a period of one year after termination of their employment with Sweatshop. Assume that in your jurisdiction, noncompetition agreements are generally enforceable under a "rule of reason," and injunctions against violating them are available in an appropriate case. Management asks your advice as to the legal effect and enforceability of the proposed noncompetition agreements under principles of contract law. What do you advise management?

D RESTITUTION AS A REMEDY UPON BREACH OF CONTRACT

Over the course of your study of contracts, you have seen several circumstances where courts require a party to account for the benefits it has received from the other party. This remedy, disgorgement of the benefits received, is called "restitution." The right to restitution is not always grounded in contract. As we see from our study of unjust enrichment in Chapter 12, sometimes the circumstances under which the benefit was given may have nothing to do with contract at all. At other times, restitution may be appropriate where a contract is unenforceable for some reason, such as indefiniteness, a defect in the bargaining process, or failure to satisfy the statute of frauds. In this section we look at situations where there is an enforceable contract and restitution is the remedy sought upon its breach.

Both expectation and reliance damages look to compensation of the aggrieved party. Expectation damages seek to put the aggrieved party in the position she would have been in had the contract been performed. Reliance damages aim to reimburse her for any losses she may have suffered in reliance on the contract and thus place her in the position she would have occupied had there been no contract. Restitution focuses on the benefit received by the breaching party. With the goal of preventing unjust enrichment, when a court orders restitution it requires a party to disgorge benefits received under the contract.

Restitution, as a contract remedy, arises in at least two distinct situations. In the first, the nonbreaching party seeks to unwind the contract in lieu of enforcing it. This remedy, sometimes called rescission, is not available in all situations in which there has been a breach of contract. If it is allowed, however, the contract is avoided, and the parties are obligated to make mutual restitution of any benefits received under the contract. Second, restitution may be relevant in a breach of contract situation where it is the breaching party who seeks restitution, rather than the nonbreaching party. We begin by examining rescission, and then consider restitution to the party in breach.

1. Rescission and Restitution

Generally, rescission of a contract is completely alternative to damages; a party electing to rescind a contract is not entitled also to collect damages for its breach. In the usual case, rescission and mutual restitution provide a less generous measure of recovery than enforcement of the contract. As we will see, however, the relative advantages of contract rescission and contract enforcement depend on the circumstances, and sometimes rescission is the plaintiff's preferred remedy.

WORCESTER HERITAGE SOCIETY, INC. v. TRUSSELL

31 Mass. App. 343, 577 N.E.2d 1009 (1991)
Massachusetts Appeals Court

ARMSTRONG, Judge.

The plaintiff (the society), a private, nonprofit organization dedicated to the preservation of historically significant buildings in Worcester, appeals from a judgment of the Housing Court which refused it a rescission of a contract and reconveyance of a house which it had conveyed to the defendant (Trussell) in 1984. The house at that time was vacant and uninhabitable, with no heat, electricity, or plumbing, was in severe disrepair, and had recently been damaged by fire. The sale was for $20,100, Trussell agreeing to abide by historic preservation restrictions and to do a complete historic restoration. The exterior portion was to be completed in one year, failing which the society could, at its option, engage workers to complete the exterior restoration at Trussell's expense. No time limit was specified for interior restoration. There was no requirement that the house be opened to public viewing or that the house be occupied.

Trussell, prior to the conveyance, gave the society, as required, evidence of his financial ability to invest the purchase price plus $45,000, the then estimated cost of the restoration. About a year and a half after the transfer, however, Trussell lost his job, with the result that work on the house, which had proceeded less rapidly than anticipated, was further slowed. The society sued for rescission in 1986 but then agreed, by way of a stipulation, to stay its hand for a further period. The case was not tried until 1989.

The society put in evidence that the exterior work was at that time still uncompleted, particularly on the rear side of the house, where sash was missing on one or two windows and a porch was supported on jacks. Trussell testified that he had scraped forty to fifty percent of the exterior to bare wood; replaced most of the clapboards on the south, sun-exposed side; prime-coated the entire house and finish-coated sixty percent of it; replaced most of the sash (most of the windows were boarded up before the sale); done roof repairs (taking some portions down to the carrying timbers); gutted most of the interior of the house, including all plaster, and carted the materials away. He acknowledged having done no restoration of the interior. The needed work, he estimated, would cost $100,000, far in excess of what had been estimated at the time of the sale. In general, he painted a picture, which the judge accepted, of meticulous, steady progress on the house, primarily by his own work, but hampered by shortage of funds which he hoped would soon be alleviated by settlement of his father's estate. The judge found the exterior work to be sixty-five to seventy-five percent complete. Acting "in [his] discretion," he refused rescission (the only remedy sought in the complaint) and suggested that the society, if it continued to be dissatisfied with the exterior progress, employ the self-help remedy set out in the contract.

There was no error based on the findings. There is ample authority for refusing rescission where there has been only a breach of contract rather than an utter failure of consideration or a repudiation by the party in breach. "In the absence of fraud, nothing less than conduct that amounts to an abrogation of the contract, or that goes to the essence of it, or takes away its foundation, can be made a ground for rescission of it by the other party." *Runkle v. Burrage*, 202 Mass. 89, 99, 88 N.E. 573 (1909). "Ordinarily equity will not set aside a contract at the suit of a party thereto on the sole ground of nonperformance by the other party of one of his agreements therein contained, in the absence of an agreement for termination upon breach by such nonperformance, where the breach is not of such a material and substantial nature as to excuse the party suing from proceeding with the contract, but will leave the party suing to his remedy by way of damages." *Barry v. Frankini*, 287 Mass. 196, 199-200, 191 N.E. 651 (1934). "The right to rescind a contract on the ground of failure of consideration exists only where the failure of consideration amounts to an abrogation of the contract, or goes to the essence of it, or takes away its foundation." *DeAngelis v. Palladino*, 318 Mass. 251, 257, 61 N.E.2d 117 (1945). See 5 *Corbin on Contracts* (1964) §1104, at 561-562 ("In the case of a breach by nonperformance ..., assuming that there has been no repudiation, the injured party's alternative remedy by way of restitution depends upon the extent of the non-performance by the defendant.... The injured party ... can not maintain an action for restitution of what he has given the defendant unless the defendant's non-performance is so material that it is held to go to the 'essence' ...").

Trussell's actions certainly have not amounted to a repudiation of the contract; the judge found that he intends to complete the restoration, although the time fixed in the contract for completion of the exterior has been greatly exceeded and may not have been realistic from the start. There has not been a total failure of consideration, Trussell having paid the purchase price and invested some additional sums and much labor in the restoration work. The visibly uncompleted portions of the exterior restoration are at the rear side of the house, the front appearing ... quite presentable. The society's concern was focused primarily, as its director testified, on the exterior appearance of the houses it rescued (explaining the cursory treatment of interior renovation in the contract and the absence of a time limit therefor or of any provision for opening the house to public view). The provisions of the purchase and sale agreement that time was of the essence applied to the closing date of the conveyance, not to the restoration provisions.

Courts have traditionally applied discretion in affording relief by way of rescission, as they have with most equitable remedies. Thus, the judge could properly take into account the "sweat equity" (in the judge's phrase) that Trussell had put into the restoration, which might be forfeit if a rescission were ordered. He could also properly take into account the fact that the contract expressly contemplated the possibility of delay in completion of the exterior work and empowered the society in that circumstance to engage a contractor to complete the exterior work and charge all costs (including architectural fees and attorney's fees) to Trussell. It was not shown that this remedy would be ineffectual. Judgment affirmed.

■ QUESTIONS

(1) What relationship, if any, does this case suggest between an aggrieved party's ability to obtain rescission and the concept of material breach?

(2) The contract called for the renovations to be completed within one year of the contract, which would have been 1985. By the time of suit in 1989—five years later—they were still not finished. The trial court estimated that it was about 65 to 75 percent complete. Why shouldn't this qualify as non-performance that is so material that it "goes to the essence" of this contract? Would it have so qualified if the renovation had been 45 percent complete? How relevant is the extent of completion? What other factors should be taken into account?

(3) What is the significance of the term providing that if Trussell did not complete the exterior renovation in a year, the Society had the right to complete the work at his expense? Why do you think that the Society did not avail itself of this right?

(4) It appears that the Society did not claim damages for breach of contract. If it had done so, how would those damages be measured?

The Worcester Heritage Society did not obtain rescission in this case. If rescission had been allowed, the court would have ordered mutual restitution; that is, the benefit conferred by each party under the contract would be returned to the other. Sometimes the court may order a party to return the actual property received; for instance, in this case it might have ordered Trussell to return the house to the Society. When the actual property can be returned, a court avoids difficult questions of valuation. When the benefit consists of something that cannot be returned, valuation is more difficult to avoid. For instance, if the court had allowed restitution in this case, it likely would not only require Trussell to return the property he received from the Society, but it would also require the Society to compensate Trussell for the benefits it received from him. But the labor and materials Trussell put into the house could not be returned. How is the court to measure the degree to which the labor and materials benefitted the Society?

The cases reveal several alternative measures of nonmonetary benefits. One measure of the value of a benefit would be its market value—what the party would have to pay in order to receive the benefit on the open market. The contract price may be some evidence of the market value of a benefit, but it is not necessarily determinative. Another measure of the reasonable value of a benefit would be the extent to which the recipient has been enriched. The net amount by which the benefit increased the recipient's wealth may be less or greater than the market value of the benefit, depending on the circumstances. It also may differ depending on whether the recipient's wealth is judged from an objective or a subjective point of view.

In choosing among the different methods of valuation, courts are swayed by many factors. Sometimes the conduct of the parties comes into play. If the behavior of the breaching party is particularly egregious, the court may choose the measure that favors the nonbreaching party. If the nonbreaching party is not itself entirely innocent of misbehavior, the court may choose a measure that is more neutral. Likewise, although restitution is concerned primarily with avoiding unjust enrichment, the court may take the apparent contract damages to the nonbreaching party into account. If one measure of the benefit is wildly disproportionate to what damages would be if the nonbreaching party sought to enforce the contract, the court may choose another measure that is less so.

To measure the benefit to the breaching party, it is particularly important to focus on what precise types of benefits are at issue. A party may gain many benefits when it breaches a contract. Generally, only those benefits that flow from the performance of the nonbreaching party need be restored. To illustrate, imagine that Carla Connoisseur enters into a contract with Al Artist, in which Al will create a modern sculpture for Carla.[11] Under the contract, Carla makes a substantial down payment. When Al finishes the sculpture, he learns that he can sell it to Big City Museum for a higher price than Carla agreed to pay. Al deliberately breaches his contract with Carla and sells the sculpture to the museum. Carla forgoes any claim to expectation or reliance damages and instead argues that she is entitled to rescission and restitution. And she is. Al provided nothing to Carla under the contract, so the standard for rescission described in the *Worcester Heritage Society* case is certainly met. Al received the benefit of Carla's performance, the down payment, and he should disgorge that benefit. However, the excess profit he made when he sold the sculpture to the museum was not a result of Carla's performance but rather of Al's breach. As a result, under a standard restitution measure of damages, Al need not account to Carla for that profit.

Courts sometimes create exceptions to this rule, however. In situations where breach is particularly egregious or wrongful, or if the parties have a special relationship, courts may require that profits from the breach be disgorged, whether or not they flow from the nonbreaching party's performance. The U.S. Supreme Court did precisely that in the colorful case of *Snepp v. United*

---

[11] You may wonder whether this transaction is governed by the common law or by UCC Article 2, as it arguably involves both goods and services. For purposes of illustration, assume it is governed by the common law. Were it governed by the UCC, the resulting analysis would be similar.

States, 444 U.S. 507, 100 S. Ct. 763, 62 L. Ed. 2d 704 (1980). Mr. Snepp, a former employee of the Central Intelligence Agency, published a book about CIA activities in South Vietnam. His employment contract prohibited him from divulging classified information and also required him to submit anything he might write about the CIA for prepublication review by the CIA. Although the book apparently didn't contain any classified information, he failed to submit the book for prepublication review, in breach of his contract with the CIA. In subsequent litigation, the CIA sought, among other things, that Mr. Snepp be required to disgorge his profits from the book. The Supreme Court affirmed a district court judgment that had imposed a constructive trust on Snepp's profits. In doing so, the Supreme Court reasoned that Mr. Snepp had breached a fiduciary duty to the government, and in order to deter future breaches of this type, he was required to disgorge the benefits of his faithlessness. Three justices dissented, holding that this was an ordinary breach of contract rather than a breach of fiduciary duty. Because the profits didn't flow from the use of any classified information, they argued, the government, rather than Snepp, would be unjustly enriched if he was required to disgorge profits attributable entirely to his own legitimate activity.

■ PROBLEM 21.11

Alison Arbitrage was hired fresh out of college by Debenture Option Warrant Co. ("DOW"), a securities trading firm. When Alison accepted the job, she signed a noncompetition agreement that barred her from trading any securities she had traded at DOW for a period of one year after terminating her employment with the firm. Alison completed a six-month-long training program, and became a successful and profitable securities trader with the firm.

Three years after joining the firm, Alison left DOW to begin her own, competing business. DOW sued Alison seeking remedies for breach of her agreement not to compete. At trial, evidence showed that Alison's training cost DOW $75,000. Evidence further revealed that while she was employed with the firm she earned $1.5 million in salary and bonuses but earned $5 million in revenues for the firm. Although DOW was not able to identify specific trading business it lost as a result of Alison's breach, DOW established that Alison earned over $2 million in profits from sales of securities in violation of the noncompetition agreement.

Assume the noncompetition agreement is enforceable and that Alison materially and unjustifiably breached it to such a degree that rescission would be available. What measure of restitution would you award DOW, and why?

2. Restitution to the Party in Breach

In Chapter 19, Section B.3, we note that at common law, a party who substantially performs a contract may enforce that contract against the other party, even though the substantial performance may constitute a breach. The non-breaching party's remedy is to seek damages, not suspend its own performance. However, where the breach is total and material, in most cases the breaching party loses the right to enforce the contract. Where the breaching party has conferred significant benefits on the nonbreaching party, the inability to enforce the contract can wreak substantial hardship on the breaching party and constitute a windfall to the nonbreaching party. As a consequence, some (but not all) courts admit to the possibility that a breaching party may be able to obtain restitution of the benefits conferred under the contract on a theory of unjust enrichment.

Consider, for instance, a contract between Ron Real and Emma Estate, in which Ron agrees to convey some land to Emma. Upon signing the contract, Emma puts down a deposit of $5,000 (often called an "earnest money deposit"). The contract does not specify what the parties' remedies will be in the event of a breach of the contract. If Ron thereafter willfully and unjustifiably refuses to sell the land to Emma, Emma should be able to sue for expectation damages or, alternatively, reliance damages. As we have seen, under either measure her down payment would be taken into account in calculating the amount of her contract damages. Instead, Emma might choose to rescind the contract (as she would almost certainly be permitted to do) and receive restitution in the amount of her deposit. So whether she enforces the contract or rescinds it, her recovery will account for the amount of the deposit she has already paid. But assume it is Emma who willfully and unjustifiably refuses to purchase the land from Ron. Ron immediately sells the land to another buyer for a larger sum than Emma had promised to pay. Ron has not suffered any damages due to Emma's breach. Should Emma in these circumstances be entitled to a return of her deposit under a theory of unjust enrichment?

The traditional answer to this question was no. Courts were unwilling to use their equitable powers to assist those who were in breach, irrespective of the cause of that breach. To put it another way, it was not deemed unjust for a party who stood ready, willing, and able to perform a contract to retain the benefits received under that contract. This approach still holds considerable sway in the real estate context, but even there has begun to erode. Of late, courts have become more sympathetic to the plight of the breaching party who has conferred some benefits under a contract.

Where the nonbreaching party is enriched by the other party's partial performance, courts are increasingly willing to allow limited restitution to the breaching party. Given the traditional hostility toward aiding breachers, this is a context where equities are likely to play a significant role. Modern courts tend to favor those breaching parties who seem relatively innocent in circumstances where the nonbreaching party is clearly enriched by the partial performance. Where the equities do not favor the breaching party, modern courts still regularly deny restitution. Even where they allow restitution, the courts take into account the damages suffered by the nonbreaching party.

■ PROBLEM 21.12

Hal Homeowner entered into a contract with Fred Floors. Hal agreed to pay Fred $8,000 to refinish the hardwood floors in his house. Hal made a $2,000 down payment and agreed to pay the balance upon completion of the job. Fred estimated that his costs to complete the job, other than his own labor, would be $1,000. The day before work was to begin, Hal decided to install carpet in his house instead. He called Fred and unjustifiably repudiated the contract. Hal now seeks return of his down payment.

Under each of the following factual variations, determine how much (if any) you would award to Hal, and why:

(a) Fred immediately takes on another job that, although similar to his contract with Hal in all other respects, pays him $10,000. The replacement job fully occupies his time.

(b) Alternatively, Fred immediately takes on another job that also pays him $8,000. Fred demonstrates that he could have handled both Hal's job and the new job without difficulty.

(c) Alternatively, as soon as Hal repudiates, Fred decides to take a break from his labors. He spends the $2,000 Hal gave him and the time he would have been refinishing Hal's floors on a vacation in Bimini.

In Section B.1, we include UCC 2-718(1), which concerns liquidated damages. The remainder of Section UCC 2-718 relates to a breaching buyer's ability to obtain a return of any deposit paid to the seller. Although UCC 2-718 expressly allows restitution in some circumstances, the buyer's right to obtain the return of its deposit is not absolute. As you read the following section, consider what limitations it imposes on the breaching buyer's ability to obtain restitution, and speculate about the purpose and effect of those limitations.

UCC 2-718. LIQUIDATION OR LIMITATION OF DAMAGES; DEPOSITS

. . .

(2)   Where the seller justifiably withholds delivery of goods because of the buyer's breach, the buyer is entitled to restitution of any amount by which the sum of his payments exceeds

(a) the amount to which the seller is entitled by virtue of terms liquidating the seller's damages in accordance with subsection (1), or

(b) in the absence of such terms, twenty per cent of the value of the total performance for which the buyer is obligated under the contract or $500, whichever is smaller.

(3) The buyer's right to restitution under subsection (2) is subject to offset to the extent that the seller establishes

(a) a right to recover damages under the provisions of this Article other than subsection (1), and

(b) the amount or value of any benefits received by the buyer directly or indirectly by reason of the contract. . . .

The Rights of Nonparties

CHAPTER 22

A THIRD-PARTY BENEFICIARIES

1. The Intent to Confer Power of Enforcement on the Third Party

Contract rights and obligations normally extend only to the parties and are not binding on or enforceable by those who are not parties to the contract. The third-party beneficiary doctrine is a narrow exception to this rule. It recognizes that under specified circumstances, a nonparty may sue to enforce a contract made for his benefit. To invoke the doctrine, it is not enough for the nonparty to show merely that the contract is beneficial to him. In many cases, a contract may incidentally create an advantage to someone who was not a party to it. For example, an employee may anticipate the productive use of an office that she will occupy by virtue of a lease entered into between her employer and the lessor; a restaurant may expect increased business as a result of the construction of a nearby theater complex to be erected under a contract between a developer and a construction company; a homeowner may look forward to improved safety in his neighborhood as a consequence of new street lighting to be installed under a contract entered into between the city and a lighting contractor. However, the mere fact that these benefits are expected by the nonparty, or even contemplated by the parties to the contract themselves, does not, on its own, give these contracts the legal effect of contracts for the benefit of a third party. The crucial attribute of a contract for the benefit of a third party is not simply that it may or will have some positive effect on that third party or even that the contracting parties desired that beneficial effect. Rather, the parties when they entered the contract must have had the purpose of giving the third party the power to enforce that benefit.

It is the power of enforcement by independent action that is the hallmark of a contract for the benefit of a third party. In the first example above, even if the employer and lessor expected the employee to obtain an advantage by having the new office space, it is unlikely that they intended to give the employee the right of independent enforcement of the lease rights. Therefore, if the lessor reneged on the lease and refused to deliver the premises to the employer, the employer alone has the right to sue the lessor for breach; we would not expect the employee to have her own cause of action against the lessor. The same distinction could be made with regard to the contracts between the developer and construction company and between the city and the lighting contractor. Unless the parties to the contract intended to confer a direct cause of action on the restaurant owner or householder, it would be only the developer or the city who could sue the contractors for breach. In these examples the employee, restaurant, and householder are known as "incidental beneficiaries" to distinguish them from third parties who are given rights of direct enforcement, "intended beneficiaries." This is how Restatement, Second §§302 and 304 describe this distinction:

RESTATEMENT, SECOND §302. INTENDED AND INCIDENTAL BENEFICIARIES

(1) Unless otherwise agreed between promisor and promisee, a beneficiary of a promise is an intended beneficiary if recognition of a right to performance in the beneficiary is appropriate to effectuate the intention of the parties and either

(a) the performance of the promise will satisfy an obligation of the promisee to pay money to the beneficiary; or

(b) the circumstances indicate that the promisee intends to give the beneficiary the benefit of the promised performance.

(2) An incidental beneficiary is a beneficiary who is not an intended beneficiary.

RESTATEMENT, SECOND §304. CREATION OF DUTY TO BENEFICIARY

A promise in a contract creates a duty in the promisor to any intended beneficiary to perform the promise, and the intended beneficiary may enforce the duty.

———————

Lawrence v. Fox, 20 N.Y. 268 (1859), is widely credited as being the case that first established, or at least first coherently articulated, the principle in American law that a contract can create rights in a third-party beneficiary, enforceable by the beneficiary's direct cause of action against the promisor. Fox entered into a contract with one Holly under which Holly lent $300 to Fox. Fox agreed to repay the loan to Lawrence, to whom Holly was indebted in the same amount. (That is, the borrower agreed to repay the loan not to the lender himself, but to the lender's creditor.) When Fox failed to pay, Lawrence sued him. Fox raised the defense that Lawrence had no standing to sue because he was not a party to the contract—there was no privity between them. The court dismissed this defense on the basis that parties to a contract have the power to create a right of enforcement in a nonparty.

Lawrence, the beneficiary, was a creditor of Holly, the promisee. For some years after the decision, it was unclear whether the doctrine would apply where there was no debtor-creditor relationship between the promisee and the beneficiary. This question was resolved by the New York Court of Appeals some 60 years later in *Seaver v. Ransom*, 224 N.Y. 233, 120 N.E. 639 (1918). Like *Lawrence*, the decision was immensely influential. It established the principle that an intended beneficiary has an independent right of enforcement, whether or not the beneficiary is a creditor of the promisee. In *Seaver* a husband promised his dying wife that he would provide in his will for her niece to inherit their house or its value. When the husband later died, it was found that he had not made the promised disposition in his will. The niece sued his estate to enforce the promise that the husband had made to his wife. The court applied and extended *Lawrence*, holding that there was no reason in law or equity to confine the doctrine to cases in which the beneficiary was a creditor of the promisee. The crucial factor is that the contract was made for the benefit of the niece. She was the only person who was damaged by the breach, and no one else had any incentive to enforce the promise.

Cases and commentary following *Lawrence* and *Seaver* drew the distinction between "creditor beneficiaries" and "donee beneficiaries," recognizing that these were different types of intended beneficiaries, but both had the right of enforcement. Section 133 of the original Restatement expressly referred to the two types separately. As you can see from §302 above, the Restatement, Second, has dropped the formal distinction between creditor and donee beneficiaries while continuing to acknowledge that the intent to confer a right of enforcement may be based on an obligation owed by the promisee to the beneficiary, or on other circumstances that indicate an intent to confer the benefit. Thus, the crucial question is not so much the nature of the relationship between the promisee and the beneficiary but rather the intent to confer the independent right of enforcement. The principle that a contract can confer an independent right of enforcement on a third party is now unquestionably established. As you may expect, the difficult issue is deciding if the parties intended to grant this power—whether the third party was indeed an intended beneficiary or merely an incidental beneficiary. Some contracts may spell out this intent expressly, but often they do not. Where intent to create a contract for the benefit of a third party is not clearly articulated in the contract, this intent must be inferred. In the absence of express intent, it is likely to be easier to infer intent where the promisee owes some obligation to the beneficiary.

Kmart Corp. v. Balfour Beatty, Inc., 994 F. Supp. 634 (D. V.I. 1998), provides an example of such inferred intent in a commercial contract. Kmart, a tenant in a shopping center, sued a roofing company, Balfour Beatty Incorporated (BBI), for breach of a contract entered into between BBI and the owner of the building (Kmart's landlord). BBI moved to dismiss the suit on the grounds that Kmart was not a party to the contract. The court found that Kmart was an intended beneficiary of the contract under Restatement, Second §§302 and 304. The court based this finding on the language of the contract, interpreted in context. Kmart was the sole or major tenant of the building and had been fully involved in the design and construction of the building. The contract provided that construction schedules must comport with Kmart's requirements, the drawings to be used must be submitted to Kmart, and all warranties were to be executed in its favor. In addition, in executing the contract for the construction, the landlord was acting pursuant to a commitment that it had made to Kmart to erect the building. Under these circumstances the court held that the parties reasonably must be taken to have conferred an independent power of enforcement on Kmart.

Unlike *Lawrence, Seaver*, and *Kmart*, the next case found that the third party was not an intended beneficiary of the contract. As you read the case, consider why the conclusion in this case differs from that in the others.

MASAD v. WEBER

2009 S.D. 80, 772 N.W.2d 144 (2009)
South Dakota Supreme Court

SEVERSON, Justice.

Randall and Lori Masad (Plaintiffs) appeal the circuit court's summary judgment in favor of the South Dakota Department of Corrections (State). The circuit court ruled that Randall Masad's (Masad) negligence claim was barred by . . . [South Dakota's sovereign immunity statute] and that, as a matter of law, Masad was not a third-party beneficiary of the contract between Catering by Marlins, Inc. (CBM) and the State. . . . [The court affirms the trial court's summary judgment in favor of the state on the contract claim. But it reverses the summary judgment in favor of the state on the negligence claim on the grounds that it did not fall within the statute's grant of immunity. That is, although the plaintiffs' contract suit is dismissed, they are able to proceed with their negligence claim against the state. We omit the court's discussion of the sovereign immunity issue.[1]]

For purposes of the motion for summary judgment, the evidence relied upon by the circuit court was not seriously contested. In 2002, CBM entered into a contract with the State to provide food services for inmates in the South Dakota State Penitentiary (Penitentiary) in Sioux Falls, South Dakota. The contract covered all time periods relevant to this case. Masad was employed by CBM in 2003 as a food service director. He primarily worked in the kitchen area of the Penitentiary's Jameson Annex. . . . [In 2004, Masad was viciously attacked and severely injured by an inmate who had gained access to the prison kitchen. The inmate had a history of violence and should not have been allowed into the kitchen area. He gained access because the prison authorities had not properly supervised him.]

Plaintiffs contend that the circuit court erred in concluding that Masad was not a third-party beneficiary of the contract between the State and CBM, resulting in the State owing Masad no duty to provide for his security. They assert that Masad was a member of the class that was to be benefited by the State's agreement to provide "safety and security." Defendants respond that it is apparent from the face of the contract that the contracting parties intended for CBM, rather than each of its employees, to possess whatever contractual rights existed concerning security. . . .

SDCL 53-2-6 governs the right to enforce a contract as a third-party beneficiary. It provides: "[a] contract made expressly for the benefit of a third person may be enforced by him at any time before the parties thereto rescind it." SDCL 53-2-6. "This does not, however, entitle every person who received some benefit from the contract to enforce it." *Sisney v. State*, 2008 SD 71, 754 N.W.2d 639, 643. The [third-party beneficiary] statute is not applicable to every contract made by one person with another for the performance of which a third person will derive a benefit; *the intent to make the contract inure to the benefit of a third party must be clearly manifested.* In the language of the statute, the contract must be on[e] "made expressly for the benefit of a third person." *Id.* (emphasis added). "Thus, the rule requires that at the time the contract was executed, it was the contracting parties' intent to expressly benefit the third party. And, even then, not all beneficiaries qualify: incidental beneficiaries are not entitled to third-party beneficiary status." [*Id.*][2] For the party claiming third-party beneficiary status to prevail, he must show "that the contract was entered

---

[1] Under the doctrine of sovereign immunity, a citizen may not sue the government (state or federal) in tort unless the government has waived the immunity or consented to the suit. However, a citizen may sue the government in contract because, by entering into the contract, the government waives its immunity in relation to claims under the contract. In this case, the plaintiffs sue in the alternative in tort and for breach of contract.—EDS.

[2] The Restatement Second [§315] defines an "incidental beneficiary" as "a person who will be benefited by performance of a promise but who is neither a promisee nor an intended beneficiary." . . . [The court then quotes the provisions of Restatement, Second, §302 relating to intended beneficiaries.]

into by the parties directly and primarily for his benefit." *Id.* A mere showing of an incidental benefit is not sufficient.

The relevant sections of the contract provide:

6.19.5 Area Security

The contractor's staff shall open, close and check State food service facilities as instructed and required by the State. State shall furnish instructions and initially train contractor's full-time managers in approved procedures.

6.21.4 Facility Security

The contractor is responsible for control of keys obtained from the State and the security of those areas that are used by its representatives. Designated employees of the contractor shall be responsible for ensuring that all equipment has been turned off, windows closed, light and fans turned off, and doors locked. The contractor shall be responsible for immediately reporting all the facts relating to losses incurred as a result of break-ins to areas to the State. The State shall designate the authority who shall receive these reports and be responsible for key control.

The State and contractor shall mutually determine the additional security measures required to control unauthorized access to all food service areas included in the contract. The State and contractor shall mutually determine their responsibilities for the cost to provide initial and future additional security.

6.21.6 State Security

The State shall provide the contractor with safety and security services currently available to food service, such as night patrol, door checks, security consulting, call response, etc. This service shall not include armored car service.

If the contractor requires additional security, it shall be provided by, or coordinated through, the State for which the contractor agrees to pay prevailing charges. In addition to Security staff, the contractor may supplement with additional supervisory staff. The contractor shall follow the State's policies in dealing with improper conduct and shall report all incidences to the State. Emergency calls shall be reported to the State as promptly as possible.

Defendants argue that nothing in the contract indicates that the State made a promise directly and primarily to CBM's employees to provide them with security while working in food service areas. Plaintiffs assert that the contract was ambiguous and introduced extrinsic evidence supporting their contention that the contract was intended to benefit third parties such as Masad.

We recently addressed the third-party beneficiary concept in *Sisney v. State,* 2008 SD 71, 754 N.W.2d 639. Sisney, a state inmate who allegedly practiced the Jewish religion, filed a complaint maintaining the state food service provider breached a contract to provide food services to state prisons by failing to adequately provide kosher food, and that this breach violated his civil rights. On appeal, this Court concluded that Sisney was not a third-party beneficiary under the contract between the food service provider and the State, and therefore, had no standing to sue on the contract. We acknowledged this was a public contract and the contract did not "expressly indicate that it was intended for Sisney's direct benefit or enforcement." Instead, the contract was made for the express benefit of the State, and "the collective benefit that inmates may have received was only incidental to that of the State." *Id.* Furthermore, the provision in the contract relating to a complaint resolution process did not confer "contractual third-party beneficiary status on Sisney to *enforce* the contract." *Id.* (emphasis in original).

We came to a similar conclusion in *Trouten v. Heritage Mutual Ins. Co.*, 2001 SD 106, 632 N.W.2d 856. In *Trouten*, Kenison purchased a business liability insurance contract from Heritage to provide coverage for her business. The contract, in pertinent part, provided coverage for "medical expenses . . . for bodily injury caused by an accident . . . [o]n ways next to premises you own or rent . . . regardless of fault." Subsequently, Trouten, a third-party, slipped and fell on a sidewalk abutting the building insured by Heritage. He reported the accident and made a claim for medical and hospital expenses. When Heritage denied the claim, Trouten sued Heritage for breach of contract, including a claim of bad faith. Ultimately, the case came before this Court on intermediate appeal with one of the issues being whether Trouten could maintain a direct action suit against Heritage when he did not contract with Heritage. This Court recognized: "[W]henever two parties enter into an agreement that appears to have been made expressly for the benefit of a third party, and such agreement has a good and sufficient consideration, the agreement itself creates all the privity there need be between the person for whose benefit the agreement was entered into and the party assuming the obligation, and an action at law should lie regardless of whether there was any obligation existing between the other party to the agreement and the third party. *But, before the third party can adopt the agreement entered into and recover thereon, he must show clearly that it was entered into with the intent on the part of the parties thereto that such third party should be benefited thereby.* This intent might, in a given case, sufficiently appear from the contract itself, but it must frequently be shown by other proof." (Emphasis added.) *Accord Verni v. Cleveland Chiropractic College*, 212 S.W.3d 150, 153 (Mo. 2007) (stating that "[t]o be bound as a third-party beneficiary, the terms of the contract must clearly express intent to benefit that party or an identifiable class of which the party is a member" and "not every person who is benefited by a contract may bring suit to enforce that contract[;]" "only those third-parties who are clearly intended beneficiaries may do so"). This Court held that because the contract did not expressly or clearly imply that a third party, such as Trouten, had a right to sue Heritage directly for medical benefits, the action would not stand.

Several jurisdictions have concluded that, under analogous circumstances, the injured third party was not a third-party beneficiary of the contract at issue. The Massachusetts Court of Appeals's decision in *Lakew v. Massachusetts Bay Transp. Auth.*, 65 Mass. App. Ct. 794, 844 N.E.2d 263 (2006), considered a case with an analogous factual scenario as that before us now. Plaintiff Lakew suffered injuries from an armed robbery, which occurred while he was on duty as a parking lot attendant in a parking garage owned by the Defendant, Massachusetts Bay Transportation Authority (MBTA). Lakew obtained a jury verdict on his claims for negligence and breach of contract. MBTA appealed, asserting, among other things, that the breach of contract claim should fail as a matter of law because Lakew was not an intended beneficiary of the lease between MBTA and Lakew's employer, which provided that MBTA would supply security at fourteen transit facilities, including Lakew's worksite. The court agreed. In applying Restatement (Second) principles, it reasoned:

> [A]s a matter of law we consider it clear from the language of the lease and the circumstances of its execution that the MBTA reserved to itself the responsibility for security services in order to control the parties' risk due to potential claims by third parties for loss resulting from property damage or personal injury at the leased facilities. While such a purpose necessarily anticipates the interests of such third parties in avoiding loss, *the purpose of the arrangement is not to confer on such parties a right to enforce the contract but instead to allocate between the direct contracting parties the risk of loss, and control over facts affecting such risk.* Viewed in that manner, third parties who suffer a loss as a result of deficient security are not "intended beneficiaries" within the terms of the Restatement (Second), which looks in the first instance to whether "recognition of a right to performance in the beneficiary is appropriate to effectuate the intention of the parties." (Emphasis added.)

Therefore, the court determined that Lakew was not an intended beneficiary of the provisions of the lease between his employer and MBTA concerning security. Although we make our decision based on SDCL 53-2-6 rather than the Restatement (Second), we find this reasoning persuasive. Analogous to the lease in *Lakew*, the instant contract was not executed "to confer on such parties a right to enforce the contract," but instead to establish CBM's and the State's mutual rights and responsibilities concerning security in light of the services CBM provided.

Under the instant case, we agree with the circuit court that "[t]he contract is unambiguous as to whether, at the time it was executed, the contracting parties intended to directly benefit CBM employees such as Masad." The language of the contract indicates that the State intended for the contractual rights concerning security be possessed by CBM, as opposed to CBM and all of its employees.[3] Because the contract is unambiguous in this regard, we need not consider extrinsic evidence.

The primary purpose of the contract was to provide food services for the prisoners in the custody of the State. Plaintiffs have failed to show that the contract was entered into by the parties "directly and primarily" for Masad's, or any other CBM employee's, benefit. *Sisney v. State*, 2008 SD 71, 754 N.W.2d at 643. Any benefit to CBM's employees, such as Masad, was indirect. Therefore, we affirm the circuit court's holding that Plaintiffs have failed to meet their burden of proving Masad was a third-party beneficiary of the contract.

---

[3] This is evident in the language distinguishing between "contractor" when referring to CBM, and "representative" or "employee" to refer to CBM's employees. Specifically, the contract provided in part: "The State shall provide the *contractor* with safety and security services . . . [;]" and "If the *contractor* requires additional security, it shall be provided by, or coordinated through, the State. . . ." (Emphasis added).

■ PROBLEM 22.1

In *Wolfgang v. Mid-America Motorsports, Inc.*, 111 F.3d 1515 (10th Cir. 1997), Wolfgang, a racing car driver, was injured when he crashed his car during a practice race and it caught fire. Because the firefighting capability at the track was inadequate, he was not rescued from the burning car in time and suffered injury that could have been prevented by proper firefighting precautions. He sued the racetrack for negligence, and also sued the organizer of the event, World of Outlaws, on the theory that he was the intended beneficiary of its contract with the speedway, under which it had the right "to cancel any event due to unsafe racing conditions." Wolfgang contended that by reserving the contractual right to ensure safe racing conditions, the organizer had assumed the duty to drivers to make sure that conditions were safe. The court found that Wolfgang was an intended beneficiary of the contract between the racetrack and the organizer, and that he therefore had a direct cause of action against the organizer for compensation for his injuries. The court noted that the intent of the parties to the contract must be determined to decide if drivers were intended beneficiaries of the contract. Although the language of the contract did not expressly state that drivers were intended beneficiaries of the contract, the intent to confer this status could be readily inferred from the fact that the organizer had the contractual right to cancel events if racing conditions were unsafe. This interpretation was bolstered by the testimony of the organizer's president, in which he admitted that it had the responsibility to drivers and members of the public to ensure that racetracks were safe.

Compare the reasoning and result in *Wolfgang* with that in *Masad* and in the *Trouten* case discussed by the North Dakota Supreme Court in *Masad*. (*Trouten* involved a claim against an insurer by a third party injured on the insured premises.) Can you explain the different results in these cases? Are you persuaded that the contract language in *Wolfgang* really does evince an intent to confer enforcement rights on the drivers?

■ PROBLEM 22.2

As we saw in *Masad* (and also as indicated in the discussion of *Wolfgang* in Problem 22.1), third-party beneficiary doctrine is sometimes used under circumstances in which there might be an alternative cause of action in tort for negligence. In such cases, principles of tort liability are closely interwoven with the contract issues. To what extent may the absence or presence of tort liability affect the determination of whether the third party is an intended beneficiary? Consider this issue as you deal with the following hypothetical situation.

Under a contract with the owner of a building, an engineer designed a sky bridge across the building's atrium. The contract expressly stated that the sky bridge must be designed to withstand an earthquake of up to 8.0 on the Richter scale. A few years after the sky bridge had been erected, an earthquake measuring 7.8 on the Richter scale caused the sky bridge to collapse. Fortunately, no one was injured, but the bridge crushed an espresso stand in the well of the atrium, owned and operated by Barry Star.

The sky bridge had been designed in accordance with accepted engineering principles and it would have withstood an earthquake of up to 7.5 on the Richter scale, which is all that is required by the city building code. Therefore assume that the engineer is not liable to anyone in tort for negligently designing the sky bridge. However, the engineer did breach her contract with the building's owner. Does Barry have a cause of action against the engineer?

2. Non-Clients as Third Party Beneficiaries of a Contract Between an Attorney and a Client

When an attorney enters into a contract with a client to perform legal work for the client, the resulting professional services may well redound to the benefit of a third party. This is particularly true where the legal services involve the drafting of a will or other disposition of property from the client to the third party. If the attorney fails to act in accordance with standards of reasonable competence in advising on the will or disposition or in drawing the documents to effectuate it, the client clearly will have a cause of action for malpractice. However, it is a much more difficult issue to decide if a nonclient beneficiary of the legal services has, or should have, an independent right to sue the attorney. The malpractice claim, like the negligence claims in *Masad* and *Wolfgang*, could be both a tort and a breach of contract. For a third party to succeed in a tort action based on malpractice, he would have to show that the attorney's negligence violated a duty of care not just to the client but to the third party personally. For a third party to succeed in a contract suit, he would have to show that he was the intended beneficiary of the contract between the attorney and client.

Noble v. Bruce, 349 Md. 730, 709 A.2d 1264 (1998), decided two consolidated cases in each of which the beneficiaries of a will sued the testator's attorney on the grounds that the attorney was negligent in providing estate planning advice and services to the testator. The beneficiaries alleged that as a result of the attorney's incompetence, the bequests attracted significant estate and inheritance taxes that could have been avoided. The beneficiaries sued the attorney in tort for negligence, and alternatively in contract. Although there was no contractual relationship between the beneficiaries and the attorney, the beneficiaries argued that they were intended third-party beneficiaries of the contract between the testator and the attorney.

On the tort claim, the court followed the established rule that a nonclient cannot sue an attorney in tort for economic loss caused by the attorney's negligence. This rule is based on the policy that to allow a nonclient to sue an attorney for negligence exposes the attorney to uncontrollable risks of liability and undermines the attorney's duty of undivided loyalty to the client.

The court rejected the contract claim as well. In part, the court's decision was based on its interpretation of the contract between the testator and the attorney. There was no indication in the terms of the contract, or from the circumstances, that the parties had any intention of conferring an independent right of enforcement on the testamentary beneficiaries. The mere fact that the beneficiaries were intended to benefit from the will did not, in itself, lead to the inference that they were also intended beneficiaries of the contract. The court also stressed that its decision was based on strong public policy concerns, similar to those applicable to negligence claims. Recognition of liability to nonclients, in the absence of clearly expressed contractual intent, could undermine the attorney-client relationship. Concerns about potential liability to nonclients could motivate attorneys to focus too strongly on avoiding this liability, to the detriment of the client's interests. In addition, the possibility of being accountable to nonclients could create a conflict of interest and compromise the attorney's duty of loyalty to the client. This would be particularly true where the client's wishes were not exactly in accord with the best interests of the beneficiary. Furthermore, an attorney sued by a beneficiary may find that the only way to defend the suit is to reveal client confidences.

■ PROBLEM 22.3

One of the most important duties owed by a lawyer to a client is the duty of confidentiality. A lawyer may not reveal information relating to the representation of a client unless the client consents to the disclosure. Even if this duty is not expressed in the representation agreement, it is unquestionably implied into the agreement as a matter of law.

Polly Tician, a senior government official, consulted Lex Lawless, an attorney, for advice on a substantial cash payment that Polly planned to make to Parry Moore. Polly, who was a strong public advocate of "family values," told Lex that she had been having an affair with Parry, which she had just ended. She had agreed to make the cash payment to Parry in exchange for his promise to keep silent about the affair. Lex advised Polly that there was nothing illegal about making the cash settlement and he counseled her to make it as soon as possible. Unfortunately, a couple of days later, before Polly had made the payment to Parry, the affair was reported in the press. Polly was forced to resign her office in disgrace. The press had obtained knowledge of the affair because Lex could not resist telling a friend about this juicy piece of gossip and, despite promising Lex to keep the information secret, the friend disclosed it to the press. Because the affair was now public knowledge, the payment of the cash settlement to Parry was pointless, and Polly never made it.

Assume that Parry would have no cause of action against Lex in tort, or on any other theory apart from third party beneficiary doctrine. Could Parry make a viable argument that he was the intended beneficiary of the contract (and, specifically, Lex's obligation of confidentiality under the contract) between Lex and Polly?

3. Members of the Public as Third-Party Beneficiaries of Government Contracts

Private parties usually enter into contracts to serve their own interests. Therefore, where most contracts between private parties are concerned, any benefit to a third party is more likely to be incidental than intended. However, government activity is intended to serve the general public welfare, so one might assume that it would be easier to find that members of the public are intended third-party beneficiaries of government contracts. *Sussex Tool & Supply, Inc. v. Mainline Sewer & Water, Inc.*, 231 Wis. 2d 404, 605 N.W.2d 620 (Wis. App. 1999), demonstrates the folly of making such an easy assumption. The Village of Lannon hired Mainline to install a sewer and water system. Under the terms of the contract, Mainline promised to "provide vehicular access at all times to the properties affected by this project."

Mainline did not maintain the access as required by the contract. After the project was completed, Sussex Tool, whose business had not been accessible during portions of the project, sued Mainline for profits allegedly lost from the disruption of its business. (Sussex Tool also unsuccessfully sued the village. That claim need not concern us.) One of the bases for Sussex Tool's suit against Mainline was that Sussex Tool was a third-party beneficiary of the contract between Mainline and the village. The court of appeals upheld the trial court's dismissal of this cause of action. It held that Sussex Tool was merely an incidental beneficiary of the contract. Government contracts are invariably made on behalf of the public, so intent to benefit members of the public is routinely present. However, this does not mean that members of the public are intended beneficiaries of government contracts with a right to enforce them. A member of the public can acquire the status of an intended beneficiary only if the language of the contract or its context makes clear the intent to confer an independent right of enforcement on members of the public who benefit from it. The contract in this case indicated no such intent.

■ PROBLEM 22.4

In the course of its opinion in *Sussex Tool*, the court distinguished an earlier case, *State ex rel. Journal/Sentinel, Inc. v. Pleva*, 151 Wis. 2d 608, 445 N.W.2d 689 (Wis. App. 1989), *aff'd*, 155 Wis. 2d 704, 456 N.W.2d 359 (Wis. 1990). In *Pleva*, the city of Milwaukee leased its lakefront to the Milwaukee World Festival, Inc. The lease provided that the festival must hold all its meetings in accordance with Wisconsin's open meeting law. When the festival failed to do so, the newspaper sued for an order of specific performance. The court held that the newspaper had standing to sue as a third-party beneficiary. In *Sussex Tool*, the court distinguished *Pleva* on the basis that the newspaper in *Pleva* sought specific performance to enforce the lease's open meeting provision in the interests of the public at large, while Sussex Tool merely sought compensatory damages for itself.

(a) Would the court have found a contract for the benefit of Sussex Tool if it was not claiming damages for lost profits following the construction but rather was suing for an injunction during the course of construction to compel Mainline to maintain access to the affected properties? If the answer is affirmative, how can this be explained? Can it be that the choice of remedy may have an impact on the question of whether the parties intended their contract to benefit third parties?

(b) In *Sussex Tool*, the court cited Restatement, Second §313(2), which provides that a promisor who contracts with the government for public works or services is not contractually liable to members of the public for consequential damages resulting from its performance or failure to perform unless the terms of the promise provide for such liability or the government is liable to the public for the damages, and a direct action against the promisor is consistent with the terms of the contract.

In *Sussex Tool*, neither of these grounds was satisfied. There was no clear contractual language, and the village was not liable to Sussex Tool. (Sussex's claims against the village based on negligence and statutory duty were dismissed.) Had the village been liable to Sussex Tool, would this have made a difference to the resolution of the case?

(c) It was noted above that the court examines the language of the government contract in context to decide whether a member of the public is an intended beneficiary of the contract. Many government contracts are entered into under statutory authority, granted to the government agency by the legislature. To what extent might the statute authorizing the contract be relevant to the determination of whether a member of the public is an intended beneficiary? What would you look for in the statute to resolve this issue?

4. Vesting of Rights in the Beneficiary and the Power of the Original Parties to Modify the Contract

After parties have made a contract, they can usually agree to modify its terms or even to cancel it completely. However, where the contract creates a right of enforcement in a third-party beneficiary, the original parties' right to agree between themselves to adjust or terminate the contract must end at some point. If it never did, the beneficiary's right of enforcement would always be vulnerable to change or annulment. The general rule is that the parties to the contract can agree to modify or terminate it at any time until the benefit vests in the third party. However, once the benefit has vested—that is, has accrued to and become settled upon the beneficiary, the parties to the contract lose the power to alter or eliminate it. As part of its distinction between creditor and donee beneficiaries, the original Restatement provided different rules on the vesting of benefits in those two classes of beneficiaries. The benefit conferred on a donee vested immediately on execution of the contract, while a creditor beneficiary's rights vested only upon acceptance or reliance. Restatement, Second §311 eliminates that distinction and sets out a rule applicable to all intended beneficiaries:

RESTATEMENT, SECOND §311. VARIATION OF A DUTY TO A BENEFICIARY

(1) Discharge or modification of a duty to an intended beneficiary by conduct of the promisee or by a subsequent agreement between promisor and promisee is ineffective if a term of the promise creating the duty so provides.

(2) In the absence of such a term, the promisor and promisee retain power to discharge or modify the duty by subsequent agreement.

(3) Such a power terminates when the beneficiary, before he receives notification of the discharge or modification, materially changes his position in justifiable reliance on the promise or brings suit on it or manifests assent to it at the request of the promisor or promisee....

■ PROBLEM 22.5

On March 1, Foxy bought some used furniture from her friend Holly for $5,000. Foxy undertook to pay Holly for the furniture by April 1. Foxy did not pay Holly on the due date. Holly became agitated and began to nag about payment. Foxy did not have the money to pay Holly, so she reluctantly decided to sell her only asset of value, a diamond pendant left to her by her mother. On April 20 she entered into a contract with Larry under which she sold him the diamond pendant for $5,000. Foxy delivered the pendant to Larry upon execution of the contract, and Larry undertook to pay the $5,000 on April 30. The contract between Larry and Foxy specified that Larry would not make the payment to Foxy, but would instead pay the money to Holly. On April 21, Foxy told Holly that she had arranged for Larry to pay the $5,000 to Holly by April 30. Foxy asked Holly whether she would accept that arrangement, and Holly said that she would.

On April 28 Larry told Foxy that he had just obtained an appraisal of the pendant, which was worth only $4,000. He asked Foxy whether she would agree to reduce the price to $4,000. Foxy agreed. On April 30, Larry paid $4,000 to Holly. Does Holly have the right to demand an additional $1,000 from Larry?

5. Defenses Available to the Promisor Against the Beneficiary

The contract between the promisor and promisee that creates the rights conferred on the beneficiary also circumscribes them. This means that the beneficiary becomes entitled to no more than the performance promised, delimited by any qualifications and conditions provided for in the contract. It also means that the beneficiary acquires the right to that performance subject to any contractual defenses that may have been raised by the promisor if enforcement of the promise had been sought by the promisee. Therefore, if, for example, the contract had been induced by fraud, duress, or mistake; or if the promisee had breached in rendering her own performance; or if the performance had become impracticable; the promisor can avail himself of these defenses in a suit by the beneficiary. In addition, the promisor can raise against the beneficiary any claim or defense that arises from the beneficiary's own conduct.

The rule on vesting is, in a sense, an exception to the general principle that a beneficiary acquires no greater rights than the promisee had. A subsequent contract between the promisor and promisee to modify or cancel the original contract binds the parties and may be raised by the promisor against the promisee. However, the subsequent contract does not bind the beneficiary if the contract was entered into after the right has vested.

The promisor may only raise a defense against the beneficiary if it arises out of the contract itself. He cannot assert a defense against the beneficiary that stems from a different transaction with the promisee and that would be in the nature of a counterclaim rather than a defense based on the contract.

■ PROBLEM 22.6

As in Problem 22.5, Foxy sold her diamond pendant to Larry for $5,000, and the parties agreed that Larry would pay the price to Holly on April 30. Foxy told Holly of this arrangement, and she agreed to accept it.

(a) Larry took the pendant to have it appraised for insurance purposes. On April 25 the appraiser told him that the stone was not a diamond but cut glass. On further inquiry, Larry established that Foxy had known this at the time of sale and that she had fraudulently misrepresented the stone to be a diamond. Larry returned the pendant to Foxy and refuses to pay anything to Holly. Is he liable to Holly for $5,000?

(b) Contrary to the facts in Question (a), the diamond is genuine and worth the full price of $5,000. While backing out of Larry's driveway after delivering the pendant to him, Foxy negligently drove into an expensive marble gatepost at the foot of Larry's driveway. It will cost $5,000 to repair the gatepost. Is Larry still liable to Holly for $5,000?

---

6. The Promisee's Rights of Enforcement

We have seen that an intended beneficiary acquires an independent right of enforcement against the promisor. What impact does this have on the enforcement rights of the promisee who would normally (in the absence of a contract for the benefit of a third party) be the person to enforce the promisor's obligation? Restatement, Second §305(1) provides: "A promise in a contract creates a duty in the promisor to the promisee to perform the promise even though he also has a similar duty to an intended beneficiary." Subsection 305(2) makes it clear that although the promisor may owe the duty to both the promisee and the beneficiary, the duty to the promisee is discharged to the extent of performance to the beneficiary. Restatement, Second §307 provides that either the promisee or the beneficiary may seek specific performance of the promise where that remedy is appropriate. This leaves open the question of whether the promisee may sue the promisor for damages. Although the Restatement, Second, has largely dispensed with the distinction between donee and creditor beneficiaries, this distinction retains significance in this area, as the next case shows.

In re MARRIAGE OF SMITH & MAESCHER

21 Cal. App. 4th 100, 26 Cal. Rptr. 2d 133 (1993)
California Court of Appeal

WORK, Associate Justice.

Donald Maescher appeals an order requiring him to reimburse his former wife, Daphne Smith, for education expenses she advanced to their son Peter for his senior year of college. He contends their marital separation agreement defining his obligation to pay college expenses created a third party beneficiary contract for the breach of which only Peter could recover damages. . . . Because we conclude the law of third party beneficiary contracts gives a promisee only a remedy of specific performance and, at best, nominal damages in a case such as this involving a donee beneficiary, the court erred in awarding Smith the moneys voluntarily loaned Peter. . . .

When Massachusetts residents, Maescher and Smith, entered into a marital separation agreement in 1976 after almost 11 years of marriage, they had two minor sons, Peter and Christopher, aged seven and five, respectively. Their agreement expressly provided that Massachusetts law would govern it and its construction. The Massachusetts judgment of divorce incorporated the agreement by reference, including a provision for child support payments. . . . [The agreement provided that the husband, Maescher, would pay monthly support for each child to his wife, Smith, until that child reached the age of 18. However, if the child attended college, Maescher agreed to provide for the child's undergraduate college education at an accredited college selected with his consent.]

Peter enrolled at Syracuse University in 1986 and Maescher paid his expenses for room, board, books, and tuition for the first three years. However, after becoming concerned with Peter's poor academic performance, Maescher told him he would initially pay only his room and incidental expenses for his senior year and would reimburse him for his tuition and other expenses only if he attained a "B" average his senior year.[4] Maescher told Peter he would have to obtain alternative financing and suggested a student loan. After Peter was denied financial assistance by the university, Smith personally loaned him the remaining money necessary to pay his tuition and other expenses for his senior year. . . . Although Peter was short of sufficient credits to graduate (a situation of which Maescher apparently was unaware), Syracuse University allowed him to participate in graduation ceremonies in May 1990, even though he received passing grades in only three of the eleven classes he entered during his senior year. He failed the only class he attended of the six he signed up for that spring

---

[4] By letter dated July 10, 1989, Maescher advised Smith of his intent, and that Peter would have to obtain a student loan or rely on the "largesse of his mother."

semester, and Maescher then presented a gift of $10,000 to Peter which he suggested be used to repay Smith for her loan to him. Smith refused the money when offered by Peter, and she suggested he use it for other purposes. . . . On January 9, 1991, Smith filed a complaint to . . . recover $11,109 for amounts she advanced to Peter for his senior year of college. . . . [T]he court . . . granted her request for $11,109 in college expenses advanced to Peter. . . . [Maescher also stopped making support payments to Smith for Peter and his brother after each of them turned 18. As part of this suit, Smith sought to recover arrears in support payments. The portion of the opinion relating to the support payments is omitted.]

We first address Maescher's contention that the court erred in awarding Smith $11,109 for the money she loaned to Peter for his senior year of college. The court relied upon the language of the separation agreement in awarding these damages to Smith. The parties agree the separation agreement made Peter an intended third party beneficiary as to college expenses. The pivotal issue in this dispute is whether Smith may maintain a damage action for breach of the third party beneficiary contract. Maescher contends only Peter may enforce the contract. Although he correctly states intended third party beneficiaries may enforce contracts, he cites no authority that *only* third party beneficiaries may enforce the contract. Rather, it is clear the promisee also has a right to enforce the contract. . . . Since Massachusetts law governs the agreement, we look particularly to generally accepted contract principles and Massachusetts case law. The Restatement Second of Contracts [§307] acknowledges the right of a promisee to at least one form of remedy (i.e., specific performance). . . . Maescher cites no Massachusetts cases, and we find none, which preclude a promisee from enforcing a third party beneficiary contract. To the contrary, Massachusetts case law appears to fully support a promisee's right to enforce the contract. As one Massachusetts court stated: "Whatever the standing of a child to enforce provisions in a contract made for its benefit . . . , it is clear that a party to such a contract may enforce it." (*Mills v. Mills*, 4 Mass. App. 273, 345 N.E.2d 915, 918 (1976)). Further, third party beneficiaries are not indispensable parties to a promisee's action to enforce the contract. Thus, we conclude Smith, as a promisee, has a right to enforce Maescher's promise to pay for Peter's college education.

However, the trial court apparently jumped from this premise to conclude Smith was entitled to bring an action for damages. Whether she may recover damages depends on whether Peter was an intended "creditor" or "donee" beneficiary. The former type of beneficiary receives payment from the promisor of a debt or other obligation owed the beneficiary by the promisee, whereas the latter type does not and essentially receives a "gift" in the form of the promisor's obligation to it. (Rest. 2d Contracts, §302, com. b & com. c.) If a promisor does not pay the promisee's debt to the creditor beneficiary, then the promisee will remain liable to the beneficiary for the full amount of the debt and could directly suffer damages in this full amount. In contrast, if the promisor does not perform its obligation to the donee beneficiary, the promisee will not be liable to the beneficiary for such performance and presumably will suffer only nominal damages. In both cases, however, as we noted above, the promisee may have a right to enforce the contract by obtaining specific performance against the promisor. As the Restatement Second of Contracts, section 305, comment a, states:

> The promisee of a promise for the benefit of a beneficiary has the same right to performance as any other promisee. . . . If the promisee has no economic interest in the performance, as in many cases involving gift promises, the ordinary remedy of damages for breach of contract is an inadequate remedy, since only nominal damages can be recovered. In such cases specific performance is commonly appropriate. In the ordinary case of a promise to pay the promisee's debt, on the other hand, the promisee may suffer substantial damages as a result of breach by the promisor. So long as there is no conflict with rights of the beneficiary or the promisor, he is entitled to recover such damages.

A promisee cannot recover damages which may be suffered by the intended third party beneficiary, although the promisee may sue for specific performance of the promisor's obligation. . . . Neither California nor Massachusetts case law appears to have dealt with these specific issues, so we adopt and apply the principles set forth in the Restatement Second of Contracts.

The record contains no evidence supporting a conclusion Smith had a legal obligation to pay Peter's college expenses if Maescher did not. . . . [T]here is nothing . . . [in law] or in the judgment of divorce requiring Smith to pay for Peter's college education expenses, nor, for that matter, any maintenance after he became 18. Nor do they require Maescher to pay such expenses, except for the specific contractual language of the separation agreement incorporated into the judgment of divorce. Thus, while Maescher's obligation to pay Peter's college expenses arises out of the separation agreement, Smith has no legal obligation to pay such expenses. Accordingly, if Maescher were to fail to pay Peter's college expenses, Peter would have no legal recourse against Smith for payment. Thus, Peter is clearly a donee beneficiary and had a direct cause of action against Maescher for violation of that provision.

The record lacks evidence showing Smith incurred legal damages by Maescher's presumed breach of the separation agreement. Certainly, the record shows she loaned Peter the remaining money (i.e., $11,109) necessary to attend his senior year of college, but she *voluntarily* made that loan without any legal obligation to do so. She has not claimed Peter assigned her his rights against Maescher. Thus, Smith has no right to collect the loaned money from Maescher.[5] Since Peter is not a party to this action, the court had no legal authority to award Smith $11,109 in damages against Maescher. As a result,

---

[5] One who voluntarily pays the debts of another generally has no right to seek recovery from that person whose debts were paid, absent any agreement to the contrary.

we reverse this portion of the order. . . . The order awarding Smith $11,109 in damages for college expenses . . . is reversed.

■ QUESTIONS

(1)　The court has little trouble in finding Peter to have been an intended beneficiary. Could a plausible argument have been made that he was not an intended beneficiary? What impact would such a finding have had on the outcome of the case?

(2)　Smith would apparently have had a better chance of success had she sued for specific performance. (By the way, why is a suit to recover a payment promised under a contract not for specific performance?) Presumably, had she sued for specific performance, Maescher would have been ordered to pay the $11,109 to Peter. But remember that Peter has already received that amount from his mother, and he also received a gift of $10,000 from his father. Therefore, it sounds as if Peter would have received just over three times his fourth year's tuition, even though (as the facts seem to suggest) he may have flunked out of college. Is there something wrong here?

(3)　The basis for allowing damages to a promisor where the beneficiary is a creditor is that if the promisor does not pay, the promisee remains liable. By contrast, because a gift cannot be enforced against the promisee, nonpayment of the gift does not result in damages to the promisee. However, in this case, Smith did suffer financial loss. Does this mean that the distinction between a creditor and a donee beneficiary is inappropriate in this case?

B ASSIGNMENT AND DELEGATION

1. The Transfer of Contract Rights and Duties

In most situations, when parties perform under a contract, each of them renders performance to the other. However, it sometimes happens that one of the parties may wish to dispose of her rights or duties under the contract—to transfer them to someone else who was not an original party to the contract. She may wish to transfer only her rights under the contract, or she may wish only to deputize someone else to perform her duties, or she may wish to do both—to dispose of her rights and duties. This section deals with the law governing such transfers.

It is useful to get the terminology straight from the outset: The transfer of a right is called "assignment," and the transfer of a duty is called "delegation." When a right is assigned, the party who transferred the right is the obligee (the person who is owed the right) under the original contract and, upon assignment, is called the assignor. The person who acquires the right is called the assignee. The party who owes the right under the original contract, and whose obligation now runs to the assignee, is called the obligor. For example, a builder entered into a contract with a homeowner under which the builder undertook to remodel the homeowner's bathroom for $10,000. A week later, the builder assigned his right to payment of the $10,000 to a friend in exchange for a used truck. The builder is the assignor, his friend is the assignee, and the home-owner is the obligor. When a duty is delegated, the person who transfers the duty is called the obligor (or is sometimes referred to as the delegator), and the person to whom the duty has been transferred is called the delegate. The party to the original contract to whom the delegated duty is owed is called the obligee. If, in the above example, the builder had delegated his duty to perform the remodeling job to another contractor, the builder would be the obligor, the other contractor would be the delegate, and the homeowner would be the obligee.

Instead of assigning only his rights or delegating only his duties, the builder may have decided to transfer the whole package of his rights and duties under the contract to the other contractor—that is, to have the other contractor do the remodeling job and to get paid directly by the homeowner. This is sometimes referred to as an assignment of the contract, but it is more correctly described as both an assignment of the contractor's rights and a delegation of his duties.

2. Assignment: General Principles

We begin by dealing with the assignment of rights under a contract. We wait until Section B.6 to consider the delegation of duties under a contract, either in conjunction with the assignment of rights or alone. As you might expect, a party's attempt to substitute someone else to perform his obligations raises different issues from the transfer of his right to receive performance.

Assignment is the present transfer of a right, so the right passes from the assignor to the assignee. An effective assignment extinguishes the right in the assignor, and it can thereafter be enforced only by the assignee. Although we are concerned here with the assignment of contract rights, it is possible to have an assignment of rights other than those created by contract. For example, the right could arise from tort or from some other source.

Whatever the source of the right, its assignment is commonly effected by a contract between the assignor and assignee under which the assignor transfers the right to the assignee in exchange for payment or some other agreed con-sideration. Although assignment by contract is usual, it is not the only way in which a right may be assigned. For example, the holder of a right may transfer it gratuitously—that is, the assignor may make a gift of the right for which he gets no consideration from the assignee. It is even possible for a right to be taken from the transferor involuntarily and without his agreement. For example, a creditor of the holder of a right may use the court process of garnishment to force transfer of the right to satisfy a judgment debt. Our focus is on a contract between an assignor and an assignee under which the assignor transfers rights that he has under a contract with the obligor. Therefore, for present purposes it is useful to think of assignment as involving two separate contracts. The first is the contract between the assignor and the obligor that creates the right. (In the above example, this is the contract between the builder and the homeowner to remodel the bathroom.) The second is a contract between the assignor and the assignee, under which the right is transferred. (In the example, this is the contract between the builder and his friend under which the right to payment was exchanged for the truck.)

Notice that the sets of relationships described here are quite different from those created by a contract for the benefit of a third party, in which the parties to the original contract intend from the outset to confer a right of enforcement on the third party. Here, the assignee does not acquire rights by virtue of some special provision in the original contract but rather through a later transaction with one of the original parties under which he takes over that party's contract rights.

For many centuries, the common law regarded contract rights as very different from rights in land or chattels. While land and chattels were property, contract rights were conceived of as merely the incidents of a personal relationship, not as assets that could be sold or transferred. Such a distinction may have been tenable in a primitive, land-based society, but it became less viable as the economy became more complex and the economic value of intangible rights became more prominent. The economy began to depend upon commerce not only in goods and land but in rights themselves. First the courts of equity, and later the courts of law, came to recognize that the owner of a right should be able to deal with it as property—to sell it, to use it as collateral for a loan, or to give it away as a gift. In modern law it has long been established without question that an intangible right, including the right to performance under a contract, is an economic asset that constitutes property. Surely an intangible right is different from land or goods, which have physical existence, but it is nevertheless property that can be sold or otherwise transferred. The concept of rights as property is reflected in the name by which they came to be known: "chose in action." "Chose" is a French word meaning "thing." By calling a right a "thing," the law designates it as something that can be owned. The phrase "chose in action" distinguishes intangible property from tangible personal property, known as a "chose in possession."

In the modern economy, contract rights are routinely dealt with in commerce, either because the owner wishes to realize their value by selling them or because he wants to use them as security in a credit transaction. For example, a retailer, such as a furniture dealer, sells goods to a customer on credit. At this point, the retailer has a contract with the customer under which the customer has agreed to pay for the goods sometime in the future, commonly in monthly installments. The retailer may not wish to wait for the customer's monthly payments to trickle in because it needs cash immediately to operate its business. To raise these funds, the retailer makes a second contract with a finance company under which the retailer sells its contract right against the customer (the customer's debt) to the finance company for cash. The finance company pays the retailer an agreed amount (the price of the contract right will typically be less than the face value of the claim to take into account factors such as the risk that the customer will default) and takes transfer of the retailer's contract right to collect the debt from the customer. On completion of this transaction, the finance company has bought the right to the customer's performance under the furniture contract, and the customer is notified to make payments directly to the finance company. Upon being notified of the assignment, the customer is obliged to make payments to the finance company, not to the retailer.

In the above example, the assignment was a sale, but the transfer, like the transfer of tangible property, could be for any other purpose that the assignee and assignor desire. For example, the retailer may not wish to sell the contract right but merely to use it as collateral to secure a loan from the finance company. In that case, the assignment could be made as security in the same way that a house or car can be used to secure a loan. The retailer still owns the contract right, but it grants a security interest in the right to the finance company. If the retailer defaults on its loan, the finance company can take over the right and use the proceeds to settle the retailer's debt.

Because contract rights are property, the general rule is that they can be freely transferred by their owner. However, this type of property has an important feature that distinguishes it from a house or car—the right transferred implicates someone beyond the parties to the transfer. That is, of course, the obligor—the person who has the obligation to perform the duty. In the above examples, the third party is the customer who bought the goods from the retailer. This adds some complexity to the transfer of rights that is not present in the transfer of tangible property. Restatement, Second §317 describes the assignment of a right and sets out some of the qualifications that are engendered by the nature of the property transferred.

RESTATEMENT, SECOND §317. ASSIGNMENT OF A RIGHT

(1) An assignment of a right is a manifestation of the assignor's intention to transfer it by virtue of which the assignor's right to performance by the obligor is extinguished in whole or in part and the assignee acquires a right to such performance.

(2) A contractual right can be assigned unless

(a) the substitution of a right of the assignee for the right of the assignor would materially change the duty of the obligor, or materially increase the burden or risk imposed on him by his contract, or materially impair his chance of obtaining return performance, or materially reduce its value to him, or

(b) the assignment is forbidden by statute or is otherwise inoperative on grounds of public policy, or

(c) assignment is validly precluded by contract.

Notice that while Restatement, Second §317(2) deals specifically with contract rights, §317(1) is more general and is not confined to contract rights. There are three points to note about §317(1):

First, §317(1) sets out the general principle that all rights, whether created by contract or otherwise (such as a right to damages for tort or a right arising from a statute) may be assigned. This general rule is subject to some exceptions based on public policy, so that the assignment of certain kinds of tort claims or statutory rights may be prohibited by statute or common law.

Second, §317(1) describes assignment only in terms of the assignor's manifestation of intention to transfer the right. This language recognizes that assignment does not have to be effected by contract; it can be achieved by the assignor's unilateral act, as would happen when the right is transferred gratuitously. The promise of a gratuitous assignment, like any other promise of gift, is not enforceable because it lacks consideration. The assignment of a right (again, like the conveyance of a gift of tangible property) therefore only becomes effective and binding (irrevocable by the assignor) once it has been executed. The question of whether the gift has been executed can be more difficult where the gift is an assignment of rights rather than the transfer of tangible property. It is usually easy to tell if a gift of tangible property has been executed, because there will usually be some observable evidence of transfer, such as a change of physical possession or (if title to the property is required to be recorded), a transfer of title. However, one cannot physically deliver an intangible right in the same way. The law generally treats the gift of a right as executed either when some document representing the right is delivered to the assignee or the assignee acts in reliance on the assignment.

Third, by speaking in general terms about a manifestation of assent, §317(1) indicates that no special formalities are needed for an assignment. The intent to assign can be shown by oral or written words or by conduct. (However, if the contract of assignment is of a type that is subject to a statute of frauds, there must be a signed writing to satisfy the statute.)

If the right to be assigned derives from the sale of goods, the assignment is covered by UCC Article 2 rather than by Restatement, Second §317. Article 2 has provisions that are largely similar to §317 in general effect, although somewhat different in nuance:

UCC 2-210(2) . . . ASSIGNMENT OF RIGHTS

Except as otherwise provided in Section 9-406,[6] unless otherwise agreed, all rights of either seller or buyer can be assigned except where the assignment would materially change the duty of the other party, or increase materially the burden or risk imposed on him by his contract, or impair materially his chance of obtaining return performance. A right to damages for breach of the whole contract or a right arising out of the assignor's due performance of his entire obligation can be assigned despite agreement otherwise.

In most cases, the obligor is likely to be indifferent about whether his obligation of performance has been assigned by the obligee. As long as the obligor receives what he has bargained for under the contract, he does not much care whether he must render performance to the original obligee under the contract or to some other person selected by the obligee. Therefore, upon being notified that the right has been assigned, the obligor usually makes no objection and performs in favor of the assignee. However, sometimes the obligor objects on the basis that the assignment diminishes or defeats his own rights under the contract. Where a plausible claim of such prejudice is asserted, the court must balance the policy of free assignability of rights against that of protecting the reasonable contract expectations of the obligor.

Managed Health Care Associates, Inc. v. Kethan, 209 F.3d 923 (6th Cir. 2000), illustrates the application of the general principles of assignment in relation to a noncompetition clause in an employment agreement. In December 1991, Ronald Kethan entered into an employment agreement with MedEcon Services, Inc., an organization that made group and bulk purchases of medical supplies for a consortium of healthcare facilities. The contract contained a noncompetition clause, which provided that Kethan would not "... during the term of this agreement and for a period of two (2) years after the termination thereof ... directly or indirectly ... solicit or cause any past, present or future ... customers ... of the Company or of any of ... [its] subsidiaries or affiliates ... to transfer all or part of their business ... or render competitive services to any such customers ... [or] engage in any of the kinds of business activities in which

---

[6] As noted previously, contract rights, like other property, may be used as collateral to secure a debt; that is, the right is not sold outright for cash; it is transferred to a lender to secure a loan. If the assignor fails to repay the loan, the lender (assignee) may take over the right and use the proceeds to satisfy the unpaid debt. UCC Article 9 generally governs the use of personal property (including intangible rights) as collateral but also contains provisions that relate to outright assignments of rights—in particular, rights to payment for goods sold. Section 9-406, mentioned at the beginning of Section 2-210(2), makes ineffective many contract terms that purport to restrict a party's ability to assign a right to payment. As a result, assignments of rights to payment for goods are routinely enforced if they comply with Article 9. Article 9 and its provisions regarding rights to payment are beyond the scope of this book. They are covered in a course on secured transactions.

the Company or any of the Subsidiaries or Affiliates have been or is now engaged within [specified states]. . . ." The contract did not directly address the issue of whether Kethan's obligations could be assigned.

From 1992 through 1998, Kethan worked as a salesman and an agreement administrator for MedEcon. He formed strong business relationships with many of MedEcon's customers and became particularly close to one customer, First Choice Cooperative, whose account he administered. In 1998, MedEcon's assets were bought by a competing group purchase organization, MHA. MedEcon's employment agreement with Kethan was included in the bundle of assets bought by MHA. Kethan never consented to the assignment. He continued to work for MHA as an at-will employee for about three weeks. He performed the same job, received the same salary and benefits, and reported to the same supervisor as before. He then resigned and went to work for First Choice.

MHA sued Kethan and First Choice, seeking an injunction to prevent Kethan from violating the noncompetition clause that he had signed when employed by MedEcon. The district court held that the noncompetition agreement was enforceable only by MedEcon and that it was not assignable by MedEcon to MHA without Kethan's consent. It therefore denied MHA's request for an injunction. The court of appeals reversed, holding that the noncompetition clause was assignable. It remanded the case for the district court to decide the merits of the motion for an injunction. The court stated the general principle that a contract is generally assignable unless the terms of the contract or public policy make it nonassignable, or it is clear that the personal relationship between the parties is a crucial feature of the contract. The court found none of these barriers to assignment. The contract had no express provisions forbidding assignment. There was no public policy against the assignment of a noncompetition clause that protects the legitimate interests of the employer and is reasonable in scope, geographic extent, and duration. The clause involved in this case satisfied these standards. Kethan, taking advantage of the opportunity gained while in the employ of MedEcon, left to work for a client with whom he had formed a special relationship, and took the client's business with him. The court considered that this was precisely the type of situation that the noncompetition clause was fairly designed to avoid. The court also rejected the argument that the contract in this case was nonassignable because it was for personal services. The court said that the noncompetition clause did not involve personal services. Rather, it only required that Kethan abstain from certain activities.

■ **PROBLEM 22.7**

Assume that Kethan had a two-year employment contract with MedEcon. Six months after his employment commenced, MedEcon sold its assets (that is, its business) to MHA. As part of the sale, it assigned its rights under the employment contract to MHA. Assume that MHA's management style is very different from that of MedEcon. MedEcon had been very employee-oriented and had taken great pains to keep its workers happy by maintaining a supportive, friendly, and nurturing work environment. It placed vases of flowers in the common areas, provided coffee and donuts, tolerated pets in the office (as long as they did not chew up corporate documents), and insisted that supervisors were always respectful to subordinates.

By contrast, MHA cares only about the bottom line. Its supervisors are discouraged from fraternizing with associates and are expected to take ruthless action to ensure that high levels of production are maintained. It does not waste money on flowers, donuts, or coffee. In fact, it does not even allow employees to bring their own donuts or coffee onto the premises because it forbids eating during working hours. Pets are not allowed, and the only animals found on company premises are the guard dogs trained to sniff employees for contraband food and drugs. MHA's offices are dark and chilly because it keeps heating and lighting at minimum levels to save costs.

Assume that the only contract rights that employees have are to be paid, not to be discriminated against unfairly, and to have sanitary and safe working conditions. MHA's rigorous regime does not offend any of these rights. Beyond these basic rights, the office environment is purely within the employer's discretion. Does Kethan have grounds to object to the assignment?

3. Assignments That Violate Public Policy

In Section A.2 we discussed *Noble v. Bruce* in which the court declined, on public policy grounds, to allow a malpractice suit against an attorney by a non-client, either on tort grounds or as a third party beneficiary. The next case discusses the public policy implications of a client's assignment of a malpractice claim against her attorney.

GURSKI v. ROSENBLUM AND FILAN, LLC

276 Conn. 257, 885 A.2d 163 (2005)
Connecticut Supreme Court

KATZ, Justice.

[Susan Lee sued Walter Gurski, a podiatrist, for malpractice. She claimed that his negligent treatment of her feet injured her. Gurski was represented in the suit by the law firm of Rosenberg and Filan, LLC ("the law firm"). Lee eventually got judgment against Gurski. Gurski alleged that he lost the suit because the law firm had acted negligently in representing him. He therefore claimed to have a cause of action against the law firm for malpractice.

Gurski did not have the funds to pay Lee's claim, so they entered into an agreement under which Gurski assigned his malpractice claim against the law firm to Lee in full settlement of her claim against him. Lee sued the law firm in Gurski's name. The jury found that the law firm had committed malpractice in representing Gurski and awarded damages. The law firm moved for a directed verdict and then for a judgment notwithstanding the verdict, both of which the trial court denied.]

. . . The law firm claims, inter alia, that the trial court improperly denied its motion for a directed verdict and its motion for judgment notwithstanding the verdict because . . . Gurski's action against the law firm had been an invalid assignment of a legal malpractice action and thus void as against public policy. . . . In deciding this question, we begin with certain general principles that typically guide our inquiry as to the issue of assignability. In *Rumbin v. Utica Mutual Ins. Co.*, 254 Conn. 259, 267-68, 757 A.2d 526 (2000), we recognized, with respect to assignment of contract claims, "the modern approach to contracts reject[ing] traditional common-law restrictions on the alienability of contract rights in favor of free assignability of contracts. . . . Common-law restrictions on assignment were abandoned when courts recognized the necessity of permitting the transfer of contract rights. The force[s] of human convenience and business practice [were] too strong for the common-law doctrine that [intangible contract rights] are not assignable. . . ."

We have taken a contrary position, however, with respect to whether a tort claim can be assigned, at least when the claim is based on personal injury. In *Dodd v. Middlesex Mutual Assurance Co.*, 242 Conn. 375, 384, 698 A.2d 859 (1997) . . . we acknowledged certain well settled principles as to such assignments: "Under common law a cause of action for personal injuries cannot be assigned, and in the absence of a statutory provision to the contrary a right of action for personal injuries resulting from negligence is not assignable before judgment. . . . It seems that few legal principles are as well settled, and as universally agreed upon, as the rule that the common law does not permit assignments of causes of action to recover for personal injuries. . . . The reasons underlying the rule have been variously stated: unscrupulous interlopers and litigious persons were to be discouraged from purchasing claims for pain and suffering and prosecuting them in court as assignees; actions for injuries that in the absence of statute did not survive the death of the victim were deemed too personal in nature to be assignable; a tortfeasor was not to be held liable to a party unharmed by him; and excessive litigation was thought to be reduced."

Because an action for legal malpractice can be pleaded either in contract or in tort, neither *Dodd* nor *Rumbin*, nor their labels, are helpful in the present case.[7] Therefore, rather than strain to fit each legal malpractice claim into a category often determined by counsel based on concerns not relevant to the inquiry at hand, we think the better approach is to resolve the issue uniformly on the basis of public policy. *See Picadilly, Inc. v. Raikos*, 582 N.E.2d 338, 341 (Ind. 1991) (noting that several jurisdictions have recognized that legal malpractice could be characterized as either assignable contract actions or nonassignable personal injury actions and instead have determined issue on basis of public policy).

Although this appeal raises an issue of first impression in Connecticut, many other jurisdictions have considered whether a legal malpractice claim may be assigned. A majority of those jurisdictions have concluded that legal malpractice claims are not assignable based on several overlapping public policy considerations. Many of those courts discuss the unique and personal nature of the relationship between attorney and client and the need to preserve the sanctity of that relationship as a reason for prohibiting the assignment. . . . In that same vein, courts also have pointed to the incompatibility of the assignment and the attorney's duty of loyalty and confidentiality in rejecting assignments of legal malpractice claims. . . . Courts also have cautioned that permitting the assignment of legal malpractice claims would encourage the commercialization of such claims and in turn spawn increased and unwarranted malpractice actions. . . . In rejecting the assignment of a legal malpractice claim as against public policy, courts also have expressed concern that allowing an assignment would make attorneys hesitant to represent insolvent, underinsured or judgment proof defendants for fear that the malpractice claims would be used as tender. . . . The final consideration cited by several jurisdictions barring assignment of legal malpractice claims pertains specifically to an assignment of such a claim to the adverse party in the underlying action and the potential for a reversal of roles that could undermine the legitimacy of malpractice judgment.

In examining all of the aforementioned considerations, we are not persuaded that every voluntary assignment of a legal malpractice action should be barred as a matter of law. Indeed, there is a significant minority view that rejects a per se bar on assignments, questioning the rationale of some of the public policy considerations cited by the majority view and favoring instead a case-by-case determination when meritorious public policy concerns actually are implicated. . . . Notably, however, of those jurisdictions that permit the assignment of a legal malpractice claim on a case-by-case basis, two jurisdictions, Texas and Washington, preclude assignment of legal malpractice actions when, as here, the assignment is to an adverse party in the underlying action. . . . Thus, although not instituting a per se rule precluding a voluntary assignment, these courts have echoed the policy concerns cited by the majority

---

[7] Indeed, it would make no sense to craft a rule, ostensibly based on public policy considerations, regarding the assignability of a legal malpractice action that the parties simply could avoid based on how they frame their pleadings.

jurisdictions that disapprove of an assignment to an adverse party in the under-lying action because it would necessitate a duplicitous change in the positions taken by the parties in the antecedent litigation.

Perhaps the best discussion of the problems associated with an assignment under these circumstances is in *Zuniga v. Groce, Locke & Hebdon*, 878 S.W.2d 313 at 318 (Tex. App. 1994). In barring the assignment of the malpractice claim arising from litigation, the Texas Court of Appeals recognized therein that, "[t]he two litigants would have to take positions diametrically opposed to their positions during the underlying litigation because the legal malpractice case requires a 'suit within a suit.' . . . For the law to countenance this abrupt and shameless shift of positions would give prominence (and substance) to the image that lawyers will take any position, depending upon where the money lies, and that litigation is a mere game and not a search for truth. . . . It is one thing for lawyers in our adversary system to represent clients with whom they per-sonally disagree; it is something quite different for lawyers (and clients) to switch positions concerning the same incident simply because an assignment and the law of proximate cause have given them a financial interest in switching."

This counterintuitive claim and reversal of roles, requiring the assignee to bring a claim for legal malpractice when she was the very party who benefited from that malpractice in the underlying litigation, would engender a perversion that would erode public confidence in the legal system. Permitting an assign-ment of a legal malpractice claim to the adversary in the underlying litigation that gave rise to the legal malpractice claim also creates the opportunity and incentive for collusion in stipulating to damages in exchange for an agreement not to execute on the judgment in the underlying litigation. Thus, the Texas and Washington courts, although adopting the minority position against a per se bar, nonetheless have agreed with the majority view that these policy considera-tions were compelling reasons to bar the assignment of a legal malpractice claim to an adversary in the underlying litigation that gave rise to the legal malpractice claim.

In the present case, Lee sued Gurski in the underlying action alleging that Gurski had been negligent in his treatment of her. In Gurski's legal malpractice action, in order to prevail, he would have had to prove that he had not been negligent and that he would have prevailed in Lee's medical malpractice action against him but for his law firm's negligence. Once Gurski assigned any or all of the interest in the malpractice action to Lee, however, the interests of these two former adversaries merged, and Lee had a vested interest in the jury's determi-nation that Gurski had *not* been negligent.

Under these circumstances, we agree with the reasoning of the Texas and Washington courts that public policy considerations warrant the barring of an assignment of a legal malpractice action to an adversary in the underlying litigation. . . . [I]ndependent of other public policy considerations—allowing assignments would: convert a legal malpractice action into a commodity; under-mine the sanctity of the attorney-client relationship; result in decreasing the availability of legal services to insolvent clients; impact negatively on the duty of confidentiality and further the commercialization of malpractice claims that in turn would spawn an increase in unwarranted malpractice actions—we conclude that the assignment of a malpractice action to an adverse party in the underlying action creates a distortion that the profession cannot endure and thus should not tolerate. . . .

The judgment is reversed and the case is remanded with direction to render judgment for the law firm.

■ QUESTIONS

(1) The court identifies several policy reasons why malpractice claims should not be assignable at all and notes that the majority of courts have held, based on those policy reasons, that malpractice claims are absolutely nonassignable. However, it declines to follow the majority approach. Why does the court not follow the majority view? Do you think that the court made the correct decision?

(2) Although liability to a third-party beneficiary arises under circumstances very different from liability to an assignee, it is interesting to see that similar public policy issues arise in both situations. Why do you think that is so?

(3) Although the court refuses to find that the assignment of a malpractice claim is contrary to public policy in all cases, it refuses to allow the assignment to an adverse party. The effect of this is that Gurski, who cannot pay Lee's judgment against him, is prevented from settling the suit by assigning his claim against the law firm to Lee. Is this fair? After all, it seems that the firm was in some way responsible for Gurski losing the suit in the first place. Do you think that this consideration should trump the policies against allowing the assignment?

4. Anti-Assignment Clauses

The third basis for precluding assignment under Restatement, Second §317 is that the contract itself validly forbids it. This provision is expanded upon by Restatement, Second §322:

RESTATEMENT, SECOND §322. CONTRACTUAL PROHIBITION OF ASSIGNMENT

(1) Unless the circumstances indicate the contrary, a contract term prohibiting assignment of "the contract" bars only the delegation to an assignee of the performance by the assignor of a duty or condition.

(2) A contract term prohibiting assignment of rights under the contract, unless a different intention is manifested,

   (a) does not forbid assignment of a right to damages for breach of the whole contract or a right arising out of the assignor's due performance of his entire obligation;

   (b) gives the obligor a right to damages for breach of the terms forbidding assignment but does not render the assignment ineffective;

   (c) is for the benefit of the obligor, and does not prevent the assignee from acquiring rights against the assignor or the obligor from discharging his duty as if there were no such prohibition.

———

UCC 2-210(4) has a provision parallel to Restatement, Second §322(1): "Unless the circumstances indicate the contrary a prohibition of assignment of 'the contract' is to be construed as barring only the delegation to the assignee of the assignor's performance."

■ PROBLEM 22.8

In *Liberty Life Assurance Co. of Boston v. Stone Street Capital, Inc.*, 93 F. Supp. 2d 630 (D. Md. 2000), Liberty Mutual Insurance Company entered into a settlement agreement with James White, who had been injured in an automobile accident. The settlement was a "structured settlement"—it did not pay the claim in a lump sum, but by periodic payments over time. Under the settlement, White received an initial payment of $162,500 and was to receive additional monthly payments of $1,000 for the rest of his life.

To fund the payments, Liberty Mutual followed the common practice of assigning the payment obligation to another insurance company, Keyport Life Insurance Company. Keyport, in turn, purchased an annuity from Liberty Life Assurance Company to fund the settlement. In essence, Liberty Mutual paid a lump sum to Keyport in exchange for Keyport's assumption of liability under the settlement. Keyport then used this lump sum to purchase the annuity from Liberty Life. The reason for this financial arrangement was that it resulted in favorable tax consequences for both Liberty Mutual and Keyport. Liberty Mutual could immediately deduct the full amount of its payment to Keyport from its current income. Keyport would not have to pay tax until it received the annuity payments from Liberty Life. Because it could offset its payment to White against this income, it would not actually have to pay any tax on it at all. The settlement agreement mentioned the Internal Revenue Service regulations that afforded this advantageous tax treatment, and made it clear that Liberty Mutual had the right to enter into such a transaction.

Although the agreement allowed Liberty Mutual to assign its payment obligation, it prohibited White from assigning his right to the periodic payments. It stated that White "... acknowledges that the Periodic Payments cannot be accelerated, deferred, increased, or decreased ... nor shall ... [White] have the power to sell, mortgage, encumber, or anticipate the Periodic Payments, or any part thereof, by assignment or otherwise."

However, White did not want to wait for the periodic payments, so he sold the right to the annuity payments to Stone Street Capital, Inc. Stone Street paid White the present value of the settlement and took assignment of his right to the annuity payments.

Liberty Life and Keyport sued White and Stone Street for a declaratory judgment that White's assignment of his rights to Stone Street was invalid. The court held that the anti-assignment clause in the settlement precluded the assignment. The court applied the principles set out in Restatement, Second §317(2)(a), and found that the assignment materially increased the burden and risk imposed on the obligor. This was because White's assignment of his right to payment placed in doubt whether Liberty Mutual and Keyport would be able to obtain the tax advantages of their transaction. IRS regulations set out very exacting requirements for the favorable tax treatment, and there was at least some question of whether White's assignment of his payment right made the transaction ineligible for that treatment. The court found that the creation of this uncertainty materially increased the risk and burden on Liberty Mutual and Keyport.

The court also found that White's assignment offended Restatement, Second §317(2)(c) because the right to assign was validly precluded by contract. It noted that §322(2)(b) provides that unless a different intent is manifested, a contractual prohibition of assignment gives the obligor a right to damages for breach but does not render the assignment ineffective. This has led courts to distinguish a party's right to assign from its power to assign, so that a party may be able to effect a valid assignment, even if doing so constitutes a breach of contract that gives rise to a claim for damages. Many courts have held that a contract effectively precludes the power to assign only if the contract uses clear language making the assignment void.

The court found that although the settlement agreement did not expressly declare that an assignment by White would be void, the contract's use of the word "power" clearly indicated an intent to deprive White of both the right and the power to assign. In addition, the reference to the IRS regulations in the agreement showed that the parties intended to preclude White's effective assignment of his rights so as to secure the contemplated tax advantages.

(a) Although the court in *Liberty Life* applies the grounds for nonassignability under Restatement, Second §317(2)(a) and (c) as separate and distinct, they are obviously not treated in isolation from each other. The court uses the ground in §317(2)(a) to bolster its finding under §317(2)(c). Do you think that the court would have upheld the anti-assignment clause if the assignment had not resulted in any potential for adverse tax consequences?

(b) The court distinguishes anti-assignment provisions that preclude the power to assign from those that merely remove the right, but not the power, to assign. What is the difference? What remedy does the plaintiff-obligor get where the assignment is void? What would its remedy be if the assignment was not void but nevertheless a violation of the anti-assignment clause?

5. The Effect of Assignment, Notice of Assignment, and the Obligor's Defenses Against the Assignee

As mentioned previously, an assignment is commonly effected by a contract between the assignor and the assignee under which the assignee gives some consideration to the assignor in exchange for the transfer of a right. As a result of this bargain, the assignee acquires the right to substitute for the assignor as the person entitled to receive and to enforce the assigned performance of the obligor. However, until the obligor is informed about the assignment, the agreement between the assignee and assignor creates rights between them only; it does not yet bind the obligor to perform in favor of the assignee instead of the assignor. The obligor becomes bound to the assignee only when she is given notice of the assignment so that she has reason to know that her performance is no longer due to the assignor, but to the assignee. Therefore, if she renders her performance to the assignor before being notified of the assignment, her obligations are discharged to the extent of that performance, and she does not have to perform again to the assignee. However, once she is notified of a valid assignment, the assignee is substituted for the assignor as the party entitled to her performance, and only performance to the assignee discharges her duty. If she disregards the assignment and performs in favor of the assignor (and the assignor does not remit that performance to the assignee) the obligor remains liable to the assignee.

It is important to recognize that the assigned right comes with whatever baggage may have been attached to it under the underlying contract. We have already seen that the obligor may object to the assignment if it impairs her rights under the contract by materially changing her duty, damaging her right to return performance, increasing her burden or risk, or violating an effective anti-assignment provision. However, even where the assignment is not precluded on these grounds, it is still subject to the general principle that the assignor cannot transfer greater rights than he has. This means that the obligor can assert against the assignee any defense that she could have raised against the assignor had the right not been assigned.[8] Generally, the defense must be related to the right assigned—that is, it must arise out of the contract that gave rise to the assigned right. In addition to any defenses, the obligor may assert any claims that are related to the assigned right. However, these claims may only be asserted defensively against the assignee in reduction of the assignee's claim because (unless the assignment is accompanied by a delegation of duties) the assignee has not undertaken any duties to the obligor and is not liable to pay damages to her. The obligor can raise unrelated defenses or claims against the assignee only if they accrued before the obligor received notice of the assignment. The following problem illustrates these concepts.

■ PROBLEM 22.9

(a) On July 1, Woody Walls entered into a contract with Syd R. Plank under which Syd undertook to replace the siding on Woody's home for $20,000. The work was to be completed by not later than July 20, and the price was to be paid upon completion of the job. On July 5, Syd assigned his right to payment under the contract to Payout Finance Co. in settlement of an outstanding loan. Syd began work on July 10 and completed it on July 15. Woody paid Syd the $20,000. On July 19 he received notice from Payout informing him that Syd had assigned his payment right to Payout, and that Woody should make payment directly to Payout. Does Woody have cause for alarm?

(b) Change the facts of Question (a) as follows: On July 6, Woody received the notice of assignment from Payout. Syd began the work on July 15 and completed it on July 20. Woody was dissatisfied with the job, which he claimed was shoddy and unworkmanlike. This led to a violent argument between Woody and Syd, culminating in Syd's hitting Woody on the head with a piece of siding board. After recovering from

---

[8] There are exceptions to this general rule that an assignee takes the right subject to claims and defenses that could be asserted by the obligor against the assignor. These exceptions apply where the right is incorporated in certain types of commercial paper such as negotiable instruments and documents. We do not deal with this subject here; we leave it to courses on commercial law.

his injuries, Woody had the work inspected by experts, who have concluded that some of the siding was improperly installed and must be redone at a cost of $5,000. Woody also has a claim of $50,000 against Syd for medical expenses and pain and suffering. It is now July 30. Syd has gone out of business and has disappeared. Payout has demanded payment of the $20,000 from Woody. How much of this claim, if anything, is Woody obliged to pay to Payout? Is Payout obliged to pay anything to Woody?

(c) Change the facts of Question (b) to the following extent: At the time of contracting on July 1, Woody and Syd agreed that on completion of the job, Woody would pay the price of $20,000 to Payout Finance Co., Syd's creditor. On July 2, the parties notified Payout of this provision, and Payout agreed to it. The parties concede that Payout is an intended beneficiary of the contract whose rights vested on July 2. The remaining facts are the same as in (b). How much of the $20,000, if anything, is Woody obliged to pay to Payout? Is Payout obliged to pay anything to Woody?

6. The Delegation of Contractual Duties

So far, we have talked only about the transfer of contract rights. However, a party to a contract may wish to transfer not only his rights under the contract but also his duties. Alternatively, he may wish to keep his rights but to arrange for someone else to perform his duties. As mentioned earlier, the transfer of duties under a contract is called delegation. The delegation of duties under a contract is quite different from the assignment of rights. Although we have seen exceptions, in most cases the assignment of rights alone is not likely to have any significant impact on the other party to the contract—all it means is that he must render performance to the new person designated. For example, it usually will make no difference to the buyer of a used car on credit that she has to write out her installment check to the dealer with whom she contracted or to a finance company to which the dealer assigned the right to payment. However, the delegation of one party's duties can have a significant impact on the other party to the contract. Assume that one of the terms of the contract between the buyer and dealer was a warranty and service commitment under which the dealer was obliged to repair any defects in the car for a year. The buyer may be unhappy if, one month after the contract, the dealer sought to substitute someone else as the repairer. The buyer would be even less happy had she chosen to buy the used car from that dealer because of his reputation for reliable service.

For this reason, the delegation of contractual duties is more circumscribed than the assignment of rights. The most striking difference is that, unlike assignment, delegation does not result in a complete substitution of the delegate for the obligor. The obligor remains ultimately liable for any breach; that is, although the general rule is to permit the delegation of duties unless this violates the contract or public policy, the obligor remains accountable for the performance and can be sued by the obligee for breach if the delegate fails to perform or performs improperly. It is possible that the obligee may vary this result by an agreement known as a "novation." In a novation, the obligee agrees to accept the delegate as a complete substitute for the obligor and to release the obligor from her duties under the contract. A novation is not inferred merely from the fact that the obligee accepts performance by the delegate. The obligee's intent to enter into a novation must be clearly and expressly manifested.

While the obligor remains liable to the obligee, delegation does not in itself give the obligee the right to enforce the contract directly against the delegate. Therefore, the basic rule is that if the delegate fails to perform or performs improperly, the obligee's cause of action is against the obligor, not the delegate. However, this basic rule is subject to a significant exception: If, as is commonly the case, the duty is delegated under a contract between the obligor and the delegate, the delegate's promise to the obligor to perform the obligor's duty will likely qualify as a contract for the benefit of the obligee. This means that the obligee becomes an intended beneficiary of the contract that transferred the duty, and the obligee can enforce the duty directly against the delegate.

Because the delegation of duties is more likely than an assignment to have a negative impact on the obligee's contract expectations, courts tend to be more solicitous of the obligee's efforts to provide in the contract for a prohibition on delegation. Therefore, a contractual provision that makes duties nondelegable is more likely to be enforced according to its terms. (That is, a court is less likely to interpret it restrictively.)

If delegation is permissible, the obligee cannot lawfully refuse to accept performance by the delegate. Such a refusal is a repudiation. However, if delegation is improper, the obligee is entitled to decline to accept the delegate's performance, and if the obligor persists in refusing to perform herself, that refusal constitutes a repudiation.

The general rules governing delegation are set out in Restatement, Second §§318 and 328 and in UCC 2-210. Notice that the terminology is reversed when we move from assignment to delegation: Because it is a duty that is being transferred, it is now the transferor (delegator) who is the obligor, and the other party to the original contract, to whom that duty is owed, is called the obligee.

RESTATEMENT, SECOND §318. DELEGATION OF PERFORMANCE OF DUTY

(1) An obligor can properly delegate the performance of his duty to another unless the delegation is contrary to public policy or the terms of his promise.

(2) Unless otherwise agreed, a promise requires performance by a particular person only to the extent that the obligee has a substantial interest in having that person perform or control the acts promised.

(3) Unless the obligee agrees otherwise, neither delegation of performance nor a contract to assume the duty made with the obligor by the person delegated discharges any duty or liability of the delegating obligor.

RESTATEMENT, SECOND §328. INTERPRETATION OF WORDS OF ASSIGNMENT . . .

(1) Unless the language or the circumstances indicate the contrary, . . . an assignment of "the contract" or of "all my rights under the contract" or an assignment in similar general terms is an assignment of the assignor's rights and a delegation of his unperformed duties under the contract. . . .

UCC 2-210(1), (5), AND (6). DELEGATION OF PERFORMANCE . . .

(1) A party may perform his duty through a delegate unless otherwise agreed or unless the other party has a substantial interest in having his original promisor perform or control the acts required by the contract. No delegation of performance relieves the party delegating of any duty to perform or any liability for breach. . . .

(5) An assignment of "the contract" or of "all my rights under the contract" or an assignment in similar general terms is an assignment of rights and unless the language or the circumstances (as in an assignment for security) indicate the contrary, it is a delegation of performance of the duties of the assignor and its acceptance by the assignee constitutes a promise by him to perform those duties. This promise is enforceable by either the assignor or the other party to the original contract.

(6) The other party may treat any assignment which delegates performance as creating reasonable grounds for insecurity and may without prejudice to his rights against the assignor demand assurances from the assignee (Section 2-609).[9]

■ PROBLEM 22.10

Seller sold her house to Buyer. Shortly before the sale, Seller had bought a hot tub, which was set up on the deck of the house. (It is a freestanding portable hot tub, not attached to or incorporated into the deck.) Seller had

---

[9] Restatement, Second §317, comment d, recognizes a similar right to assurances under common law.

bought the hot tub on credit, using funds borrowed from Finance Co. At the time that Seller sold the house to Buyer, there was still a balance of $5,000 due on the hot tub. When buying the house, Buyer had also bought the hot tub from Seller. Instead of paying cash for the tub, Buyer paid a small amount to Seller to cover the difference between the loan amount and the value of the tub. To make up the balance of the price, Buyer agreed to take over Seller's obligation to Finance Co. and to continue making installment payments on the loan until it had been fully paid off. Seller wrote a letter to Finance Co. informing it that Buyer had bought the house and hot tub and would be responsible for making the remaining payments. In response, Finance Co. sent Buyer a payment coupon book, showing his name as the customer. Finance Co. asked Buyer to enclose one of the coupons with each monthly payment that he remitted. A month after the sale of the house, Buyer defaulted on his payments to Finance Co.

(a) Does Finance Co. have a direct cause of action against Buyer?

(b) Assume that Finance Co. discovered that Buyer could not pay the balance due on the tub. He also has no assets that can be seized in execution to settle the debt. (The house is his only property of value, and it is heavily mortgaged and otherwise exempt from creditors' claims under state law.) Finance Co. claimed payment of the balance from Seller. Is Seller liable to Finance Co.?

■ PROBLEM 22.11

(a) Deli Gator is a chef from New Orleans famous for her gator burgers. Eva Glades was planning a large dinner for March 1 in support of the Wetlands Drainage and Paving Society, a cause about which she was very passionate. On February 15, she called Deli to place an order for 1,000 gator burgers, to be delivered C.O.D. by 6 P.M. on March 1. Deli accepted the order. On February 20, Deli was awarded a large and lucrative contract to supply gator burgers for a huge convention. She realized that she did not have the capacity to fill Eva's order as well. She contacted her competitor, Croc O'Dile, who agreed to "take over" her contract with Eva. At 5:30 P.M. on March 1, Croc arrived at Eva's with 1,000 of his burgers. Eva refused to accept delivery, insisting that she had ordered genuine Deli Gator burgers and would take nothing else. Croc assured Eva that his burgers were made from the choicest and most succulent gator meat and that they were equal to Deli's burgers in quality, taste, and appearance. (This happens to be true. At last year's county fair, blindfolded connoisseurs could not tell the difference.) Eva was unmoved and persisted in rejecting the burgers. Was Eva justified in her refusal? Who has what rights against whom?

(b) Change the facts of (a) as follows: On February 20, when Croc took over the contract from Deli, he called Eva to tell her that he would be supplying the burgers instead of Deli. Eva said she had no objection. She asked if she was supposed to pay him or Deli, and he replied, "I bought your contract from Deli and paid her out. She is no longer involved, and you must pay me direct." Eva said "Fine." Croc turned out to be very unreliable and failed to deliver the burgers to Eva on March 1. When it became clear that Croc would not show up and attempts to reach him were unsuccessful, Eva made heroic efforts to find another supplier. She was able to buy the burgers elsewhere, but it cost her $2,000 more than the price under the contract with Deli. What rights does Eva have, and against whom?

■ PROBLEM 22.12

As in Problem 22.11, Eva was planning her dinner for March 1. On February 1, Eva had hired the famous crooner, Marsh E. Boggs, to provide the entertainment at her party for a fee of $5,000. In terms of the contract, Marsh was to be paid on February 28, one day in advance of the party. On February 10, Marsh accepted an offer for a more advantageous booking. Marsh's younger brother, Newt, was also a singer. He was short on work, so Marsh assigned the contract to him.

(a) Does Eva have grounds to object?

(b) Assume that Eva did not object. On February 28, she paid the $5,000 to Marsh as required by the contract. Marsh blew the money at the races and has disappeared. Newt asserts that Eva's payment to Marsh was not proper performance under the contract and insists that she must pay him, otherwise he will not sing at the dinner and will sue her for his damages. Is he correct?

■ PROBLEM 22.13

As before, Eva's party was planned for March 1. Because Eva had invited a large number of people to her party, she realized that she would need someone to help serve the food and clean up afterwards. On February 2 she hired Home Services, Inc. to provide staff for this purpose. She chose Home Services because it was bonded and insured, and several of her friends had used the company in the past and had recommended it. On February 4, Home Services notified Eva that it had assigned the contract to Domestic Catering Services, Inc. Eva has never heard of the company, and she is unhappy about dealing with it or having its employees in her home. Consider whether Eva may refuse to accept performance from Domestic Catering under the following separate circumstances:

(a) When it told Eva of the assignment, Home Services explained that it had to assign the contract because it had too much work. It assured her that it would continue to take full responsibility for the service and that one of its supervisors would check in at her party a couple of times during the evening to make sure that everything was going smoothly.

(b) Would your answer change if the reason for the assignment given by Home Services was that its owner had suddenly decided to retire? He had just closed the business and had gone off to his condo in the Bahamas.

(c) The facts are the same as in (a), but the contract between Eva and Home Services was contained on a printed form provided by Home Services. One of the printed terms stated, "This contract is personal to the parties and neither may transfer any rights or duties without the express written agreement of the other."

This part of the book includes several multiple choice questions for each chapter. Every question is followed by an explanation of which answer or answers we believe to be the best. The purpose of the questions is to give you an opportunity to review the material that you are learning, and to self-assess your understanding of the principles and concepts addressed in each chapter. We suggest that you work on these questions after you have completed each chapter. To make the best use of the questions, attempt to answer the question before you consult the related answer and explanation. In some cases, there is only one correct answer. In others there may be more than one correct answer. Choose the answer that you consider to be the most accurate, persuasive, and certain based on the information contained in the question, and articulate for yourself why you selected that answer. After you have answered a question, compare our explanation. This will help you to evaluate whether you have understood and properly analyzed the applicable doctrine and principles.

■ CHAPTER 1. INTRODUCTION TO CONTRACTS

Question 1

Margaret, a consumer, had visited the website of Sailing Sales, Inc. and had booked and paid for an expensive all-inclusive cruise. The booking was subject to Sailing's standard terms that were accessible by clicking on a link on Sailing's website. Margaret did not click on the link so she did not know what the standard terms were. One of them stated that all bookings were final and non-refundable. Two weeks after booking the cruise, Margaret changed her mind and wished to cancel her booking. Sailing refused to refund her payment and Margaret sued to recover it.

Margaret's attorney, Sue Smartly, based Margaret's suit on the theory that the standard no-refund term was not enforceable against Margaret because the website was not set up in a way that gave the consumer adequate notice of the standard terms. Although this question had not been addressed in this state, several state Supreme Court decisions in other states had established this principle. In the trial of the suit, the trial court agreed with Sue's argument and granted judgment in favor of Margaret.

A month later, Sue represented Jamie, another consumer who had made a booking with Sailing Sales on the same website, with the same link to the standard terms, and had sought a refund after cancelling the booking. Sue commenced suit against Sailing for a refund in the same county in which Margaret's case had been decided, but a different judge was assigned to Jamie's case. Sue made the same argument in this case as she had made in Margaret's case—that the no-refund term was unenforceable because it was not properly noticed on

Sailing's website. In support of her argument, Sue cited the decision in Margaret's case as well as the decisions in the courts of other states as a precedent. However, the trial judge in this case disagreed with Sue's argument and with the decisions in Margaret's case and in the other courts. This judge held that since the standard terms were accessible on the website, Jamie was responsible for reading them and could not evade them by claiming that he had not read them.

(A) The judge in Jamie's case was not bound by the decisions of the Supreme Courts of other states, but erred in failing to follow the precedent set in Margaret's case, which was decided in the same jurisdiction.

(B) The judge in Jamie's case was not bound by the decision in Margaret's case, but erred in failing to follow the precedent set in the Supreme Courts of other states.

(C) The judge in Jamie's case erred in not following binding precedent set by both Margaret's case and the Supreme Courts of other states.

(D) Neither the decision in Margaret's case nor the decisions of the courts of other states bind the judge in Jamie's case.

Question 1 Answer

(D) is the correct answer. The decision of a trial court is persuasive but does not create precedent that is binding on a subsequent court dealing with the same legal question. Similarly, although decisions of the Supreme Courts of other states may be persuasive, they are not binding precedent.

Question 2

The decision of the court in Margaret's case and in the decisions of the Supreme Courts of other states are supported by five prominent and well-respected treatises on contract law as well as by six law review articles. In addition, Sue is a very prominent contracts lawyer with a reputation for accurate and correct legal analysis. By contrast, there is scant support for the decision of the court in Jamie's case.

(A) This makes no difference. The binding precedent was set in the previous case, and the answer is still that the judge in Jamie's case erred in failing to follow it.

(B) This makes no difference. The binding precedent was set in the previous case and in the decisions of the Supreme Courts of other states, and the answer is still that the judge in Jamie's case erred in failing to follow it.

(C) This makes no difference. The judge in Jamie's case is still not bound by precedent.

(D) The judge in Jamie's case may not have been bound by a single decision in a prior case, but once there is such overwhelming authority in favor of Jamie's position, the judge is bound to follow it.

Question 2 Answer

(C) is correct. The treatises and law review articles may also be persuasive authority but do not bind the court.

Question 3

The facts are as in Questions 1 and 2. Sue represented Jamie in appealing the trial court's decision to the state Court of Appeals, which agreed with Sue's argument and held that Jamie was entitled to judgment for a refund of his payment. Based on the facts set out in Question 1, the best articulation of the rule of this decision is:

(A) A customer who enters into a transaction on a website is not bound by standard contract terms that are accessible only by a link on the website.

(B) A customer who enters into a transaction on a website is not bound by standard terms unless those terms are fair and reasonable. A no-refund term is not fair and reasonable.

(C) Standard terms on a website are not binding on a customer who enters into a transaction on the website unless those terms are clearly noticed and accessible.

(D) It is not permissible for the operator of a website to include standard terms on the website unless the operator specifically brings those terms to the attention of the customer and obtains a signification of the customer's assent to them.

Question 3 Answer

(C) is the correct articulation of the rule. (A) is too broad a statement because the customer could be bound by terms that are accessible via a link provided that the website displays the link in a way that it would come to the attention of a reasonable customer. (B) is incorrect because the court did not deal with the substance of the term—just with the question of whether it was properly noticed and accessible. (D) is incorrect because it goes much further than what the court required. The court invalidated the standard term because of inadequate notice, but did not require that the customer must expressly signify assent to it.

Question 4

In the course of its opinion in Jamie's case, the Court of Appeals made the following statement: "It would have been a better practice for the defendant to ensure that its customer signified assent to the standard terms. This could be done by presenting the terms to the customer automatically before the order is placed and requiring the customer to manifest assent by some action, such as by clicking an 'I agree' button on the website, before being able to place the order. A website set up in this way would eliminate the problem of having to decide if the customer has had proper notice of the terms."

(A) This statement is dictum, which has persuasive, not binding, force.

(B) This statement is the rule of the case, which is binding precedent on all courts in the state.

(C) This statement is the rule of the case, which is binding precedent on courts of lower stature in the state. It binds the Court of Appeals, in a sense. That court will consider itself bound by its own precedent, but it has the power to overturn its prior decision if it later considers it to be wrong.

(D) This statement is the rule of the case, which is binding precedent on the Court of Appeals and courts of lower stature in that state.

Question 4 Answer

(A) is correct. In deciding the case, the Court of Appeals held merely that a customer is not bound by standard terms if the link is inadequately noticed and the terms are not reasonably accessible. Its discussion on how a website operator might avoid the problems that arose in this case is not necessary to the disposition of the case and is dictum. Had it been the rule of the case, (B) would be incorrect because the decision of the Court of Appeals would not bind the state Supreme Court, and (D) would be incorrect because the precedent does not absolutely bind the Court of Appeals. (C) would be correct if this had been the rule of the case because the court would consider itself bound by its own precedent, and would be most reluctant to depart from it unless convinced that it is wrong.

Question 5

As in Question 1, Sue represents Jamie, who wishes to recover his payment to Sailing Sales after cancelling his booking. Sailing Sales has refused to give Jamie a refund and Sue has commenced suit on his behalf in the local federal district court.

(A) Sue may not bring suit in federal court because contracts are governed by state law and can be litigated only in state court.

(B) State and federal courts have concurrent jurisdiction over contract disputes, so Sue may freely choose whether to sue in federal court or state court.

(C) Sue may bring suit in federal court provided that she can establish grounds for federal jurisdiction. The federal court will decide the case by applying the law of the state that governs the transaction.

(D) Sue may bring suit in federal court provided that she can establish grounds for federal jurisdiction. The federal court will decide the case by applying the federal law of contract.

Question 5 Answer

(C) is correct. Normally, state courts, not federal courts, have jurisdiction to hear contract cases. However, a federal court may have jurisdiction to hear the case provided that there are grounds for federal jurisdiction. One of the most common grounds that applies in contract disputes is diversity of citizenship. Even if the federal court has jurisdiction to hear the case, it must apply the law of the state that governs the transaction. There is no general federal law of contract.

Question 6

Alvin was due to fly out of the city airport on Friday at 9 A.M. for a trip to China. He asked his friend Sarah if she would take him to the airport. She agreed to do so and they arranged that she would pick him up at his house on Friday at 6:30 A.M. Sarah failed to show up on Friday at 6:30 A.M. and did not answer her phone when Alvin tried to call her. Alvin then tried to find a cab to take him to the airport, but all the taxi companies were busy and Alvin was not able to get a cab until 7:30 A.M. By that time the morning rush hour had begun, so Alvin did not get to the airport in time and missed his flight. Alvin incurred substantial costs—not only did he have to pay the cab fare, but he forfeited the non-refundable airfare and had to book a new flight to China. Alvin would like to recover these losses from Sarah.

(A) Alvin and Sarah had no contract, so Alvin has no claim for breach of contract damages against Sarah.

(B) Alvin and Sarah had a contract which Sarah breached. Alvin can recover damages from Sarah, consisting of his cab fare and non-refundable airfare.

(C) Alvin and Sarah had a contract which Sarah breached. Alvin can recover damages from Sarah, consisting of his cab fare and his non-refundable airfare. In addition, Alvin can recover emotional distress damages to compensate him for the frustration and distress caused by his struggle to find a cab, deal with traffic, and lose his flight.

Question 6 Answer

(A) is correct. A contract is an exchange relationship and the arrangement between Alvin and Sarah does not qualify as a contract because there is no indication that Alvin had given Sarah or promised Sarah anything in exchange for taking him to the airport. This is therefore not a contract, but an informal arrangement in which Sarah is doing a favor for Alvin. (The nature of the exchange relationship will be discussed more fully when we deal with consideration doctrine in Chapter 9.) Had this been a contract, (B), not (C), would have been the correct answer—Alvin would have been able to recover his economic losses resulting from Sarah's breach, but emotional distress damages are not available for breach of contract except in very limited circumstances.

Question 7

Archie Tect, a famous architect, agreed to design a new house for Homer. The parties signed a letter of engagement that described the project and set out the terms of their arrangement. It is a mark of great distinction to have a home designed by Archie, and Homer, a wealthy and prominent member of the community, was very excited that Archie had agreed to build him a spectacular home that would signal his importance and let the world know that he was a man of great taste and influence. A short while after they made this agreement, Archie told Homer that he had taken on too many projects and did not have the time to design a house for Homer.

(A) Homer and Archie have no contract, so Homer has no remedy against Archie.

(B) Homer and Archie have a contract, so Homer can recover damages from Archie provided that he can prove that he suffered an economic loss as a result of Archie's breach of the contract.

(C) Homer and Archie have a contract and because Archie's services are unique, this is an appropriate case for granting Homer the remedy of specific performance.

(D) Homer and Archie have a contract and because damages would not be an adequate remedy to compensate Homer for Archie's breach, this is an appropriate case for granting Homer the remedy of specific performance.

Question 7 Answer

(B) is correct. The facts state that the parties agreed that Archie would build a house for Homer and that they executed a letter of engagement. Although these facts are skimpy, the question does indicate that the agreement had the hallmarks of a contract. Therefore, there is no basis to conclude, as (A) does, that they have no contract. Archie breached the contract, so Homer is entitled to a remedy. However, he will only be able to obtain the remedy of specific performance—thereby compelling Archie to design the house for him—if he can satisfy the criteria for equitable relief. It may well be, as stated in (C) and (D), that Archie's services are unique and that damages will not compensate Homer adequately for losing Archie's services. However, this is not the only consideration. In addition, the court will take into account the equities between the parties, the difficulty in supervising performance, the impact of the order on third parties, and the public interest. These factors weigh against an order of specific performance. Courts are most reluctant to order specific performance of personal service contracts because they are difficult to supervise and seem rather too much like personal servitude. In addition, the question suggests that Archie has overcommitted, so an order to perform this contract could cause him to breach others. These considerations will likely preclude specific performance. However, if Homer suffers an economic loss, say by having to pay more for the services of another architect, he should be able to recover that loss as expectation damages.

■ CHAPTER 2. SALES OF GOODS

Question 1

Clay Potts is a professional potter. He makes large ceramic plant pots in his workshop and then sells them at craft fairs. His materials cost very little, so most of the price that customers pay for his pots represents his skill and labor in making them.

(**A**) Clay's sales of pots to customers are sales of goods subject to UCC Article 2.

(**B**) Clay's sales of pots to customers are hybrid transactions consisting of both labor and materials. However, they fall within UCC Article 2 because the sale of the pots is the predominant purpose of the contract.

(**C**) Clay's sales of pots to customers are hybrid transactions consisting of both labor and materials. However, they do not fall within UCC Article 2 because Clay's labor in creating the pots predominates over the relatively low cost of materials.

Question 1 Answer

(**A**) is correct. Most goods involve a process of manufacturing and in many cases the labor and skill in making the goods outweighs the cost of the raw materials used to make them. Therefore, if a predominant purpose test was used to determine if manufactured goods constituted "goods" under Article 2, many items that are obviously goods would not be covered by Article 2. UCC 2-105(1) clarifies this by defining "goods" to include "specially manufactured goods." Where the purpose of the transaction is the sale of a tangible, movable end product that meets the definition of "goods" in UCC 2-105(1), this is a sale of goods and not a hybrid transaction.

Question 2

Clay Potts is not a professional potter. He has a full-time job working in a bank during the week. As his hobby, he makes ceramic plant pots in his home workshop on the weekends. He occasionally sells some of the pots to friends when they see and admire his work.

(**A**) UCC Article 2 does not apply to these transactions because the pots are not predominantly goods.

(**B**) UCC Article 2 does not apply to these transactions because Clay is not a merchant.

(**C**) UCC Article 2 does apply to these sales. Although Clay occasionally sells the pots to friends, he probably does not qualify as a merchant under UCC 2-104(1).

(**D**) UCC Article 2 does apply to these sales. Because Clay sells the pots to friends, he likely qualifies as a merchant under UCC 2-104(1).

Question 2 Answer

(C) is correct. As explained in question 1, pots are goods, and sales of pots are not hybrid transactions. UCC Article 2 therefore applies to the sales. UCC 2-104(1) defines a merchant either as a person who deals in goods of that kind or who by his occupation holds himself out as having knowledge or skill peculiar to the practices or goods involved in the transaction. Official Comments 1 and 2 to UCC 2-104 emphasize that the definition is meant to distinguish professionals who buy or sell goods in the course of their business from casual and inexperienced buyers and sellers. By selling the pots to his friends on occasion, Clay does sometimes deal in his pots, so an argument could be made that (D) is correct. However, given the emphasis on the professional status of a merchant, it is more likely that Clay would not qualify as a merchant because he is not a professional in the business of selling pots and does not hold himself out to the public as such. The fact that he is a businessman in his full-time job does not make him a merchant in relation to his hobby.

Question 3

The facts are the same as in Question 2, but Clay never sells the pots to his friends or anyone else. He keeps most of the pots for himself but he gives some of them to friends and donates most of them to charitable organizations for charity auctions and thrift shops.

    (A) UCC Article 2 does not apply to Clay's gifts and donations because the pots are not predominantly goods.
    (B) UCC Article 2 does not apply to Clay's gifts and donations. The pots are goods but the transactions relating to the pots are not sales.
    (C) UCC Article 2 does apply to these transactions, which are sales of goods. Although Clay enters many transactions in which he deals with these goods, he probably does not qualify as a merchant under UCC 2-104(1).
    (D) UCC Article 2 does apply to these sales. Because Clay enters many transactions in which he deals with these goods, he likely qualifies as a merchant under UCC 2-104(1).

Question 3 Answer

(B) is correct. The transactions do involve goods. However, a sale is defined in UCC 2-106(1) as the passing of title from the seller to the buyer for a price. The price need not be in money, but there must be something of value given by the buyer to the seller in exchange for the goods. These transactions are donations to friends and organizations and therefore are not sales subject to UCC Article 2.

Question 4

Scopes, Inc. sells, repairs, and services telescopes. It entered into a contract with a university to repair a telescope used in the astronomy department's observatory.

The repair required the supply of complex precision parts that cost $200,000, and the charge for the labor of highly-trained technicians was $185,000. The repair contract was in writing and it contained a 90-day warranty on all parts used and labor performed in the repair. A month after the repair was completed, the telescope ceased working. The university claims that this was because the repair was defective, but Scopes claims that the reason for the breakdown was that students in the astronomy department had mishandled and abused the instrument.

(A) This hybrid transaction falls within Article 2 because the parts cost more than the labor, making the predominant purpose of the contract a sale of goods.

(B) This hybrid transaction falls within Article 2. Where the cost of parts and labor are about equal, the default rule is that the transaction is subject to Article 2.

(C) This hybrid transaction does not fall within Article 2. Although the parts cost slightly more than the labor, the parts would be useless without the skill of installing them properly, so labor is the predominant purpose of the contract.

(D) We cannot decide on the predominant purpose of the contract based on these facts, but the facts do not suggest any reason why resolution of the dispute would depend on whether it is subject to Article 2 or the common law.

Question 4 Answer

(D) is correct. The cost of the goods and labor are closely equivalent. Scopes both sells and repairs telescopes and the facts do not allow us to conclude that either repair or sale is the basic nature of its business. There are also no facts that help to evaluate the other factors identified in *Audio Visual Artistry*. We therefore cannot make a determination of the predominant purpose of the contract based on these facts. However, since the dispute involves a factual question of the cause of the telescope's malfunction, and does not appear to involve any rule of law that would be different at common law and under the UCC, there is no apparent reason to determine scope.

Question 5

At the end of his first year of law school, Lex Lawless sold his contracts casebook to a classmate for $50.

(A) Lex only sells his books after he has used them, to recoup some of what he spent on them. He is therefore not in the business of dealing with law books, so UCC Article 2 does not apply to this transaction.

(B) This transaction is not a sale of goods because the book has no value as a physical object consisting of nothing more than paper. Its true value is in its content, which is intellectual property—an intangible right and not a "good."

(C) This transaction is a sale of goods subject to UCC Article 2.

(D) This transaction is a sale of goods, but Article 2 does not apply to it because Lex is an occasional seller and not a merchant.

Question 5 Answer

(C) is correct. Although the value of the book is in its content, once the content is incorporated into a physical object, such as a book, the sale of that object falls within UCC Article 2. (B) is therefore incorrect. (A) and (D) say basically the same thing in different words. If you selected either of these answers you made the mistake of thinking that Article 2 applies only to merchants. Article 2 applies to all sales of goods. The question of whether one or both parties are merchants is only relevant to those sections of Article 2 that have a special rule that covers merchants.

■ CHAPTER 3. CONTRACTUAL ASSENT AND THE OBJECTIVE TEST

Question 1

Question 1 for Chapter 1 dealt with Margaret, a consumer, who booked and paid for an expensive all-inclusive cruise on the website of Sailing Sales, Inc. The booking was subject to Sailing's standard terms that were accessible by clicking on a link on Sailing's website. One of those terms stated that all bookings were final and non-refundable, but Margaret did not know about it because she did not click on the link. Two weeks after booking the cruise, Margaret changed her mind and wished to cancel her booking. Sailing refused to refund her payment and Margaret sued to recover it.

The question for Chapter 1 focused on the doctrine of precedent, and indicated two contrary court decisions on the substantive issue of whether Margaret should be bound by the no-refund term. The focus of this question is to consider which result is better under the principles introduced in Chapter 3.

(A) Margaret should be able to recover her payment despite the no-refund term. The standard terms of the website should not be enforceable against Margaret because the website was not set up in a way that gave her adequate notice of the standard terms.

(B) Margaret may be able to recover her payment despite the no-refund term. To decide this issue we must determine if the link to the terms would give adequate notice of the terms to a reasonable person in Margaret's position.

(C) Margaret should not be able to recover her payment because she is bound by the no-refund term. The link was visible on the webpage and she had a duty to click on it to read the standard terms.

(D) Margaret should be able to recover her payment despite the no-refund term because the term is unfair and one-sided.

Question 1 Answer

(B) is correct. To determine whether Margaret had a duty to read the term and should be bound by it despite not knowing about it, a court would apply the objective test to decide if the link to the term was exhibited in such a way that it would have given notice of the term to a reasonable person in Margaret's position. Answers (A) and (C) might ultimately be correct, but they are conclusory and we cannot reach those conclusions without applying the objective test. (D) is also wrong because it is conclusory. As the notes following *James* indicate, the doctrine of unconscionability may allow a court to avoid a term that is unfair and one-sided. However, there is no indication in the facts that the no-refund term is unfair under the circumstances, and we would need more information to make this determination.

Question 2

Super Market, Inc. is conducting a promotion under which its customers get stickers each time they buy products from the store. The customer then places these stickers on matching spaces on game cards and when all the spaces on the card are full, the customer can submit the card to Super Market for a prize. The back of the game card states, "To see the rules of this game, ask any cashier for a copy of them or go to our website, www.supermarket/games.com." The rules are the usual rules that commonly govern promotions of this kind and they are in fact available in print form from cashiers or on the webpage and may be accessed from either of those two sources by a customer who goes to the trouble of finding out what they are. However, a poll of customers has shown that only 5% of customers who play the game have done either of these things. While most customers assume that the game is governed by rules, the great majority have never seen the rules and have no idea what those rules are.

(A) Nevertheless, the customers are bound by the rules.

(B) Because 95% of customers do not take the opportunity to access the rules, it must be concluded that Super Market's notice of the rules is inadequate and the rules will not bind customers.

(C) The rules will bind the 5% of customers who took the opportunity to access them, but not the 95% of customers who did not.

(D) This question cannot be answered because the facts do not state what the rules are.

Question 2 Answer

(A) is the best answer. Because all promotions are subject to rules and the rules governing this game are common and unexceptional, a reasonable customer would expect that the game is subject to rules of this kind. Therefore, the notice at the back of the game card that informs customers of the existence of the rules and of the simple means of accessing them should be enough to make the rules binding on all customers. (B) suggests that because 95% of customers do not read the rules, a reasonable customer would not know of them. However, the mere fact that a huge majority of customers do not bother to read the rules does not mean that a reasonable customer would not know that the game is subject to rules. (C) is based on the general principle that even if standard terms are not adequately noticed, they will still bind a person who has actual knowledge of them. However, if we conclude that there is adequate notice, (C) is too restrictive. (D) suggests that the nature of the rules is relevant to the question of whether they are binding. This may be true if the rule in question is so unusual that it is contrary to the reasonable expectations of customers. However, there is nothing in the facts to indicate that such a rule is included in the standard terms governing this game.

Question 3

Which of the following statements is most accurate?

(A) The Federal Arbitration Act requires parties to arbitrate disputes whenever one of the parties demands that the dispute be settled by arbitration.

(B) The Federal Arbitration Act requires parties to arbitrate disputes only when both parties understand that they have agreed to arbitrate the dispute.

(C) The Federal Arbitration Act requires parties to arbitrate disputes only where parties have actually agreed to arbitrate the dispute.

(D) The Federal Arbitration Act requires parties to arbitrate disputes where parties have manifested assent to a valid arbitration provision.

Question 3 Answer

(D) is the most accurate statement. The Federal Arbitration Act upholds the validity of an arbitration agreement unless there are grounds to invalidate it under principles of contract law. Under the objective test, a manifestation of assent to an arbitration provision binds a party provided that there are no other grounds under contract law to invalidate the provision. (C) is incorrect in that it requires actual (subjective) agreement to the provision. (A) is incorrect because there must be an agreement to arbitrate and (B) is incorrect because it does not recognize the requirement that the arbitration provision be valid under contract law.

Question 4

When a customer orders goods on a website, she places the goods in a virtual shopping cart. When she has finished selecting the goods, she must go to the shopping cart to complete her purchase by submitting the order, entering a delivery address and payment information, and finally confirming that the order and other information are correct. After the customer completes the first step of submitting the order, a text box appears automatically on the computer screen which contains standard terms governing the transaction. The box contains about half a page of terms and the customer must scroll down the box to read them all. There is also a button on the box that allows the customer to read the terms in a full-page format or to print them. The customer cannot proceed to complete her order until she has clicked on a button on the text box that states "I acknowledge that I have read and understand these terms." These standard terms are best characterized as:

(A) Shrinkwrap terms.
(B) Boxtop terms.
(C) Browsewrap terms.

(D) Clickwrap terms.

(E) None of the above.

Question 4 Answer

(E) is the best characterization, based on the definitions of these terms in Sections C.3 and C.4 of Chapter 3. Courts usually use the word "shrinkwrap" to describe terms that are within the packaging (whether of a physical object or software) so that they are not seen by the buyer until the package is opened. "Boxtop" refers to terms visible on the packaging itself. Terms that are set out on a website are called "browsewrap" if the customer has to click on a link to see them, but need not manifest assent to them before completing the transaction, and "clickwrap" if the terms are presented on the website in a way that the customer must signify assent to them before completing the transaction. The terms here would clearly be clickwrap if the customer manifested assent to them by clicking on the button. However, clicking on the button on this website is merely the customer's acknowledgment of having read and understood the terms. This process does not neatly fit into the definition of "browsewrap" either because the terms are presented automatically to the customer, who does not have to click on a link to see them. Probably the best characterization is that website has established a hybrid between clickwrap and browsewrap that allows the website operator to establish that the terms were well-noticed to the customer, but not to establish that the customer manifested assent to them. Although some courts may conclude that a customer manifested assent to the terms by placing an order under these circumstances, this result is by no means certain. As a practical matter, once the website operator has gone to the trouble of including a button for the customer to click, it makes no sense to fall short of having the button operate as an "I agree" button that expressly and specifically manifests the customer's assent to the terms.

Question 5

Say that in *Leonard v. PepsiCo* the commercial featured a Ferrari Berlinetta rather than a Harrier jet. Apart from this, the commercial was exactly the same as described in the case except that the student arrived at the school in the Ferrari, the military music was replaced by loud pop music, and the words that appeared after the drum roll were "FERRARI BERLINETTA, 2,000,000 PEPSI POINTS." The retail price of the Ferrari is about $300,000. Leonard, who has no sense of humor, genuinely believed that the Ferrari was offered as a real prize and he therefore spent $200,000 to buy the needed Pepsi drinks and additional Pepsi points.

(A) This should change the result of the case because the joke is no longer obvious to a reasonable viewer—although a student would not be likely to fly a military jet to school, driving to school in a Ferrari is somewhat plausible.

(B) This should change the result of the case because Leonard honestly believed that the offer of the Ferrari was genuine and it misled him into spending $200,000 to buy the necessary Pepsi points.

(C) This should not change the result of the case. Even with these changed facts, there is sufficient indication that a reasonable person would have understood the commercial to be a joke.

(D) This should not change the result of the case because Pepsi intended the inclusion of the Ferrari in the commercial to be humorous and not to be taken seriously.

Question 5 Answer

(C) is the best answer. Replacing the jet with the Ferrari eliminates some of the factors that the court identified as signaling to a reasonable person that the jet was included as a joke. Although there are arguments to the contrary, there remain clear indications that would lead a reasonable person to understand that there was no serious offer of a Ferrari for 2,000,000 Pepsi points—the tone of the commercial is still humorous, hyperbolic, and absurd, and the retail price of the car is $100,000 more than the cost of the 2,000,000 Pepsi points. (A) is therefore not a convincing answer. (B) and (D) are both wrong because they both focus on the subjective understanding of one of the parties rather than on the objective meaning of the commercial.

■ CHAPTER 4. THE OFFER

Question 1

Buyer operates a factory. One of its machines needed replacement, so Buyer sent a letter to several manufacturers setting out the technical specifications of the machine and requesting bids on its price. Seller, one of the manufacturers who received this letter, replied by sending an e-mail to Buyer with the subject heading, "Your request for a bid." The body of the message stated, "Thank you for requesting a bid from us. We have a machine that meets your specifications in stock and can supply it for $100,000, including delivery and installation. We would be able to deliver and install the machine on any date convenient to you after receiving your order. We hope that you find this acceptable and we look forward to doing business with you."

(A) Buyer made an offer to Seller by sending the letter requesting a bid.

(B) Seller made an offer to Buyer in its e-mail.

(C) No offer has been made yet by either party because the terms of the transaction have not been settled.

(D) No offer has been made yet by either party because neither a request for bids nor a price quotation can constitute an offer.

Question 1 Answer

(B) is the best answer. An offer is a manifestation of willingness to enter a bargain which would justify a reasonable recipient in understanding that its assent to the proposed bargain is invited and would result in the formation of a contract. The question of whether a communication constitutes an offer is determined by interpreting the language of the communication in context. Although the language of the e-mail does not use the word "offer," it sets out the terms on which Seller is willing to deal with Buyer and can be reasonably understood to give Buyer the power to bind Seller to a contract. (A) is wrong. A letter to a manufacturer requesting a bid would not qualify as an offer because it is clear that Buyer is calling for price information before ordering the machine and does not manifest an intent to be bound in a contract by Seller's response to the letter. (C) is probably incorrect as well. On its face, the e-mail does set out the terms on which Buyer is willing to enter the contract. To the extent that it does not specify certain terms (such as the time for payment or whether the machine is warranted) these terms could probably be supplied by trade usage or by default terms recognized in law. (D) is wrong. Either a request for bid or a price quote can be an offer if expressed in a way that manifests intent to a reasonable recipient that an offer is intended.

Question 2

Homeowner invited Home Cleaning Services, Inc. to visit his home and give him a quote on how much it would charge to clean his house every two weeks. The

HCS representative came over to his house, inspected it, told him it would charge $150 for each cleaning, detailed the tasks that would be performed for that price, and indicated when it could schedule the services. Homeowner said that he would think about it and let HCS know.

(A) HCS has made an offer to Homeowner.

(B) Homeowner has made an offer to HCS.

(C) No offer has been made because there has not been any formal written proposal.

(D) No offer has been made because a price quotation cannot be an offer.

Question 2 Answer

(A) is the best answer. As noted in the answer to Question 1, a price quote can be an offer, so (D) is wrong. Based on the test of an offer set out in Question 1, Homeowner could reasonably understand that the price quote invited him to form a contract upon acceptance. The facts do not support (B) because a mere request for information on the cost of a service cannot create the reasonable understanding that HCS could bind Homeowner to a contract merely by giving a price quote. (C) is wrong because an offer to provide services can be oral and does not need any formalities.

Question 3

A clothing store sent an e-mail advertising a sale to all customer e-mail addresses on its list. The e-mail stated, "Every item in our store will be reduced by 25% from 10 A.M. to 8 P.M. next Saturday, April 28. Quantities are limited to stock on hand, so come in early to avoid disappointment."

(A) This e-mail cannot be an offer because the reasonable recipient of a mass e-mail must realize that the sender does not intend the advertisement to be an offer.

(B) This e-mail cannot be an offer because the sale is limited to stock on hand.

(C) This e-mail cannot be an offer because it was sent to a large number of recipients.

(D) This e-mail could be an offer provided that a reasonable reader of the e-mail would understand it as such.

Question 3 answer

(D) is correct. Although courts may operate on the assumption that an advertiser does not usually intend the advertisement to be an offer, it could constitute an offer if its wording and the context (including reasonable expectations in the marketplace) would justify a recipient in understanding it to be one. For this reason, (A) is wrong. (B) is wrong. Limiting sales to stock on hand does not preclude the e-mail from being an offer, and because it contains words of limitation it may actually point to its being an offer, as stated in *Leonard.* (C) is wrong. An advertisement could be an offer if it can be reasonably interpreted as such, even if the advertiser disseminates it widely.

Question 4

During her campaign for re-election, the mayor of the city claimed in an interview with a television reporter that she had completely eliminated the problem of homelessness in the city. The reporter expressed skepticism and said that he had often seen people sleeping under bridges and in parks. The mayor declared, "No, you are wrong. I will state again that there are no longer any homeless people in our city. To show how confident I am in saying this, I will give $100 to any homeless resident of this city who comes to my office tomorrow." The next day 200 people showed up at the mayor's office and proved that they lived in the city and were homeless.

(A) The mayor did not make an offer because a reasonable person would understand her statement to be mere political puffery and would not take it seriously.

(B) The mayor did not make an offer because no reasonable person would understand a statement made during a television interview to be an offer.

(C) The mayor made an offer which was accepted by all 200 people. The mayor is therefore obliged to pay $100 to each of them.

(D) The mayor made an offer which was accepted by the first person to show up at her office on the following day. The mayor is therefore obliged to pay $100 to that person.

Question 4 Answer

(C) is the most persuasive answer. The mayor was foolish enough to make a statement that could be reasonably understood by viewers of the TV interview to give the power of acceptance to all homeless people in the city who showed up at her office on the appointed day. The mayor may have intended her statement to be rhetorical or political puffery, but (A) is too dogmatic in asserting that a reasonable person would understand it as such. (B) is wrong. The statement is not disqualified from being an offer merely because it was made in a TV interview. (D) is not as plausible an interpretation as (C) because the mayor did not confine her offer to the first homeless person to show up at her office, but extended it to all homeless people.

Question 5

Seller wished to sell his car. He left the car in a parking lot with a sticker on the front windscreen which read, "Offered for sale, as is, $16,000 cash" and included Seller's phone number.

(A) Seller has made an offer because the sign used the word "offered."

(B) Seller has made an offer because the sign states all relevant terms and leaves nothing to be negotiated.

(C) Seller has not made an offer. A sign on a car can be nothing more than a solicitation of offers.

(D) Seller might have made an offer, but to answer this question we need more information on the reasonable expectations in the marketplace.

Question 5 Answer

(D) is the best answer. Seller may have made an offer, as indicated in (B), because the sign does appear to state all relevant terms and leaves nothing to be negotiated. However, the reasonable expectations of the marketplace could be crucial to decide if a reasonable person seeing the sign would be justified in concluding that Seller could be bound in contract by a signification of acceptance. The fact that Seller used the word "offered" on the sign could be a factor that points to the sign being an offer, but (A) is too emphatic. Similarly, (C) is also too emphatic. A sign on a car could be an offer if so reasonably understood in the marketplace.

■ CHAPTER 5. ACCEPTANCE

Question 1

Factory had imported a new machine and needed to have it installed. On May 1, Factory wrote a letter to Engineering Co., setting out the technical specifications of the machine and requesting a bid for its installation. Engineering Co. responded by sending an e-mail to Factory on May 2 with the subject heading "Offer." The body of the message stated, "Thank you for requesting a bid from us. We are happy to offer to install your machine for the price of $100,000. We would be able to do the installation on any date convenient to you after receiving your order. We hope that you find this acceptable and look forward to doing business with you." On May 3, Factory responded by sending an e-mail with the subject heading "Acceptance of your Offer." The body of the message stated, "We do wish to have you install the machine for $10,000. Can you do the installation this week?" The price of $10,000 written in Factory's e-mail was a typographical error. Factory had meant to write "$100,000."

    (A) Factory has accepted Engineering Co.'s offer despite the typographical error.
    (B) Factory has not accepted Engineering Co.'s offer because of the typographical error.
    (C) Factory has not accepted Engineering Co.'s offer because of the request to install the machine this week.
    (D) Factory has not accepted Engineering Co.'s offer because of the typographical error and the request to install the machine this week.

Question 1 Answer

(B) is correct. In context, Engineering Co.'s e-mailed price quote probably constitutes an offer. Even though Factory unintentionally misstated the price, this error prevents the e-mail from being a manifestation of assent to the offer, much in the same way that the buyer's signature in the "counter to counteroffer" space in *Roth* prevented the buyer's response in that case from being an acceptance. (C) and (D) are wrong because the request to install the machine this week would not have precluded contract formation—the offer contemplates that Factory would select the installation date.

Question 2

The facts are as stated in Question 1. On May 7 (five days after receiving Engineering Co.'s e-mail), Factory wrote a letter to Engineering Co. stating, "Thanks for your e-mail. We do wish to have you install the machine for $100,000. We need it installed by May 12."

(A) This is likely an effective acceptance.

(B) This is not likely an effective acceptance because Factory should have responded by e-mail, not by mail.

(C) This is not likely an effective acceptance because Factory apparently varied the terms of the offer with its demand for installation by May 12.

(D) This is not likely an effective acceptance because Factory waited too long to respond.

Question 2 Answer

Although an argument can be made for (D), **(A)** is the best answer. Again, Engineering Co.'s e-mail probably constitutes an offer. The offer does not specify a time for acceptance, so it must occur within a reasonable time. Although the determination of a reasonable time is a question of fact, to be determined under all the circumstances, there is no indication in the facts that the transaction is one in which a response would have to be made sooner than five days after the offer. Therefore, the conclusion in (D) does not seem to be justified. There is no basis for (B) because the mode of acceptance is not specified and the communications began with a letter, so there is no convincing basis for arguing that mail is not impliedly authorized. (C) is wrong. As stated in the answer to Question 1, this is not a variation of the offer, which contemplates that Factory will select the delivery date.

Question 3

The facts are as stated in Question 1, except that Engineering Co.'s e-mail contained the additional sentence, "Please note that this price quotation is good for 10 days." On May 17 (fifteen days after receiving Engineering Co.'s e-mail), Factory responded by letter, "Thanks for your e-mail. We accept your offer to install the machine for $100,000."

(A) Factory's letter is an effective acceptance.

(B) Factory's letter is not an effective acceptance because mail is not a permissible mode of acceptance.

(C) Factory's letter is too late to be an acceptance, so it operates as an offer.

(D) Factory's letter lacks sufficient detail to be an acceptance or an offer.

Question 3 Answer

(C) is the best answer. By stating that the price quotation was good for 10 days, Engineering Co. signifies that the offer to install the machine at that price lapses 10 days after the offer was made. Therefore, Factory had lost the power of acceptance when it sought to accept on May 17, so its letter is an offer to revive the transaction which Engineering Co. may choose to accept, if it is still willing to install the machine for the price that it originally quoted. Therefore (A) is wrong. (B) is wrong for the reason stated in the answer to Question 2. (D) is wrong. The terms of the contract are contained in Engineering Co.'s offer, so Factory's response needs no detail at all.

Question 4

The facts are as stated in Question 1, except that Engineering Co.'s e-mail contained the additional statement, "This offer, with its complete terms, is contained in the attached document. To accept this offer, please print out the document, sign it, and mail it to us by May 10." Which of the following responses is most likely to be an effective acceptance?

(A) Factory responded by e-mail on May 4, stating, "Thanks for your offer. We accept."

(B) Factory responded by e-mail on May 11, stating, "We read the attachment to your e-mail, which is acceptable to us, so we accept your offer."

(C) Factory printed out the attachment, scratched out an arbitration provision, initialed the change, and signed the document, which Factory mailed to Engineering Co. on May 4. Engineering Co. received it on May 6.

(D) Factory printed out the attachment, signed it, and mailed it to Engineering Co. on May 10. Engineering Co. received it on May 12.

Question 4 Answer

(D) is the correct answer. Factory has conformed exactly with the method of acceptance specified by Engineering Co. and has accepted in time. The language of the offer does not exclude the mailbox rule, which makes the acceptance effective on its mailing on May 10, even though it was received only on May 12. By contrast, the other methods of acceptance are not the most likely to be effective and some are completely ineffective. Factory's effort at acceptance by e-mail described in (A) might be effective, but it is not the most likely alternative to be effective. Even though an argument could be made that the offer does not expressly declare its procedure to be the exclusive means of acceptance, an e-mail acceptance does not conform at all to the stated procedure and might therefore be inadequate. The e-mail in (B) is closer to what Engineering Co. has asked for, but still not exactly in compliance with the mode and is too late. In (C), Factory did conform to the mode of acceptance and responded in time, but by striking out the arbitration provision Factory did not accept the terms offered and instead made a counteroffer.

Question 5

Question 4 for Chapter 4 described a television interview in which the mayor, running for re-election, claimed that she had completely eliminated the problem of homelessness in the city. When the reporter expressed disbelief, the mayor declared, "No, you are wrong. I will state again that there are no longer any homeless people in our city. To show how confident I am in saying this, I will give $100 to any homeless resident of this city who comes to my office tomorrow."

(A) The mayor has made an offer for a bilateral contract.

(B) The mayor has made an offer for a unilateral contract.

(C) The mayor has made an offer that may be accepted either by promise or performance.

(D) The mayor has not made any offer at all.

Question 5 Answer

(B) is correct. As explained in the answer to Question 4 for Chapter 4, the mayor did make an offer, so (D) is incorrect. The offer states that the payment will be made to all homeless people in the city who show up at her office at the appointed time. The act of showing up at the office on the date specified is the performance required under the contract. The nature of the contract is such that it would make no sense to see it as calling for contract formation by a promise to show up. Nor does it make sense to conclude that a contract is formed when performance begins because that would bind a homeless person to complete the journey to the mayor's office once he or she embarks on it. It is therefore, by nature, an offer for a unilateral contract, even though it does not state in so many words that it can be accepted only by full performance. Because the offer cannot be accepted by anything less than full performance, both (A) and (C) are incorrect.

Question 6

The facts are the same as in Question 5. Assume that the mayor did make an offer in her television interview. Joe had been evicted from his apartment a few days before the mayor made her statement on television, and he has been homeless since then. Joe knew nothing about the mayor's statement on the television. However, by coincidence, on the day that the mayor had appointed for people to come to her office, Joe went to the city hall to protest to the mayor about the inadequacy of the city's efforts to provide enough shelters to house the city's homeless population. He saw the mayor and voiced his protest. He later heard of the mayor's television statement.

(A) Joe has not accepted the offer because there was no meeting of the minds—he had no intent to accept it when he went to the city hall.

(B) Joe manifested apparent intent to accept the offer, so under the objective test, he has accepted the offer even though he did not know about it.

(C) Joe's action is an inadvertent manifestation of acceptance. Even under the objective test, an action that inadvertently manifests intent to accept an unknown offer can never be treated as an acceptance.

(D) Joe's action is an inadvertent manifestation of acceptance. Although an offeree cannot be bound if he or she inadvertently manifests intent to accept an unknown offer, sometimes the offeree can elect to have the action be treated as an acceptance.

Question 6 Answer

(A) is wrong because it suggests that assent is determined subjectively. (B) is wrong because it states the objective test too absolutely and fails to recognize that courts recognize an exception to the objective test where conduct inadvertently manifests acceptance of an offer unknown to the actor. Both (C) and (D) recognize this, but **(D)** is the better answer because (C) is too absolute in stating that an inadvertent manifestation of acceptance can never be treated as acceptance. The purpose of the doctrine is to protect a person who does not know of an offer from being bound by an action that happens, by chance, to appear to be an acceptance of the offer. Where a person does not know of an offer and cannot reasonably be held accountable for the apparent meaning of the act that seems to manifest of assent, it would be unfair to apply the objective test to bind the party to the unintended acceptance. However, the doctrine makes no sense where the party who inadvertently manifested assent later discovers that he has apparently accepted an offer that serves his interests and he wishes to have the benefit of the contract performance. In such a case, it is better policy to hold the offeror accountable for setting up the situation that gave rise to the apparent contract. Courts are particularly likely to allow inadvertent assent to act as acceptance when the offeror is a public entity or official.

Question 7

On March 1, Offeror mailed an offer to Offeree. The offer stated, "This offer will lapse at 5 P.M. on March 10 unless a written acceptance is received before that time." On March 4 at 10 A.M. Offeree mailed a written acceptance to Offeror. At noon on March 5, Offeror sent a text message to Offeree revoking the offer. Offeree received the message immediately. Offeror received Offeree's acceptance when the mail was delivered to him at 4:30 P.M. on March 5.

   (A) The text message was an effective revocation and it terminated the offer because it was received by Offeree before Offeror received the acceptance.

   (B) The text message was not an effective revocation because the offer was sent by mail and the revocation must be sent in the same way. The offer had therefore not terminated by the time it was accepted at 4:30 P.M. on March 5.

   (C) The text message would have been an effective revocation if it had been received by Offeree before the offer was accepted. However, the revocation only took effect at noon on March 5 and the acceptance took effect on mailing at 10 A.M. on March 4. The offer was therefore accepted before Offeror sought to revoke it.

Question 7 Answer

There is a good argument that **(A)** is correct because it is reasonable to interpret the offer as excluding the mailbox rule, so the revocation, which was communicated to Offeree at noon on March 5 took effect before the acceptance was received at 4:30 P.M. on that day. However, there is also a good argument that **(C)** is correct: The language of the offer specifies only that acceptance must be received by the lapse date to bring the contract into existence. It does not actually say that receipt of the acceptance is required to preclude revocation before that date. Therefore, an acceptance sent before the lapse date, while effective for contract formation only if received by 5 P.M. on March 10, could be effective on mailing for purposes of precluding revocation. This may be a strained interpretation, but not an implausible one. (B) is wrong. A revocation is effective as soon as the offeree knows about it. It need not be sent in the same medium as the offer.

■ CHAPTER 6. CONFLICTING STANDARD TERMS, THE BATTLE OF THE FORMS, AND LATE NOTICE OF STANDARD TERMS

Question 1

Buyer, a consumer, called Seller, a retailer, by phone and ordered goods. During the phone call, Seller agreed to ship the goods as ordered. This was the first time that Buyer had bought goods from Seller. When taking Buyer's order, Seller asked for her e-mail address. After the phone call, Seller sent an e-mail to that address confirming the order. The e-mail correctly described the order but it also included a term that Seller includes automatically in all e-mail confirmations. The term stated that any dispute relating to the transaction would be settled by binding arbitration. Seller had not mentioned this term during the phone call.

(A) By including the arbitration provision in the confirmation, Seller made a counteroffer to Buyer.

(B) Seller's e-mail is an acceptance of Buyer's offer despite the arbitration provision. The arbitration provision is a proposal for an additional term which becomes part of the contract provided that it does not materially alter the offer.

(C) Seller's e-mail is an acceptance of Buyer's offer despite the arbitration provision. The arbitration provision is a proposal for an additional term which becomes part of the contract provided that Buyer does not object to it within a reasonable time.

(D) Seller's e-mail is not an acceptance of Buyer's offer and the arbitration provision does not become a term of the contract.

Question 1 Answer

(D) is correct and the other answers, characterizing the e-mail as an acceptance, are wrong. Seller's e-mail is not an acceptance of Buyer's offer, which Seller accepted orally during the phone call. The e-mail was therefore merely a confirmation of the order with an additional term. Under UCC 2-207(2), a term in a confirmation that is additional to what was agreed upon is treated as a proposal for addition to the contract and does not become part of the contract unless both parties are merchants, which Buyer is not.

Question 2

Buyer, a retailer, called Seller, a wholesaler, by phone and ordered goods that Buyer needed as inventory for its store. During the phone call, Seller agreed to ship the goods as ordered. This was the first time that Buyer had bought goods from Seller. After the phone call, Seller mailed a written confirmation to Buyer, The confirmation correctly described the order but it also included a preprinted term that Seller includes in all its confirmations. The term stated that any dispute relating to the transaction would be settled by binding arbitration. Seller had not mentioned this term during the phone call.

(A) By including the arbitration provision in the confirmation, Seller made a counteroffer to Buyer.

(B) Seller's confirmation is an acceptance of Buyer's offer despite the arbitration provision. The arbitration provision is a proposal for an additional term which becomes part of the contract provided that it does not materially alter the offer and Buyer does not object to it within a reasonable time.

(C) Seller's confirmation is not an acceptance of Buyer's offer. Nevertheless, the arbitration provision is a proposal for an additional term which becomes part of the contract provided that it does not materially alter the offer and Buyer does not object to it within a reasonable time.

(D) Seller's confirmation is not an acceptance of Buyer's offer and the arbitration provision does not become a term of the contract.

Question 2 Answer

(C) is correct. As in Question 1, the contract was formed orally during the phone call, so the confirmation is not an acceptance, but merely a confirmation of the contract. Unlike Question 1, both parties to this transaction are clearly merchants as defined in UCC 2-104. Under UCC 2-207(2) where both parties are merchants, an additional term in a confirmation is treated as a proposal for an addition to the contract which becomes part of the contract provided that none of the exceptions in UCC 2-207(2) apply. There are no facts to indicate that Buyer objected to the term in advance or expressly limited the offer to its terms. Therefore, the term will become part of the contract provided that it does not materially alter the offer and Buyer does not object to it within a reasonable time after getting notice of it.

Question 3

Buyer and Seller are both merchants. Buyer ordered goods from Seller, using its order form. The order form contained no preprinted terms. It just set out the particulars of the goods ordered, the delivery term, and the price. Upon receiving the order, Seller immediately sent its order acknowledgment form to Buyer in which it agreed to deliver the goods ordered for the price and at the place stipulated in the order form. The acknowledgment also contained a preprinted forum selection clause that required any dispute arising out of the transaction to be litigated in the courts of Seller's state. Buyer's order form had no provision relating to forum selection. Neither party has yet performed. Assume that Seller's forum selection clause is a material alteration of the offer.

(A) The parties have a contract which has no forum selection provision.

(B) The parties have a contract and Seller's forum selection clause is part of that contract.

(C) Seller's acknowledgement does not operate as an acceptance, so the parties have no contract.

Question 3 Answer

(A) is correct. Seller's confirmation is a definite and seasonable expression of acceptance under UCC 2-207(1), so the parties do have a contract. Seller's forum selection clause is treated by UCC 2-207(2) as a proposal for addition to the contract. Both parties are merchants, so Seller's term could become part of the contract under UCC 2-207(2), but it falls away because it materially alters the offer.

Question 4

Buyer and Seller are both merchants. Buyer ordered goods from Seller, using its order form. The order form contained preprinted terms, one of which was a forum selection clause that required any dispute arising out of the transaction to be litigated in the courts of Buyer's state. Upon receiving the order, Seller immediately sent its order acknowledgment form to Buyer in which it agreed to deliver the goods ordered for the price stipulated in the order form. The acknowledgment also contained preprinted terms, one of which was a forum selection clause that required any dispute arising out of the transaction to be litigated in the courts of Seller's state, which is different from Buyer's state. Assume that Seller's forum selection clause is a material alteration of the offer. Seller delivered the goods and Buyer accepted them. Neither party had read the terms on the other's form. A dispute has now arisen about the quality of the goods.

    (A) The parties have a contract. Buyer's forum selection clause is part of the contract and Seller's is not.

    (B) The parties have a contract. Seller's forum selection clause is part of the contract and Buyer's is not.

    (C) The parties have a contract. Buyer's and Seller's forum selection clauses cancel each other out so that there is no forum selection clause in the contract.

    (D) Seller's acknowledgement does not operate as an acceptance, so the parties have no contract.

Question 4 Answer

(A) is the correct answer in many jurisdictions. Had the writings of the parties not established a contract, but the parties had performed, UCC 2-207(3) would apply to eliminate both Buyer's and Seller's conflicting forum selection clauses, and a contract would have been formed on the terms on which the forms agreed, supplemented by gap fillers. The effect would have been as described in (C). However, the exchange of forms did result in contract formation because Seller's confirmation is a definite and seasonable expression of acceptance under UCC 2-207(1) and Seller's forum selection clause is treated by UCC 2-207(2) as a proposal for addition to the contract which falls away because it would materially alter the contract. Because UCC 2-207(3) does not apply, and because Seller's forum selection clause does not become part of the contract under UCC 2-207(2), the contract is subject to Buyer's clause. Because UCC 2-207(2) does not expressly mention different terms, some courts refuse to apply it to different terms and instead use a "knockout" approach under which they eliminate conflicting terms and replace them with gap fillers. In these jurisdictions, (C) would be the correct answer.

Question 5

Two of the following propositions are arguable interpretations of the opinion in *ProCD v. Zeidenberg* and two are not. Which are the two arguable propositions?

(A) Under UCC 2-207, a seller of software on a disk can add terms to the contract by including them in the software so that they are exhibited to the buyer on opening the program.

(B) Although a contract can be formed at the time of buying software on a disk at a store, it can also be formed by an offer that is made to the buyer on the disk when the program is opened. The buyer then accepts this offer and completes the sale by not returning the software within the time specified in the offer.

(C) Where software on a disk is sold subject to the buyer's right to return it after taking it home, the contract is formed not at the time that it is bought at the store, but when the buyer fails to exercise the right not to keep the software.

(D) Software does not qualify as goods, and therefore UCC Article 2 does not apply to this transaction.

Question 5 Answer

(B) and **(C)** are arguable interpretations of the opinion. (A) is not, because the court determines that offer and acceptance occurred at the time the buyer saw the terms on the software and kept it despite the right to return it. The court therefore does not see the terms as having been added after contract formation and does not therefore say that terms can be added in this way. (D) is also not an arguable interpretation of the opinion. The opinion refers to UCC 2-204 and, as the note following the case indicates, the court assumed that Article 2 applied but declined to apply UCC 2-207 because only one form was used.

Question 6

Buyer bought a skateboard online from Bonebreak Boards, Inc., a skateboard manufacturer. The skateboard was delivered to Buyer in a box a few days later. When Buyer opened the box, there was a single piece of paper attached to the skateboard. Buyer discarded it without reading it. Had he read it he would have seen that it contained two terms:

1. The use of a skateboard can result in serious injury. You use this skateboard at your own risk. By using this skateboard you agree to absolve Bonebreak Boards of all responsibility and liability for any injury that you may suffer as a result of your use of the skateboard.
2. Return policy: An unused skateboard may be returned for a refund within 30 days of purchase.

These terms were not set out anywhere on Bonebreak's website or otherwise revealed to Buyer at the time that he placed his order. Two of the following propositions are arguable on the basis of *ProCD v. Zeidenberg* or *Defontes v. Dell*. Which are the two arguable propositions?

(A) This term does not bind Buyer. He is not a merchant and the term therefore does not become part of the contract under UCC 2-207.

(B) This term does not bind Buyer because Bonebreak did not clearly notify him that he had the right to reject the term and return the goods.

(C) This term is binding on Buyer because it is a reasonable limitation of liability for injury caused by Buyer's negligent use of the skateboard.

(D) This term is binding on Buyer if he uses the skateboard or does not return it within 30 days.

Question 6 Answer

(B) reflects the decision in *Defontes v. Dell* and **(D)** accords with *ProCD v. Zeidenberg*. Although some courts have declined to follow *ProCD*, which would support the conclusion reflected in (A), *Defontes* rejected those cases and held that *ProCD* was better reasoned in holding that a rolling contract binds the customer who accepts it by failure to reject the goods and terms within the time allowed. However, *Defontes* held that the term only binds customers if they are given clear and conspicuous notice of the right to reject. Bonebreak's shrinkwrap terms fall short of the standard of notice required by *Defontes*. The right to reject the terms by returning the goods is vaguely stated and must be inferred from the statement in the liability disclaimer that tells customers that use of the skateboard constitutes agreement to the disclaimer, read with the return policy in the second clause. (C) is not the best answer because it disregards the issue of whether Buyer manifested assent to the term and focuses only on the issue of whether the disclaimer is reasonable. Unless the customer otherwise had adequate notice of the term and the right to reject it, the mere fact that the term may be reasonable does not, by itself make it part of the contract.

Question 7

As in Question 6, Buyer bought a skateboard online from Bonebreak Boards, Inc., a skateboard manufacturer. The skateboard was delivered to Buyer in a box a few days later. The following language was printed on the outside of the box in large letters: "The use of a skateboard can result in serious injury. You use this skateboard at your own risk. By using this skateboard you agree to absolve Bonebreak Boards of all responsibility and liability for any injury that you may suffer as a result of your use of the skateboard." This statement was not contained on Bonebreak's website or otherwise revealed to Buyer at the time that he placed his order. The website made it clear that the sale of the skateboard was final and Buyer could not return it for a refund. Buyer was aware that the sale was final when he placed his order.

(A) The disclaimer does not bind Buyer. He is not a merchant and the term therefore does not become part of the contract under UCC 2-207.

(B) The disclaimer does not bind Buyer because Bonebreak did not clearly notify him that he had the right to reject the term and return the goods.

(C) The disclaimer is binding on Buyer because it is a reasonable limitation of liability for injury caused by Buyer's negligent use of the skateboard.

(D) The disclaimer is binding on Buyer if he uses the skateboard or does not return it within 30 days.

Question 7 Answer

With this change of the facts, **(A)** is the correct answer. (B) and (D) are no longer correct because this is not a rolling contract—Buyer has no right to reject the boxtop terms after reading them on the box, delivered after the order was placed. Therefore, Buyer and Bonebreak entered the contract at the time that Buyer placed his order for the skateboard on the website and the terms on the box must be treated under UCC 2-207(1) as proposals for addition to the contract. Because Buyer is a consumer and a casual buyer, not a merchant, the terms do not become part of the contract under UCC 2-207(2) and fall away unless Buyer agrees to them. Mere use of the skateboard is not likely to be treated as a signification of assent. (This boxtop term would likely have bound Buyer had he been given notice of it at the time of contracting.)

■ CHAPTER 7. PRELIMINARY, INCOMPLETE, AND INDEFINITE AGREEMENTS

Question 1

A Type I preliminary agreement is:

(A) An actual, binding contract.
(B) Not yet a binding contract, but an agreement to enter into a binding contract.
(C) An agreement to agree.
(D) An agreement to negotiate in good faith.

Question 1 Answer

(A) is correct. In *Brown v. Cara* the court characterized a Type I preliminary agreement as a complete agreement that reflects agreement on all issues perceived to require negotiation and binds them to their ultimate objective. All that remains is for the parties to formalize the agreement in a signed writing.

Question 2

A Type II preliminary agreement is:

(A) An actual, binding contract.
(B) Not yet a binding contract, but an agreement to enter into a binding contract.
(C) An agreement to agree.
(D) An agreement to negotiate in good faith.

Question 2 Answer

(D) is correct. As explained in *Brown* and the note following it, a Type II preliminary agreement comes into effect where the parties have not yet entered a binding agreement in their negotiations, but it is clear from the circumstances that they have committed to continue to negotiate in good faith in a genuine effort to reach their ultimate contractual objective.

Question 3

An agreement to agree is:

(A) An actual, binding contract.
(B) Not yet a binding contract, but an enforceable agreement to enter into a binding contract.
(C) An agreement to negotiate in good faith.
(D) Of no binding legal effect at all.

Question 3 Answer

(D) is correct. Courts use the term "agreement to agree" to refer to an agreement that defers a material term for later resolution and therefore cannot qualify as a contract until that term is settled. Because the parties have not yet resolved this essential term, their agreement is too tentative to be treated as a contract.

Question 4

A letter of intent:

(A) Is a binding contract expressed in the form of a letter.
(B) May or may not be a binding contract.
(C) Is an offer.
(D) Is a Type II preliminary agreement.

Question 4 Answer

(B) is correct. A letter of intent is a form of preliminary agreement. It usually sketches out the terms on which the parties are willing to transact business but contemplates execution of a more formal writing in the future and possibly also further negotiations to settle terms that have not been addressed. The letter would have to be interpreted under all the relevant circumstances to decide if the parties intended it to be a binding Type I preliminary agreement, a Type II preliminary agreement committing them to negotiate in good faith, or merely a non-binding preliminary understanding.

Question 5

Lessee and Lessor entered into a five-year lease, which Lessee had the option to renew for a further five-year period. The rent payable for the first five years of the lease was stated in the lease. The renewal option stated that if Lessee decided to exercise the option, the rent for the option period would be "in an amount to be determined by Lessor in its reasonable discretion." After Lessee exercised the renewal option, Lessor proposed a rent that Lessee regarded as excessive.

(A) The exercise of the renewal option did not give rise to a valid contract because the parties deferred agreement on the rent for the option period.
(B) The exercise of the renewal option did not give rise to a valid contract because the rent provision is too indefinite.
(C) The exercise of the renewal option did give rise to a valid contract under which Lessor has the right to determine the rent, subject to a standard of reasonableness.
(D) The exercise of the renewal option did give rise to a valid contract. Because the parties dispute the amount of rent to be paid, the court must fix a reasonable rent for the renewal period.

Question 5 Answer

(C) is correct. The parties did not defer agreement, as stated in (A), because they did not leave the rent for future negotiation, but manifested the intent to give Lessor the right to determine the rent. Lessor's discretion to determine the rent is subject to the requirement that it act reasonably in doing so. Therefore, to resolve the dispute over the rent, the court must determine if Lessor has acted reasonably deciding on what rent to charge. This is not the same as the court fixing the rent, as indicated in (D) because the court's role is to decide if Lessor is reasonable, not in taking over the function of fixing a reasonable rent itself. (B) is wrong. Although the rent provision is not stated as a concrete figure or formula, which would be clearer, it should not cause the renewal contract to fail for indefiniteness. Because the lessor is given the discretion to set the rent, the mechanism for supplying the omitted term is clear enough to indicate what the parties intended and to allow the court to determine what the rent term should be.

■ CHAPTER 8. STATUTE OF FRAUDS

Question 1

A friend of yours has agreed orally to purchase a home from a relative, and is vaguely aware that the statute of frauds might be relevant to the transaction. In particular, your friend is curious what effect the statute of frauds might have if the seller sought to avoid the transaction. Which of the following is an accurate statement?

(A) The statute of frauds does not apply to this transaction unless one of the parties is a merchant.

(B) Unless both parties sign a written document embodying the terms of the purchase and sale, the parties will not have a contract.

(C) If either party begins to perform, part performance will allow enforcement of the contract even if the statute of frauds is not otherwise satisfied.

(D) Any writing which satisfies the statute of frauds will also establish the existence and terms of a contract between the parties.

(E) Even if the seller signed a writing which is sufficient to satisfy the statute of frauds, to enforce the contract the buyer may still need to establish the existence and terms of that contract.

Question 1 Answer

The correct answer is **(E)**. It is possible that a writing could satisfy the statute of frauds without conclusively demonstrating the existence and terms of a contract. (A) is wrong because merchant status is irrelevant to a real estate transaction. (B) overstates the requirements of the statute of frauds in many states; the seller's signature to an adequate writing would be required to enforce the contract against the seller, but not the buyer's. (C) overstates the scope of the part performance exception and is therefore not accurate unless it takes into account that courts tend to apply it narrowly. Apart from any other restrictions, courts require that the performance not be consistent with any explanation other than the parties entered a contract. (D) is incorrect because satisfaction of the statute of frauds is analytically distinct from the existence and terms of the parties' contract as explained in answer (E).

Question 2

On July 1, Crystal Clutter, the proprietor of Crystal's Lighting Store, visited the studio of Arty Glass for the purpose of buying some inventory for her store. She decided to buy a large chandelier that Arty had made. The price of the chandelier was $7,000. (The materials used in making the chandelier constitute only about 45 percent of the price. The balance represents the value of Arty's labor and skill in making the chandelier.) The parties arranged that Arty would pack the chandelier and deliver it to Crystal's store by July 20. Crystal would pay for the chandelier on delivery. Arty recorded the transaction on an invoice slip that bore his name and address at the top of the page. He wrote, "Sold to Crystal's Lighting Store, one chandelier, inventory no. 2543. Price $7,000. Cash on Delivery. To be delivered by July 20 to the following address." He then wrote the address of Crystal's Lighting Store on the invoice. Arty gave Crystal a copy of the invoice and she left the studio. On July 11, before Arty had begun to pack the chandelier, Crystal called him and told him that she had changed her mind and no longer wished to buy it. Arty claims that the parties have an enforceable contract. Crystal denies it.

(A) Crystal and Arty have an enforceable contract. It is a sale of goods subject to the statute of frauds under UCC 2-201, but the statute is satisfied because Arty's note likely qualifies as a sufficient record as against Crystal under UCC 2-201(1).

(B) Crystal and Arty have an enforceable contract. It is a sale of goods subject to the statute of frauds under UCC 2-201, but the statute is satisfied. Although Arty's note does not qualify as a sufficient record as against Crystal under UCC 2-201(1), it is enforceable against her under UCC 2-201(2).

(C) Crystal and Arty have an enforceable contract. It is a sale of goods subject to the statute of frauds under UCC 2-201. There is no sufficient record, but the contract likely satisfies the test of UCC 2-201(3)(a).

(D) Crystal and Arty have an enforceable contract. The contract is not subject to the statute of frauds under UCC 2-201 because the predominant purpose of the transaction is not a sale of goods, but services. This is because the labor in making the chandelier constitutes 55% of its price.

(E) Crystal and Arty may have a contract, but Arty cannot enforce it because it is a sale of goods subject to the statute of frauds under UCC 2-201 and there is no record sufficient to satisfy the statute as against Crystal.

Question 2 Answer

The correct answer is **(B)**. Both parties are merchants and all the elements of UCC 2-201(2) are satisfied. (A) is wrong because Crystal did not sign the record, so UCC 2-201(1) is not satisfied as against her. (C) is wrong because there is no indication that the goods are specially manufactured for Crystal. (D) is wrong because this is not a hybrid transaction but the sale of a tangible end-product that is goods. Almost all goods are manufactured before they are sold and some portion of the price of goods almost always covers the costs of making them. (E) is wrong because the contract is enforceable as explained in answer (B).

Question 3

Susan Smith lived next to John Jones. Susan's car broke down, and she saw that John had a "for sale" sign on the truck parked in his driveway. Susan offered to buy the truck for $6,000, with delivery to be the next day. John agreed. Neither party signed anything. Later that afternoon John decided he could sell the truck for more money, and called Susan to tell her that their deal was off. Which of the following is the most persuasive?

(A) The parties have an enforceable contract, because John accepted Susan's offer.

(B) The parties have an enforceable contract, because John admitted the existence of a contract when he told Susan that their "deal" was off.

(C) The parties may have a contract, but it may not be enforceable under the UCC's statute of frauds.

(D) The parties do not have a contract because John does not intend to be bound.

(E) The parties do not have a contract because they have not agreed to sufficiently definite terms.

Question 3 Answer

The correct answer is **(C)**. If there is a contract between the parties, it is subject to UCC 2-201 because this is a sale of goods for more than $500. The facts do not reveal any writing or other action that would satisfy the requirements of the statute. (A) is incorrect because although the parties may have a contract, it is not certain that the requirements of the statute of frauds have been met, so any contract may not be enforceable. (B) is wrong because John's admission, if there was one, was not sufficient to meet the requirements of UCC 2-201. It is not a writing, so is insufficient under UCC 2-201(1). Likewise, it is not in a pleading, testimony, or otherwise in court, so is insufficient under UCC 2-201(3)(b). (D) is incorrect. Although John may never had intended to be bound (the facts do not expressly say this), he did not manifest that intention until after the contract was arguably entered, and so it is irrelevant. (E) is arguably correct, but given the UCC's flexible approach to contract formation under UCC 2-204, it is far from certain. Accordingly, (C) remains the best answer.

Question 4

Ellie Gant is the proprietor of an art gallery. She sells a lot of glasswork made by Arty Glass, a glassblower. Ellie's customers are fascinated by the techniques used by Arty in making his glass pieces, and many have asked Ellie to arrange lectures by Arty in which he explains his techniques. Ellie decided that the lectures would be a good idea, and that advertising them might generate greater interest in her gallery and increase her sales. She called Arty on February 1, 2017 and proposed to him that he come to her gallery periodically to deliver a lecture on glassblowing, illustrated with slides and videos that demonstrate his technique. Arty was enthusiastic about doing this, and they agreed that he would deliver a two-hour lecture from noon to 2 P.M. on the first Saturday of every month, beginning on March 4, 2017 (the first Saturday of that month) and ending on February 3, 2018 (the first Saturday of that month). The parties settled on the themes for each of the lectures and agreed that Ellie would pay Arty $500 for each lecture, payable when he arrived to give the lecture. After the phone conversation, Ellie sent an e-mail to Arty which read, "I am thrilled that we have set up this lecture series for the first Saturday of the month through February 2018 and confirm that I will pay you $500 for each lecture. I look forward to seeing you on March 4." Ellie did not type her name on the e-mail, but her name does appear with her e-mail address at the head of the e-mail. Before the date of the first lecture on March 3, Arty called Ellie and told her that he had changed his mind and did not want to do the lectures. Ellie threatens to sue Arty for breach of contract, but Arty denies that the parties have an enforceable contract.

(A) Ellie may enforce the agreement against Arty. Their oral agreement is enforceable because the agreement is not subject to the statute of frauds.

(B) Ellie may enforce the agreement against Arty. Their oral agreement is enforceable. Although it is subject to the statute of frauds, Ellie's e-mail to Arty constitutes a record sufficient to satisfy the statute.

(C) The oral agreement between Ellie and Arty is subject to the statute of frauds. Ellie may enforce it against it Arty provided that both parties are merchants.

(D) The oral agreement between Ellie and Arty is subject to the statute of frauds, and Ellie may enforce it against Arty provided that Ellie's name at the head of her e-mail qualifies as a signature.

(E) Ellie may not enforce the agreement against Arty. Their oral agreement is subject to the statute of frauds and is unenforceable because there is no record that satisfies the statute of frauds.

Question 4 Answer

(E) is correct. This is a contract that cannot, by its terms, be performed within a year of its execution because performances are required on set dates through the period of just over a year and neither party could accelerate performance without breaching it. The statute of frauds does therefore apply and there is no record signed by Arty that would satisfy it. (A) is therefore incorrect. (B) is incorrect. Even if the e-mail was sufficient as against Ellie, Arty is the party to be charged and he has not signed any record. (C) is incorrect. This is not a sale of goods, and the parties' status as merchants is not relevant. (D) is incorrect for the same reason as (B).

Question 5

Sam Seller and Ben Buyer orally agreed to the purchase and sale of certain goods for $750. Ben paid the purchase price in cash at the time the parties reached agreement, but Sam never delivered the goods. Ben sues Sam for breach of contract in small claims court. Without knowing more, which of the following is the most persuasive?

(A) The statute of frauds is satisfied as against Ben, but not as against Sam.

(B) The statute of frauds is satisfied as against both Ben and Sam.

(C) The contract will not be enforceable against either party under the statute of frauds, because neither Sam nor Ben signed a writing sufficient to indicate that a contract for sale was made between the parties.

(D) The statute of frauds will not apply because Ben performed the contract within a year of its execution.

(E) The statute of frauds will not apply unless both parties are merchants.

Question 5 Answer

The correct answer is **(B)**. This is a sale of goods for more than $500, so UCC 2-201 applies. Ben's payment of the price in cash and Sam's acceptance of that payment satisfy the statute as against both parties under UCC 2-201(3)(c). (A) is therefore incorrect. (C) is also incorrect, because a signed writing is not necessary if an exception to the writing requirement is satisfied. (D) is correct insofar as it implies that the one-year provision of the statute of frauds in effect in most states will not apply, but it also suggests that other statutes of frauds (such as UCC 2-201) will not apply, which is incorrect. (E) is incorrect because merchant status is not required for UCC 2-201 to apply. The exception in UCC 2-201(2) only applies between merchants, but that is not the exception at issue here.

■ CHAPTER 9. CONSIDERATION

Question 1

During Joe College's freshman year, his wealthy uncle Ron Rich wrote him a letter in which he promised to pay off Joe's student loans if Joe studied hard and graduated with at least a B average. Joe in fact studies hard and graduates with a degree in biology and a straight A average. He is admitted and is offered scholarships at several selective medical schools as a result. Ron Rich dies before he pays anything toward Joe's student loans. The uncle's estate refuses to honor his promise to Joe. Without more, which of the following is the most persuasive?

(A) Ron Rich's promise is supported by consideration because Joe College incurred a legal detriment that was bargained for.

(B) Ron Rich's promise is not supported by consideration, because Joe College did not incur a detriment but instead was benefitted by his hard work.

(C) Ron Rich's promise is not supported by consideration, because Ron Rich was not benefitted by Joe College's hard work.

(D) It would be against public policy to enforce such a promise against an estate.

Question 1 Answer

(A) is the best answer. This question presents a modern version of *Hamer v. Sidway*. By applying himself to his studies instead of the other activities he might have chosen during his college years, Joe has incurred a legal detriment. It is irrelevant that he might have benefitted in some real sense from his hard work, so long as his performance constituted a legal detriment. Accordingly, (B) is incorrect. Further, it seems the legal detriment was bargained for, that is, the promise and the legal detriment, in Holmes' terms, stand in a "relation of conventional reciprocal inducement." Although we don't know Joe's actual motivations for studying hard, conventionally a promise like the one his uncle made might have encouraged him to do so. We can thus conclude that such a promise typically would induce the legal detriment. The converse is also true. Someone in the uncle's position might well make such a promise to encourage the nephew to study, so, in other words, we can assume that the legal detriment induced the promise as well. Because the uncle received what he likely sought, it's fair to say that he was benefitted in the legal sense, even if he didn't receive any concrete economic benefit from Joe's hard work, so (C) is incorrect. (D) alludes to the statement in *Congregation v. Deleo* that it would be against public policy to enforce a promise such as the one involved in that case against an estate. Although the court doesn't explain its reasoning on that point, its primary concern seems to be that the promise was oral, and here it is written. Further, the court concluded in the *Deleo* case that no consideration was present, and here there is consideration. So without more facts, it is overconfident to conclude that public policy would prevent enforcement of the uncle's promise under these circumstances.

Question 2

Sally Smith promises that if Jerry Jones comes by her house on Tuesday morning, she will pay him $75. Jerry drops by Sally's house on Tuesday morning, but Sally refuses to pay him the promised $75. Which of the following facts (if true) is MOST likely to lead to the conclusion that Sally's promise was supported by consideration?

    (A) Before Sally made her promise, Jerry had done some landscaping work for her.

    (B) It would benefit Sally to have Jerry drop by her house.

    (C) It would be inconvenient for Jerry to drop by Sally's house.

    (D) It would benefit Jerry to drop by Sally's house.

Question 2 Answer

(B) is the best answer. The issue in this question is whether any legal detriment Jerry suffered was bargained for. For the consideration to be bargained for, it must appear that the promise induced the legal detriment and the legal detriment induced the promise. So long as Jerry had no pre-existing legal obligation to come to Sally's house, he would incur a legal detriment by doing something he wasn't otherwise obligated to do. Whether it was inconvenient for Jerry to drop by Sally's house or alternatively, would benefit him, is irrelevant to the question of whether he suffered a legal detriment. (A) is incorrect. The landscaping work Jerry did in the past probably constituted a legal detriment, but it can't be consideration for Sally's promise because it wasn't induced by the promise—the promise had not yet been made at the time he did the landscaping work. In the confusing language courts often use, the landscaping work constituted "past consideration" and thus is insufficient. Although consideration doctrine doesn't require that the promisor receive a benefit, a benefit to the promisor may be one factor that helps distinguish bargained for consideration from a condition to a gift. The question does not state the reason why Sally told Jerry to come by her house to receive the payment, so it is conceivable that Sally was proposing to give a gift of $75 to Jerry and the only reason she told him to come to her house was to deliver it to him. If that is so, Jerry's detriment did not benefit Sally, and his coming to the house may therefore be just a condition of getting the gift, and not consideration. If, however, the visit benefitted Sally, one assumes she might have made her promise to induce Jerry to come by. (B) is the best answer because it states a factor that is relevant to the question of whether any legal detriment was bargained for, while (A), (C), and (D) do not.

Question 3

Under applicable law, all charitable organizations are required to make their financial records available to the public. Dan Donor expressed an interest in looking at the records of Cheap Charity Co. (a charitable organization dedicated to educating the public on principles of thriftiness). Cheap Charity Co. agreed to let Dan review its records, so long as Dan paid it $100 to reimburse it for the personnel costs associated with gathering and making the relevant records available. Dan agreed, but after reviewing the records refused to pay the $100 charge. Which of the following is the most persuasive?

(A) Dan is obligated to pay Cheap Charity Co. $100, because his promise to pay is supported by legally sufficient consideration.

(B) Dan probably is obligated to pay Cheap Charity Co. $100, because courts generally do not inquire into the adequacy of consideration.

(C) Dan probably is not obligated to pay Cheap Charity Co. $100, because his promise is illusory.

(D) Dan probably is not obligated to pay Cheap Charity Co. $100, unless Cheap Charity Co. did more than the law required.

Question 3 Answer

(D) is the best answer. If Cheap Charity Co. has a preexisting legal duty to make its records available to Dan, it incurs no new legal detriment in allowing him to view them. Assuming the law doesn't authorize organizations to charge a fee, absent more there wouldn't be any consideration for Dan's promise. If, however, Cheap Charity Co.'s performance differs from what is required by law in a way which reflects more than a pretense of a bargain, the difference may itself constitute a legal detriment sufficient to constitute consideration. Without knowing more about whether Cheap Charity Co.'s performance mirrors what was already required of it at law, (A) is over-confident. (B) alludes to the principle that so long as legally sufficient consideration is present, courts generally don't inquire into the relative value of the legal detriments undertaken by the parties. Since it is the legal sufficiency of Cheap Charity Co.'s detriment that is at issue, not its relative value, this principle is inapposite. (C) questions the legal sufficiency of Dan's promise, which is not at issue.

Question 4

Cal Careful trips on a crack in Larry Lizard's sidewalk and hurts his arm. Larry rushes outside and tells Cal that he will give Cal $500 when he gets paid at the end of the month if Cal agrees not to sue him. Cal agrees. As it turns out, Cal suffered a minor sprain and soon feels better. At the end of the month Larry refuses to pay him anything. Which of the following is the most persuasive?

(A) Any claim Cal had proved to be invalid, so Cal provided no consideration for Larry's promise.

(B) If at the time of their agreement Cal had a reasonable and good faith belief in the possible validity of his claim against Larry, he provided consideration for Larry's promise.

(C) There is no consideration for Larry's promise, because at the time of their agreement Larry had a preexisting legal duty to maintain his sidewalk.

(D) There is consideration for Larry's promise, because it would benefit him not to have Cal take him to court.

(E) There is consideration for Larry's promise, because courts generally do not inquire into the adequacy of consideration.

Question 4 Answer

(B) is the best answer. At issue in this question are the circumstances under which settlement of a claim will be deemed to be supported by consideration. Even if a claim turns out in retrospect to be unfounded, under some circumstances the promise to give up that claim will be sufficient to provide consideration for the potential defendant's return promise. So even if Cal's potential claim against Larry turns out to be invalid, giving it up may constitute consideration for Larry's promise to pay in appropriate circumstances. So, (A) is incorrect. *Fiege v. Boehm* states "forbearance to assert an invalid claim by one who has not an honest and reasonable belief in its possible validity" is insufficient consideration for a contract. If, on the other hand, the party agreeing to give up the claim has a reasonable and good faith belief in its potential validity, consideration is present. These are the assumptions specified in (B). As an aside, we note the tests articulated in Restatement, Second §74 may allow enforcement of settlement agreements in an even broader range of circumstances than those specified in (B). Under the tests articulated in this section, if the invalidity of the claim was in fact subject to question at the time of the settlement agreement, a promise to surrender that claim can constitute consideration. Even if there was no doubt under the facts or the law that the claim was invalid, if Cal nonetheless believed that it might fairly be determined to be valid, giving it up could constitute consideration. If true, (C) establishes Cal's right to bring a claim, and reinforces the legally sufficiency of his promise to give up that claim, not the converse. (D) may rest on a true statement—Larry would gain a practical benefit if he was relieved of the inconvenience of having to defend himself in court—but at issue in this question is the legal sufficiency of Cal's promise, not whether it induced Larry's promise to pay. Even a completely vexatious and frivolous lawsuit might inconvenience Larry, and he might benefit in a practical sense if Cal were to give it up. But it doesn't follow that surrender of such a claim would be legally sufficient consideration for Larry's promise. Likewise, (E) cites an accurate statement of the law—courts generally do not inquire into the adequacy of consideration; that is, they generally do not inquire into the relative value of the legal detriments exchanged by the parties. However, they do inquire into the legal sufficiency of any alleged consideration, so (E) standing alone is not persuasive.

Question 5

Realty Co. and Business Co. signed a five-page lease agreement in which Business Co. agreed to lease some office space from Realty Co. for a period of five years. Among other things, the lease agreement stated "Business Co. shall have no obligation to move into the space under this lease or pay rent unless after inspection Business Co. finds the leased premises to be satisfactory." After both parties signed the lease agreement, Realty Co. found another tenant who was willing to lease the space at a higher rent. Which of the following is the most persuasive?

(A) The lease agreement is not enforceable as a contract, because Business Co.'s obligations under the lease are illusory.

(B) The lease agreement is not enforceable as a contract, because Business Co. had a pre-existing duty to inspect the leased premises, and has not yet done so.

(C) Realty Co.'s obligation to lease the space is supported by consideration, because Business Co. has an implied obligation to exercise its discretion reasonably or in good faith.

(D) Realty Co.'s obligation to lease the space is supported by consideration, because it did not intend to make a gratuitous gift.

Question 5 Answer

(C) is the best answer. If Business Co. were deemed to retain complete discretion over any obligation to go forward, (A) would be the best answer. Under this interpretation, Business Co. wouldn't really commit itself to do anything by signing the lease agreement. Where the parties otherwise manifest an intention to be bound, however, most courts would constrain Business Co.'s discretion, and require it to make a reasonable or good faith determination of whether the leased premises were satisfactory. Although the choice of standard may depend on the circumstances, few courts are likely to interpret the agreement to allow Business Co. to be arbitrary in the exercise of its discretion. (B) reflects a misunderstanding of the relationship between preexisting legal duties and consideration doctrine. (D) focuses on Realty Co.'s motives in entering the lease, rather than on the nature of the legal detriment provided by Business Co.

■ CHAPTER 10. PROMISSORY ESTOPPEL

Question 1

Ken Kirksey is a wealthy investment banker. When he has the time, he likes to go hiking with his childhood friend, Ron Ricketts. Ken knows that Ron has long wanted to go trekking in the Himalayan mountains, and has been saving for years to afford the trip. This year, on Ron's birthday, Ken urges him to sign up for a Himalayan trekking adventure right away, and promises to pay $10,000 towards the cost of the trip to help him do so. Although he would love to join him, Ken says, he won't be able to take enough time off work, so he encourages Ron to go on his own. Ron thanks him profusely for his generosity. Ken subsequently rues his promise, and informs Ron that he won't pay anything towards the trip. Ron wonders if Ken is potentially liable to him under a theory of promissory estoppel. Which of the following would support recovery under that theory?

(A) Before Ken made his promise, he knew that Ron had spent over $5,000 on travel gear for a potential Himalayan adventure.

(B) Ken had paid for several solo hiking trips Ron had taken in the past.

(C) After Ken made his promise, Ron purchased non-refundable airline tickets to Nepal.

(D) All of the above.

(E) None of the above—Ron will not be able to recover under a theory of promissory estoppel.

Question 1 Answer

(D) is the best answer. Although Ron's success in litigation is not assured, a court may allow recovery under a theory of promissory estoppel if it is convinced that injustice would result if the promise were not enforced. All of the factors listed in (A) through (C) weigh in Ron's favor. (C) shows a costly action that Ron took, and in context it is reasonable to suppose that Ken's promise induced him to take such a step. (A) suggests that Ken knew that Ron was serious about his intentions, someday, to take a trip to the Himalayas, so one might conclude that Ken's promise was one which he reasonably should have expected to induce action or forbearance on Ron's part. Given that Ron has already spent money in furtherance of his dreams, Ken perhaps should have reasonably expected his promise to induce him to spend more. Further, the fact, as indicated in (B), that Ken had paid for Ron's trips in the past made his promise the more credible, and increases the likelihood that Ron may have relied on it and supports his reasonableness in doing so. Of course, there are no guarantees, but promissory estoppel is a highly contextual theory of liability, and all of the factors listed in (A) through (C) are likely to be relevant should Ron pursue his claim.

Question 2

Phil Anthropist signed a written pledge card, in which he promised to make a $5,000 donation to the Anystate Symphony "in consideration of my love of music and my moral obligation to support the arts." Phil died before he could fulfill the terms of his pledge. Which of the following is the most persuasive and certain?

(A) Although it isn't supported by consideration, the pledge will be enforceable against Phil's estate.

(B) If Anystate Symphony incurred costs in reliance on Phil's pledge, it is likely that it will be able to enforce the pledge against his estate.

(C) Anystate Symphony probably can enforce the pledge against Phil's estate, because the pledge is supported by consideration.

(D) Anystate Symphony probably cannot enforce the pledge against Phil's estate, because the pledge is not supported by consideration.

(E) Anystate Symphony probably cannot enforce the pledge against Phil's estate, because enforcement would impose an unwarranted legal rigidity on a moral or ethical obligation.

Question 2 Answer

(B) is the best answer. Charitable pledges are particularly fruitful grounds for the theory of promissory estoppel, and courts regularly enforce pledges if the promisees have relied on them to their detriment. Some courts who follow Restatement, Second §90(2) are willing to enforce charitable pledges even if there is neither consideration for nor reliance on the pledge. Not all courts are willing to go this far, as suggested by the analysis in *In re Morton Shoe*, so (A) is overconfident. Further, recovery under a theory of promissory estoppel is more straightforward than recovery under a theory of contract supported by consideration. Neither the donor's love of music nor any felt moral obligation to support the arts would normally constitute the type of legal detriment that could constitute consideration for the pledge. Nonetheless, upon receipt of the pledge some courts might imply a promise on the Symphony's part to perpetuate the donor's name—as in *Allegheny College v. National Chautauqua County Bank of Jamestown*. Absent express instructions from the donor on what to do with the pledged funds, however, some courts would be hesitant to imply such a promise, and would find consideration lacking. *Congregation v. Deleo* (from Chapter 9) for instance, refused to find consideration in the absence of such instructions. Since the consideration analysis in this context varies from jurisdiction to jurisdiction and from case to case, either (C) or (D) could be correct, so neither is certain. (E) quotes the justification for not enforcing the promise of confidentiality from a newspaper to its source in *Cohen v. Cowles Media Co.* as a contract supported by consideration. It isn't clear that the reasoning of *Cohen* would carry over to the context of charitable pledges. Even if it did, *Cohen* nonetheless enforced the promise under the more flexible theory of promissory estoppel. At bottom, (E) overstates the case when it suggests that the pledge will not be enforceable under any theory.

Question 3

Mammoth Corporation is considering entering into a major contract with Amalgamated Industries. Before the parties start to negotiate, the president of Mammoth tells the president of Amalgamated that he needs to know whether Amalgamated is serious about the deal, because Mammoth is going to have to hire lawyers, investment bankers, and other professionals to help it put the deal together. The president of Amalgamated states, "We're as serious as serious gets. Let's all get busy and put this thing to bed." After months of contentious discussions, Amalgamated breaks off negotiations, and Mammoth seeks remedies. Which of the following is the most persuasive?

(A) Absent additional facts, it is unlikely that Amalgamated owes Mammoth any enforceable obligation.

(B) The parties probably had an agreement to negotiate in good faith, and Amalgamated was probably in breach when it broke off negotiations.

(C) By beginning to negotiate, Amalgamated accepted Mammoth's offer and implicitly promised to complete negotiations. Amalgamated probably breached this promise when it broke off negotiations.

(D) By beginning to negotiate, the parties entered into an option contract, and it was too late for Amalgamated to back out of the negotiations.

(E) Mammoth should be able to recover from Amalgamated on a theory of promissory estoppel.

Question 3 Answer

(A) is the best answer. This question calls for a subtle distinction among the different forms of liability that might arise during contractual negotiations. Although courts sometimes find that promises in the initial stages of negotiations give rise to some level of liability, that holding is unlikely under the facts of the question. For instance, there are no indications of unequal bargaining power or other inequitable conduct along the lines of that found in *Hoffman v. Red Owl Stores, Inc.* Instead, the facts of the question more closely resemble those of *Garwood Packaging, Inc. v. Allen & Company, Inc.,* and are even less compelling than those of the case. Amalgamated's assurances in the question are vague and nonspecific. Other than the inconvenience and costs of the negotiations themselves, there is no indication that Mammoth incurred costs in reliance on the assurances, certainly nothing as extensive as the costs incurred by the unsuccessful plaintiff in *Garwood.* It is highly likely that a court would decline to use promissory estoppel to enforce the assurances as promises absent additional facts, so (E) is incorrect. No other theory of liability seems appropriate here either. As we studied in Chapter 7, courts are sometimes willing to imply enforceable agreements to negotiate in good faith. This approach remains controversial in many jurisdictions, however, and even in those where it is available generally, it is unlikely to apply in circumstances like these. Generally a court will require much more in terms of commitment, and at a minimum will want to see a greater degree of consensus on the structure of the negotiations or the basic outlines of the proposed transaction, before it will imply an enforceable agreement to negotiate in good faith. The conclusion stated in (B), therefore, is unlikely. (C) states the rule of law that would be applicable if beginning performance was a reasonable way to accept an offer. It is inappropriate to apply that rule here, because there is no offer open for acceptance. (D), alternatively, states the rule of law that is appropriate when an offer is an offer to enter into a unilateral contract. As we saw in Chapter 5, if the only way to accept an offer is to complete performance, then the beginning of that performance might be deemed to create an option contract, and it might be too late for the offeror to revoke its offer. There is no reason to believe there is an offer here, much less the specific kind of offer that calls for performance as the sole means of acceptance.

Question 4

Paul Perfidious promises to sell his house to Ned Newbie, with the transaction to close in sixty days' time. Although the parties talk at length about the specific terms of their agreement, they never commit anything to writing. Ned proceeds to purchase expensive custom-made living room furniture, specifically designed to fit the seating area in Paul's house. Ned also gives the required thirty-day notice to terminate the lease on his apartment, so he will be ready to move into his new house as soon as the transaction closes. As the agreed date for the sale approaches, Paul regrets his decision to sell, and calls Ned to let him know he has taken the house off the market. Ned wonders whether Paul's promise to sell his house should be enforceable under a theory of promissory estoppel. Which of the following is the most persuasive and accurate?

(A) Ned will not be able to enforce Paul's promise under a theory of promissory estoppel, because promissory estoppel is only applicable in situations where consideration is absent.

(B) Ned will not be able to enforce Paul's promise under a theory of promissory estoppel, because enforcement of the promise is barred by the statute of frauds.

(C) Any contract between Paul and Ned may be unenforceable under the statute of frauds, but Ned may be able to obtain some remedies under a theory of promissory estoppel.

(D) Ned's reliance on Paul's promise substitutes for consideration, so Ned should be able to attain specific performance of Paul's promise.

Question 4 Answer

(C) is by no means certain, but is the best answer among the alternatives. Since the agreement between Paul and Ned contemplates the transfer of an interest in land, it will be subject to the statute of frauds in effect in the relevant state. Accordingly, since as far as we know Paul hasn't signed anything, the contract will be unenforceable against him unless an exception to the statute of frauds obtains. In some states, Ned's actions in reliance on the contract might be sufficient to satisfy the part performance exception to the statute of frauds. In other states, it might not. In the alternative, Ned could argue that his reliance should operate to remove the barrier of the statute of frauds under a theory of promissory estoppel, akin to the principle reflected in Restatement, Second §139. It seems clear that Paul's promise to sell his house induced Ned to purchase the living room furniture and terminate his apartment lease. Whether Paul should have reasonably expected Ned to take such actions is open to debate. Likewise, whether the nature of reliance was such that a court would deem it unjust not to enforce Paul's promise is uncertain. Assuming Ned could make out all of the elements of Restatement, Second §139, some courts would be willing to enforce Paul's promise, at least to some degree, notwithstanding the statute of frauds. Not all courts have accepted the invitation of Restatement, Second §139, however. Ned's potential to succeed on this theory may vary greatly from jurisdiction to jurisdiction. (A) confines the doctrine of promissory estoppel too narrowly. Although courts have differed in their willingness to apply the theory in the broader context of a bargain, there is no question that some courts have been willing to do so. *Tour Costa Rica v. Country Walkers, Inc.* is an example of a case where a court allows recovery under a theory of promissory estoppel, even though consideration is arguably present. Some jurisdictions do not allow promissory estoppel to overcome operation of the statute of frauds, but (B) overstates the case by suggesting no jurisdiction would be willing to do so under any circumstances. In contrast, (D) overstates the case in the other direction, suggesting that Ned will be able to obtain specific performance. Although in many jurisdictions specific performance is available rather routinely to a buyer who establishes that a seller has breached its contract to sell land, it is unclear whether courts would be willing to allow specific performance on a theory of promissory estoppel. Some courts, although willing to enforce Paul's promise generally, would limit Ned's remedy as justice requires to his expectation or even his reliance damages.

Question 5

Change the facts of Question 4 as follows. This time, assume that Paul Perfidious is Ned Newbie's wealthy uncle. Paul learns that Ned has lost his job and is destitute. He writes a letter to Ned as follows: "I have long been planning to retire, and have recently decided to do so and travel the world. I know your situation is one of grief and difficulty. You have always been kind to me, Ned, and I appreciate all of the things you have done for me over the years. If you are able to terminate your current apartment lease and get out of your obligation to pay rent, I promise I will give you my house in sixty days' time. I will have no further need for it, and I feel like I want you to do well." Ned receives the letter, immediately gives notice on his apartment, and purchases (on credit) some expensive custom-made living room furniture, specifically designed to fit the seating area in Paul's house. Paul passes away before he can honor his promise, and Ned seeks to enforce the promise against Paul's estate. Assume Ned is able to persuade a court that Paul's promise should be enforceable against his estate under a theory of promissory estoppel. Which of the following is the most persuasive?

(A) Ned's remedy will be limited to restitution for the value of the things he had done for Paul over the years.

(B) Ned will be able to obtain compensation for the costs he incurred in reliance on Paul's promise, so long as he can establish that they were reasonable under the circumstances.

(C) Ned will be able to obtain compensation equal to the value of Paul's house.

(D) Ned will be able to obtain specific performance of Paul's promise to give Ned his house.

Question 5 Answer

(B) is the best answer, although some courts might be willing to award Ned the damages described in (C). Given the likely disparity between the value of Paul's house and the relatively limited costs Ned incurred in reliance on Paul's promise, it's likely that a court would conclude that justice requires that his remedy be limited to his reliance damages. (B) describes his reliance damages, while (C) posits an expectation measure of his loss. Neither restitution nor specific performance is a common remedy under promissory estoppel. Accordingly, without more neither (A) nor (D) is persuasive.

■ CHAPTER 11. OPTIONS AND FIRM OFFERS

Question 1

Dick makes a written offer to Jane to sell her his house. Dick's offer, by its terms, states that it shall remain open for acceptance until Friday at 5:00 p.m. Without more, which of the following is accurate?

(A) If not previously terminated, the offer will lapse on Friday at 5:00 p.m.

(B) Any attempt to revoke the offer prior to Friday at 5:00 p.m. will be ineffective.

(C) Even if Jane makes a counteroffer, Jane will continue to have the power to accept Dick's offer until Friday at 5:00 p.m.

(D) All of the above.

(E) None of the above.

Question 1 Answer

(A) is the best answer. Even if use of the word "shall" connotes commitment on Dick's part, without more, any promise to keep the offer open is a legal nullity. As far as we know it isn't supported by consideration. Nor does Dick recite a purported consideration for making the offer. There is no other reason under the facts to believe that any promise to keep the offer open would be enforceable. Accordingly, both (B) and (C) are incorrect. So long as the offer hasn't yet been accepted, Dick may revoke it and terminate the power of acceptance. The effect of a counteroffer would be to terminate the power of acceptance as well.

Question 2

As in Question 1, Dick makes a written offer to Jane to sell her his house. A court concludes that the offer constitutes a binding option contract. A consequence of this characterization is:

(A) Dick is obligated to sell his house to Jane on the terms specified in the offer.

(B) Jane is obligated to purchase Dick's house on the terms specified in the offer.

(C) Dick may not revoke his offer to sell his house to Jane.

(D) Jane paid Dick for his promise not to revoke his offer.

Question 2 Answer

(C) is the best answer. An option contract is preliminary to, but distinct from, the ultimate contract it contemplates. The consequence of concluding that an offer constitutes an option contract is that the offeror loses its usual right to revoke the offer at will. The offeree is not obligated to accept the offer—so (A) overstates the consequences of characterizing the offer as an option contract.

Unless and until the offeree does accept the offer, the offeror is not obligated to go forward with the ultimate contract either, so (B) is likewise incorrect. (D) states a rationale for the court's conclusion that the offer was an option contract. However, it is not a consequence of characterizing the offer as an option.

Question 3

General Contractor Co. planned to bid on a project to build a new school. It sent out letters inviting local subcontractors to submit bids to complete various aspects of the job. In its invitation, it detailed the work to be done in some detail, and stated "to allow us to estimate our own bid, all bids for subcontracts must be held open for a period of sixty days." T&R Excavating, Inc. submitted a bid to complete the excavation work for the project for $50,000. At the bottom of its one-page bid, it stated "this bid is a price quotation and is for informational purposes only; it does not constitute a firm offer and it should not be relied upon." General did not notice this statement at the bottom of T&R's form, and used the $50,000 figure T&R quoted in computing its own bid. General was awarded the school job; however, citing increased costs T&R refused to do the excavation work for anything less than $75,000. Which of the following is the most persuasive?

(A) T&R's bid was an offer, and General accepted it when it used T&R's bid in computing its own bid for the school job.

(B) T&R's bid was an offer, and T&R was not entitled to revoke it for a period of sixty days.

(C) T&R's bid was an offer, and to the extent General relied on it in computing its own bid, T&R may not be entitled to revoke it.

(D) T&R's bid was an offer, but T&R was entitled to revoke it at any time prior to acceptance.

(E) Absent additional facts, T&R's bid did not constitute an offer.

Question 3 Answer

(E) is the best answer. This question harkens back to *Fletcher-Harlee Corp. v. Pote Concrete Contractors, Inc.* in Chapter 4. It is a reminder that a communication that makes it clear that no commitment is intended cannot constitute an offer. All of the other answers depend on T&R's bid being an offer, which it is not.

Question 4

As in Question 3, General Contractor Co. planned to bid on a project to build a new school. It sent out letters inviting local subcontractors to submit bids to complete various aspects of the job. In its invitation, it set out the work to be done in some detail, and stated "to allow us to estimate our own bid, all bids for subcontracts must be held open for a period of 60 days." T&R Excavating, Inc. submitted a bid to complete the excavation work for the project for $50,000. T&R's bid was silent on whether and how long it would be held open. General used the $50,000 figure T&R quoted in computing its own bid. General was awarded the school job; however, citing increased costs, T&R refused to do the excavation work for anything less than $75,000. Which of the following is the most persuasive?

(A) T&R's bid was an offer, and General accepted it when it used T&R's bid in computing its own bid for the school job.

(B) T&R's bid was an offer, and T&R was not entitled to revoke it for a period of 60 days.

(C) T&R's bid was an offer, and to the extent General relied on it in computing its own bid, T&R may not be entitled to revoke it.

(D) T&R's bid was an offer, but T&R was entitled to revoke it at any time prior to acceptance.

(E) Absent additional facts, T&R's bid did not constitute an offer.

Question 4 Answer

Under modern doctrine, **(C)** is probably the best answer, although depending on the facts and the jurisdiction, some courts might find (A) or (D) persuasive instead. The question poses a situation similar to the ones involved in *Drennan v. Star Paving Co.* and *James Baird Co. v. Gimbel Bros.* (summarized in Problem 11.2). Typically, a contractor isn't deemed to accept a bid merely by using it in computing its own bid. There may be some exceptions to this, however, especially if some rule of law or custom in the relevant industry requires a successful contractor to award a subcontract to the lowest bidder. Should this exceptional situation obtain, a court might conclude that General accepted T&R's bid and was obligated to award the subcontract to T&R, subject only to the condition that General receive the contract on the overall job. This argument was rejected by *Drennan* and by *Baird*, and absent additional facts there is no reason to believe it would be persuasive here, so (A) is not the best answer. Some might argue that since General's solicitation stated that all bids must be held open for a period of sixty days, T&R implicitly promised to do so when it submitted a bid in response to the solicitation. Nonetheless, generally speaking, a mere promise to keep an offer outstanding for a stated period of time is ineffective absent consideration or reliance. (B) requires neither consideration nor reliance, and so overstates the case. (C) reflects the holding in *Drennan v. Star Paving Co.,* while (D) takes the more conservative approach adopted by *James Baird Co. v. Gimbel Bros.* While the approach of *Drennan* has not been universally adopted, it is now enshrined in Restatement, Second §87(2), and is probably more reflective of the modern trend.

Question 5

Sally Sedan signs a writing in which she offers to purchase an antique car at a specified price from Dan Dealer. Assume that the terms of the offer in context are fair and reasonable. The offer by its terms states that it will remain open for a period of 30 days, and Sally separately initials this statement. Without more, which of the following is the most persuasive and certain?

(A) Unless the writing recites a purported consideration for the making of the offer, Sally may revoke the offer at will.

(B) If Sally is a merchant, the offer will be irrevocable for the period stated.

(C) If Dan is a merchant, the offer will be irrevocable for the period stated.

(D) If Dan relies to his detriment on the offer, it will be irrevocable for the period stated.

Question 5 Answer

(B) is the best answer, although in some circumstances (D) may be correct as well. Since the offer contemplates a sale of goods, UCC 2-205 is relevant. This section makes certain offers to buy or sell goods irrevocable, even if the offeree provides no consideration for the making of the offer. In order for the section to apply, however, certain requirements must be met. First, the offer must be by a merchant, which is the requirement highlighted by (B). Second, the offer must give assurance that it will be held open, which the question says it does. Third, UCC 2-205 makes the offer irrevocable for the period stated—here, 30 days—so long as that period doesn't exceed three months, which it doesn't. Finally, if the promise to keep the offer open is on a form provided by the offeree, it must be separately signed by the offeror. We have no indication that Dan provided the form that Sally signed. But even if he did, the question indicates that she separately initialed the term in question, and her initials will almost certainly qualify as a signature. At bottom, so long as Sally is a merchant, the requirements of UCC 2-205 are met and the offer will be irrevocable for the period stated. Dan's merchant status is irrelevant under UCC 2-205, so (C) is inapposite. (A) invokes a situation where an offer might be irrevocable—it mirrors the requirements of Restatement, Second §87(1)—but it fails to recognize that UCC 2-205 provides an alternative mechanism for making a firm offer in the context of sales of goods. (D) is arguably persuasive, but is by no means certain. Since UCC 2-205 provides a relatively straightforward mechanism for merchants to make their offers irrevocable, some courts would be disinclined to use promissory estoppel to achieve the same result in circumstances where the elements of the statute were not met. Even if a court were generally willing to use promissory estoppel to supplement UCC 2-205, it is likely that the court would require more than a mere showing that Dan relied to his detriment on the offer. For instance, if the court were to follow a rule akin to that outlined in Restatement, Second §87(2), it would want to examine whether Sally reasonably should have expected Dan to rely on the offer, whether his reliance was of a substantial character, and to what extent it would be necessary to consider the offer binding as an option contract in order to prevent injustice. The bare facts of the question do not illuminate whether a court would be likely to find any of these factors to be present.

■ CHAPTER 12. OBLIGATION BASED ON UNJUST ENRICHMENT AND MATERIAL BENEFIT

Question 1

The term "quasi-contract" refers to:

    (A) An actual contract, not expressed, but inferred from the circumstances.
    (B) The basis of a claim for unjust enrichment.
    (C) The basis of a claim for restitution.
    (D) The basis of a claim for *quantum meruit*.

Question 1 Answer

(B) is correct. (A) is wrong because "quasi-contract" does not refer to an actual contract, whether express or implied from the circumstances, but is the basis of a claim for unjust enrichment. (C) and (D) are wrong. Restitution refers to a type of remedy, not the basis of the claim, while *quantum meruit* is one way of measuring recovery under the remedy. Although restitution based on *quantum meruit* is a remedy available for quasi-contract (unjust enrichment), neither the remedy of restitution nor the measurement based on *quantum meruit* are confined to quasi-contract. Either or both may be available in some circumstances for breach of an actual contract.

Question 2

While sitting on his porch one morning, Guy Good saw his neighbor's dog run into the street. A passing car hit the dog and drove on without stopping. Guy tried to find his neighbor to tell her, but she was not home. Guy therefore took the injured dog to a veterinary clinic. Before it would treat the dog, the clinic insisted that Guy agree to pay for the treatment, which he did. The treatment cost $600.

    (A) Guy should be able to recover from his neighbor the $600 charged by the veterinary clinic on the basis of quasi-contract.
    (B) Guy should be able to recover from his neighbor the $600 charged by the veterinary clinic on the basis of contract implied in fact.
    (C) Guy should not be able to recover from his neighbor the $600 charged by the veterinary clinic, either on the basis of quasi-contract or contract implied in fact. The neighbor did not agree to Guy's services, and he acted as a volunteer.
    (D) Guy should not be able to recover from his neighbor the $600 charged by the veterinary clinic, either on the basis of quasi-contract or contract implied in fact. The neighbor did not agree to Guy's services, and he acted as an officious intermeddler.

Question 2 Answer

(A) is likely correct. Guy responded to an emergency situation in which he was not able to get his neighbor's authorization before incurring the cost of treating the dog. Although some courts require that the emergency involves a threat of human death or bodily harm, and not to property, this seems like too restrictive an approach. A person should not be treated as an officious intermeddler where it is clear that failure to intervene will cause significant property damage, especially where the property is a living animal. Therefore (D) reflects too narrow an approach. (C) is also too restrictive. Although Guy did not manifest intent to claim reimbursement of his expense, this does not make him a volunteer if it can be inferred from the circumstances that he had a reasonable expectation of reimbursement. It would not be reasonable to expect that Guy would pay for his neighbor's veterinary expenses. (B) is wrong. Guy had no communication with the neighbor, so there could not be an actual contract.

Question 3

In addition to the facts in Question 2, Guy spent four hours of his morning driving the dog to and from the clinic and waiting at the clinic while the dog's injuries were being treated.

   (A) Guy should be able to recover from his neighbor the value of his four hours' time spent on the basis of quasi-contract.
   (B) Guy should be able to recover from his neighbor the value of his four hours' time spent on the basis of contract implied in fact.
   (C) Guy should not be able to recover from his neighbor the value of his four hours' time spent, either on the basis of quasi-contract or contract implied in fact. The neighbor did not agree to Guy's services, and he acted as a volunteer.
   (D) Guy should not be able to recover from his neighbor the value of his four hours' time spent, either on the basis of quasi-contract or contract implied in fact. The neighbor did not agree to Guy's services, and he acted as an officious intermeddler.

Question 3 Answer

(C) is the best answer. Although there is a reasonable expectation that Guy would recover his out-of-pocket costs, the time spent in dealing with the emergency is more likely to be seen as altruistic and gratuitous.

Question 4

Change the facts in Question 2: The veterinary clinic did not insist that Guy pay for the treatment. Instead, it billed the neighbor after it treated the dog. The price of $600 is the customary charge for the services that the clinic provided.

(A) The veterinary clinic should be able to recover the $600 fee from Guy's neighbor on the basis of quasi-contract.

(B) The veterinary clinic should be able to recover the $600 fee from Guy's neighbor on the basis of contract implied in fact.

(C) The veterinary clinic should not be able to recover the $600 fee from Guy's neighbor, either on the basis of quasi-contract or contract implied in fact. The neighbor did not agree to the clinic's services, and it acted as a volunteer.

(D) The veterinary clinic should not be able to recover the $600 fee from Guy's neighbor, either on the basis of quasi-contract or contract implied in fact. The neighbor did not agree to the clinic's services, and it acted as an officious intermeddler.

Question 4 Answer

(A) is the best answer for the same reason stated in the answer to Question 1. The clinic's claim for its services are distinguishable from Guy's claim for his services in Question 2 in that the clinic is not likely a volunteer. The reasonable expectation is that a business does not perform services gratuitously. Further, given the need to treat the dog immediately, it was not reasonable to expect the clinic to obtain the neighbor's assent before providing the services, so it is not an officious intermeddler either.

Question 5

Tanya's basement flooded during the rainy season. She therefore hired a contractor to install a drainage system, which diverted rainwater from her house into a nearby stream. The work was expensive and cost Tanya $60,000. The drainage system also benefitted the property of Tanya's neighbor, Phil, by curing a flooding problem on that property. Prior to installing the drainage system, Tanya had not asked Phil to contribute to the cost of the drainage system, but she now feels that Phil should pay half the cost, since the work benefits him as well.

(A) Tanya should be able to claim $30,000 from Phil, who has received a substantial benefit as a result of the installation of the drainage system.

(B) Phil is a "free rider" who has been unjustly enriched by the installation of the drainage system. Tanya should therefore be able to claim $30,000 from Phil.

(C) Phil has been unjustly enriched by the installation of the drainage system. Although Tanya may not be able to claim the full $30,000 from Phil, she should be able to recover at least the *quantum meruit* value of the benefit conferred on Phil.

(D) Tanya has no unjust enrichment claim against Phil.

Question 5 Answer

(D) is correct. As pointed out in *Birchwood Land Company*, Phil's property was incidentally benefitted by Tanya's construction work. Tanya cannot impose liability on him without his consent, and the benefit must be seen as voluntarily conferred.

■ CHAPTER 13. POLICING CONTRACTS FOR IMPROPER BARGAINING

Question 1

Seller's car had been involved in a serious collision and had been badly damaged. Seller had the car repaired, but the repairer could not completely straighten the chassis, which had been bent. Seller was not aware that the chassis was still bent. About a year later, Seller sold the car to Buyer. Seller did not tell Buyer that the car had been in a collision and had been extensively repaired. Seller gave Buyer the car's maintenance records at the time of the sale. However, these records did not include any documentation relating to the repair. Seller had deliberately removed them because he did not want Buyer to know that the car had been in a collision. Because the car appeared to be in excellent condition, Buyer could not tell that there was anything wrong with it and did not think to ask Seller if the car had ever been damaged and repaired. Buyer only discovered the bent chassis after the sale, when he took the car for a service and the mechanic noticed it.

(A) Seller has committed fraud, which entitles Buyer to avoid the contract if he can establish materiality and justifiable reliance.

(B) Seller has committed fraud, which entitles Buyer to avoid the contract if he can establish justifiable reliance. Buyer is not required to establish materiality.

(C) Seller has committed fraud, but there is no basis for avoiding the contract because the car is goods. Article 2 has no provision allowing avoidance for fraud, which therefore applies only in contracts under common law.

(D) Seller did not commit fraud because he did not know that the chassis was bent.

Question 1 Answer

Either **(A)** or **(B)** is correct. (B) is correct under Restatement, Second §164, because it does not include materiality as an element of fraud. However, (A) is also correct because many courts do not follow this approach and require materiality to be proved. (C) is wrong. Although Article 2 has no provision governing fraud, the common law doctrine applies to sales of goods under UCC 1-103(b). (D) is wrong in stating that Seller did not commit fraud. Although Seller did not know about the bent chassis, he took affirmative action to hide the collision and repair by deliberately removing the repair records. Buyer could claim fraud by non-disclosure as an alternative to active fraud, but active fraud gives Buyer a stronger case for avoidance.

Question 2

Change the facts of Question 1: Seller did not deliberately remove the records of the repair. They had been filed in his insurance file, not with the maintenance records, and he forgot about them.

(A) Seller has not committed fraud because he did not deliberately remove the records.

(B) Seller has made no assertion, so he has not committed active fraud. However, his failure to disclose the collision and repair will entitle Buyer to avoid the contract if he can establish that Seller had a duty to disclose and that he justifiably relied on the nondisclosure.

(C) Seller has made no assertion, so he has not committed active fraud. However, he failed to disclose the collision and repair. If this is a material fact, Buyer will be entitled to avoid the contract if he can establish that Seller had a duty to disclose and that he justifiably relied on the nondisclosure.

(D) Seller may have committed fraud, but there is no basis for avoiding a contract in this case because the car is goods. UCC Article 2 has no provision allowing avoidance for fraud, which applies only in contracts at common law.

Question 2 Answer

The correct answer is now **(B)** or **(C)**. (B) is correct under Restatement, Second §164, which does not include materiality as an element of fraud, but (C) is correct under the case law that does require it. (A) is not correct. Although Seller has not actively tried to conceal the repair, he may still be liable for fraud by nondisclosure. Seller failed to disclose the collision and repair. If this disclosure is required under Restatement, Second §161, Buyer can claim avoidance for fraud. (D) is wrong, as explained in the answer to Question 1.

Question 3

Carr is employed as a sales representative by Pedal Power, a bike store. Carr was the only employee of the store who drove to work. All the other employees rode to work by bike. One day, the manager of the store told Carr that she would fire Carr unless he signed an agreement in which he promised to ride a bike to work instead of driving. Carr protested, pointing out that his employment contract specified that he could only be fired for good cause, and driving to work was not good cause. The manager disagreed. She told Carr that she had consulted the store's lawyer, who had researched the question and had advised her that she would be entitled to dismiss an employee for this reason. Because of a recession, other employment opportunities were scarce and Carr did not wish to lose his job, so he signed the agreement. He later found out that the manager had never consulted the store's lawyer on this question and that she would not have been legally entitled to dismiss him for refusing to sign the agreement.

(A) These facts indicate that Carr may have grounds to avoid the agreement for fraud, but not for duress.

(B) These facts indicate that Carr may have grounds to avoid the agreement for duress, but not for fraud.

(C) These facts indicate that Carr does not have grounds to avoid the agreement for either duress or fraud.

(D) These facts indicate that Carr may have grounds to avoid the agreement for either duress or fraud.

Question 3 Answer

(D) is correct. The facts suggest that there has been both a fraudulent misrepresentation (the manager's false assertion that she had obtained legal advice that supported dismissing Carr) and an improper threat to dismiss Carr in breach of their employment agreement. There is a reasonable argument that Carr can establish the other elements of fraud (materiality and justifiable inducement) and duress (no reasonable alternative but to enter the contract). However, Carr would have to select either one of these causes of action because their elements are inconsistent: To claim duress, he must show that he had no reasonable alternative but to agree, and to claim fraud he must show that he was induced by the misrepresentation to enter the contract—that he would not have entered the contract but for the misrepresentation. This conflict between the elements of fraud and duress appears to have escaped the court in *Germantown Manufacturing*, which found that Ms. Rawlinson had shown meritorious defenses of both fraud and duress. (In case you are wondering, because the store did not have the right to fire Carr, he may also have grounds to challenge the validity of the contract for lack of consideration. The store appears to have suffered no legal detriment in exchange for his promise.)

Question 4

Builder entered into a contract with Owner to remodel the kitchen in Owner's home for $60,000. The remodeling required the complete demolition and rebuilding of the interior of the kitchen. After the contract was executed, Builder went to a contractor's convention. From what he heard at the convention, he realized that most contractors made a much higher profit on their jobs than he did. He had been undercharging for kitchen remodels and should have charged Owner $70,000. The contract between Builder and Owner states a firm price of $60,000 for the completed job. Nevertheless, Builder told Owner that he would not do the remodeling job unless owner agreed to a $10,000 price increase. Owner reluctantly agreed.

(A) Owner is probably bound by the contract modification.

(B) Owner is probably not bound by the contract modification on grounds of duress.

(C) Owner is probably not bound by the contract modification on grounds of fraud.

(D) Owner probably cannot avoid the modification on grounds of duress, but it is likely invalid for lack of consideration.

Question 4 Answer

(D) is the best answer. There is no indication that Builder suffered any additional detriment in exchange for Owner's promise to pay the increased price. (B) is not a good answer. Although Builder has made an improper threat to breach the contract if Owner does not agree to the price increase, Owner would have difficulty in showing that she had no reasonable alternative but to agree. She was not under any particular pressure to continue with this transaction and could simply have found another builder to do the remodel. She would likely have had to pay more for the substitute transaction, but she could have recovered this additional cost from Builder as expectation damages. (C) is also not a good answer because there is no indication that Builder made any false representation to Owner.

Question 5

The facts are the same as in Question 4.

(A) These facts indicate that the modification is both procedurally and substantively unconscionable.

(B) These facts indicate that the modification is substantively but not procedurally unconscionable.

(C) These facts indicate that the modification is procedurally but not substantively unconscionable.

(D) There is no basis on these facts to find either procedural or substantive unconscionability.

Question 5 Answer

(C) is the best answer. Builder has sought to coerce owner into modifying the contract by threatening to breach it if owner refuses. A threat that qualifies as improper for duress purposes is probably also enough to constitute unfair bargaining for unconscionability purposes. However, it seems that the modified price may not be substantively unfair because it sounds like it is no more than the market price of the project. Therefore, Owner could have difficulty establishing that the modified contract is substantively unconscionable.

Question 6

Tiny Little set up a new retail business. He bought a cash register online from Big Business Machines, Inc. (BBM). To place his order for the cash register, Tiny had to click a button that signified his agreement to BBM's standard terms, which were readily accessible by scrolling down the text box containing the "I agree" button that Tiny had to click to signify assent to the terms. Tiny read the standard terms. One of them was a forum selection clause that required all disputes arising out of the transaction to be litigated in the courts of BBM's home state, which is hundreds of miles away from Tiny's state. Tiny did not think much about this, and so he clicked the "I agree" button and ordered the cash register.

BBM shipped the cash register to Tiny and he used it. He did not realize that a defect in the cash register caused it to miscalculate the change due in transactions, so Tiny was consistently giving customers too much change. When he finally noticed the problem, he demanded that BBM repair the defect and refund to him the amount that he had lost by giving customers too much change. BBM agreed to the repair but refused to compensate Tiny for the losses he had suffered. Tiny sued BBM in the small claims court in his city to recover these losses. BBM moved to dismiss the suit on the grounds that Tiny had agreed to its standard forum selection provision.

(A) The contract between Tiny and BBM is a contract of adhesion and the forum selection clause is unenforceable.

(B) The forum selection clause is unconscionable and unenforceable.

(C) The contract between Tiny and BBM may be a contract of adhesion and unconscionable, but Tiny cannot make this argument because this is a business transaction, not a consumer transaction.

(D) The contract between Tiny and BBM is a contract of adhesion but Tiny will probably have trouble establishing that the forum selection clause is unenforceable.

Question 6 Answer

(D) is most likely the correct answer. This probably qualifies as a contract of adhesion because it is presented to individual customers by a larger, more powerful corporation and is likely proffered on a take-it-or-leave-it basis. If the customer wants the transaction, he probably has no choice but to adhere to the terms. (Of course, if a similar item could be bought from another seller without the forum selection clause, the ability to choose another seller would weaken the argument of adhesion.) However, adhesion on its own is not enough to permit avoidance of the contract or an adjustment of its terms. Even if a contract is adhesive, Tiny must show that the adhesive nature of the contract allowed BBM to take advantage of its dominance to impose an unfairly one-sided contract or term on him. There is no indication of procedural unconscionability—the terms were clearly presented, without any form of sales pressure, and Tiny did in fact read them and acquiesce. It is also unlikely that a court would find a forum selection provision to be substantively unconscionable if the forum selected is reasonable. Therefore, (A) and (B) are wrong. (C) is wrong in stating that only a consumer may raise the issue of adhesion or unconscionability. The argument is available to any party, irrespective of identity. However, a larger, more sophisticated and powerful commercial entity may have more difficulty in establishing its elements.

Question 7

When Patient checked in at the hospital for surgery she was presented with several forms to sign. One of the forms consented to the surgical procedure. It contained a provision in which Patient agreed to arbitrate any claim against the hospital, arising from the surgery. The provision stated that the arbitration would be conducted by a panel of three doctors appointed by the hospital. The surgery was not successful and Patient sued the hospital for malpractice. The hospital sought to dismiss the suit on the grounds that Patient had agreed to arbitrate the claim. The court held that the arbitration agreement was procedurally unconscionable because it was presented to Patient just before she was to undergo surgery, giving her no meaningful choice but to acquiesce. The court also found that the agreement was substantively unconscionable because an arbitration panel of three doctors appointed by the hospital would likely not be impartial. If the court followed *Zuver v. Airtouch Communications* the most likely result would be:

   (A) The court would enforce the arbitration provision, but would amend it to substitute a more impartial arbitration panel.
   (B) The court would enforce the arbitration provision as it stands, without any changes.
   (C) The court would sever the arbitration provision and allow Patient to continue the suit in court.
   (D) The court would avoid the entire consent agreement, including the arbitration provision.

Question 7 Answer

In *Zuver* the court deleted those provisions of the arbitration agreement that it found substantively unconscionable and enforced the rest of the agreement. The important difference between the facts of this question and *Zuver* is that the court in this question found procedural unconscionability, whereas the court in *Zuver* found that the mere fact that the contract was adhesive was not enough to make it procedurally unconscionable. This would suggest that maybe (C) is the best answer because the existence of procedural unconscionability makes this a stronger case for complete severance of the arbitration provision. However, we think that **(A)** is the more likely result because the court emphasizes the public policy in favor of arbitration and expresses reluctance to upset the agreement more than absolutely necessary. Therefore, the court would probably conclude that altering the panel, rather than severing the provision entirely, best gives effect to the parties' manifested intent. Of course, a different court may be less sympathetic to the hospital and may conclude that the penalty for its overreaching should be severance of the arbitration provision entirely.

■ CHAPTER 14. ILLEGALITY, VIOLATION OF PUBLIC POLICY, AND LACK OF CONTRACTUAL CAPACITY

Question 1

Lex, an attorney, entered into a contract with a client to represent the client in a criminal case. The client agreed to pay Lex a contingent fee of $10,000 provided that Lex was successful in obtaining an acquittal in the case. The state's rules of attorneys' professional conduct and a state statute prohibited an attorney from charging a contingent fee in a criminal case, so the contract was illegal. The client knew this, but agreed to the contingent fee anyhow because she did not want to be liable for attorney's fees unless she was acquitted of the crime. Lex did succeed in obtaining an acquittal but the client has refused to pay his fee.

(A) Lex is precluded from suing for any fee under the *in pari delicto* rule.

(B) Lex is precluded from suing for the agreed fee under the *in pari delicto* rule, but may sue the client for a reasonable fee on principles of unjust enrichment.

(C) Lex is not barred from suing for the fee under the *in pari delicto* rule because the client knew the fee violated the law and colluded with Lex in the violation.

(D) Lex is not barred from suing for the fee under the *in pari delicto* rule, but the client can avoid the contract on grounds that it is unconscionable.

Question 1 Answer

Although there could be an argument for (B), we do not think it would succeed. **(A)** is the better answer. If Lex sued the client for the fee, the client would likely succeed in raising the *in pari delicto* rule as a defense to the suit. Although the client knew that the contingent fee violated the rules of professional conduct, Lex, as the attorney subject to the rule, bears greater responsibility for the violation. It also accords best with public policy to deny recovery of any fee to Lex to discourage lawyers from violating the rules and to protect the client from a lawyer whose objectivity might be influenced by a personal stake in the outcome of the criminal case. (B) suggests that even if the court does not allow the lawyer to enforce the contract, it might allow *quantum meruit* recovery to prevent the unjust enrichment of the client. In some cases, a court that refuses to enforce an illegal contract might be more amenable to a restitutionary claim. However, in this case Lex's greater guilt and the public policy of holding lawyers to the rules of professional conduct make it unlikely that a court would be sympathetic to a claim for restitution. (C) is wrong for the reasons stated above—even if the client knowingly collaborated in the illegal arrangement, both the balance of guilt and public policy weigh against Lex. (D) is wrong. The *in pari delicto* rule does bar Lex's recovery, and there is no indication that the contract was unfairly bargained (procedurally unconscionable) or substantively unfair and one-sided.

Question 2

Lexie and Lawson, both attorneys, entered into an agreement under which Lexie employed Lawson as an associate in her law firm. The employment agreement contained a noncompetition provision that barred Lawson from practicing law in the city for two years after leaving the firm. The state's rules governing the professional conduct of attorneys states that an attorney shall not participate in a partnership or employment agreement that restricts the right of an attorney to practice law.

(A) The noncompetition provision is enforceable because it was fairly bargained and protects Lexie's legitimate interest in preventing Lawson from poaching her clients.

(B) The noncompetition provision is unenforceable under the *in pari delicto* rule.

(C) The noncompetition provision is unenforceable under the rules of professional conduct governing attorneys.

(D) The noncompetition provision is unenforceable unless the restraint satisfies the "rule of reason."

Question 2 Answer

(B) is the best answer. The parties are both attorneys, so they are both subject to the rules of professional conduct and are at least equally guilty in violating them. (Lexie, as the employer, may in fact bear even greater guilt.) In addition, the rule encompasses the strong public policy against imposing restrictions on an attorney's ability to practice because this would prevent clients from being able to use the attorney of their choice. Although the ultimate effect of the rule of professional conduct may be to render the agreement unenforceable, (C) is inaccurate. The rules of professional conduct forbid attorneys from making such agreements and violation of the rule could lead to discipline. However, the rule does not actually invalidate the agreement, so that the court must determine its enforceability by applying the *in pari delicto* rule. (D) is wrong. The "rule of reason" is not used where the agreement is prohibited under the rules of professional conduct. (A) is wrong. Even though the provision may have been fairly bargained and may prevent Lawson from taking Lexie's clients with him if he leaves, the provision is unenforceable for the reasons stated above.

Question 3

Abel, a genius, developed a computer program when he was 16 years old. Just before his 17th birthday, he sold the program to a technology company for $1 million, which he was paid upon execution of the contract. This was a fair price for the program. A month later, he changed his mind and wished to avoid the contract. The age of majority in the state is 18.

(A) Abel may not avoid the contract because he has already received the $1 million payment for the program.

(B) Abel may not avoid the contract because he received a fair price for the program and was not exploited.

(C) Abel may not avoid the contract because he is a genius and had the sophistication to enter into the transaction.

(D) Abel may avoid the contract.

Question 3 Answer

(D) is correct. Because Abel was still a minor when he sought to avoid the contract, his right of avoidance is absolute. It does not depend on the fact that he had been paid for it, that the price was fair, or that he was clever and sophisticated. The answer might have been different if this had been a contract for necessaries. Upon avoidance, Abel will have to return the $1 million, or at least as much of it as has not yet been spent.

Question 4

Abel, a genius, developed a computer program when he was 17 years old and he sold the program to a technology company for $1 million one month before his 18th birthday. This was a fair price for the program and it was paid to him upon execution of the contract. Six weeks later, Abel changed his mind and wished to avoid the contract. The age of majority in the state is 18.

(A) Abel may not avoid the contract because he lost the opportunity to avoid it when he became a major.

(B) Abel may avoid the contract because he was a minor when he made it.

(C) Abel may avoid the contract because he did not expressly ratify it after becoming a major.

(D) Abel may avoid the contract unless he is deemed to have ratified it by conduct or inaction after becoming a major.

Question 4 Answer

(D) is correct under the generally-applicable common law rule that a person becomes bound by a contract entered into while a minor if he ratifies it, either expressly, impliedly, or by inaction after attaining majority. (C) would be correct only in those states (such as Maine) that have deviated from this rule and recognize only express ratification. (A) is wrong because a minor does not automatically lose the right of avoidance on reaching majority, and (B) is wrong because it ignores the possibility of post-majority ratification.

Question 5

Abel, a genius, developed a computer program when he was 21 years old. A few months later he sold the program to a technology company for $1 million, which he was paid upon execution of the contract. A month later he changed his mind and wished to cancel the sale. He can show, by the testimony of a psychiatrist, that he suffers from depression and was in a depressed state at the time that he entered the contract. This made him pessimistic about the potential usefulness and value of the program. Abel claims that had he not been depressed, he would never have sold the program, but would instead have developed and exploited it himself. The representatives of the technology company had not known Abel before they met with him to negotiate the contract, and he appeared to be rational during the negotiations.

(A) Abel can avoid the contract on the basis of a cognitive mental disorder.

(B) Abel can avoid the contract on the basis of a motivational mental disorder.

(C) Abel cannot avoid the transaction on the basis of mental incapacity.

(D) Abel cannot avoid the transaction on the basis of mental capacity unless he can show that the terms of the contract were unfair.

Question 5 Answer

(C) is the best answer. Although Abel was suffering from depression at the time of the contract, depression is not likely to render a person incapable of reasonably understanding the nature and consequences of the transaction (as might a cognitive mental disorder) and is more appropriately classified as possibly affecting his ability to act in a reasonable manner in relation to the transaction (a motivational mental disorder). However, even if Abel was suffering from a motivational disorder, Restatement, Second §15 requires in addition that he establish that the other party had reason to know of his condition. The facts indicate that there was nothing in the circumstances or in his conduct that would have alerted the company to his condition.

▉ CHAPTER 15. CONTRACT INTERPRETATION AND CONSTRUCTION

Question 1

Ollie Organ is a professional organizer. Betty Business and Ollie Organ orally agree that Ollie will come to her office at 9:00 a.m. each weekday for a month, and will spend one hour helping her organize her files. Betty agrees to pay Ollie $75 at the end of each visit. The first Monday, Ollie arrives at 9:10 a.m., but spends an hour as agreed organizing the office. Betty pays him $75 without complaint. On Tuesday, he is twenty minutes late, but again spends an hour as agreed organizing the office. Betty isn't pleased, but says nothing and again pays him for his work. He arrives on a timely basis for the rest of the week and Betty pays him $75 after each visit. The following Monday, Ollie again arrives at 9:10 a.m. Betty is fed up with Ollie's lack of timeliness, and decides she no longer trusts his abilities as an organizer. She believes he has breached their agreement, and seeks to terminate it. Based on these facts alone, which of the following is the most persuasive?

(A) Ollie may not be in breach, because usage in the trade suggests start times may be approximate.

(B) Ollie may not be in breach, because the parties' course of dealing suggests start times may be approximate.

(C) Ollie may not be in breach, because the parties' course of performance suggests start times may be approximate.

(D) Since the parties expressly agreed to a start time of 9:00 a.m., Ollie is in breach.

Question 1 Answer

(C) is the best answer. Especially where an agreement is informal, as this one appears to be, courts often consult contextual evidence to determine the content of the parties' contract and the meaning of any express terms they may use in communicating with each other. Evidence that consists of a usage of trade, course of dealing, or course of performance tends to be particularly persuasive of what the parties might have reasonably expected under the circumstances. A "usage of trade," referenced in (A), generally refers to a practice that is regularly observed in a particular place or industry, transcending the specific parties involved in a particular dispute. There may well be usages of trade relevant to this situation, but none are revealed by the question. The phrase "course of dealing," invoked in (B), generally refers to patterns of behavior between the specific parties to the dispute which they observe in transactions prior to the one at issue. Suppose for instance that Betty Business is a technology consultant, and she first met Ollie Organ when he hired her to set up the computer network at his office. Suppose further they had agreed that she would arrive at his office at a specific time and she was repeatedly late. If neither party remarked on her lateness nor objected to it in any way, they might both be justified in understanding that strict adherence to appointment times wasn't particularly important in their dealings with each other. This shared understanding, drawn from a prior interaction, might carry over to the transaction at issue. Here, we don't have any information about past dealings between Betty and Ollie, so the phrase "course of dealing" is inapposite. There's a small chance that a court might consider each organizing visit to constitute a separate contract, in which case the interactions on previous visits might establish a "course of dealing" for the most recent one. This in an awkward interpretation of the facts, however. Ollie's work seems to be part and parcel of the same task, and was arranged on the same terms through a single agreement. Instead, the phrase "course of performance" is more apt. Since Betty repeatedly accepted Ollie's late arrival without objection, some courts might consider her actions sufficient to establish a "course of performance" under which start times were approximate.

Question 2

As in Question 1, Ollie Organ is a professional organizer. Ollie and Ed Engineer sign a written contract in which Ollie agrees to organize Ed's files on specified terms and conditions. Once Ollie begins to work, Ed insists that Ollie take a look at the files on his computer and include them in the scope of his organizational tasks. Ollie insists that he had only agreed to organize Ed's paperwork, and any organization of his computer files would require payment of a fee in addition to the one the parties had specified in their written contract. Ultimately, the dispute ends up in court in a jurisdiction that applies the "plain meaning" approach to contract interpretation. Which of the following is the most accurate description of what such an approach requires?

(A) In determining what the words in the written document mean, the fact-finder should be guided by the plain meaning of those words.

(B) The judge will determine the meaning of the parties' contract based on the words contained in the writing alone. Under no circumstances will the judge or the fact-finder consult any evidence outside of the "four corners" of the signed document.

(C) Unless the words in the agreement have a plain meaning, the parties will not have an enforceable contract.

(D) The judge will determine whether the words in the writing are ambiguous, but in doing so will not consult evidence of meaning drawn from the dealings between the parties.

Question 2 Answer

(D) is the best answer. Under a "plain meaning approach," a judge will determine whether the words in the writing are ambiguous based on the judge's own intuitions, the dictionary meanings of the words themselves, and any clues that are revealed by an examination of the written document. If the judge determines the words are unambiguous, the judge will apply their unambiguous meaning. If instead the judge determines the words are ambiguous, the fact-finder may consult evidence drawn from a variety of sources and determine what the most reasonable meaning would be under the circumstances. (A) is incorrect, because it allocates the judge's responsibilities under the plain meaning approach to the jury. If the judge determines that the words contained in the document are unambiguous, (B) might accurately describe the plain meaning approach. It ignores the possibility that a judge could determine that the words don't have a single, unambiguous plain meaning, and that the judge or fact-finder could consult other evidence to resolve the ambiguity. (C) is incorrect. If the judge and the fact-finder are unable to ascertain whether the parties agreed to sufficiently definite terms, it may be that any agreement between the parties would not be enforceable as a contract. But this is not a consequence of the "plain meaning" approach to contract interpretation; it is a broadly applicable principle of contract law.

Question 3

Vendors frequently supply standard terms to govern all like contracts to which they are a party. In interpreting such contracts, some courts apply the *contra proferentum* principle. Which of the following describe this principle (more than one answer may be correct)?

(A) So long as they are unambiguous, the standard terms will be interpreted in accordance with their objectively reasonable meaning.

(B) Any ambiguity in the standard terms will be interpreted against the drafting party.

(C) If ambiguous, the standard terms will be interpreted in accordance with the reasonable expectations of the non-drafting party.

(D) Whether or not they are ambiguous, the standard terms will be interpreted in accordance with the reasonable expectations of the non-drafting party.

Question 3 Answer

Depending on the jurisdiction, either **(B)** or **(C)** may be an accurate description of the principle. In its starkest form, courts interpret any ambiguity in standard terms against the drafter, as provided by (B). Probably the more common approach, however, is to adopt the non-drafting party's interpretation of the term only to the extent that interpretation is reasonable. This is the approach suggested by (C). (A) describes a general principle of contract interpretation, unrelated to the *contra proferentum* principle. (E) describes the relatively controversial approach the majority in *Atwater Creamery Co. v. Western National Mutual Insurance Co.* uses to interpret a standard contract. This approach is largely limited to the insurance context, although it is occasionally used in other contexts where the vendor is acting as a fiduciary or otherwise occupies an unusual position of power or trust.

Question 4

Parties sometimes argue that their contracting partners have breached an obligation of good faith. In relation to the notion of good faith, which of the following is an accurate statement?

(A) Parties to a contract have an obligation to act in good faith only if their agreement so provides.

(B) Parties have a general obligation to act in good faith in the performance and enforcement of a contract governed by common law; however, there is no such obligation in contracts governed by UCC Article 2.

(C) Parties have a general obligation to act in good faith in the performance and enforcement of contracts governed by UCC Article 2; however, there is no such obligation in contracts governed by common law.

(D) Parties have a general obligation to act in good faith in the performance and enforcement of contracts whether such contracts are governed by common law or by UCC Article 2.

(E) Unless their contracts provide otherwise, parties have a general obligation to act in good faith in the performance and enforcement of contracts.

Question 4 Answer

(D) is the best answer. Except in a few isolated jurisdictions, courts construe contracts to impose a duty of good faith on the parties even if their agreement is silent. (A) is thus incorrect. The general duty of good faith arises both at common law and under the UCC, as reflected in Restatement, Second §205 and UCC 1-304. So, neither (B) nor (C) is accurate. Although the terms of the parties' agreement strongly shape what good faith in the performance or enforcement of that agreement might require, the duty of good faith cannot be disclaimed altogether. Accordingly, (E) is also incorrect.

Question 5

Billy Beer hosted a dinner for some business associates at a nice restaurant. When the server came to take drink orders, Billy, who is usually a beer drinker, asked the server to recommend a bottle of wine. She recommended several; when Billy asked the price of one of the bottles, she said "thirty-seven fifty." Billy ordered the bottle of wine, and along with two of his companions drank it with pleasure. When the bill came for the meal, it reflected a charge of $3,750 for the wine. Billy said he thought the bottle cost $37.50, not $3,750. Billy was unable to resolve the situation with the restaurant manager, and refused to pay anything for the wine. Which of the following is the most persuasive?

(A) Since the restaurant was a nice restaurant, Billy was unreasonable in his belief that the wine would cost $37.50. Accordingly, he owes the restaurant $3,750 for the wine.

(B) The server should have been clearer in her statement about the cost of the wine. Accordingly, Billy's interpretation should prevail, and he owes the restaurant $37.50 for the wine.

(C) So long as neither party knew the meaning attached by the other, and assuming neither party was more at fault for the misunderstanding, no contract resulted and Billy owes nothing for the wine.

(D) So long as neither party knew the meaning attached by the other, and assuming neither party was more at fault for the misunderstanding, no contract resulted, but Billy may owe the restaurant the reasonable value of the wine.

Question 5 Answer

(D) is the best answer. Where parties attach different meanings to their expressions of agreement, under general principles of contract interpretation courts will apply the meaning that is most reasonable under the circumstances. However, as suggested by *Konic International Corp. v. Spokane Computer Services, Inc.*, where the difference is material, where neither party knows or has reason to know the meaning attached by the other, and where neither party is more at fault for the misunderstanding, a court may conclude that no contract resulted from the parties' manifestations of assent. Although arguments could be made to support either (A) or (B), absent greater understanding of the context of the misunderstanding, it is difficult to conclude that one interpretation is objectively more reasonable than the other or that one party was more at fault. (Of course, contextual evidence, such as the usual, customary, and reasonably expected range of wine prices in a restaurant of the kind involved, or the prices of other wines offered by the restaurant on its wine list, or the degree to which other patrons had complained about the restaurant's wine prices in the past, could point in the direction of either (A) or (B) being more persuasive.) In *Konic*, the court concluded that no contract resulted from the parties' manifestations of assent. Because the surge protector in that case could be returned, Spokane Computer Services, Inc. was not required to pay for it. Here, since the bottle of wine cannot be returned, if a court found no contract resulted, it nonetheless would be likely to order Billy to pay restitution to the restaurant. In such a case, neither party's subjective understanding of the price of the wine would control; instead, the court would order restitution according to a *quantum valebant* standard (that is, as much as the goods were worth). The theory of recovery would be unjust enrichment, not contract. Accordingly, (D) is a better answer than (C).

■ CHAPTER 16. THE PAROL EVIDENCE RULE

Question 1

Sara Secret and Larry Lie enter into an agreement governed by the common law, and both sign a writing to memorialize the terms of that agreement. After the agreement is signed, a dispute arises between them and they end up in litigation. The court concludes that the signed writing is fully integrated under applicable legal principles. Notwithstanding, Sara seeks to introduce evidence supporting her claim and drawn from the negotiations that led up to the parties' agreement. With respect to the evidence Sara seeks to introduce, which of the following are accurate (more than one answer may be correct)?

(A) Sara will be able to introduce the evidence, so long as the judge finds it to be credible.

(B) Sara will be able to introduce the evidence, so long as the writing contains terms that are ambiguous.

(C) Sara will not be able to introduce the evidence to explain the terms contained in the writing.

(D) Sara will not be able to introduce the evidence to supplement the terms contained in the writing.

(E) Sara will not be able to introduce the evidence to contradict the terms of the writing.

Question 1 Answers

(D) and (E) are the best answers. If a writing is integrated, the parties may not introduce evidence of matters that occurred prior to the writing or contemporaneously with the writing for the purpose of contradicting the written terms. If the writing is not only integrated but fully integrated, the parties may not introduce any such parol evidence to supplement the terms of the writing either. Whether Sara's evidence is credible might be relevant (in some jurisdictions) to the question of whether the writing is integrated and if so, to what degree. But even if the judge finds the evidence credible, it doesn't necessarily follow in all jurisdictions that the fact-finder will be allowed to hear it. Since the question asks us to assume that the judge found the writing to be fully integrated, as discussed above, a likely consequence is that the fact-finder will *not* be allowed to hear the evidence under many circumstances. So (A) misstates the nature and consequences of the judge's inquiry under the parol evidence rule. (B) may be correct if Sara is introducing the evidence for the purpose of explaining the ambiguous terms. If, however, she seeks to supplement or contradict the writing, the evidence will not be admissible for that purpose. Of course, whether any given evidence explains or alternatively supplements or contradicts a writing is itself a question of some subtlety and the answer may be uncertain. But (B) as written suggests that Sara can introduce parol evidence for any purpose whenever the writing is ambiguous in some respect, and that conclusion is overbroad. (C), in contrast, is overly narrow. Even a fully integrated writing may contain some terms that are ambiguous. (If ambiguities run throughout the writing, a court may conclude that the writing wasn't intended by the parties to be fully integrated. But under the assumptions of the question, that didn't happen here.) To the extent a judge concludes that a particular term is ambiguous, under principles of contract interpretation it may allow the fact-finder to hear parol evidence relevant to the possible meaning of that term. So although it is not assured that Sara will be able to introduce her evidence for purposes of explaining the written terms, it isn't accurate to state she will never be able to do so.

Question 2

Larry Law learns that the case law in a given jurisdiction establishes a "four corners" approach to the parol evidence rule. He is curious what this means. In circumstances where parties have signed a writing reflecting the terms of their agreement, which of the following best explains the "four corners" approach to the parol evidence rule?

(A) The fact-finder will be allowed to hear evidence of the meaning of the writing if and only if the language of the writing is ambiguous on its face.

(B) The fact-finder will be allowed to hear evidence of prior or contemporaneous oral agreements if they relate to matters described within the "four corners" of the writing.

(C) The fact-finder will not be allowed to hear evidence of prior or contemporaneous oral agreements if they relate to matters described within the "four corners" of the writing.

(D) The judge will determine whether the writing is a fully integrated writing, a partially integrated writing, or not integrated at all without consulting factual evidence outside the "four corners" of the writing.

(E) The fact-finder may consider factual evidence that explains the writing, but not evidence that supplements or contradicts it.

Question 2 Answer

(D) is the best explanation of the "four corners" approach to the parol evidence rule. The "four corners" approach relates principally to the method the judge uses to determine whether the signed writing is integrated, and if so, to what degree. A judge applying the "four corners" approach purports to make this decision based on the form and content of the writing alone. (A) describes the "plain meaning" approach to contract interpretation, not the "four corners" approach to the parol evidence rule. (B) and (C) focus on what evidence should or should not be admitted once a court has determined the degree to which a writing is integrated. As noted above, the factor that distinguishes a "four corners" approach to the parol evidence rule is the method the judge uses to determine the degree to which the writing is integrated. (E) sketches possible consequences of the conclusion that a writing is fully integrated. It doesn't explain how a "four corners" approach to the question of integration differs from other, more contextual approaches.

Question 3

Another jurisdiction follows the "contextual" approach to the parol evidence rule at common law. The parties to a transaction that involves both the sale of goods and the provision of services have signed a writing reflecting the terms of their agreement. They are uncertain whether the transaction will be governed by the common law or by UCC Article 2. Which of the following are accurate (more than one may be correct)?

(A) Parol evidence is more likely to be admissible in disputes governed by the common law than those governed by the UCC.

(B) Parol evidence is less likely to be admissible in disputes governed by the common law than those governed by the UCC.

(C) Whether governed by the common law or the UCC, a judge is likely to consider parol evidence in determining the degree to which the parties intended the signed writing to incorporate the final and complete version of what they agreed.

(D) Whether a dispute is governed by the common law or the UCC, the fact-finder is likely to find parol evidence to be credible.

(E) Whether a dispute is governed by the common law or the UCC, the judge is likely to allow the fact-finder to hear contextual evidence that contradicts or supplements a written agreement.

Question 3 Answer

(C) is likely to be accurate whether a court applies a "contextual," common law approach or UCC Article 2. All of the other answers are either uncertain or incorrect. As noted in the answer to Question 2 above, a principal difference between a "contextual" approach to the parol evidence rule and a "four corners" approach relates to the method a court uses to determine the degree to which the writing is integrated, or, in UCC terms, whether it is a final expression with respect to the terms contained therein and if so, whether it is also a complete and exclusive statement of the terms of the parties' agreement. The UCC's version of the parol evidence rule is highly contextual, so there may not be any differences of substance between a "contextual" common law approach and the UCC's approach. If anything, the UCC's version is less likely to exclude parol evidence than the common law, so (B) is a better answer than (A). To the degree that courts have adapted the common law to closely resemble the UCC, however, one can't be confident that any significant differences between the two bodies of law persist. Even if a court applies a highly contextual approach to the parol evidence rule, there is no guarantee that any given evidence will prove credible or for that matter, be admissible. Accordingly, the consequences described in (D) and (E) do not follow.

Question 4

Major Manufacturer enters into a written contract with Dedicated Distributor, whereby Major agrees to sell goods to Dedicated, and Dedicated agrees to act as Major's exclusive distributor for those goods within a specified territory. Both parties are represented by counsel, and both parties sign a written memorial of their contract. A boilerplate clause in the writing says "this agreement supersedes all prior proposals, negotiations, agreements and understandings relating to the subject matter hereof." Six months later, Major gives Dedicated notice that the contract will be terminated in thirty days. Major argues it is entitled to terminate the contract at any time without cause on reasonable notice. Dedicated argues Major has no right to terminate the agreement, but instead can do so only if Dedicated is in breach. The written agreement is silent on the circumstances under which the agreement may be terminated or cancelled. Major's argument is most likely:

(A) Persuasive, if parties in the relevant trade or industry typically understand that exclusive distributorship agreements can be terminated without cause upon reasonable notice.

(B) Persuasive, if the parties agreed to such a termination right orally before the contract was signed.

(C) Not persuasive, because such a termination right would necessarily contradict the terms of the written agreement.

(D) Not persuasive, because the written agreement is likely to be a complete and exclusive statement of the terms of the parties' agreement, and therefore cannot be supplemented.

(E) Not persuasive, because if the written agreement is a complete and exclusive statement of the terms of the parties' agreement, it is not appropriate to consult extrinsic evidence to explain it.

Question 4 Answer

(A) is the best answer. It is likely that this transaction will be governed by UCC Article 2. (Although one could make the argument that this is predominantly a sale of Dedicated's distribution services, absent additional facts, that argument would not be likely to prevail.) Accordingly, UCC 2-202 will apply to the transaction. The facts of the question strongly suggest that the written contract was intended not only as a final expression of their agreement with respect to the terms that are included in it, but also as a complete and exclusive statement of the terms of their agreement. Since both parties are represented by counsel and the agreement contained a merger clause, this conclusion would be very difficult to overcome, and we don't have any facts to suggest we would escape it in this case. Accordingly, the writing can be explained or supplemented by course of performance, course of dealing or usage of trade, but cannot be supplemented by additional terms drawn from other sources. (A) describes a relevant usage of trade, recourse to which would be permissible under UCC 2-202(a). (B) describes evidence of a prior oral agreement, which would be excluded under UCC 2-202(b). While true that Major could not introduce parol evidence to contradict the terms of the writing. (C) makes a conclusion that is not justified by the question. There is no guarantee that a court applying the UCC would conclude that a termination right necessarily contradicted the provisions of a written agreement if it was silent on that point. (D) and (E) are incorrect because they both rule out recourse to parol or extrinsic evidence of any sort under the circumstances described, and so are overbroad.

Question 5

A dispute arises under a fully integrated contract governed by the common law. Which of the following should be kept from the trier of fact under the parol evidence rule?

    (A) Evidence that establishes that one of the parties did not have mental capacity at the time the parties entered the contract.

    (B) Evidence that establishes that the contract was induced by undue influence.

    (C) Evidence that establishes that a breach was a material breach.

    (D) All of the above.

    (E) None of the above.

Question 5 Answer

(E) is the best answer. The parol evidence rule helps to determine what the terms of a contract are, assuming the parties have an otherwise enforceable contract. (A) and (B) both describe matters that go to the enforceability of the contract, not its terms, and as such the parol evidence rule is inapposite. Likewise, (C) describes a question that arises once the terms of the contract have been established, and so the parol evidence rule has no application. As an aside, the proper scope of the parol evidence rule becomes quite muddled when one of the parties seeks to introduce evidence that a contract was induced through misrepresentation or fraud. Although allegations of misrepresentation or fraud typically go to the enforceability of the contract, not its terms, there are courts that nonetheless extend the parol evidence rule to bar the proffered evidence under some circumstances. (Other courts reason instead that the party relying on a parol representation is not entitled to relief because it was not justified in doing so, given that the writing either didn't include the representation or even contradicted it. Whether this line of reasoning presents a question of law for the judge or a factual issue properly submitted to a jury may differ from jurisdiction to jurisdiction.) None of the answers to Question 5 invoke misrepresentation or fraud, so we need not entangle ourselves in that issue for purposes of the question.

■ CHAPTER 17. MISTAKE AND EXCUSE DUE TO CHANGED CIRCUMSTANCES

Question 1

Tom Taylor and Carrie Caldwell signed a written lease agreement. Under the terms of the lease, Tom agreed to pay Carrie $2,000 per month to lease Carrie's warehouse for a period of five years, beginning in two weeks' time. Without the knowledge of either party, a few hours before they signed the lease the warehouse was totally destroyed by fire. Assuming the lease itself is silent as to the responsibilities of the parties under these circumstances, which of the following is the most persuasive:

(A) Either Carrie or Tom may be able to avoid the lease on the basis of mutual mistake, because both parties assumed the warehouse was still in existence at the time the lease contract was entered.

(B) Carrie may be excused of her obligations under the lease on the basis of commercial impracticability, because the fire made it impracticable to deliver the leased premises as agreed.

(C) Tom may be excused of his obligations under the lease on the basis of frustration of purpose, because he no longer has any use for the leased premises if the warehouse has burned to the ground.

(D) Neither party will be able to avoid or be excused from obligations under the lease under any theory.

Question 1

(A) is the best answer. Because the fire and attendant destruction of the warehouse were facts in existence at the time the lease was entered, mistake is the most appropriate doctrine under these circumstances. (B) and (C) suggest doctrines that are analogous to mistake, but which are not relevant under the specific facts of the question. Commercial impracticability and frustration of purpose both relate to things that occur after the relevant contract is entered, so neither is an appropriate grounds for excuse under these circumstances. Avoidance under mistake doctrine is not a sure thing, because among other things a court would have to determine whether either party bore the risk of the mistake. However, there are no facts in the question to help us analyze this issue, so (D) is overconfident.

Question 2

Trinity Thrift Store sells donated items and uses the funds it receives to support its public service mission. A sign by the cash register states that customers should check their purchases carefully, because all sales are "as is." Sam Scavenger was shopping at Trinity Thrift Store one day and saw a beautifully etched metal cup on sale for $25. He thought it would make a nice decorative accent for his office, bought it with his credit card, and took it in to work. The next day, one of his office-mates recognized the cup as a valuable and rare antique silver chalice, and estimated that it was worth at least $750,000. Sam is delighted with his windfall, but is worried that Trinity Thrift Store might seek to avoid the sale should it learn what happened. Which of the following is the most persuasive?

(A) Trinity Thrift Store should be able to avoid this contract, because it was a mistake to only charge $25 for such a valuable item.

(B) Trinity Thrift Store should be able to avoid this contract, because the risk of mistake was allocated to Sam Scavenger by the sign at the cash register.

(C) Trinity Thrift Store should not be able to avoid the contract on the grounds of mistake, because Trinity Thrift Store bore the risk of the mistake.

(D) Trinity Thrift Store should not be able to avoid the contract on the grounds of mistake, because this is a sale of goods governed by UCC Article 2, and mistake is a common law doctrine.

Question 2 Answer

(C) is the best answer. Although it might have been a mistake in common parlance to sell a valuable item for such a low price, the legal doctrine of mistake only operates to relieve parties of their contractual obligations in exceptional circumstances. Accordingly, (A) is not persuasive. Although UCC Article 2 does not contain specific provisions relating to the doctrine of mistake, the general principles of mistake doctrine supplement the specific rules of UCC Article 2 by virtue of UCC 1-103(a). Therefore (D) is incorrect. Some courts might decide that there was no mistake of fact here, but rather one of judgment or value. As such, they might decline to avoid the contract under mistake doctrine. Other courts might reach the same result, but phrase their analysis in terms of risk allocation. (B) suggests Sam Scavenger bore the risk of the mistake, while (C) suggests Trinity Thrift Store did. Both the "as is" sign posted by the cash register and the general context of thrift store sales weigh against avoidance of the transaction. *Cherry v. McCall* suggests that absent fraud or some other invalidating cause, a buyer should not be able to avoid a contract on the basis of mistake doctrine when the buyer purchases the property "as is" and it turns out to be worth a lot less than the buyer might have hoped. The question presents the opposite situation: Sam purchased the property "as is," and it turned out to be worth a lot more than he expected. If a court holds the purchaser to a contract when the facts turn out to be unfavorable, it is likely to allow the purchaser to reap the benefits of the contract when the facts turn out to be in his favor. *Estate of Nelson v. Rice* reinforces this analysis, suggesting that a seller who puts property up for sale, knowing that he or she doesn't have full knowledge as to the nature and value of that property, bears the risk that the property might turn out to be worth far in excess of what it might have supposed. To put it in terms of Restatement, Second §154, both parties in the question were arguably aware, at the time the contract was made, that they had only limited knowledge with respect to the facts to which the mistake relates, but treated their limited knowledge as sufficient. Accordingly, Trinity Thrift Store should be deemed to bear the risk of the mistake, and (C) is the best answer.

Question 3

Business Co. and Industry, Inc. negotiated a major business transaction, in which Business Co. was to provide services to Industry, Inc. Business Co.'s lawyers worked late into the night drafting documents to reflect the terms to which the parties agreed. Unfortunately, they neglected to insert the price the parties negotiated for Business Co.'s services, and throughout the document the price was listed as "$[to be determined]." Although lawyers on both sides reviewed the final document carefully, no one noticed the omission of the price term. After the written contract was signed, Industry, Inc. decided it didn't want to go forward with the transaction. Executives at Industry, Inc. acknowledge that the parties orally agreed to an annual payment of $100,000, but insist that Industry, Inc. should not be bound because the final signed document does not specify a price term. Which of the following is the most persuasive?

(A) Since it lacks a price term, any agreement between the parties is insufficiently definite to constitute an enforceable contract.

(B) Evidence of the alleged oral agreement is inadmissible under the parol evidence rule.

(C) The contract is avoidable by either party on the grounds of mutual mistake, so Industry, Inc. should not be bound.

(D) To the extent Business Co. is able to establish that the parties did in fact agree to a price, a court may reform the contract to reflect the price agreed by the parties.

Question 3 Answer

(D) is the best answer. The question poses a mistake in expression. If a court concludes that there has been a mistake in expression such that the written document signed by the parties doesn't reflect their "true" agreement, the conventional remedy would be to order reformation. Courts are sometimes hesitant to order reformation when it would require the court to create language to cover a situation that the parties arguably didn't anticipate. This is not one of those situations, however, and assuming Business Co. can establish that the mistake was in essence a simple error for which both parties are equally responsible, reformation should be available. In the unlikely event a court were unwilling to reform the document to reflect the "true" agreement of the parties, it might decline to enforce the contract altogether, either on the grounds specified in (A) or as described in (C) under the doctrine of mutual mistake. Finally, as discussed in Chapter 16, the parol evidence rule generally doesn't bar evidence necessary to establish grounds for avoiding or reforming an otherwise enforceable contract. Accordingly, (B) is incorrect.

Question 4

Darla Design contracts with Business Co. to create its corporate website. Before she starts to work on the website, she is struck by a car and is hospitalized for a period of months. Business Co. locates another designer to complete its website. When Darla returns to good health, Business Co. seeks to recover the difference between what it had to pay the replacement web designer and what it had agreed to pay Darla for the work. Which of the following is the most persuasive?

(A) Darla's accident has rendered her performance under the contract impracticable, and her performance is probably excused.

(B) Although Darla's performance under the contract is probably excused, she still owes Business Co. damages to compensate it for the extra expense it incurred in hiring a substitute designer.

(C) Darla probably isn't excused of her obligation to perform. Accordingly, she probably owes Business Co. damages to compensate it for the extra expense it incurred in hiring a substitute designer.

Question 4 Answer

Although not certain, **(A)** is the best answer. The contract between Darla Design and Business Co. is a personal services contract. Death or other incapacity of the person who owes services under such a contract typically excuses that person's performance, unless the language or the circumstances indicate the contrary. Although some courts inquire into whether the incapacity was the fault of the person seeking excuse, there is no indication from the facts that Darla was in any way at fault for her accident. (Some courts allow excuse even when fault is alleged, as in *CNA International Reinsurance Co. v. Phoenix.*) It may be that there is language in the parties' agreement or other circumstances to suggest that Darla should not be excused (and thus should not be relieved of her obligation to pay damages when she is unable to perform). If this were the case, (C) would be the best answer, but the question doesn't reveal any facts to support this argument. (B) is incorrect. If Darla is excused from performance, the consequence is she is no longer deemed in breach and as a result does not owe damages.

Question 5

Design Co. contracts with Business Co. to create its corporate website. Design Co. assigns one of its employees, Darla Design, to work on Business Co.'s website. Before she starts to work on the website, she is struck by a car and is hospitalized for a period of months. All of Design Co.'s other designers are busy with other jobs, and Design Co. informs Business Co. that it won't be able to design the website after all. Business Co. locates another design firm to complete its website. Business Co. seeks to recover the difference between what it had to pay the replacement design firm and what it had agreed to pay Design Co. for the work. Which of the following is the most persuasive:

(A) Darla's accident has rendered Design Co.'s performance under the contract impracticable, and its performance is probably excused.

(B) Although Design Co.'s performance under the contract is probably excused, it still owes Business Co. damages to compensate it for the extra expense it incurred in hiring a substitute design firm.

(C) Design Co. probably isn't excused of its obligation to perform. Accordingly, it probably owes Business Co. damages to compensate it for the extra expense it incurred in hiring a substitute design firm.

Question 5 Answer

Here, **(C)** is probably the best answer. Absent additional facts, it appears that this is no longer a personal services contract. Darla's involvement isn't critical to the parties' arrangement; there is no reason to believe another designer at the firm couldn't have satisfied Design Co.'s obligations under the contract. The fact that an employee—even an important employee—has become unavailable is the type of occurrence that happens on a regular basis in business. In terms of the language of Restatement, Second §161, a court would likely conclude that the non-occurrence of this event was not a basic assumption on which the contract was made. Accordingly, even though it might be highly impractical for Design Co. to complete the job without Darla's involvement, it is quite likely that a court would still hold it liable for damages in the event of breach. Accordingly, under the facts of this question, (A) is not persuasive. As in Question 4, (B) is incorrect. If excuse were available, it would relieve Design Co. not only of its obligation to perform, but also of its responsibility for damages in the event it was unable to perform. But as noted, excuse is unlikely in this instance.

■ CHAPTER 18. CONDITIONS AND PROMISES

Question 1

Tenant had five years left on his lease of attractive retail premises but had decided to retire and sublet the premises. He advertised the sublease and was approached by Subtenant who offered to sublease the premises at a rent of ten percent more than Tenant was paying to the landlord. Tenant was interested in the offer, but did not wish to commit to it until he was able to get the landlord's asset to the sublease. The parties entered into an agreement under which Tenant agreed to sublet the premises to Subtenant "on condition that the landlord of the premises authorizes the sublease within two weeks of the date of this agreement."

    (A) The landlord's authorization of the sublease is a promissory condition precedent to Tenant's obligation to sublet the premises to Subtenant.
    (B) The landlord's authorization of the sublease is a promissory concurrent condition to Tenant's obligation to sublet the premises to Subtenant.
    (C) The landlord's authorization of the sublease pure condition precedent to Tenant's obligation to sublet the premises to Subtenant.
    (D) The landlord's authorization of the sublease is pure condition, subject to Tenant's ancillary promise to use best efforts to secure the authorization.

Question 1 Answer

(D) is correct. The landlord's authorization is out of Tenant's control, and he therefore does not likely promise that it would be given. In fact, such a promise would defeat the purpose of the condition. However, even if no ancillary promise is expressly stated, the nature of the condition readily gives rise to the implication that Tenant must at least make reasonable efforts (such as requesting the authorization in good time) to get the landlord's authorization. (A) is therefore incorrect in describing this as a promissory condition. Because the condition must be satisfied before Tenant's obligation arises, it is precedent, so (B) is incorrect. The condition is pure, in the sense that Tenant does not promise to get the landlord's consent, but, as explained above, it is subject to an ancillary promise, so merely describing it as pure, without this qualification makes (C) inaccurate.

Question 2

The facts are as set out in Question 1. Two weeks and one day after the agreement was executed, Tenant received the landlord's authorization to sublet the premises.

    (A) The condition is satisfied, so Tenant is obliged to sublease the premises to Subtenant.

(B) The condition is substantially satisfied, so Tenant is obliged to sublease the premises to Subtenant.

(C) The condition is not satisfied, so Tenant is not obliged to sublease the premises to Subtenant.

Question 2 Answer

(C) is correct. The agreement uses clear words of condition ("on condition that") so the condition is express. Where the parties provide a condition by express language, courts require strict compliance with the condition and do not regard substantial satisfaction as sufficient. Therefore (A) and (B) are wrong.

Question 3

The facts are as set out in Question 1. Tenant received the landlord's authorization in good time but nevertheless refused to sublease the premises to Subtenant.

(A) Tenant's refusal to perform constitutes the non-fulfillment of a promissory condition. Subtenant is therefore entitled to withhold his own performance and may sue Tenant for any damages suffered.

(B) Tenant's refusal to perform constitutes the non-fulfillment of a pure condition. Subtenant is therefore entitled to withhold his own performance but may not sue Tenant for any damages suffered.

(C) Tenant's refusal to perform constitutes a breach of pure promise. Subtenant is therefore entitled to sue Tenant for any damages suffered.

(D) No contract has been entered yet because Tenant never accepted Subtenant's offer. Tenant therefore could not yet have breached any contract.

Question 3 Answer

(A) is correct. The condition of the landlord's authorization has been fulfilled, so Tenant is obliged to proceed with the sublease. Tenant's promise to do so is also a construed condition of Subtenant's performance because the parties' promises under the contract (Tenant's promise to provide the premises in exchange for Subtenant's promise to pay rent) are dependent. Therefore, Tenant's failure to perform is both a breach of his promise and non-fulfillment of the condition to Subtenant's performance. This entitles Subtenant both to withhold his own performance and to sue for damages. (B) is wrong. The condition is question here is Tenant's construed promissory condition to sublet the premises to Subtenant. This is therefore not a pure condition. (C) is wrong. Because the parties' promises are dependent, Tenant's promise is not pure. (D) is wrong. The parties have already entered a conditional contract, so they have passed the stage of offer and acceptance.

Question 4

A contract for the construction of a building divided the performance into stages by providing that the owner would pay the builder in installments as the work progressed. The contract provided for a final payment to be made by the owner after the building was finished.

(A) The owner's promise to pay the final payment is a promissory condition because it is subject to the condition that the building is finished.

(B) The owner's promise to pay the final payment is a pure promise.

(C) The owner's promise to pay the final payment is a condition precedent to the builder not suing for the unpaid balance.

(D) The owner's promise to pay the final payment is a concurrent promissory condition to the completion of the building.

Question 4 Answer

(B) is correct. The owner's promise to make the final payment under the contract is not a condition, express, implied, or construed, of any further performance under the contract. It is therefore a pure promise. The owner does not have to make this payment until the building is finished, so the owner's pure promise to make the final payment is subject to the condition that the building is completed. (A) is wrong. The payment is subject to the condition that the building is completed. This makes it a promise subject to a condition, not a promissory condition of some further performance by the builder. (C) is wrong. Although the builder would be entitled to sue the owner for non-payment, this is a matter of enforcing the contract, not a condition to any performance under it. (D) is wrong. The contract makes it clear that the completion of the building must come before payment so it is a condition precedent to payment, not a concurrent condition.

Question 5

The contract is as in Question 4, except that it provided that the owner's final payment was conditional on the owner's architect certifying that the building had been properly completed in accordance with the plans and specifications. Immediately after the building was finished, the owner fired the architect, so no certificate was issued.

(A) By firing the architect, the owner waived the condition of the architect's certificate, so the builder is entitled to payment.

(B) Because the owner fired the architect, he is estopped from asserting non-fulfillment of the condition of the architect's certificate, so the builder is entitled to payment.

(C) The owner engaged in obstructive conduct by firing the architect, so the condition of the architect's certificate is deemed fulfilled and the builder is entitled to payment.

(D) Because no certificate was issued, the condition precedent to payment is not satisfied and the builder is not entitled to payment.

Question 5 Answer

(C) is the best answer because the owner prevented fulfillment of the condition by firing the architect and a party should not be allowed to resist payment by obstructive conduct. (An alternative argument could be that the owner breached an implied ancillary obligation to make reasonable efforts to procure the certificate.) (A) could be correct because firing the architect could signify a waiver—a voluntary relinquishment of the right to a certificate as a condition of payment. However, because a waiver is a unilateral relinquishment of a right, courts will not allow it unless the term waived is non-material and we cannot tell from the facts if this was a non-material term. (B) could be correct. Firing of the architect could estop the owner from claiming a right to a certificate because it could be construed as conduct that reasonably indicates an intent not to rely on the certificate. However, estoppel requires reasonable reliance on the conduct by the builder and the facts do not indicate any such reliance. (D) is not a justifiable answer because a party cannot refuse to perform on the basis of non-fulfillment of a condition that he has prevented from being satisfied.

■ CHAPTER 19. MATERIAL BREACH, SUBSTANTIAL PERFORMANCE, AND ANTICIPATORY REPUDIATION

Question 1

On March 15, Flora entered into a contract with Luscious Landscapes, Inc. (LL) under which LL undertook to install an irrigation system in Flora's garden for a price of $7,000. The contract provided that LL would begin work on April 1 and would complete the job by April 7. LL did not show up at Flora's home on April 1. When she called to find out why, LL's representative told her that they were running behind schedule and that they would not be able to start her job until April 4.

(A) LL has not yet breached the contract. It is entitled to begin work after April 1 provided that it is able to complete it by April 7.

(B) LL has breached the contract, so Flora is entitled to terminate it and claim any expectation damages that she suffers.

(C) LL has repudiated the contract but it may retract its repudiation by completing the work by April 7.

(D) LL has breached the contract. If the breach is material and total, Flora may terminate the contract but if it is not material she may not do so. In either event, she would be entitled to claim damages if the breach causes her economic loss.

Question 1 Answer

(D) is correct. The contract specifies that work must begin on April 1, so LL did breach by failing to begin work on that date. However, we cannot tell from the facts whether the late start is itself a material breach, or, if it results in delay in completion, whether that delay would be a material breach. If the breach is not material, Flora may not terminate the contract. Whether or not it is material, Flora would be entitled to damages if she can show that the breach caused her economic loss. (A) is wrong because the late start is a violation of the contractual commitment and therefore a breach, even if it may not be a material breach. (B) is wrong. Even though the late start is a breach, it would not entitle Flora to terminate the contract unless it is material and total. (C) is wrong. This is not a repudiation because the breach occurs at the time of performance, not before it.

Question 2

On March 15, Flora entered into a contract with Luscious Landscapes, Inc. (LL) under which LL undertook to install an irrigation system in Flora's garden for a price of $7,000. The contract provided that the irrigation system would be completely installed and operational by no later than April 7 and that "time of completion is of the essence." LL called Flora on March 25 and told her that they had fallen behind in their work for other customers and would not be able to install her irrigation system until May 15.

(A) LL has breached the contract, so Flora is entitled to terminate it immediately and claim any expectation damages that she suffers.

(B) LL has repudiated the contract, so Flora is entitled to terminate it immediately and claim any expectation damages that she suffers.

(C) LL has repudiated the contract. Flora may terminate it and claim any expectation damages that she suffers after she has demanded a retraction and LL fails to retract the repudiation within a reasonable time.

(D) LL has neither materially breached nor materially repudiated the contract because it has expressed willingness to complete the installation within a reasonable time.

Question 2 Answer

(B) is correct. By stating that it will not perform as promised prior to the date of performance, LL has repudiated the contract. The proposed change in completion date is most likely material. Where the parties have specified in the contract that time of completion is of the essence, a court is likely to enforce the express intention of the parties to treat that term as material. Because LL materially repudiated the contract, Flora is entitled to terminate it immediately and will be entitled to claim any damages suffered. (A) is wrong—a breach only occurs when performance is due. An advance statement of intent not to perform is a repudiation. (C) is wrong. Although Flora could give LL an opportunity to retract, she is not obliged to do so. (D) is wrong for the reason stated in (A).

Question 3

On March 26, Flora entered into a contract with Luscious Landscapes, Inc. (LL) under which LL undertook to install an irrigation system in Flora's garden for a price of $7,000. The contract provided that LL would begin work on April 1 and would complete the job by April 7. It required Flora to pay a deposit of $3,500 to LL on execution of the contract and to pay the balance of the price on completion of the job on April 7. Flora gave LL a check for $3,500 on March 26. LL deposited the check on that day, but received notice from its bank on March 30 that Flora's bank had refused to honor the check because she had insufficient funds in her bank account. It is now April 1.

(A) LL is not obliged to begin work on April 1 because Flora has breached the contract.

(B) LL is not obliged to begin work on April 1 because Flora has repudiated the contract.

(C) LL is not obliged to begin work on April 1 and may terminate the contract because Flora has either breached or repudiated the contract.

(D) Flora has neither breached nor repudiated the contract, but the dishonored check gives LL grounds to demand an adequate assurance of performance before it begins work.

Question 3 Answer

(A) is correct. Flora's payment of the $3,500 deposit is a construed promissory condition precedent to LL's performance. Her breach of this promissory condition is likely material because the parties have set up the contract to assure LL of advance payment of half the price before it begins work. Flora's breach therefore excuses LL from rendering its own performance on April 1. However, even though LL may suspend its own performance, it is possible that Flora may be able to cure the breach by paying the $3,500 from some source other than the bank account on which she issued the check, provided that the late payment is not itself a material breach. For this reason, (C) is wrong. (B) is wrong because Flora has breached, not repudiated because her failure to perform was on the date due for the performance, not before it. (D) is wrong because Flora did breach the contract, so adequate assurance of performance is not apposite. (Do not confuse adequate assurance of performance—which may be demanded before the time for performance—with cure, which involves rectifying a breach that has occurred.)

Question 4

Flora entered into a contract with Luscious Landscapes, Inc. (LL) under which LL undertook to install an irrigation system in Flora's garden for a price of $7,000, to be paid upon completion of the job. LL began work on the date scheduled and completed it in time. However, it designed the system poorly. As a result, the system floods some parts of the garden while leaving other parts dry. It also wastes a lot of water by discharging too much spray onto paved areas and the street. The only way to rectify these problems is to dig up the pipes and sprinkler heads and to relay them properly. The cost of doing this is $8,000. The existence of a functioning sprinkler system adds about $2,000 to the market value of a house. Flora has refused to pay LL for the work.

(A) The cost of rectifying the defects in the system are excessive, so Flora can claim damages of no more than $2,000—the diminution in the market value of her house. Flora must therefore pay LL $5,000, the difference between the contract price and the diminution in the value of her property.

(B) The cost of rectifying the defects in the system are excessive, so Flora can claim damages of no more than $2,000 – the diminution in the market value of her house. Flora is not obliged to pay anything to LL and can claim damages of $2,000.

(C) The sprinkler system is valueless, so Flora is not obliged to pay anything to LL and can claim damages of $8,000, the cost of rectifying the defective system.

(D) Flora is entitled to the cost of rectifying the defective system, so she is not obliged to pay anything to LL and can claim damages of $1,000, the difference between the contract price and the cost of rectifying the defective system.

Question 4 Answer

(D) is correct. The usual measure of damages for a breach is the cost of rectifying the defective work. Diminution in market value would only be an appropriate substitute where the cost of rectification is so excessive that it would overcompensate Flora and impose an unfair forfeiture on LL. Flora contracted for a functioning irrigation system but received no benefit of her bargain because she has been left with an unusable one. This is a very different situation from that in *Jacob & Youngs, Inc. v. Kent* in which the house was fully functional and it was not necessary to allow the owner damages based on the expensive replacement of the pipes. Flora is therefore not confined to diminution in market value, as suggested by answers (A) and (B), and is entitled to the cost of rectifying the defect, $8,000. However, she would be overcompensated if these damages were not offset against the contract price of $7,000 because she would then receive the sprinkler system for free. (C) is therefore incorrect.

Question 5

Buyer bought a bed online from Seller. The bed was sold unassembled. Seller's order confirmation specified that the bed would be delivered no later than seven business days after the order was placed. Buyer received the box containing the bed components five days later. Buyer unpacked the box immediately and checked the parts. He discovered that the headboard, which should have been included, was missing. This was an inadvertent omission by Seller.

(A) Buyer may reject the bed and cancel the sale only if the failure to include the headboard is a material breach of contract.

(B) Buyer may reject the bed and cancel the sale even if the failure to include the headboard is not a material breach of contract.

(C) Buyer may reject the bed even if the failure to include the headboard is not a material breach of contract. However, if Seller offers a timely cure, Buyer is obliged to accept it.

(D) Buyer may not reject the bed because Seller's failure to include the headboard was an inadvertent error, made in good faith.

Question 5 Answer

(C) is correct. This is a sale of goods, so the perfect tender rule of UCC 2-601 applies, and Buyer is entitled to reject nonconforming goods, irrespective of whether the nonconformity is material. (A) is therefore wrong. However, (B) is wrong because Buyer may not immediately cancel the sale. Seller has the right to cure under UCC 2-508(1) by substituting a conforming tender (delivering the headboard) before the 7 day delivery period expires, provided that Seller acted in good faith in delivering nonconforming goods, gives Buyer timely notice of intent to cure, pays the expense of curing, and compensates Buyer for any loss suffered. (Seller may even have the right to cure beyond the seven-day period under UCC 2-508(2) if it had reasonable grounds to believe late delivery would be acceptable.) (D) is wrong. Buyer has the right to reject the nonconforming tender irrespective of Seller's good faith, but Seller's right to cure may ultimately overcome the legal effect of rejection.

■ CHAPTER 20. INTRODUCTION TO CONTRACT DAMAGES AND THE "BENEFIT OF THE BARGAIN"

Question 1

Fred Family puts his house on the market, and states that his asking price is $350,000. Hardy Bargainer is interested in buying it. He negotiates relentlessly with Fred, and finally persuades Fred to agree to sell the house for $200,000. The parties sign a written contract to that effect. Before the transaction can close, Fred has second thoughts and decides he shouldn't have given in to Hardy's high-pressure tactics. If he is going to sell his house at a bargain price, he decides, he would rather sell it to a relative. Fred's nephew Ned Family happily purchases the house for $250,000. Hardy puts in offers on several equivalent houses, but all of them were sold to buyers who agreed to pay more than $300,000, a price Hardy couldn't afford and wasn't willing to pay. Hardy decides to remain in his small apartment. Assuming Hardy can establish that the contract is enforceable generally and Fred unjustifiably breached it, which of the following best approximates Hardy's direct damages?

(A) $150,000; that is, the difference between Fred's asking price and the price Hardy was able to negotiate.

(B) $100,000; that is, the approximate difference between the price for which equivalent houses are selling on the market and the price Hardy agreed to pay.

(C) $50,000; that is, the difference between the contract price and the price obtained in the substitute transaction with Ned Family.

(D) Nothing, because Hardy didn't enter into a substitute transaction.

Question 1 Answer

(B) is the best answer. The question suggests that Hardy obtained a particularly good deal on the house. Even though he didn't enter into a substitute transaction, he nonetheless should be entitled to receive compensation for the loss of the benefit of this advantageous bargain. (D) is therefore incorrect. An appropriate measure of Hardy's loss is the difference between the market value of the house and the bargain price he was able to negotiate. There is no reason to believe that either Fred's asking price or the price Ned agreed to pay bore any relationship to the market value of the house. Accordingly, neither (A) nor (C) is persuasive. In contrast, the fact that several equivalent houses sold for over $300,000 is some evidence of market conditions, and may be sufficient to establish at least an approximate market value for Fred's house.

Question 2

Paula Piano contracts with Ted Tuner to tune her concert grand piano for $1,000. Paula Piano pays for the job in advance. Ted Tuner completes the job on a timely basis, but the next day the piano is again out of tune. Ted Tuner refuses to perform any additional services without further payment. Paula Piano hires a reputable company to inspect the piano. It determines that Ted Tuner overtightened the piano's strings, and estimates that it will cost $1,500 to repair the damage Ted Tuner did and retune the piano correctly. Assuming this report is accurate and assuming further that Paula Piano can establish that Ted Tuner unjustifiably, materially, and totally breached the contract, the best measure of Paula Piano's direct damages is:

(A) $1,000, the price Paula Piano paid Ted Tuner.

(B) The difference in market value between a properly tuned piano and the piano in its current condition.

(C) The profit (including reasonable overhead) that Ted Tuner made on the transaction.

(D) $1,500, the cost to repair the damage and redo the job.

(E) $500, the difference between the cost to repair the damage and redo the job and the contract price of $1,000.

Question 2 Answer

(D) is the best answer. Where a party performs in a deficient manner, the usual measure of damages is the cost of remedying and completing the performance. (A) suggests a restitution measure. There is no reason to believe that Paula's recovery would be limited to this amount. Sometimes the measure described in (B) closely tracks the cost of remedying and completing the performance. Other times, especially where quality work would have to be destroyed in order to repair deficient performance, the cost of remedying the problem and completing the performance dwarfs any diminution in market value caused by the deficient performance. Typically, any limitation on the plaintiff's damages to the smaller market-based measure would require a showing that the cost of remedying the defect and completing the performance is inappropriate. For instance, the measure might not be appropriate if it would work an unfair forfeiture (the test applied by *Jacob & Youngs, Inc. v. Kent* in Chapter 18) or would otherwise exceed the bounds of reasonableness (the test enunciated in *Landis v. William Fannin Builders, Inc.*) There are no facts to indicate it either of these tests would be satisfied here. (C) focuses on Ted's lost profits. It is Paula's lost expectation that is at issue, so (C) is incorrect. (E) states a measure that might have been appropriate had Paula not already paid Ted. It doesn't capture the full extent of Paula's lost expectation in light of her having paid Ted in advance.

Question 3

Karrie Kitchen caters receptions, parties, and other events. She enters into a contract to cater the holiday party at Big Law LLP for $30,000. Karrie calculates that the $30,000 fee will allow her to purchase $10,000 worth of food and beverages, pay $5,000 to hire a staff of servers specifically for this event, and leave $15,000 to help cover her own salary, utilities, and other expenses associated with her catering business. Big Law LLP promises to pay the full amount due at the end of the party. As the holiday season approaches, all of the lawyers at Big Law LLP are busy negotiating and documenting a major corporate transaction. Big Law LLP decides no one is likely to attend, so it cancels its holiday party and unjustifiably repudiates its contract with Karrie. At the time of the repudiation, Karrie had not yet purchased any food or beverages for the event, nor had she hired any serving staff. Even with advance notice, Karrie wasn't able to replace Big Law LLP's business by taking on another job. She spends the night of the party playing video games in the office of her catering kitchen. Karrie is curious whether Big Law LLP owes her any damages, and if so, what they might be. Which of the following is the most persuasive?

(A) Karrie didn't suffer any damages, so Big Law LLP doesn't owe her anything.

(B) Karrie is entitled to the difference between the contract price and what she would have obtained from a substitute transaction. Since she wasn't able to arrange a substitute catering job, Big Law LLP owes her the full contract price of $30,000.

(C) Karrie is entitled to damages to the extent she can establish that Big Law LLP agreed to pay more for the party than the market value of the goods and services she was to provide.

(D) Karrie is entitled to damages in the amount of $15,000, that is, the amount of profit she expected to earn from the contract.

Question 3 Answer

(D) is the best answer. (A) fails to recognize that Karrie lost the opportunity to earn a profit from the transaction, and so is incorrect. The question describes a situation where neither a measure of damages based on a substitute transaction (alluded to in (B)) nor a market measure (as suggested in (C)) is likely to fully compensate Karrie for her lost expectation. Instead, a court is likely to consider Karrie to be a "lost volume" plaintiff, and compensate her for the profits she would have earned from the transaction. She wouldn't be able to recover the entire contract price, because she saved some expenses by not having to perform. An appropriate measure of her profit, then, would subtract out those expenses (here, the costs of the food, beverages, and servers). Even if accounting practices might figure her net profits after allocating a portion of her overhead, she would not be required to subtract any expenses from her damage calculation unless she actually saved those expenses due to the breach. Accordingly, the fact that she planned to allocate a portion of the price to cover her salary, utilities and other expenses associated with her business is irrelevant to the calculation of her damages.

Question 4

Karrie Kitchen, from Question 3, contracts to purchase 100 cases of strawberries from Fred Fruit for $2,500 and makes a down payment of ten percent. Fred unjustifiably fails to deliver the strawberries as agreed. If Karrie incurs one or more of the following, which would constitute potentially compensable incidental damages (more than one answer may be correct)?

(A) The down payment Karrie made when she contracted to purchase the strawberries from Fred Fruit;

(B) The amount by which the price of replacement strawberries exceeds $2,500;

(C) The charges Karrie incurs to locate another strawberry supplier and to have the replacement strawberries trucked to her on an expedited basis;

(D) The profits Karrie loses if she isn't able to serve strawberries at a celebrity wedding she had planned to cater;

(E) The costs and attorneys' fees Karrie incurs seeking remedies against Fred Fruit in court.

Question 4 Answer

(C) is the best answer. In a transaction in goods governed by UCC Article 2, an aggrieved buyer can claim incidental damages, which are defined in UCC 2-715 to include any commercially reasonable charges, expenses, or commissions in connection with effecting cover. So long as they were commercially reasonable, the costs specified in (C) would qualify. Any calculation of damages owing to Karrie would take account of the down payment described in (A), but such a down payment is not an expense incident to the breach. The amount by which the price of replacement strawberries exceeds the contract price would constitute Karrie's direct damages, not incidental damages. Lost profits, described in (D), if compensable at all, would constitute consequential damages, not incidental damages. Although in theory the litigation costs specified in (E) may constitute expenses incident to the breach, under our legal system they are not compensable unless the parties' agreement provides otherwise, and even then may not be fully recoverable.

Question 5

Karrie Kitchen from Question 3 was invited to audition for a new reality television show in which participants compete in a cooking competition, and the winner is asked to become the head chef at a famous restaurant. Karrie is very excited about the audition, because a chance to participate in the show is the break she thinks she needs for her career to take off. Karrie doesn't want to risk being late for the audition, so the day before it is scheduled she calls Reliable Taxi Co. to arrange a ride. She tells Reliable Taxi Co. that it is absolutely essential that she arrive on time. Reliable Taxi Co. tells her when she needs to leave in order to be sure to arrive early at her stated destination, and tells her what it will charge for the ride. The parties contract for the transportation services as discussed, and she agrees to pay once she arrives at her destination. The next morning, the driver sleeps through his alarm. When it appears that the driver is running late, Karrie calls the producers of the show who tell her that if she misses her audition she will not be able to reschedule and will lose her chance to be considered for the show. The driver finally shows up, but arrives an hour after the appointed time. Karrie knows it is already too late to make her audition, and refuses to get in the car or pay Reliable Taxi Co. anything. Karrie seeks to recover the profits she lost due to her inability to participate in the television show. Assuming Reliable Taxi Co. unjustifiably failed to arrive on time, without more, which of the following is the most persuasive?

(A) Karrie probably is not entitled to the damages she seeks, because it is unlikely that she will be able to prove her losses with reasonable certainty.

(B) Karrie probably is entitled to the damages she seeks, because her losses stemmed from general requirements.

(C) Karrie probably is entitled to the damages she seeks. Although her losses stemmed from particular requirements, Reliable Taxi Co. had reason to know of those requirements.

(D) Karrie probably is entitled to the damages she seeks, because she attempted to mitigate her damages by calling the producers of the show.

Question 5 Answer

(A) is the best answer. To be compensable, any losses Karrie suffers must be established with reasonable certainty, and must have been within the reasonable contemplation of the parties at the time the contract was entered. In addition, if Reliable Taxi Co. establishes that Karrie could have avoided the negative consequences of breach had she taken reasonable action when she learned of it, she will not be able to recover the damages she could have avoided. It is highly unlikely that Karrie will be able to establish damages of this sort with reasonable certainty. Future profits of a new enterprise can be very difficult to establish. Karrie's alleged losses are all the more speculative, because her chances of surviving the audition and making it on to the show at all were uncertain. If she can't establish her damages with reasonable certainty, she can't recover them, even if she overcomes any other potential limitations on their recovery. Even if she can establish them with reasonable certainty, she faces significant barriers persuading a court of any of the propositions included in (B), (C), or (D). If the losses stem from general requirements as suggested by (B), they will be deemed to be within the reasonable contemplation of the parties as a matter of course. One might argue that on-time delivery is a general requirement, typical of anyone who contracts for the services of a company with a name like "Reliable Taxi Co." However, her claim stems from the particularly high stakes she thinks are associated with the audition, so it is likely that a court would characterize her requirements as particular, rather than general, ones. Thus (B) is uncertain. (C) is uncertain as well. Courts differ in the degree to which they require a party to bring home particular requirements to a contracting partner before they conclude the requirements were within the reasonable contemplation of the parties. It is unclear whether the bare statement that it is essential that she arrive on time would suffice. Even if she established damages with reasonable certainty, some courts might find (C) persuasive, while others might not. Likewise, whether her efforts to mitigate damages were reasonable under the circumstances is subject to question. Perhaps, for instance, she had an opportunity to arrange alternate transportation and still arrive on time. Without more, (D) is conclusory and not persuasive.

■ CHAPTER 21. CONTRACT REMEDIES IN THE BROADER CONTEXT

Question 1

Ima Innocent and Ed Evil enter into a contract under which Ed agrees to fix the brakes on Ima's car. Ed does not have the correct part, so he deliberately and knowingly uses a part that is not designed for Ima's car and which he knows will not work properly. As a result of the faulty repair, Ima's brakes fail and she is injured. Ima sues Ed, alleging both breach of contract and commission of a tort. Assume that Ed's conduct does constitute both a breach of contract and a tortious act. Without more, which of the following is the most likely to be accurate?

(A) Because the breach also constituted a tort, Ima should be able to recover damages for pain and suffering and emotional distress as well as punitive damages.

(B) Ima will be likely to recover damages for pain and suffering and emotional distress but will only be able to recover punitive damages if the breach constitutes the kind of tort for which punitive damages are recoverable.

(C) Because the tort also constitutes a breach of contract, Ima's remedy will be limited to the contract remedy of economic, compensatory damages.

Question 1 Answer

(B) is the best answer. The question implicates the complicated relationship between contract remedies and tort remedies. Once there has been physical injury resulting either from intentional or negligent tortious conduct, the plaintiff can claim pain and suffering and emotional distress damages, even if that tort also constitutes a breach of contract. However, punitive damages can be recovered only if the plaintiff establishes grounds for taking the extraordinary step of increasing damages beyond compensation for the purpose of punishing the defendant. Ed would not automatically incur liability for punitive damages, even if his breach of contract was deliberate. His actions must be particularly egregious, willful, and wanton. Ed's conduct in this case may qualify, but it may not. If punitive damages would be available as a remedy for Ed's behavior, some courts would only award them as part of Ima's tort lawsuit, so if her tort law claim was barred by the statute of limitations or otherwise unavailable, she would not be able to recover them. In other jurisdictions, so long as she makes out the required tort-like behavior, she would be able to recover them as an element of her contract damages. Since (B) appropriately circumscribes the circumstances in which Ima might be able to obtain punitive damages, it is the best answer, while both (A) and (C) state propositions that are overly broad. (A) too readily assumes that punitive damages are available. (C) is incorrect in that the fact that the tortious conduct is also a breach of contract will not restrict Ima's ability to claim tort damages.

Question 2

Windy Waters Co. operates a not-for-profit summer camp for teenagers. Carla Canoe and Windy Waters entered into a contract pursuant to which Windy Waters agreed to pay Carla $4,000, in advance, in exchange for Carla's agreement to serve as a canoe instructor during the ten-week summer season. The written agreement signed by both parties included the following term: "Carla Canoe acknowledges that Windy Waters will suffer damages that are difficult to estimate should Carla not complete her full ten weeks of service. Accordingly, should Carla leave her position before the end of the ten-week term, Windy Waters shall be entitled to $10,000 in liquidated damages as its sole remedy for breach." Windy Waters explained this term carefully to Carla, and asked her to initial it separately to indicate that she had read it and understood it. Three days before her ten-week commitment is over, Carla decides to return to the city and unjustifiably breaches her contract with Windy Waters. Windy Waters asks one of its sailing instructors to take over Carla Canoe's responsibilities, and pays him an additional $100 to do so. Windy Waters suffers no other economic losses due to Carla's departure. Nonetheless, Windy Waters seeks to recover $10,000 for Carla's breach. Without more, which of the following is the most persuasive?

(A) The contract clause is an enforceable limitation on remedy. Even though it is valid, it has no effect on Windy Waters' recovery of its actual damages because $100 is less than the limitation of $10,000.

(B) The contract clause is probably unenforceable as a penalty.

(C) Since Carla freely and knowingly agreed to the contract clause, she is probably liable for $10,000 in liquidated damages.

(D) The liquidated damages provision is probably enforceable because it recites that Windy Waters' damages would be difficult to estimate.

Question 2 Answer

Although not certain, **(B)** is the best answer. If $10,000 is reasonable in light of Windy Waters' anticipated or actual loss and in light of the difficulties of proof of loss, under the test articulated in Restatement, Second §356 the contract clause might be enforceable as a valid liquidated damages clause. If, however, it fixes damages at a level that is unreasonably high, it will be unenforceable as a penalty. Without more, $10,000 seems an unreasonable amount, especially in view of the fact that Windy Waters only paid Carla $4,000 for a full summer of work. Carla had a relatively limited role at the camp, and even if she had left earlier than she did, it isn't obvious that there would have been significant economic consequences associated with her departure. The facts of the question are distinguishable from *Kent State University v. Ford*, where the plaintiff was able to persuade the court that there were substantial, if not easily quantifiable, losses associated with the departure of a basketball coach before the expiration of his contract term. It seems reasonable, in context, to assume that the clause is included in Carla's contract for the purpose of deterring and penalizing breach, rather than compensating Windy Waters. Accordingly, it is likely that a court would decline to enforce it. (A) suggests that the clause should be interpreted to be a limitation on remedy, rather than a liquidated damages provision. There is no justification for this interpretation. The facts of the question can be distinguished from *Wedner v. Fidelity Security Systems, Inc.* There, the contract provided that the service provider would not be liable for any loss or damage to goods, however should it be deemed liable for any reason, its liability would be limited to the yearly service charge payable as "liquidated damages." In context, the court interpreted this provision to be a limitation on the remedy as opposed to a true liquidated damages clause. Here, the intention (and certainly the effect) of the clause is not to limit Windy Waters' damages, but instead to fix them at a specified amount. It's likely that a court would interpret the clause to be a liquidated damages clause, and so subject it to the scrutiny reserved to those types of contract provisions described earlier. Generally, this is a context where the compensation policy of contract law prevails over any competing policy based on freedom of contract. A term that fixes liquidated damages at an amount that is unreasonably large will be unenforceable, even if the term was freely agreed upon by the parties. Accordingly, (C) is unpersuasive. Likewise, if Windy Waters could prove that it would have been difficult to estimate its losses at the time the contract was entered, that showing might improve its chances of enforcing the contract clause as written. However, a mere recitation in the contract that its damages would be difficult to estimate is unlikely to suffice, so standing alone, (D) is unpersuasive as well.

Question 3

Deli Co., a small restaurant, purchased a new oven from Appliance Co., a major manufacturer of commercial appliances. Appliance Co. provided a form contract to govern the sale. Before signing the contract, Deli Co. negotiated the price, a trade-in credit for its old oven, and delivery terms. It did not object to a clause in the contract which excluded all liability for consequential damages caused by any defect in the oven. The oven was delivered and installed, and Deli Co. paid the price. A month after installation, due to a defect in the oven's wiring, there was a fire in the restaurant. There was significant damage to the premises and Deli Co. had to close its restaurant for over a month to complete repairs. Deli Co. sought damages from Appliance Co. for the cost of repairs to the restaurant as well as the profits it lost while the restaurant was closed. Assuming the oven didn't conform to the terms of the contract when it was delivered, which of the following is the most persuasive?

(A) Deli Co. is probably not entitled to recover the damages it seeks, because they are consequential damages of the defect and the language in the contract is likely to be enforceable.

(B) Deli Co. is probably not entitled to any damages for the defect, because it accepted and paid for the oven.

(C) Deli Co. is probably entitled to recover the damages it seeks, because they are incidental to the defect, and thus are not precluded by the language in the contract.

(D) Deli Co. is probably entitled to recover the damages it seeks, because they are direct damages of the defect, and thus are not precluded by the language in the contract.

(E) The clause excluding liability for consequential damages likely constitutes an unenforceable limitation on remedy.

Question 3 Answer

(A) is the best answer. The transaction is a sale of goods, so UCC Article 2 will govern. As discussed in Section C of Chapter 20, under UCC 2-714, even where a buyer has accepted goods, it may recover damages for any non-conformity in the goods, and in a proper case may also recover incidental and consequential damages. So the mere fact that Deli Co. has accepted and paid for the goods will not foreclose a remedy, and (B) is thus incorrect. The damages Deli Co. seeks are for injury to its property as well as lost profits. These types of damages are properly characterized as consequential damages, rather than incidental damages (as suggested by (C)) or direct damages (as suggested by (D)). Incidental damages would include such things as the cost of inspecting the oven to determine the cause of the fire, while direct damages would encompass the difference in value between a conforming oven and one with defective wiring. So the ultimate issue posed by the question is whether the limitation on recovery of consequential damages included in the contract is enforceable. UCC 2-719(3) provides that consequential damages may be excluded unless the exclusion is unconscionable. Since Deli Co. was able to negotiate the terms of its agreement with Appliance Co., there doesn't appear to be much procedural unconscionability here. Likewise, although in retrospect the operation of the exclusion may seem harsh, courts are unlikely to consider it substantively unconscionable. The language of UCC 2-719(3) reinforces this conclusion, as it sets up the presumptions that limitations of liability for personal injury in the consumer context are unconscionable, while limitations on commercial losses are not. Thus, under the facts of the question, (A) is more persuasive than (E).

Question 4

Two parties enter into a contract. Upon breach, the aggrieved party seeks specific performance. As a general matter, under which of the following circumstances will specific performance NOT be available (more than one answer may be correct)?

(A) A buyer seeks to enforce a contract to purchase real estate for $300,000;

(B) A seller seeks to enforce a contract to sell real estate for $300,000;

(C) An employer seeks to enforce a six-month employment contract against an employee who is attempting to quit;

(D) An employer seeks to enforce a noncompetition agreement against a departing employee who is seeking employment with a competitor;

(E) A buyer seeks to enforce a contract to purchase an antique clock owned by a collector.

Question 4 Answers

(B) and **(C)** are the best answers. Generally, specific performance is only available if damages would be inadequate to compensate the plaintiff. Further, a court in a specific instance may decline to order specific performance if the equities do not merit it. Accordingly, it is difficult to generalize about the circumstances under which specific performance will be available. There are a number of circumstances, however, where specific performance generally is not available, and (B) and (C) describe two of them. Although specific performance is rather routinely available to buyers of real estate, as described in (A), sellers of real estate seldom are entitled to the remedy. Since the performance the seller expects under the contract is payment, it is usually quite straightforward to compensate the seller for the buyer's breach through the award of money damages. Contempt of court and the other consequences that attach to an injunction are not appropriate where the performance at issue is the payment of money. (B), therefore, describes a situation where specific performance is not available. Even if damages would be inadequate to compensate the plaintiff, (C) describes a situation where courts decline to order specific performance. It is generally considered unfair and impractical to order an individual to perform a personal services contract. Under some circumstances, courts may be willing to issue a prohibitory injunction preventing actions that are inconsistent with the contract (for instance, against accepting a position with another employer), but typically these types of injunctions are available only when the employee is party to an enforceable noncompetition agreement or the like. In such an instance, the injunction would be the equivalent of ordering specific performance of the noncompetition agreement, as suggested in (D). It is an overstatement to say that specific enforcement of a noncompetition agreement is always available—many courts, for instance, will scrutinize the agreement under the "rule of reason" and even if reasonable, will deny an injunction if damages are adequate to compensate the plaintiff. However, specific performance is sometimes available as a remedy for breach of these kinds of agreements, so (D) is not a good answer. The contract described in (E) would be governed by UCC Article 2. UCC 2-716(1) provides that specific performance may be decreed "where the goods are unique or in other proper circumstances." A specific antique clock owned by a collector is the type of item that is likely to qualify as "unique," so specific performance might well be available. Again, by stating that specific performance "may" be decreed, the statute affords the court some discretion in awarding the remedy. Nonetheless, (E) describes a situation where specific performance might obtain, so it too is not a good answer.

Question 5

In circumstances where there has been a breach of contract, one of the parties may seek restitution for the benefits conferred on the other party to the contract. Which of the following is an accurate statement?

(A) Rescission of the contract, accompanied by mutual restitution of the benefits conferred under it, is always available as a remedy to the aggrieved party.
(B) Restitution is always available to the party in breach.
(C) Restitution is never available to the party in breach.
(D) None of the above.

Question 5 Answer

(D) is the best answer. Often, the aggrieved party's expectation or reliance damages will exceed any recovery it might obtain through rescission. Accordingly, it may prefer to enforce the contract through recovery of expectation or reliance damages rather than obtain restitution. That is not to say, however, that rescission and restitution will always be available. For instance, the court in *Worcester Heritage Society, Inc. v. Trussell* was unwilling to order rescission and mutual restitution under the facts of that case, stating that it is appropriate to confine rescission to instances where there has been "an utter failure of consideration or a repudiation by the party in breach." Some jurisdictions don't allow the party in breach to obtain restitution, reasoning that restitution is an equitable remedy and should not be available to someone who has failed to perform its contractual obligations. This strict view is probably in the minority, as it is becoming more common to allow some measure of restitution to a breaching party under appropriate circumstances. Further, UCC 2-718(2) and (3) may allow restitution to a breaching buyer of goods under the conditions described in those provisions. At bottom, restitution is sometimes available to the party in breach, but sometimes it is not. So neither (B) nor (C) accurately captures the applicable legal principles.

■ CHAPTER 22. THE RIGHTS OF NONPARTIES

Question 1

Benny Fishery was employed as a late-night cashier in a supermarket. The supermarket had a contract with Security Services, Inc. (SS), under which SS undertook to provide a security guard at the supermarket during its night-time opening hours. At 11:30 p.m. on the night of June 10, Benny was attacked and injured in an armed robbery. On that night, SS had failed to provide the security guard as required by its contract with the supermarket. Benny argues that the robbery and his consequent injury would have been prevented had the guard been present.

(A) Benny is an intended beneficiary of the contract between the supermarket and SS and therefore has an independent contractual cause of action against SS for breach of contract.

(B) Benny is an incidental beneficiary of the contract between the supermarket and SS and therefore has an independent contractual cause of action against SS for breach of contract.

(C) Benny is an incidental beneficiary of the contract between the supermarket and SS and therefore has no independent contractual cause of action against SS for breach of contract.

(D) Benny is a creditor of the supermarket, which owes him wages for his work. As a creditor beneficiary, Benny has an independent contractual cause of action against SS for breach of contract.

Question 1 Answer

(C) is most likely the correct answer based on *Masad v. Weber* and the *Lakew* case discussed in that opinion. The supermarket's principal goal in entering into the contract with SS was to protect its own property and interests. Although its employees and customers also benefit from the security arrangement, there is nothing in the contract to suggest that the parties intended them to have a direct cause of action against SS for breach of the contract. Benny is therefore best regarded as an incidental beneficiary, not an intended beneficiary. However, the question of the parties' intent is a matter of interpretation, so it is conceivable that a court might find Benny to be an intended beneficiary, so answer (A) is not clearly wrong. (B) is clearly wrong because it misstates the law. If Benny is classified as an incidental beneficiary, he does not have an independent right of action under the contract. (D) is wrong. The term "creditor beneficiary" is merely used to describe a type of intended beneficiary. The crucial question remains whether the parties' intent was to confer a cause of action on the third party. If the third party is a creditor of the promisee, this may be a good indication that he is an intended beneficiary, as happened in *Lawrence v. Fox* but this is not dispositive, especially where settlement of the debt is not the purpose of the contract.

Question 2

Lexie Lawless, an attorney, undertook to defend Emma Bezzel, a bookkeeper, in a criminal case in which Emma was charged with embezzling money from her employer. Lexie handled the case so incompetently that she clearly committed malpractice. As a result, Emma was convicted and sentenced to a year's imprisonment. Emma's husband claims that Lexie's incompetence has caused him financial loss because Emma can no longer contribute to the family income. He has sued Lexie for malpractice based on her failure to perform properly under her contract with Emma.

(A) Emma's husband is an intended beneficiary of the contract between Lexie and Emma and therefore has an independent cause of action for malpractice against Lexie, based on Lexie's breach of her contract with Emma.

(B) Emma's husband is an incidental beneficiary of the contract between Lexie and Emma and therefore has no independent cause of action for malpractice against Lexie, based on Lexie's breach of her contract with Emma.

(C) Emma's husband is an incidental beneficiary of the contract between Lexie and Emma and therefore has no independent cause of action for malpractice against Lexie based on Lexie's breach of her contract with Emma. However, Emma's husband can sue Lexie for malpractice in tort for negligently representing Emma.

(D) Had this contract not involved the provision of legal services, Emma's husband would have qualified as an intended beneficiary of the contract. However, public policy considerations preclude this conclusion in the context of an attorney-client relationship.

Question 2 Answer

(B) is the best answer. An attorney's successful representation of a client in a criminal case will likely confer some benefit on the client's family or dependents, but unless it is clear from the representation contract that the parties intend to confer a right on those beneficiaries to sue the attorney for malpractice, they are best treated as incidental beneficiaries. Under some circumstances (A) could be an arguable answer, but it does not seem so on these facts because no such intent is apparent here. In addition, in a contract for legal services, courts are particularly reluctant to find intent to confer a right of action on a non-client because of the impact this may have on the attorney-client relationship. (C) could be a correct answer under some circumstances, but for a non-client to sue an attorney in tort for malpractice, the non-client would have to show that the attorney owed a duty of care to him. These facts do not support that conclusion. (D) does identify the policy of approaching attorney-client contracts more cautiously, but because there are no facts to indicate an intent to confer a direct cause of action on Emma's husband, the result likely would be the same even if the contract not involved the provision of legal services.

Question 3

As in Question 2, Lexie Lawless incompetently defended Emma Bezzel in the criminal case in which Emma was charged with embezzling money from her employer. As a result, Emma has a cause of action against Lexie for malpractice, based on Lexie's contractual duty to represent Emma competently. Emma decided that she did not wish to sue Lexie herself, so she transferred her claim against Lexie to her husband.

(A) Emma's husband is now clearly an intended third party beneficiary of the contract between Emma and Lexie.

(B) Emma's husband is still not an intended beneficiary of the contract between Emma and Lexie, but he may be able to sue Lexie for malpractice as the assignee of Emma's malpractice claim.

(C) Emma's husband is still not an intended beneficiary of the contract between Emma and Lexie. He also has no right to sue Lexie for malpractice as the assignee of Emma's malpractice claim because he gave Emma no consideration for transferring the claim to him.

(D) Emma's husband is still not an intended beneficiary of the contract between Emma and Lexie. He also has no right to sue Lexie as the assignee of Emma's malpractice claim because it violates public policy for a client to assign a malpractice claim to a non-client.

Question 3 Answer

(B) is the best answer. The assignment does not change the fact that Emma's husband was an incidental beneficiary of the contract, so (A) is wrong. However, he now acquires the right to sue under the contract by the assignment. A party to a contract may assign her rights under it unless that assignment clearly violates public policy. While *Gurski v. Rosenblum and Filan, LLC* indicates that an assignment of an attorney malpractice claim could violate public policy, that case involved the assignment of the claim to an adversary in the underlying litigation. The same concerns may not be present when the claim is assigned to a family member. Therefore, while (D) could be a correct answer under some circumstances in some jurisdictions, it is stated too broadly. (C) is wrong. An assignment can be gratuitous and does not need consideration, provided that it is executed and not merely a promise to assign the right in the future.

Question 4

Lexie Lawless, an attorney, undertook to defend Emma Bezzel, a bookkeeper, in a criminal case in which Emma was charged with embezzling money from her employer. A week before the trial was to begin, Lexie agreed to represent an important client in a multi-million dollar negotiation. Lexie could not handle both Emma's trial and the negotiation, so she handed Emma's file over to Justin, another attorney, who agreed to take on Emma's defense in exchange for receiving the fee to be paid by Emma for the representation. (Lexie and Justin are both sole practitioners and are not associated in the same firm.)

(A) This is an assignment of rights and delegation of duties under Lexie's contract with Emma, but it cannot be accomplished without Emma's consent.

(B) This is a valid assignment of rights and delegation of duties under Lexie's contract with Emma, which does not need her consent. Justin has been fully substituted for Lexie as the party to the representation agreement.

(C) This is a valid assignment of rights and delegation of duties under Lexie's contract with Emma, which does not need her consent. However, if Justin commits malpractice, Emma can sue Lexie for breach of the contract.

(D) This is a valid assignment of rights under Lexie's contract with Emma, but it is not a valid delegation of Lexie's duties, which Lexie cannot transfer to Justin.

Question 4 Answer

(A) is correct. The attorney-client relationship is a special one, in which the client is entitled to expect that the attorney with whom she contracted will perform the duties under the contract. Lexie therefore cannot assign this contract to another lawyer unless Emma agrees to accept the substitution. (This would involve Emma's agreement to terminate her contract with Lexie and a new representation contract between Emma and Justin.) Lexie's duties under the contract cannot be delegated because the parties contemplate performance by her, and because it would violate public policy to permit her to transfer those duties without Emma's consent. (B) is therefore wrong. It might be possible for Lexie to assign her right to the payment of fees under the contract, provided that she does not delegate her duties and that the assignment of that right does not compromise the representation. In that situation (D) might be correct. However, in this case Lexie is not seeking only to assign her right to payment of the fees. (C) is wrong. In a valid delegation, Lexie would remain liable for any breach of the contract by Justin. However, this is not a valid delegation.

Question 5

Buyer bought a new car on credit from Dealer. Dealer financed the credit purchase itself and the contract provided that Buyer would pay for the car by monthly installments over four years. A year after the contract was executed, Dealer sold the installment contract to Bank. Bank notified Buyer immediately in writing that payments under the contract must be made to Bank, not Dealer. However, Buyer overlooked the notice and continued to make payments to Dealer for three months. He realized his mistake only when he received a notice from Bank claiming that he was in default in his payments. Dealer never transmitted those payments to Bank and has now become bankrupt, so there is no prospect of recovering the payments from Dealer.

(A) Bank has no right to demand that Buyer pay it the three months' payments. This is a sale of goods under UCC Article 2, and rights under such contracts may not be assigned.

(B) Bank has no right to demand that Buyer pay it the three months' payments because Buyer never consented to the assignment.

(C) Bank has no right to demand that Buyer pay it the three months' payments because Buyer has in fact paid those installments and it would be unjust to require him to pay them again.

(D) Bank has the right to demand that Buyer pay it the three months' payments, even though Buyer had already paid those installments to Dealer.

Question 5 Answer

(D) is correct. The assignment of the right to payment under the credit arrangement is valid and Buyer did receive notice of the assignment. He is therefore obliged to pay the assignee, and payments to the assignor do not discharge his duty. (A) is wrong. UCC 2-210 expressly recognizes the assignment of rights under a sale of goods unless the qualifications in that section apply. They do not apply in this case. (B) is wrong. It is not necessary that an obligor assent to the assignment. (C) is wrong. Although it may be unfortunate that Buyer has to pay the installments twice, he bears the risk of having to do so if he disregards or overlooks the notice of assignment and continues to pay the assignor. There is no indication in the facts that the notice was inadequate.

Principal cases and the page on which they begin appear in bold. If a case, excerpt, or discussion spans more than one page, just the first page is listed. Please note that this table does not include references to the assessment questions at the end of the book.

If the materials quote or excerpt a secondary source at length, both the name of the source and page on which the quote or excerpt begins appear in bold. If the quote, excerpt, or discussion spans more than one page, just the first page is listed. Please note that this table does not include references to the assessment questions at the end of the book.

Books and Treatises

Articles

Miscellaneous Model Rules and Statutes

INDEX

Please note that this index does not include references to the assessment questions at the end of the book.

Equitable estoppel, 343, 376, 480, 756-757, 759-760, 764, 944-945

Equity, *See also* Estoppel; Injunctions; Promissory Estoppel, Specific Performance; Unconscionability

  balance of equities, 414, 522-523, 524, 529, 931, 933, 937, 940, 942-945

  clean hands doctrine, 414-415, 935

  court of, 488-489, 923, 926, 929

  excuse of condition, 764, 765

  generally, 23-28

  inadequate legal remedy, 926-927, 928-930, 931-933, 936, 937, 940

  jury trial, 490

  law distinguished, 926-927

  mistake doctrine, equitable derivation, 679, 683, 701

  substantial performance, 787

  unjust enrichment. *See* Unjust enrichment

Estoppel. *See* Equitable estoppel; Promissory estoppel

Evidence. *See* Burden of proof; Parol evidence; Statute of frauds

Exchange. *See* Consideration

Exclusive dealings contract. *See* Agency; Consideration

Exculpatory clause. *See* Damages; Illegality and public policy; Warranties

Executed gift. *See* Consideration

Execution. *See* Damages

Exemplary damages. *See* Damages

Expectation damages. *See* Damages

Express and implied terms. *See* Conditions; Promise; *specific subject headings*

Extortion. *See* Duress; Modification of contract

Fair dealing. *See* Good faith

Firm offer. *See* Offer and acceptance; Options and firm offers

Foreseeability. *See* Damages

Forfeiture. *See* Damages; Specific performance

Formalism. *See* Classical contract law

Formalities. *See* Consideration; Modification of contract; Parol evidence; Statute of frauds

Formation of contract. *See* Indefiniteness; Offer and acceptance

Form contracts. *See* Standard contracts

Forum selection clause, 80, 87-88, 190-191, 495-500, 550-551, 605

Fraud. *See* Fraudulent misrepresentation; Statute of frauds

Fraudulent misrepresentation

  affirmative false statement, 428-429, 432, 434-436, 438-439, 447, 462

  "as is" provision, effect, 695

avoidance (rescission), 427-428, 432, 464, 467

caveat emptor, 445, 447, 449-450

concealment, 429, 437-438, 695

damages for, 434, 435-436, 437, 464-465

disclaimer, effect, 458, 461-462, 463

elements, generally, 428-430, 435, 441, 447-448

in factum, 465-466, 473

intent to deceive, 430, 434, 438

justifiable reliance (inducement), 431, 435, 436, 441-442, 445, 448, 450, 453, 455, 458, 462-463, 473, 553, 667-668

knowledge of falsity, 430, 441, 452-453, 473

materiality, 430-431, 437, 438, 441, 443, 446-449, 453, 463-464, 473

merger clause, effect, 459-463, 464

by minor, 547, 552-553

misrepresentation of fact, 428-429, 441, 453-454, 455-456, 687

misrepresentation of intent, 456-457

misrepresentation of opinion, 429, 451-456

mistake, duty to correct, 439, 442-443

negligent misrepresentation distinguished, 431, 463-464, 671-672

nondisclosure, 429, 438-448

nonparty misrepresentation, 430

parol evidence exception, 667-673

promise fraudulently made, 428, 457

psychological (non-physical) impairment of property, 448-449

punitive damages, 464-465,907

reckless assertion, 435, 436, 448

restitution, 432

sale of goods, 428

scienter, 430, 434, 435, 436, 441, 447-448

statutory disclosure requirement, 446-447

tort nature, 428, 439, 444, 464-465

void contract, 466

Freedom of contract, 13-14, 313, 319, 520, 607, 672, 908, 911

Frustration of purpose, 705, 716-723

Gap fillers. *See* Good faith; Price; Sale of goods; Warranties

Good faith

  compromise of doubtful claim, 314-316, 324-330

  condition of satisfaction, 335-336, 749-750

  defined, 618, 621-622, 623-624

  discretion circumscribed, 246, 608, 614-615

  exclusive dealings, 251-252, 336-338, 614-615

  general obligation (implied covenant), 251-252, 614, 616-617, 618-625, 908

  improper threat, 468

  mental incompetence cases, 564-565, 567